Windows XP™ Secrets®

Curt Simmons

Hungry Minds™

Best-Selling Books • Digital Downloads • e-Books • Answer Networks •
e-Newsletters • Branded Web Sites • e-Learning

New York, NY ✦ Cleveland, OH ✦ Indianapolis, IN

Windows XP™ Secrets®

Published by
Hungry Minds, Inc.
909 Third Avenue
New York, NY 10022
www.hungryminds.com

Library of Congress Control Number: 2001095936

ISBN: 0-7645-4852-2

Printed in the United States of America

10 9 8 7 6 5 4

1B/QU/RR/QR/IN

Distributed in the United States by Hungry Minds, Inc.

Distributed by CDG Books Canada Inc. for Canada; by Transworld Publishers Limited in the United Kingdom; by IDG Norge Books for Norway; by IDG Sweden Books for Sweden; by IDG Books Australia Publishing Corporation Pty. Ltd. for Australia and New Zealand; by TransQuest Publishers Pte Ltd. for Singapore, Malaysia, Thailand, Indonesia, and Hong Kong; by Gotop Information Inc. for Taiwan; by ICG Muse, Inc. for Japan; by Intersoft for South Africa; by Eyrolles for France; by International Thomson Publishing for Germany, Austria, and Switzerland; by Distribuidora Cuspide for Argentina; by LR International for Brazil; by Galileo Libros for Chile; by Ediciones ZETA S.C.R. Ltda. for Peru; by WS Computer Publishing Corporation, Inc., for the Philippines; by Contemporanea de Ediciones for Venezuela; by Express Computer Distributors for the Caribbean and West Indies; by Micronesia Media Distributor, Inc. for Micronesia; by Chips Computadoras S.A. de C.V. for Mexico; by Editorial Norma de Panama S.A. for Panama; by American Bookshops for Finland.

For general information on Hungry Minds' products and services please contact our Customer Care department within the U.S. at 800-762-2974, outside the U.S. at 317-572-3993 or fax 317-572-4002.

For sales inquiries and reseller information, including discounts, premium and bulk quantity sales, and foreign-language translations, please contact our Customer Care department at 800-434-3422, fax 317-572-4002 or write to Hungry Minds, Inc., Attn: Customer Care Department, 10475 Crosspoint Boulevard, Indianapolis, IN 46256.

For information on licensing foreign or domestic rights, please contact our Sub-Rights Customer Care department at 212-884-5000.

For information on using Hungry Minds' products and services in the classroom or for ordering examination copies, please contact our Educational Sales department at 800-434-2086 or fax 317-572-4005.

For press review copies, author interviews, or other publicity information, please contact our Public Relations department at 317-572-3168 or fax 317-572-4168.

For authorization to photocopy items for corporate, personal, or educational use, please contact Copyright Clearance Center, 222 Rosewood Drive, Danvers, MA 01923, or fax 978-750-4470.

Hungry Minds is a trademark of Hungry Minds, Inc.

Credits

Acquisitions Editor
Nancy Stevenson

Project Editor
Kevin Kent

Technical Editor
Jim Aspinwall

Copy Editors
Rich Adin
Jennifer Mario

Editorial Managers
Ami Frank Sullivan
Kyle Looper

Senior Vice President, Technical Publishing
Richard Swadley

Vice President and Publisher
Mary Bednarek

Project Coordinator
Maridee Ennis

Proofreader
Nancy Reinhart

Indexer
Johanna VanHoose Dinse

About the Author

Curt Simmons is a technology author and trainer focusing on Windows operating systems and Internet technologies. He is the author of over 20 books, including many high-level networking titles. Curt is a Microsoft Certified Systems Engineer, a Microsoft Certified Trainer, and a Chauncey Group Certified Technical Trainer. When not tinkering with new operating systems and technologies, Curt spends his time with his wife and kids.

Acknowledgements

I would like to thank everyone at Hungry Minds, Inc., for giving me the opportunity to write this book. Thanks to Nancy Stevenson, my acquisitions editor, for the green light and to Kevin Kent, the project editor, for his guidance and editorial work. Thanks also to Rich Adin and Jennifer Mario, who made sure the words were right. Thanks to Jim Aspinwall for the fine technical review, and as always, thanks to my agent, Margot Maley. Finally, thanks to my wife and children for supporting me during the long hours spent writing this book.

Preface

Welcome to *Windows XP Secrets,* your one-stop guide to Microsoft's latest operating system. In this Preface, you learn about . . .

- ◆ The purpose of this book
- ◆ The structure and contents of this book
- ◆ How to use this book

Windows XP — The operating system for everyone

Welcome to the eleventh book in the Windows *Secrets* series from Hungry Minds, Inc. This introduction gets your feet on solid ground and your exploration of Windows XP on the right track. With this book, you can unlock the secrets of Windows XP and configure this new and dynamic operating system in a way that's right for you.

If this is your first Windows *Secrets* book, you hold in your hands the best secrets, little-known tricks, and lifesaving workarounds available in Windows XP Professional and Windows XP Home Editions. Using the information in this book, you can work and play faster, smarter, and easier with Windows XP.

If you've used previous books in the Windows *Secrets* series, you know you'll find within this book those hard-to-find facts and techniques that Microsoft doesn't seem to get around to putting in its own books on the subject.

Windows XP Secrets gives you the information you need to make the most of Windows XP. If you are coming from Windows 2000, Windows XP will be very familiar. If you are coming from Windows 9*x* or Me, you'll recognize many aspects of the operating system but quickly realize how different Windows XP is. Built on the Windows 2000 code base, Windows XP combines the best features of Windows 2000 and Windows Me and includes new tools, features, and a sleek, new interface.

In this book, you find only the best, most hard-to-find information on Windows XP. Information in this book has been collected through beta testing of the product, and with the information you find here, you can unravel the secrets of Windows XP in no time.

What this book doesn't cover

There are many gems in this book, but there are a few things that you *won't* find within. For example, I don't cover the easy stuff. If XP's help system or printed manual covers a topic, it's probably not in here. I left out the obvious stuff so you get more "secret" stuff. Sure, I give you some steps that you can find in the operating system's help files, but most of what you find here is beyond the obvious. This book is for the intermediate to advanced computer user, so if you are just getting started with Windows, you can learn much here, but you may need an additional book for the beginner. On the other end of the scale, this book does not provide an extensive look at Windows XP in a Windows 2000/XP domain. Though this book does cover some useful aspects of Windows XP's networking features, if you are needing to use Windows XP in a domain environment where Group Policy, IP Security, and related networking concepts are often implemented, you'll need a different book that focuses on networking and administration of Windows XP. However, if you are a typical home or office user, then this book is exactly what you need.

What is in this book

Windows XP Secrets is organized into seven parts. Each part is further organized into a number of chapters to give you a convenient way to get just what you need out of this book.

Part I: Installation and Drive Configuration Secrets

Part I covers upgrading and clean installing Windows XP, as well as advanced setup options that are available to networking environments. It also explores Windows XP drive configuration and disk quotas.

Part II: XP Interface and Settings Secrets

Part II explores the new XP interface and shows you all the tips and tricks to get your system to look just the way you want. You find out about Display configuration, the new XP Start menu, and shortcuts, as well as folder options, the Recycle Bin, and the Microsoft Management Console.

Part III: Software Secrets

Part III explores how Windows XP handles software compatibility and incompatibility. You learn about adding and removing components, about managing software applications, and about digital media.

Part IV: Hardware Secrets

Making Windows XP work with all the different kinds of hardware out there can be a challenge. In this part, you learn how to manage hardware on Windows XP, including information on managing your computer with the Control Panel, understanding the Registry, as well as using printers and other peripherals.

Part V: Internet and Dial-Up Communication Secrets

Windows XP is designed to work seamlessly with the Internet, and there are a number of new tools and features that make working and playing on the Internet easier. In this part, you learn about dial-up and broadband configurations, Internet Explorer, Outlook Express, and Web publishing.

Part VI: Windows XP Networking Secrets

In Part VI, you learn about the secrets of Windows XP networking. You start out with an overview of networking technologies. Then you see how to make the most of Windows XP on small office and home networks, as well as more complicated connections, such as Virtual Private Networks (VPNs), Remote Desktop, Internet Connection Sharing (ICS), Internet Connection Firewall (ICF), and a host other technologies.

Part VII: Optimization and Troubleshooting Secrets

Finally, the book wraps up by exploring the optimization and troubleshooting options and features that are available to you but not readily apparent. This section shows you how to get your computer running in peak condition and how to resolve common problems.

How to use this book

Windows XP Secrets is designed to help you get the information you need quickly and easily. This is a reference book designed to provide the information you are looking for at the time when you need it. Therefore, feel free to skip around. Use the table of contents and the book's index to find the information that you need.

However, if you are really trying to immerse yourself in Windows XP technology, this book is organized logically and can be read cover to cover. Each chapter stands on its own, but chapters are organized around each other and are designed to be easy to read and easy to understand. If you are an advanced user, you can jump to the information you need quickly and easily. If you need more basic information, you can read the book in order and learn a wealth of information.

To help you along the way, you'll find the following features in each chapter:

◆ **In This Chapter** — Each chapter begins with a brief introduction and bullet list of the topics you will learn about in the chapter. Use this information to determine if the chapter has the information that you might need.

- ◆ **Summary** — Each chapter contains a summary that gives you a quick, bullet-by-bullet review of the information contained in that chapter.

- ◆ **Steps** — Where appropriate, I provide you with step-by-step instructions to help you quickly and easily accomplish tasks.

- ◆ **Screen shots** — A picture is worth a thousand words, and that much can also be true in computer books. I include pertinent screen shots of the XP interface throughout the book to help you stay on track and get the information you need easily.

Also, you'll find a few icons throughout the chapters that flag some tidbit of text for your attention. You'll find these helpful:

CAUTION: The **Caution** icon warns you about side effects you should watch out for or precautions you should take before doing something that may have a negative impact on your system.

CROSS-REFERENCE: The **Cross-Reference** icon points you to places both inside and outside of this book where you can get more information about a particular topic.

NOTE: The **Note** icon points out items of interest or importance that I want to call your attention to. You can think of notes as friendly pieces of advice.

SECRET: The **Secret** icon marks items that are not documented in the manual you get with Windows XP or are little-known facts that are not obvious for most Windows XP users. This information may be written down *somewhere* by Microsoft, but not in a way that's easy for users to find.

TIP: The **Tip** icon indicates a technique that may involve items on the menu or in the manual, but the trick is not obvious or well explained by Microsoft.

Understanding Windows commands

Although Windows relies on the mouse for most things, there are times when a good old typed-in command is just the thing you need to get the result you want.

In this book, the following styles show you what to type, and when.

```
notepad {/p} filename
```

When you need to type a command, it's shown in a special font, as in the previous line.

Optional parameters are shown in curly braces {like this}.

Items to be typed exactly as shown are in roman type, such as the /p in {/p}. (For example, /p indicates that Notepad is to print the filename that follows.)

Terms that should be replaced with real words or numbers are shown in *italics,* such as *filename.* In this case, you don't type the letters f-i-l-e-n-a-m-e. You substitute the name of the file you want to operate on, such as readme.txt.

To open the `readme.txt` file in the `C:\Winnt` folder, for example, you would click the Start button, click Run, and then type the following and click OK:

```
notepad c:\windows\readme.txt
```

To print the same file, you would type the following instead:

```
notepad /p c:\windows\readme.txt
```

There are usually several different ways to represent the name of a file, and each way can describe the same file. For example, if you are at a command prompt and are currently in the `c:\winnt` folder, all of the following commands work the same way to open the `setuplog.txt` file:

```
notepad c:\windows\setuplog.txt
notepad c:\windows\setuplog
Notepad Setuplog
NOTEPAD SETUPLOG.TXT
```

Special keys on your keyboard are shown in the book with an initial capital letter. This includes Enter, Backspace, Tab, Alt (alternate), Ctrl (control), Esc (escape), and so on.

If I want you to hold down one special key while you press another, a plus sign (+) appears between the two keys. For example, *Ctrl+A* means *hold down the Ctrl key, press and release the A key, and then release the Ctrl key.*

If I want you to press and release each of a series of keys in turn, commas appear between the keys. For example, *press Alt, F, O* means *press and release the Alt key, then press and release the F key, and then press and release the O key.* (This runs the File ⇨ Open command in most Windows applications.)

Sometimes the mouse is all you need to run a command, but you can also run it with a keyboard combination. I don't necessarily spell out the keyboard equivalent, but if there is one, you can use it if you like. For example, when I say *choose File ⇨ Open* you could pull down the File menu and then choose Open with your mouse. Alternatively, you could press Alt, F, O to do the same thing. The choice is yours.

Are you ready?

Are you ready to eXPerience all that Windows XP has to offer? Welcome to the power of Windows 2000 and the friendliness of Windows Me, plus a whole bunch of new things to boot. As you work with Windows XP and use this book as your companion, remember to enjoy the learning journey and find ways that make Windows XP the best operating system for you.

Contents

Part V: Internet and Dial-Up Communication Secrets 347

Part VII: Optimization and Troubleshooting Secrets .. 597

Chapter 24: Optimizing Windows XP 599

Chapter 25: Troubleshooting Tools in Windows XP 621

<u>Part I</u>

Installation and Drive Configuration Secrets

Chapter 1

Installing and Upgrading to Windows XP

In This Chapter

Windows XP, like previous versions of Microsoft Windows, can be installed as an upgrade over certain versions of Windows or as a clean install. Across the board, the installation of Windows XP is rather easy and "hands-off" throughout most of the setup routine. In this chapter, you explore the setup process and the steps you should take to get ready for a Windows XP installation, including . . .

- ♦ Getting ready to install Windows XP
- ♦ Performing an upgrade or a clean install
- ♦ Solving installation problems

Which XP Version Do You Need?

If you have picked up this book and you have not yet purchased Windows XP, there are a few things you should know about the XP family. First, there are two versions of Windows XP — the Home edition and the Professional edition. At first glance, it may seem that the Home edition should always be used by someone with a home computer, while the Professional version is more for office use and businesses. While that statement is true, Windows XP Professional edition is often used by home users, as well — and rightly so. Windows XP Professional has a number of features that are not available or even necessary on the Home edition.

If you are still trying to decide which version might be right for you, you need to take a look at a few different issues. First, if you are buying a new computer from an Original Equipment Manufacturer (OEM), it will probably arrive to you with Windows XP already installed. You may need to complete a few setup questions, but basically, the computer is good to go. So, when you purchase this computer, you need to decide what operating system you want to buy. Typically, Windows XP Professional is more expensive than the Home edition, so weigh your needs carefully.

If you have an existing computer that you want to upgrade or clean install to Windows XP, take a hard look at XP's needs and requirements before buying that installation CD. In short, do you homework first, and this chapter is just what you need to get you on your way.

As you are deciding which version is best for you, keep the following bullet points in mind. They make a number of distinctions between Windows XP Professional and Home editions clear.

- ♦ Windows XP Home edition contains the tools and features that give you a rich computing experience, home networking capabilities, and full-featured Internet tools. For the average home user with one or two computers, the Home edition is all you need.

- ♦ Windows XP Professional has every feature of the Home edition, but it contains more advanced networking and user management features. Windows XP Professional can function in a Windows 2000 domain and contains all of the features necessary for corporate and business networking.

- ◆ Once you install Windows XP Professional, you cannot downgrade to Windows XP Home edition.
- ◆ If you need more advanced networking components and features, even if you are using Windows in a workgroup, the XP Professional version will be your best choice.

Unless you are a home user that has no intention of using advanced networking features and user management features, the Professional edition is always you best bet because it gives you everything you might need both now and in the future.

Getting Ready for Installation

Windows XP is built on the Windows 2000 code base, so it makes sense that the easiest upgrade path is from Windows 2000 Professional to Windows XP. Both of these versions of Windows share the same Registry database and structure, and they each have the same file system and folder architecture. However, you can also easily upgrade Windows 98 and Windows Me to Windows XP, provided that your computer meets the hardware requirements to run XP — and these requirements are more stringent than previous requirements. To make certain that your computer can meet the demands of Windows XP, you should carefully plan and check the hardware requirements, which you learn about in the next section.

Checking minimum hardware requirements

First, you need to see if your computer is up to the task. Table 1-1 shows the minimum hardware requirements recommended by Microsoft, as well as a consensus opinion of what you really need to run Windows XP with adequate performance.

Table 1-1: Hardware Requirements for Windows XP

Component	Microsoft Requirements	Realistic Minimums
Processor	233 MHz Pentium or higher	400 MHz Pentium II or higher
RAM	64MB minimum; 128MB recommended	128MB is the bare minimum — get as much as possible
Hard Drive	1.5GB	4GB +
Video	VGA or better	SVGA
Peripherals	Standard keyboard, mouse, CD-ROM drive, and the like	Same

The realistic minimums have come from discussions in newsgroups, as well as from reviews of beta versions of the operating system. In practical terms, the hardware on your computer needs to be beyond the minimum values in order to see effective performance. Windows XP is a heavyweight operating system, and it needs the hardware to carry the load. If the computer is barely meeting the minimum requirements listed in Table 1-1, your system will not be able to handle the demands of XP. Sure, you may get it installed and be able to boot the system, but you are likely to experience severe performance problems. Your system needs to be closer to the Realistic Minimums values presented in Table 1-1 — these values will give you a system that can handle XP and perform in a satisfactory manner.

Backing up

If you are upgrading an existing computer, the first thing you want to do is back up all your data. If you are upgrading — rather than doing a clean install — all your programs and files should be waiting for you there at the end, but don't count on it. Any number of bad things can happen during an upgrade, and there is always a chance that you can lose files. So back up all your data files, such as your word processing documents, spreadsheets, and the like, first. Even if your critical data is found on a different volume or partition from the boot volume, I would still recommend a backup to removable media or at least to another physical disk.

There are many other valuable pieces of information scattered elsewhere on your hard drive, so you should make sure you back those up, as well. This includes your e-mail address book, Web site passwords stored in cookie files, preferences stored in .INI files, Registry .DAT files, and so forth. Depending on the size of your hard drive and the type of backup media you use, it might be best to do a complete backup. The easiest way to backup data on your Windows computer is to use the Windows backup utilities. See your Windows' version documentation for instructions.

Collecting drivers

Windows XP ships with an extensive list of drivers for most common hardware devices — in fact, XP has the most extensive driver database ever included in a Microsoft operating system. To see if your hardware is supported, check the Hardware Compatibility List (HCL) located in the \Support folder of the Windows XP Professional CD-ROM or on the Web at www.microsoft.com. If your device is not on the list, you need to locate the disks or CD-ROMs that came with it or contact the hardware manufacturer to see if they have a Windows XP driver available. If the devices are Plug and Play, then you (probably) won't need to get drivers.

> **TIP:** If you need an updated driver, they are often available for download from the hardware manufacturer's Web site.

If you are not sure what drivers you may need, don't worry. In one of the first installation steps, the Setup Wizard scans your hardware for problem devices. If your system hardware is okay, Windows XP will install. If not, the areas of conflict will be identified for you.

> **TIP:** Any last minute changes, cautions, or warnings from Microsoft will be included in a number of files that usually can be found in the root directory of the Windows XP CD-ROM. These include the Read First Notes, the Setup text file, the Advanced Setup text file, and the Release Notes. There may be valuable information about incompatibilities, or about things you should not do while installing, and the information is typically more current than the information contained in the printed material accompanying the CD-ROM.

> **CAUTION:** While there are safeguards built into the Windows XP Setup Wizard that should prevent you from incapacitating your computer, you should still make sure you have an Emergency Boot Disk from your current operating system. Depending on how — or when — the Windows XP setup was interrupted, this might allow you to restore your computer to something resembling its previous state should a problem occur.

Planning Your Installation

When you actually begin the installation process, one of the first questions you will be asked is whether you want to upgrade your existing operating system or perform a new (or clean) installation. What you decide here has important ramifications on your workload immediately after the operating system installation is complete. When you upgrade, you replace your existing operating system files with the Windows XP files. However, your applications, settings, and data files should remain intact, and will be ready for use when Setup is over. On the other hard, during a new installation, Windows XP is installed into a new folder, leaving your old operating system files in place. You must then reinstall all of your applications and reset all of your preferences so that the new operating system knows about them.

In general, you should perform an upgrade if you answer yes to *all* of the following questions:

♦ Does your current operating system support an upgrade to Windows XP? (To directly upgrade, you must be currently running Windows 2000, Windows NT 4.0, Windows Me, or Windows 98.)

♦ Do you want to replace your previous Windows operating system files with Windows XP? (This saves hard drive space.)

♦ Do you want to keep your existing data and preferences? (An upgrade should allow all your applications to remain in place.)

There are four questions to answer if you are considering a new installation. If you answer yes to *any* of these, then you should perform a new installation:

♦ Do you have an empty hard drive? (No operating system is installed.)

♦ Does your current operating system not support an upgrade to Windows XP? (DOS, Windows 3.1, Windows 95.)

♦ Do you want to get rid of your existing data and preferences and make a fresh start?

♦ Do you want to have a dual-boot configuration with Windows XP and your existing operating system version? (You need two disk partitions to do this.)

The Windows XP files can take as much as 650MB of space for a full installation on your hard drive. Space limitations may play a factor in your decision on whether to do an upgrade or a clean installation, if you don't think you have room for two operating systems.

> **TIP:** While it may seem a bit drastic, some experienced computer users swear by a housecleaning procedure, whereby once every six months or so, they back up their data files, reformat their hard drives, and then reinstall their operating system and all their applications from scratch. They say this "spring cleaning" helps clear out a lot of unneeded settings, files, and assorted clutter, and helps their computer run more quickly and efficiently. If this sounds like a good idea, then a new install might be for you.

Choosing a File System

Another decision you may need to make is to determine what file system you will use on your hard drive. The file system is the way your files are organized on your hard drive. Windows XP can work with the NT file system (NTFS), as well as the two legacy systems, File Allocation Table (FAT), and File Allocation Table (32-bit) (FAT32). If your hard drive is already using NTFS, you have no decision to make, because once you have gone to NTFS, you can't go back without reformatting your hard drive.

NTFS is the native file system for Windows XP, and it is the system that Microsoft recommends you use with Windows XP. It has both advantages and disadvantages over FAT systems. NTFS provides for more secure files, better disk compression, and better scalability to larger drives. It also uses large hard drives more efficiently than does FAT. The major disadvantage is that only Windows NT, Windows 2000, and Windows XP recognize it. Other operating systems, such as Windows 95 and 98, cannot read from or write to NTFS partitions.

> **TIP:** On a large hard drive, NTFS partitions are more efficient. If you use FAT32 on a 2GB hard drive, each cluster on the drive will be 32K in size. Because two files cannot share a cluster, even a 1K file will occupy 32K of space on a drive. If a drive is formatted as NTFS, each cluster is 2K. The smaller clusters are more efficient — converting a 2GB drive from FAT to NTFS could easily free up 300MB of space on a drive.

To add to the confusion, the version of NTFS that ships with Windows NT 4 is NTFS 4. When Windows XP is installed, it upgrades this version to NTFS 5. The only version of Windows NT that can read NTFS 5 partitions is NT 4.0, Service Pack 4. If there is any chance you will have to go back to Windows NT, you must have installed Service Pack 4 first, or you will not be able to read from your drive. The only way you can recover from this is to reformat your drive.

> **TIP:** If you plan to use a dual-boot system with Windows XP and an earlier operating system (Windows 3.1, Windows 95, Windows 98, OS/2, or Windows NT Service Pack 3 or earlier) occupying different partitions, you should use FAT, or you should use FAT32 if the second operating system is Windows 95 OSR2 or Windows 98. The older operating systems will not be able to access NTFS 5 partitions. If you want to dual boot with Windows XP and Windows 2000, use NTFS. See Chapter 2 for more information about dual-boot systems.

Upgrading to Windows XP

After you have backed up your data, collected any drivers you need, and decided on the type of installation and file system, it's time to actually perform the upgrade. Don't worry, though; you haven't reached the point of no return yet. You have a number of opportunities to change your mind during the early stages of the upgrade process.

Installing from the CD-ROM

The installation process is simple if you are upgrading from the CD-ROM. Boot your computer using your existing operating system. Then insert the Windows XP CD-ROM disc into the drive. It should start automatically and give you a What do you want to do? screen, shown in Figure 1-1. As you can see, your options are to install XP, to install optional Windows components, to perform additional tasks, or to check your system for compatibility. Later chapters explore the options in Windows components and the additional tasks that you can perform (which is essentially a series of wizards). The Check system compatibility option helps you to determine whether your system is capable of running the Windows XP operating system. When you click the Check system compatibility option, a second What do you want to do? window appears where you can choose to visit the compatibility Web site or to have XP check your system automatically.

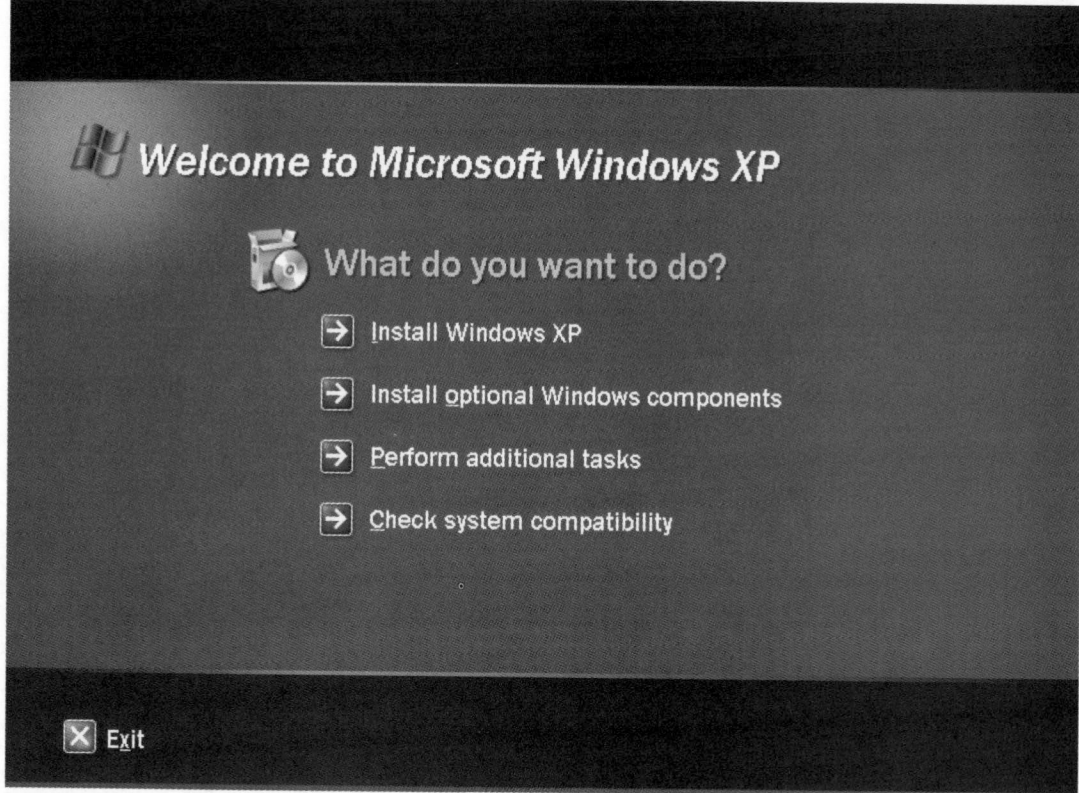

Figure 1-1: What do you want to do? window

If you choose to check the system automatically, a connection to the Internet is launched and the Windows Upgrade Advisor checks for any new updates to the setup program that need to be download. It then checks your system for problems or incompatibilities. If setup finds any problems or incompatibilities (or none), a window appears telling you the results, as shown in Figure 1-2.

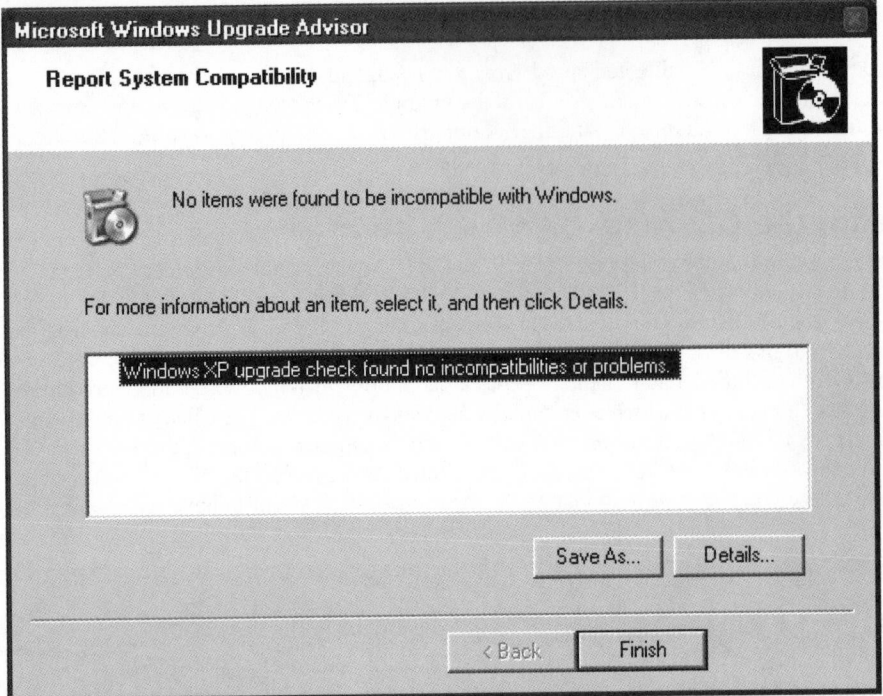

Figure 1-2: Compatibility results

When you are ready to install XP, choose the Install Windows XP option on the What do you want to do? screen. You will see the Welcome screen for the Windows XP Setup Wizard, as shown in Figure 1-3.

If the Windows XP CD-ROM disc does not automatically start, click Start ⇨ Run and type the following command in the Open text box (where d: is the letter that actually represents your CD-ROM drive):

```
d:\setup.exe
```

Use the drop-down menu to select Upgrade and click Next. You will see the Microsoft License Agreement as shown in Figure 1-4. To move on to the next step, you must select "I accept this agreement." (Fortunately, you only need to accept the agreement. You don't have to show that you understand it.)

If your current drive is partitioned as a FAT or FAT32 partition, you are asked if you want to upgrade to NTFS. (If you already have an NTFS partition, you won't see this step. Instead, you will be automatically upgraded to NTFS 5 later in the installation process.)

The next window asks you to enter your product key, which is found on the back of your CD-ROM jewel case. Enter the product key in the provided boxes (it's not case sensitive), and click Next.

The Dynamic Update window appears, prompting you to connect to Microsoft and to download any updated files that may be needed for your installation. You should allow setup to perform this download check, so click Yes and then Next.

From this point on, setup is automatic. You can sit back and read the advertising screens as they appear, or just leave Windows XP to its own chores. Setup reboots occur automatically and without intervention from you. Toward the end of the installation routine, you will be prompted to Activate windows, which you can choose to do at this time or you can wait. The next section gives you more information about activation.

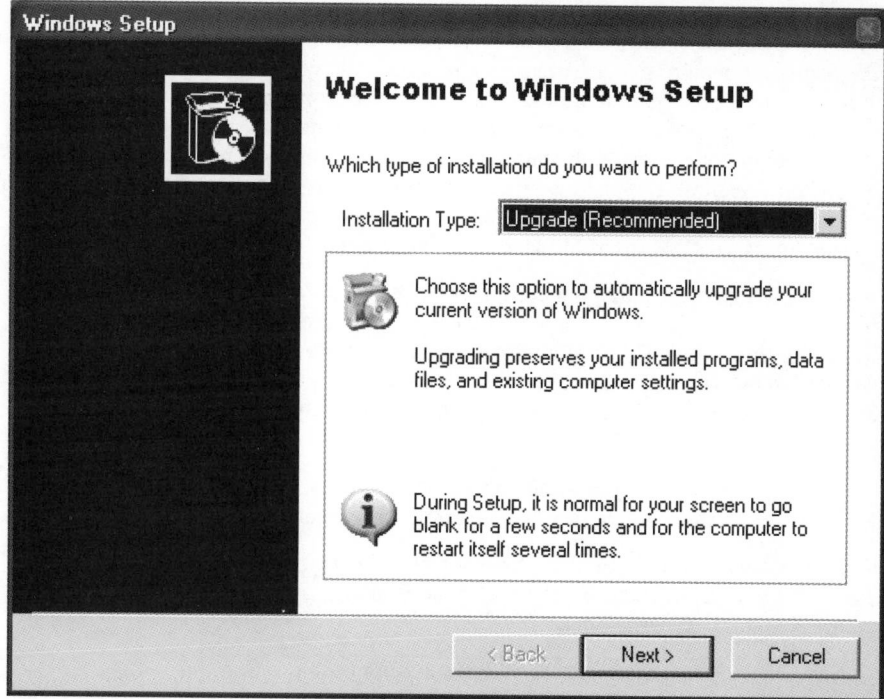

Figure 1-3: The Windows XP Setup Wizard. If you are upgrading from a supported operating system, upgrading, rather than a clean install, is usually the recommended option.

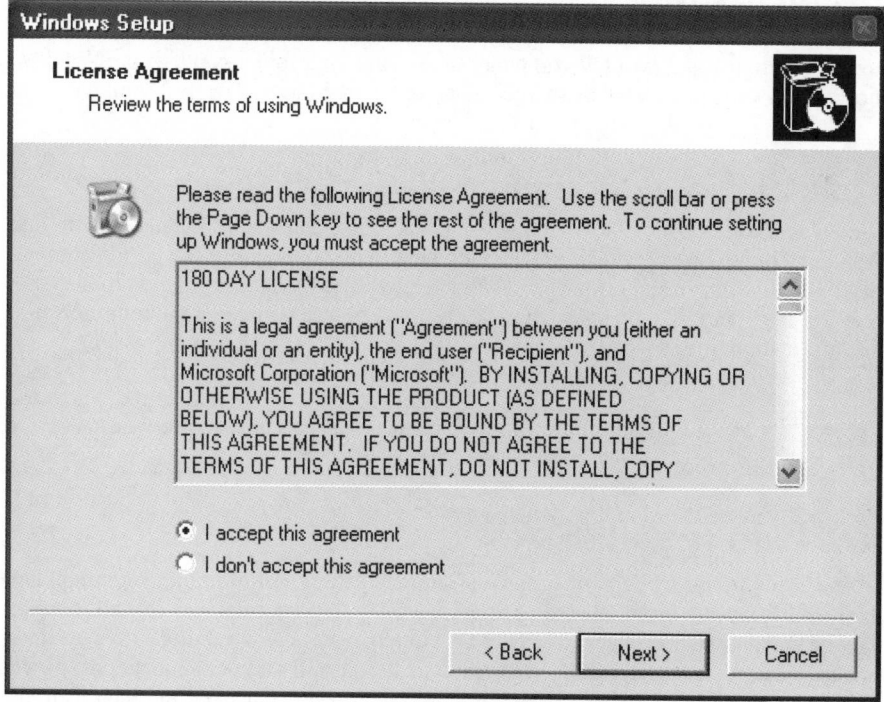

Figure 1-4: The Microsoft License Agreement for Windows XP. You must agree to continue the installation.

Activating Windows XP

Activation is a new Windows XP feature that activates your product code with Microsoft. Activation is completely anonymous — there is no registration information collected from you. The purpose of activation is to help prevent piracy. During activation, the computer's ID and/or serial number along with hardware information about your computer is transmitted and recorded. This prevents multiple computers from using the same CD-ROM and installation key. Once activation occurs, a confirmation is sent to your computer and the operating system is activated. In short, it forces people to stick to their licensing agreement instead of using one CD-ROM to install XP on 100 computers.

Activation is quick and easy. Using a modem, your computer makes a call to your Internet service provider (ISP) and then connects to Microsoft. Activation takes only a moment and if you are having problems, you can call and activate your XP system with a technician. If you are not connected to the Internet at the time of installation, you can delay activation until your computer is online, or if you prefer, you can also call a Microsoft telephone number and activate the operating system that way. See your computer's documentation for details.

Also, depending on your computer, activation may already be done for you if you are buying a new machine with Windows XP preinstalled. Again, check your computer's documentation for instructions.

The hitch is that activation is required — if you don't activate XP, it will typically stop functioning after 30 days until you activate the software. You can choose activate Windows XP at the end of the setup routine or later by choosing Start ⇨ All Programs.

> **NOTE:** If you purchased your computer with a preinstalled copy of Windows XP, it is possible that activation may not be necessary. Check your computer documentation for details.

Upgrading over a network

Instead of installing from a CD-ROM disc, you can upgrade your computer over your network (where applicable). Your network administrator will tell you which shared network folder contains the Windows XP setup files. Typically, you will connect to the shared folder and launch setup.exe. From that point, installation appears as though it is running from you CD-ROM drive.

Connecting to a network during installation

If you want to connect to a network during the Windows XP installation, you also might need to provide some network information. During an upgrade, if you already belong to a domain, your existing computer account will be used. If you don't have an account, you will need to provide that information to the wizard. You should determine your domain and account information before you begin the setup process. If you don't have this information, join a workgroup instead of a domain. You can join an existing workgroup, provide a new workgroup, or just use the default workgroup name that the wizard suggests.

> **TIP:** You can change all of your network settings later, or you can set up new network connections. If you are not sure what answer to provide, it should be safe for you to accept the default suggestions and move on.

Performing a Clean Install

There are two different starting points when performing a clean installation. For example, you might have a hard drive with no operating system installed at all, providing you with no normal way to start the computer. Or, it might be that an existing operating system is already installed. If you perform a clean install on a PC that already has Windows installed, you will need to reinstall all your applications, as well as reconfigure the system to your liking. A clean installation does not preserve any settings, applications, or data. So, make sure you save any important data or perform a data backup before performing a clean installation.

Running the installation

You can perform a clean installation of Windows XP so that XP is installed into a different folder than the previous operating system folder (in a case where there is a previous operating system). When a clean installation is performed, you need to reinstall all of your applications and reconfigure any desired settings. If your computer has a blank hard drive (a hard drive with no bootable operating system), to begin installing XP, you need to start the computer by using the Windows XP installation CD-ROM. Consult your computer documentation for more information about booting from your CD-ROM. The following steps walk you through the clean installation process.

STEPS

Clean install

1. Insert the Windows XP CD-ROM disc into the CD-ROM drive.

2. Start your computer as usual.

3. If the Windows XP Setup Wizard automatically starts, you can skip the rest of these steps, and move to the next section.

4. If the Setup Wizard doesn't start automatically, and you are running Windows 95, 98, Me, NT 4.0, or 2000, choose Start ⇨ Run. If you are running Windows NT 3.51 or Windows 3.1, choose File ⇨ Run from the Program Manager.

5. In Windows 95, 98, NT 3.51 or NT 4.0, Me, and 2000 type the following command in the Open text box (where d: is your CD-ROM drive letter):

```
d:\setup.exe.exe
```

6. In Windows 3.1, type the following command at the DOS prompt (where d: is your CD-ROM drive letter):

```
d:\setup.exe
```

7. Press Enter to start the Setup Wizard.

Clean install information

A clean install does not use any of your existing information, so you have more questions to answer during the Setup Wizard than if you had upgraded. As with an upgrade, you have to agree to the License Agreement, and you then need to decide which file system to use. Following those steps, you are asked to select your preferences for the following options:

♦ In the Setup Options window (shown in Figure 1-5) — You can choose your language and accessibility options. You can also choose Advanced options to change the default manner in which setup handles files.

♦ NTFS File system — If the drive you are currently installing is a FAT or FAT32 drive, you can choose to upgrade the drive to NTFS. Choose Yes or No, but if you want to use a dual-boot scenario, choose No.

♦ Dynamic Updates — You are prompted to allow Windows XP to access the Internet in order to check for updated setup files. You should choose to use this option.

After this portion of setup is complete, the automatic process begins and reboots the computer into a DOS-based setup mode. You need to answer some additional questions, such as "Do you want to setup now or enter repair mode." You may be prompted to repair older versions or choose an installation location. Just follow the prompts that appear.

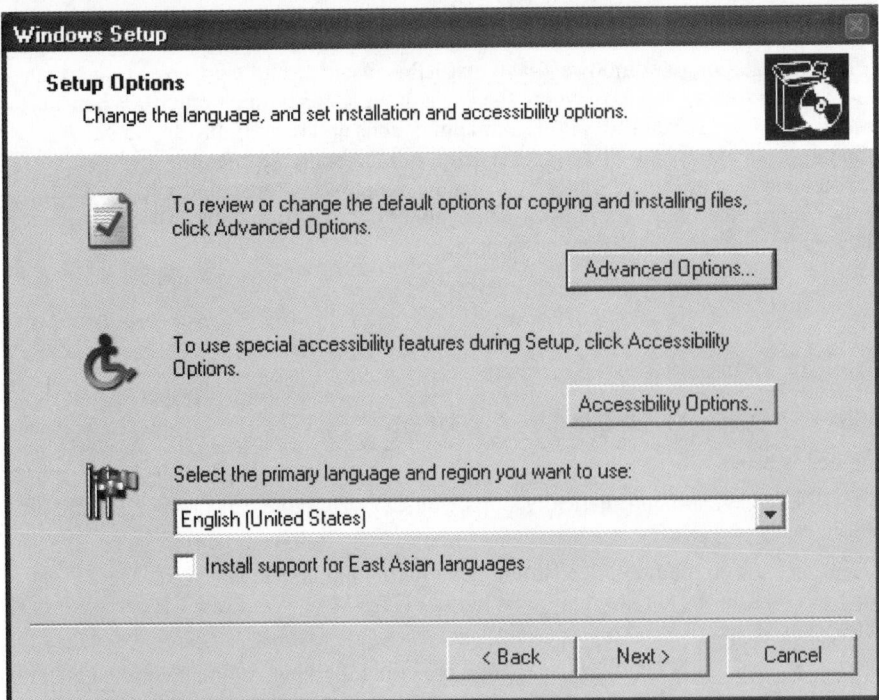

Figure 1-5: Setup Options window

At this point, installation continues without any further assistance from you. As setup nears completion, some additional screens appear once again requesting information. They are as follows:

- Regional and Language Settings — choose region and the language you prefer.

- Enter your name, a computer name, and enter an administrator password. You will need this password to logon to XP for the first time, so remember it!

- Complete the modem dialing information by entering your area code and other requested information.

- Date and Time Settings — Choose the current date and time.

After you enter this information, installation continues. If you have a network adapter card on your computer, the Network Settings window appears, where you can choose typical network settings or manually configure them (you can always make changes later as well). You'll also see a workgroup or domain selection window. If you are not in a domain, just leave the workgroup setting as is. If you are in a Windows 2000/XP domain, enter the required information.

Running Setup from the Command Line

You also can install Windows XP from the command line. You might want to choose this route so that you can customize your installation, or so that you can perform an unattended installation. If you are upgrading from the Windows 2000, Windows NT, or Windows 98/Me command prompt, the syntax of the command-line prompt is as follows (where d: is your CD-ROM drive letter):

```
d:\i386\winnt32.exe {options}
```

TIP: Winnt32.exe can be run from the command prompt or Windows Explorer, within Windows, or the Run line. Winnt.exe can be run only from DOS.

Table 1-2 outlines the command-line switches for the winnt32 setup.

Table 1-2: Command-Line Switches for WINNT32 Setup

Command Line Switch	Explanation
/s:*sourcepath*	Points to the location of the Windows XP installation and CAB files. You can have multiple source parameters, such as when you need to copy files from multiple drives or servers.
/syspart:*drive*	Lets you copy the Setup startup files to an active partition on your hard drive. You can install that drive in another computer so that when that computer starts, Setup resumes with the next step. You must also use the /tempdrive switch if you use the /syspart switch. Example: /syspart:d:
/tempdrive:*drive*	Tells the Setup program to put its temporary files on the specified drive, and then to install on the specified drive.
/copydir:*foldername*	Creates an additional folder within the Windows XP folder. Files within the source folder of the same name will then be copied to the location specified. You can use the new folder to hold custom files. (This switch is used in place of the /r switch.) Example: /copydir:oemfile
/copysource:*foldername*	Creates an additional folder, like /copydir above, but this temporary folder is deleted after setup is complete.
/cmd:*command*	Executes the specified command prior to the final setup step, after the computer restarts the second time. Example: /cmd:special.bat
debug[*n*][:*filename*]	Creates a debug log of the level specified by n. The default level is 2, or Warning. Example: /debug[2][:debug.log]
/i:Dosnet.inf	The filename, without a path, of the setup information file. The default filename is Dosnet.inf.
/x	Prevents setup from creating setup boot floppies.
/unattend	Upgrades your previous version of Windows. All user settings from your previous installation are maintained, which means that no user input is needed during setup.
/unattend[*num*]:*answerfile*	Performs a new installation of Windows XP. Answers to setup questions will be taken from the specified answer file. The value of [*num*] is the number of seconds after setup finishes copying files and the time setup restarts.
/r:*directory*	Adds an additional directory in the directory tree where Windows XP is installed. This can be used multiple times. It creates an empty directory, unlike /copydir:*foldername*.
/e:*command*	Executes the specified command after setup has completed and Windows XP has been installed.
/udf:id [,UDF_file]	An identifier (ID) for setup to use to specify how a Uniqueness Database File (UDF) can change an answer file.

Be Prepared

By now, you should have a computer running a functional Windows XP operating system. You will soon be making changes as you install hardware and software, as well as changing the configuration to fit your working style. Although it is touted as the most stable version of Windows yet, there is still a chance that some changes you make could temporarily render your computer helpless. Accordingly, Windows XP includes the System Restore feature that was first introduced in Windows Me. System Restore is a great tool that can get you out of a number of jams, and you can learn more about it in Chapter 25. You should create an Emergency Repair Disk in Windows XP. The Emergency Repair Disk will help you fix problems with your system files, your Registry, and your hard disk structure. The Emergency Repair Disk is part of the Windows Backup program, shown in Figure 1-6, and is generated using the Automated System Recovery Wizard.

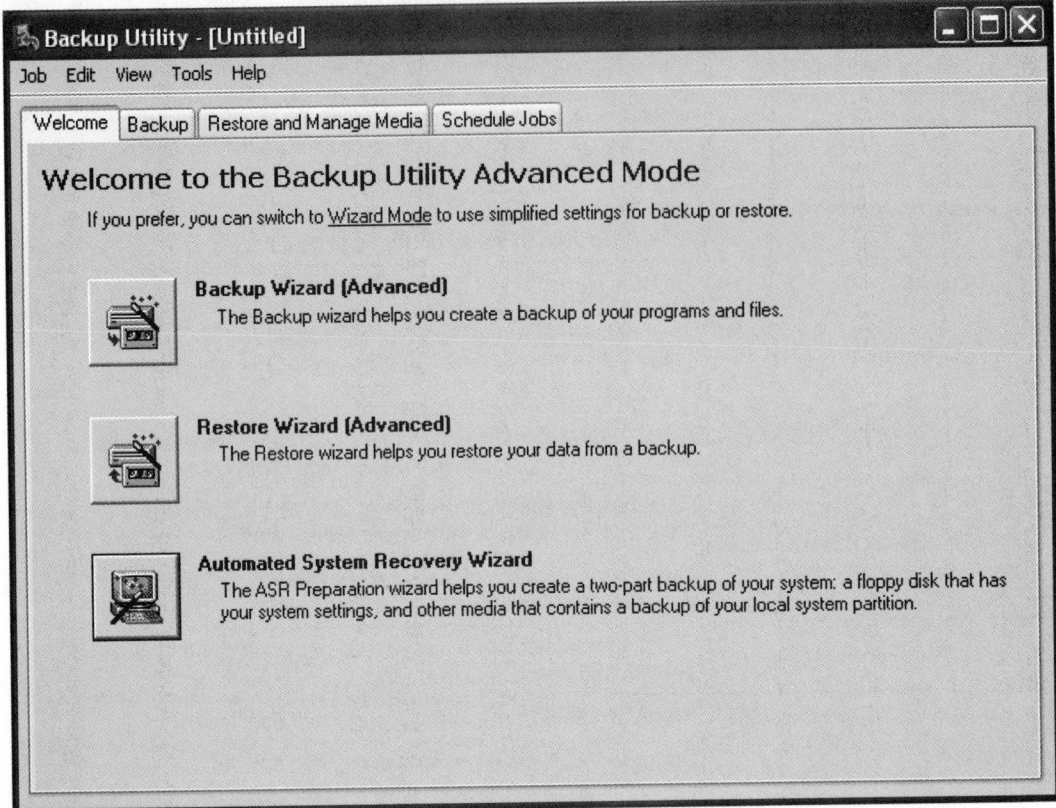

Figure 1-6: The Emergency Repair Disk is part of the Windows Backup program.

The following steps walk you through the Automated System Recovery Preparation Wizard.

STEPS

Automated System Recovery

1. Before you begin, you need a blank, formatted 1.44MB floppy disk in order to create the recovery boot disk and a location to store the backup files (hard drive, CD-ROM, Zip drive, or so on).

2. Choose Start ⇨ All Programs ⇨ Accessories ⇨ System Tools, and then click Backup.

3. The Backup Wizard appears. Click the Advanced link. Then, click the ASR Preparation button on the Welcome tab.

4. Click Next on the wizard Welcome screen.

5. The Backup Destination window appears, as shown in Figure 1-7. Choose a location to create a backup file (such as a tape drive, Zip drive, or so on). Later, you will need a floppy disk.

6. Click Finish. The ASR Preparation Wizard creates a snapshot file of your system and records it to your floppy disk, as you can see in Figure 1-8. The actual backup files are stored in the location you specify and the floppy disk is used to start the system.

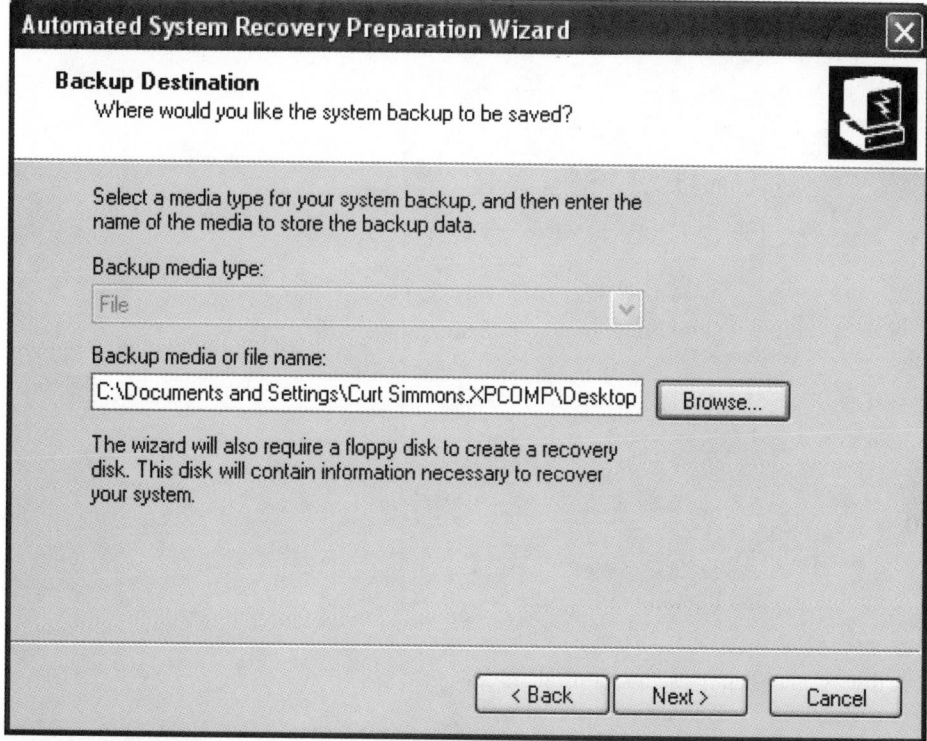

Figure 1-7: Media selection

TIP: If you change your computer's configuration, you will want to run the ASR Preparation Wizard again. The old disk will be able to take you back only to your old configuration, which will no longer be valid.

Solving Setup Problems

Microsoft has included a series of troubleshooting steps to help you with installation issues. They are installed under Start ⇨ Help, but without a successful installation of Windows XP, they won't be much use to you. If you have access to another computer that has a successful Windows XP installation, you can run the Windows Troubleshooter by choosing Start ⇨ Help.

Included with a number of Windows XP hardware and software troubleshooting guides is the System Setup Troubleshooter, which suggests remedies for problems with your Windows XP setup. Figure 1-9 shows the potential problem points for which you might find solutions. (Note: The help system assumes that your computer has passed the System Compatibility Check at the beginning of the setup process.)

TIP: If you are having problems finding the troubleshooter, I'm not surprised. It seems as if Microsoft made the troubleshooter a secret! Open Help and Support and search for Troubleshooters. In the provided list of matches, click List of Troubleshooters to find the System Setup Troubleshooter.

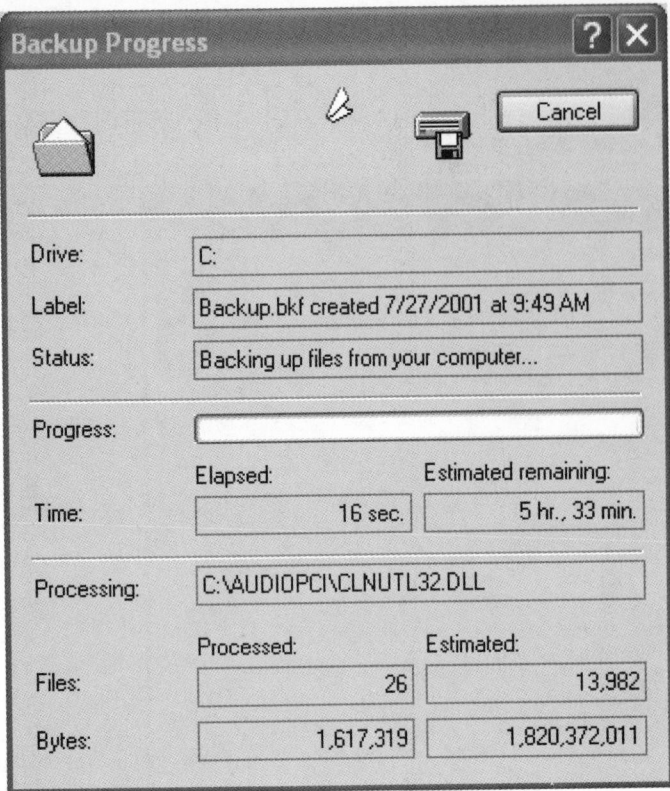

Figure 1-8: ASR Copy Process

Try the steps that follow, and then try again to install after each step.

STEPS

Troubleshooting intermittent problems

1. If you are having intermittent problems when installing Windows XP, the first suggestion is to temporarily disable your system cache memory. The system cache memory creates a reservoir of cached information as installation is taking place, and this cache may be clogging up the system and keeping setup from running. Instructions on how to do this are specific to various computer models, so you should consult your hardware guide or manufacturer for this information.

2. Make sure your RAM modules have the correct specification and that they are correctly installed. (Problems here would have appeared using your previous operating system, too.)

3. Check whether your computer is infected with a boot sector virus.

4. If your system is clean, you might need to add a wait state to your RAM settings. This is typically done through BIOS or CMOS settings, and, again, differs by computer. A wait state forces the RAM, or other system components, into an idle state for a period of time. This enables setup to run without the computer trying to hold setup information in memory, which can essentially clog up the system.

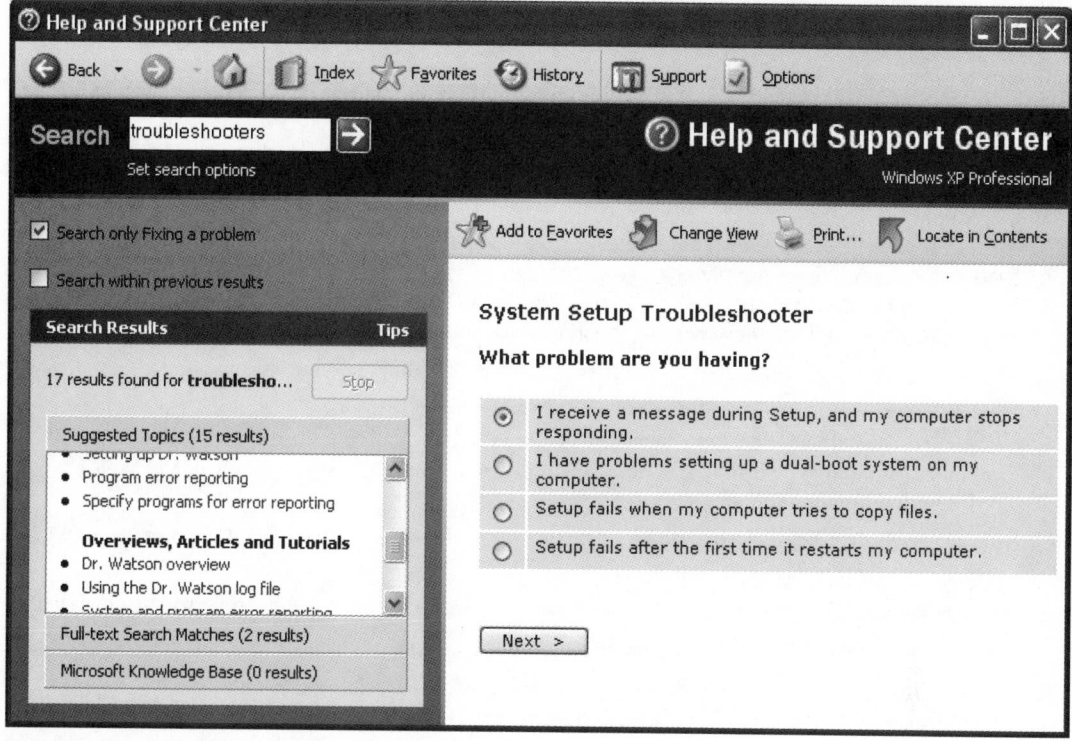

Figure 1-9: Windows XP System Setup Troubleshooter

STEPS

Troubleshooting setup failures when copying files

1. Make sure your hard drive and CD-ROM have the correct drivers, and that they are properly configured. This should be done at the CMOS or BIOS levels, not with your previous operating system's Control Panel application. If you manage these settings at the CMOS or BIOS levels, the settings will stay attached to the hard ware during installation, whereas those settings may be lost if you manage them from a previous operating system (which is currently in the process of being upgraded or removed). You can think of the CMOS or BIOS settings as more a "hard wired" configuration.

2. Make sure that all drive jumper settings are correct. If your drives are connected to the primary IDE channel, and your secondary IDE channel is enabled in your CMOS, move your CD-ROM drive cable to the secondary channel and configure it as a master.

3. If that doesn't work, ensure that there are no hardware conflicts on your system, and check that you are using the correct IDE controller settings in the system BIOS.

4. The next step, if the files still won't copy, is to check whether your system's motherboard, controller, or hard disk has problems with a high-speed data transfer, also called PIO mode. You might need to lower this setting in your CMOS configuration.

5. If you are still having problems, you might need to disable your system cache memory, which may be causing a conflict during Setup.

6. Ensure that your RAM modules are the correct specifications and that they are correctly installed.

7. Try adding a wait state to your RAM, again through your CMOS settings.

8. Make sure that all your drive cables are connected and working properly.

STEPS

Troubleshooting setup failures during questions or after first reboot

1. Make sure your hard drive and CD-ROM have the correct drivers, and that they are properly configured. This should be done at the CMOS or BIOS levels, not with your previous operating system's Control Panel application.

2. Make sure that all drive jumper settings are correct. If your drives are connected to the primary IDE channel, and your secondary IDE channel is enabled in your CMOS, make sure that you move your CD-ROM drive cable to the secondary channel and configure it as a master.

3. If that doesn't work, ensure that there are no hardware conflicts on your system, and check that you are using the correct IDE controller settings in the system BIOS.

4. If setup is still failing, check whether your system's motherboard, controller, or hard disk has problems with a high data-transfer speed or PIO mode. You may have to lower this in your CMOS configuration.

5. If you are still having problems, you might need to disable your system cache memory, which may be causing a conflict during setup.

6. Ensure that your RAM modules are the correct specifications and that they are correctly installed.

7. Check whether your computer is infected with a boot sector virus.

8. If your system is clean, you might need to add a wait state to your RAM settings. This is typically done through BIOS or CMOS settings, and again, differs by computer.

STEPS

Troubleshooting setup failure when looking for the CD-ROM

1. Make sure that your hardware configuration lets you boot from the CD-ROM drive.

2. If it does, you need to check the Windows XP Hardware Compatibility List to make sure your drive and drive controller are supported. If they are not on the list, you need to contact the manufacturer for drivers.

3. If they are supported, make sure your hard drive and CD-ROM have the correct drivers, and that they are properly configured. This should be done at the CMOS or BIOS levels, not with your previous operating system's Control Panel application.

4. Make sure that all drive jumper settings are correct. If your drives are connected to the primary IDE channel, and your secondary IDE channel is enabled in your CMOS, make sure that you move your CD-ROM drive cable to the secondary channel, and then configure it as a master.

5. Check to make sure your CMOS boot order is set correctly. At startup, the CD-ROM should be accessed before the hard drive if you want to boot from it. As a quick test, the CD-ROM's busy light should flicker before your hard drive starts.

6. Ensure that there are no hardware conflicts on your system, and check that you are using the correct IDE controller settings in the system BIOS.

7. If there are no conflicts, check whether your system's motherboard, controller, or hard disk has problems with a high data-transfer speed or PIO mode. You may have to lower this in your CMOS configuration.

8. Check whether your computer is infected with a boot sector virus.

9. Make sure all your cables are connected properly.

Summary

In this chapter, you explored the most common situations in a Windows XP installation. You learned about . . .

♦ The necessary installation preparation steps: hardware requirements, backup, collecting drivers, and so forth

♦ The criteria for determining whether to upgrade or do a clean install

♦ The file system options available in Windows XP

♦ The upgrade process

♦ Performing a clean installation

♦ Running installation from the command line

♦ Using the ASR Preparation Wizard

♦ About some troubleshooting steps

Chapter 2

Advanced Windows XP Installation

In This Chapter

The two branded products of Windows XP — Home and Professional — follow the same installation and setup routine. For the most part, the two operating systems are the same except that Professional has more tools and networking capabilities, as well as administrative tools and features, than the Home edition has. Also, XP Professional contains some advanced setup features that are provided for different types of network installations. The idea is to make the IT professional's job easier if he or she has to install 1000 XP Professional workstations. These tools enable you to automate the process and provide streamlined configurations. If you are not working with XP Home or Professional edition dual-boot configuration or XP Professional in a network environment, these various solutions will not be helpful to you, but if you are, these may just be the track to installing XP efficiently and accurately in your network. However, you'll find some helpful troubleshooting at the end of this chapter that may be use to you. In this chapter, you learn about . . .

- ♦ Dual-boot configurations
- ♦ Using unattended installations
- ♦ Additional advanced installation options
- ♦ The Recovery Console and troubleshooting installations

Installing a Dual-Boot System with Windows XP

A dual-boot computer contains two or more operating systems that are installed in different disk partitions/volumes. (When a "dual-boot" system contains more than two operating systems, it is sometimes called a "multiboot" system. However, for simplicity's sake, I refer to all dual or multiboot systems as dual-boot systems.) During boot, you are given a menu option to boot into the operating system that you want. For example, you might have a dual-boot system with Windows XP and Windows 98, or maybe Windows XP and Linux. The reason, of course, is to use more than one operating system on the same computer instead of having multiple computers that each contains a single operating system.

Why would someone want a dual-boot computer, you might ask? That's good question, and there are some important reasons a dual-boot system might be right for you:

- ♦ **IT testing** — Various power users most definitely want to be able to dual-boot their systems. Some are high-end developers and IS administrators who need to work on a variety of platforms.
- ♦ **Software compatibility** — As you are well aware, one piece of software that works great with one version of Windows may not work with the next. Your only options are to discard the software or to upgrade to a new version. A dual-boot system works around this problem. You can use your older applications with an older operating system so that you don't lose them by moving to a new operating system.

NOTE: Windows XP contains an application compatibility program that may enable you to run older programs that are not compatible with Windows XP. See Chapter 8 to learn more; this may be a better solution than a dual-boot configuration.

◆ **The best of both worlds** — Some people like a dual-boot system because they get to use different operating features instead of being stuck with a single OS.

Most often, dual-boot configurations are used to support two different operating systems and different software. I use Windows 2000 Server and Windows XP Professional on the same computer by using a dual-boot configuration. This configuration works well and enables me to test and work with each operating system without having separate computers. Software compatibility is another important issue. Perhaps you have a custom program that was written for Windows 95. You want to keep using that program, but you also need the power of XP. A dual-boot scenario can help you meet that goal. Keep in mind that you can configure a dual-boot scenario with either version of Windows XP and another version of Windows (or even Linux).

Be forewarned, however: setting up a dual-boot system is not a simple process, and it will take you into a dark part of the Windows forest where the wizards are scarce and help is expensive. Also, if you have an OEM computer, don't expect the technical support line to get you out of dual-boot jam or disaster.

Still, despite the potential for problems and the lack of help, a dual-boot system has a number of advantages. Windows XP can dual-boot with these operating systems:

◆ Windows 2000

◆ Windows NT 4.0

◆ Windows Me

◆ Windows 9x

◆ Windows 3.1 and Windows for Workgroups 3.11

◆ MS-DOS

◆ OS/2

Windows XP also can be dual booted with other operating systems, but only through the use of other companies' products; Windows XP does not provide a way to dual boot between them. Operating systems in this category include:

◆ UNIX

◆ NetWare

◆ Linux

> **CAUTION:** To create a dual-boot system, you need at least two different partitions on your computer's hard drive. These can be configured with Fdisk or with a third-party application such as Partition Magic. Remember that these are advanced options, and if you have an OEM computer (Compaq, Dell, Gateway, HP, and the like), technical support from these companies will not help in the event of problems. Also, you may need to gather drivers for the OEM computer's hardware, which can be more than difficult. Just think carefully and study your options before committing to a dual-boot scenario.

Creating volumes

In a dual-boot environment, Windows XP can have either its own hard drive or have its own disk volume/partition. Therefore, the first step in the dual-boot installation process is to decide where on your hard drive (or its primary partitions) you want your operating systems to be installed. You need to use Fdisk or Partition Magic to create the partitions. If your system has multiple hard drives and currently runs Windows XP, 2000, or NT, you can use the Disk Management program included with these operating systems to create the volumes needed. See Chapter 3 to learn more about disk management.

> **TIP:** Make sure the partitions are not too small. For XP, you should allow at least 1 GB for the partition. Also, some programs — even if installed on another drive or partition — might insist on installing some files into the Windows XP directory.

Choosing a file system

After you determine where you want to install Windows XP and your other OS(s), the next step is to decide what file system to use.

In general, to obtain the full benefits of Windows XP security and file compression, you need to use the NTFS file system. However, there are other factors to consider when you are setting up a dual-boot system.

The biggest factor you need to consider involves backward compatibility. If you use the NTFS file system — which the Windows XP Setup program will upgrade to NTFS 5 — only Windows 2000 and XP will be able to read files created on that partition. Windows NT 4.0 Service Pack 4 or later will be able to read files on NTFS 5, but earlier operating systems will not.

CROSS REFERENCE: You can learn more about file system differences in Chapter 3.

Here are some general file system guidelines:

♦ If you want to dual boot between Windows XP and MS-DOS, Windows 3.1, Windows 3.11, OS/2, Windows 9x or Me, Windows NT 3.51, or Windows NT 4.0 with Service Pack 2 or earlier, then you must use FAT16 or FAT32. In order to use FAT32, you can't use any operating system earlier than Windows 95 OSR2. Your partition must be 2GB or less in size.

♦ If you want to dual boot between Windows XP and Windows 95 OSR2, Windows 98, or Windows Me, you should use FAT32. You need a hard drive of at least 512MB.

♦ If you will be dual booting between Windows XP and Windows 2000, you should use NTFS.

TIP: If you do convert to NTFS 5, you cannot go back to any of the earlier file systems without first backing up all your files, reformatting the partition, and then restoring all your files from your backup.

SECRET: If you have an NTFS file system, earlier versions of Windows (such as Windows 95 OSR1) on a dual-boot system will not be able to access the NTFS partitions of their own local hard drive. But, if you have set up a peer-to-peer computer network between a Windows XP PC and a PC running an earlier version of Windows (such as Windows 95 OSR1), the older version of Windows *will* be able to access the files on the NTFS portion of the Windows XP PC's hard drive over the network because of the operating system's network redirector software. You can learn more about peer-to-peer networking in Chapter 20.

Advantages of NTFS

If you use either FAT or FAT32 instead of NTFS 5, you will not be able to use the following Windows XP features:

♦ Increased security settings. Under NTFS, you can assign permissions to individual files and folders.

♦ Recovery log of disk activities. According to Microsoft, users should rarely need to run any disk repair program on an NTFS volume.

♦ Flexible formatting options, volume extensions, striped volumes, encryption, volume extensions without restart, disk quotas, distributed link tracking, mount points, and full text and property indexing.

Advantages of FAT

Of course, the major advantage to FAT16 and FAT32 is that they are the only file structures the older operating systems understand. Also, on a smaller hard drive, FAT can provide faster performance, both because the FAT file structure is simpler, and because the FAT folder size is smaller for an equal number of files.

Dual-boot considerations

There are many variables to consider when contemplating a dual-boot configuration. Table 2-1 lists some of the dual-boot issues that might affect you, depending on your situation and needs.

Table 2-1: Dual-Boot Considerations

Factor	Considerations
Partitions	Each operating system should ideally have its own drive or disk partition, and the operating system boot files normally must be located on the first physical hard drive in order to be bootable.
Applications	Because dual-booting requires a clean installation of your applications under Windows XP, you need to reinstall all your applications afterward.
Installation order	If your system is to be configured with MS-DOS or Windows 95 and Windows XP, you should install Windows XP last to avoid overwriting important XP files. Generally, you want to install dual-boot operating systems in the chronological order of their creation, except in the case of OS/2, which must be installed last.
File system	Your choice of file systems (FAT, FAT32, or NTFS) will be determined by your mix of operating systems.
Existing dual-boot systems	If you plan to add Windows XP to a system that is already set up to dual-boot between MS-DOS and OS/2, the Windows XP Setup program will configure your system so that you can dual boot between Windows XP and the operating system you most recently used before you ran Windows XP setup. If you are already dual-booting with other operating systems such as Windows 98 and Windows 2000 you must have a different installation volume/partition in order to add Windows XP to the dual-boot configuration.
Compressed drives	Windows XP can be installed on a compressed drive only if it uses the NTFS file compression utility. If you plan to dual boot with Windows 95 or 98, you don't have to decompress DriveSpace or DoubleSpace volumes, but the compressed volumes won't be available while you are running Windows XP. Also, Windows XP cannot be installed on a DriveSpace or DoubleSpace volume.
Hardware settings	Microsoft warns that the first time you use Windows 95 or 98, it might reconfigure your hardware settings, which might cause problems with Windows XP. More than likely, you will experience device conflict problems.
Application sharing	For applications to be able to run under both operating systems, they must be installed in each operating system. If you want to preserve settings in an application across operating systems, it is recommended that you reinstall each application under each operating system into the same folder. Of course, installing applications under each operating system consumes a lot of disk space because you have the same application installed over and over; that's something to be aware of.

Dual-boot scenarios

Each possible Windows XP dual-boot scenario has its own tricks and wrinkles, as you'll see below. Before you begin, though, I urge you to prepare for the unexpected.

You should make sure you have good backups of all your data. It's also a very good idea to have a Windows XP startup floppy disk on hand so that you can boot the PC if your hard drive gets toasted. For more information on creating an emergency boot disk, see Chapter 1.

SECRET: If your hard disk has partitions containing Windows XP, Windows 2000, Windows NT, Windows 98 or 95, Windows 3.x, DOS, or OS/2, you can choose which operating system your PC boots up to by changing the active partition.

How does dual booting work in Windows XP?

The dual-boot function in Windows XP is managed by `Bootsect.dos`. This hidden, read-only system file is recreated each time the Windows XP Setup program is run.

When you install Windows XP on a *x*86-based computer, Windows XP copies the boot sector for the active partition of the computer to the file `Bootsect.dos`. Windows XP Setup then replaces the boot sector on the active partition with its own boot sector.

When you start your computer and Windows XP is on the active partition in a multiboot system, Windows XP automatically starts the NT Boot Loader (NTLDR). The Boot Loader enables you to choose between installed operating systems. The NT Boot Loader checks the entries in the `boot.ini` file and presents that information to you in a menu where you can choose the operating system that you want. You can also edit `boot.ini` to meet your needs, and I'll explore that later in the chapter.

Booting from the root

To boot into Windows XP, Windows XP's system partition (which contains all the files necessary to load Windows XP — `Boot.ini`, `Bootsect.dos`, and `Ntdetect.com`) must be located on the active partition of the computer's first hard drive.

To install and load one or more additional operating systems on your *x*86-based PC, you must change the active partition so that each OS's partition is the active partition at the time of installation.

Use Windows XP's Computer Management snap-in (see Figure 2-1), which you can access through the Administrative Tools folder in Control Panel, to designate a new active partition.

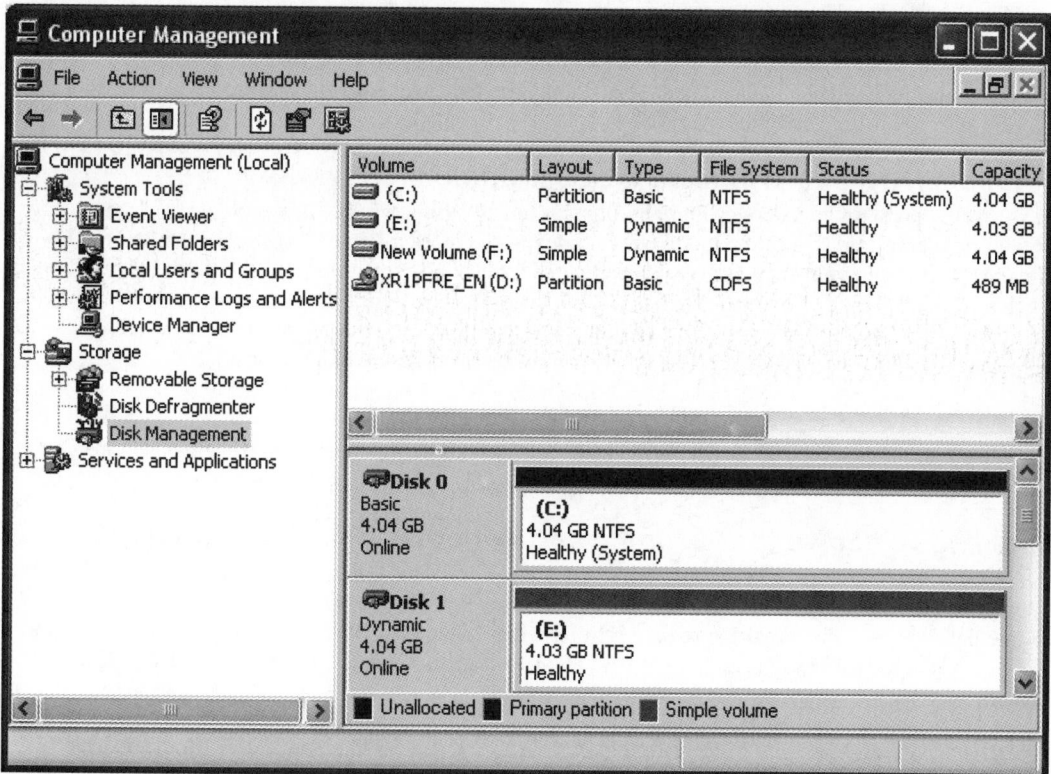

Figure 2-1: The Computer Management snap-in

STEPS

Using the Disk Management snap-in to set the active partition

1. Choose Start ⇨ Control Panel. Open Administrative tools and open Computer Management.

2. Expand Storage in the left pane so that you can see Disk Management.

3. In Disk Management snap-in, click a logical drive or primary partition.

4. Right-click the desired partition and click Mark As Active.

> **SECRET:** You cannot mark a logical partition as active. There can be only one active partition per disk. Also, if your Windows XP computer uses dynamic volumes, you cannot mark dynamic volumes as active unless you reconvert the dynamic disk back to basic.

The only problem with this method is that you need to be running Windows XP to use it. If you can't run Windows XP, you can use the MS-DOS Fdisk.exe program to accomplish the same thing.

STEPS

Using DOS Fdisk to set the active partition

1. Boot your system to the MS-DOS prompt by using a startup disk that contains Fdisk.exe.

2. Type **a:fdisk** at the DOS prompt and press Enter.

3. Type the numeral **2** in the Enter Choice box.

4. Make sure one of the columns has an A in the Status column, indicating that it is the active partition.

5. To change the active — or system — partition, type the number of the partition you want to set as the active partition, and then repeat Step 4.

Installing DOS and Windows XP dual-boot

Do yourself a favor and install MS-DOS before you install Windows XP; if you do, you'll find getting the dual-boot configuration set up much easier. Use the steps described above to change one of the primary partitions on your hard drive to the active partition, and then install MS-DOS to that partition as directed by your MS-DOS manual. Then, install Windows XP to another partition on your hard drive, which the Windows XP Setup program will change to be the active or boot partition as described above. Any partitions you want MS-DOS to be able to see must be formatted as FAT or FAT32.

Installing Windows 3.x and Windows XP dual-boot

Again, it's best to install the older OS, Windows 3.x, first into a separate partition. Any partitions you want Windows 3.x to be able to see must be formatted as FAT.

Installing Windows 95, 98, or Me and Windows XP dual-boot

You can dual boot Windows 9x and Me with Windows XP. This configuration is rather easy and works great, but if you want any of the 9x/Me operating systems to be able to access files on the XP volume/partition, you must make sure the partition where you install Windows 95 or 98 is formatted to FAT16 for Windows 95 OSR1, and either FAT16 or FAT32 for Windows 95 OSR2 and Windows 98/Me.

Installing Windows NT or Windows 2000 and Windows XP dual-boot

Like Windows 9x/Me, you can install Windows NT or Windows 2000 to dual boot with Windows XP. The process works in the same way, but you can use NTFS on your partitions because Windows 2000 and XP use the same version of NTFS, and Windows NT 4 can be upgraded to NTFS 5. However, if you want to dual boot between XP and NT 3.x (which you probably don't), you'll need to use FAT32.

Installing OS/2 and Windows XP dual-boot

Here's another place where the general rules don't apply. Even though OS/2 is one of the oldest OSs, you should install it last in a dual-boot installation sequence because OS/2 may give you some volume/partition problems if the other operating system(s) are not installed first. Thus, if you want to be able to boot to Windows 95, Windows XP, and OS/2, you'd install Windows 95 first, Windows XP next, and OS/2 last.

Installing UNIX, NetWare, or Linux and Windows XP dual-boot

The same general rule applies here: install UNIX or another non-Microsoft operating system in a separate partition from the one that contains Windows XP. You can then use either the other operating system's boot manager, or a third-party partitioning and boot management tool (such PowerQuest's Partition Magic, IBM's Boot Manager, or V Communications' System Commander) to choose the partition you want to boot to. Be careful, though. If your dual-boot environment includes any NTFS 5 partitions, make sure that the third-party tool can handle NTFS 5.

Windows XP Setup program and dual-boot

You've installed one or more operating systems on one or more partitions of your hard drive, which you make active as needed. Now, you want to install Windows XP. Piece of cake.

You can designate the partition where you want to install Windows XP as the active partition, as discussed earlier. Setup and installation is one of the places in which Microsoft made a great effort to make things easier — and it shows.

When the Windows XP Setup program runs, it checks your existing hard drive configuration. Depending on what it finds, you might have these options during setup:

♦ If Setup finds an unpartitioned hard drive, you will be given the opportunity to create and size a partition for Windows XP.

♦ If the hard drive has a partition with insufficient room for Windows XP, but there is enough unpartitioned disk space available, you will be able to use the unpartitioned space for the installation.

♦ If the hard drive has a partition that is big enough for Windows XP, you can use that.

♦ You can delete an existing partition to create more unpartitioned disk space for a Windows XP installation.

CAUTION: Deleting a partition will erase any data on that partition. Make sure you move or back up any data that you do not want to lose before deleting a partition.

TIP: During Windows XP setup, create only the partition you need for Windows XP. After it has been installed, you can use the Windows XP Disk Management snap-in to make changes or to create new partitions.

Installing — and reinstalling — your applications

After you've successfully installed two or more operating systems, you get to reinstall all your applications — not just once, but once for each operating system you have installed. Depending on the operating systems you have chosen, you may need to reinstall your Office applications under each operating system. This means you will have more than one copy of the application that you can run with the current dual-boot system. Because operating systems store applications and configure them differently, you are likely to have problems if you install an application under one system and try to access it from the other operating system. In some cases, however, this actually will work fine, and it all depends on the application and which operating systems are you are dual booting. As you can see, trial and error may have to be your friend to get things working the way that you want.

SECRET: Here's one the folks in Redmond find very restful. If you install a Windows program to a common folder on a dual-boot Windows XP computer, you can run the exact same program under different versions of Windows on the same computer in some cases. This option enables you to install the application only one time, but I can't promise that it will work. Your are much less likely to have problems if you are dual booting later versions of Windows, such as 2000 and Me.

Editing Boot.ini

After you have your dual-boot system configured, you see a boot menu that appears when you start the computer. This enables you to choose the operating system that you want to boot. However, what if you are given only 2 seconds to choose, or what if the operating system you use most is second in the list, which means it is never selected by default?

You can change these settings by editing a hidden attribute file called `boot.ini`. `Boot.ini` is so hidden that you can't even see it when folder options are set to "show hidden files and folders," but you can easily open `boot.ini` with Notepad by simply choosing Start ⇨ Run and typing **C:\boot.ini**. In Windows XP, however, there is even an easier way of making these changes. Access System Properties in Control Panel, or right-click My Computer and click Properties, then click the Advanced tab and click the Settings button under Startup and Recovery. The Startup and Recovery window appears, as shown in Figure 2-2.

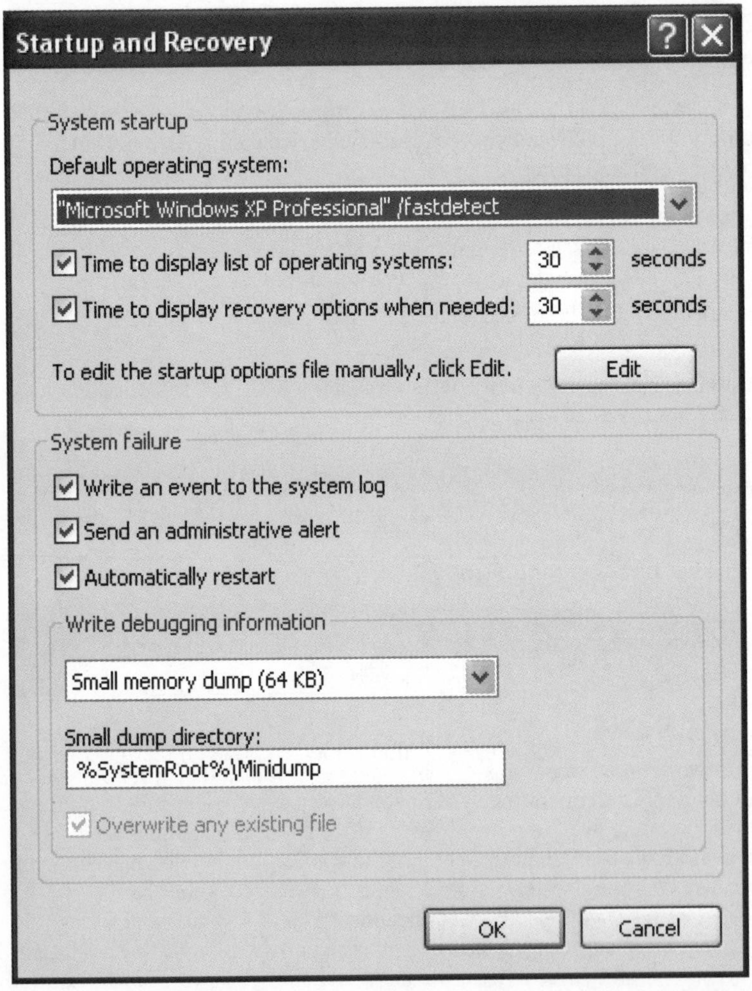

Figure 2-2: Startup and Recovery

The System startup section enables you to make changes to boot.ini without dealing with the Notepad version. Under the default operating system drop-down menu, choose which operating system is the default one (the one that boots if you make no selection on the boot selection menu). Typically, the time to display the operating system menu, as well recovery options such as safe mode, is 30 seconds. You can change these values as you like. Essentially, changing these settings edits boot.ini for you. However, you can click the Edit button to open boot.ini in Notepad, as shown in Figure 2-3, so that you can make additional changes.

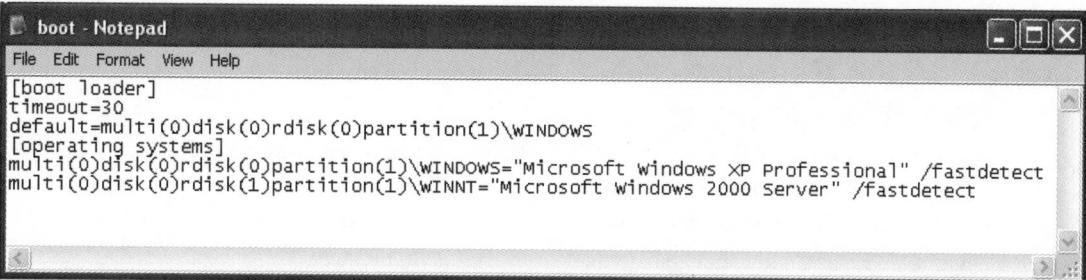

Figure 2-3: Boot.ini

CAUTION: Be very careful when editing boot.ini. Incorrect changes made to this file may stop Windows from booting at all, so proceed with caution. Make sure you know what you are doing before you manually make changes to this file.

As Figure 2-3 shows, my system boots Windows XP Professional and Windows 2000 Server. You can see in the file that my default loading system is Windows XP and that I have a timeout value of 30 seconds. I can manually change these settings in this file and save them, or I can make the same changes more easily and safely on the Startup and Recovery tab.

A location string, known an Advanced RISC Computing (ARC) path, represents each operating system. This path points to the boot partition of the operating system that is used to start the booting of that particular system. IDE, EIDE, ESDI, and some SCSI disks use the following path to access the boot partition:

```
multi(0)disk(0)rdisk(0)partition(1)\Windows  (or WINNT)
```

If multiple SCSI disks are in use, the path appears as follows:

```
scsi(0)disk(0)rdisk(0)partition(1)\Windows  (or WINNT)
```

In case you are terribly curious about ARC paths, here's what the pieces mean:

- ◆ **Multi** — This parameter identifies the disk controller.

- ◆ **Disk** — The disk parameter is not used with multi and should always be 0. When used with SCSI, it is the SCSI ID of the disk.

- ◆ **Rdisk** — The original number of the controller starting with zero. In the SCSI form, it is the logical unit number of the disk.

- ◆ **Partition** — Identifies the partition on which the boot partition is located. The numbering always begins with 1.

Installing the Windows XP Resource Kit

The Windows XP Resource Kit contains a collection of management tools, support utilities, and documents that can help you manage and configure your Windows XP computer. You'll find the Resource Kit on your installation CD-ROM. It is not installed during the default Windows XP installation, so you need to install it separately after you have Windows XP up and running.

Among other things, the Resource Kit contains DiskProbe and Setup Manager (which eases the task of unattended Windows XP installations), which is explored later in this chapter. The general tool groups in the Resource Kit are Deployment, Diagnostics, Computer Management, Network Management, and Storage Management.

To install the Resource Kit, follow these steps:

STEPS

Installing the Resource Kit

1. Start your Windows XP computer.
2. Insert the Windows XP CD-ROM into the CD-ROM drive and wait for the AutoRun screen. If the AutoRun screen doesn't appear, see Step 6.
3. When the AutoRun screen appears, click Perform Additional Tasks, and then click Browse this CD.
4. Using the Browse window, navigate to the \Support\Tools folder.
5. Click SupTools.msi, and then follow the installation instructions.
6. If the AutoRun screen doesn't appear after you insert the CD-ROM, choose Start ⇨ Run.
7. Type the following command into the Open text box on the Run dialog box (where D: is your CD-ROM drive letter):

```
D:\SUPPORT\TOOLS\SUPTOOLS.MSI
```

The setup program will install the Resource Kit tools onto your hard drive (see Figure 2-4). The default installation directory is \Program Files\Resource Kit, and the tools will occupy about 8MB of disk space. It will also add shortcuts to your Start ⇨ Programs menu.

SECRET: If you have problems installing the tools, copy the entire \Support\Reskit\ folder to a temporary folder on your hard drive, and then run setup from your hard drive.

The tools that come with the Resource Kit are accessed through the Microsoft Management Console (MMC), which is a shell program that you use to manage various utility and configuration programs that either come with Windows XP or that can be added later.

CROSS-REFERENCE: You can learn all about the MMC in Chapter 7.

Unattended Installation

One of the greatest weaknesses of Windows NT 4, the immediate predecessor of Windows 2000, was the headache it gave system administrators trying to install it across extensive networks. With Windows 2000 Server and now Windows XP Professional, unattended installations are now much easier and actually, well, unattended.

So what was the problem with NT networks? With Windows NT 4, you had to individually run setup on each machine on a network, which consumed 45 to 60 minutes of IS time for each machine to which you installed NT or upgraded to NT.

Among the endearing qualities of Windows NT 4 was the fact that every time you added new hardware you had to rerun every service pack you'd ever applied to a machine! Say what? (Well, actually, the system administrators I know said a lot more than *what*.)

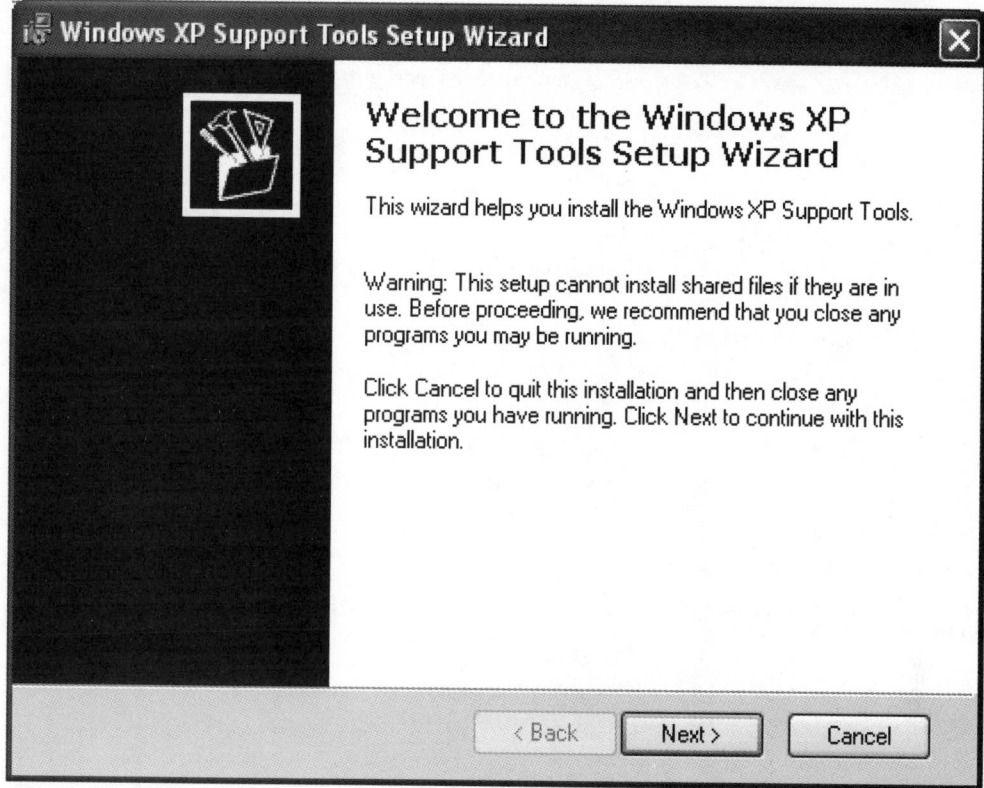

Figure 2-4: Starting the Resource Kit installation

Some of these expressions were apparently communicated back to Microsoft, because Windows 2000 offered a much richer array of automated installation tools, which are also available in Windows XP:

♦ Fully automated installation scripts with Setup Manager

♦ Disk imaging with System Preparation Tool

♦ Remote Installation Server

♦ Electronic software distribution with Systems Management Server 2.0

To use these tools, you need to extract the Deploy.cab file found on the Windows XP installation CD-ROM. It is important to note that some of these options are available only when used in conjunction with Windows 2000 Server and are designed for widespread Windows XP deployment. To open these tools, follow these steps:

STEPS

Installing Deployment Tools

1. Start your Windows XP computer.

2. Create a new folder in a desired location on your hard drive and name it **Deployment**.

3. Open the Windows XP installation CD-ROM and navigate to Support\Tools.

4. Locate the Deploy.cab icon, as shown in Figure 2-5.

Figure 2-5: Deploy.cab contains deployment tools.

5. Double-click the Deploy icon, then choose Edit ⇨ Select All.

6. Drag the selected items to the folder on the hard drive you created. The tools now appear in this folder.

Automatic installation by scripting

One of the best deployment features is the fully scriptable installation now available through the Setup Manager Wizard shown in Figure 2-6.

During an installation, the Windows XP setup routine poses several questions to you, the user. You answer the questions and Windows XP installs the system based on your responses. Setup Manager enables you to answer those questions to file, then install Windows XP so that the answers it needs are accessed from this file. This feature provides a totally hands-off installation procedure. That may not sound like much, but imagine if you had to install 1000 computers!

So, answer files are used to answer questions during Setup. With an answer file, you can provide all of the "answers" setup needs, and you can even provide information about hardware, such as sound cards. Better still, the Windows XP Setup program won't abort if a peripheral such as a modem doesn't install properly.

The Windows XP Setup Manager Wizard walks you through the process of creating an answer file without requiring you to actually write any script yourself. Answer files can be used to both upgrade and create new systems.

Figure 2-6: Windows XP's Setup Manager Wizard automates the creation of answer files.

By creating automated installation scripts with answer files, system administrators can avoid having to physically send a technician to every desktop to spend as long as an hour there.

STEPS

Using Setup Manager to create an answer file

1. Start the Setup Manager from the folder you created for the `Deploy.cab` tools. Click Next on the Welcome screen.

2. Choose Create a new answer file. You also can choose to edit an existing answer file, or you can create an answer file that duplicates the settings of the XP PC you are now using to run the Setup Manager.

3. Choose whether the answer file is for an unattended installation, Sysprep Installation, or Remote Installation Service by selecting the correct the radio button. For these steps, I chose the unattended installation option. Click Next.

4. Choose the Platform (Windows XP), and then click Next.

5. Select the level of user interaction desired, as shown in Figure 2-7. The user interaction levels available are as follows:

- **Provide defaults** — This option provides the default setup options so that the user can review them. In other words, this option is not fully unattended because you still have to "ok" what setup is doing.

- **Fully automated** — Setup does not prompt the user for any answers; everything is taken from the answer file.

- **Hide pages** — All answers are taken from the answer file, and the setup wizard screens do not even appear to the user.

- **Read only** — This option shows the setup pages, but users cannot interrupt and change settings that have been configured in the answer file.

- **GUI attended** — Using this option, the text-based portion of setup is unattended, but the GUI portion remains the same (which is barely any different than setup would be without any answer file).

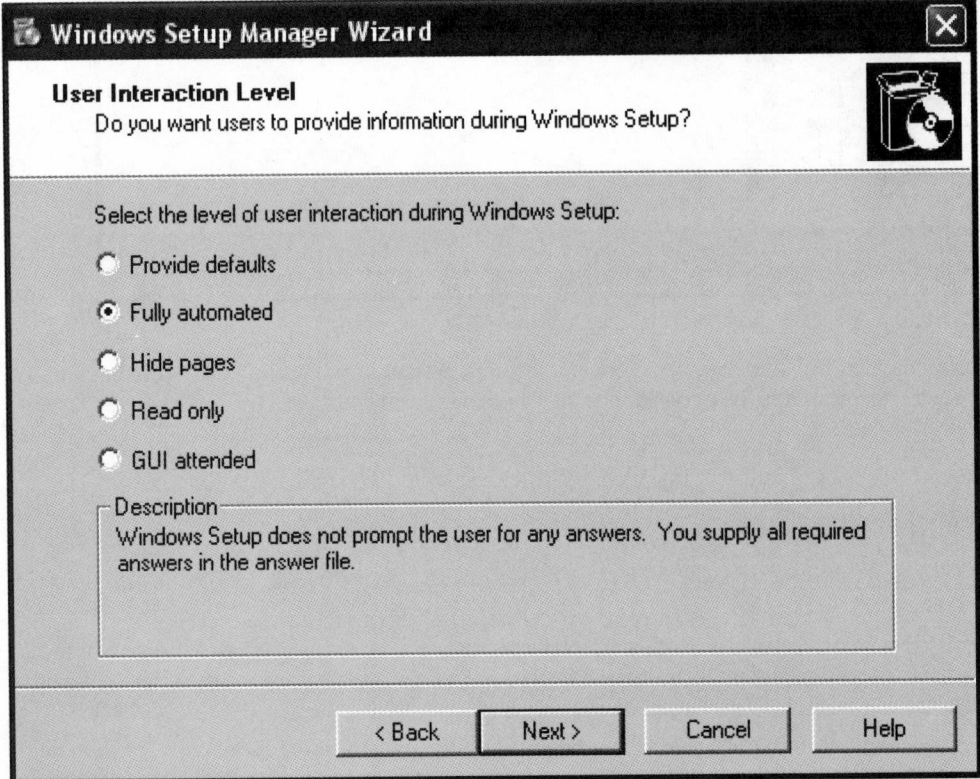

Figure 2-7: User Interaction Level

6. The Distribution Folder window appears. Choose whether to create or modify a distribution folder or to install from CD-ROM. The distribution folder option copies the XP installation CD-ROM contents to the folder. Make your selection and click Next.

7. Accept the end user license agreement and click Next.

8. As Figure 2-8 shows, the Window changes in order to customize the software. You can respond to each option by clicking Next, or you can just navigate through the tree structure on the left side of the window. As you can see, the options presented here are the same options that appear during a typical setup, except that you are answering the questions in advance. Complete the setup options as desired. Once you are done, click Finish, and then note where the unattended.txt file will be created.

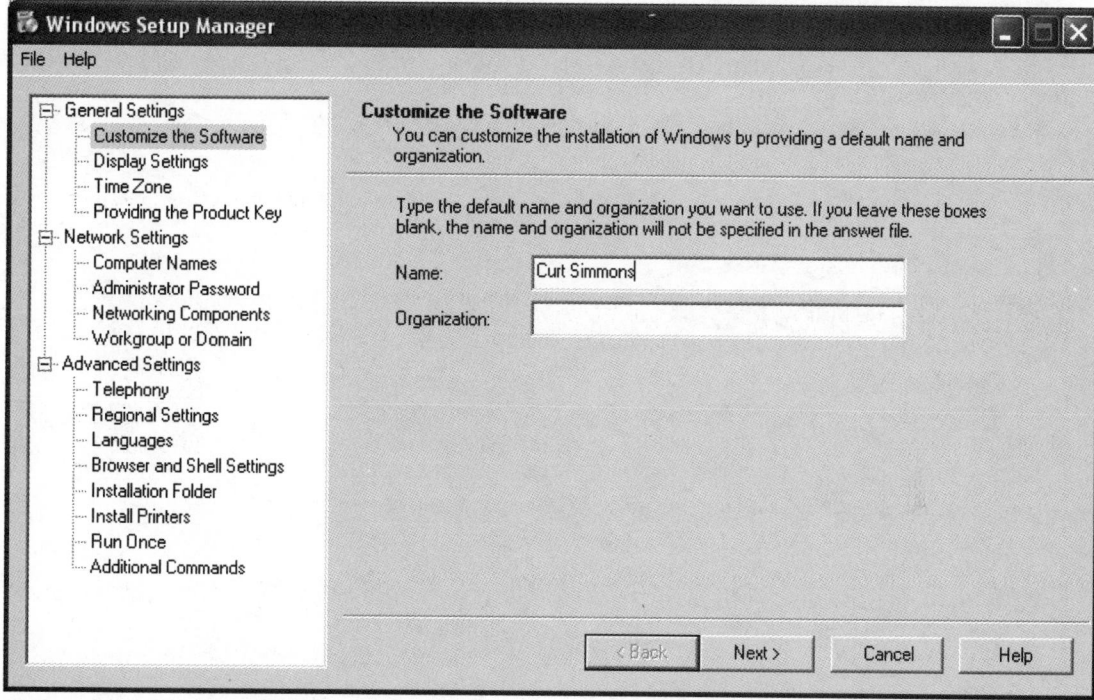

Figure 2-8: Customization window

To perform an unattended installation of Windows XP, you would type the following command:

```
winnt[32] /unattend:<answer file> /s:<install source> [/syspart:<target drive>]
```

where the parameters are as listed in Table 2-2.

Table 2-2: Unattended Install Parameters

Parameter	Explanation
`<answer file>`	The file containing the answers to the installation questions.
`<install source>`	The location of the Windows XP installation files.
`/syspart`	This copies all of the boot and temporary files to a target drive and then marks the target as active. You use this switch if the target drive is to be duplicated and then put into another computer as the primary drive.

Obviously, your answer file must be carefully constructed so that it supplies the correct answers to installation questions. A sample answer file called unattend.txt can be found in the \I386 folder on the Windows XP CD-ROM.

A sample file uses the following format:

```
; Sample Unattended Setup Answer File
;
; This file contains information about how to automate the installation
; or upgrade of Windows NT Workstation and Windows NT Server so that the
; Setup program runs without requiring user input.
;
; For information on how to use this file, read the appropriate sections
; of the Windows NT 5.0 Resource Kit.
[Unattended]
Unattendmode = FullUnattended
OemPreinstall = NO
TargetPath = WINNT
Filesystem = LeaveAlone
[UserData]
FullName = "Your User Name"
OrgName = "Your Organization Name"
ComputerName = "COMPUTER_NAME"
[GuiUnattended]
TimeZone = "004"
; Sets the Admin Password to NULL
AdminPassword = *
; Turn AutoLogon on
AutoLogon = Yes
;For Server installs
[LicenseFilePrintData]
AutoMode = "PerServer"
AutoUsers = "0"
[GuiRunOnce]
; List the programs that you want to launch when the machine is logged into for
the first time
; "Notepad %WINDIR%\Setuperr.log"
[Display]
BitsPerPel = 4
XResolution = 800
YResolution = 600
VRefresh = 70
[Networking]
; When set to YES, setup will install default networking components. The
components to be set are
; TCP/IP, File and Print Sharing, and the Client for Microsoft Networks.
InstallDefaultComponents = YES
[Identification]
JoinWorkgroup = Workgroup
```

Automatic installation by disk imaging

The System Preparation Tool (also in `Deploy.cab`) provides for the use of the same disk image across multiple Windows XP machines — even where the hardware is not uniform. The reason that disk image deployment can work across a relatively heterogeneous network is that the Windows XP Setup program automatically runs the process of detecting and installing hardware after the operating system files have been copied to the target machine.

The great thing about System Preparation is that it enables you to install one machine, configure the desired settings, install the desired applications, and then make an "image" of that installation that can be copied and installed on other machines. In both large and small networks, the result is saved installation time and systems that have the same configuration. In the past, this kind of disk imaging was a problem because each Windows NT computer has a unique security identifier (SID). An image would copy the SID and install the same SID on each machine, which would not work in a Microsoft network.

That problem has been alleviated with `Sysprep.exe`, a tool first introduced in Windows 2000. `Sysprep` generates a unique SID for each installation right after the imaging has been done on the new machine. A minisetup program runs (about 5 minutes) that that generates the SID and finishes the installation. This all sounds great and it is, but there are three serious caveats that you must consider:

- ♦ First, the machines that you are copying the image to must have the same drive controls, hardware abstraction layers, and BIOS versions. Although differing sound cards, video cards, and other types of hardware are unimportant because they are detected and installed after setup, the imaging process essentially dumps the contents of the source computer's drive/volume onto another computer, and unless the drive controls, system hardware, abstraction layers, and BIOS configuration are the same, you will have trouble. So, you can see that `Sysprep` is great for installing to computers that are basically identical, but not for installing computers that have different hardware standards and are created by different vendors.

- ♦ `Sysprep` is simply a preparation tool. It prepares the drive for imaging, generates the image, and runs the minisetup routine. It does not actually provide the disk duplication process. For that, you'll need a third party product such as PowerQuest's Drive Image or Symantec's Norton Ghost. Without one of these third-party applications to actually perform the imaging, `Sysprep` is useless.

- ♦ Some security settings on your source computer may be modified during the `Sysprep` configuration, so make sure you want to create the drive image before running the utility. If your source computer has already joined a Windows 2000 domain, it will need to rejoin the domain because `Sysprep` will remove the SID from the machine. Any new SID must rejoin the domain.

> **CAUTION:** The only way to make sure that disk image deployment of Windows XP will work is to rigorously test it beforehand. There can be many unexpected pitfalls. For instance, the mass storage controller on both the master and the target images must be the same. You'll come to grief if one PC has a Symbios Logic controller and the other has an Adaptec controller.

Running Sysprep.exe

Once you are sure that `Sysprep` is the tool you need to install a group of Windows XP computers and you have third-party software that can manage that actual drive imaging, you are ready to use `Sysprep`. On the source computer, install and configure Windows XP and install any desired applications that you want imaged as well.

If you haven't already done so, open the `Deploy.cab` folder found in `Support\Tools` folder on your installation CD-ROM and copy all of the contents to a desired folder on your computer's hard drive.

> **SECRET:** `Sysprep.exe` requires the `SetupCL` utility, also found in the `Deploy.cab` folder. It is important that you copy all of the cab files to your local computer's folder in order for `Sysprep` to function correctly.

After you have completed these actions, you are ready to run the `Sysprep` utility. The following steps walk you through this process.

STEPS

Running Sysprep.exe

1. In the folder in which you extracted the `Deploy.cab` files, double-click `Sysprep`. Click OK to the message that appears telling you that security settings on the computer may be modified.

2. The System Preparation Tool window appears, as shown in Figure 2-9. After you have finished testing the system and have finished installing applications, click the Reseal button, which will clean up the computer and prepare it for imaging. This action regenerates a SID on the next reboot, which is necessary only if you plan on imaging after shutdown. You can avoid the new SID generation by clicking the NoSIDGen check box option. After you have resealed the computer, you are ready to begin the drive preparation. Open Sysprep again and click the Factory button to begin the drive image creation. Your computer will reboot.

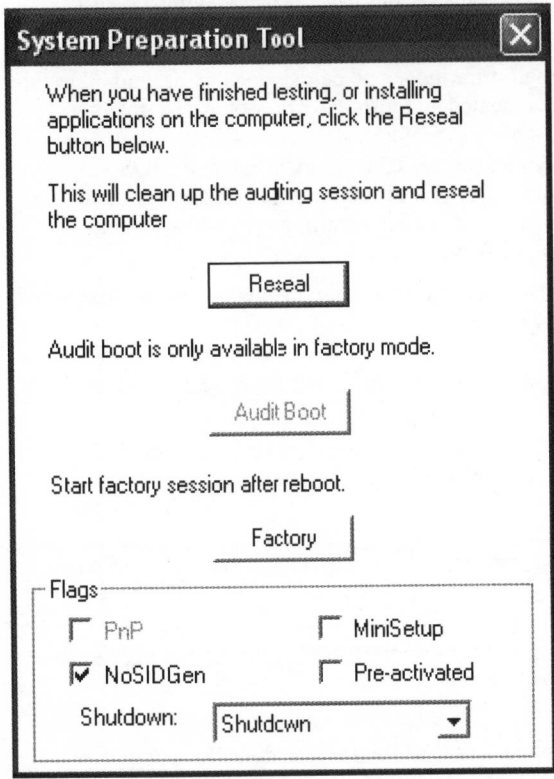

Figure 2-9: Sysprep.exe

3. After rebooting, use your third-party imaging software to create the drive image. When you run the image on the target computer, minisetup will run and assign a SID and ask the user for basic setup information. This process takes about 5 minutes. Once complete, the Sysprep folder and its contents are deleted and the computer is rebooted.

Creating an answer file for Sysprep

You can also create an answer file for the minisetup portion of Sysprep for a completely hands-off imaging and setup process. To create an answer file that can be used with Sysprep, follow these steps.

STEPS

Creating an answer file to use with Sysprep.exe

1. Launch Setup manager and begin the process of creating a new answer file. On the Product to Install Wizard screen, shown in Figure 2-10, choose Sysprep Install. Complete the setup manager so that the unattended file is created. Notice that the file is called Sysprep.inf. Sysprep requires this file name, so do not rename this answer file.

2. Place the `Sysprep.inf` file in the `Sysprep` folder before you run `Sysprep.exe`. The `Sysprep.inf` file automates minisetup.

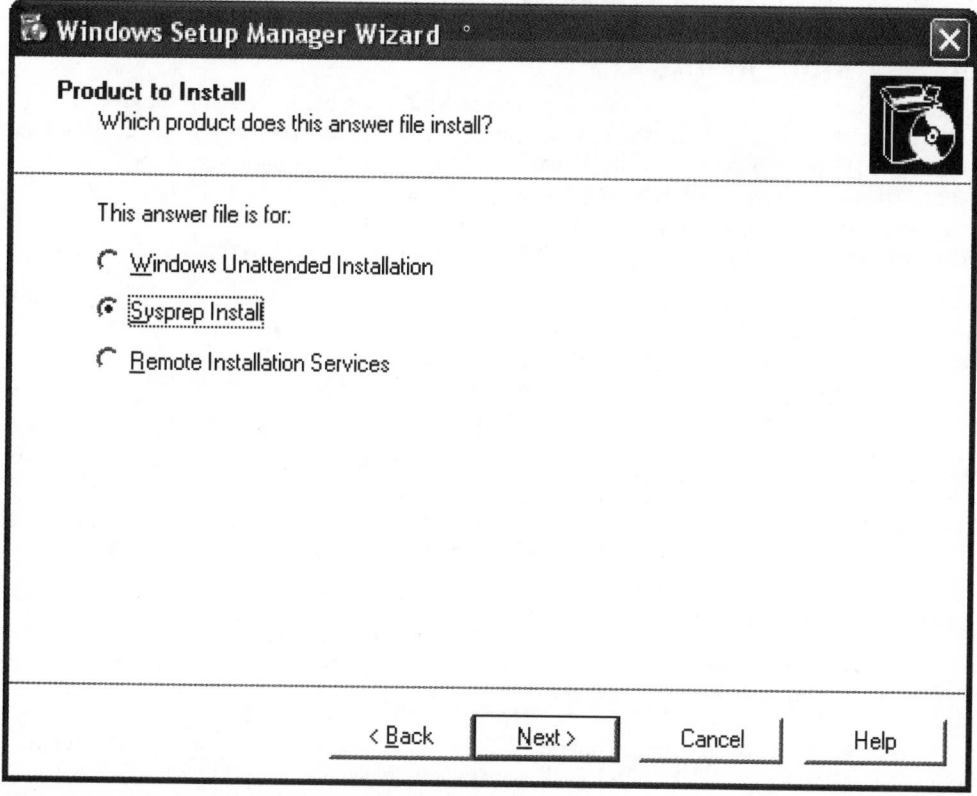

Figure 2-10: Setup Manager can be used to create a Sysprep.inf file.

Automatic installation by remote installation server

Microsoft has leveraged the Windows 2000 Active Directory feature to make possible a new method of automatic installation in Windows 2000, as well as in XP — remote installation server (RIS). Remote OS installation can use Microsoft's Preboot Execution Environment (PXE) remote boot technology and server-based services to install copies of Windows XP Professional on workstations throughout an enterprise.

> **NOTE:** Because Windows XP Home edition does not have the advanced networking capabilities of Windows XP Professional, it is not a candidate for a RIS installation.

> **TIP:** Remote Installation Server deployment of Windows XP is only suited to organizations that already have an Active Directory infrastructure, where the target machines are new and support PXE, which is explained in more detail later in this section.

Because RIS is a server-based networking product, it is inappropriate for small office or home use — your network must be using the Active Directory and Windows 2000 Server in order to use RIS. (I should note that the next version of Windows Server (2002/XP) will support the features of RIS as well, but since that version is not available at the time of this writing, I'll refer only to Windows 2000 Server.) RIS is an effective method for widely deploying Windows 2000/XP Professional for network environments, and it is a preferred method over `Sysprep`. You use Windows 2000 Server to set up and administer RIS installations of Windows XP, which is not something you are able to do from your Windows XP computer. Obviously, this section of the chapter is not for everyone, but if you are an administrator or desire to be one, or if RIS is use in your work environment and you are curious about it, then read on.

RIS and its requirements

Remote installation service runs on a Windows 2000 Server. The server holds the setup files for Windows XP (or Windows 2000) and distributes those files to RIS clients along with a unique SID. Like Sysprep, this method of installation is completely hands-off from an administrator's point of view. Because setup occurs over the network from the RIS server, the administrator is free to deal with other tasks, instead of spending time managing installations. Because you do not need third-party disk imaging software, RIS is the preferred method of Windows XP deployment, rather than Sysprep.

However, RIS is not without its limitations. First, it can be used only in networks running Windows 2000 (or later) using the Active Directory. Dynamic host configuration protocol (DHCP) and domain name system (DNS) must also be used in your network in order for RIS clients to contact the RIS server for service, so this solution typically isn't practical for the smaller network.

To deploy Windows XP using RIS, the client computers must be able to communicate with the RIS server so that the XP installation files can be downloaded. If the computers are equipped with a network adapter that supports the PXE ROM, then the computer can contact the RIS server on its own. When you start the computer, the PXE ROM asks if you want to start the computer from the network. If you answer "yes," then the PXE ROM contacts the DHCP to lease an Internet protocol (IP) address, and then the DNS server is contacted for name resolution with the RIS server. After the client has the RIS server's IP address, it can directly contact the RIS Server and installation can begin.

> **NOTE:** The PXE ROM is read-only memory information that your computer reads in order to attempt a network boot. Without the PXE ROM, a computer cannot boot over the network.

Unfortunately, not a lot of network adapters support PXE ROM, so unless you have specifically bought computers for a RIS rollout, you may be out of luck. However, you can use Windows 2000 Server to create an RIS boot disk to start the computer and to contact the RIS server, provided that these clients use a PCI network adapter card. RIS only supports PCI network adapter cards at this time.

> **TIP:** Upgrades are always in the works, so you might see more flexible options appear in later releases of a Windows Server product.

Setting up the RIS server

To set up the RIS server, you must install it on a Windows 2000 server, then set up the software. You need administrative rights to Windows 2000 Server to accomplish the following tasks. Obviously, this is not a server administration book, but I'm including steps and screenshots from Windows 2000 Server to show you how the process works, and this is good reading for those of you who want to move into the world of network administration.

The Windows 2000 Server that will become the RIS Server must have at least two disk volumes, and preferably two physical hard disks. One volume or disk holds the Windows 2000 files while the other holds the RIS installation folder and Windows XP image. You must use NTFS on this volume and you must have enough free disk space on the volume or disk to store the image.

To install the RIS server, use Add/Remove Programs in Control Panel to select Add/Remove Windows Components. When the selection window appears, choose Remote Installation Service and finish the installation. The Windows XP installation CD-ROM may be needed to complete the process and any current service packs may be needed, as well.

After the RIS Server software is installed on Windows 2000 Server, the server must be authorized by the Active Directory. Authorization is an Active Directory security feature that prevents RIS servers and other types of servers (such as DHCP) from coming online and servicing clients that are not authorized. Essentially, the Active Directory has to "bless" their existence on the network before they can be used.

To authorize the RIS server, you use the DHCP console. In the DHCP console, choose your RIS server, and then choose Action ⇨ Manage Authorized Servers. In the Manage Authorized Servers dialog box, click Authorize, as shown in Figure 2-11.

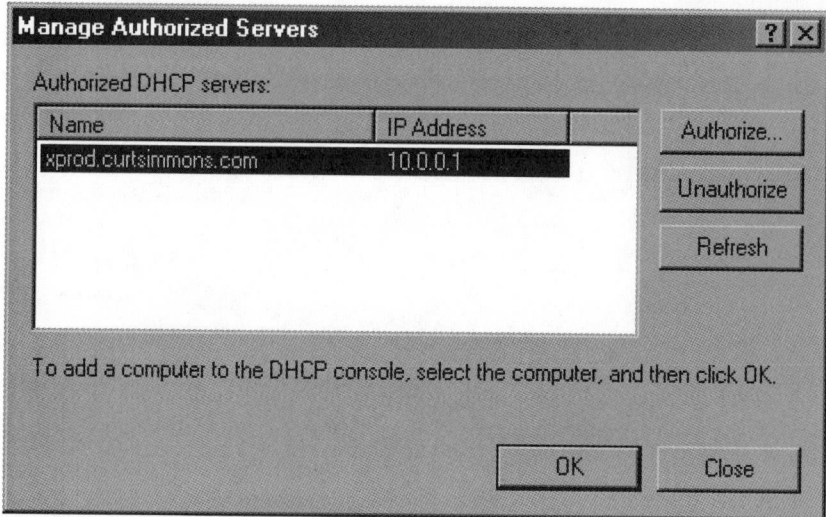

Figure 2-11: Authorize the RIS Server via DHCP.

After Active Directory authorizes the RIS server, the actual RIS setup can occur. The following steps walk you through the process of setting up RIS.

STEPS

Creating an answer file to use with RIS

1. Choose Start ⇨ Run. Type **risetup** and click OK.

2. The Remote Installation Services Wizard appears. Click Next on the Welcome screen.

3. The Remote Installation Folder Location window appears, as shown in Figure 2-12. You must select an NTFS volume/disk that is separate from the volume/disk on which Windows 2000 Server is installed. Make sure that the volume/disk you select is large enough to handle all of the Windows XP files that will be copied.

4. In the Initial Setting window, choose whether the server will begin responding to RIS clients after setup or whether it will have to wait until you choose for it to begin responding. Make your selection and click Next.

5. Specify the source location of the Windows XP installation files (CD, network drive, or local drive) and click Next.

6. Once the copy process is complete, give the installation a name, or just accept the default name.

7. Enter the help text that will be seen by network users if desired and click Next.

8. Review the settings and click Finish. The files are copied to the RIS installation folder.

Once installation is complete, clients can begin contacting the RIS server for service if you have allowed the RIS server to service clients. The properties for the RIS server can be managed in the Active Directory, and you can enable or stop the RIS server from servicing clients at any time.

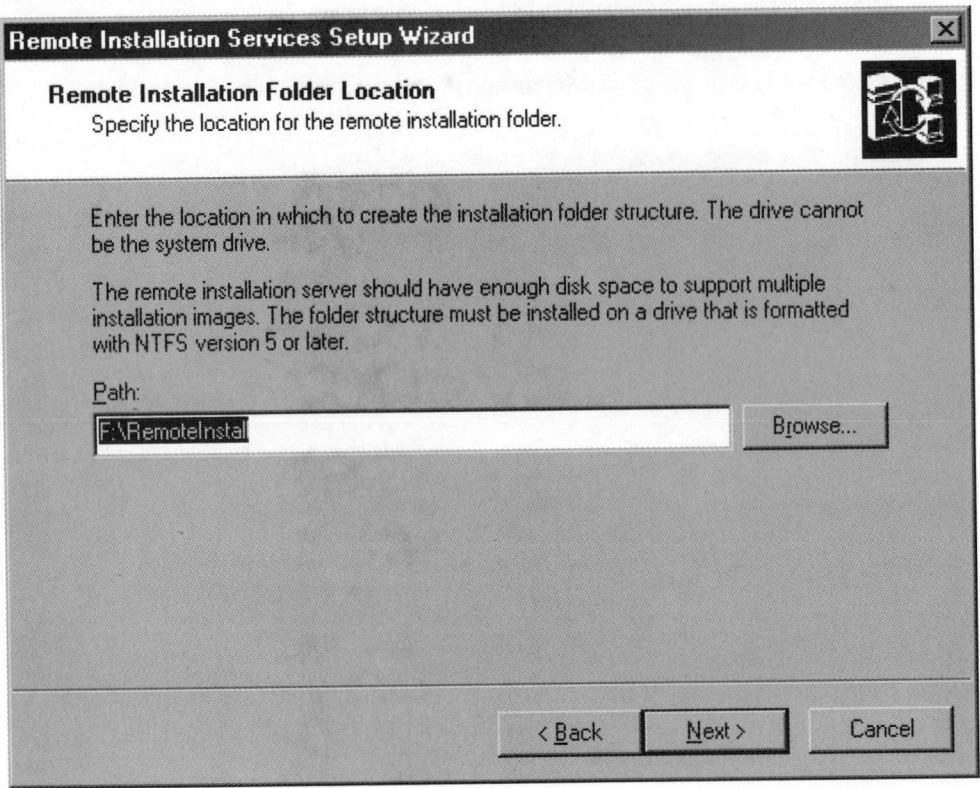

Figure 2-12: Remote Installation Folder selection

Automatic installation by electronic software distribution

And for the really Big Boys — those who have bought into Microsoft's Systems Management Server (SMS), Windows XP offers even more bells and whistles. In addition to rolling out Windows XP Professional, SMS 2.0 provides detailed software and hardware inventory and monitoring, as well as remote troubleshooting tools. The use of SMS is, of course, an advanced administration topic that is beyond the scope of this book, but a number of high-level networking books address the subject if you are interested in learning more.

Setting Up the Recovery Console

Once installation is complete, you should set up the Recovery Console, a command-line utility that appears as an "advanced" startup menu option. The Recovery Console is available when you boot the computer and hold down the F8 key. It appears with Safe Mode and the related options.

CROSS REFERENCE: The Recovery Console is available in both Windows XP Home and Professional editions. You can learn more about the available Recovery Console commands in Chapter 25.

The Recovery Console is used to repair Windows if you have problems starting it, and you can perform a number of additional tasks, such as format drives, start and stop services, access folders and files, and related tools. To make Recovery Console available as a startup option, however, you need to install it. To do so, you need to run this command from the Windows XP installation CD-ROM, where D: is the drive letter of your CD-ROM:

```
D:\i386\winnt32.exe /cmdcons
```

After you have installed the Recovery Console, boot into advanced options (F8) and check it out. You can type help at the command prompt to learn about the Recovery Console commands.

> **SECRET:** Although the Recovery Console receives a lot of press and is a great tool, you should use Safe Mode first if your computer will not start — this is the easiest way to resolve problems in Windows XP. The Recovery Console has many commands and options that can be helpful, but in many cases, a simple Safe Mode boot will do the trick too. So, always start with the easiest tool, and then move forward.

Solving Common Installation Problems

The Windows XP setup routine is the most stable routine Microsoft has ever produced. You are unlikely to experience problems at all during a typical installation or upgrade, but if you do, there are a few typical failure points you should be aware of. Check out the following sections for more information about these issues and how to tackle them.

Setup stops responding

If setup stops responding, particularly during the second half of installation, then a hardware device is the most likely culprit. Under most circumstances, you can simply turn the computer off and turn it back on in order to continue installation. If this doesn't work, try to use Device Manager to disable all devices that are not System devices. If you are performing a clean installation and cannot access Device Manager, consider turning the computer off and taking a quick hardware inventory. Remove any hardware from the computer that might be questionable.

> **TIP:** This problem can typically be avoided by doing a little hardware homework before installation ever begins.

If hardware does not seem to be the problem, consider turning off your system's cache memory by using your hardware's startup options. See your computer documentation for details on accessing system cache. After it is turned off, try starting setup again. This will make setup take up to three times longer to complete, but it might get you through a troublesome installation.

There may be other sources to this problem as well, such as:

◆ Upgrade incompatibilities with Windows 98 — If you are upgrading from Windows 98 and are having problems, you might consider trying a clean install. You will lose your settings and documents from Windows 98, but there may be driver problems that are causing the upgrade to fail.

◆ Boot sector virus — If possible, scan your hard drive for a boot sector virus and make sure it is clean.

◆ Make sure the computer meets the minimum hardware requirements.

◆ Uninstall any antivirus software from the computer and try setup again.

◆ Try turning off USB support.

Setup fails during file copy

File copy failure can occur as a result of the problems described in the previous section, but failure can also occur if there are problems with the CD-ROM drive or a faulty installation disk. If you are using multiple CD-ROMs, setup may be looking at the wrong CD-ROM, or there may be cable attachment problems with remote CD-ROMs. A hardware conflict between two devices could also affect file copy. In short, there are a number of potential issues to consider and it is best to tackle them one at a time in order to find a resolution.

Upgrade problems

If you experience problems upgrading to Windows XP, make sure that you have checked out your computer's hardware and that the version of Windows you are attempting to upgrade is upgradeable. Under most circumstances, upgrade failure is caused by hardware incompatibilities, so this is your first area to consider. Also, if the operating system you are upgrading experienced many problems prior to upgrade, you should consider a clean install just to make sure that Windows XP does not inherit any of these problems. Also, you should make sure that the computer's BIOS is up-to-date. Check the computer manufacturer's Web site to see if an updated BIOS is available.

Dual-boot problems

Most problems with dual-boot configurations boil down to a few important planning issues, such as the following:

- ◆ Make sure you have two volumes/partitions so that an operating system can reside on each one.
- ◆ Make sure you are using the correct file system(s).
- ◆ Make sure the volume/partitions are large enough for the operating systems.
- ◆ Make sure the computer's hardware is compatible with the operating systems.
- ◆ Make editorial changes to boot.ini as necessary to adjust boot loader behavior.

Problems with networking services

During Windows XP setup, you can join a domain or configure the computer to function in a workgroup. If you have problems configuring these options, particularly in joining a domain, the TCP/IP settings are typically the problem. The easiest way to resolve the issue is to complete the installation and then reconfigure TCP/IP for network connectivity. See Chapters 19 and 20 to learn more about TCP/IP configuration.

Problems with Hardware

If you are upgrading your operating system, it is very important that you stop and take a look at your computer's hardware. Your computer's hardware must be able to support the demands of Windows XP, and the odds are quite good that you will need newer drivers in order to make the best use of the hardware. Don't assume that hardware working under Windows 2000/NT or 9x will work under Windows XP. Do your homework!

If you need to buy new hardware or upgrade system components, such as RAM, you should get a reputable person to do the installations, and you need to buy quality components. Cheap cards and RAM may save you money at the moment, but you usually get what you pay for.

Summary

In this chapter, you learned about several advanced Windows XP installation issues, including . . .

♦ Installing Windows XP on a dual-boot system

♦ Installing the Windows XP Resource Kit and `Deploy.cab`

♦ Applying various tactics for unattended Windows XP Professional installation

♦ Using `Sysprep.exe` and RIS

♦ Installing the Recovery Console

♦ Solving common installation problems

Chapter 3

Windows XP Drive Configuration

In This Chapter

Hard disk, or drive, configuration has long been an important part of managing a computer system. After all, every piece of information stored on your computer is stored on a hard drive. If you have used Windows 2000, drive configuration in XP will be nothing new to you; however, if you come to XP from the 9x/Me generation, you'll find that hard disks work differently and are managed in different way under Windows XP. This chapter teaches you all about hard drive configuration and management. Specifically, you will learn about . . .

- ♦ Using NTFS file system, and some of its advanced safety features
- ♦ Using new kind of disks — dynamic drives — that give your more flexibility and error protection
- ♦ Checking your drives for errors
- ♦ Defragmenting your drives
- ♦ Enabling compression and encryption support

Drives and File Systems

All of your programs and all of your data reside in files on your drives. These drives might be hard drives, floppy drives, or removable drives. What keeps them all from turning into random bits of data is the *file system*. Windows XP is designed to use the New Technology File System (NTFS 5), although it also supports both the FAT16 and FAT32 file systems found in earlier versions of Windows, as well as MS-DOS and OS/2 systems. However, some of the more advanced features of Windows XP, such as disk management, file system security, disk quotas, and the like, all require NTFS.

> **NOTE:** Unless otherwise noted, this book assumes that you are using the NTFS file system on your hard drives. However, the NTFS file system is not supported on floppy drives, nor is it used on most removable disks. So, even on a Windows XP computer, you will typically still have some FAT drives.

NTFS

NTFS 5 is an upgrade to the NTFS 4 system found in Windows NT 4.0. The NTFS system provides a number of important technologies, including:

- ♦ Multiple data streams
- ♦ Reparse points
- ♦ The Change Journal
- ♦ Encryption at either the file or folder level
- ♦ Compression at either the file or folder level

> **TIP:** The Change Journal is a particularly significant safety feature. It is a persistent log of all changes made to files on a particular volume. The Change Journal keeps track of when files are added, deleted, and modified. This is a benefit to file system indexing, replication, and remote backup services.

NTFS 4 and NTFS 5

If you upgrade to Windows XP from Windows NT 4.0, and your drive was already using NTFS 4, you will automatically be upgraded to NTFS 5 during the Windows XP setup. If you are upgrading from Windows 9x or Me, you will be given an option to use the NTFS file system when you install Windows XP.

> **CAUTION:** There is enough difference between the two file systems that some of the Windows NT 4.0 disk utilities, such as CHKDSK and AUTOCHK, will not work on NTFS 5 volumes. These tools do check the NTFS version before they start their work, so you should not be able to inadvertently mangle your file structure. If you want to use these utilities, you must use updated versions of these tools.

NTFS cluster size

NTFS organizes a drive into clusters, and then uses these clusters to allocate files. The default cluster size depends on the size of the volume. Table 3-1 lists the NTFS default cluster sizes.

Table 3-1: NTFS Default Cluster Size

Volume Size	Cluster Size	Sectors per Cluster
Less than 512MB	512 bytes	1
513MB–1024MB	1K	2
1025MB–2048MB	2K	4
2049MB–4096MB	4K	8
4097MB–8192MB	8K	16
8193MB–16,384MB	16K	32
16,385MB–32,768MB	32K	64
Greater than 32,768MB	64K	128

While these are the default sizes, you are not limited to these sizes. If you use the Format command at the Command Prompt, you can specify any of the cluster sizes listed in Table 3-1.

> **CAUTION:** Of course, when you use the Format command, all the existing data on a drive is erased, so make sure you know what it is you are formatting.

Why does cluster size matter? Two files cannot share a cluster. If you use 8K clusters, even a file that is only 1K in size, such as a shortcut, will take up 8K on the disk, of which 7K is empty, wasted space.

NTFS and security

One of the major reasons for implementing NTFS is the security features that it provides. With FAT, you are limited to basic share and user level security. However, with NTFS, security on all shared items and even operating system security is much more advanced. For example, you can not only control what network users can access, but you can also control exactly what they can and cannot do with a particular share.

On the OS local home front, NTFS security provides rich user support and a tightly controlled operating system that requires user authentication in order to gain access. Because of the security features alone, NTFS is currently the file system of choice Windows NT/2000 networks.

NTFS and long filenames

Just like Windows 95, Windows 98, Windows Me, Windows NT 4.0, and Windows 2000, you can use long filenames in Windows XP. Windows XP also generates the older 8.3 filenames automatically, to ensure that older applications can also find your files. When creating a short filename from a long filename, NTFS takes the following steps:

♦ NTFS uses the Unicode character set for filenames. Because Unicode has a number of characters that MS-DOS cannot handle in filenames, these characters — along with any spaces — are removed when the filename is converted to an 8.3 filename.

♦ If the filename is longer than eight characters, the name is truncated to six characters, and a ~1 is then appended to the filename. If another file exists whose first six characters are the same as a previous file, a ~2 is appended to the filename.

♦ If still more duplicates are created, NTFS then appends ~3, ~4, and so forth. When it reaches ~9, it truncates the long filename to the first two letters, and then mathematically transforms the next four letters. It also will append a ~1, a ~2 to the filename, and so on.

Converting to NTFS

If you upgrade from Windows NT 4.0 to Windows XP, and you are using the NTFS 4 file system, the upgrade process automatically converts you to the NTFS 5 file system. (If you upgraded from 2000, the conversion was not necessary.) If you are using a FAT or FAT32 file system, you are asked if you want to convert to NTFS. If you say no, there is still time to change your mind. A new Command Prompt command — `Convert.exe` — will allow you to convert an existing drive's file system to NTFS 5.

The Convert utility is a one-way street: you can't convert from NTFS back to FAT. Convert can be used only one time on a drive. To use Convert, choose Start ➪ Run and type **CMD**, and then press Enter. Then, type the following command:

```
c:\convert drive: /fs:ntfs {/v}
```

where *drive:* is the drive you want to convert. You cannot use this command on your current drive, because the drive must be locked. If you specify the current drive in the command, you are asked if you want the drive converted the next time you restart the computer. The optional /v switch enables verbose mode. It displays progress messages during the conversion process.

If you try the automatic conversion at startup route by specifying the current drive, there is a chance that the conversion might fail. If it does, there is a way to check for clues as to what went wrong by using the Event Viewer.

STEPS

Checking on NTFS conversion failure

1. Choose Start ➪ Control Panel➪ Administrative Tools.
2. Open Computer Management and click the Event Viewer.
3. In the Console Tree, select Application Log.
4. In the details pane, look for error messages with Winlogon as the source. (Make sure that the log is sorted by date, in descending order, so that the most recent messages are at the top of the list.) It should specify the reason that the conversion failed.

Basic and Dynamic Drives

In addition to having two different file systems (NTFS and FAT), Windows XP provides a kind of storage system that may be new to you — *dynamic drives* — which were first introduced in Windows 2000. You can change existing hard drives on Windows XP computers into dynamic drives. These drives can hold a wide variety of different volumes (see Table 3-2). The legacy type of hard drive system that is commonly used in Windows 95, Windows 98, Windows Me, and Windows NT systems, is now referred to as a basic drive. It can contain the familiar primary and extended partitions, and logical drives commonly used in earlier versions of Windows.

> **NOTE:** Basic and dynamic drives can coexist with FAT, FAT32, and NTFS file systems. A basic drive can be an NTFS disk, or it can be a FAT or FAT32 disk. Similarly, a dynamic drive can support FAT, FAT32, or NTFS.

Though basic and dynamic drives can coexist, it is important to remember that only Windows 2000 and Windows XP systems can access dynamic drives. Given the incompatibilities involved with dynamic drives, why would you want to use them? There are two basic reasons: safety and flexibility. They have a number of extended capabilities, and support many different types of volumes that help provide fault-tolerance. In addition, you can change and resize drives without rebooting the computer.

> **CAUTION:** You can upgrade a basic drive to a dynamic drive using the procedure explained in the section on disk management later in this chapter. But before you do, realize that such an upgrade is a one-way street. The only way to go back to a basic drive is by repartitioning the drive. Why is this significant? Because the only operating systems that can access a dynamic drive are Windows XP and Windows 2000.

A volume on a dynamic drive is roughly equivalent to a partition on a basic drive. With basic drives, you can take one physical hard drive and split it into two or more partitions, which might be primary partitions or extended partitions. From the point of view of the operating system, they are separate drives.

A volume on a dynamic drive also gets its own drive letter, just like a partition. A volume can be split, as long as there is sufficient free space on the disk. These volumes can have any one of the layouts described in Table 3-2.

Table 3-2: Dynamic Drive Types

Volume Type	Description
Simple Volume	Created from free space on a single drive. It is closest in concept to primary partitions on basic drives.
Spanned Volume	A volume is not limited to existing on one physical drive. It can be made up of space from multiple physical drives, up to a maximum of 32 drives. You can extend a spanned volume onto additional drives, as long as you are below the maximum. These volumes cannot be mirrored.
Mirrored Volume	A volume whose data is duplicated on two different physical drives. This is done to provide fault-tolerance; if one drive fails or develops a bad sector, you can retrieve the missing data from the redundant volume. Mirrored volumes are sometimes called RAID-1 volumes.
Striped Volume	In a striped volume, the data is interleaved across two or more physical drives, with the data allocated evenly. These volumes cannot be mirrored, nor can they be extended. These sometimes go by the name of RAID-0 volumes.
RAID-5	To achieve fault-tolerance, data on a RAID-5 volume is striped across three or more physical drives. Then, a calculated value called Parity is also striped across the disk array. If one of the physical drives fails, the missing data can be recreated from the parity and the remaining data. These drives cannot be extended or mirrored.

If there are no basic drives on the computer, one of the volumes becomes the system volume, which is the volume containing the hardware-specific files used to boot a Windows XP computer. The boot volume is where the other Windows XP operating system files — those in %Systemroot% and %Systemroot%\System32 — are located.

NOTE: Dynamic drives are not supported on laptop computers; the option to upgrade from a basic drive to a dynamic drive should not be available on them. However, some laptop computers that are not ACPI- or APM-compliant may, nonetheless, have the conversion option enabled. You can edit the following Registry key to make sure that it has a value of 1: `HKEY_LOCAL_MACHINE\System\CurrentControlSet\Control\IDConfigDB\CurrentDockIn fo\DockingState`. Easier still, just remember: no dynamic drives on laptops.

Drive Management

There are two ways in which you can access most of the drive management functions in Windows XP. The first is a traditional way familiar to users of Windows 95, 98, and Windows NT — through My Computer. The second is the format that Microsoft is using for its utilities: the Microsoft Management Console (MMC), which you are already familiar with if you are moving from Windows 2000. You can find the MMC by opening Computer Management, which is found in Administrative Tools in the Control Panel. Click the Storage node to see disk management.

CROSS-REFERENCE: For more detailed information on using the Microsoft Management Console, see Chapter 7.

Drive properties

Click My Computer, right-click the drive you want to examine, and then select Properties from the context menu. This displays the familiar Local Disk Properties dialog box, as shown in Figure 3-1.

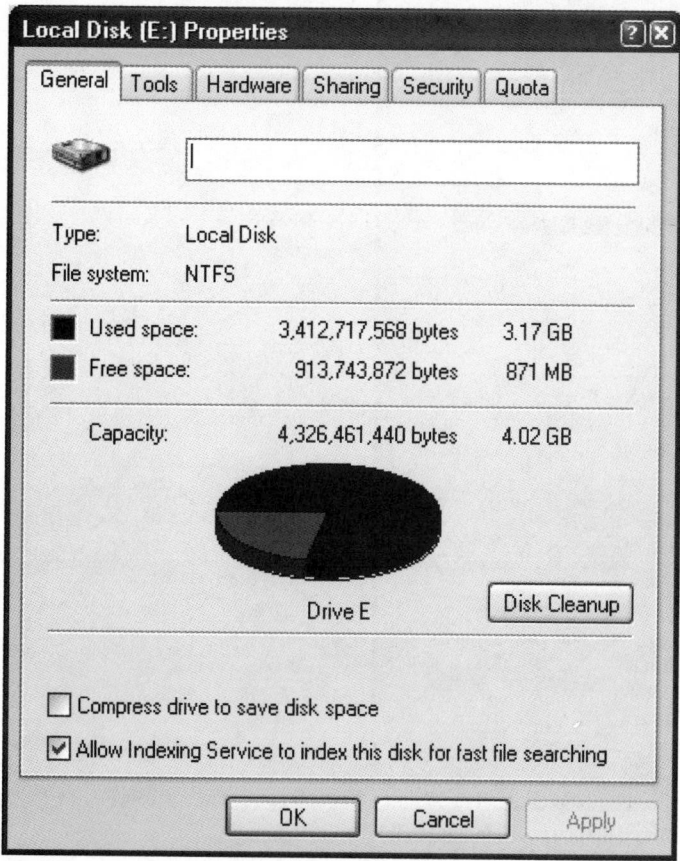

Figure 3-1: The Local Disk Properties dialog box has new compressing and indexing options, as well as the Disk Cleanup button.

The Local Disk Properties dialog box looks quite similar to its counterparts in Windows 9x, Me, NT, and 2000. It displays — both numerically and graphically — the size of the drive, as well as the amount of free space left. It also displays the file system used on the selected drive (FAT or NTFS).

Initially, the disk's label will probably say something generic, such as Local Disk. You can type a new name into the Label text box. This new name will then be reflected in the window's title bar, within the My Computer window, and in the Windows Explorer. If you are using the NTFS file system, the drive name can be up to 32 characters in length. If you are using the FAT file system, you are limited to 11 characters. In both cases, you still can identify a drive by its drive letter.

Disk Cleanup

Disk Cleanup was a feature first seen in the Windows 98 Disk Properties dialog box and was also available in Windows Me and 2000. It is a way to quickly free up space on your drives. Everything it does, you also could do manually, if you took the time to search through your hard drive looking for files to delete or compact. However, Disk Cleanup performs this task more quickly, and it does a more thorough job. In Windows XP, you can access Disk Cleanup from the General tab of the disk's properties dialog box.

When you click the Disk Cleanup button, it first scans your disk looking for files that can be deleted. It then reports its findings in a report similar to the one shown in Figure 3-2.

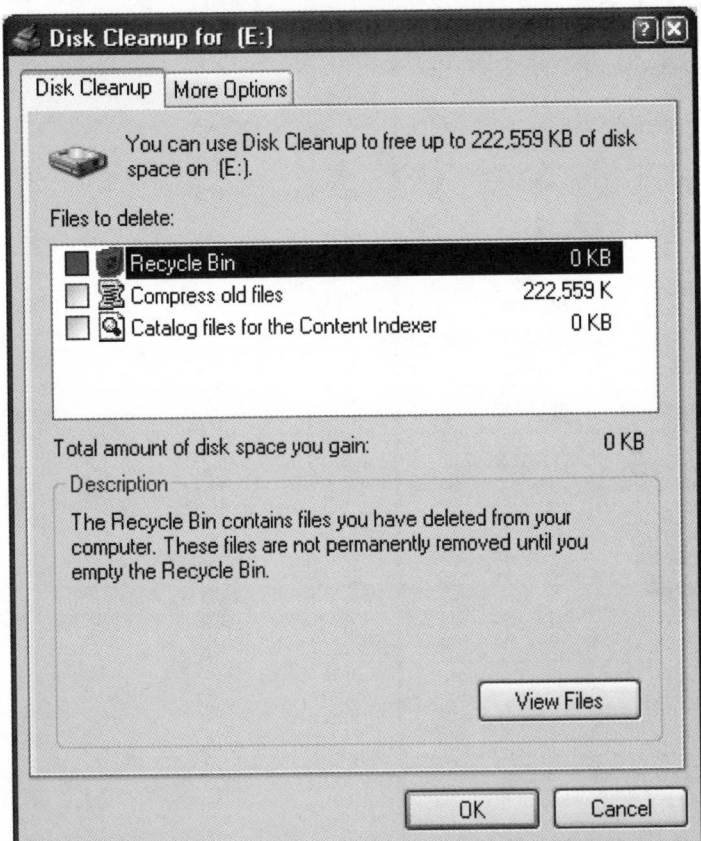

Figure 3-2: Disk Cleanup will first scan your drive and tell you how much space it will potentially free up.

It looks for files in four major categories:

- **Temporary Internet Files** — It will empty your Internet Explorer 6 cache folder for you. You can do this yourself by starting Internet Explorer and choosing Tools ⇨ Internet Options, and then clicking Delete Files on the General tab. (You also can clear your browser cache by using the Internet applet in the Control Panel.) If you highlight Temporary Internet Files in Disk Cleanup and then click View Files, you will see which files will be deleted.

- **Offline Web Pages** — If you have set up some Web pages for offline viewing, and any of those pages are stored on your computer, you can delete them. The settings for offline pages will be saved so that you can later refresh the pages.

- **Recycle Bin** — If you haven't emptied the Recycle Bin lately, Disk Cleanup will empty it for you.

- **Compress Old Files** — To save even more space, Disk Cleanup will compress rarely used files for you. (See "Compression" later in this chapter for more information on compressing files.)

In addition to these four basic categories, you can select the More Options tab, shown in Figure 3-3, and let the Windows Components Wizard assist you in removing some of the Windows XP optional components, installed programs, and system restore points that you might no longer need. The Installed Programs button takes you to the Add/Remove Programs dialog box, from which you also can access from the Control Panel.

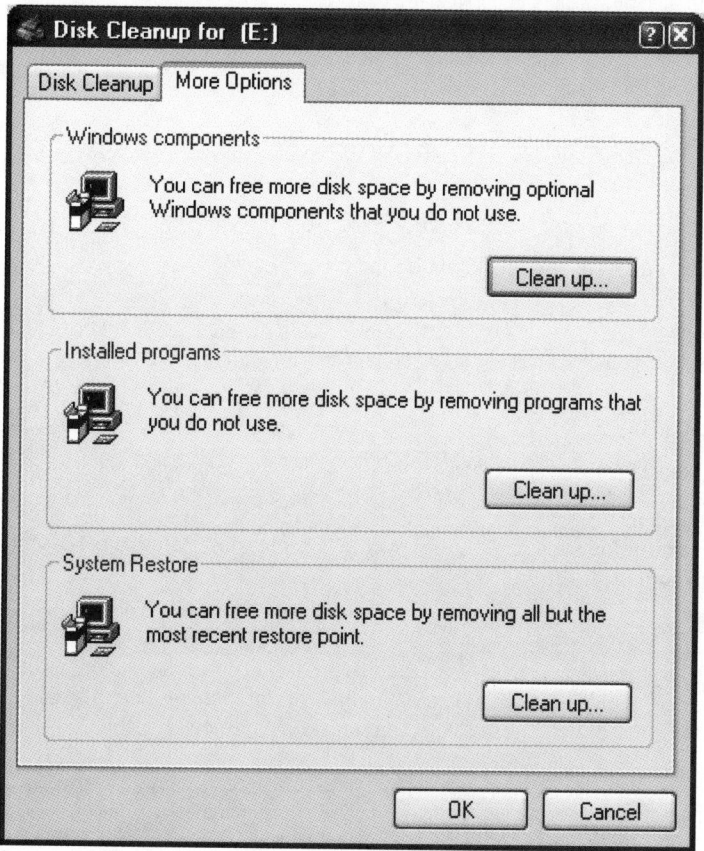

Figure 3-3: You can remove more items from your system using More Options.

After you decide what you want to throw out or compress, select those options and click OK.

> **TIP:** In practical terms, Disk Cleanup helps you remove files and applications you don't use. In order to greatly increase disk space, the application removal portion of Disk Cleanup is the most important because you are more likely to gain disk space by removing applications. Of course, you can also perform this action manually using Add/Remove Programs in Control Panel.

Compression

When you are using an NTFS drive, you will see an option in the lower portion of the dialog box that enables you to compress the drive. You also can compress individual folders or files. (Compression can be toggled on or off.)

If a file or folder is compressed, any Windows-based application should be able to read from and write to it without running another program to decompress it. This step is taken automatically, and the file or folder is automatically recompressed when changes are made. This compression is similar to the MS-DOS DoubleSpace and DriveSpace utilities. However, on an NTFS drive you can compress individual files or folders, whereas the MS-DOS programs only worked on drives.

> **TIP:** If you have a cluster size larger than 4K (see Table 3-1), you will not be able to use NTFS compression. According to Microsoft, compression is efficient at cluster sizes smaller than 4K. But when clusters are larger, the savings in disk space is not worth the performance hit. On an NTFS volume with clusters larger than 4K, compression is not available.

STEPS

Compress a drive

1. Open My Computer.
2. Right-click the drive you want to compress. Select Properties.
3. Select the "Compress drive to save disk space" check box on the General tab.
4. To turn off compression, clear the compression option check box.

> **TIP:** If you move a compressed file or folder, it keeps its compression state no matter what the compression status of its destination folder is. A compressed file stays compressed; an uncompressed file remains uncompressed. On the other hand, when you copy a file, its compression status changes to reflect the destination folder. If you copy an uncompressed file to a compressed folder, it also becomes compressed. If you move a compressed file from an NTFS volume to a FAT volume, it is automatically uncompressed, because the FAT volume does not support NTFS compression.

There is also a command-line utility called `Compact.exe` in the `c:\windows\System32` folder that enables you to compact specific files and folders, as well as to view the compression status of particular files and folders. The syntax of the program is as follows:

```
c:\winnt\System32\compact {folder or filenames} {options}
```

If you run Compact without any of its optional parameters, it will tell you the compression status of all the files in your current folder. You can specify files or folders it should work on using wildcards or multiple filenames. Leave spaces between the filenames or between multiple parameters. Table 3-3 lists `Compact.exe`'s parameters.

> **TIP:** Speaking of compression, keep in mind that Windows XP natively supports folder compression. When you create folders, you can choose to create compressed folders where data can easily be stored. The process is transparent to you, and you can open the compressed folders and read the contents just as you would any other folder, but the folder consumes much less disk space when it is compressed.

Table 3-3: Compact.exe Parameters

Parameter	Meaning
/C	Compresses the specified files and marks the specified folders, so that any files that are added to the folders will also be compressed.
/U	Uncompresses the specified files and marks the specified folders, so that files added afterward will not be compressed.
/S	Any specified action on a folder is extended to all subfolders.
/A	Displays all hidden or system files, which normally won't be displayed.
/I	By default, Compact.exe stops on errors. This parameter forces it to continue.
/F	By default, if a file is already compressed, it is skipped during compression. If you use /F, you force compression.
/Q	Causes Compact.exe to report only the essential information.

Drive tools

Select the Drive Properties dialog box Tools tab to see the three tools available for working on drives: Error Checking, Backup, and Defragmentation.

Error Checking

Checking for disk errors is similar to using the Scandisk program provided in earlier versions of Windows, although you will not find Scandisk.exe included with Windows XP. When you check your drives for errors, you have the option to automatically fix errors, as well as scan for and recover bad sectors.

The major difference in Windows XP comes from the NTFS file system. With NTFS, a log of all file transactions is stored on the disk, all bad clusters are automatically replaced, and the key information for all files is copied and stored. In the event you have disk problems, you can use this log as a recovery tool, which should ensure that the disk is returned to a consistent state.

NTFS volumes are managed by means of a Master File Table (MFT) and metadata that maintains the file system structure. The MFT contains one record for each file and folder on the drive, and it is also mirrored in a second version, called MFTMirr, which ensures that if the MFT is damaged, a backup copy is available.

As you can see in Figure 3-4, Error Checking is a simple utility that enables you to automatically fix file system errors and attempt recovery of bad sectors.

Backup

Backup leads you to the Microsoft Backup utility. You also can access the Microsoft Backup utility by choosing Start ➪ All Programs ➪ Accessories ➪ System Tools ➪ Backup. If you have no other backup programs or procedures, you can use Backup to make copies of your data. Backup also can be used to create Emergency Recovery Disks and to back up your system state.

TIP: There are no hard and fast backup rules — your backup plan depends on your needs and the amount of data tha needs to be backed up. As a general rule, you should perform a full backup every week or so if you use your computer on a regular basis. If you are creating/editing a lot of files, a backup of those folders should be performed every time you make changes.

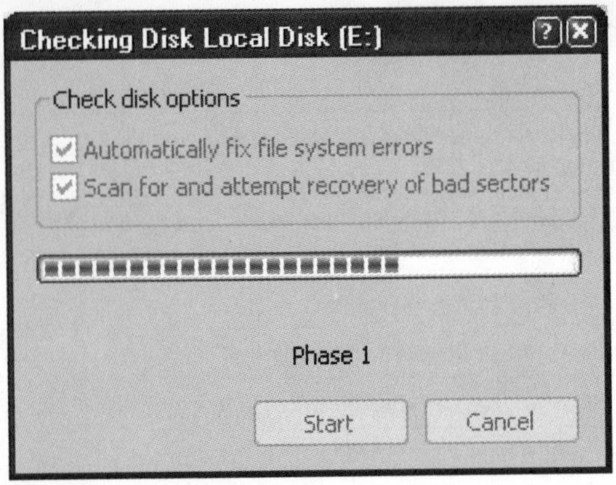

Checking Disk Local Disk (E:)

Check disk options
- ☑ Automatically fix file system errors
- ☑ Scan for and attempt recovery of bad sectors

Phase 1

Start | Cancel

Figure 3-4: Error Checking tool

Defragmentation

From the Drive Properties dialog box Tools tab, you can access the Windows XP Defragmentation utility. (You also can access this utility from the Computer Management Console by selecting the Storage node, as discussed earlier.) Fragmentation refers to the way in which files are stored on a drive. When a file is saved, it is placed in the first available open space on a hard drive. If the file will not completely fit into that open space, the remaining portion of the file is then written to the next empty space, and so forth. Over time, as files are added and deleted, the files on your hard drive become increasingly fragmented.

You can see how fragmented your drive is by performing an analysis. Follow these steps:

STEPS

Fragmentation Analysis

1. Choose Start ⇨ All Programs ⇨ Accessories ⇨ System Tools ⇨ Disk Defragmenter.

2. Select the drive that you want to analyze in the drive pane and click Analyze.

3. Analysis takes place and you see a colored coded graph appear.

4. After the analysis has completed, you are given an Analysis Report, as shown in Figure 3-5. It also provides you with a recommendation as to whether you should defragment your drive. You do not have to follow the advice. You can run the defragmentation utility, even if the analysis says it is unnecessary.

The main Defragmentation dialog box, which is available by clicking the Defragment Now button on the Tools menu of the disk's properties sheets has a banded display that shows the status of the sectors on your hard drive. Table 3-4 outlines the colors and their meanings.

Table 3-4: Defragmentation Display

Color	Meaning
Green	System files used by the NTFS system for the MFT table and logs. These will not be moved. You only see these green areas on NTFS volumes.
Blue	Contiguous files, stored in one piece.
Red	Fragmented files, stored in nonadjacent areas of the drive.
White	Free space.

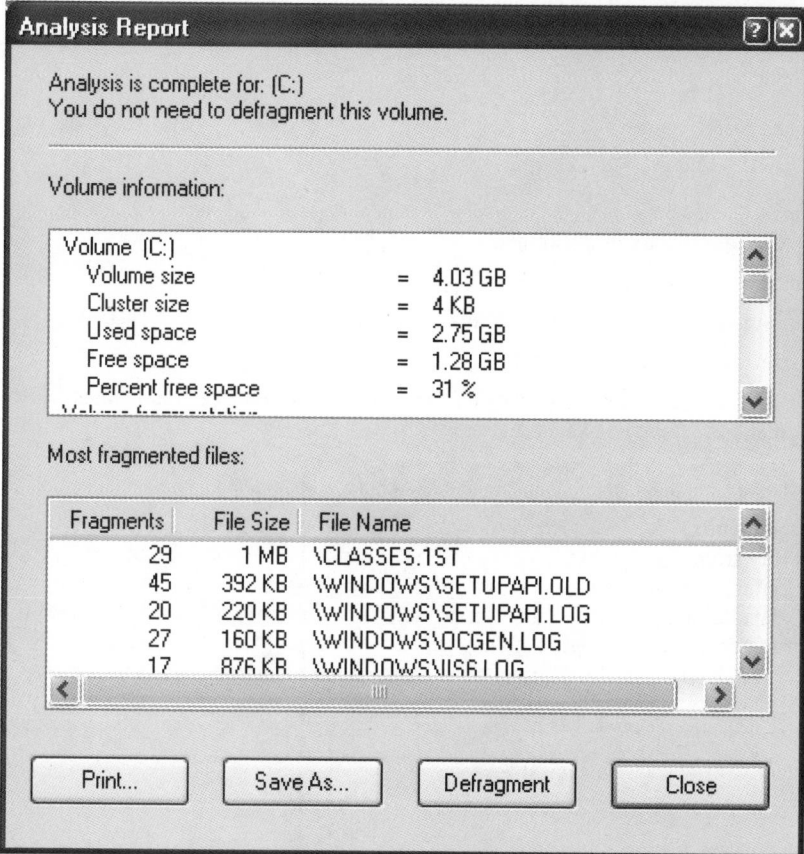

Figure 3-5: Anaysis report

As the table indicates, the more red you see, the more fragmentation you have, and the more likely you are to benefit from defragmentation.

SECRET: The system files, shown in green, are not moved during defragmentation. The greater the percentage of space they take up on a volume, the less likely that fragmentation will show much in the way of results, because it has to work around these large, unmovable blocks.

Click Defragment if you want to proceed with the actual defragmentation. It may take awhile, depending on how much fragmentation there is, how much free space is available, and how fast the computer is.

NOTE: Defragmenting a drive is a lot like organizing a closet. If you go through it first and throw out all the stuff that hasn't been used in a long time, the end result will be much better. Of course, you don't have to "throw out" files. They can be backed up and stored on a tape drive, Zip drive, or other high-capacity storage device using the Backup utility or through a manual copy process. The point is to regularly take a look at your computer and lose any files or applications that you no longer need.

If your MFT file outgrows its reserved space and becomes fragmented, it may cause a performance hit. You can see if your MFT file is highly fragmented.

To do so, follow these steps:

STEPS

Examining MFT fragmentation

1. Open My Computer.
2. Right-click the drive you want to examine and then select Properties.
3. Select the Tools tab and then select Defragment now.
4. Select the drive you want to analyze and then click Analyze.
5. When the analysis is complete, click View Report.
6. In the upper pane labeled Volume information, scroll down until you find the section labeled Master File Table (MFT) fragmentation (see Figure 3-6).

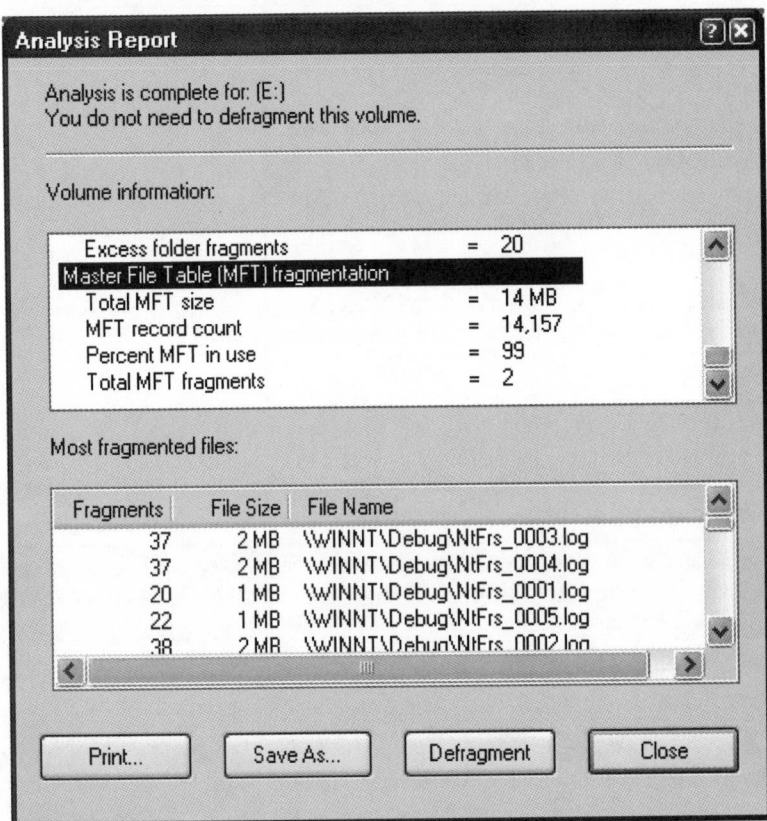

Figure 3-6: This portion of the Analysis Report appears if your Master File Table (MFT) is fragmented.

SECRET: If your drive has a high number of very small files, it is more likely to use up its MFT space and become fragmented than a drive having a small number of very large files. The Disk Defragmenter won't put the MFT back together again. However, there is a way to reserve extra space for the MFT, which will make it less likely that the MFT becomes fragmented in the first place. The next few paragraphs discuss this method.

The method applies to NTFS drives in general, not just for Windows XP. It does not work retroactively, but is to be used when you first bring a volume online. The fix involves adding a new Registry parameter to the following registry key:

```
HKEY_LOCAL_MACHINE\SYSTEM\CurrentControlSet\Control\FileSystem
```

The new parameter — NtfsMftZoneReservation — gives more control over how much of a volume NTFS will keep reserved for the MFT. The new value is a REG_DWORD that can range from 1 to 4. If it is set at 1, the default value, the least amount of space is reserved, whereas setting it at 4 reserves the most space.

CROSS-REFERENCE: Microsoft details this setting in the following technical document located on their Web site at: `http://support.microsoft.com/support/kb/articles/q174/6/19.asp`.

If you feel like experimenting with this setting, here is what you should do:

STEPS

Reserving more space for the MFT

1. Choose Start ⇨ Run, and type **regedit** in the Open text box. Then press Enter or click OK.
2. Navigate to the following subkey:

```
HKEY_LOCAL_MACHINE\SYSTEM\CurrentControlSet\Control\FileSystem.
```

3. Choose Edit ⇨ New ⇨ D_Word Value.
4. Name this key **NtfsMftZoneReservation**, and then press Enter.
5. Right-click the new value, and then select Modify from the context menu.
6. Type your new value, which can be between 1 and 4. Click OK.
7. Close the Registry Editor.

The Paging File also referred to as the *Virtual Memory Paging File* refers to a portion of your hard drive that is set aside for use as RAM when your actual memory is depleted. You can set the size of this file through the Control Panel's System applet. Microsoft recommends that you set the size of your paging file to 1.5 times the amount of your installed RAM.

The paging file is, however, like any file on your computer. As changes are made, segments of the paging file can get scattered on the hard disk, which requires more time for Windows XP to read the file. Since you are dealing with virtual memory, the more time it takes to read that virtual memory, the slower your system performs. Like regular defragmentation, defragmenting the paging file reorganizes it and makes it faster for Windows XP to read — which results in faster performance for you.

STEPS

Defragmenting your paging file

1. Choose Start ⇨ Control Panel, and then click System.
2. Select the Advanced tab, and then click Settings under Performance.
3. Click the Advanced tab, and then click Change under Virtual Memory. This takes you to the Virtual Memory dialog box, as shown in Figure 3-7.

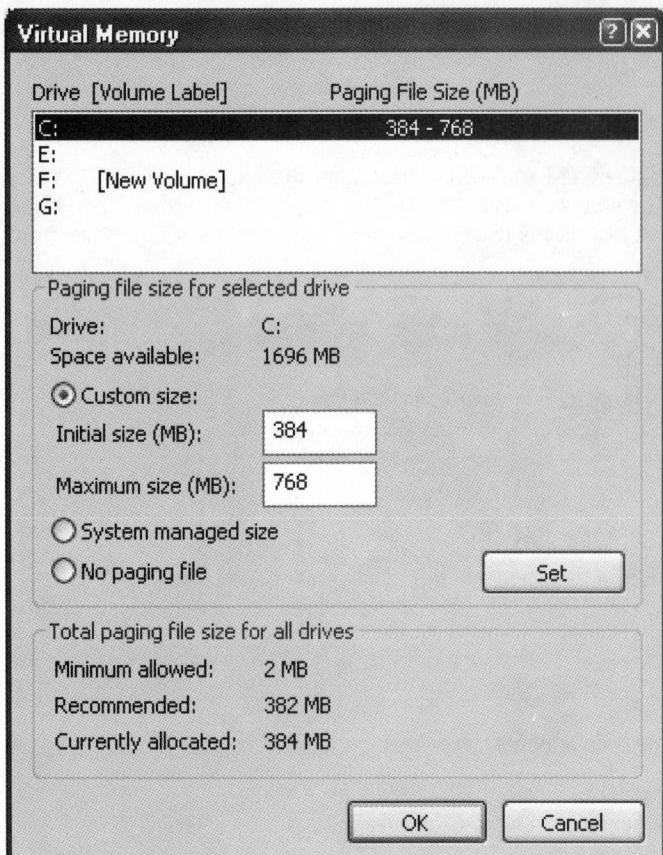

Figure 3-7: Virtual Memory

4. Select another drive for your paging file from the upper panel. Set a minimum and maximum size for the paging file.

5. Select the drive on which the current paging file is located. Change the minimum and maximum values for the original paging file to zero.

6. Click OK to close all of the dialog boxes.

7. Reboot your computer.

8. Open My Computer, right-click the drive holding your new paging file, and then choose Properties from the context menu. Select the Tools tab.

9. Now follow Steps 1 through 3 above to access the Virtual Memory dialog box. Change your settings back to their original settings by restoring the paging file on your original disk.

10. Go to the temporary paging file you created earlier, and reduce its minimum and maximum settings to zero.

11. Reboot your computer to restore the paging file to its original drive.

Other Drive Properties tabs

There are a number of other tabs in the Drive Properties dialog box. Many of these are discussed elsewhere in the book and often can be reached by other paths.

Hardware

This takes you to the Hardware Properties dialog box for your disk drives. You also can access this dialog box by going to Start ⇨ Control Panel ⇨ Administrative Tools ⇨ Computer Management ⇨ Device Manager, and then right-clicking the drive whose properties you want to view. Hardware management is discussed in Chapter 11. Most drive-management functions are now handled through the Computer Management Console, which is discussed later in this chapter.

Sharing and security

The Sharing tab, in conjunction with the Security tab, is where you can control access to your drives and folders. From this location, you can share the entire disk with others on your network and set permissions so that only certain people can access the drive over the network (see Figure 3-8). You can learn more about networking and sharing drives and folders in Chapter 20.

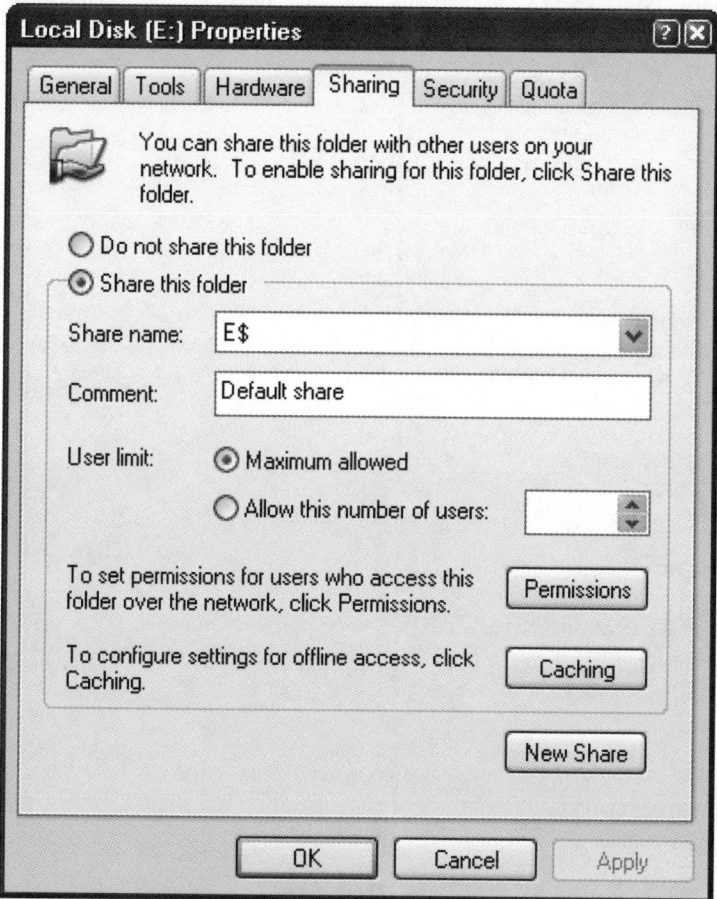

Figure 3-8: You can share access to your drives from the Sharing tab.

Disk quotas

If you are using the NTFS file system, and if you are logged on as Administrator, you will see a Quota tab in the Disk Properties dialog box. This enables you to set limits on the amount of disk space that user files can occupy. Although quotas are most often used in a storage volume on a networked drive, they also can be used on a standalone computer or on a peer-to-peer network in order to manage drive consumption. For example, suppose that your Windows XP computer resides on a home or small office network. Other network users access your 20GB hard drive in order to store information. Disk Quotas can be implemented to control how much disk storage space these users consume (and to provide you a great way to keep track it all).

By default, disk quotas are disabled. To enable them, follow these steps:

STEPS

Using Disk Quotas

1. Open My Computer.

2. Right-click the drive on which you want to establish quotas and then click Properties.

3. Select the Quota tab, as shown in Figure 3-9. You should see a message that disk quotas are disabled, and most of the available options will be grayed out. Select Enable quota management to enable the other settings in the dialog box.

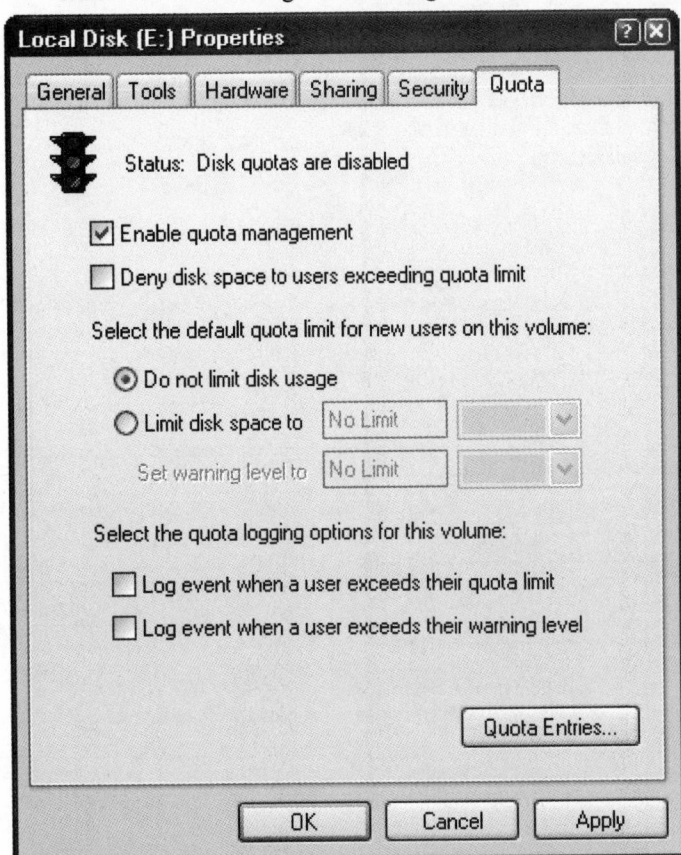

Figure 3-9: If you enable disk quotas, you also should set a warning level sufficiently below the quota so that users will not be caught unaware as they near their limit.

4. Select Limit disk space to, and then set an overall limit. You have quite a bit of flexibility here. Quotas can be set to any numerical quantity of kilobytes, megabytes, gigabytes, terabytes, and pb (which must be a really big number — what's it stand for, Plenty Byte?). Actually, it stands for "petabyte" which equals 1 quadrillion bytes, or 1,125,899,906,842,624 bytes (whew!).

5. Set a warning level that is sufficiently below the quota limit so that a user will know they are approaching that limit and have plenty of time to take corrective action.

TIP: If users regularly save files of 1MB, for example, the quota warning level should be set much higher than 1MB below the quota limit. You don't want them to hit the warning limit at the same time they exceed the quota.

6. Click OK. The drive will be rescanned to calculate each user's amount against the quota.

TIP: When quotas are enabled, they apply only to new users who are added to the system after the setting is changed. Quotas will not be set against existing users, by default. However, if you access the Quota Entries window, you can establish quotas against the existing users.

Diskuse

The Windows XP Resource Kit provides a command-line tool that you can use to view a directory tree and report the amount of disk space used by different users. This utility might be helpful in seeing the initial amount of disk space used so that you can set realistic quotas.

To use this utility, choose Start ⇨ Programs ⇨ Command Prompt and type the following command:

```
c:\diskuse path {options}
```

Table 3-5 lists the possible parameters for this utility.

Table 3-5: Diskuse Parameters

Parameter	Description
Path	The path to the directory in which you want to calculate disk use. It can be a full pathname, such as c:\winnt, a relative pathname, or it can be a Universal Naming Convention (UNC) name. This will not search subdirectories. To include them in the calculation, use /s.
	Options
/f:filename	Send results to a file rather than to the screen.
/e:filename	Store errors in a file rather than on the screen.
/u:username	Report disk usage for the given username.
/s	Include subdirectories in the report.
/t	Output the results in the form of a table.
/w	Output the results in Unicode output format.
/q	Run Diskuse in quiet mode.
/v	Run Diskuse in verbose mode. In addition to totaling the disk usage, it gives a list of filenames.
/r:filename	Measures disk usage against restrictions stored in the specified filename.
/o	Reports users who are over the limits set in the restrictions file.
/n:#	Display the number (#) of files per user.
/x:#	Display files larger than # bytes.
/d:a|c|w	Display the access, creation, and write dates.
/?	Displays the help file.

If you do not specify a pathname, the disk usage in the current directory will be reported. You can view the output onscreen, or you can use the optional /f: parameter to specify a filename in which to store the results.

Web sharing

If you have installed Internet Information Server (IIS) — an optional component in Windows XP — you will see one additional tab in your Drive Properties window for Web Sharing. This feature enables you to share folders on your local intranet so that users can more easily access them. Typically, you do not use this component unless you are configuring your computer to be an intranet Web server.

Storage

With Microsoft's push to get more of the management utilities into the MMC framework, it is not surprising to see a number of important disk utilities within the Computer Management Console. In some cases, this amounts to an alternative path to the same tool, as in the case of the Disk Defragmenter. But in other cases, there are some disk management tools that you cannot reach from anywhere else. It also might not be surprising to find, in future updates of Windows, that the only way to reach these tools is through a management console.

STEPS

Opening Storage Tools

1. Choose Start ➪ Control Panel and then click Administrative Tools.
2. Click Computer Management.
3. In the console tree, expand the Storage node.
4. The most important new tool is Disk Management. Select it in the console tree.

Disk management

The Disk Management snap-in can combine both a text and graphical view of all the drives on a computer, including hard drives and removable drives. Click View on the console menu to choose from Disk List, Volume List, or Graphical View for both the upper and lower sections of the Disk Management dialog box.

The Disk Management snap-in, as shown in Figure 3-10, shows the relationship between disks and volumes. A disk is a physical unit. It is what you can buy in a store and install in your computer. You can take a disk and split it into partitions (on a basic drive) or volumes (on a dynamic drive), which are essentially the same thing. They are portions of a physical disk that can function as separate disk drives, with their own drive letters. Note that Zip, Jaz, Orb, CD-ROM, and DVD drives are also listed here.

The colors above each drive (which you cannot see in the figure) indicate the type of partition or volume. The default colors are:

♦ **Black** — Unallocated space
♦ **Dark Blue** — Primary partition
♦ **Green** — Extended partition
♦ **Light green** — Free space
♦ **Blue** — Logical drive

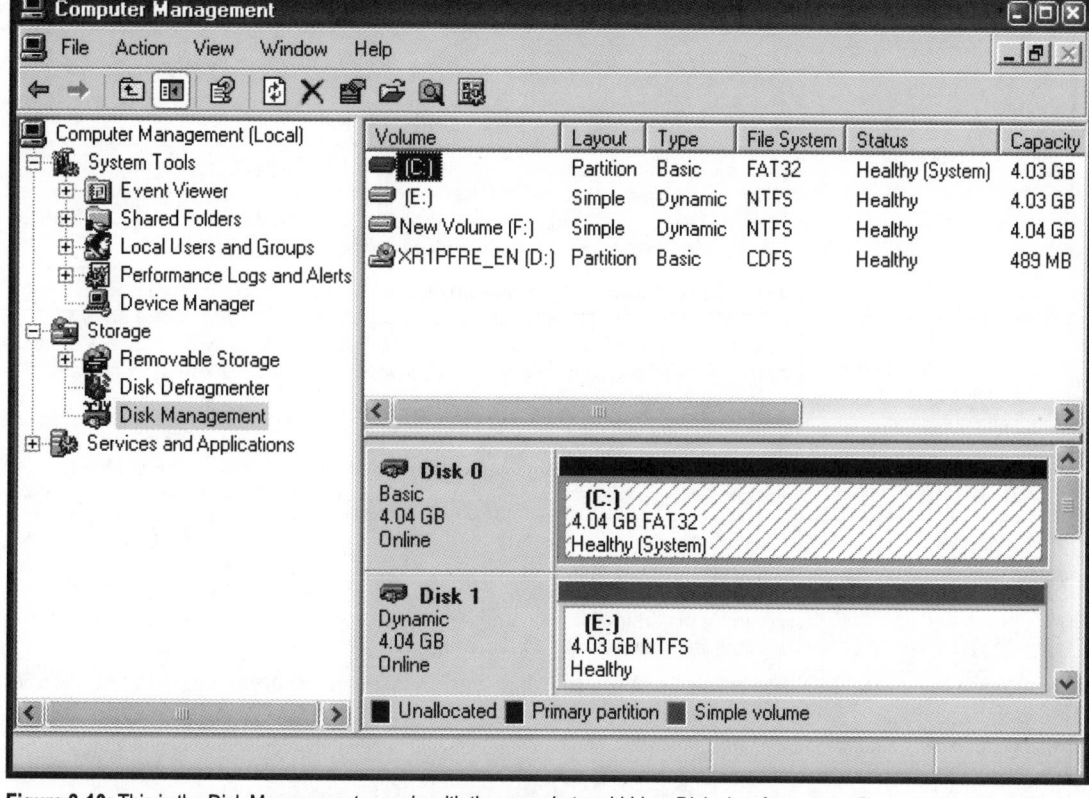

Figure 3-10: This is the Disk Management snap-in with the console tree hidden. Disk size, free space, file system, and health of the drive are some of the variables that can be seen from this screen.

- ♦ **Olive** — Simple volume
- ♦ **Purple** — Spanned volume
- ♦ **Cadet Blue** — Striped volume
- ♦ **Brick** — Mirrored volume
- ♦ **Cyan** — RAID-5 volume

SECRET: If you don't like the default color arrangement, you can change it. From the Disk Management console, choose View ⇨ Settings, and then assign your own color settings.

Disk Management reports most of the information that you can see from the Disk Properties dialog box. It reports the file system, capacity, and free space in the disk listing in the upper portion of the dialog box. In the graphical view in the lower portion of the dialog box, it shows which drive is the system drive, which is where your Windows XP files are located. One important piece of information that Disk Management can display (that Disk Properties cannot) is the status of your disks and your volumes. Disk status is shown in the gray boxes in the left portion of the graphical view. Each option is described in Table 3-6.

Table 3-6: Disk Status

Disk Status	Description
Online	This is the normal status for a disk. It means that everything is okay — it can be accessed and there are no known problems.
Online (errors)	If a disk is a dynamic drive, it might be listed this way. It is working, but I/O errors have been reported. Some errors may be transient, and may have occurred because the disk was powered down. Right-click the disk and select Reactivate disk, and the status should change back to online.
Offline	This status is also only for dynamic drives. The disk might have been corrupted, or it might have been powered down. If the disk name says Missing, that means the disk was recently online, but now Windows XP can't find it. If there are controller, cable, or power problems, fix them, and then select Reactivate disk.
Foreign	This status is also only for dynamic drives. It means that this disk has been moved from another computer, but it has not been set up for use. Use the Import Foreign Disks option so that the disk can be recognized.
Unreadable	This is not good. The disk might have become corrupted, or it might have suffered a hardware failure. This can occur with both basic drives and dynamic drives. In some cases, this will be displayed when a disk is first spinning up, before it is ready to use. Choosing Action ⇨ Rescan should change its status back to online.

In addition to reporting on the status of disks, Disk Management also will report on the status of volumes. Each volume on a drive has its own status descriptions, which are described in Table 3-7. (These are different from the status descriptions for disks.)

Table 3-7: Volume Status

Volume Status	Description
Healthy	The normal volume status. It means that the volume is accessible and has no known problems. Both basic and dynamic drives can be healthy.
Healthy (at risk)	This is a status only for volumes on dynamic drives. It means you can access the volume, but that there are I/O errors. The underlying disk is probably reporting online (errors) status. Reactivating the disk should also change the volume status to Healthy.
Initializing	This status is only for dynamic drives. When initialization has finished, the volume should change to Healthy status.
Resynching	This is reported on both basic and dynamic mirrored volumes. The two mirrors are being resynchronized so that each has identical contents. When the action is complete, status should change to Healthy. You can access a mirrored drive while it is resynchronizing, but don't change its configuration.
Regenerating	This is reported for both basic and dynamic RAID-5 volumes. It means that data and parity are being regenerated. When the process is complete, status should change to Healthy.
Failed Redundancy	This applies to both basic and dynamic RAID-5 or mirrored volumes. It means that you no longer have fault-tolerance because one of the disks is offline. You can continue to use the remaining disk, but if it fails, you will have no backup.
Failed Redundancy (at risk)	The same status as above, except that there are also I/O errors on the underlying disk. This applies only to dynamic drives.

Volume Status	Description
Failed	This applies to both basic and dynamic volumes. It means the volume can't be started. If it is a dynamic volume, the Reactivate volume option should bring the underlying disk back online. If it is a basic volume, you can only check whether the disk is turned on and that all the cables are plugged in. Otherwise, hope that the backup is current.

Disk management actions

You can perform most disk management actions by right-clicking one of the partitions or volumes in the graphical disk view. If you right-click a hard drive, you will be able to perform many common functions, such as:

♦ **Open** — This opens the contents of the drive in a single-pane in My Computer view.

♦ **Explore** — This opens the contents of the drive in the double-pane Windows Explorer view.

♦ **Properties** — This takes you to the same dialog box that you see when you right-click a drive in My Computer and then select Properties from the context menu.

In addition to some of the more common functions that you can perform when you right-click a partition or volume, there are other advanced tools, too.

Upgrade from a basic to dynamic drive

If you decide that you want to convert one or more of your basic drives to a dynamic drive, follow these steps:

STEPS

Upgrade to a Dynamic drive

1. Make sure that you close any programs that are running on the disks you want to upgrade and that the disk has at least 1MB of unallocated space.
2. Choose Start ⇨ Control Panel ⇨ Administrative Tools ⇨ Computer Management.
3. Expand Storage in the console tree.
4. Select Disk Manager.
5. Right-click the disk you want to upgrade, and then select Convert to Dynamic Disk, shown in Figure 3-11. Then, follow the rest of the instructions that appear on your screen.

NOTE: You cannot convert removable media drives, such as Zip, Jaz, or Orb drives, to dynamic drives. Also, you can't upgrade a basic drive if the sector size of the disk is greater than 512 bytes.

In some cases, you can't close all the programs running on a disk before you upgrade. If you want to convert your system disk, for example, the Computer Management Console must be running. In these cases, you must reboot your computer for the upgrade to take place. You probably want to do that right away, because certain events, such as those listed below, can cause the update to fail:

♦ Disconnecting all existing dynamic drives while the system is rebooting

♦ Replacing a disk or set of disks that will be upgraded

♦ Changing the disk layout of a disk that is being upgraded

♦ I/O errors on the disk during the upgrade

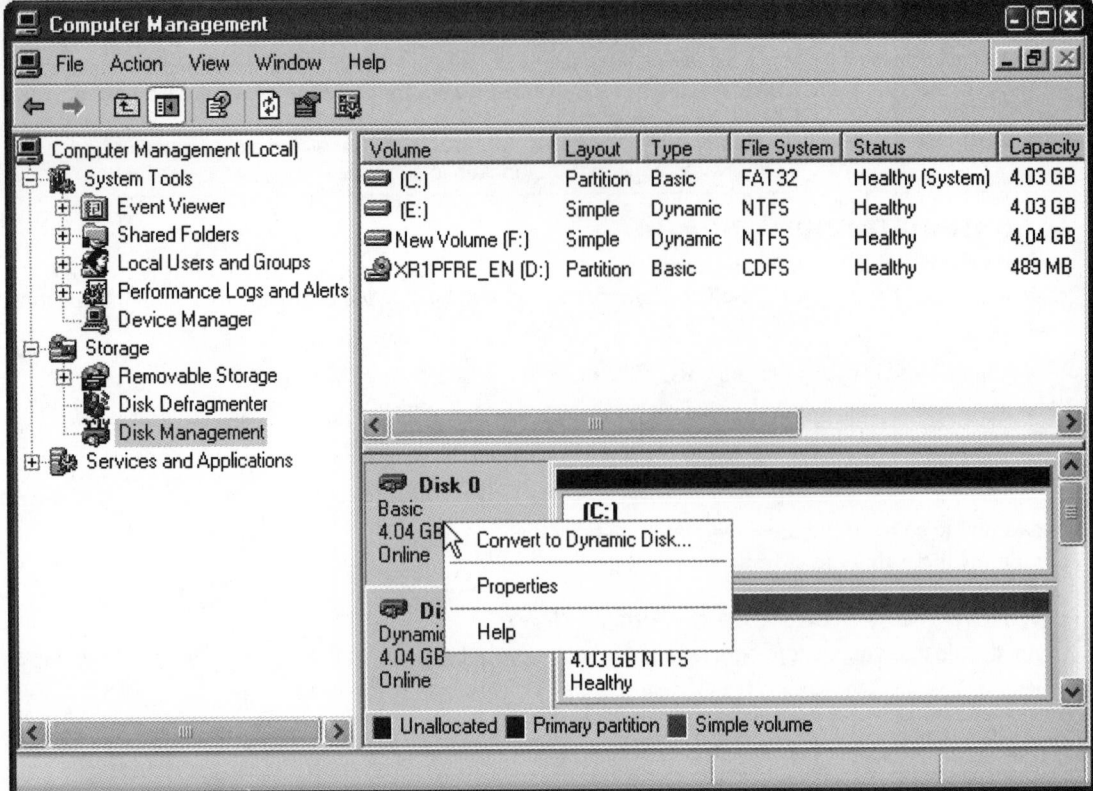

Figure 3-11: Upgrading a basic disk to dynamic

Refresh and Rescan

When viewing your disks through the Disk Management tool, the current state of the system might not always be reflected in the display. There are two different tools with which you can update your display to better reflect your disks: Refresh and Rescan. Refresh is the less thorough of the two. It refreshes the GUI (graphical user interface) display to show any changes in the volume information. Rescan does a deeper examination of your hardware. It looks for new or missing disks and re-enumerates them. Of the two, Refresh is faster than Rescan because it does less.

Mark partition active

When you mark a partition as active, the partition becomes the partition from which your computer boots when you power it up. Your active partition must be a primary partition on a basic drive. If you have only the Windows XP operating system on your computer, the partition can be the same as the system partition — where your Windows XP files are located.

Modify drive letter

If you don't like the way in which your drives are lettered, you can change the letters by following these steps:

STEPS

Changing drive letters

1. Choose Start ⇨ Control Panel ⇨ Administrative Tools.

2. Click Computer Management.

3. Expand Storage in the console tree, and then select Disk Management.

4. Right-click the drive whose letter assignment you wish to change. Select Change Drive Letter and Paths.

5. Select the drive letter in the box and click Change.

6. As shown in Figure 3-12, click the arrow to the right of the list box to choose an available drive letter.

7. Click OK, and then click Close.

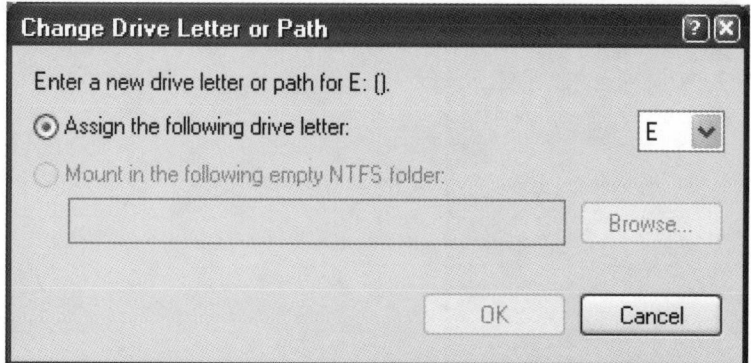

Figure 3-12: You can assign a new drive letter from the list box. Only available drive letters will be listed.

The list of drive letters that you can assign includes only available letters, not those that are already assigned. After you switch the letters following the steps above, the drive will be assigned the new letter. However, the old letter is also still assigned to this drive until you reboot. This means that if you wish to flip-flop drive letters, you first have to assign one drive to a third, unused letter, and then restart your computer. After you restart, take these steps again, this time assigning the second drive to the now-free letter. Then repeat the steps again, switching the first drive to the second drive's now free drive letter.

There may be some unintended consequences if you switch drive letters — especially hard drive letters. If you switch drive letters, and you had shortcuts pointing to those drives, the shortcuts will no longer work. You have to edit them so that they point to the new, correct drive letter. Entries on your Documents menu might also be affected. If you have moved the My Documents folder, and it is located on a drive that has had its drive letter changed, you will have to point to the new drive. While it is true that third-party utilities such as Norton Utilities can refer such broken references, it's best to avoid the problem from the start if possible.

> **CAUTION:** Also, note that if you have several drives, such as D:, E:, F:, and G: and you want to make a new drive E:, you would have to bump F and G down a letter if you want the drives to stay in their existing order. So, be careful when you changing drive letters and try to avoid doing so if possible.

Format

You can format any disk partition from the shortcut menu. Of course, if you format a drive, all the files on the drive are deleted. Be careful with the formatting commands. For both hard drives and floppy drives, clicking Format first takes you to a dialog box where you can abort any Format command that you issue.

STEPS

Formatting a hard drive

1. Choose Start ⇨ Control Panel ⇨ Administrative Tools.

2. Select Computer Management, expand the Storage node, and then select Disk Management.

3. Right-click the drive you want to format and select Format. The Format dialog box appears, as shown in Figure 3-13.

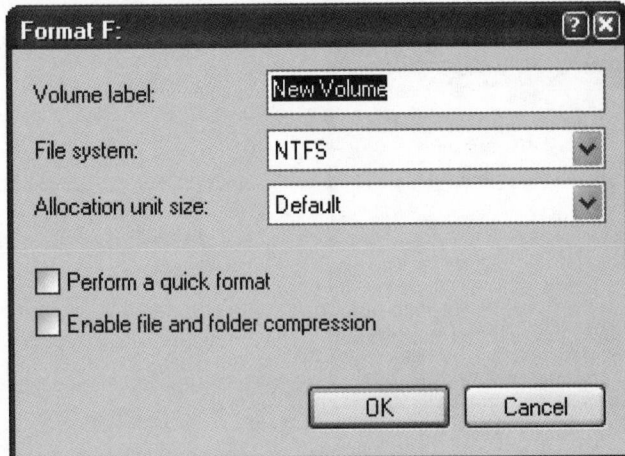

Figure 3-13: You have a number of choices to make in the Format dialog box, including the file system, the cluster size, and the volume label (hidden in this view).

4. Before formatting, you have a number of choices to make. You need to decide which file system to use (NTFS or FAT), the cluster size (the default cluster size for your size drive can be found in Table 3-1 at the beginning of this chapter), the volume label (which can be left blank), and whether you want to enable file and folder compression.

5. Click OK to begin the formatting. If you decide you don't want to lose all the files on this drive, click Cancel.

> **TIP:** The Quick Format option deletes the file allocation table and root directory on a drive, but it does not scan the entire disk for bad sectors. You can perform a quick format only on a previously formatted disk, and you should use it only if you are sure the disk is in good condition. If you perform a quick format and bad sectors exist, some of your data might get written to those bad sectors, resulting in a loss of files.

You cannot format a floppy disk from the Drive Management snap-in. Instead, you format floppies from My Computer or from the Windows Explorer.

STEPS

Formatting a floppy disk

1. Insert the disk you want to format into your floppy drive.

2. Open My Computer or the Windows Explorer.

3. In My Computer, right-click your floppy drive and then select Format. In the Windows Explorer, right-click your floppy drive in the folder pane, and then select Format.

You can also issue a Format command from the command prompt for both hard drives and floppy disks. To use it, choose Start ⇨ Run ⇨ Command, and then type the following command:

```
format drive: {options}
```

To use the Format command on a hard drive, you must be logged on as a member of the Administrator's group. Table 3-8 lists the Format command parameters.

Table 3-8: Format Command Parameters

Parameter	Meaning
`drive:`	The drive you want to format. This must be a valid drive letter on your system. If you do not specify any of the optional switches below, then the existing settings will be repeated.
Optional Parameters	
`/fs: filesystem`	The file system to use while formatting. This can be either NTFS or FAT. If you are formatting a floppy or Zip disk, this can be FAT only.
`/v: name`	The volume label for the drive. If you don't specify this value, Windows XP will prompt you for a volume label after formatting. If the disk might also be used by an MS-DOS system, there is an 11-character limit for the volume name; otherwise, the limit is 32 characters.
`/a: size`	This is the cluster size, measured by the number of bytes per cluster. Allowable values are 512, 1024, 2048, or 4096. If you do not specify this, then cluster size will depend on disk size, and will be set to the default in Table 3-1.
`/q`	Performs a quick format. See the information in the previous Tip.
`/f: size`	Specifies the size of the floppy disk. The values are: 160, 180, 320, 360, 720, 1200, 1440, 2880, 20.8MB (magneto-optical disk). The physical disk must be able to handle the size you choose here.
`/t:# of tracks` `/n: # of sectors`	Rather than specifying the size of the disk with the preceding command, you can say how many tracks and sectors to use. These two commands must be used together, and they can't be used with the `/f:` command.
`/c:`	Sets compression on by default for all new files. (For NTFS drives only.)
`/1`	For a floppy disk, formats only one side.
`/4`	For a floppy disk, formats a disk in a 1.2MB disk drive as a 360K disk (the same format as a 5.25-inch floppy disk).
`/8`	This will format eight sectors per track on a 5.25-inch floppy disk. This ensures compatibility with versions of MS-DOS earlier than 2.0.

Chkdsk

For those of you whose computer experience stretches back to the days of MS-DOS, the mention of Chkdsk might bring you a warm feeling of nostalgia. (Depending on your memories of DOS, it might also send shudders down your spine.) Chkdsk is a command-line utility that checks the status of a disk, checks for errors, and optionally allows you fix those errors. Chkdsk ships with Windows XP.

> **TIP:** Chkdsk is able to run on hard drives, removable drives (such as Zip drives), and floppy drives. However, it is not able to run on CD-ROM or DVD drives. You will get a different report based on the file system used on the drive you are checking. Reports on NTFS drives are more detailed.

To run Chkdsk on a hard drive, you need to access the command prompt, type the following command, and then press Enter:

```
c:\chkdsk {drive:path\filename} {options}
```

Chkdsk uses the optional parameters listed in Table 3-9.

Table 3-9: Chkdsk Parameters

Parameter	Meaning
drive:	The drive you want Chkdsk to examine. If this value is left blank, Chkdsk checks the current drive, which would be the C: drive in the example given before this table.
path\filename	Chkdsk will check the specified path and filename for file fragmentation. You can use wildcards here.
/f	Causes Chkdsk to fix the errors it finds. It can do this only if the disk is locked. If you can't lock the disk, it will ask if you want it checked the next time the computer starts.
/v	Enables verbose mode. It will display every filename in every directory that it checks.
/r	Locates any bad sectors on the disk and recovers any information it can. The disk must be locked for this option.
/l{:filesize}	On an NTFS drive, it will set the size of the log file to the size specified. If you don't specify a filesize, it will report the current size.
/x	On an NTFS drive, it forces the volume to dismount, which makes all open handles to the volume invalid. This also will automatically process /f actions.

Output from Chkdsk differs depending on the file system in use on the disk that you are checking. Figure 3-14 shows the output from running Chkdsk on a floppy drive that uses the FAT file system.

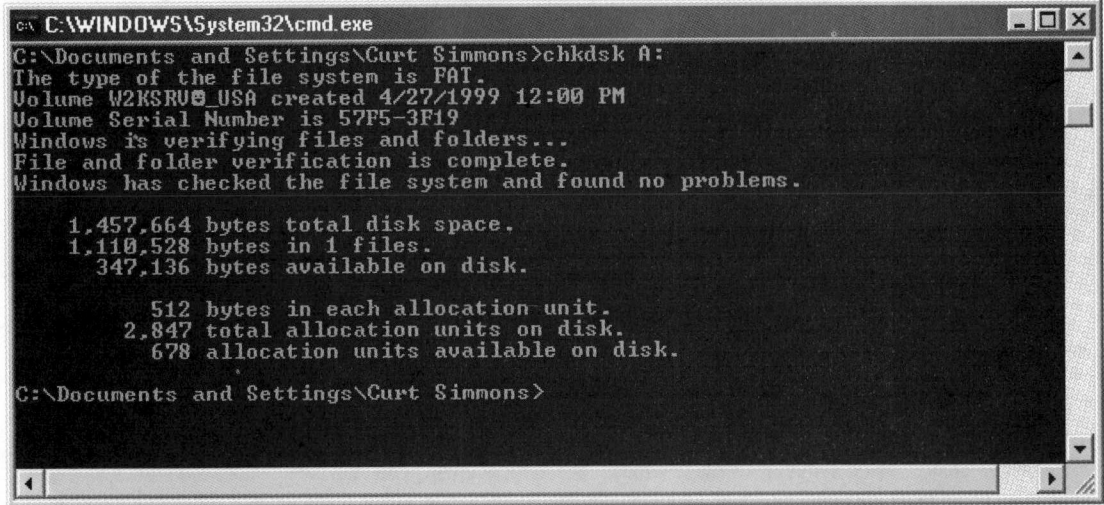

Figure 3-14: Running Chkdsk on a FAT disk gives you a display similar to what you would see when you run Chkdsk on a DOS or Windows 3.1 system.

Typing the same Chkdsk command on an NTFS drive gives much more feedback — verifying files, indices, and security descriptors as shown in Figure 3-15. Both reports come from running Chkdsk with only the drive letter as an argument.

The important item to keep in mind about Chkdsk is that it is a lower-level utility that can provide you with more information about disk status and configuration than the existing operating system tools interface. If you really want a complete report about a disk, use this tool to find what you need.

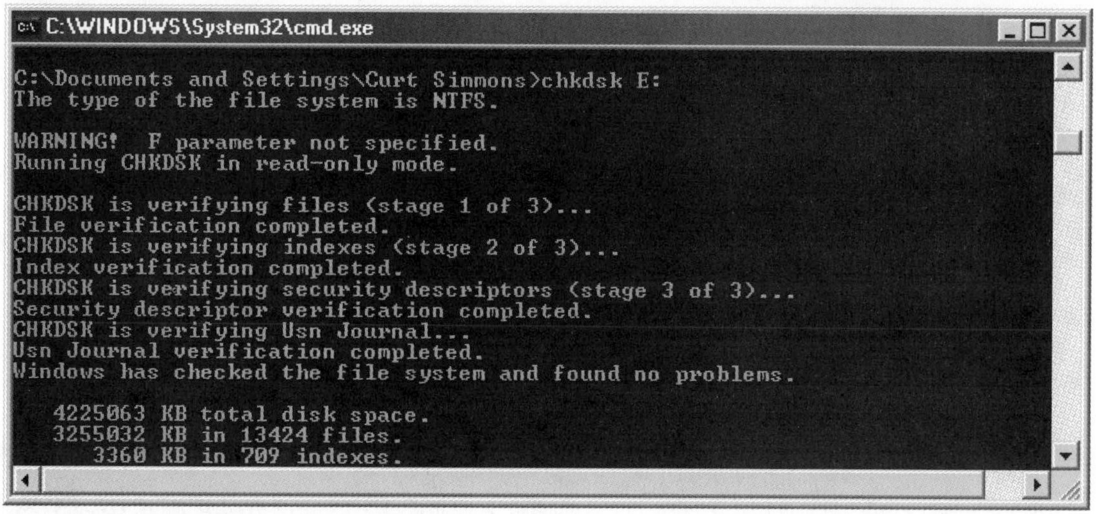

```
C:\WINDOWS\System32\cmd.exe                                    _ □ X

C:\Documents and Settings\Curt Simmons>chkdsk E:
The type of the file system is NTFS.

WARNING! F parameter not specified.
Running CHKDSK in read-only mode.

CHKDSK is verifying files (stage 1 of 3)...
File verification completed.
CHKDSK is verifying indexes (stage 2 of 3)...
Index verification completed.
CHKDSK is verifying security descriptors (stage 3 of 3)...
Security descriptor verification completed.
CHKDSK is verifying Usn Journal...
Usn Journal verification completed.
Windows has checked the file system and found no problems.

   4225063 KB total disk space.
   3255032 KB in 13424 files.
      3360 KB in 709 indexes.
```

Figure 13-15: Running Chkdsk on an NTFS drive

About Disk Indexing

If you take a look at the General tab of a disk drive's properties, you'll see an "Allow Indexing Service to index this disk for fast file searching" option. This check box enables the Indexing Service to catalog the disk so that when you perform a search, it can find the item on the disk by using the disk's catalog. That all sounds great, and if you have to perform a lot of search functions, then it can be. However, in order for Indexing Service to keep up with the changes and new files to your disk, it has to run in the background, which consumes system resources. Here is one instance where you can turn a feature off and save system resources. If you believe that the Indexing Service is that important to your needs, certainly leave it enabled, but if you rarely use the Search feature, then clear this check box to give your system a little performance boost.

Final Disk Usage Tips

The computer's hard disk is not something you will need to spend a lot of time configuring or worrying about. Once you have a configuration that works, it's really all about maintenance. As you work with your computer, however, it is important to make the best use of the computer's hard disk in order to make the most of storage space and performance. As you work with Windows XP, keep the following points in mind:

♦ If at all possible, use NTFS. NTFS provides you the best file system, best security features, and makes the best use of disk storage space.

♦ Keep disk volumes to a minimum. You may have four hard drives and be capable of creating 50 different volumes, but you should question if that configuration will help you. Volumes, in and of themselves, consume disk space for organization purposes, not to mention that too many volumes becomes more confusing than helpful. To keep your system and storage organized do not create volumes that you do not need.

♦ Get in the habit of running regular backups, defragmentation, and error checking. These procedures can be run during off hours, and they ensure that data is never lost and that your hard disk is always performing in peak condition.

♦ Use dynamic drives over basic drives. Dynamic drives give you more configuration and management flexibility.

- Although you can share entire disks or volumes on a network, from a security point of view, you should share only folders that are really needed on that network.

- Use disk quotas to control how much storage space users are consuming on your system's hard disk if multiple users are storing data.

Summary

Windows XP provides advanced management tools that enable you both configure and manage drives on your Windows XP computer: This chapter explored the following points:

- Windows XP, like Windows 2000, supports dynamic drive configurations and disk volumes. These features enable easy management and easy reconfiguration as necessary.

- Disk tools, such as error checking, disk quotas, defragmentation, and backup enable you to protect data while making the best use of your computer's hard disk.

- With Windows XP, you can easily format and compress drives as well as folders as needed in order to reconfigure drvies and conserve disk space.

Part II

XP Interface and Settings Secrets

Chapter 4

Display and Taskbar Configuration

In This Chapter

After Windows XP is installed, your first view of the operating system will be different than your first view of previous versions of Windows. By default, there are no icons on the desktop except for Recycle Bin, and the Start Menu looks and works somewhat differently than in the past. Overall, the default interface is more graphics driven, which is supposed to make Windows easier for new users while also making it flexible for advanced users. That statement, of course, is matter of opinion, but the good news is that you can configure display and taskbar settings in a number of different ways, which you learn to do in this chapter. In this chapter, you learn about . . .

+ Using the Windows XP interface
+ Applying themes in Windows XP
+ Modifying the Windows XP theme or the Classic theme
+ Configuring desktop icons and their management
+ Configuring the taskbar and related toolbars

The Windows XP Desktop

Ah, the desktop — that place in Windows where you find your main icons and where you even place your stuff for easy access. When Windows XP is first booted, it is often a shock to see the empty desktop with only the Recycle Bin present. Of course, your typical desktop items such as My Computer are not gone; rather, they have been relocated to a different place in Windows — the Start Menu primarily. The idea behind this new look is to keep your desktop clean while making the usual desktop icons you might need readily available on the Start Menu. As applications are installed and shortcuts to those applications placed on the desktop, you can easily open applications from the desktop or move those shortcuts to the Start Menu. In the end, you have more customization options so that Windows XP looks exactly the way you want it to.

The new Windows XP interface is in fact a theme. Themes first became very popular in Windows 98 when Microsoft included a host of additional themes. The themes change not only the Windows desktop, but also the icons, sounds, and basic system settings. In short, a theme controls every aspect of how your operating system looks and "feels." Themes have certainly not gone away in Windows XP, and the XP interface you first see is simply a theme — a theme that is customizable.

The XP theme and the bulk of the Windows desktop appearance settings are configured using Display Properties, a properties dialog box with which I am sure you are familiar. However, XP's Display Properties has changed somewhat, and in this section, I show you how to reconfigure the XP display in a manner that is pleasing to you. I assume that you've worked with Display Properties before, so I don't go into the basics here, but I do show you how to make changes, along with outlining what you can and can't do.

The Display Properties dialog box in Windows XP is found under Display in Control Panel, or you can simply right-click an empty area of the desktop and click Properties. Either way, you arrive at the Display

Properties dialog box, and the following sections explore what you can do and how you can change the appearance and settings of your system.

Themes

The first tab you see under Display Properties is the Themes tab. Because the default XP interface is a theme, it's no surprise that the theme concept now has its own tab in Display Properties. The only thing you can do on the Themes tab, shown in Figure 4-1, is use the drop-down menu to select a different theme, or create a new theme. The drop-down menu provides you with the default XP theme, but you can also choose the Windows Classic theme, which makes XP look like Windows 9x/Me/2000. Or you can choose My Current Theme, which is simply a naming convention that is used for your current theme, which you can modify. Of course, you can select any theme and make changes to it by using the remainder of the display properties tabs setting options. In this case, Windows automatically saves your settings by naming the theme with a (Modified) listing. For example, the default theme is Windows XP. If you make setting changes, the theme is not overwritten, is simply renamed as Windows XP (Modified). This feature prevents you from accidentally overwriting the XP or Windows Classic default themes. Either way, you can adjust the theme that you want to use or create your own by selecting a theme, clicking Save As, and giving the theme a name. You can then make configuration changes as desired. If you have checked out the XP theme and decided that it is not right for you, you can easily select the Windows Classic theme, which you can modify to suit your taste.

TIP: Themes that you modify or create are saved in My Documents as a theme file. The file is essentially a listing of settings the system reads in order to create the theme. You can view the settings by opening the theme file with Notepad or any text editor.

Desktop

The Desktop tab, shown in Figure 4-2, enables you to choose a background picture or pattern for use on your desktop. You can choose from a variety of default pictures or graphics files in the list, or you can Browse and select your own. The desktop display is rather versatile — you can choose to display virtually any kind of picture file, even an HTML page from the Internet if you like. If you do not want to use a picture or graphics file at all, just select the None option in the list and use the Color drop-down menu to select a background color. You can be creative here, so try several different settings to find the one that is right for you.

NOTE: If you are having problems with a picture or pattern being distorted, use the Position drop-down menu and change the item from Stretch to Center.

The Customize Desktop button at the bottom of the Desktop tab enables you to make a number of additional desktop appearance changes. Clicking the Customize Desktop button brings up two tabs, the General tab and the Web tab. There are a few different settings on the General tab, shown in Figure 4-3, which are as follows:

♦ **Desktop icons** — By default, only the Recycle Bin appears on the XP theme interface, but you can change that behavior by selecting My Documents, My Computer, My Network Places, or Internet Explorer if you want those icons back on the Desktop. Of course, you can put more than these on the desktop by using shortcuts, which are explored in Chapter 5, but if you want these icons back, just check the options.

♦ **Icon selection** — The default item icons are shown in the middle portion of the window. If you do not want to use a default icon, just select it and click the Change Icon button. An icon list appears where you can select a number of other icons found in C:\Windows\System32, or you can browse and select your own icons from among those that you have downloaded or created. You learn more about creating icons later in this chapter.

Figure 4-1: Use the Themes tab to make changes to the default XP theme, to use Windows Classic theme, or to create your own theme.

- ◆ **Desktop cleanup** — Windows XP includes a new Desktop Cleanup Wizard. By default, the wizard is configured to run automatically every 60 days, but if you don't want the wizard to run, you can turn it off by clearing the check box option. Basically, the wizard just looks for shortcuts and files to move to an unused items folder. The cleanup wizard is okay, but you, like me, may get annoyed that it moves things around, so I prefer to skip it.

The Web tab enables you to display a Web page on your desktop. While you can display an HTML file by simply using the background selection options, you can display an actual live Web page using the Web tab. If you click New, you see the option to add a new Web page by entering the URL, or you can visit the Microsoft Desktop Gallery and select Web-based items from that site. If you have used Windows 98/Me, these options are certainly familiar.

SECRET: If you don't want items to move around on the desktop, click the Lock Desktop Items check box on the Web tab. This will prevent you from accidentally moving items around, and is a good setting if other people, such as your kids, use the computer.

After you choose a Web page to display, you can choose to Synchronize that Web page with the Internet by clicking Synchronize. This enables Internet content that has changed on the Web site to be updated with your desktop version. Of course, clicking Synchronize over and over in order to get new content would not be much fun, so there is an automated way to do this as well. The following steps show you how to automate synchronization.

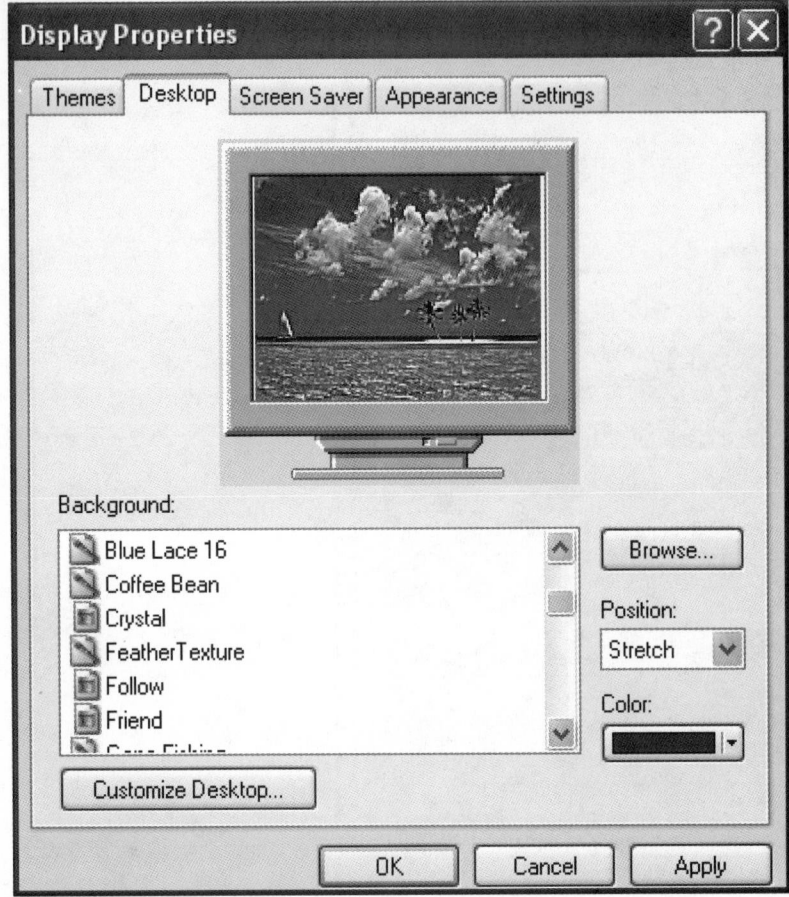

Figure 4-2: Use the Desktop tab to select and customize a desktop picture or pattern.

STEPS

Automatic synchronization of Web page desktop display

1. On the Web tab, select the desired Web page and click the Properties button.

2. Click the Schedule tab, and then click the Use the following schedule radio button. Click Add.

3. In the New Schedule dialog box, shown in Figure 4-4, create a schedule for content download. This can be as frequent as you like, and if you do not have a persistent Internet connection, you can choose to have Windows automatically connect for you by clicking the check box option.

4. Click the Download tab, which is shown in Figure 4-5. The settings here enable you to control the content that is downloaded to your computer. You can configure the link depth and hard drive space usage settings by using this page, and you can click the Advanced button and deselect some items that might take up too much room (such as Java applets). Make your selections and click OK.

Desktop Items

General | Web

Desktop icons

☐ My Documents   ☐ My Network Places
☑ My Computer   ☐ Internet Explorer

My Computer   My Documents   My Network   Recycle Bin   Re
                              Places   (full)

Change Icon...   Restore Default

Desktop cleanup

Desktop cleanup moves unused desktop items to a folder.

☑ Run Desktop Cleanup Wizard every 60 days

Clean Desktop Now

OK   Cancel

Figure 4-3: Desktop Items General tab

New Schedule

Please specify settings for your new schedule.

Every 1 ⬍ days at   7:40 AM ⬍

Name: My Scheduled Update

☑ If my computer is not connected when this
   scheduled synchronization begins,
   automatically connect for me

OK   Cancel

Figure 4-4: Create a Schedule

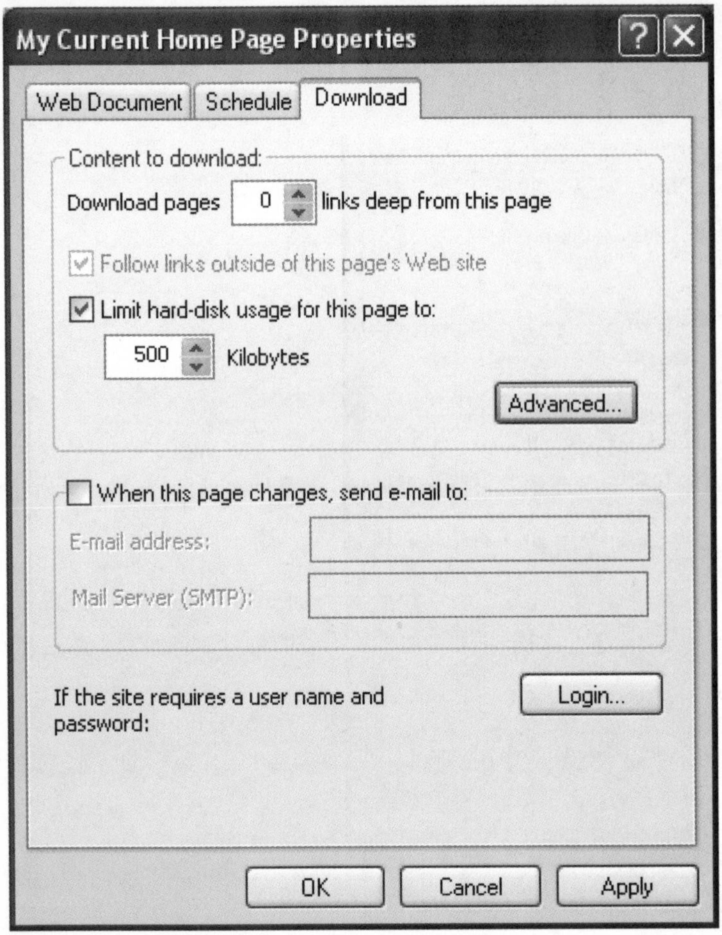

My Current Home Page Properties [?][X]

Web Document | Schedule | Download

Content to download:

Download pages [0 ▲▼] links deep from this page

[✓] Follow links outside of this page's Web site

[✓] Limit hard-disk usage for this page to:

[500 ▲▼] Kilobytes

[Advanced...]

[ ] When this page changes, send e-mail to:

E-mail address: [   ]

Mail Server (SMTP): [   ]

If the site requires a user name and password: [Login...]

[OK]   [Cancel]   [Apply]

Figure 4-5: Download tab

TIP: The more lenient you are with these settings, the more content you will see on your desktop. If you are worried about drive-consumption space, it may be best not use to use an HTML page on your desktop. However, if you are only interested in the content a site provides and not the graphics, click the Advanced tab and clear the Images check box so that images are not downloaded to your computer.

Screen Saver

The Screen Saver tab in the Display Properties dialog box enables you to choose a screen saver and the timeout interval that must occur before the screen saver activates. If you like, you can choose the password protect option, which locks your computer when the screen saver activates. You must use your account password to reenter the system. This is a great security feature, which keeps other people from snooping around your computer when you step away from it. If you are in a workgroup setting, I particularly recommend that you enable this feature. You can also configure Power options here, which are explored in Chapter 10.

Appearance

The Appearance tab gives you a number of specific settings that you can adjust. As Figure 4-6 shows, the Appearance tab provides a simpler front end to these settings. You can choose to use Windows XP or Windows Classic style windows and buttons, choose a default color scheme, and choose a font size (normal, large, extra large).

Figure 4-6: Appearance tab

Don't worry — the Appearance options that were found on this tab in Windows 9x/Me/2000 are still here, but you have to click the Advanced button to access them. This action opens the Advanced Appearance window where you can individually adjust the color and font settings for Windows items, such as active title bar, desktop, caption buttons, menu, scroll bar, and a host of others. When you select a setting, the default settings appear in the in the drop-down menus and selection buttons. Just use these menus and buttons to change the appearance of items, as shown in Figure 4-7.

For the most part, the default settings are probably fine, but it important to remember that these settings give you a fine level of control over appearance. For example, you can adjust how items fit on the desktop by changing the Icon Spacing settings or you can change the color and size of the active window's border. Whatever the appearance setting might be, you can configure it here. Just experiment with the settings until you find the ones that are right for you. (I often use these settings to change the desktop background color because you have more options here. Also, I recommend you take a look at the fonts on your windows settings. If you like what you see, leave it as is, but you may find a font that is easier for you to read, so definitely check those out.)

The final setting options on the Appearance tab concerns effects. If you click the Effects button, the Effects window appears, shown in Figure 4-8, which gives you just few selection items. For example, the default XP behavior is to provide a fade-out appearance for menus and tooltips. This is cool, but it does take up a lot of time, so you can change it here. You can also adjust the additional settings on this window, which are all self-explanatory.

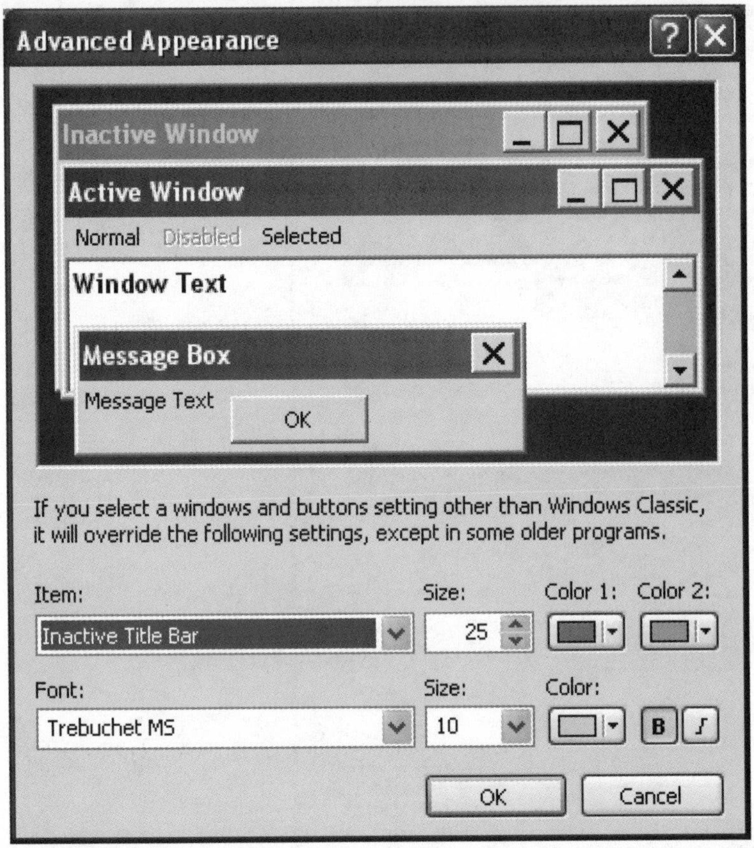

Figure 4-7: Advanced Appearance

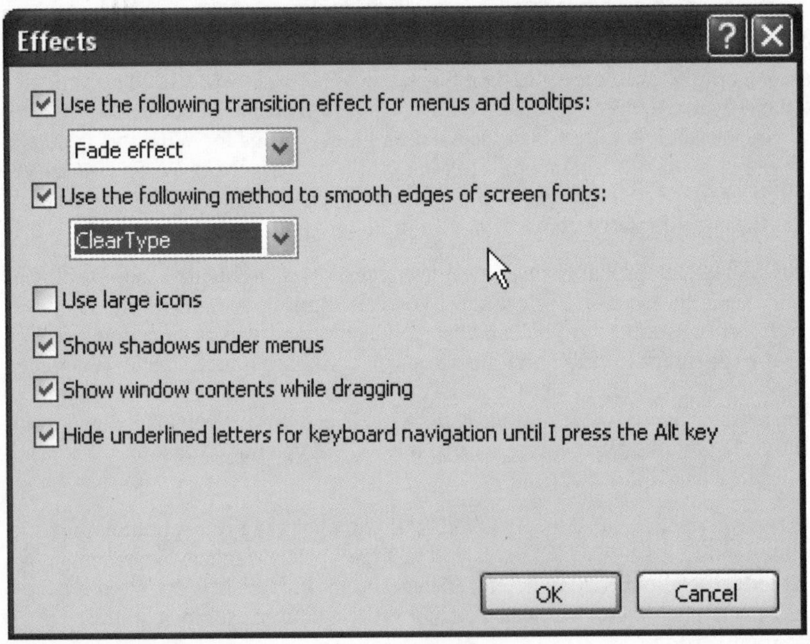

Figure 4-8: Effects settings

SECRET: These visual settings are all nice, but they require more processing power from your computer. If you are having performance problems, don't use these, and also see Chapter 24 for more information about how to conserve system resource usage by reducing XP's visual effects.

Settings

Finally, the Settings tab provides you with settings for your computer's display adapter. You can adjust the screen resolution and color quality here. You can also launch the Video Display Troubleshooter and access advanced settings for the video card. The advanced settings are self-explanatory, but here are some things to note:

♦ If your video card's resolution makes screen items too small to view, you can change the DPI settings on the General tab to a larger setting. This may make the screen items easier to see under the current video card.

♦ By default, modes that the video card cannot support are hidden from the selection options on the Settings tab. You can change this behavior by clearing the check box on the Monitor tab; this is not recommended because attempting to use unsupported modes may cause damage to the video card.

♦ Use the Color Management tab to choose a color profile for the monitor. Under most circumstances you do not need to do this, but if you are having problems with the monitor appearance, you can try some of these settings to see if there is any improvement.

Adding Items to the Desktop and Creating Your Own Desktop Content

It is easy to put new items, represented by icons, on the desktop. You can place new (empty) folders, new shortcuts, or new (blank) documents on the desktop. By default, you can create new documents of these types: Internet Document (HTML), Text, WordPad, Bitmap Image, Briefcase, and Wave Sound. If you like, you can add more document types to the list, or remove document types from the list. Just right-click any empty desktop area, point to New, and make your selection.

When you create a new shortcut (right-click the desktop, point to New on the context menu, click Shortcut), a wizard starts that guides you through the process of linking your new shortcut to an application. When you install new applications, they often add their own document type to the New menu. Follow the wizard screens to add the shortcut, and also see Chapter 5 to learn more about shortcuts.

TIP: Placing new blank documents on the desktop is a pretty nifty feature and contributes to the document-centric character of Windows. When you click a new document icon on your Desktop, Windows brings up the appropriate application and opens the blank document within it so that you can edit the document. To add new document icons to the Desktop, right-click the Desktop, point to New, and then click the document type that you want to add.

The new documents don't necessarily have to be empty or unformatted. You can create forms or certain subtypes of documents, such as "my standard format letter," and use them as a basis for creating new documents.

Pasting and undoing actions

The Paste command on the desktop context menu lets you copy (or move) a file (or application, folder, or shortcut) to the desktop. For example, if to copy a file to the desktop, first select a file in a folder window or in the Explorer. Then right-click the file and choose Copy, which means "copy this file to someplace as soon as I tell you where." Finally, right-click the desktop and choose Paste to tell Windows, "this is where I want you to copy the file." Windows includes the Paste command in context menus for a variety of other (yet to be investigated) desktop icons.

Your desktop context menu might include an Undo command below the Paste command. The specific Undo command that appears depends on what actions you took in folder windows. If you have just renamed a file, for example, you will see the Undo Rename command. If you have just deleted a file, you will see the Undo Delete command.

The Undo command shows up in the desktop context menu (and in most context menus) whenever you have taken an action that can be undone. If you remember what it was that you did and you want to undo it (as long as you haven't quit and restarted Windows), here's your chance.

Animating your desktop

You can place animated GIF files on your desktop and let them play over and over and over again. Animated GIF files are graphics files that contain multiple images that are displayed one after another to simulate motion. You can create animated GIF files with Paint Shop Pro. You'll find the latest version of Paint Shop Pro at www.jasc.com. You can also use the GIF Construction Set found at www.mindworkshop.com/alchemy/gifcon.html.

To enable your desktop to play animated GIF files, you need to take the following steps:

STEPS

Putting animated GIFs on your desktop

1. Right-click your desktop and click Properties.
2. Click the Desktop tab, and then click New.
3. In the New Desktop Item window, click Browse. Locate the item that you want to include and click Open; then click OK.

After the GIF icon appears on your desktop, you can drag it to the desired location and even access a menu above the icon to manage it. You can choose to split the desktop with the icons, or to cover the desktop with the GIF image. This may, however, cause distortion.

Macintosh, Anyone . . .

Just for fun, check out www.yaromat.com/macos/index.htm. I won't tell you what you'll see there because that would spoil the fun. It won't hurt.

If you really do want to make your Windows computer look more Mac-like (and why not), download some of the icons and other things that you can find at www.gjeffrey.com/mac/downloads.html. This will make those of you who have switched from the Mac to the dark side a bit more comfortable with your choice. Sort of like old home week!

Some folks didn't like the iMac, so they created the iHate iMac site. You can download their iMac Recycle Bin icon and desktop from www.iamlost.com/imac.

If you are interested in having the Macintosh user interface on your Windows computer, you might want to give the freeware MacVision a try. It transforms your desktop and your taskbar into the Macintosh desktop and Finder bar. MacVision essentially replaces you taskbar with a MacOS Finder bar. The MacOS Finder bar emulator program works just like the Macintosh Finder bar, so you'll get a feeling of mixed Windows and Macintosh worlds here. Whether you want to do this or not depends on your love of the Macintosh OS, but you can check it out at http://members.aol.com/JMB1984/MacVision if you are interested.

New Icons for Desktop Items

As noted earlier, you can replace icons for any items that you choose to view on your desktop, such as My Computer or My Documents. You can choose new icons to replace the default ones that come with your desktop. There are also many themes available for downloading on the Internet (lots with copyright infringement warnings written all over them). See the selection at CNET, which you will find at http://downloads.cnet.com. There's a bunch of other interesting downloads there as well, so spend a few moments browsing.

If you want to choose your own new icons instead of using the default Windows icons, you need to do manually what the themes application does automatically: You have to edit the Registry. Of course, to do this you also have to find a source of new icons.

Icons are stored in some executable files (files with .exe extensions), in some dynamic link libraries (files with .dll extensions), in icon files (files with .ico extensions), and in special icon libraries.

You can change the icons by accessing the General tab of Customize Desktop, found on the Desktop tab of Display Properties. You can also use the File Types tab of the Folder Options dialog box to search an individual file for icons.

STEPS

Looking at icons

1. Open My Computer. Choose View ⇨ Folder Options, and then click the File Types tab.
2. Click any file type in the Registered File Types list. Click the Advanced button.
3. Click the Change Icon button. The icons you see under Current Icon are contained in the file listed in the File Name field. To see icons in other files, click Browse. You can now search for another file that contains icons.

Be sure to click Cancel when you are done looking at icons.

Making your own icons

You can easily make your own icons, just by using MS Paint. Here's how:

STEPS

Making your own icons

1. Choose Start ⇨ Programs ⇨Accessories ⇨ Paint.
2. In the Paint window, choose Image ⇨ Attributes. Make the Height and Width 32 pixels, and click OK.
3. Choose View ⇨ Zoom, and then Show Grid.
4. Choose View ⇨ Zoom ⇨ Custom. Choose 800% and click OK.
5. Create your new icon. Save it as a .bmp file. You can change its extension later to .ico, if you like.
6. You can now treat this file as a regular icon file. Following the "Looking at icons" steps in the previous section, you can point to it and use it on your Desktop.

High Color icons

Although icons were originally limited to 16 colors, you can now have 16-bit (High Color, or 64 thousand colors) or 24-bit (True Color, or 16 million colors) color icons. If you create your own icons with MS Paint, you can choose the color depth.

To display High Color or True Color icons, you need a video card with enough memory at a given resolution. Right-click the desktop, click Properties, and then click the Settings tab. Check the Color drop-down list to find out what your color depth is. If you have enough memory, you'll see High Color (16 bit) and/or True Color (24 bit) in the list. If you don't see these values, reduce your screen resolution using the Screen Area slider. Then choose either High Color or True Color from the drop-down list and click OK.

After you've set your color depth to High Color or True Color, you can enable your desktop to display High Color or True Color icons. Right-click your desktop, click Properties, click the Effects tab, and mark Show icons using all possible colors.

If you choose High Color or True Color, you also get gradient fills in the title bars of your dialog boxes.

> **CAUTION:** You can experience some performance degradation when you choose True Color, depending on your graphics card and system resources.

Getting rid of unattached desktop icons

By unattached desktop icons I mean icons that got there when you installed a piece of software, but didn't go away when you deleted that software. If right-clicking the icons and clicking Delete doesn't work, and you can't see what is creating them, then there is a spot in the Registry where you might just find them.

Open your Registry Editor and navigate to `HKEY_LOCAL_MACHINE\SOFTWARE\Microsoft\Windows\CurrentVersion\explorer\Desktop\NameSpace`. There you'll find a set of Class IDs, as shown in Figure 4-9.

Before making any changes in this key, back it up. Highlight NameSpace in the left pane, and choose Registry ⇨ Export Registry File. Enter the name for this text backup of this branch, perhaps **NameSpace**, and click Save. If later you discover that you deleted something that you'd rather not have deleted, you can get it back by importing this file.

You can highlight each of these Class IDs and see if there is a corresponding application name displayed in the right pane. If there is a name that corresponds to the software that has been deleted from your computer, you can highlight the Class ID and then delete it.

If you have installed Outlook 98, 2000, or 2002, it has a Class ID in the NameSpace for its desktop icon (the Class ID starts with 00020D75) but no name in the right pane.

If you're considering deleting a Class ID and want to search first to see whether there are other instances of it in the Registry, you can do that. If you find other instances of this Class ID, you can see if they refer to program executables that are now deleted. If so, you can delete these branches of the Registry. Deleting the Class IDs from the NameSpace deletes the icons from the desktop.

Getting icons from the Web

Of course, the Internet is a fun and useful place to locate all kinds of free icons that you can use with Windows XP. These icons enable you to customize your interface in a way that you like. There are lots of sites to choose from, and you can easily locate them by using any search engine, but here are a few to get you started:

- www.yoink.com/iconcity
- www.dotico.com

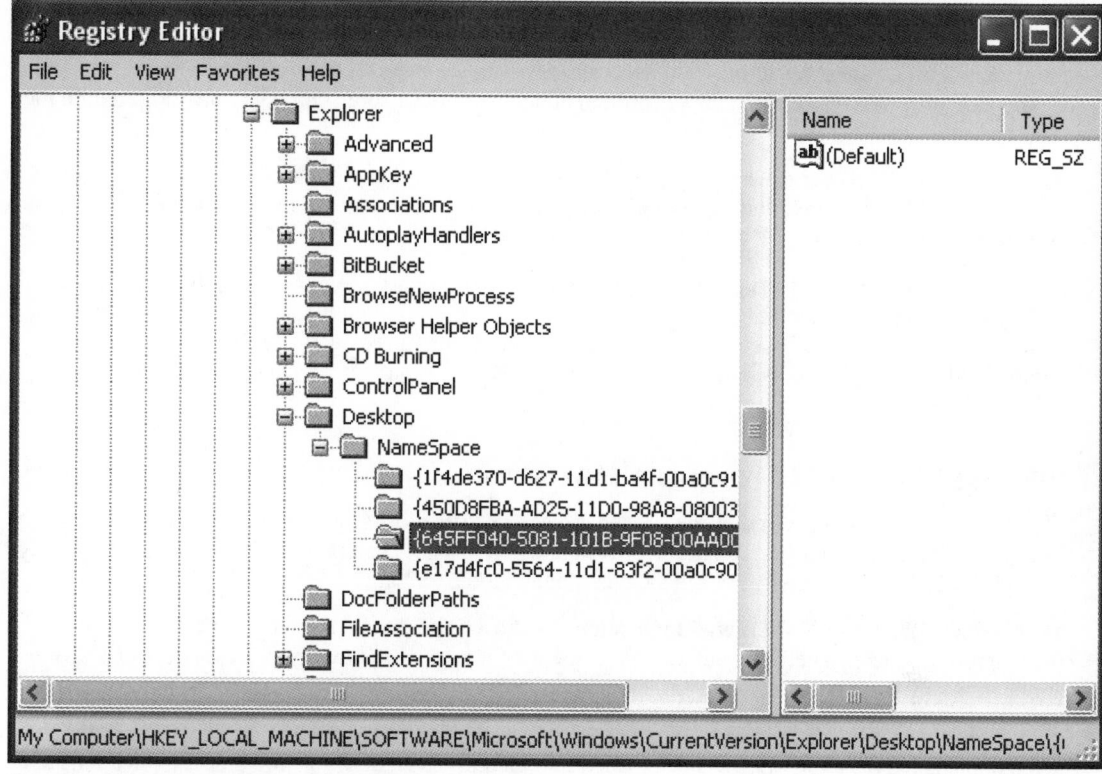

Figure 4-9: The Registry location of the NameSpace Class IDs

♦ `www.zeldman.com/icon1.html`

♦ `www.madsciencelaboratories.com/icons.html`

Increasing the size of your icon cache

If you find that the icons on your taskbar keep changing, such as shrinking in size or disappearing altogether, it may be because your icon cache is too small to keep copies of all the icons. You can increase the size of your icon cache by taking these steps:

STEPS

Increasing your icon cache size

1. Choose Start ⇨ Run, type **regedit**, and press Enter.

2. Navigate to
   `HKEY_LOCAL_MACHINE\SOFTWARE\Microsoft\Windows\CurrentVersion\explorer`.
   Highlight this key in the left pane of your Registry editor.

3. Right-click the right pane, and choose New ⇨ String Value.

4. Rename the string value **MaxCachedIcons**.

5. Double-click MaxCachedIcons in the right pane, type the value **2048**, and click OK.

Managing Scraps

Some Windows-aware applications can place *scraps* on the desktop (or in any folder window). You can try this out using WordPad. Open up a WordPad document. Select some text. Drag and drop it onto the desktop.

An icon with the name Scrap appears on the desktop. This is a document that can be read by WordPad. It is made up solely of the text that you dropped on the desktop. Click its icon on the desktop, and WordPad launches.

Scraps give you an easy way to pile up a bunch of notes or graphics on your desktop (or in any other folder) and then make something of them later. For example, you might want to put a scrap containing your company logo on the desktop, and then paste it into documents as you edit them. Scraps give you an alternative to the Clipboard, and the advantage of using them is that you can keep multiple pieces available at one time.

The Taskbar and Its Toolbars

The first time you start up Windows, the taskbar displays little more than the Start button, the Quick Launch toolbar, and a digital clock in the tray — and perhaps not even this much, depending on your XP configuration. In fact, you may not see a Quick Launch toolbar at all.

The taskbar is the home of the *active* applications — those applications that you started by clicking a file or an application icon. There is a button on the taskbar (or an icon in the tray) for every major active application or window (it is possible for applications to hide their taskbar icons).

An application or a document needs to be read into memory from the hard disk before it can act or be acted upon. An application that has been loaded into memory is an *active* application. Applications that are stored on your computer's hard disk but haven't been loaded into memory are *inactive*. A document is loaded into memory with its application. There aren't any stray documents out there in memory without their associated applications.

Some applications don't put buttons on the taskbar or icons in the tray. These "hidden" applications run in the background and aren't looking for any user input. You can hide the taskbar buttons of whatever applications you choose. You can also move taskbar buttons over to the tray, where they are displayed as small icons. The following sections explore taskbar and toolbar configuration options that are available to you.

Configuring the taskbar

You can right-click an empty area of the taskbar and click Properties to access the Taskbar's single properties dialog box, which is shown in Figure 4-10.

As Figure 4-10 shows, you have a few basic check box options that determine how the taskbar behaves, such as auto-hide, feature grouping, and the option to show Quick Launch. You also see a section for the Notification Area, formerly called System Tray, where you can choose to hide icons that are inactive. If you want to change this behavior per item, you can click the Customize button and determine how Notification Area icons are managed. For example, Figure 4-11 shows that I am using the available menu to hide the Windows Messenger when it is inactive. Your other choices are Always hide and Always show. The point here is that XP attempts to keep your taskbar clean by not showing icons that aren't doing anything. If your previous Windows PC was anything like mine, you ended with a long System Tray full of junk that wasn't telling me anything. This feature enables nonactive icons to hide, but you can edit them as desired.

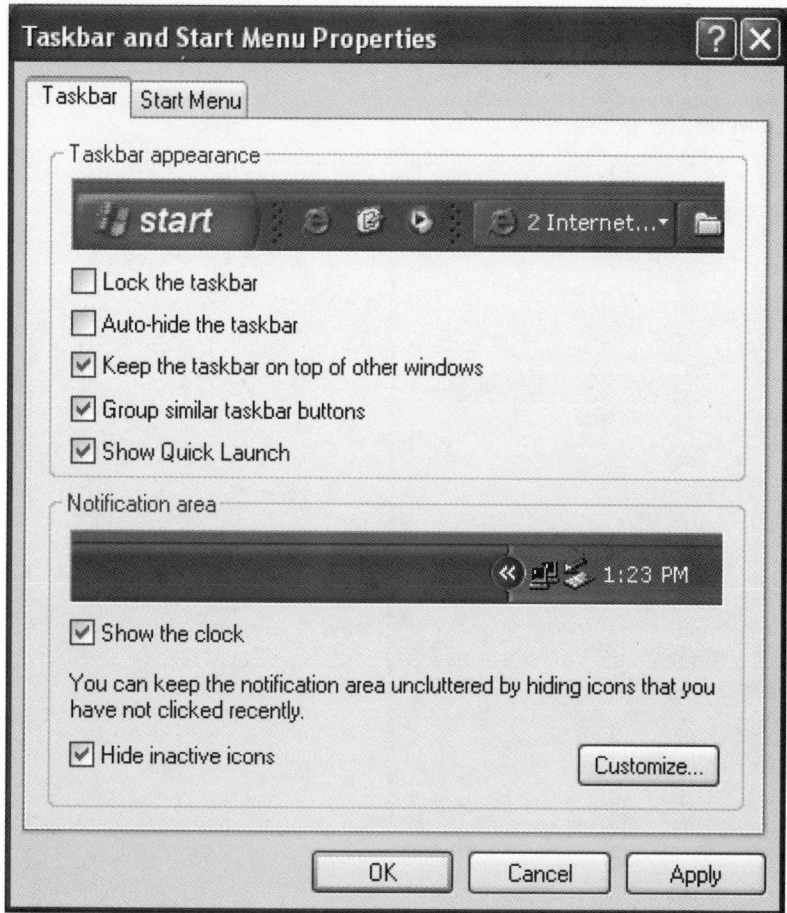

Figure 4-10: Taskbar properties

Using taskbar toolbars

Windows comes with a set of default toolbars. These toolbars resemble the taskbar and are connected to it. Right-click your taskbar, point to Toolbars, and click Address, Links, Desktop, or Quick Launch to display one of the default toolbars, or click New Toolbar to define your own (see the "Toolbars" section later in this chapter). If you want to hide a toolbar, clear the check mark next to its name in the Toolbars submenu. (You can't temporarily hide a user-defined toolbar. When you clear its check mark, the toolbar is removed.)

Taskbar buttons

Each taskbar button includes the application's or window's icon and name. If there is an associated document or file with the application, its name is supposed to appear first on the button (according to the Windows software design guidelines). The icons on the taskbar button are smaller versions of the icons you see on the desktop.

Windows and multidocument applications place the name of the application first on the taskbar button. For example, if you open a copy of Microsoft Word, you'll see a button labeled Microsoft Word on the taskbar, and you will be hard-pressed to see the name of the open document. If you open the Windows Notepad without a document, Untitled appears as the first name on the taskbar button.

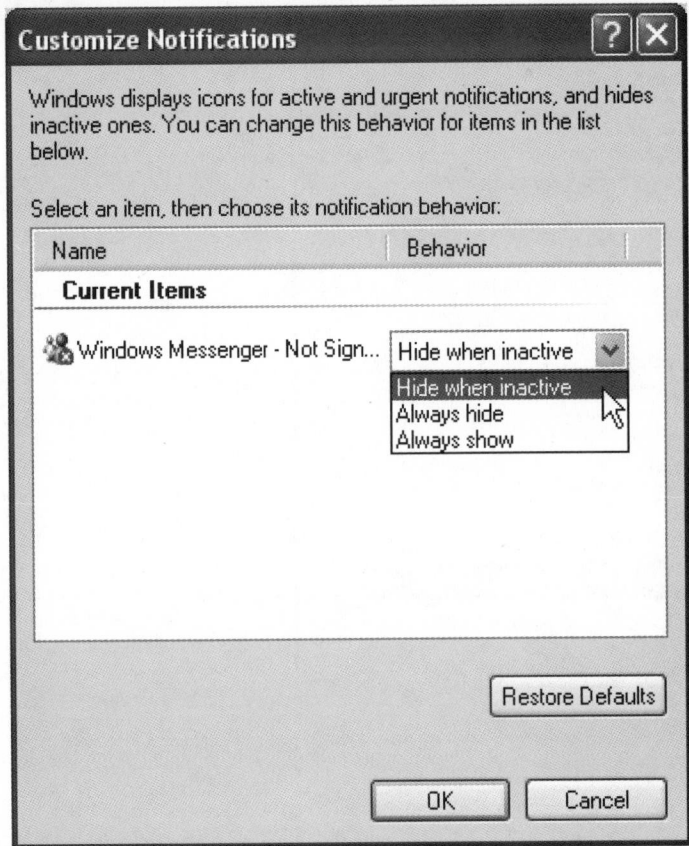

Figure 4-11: Customize Notification Area icon behavior

> **TIP:** Every user-interactive active application or window is represented on the taskbar, regardless of whether the application is currently minimized, restored, or maximized. (The only exceptions are applications that run behind the scenes, which don't need taskbar buttons, and those that have icons in the tray instead of taskbar buttons.) *This means that the taskbar is a task switcher.* It does not matter whether the active application has been minimized or is now buried under other application windows on the desktop; you can bring it to the top by clicking its button (a single click at that) on the taskbar.

The taskbar is one of Window's most fundamental "ease of use" improvements over the old Windows 3.1*x* interface. It is also an advantage that Windows has over the Apple Macintosh. This feature makes it almost impossible to lose track of which documents and programs are open, even when they are stacked on top of each other.

> **NOTE:** The single-click operation of the taskbar makes it easy to switch between *tasks* — which are simply active applications or windows. Combine this with Windows's enhanced resource management, and it is easy to find yourself using multiple active applications and opening multiple instances of your Explorer or My Computer windows. Windows makes multitasking (defined from the user's perspective as quickly jumping among active applications and windows) easy enough to be useful.

To toggle between minimizing and restoring an application window, just click the application's taskbar button, and then click again.

Sizing the taskbar

The taskbar starts out thin, but you can make it bigger — in fact, you can make it as large as one-half of the desktop.

Move your mouse pointer to the top edge of the taskbar so that the mouse pointer turns into a resize arrow. Hold down the left mouse button and drag the taskbar's edge upward. The taskbar increases in height in button-height increments.

Windows sizes the buttons on the taskbar automatically. All the buttons are the same size, no matter how long the names of the application and its associated document are. If the names are too long to fit in the button, Windows truncates them and places an ellipsis after them, if there is room.

You can see the full name of the application and document associated with a given button by placing your mouse pointer over the button and waiting for less than a second. A ToolTip (a small pop-up box with text) appears next to your mouse pointer. This happens only if the full name of the application and its associated document can't fit on the button face.

SECRET: As you open additional applications, the taskbar buttons shrink, unless you increase the size of the taskbar. When the buttons become so small that they are just big enough to contain the 16 x 16-pixel icons within them, they get no smaller. If you add more active applications at that point, all the icons will not be displayed at the same time on the taskbar. In this situation, a *spin control* appears on the taskbar. You can spin the control to see icons that are not currently in view.

The taskbar is attached to an edge of the desktop. If it is on the bottom, you can't narrow it by detaching it from the right or left edge. The resize arrow appears only when the mouse pointer is near the top of the taskbar. It is also possible to shrink the taskbar so that it only appears as an edge-line across the bottom of the screen. Of course, using this configuration is pointless and really aggravating, but it can be a fun practical joke to play on a good-natured family member or colleague.

Moving the taskbar

The taskbar doesn't have to be on the bottom of your desktop. You can move it to any other edge (the top, bottom, left, or right side of the screen).

To move the taskbar, position the mouse pointer over it, but not over any of the buttons on the taskbar, nor over the line at the left (or top) end of the taskbar button area. Press down the left mouse button and drag toward one of the other desktop edges. Release the mouse button when the outline of the taskbar is positioned on the desired edge.

SECRET: If you dock your taskbar on the right side, you can get to the buttons on the taskbar with an easy movement of the mouse. If the taskbar is hidden, however, it may be a bit too easy and end up as quite a bother. Here's why: If your document is anywhere near the right edge of your screen and you move the mouse quickly to the right to scroll, you are likely to overshoot the scroll bar and move to the desktop edge. Up pops the taskbar, which you didn't want. Now you have to move the mouse at least 10 pixels to the left of the taskbar to get the taskbar to disappear — a waste of time.

The advantage of placing the taskbar on the right is that it is easy for you to get to it. And if Auto hide is off, the taskbar stays in view, so you don't have to worry about making it pop up accidentally. However, there are disadvantages to placing the taskbar on the right. If Auto hide is turned on, you have to be accurate with your mouse to avoid inadvertently displaying the taskbar. Furthermore, a vertical taskbar with horizontal buttons is most likely fatter than a horizontal taskbar with horizontal buttons, because the buttons have to be wide enough to display the names (although this is only an issue if Auto hide is off).

One advantage of leaving the taskbar on the bottom or moving it to the left is that you can have Auto hide on and still not accidentally pop up the taskbar so often that it becomes annoying. And if you are left-handed, it might feel natural to attach the taskbar to the left edge of the desktop. However, docking the taskbar on the left side will probably be a difficult adjustment for most people, and if you place it on the bottom, the Start menu on the taskbar pops up instead of dropping down.

Placing the taskbar on the top edge of the desktop makes it feel like a menu bar or a toolbar, and moving the mouse to the top of your screen is a "natural" movement for Windows users. The Start menu also drops down from the Start button in a familiar manner. If you have the real estate, put the taskbar on the top edge and keep Always on top turned on and Auto hide turned off. This option will probably feel comfortable to you. (Just remember that if you turn on Auto hide, you'll have the problem of mouse overshoot when you choose menu items, although it won't be nearly as bad as if the taskbar is at the right.)

Test out each location to figure out which one works the best for you. Be sure to give yourself a reasonable amount of time to try each one.

> **SECRET:** Windows applications may be partially covered by the taskbar if they are at their restored size and the taskbar is attached to the top edge of the desktop with Always on top turned on and Auto hide turned off. When Windows applications are maximized, they are not obscured by the taskbar.

That Windows applications can't seem to find the taskbar when they are at their restored size can be quite annoying. If a window's title bar is covered by the taskbar, you have to use the keyboard to lower the window enough to bring the title bar into view. (Press Alt+spacebar, M, press the down arrow repeatedly to move the window down, and then click once.) You could also just maximize the application's window by pressing Alt+spacebar, X.

Resizing and moving windows on the desktop

By using the taskbar, you can cascade, tile, or minimize all the sizable windows on the desktop. Right-click the taskbar and choose one of the sizing options.

Minimize All Windows is a very powerful function, because it is paired with Undo Minimize All. (When you right-click the taskbar after choosing Minimize All Windows, the context menu contains an Undo Minimize All command.) You can clear your desktop with one command, and then place everything back where it came from with the opposite command. This is a very handy feature if you want to get to some icons on your desktop that are covered up by your application windows.

It is even easier to use the Show Desktop button on the Quick Launch toolbar. This button is also a toggle switch. Click it once to clear your desktop of all open windows. Click it again to restore them.

Toolbars

Toolbars add another way to get at your documents, Web pages, and applications easily and from the desktop if you like. Applications don't have to be active to be on a toolbar (unlike the taskbar). You can think of toolbars as folder windows with special properties. For the most part, they just contain shortcuts to documents, URLs, and applications. You can leave the toolbars connected to the taskbar, or move them to any location on your desktop. To display a toolbar, right-click an empty part of the taskbar, click Toolbars, and then click the toolbar.

One of the four default toolbars is the Address toolbar. If you type a URL or a folder name in the Address field of the Address toolbar and press Enter, a window appears on the desktop that displays the contents of that folder or the Web page associated with the URL.

You can move a toolbar by dragging and dropping it. To do this, move your mouse pointer over the line at the far left (or top) edge of the toolbar. When you see the resize arrow, drag the toolbar to one of the edges of the screen to dock it on that side, or drag it into the middle of the desktop to make it float. This technique also works to adjust the relative positions of the taskbar and the toolbars if they are sharing the same edge of the screen.

You can create a new toolbar that contains the contents of a folder. One way to do this is to just drag the folder icon (or a shortcut to the folder icon) to the very edge of your desktop and drop it there. You can do this with My Computer, My Documents, and My Network Places, as well as with any icons that represent folders containing documents and/or applications.

Another way to create a toolbar for the contents of a folder is to use the New Toolbar dialog box. To see an example of this, follow these steps:

STEPS

Creating a new toolbar

1. Right-click an empty area of the taskbar and choose Toolbar ⇨ New Toolbar.

2. In the New Toolbar window, which is shown in Figure 4-12, select a desired folder or enter a URL. You can also choose to make a new folder from this location. Make your selection and click OK. The new toolbar now appears on the taskbar.

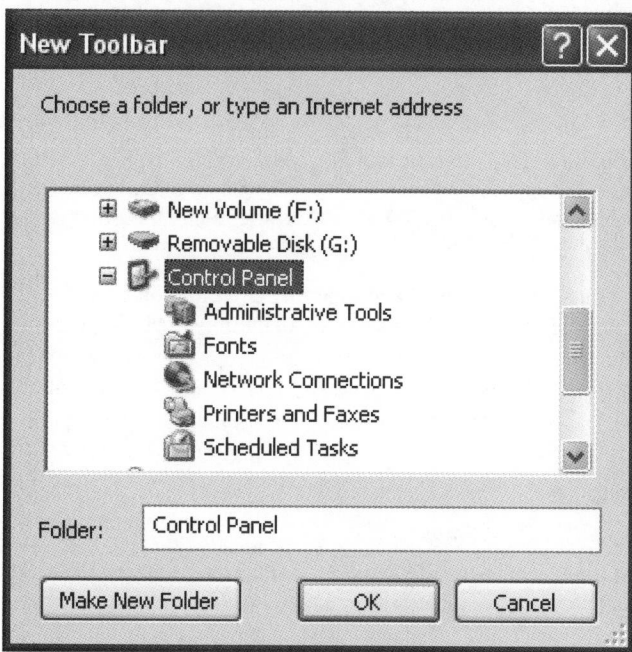

Figure 4-12: New Toolbar selection

Of course, even though you can create the toolbar out of any existing folder, it is best to use folders that only contain shortcuts. If you want to add shortcuts to the toolbar that you just created (and its corresponding folder), just drag and drop them to the toolbar.

You can also drag and drop shortcuts to the Links toolbar and the Quick Launch toolbar. The Links toolbar appears both on your desktop and in your Explorer window. Any shortcuts you drag and drop onto it show up on the toolbar in both places.

If you want to remove the toolbar you created in the "Creating a new toolbar" steps, right-click the taskbar, click Toolbars, and clear the check mark next to the toolbar (or right-click the toolbar and click Close Toolbar). You can't temporarily hide toolbars that you create, unlike the four preexisting toolbars. Once you close the toolbar, it's gone.

Moving toolbars to other locations

The default Windows configuration displays a single toolbar (the Quick Launch toolbar) attached to the taskbar. However, you can display multiple toolbars and place them on any edge of the desktop (or in the middle of it, if you like). For example, you might want to place the Desktop toolbar on the side of your desktop so that your desktop icons are always accessible.

To do this, take the following steps:

STEPS

Making the desktop icons always accessible

1. Right-click the taskbar, point to Toolbars, and click Desktop.

2. Point to the vertical bar at the far-left edge of the Desktop toolbar (which is now partially covering your taskbar), and drag and drop the toolbar to the left or right edge of your Desktop.

3. Resize the toolbars as desired.

Easy access with toolbars

It can be quite time-consuming to navigate around to find the files that you are working on. That's why there is a My Documents shortcut on your Start Menu, why you can create shortcuts to any of your documents, and why there is a list of recently opened documents on your Start menu and the File menu in your applications.

Another very clever way to get to your documents and programs, and to almost anything on your computer, is to use menus cascading from a toolbar. To see how this works, open up your Desktop toolbar by taking these steps:

STEPS

Opening a My Desktop toolbar

1. Right-click your Taskbar and choose Toolbars ⇨ Desktop.

2. Drag the sizing bar at the left end of the toolbar to move the Desktop toolbar over to the right (assuming you have a horizontal taskbar) so that only the word Desktop and a chevron arrow show.

3. Click the arrow; the Desktop contents are displayed in a menu, as shown in Figure 4-13.

Figure 4-13: Menu options become available in the toolbar

4. Click the My Computer icon in your Desktop menu. The contents of your computer are displayed in a new menu.

5. Click your Hard Drive icon. You get a menu containing the items found in your root directory (except for the hidden files).

6. Continue opening up menus of folders on your hard disk to get to any folder or file that you wish.

You can get to any application or file just by navigating down-cascading menus. But there is a way to make this easier, as the following steps show.

STEPS

Opening your hard disk toolbar

1. Right-click your taskbar and choose Toolbars ⇨ New Toolbar.

2. In the New Toolbar dialog box, highlight your main hard disk and click OK.

3. Drag the sizing bar at the end of the new hard disk toolbar to the right so that you see only the name of the hard disk and a chevron arrow.

4. Click the arrow to display the contents of your root directory (minus the hidden files).

5. Click a folder on your hard disk menu to display the contents of the folder as a menu.

6. Click subfolders to display their contents.

You can set up toolbars for multiple hard disks. You can create a toolbar using My Computer instead of your hard disk. You can also create toolbars for the Control Panel folder, the Network Connections folder, and so on. Pretty much any folder can become a menu.

> **CAUTION:** These menus are not menus of shortcuts, so you'll need to be careful not to delete items from the menus. If you do, you'll delete the actual item itself, and not just a shortcut to it.

Toolbars as Web pages

Because the Windows user shell is an object-oriented program, you'll find that certain items can take on the characteristics of other items, even when it doesn't seem that useful. For example, you can store an entire Web page in a toolbar.

At first glance, this doesn't seem very helpful, but for Web pages that provide constant text information, such as stock news, this may be helpful. For example, you can display a Web page on your computer that reports news, stocks, financial information, and other information that changes constantly. While the information here is not a real-time data stream from the Internet, these pages provide you a quick way to refresh Web content and get up-to-date information.

To put a Web page on a toolbar, take these steps:

STEPS

Putting a Web page on a toolbar

1. Right-click your taskbar and choose Toolbars ⇨ New Toolbar.

2. Type the URL of a local or Internet resource, as shown in Figure 4-14.

3. Click OK.

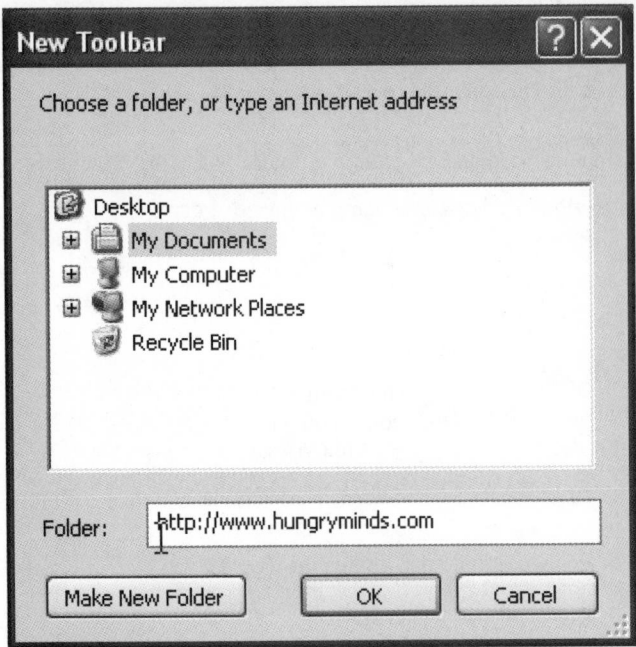

Figure 4-14: Enter a URL

Tabbing through your taskbar buttons

How about a little taskbar shortcut that can be really helpful when you have a bunch of items open on the taskbar? Hold down the Win key as you press the Tab key repeatedly. Each button on your taskbar appears to be pressed. Press Enter to bring the associated document or application to the foreground. If you need to switch between items, you can use this keyboard shortcut and avoid grabbing your mouse each time you need to move something into the foreground. Check it out!

Using the Address bar to run your programs

You can open any program on your computer by simply typing its name in any folder address bar or at the Run dialog box. So, why not put an address bar on your taskbar — then you can open any program directly from your desktop without wading through a bunch of menus?

Right-click your taskbar and choose Toolbars ⇨ Address to display an Address bar on your Desktop. The Address bar is a toolbar whose main purpose is to call up Internet Explorer when you type or paste in a URL. It looks and works just like the Internet Explorer Address bar. Despite its name, the Address bar is also a command-line processor. You can type a filename and the associated application will open and display the file. You have to type the complete pathname as well as the filename, and there is no Browse button, as there is in the Start ⇨ Run dialog box.

Putting Find on the Quick Launch toolbar

If you have a lot of documents and other files on your computer, and you seem to be using the Find option frequently to locate them, you can easily put Find on your Quick Launch toolbar where you can more easily search for what you need. You can easily put Find on your Quick Launch toolbar. Here's how:

STEPS

Putting Find on the Quick Launch toolbar

1. In Explorer, choose Tools ⇨ Find ⇨ Files or Folder.
2. Make any changes to the Find dialog box necessary to make this your general Find.
3. Choose File ⇨ Save Search. This saves the Find settings as a shortcut on the desktop.
4. Change the name of the Find shortcut on the desktop if you like. Otherwise, just drag and drop it onto the Quick Launch toolbar. Delete the shortcut from the desktop.

Moving the Quick Launch icons around

You can move the icons in the Quick Launch toolbar just by dragging them to a new location on the toolbar, and dropping them when the black line appears between icons. You can also do this with other toolbars as long as they are folders of shortcuts. You can't do it for a My Computer toolbar; you can do it with a Favorites toolbar.

The order in which the toolbar items appear in these menus is kept in the Registry. This is why you can rearrange their order on the toolbar.

Using a Foobar

Foobar is a launch bar with a series of little applets attached to it, as shown in Figure 4-15. *Quick* is the key word here — applets that start and end fast, and do a little bit well.

Figure 4-15: Foobar is a collection of helpful little applets that appear as buttons on the launch bar.

You can keep your passwords (not integrated with Windows), write sticky notes, store a contact list (not integrated with the Windows Address Book), keep track of the time spent on various activities, keep a To Do list, open your favorite documents, run your favorite applications, and set some reminders. At first glance, the Foobar may not seem that useful; after all, Windows XP includes productivity tools that offer more features than the ones provided here. However, the key point is that these little utilities are readily available and simple to use, rather than opening an entire application just to get what you need. For example, store addresses here quickly and grab them quickly when you need them, rather than opening Address Book, finding the address, and so on. Check it out and see if it is helpful to you. You can find Foobar at `http://matrixsoftware.com`.

Navigating on the Desktop

In this section, you learn some tricks for making your desktop easier to use.

Clearing the desktop

You can easily clear the desktop to get at any of your desktop shortcuts. Hold down the Win key and press D. This is a toggle, so all your open windows come back when you do it again.

Win+M also works to clear the Desktop, but it isn't a toggle. You have to press Win+Shift+M to bring back the windows.

Quickly showing the properties of desktop and Explorer icons

You ordinarily right-click an icon and click Properties to display its properties. But you can do this even more quickly by pressing the Alt key as you click the icon. Try this with your My Computer, Internet Explorer, My Documents, and other icons.

Solving Common Desktop and Taskbar Problems

Windows XP provides a highly configurable desktop and taskbar — this simply means that you have a lot of options available to make Windows XP look the way you want it to. However, like any operating system component, you may get stuck from time to time, so I've compiled a few common problems and solutions you are likely run into when you are configuring the Windows XP desktop and taskbar.

Using the Windows Classic theme

The Windows Classic theme removes the XP-type components from Windows and makes Windows look like an older version, such as 9x, Me, and 2000 — sort of. In truth, the theme is removed and the Windows Classic theme is used, but that does not mean that everything will look just the way it did in previous versions of Windows. In fact, using the classic theme does not put your icons back on the desktop, the Start menu does not quite look the same as it did, and folders still appear as Web pages. You can individually tweak these items as needed, and if you really want to go back to the classic look for a particular folder, go to Tools ⇨ Folder Options and choose Use Windows Classic folders to lose the Web appearance.

Advanced appearance settings do not work

If you are individually configuring advanced appearance settings, such as active title bar, tooltip, or selected items, those settings may be overwritten if the Windows XP theme is in use and the Windows XP style option is used on the Windows and buttons category on the Appearance tab (see Figure 4-16). To make sure that your custom settings are not overwritten, change this setting to Windows Classic style.

Secure Web site content display

If you want to display Web content on your desktop from a secure site that requires a login, you can configure XP to automatically login when a scheduled synchronization occurs. This provides a hands-off way for you to access this secured content so that it is readily available on your desktop. First, access the Desktop tab of Display Properties. Click Customize Desktop, and then add the URL to the list on the Web tab. Then select the URL and click Properties. Set up a schedule as desired and on the Download tab, click the Login button. Enter the username and password required to login in the provided dialog box, as shown in Figure 4-17, and click OK.

Font size

If you need to have the display's fonts appear in a larger size for easier viewing, you do not have to configure each advanced appearance item's font size. You can more easily access the Appearance tab of Display Properties and choose the Large option under Font Size. If some items still do not appear large enough, then access the Advanced properties and change the font size for the item that is too small.

Desktop icon placement

By default, there is an invisible grid under the Windows XP desktop that divides the desktop into logical blocks. Icons are stored within those grid blocks, and you may find it annoying that when you place an icon in a certain location, it may jump to the left or right a bit.

Figure 4-16: Change Windows and Buttons to Windows Classic style

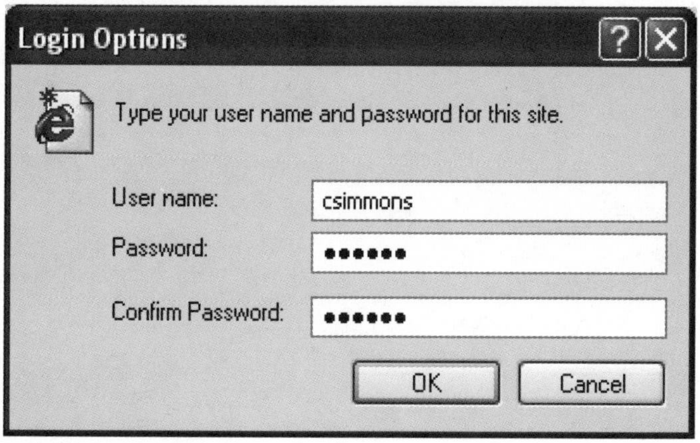

Login Options

Type your user name and password for this site.

User name: csimmons

Password: ●●●●●●

Confirm Password: ●●●●●●

OK   Cancel

Figure 4-17: Login Options

You can stop this grid behavior by simply right-clicking an empty area of your desktop and pointing to Arrange Icons by. You'll see an option that says Align to grid. Clear this check mark and you will be able to place icons anywhere you want. Also, notice that you have some other icon organization options on this menu, which are self-explanatory.

NOTE: The point of the Align to grid feature is to keep your icons organized in rows. Without the Align to grid option turned on, your desktop can get rather messy. Of course, if you are like me, a messy desktop probably makes you feel right at home.

Taskbar movement

The taskbar can be moved from edge to edge on your desktop, provided that the taskbar is not locked into place. If you can't move the taskbar, simply right-click an empty portion of it and clear the Lock the taskbar setting option.

Summary

In this chapter, you learned to configure the Windows XP desktop and taskbar. Windows XP gives you a streamlined, easy-to-use and easy-to-configure interface that is designed to make computing faster for advanced users and easier for new users. The XP Interface settings, however, can be changed to mimic the Windows Classic style by using a Classic theme. In the same manner, the taskbar has been streamlined to provide you easy access to open programs and Notification Area icons that are active and important. You can configure a number of toolbars to assist you, and you can move the taskbar around the Windows interface as necessary. This chapter explored . . .

♦ Configuring the Windows XP desktop using Desktop Properties

♦ Modifying Windows XP themes

♦ Enhancing Windows XP's appearance with settings and options

♦ Using the desktop and managing information on it

♦ Configuring the taskbar

♦ Using taskbar menus

♦ Moving and customizing the taskbar

Chapter 5

Configuring the Start Menu, Shortcuts, and Search Functions

In This Chapter

The Windows XP Start menu has received a lot of attention, and it should because it is now the default way to access everything. The Start menu has been redesigned to be more useful, more flexible, and smarter. Whether you agree with these design issues is certainly a matter of opinion, but the good news is that you can configure the Start menu in a number of ways, and you can even return it to classic Windows functionality. In this chapter, you take a look at Start menu configuration, shortcut usage, folder menus and options, and finally, Windows XP's new File and Settings Transfer Wizard. In this chapter, you learn about . . .

♦ Configuring the Start menu

♦ Using Windows XP Search

♦ Configuring folder menus

♦ Using the File and Settings Transfer Wizard

Windows XP Start Menu

With a first look at the Windows XP interface, you find that the Start menu looks and acts differently than it does in previous versions of Windows, as shown in Figure 5-1. Sure, it basically performs the same role — it gives you easy access to the programs and files — but it contains more information than previous Start menus and attempts to help you get to stuff faster.

As you can see in Figure 5-1, the XP Start menu is divided into two columns with division bars in various places in the columns. On the right column, you see access to several common Windows folders, such as My Documents, My Pictures, My Computer, and so on. You can click any of these items to open them, but you can also right-click the item to see its typical menu options. For example, if you right-click My Computer, you can choose Open, Explore, Map Network Drive, Properties, and more. Typically, you would be able to access only the actual shortcut's properties in this manner, but the Start menu contains the actual folder options here, which is nice. Also, you can choose the "Show on Desktop" option to place an icon copy of the item on the desktop. The copy, however, does not appear as a typical shortcut, but rather it looks like the actual icon, such as you would typically see with My Computer, My Documents, and other similar icon representations.

In the next portion of the right column, you see access to Control Panel, Printers and Faxes, Help and Support, Search, and Run. You can't do anything with these items except use them from this interface, but you can change them and remove them if you like, which I address later in this section.

In the left column, you see Internet Explorer and Outlook Express followed by a line. These items are considered a part of Start menu and permanently remain there unless you right-click the items and click Remove From This List. This removes only the shortcut from the Start menu, not the actual programs themselves. You can also access Properties sheets for these programs by right-clicking the icons and clicking Properties.

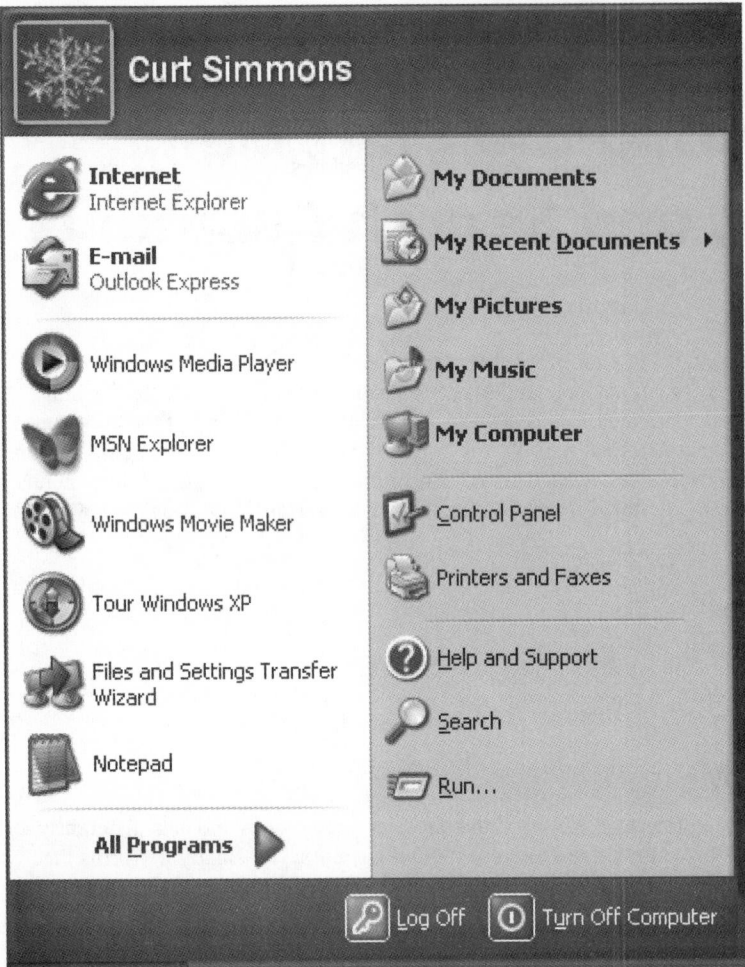

Figure 5-1: The XP Start menu

In the second portion of the left column, you see a number of other applications, such as MSN Explorer and Windows Movie Maker, that Microsoft would like for you to use (of course). As you open other applications, they also appear in this list. In other words, the Start menu attempts to remember programs that you open and post them on the Start menu so you can get to those items more quickly. The area above these items that holds Internet Explorer and Outlook Express is called the *Pinned Items list,* because its items are a permanent part of the Start menu. The programs below the line are called Frequently Used Programs and appear only if you use them. By default, only six programs can be displayed on this list. As you use new programs, older ones listed here that you are not using are removed. You can change this default value, which I show you how to do later in this section, and you can also move a frequently used program to the Pinned Items list by simply right-clicking the program and clicking Pin to Start Menu.

You can also click the All Programs link to access your typical Start menu folders, such as Accessories, Games, and other programs you have installed. Of course, you can apply plenty of other tips and tricks, and I cover those in a moment.

So now that you have reviewed the basics, it's time to take a look at how you can configure and customize the Start menu to suit your needs.

Configuring the Start menu

You can easily configure the Start menu by right-clicking the Start menu button and choosing Properties. You can also right-click any empty area of the Start menu itself and access the same Properties dialog box. Either way, the Taskbar and Start Menu Properties dialog box, shown in Figure 5-2, gives you to the option to either use the XP Start menu or the Classic Start menu. I'll address both of these options in the following two sections.

Figure 5-2: Taskbar and Start Menu Properties

XP Start menu

If you want to continue using the XP Start menu, just click the Customize button to configure the options. You see a General and an Advanced tab appear. The General tab, shown in Figure 2-3 is rather self-explanatory. From the Customize Start Menu dialog box, you can . . .

- ◆ Change icon size from large to small.
- ◆ Change the default number of programs that appears on the Start menu. This refers to the Frequently Used Programs. By default, only six are shown, but you can change the value to up to 30. You can also clear the current list by clicking the Clear List button.

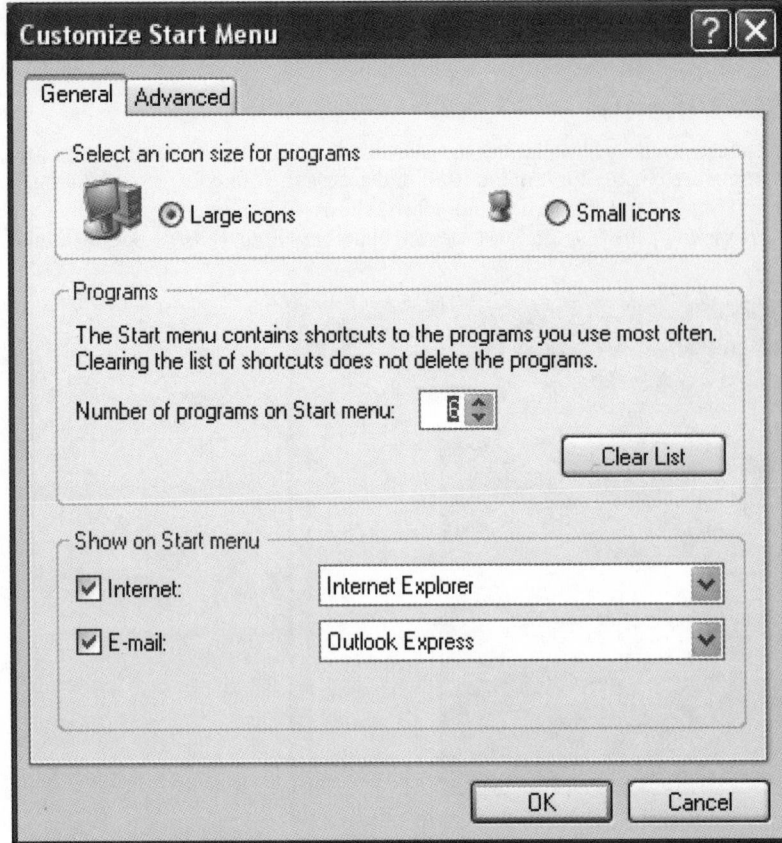

Figure 5-3: Customize Start Menu dialog box, General tab

♦ You can choose to show a browser and e-mail client on the Start menu (pinned). By default, these are Internet Explorer (IE) and Outlook Express. You can change them by using the drop-down menu and choosing different programs, which should appear here. (The key word is *should* — if the browser or e-mail client you want doesn't appear here, you can fix that by adding a shortcut to the Start Menu, which is explored later in this chapter.)

The Advanced tab, shown in Figure 5-4, gives you a number of options that enable you to more finely control the content that appears on the Start menu and how that content is handled. There are a number of important settings here, which are reviewed in the following list:

♦ **Open submenus** — By default, submenus appear when you pause on them with your mouse (prevents clicking).

♦ **Highlight newly installed programs** — When you install a new program, it is highlighted in the Start menu, I suppose so you can easily find it. You can use this feature or clear the check box to disable it if it gets on your nerves.

♦ **Start menu items** — There are a number of items here you should look through:

  • **Control Panel** — You can display it as a link, as a menu, or not at all. I find the menu option most helpful because you can easily access any Control Panel applet directly from the pop-out menu instead of having to actually open the Control Panel folder.

  • **Dragging and dropping** — Leave this one enabled so you can easily drag and drop new items to the Start menu.

  • **Favorites** — You can choose to display favorites.

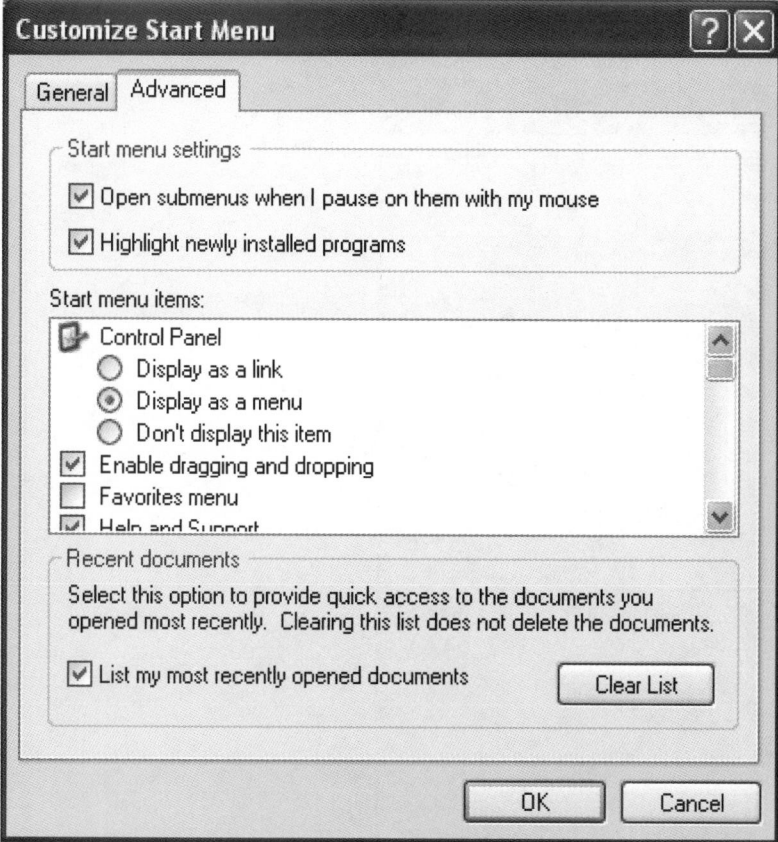

Figure 5-4: Customize Start Menu dialog box, Advanced tab

- **My Computer** — You can display it as a link, as a menu, or not at all (menu is recommended).
- **My Documents** — Same options here.
- **My Music** — Same options here.
- **My Network Places** — You can choose whether to display it.
- **My Pictures** — Display as a link, as a menu, or not at all.
- **Network connections** — Display as Connect to menu, Don't Display, or Link to Network Connections folder. The Display as Connect to menu option gives you the fastest access to your connections.
  - **Printers and Faxes**, **Run command**, **Scroll programs**, **Search** — You can choose to show or not show any of these.
  - **Administrative tools** — You can choose to display all administrative tools on the All Programs menu, on both the All Programs and Start menus, or on neither.
- ♦ **Recent documents** — You can choose whether to have the Start menu display your recently used documents, and you can clear this list.

Classic Start menu

You can choose to use the Windows Classic Start menu by clicking the radio button option in the Taskbar and Start Menu Properties dialog box. You can then click Customize to make changes. As you can see in Figure 5-5, the configuration options look similar to those found in previous versions of Windows. You can choose what folders and options you want to include by clicking the check boxes. Use the Add and Advanced options to add more shortcuts to the Start menu and manage file and folder content.

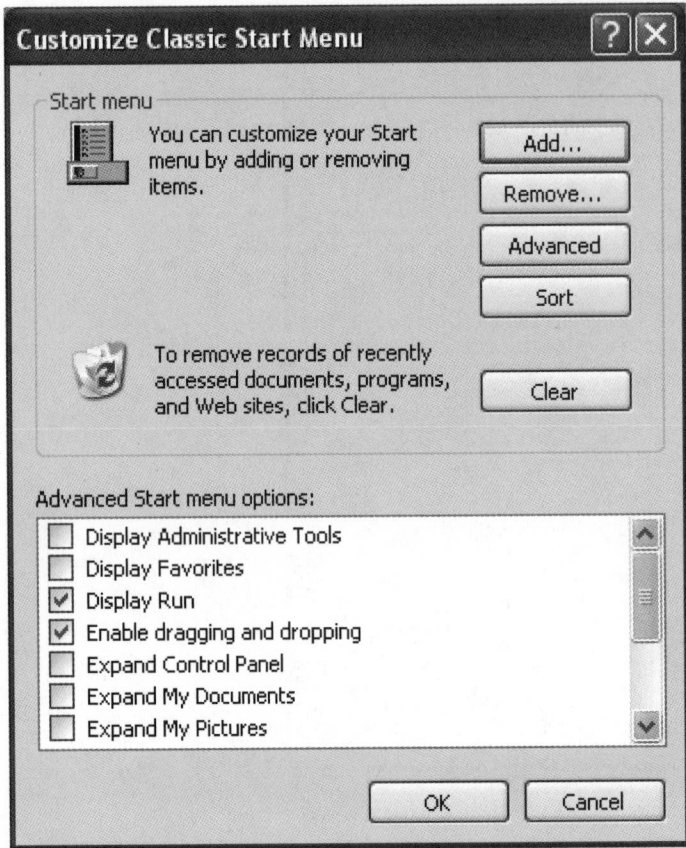

Figure 5-5: Classic Start menu properties

Customizing the Start menu

Once you configure the basic options for the Start menu using the Properties pages, you can then customize the Start menu to meet your needs. Mainly this involves putting content on the Start menu so that you can easily access it. The more programs or folders you place on the Start menu that you regularly use, the easier it is to access them while keeping your desktop clean.

You can place any item on the Start menu by simply dragging and dropping the item on the Start button. This includes programs, drives, documents, and even URLs. Items that you drag and drop on the Start menu are automatically pinned to it. Of course, you can remove those items at any time you want by simply right-clicking the item and choosing Delete from the pop-up menu.

When you drag and drop an item, the shortcut for that item is automatically created and placed on the Start menu. This way, you never actually move an item to the Start menu, you simply create a shortcut for it. In other words, dragging and dropping as described merely creates shortcuts on the Start menu; you do not actually move these items from their original home.

SECRET: Keep in mind that a shortcut is a pointer to another item. It tells Windows where to go to find the item, and if you delete or move that object, the shortcut essentially becomes a dead link. In order to fix the problem, you'll need to edit the target location for the object in the shortcut's properties. See the next section for details.

Creating and Repairing Shortcuts

As noted in the previous section, you can customize the Start menu by deciding what items should appear on the menu. This is done through shortcuts, which are addressed in this section. You can create a shortcut for an item by right-clicking the item and choosing Create Shortcut. You can also use the Create Shortcut Wizard by right-clicking an empty area of the desktop and choosing New ⇨ Shortcut. In the Create Shortcut window, enter or browse for the location of the item, as shown in Figure 5-6.

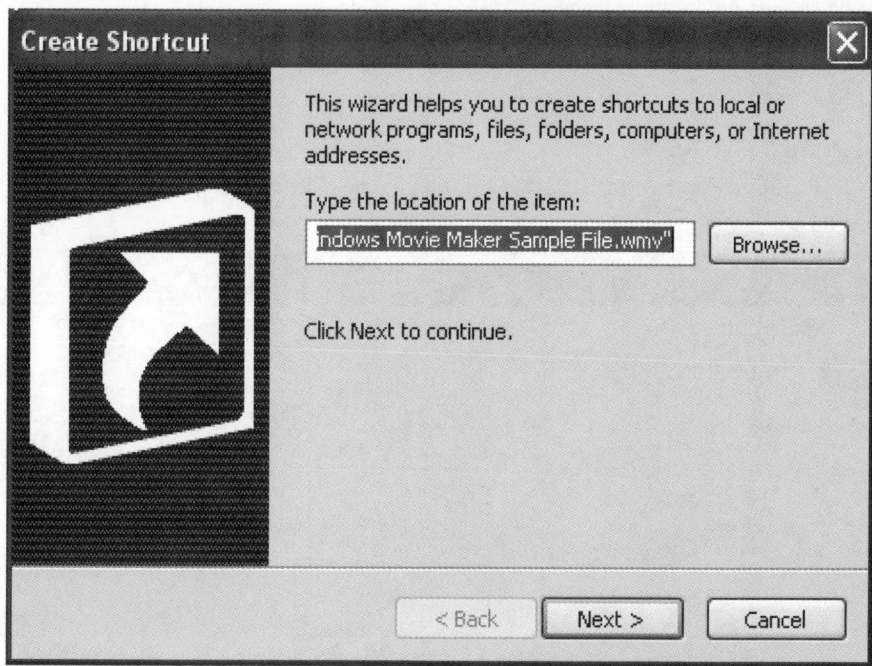

Figure 5-6: Create Shortcut Wizard

Windows XP reads the file extension or item extension and attempts to match an icon with the item in order to create the shortcut. Once the shortcut is created, however, you can easily change the icon to something else by right-clicking the shortcut and choosing Properties. Access the Shortcut tab and click Change Icon.

Once you are happy with the shortcut, you can simply drag it to the Start button to pin it to the Start menu.

As you work with shortcuts, keep in mind that you can store any number of helpful items on Start menu. Consider putting commonly used Control Panel applets directly on the Start menu — or dial-up connections or documents. You can drag and drop folders, as well. Create a custom folder and put a group of shortcuts in it, then drag and drop the folder on the Start menu. As you can see, there are many possibilities.

As noted previously, if a shortcut path changes, you can edit the shortcut in order to repair it. Keep in mind that shortcuts are simply links to other items on your system. When you click a shortcut, Windows XP reads the link information and retrieves the desired object (or program) from its real location. If you move or delete an item, the target location is no longer accurate; therefore the shortcut will not work. If you move an item and you want to keep your shortcut available, you can easily edit the target location by right-clicking the shortcut, clicking properties, and editing the target location on the Shortcut tab. Or, you may find it just as easily to delete the old shortcut and create a new one.

Managing Folder Menus

When you click All Programs in the Start menu, you see the typical Windows menus that you are familiar with, such as Accessories, Games, and a variety of other folders and programs. You can easily change the contents of what you see under All Programs, because you are basically looking at a folder structure with shortcuts. For example, under Accessories, you find System Tools, but System Tools are not actually stored here — you are just seeing shortcuts. Because of this design, you can manually change the menus to suit your needs. To do so, just follow these steps:

STEPS

Configuring folder menus

1. Navigate to `C:\Documents and Settings\yourusername\Start Menu\Programs`.

2. You'll see typical folders and programs here, shown in Figure 5-7.

Figure 5-7: Programs folder

3. Open folders and add/remove shortcuts as desired. You can create new shortcuts and simply drag and drop them here. You can also add your own custom folders to the Programs folder so that they appear on the Start menu.

XP Shutdown/Restart/Logoff Features

As always, you can shut down, restart, or log off using the Start menu. Because this is such a simple operation, I won't bore you with the details, but I would like to mention a couple of features that are new in XP.

First, Windows XP has a hibernate feature. Hibernate is a part of the APM features of Windows XP, and it is a good setting to use for several reasons. Hibernate works like shutdown in that the power to your computer is turned off. The difference is that hibernate stores everything that is in memory on your hard drive. When the computer restarts, the information is read back into memory. So, the cool feature is that you can use hibernate without saving everything and closing down your applications. Of course, your computer has to support the hibernation feature, and you can quickly find out if the feature is supported by choosing Start ⇨ Control Panel ⇨ Power Options. You'll see a Hibernate tab, as shown in Figure 5-8. Make sure that "Enable hibernation" is checked. Also, if you want password protection for when the computer comes out of hibernation, the click Prompt for Password check box under the Advanced tab of Power Options Properties.

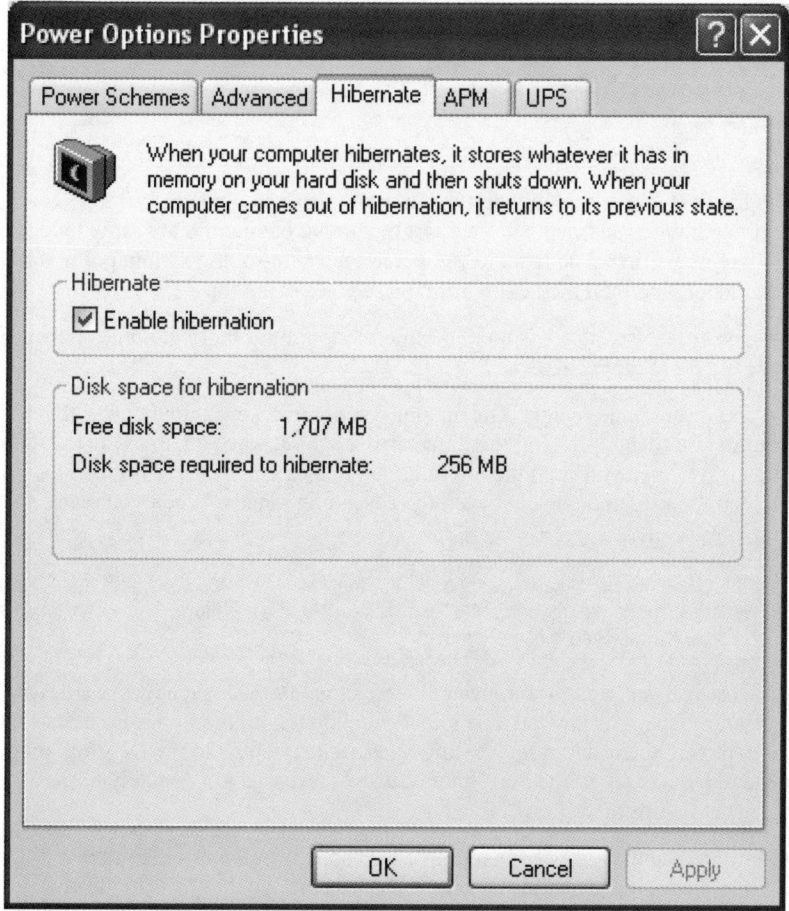

Figure 5-8: Hibernate tab

The second new feature I want to mention is fast user switching. Fast user switching is an available option when you choose Start ⇨ Log Off. The fast user switching feature is just that — you can basically switch users without logging off. When you switch users, the logon screen appears so the user can pick his or her username and enter a password, and then the desktop returns. No applications are closed during the switch. This feature is great when several people use a computer and one needs the machine for a few minutes only. You can switch over to that user and then switch back without closing applications or work.

Remember these caveats about fast user switching:

♦ In order to use fast user switching, you must be logged on as a local administrator of the machine, and you must enable the feature on the User Accounts dialog box found in the Control Panel.

♦ You can't use fast user switching if the XP computer is a member of a Windows domain.

♦ Serial keys (accessibility feature) do not work when fast user switching is enabled.

Running the Start Menu with the Keyboard

You can run the Start menu with your keyboard. The most important keyboard combination is Ctrl+Esc, which displays the main Start menu. The Windows key on Windows keyboards also displays the Start menu.

TIP: If you press the Ctrl button while you click the Maximize button in the upper-right corner of a folder or Explorer window, the window expands to full screen and the taskbar disappears. If you have opened a window in full-screen mode, pressing Ctrl+Esc or the Windows key still displays the Start menu.

You can choose menu items on the Start menu by pressing the letter key that corresponds to the underlined letter in the name. If you have added items to the Start menu that begin with the same letter, the letter key will take you to these items first. The letter keys operate in round-robin fashion, going to the first item that starts with that letter, and then the next, until it starts over at the top again.

The letter keys work in all the submenus also. There is no underlined letter in the shortcut names under the Programs menu, so you type the first letter of the item.

The arrow keys can also move you through the menus. The up and down arrow keys move you within a menu. When you get to the bottom of a menu, pressing the down arrow again takes you up to the top. (By the same token, pressing the up arrow when you're at the top of a menu takes you to the bottom.) The right and left arrow keys move you forward and back between the cascading menus. When you reach a menu item that you want to run, press Enter.

SECRET: If you press Ctrl+Esc and then Esc, the Start menu disappears, but the focus stays on the Start button. When the Start button has the focus, you'll see the focus rectangle on it. You can confirm the Start button still has the focus by pressing Enter after you've pressed Ctrl+Esc, Esc. The Start menu will reappear.

Once the Start button has the focus, you can press Tab repeatedly to change the focus clockwise from the Start button to other objects on your display. If you have a toolbar immediately to the right of the Start button, the focus will shift there, then to the taskbar, then to any other toolbars, then to the Desktop, then to any of Active Desktop items, and then back to the Start button. If the taskbar is immediately to the right of the Start button, the focus will shift there first.

If the focus is on the taskbar, you can use the arrow keys to move the focus from button to button. To restore an application or bring it to the top of the windows on the Desktop, move the focus to the taskbar button for that application and press Enter.

If the focus is on an icon on the Desktop, you can use your arrow keys to move among the Desktop icons to focus on the application, folder, or file you want to open. Press Enter when the focus is on the desired icon.

If the Desktop has the focus, the taskbar border will display the Inactive Window Border color, and an icon on the Desktop will be highlighted.

If you define hot keys for the shortcuts on the Start menus, you can start an application immediately without going through the Start button, just by pressing its hot key combination.

Quick Launch

The Quick Launch bar, which has been around since the days of Windows 95, gives you a quick access bar next to the Start Menu. The Quick Launch bar typically holds Internet Explorer, Outlook Express, and other applications, depending on what is installed. The idea is to give you an easy location to start programs that you use often.

By default, the Quick Launch bar no longer appears on the taskbar in Windows XP — you have to turn it on by clicking the Show Quick Launch check box option on the Taskbar properties tab.

Like the Start menu, you can drag and drop shortcuts onto the Quick Launch bar in order to customize it. You can also drag the Quick Launch bar off the taskbar and position it at the top of the screen so that it acts more like a custom toolbar where you can easily access programs that you use frequently.

The XP Search Tool

Windows XP includes a search capability, something that was first introduced with Windows 98. You can get to this search function in a number of ways. If you want to search for files or folders, right-click the Start button, the My Computer icon, or any folder icon, and then choose Search in the context menu. You can also click the Search button in any Explorer or folder window.

> **TIP:** The easiest way to find a file or folder? Press F3 when the focus is on the Desktop, a folder window, an Explorer window, or the taskbar. Also, if you don't like the little animated dog character you now see, you can turn off the feature by scrolling to the bottom of the search menu and clicking the option.

Windows XP expands the capability of the search option from what was originally available in Windows 95. You can now search for people using directory services on the Internet or your Windows Address Book. You can also connect to Internet search engines to search for topics, words, or phrases found on Web sites or in newsgroups.

> **NOTE:** Just because the command is called *Search* doesn't necessarily mean the usefulness of this function is limited to finding things. For example, you can use Search as a filter to list all the executables in a folder or in a set of folders in one window.

You can find files and/or folders that match the criteria you set in the Search Results dialog box (right-click the Start button and choose Search). Windows gives you a significant number of options to define your search strategy.

File or folder name

If you are looking for a specific file or folder and you know its name, type the name in the search field, as shown in Figure 5-9. You can search for multiple folders, files, or file types. Just separate their names by commas, as in

```
*.bat, *.sys, *.txt, bill?.*
```

Take notice of the asterisk in the figure and the ones in the search example I gave before the figure. These are wild cards, and with wild cards you can type a partial name for you search. The wild cards are ? and *. The question mark stands for one letter and the asterisk for one or more letters. Table 5-1 shows these and other options for your searches. Note that *abc* stands for any three letters.

Figure 5-9: Type a file or folder name or partial name. If you know the general area (folder or drive) where the file or folder is located, choose a drive from the "Look in" drop-down list.

Table 5-1: Search Options

Entered in Name Field	Search Location
*	All files and folders
.	All files and folders
*.	All files
.	No files or folders (a file can't be named "dot")
.exe	No files or folders (because a filename cannot start with a period)
abc	All files and folders with abc in the name (including extensions)
exe	All files and folders with exe in name or extension; most likely executable files

Entered in Name Field	Search Location
*.exe	All files with *exe* in extension only
abc	All files and folders with *abc* in name
*abc	All files with *abc* as last letters in name (not including extension)
*abc?	All files with *abc* as second to last letters in name (not including extension)
?abc	All files and folders with *abc* as at least second letters in name if not later
?abc*	All files and folders with *abc* as the second through fourth letters in name
??abc	All files and folders with *abc* as at least the third letters in name, if not later
?abc?	All files and folders with at least one letter in front of *abc* and at least one behind in name
?a?.*	Three-letter filename with middle letter of name given and extension unknown

Notice that unlike searching in DOS for filenames, you can have an asterisk or question mark in front and still get meaningful results. In fact, the search algorithm is much more flexible and powerful than what was available with DOS or earlier versions of Windows.

In the "Look in" field, enter the general location for the file or folder. If you know a file or folder is on a certain disk drive, choose that drive letter. If you want to narrow it down further, click Browse to choose a folder, or include a pathname in the search field.

SECRET: Search searches for your files in hidden subfolders if you have marked the "Show hidden files and folders" option button in the View tab of the Folder Options dialog box (choose Tools ⇨ Folder Options in an Explorer or folder window). Search will not find your fonts in the Fonts folder (which has the System attribute set, but is not hidden) if the "Look in" field in your search dialog box is set to \Windows and not to Windows\Fonts.

You may find it convenient to "root" two or more searches at different starting points. In the "Look in" field, just separate multiple roots with semicolons. For example, you could type **C:\Windows; D:** to start searching at two folders on separate drives. In Figure 5-10, you can see this search in progress.

Text string

You can search for files that contain a given text string by typing it in the "A word or phrase in the file" field. The search method has to search through each file to find out if it contains the string.

Microsoft Office contains its own indexer, called Find Fast, which lets you use the File Open dialog box of any Office application to quickly search for documents based on a text string. If you have installed Microsoft Office, you may want to use this method of searching for text strings in documents instead.

If you leave the name field blank, your search will go through all the files that match the criteria you set in the "Look in" and "A word or phrase in the file" fields.

TIP: You can disable Windows XP indexing on your drives in order to speed system performance, but your searches will work much slower. See Chapter 3 to learn more about the Indexing Service.

File size and advanced restrictions

You can search for files that are of a certain file type or are at least as big as or greater than a certain size. Click the arrows for advanced options and size to restrict the search field using file size and other restrictions (see Figure 5-11).

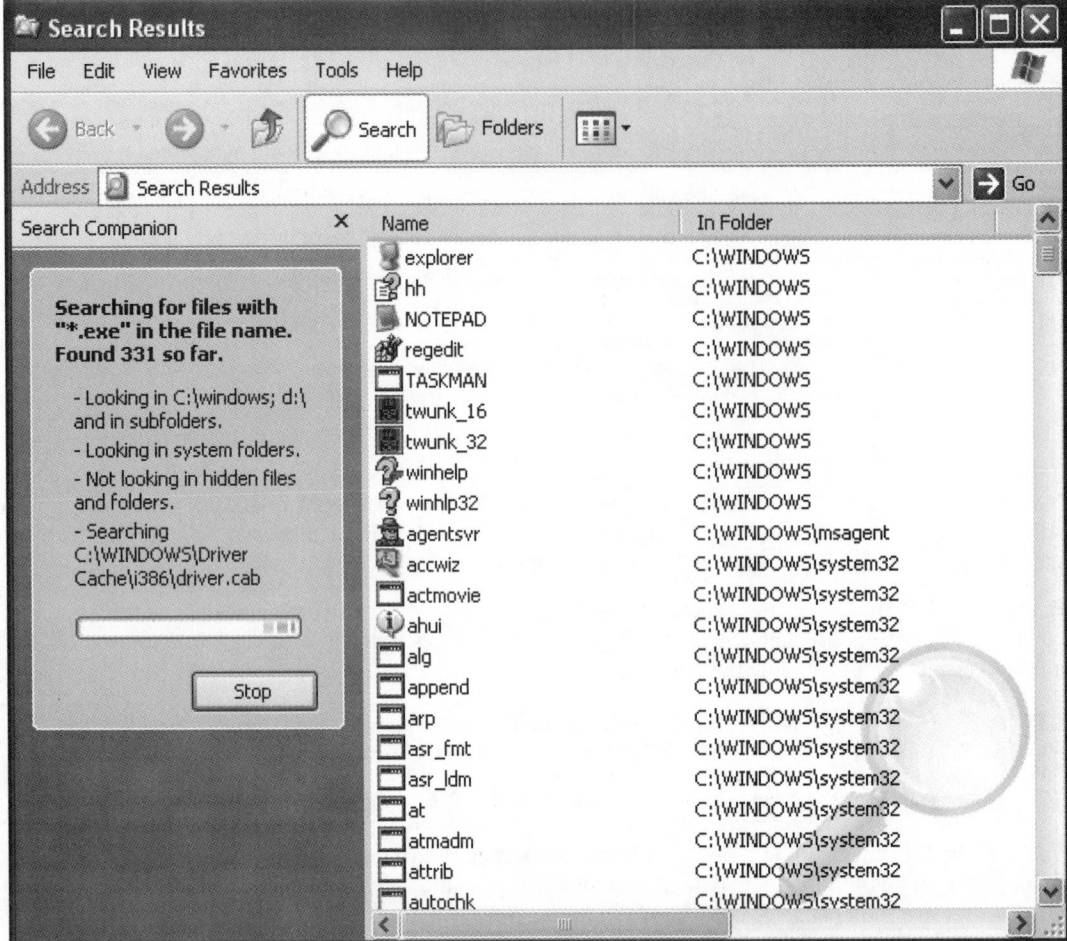

Figure 5-10: Separate drive letters with semicolons to search multiple drives. By indicating the folder to start in, you can make one search start at several different points.

You use the File Type option to limit the search to files of a certain type — for example, all text files, all Microsoft Word files, or all Quattro Pro files. Moreover, if you have some idea of how large the files you're looking for are, you can use size as a search criterion.

Saving the search

Windows retains your search criteria after you've performed the search. If you don't like the results of a search, you can modify the criteria and do another one. If you want to use a particular set of search criteria as the basis of future searches, you can save it as an icon on your Desktop. To do this, make sure the criteria you want to save are specified in the Search Results dialog box, and choose File ⇨ Save Search.

When you want to perform a search that you've saved as an icon, click the icon (or a shortcut to it). Windows displays the Search Results dialog box with all the search criteria specified. Optionally modify the criteria and then click Search Now to perform the search.

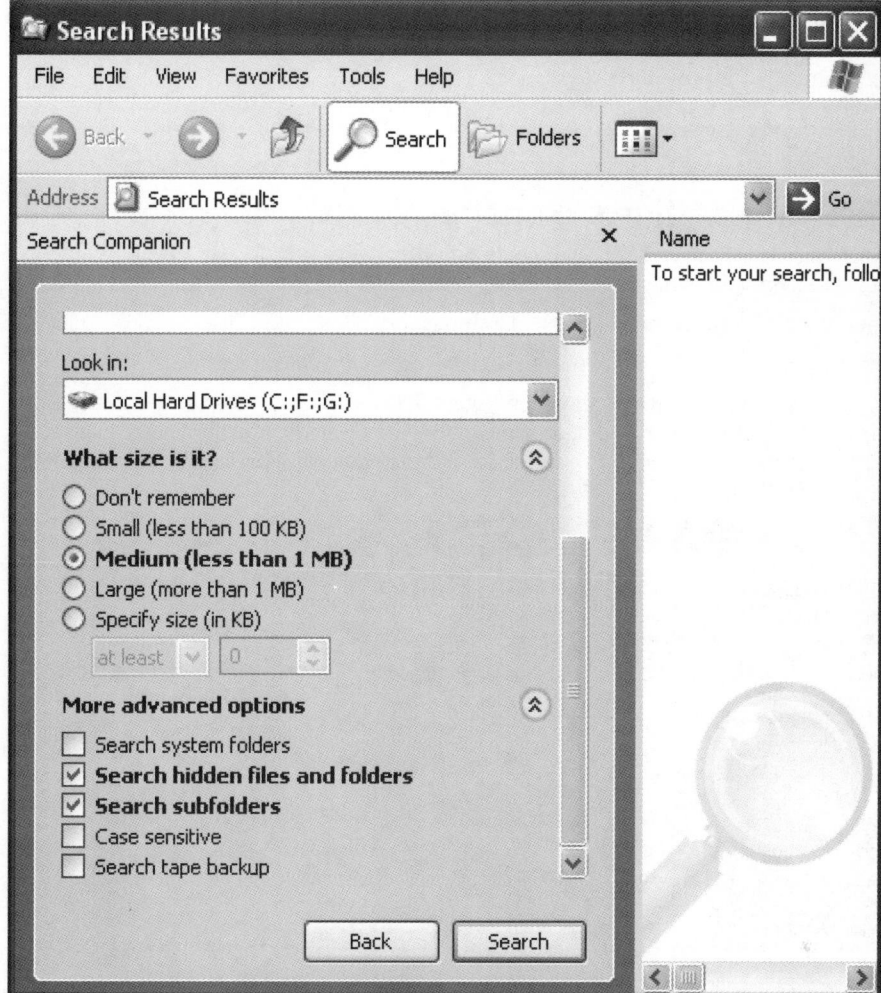

Figure 5-11: Size and advanced options for searches

Files and Settings Transfer Wizard

Windows XP introduces a new wizard that makes the transfer of files and settings from computer to computer much easier. In the past, if you needed to move to a new computer, you had to manually port over your documents to that machine, reconfigure Internet Explorer, your settings, and basically anything else that you wanted. This process was time consuming at best, so Windows XP includes a way to move files and settings from another Windows computer to your new XP computer. With the Files and Settings Transfer Wizard, you can . . .

♦ Move all of your documents and document folders

♦ Move system settings, such as display properties, taskbar configuration, and most any other personal settings

♦ Move Internet Explorer and Outlook Express configurations

♦ Move dial-up and other types of network connections

Your can transfer files and settings from computers running Windows 9*x*, Me, 2000, NT 4.0, and XP (32-bit only). For the transfer, you need some kind of connection between the old computer and the new computer, such as a network connection or a direct cable connection. You can also use a Zip disk or some other type of removable media that is large enough to handle all of your documents and settings. When you are ready to run the transfer, follow these steps:

STEPS

Using the Files and Settings Transfer Wizard

1. On the old computer (on which you save documents and settings for transfer), insert the Windows XP installation CD-ROM, and then choose Perform Additional Tasks from the menu that appears.

2. From the second menu, choose Transfer Files and Settings.

3. The Files and Settings Transfer Wizard appears. Click Next on the Welcome screen.

4. The transfer method window appears, as shown in Figure 5-12. You can choose to transfer settings by a network connection, removable media, or some other type of media transfer. You can also choose to just save the transfer file to a disk on the local drive and deal with transfer it later. Make your selection and click Next.

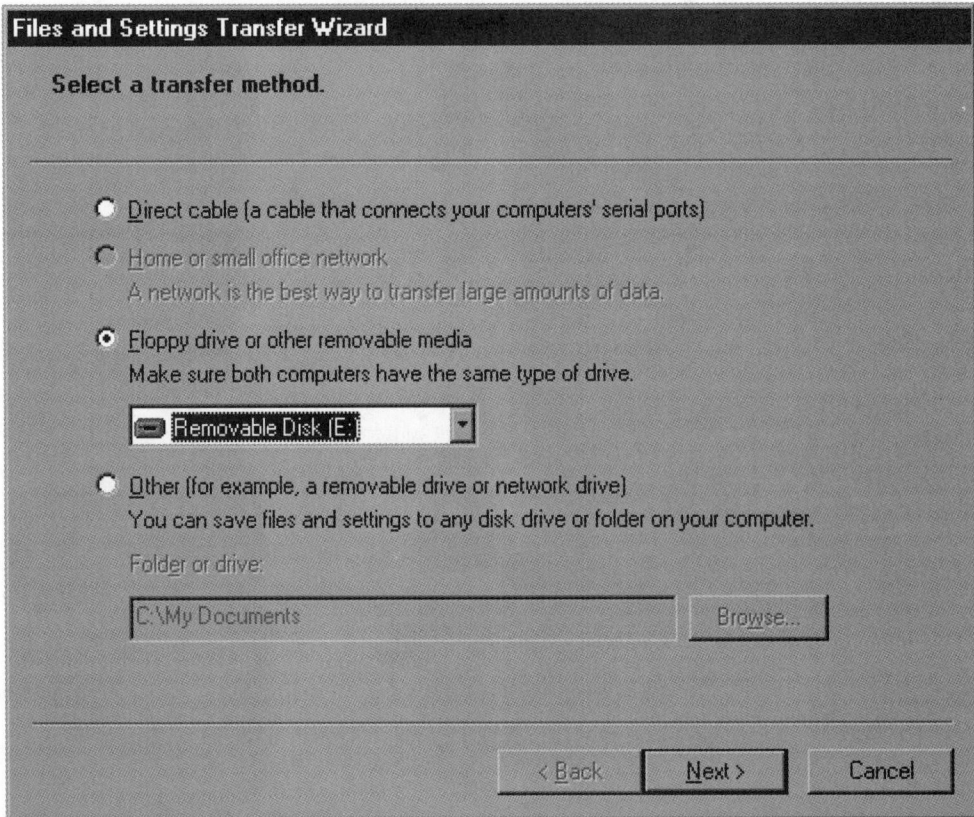

Figure 5-12: Select a transfer method.

NOTE: The wizard will give you the opportunity to choose what you want to transfer. For example, you may just want to transfer settings only. In this case, a floppy disk is typically all you need, because the settings are compressed into one DAT file. In fact, a typical settings transfer file is about half a megabyte. Of course, if you transfer documents, you'll need more space.

5. The transfer window appears, as shown in Figure 5-13. You can choose to transfer settings only, files only, or both. You can also select the custom check box so that you can explicitly select what you want to include. Make your selection and click Next.

6. If you choose to select the options, a window appears, shown in Figure 5-14, in which you can review all of the settings and documents the wizard has selected for transfer. You can then manipulate the list by adding and removing items as you wish. The list is quite long, but it can save you some transfer time if you edit out the items you don't want. Make your selections and click Next.

7. The wizard collects and compresses the data you want to transfer. Once the wizard is finished, click the Finish button.

8. On the Windows XP computer that you want to transfer the settings to, choose Start ⇨ All Programs ⇨ Accessories ⇨ System Tools ⇨ Files and Settings Transfer Wizard. Click Next on the Welcome screen.

9. In the Which Computer is this window, select New Computer, and then click Next.

10. In the XP CD window, choose the "I don't need the Wizard disk" option since you have already created the files and settings document using the CD-ROM. Click Next.

11. In the next window, enter the location where the files are coming from (floppy, direct cable, and so on) and click Next.

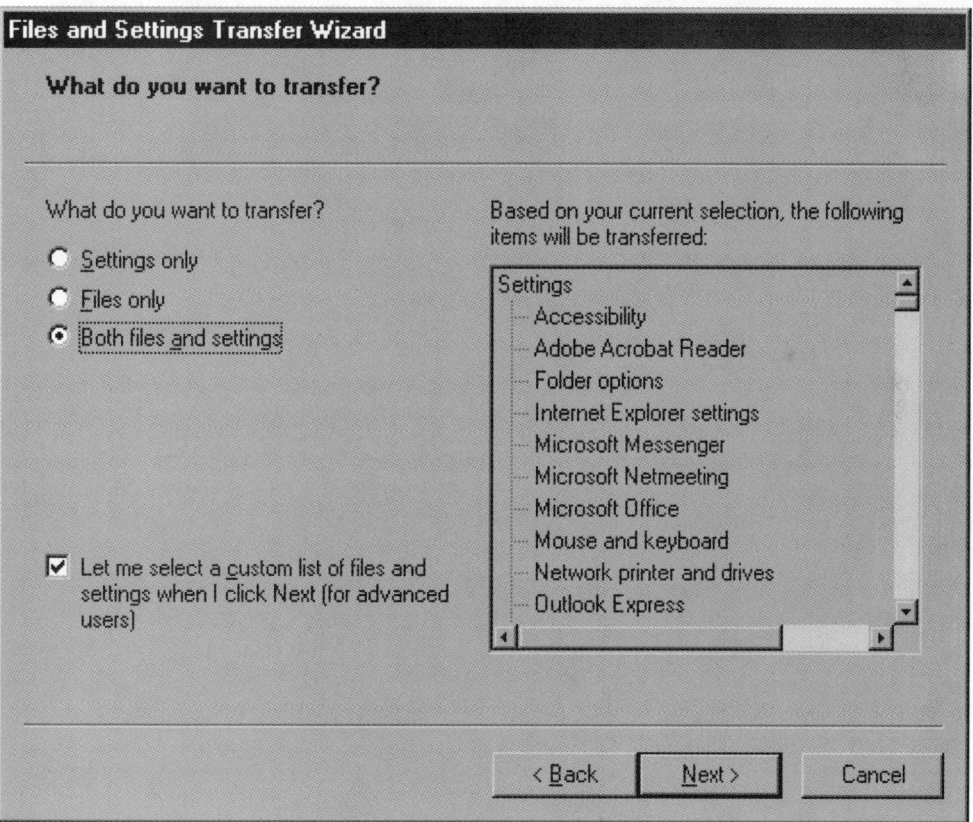

Figure 5-13: Transfer options

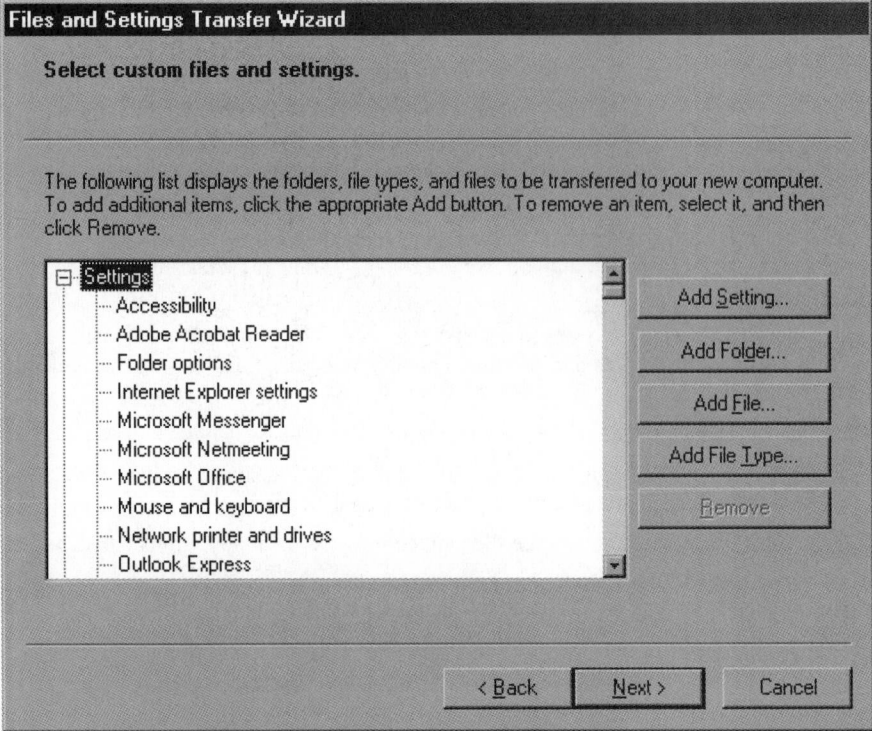

Figure 5-14: Manual transfer selection

12.   The transfer process begins. This may take some time, depending on the amount of data being transferred.

13.   When the transfer completes, just click Finish.

Third-Party User Interface Tools

At the time of this writing, XP is a brand-new release, so there aren't many third-party "tweaking" tools. However, things are always in development or on the upgrade path, so with time you may find plenty of tools that help you tweak and configure XP in just the way you want. I'm including a few tools here that I have used that work fine with XP. As you are looking, you can search the Internet for new tools, and you might consider checking out www.zdnet.com, www.download.com, and www.tucows.com for the latest.

TweakUI

TweakUI is a Microsoft product designed for power users, so it's not really a third-party product. With TweakUI, you can manipulate and customize all kinds of Windows interface items and introduce a number of helpful controls. At press time, the TweakUI version for Windows XP has not been released, but you can keep a watchful eye by searching Microsoft.com. Although some users have had success with earlier versions of TweakUI on Windows XP, I'm not recommending that approach because of possible problems. Your best bet is to get the XP version (if it's available as you are reading this).

Tweaki

Tweaki for Power Users is a shareware program available from www.jermar.com. The current version supports Windows 2000 and 9x/Me, and it works for me on Windows XP. The basic interface enables you to perform a number of tweaks and interesting configuration options using a simple console, shown in Figure 5-15.

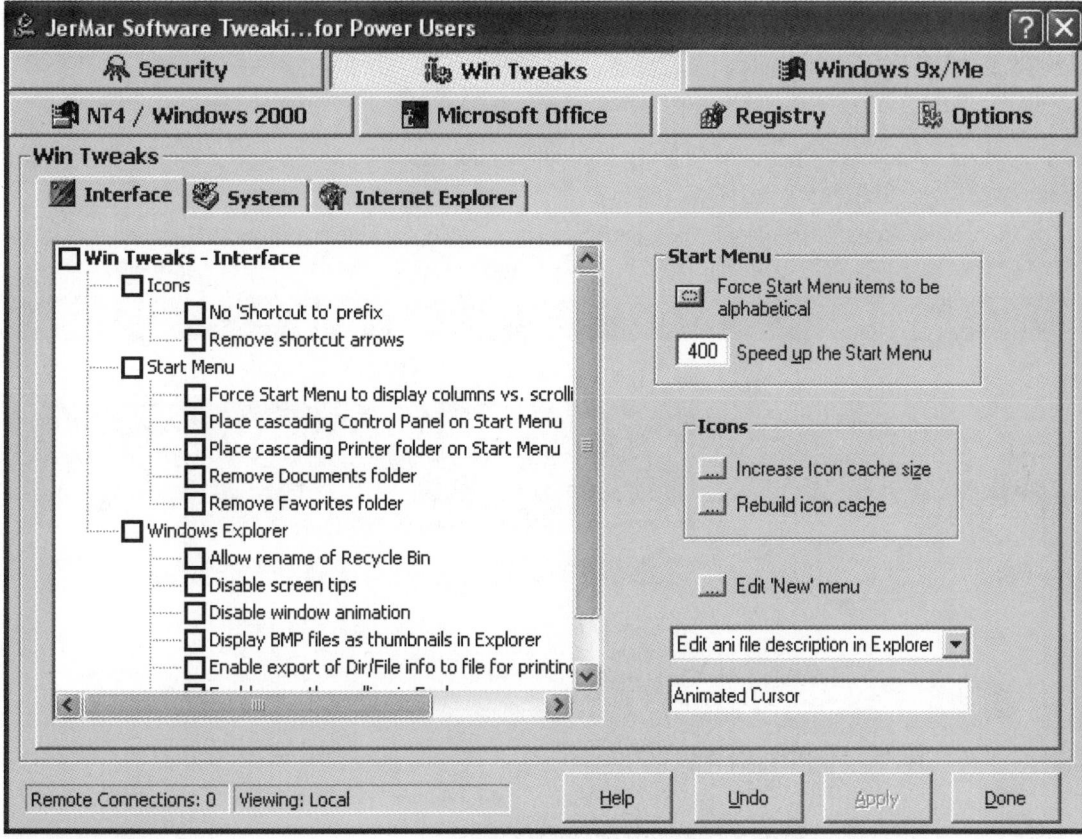

Figure 5-15: Tweaki

The interface for Tweaki is self-explanatory, but here are a few of the options and features to get you started. You can click the tabs at the top of the screen and access various systems or components, which are:

♦ **Security** — Make security changes to the interface, system settings, and Internet Explorer. A number of disable features can turn off various program options.

♦ **Win Tweaks** — Make changes to the Windows interface, such as icon appearance, the Start menu, and Windows Explorer (you can even rename the Recycle Bin). You can also make changes to system components. For example, you can disable autoplay on the CD-ROM and make other general changes. You can also make behavior changes to Internet Explorer.

♦ **NT4/Windows 2000** — Make changes to a number of system divisions, such as the performance, server, network, debug, and Windows 2000-specific divisions. As you will see, some of these do not apply to Windows XP, but you can browse through them.

♦ **Registry** — Easily locate registry items.

♦ **Options** — Configure a number of items such as password protection, user preferences, and remote connections to other desktops. Also, use the Check for Upgrade button to get the latest version.

> **TIP:** You can save some CPU cycles by disabling Windows animation under the Windows Explorer option, as shown in Figure 5-15. You can also take some other actions to reduce Windows animation and give the system a performance boost in doing so. See Chapter 24 for details.

Registry Guide

The Windows Registry Guide is a help file that gives you a bunch of tips and tricks for tweaking the registry. In the 3.0 versions, you find a section on Windows NT/2000 tweaks, and these work fine for Windows XP, as well. You'll find divisions for enhancements to the Windows Registry, such as changing the color of compressed files, renaming My Computer, automatic rebooting in the case of a blue screen, and a number of others.

The file has additional divisions for files, performance, security, troubleshooting, and tips and tricks, as you can see in Figure 5-16. The Windows Registry Guide is downloadable from www.zdnet.com.

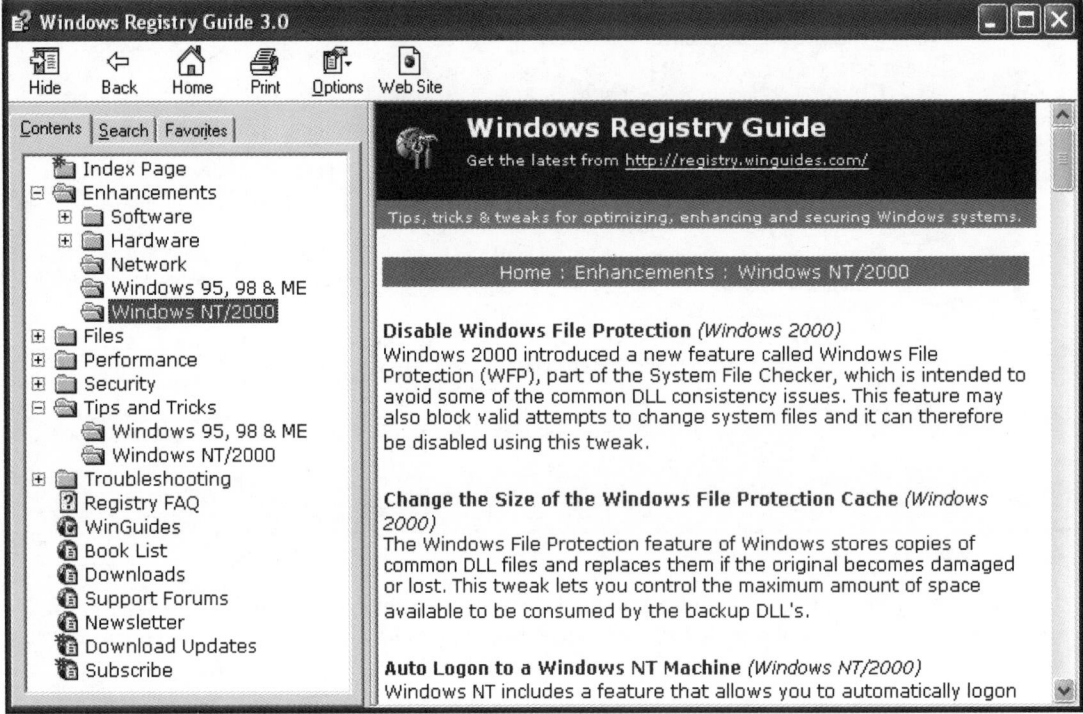

Figure 5-16: Windows Registry Guide

Summary

In this chapter, you examined several Windows XP interface and management issues. You examined the Start menu and looked at how to customize the content found there. You also explored Windows XP Search features, as well as the Files and Settings Transfer Wizard. Finally, I pointed out a few tools that can help you further tweak your Windows XP interface. In summary . . .

♦ The Windows XP Start menu can function in either XP or Classic mode, depending on your needs or preference.

♦ The XP Start menu provides diverse and easy access your drives, programs, files, and folders. Additionally, the Start menu remembers what programs you access and posts them on the Start menu.

♦ The Windows XP system has the best search features available on any Windows operating system, allowing complex, yet tightly controlled searches.

♦ The Files and Settings Transfer Wizard gives you an easy way to transfer files and settings from one computer running a previous version of Windows to another computer running Windows XP.

♦ A number of third-party tools are available that can help you configure and manage the XP interface and Windows Registry.

Chapter 6

Folders, the Recycle Bin, and My Documents

In This Chapter

Windows XP continues the tradition of Windows Me by making folder design easy to use (and to configure) to meet your specific needs. In fact, folders in Windows XP take on the new XP interface design, but you can adjust and tweak folder appearance, including the appearance of the My Documents folder, in a number of ways. As in previous versions of Windows, the Recycle Bin returns in Windows XP as the only default icon on your desktop. Like folder views, the Recycle Bin basically looks and works in the same way as it did in Windows Me. If you are a previous Windows user, you won't find too many new surprises in these items, so this chapter focuses on . . .

♦ Customizing Windows XP folders

♦ Configuring the Windows XP Recycle Bin

♦ Making the best use of My Documents

XP Folders

The default XP theme provides a folder structure similar to that with which you became accustomed in Windows 98/Me/2000. By default, folders appear as dual pane windows that look more like a Web page. This Web-based appearance first started appearing in Windows 98, and with XP, it's understood that you will use the Web view. While you can switch to a "classic" view, you basically lose a number of XP's interface features when you do so.

By default, the dual pane view, as seen in the My Computer example in Figure 6-1, gives you typical menus; a toolbar that looks a lot like Internet Explorer; an information area that contains information that resides in the folder; and a left pane, or Explorer bar, that contains links to tasks and more information. Typically, you'll see a section of tasks related to the content in the window, and related places on the computer. In addition, sometimes you will see a Details box that provides more information about the item that is selected in the right pane.

If you are happy with this default XP approach to folder views, then there is nothing for you to configure. However, if you want to make some changes, there are plenty that can be made; this chapter explores those options.

> **TIP:** A frustrating thing about XP folder views is that the various panes are not readily resizable. In other words, you can't stretch the left pane over the Explorer pane and vice versa. This is a real drag (no pun intended) and makes using the XP folder view seem less versatile than previous versions of Windows.

Windows 98 introduced the notion of "one click" — the Web-based look and feel of Windows whereby each icon or folder acts as an Internet link that you can simply click and open. The single click option saves all those double-clicks, and Microsoft was sure one click would be a big hit.

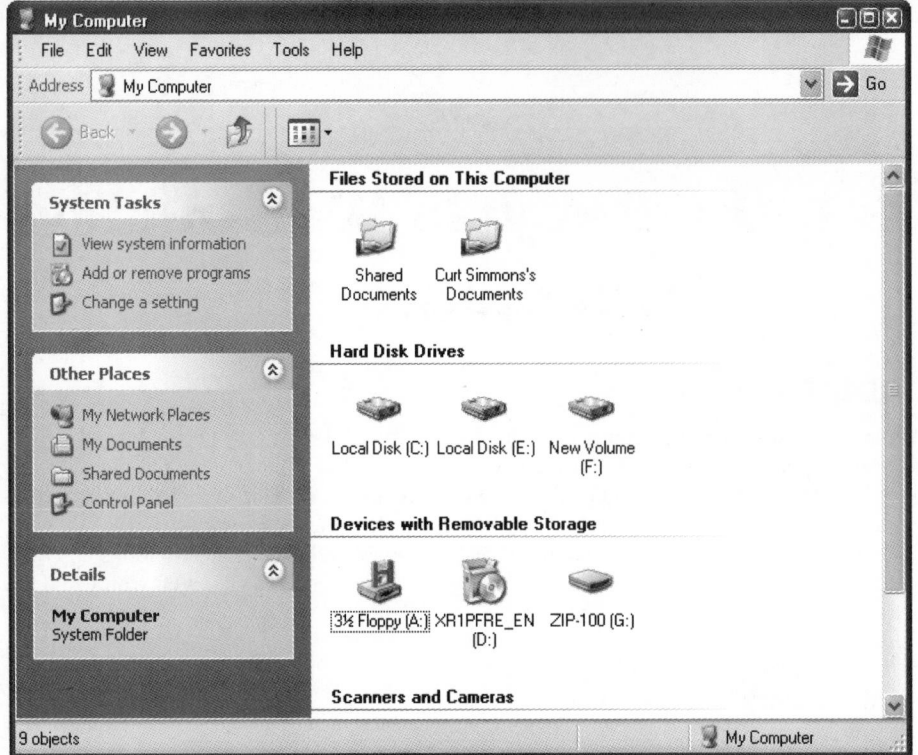

Figure 6-1: Typical XP folder view

However, like My Briefcase a few years ago, many users found one click more aggravating than helpful and the one click feature is not enabled by default in the XP interface. You can, however, easily enable it, if you like this feature.

In this chapter and others, I use the term *click* as a stand-in for both methods. When I refer to a click, keep in mind that you can use a double-click instead, if you have configured your computer to use the *Classic style* interface (this is the Windows 9x interface). I also state that you can rest your mouse pointer over an icon to select it. If you have chosen the Classic style interface, you'll need to click the icon to select it.

You can choose between single-clicking or double-clicking in the My Computer window, by choosing View ⇨ Folder Options, and clicking either the Single-click or Double-click radio buttons on the General tab, as shown in Figure 6-2. If you choose to single-click, you can also choose whether to underline icon titles, which is consistent with the Web browser look and feel, or underline titles only when you point to them.

The My Computer Window

Formerly a mainstay of the desktop, My Computer now resides on your Start Menu. This is not to say that My Computer is no longer important — it still remains the primary location to access and manage drives, but in an effort to make the desktop cleaner, Microsoft has removed all icons from the desktop except Recycle Bin.

TIP: You can drag an icon found on the Start Menu to the desktop in order to make a shortcut to it. For example, if you still want to see My Computer on the desktop and you want to use the default XP view, just drag My Computer off the Start Menu to the desktop. A shortcut will be created on your desktop; now you can access My Computer from either the desktop or the Start Menu. This feature is true of virtually any folder on your system.

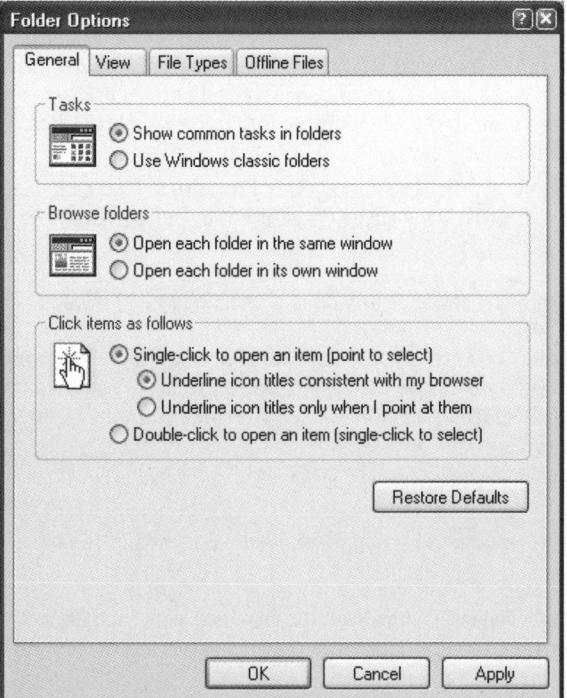

Figure 6-2: Folder Options, General tab

The XP My Computer interface is somewhat different than that seen in previous versions of Windows. In the past, this area only provided a place to access your floppy drive, hard drive, and the like. In Windows XP there are some additional items here, and they are organized in a category view by default. They are:

- ♦ **Files Stored on This Computer** — The title of this section is rather misleading. After all, what actually appears here is *shared folders* on your computer — not every file that is stored on your computer. If you have nothing shared out, this category many not appear at all.

- ♦ **Hard Disk Drives** — All hard disk drives installed on your computer appear here.

- ♦ **Devices with Removable Storage** — All floppy drives, CD-ROM drives, ZIP drives, and other removable storage drives appear here.

- ♦ **Scanners and Cameras** — If you have any scanners and cameras installed on your computer, they appear here.

- ♦ **Other categories** — Depending on your computer's hardware, you may have other categories appear, such as tape drives.

Folders

Microsoft has replaced the term *directory* (a term from DOS, Windows 3.1*x,* and many operating systems before DOS) with *folder* — a more office-oriented name. The folder concept has been around since Windows 95 and is friendlier than "directory." Also, folders can do much more than DOS directories. Some special folders, such as the folders in the My Computer window, have additional capabilities. You can place folders (or better yet, shortcuts to folders) on the Desktop, and they can contain folder windows of their own.

You can place a folder icon (or a shortcut to a folder icon) on the Desktop or in a folder window. Folders can contain other folders, just as DOS directories can contain subdirectories. To locate your files, you click a folder icon to display a window containing other folder icons.

Item properties

Items that are stored in folders have properties dialog boxes. For documents, this dialog box usually just gives you information, but for other items, you see a full set of properties sheets where configuration can take place. For example, when you right-click a drive icon in the My Computer window, you can click Properties to see the disk properties dialog box, as shown in Figure 6-3.

To view or change the properties of a drive, right-click the drive icon and click Properties. You can change the drive's volume label, you can also check the drive for errors, back it up, or defragment it by clicking the Tools tab.

CROSS-REFERENCE: Check out Chapter 3 for more details on defragmenting disks or checking them for errors.

You can share your drive with others on your network by setting your share configuration in the Sharing tab. If the drive is an NTFS drive, you will also see a compression check box option so that Windows XP can compress drive contents in order to conserve disk space. You can also remove files you may not need by clicking Disk Cleanup and choosing what to remove.

Opening a new window

Click a drive icon in the My Computer window to open a window that displays the contents of the drive. The contents will consist of folder and file icons, as shown in Figure 6-4.

Each icon has an associated window. If you use the "classic" Windows settings, when you click an icon in one of these windows, you will open yet another window. My Computer has its own window, and all your disk drives have their own windows.

You can continue to click folder icons to move hierarchically through the folders stored on your drive. Folders can contain subfolders, which, in turn, can contain more subfolders. You can move sideways by returning to a parent folder and then moving to a different subfolder.

If you view your computer's contents through one window, you can also go backward and forward along the path that you have traveled. Click Back (left-pointing) to go back to the previous view that you chose. If you've gone back, click Forward (right-pointing) to move forward to where you were before you went back. (If you don't see the toolbar, choose View ⇨ Toolbars ⇨ Standard Buttons.)

Closing a folder window

The three buttons in the upper-right corner of a window enable you to minimize, maximize, or restore, and to close a folder window, respectively, from left to right.

SECRET: Hold down the Shift key as you click Close to close not only the window with the focus, but all its parent windows as well. If you opened a number of windows to get to the current one, this method gives you an easy way to get rid of all the preceding windows. If you want each window to open within the same window (or not), you can choose either option on the General tab of Folder Options in Control Panel.

Change Your Window View

Many different options are available in Windows XP under the View menu item. If you used Windows 98/Me/2000, none of these items are new. You have multiple toolbars, an Explorer bar, and a number of different icon view choices.

You can choose how the drive icons, folder icons, and other icons are displayed in a window by choosing among five views:

♦ **Thumbnails** — This option presents larger icons for each item in the folder. You may like this view, but it does tend to take up a lot of room.

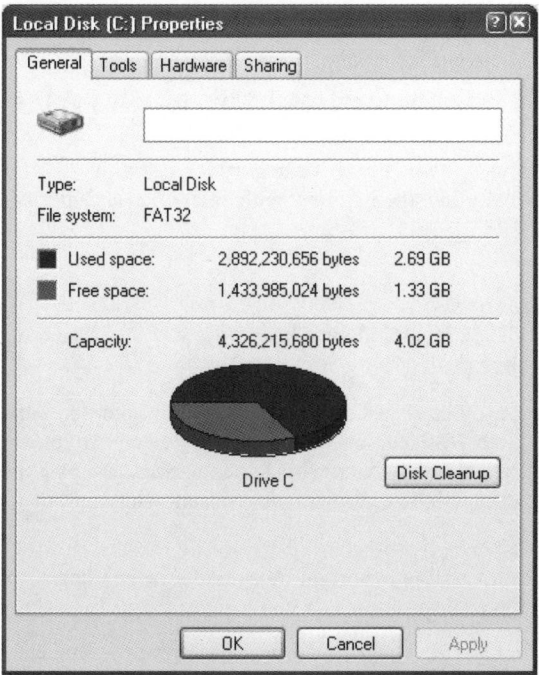

Figure 6-3: The General tab of the Properties dialog box for a disk drive

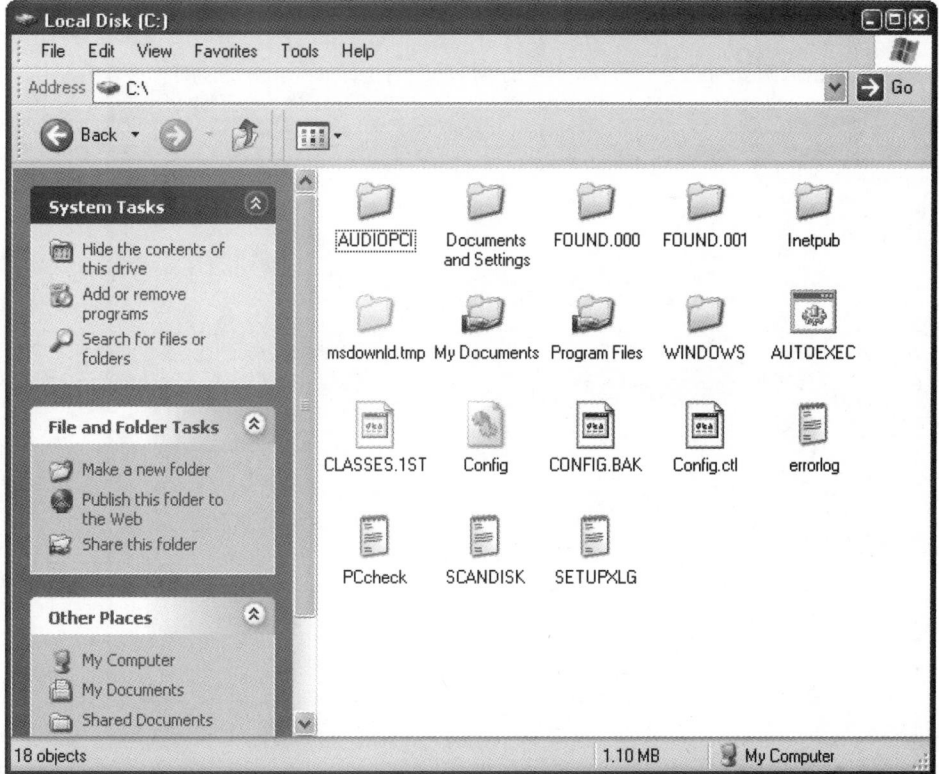

Figure 6-4: Drive contents

♦ **Tiles** — This option looks like Thumbnails, but the icons are smaller.

♦ **Icons** — This view provides a typical icon-based view of each item.

♦ **List** — This view provides an icon for each item, but the items are listed. This is an easy way to see everything in the folder.

♦ **Details** — This option provides yet another icon view, typically in a category format with additional information about each item. It is basically like the list view with categories and more information.

Order the icons

You can specify the order in which your icons are displayed in a window. Choose View ⇨ Arrange Icons and then click the desired option in the submenu that appears.

If you are viewing the top-level My Computer window (you have just clicked the My Computer icon on the Desktop), your choices are by Name, by Type, by Size, by Free Space, and by File System. If you are viewing other drive and folder windows, the choices are usually by Name, by Type, by Size, and by Date. However, the exact set of options that you see in the Arrange Icons submenu depends on what kind of folder you are currently viewing.

If you are using Details view, you can also choose which variable to sort on by clicking the heading buttons (Name, Size, Type, and so on.) located at the top of the columns. If you want to toggle between ascending and descending order, click the heading button a second time. For example, Figure 6-5 shows that I have the items in My Computer listed by free space (total size).

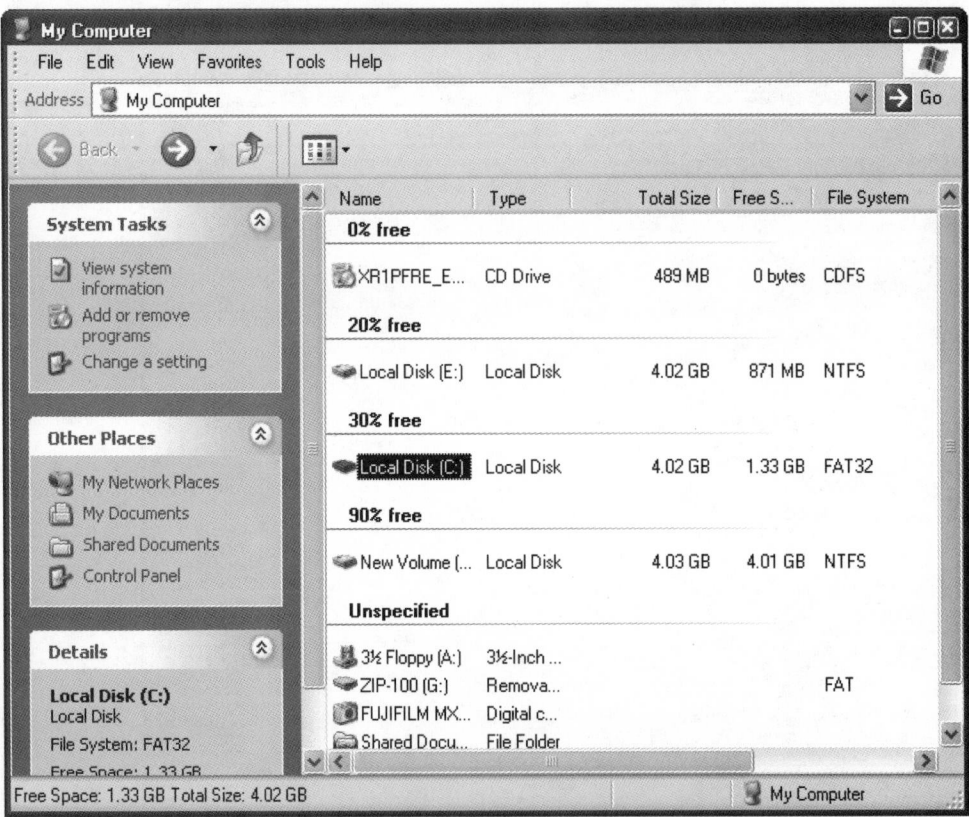

Figure 6-5: Toggle organization when using Details by clicking the column headings

TIP: If you want to switch out of Details view but can't seem to make the categories go away, choose View ⇨ Arrange Icons By ⇨ Show in Groups to turn it off.

Line up your icons

As with the Desktop, every folder window contains an invisible grid, although Windows only uses the grid in the Large Icons and Small Icons views. The size of the grid depends on the size of the icons, the font size (magnification), and the display resolution. You can snap your icons to the center of the cells in the grid by right-clicking the client area of the folder window and choosing View ⇨ List.

Changing the columns in Details view

When you choose the Details view of a folder window (View ⇨ Details), heading buttons appear above each column. At the edge of each of these buttons is a black spacer line. When you rest your mouse over the line, the mouse pointer becomes a vertical line with two horizontal arrows.

You can change the order of the columns by dragging a column header to the left or right. Just place your mouse pointer over a heading button, press and hold down the left mouse button, and drag the column header to the desired position. For example, I often move the Modified column, putting it just to the right of the Name column to make it easier to see when each file was modified.

You can change a column's width by dragging the spacer line on the right edge of the column's heading button to the left or right. If you drag the spacer line for Name to the right, for example, the Name column widens, and the remaining columns shift over to the right.

TIP: If you want to temporarily hide a column in Details view for a given folder window, drag the spacer line at the right edge of the heading button to the left edge of the column. You can redisplay the column — even though you can't see it — by dragging the now-invisible heading button's edge to the right.

Each folder window has its own properties. Before you adjust the width of the columns in a window, they have the default properties. After you change the column widths, Windows retains the new settings and uses them the next time you open that particular folder. This is true even if you open the folder window through My Computer and make changes to it, and then reopen the same folder in Explorer view.

SECRET: Do you want to adjust a column's width in Details view so that none of the entries in the column are truncated? Rest your mouse pointer over the spacer line and double-click. Windows widens (or narrows) the column just enough to fit the widest entry. This is the same method you use to AutoFit columns in Excel and Access.

Finally, you can actually change the Details items that appear. Just choose View ⇨ Choose Details. A list appears where you can select or deselect the Details items that appear when using Details view.

Windows toolbars

In Windows 95, the My Computer window and Explorer window came with only one toolbar. In Windows Me and 98, these windows came with three toolbars, Standard Buttons, Address Bar, and Links. The same is true in Windows XP, and you can even customize the toolbars if you like.

The Standard Buttons toolbar has a standard version and an Internet Explorer version (which is often referred to as the *Internet toolbar*). You can decide which toolbars to display (if any), how they should be positioned, how wide they should be, and whether text will accompany their icons — in short, you have lots of flexibility.

Windows Me and 98 combine the Internet Explorer browser window with the regular Windows 95 windows such as My Computer. Therefore, Microsoft had to come up with a way to combine the toolbars applicable to each window.

> **TIP:** The idea behind the toolbars is Internet integration. You can easily work within a local folder and use the Address Bar to jump to another folder or go to a Web address. You can use the Favorites menu to add favorites and to adjust links just like you do in Internet Explorer. This continued "seamlessness" between your computer and the Internet is a trend that you will continue to see.

If you have a small screen (like that on a portable), the toolbars can hog a bunch of precious real estate. Thankfully, they are flexible enough that you can decide just how much space to allot to them and how many to use.

In Figure 6-6, all three toolbars are enabled. I have the Standard toolbar available, the Address Bar (which looks like Internet Explorer), and the Links option (which also looks like Internet Explorer).

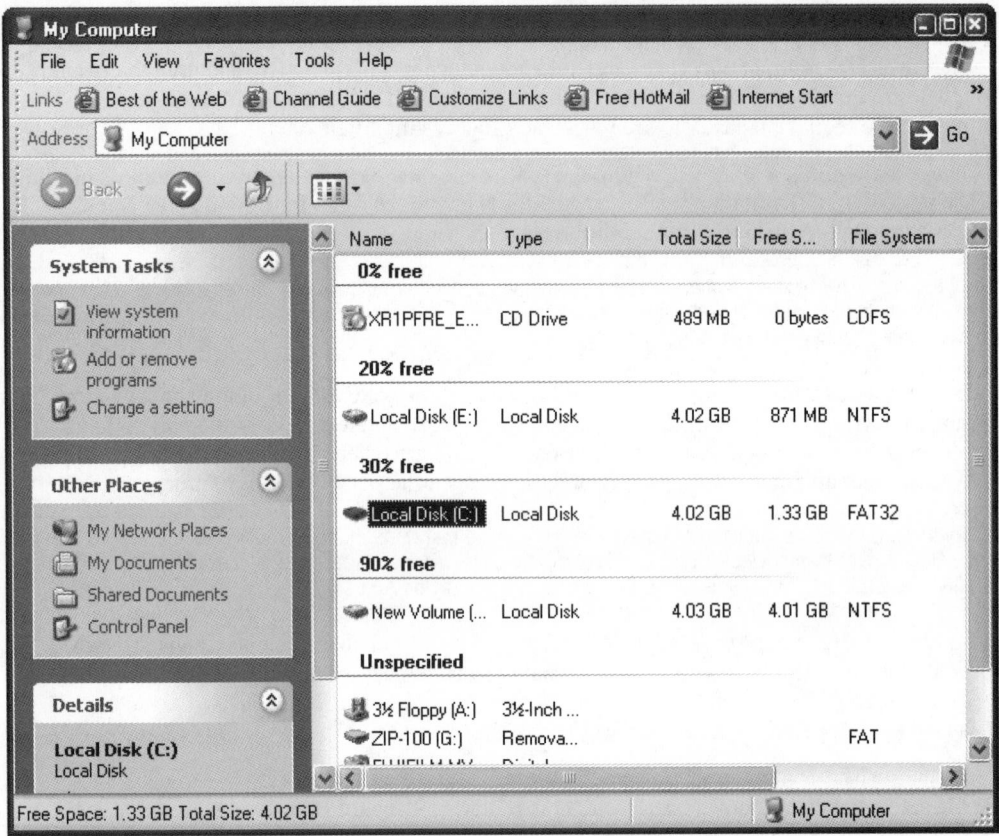

Figure 6-6: Toolbar options

By default, toolbars are locked into place. This means that you add the desired toolbars to your folder, they are placed on the window by the system, and you can't move them. However, you can choose View ⇨ Toolbars ⇨ and clear the Lock the Toolbars option so that you can rearrange the toolbars by dragging them around the window. For example, consider Figure 6-7, where I have dragged and dropped my toolbars into new locations.

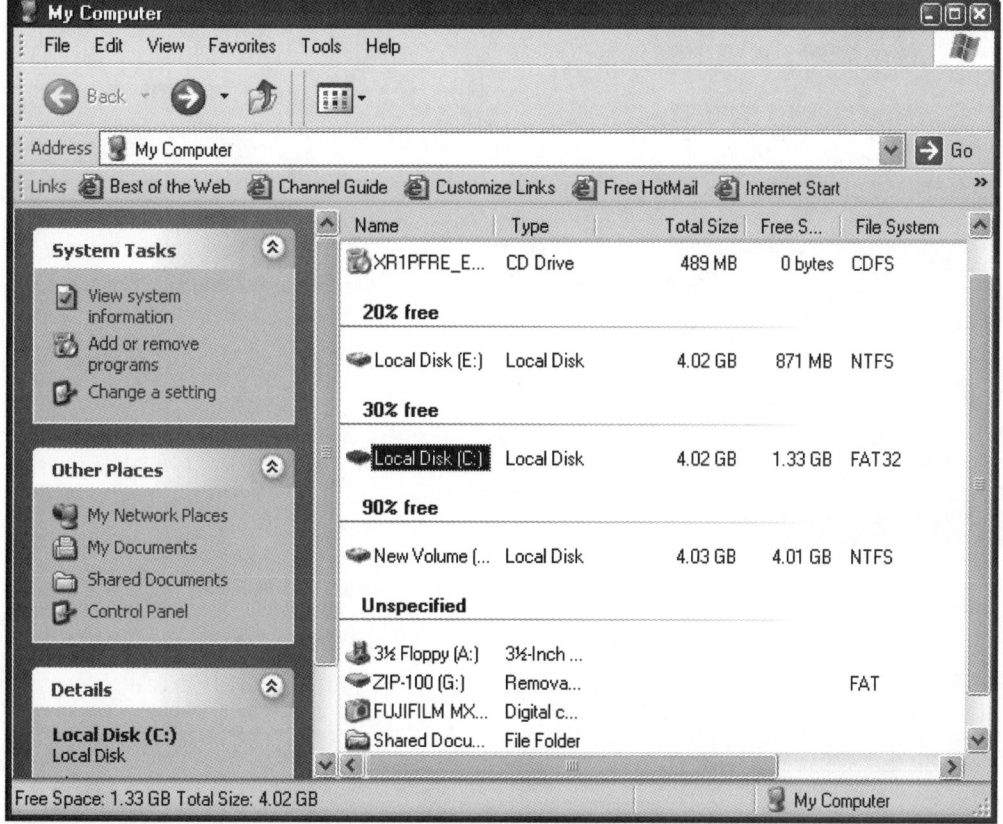

Figure 6-7: Toolbar arrangement options

SECRET: Windows retains the toolbar settings for your My Computer window, so the next time that you open a folder window, you'll see the same toolbars in the same positions. The Windows Explorer and the Internet Explorer windows also retain their own toolbar settings. You can use these three windows interchangeably to perform similar functions, but establish unique toolbar settings in each one.

The Explorer bar

Choose View ⇨ Explorer Bar in a My Computer window, and you'll see a submenu. When you mark one of these options, a new pane appears on top of the default XP pane (tasks, other places, and so on). The Explorer Bar works just as it did in previous versions of Windows, but it actually resides on top of the default XP pane — in other words, you can't remove the XP pane but you can place other Explorer Bar items on top of it.

SECRET: Actually, if you want to remove the Tasks pane from a folder altogether, you can do so with Folder Options, which I discuss later in this chapter.

The content of the pane varies depending on which option you choose (Search, Favorites, History, or Folders). Figure 6-8 shows what the My Computer window looks like if you choose View ⇨ Explorer Bar ⇨ History.

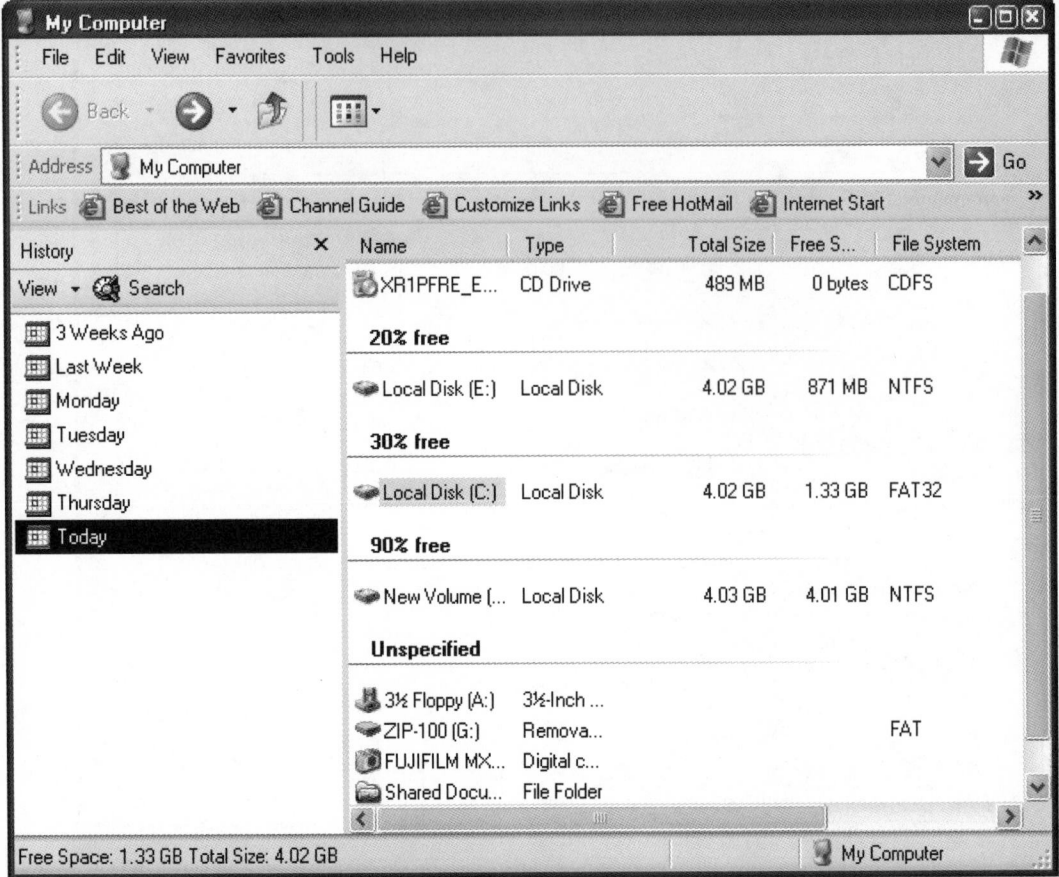

Figure 6-8: A Windows folder window with the History Explorer bar

Customizing toolbars

You can customize the toolbars found in your folders so that they look the way you want and so that they contain the items that you need to use. Simply open the desired folder and choose View ⇨ Toolbars ⇨ Customize. This action opens the Customize Toolbar interface, as you can see in Figure 6-9.

This interface provides the available toolbar buttons window and a window showing the current toolbar buttons. Simply select the item that you want to add or remove and click the appropriate button. You can add or remove as many or as few icons as you want in order to get the toolbar configuration you need, and you can change these settings easily and at any time.

Customizing a folder

Folders that you create have a customization feature by which you can customize how the folder looks and what icon represents that folder. However, default Windows folders, such as My Computer and My Documents, cannot be changed using the XP interface theme.

To customize a folder, just right-click the folder and click Properties. Then click the Customize tab, as shown in Figure 6-10.

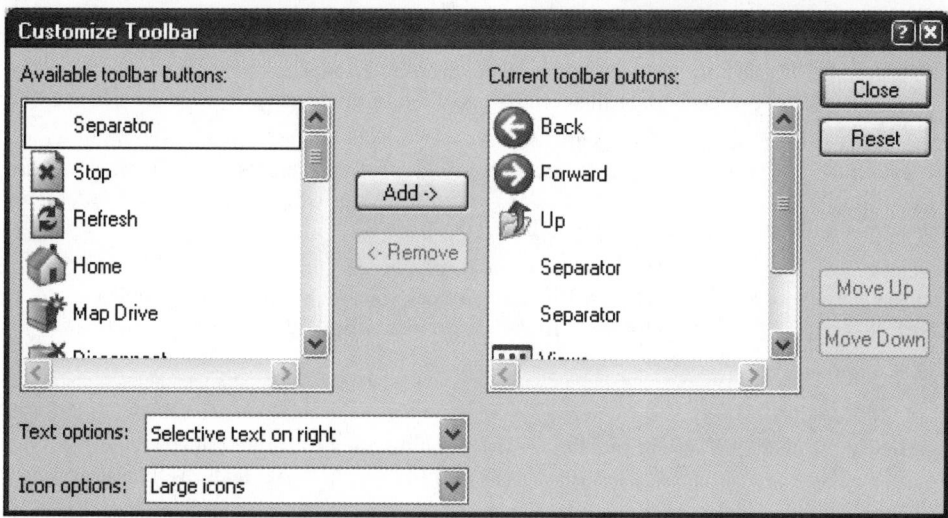

Figure 6-9: Customize Toolbar

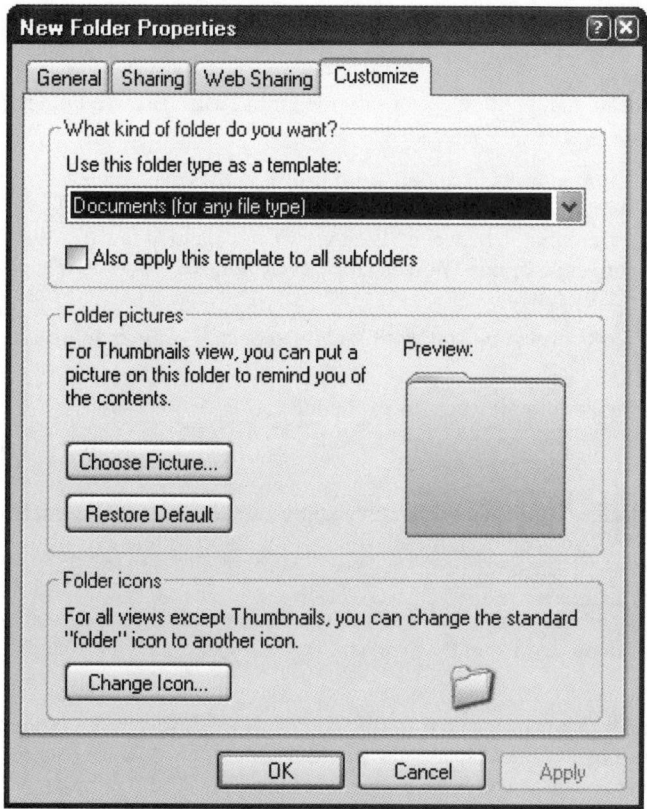

Figure 6-10: Folder customization

You have three configuration options:

- **Type of folder** — Choose a folder template from the drop-down menu, such as documents, pictures, or music. You can also apply this template to all subfolders as well.

- **Folder pictures** — You can use plain manila folders, or you can choose a picture (anything you want) to put on the folder. For example, if you have a folder full of pictures, you can put a picture on the folder itself. The purpose of this feature is to remind you of what is in the folder, and there are a number of interesting things you can do here.

- **Folder icons** — You can change the folder icons to basically anything you want. Click the Change Icon and select an icon you want, or click Browse to select your own. There are many Web sites that offer free icons — just search for "free icons" on your favorites search engine.

Folder Options

I mentioned earlier in the chapter that you can change from double-click to single-click or vice versa by using Folder Options. However, folder options give you a number of additional features that determine how your folders look and operate.

Choosing Tools ⇨ Folder Options in any folder window lets you set a number of Desktop, Explorer, My Computer, and Internet Explorer options. There are a number of different features available, and the following sections review them for you.

General

On the General tab, you can choose some basic radio button options divided into Tasks, Browse Folders, and Click Items. Your options are:

- **Tasks** — You can choose to "show common tasks in folder" or to use Windows classic view. Essentially, these two buttons enable you to either show the Explorer Tasks pane in each folder or remove it. In the past, these settings differentiated between "Web view" and classic view (no Web view), but the removal of Web is no longer an option. You can, however, remove the sometimes helpful, sometimes aggravating, left Tasks pane.

- **Browse Folders** — This enables you to choose how you want folders to open — either within themselves or each in its own window.

- **Click Items** — You can use single-click or double-click, as explained earlier in this chapter.

View

For some users, the improvement to the interface in Windows that they appreciate the most is that each folder can now maintain its own settings. Now you can design each folder window to be however you like it.

The view settings that you have control over are the icon views in a folder window (Large Icons, Small Icons, List, or Details), the icon order (By Name, By Type, By Size, and By Date), and the widths and order of the columns in Details view.

Now you can display each folder in a manner that is best suited for the contents of that folder. You might display a folder full of shortcuts to applications in Large Icons view sorted by name. If a folder contains pictures, you might choose Thumbnail view so that you can see previews of the files. And if a folder contains documents, you might display it in Details view sorted by date.

To modify how Windows handles view settings, choose Tools ⇨ Folder Options and click the View tab. If you want each folder to remember its view settings, just make the changes you want and click OK. To force the view settings for all folders to be the same as the current folder, click Apply to All Folders. To force all folders back to the default view settings, click Reset All Folders, as shown in Figure 6-11.

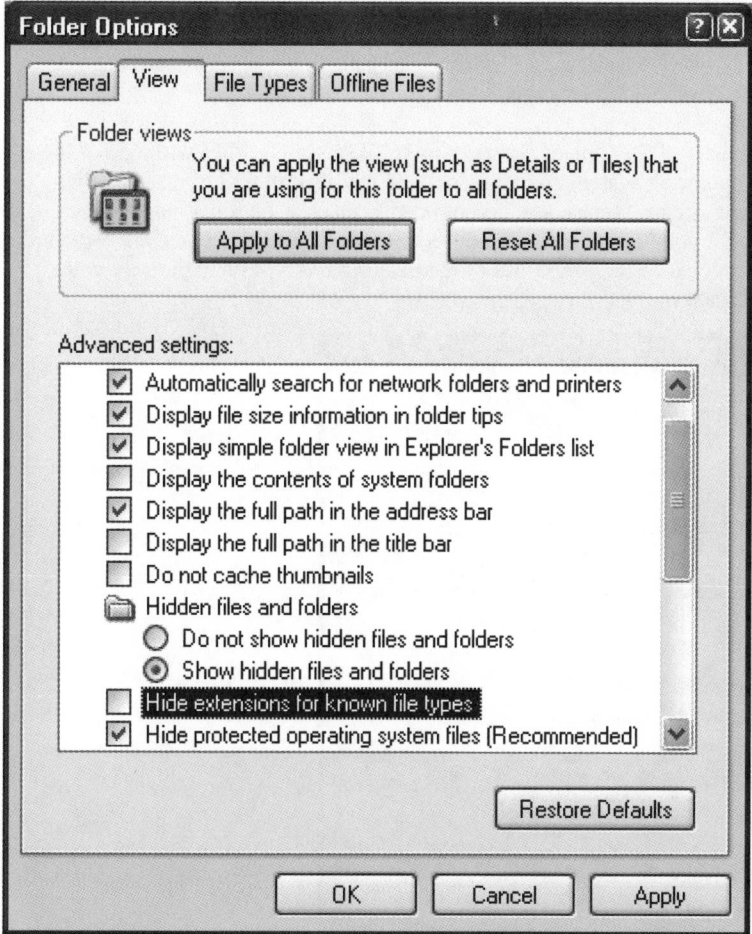

Figure 6-11: View tab

The Advanced settings window has a number of additional setting options that control how your folders behave and what they display. You should take a look at this list for anything you might want to enable, but let me point to a few goodies:

◆ If you are using the Address Bar in the folder, consider enabling the Display the full path in the title bar option. This will allow you to see exactly where in the Windows folder structure a file is located.

◆ Under hidden files and folders, click the Show hidden files and folders radio button to see everything on your computer. Use caution, though, when handling hidden files and folders because they are often system specific and are not designed to be tampered with.

◆ It seems as though Windows XP wants users to forget about file extensions. When you first install Windows, it doesn't show files with certain extensions in folder windows or in Explorer windows. And it doesn't show the three-letter extensions for files of registered file types. You can tell Windows to display these missing files and extensions by clearing the Hide extensions for known file types check box.

◆ If you miss the existence of Control Panel in My Computer, you can put it back with the Show Control Panel in My Computer check box option.

♦ The Show encrypted or compressed NTFS files in color feature can help you keep track of what is compressed on your computer and what is not compressed.

File types

The File Types tab lists every registered file type on your computer. Essentially, files with one of these file types are recognized by the operating system and an associated application will try to open them, as shown in Figure 6-12. Under most circumstances, you do not need to change anything here. However, if you are trying to use a file type that your computer does not seem to recognize, you can click New and add it to the system. Also, you can change the properties of the existing file types and the way your system handles them, which is shown in the following steps.

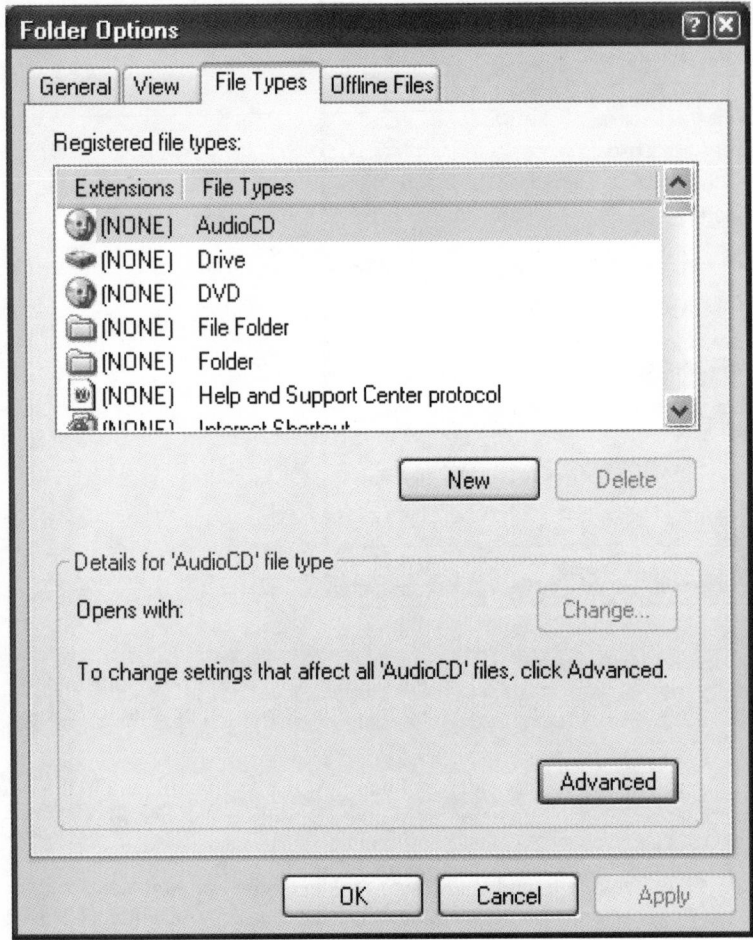

Figure 6-12: File Types window

STEPS

Changing file type properties

1. On the File Types tab, select the file type that you want to edit and then click Advanced.

2. The Edit File Type window appears, as shown in Figure 6-13. As you can see, you can change the default icon or you can change the action. As Figure 6-13 shows, the default action for an AudioCD file is for the computer to play the CD. You can use the New, Edit, or Remove buttons to change

this behavior. Also, you can determine whether or not you receive a confirmation message after a download occurs for this file type, and whether or not to show an extension. When you're done, just click OK.

> **TIP:** Without question, you do not need to browse all of the file types and begin making changes. The point to remember here is that if you need Windows XP to handle some kind of file type in certain way, you may be able to accomplish that goal on the file type properties dialog box. One thing you might consider is enabling the "Confirm open after download" check box so that any files that you download are never opened automatically by the system without your consent. To configure this option, scroll through the file types and select those typically downloaded (HTML. JPEG, MPEG, and so on).

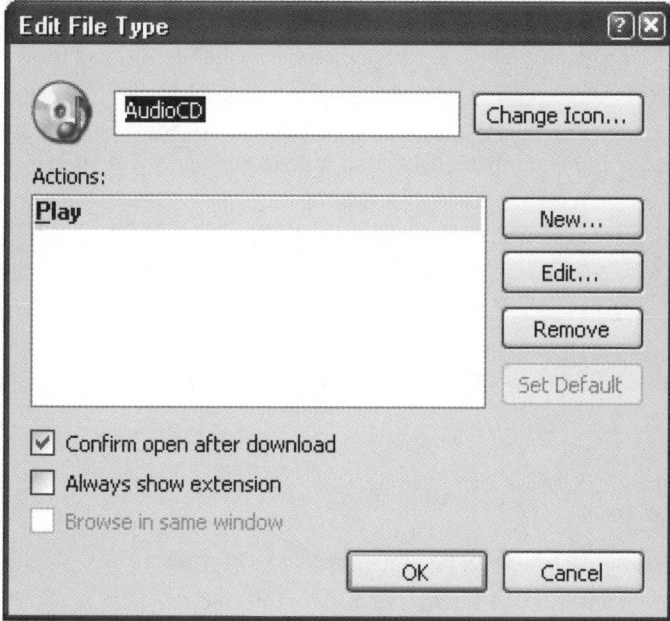

Figure 6-13: Edit File Type

Offline files

Offline files enable your computer to cache network documents so that you can view them when you are not connected to the network. See Chapter 20 to learn more about enabling and connecting to offline files.

The Recycle Bin

The Recycle Bin doesn't recycle anything but your disk space. If you want to stretch the analogy a bit, you could say that if you delete unused files, you won't have to go out and buy new hard disks, but that is stretching it.

My take on the use of this symbol for the trashcan is that Microsoft realized people would rather have a Recycle basket on their Desktop than a trashcan. It is cooler. Right? And, of course, it is more politically correct.

So why the Bin part of Recycle Bin? During the early stages of the development of the Recycle Bin — in beta testing of Windows 95 (then code-named Chicago) — its name was Recycle.bin. This is a pun. In a UNIX file system, *bin* is a standard subdirectory in which the *binary* files (executable programs) are stored. Combine the trash-receptacle meaning of the word *bin* with its UNIX-world meaning, and the nerds at Microsoft got *.bin* on the Chicago Desktop. An art director or somebody in marketing made them get rid of the period and capitalize the *b*.

The Recycled folders

The Recycle Bin is an alias (a stand-in) for the special folders labeled Recycled. You can use the Explorer to see these folders — you'll find one on every hard disk and every logical drive on the hard disk. (If you have divided the hard disk into multiple drives, such as C, D, and so on, you will see a Recycled folder on each logical drive.) The Recycle Bin icon is displayed on the Desktop for easy access. The Recycled folder icons are attached to the hard disk drive icons along with your other folders. (The Recycled folders are, indeed, folders, even though they don't have the standard folder icons.) They are designated as file type Recycle Bin.

If you click the Recycle Bin icon or any of the Recycled folder icons, you find that they all display the same contents. Opening the Recycled folder icon attached to one hard disk shows the files deleted from your other local hard disks as well.

Microsoft made it a point to put the Recycle Bin on the Desktop and made it hard to remove. The Recycle Bin stores all the files that have been deleted from your hard disks. You have to go to only one place to find all your deleted files.

> **SECRET:** You can change the name of the Recycled folders; it just doesn't do any good. If you change the name *Recycled* to *Wasted*, the next time you start Windows, it creates a new Recycled folder. You end up with two recycle receptacle icons, both of which display the same list of deleted files when you click them.

If you were following along and really created a Wasted folder, now I have to bail you out. You have a Recycled folder and a Wasted folder. How do you erase or get rid of the Wasted folder? It's not so easy.

STEPS

Getting rid of the "Wasted" folder

1. Choose Start ⇨ Programs ⇨ Accessories ⇨ MS-DOS Prompt to open a DOS window.

2. Change directories to the \Wasted directory. (You'll find it in the root directory.)

3. Type **dir /a** to see if any files are stored in the Wasted directory. You are going to purge these files, so be sure to restore any that you might want to keep before you take the next step. To restore any of these files, right-click the Wasted folder, click Open, right-click any file that you want to restore, and click Restore.

4. Type **Attrib -r -s -h Desktop.ini**.

5. Type **del *.*** and press the Enter key.

6. Change directories to the root directory of the hard disk partition that contains the Wasted directory (**cd **).

7. Remove the Wasted directory by typing **rd Wasted** at the DOS prompt.

The Recycled folders are system resources. Windows regenerates them if you change the name of a Recycled folder. It doesn't want you to mess with these resources because it needs them to manage deleted files.

> **SECRET:** The Recycled folders are, indeed, folders, but they are special ones. When you display the contents of a Recycled folder in Details view, you'll see an additional column named Original Location, which tells you where the folder/document originally resided in the operating system before it was placed in the Recycle Bin. Also, Recycled folders don't use the folder icon. Furthermore, the Recycled folders are hidden so that you can't see them if you go to DOS and type **dir** (although you can see them if you type **dir /a**).

Windows puts the deleted files in these folders, but it stores them under new names (although you don't see this). Each Recycled folder contains an additional file named Info. Again, you don't see this file (unless you type **dir /a** at the DOS prompt). Windows combines the deleted files and the Info file to create entries that look like the original deleted filenames with the addition of a column that lists their original location on the system before it was moved to the Recycle Bin.

What is really unusual about these Recycled folders is that their folder windows display the names and icons of all the deleted files, not just the ones stored in that particular folder or deleted from that particular logical disk drive. The files deleted from a particular drive, however, are actually stored in the Recycled folder on that drive. You can see this for yourself by going to the DOS prompt, changing directories to the Recycled folder on a particular drive, and typing **dir /a**.

The code that makes the Recycled folders special is stored in a dynamic link library named Shell32.dll. This file is referenced in the Desktop.ini file.

The recycle receptacle icons

Both the Recycle Bin and the Recycled folders use a recycle bin as their icon. If there are no files in the Recycle Bin, the icon shows an empty bin. If there are any deleted files in the Recycle Bin, the icon displays white paper stuffed into the bin.

If you delete a file and the Recycle Bin was previously empty, the Recycle Bin icon on the Desktop changes to its "stuffed with white paper" state. If you click the Recycle Bin icon to open it and then drag a file to the Recycle Bin folder window, the Recycle Bin icon in the title bar changes from the empty state to the "stuffed with white paper" state.

You can delete items in the Recycle Bin by right-clicking the item's icon and clicking Delete.

> **SECRET:** You can change the icons that represent an empty or a full Recycle Bin. Use your Registry Editor to navigate to the following: HKEY_CLASSES_ROOT\ CLSID\ {645FF040-5081-101B-9F08-00AA002F954E}. Highlight DefaultIcon in the left pane. Double-click first on *empty* and later on *full* in the right pane. Type the path and filename for the files that contain the icons that you want to use to represent the Recycle Bin in both states.

What does the Recycle Bin do?

Unless you have configured the Recycle Bin to remove files immediately on delete (see "Removing files immediately when deleted" later in this chapter), the Recycle Bin stores the files (and shortcuts, which are stored as files) that you have deleted from your local hard disks using Explorer or a folder window.

The deleted files remain in the Recycle Bin until you issue the Empty Recycle Bin command (by right-clicking the Recycle Bin icon and choosing Empty Recycle Bin, or by choosing File ⇨ Empty Recycle Bin in the Recycle Bin window). If you want to restore a file (or files) in the Recycle Bin (prior to emptying the Recycle Bin), you can select it, and then choose File ⇨ Restore (or right-click the file and choose Restore), or just click the link in the Tasks box, as shown in Figure 6-14. The selected file is returned to its original folder, even if the folder has been deleted. Windows restores the folder simultaneously.

> **CROSS-REFERENCE:** Restoring files that you have sent to the Recycle Bin is discussed later in this chapter in "Restoring deleted files."

You also see deleted folders in the Recycle Bin. You can restore a folder (and any subfolders it contains) by right-clicking the folder icon in the Recycle Bin and choosing Restore from the context menu. And unlike the pre-Internet Explorer 4.0 version of Windows 95, Windows XP lets you restore empty folders. Such a capability is useful because some transaction software uses empty folders as temporary storage and requires that these folders be available always.

You can send files or folders to the Recycle Bin in several ways. You can select a file/folder in a folder window or the Explorer and press Delete. You can right-click a file/folder and click Delete on the context menu. You can also drag and drop a file/folder to the Recycle Bin icon on the Desktop or in the Explorer, or to the Recycled folder icons in the Explorer and folder windows.

What does it mean to delete an Item?

To *delete* a file means to move it to the Recycle Bin. The fact that deleted files are stored in the Recycle Bin means that they aren't "really" deleted. They are still taking up space on your hard disk.

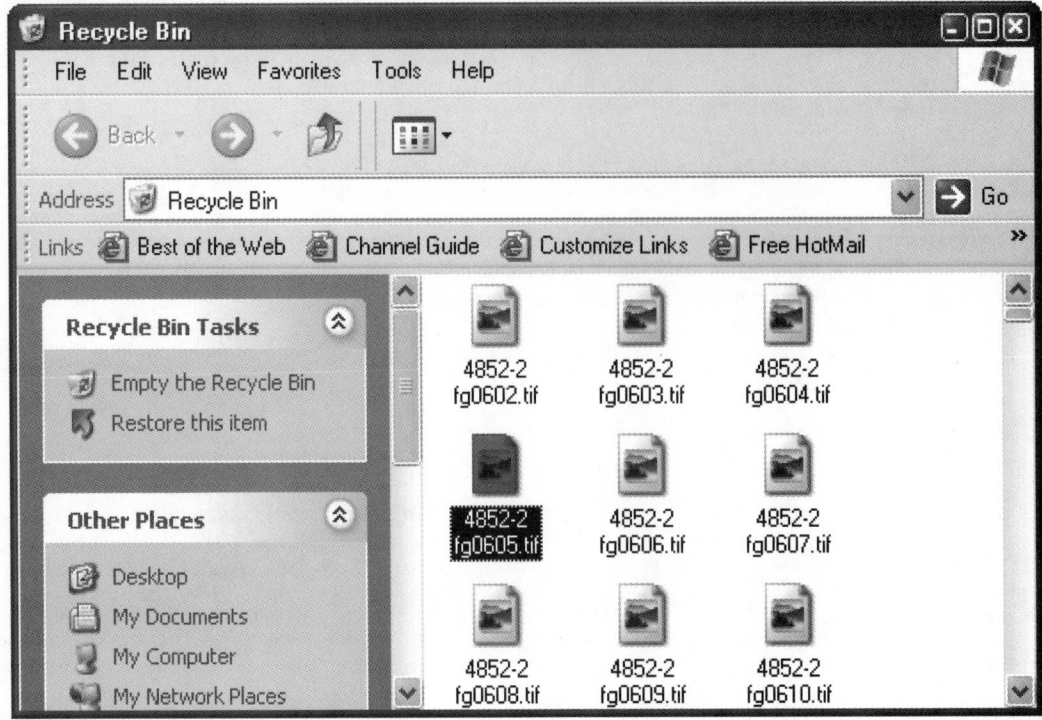

Figure 6-14: Recycle Bin

What is great about the Recycle Bin is that it allows you to organize and clean up your file system without having to make a decision that you may regret a few minutes later. If you delete something and then realize it's more important than you had thought, you can restore it easily.

The Recycle Bin provides a tradeoff between the safety and convenience of not deleting the file until later and the valuable disk space taken up by these deleted items. It is up to you to decide when to empty it.

When you empty the Recycle Bin or delete files in a DOS session, the names of the deleted files are altered so that they don't show up in the file listings in the Explorer, folder windows, or DOS directory lists. The disk space taken up by the files is now available to be written over by new files. If they haven't been written over yet, you can recover these files by using low-level tools. For additional information, see the section entitled "Undelete and Unerase" later in this chapter.

To summarize, there are three levels of delete. If you delete a file in a folder or Explorer window, it is stored in the Recycle Bin. If you delete it from the Recycle Bin, or delete it in a DOS window, it is deleted from the file management system. If you use low-level tools to wipe the space on the hard disk that it occupied, it can't be recovered. Still, a slightly earlier version of the file may be intact on the hard disk in some other location — in which case, that earlier version would be recoverable.

Emptying the Recycle Bin

As you have seen, dropping a file into the Recycle Bin or pressing the Delete key after selecting an icon does nothing more than move the file to the Recycle Bin. It certainly doesn't delete it — unless you choose the Remove files immediately when deleted option in the Recycle Bin Properties dialog box (right-click the Recycle Bin icon and choose Properties).

To delete the items in the Recycle Bin, click the Recycle Bin icon on the Desktop and then choose File ⇨ Empty Recycle Bin in the Recycle Bin window. All the files in the Recycle Bin are purged.

If you want to purge only some of the items in the Recycle Bin, select those items first, and then choose File ⇨ Delete. Or, you can right-click the items that you want purged and click Delete in the context menu.

Deleting files from common file dialog boxes

You can delete files from the common file dialog boxes that are used by Windows-aware applications. If you choose File ⇨ Open (or File ⇨ Save As) to display the Open (or Save As) dialog box, you can right-click a file and choose Delete from the context menu, or select the file and press Delete. The deleted file is stored in the Recycle Bin.

The Windows common file dialog boxes work a lot like folder windows. You can drag and drop files to and from them. You can rename files. You can create new folders or files. You can't, however, select multiple files or folders.

You can't delete files in the older common file dialog boxes, such as those used by the old Windows 3.1*x* Write. Microsoft now refers to these as *Win-1* common dialog boxes.

Deleting shortcuts

If you delete a shortcut, only the shortcut goes to the Recycle Bin, not the target (whether it be a file, application, or folder). The original item stays right where it was and continues to work fine. You are only deleting the shortcut file itself — which has an extension of lnk, pif, or url — not the target of the shortcut.

Right- or left-drag to the Recycle Bin

There are many ways to delete a file. You can drag the file to the Recycle Bin icon, to a Recycled folder icon, or to an open Recycle Bin or Recycled folder window. If you left-drag the file icon, it is moved to the Recycle Bin. If you right-drag it, you are given the choice to move the file or cancel the move.

You can drag files back out of the Recycle Bin and place them in any folder, not just in their original location. If you right-drag a file out of the Recycle Bin to a folder window, you are given the chance to move the file or cancel the move.

If you right-click a file icon and click Delete in the context menu, or if you highlight a file icon and press the Delete key, you will be asked to confirm your deletion. It doesn't matter whether the Recycle Bin has been set to remove files immediately when deleted or not; you will still be asked for confirmation of the deletion.

If you drag a file (either left- or right-drag) to the Recycle Bin, you will not be asked for confirmation unless you've set the Remove files immediately when deleted option. The Windows designers assumed that if you were willing to go to all the trouble of dragging a file to the Recycle Bin, you meant it.

You can turn off the delete confirmation message by following these steps:

STEPS

Turning off delete confirmation

1. Right-click the Recycle Bin icon on your Desktop.
2. Click Properties in the context menu.
3. Click the Global tab (if necessary).
4. Clear the Display delete confirmation dialog box check box, as shown in Figure 6-15.

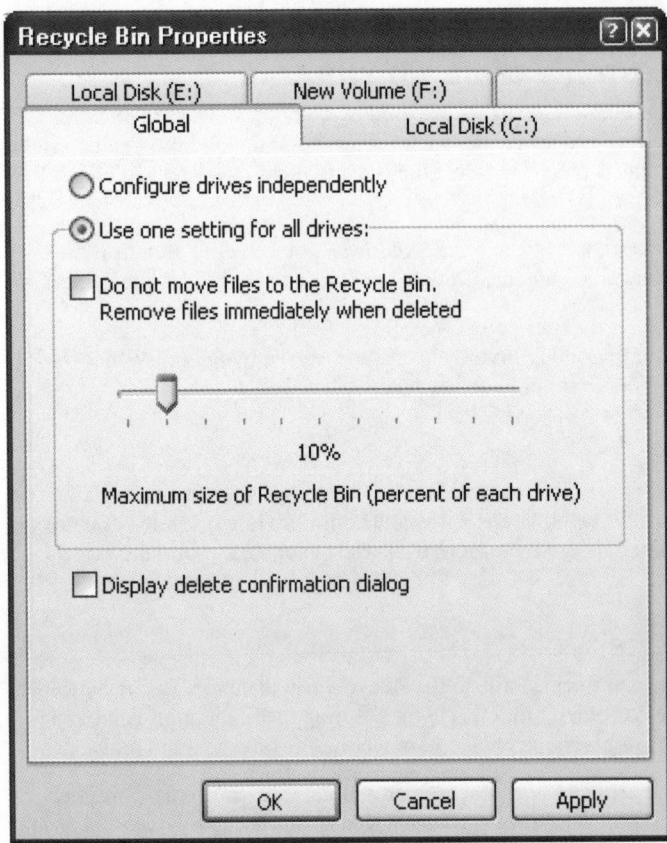

Figure 6-15: Recycle Bin Properties, Global tab

Shift+Delete

You can delete files without sending them to the Recycle Bin — in other words, purge them — by highlighting their filenames, holding down Shift, and pressing Delete. (You can also hold down Shift while clicking Delete in a context menu.) The files won't be sent to the Recycle Bin because by deliberately holding down the Shift key, you are telling Windows that you want these files purged. Don't confuse this use of Shift+Delete with the use of Shift+Delete in word processors to send selected text to the Clipboard. Most word processors also support Ctrl+X to cut to the Clipboard, so if you use this key combination, you won't mix up the meaning of Shift+Delete.

Deleting your hard disk

If you right-click a hard disk drive icon in the Explorer or in a folder window, you won't find Delete on the context menu. It's not a good idea to delete a hard disk, and, in fact, you can't. But you can delete — or move to the Recycle Bin — all the files on the hard disk by dragging the drive icon to the Recycle Bin.

I don't suggest you do this, especially if the space taken up by the current files on the hard disk is greater than the space set aside for deleted files in the Recycle Bin. If you delete a hard disk, you are moving all the files on the hard disk to the Recycle Bin. This is not possible if the Recycle Bin doesn't have room for them.

All this can get quite confusing. The Recycled folders are attached to a hard disk, but they show all the files that have been deleted or moved to the Recycle Bin, no matter which hard disk (or disk partition) they were deleted from. If you drag a hard disk drive icon to the Recycle Bin, are you also deleting the files stored in the Recycled folder? The next section addresses this question.

Deleting My Computer or other key components

You can drag My Computer, My Network Places, and the Recycle Bin and drop them on the Recycle Bin folder window. But when you do, you will just get a beep. Thankfully, Windows won't let you delete these things.

The same is true of the Printers folder, the Control Panel, the Fonts folder, and the Dial-Up Networking folder. You just get a beep. You can try deleting one of these folders with a right-drag, which feels safer because right-dragging normally gives you a context menu confirming the move. But either way, Windows won't let you delete these folders because they are key system components.

Deleting files on removable media

Files on removable media, such as floppy disks, Zip disks, CD-RWs, and so on, are not moved to the Recycle Bin when you delete them. (In fact, files you delete from any removable media are not sent to the Recycle Bin.) You can drag the removable drive icon to the Recycle Bin (icon or folder window), and all the files will be purged after you are first advised of that fact and allowed to change your mind. The message box that appears displays an icon of a file being shredded as a way of indicating that your files will be very difficult to recover if you continue.

If you highlight a file that is stored on a removable disk and press Delete, you will get the same notification. Windows just doesn't provide as much safety for files on removable disks as it does for files on your local hard disks, although it does ask every time for confirmation of the deletion (purge).

Restoring deleted files

It is easy to get files back from the Recycle Bin. Just click the Recycle Bin icon on the Desktop to open the Recycle Bin folder window. Right-click the item that you want to restore, and then click Restore. The file is restored to its original location. If the folder that it was stored in has been deleted, the folder is also restored.

TIP: If deleting a file was the last file management action you carried out, you can choose Edit ⇨ Undo Delete in the Recycle Bin window, or right-click the window and choose Undo Delete from the context menu.

You can also just drag the files out of the Recycle Bin and move them to wherever you want. Dragging only moves files in and out of the Recycle Bin, no matter whether you right-drag or left-drag. If you right-drag, you won't see options for Copy, Create Shortcut(s) Here, or any other command you usually see in a context menu when you right-drag and drop.

SECRET: Do you want to check out a graphic or text file that you have already put in the Recycle Bin? Maybe you want to edit it after you deleted it. As long as you haven't emptied your Recycle Bin, you can drag and drop the file from the Recycle Bin onto your application icon. After you're done viewing the file you don't have to worry about deleting it, because it wasn't undeleted in the first place.

If you edited a file that's currently in the Recycle Bin and want to save its new version, save it to another folder. The name of the file in the Save As dialog box will default to its Recycle Bin name, which is not its original name (even though the original name is shown in the Recycle Bin window). This name is used internally by the Recycle Bin to track the deleted files. You may want to change it if you save the edited file to a new folder.

CAUTION: Unlike moving, copying, or deleting a file, emptying the Recycle Bin is not a recoverable action. You won't find Unempty the Recycle Bin on the context menu. (If the emptied files haven't yet been overwritten by other files, however, you may still be able to get them back with an Undelete utility, as I discuss later in this chapter.)

Removing files immediately when deleted

You can set a Recycle Bin property to remove files immediately when deleted. When you delete a file, it is not moved to the Recycle Bin but is immediately purged from the file system.

When this option is set, if you drag files to the Recycle Bin or highlight them and press Delete, Windows confirms the file deletion because now they will be purged. This is also true if you right-click a file and choose Delete.

To set the properties of the Recycle Bin, right-click the Recycle Bin icon or the Recycle Bin folder window and choose Properties. Access the Global tab and click the check box so that files are removed immediately.

CAUTION: If you use this option, you have no safety net at all. Files are automatically deleted and you cannot get them back later if you make a mistake. Because there is no fail-safe here, I recommend that you do not use this setting.

The Recycle Bin and networks

If you are connected to a local or wide area network does the Recycle Bin show you all the deleted files? Are you going to see all the deleted files on all the servers in your Recycle Bin? Nope.

You see only the files that you deleted from your local hard disks. It doesn't matter if the server resources (a hard disk or folder) are mapped to a local drive letter or not. You can click a Recycled folder on the host or server computer and you still will see only the files that you deleted from your local hard disks.

If you delete a file on the host, it is the same as if you deleted a file from a floppy disk — it is purged. The deleted file is not saved to the Recycle Bin. The final point — be careful when deleting files from a host because you do not have the Recycle Bin as a fail-safe.

Undelete and Unerase

If a file is purged, it is no longer recognized by the Windows file management system. Files are purged when you choose Empty Recycle Bin, when you hold down Shift and press Delete to delete a selected file, or when you delete a file and the Recycle Bin Properties dialog box has been set to remove files immediately when deleted.

When a file is purged, all that happens is that the first letter of its filename is changed so that it is no longer recognized as a legitimate filename by the file management system. The space taken up by that file is now available for use when other files are written to the hard disk.

Symantec provides Norton Utilities for Windows. These utilities are integrated with the Windows Desktop and user interface, and they include an unerase capability. If you have installed Norton Utilities for Windows, when you right-click the Recycle Bin icon, you'll see some new commands in the context menu. Norton Utilities provides additional backup for deleted files by taking over the functions of the Recycle Bin.

Norton Utilities lets you unerase files that have been purged without having to use the Undelete utility in MS-DOS mode. Unerase has to deal with the same issues as Undelete: The deleted file's name has been altered, so although the hard disk space may still contain the purged file's contents, the space has been marked available. Use Norton Utilities' Unerase as soon as you can after you inadvertently purge a file to increase your chances of recovering it.

If you have multiple hard drives . . .

You can configure the amount of drive space that Recycle Bin uses (10 percent by default) on each hard drive, if your computer has more than one physical hard drive. If you want to adjust the amount of space used on each, you can easily make these changes by simply accessing the Recycle Bin's properties. On the Global tab, click the radio button option to configure drives independently. Then, click the tab for each drive that appears, as shown in Figure 6-16. You can then use the tab to configure the space usage on that particular drive as needed.

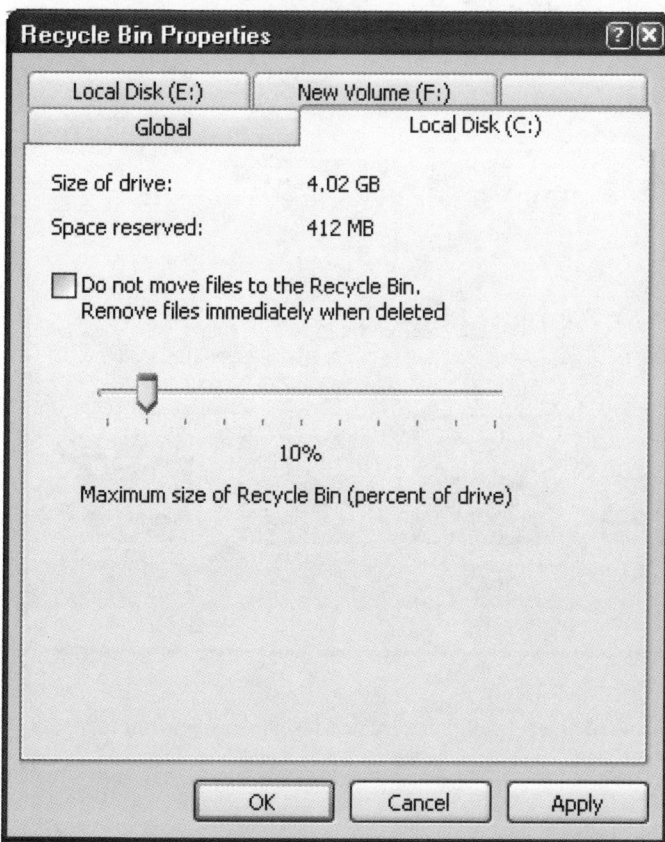

Figure 6-16: Recycle Bin drive usage

My Documents

Earlier in this chapter, you explored the folder options and features found in Windows XP. That discussion also applies to the My Documents folder, which by default also has subfolders of My Music and My Pictures and may have My Videos if you have video files on the computer.

The good news about My Documents and its subfolders is that Windows XP is aware of the kinds of files you store in the folders and attempts to make those files more accessible to you. For example, as you can see in Figure 6-17, the sample pictures folder not only provides you with the files in the folder, but it presents them to you in a "filmstrip" view that enables you to click through files to see them more clearly. If you look in the Picture Tasks pane on the left side of the screen, note that you can view the pictures in a slide show format, order print copies on the Internet, and perform related tasks. The point is that Windows XP is highly "file aware" and attempts to make your use of files more visual easy. The same is true with movie files — you can directly view movie files from the folder they are stored in.

As with any folder, you can use the View menu to make appearance changes to My Documents and its subfolders, and you can access Folder Options to make more global appearance changes. You can create additional folders inside of My Documents or any existing subfolders, and you can share those folders on a network. See Chapter 20 to learn more about sharing.

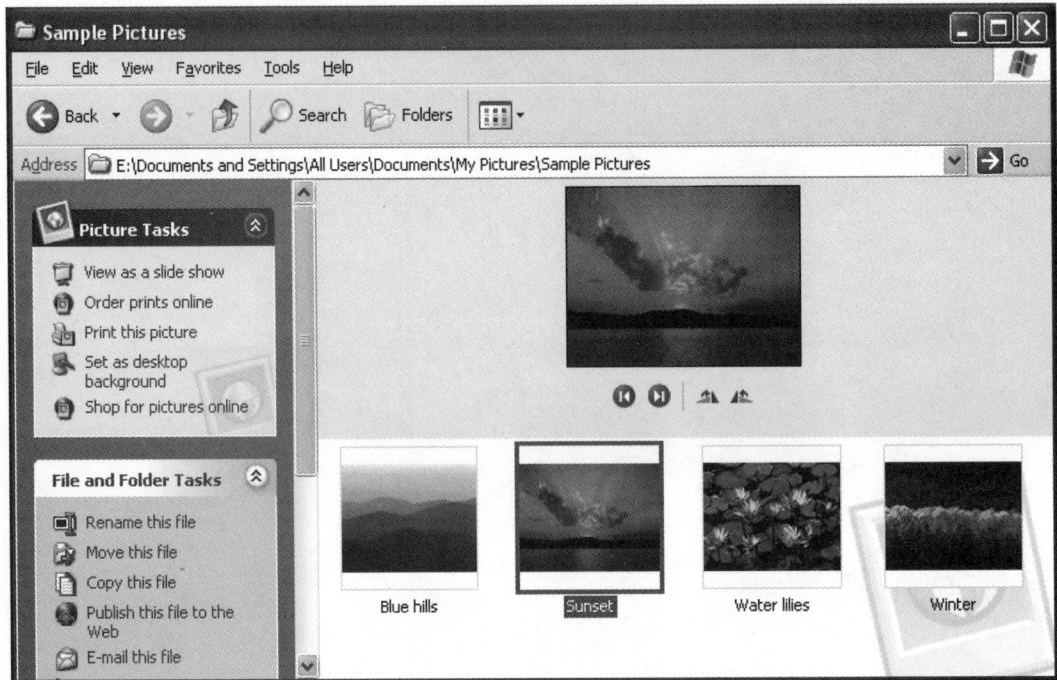

Figure 6-17: My Documents — My Pictures

Overall, My Documents is very straightforward and self-explanatory and it serves as a useful repository for all kinds of data.

Summary

In this chapter, you explored Windows XP's folder configuration features, the Recycle Bin, and the My Documents folder. Windows XP attempts to make your work easier and faster through a number of helpful folder features and gives you the ability to manage the removal of documents and folders with Recycle Bin.

Windows XP enables you to . . .

- ◆ Access the View menu on any folder to change the appearance of the folder concerning icons and toolbars.
- ◆ Use Folder Options in Control Panel or on a folder's Tools menu to use the classic folder view, one-click, and related settings. You can also manage file types from this location.
- ◆ Easily manage the removal of items with the Recycle Bin's features.
- ◆ Use My Documents serves as an easy place to store and view documents of all types.

Chapter 7

The Microsoft Management Console

In This Chapter

In the days of Windows 2000, Microsoft introduced a tool that had appeared previously in certain server products used with Windows NT. This tool, called the Microsoft Management Console (MMC), is a graphical user interface used to open all kinds of tools and features in a streamlined, easy way. The MMC is still alive and well in Windows XP, and even though you might not realize it, you are already using the MMC as you use Windows XP. However, the MMC holds many secrets that can make your work and play with Windows XP easier, faster, and more customizable. In this chapter, you'll learn all about the MMC. Specifically, you learn about . . .

- ◆ Using the MMC
- ◆ Using the MMC snap-ins available with Windows XP
- ◆ Creating your own MMC consoles
- ◆ Creating taskpad views

What Is the Microsoft Management Console?

The Microsoft Management Console is a shell program that provides a common framework for administrative tools. Just as the Windows Explorer provides a common way to view and manage files and folders, the MMC is a common way in which to view and manage networks, computers, services, and system components. By using the MMC, all servers, system components, networks, and anything else you view with the MMC has a streamlined appearance that makes the mastery of any new tool much easier.

The MMC itself provides no administrative functions. Instead, it is a container for the tools you use to perform administrative functions. These tools are called *snap-ins*, and they are available from both Microsoft and other software vendors. In addition to snap-ins, MMC consoles can hold ActiveX controls, links to Web pages, folders, and so forth. The MMC itself can be thought of as the engine that runs the snap-ins.

Windows XP includes a number of MMC consoles that have already been configured with some of the more important system administration tools. One of the most important of these tools is the Computer Management Console, which you have most likely used at this point. You can find the Computer Management Console, as shown in Figure 7-1, in your Administrative Tools folder in Control Panel. As you can see in the figure, the Computer Management Console is made up of several tools residing in the left pane and when a tool is selected, it appears in the right pane.

Many of the individual tools within the Computer Management Console are covered later in this chapter. One thing you will immediately notice is that regardless of the tool you want to the use the MMC brings a common look and feel to the tools. By default, any of the MMC consoles — such as the Computer Management Console — have two panes, resembling the Windows Explorer.

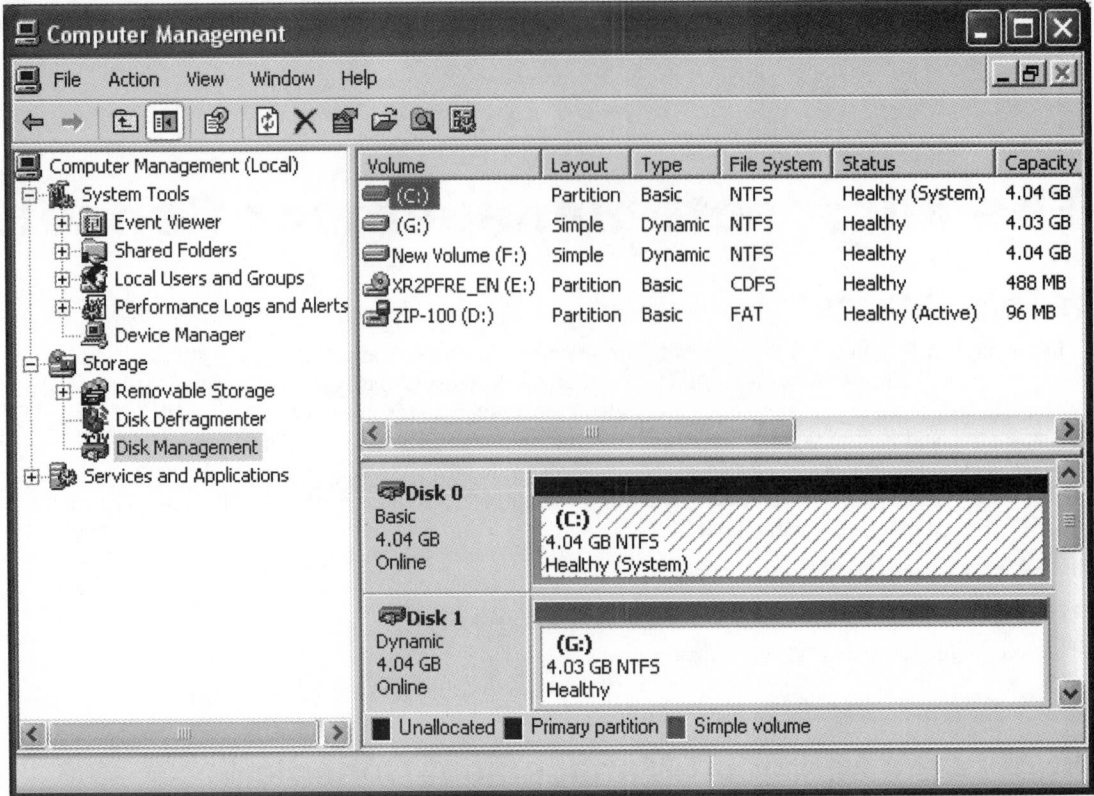

Figure 7-1: Computer Management is an example of the MMC and snap-ins.

The left pane is the console tree, and it displays the tools and other items available in the console. Just like the Windows Explorer, you will see a hierarchical arrangement of tools, further arranged in nodes. To expand a node, click the plus sign to the left of a node, just like you would expand a folder in the Windows Explorer. Each console tree might contain a number of levels, and each one can be expanded in turn.

NOTE: Often, an item in the console tree will have a plus sign next to it. When you click the plus sign to expand the tree, the plus sign will disappear, and you will see that there are no subfolders beneath it.

The right pane is the details pane. When you select an item (a snap-in) in the console tree, its contents display in the right pane. What you see in the details pane also depends on the selected snap-in.

Most MMC consoles contain only three primary menu commands: File, Action, and View. These are context-sensitive menus, and each displays different menu commands depending on the selected snap-in. With these two commands are a number of toolbar icons. The exact icon selection also differs depending on the tool that is selected.

SECRET: The Computer Management Console offers so many useful tools that you really should create a shortcut to it on your Desktop for quick and easy access. It may well be that the Computer Management Console is *the* most important new tool in Windows XP.

STEPS

Creating a shortcut to the Computer Management Console

1. Choose Start ⇨ Control Panel.

2. Open the Administrative Tools folder.

3. Right-click Computer Management, and then select Create Shortcut from the context menu.

4. A shortcut labeled Computer Management (2) will appear in the Administrative Tools folder. Click and drag it to your Desktop.

5. If you want, you can right-click the icon on your Desktop and then select Rename so you can delete the (2) appended to the shortcut's name.

6. If you want the shortcut to appear on your Start menu, drag and drop the Computer Management shortcut onto your Start button.

Running MMC and consoles from the command prompt

Consoles that are used in the MMC have the extension .msc (management saved console). You can run the Computer Management Console by choosing Start ⇨ Run and then typing the following in the Open text box:

```
C:\windows\system32\compmgmt.msc
```

As an alternative to typing the exact path, you also can type the command as:

```
%systemroot%\system32\compmgmt.msc
```

In both cases, the Computer Management Console will open, just as if you had opened it from Control Panel. (If you created a shortcut to the Computer Management Console using the preceding steps, right-click the shortcut and select Properties. You will see that the target resembles the latter example.)

Instead of opening one of these consoles from the command prompt, you can first open MMC itself, either to create a new console or to modify an existing console. The syntax for this command is as follows:

```
mmc {path\filename.msc} {/a} {/s}
```

The MMC parameters are outlined in Table 7-1.

Table 7-1: MMC Command-Line Parameters

Parameter	What It Means
{path\filename.msc}	Starts MMC and opens the specified .msc file. If this parameter is left blank, MMC will start with a new, empty console.
/a	Opens the console file in author mode so that you can make changes to it.
/s	Turns off the splash screen that you would normally see when starting MMC. In Windows XP, the splash screen is automatically suppressed when you open an existing console file.

If you want to locate all of the MMC console files that currently exist on your system, you can do so with a quick and easy search. Just use the following steps.

STEPS

Searching for console files

1. Choose Start ➪ Search ➪ For Files and Folders.

2. In the search box, type ***.msc.**

3. Click Search.

4. If you want to open one of the consoles listed in Search Results dialog box, choose the filename.

> **TIP:** If you run only the MMC command with no arguments, the Computer Management Console opens with an empty MMC window. From there, you can use the Console ➪ Open command to open any existing console files.

Creating a new console

You can easily create your own console file. You might want to do this so that you can gather your own collection of snap-ins in a customized format, rather than relying on one of the preconfigured consoles that accompanies Windows XP. (Also, as the snap-in model for computer controls spreads, you may find more third-party snap-ins that you can add to the configuration tools that accompany Windows XP.)

STEPS

Creating your own console file

1. Choose Start ➪ Run and type **mmc /s** in the Open text box.

2. This opens an empty console inside the MMC window. (Until you add some snap-in tools to the console, the MMC window will be empty.) To add tools to your console, choose File ➪ Add/Remove Snap-in.

3. Click Add. This will display a list of available snap-in tools from which you can select tools to add to your new console, as shown in Figure 7-2.

4. Scroll down the list until you find System Information. Select it and click Add.

5. If your computer is on a network, you will be asked which computer you want this tool to manage. This can be either your local computer or another computer on your network. Choose Local Computer. If you will be managing another computer on the network, you will need to have appropriate permissions.

6. The list of available snap-ins will remain open. Select Device Manager, as well as Local Computer.

7. Close the Available Standalone Snap-in list to return to the Add/Remove Snap-in dialog box (see Figure 7-3). Selecting one of the snap-ins listed in the dialog box displays a description of its functions in the Description pane.

8. Click OK to return to the Console Root dialog box. You then see the two tools you selected listed in the dialog box.

9. Choose Console ➪ Save As, and save the new console as Console1.msc.

As you can see, you can browse and open any available snap-in and then save that console so that you can more easily access it. However, Windows XP also provides you with some custom consoles that have already been created for you. A good example of a preconfigured console is the Computer Management console, explored in the next section.

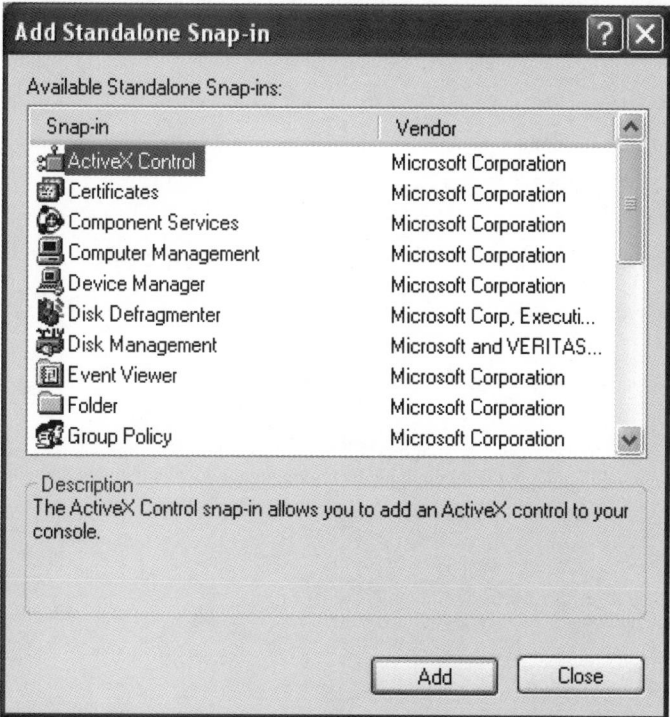

Figure 7-2: All the available snap-ins on your computer will be listed in the Add Standalone Snap-in dialog box.

Computer Management

For most users, the Computer Management Console is the most important console, holding a number of very important tools they use on a daily basis. When open and viewed at the console tree, three nodes are displayed: System Tools, Storage, and Services and Applications

In its default configuration, System Tools has five nodes, as shown in Figure 7-4.

Each System Tool is briefly described here:

♦ **Event Viewer** — Tracks many different events that occur on your computer. Events are recorded in a log that can be viewed for troubleshooting purposes.

♦ **Shared Folders** — Displays resources on your computer that are available to other users on the network, as well as what resources are in use.

♦ **Local Users and Groups** — Allows you to manage individual users and groups for a Windows XP Professional computer.

♦ **Performance Logs and Alerts** — Allows you to track hardware usage and system services.

♦ **Device Manager** — Provides a graphical view of the hardware attached to your computer, as well as the tools for managing it (see Chapter 10). The Windows XP Professional Device Manager is similar to the Device Manager in Windows 98/Me.

The tools available in the Computer Management Console play an important role in three main areas: security, information gathering, and managing your computer. The rest of this chapter discusses these different areas and the features they provide.

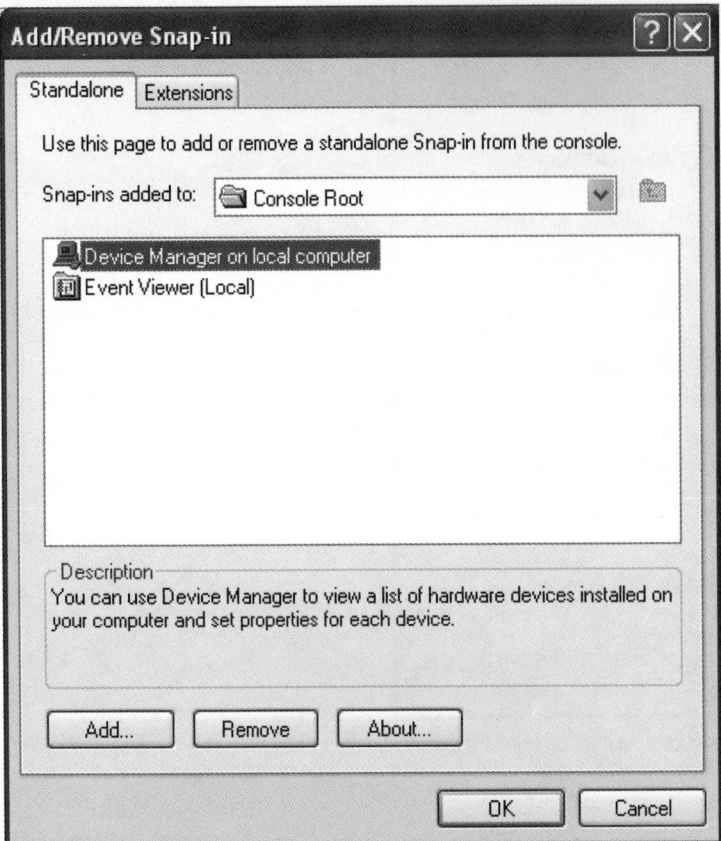

Figure 7-3: The tools you have selected are displayed in the Add/Remove Snap-in dialog box.

CROSS-REFERENCE: See also Chapter 24 where you can learn more about Event Viewer, Task Manager, and Performance Monitor.

Security

Windows XP provides many important security features, even if the computer is not connected to a Windows 2000/XP network. Snap-in tools available in the Computer Management Console, Local Users and Groups, and Shared Folders all allow you to configure a Windows XP computer in any number of ways for sharing or limiting access to data.

In small offices, where a number of users might share access to a computer or a group of computers on a peer-to-peer network, Local Users and Groups can be used to safeguard important settings or data. It also can be used in a home/office, where you might allow your staff or temporary help to update some contact and accounting information without providing any access to sensitive financial information and data files. For your home computer, you can restrict your children's access to the computer for games and word processing only, for example, while also restricting their access to your work data files and your configuration information.

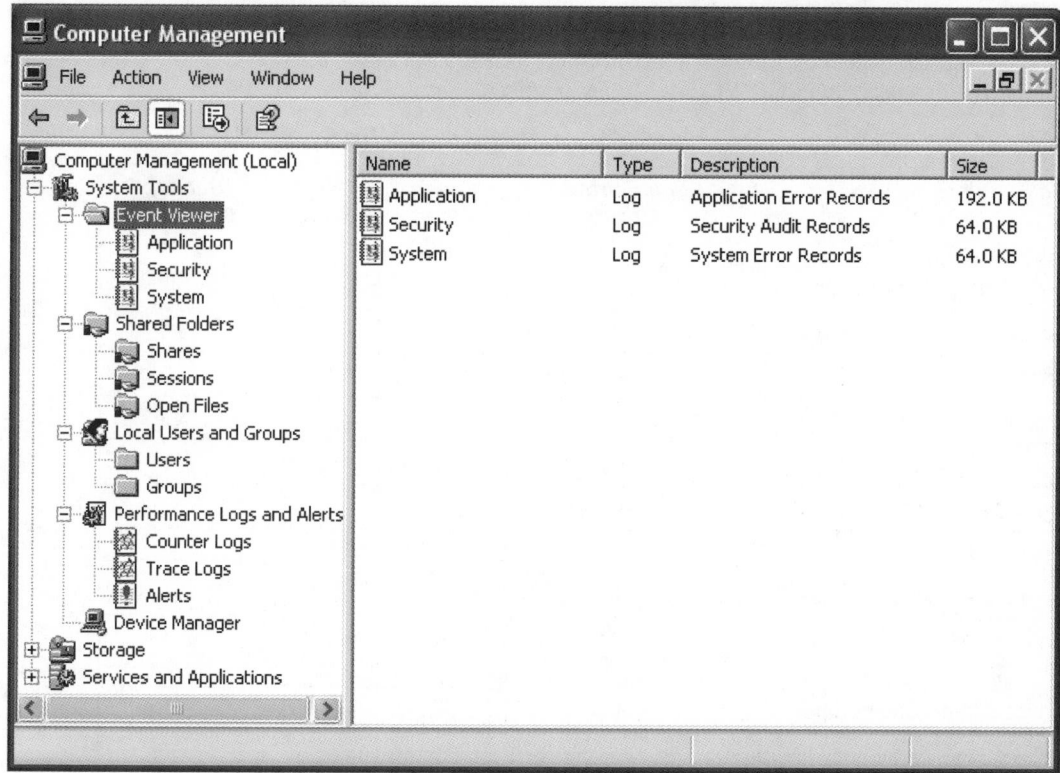

Figure 7-4: Some of the most important management and troubleshooting tools can be found in the Computer Management Console's System Tools node.

The User accounts tool is used to configure security when several individuals share the same computer. It also can be used to configure security for a computer that is installed on a simple peer-to-peer network. (When a Windows XP Professional computer is connected to a client/server network controlled by Windows 2000 Server, the Active Directory tools provide much — if not all — of the security configuration.)

SECRET: One other reason you should spend more time managing system security is directly related to the growing availability of Internet connections that are "always on," such as those provided by cable modems and DSL connections. Both of these technologies not only provide an open path *from* your computer to the Internet, but also provide an open path *to* your computer from the outside world, potentially allowing access to your computer and your sensitive data to outsiders.

Groups

When you perform a clean install of Windows XP to an NTFS-formatted drive, or when you upgrade from Windows 9*x* to Windows XP, security will be set to the default file system and Registry permissions settings. If you upgrade from Windows NT 4.0 to Windows XP, security is not set to the default settings; rather, your Windows NT settings are maintained. You can, however, change to the default settings. (See "User and group management" later in this chapter for more information.)

Of the user categories available in Windows XP, the three most important categories are Administrators, Power Users, and Users. Specific rights and permissions for all user categories are explored in more detail in Chapter 23.

NOTE: A Windows XP user assigned to the User level should be able to run any program written to conform to the Windows XP Application Specification. However, he or she cannot run legacy applications. You must be assigned to the Power User level to run legacy applications.

Default user rights

Table 7-2 lists the default user rights after performing a clean install of Windows XP Professional onto an NTFS drive, or when you install Windows XP as an upgrade from Windows 9x/2000.

Table 7-2: Default User Rights in Windows XP

Rights/Permissions	Administrators Group	Power User Group	Users Group	Backup Operators Group
Access another user's private data	X			
Access computer from network	X	X	X	X
Assign user rights	X			
Back up files and directories	X			X
Change system time/date	X	X		
Configure password policy	X			
Create a paging file	X			
Create administrative accounts	X			
Create and delete nonadministrative file shares	X	X		
Create local users and groups	X	X		
Create, manage, delete, and share local printers	X	X		
Debug programs	X			
Force shutdown from a remote system	X			
Format a hard drive	X			
Increase quotas	X			
Increase scheduling priority	X			
Install applications that modify Windows system files	X			
Install operating system	X			
Install service packs, hot fixes, and Windows updates	X			
Install system services	X			
Install, configure, load, and unload device drivers	X			
Log on interactively	X	X	X	X
Manage audit and security logs	X			
Modify firmware environment variables	X			
Modify groups or accounts created by other users	X			

Rights/Permissions	Administrators Group	Power User Group	Users Group	Backup Operators Group
Modify users and groups they create	X	X		
Profile a single process	X		X	
Profile system performance	X			
Remove computer from docking station	X	X	X	
Repair operating system	X			
Restore files and directories	X			X
Shut down the system	X	X	X	X

SECRET: By default, there are no permissions assigned to the root directory. Whatever permissions might have existed before installing Windows XP will be maintained, which means that everyone has full control. You might need to change these settings to effect a more secure system. (Changes in permissions are discussed in "Shared folders" later in this chapter.) However, do not change these settings without first exploring the consequences. Changing the default permissions can cause multiple problems throughout your system.

The reason the root directory is not secured, according to Microsoft, is because the Windows XP Access Control List Inheritance Model would recursively configure all subdirectories from the root, if there were default permissions assigned to it. If there are non-Windows XP directories located on the install partition, their security settings might change in ways you don't anticipate because of Windows XP's user management features.

Restoring default settings

If you install Windows XP by upgrading from Windows NT 4.0, your computer will not start with the default security settings. Instead, the NT 4.0 security settings will be used. If you want to use the default security settings, you must use the Security Template snap-in. Follow these steps:

STEPS

Restoring the default Windows XP security settings

1. Choose Start ⇨ Programs ⇨ Command Prompt.

2. At the command prompt, type the following commands and then press Enter after each line (*windows* is your Windows XP folder):

```
cd windows
cd system32
```

3. Still at the command prompt, type the following and press Enter:

```
Secedit /configure /cfg basicwk.inf /db basicwk.sdb /log basicwk.log /verbose
```

This command-line program can either configure or analyze the system security settings using the Security Template tool. It makes use of templates that are stored as plain-text INF files, which can be swapped, edited, or merged together to copy security settings from one computer to another.

The syntax for using this tool to configure system security is as follows:

```
Secedit /configure /DB filename {/CFG filename} {options}
```

The optional parameters for `Secedit` are listed in Table 7-3.

Table 7-3: Security Editor Configuration Parameters

Parameter	Description
/DB *filename*	Required argument; displays the path to the database for the security template that should be applied. The database files have an .sdb extension.
/CFG *filename*	Path to the security template that you want imported into the security editor database and then applied to the system. If this argument is missing, the template that is already in the database will be used.
{*options*}	Options can be any of the parameters following in this table.
/overwrite	Valid only when used with the /CFG *filename* switch. If this switch is used, the template specified in the /CFG argument will overwrite any template that is already in the database. If this switch is not used, the /CFG filename will be appended.
/area	Separate security areas exist in the system. If this argument is not used, the default is all areas. You also can specify the following areas, with each area separated by a space: SECURITYPOLICY — Local and domain policies for the system. GROUP_MGMT — Restricted group setting for any groups specified in the security template. USER-RIGHTS — Specifies the user logon rights and grants privileges. REGKEYS — Sets security on local registry keys. FILESTORE — Sets security on local file storage. SERVICES — Sets security for all defined services.
/log *logpath*	Displays the path to the log file. If the logpath value is not specified, the default path is used. Default logs are kept in the c:\windows\security\logs folder.
/verbose	Displays more detailed progress information.
/quiet	Disables all screen and log output.

The Security Editor also can be used to analyze system security settings. It compares the security settings on your computer against a stored security configuration.

To perform an analysis, use the following steps.

STEPS
Performing a security analysis

1. Choose Start ⇨ Programs ⇨ Command Prompt.

2. At the command prompt, type the following commands and press Enter after each line (*windows* is your Windows XP folder):

```
cd windows
cd system32
```

3. Type the following command and press Enter:

```
secedit /analyze /DB filename {/CFG filename} {options}
```

The parameters for the analyze command are listed in Table 7-4.

Table 7-4: Security Editor Analyze Command Parameters

Parameter	Meaning
/DB `filename`	Required argument that displays the path to the database holding the security configuration that you want to compare against. The database files have an `.sdb` extension.
/CFG `filename`	The security template that should be imported into the database. If this filename is not specified, the analysis will be conducted against the template already contained in the database.
{`options`}	Options can be any of the parameters following in this table.
/log `logpath`	Displays the path to the log file. If the path is not specified, the default is used. Default logs are kept in the `c:\winnt\security\logs` folder.
/verbose	Displays more detailed progress information.
/quiet	Disables all screen and log output.

The template files used for the /CFG command are plain text INF files, which you can modify with a text editor such as Notepad, if you want to substitute part of the settings for a different profile. You also can open these files in Notepad just to examine their settings. The DB files used in the /DB argument are binary files that cannot be viewed or edited using a text editor.

TIP: The best way to read INF files is to right-click and use the Send To shortcut to send the files directly to Notepad.

User and group management

Users and groups are managed from the Computer Management Console. Expand System Tools in the console tree, and then expand Local Users and Groups. I discuss two folders listed beneath Local Users and Groups — one holding all the users for the computer and the other holding the default groups —earlier in this chapter. For added flexibility in security, however, you can create additional groups.

NOTE: When you first install Windows XP, the administrator account and a guest account are created for you. The administrator account is the default account; it cannot be deleted, disabled, or removed. This means that you will never be locked out of your computer, provided you remember the administrator password.

Run As

If your daily computing tasks involve activities that do not require you to use your administrator account, but you often need to perform such tasks as installing programs or tweaking a few settings, you normally need to log off and then log on again as an administrator to make those changes. Depending on the security settings defined for your standard user account, you might have access to the Computer Management Console from which you can make changes to individual settings. If your security settings do not allow you to make any changes to your security settings, you will see a message telling you so.

CAUTION: When you first log on as the administrator, you can set up other user accounts. It is a good security practice to log on as something other than the administrator for your everyday computer use. If you are using your computer as the administrator, you are more susceptible to security problems. As an administrator, you have full control over the system settings, which a malicious program might exploit to bring havoc to your computer. If this happens while you are logged on as a standard user, the Windows XP security settings will prevent malicious programs from executing.

If you want to use the computer as a standard user for security purposes, but you don't want to have to constantly log off and then log on again as an administrator, use the Run As command. This command can be used from the Windows Explorer, from the command line, or from a desktop shortcut, using the following steps:

STEPS

Using the Run As command to start a program

1. Open the Windows Explorer and navigate to the folder containing the program you want to run.

2. Hold down the Shift key, and then right-click the program in the right pane.

3. Choose Run As from the context menu to open the Run As dialog box shown in Figure 7-5.

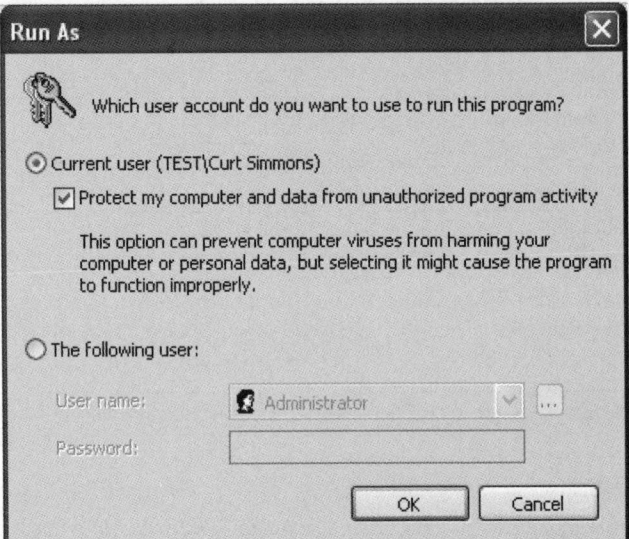

Figure 7-5: After selecting Run As from the context menu, you can select the user you want to log on as by typing in the username and password for that user.

4. Fill in the name and password. You will not be able to log on and run any programs using the identity of another user if you do not know the correct username and password.

> **TIP:** You might want to use the Computer Management Console to change settings, but you also know that you need to have an administrator account in order to change most settings. The easiest way to accomplish this while you are logged in as a standard user or a power user is to create a shortcut to the Computer Management Console on your Desktop you can use to open the console as an administrator, using the following steps.

STEPS

Creating a shortcut using the Run As command

1. Right-click the Desktop.

2. Select New, and then choose Shortcut from the context menu.

3. In the Type location of the item text box, type the following (with the quotation marks, but substituting the actual name of this computer for the *computername* value):

```
runas /user:computername\administrator "mmc %windir%\system32\compmgmt.msc"
```

4. Click Next, type a name for this Desktop shortcut, and then click Finish.

5. When you click this shortcut, you will be prompted for the password of the particular administrator you added in Step 3.

The window in which you are running the Computer Management Console — or from within the window of any other program you started using the Run As command — will not indicate the username under which you have logged on.

SECRET: You can use this same syntax for Run As to run other programs. However, there are a few applications you can't start with the Run As command: Windows Explorer, the Printers folder, and desktop items such as My Computer and the Recycle Bin. According to Microsoft, this is because these items are opened indirectly by Windows XP.

Adding users

You might want to add additional user accounts to your computer for the following:

♦ For yourself, so that you won't need to log on to the computer as administrator to perform everyday tasks.

♦ For different people who share a computer and would like to be able to maintain their own settings.

♦ For users on a peer-to-peer network so that they can access shared files or printers on this computer.

To create additional users, follow these steps:

STEPS

Setting up a user account

1. Choose Start ➩ Control Panel, and select Administrative Tools.

2. Click Computer Management.

3. Expand the console tree, and then navigate to System Tools ➩ Local Users and Groups ➩ Users.

4. On the Console menu, choose Action ➩ New User. The New User dialog box appears, as shown in Figure 7-6.

5. Type the new user's name and password in the appropriate text boxes. If you leave the option "User must change password at next logon" checked, the option "User cannot change password" and the option "Password never expires" remain disabled. (See "Usernames and passwords," later in this chapter, for tips on creating usernames and passwords.)

TIP: User accounts have a security identifier that stays with the account. This means that you can rename an account without causing the account to lose any properties, such as its password, group memberships, and user profile.

You also can delete user accounts that you have created. Once you delete a user account, all the individual settings and files are deleted, and you cannot restore them using any typical restore operation.

TIP: If you are unsure if deleting a user account will cause something to be lost that might be needed later, you can first disable a user account to lock out the account while still preserving the user account settings. Later, after you are sure that the user account is no longer needed, you can then delete it. To disable a user account, right-click the account in the detail pane, and then select Properties from the context menu. Select Account Disabled, and click OK.

When you log in, the last name of the user account is displayed. If you don't want that name displayed, you can disable the setting using the Group Policy snap-in in the MMC.

STEPS

Disabling last name display at login

1. Choose Start ➩ Run, and type the following in the Open text box:

```
mmc /s
```

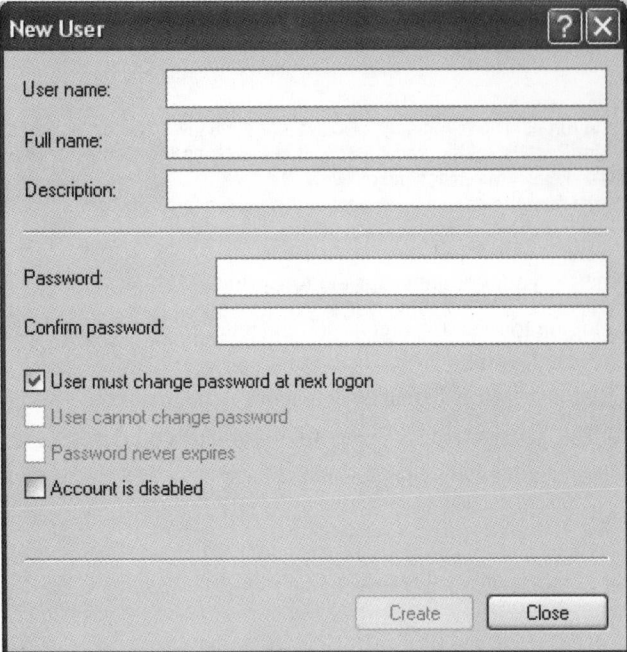

Figure 7-6: Fill in and select options for each user that you create on this computer.

2. Choose Console ⇨ Add/Remove Snap-in.

3. Click Add, and then select Group Policy to start the Select Group Policy object.

4. Select the Local Computer or, if you are on a network, another computer, and then click Finish.

5. Click Close, and then click OK to return to the Computer Management Console.

6. In the console tree, navigate to Computer ⇨ Computer Configuration ⇨Windows Settings ⇨ Security Settings ⇨ Local Policies ⇨ Security Options, as shown in Figure 7-7.

7. In the details pane, right-click the option "Interactive Logon: Do not display last name in logon," and make sure this is enabled.

8. Since you might want to use the Group Policy snap-in again, save this console using the Console, Save As command to make accessing it faster the next time you want to use it.

> **TIP:** The Group Policy snap-in is designed as a network tool, but it can be used on standalone Windows XP computers, as well. See Chapter 23 to learn more.

Usernames and passwords

Each username must be unique, not only from all other usernames, but also to any group names on the same computer. A username can be up to 20 characters long, including spaces and periods, but it cannot be *only* spaces and periods, nor can it include any of the following characters: " / \ [ ] : ; | = , + * ? < >

Unless this computer will be used by no one but you and will not have any network or Internet access, create a strong and secure password that is difficult for anyone to break. This is especially true for the administrator password, which allows access to everything on the computer. Passwords can be up to 14 characters long and can include letters and numbers. Passwords can use the symbols that usernames are restricted from using, as well as other symbols.

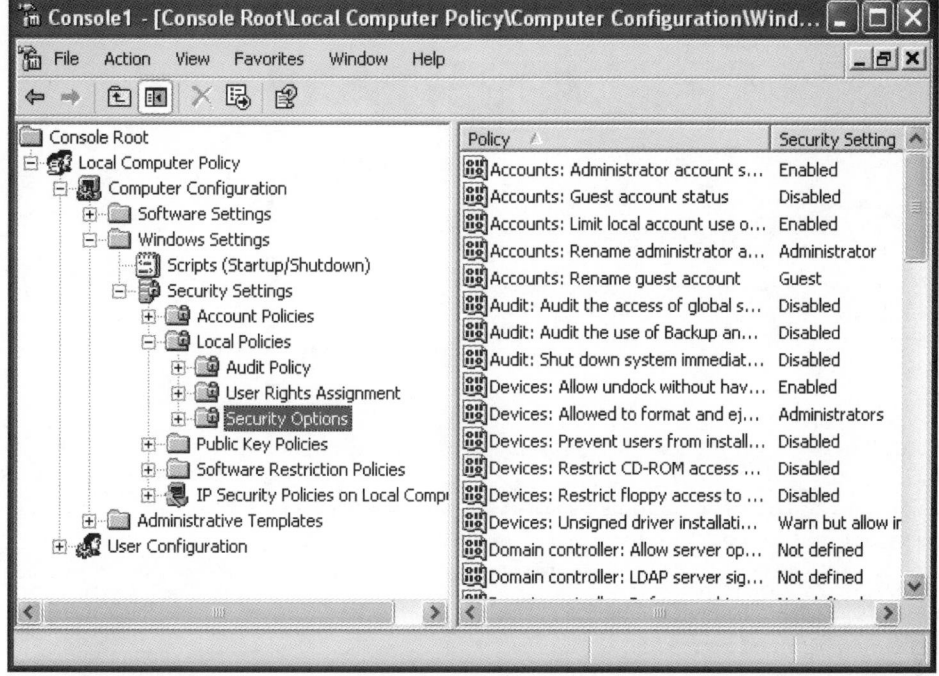

Figure 7-7: In the Group Policy snap-in, navigate to Security Options, and then enable the option Do Not Display Last Name.

Never use your name, telephone number, the names of your kids, spouse, or pets, or your social security number for your logon password. If you construct your password the right way, it will be extremely difficult — if not impossible — to hack. Combine letters, numbers, and symbols in a random fashion. For example, the password *orxt!@238cMb* would be difficult to crack — and difficult to remember, too. By the way, you're not the only person to have watched the *Seinfeld* television series, so don't use *Bosco* as your password.

Assigning users to groups

By default, when a new account is created, it is assigned to the Users group. A new account can be promoted to a higher group:

♦ If the user account was created by a power user account, that power user can log in and add the user to the Power Users group.

♦ An administrator account is the only account that can promote it to the Administrators group.

To change a group membership when you have the appropriate permissions, follow these steps:

STEPS

Adding a user to another group

1. Choose Start ⇨ Control Panel, and then click Administrative Tools.
2. Click Computer Management.
3. In the console tree, navigate to System Tools ⇨ Local Users and Groups ⇨ Users.
4. In the Details pane, right-click the user, and then select Properties from the context menu.

5. Select the Member of tab, and then click Add. This will display the Select Groups dialog box, as shown in Figure 7-8.

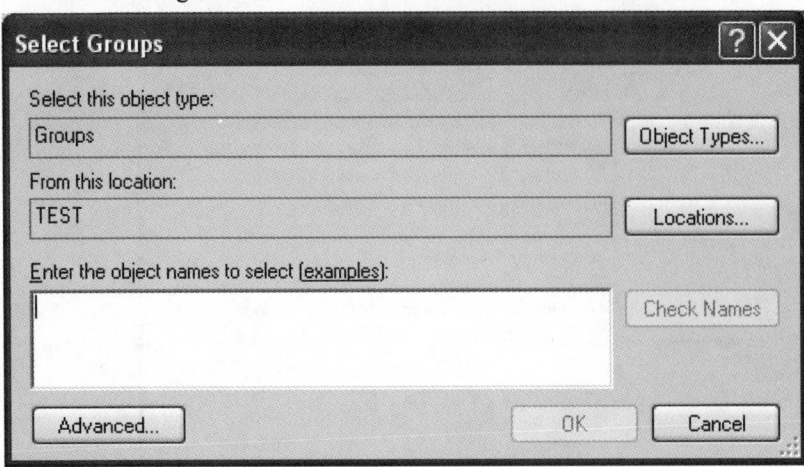

Figure 7-8: By default, new users are added to the Users group. They can be promoted to a more powerful group by another user with the appropriate permissions.

6. Click Object Types and select the group that you want to add the users to, and then click OK to return to the Member of tab.

Once you have created new accounts and assigned the accounts to groups, you can use these settings to manage permissions for various resources on this computer. You can limit access to certain shared folders (see "Shared folders" next in this chapter) and printers to certain groups or certain users, while permitting access to others.

If you decide that your security scheme needs another group, you can create more groups. To create another group, highlight Groups in the Computer Management Console tree, click Action, and then select Create Group. You will be asked to type a name and description for the group. You can then add users to the new group.

Shared folders

Shared folders — in coordination with user groups — allow you to limit access to certain folders on a Windows XP computer. They can be used either on a standalone Windows XP computer that is shared by a number of users, or when a Windows XP computer is connected to a simple peer-to-peer network. (When you are dealing with a full-sized client/server network connected to a Windows 2000 server, there are more powerful security tools available.)

The Shared Folders snap-in allows you to create new shared folders and modify permissions, view users who may be connected to the computer through a network, and see which files have been opened by remote users.

TIP: Only administrators or power users can use the Shared Folders tool on a Windows XP computer.

To view shared folders, select System Tools ⇨ Shared Folders ⇨ Shares in the console tree. Even if you have not set up shared folders on your computer, you might see that some shares already exist in the details pane. These are special shares created by Windows XP. Most of these shares are indicated by the inclusion of a dollar sign ($) appended to their name. Table 7-5 lists the special shares and their purpose.

TIP: In general, you should not change these shared resource settings. They are created by Windows XP, and you might experience problems if you delete or change them.

Table 7-5: Special Shares

Share	Purpose
{drive letter}$	A special share that allows an administrator to access the root directory of a storage device. You might see C$, D$, and so on.
ADMIN$	A resource leading to your system root — the directory into which Windows XP is installed. It is used during remote administration of the computer.
IPC$	Allows named pipes — a special segment of system RAM — to be shared. It is also used in remote administration.
PRINT$	Allows remote administration of a printer.
FAX$	Allows fax files from a fax client to be temporarily cached.

In addition to these special shares, you might want to share other drives or folders to give other users access to files contained on those drives or in those folders. To create a share, follow these steps:

STEPS

Creating a shared folder

1. In Computer Management, select System Tools ⇨ Shared Folders ⇨ Shares.

2. On the console menu, choose Action ⇨ New File Share.

3. This opens the Create Shared Folder wizard. You can select an entire drive to share, or you can expand the folder tree and select a particular folder. Click Browse to select the item for which you want to create a shared resource, and give it a share name and description. This name and description is seen by other users when they attempt a connection to the shared resource. Click Next.

4. Now you need to set the permissions for this new shared resource. You can change these permissions later, so just accept the defaults for now. Click Next.

5. Click Finish to complete the wizard. Your new shared resource should now be displayed in the Shares detail pane.

SECRET: In order to take advantage of the security features of Windows XP, the disk that holds a shared folder must be formatted with NTFS.

Gathering Information

You can use a number of tools in the Computer Management Console to gather information about your computer.

Performance logs and alerts

Windows XP automatically keeps a number of logs that let you see what has happened on your computer. You can view these logs using the Event Viewer (see "Using the Event Viewer" later in this chapter). Windows XP also can create several optional logs that you can start to monitor some aspect of either the local or remote computer, or to send alerts when a specific event has taken place. The data collected by these logs can be examined using the Performance Monitor snap-in that comes with Windows XP, or the logs can be configured to save the data in comma-separated value (CSV) files or tab-delimited text files, which you can then import into a spreadsheet or database file for further analysis.

CROSS-REFERENCE: The Performance console is capable of real-time monitoring, logging, and administrative alerting features. You can learn more about all of these features in Chapter 24.

To create a new log file, follow these steps:

STEPS

Creating a performance log

1. Open the Computer Management Console. Expand the Performance Logs and Alerts nodes, and then select Counter Log.

2. Right-click the details pane and select New Log Settings. You are asked to type a name for the log. You can use Sample1 as a name.

3. Click the Add Objects and Add Counters buttons on the General tab to select the counters you want to monitor, as shown in Figure 7-9.

4. You can adjust how often the counters will be sampled; the default is every 15 seconds. The time increment can be changed from seconds to minutes, hours, or days.

5. Select the Log Files tab. By default, log files are saved to the C:\PerfLogs folder, although you can change this to any directory you choose. You also can change the default filename.

6. Choose a file type from the drop-down list box. A binary circular file will, when full, begin to overwrite itself. You also can set an upper limit on the size of the log file.

7. Select the Schedule tab. For now, set the log file to start and stop manually, although you also can set it up on an automatic schedule.

8. Click OK to close the dialog box and return to the Computer Management Console.

You can set up more than one counter log. Any logs that are set up — including any default logs created by Windows XP — will be listed in the details pane if you have select Counter Logs in the console tree. Since you set up the new log for a manual start, its icon should be red, which means it is not running. To start it, right-click and select All tasks ⇨ Start from the context menu.

> **TIP:** You can view logs or watch counters in real time using the Performance Monitor. However, you cannot access the Performance Monitor from the Computer Management Console. It has its own separate MMC called Performance, which you can set up using the following steps:

STEPS

Viewing a counter in the Performance Monitor

1. Choose Start ⇨ Control Panel, and then click Administrative Tools.

2. Select Performance then Performance Monitor in the console tree.

3. To view current activity on your system, click the Add button. This opens a dialog box similar to the one shown in Step 3 of the Creating a performance log steps. Add the objects and counters as desired.

4. Right-click the Graph area of Performance Monitor, and select Properties from the context menu.

5. Select the General tab. In Update Time, select Periodic Update and set an interval of one second. Click OK.

The Performance Monitor now starts tracking your two performance indicators. The default view is a line graph, as shown in Figure 7-10. Beneath the graph display, you see numeric displays of the counters you are tracking. When you have multiple counters like this example displays, select one of the counters from the list on the lower edge of the Performance Monitor dialog box to display its statistics.

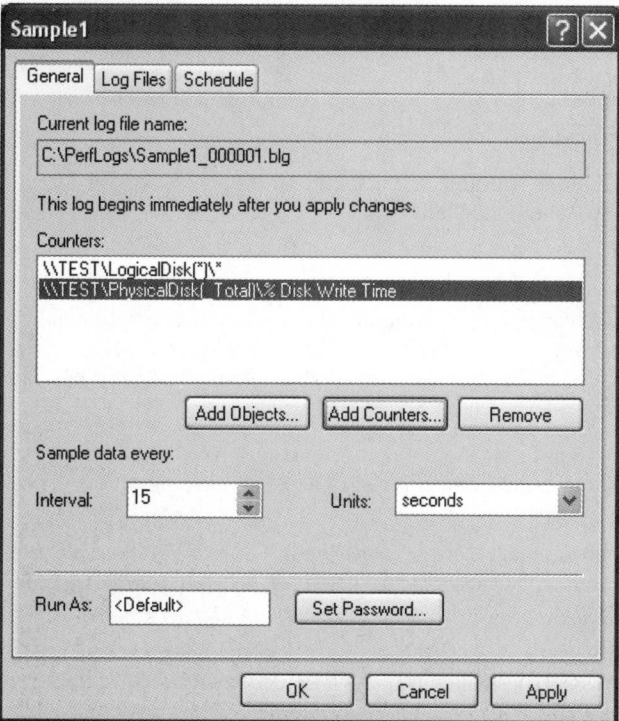

Figure 7-9: From the Select Counter dialog box, you choose the system activities you want to monitor.

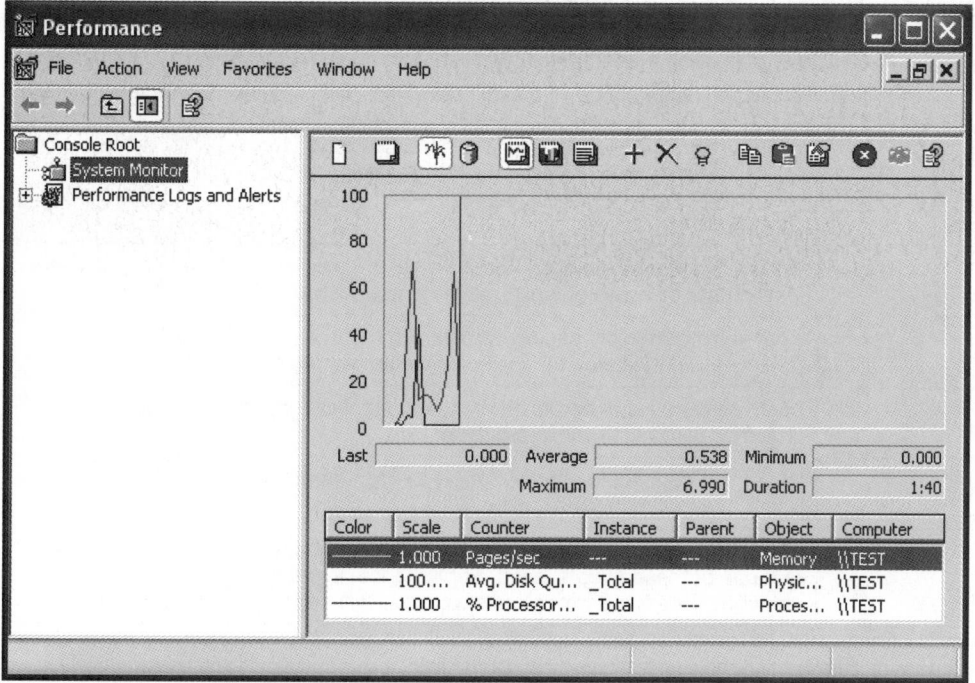

Figure 7-10: The Performance Monitor can be set up to track multiple counters. Current activity is being tracked at the heavy vertical line. When current activity reaches the right side of the graph window, it will wrap around to the left and overwrite the existing display.

SECRET: An important principle in physics says that the act of observing something alters the behavior of what you are observing. Setting up counters to run at periodic intervals causes system activity, which in turn shows up on your performance graphs. The very fact that you are monitoring your system increases the system activity beyond what it otherwise would be. So, as you are using Performance and using the data you collect to make judgments about your system, keep in mind that the use of the Performance console uses system resources as well.

To stop real-time monitoring, click the Stop button. This halts the display. To restart, click Stop again. To erase the current display, click Clear Display — the second button from the left.

Using the Event Viewer

The Event Viewer is another way in which you can gather information about your computer and its performance. The Event Viewer can be found when you expand the Computer Management System Tools node. Windows XP keeps three separate logs that record certain events on your system. These three logs are:

♦ **Application log** — Applications or programs can record events in this log. An application written to take advantage of the application log can record error messages here, for example. All users can view this log.

♦ **System log** — Windows XP system components record information in this log. For example, if a driver fails to load, or if there is a problem with a service during startup, an event will be recorded here. All users can view this log.

♦ **Security log** — Once an administrator specifies events that are to be recorded, the security log can keep a record of successful and unsuccessful login attempts, and whether resources have been used to create or delete files. By default, the security log will not be running, but it can be enabled using the Group Policy snap-in discussed earlier in this chapter. Also, only those users assigned to the Administrators group have access to the security log.

CROSS-REFERENCE: See Chapter 24 for additional information about Event Viewer and the log features.

These are the types of events that are recorded in the logs, and they can then be viewed using the Event Viewer. Figure 7-11 shows a sample application log, and Table 7-6 outlines the types of events that can be viewed.

Table 7-6: Event Log Items

Type of Event	Description
Error	What Windows XP deems to be a significant problem that could cause either a loss of data or a loss of functionality. Indicated by a red and white *x* icon.
Warning	Something that might cause a problem sometime in the future, but not at the present time. Indicated by a yellow triangle with an exclamation point.
Information	Logs the successful operation or logs an application, driver, or service. Indicated by a blue *i* within a bubble.
Success Audit	When you configure security logging to track certain events, this indicates that one of these events was successful.
Failure Audit	When you configure security logging to track certain events, this will indicate that one of these events failed. For instance, if you are tracking logins, and someone enters the wrong password, this will be recorded as a failure.

The application log tells you when the event happened and what triggered it, along with some other cryptic codes, including an event number. To see the details from a particular event, right-click the event in the details pane. Figure 7-12 displays an error that is detailed in the Event Properties dialog box.

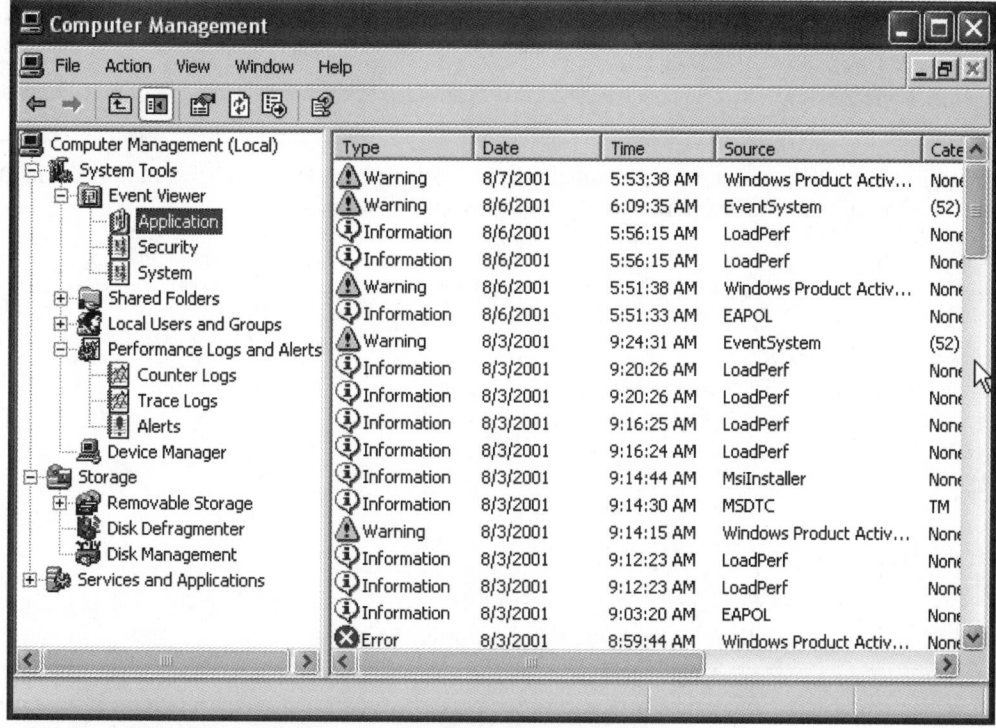

Figure 7-11: Application logs track errors, warnings, and information events.

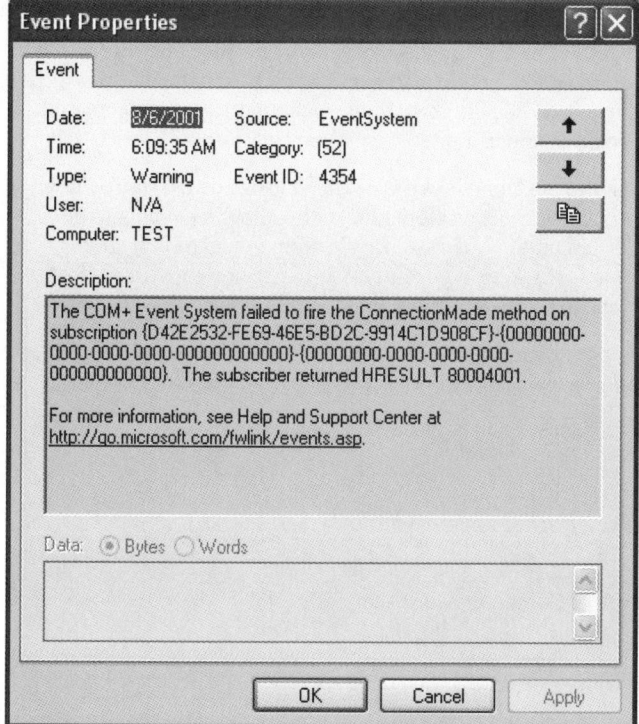

Figure 7-12: Right-click an event to view details and an explanation of what happened.

SECRET: Although the Warning "label" on a Warning event sounds important and ominous, many warnings can be safely ignored. For example, you might see this warning in your application log: "Failed to obtain Kerberos server credentials for ISAKMP/Oakley service. Kerberos authentication will not function. The most likely reason for this is lack of domain membership." Anytime you start a Windows XP computer and it is not connected to a Windows 2000 Server network domain, you will see this warning, and you can safely ignore it.

You can sort the events shown in the viewer in the same way you sort in the Windows Explorer. Clicking the column heading sorts by that column; click again to reverse the sort order.

TIP: Since you will probably be most interested in the events that just occurred, make sure the Event Log is sorted by date in descending order. (The arrow in the column header should be pointed downward.)

Event Log properties

Configuring the logs is similar for all three of the logs. To make changes in the configuration — in this example, for the application log — follow these steps:

STEPS

Configuring an application log

1. Choose Start ⇨ Control Panel.
2. Click Administrative Tools, and then select Computer Management.
3. Expand the System Tools node, and then expand Event Viewer.
4. In the console tree pane, right-click the name of the log you want to configure. Since they are similar, right-click Application for this exercise.
5. The Application Properties dialog box appears, and you can configure the log from there.

The Application Properties dialog box, shown in Figure 7-13, shows the path and filename for the log. All the logs are kept in the `C:\windows\system32\config` folder, and they all have the file extension `.Evt`. The default maximum log size is 512K, but this value can be increased or decreased. You have a number of choices when you reach this upper limit.

You can configure event log wrapping so that the log can overwrite as much as is needed (this way you are always recording events in your log). You also can set a safety margin by allowing events to be overwritten only if they are older than a specified number of days. In addition, you can set it so that nothing is overwritten, but you will need to manually keep a check on the log because it will fill to capacity. (You will receive a message when the log becomes full.)

If you set this option, you must remember to periodically empty your log file. To clear it, follow these steps:

STEPS

Manually clearing a log file

1. Choose Start ⇨ Control Panel.
2. Click Administrative Tools, and then select Computer Management.
3. Expand the System Tools node, and then expand Event Viewer.
4. Select the log you want to clear in the console tree, and then choose Action ⇨ Clear All Events.
5. You are prompted for whether you want to save the old log file. If you say yes, you will be asked to type a name for the saved log, which will be saved with an `.Evt` extension. If you say no, your log data will be permanently discarded.

The Security log

If you use the Event Viewer to view the contents of your log, you will see that the security log is empty. By default, it is disabled.

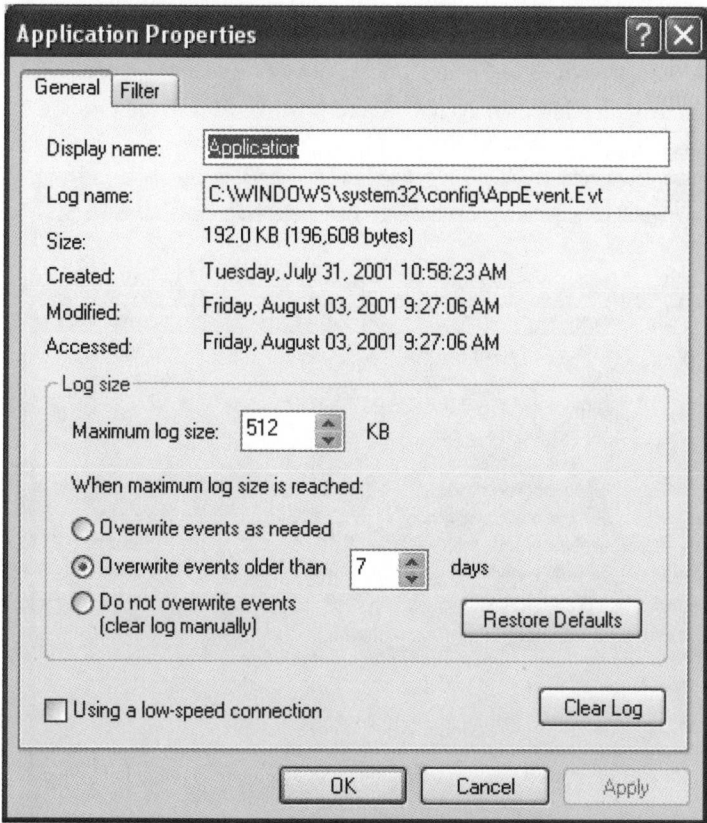

Figure 7-13: The Application Properties dialog box lets you control how large your log files become and what happens when you reach that upper limit.

If you want to start recording security events, follow these steps:

STEPS

Start the security log

1. If you created the Group Policy MMC in the "Disabling last name display at login" steps earlier in this chapter, open it and jump to Step 7. Otherwise, do the following:

2. Choose Start ⇨ Run and type the following into the Open text box and click OK:

```
mmc /a
```

3. Select the Console menu, click Add/Remove Snap-in, and then click Add.

4. Select Snap-in, click Group Policy, and then click Add.

5. For Group Policy Object, click Local Computer, and then click Finish.

6. Click Close, and then click OK. This creates the Group Policy MMC.

7. In the console tree, expand these nodes until you reach Audit Policies: Local Computer Policy ⇨ Computer Configuration ⇨ Windows Settings ⇨ Security Settings ⇨ Local Policies ⇨ Audit Policies.

8. In the details pane, select the event you want to start auditing (logging) and choose Action ⇨ Security.

9. In the Security dialog box, click your selections in Change Local Policy to, and then click OK.

10. Repeat Steps 8 and 9 if you want to audit additional events. Figure 7-14 shows the Audit Policy options.

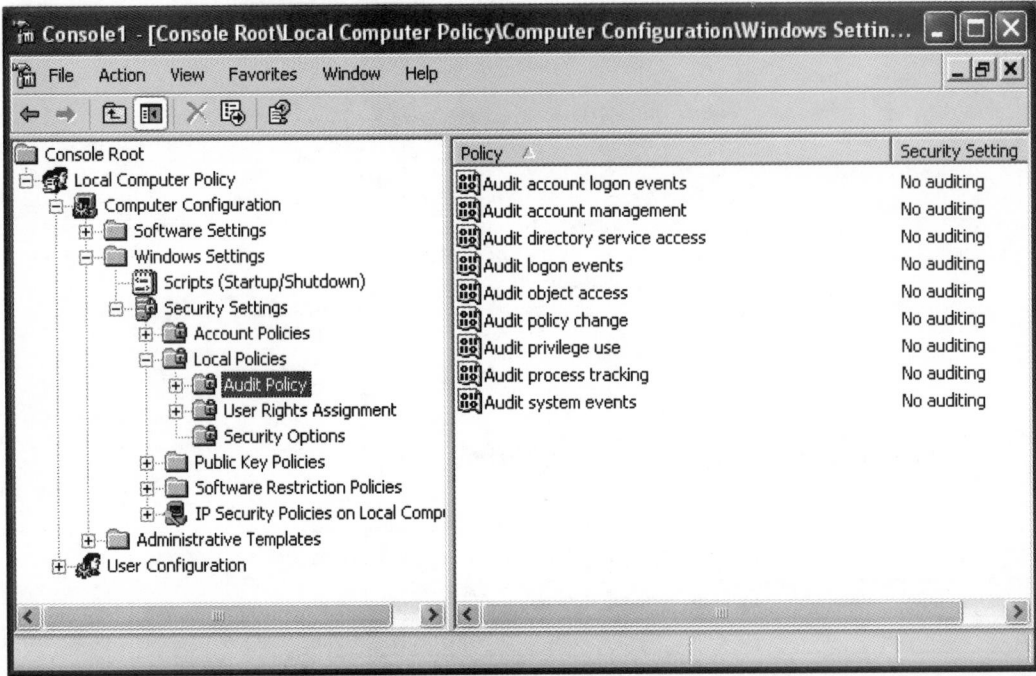

Figure 7-14: To start security logging, open the Group Policy Snap-in, and select Audit Policies. As you can see, nothing is audited by default, but you can double-click the desired entries and enable it.

Managing Your Computer

The Computer Management Console offers several more tools. I cover some, such as Device Manager and storage management, in various chapters throughout this book. (See Chapter 11 to learn more about Device Manager and Chapter 3 to learn more about storage management.) Advanced users may also want to manage Services, which is explored in the next section.

Services

Another Computer Management snap-in, Services and Applications, reports the status of services and allows you to manage them (see Figure 7-15).

TIP: By default, you have to be logged on as an administrator to be able to start and stop services.

A *service* is a background process — or "helper" program — that provides some specific support to other programs. Typically, users would not directly interact with a service the way they would with a spreadsheet or word processing application. A service runs in the background, and it helps ensure that other programs work as they should.

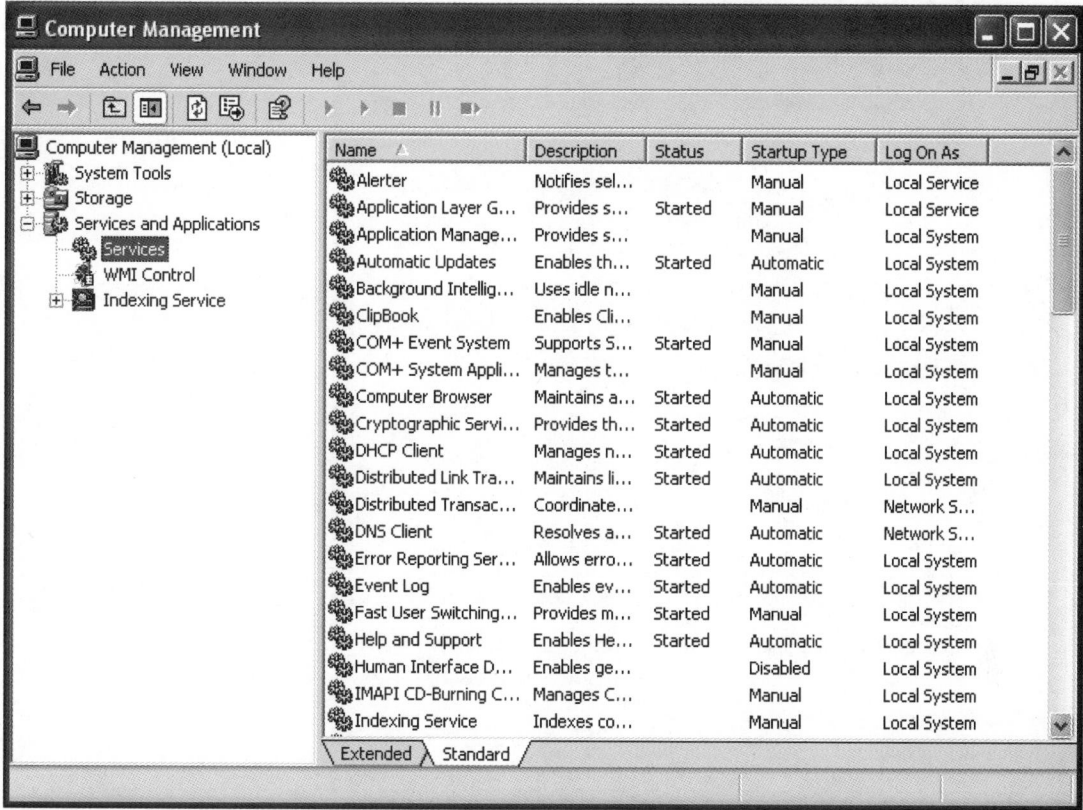

Figure 7-15: The Services snap-in is part of System Tools. It lets you manage services (start, stop, and configure) on your computer.

SECRET: Make sure that you can see all the information available with the Services snap-in. Choose View ⇨ Choose Columns, and make sure that Name, Description, Status, Startup Type, and Log On As are all selected. As in the Windows Explorer, you can sort the information in the details pane by column. The default view is to sort by name. If you want to sort by status instead — so that you can see which services are running — click the upper portion of the Status column twice. The first click sorts in ascending order and lists the services that aren't running first; their status is blank. The second click sorts the column in descending order.

The Startup Type column shows if these services are started automatically or if they are called by some other service or program. When you enable this service from the Search window, you see the indexing service running in the Services window. If you disable this service from the Search window, its status changes to Stop. To see more information about a particular service, right-click the service and select Properties from the context menu. For example, the properties for the Automatic Updates service are shown in Figure 7-16.

You can enable or disable services, or you can pause services from the General tab of the Properties dialog box. You also can use the VCR-like controls in the upper portion of the detail pane. Select a service and these controls become active, and they can be used to start or stop a service.

CAUTION: Don't stop a service unless you know it is optional. Some services perform vital system functions. You can stop the indexing service, because all it does is speed up your searches. However, you do not want to shut down the Plug and Play service, since it plays a crucial role in managing your hardware.

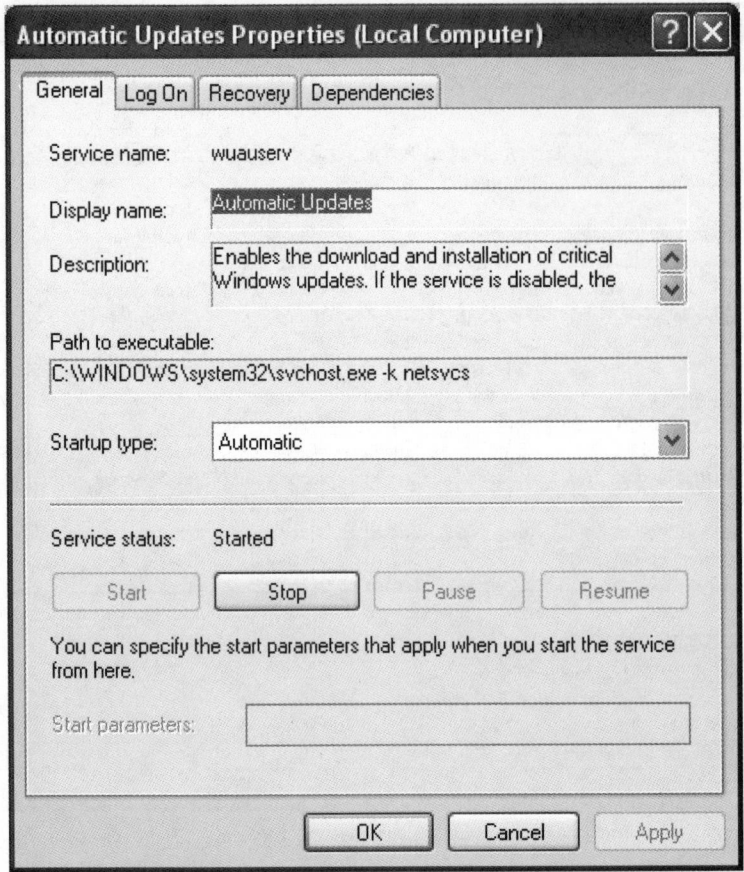

Figure 7-16: The Properties window of the Automatic Updates service.

Some services depend on other services, so shutting down one can cripple another. You can trace service dependencies by right-clicking a service, selecting Properties from the context menu, and then selecting the Dependencies tab. This tab has two panes. The upper pane shows what other services are needed by the service to function. The lower pane shows which other services need the selected service.

Many services are configured by default in Windows XP. Table 7-7 describes what many of these services do. As a general rule, unless you are sure you can do without a particular service, it is best to leave it alone.

NOTE: Your computer might have more or fewer services available than what is listed in Table 7-7, depending on your configuration.

Table 7-7: Default Services in Windows XP

Service	Provides
Alerter	Notifies specified users or computers of administrative alerts that occur on a system.
CIM Object Manager	Controls the interaction between network management applications and local or remote data or system events.
ClipBook Server	Supports the ClipBook Viewer, which adds functionality to the Clipboard.

Service	Provides
Computer Browser	Keeps track of the computers currently on the network and provides this list to programs that need it.
Content Index	Keeps a full text index of files and folders on a computer to aid in searches.
Directory Replicator	Used when you replicate directories between computers.
Event Log	Provides a list of system, security, and program events on a computer.
Logical Disk Manager	Takes care of all disk management activities, such as disk partitioning and volume creation, logical drive lettering, and formatting.
Media Services Management	Provides services for removable media hardware, such as CD-ROM drives, Zip drives, and Jaz drives.
Messenger	When the Alerter service sends messages, it uses the Messenger service.
Microsoft Fax Service	Manages incoming and outgoing faxes for both local and network clients.
Microsoft Install Service	Manages application installation. This also includes rollback and repair services.
Net Logon	If a Windows XP client participates in a domain, it handles the authentication of logon events.
Network DDE	Provides the transportation and security for network dynamic data exchange.
Network DDE DSDM	DDE Share Database Manager. This supports Network DDE.
NT LM Security Support Provider	If a program uses something other than the named pipe transport, this provides security.
Plug and Play	Handles the installation and configuration of Plug and Play devices. (See Chapter 11.)
Remote Procedure Call Service	Helps distributed programs by providing endpoint mapping and other RPC functions.
Server	Handles file, print, and named pipe sharing. Also provides Remote Procedure Call (RPC) support.
Smart Card Resource Manager	Manages Smart Card devices, which are a new hardware-based security system.
Spooler	Manages the print spooler, which stores documents that are to be printed onto the hard drive, and then sends them to the printer one by one.
Task Scheduler	Supports the Task Scheduler, which you can configure for automated activities.
Telephony	Manages telephony services and devices attached to the computer.
UPS	Manages any uninterruptible power supply that may be attached to the computer.
Workstation	Manages network connections and communications.

Device Manager

Another important tool in managing your computer is the Device Manager, which lets you manage your hardware. The Device Manager is very similar to the Windows 98 Device Manager and is covered in detail in Chapter 11.

Storage Management

Computer Management has a number of tools with which you can manage your storage devices, such as hard drives, floppy drives, and removable drives. Given the importance of these tools, they are covered in detail in Chapter 3.

Configuring Custom Consoles

Throughout this chapter, you have explored the use of the MMC and the most common snap-ins you are likely to work with, particularly Computer Management. I've also noted that you can easily create new MMCs by opening an empty MMC, adding the desired snap-ins, and saving the console. This is a great way to place all of the snap-in tools you commonly use in one location. For example, take a look at Figure 7-17. I have a custom MMC that has a shortcut to it on my desktop. I can easily access the tools I use most often through this one console. I created this console from scratch by opening an empty MMC and adding the snap-ins that I wanted to use.

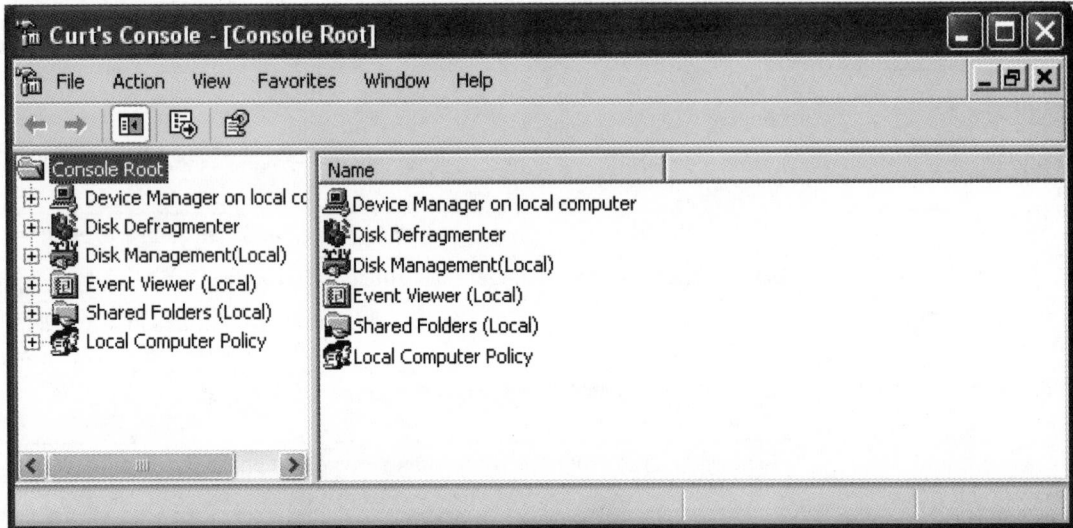

Figure 7-17: Custom MMC console containing a number of snap-ins.

From the custom MMC, you can make a number of additional configuration changes that you may find interesting and helpful. For example, use the Favorites menu to add the console to the Favorites list so that it always shows up under Favorites, no matter what folder you are working in. Use the Window menu to reorganize the appearance of the MMC. Also, choose Customize from the View menu to make basic appearance changes to the information the MMC displays, as shown in Figure 7-18.

Another item that you may find helpful is the taskpad view. A taskpad view is simply made up of icon shortcuts that enable you to define tasks for a particular snap-in. As an advanced user, you may not find taskpads that helpful to you, but consider this scenario: You need to create a custom MMC for a coworker. The coworker has minimal computing skills, but you need the coworker to be able to use the Shared Folders snap-in to disconnect all sessions when necessary. You make this task easy by creating a simple custom console for the Shared Folder snap-in, and then creating a taskpad view for the action of disconnecting all sessions. As you can see, the task appears as a link. All the user has to do is click the link to carry out the action, as shown in Figure 7-19.

Creating taskpad views is rather easy, with the help of two wizards, the Console Wizard and Task Wizard. The following steps walk you through the process of creating a taskpad view.

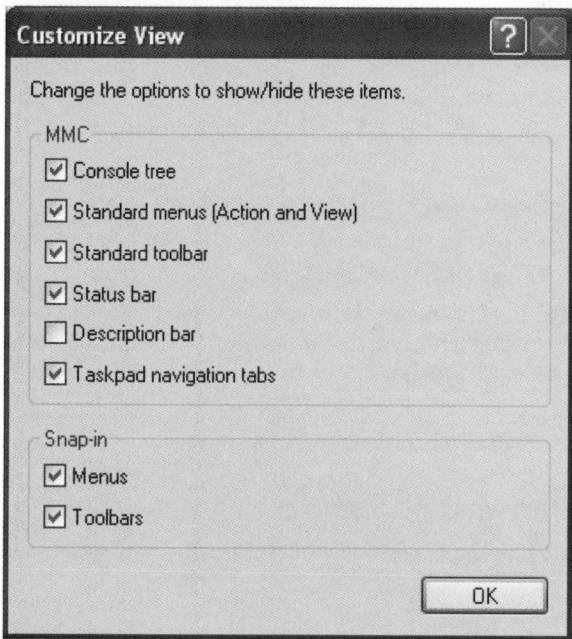

Figure 7-18: Use the Customize View window to make basic appearance changes.

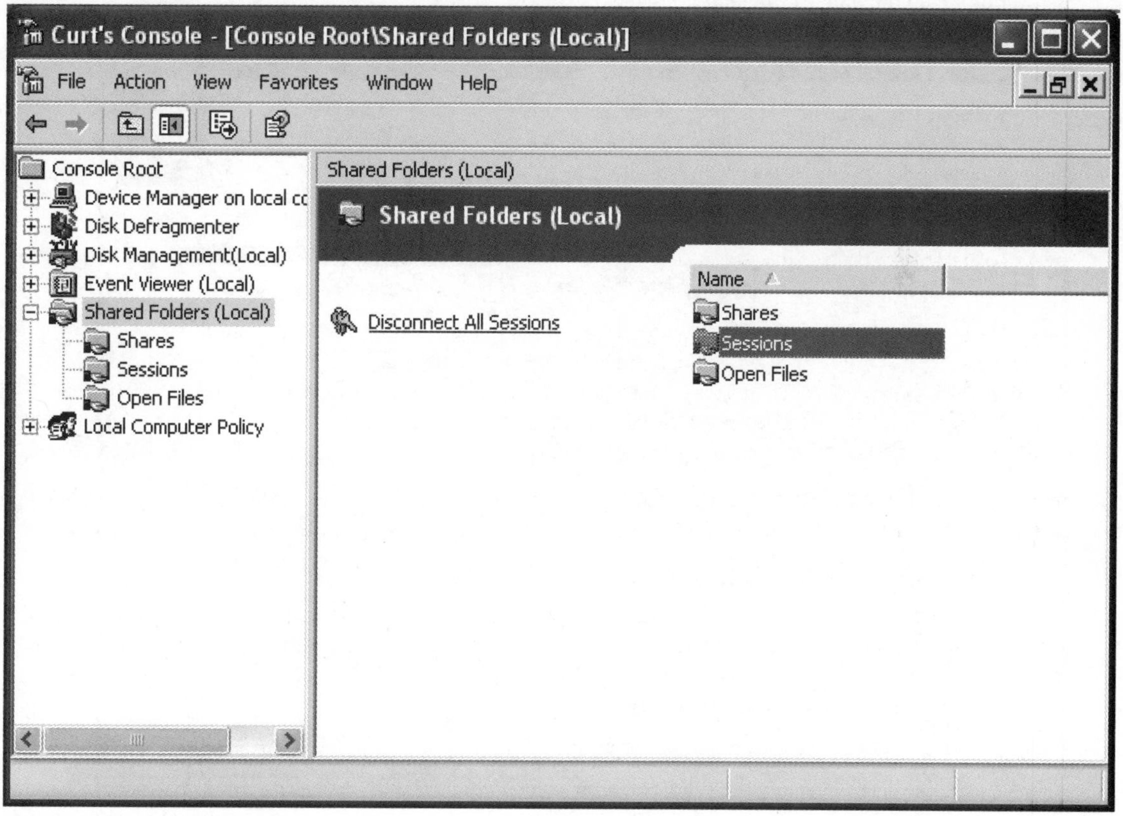

Figure 7-19: Custom taskpad view

STEPS

Creating a taskpad view

1. Create the desired MMC with the desired snap-in(s) to which the taskpad view will apply and save the console.

2. In the console, select the snap-in to which the taskpad will apply, then choose Action ⇨ New Taskpad View.

3. The New Taskpad View Wizard appears. Click Next on the Welcome screen.

4. In the Taskpad Display window, shown in Figure 7-20, choose the style for the details pane by clicking the appropriate radio button. Also, choose either text style for descriptions or InfoTip style (pop-up window). Also, choose the list size as small, medium, or large using its drop-down menu. Click Next.

5. The Taskpad Target window appears. Choose whether this taskpad will apply to the selected snap-in or all snap-ins in the console. Click Next.

6. Give a name to the taskpad and a description, if desired, and click Next.

7. On the completion window, make sure that the Start New Task Wizard check box option is selected, then click Finish.

8. The New Task Wizard appears. Click Next on the Welcome screen.

9. The Command Type window appears, as shown in Figure 7-21. You can choose to run a menu command, shell command, or navigation command for the taskpad. Make a choice for the kind of command you want to run, and click Next.

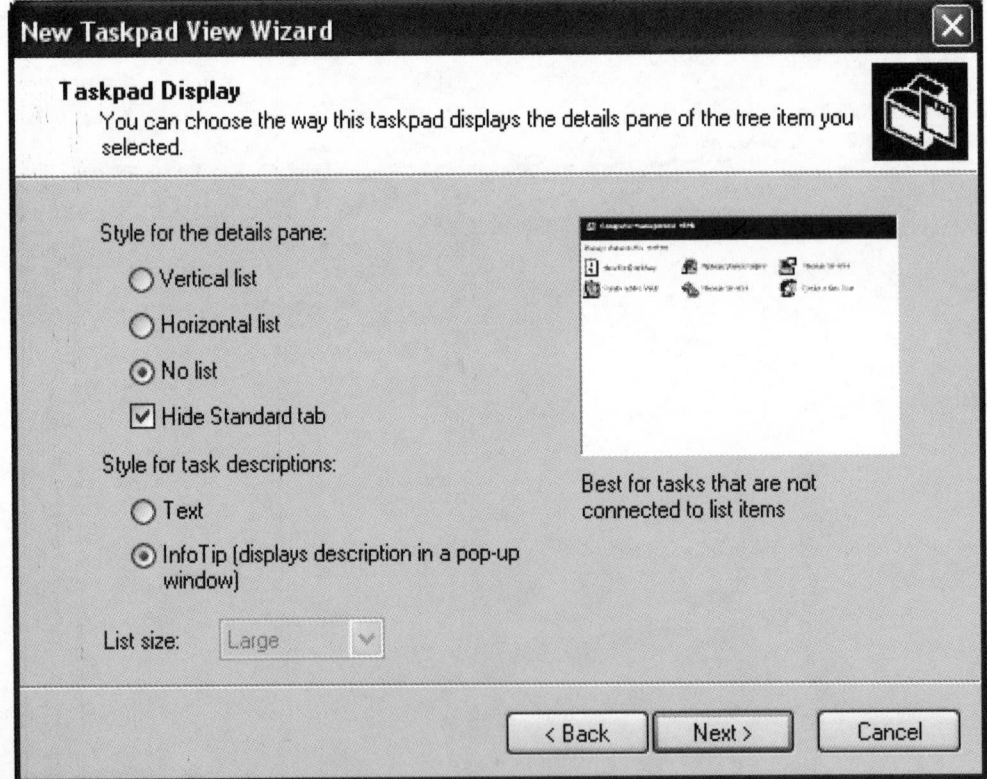

Figure 7-20: The Taskpad Display window

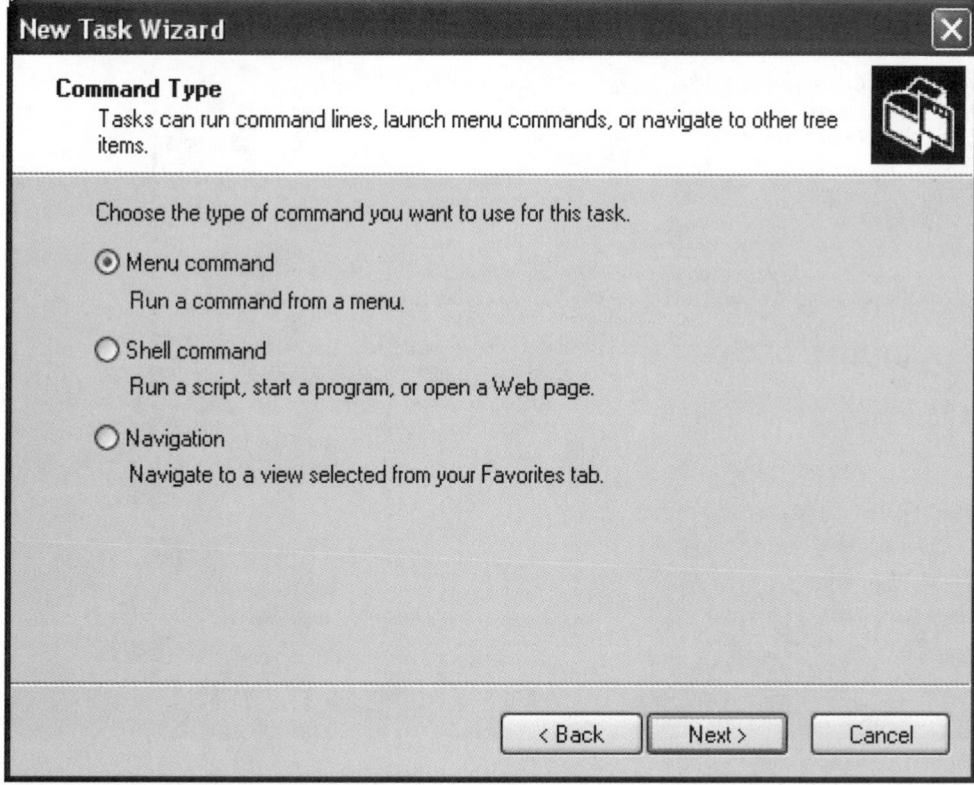

Figure 7-21: Command Type window

10. The Shortcut Menu Command window appears. Choose a source for the command from the drop-down menu, as shown in Figure 7-22. You can choose to list the task in the details pane or as a tree item. Then select the command item in the left pane and the desired command in the right pane. As you can see in Figure 7-22, I am choosing the Disconnect All Sessions task for this taskpad. Click Next.

11. The Name and Description window appears. Enter a desired task name and description and click Next.

12. The Task Icon window appears, as shown in Figure 7-23. Choose a desired icon to represent the task, or browse for a custom icon that you want to use. The icon should be something recognizable to the user for whom you are creating the taskpad. Click Next.

13. Click Finish to complete the wizard. The task you created now appears in the MMC.

Using the MMC and the features of custom consoles, you can create console management tools that help you easily manage the features and functions of Windows XP. As you work with Windows XP, keep in mind all that the MMC has to offer and use the custom console options to make your work with Windows XP easier and faster.

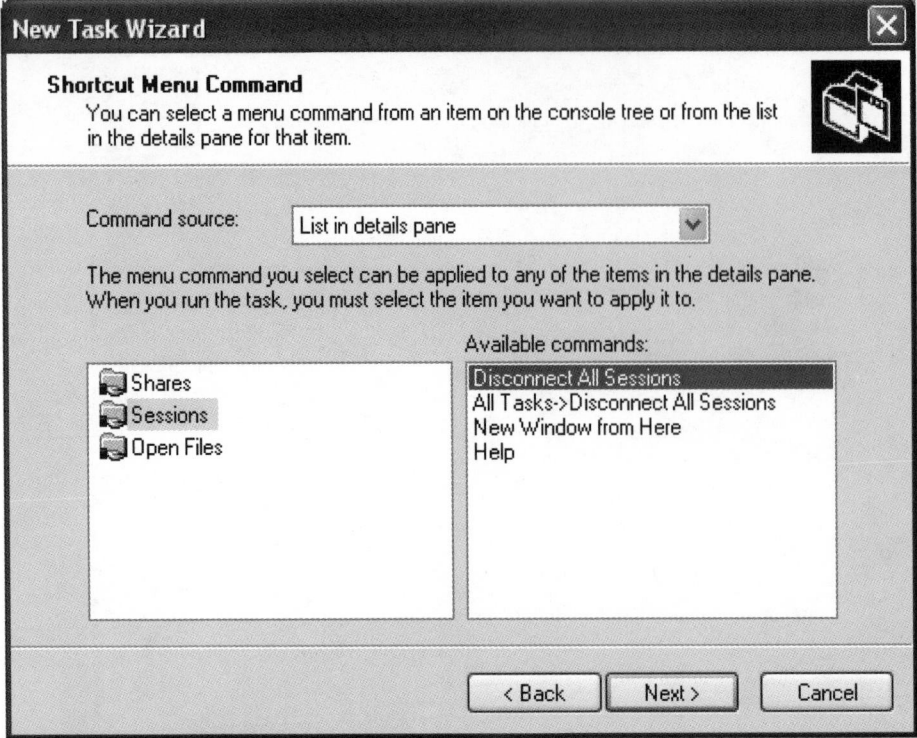

Figure 7-22: Choose the desired task.

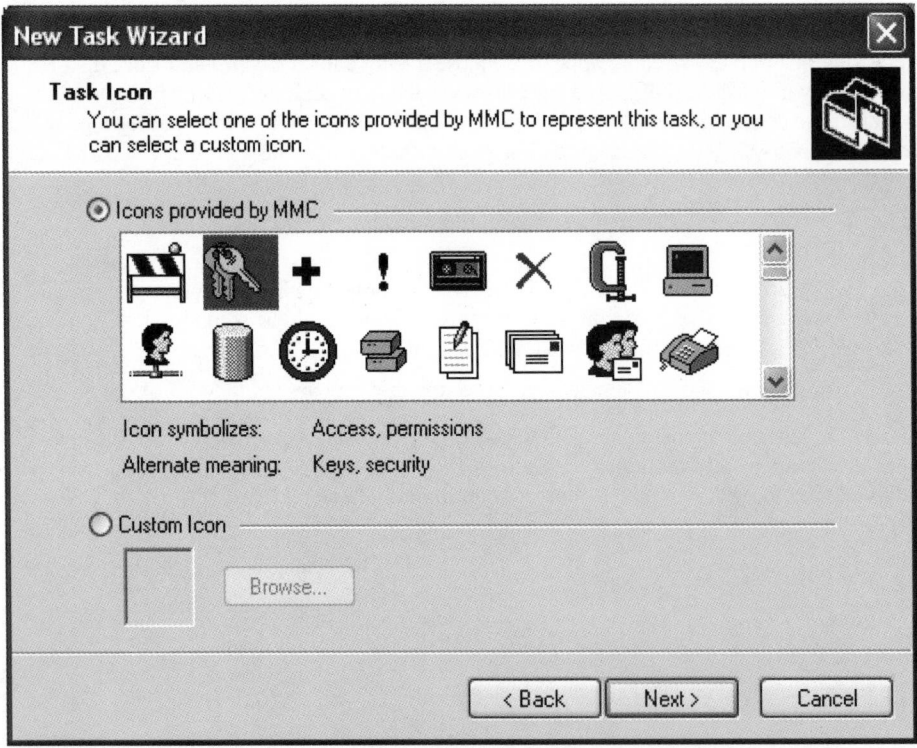

Figure 7-23: Choose an icon to represent the task.

Summary

In this chapter, you learned how to use tools within the Microsoft Management Console, the new framework for system administration tools. You can now . . .

- Customize tools within the MMC interface
- Manage security using MMC snap-ins
- Gather system information using MMC snap-ins
- Manage the computer with MMC snap-ins
- Create custom taskpad views

Part III

Software Secrets

Chapter 8

System Components and Software Management

In This Chapter

Windows XP handles software better than any previous version of Windows. In fact, software management and configuration are quite easy, and you have a few new tools to try out when you are having problems with software. In this chapter, I explore Windows components and software installation, removal, and management. If you are currently having problems with software under Windows XP, then you may find exactly what you need in this chapter. In this chapter, you learn about . . .

♦ Installing and managing system components

♦ Managing programs on your computer

♦ Managing program compatibility issues

Managing Windows Components

With the exception of some higher-level networking tools, almost everything you ever need is already installed and available on Windows XP. In Windows 9*x* and Me you had to go to Windows Setup to add components from time to time. That's changed in Windows XP. You should rarely, if ever, have to access Windows XP's Add/Remove Windows Components unless you are performing some specialized tasks. However, if you do, the process of adding and removing components from your system is rather easy.

If you have used Windows 2000, you are familiar with the Add/Remove Windows Components feature under Add/Remove Programs. Before performing the task of adding and removing components, though, first consider what is available here:

♦ **Accessories and Utilities** — Under Accessories and Utilities, you can install and remove several accessories and games, all of which are installed by default. They are as follows:

- Calculator
- Character Map
- Clipboard Viewer
- Desktop Wallpaper
- Document Templates
- Mouse Pointers
- Paint
- Freecell
- Hearts
- Internet Games
- Minesweeper

- Solitaire
- Spider Solitaire

♦ **Fax Service** — If you want to use Windows XP's souped-up fax service, install it here. The fax service is not installed by default.

♦ **Indexing Service** — The indexing service allows XP to provide full and fast text searching on your computer. This service is installed by default.

♦ **Internet Information Services (IIS)** — IIS is used to host intranet or Internet sites from your Windows XP computer. You don't need it if you have no intention of doing so, but if you choose to install it, IIS has several components, which are as follows:

- Common Files
- Documentation
- FTP Services
- FrontPage 2000 Server Extensions
- Internet Information Services Snap-in
- SMTP Service
- Visual InterDev RAD Remote Deployment Support
- World Wide Web Service

> **CAUTION:** Do not install IIS on your computer unless you plan to use it. IIS may create security holes in your computer, especially if you have an always-on connection such as cable, DSL, or satellite.

♦ **Management and Monitoring Tools** — This sounds like a big category, but in fact, you can install only Simple Network Management Protocol and WMI SNMP Provider here. Neither is installed by default, and these tools are not used on home or small office networks. Under most conditions, typical power users would not install these items.

♦ **Message Queuing** — Used primarily in larger networks, Message Queuing provides guaranteed message delivery, security, and related services. This tool is not installed by default.

♦ **MSN Explorer** — Installed by default and easily removed (thank goodness). Obviously, Microsoft advertises MSN throughout Windows XP, and if you choose to use MSN, you can use the MSN Explorer. For the rest of us, however, it cannot be used, so remove it here so that it not taking up useful hard disk space.

♦ **Networking Services** — This category allows you to install RIP Listener, Simple TCP/IP Services, and Universal Plug and Play. None of these are installed by default.

> **TIP:** If you are on a network, you should consider installing Universal Plug and Play. See Chapter 11 for details.

♦ **Other Network File and Print Services** — You can install print services for UNIX here, which are not installed by default.

♦ **Smart Tags support for Microsoft Internet Explorer** — Installed by default.

♦ **Update Root Certificates** — Allows for the automatic download of the most current root certificate. This one is also installed by default.

As you can see, unless you need some specific tools or need to use XP in a certain way (such as a Web server), there is not a lot here that you need to work with. However, if you want to install or remove any of these components the process is very straightforward. The following steps give you a quick walkthrough.

STEPS

Adding and removing Windows components

1. Open Control Panel and double-click Add/Remove Programs.

2. In the Add or Remove Programs window, as shown in Figure 8-1, click the Add/Remove Windows Components button in the left column.

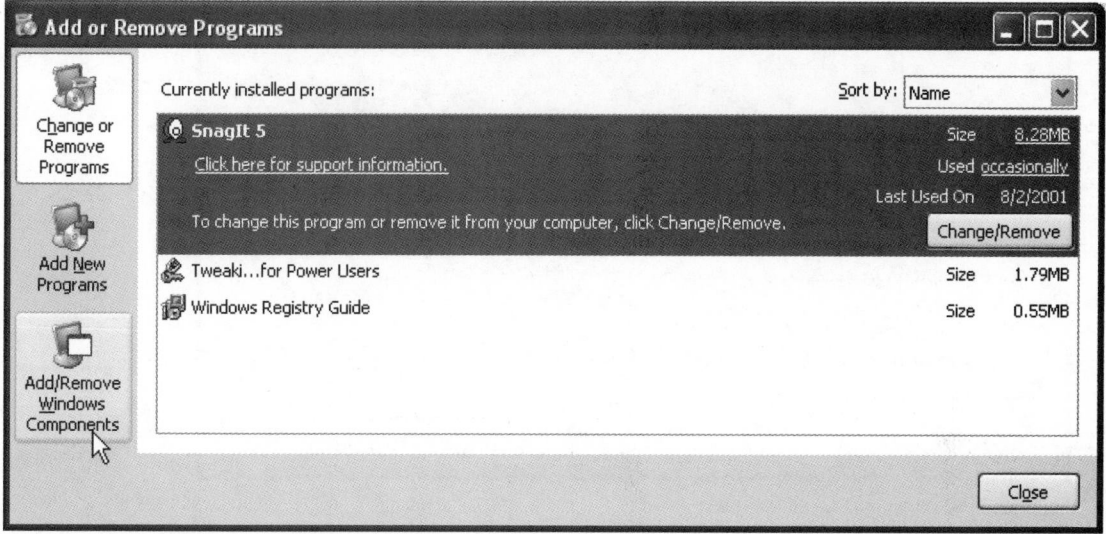

Figure 8-1: Add or Remove Programs window

3. Windows XP Setup begins and the Windows Components window appears, as shown in Figure 8-2. Check or clear an item that you want to install or remove. If an item is a category, the Details button will become available. Select the category and click Details, then click the desired check boxes to either remove or install items as desired. When you finish this selection process, click Next.

4. Setup configures the components. You may need your installation CD to complete the process.

5. Click the Finish button when it appears.

Installing and Removing Programs

Installing and removing programs in Windows XP is a rather straightforward process, as it was in previous versions of Windows. Most software installation CDs today come with an automatic launching file: You place the CD-ROM into the CD-ROM drive, and the installation window for the application automatically appears. From that point, you just follow the steps.

> **TIP:** Windows XP is built on the stability of Windows 2000 in many different ways, but one of those is through system file protection. Critical system files are stored in a hidden folder, and applications that you install on your system are not allowed to alter those files. Because system files cannot be corrupted by applications, your Windows XP system is highly stable and free from the many lockups and related application conflict problems we all came to know and love in Windows 9x.

If this doesn't happen, you can either manually launch the installation of the application by running the setup.exe program found on the installation CD or by letting Windows XP help you. For most power users, the easiest way to start the installation is to simply run $D:\setup.exe$ where D is your CD drive letter.

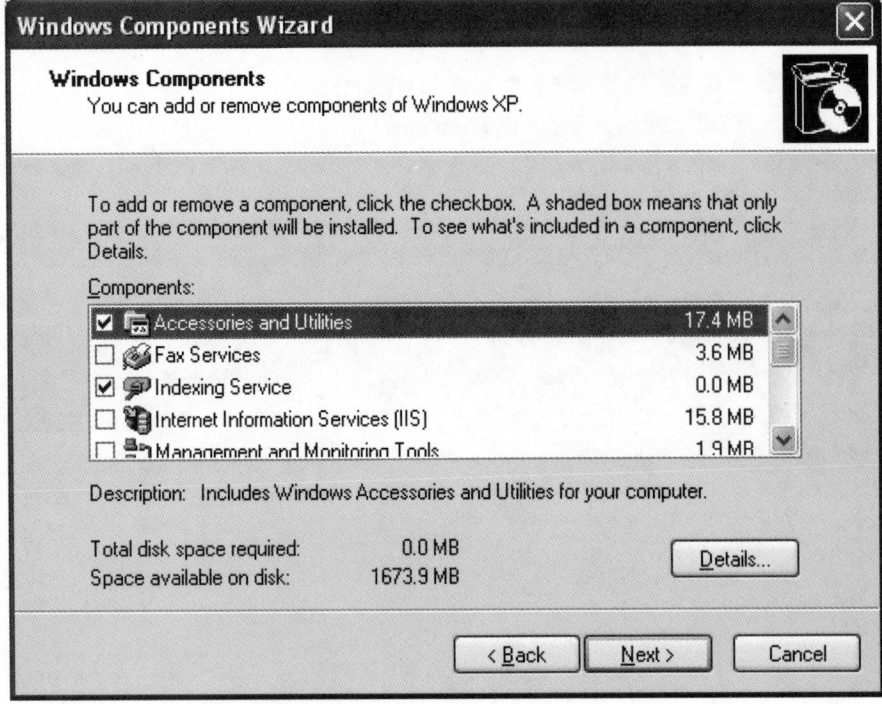

Figure 8-2: Windows Components window

However, Windows XP can help with this process should an application not have an automatic launching file or if a user does not want to look for `setup.exe`. If you return to the Add/Remove Programs window, you see a button labeled Add New Programs. If you click this button, a secondary window appears in which you can choose to install from CD or floppy, or visit the Windows Update site for software upgrades to XP. If you choose CD or floppy, a wizard appears that looks for `setup.exe` on either the floppy disk or the CD. You can then click Finish to launch the installation. Of course, this process basically adds a whole bunch of steps to simply starting `setup.exe` on your CD drive, but beginning users or those who just prefer to use their mouse may find the process helpful.

TIP: If you upgrade to Windows XP from a previous version of Windows, all applications are kept with your new system. This does not, however, mean that they will work. See "Application Compatibility in Windows XP" later in this chapter for details.

Aside from installing programs, you can remove them as needed, which can be somewhat more troublesome and interesting than installing them. You essentially have three different ways to remove a program from Windows XP:

♦ Use the program's uninstall feature

♦ Use Windows XP's remove feature

♦ Forcefully remove the application yourself

The first two options are rather easy, as you are well aware. First, most applications come with an uninstall feature. If you access the program's folder in Programs, you may see an uninstall icon. Click the icon to start the uninstallation. If there does not seem to be a program, you can often use the program's CD to uninstall the program from your system. When the uninstall process on the CD begins, it detects that the program is already installed and offers to remove it for you. Of course, different people develop software and these features may or may not exist for your particular software title.

If the application doesn't help you remove it, then Windows XP can. Return to Add or Remove Programs and select the application in the list. As you can see in Figure 8-3, you have the option to Change or Remove Programs. This option may be displayed as Change/Remove, depending on the application.

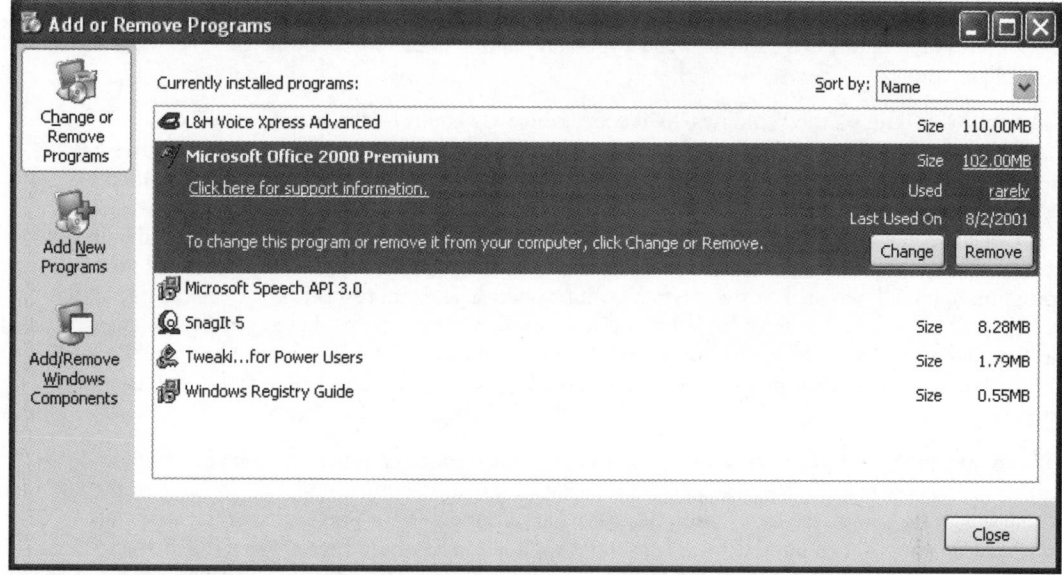

Figure 8-3: Add or Remove Programs — Change or Remove Programs option

The change option is used for program suites like Microsoft Office that have several different components you can install or uninstall. If you choose the change option, you are taken back to that program's setup window, and you need the installation CD again. If you choose the remove option, a window appears for you to confirm the deletion, and Windows removes all related files.

In a perfect world removing a program would be a snap. But what do you do if the program is installed on your system but does not appear in Add/Remove Programs and does not have its own uninstall program (which is typical of older programs)? At this point, you are forced to manually remove the program from your computer.

To manually remove a program, locate the program's folder, which is typically stored in C:\Program Files. However, some older programs may place their folders directly in the root. In either case, locate the folder, right-click it, and then choose Delete. This moves the folder and all of its components to the Recycle Bin. It's a good idea to leave the program in the Recycle Bin for a period of time until you have used other applications. Some applications are dependent on each other, and the deletion of one application's folder may remove needed shared files. Of course, removing an application in this way may leave shared DLL files in other places on your system that are no longer needed, but these typically don't cause problems.

TIP: Other third-party tools, including TweakUI, may be able to help you remove problematic applications. You can search the Internet for these tools and utilities with your favorite search engine.

Application Compatibility in Windows XP

Application compatibility has been an ongoing problem since the days of early computing. As operating systems are redesigned and rebuilt, applications that are written for one operating system may no longer work on the new operating system. This primarily occurs because the operating system code on which the application was built changes, thus resulting in zero compatibility or unstable behavior. As the application makes API calls to the operating system, the operating system may not respond in a manner that the application expects, resulting in a frozen screen.

Although compatibility continues to be an issue with operating systems and software, Windows XP includes several new features that help bridge the gap in terms of compatibility. This is one of the best new features of Windows XP, so I'll spend a moment talking about compatibility, then explore the tools available to you.

Windows XP is built on the Windows 2000 code, which was built on the Windows NT code. Because of this applications written for Windows NT and 2000 will most likely work fine under Windows XP. However, applications written for Windows 9x and Me may experience problems, because those applications were written for a completely different code base. Also, Windows 9x and Me were quite lackadaisical about application management. For instance, a program, such as a game, could gain full access to system resources and hardware. Not so in Windows XP (like 2000). Windows XP never allows a program to directly control hardware or system resources. The end result is a very stable operating system that is typically free from lockups and other application problems, but not compatible with a lot of software that was developed for Windows 9x. Because Windows XP is the first home operating system built on the 2000 code, this presents a problem. To alleviate that problem, some additional tools and features are built into XP that enable it to work with these programs.

XP's compatibility features depend on application database files that are used to interact with applications on the system. Because applications and application compatibility are outside of the operating system kernel, the application database files are used as a go-between for the applications and the operating system. In a nontechnical sense, the application database files act as a translator so that application calls can be understood and handled by the system in a way that is appropriate to the application.

There are four main application database files:

♦ **MigDB.inf** — This database file is used for migration of applications from Windows 9x and Me. It can identify and flag programs that are incompatible or require an upgrade. This file is responsible for the message that may appear during installation telling the user that a certain application may not work correctly under Windows XP.

♦ **NTCompat.inf** — This database file is used for upgrades from Windows NT and Windows 2000. It also provides incompatibility information concerning applications.

♦ **SysMain.sdb** — This database file contains matching information and compatibility fixes.

♦ **AppHelp.sdb** — Help files that can give the user clues about compatibility and how to resolve problems.

Aside from MigDB.inf and NTCompat.inf, SysMain.sdb is the primary database file that pulls the information from the MigDB.inf and NTCompat.inf files. It then looks for matches that can fix the incompatibility problems. These matches are often simple changes that allow Windows XP to give the application what it needs to function properly. The fixes, which are also called *shims,* are held in this database file, which contains about 200 at the time of XP's release.

> **SECRET:** Shims can be used by any application, but third-party developers cannot write new shims for Windows XP. This restriction is a security protection feature implemented by Microsoft. What you get out of the box is it.

With shims, Windows XP can invoke several compatibility modes. Essentially, a compatibility mode enables XP to use the identified shims for that category and (hopefully) fix the compatibility problems the application has with Windows XP. These shims emulate the operating system that is needed by the program. For example, if an application is written for Windows 98, the shims can emulate the structure of the Windows 98 Registry, the location of certain system and user folders, file paths, and related changes in the operating system that the application would not be able to handle.

The compatibility modes available in Windows XP are as follows:

- **Windows 95** — Emulates the Windows 95 environment.
- **Windows 98/Me** — Emulates the Windows 98/Me environment.
- **Windows NT 4.0** — Emulates the Windows NT 4.0 environment.
- **Windows 2000** — Emulates the Windows 2000 environment.
- **256 colors** — Reduces video card color to 256 colors for applications that can only handle 256 colors.
- **640 by 480 screen resolution** — Restricts screen resolution to 640×480 pixels for applications that can handle only that screen resolution.

SECRET: Video cards cause a lot of application compatibility problems, hence the two compatibility modes offered to deal with display and resolution. Also, notice that there are not compatibility modes for Windows 3.x and NT 3.x: it's time to leave these systems in the past! All of the above modes can be easily invoked by a typical end user.

- **System modes** — A few other modes are available that power users and administrators typically invoke. These modes are used to limit or manage security and profiles for the user in order to run programs that require a limited security context. The Limited User Account mode is available, as well as the Profiles mode, both of which can be invoked using the QFixApp or CompatAdmin tools, tools that are described and explored later in this chapter.
- **Custom modes** — You can create a custom mode for a particular application, based on the application's needs, using the CompatAdmin tool, explored later in this chapter.

SECRET: The compatibility modes and shims provided with Windows XP support around 100 of the most popular programs so that they can work with Windows XP. However, they do not support everything, and they certainly do not support any custom applications. However, you can still try to use one of these applications with a compatibility mode, and you may have good results. Be sure to use Windows XP's dynamic update and Windows update from time to time to ensure that your XP system has all of the available shims in its database.

As mentioned, there are a few tools you can use for application compatibility and to configure application compatibility for your system. The following sections explore these tools.

Program Compatibility Wizard

The Program Compatibility Wizard is the end user's tool for using a compatibility mode. It's easy to use and works great most of the time, and even for advanced users, it's best to use the wizard when possible. The Program Compatibility Wizard is available in your Accessories folder, and the following steps walk you through the process of using the wizard.

CAUTION: The program compatibility modules are not designed to work with antivirus software, backup software, or other types of software that help you manage your computer system. You need to upgrade to an XP-compatible version in order to use these types of software. Attempting to use them with Windows XP compatibility mode may cause system problems.

STEPS

Using the Program Compatibility Wizard

1. Choose Start ⇨ All Programs ⇨ Accessories ⇨ Program Compatibility Wizard.
2. The Help and Support Center opens, which houses the Program Compatibility Wizard. Click Next on the Welcome screen.
3. Choose the program that you want to run in compatibility mode. You can choose to pick from a list of programs already installed on your computer, run the program from your CD-ROM drive, or manually locate it on your computer. Make your selection and click Next.

4. The compatibility mode window appears, as shown in Figure 8-4. Choose the operating system you want to emulate, or you can choose not to apply a compatibility mode. Use this option if you just want to manage video card settings. Make your selection and click Next.

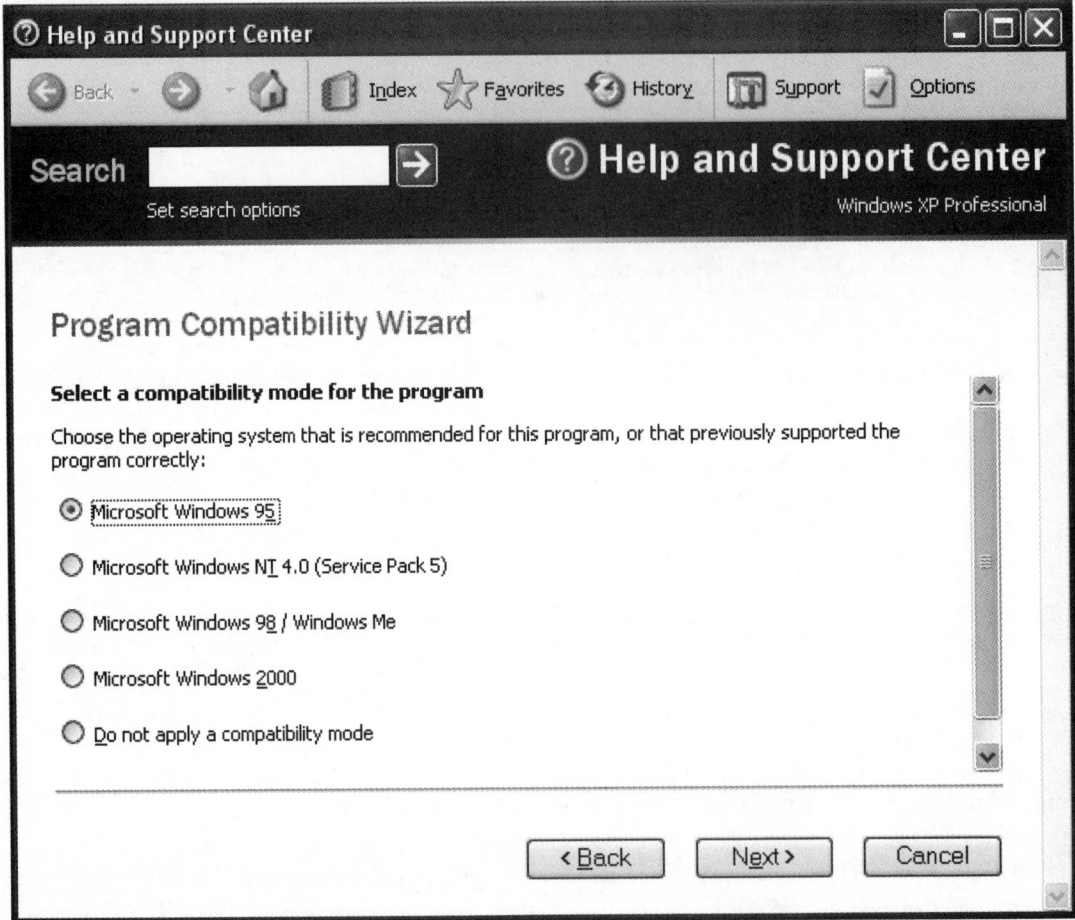

Figure 8-4: Choose an operating system.

5. The display settings window appears, as shown in Figure 8-5. Choose any display setting restrictions you need. Make sure you need the restrictions before using them, however. Typically older games and children's programs benefit from these settings. Make your selections and click Next.

6. A summary of your selections appears. To test the compatibility settings, click Next.

7. The program opens, and XP applies the desired compatibility settings. Use the program a bit and see if it works properly. When you finish, exit the program to return the compatibility wizard. If the program worked as it should, choose the Yes option and click Next. If not, choose No and try different compatibility settings. Note that if you click Yes, the program is set to always use the compatibility mode. Now you can run the program as needed without returning to this wizard.

TIP: To remove the compatibility settings, just run the wizard again and remove all of the options you selected for the particular program.

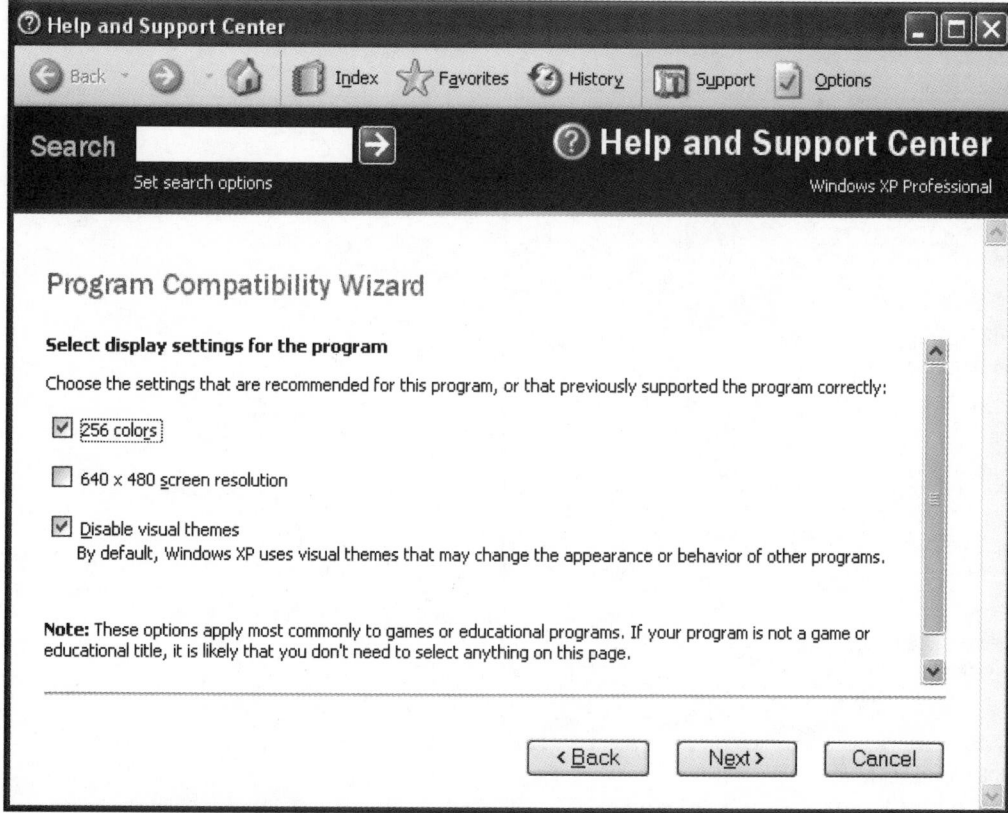

Figure 8-5: Choose display settings.

If you want to avoid the wizard and make these settings directly to the application, you can easily do so by accessing the application's executable Properties sheets. Just locate the executable icon for the program, right-click it, and click Properties. You'll see the Compatibility tab, as shown in Figure 8-6. Select the check box option and choose a compatibility mode that you want to use for the application. Then select display settings if needed. Also, you can use this tab to remove compatibility mode settings.

QFixApp

QFixApp is a utility you can use to manually solve compatibility problems with applications by applying shims to the fix from the available database. The QFixApp is available in the Application Compatibility Toolkit, which is downloadable from `http://msdn.microsoft.com`. Once you download and install the toolkit, you'll see an HTML page that outlines the documents and tools in the toolkit. If you scroll to tools, you'll see both the QFixApp and Compatibility Administration Tool, as shown in Figure 8-7.

The QFixApp tool gives you total control over an executable file by allowing you to actually examine the `SysMain.sdb` file and apply any shim to the executable. The Program Compatibility Wizard basically does this, but it applies the fixes based on one of the modes you select. With QFixApp, you can apply a mode that you desire and manually overlay any additional fix that you want. This feature is quite helpful if you have applied a mode to an application, but you are still having a particular problem. If you can isolate the likely cause of the problem, then you can use QFixApp to apply that single fix while keeping the original mode application intact. In short, you have total control over how the fixes are applied. The reverse is also true. If a fix is applied within a mode, you can individually remove fixes out of the mode for that application that may be giving you problems. The good news is that if you solve the problem for the application, you can use the Compatibility Administration Tool to deploy the fix to other XP machines on your network that are running the same program.

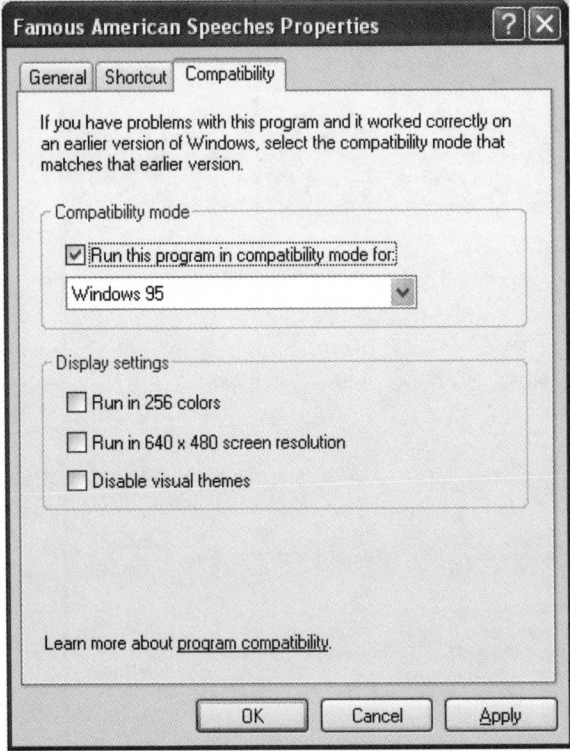

Figure 8-6: Compatibility tab

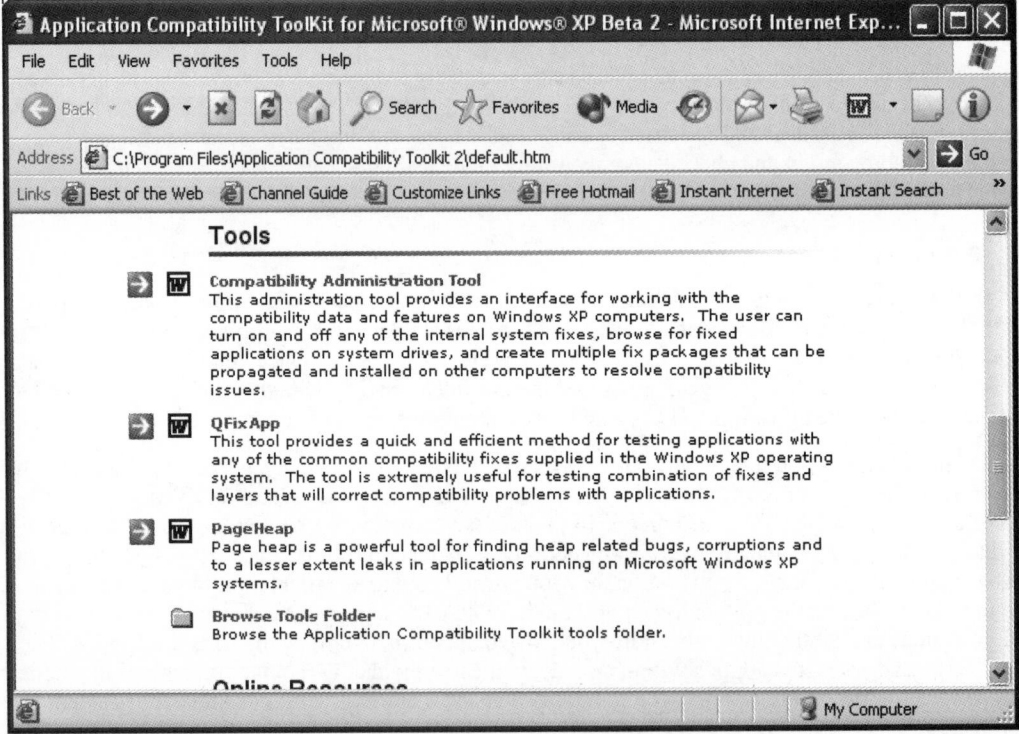

Figure 8-7: Application Compatibility Toolkit

Overall, the tool is quite straightforward and easy to use. The following steps give you a walkthrough.

> **SECRET:** Microsoft seems to go back and forth between the terms *shim* and *fix*. They mean the same thing, so don't get confused when you are working with these tools.

STEPS

Using QFixApp

1. In the Application Compatibility Toolkit, click the Open link next to QFixApp.

2. The QFixApp window appears, as shown in Figure 8-8. Browse for the executable file for the program you want to try and fix. If there are any existing fixes in the database for this application, you can choose to disable them by clicking the check box. This allows you to attempt the configuration without the use of any preexisting fixes you may have configured with the compatibility wizard.

3. On the Layers tab, you can apply one of the existing modes to the application if you so choose. For example, you can choose 256 colors, Disable themes, NT 4 with Service Pack 5, Windows 98, and others. If you don't want to use an existing layer, just click the Fixes tab.

4. In the Fixes tab, you see each available fix. If you click a fix, you can see a fix description toward the bottom of the window describing what the fix should correct with the application. Work through the list, selecting the fixes that you want to apply.

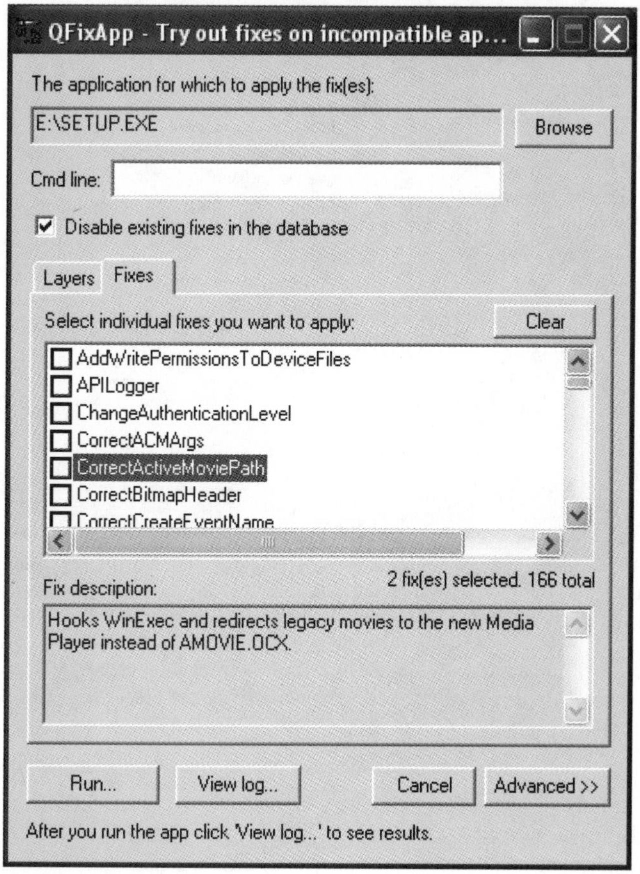

Figure 8-8: QFixApp

5. When you are ready to test the applications with the fixes you have applied, click the Run button. The application opens, and you can use it as desired. Make note of what problems still exist and what problems were solved. You can then add and remove fixes as needed until you find the right combination for the application.

TIP: You can view the log file of the fixes by clicking the "View log" button; you can see it in the AppPatch folder in your Windows directory. QFixApp adds files to the AppPatch folder as needed for the fix you have created for the application.

There are also some advanced features you can use with QFixApp. If you click the Advanced button, a secondary window appears, as shown in Figure 8-9. The options here help you apply the fixes to the correct application on your system. This is helpful if more than one .exe file has the same name, but the fix should be applied to only one. You can examine the list of attributes that appear and select the attributes that correctly describe the .exe. When you've identified the attributes, you can click the "Create fix support" button to create an .sdb file for the application. You also have the option to view XML commands for the attribute.

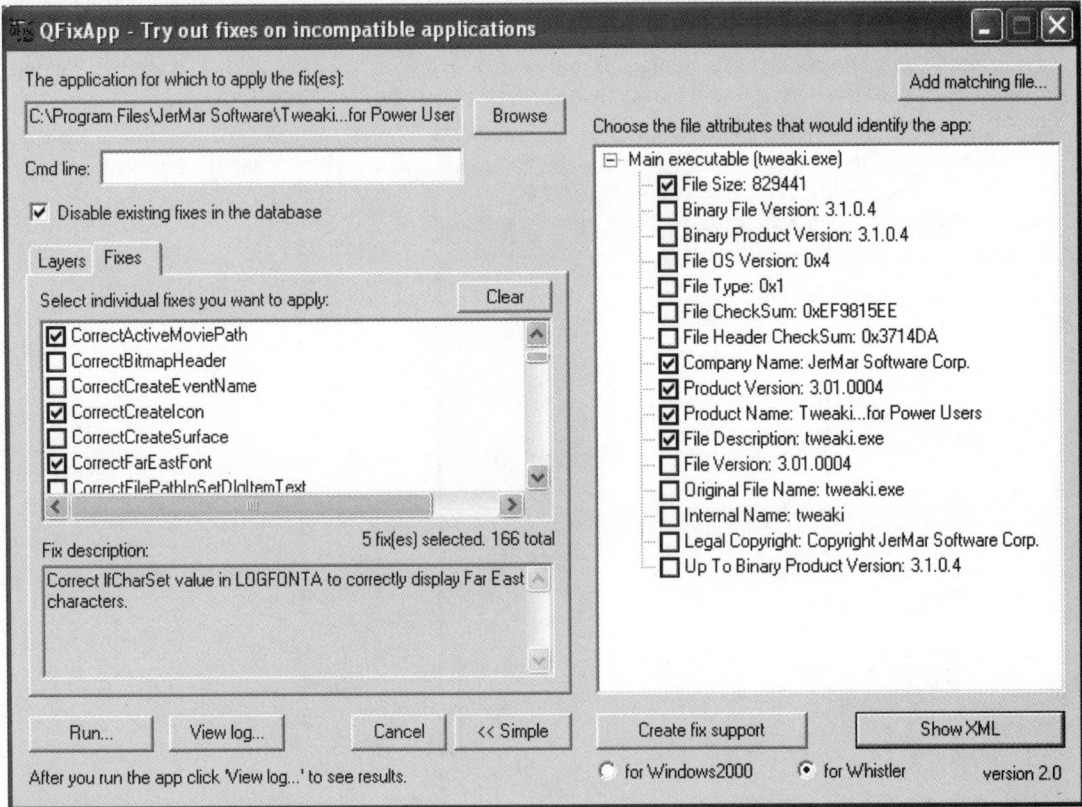

Figure 8-9: Advanced QFixApp options

Once you have identified the fixes you need for the particular application, there's not much else you can do with QFixApp. If you need to deploy the fixes on other Windows XP machines, you can use the Compatibility Administration Tool, which is explored in the next section.

Compatibility Administration Tool

The Compatibility Administration Tool (CompatAdmin.exe) is also a part of the Application Compatibility Toolkit, and as you'll see, performs much of the same functions as QFixApp. CompatAdmin.exe enables you to browse the database of fixes provided for applications in Windows

XP. Then you can assign fixes to those applications as necessary. Once you apply the fixes to the application and the application is in good working order, you can create a package with those fixes and deploy them to other Windows XP computers.

> **TIP:** A handy feature of `CompatAdmin.exe` is the search function. You can search and locate fixed applications both on your local machine and on network drives. As the name suggests, this tool is designed for administrators who have to manage fixed applications in a network environment.

The CompatAdmin tool gives you a window interface, as you can see in Figure 8-10. The left pane lists all of the applications that are supported by fixes in Windows XP. You can select one of the applications and, in the right pane, see the executable file the fix applies to and the actual compatibility fixes applied to this application by default. You also see the file-matching results ensuring that the executable is the correct one for the application.

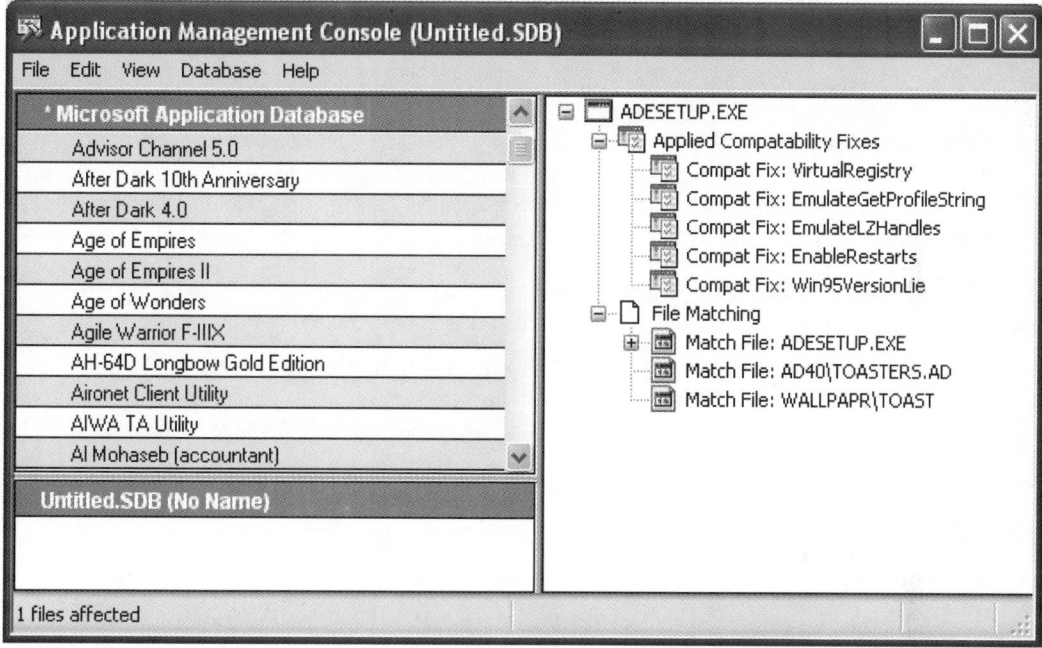

Figure 8-10: CompatAdmin.exe

There are a number of applications to view, and depending on the application, a number of fixes for that application. If you are having a hard time browsing the applications and fixes, you can control how much information is displayed using the View menu. By default, compatibility fixes, compatibility modes, Apphelp entries, and application patches are all displayed. If you just want to see how patches are applied, you can clear the check next to the other items, and the view will be a lot easier to work with.

The interface is rather straightforward, but there are several important actions you can perform with CompatAdmin. The following sections explore what you can do with this tool.

Disabling fixes

Keep in mind that that the application databases provide information about applications Microsoft has determined fixes for and the fixes that should be applied. When a user invokes the Application Compatibility Wizard, a match for that application under the desired Windows version is attempted. However, you may need to change this behavior for a particular application. As was the case with the QFixApp tool, you can use the default fixes assigned by the database and overlaid with the chosen operating system; you can remove them and apply your own; or you can simply add to the existing one. With the CompatAdmin tool, you disable the default database fix for an application, and then use

QFixApp or the CompatAdmin tool to create your own fix. Then, that fix can be run or even deployed. Disabling a fix disables it on the local system and only disables it — there is no deletion — so that you can easily re-enable the fix at a later time. The following steps show you how to disable a fix.

STEPS

Disabling a fix

1. In the Application Compatibility Toolkit, click the Open link next to `CompatAdmin.exe`.
2. In the CompAdmin tool, browse the application list and select the application.
3. In the right pane, right-click the executable (or actually any portion of the fix) and choose Disable Entry. A red exclamation point now appears over the fix.
4. You can re-enable the fix at any time by right-clicking it and choosing Enable Entry.

SECRET: If you disable several entries, you can easily view them all by choosing View ⇨ Show Disabled Entries.

Creating new databases and new fix entries

One of the most powerful options that CompatAdmin brings to the table is that you can create custom databases and custom fixes for the applications as needed. When you first open CompatAdmin, a new database is created for you and appears in the lower-right portion of the screen. By default, this database is named `Untitled.sdb`. You can use the Database menu to rename the database as desired. You can also perform a few additional actions using the database menu that specifically allow you to create custom fixes for your new database, and you can even define your own compatibility mode.

Select the database name in the lower left corner, then click the Database menu. You see the option to Create Application Fix. The following steps show you how to use CompatAdmin to create custom fixes.

STEPS

Creating a fix

1. In the Application Compatibility Toolkit, click the Open link next to `CompatAdmin.exe`.
2. Select the database name in the lower-left corner and choose Database ⇨ Create Application Fix.
3. The "Select method" window appears, as you can see in Figure 8-11. If you choose Apply Compatibility Mode, you simply select the desired executable and assign one of the preconfigured modes, such as Windows 98, 256 colors, and so on. Essentially, this option performs the same actions as using the Program Compatibility Wizard. In order to assign custom fixes to an application, use the Apply specific Compatibility Fix radio button and click Next.
4. Enter a desired name for the fix.
5. Use the Browse button to select the executable you want to apply the fix to.
6. Select the desired fixes in the provided list, shown in Figure 8-12. Note that an explanation for each fix appears in the right window. Click Next after you select all fixes that you want to apply.
7. In the identification window, browse and select the files that identify the application. There is also an Auto-Generate option so the wizard can perform this action for you, which is recommended. Make your selections and click Next.
8. Perform a test run of the application by clicking the provided button, then click Finish when you're done.

Aside from creating custom fixes from this window, you can also create your own compatibility mode. For example, suppose that your environment has several custom applications. You can create a custom fix for those applications by creating your own custom compatibility mode. Then the mode can more easily be applied to the desired applications. The following steps walk you through the creating of a custom compatibility mode.

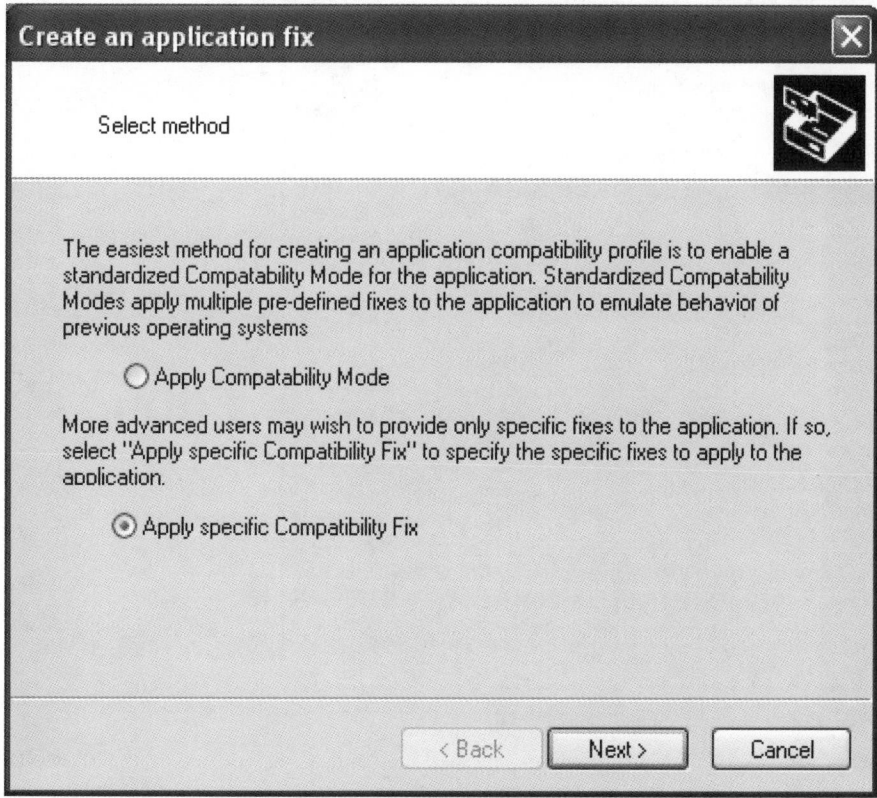

Figure 8-11: Select a method.

STEPS

Creating a custom compatibility mode

1. In the Application Compatibility Toolkit, click the Open link next to CompatAdmin.exe.
2. Select the database name in the lower-left corner and choose Database ⇨ Add Custom Compatibility Mode.
3. In the custom mode window, shown in Figure 8-13, give the mode a name in the box provided, then move any of the fixes you want for the mode to the "Shims and patches" area of the window. If necessary, you can click the Copy Mode button and select one of the existing modes (such as Windows 98, Windows 2000, 256 colors, and so on), then you can modify that mode as desired. Once you are finished, click Done.

TIP: At any time, you can return to the Database menu and edit or delete application fixes that you create or custom compatibility modes.

Deploying custom databases

Once you have created the custom fixes and/or compatibility modes for your custom database, you can then deploy that database to other Windows XP machines. In a sense, this is misleading because the console doesn't actually help you deploy the SDB database file that you created. You save it in the console, then simply copy the SDB database file to the desired Windows XP computers. You can deploy the file using a simple network share, floppy disk, or whatever works best for you.

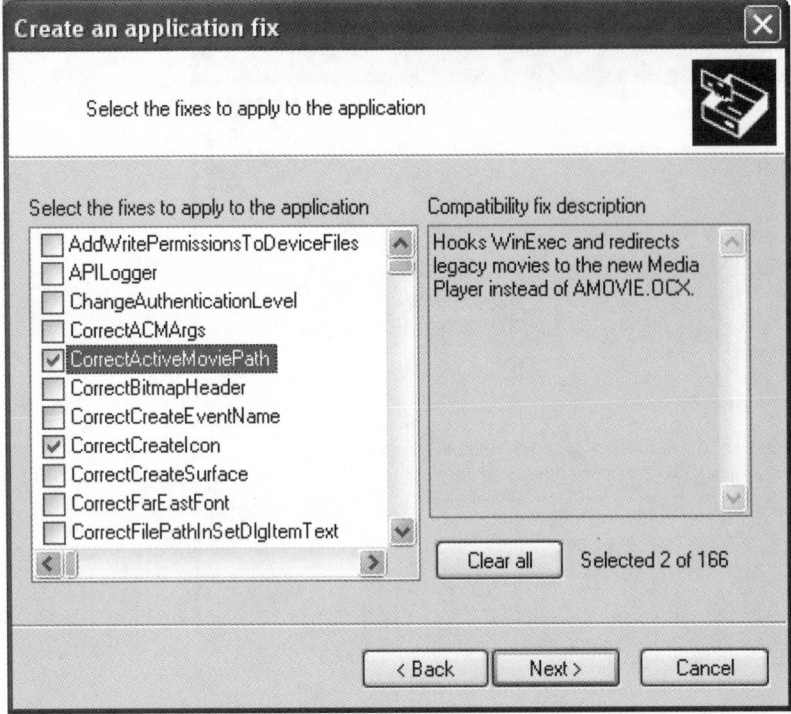

Figure 8-12: Select desired fixes.

The point is that the console doesn't provide a delivery method. Once the file is located on the other XP machines, simply run the SDB file on those machines and Windows XP will register the new database.

Searching for fixed applications

The CompatAdmin tool provides an easy way to search for fixed applications by using the search option on the View menu. Just search for the type of file that you want in the drive or network drive location desired. This tool makes it easy to locate fixed applications on your machine or across network drives.

Managing Applications and Application Performance

With any application, what we all need is for the application to work well on our computers, and this idea includes both functionality and performance. The application compatibility tools and features in Windows XP attempt to make this happen. The idea is that a user can run older (9x) applications on Windows XP without any problems. Of course, this perfect world does not exist, and there is still the possibility that certain applications will not work well or that an application may lock up. The good news is that an application lockup doesn't usually bring the XP system down as it often did in Windows 9x.

One of your best tools for managing applications on your system continues to be Task Manager. In Windows 9x and Me, you could press Ctrl+Alt+Delete and bring up a Close Program window. You have this same option in Windows XP, but instead of a simple window, you see your entire Task Manager, as shown in Figure 8-14.

CROSS-REFERENCE: See Chapters 24 and 25 to learn more about the Task Manager features found in Windows XP.

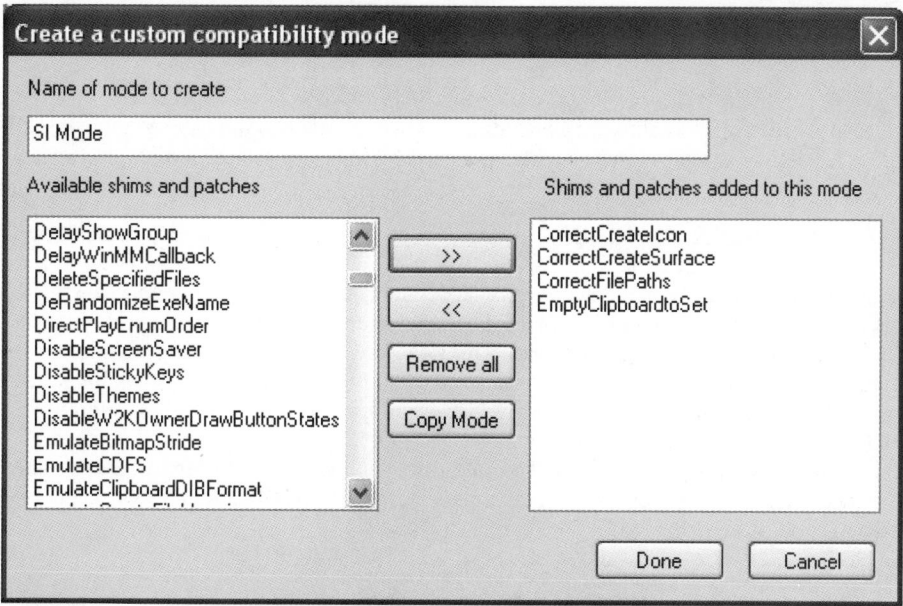

Figure 8-13: Create a custom compatibility mode.

Figure 8-14: Task Manager

You can select any offending application on the Applications tab and click End Task to halt it. Notice that if there is a problem with the application, its status will say Not Responding. Also, notice at the bottom of the window that you can see the CPU usage percentage, which might also be of help to you.

Speaking of performance, you can also click the Performance tab and see a bar and chart graphic of CPU and memory usage. This setting can also tell you whether an application is hogging all of your system cycles.

Another option in System Properties can be helpful in terms of application performance and management. First, access System Properties by choosing Start ⇨ Control Panel ⇨ System. On the Advanced tab, click the Settings button under Performance, then click the Advanced tab. As you can see in Figure 8-15, the default behavior is for the operating system to favor application performance over system performance. This means that if an application is running, it is favored for CPU and RAM usage over system processes that may be running at the same time. These settings are configured by default, and you leave them that way to get the best performance from your programs. However, in some instances, it is best to optimize performance for background services and system cache. For example, if your Windows XP computer functions as a Web server on an intranet, you need the most power and resources to support that system service — not an application. However, under most circumstances, the Programs radio button selections are what you need and should keep enabled.

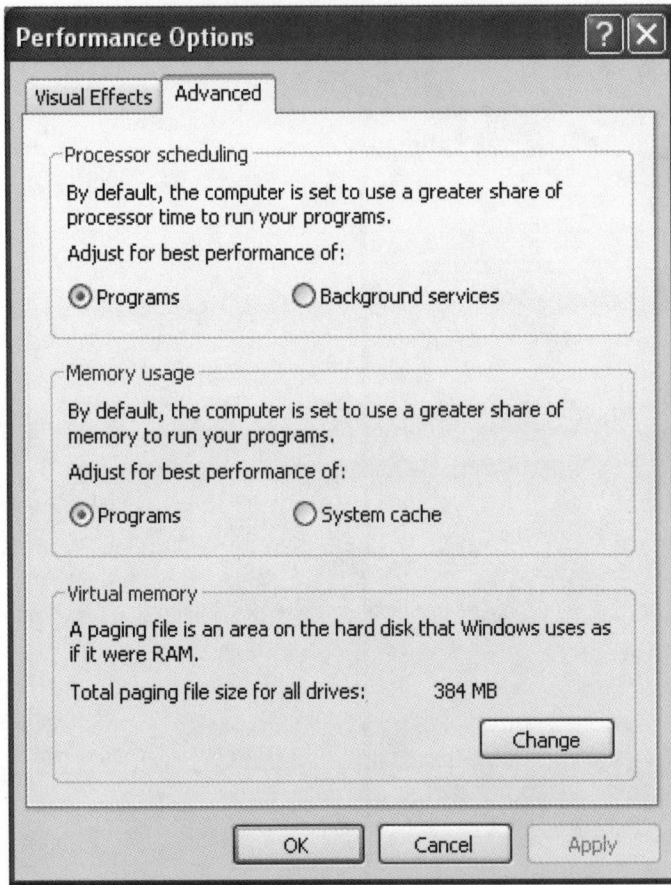

Figure 8-15: Performance Options — keep the Programs options selected.

As a general rule, Windows XP handles applications well, and you should be problem free. To make the best of application usage and performance, however, keep in mind the following guidelines:

♦ Make sure your system has the hardware resources necessary for the application you want to run. Having enough physical RAM installed is critical, and the quality of your video card may affect some applications.

♦ For best application performance, close all programs that you do not need at the moment. Use Task Manager to see what programs might be running the background. The more programs you close, the more system resources are available to the desired application.

♦ Common background processes, such as printing, consume system resources and have a negative effect on application performance. Try not to have any background processes running when you are using resource-intensive applications.

♦ Check the application's documentation for tips about performance and usability issues. Often manufacturers identify issues that you can readily address on your system.

♦ You may be able to use third-party tools to boost performance for your application. Check the manufacturer's Web site or search the Internet for possible options.

Summary

In this chapter, you explored system components and software management. Windows XP facilitates system component management by providing an easy interface through which you can add and remove Windows components as needed. Typically, you don't need to use this interface because most everything you need in Windows XP is already available. Windows XP supports the easy addition and removal of applications through interface tools, and the new compatibility features make application support the richest yet. In summary . . .

♦ Use Add/Remove Programs, Add/Remove Windows Components to manage system components.

♦ You can easily install applications using Add/Remove Programs or the program's setup file.

♦ You can remove programs in the same manner with Add/Remove Programs or the program's uninstall feature.

♦ Windows XP supports application compatibility with previous versions of Windows by allowing Windows XP to emulate the environment of a previous Windows version.

♦ Windows XP supports the management of application compatibility through the Application Compatibility Toolkit, which is downloadable from `http://msdn.microsoft.com`.

♦ Use Task Manager and system properties to manage applications and boost application performance on your Windows XP computer.

Chapter 9

Managing Media

In This Chapter

Windows Me provided vast improvements in media management and development over previous versions of Windows. You found the new Media Player 7, which was a tremendous improvement over previous versions of Media Player. Windows Me also introduced Windows Movie Maker, a new video editing tool. These tools are alive and well in Windows XP and can meet most of your digital media needs. In this chapter, you explore . . .

♦ Using digital media in Windows XP

♦ Using Windows Media Player

♦ Using Movie Maker

Digital Media in Windows XP

Digital media is certainly nothing new in Windows operating systems. You've had the ability to open picture files, listen to music, and view video clips for several generations of Windows. Windows XP, though, is the most digital media–aware operating system Microsoft has produced to date. Windows XP is able to read media types and associate programs with various types of digital media. Picture and digital camera management works better than ever before because Windows can associate file types with hardware — in other words, Windows XP knows what file format you are working with instead of being a dumb operating system that simply responds to your commands.

You're also familiar with the subfolders found under My Documents, such as My Music, My Pictures, and My Videos. As you are working with different digital media file types, Windows XP recognizes and identifies those file types and then prompts you to save them in one of these default media folders (which you can do or not do). Using the default Windows XP theme, you can open one of these media folders and view/hear the media in that folder or through Windows Media Player. The Tasks action box in the left pane presents you with actions related to that particular kind of media. For example, as you can see in Figure 9-1, the My Pictures folder enables you to view your pictures as a slide show, order prints online, or print the pictures. Each media folder has its own tasks relevant to the media.

Of course, all of these features make new users' work with Windows XP easier and more intuitive. For the experienced user, these features are nice but not really necessary. The best thing about the XP theme view is that you can readily see full images of your pictures and a sample shot from a video clip by simply opening the folder rather than having to use those aggravating little thumbnail views found in Windows 9x, 2000, and Me. You can, of course, change views and customize the media folders in a way that is pleasing to you using the View menu.

Aside from using third-party programs and media hardware to manage media on Windows XP, you are provided with two standard tools — Windows Media Player and Windows Movie Maker. The remainder of this chapter explores these two tools.

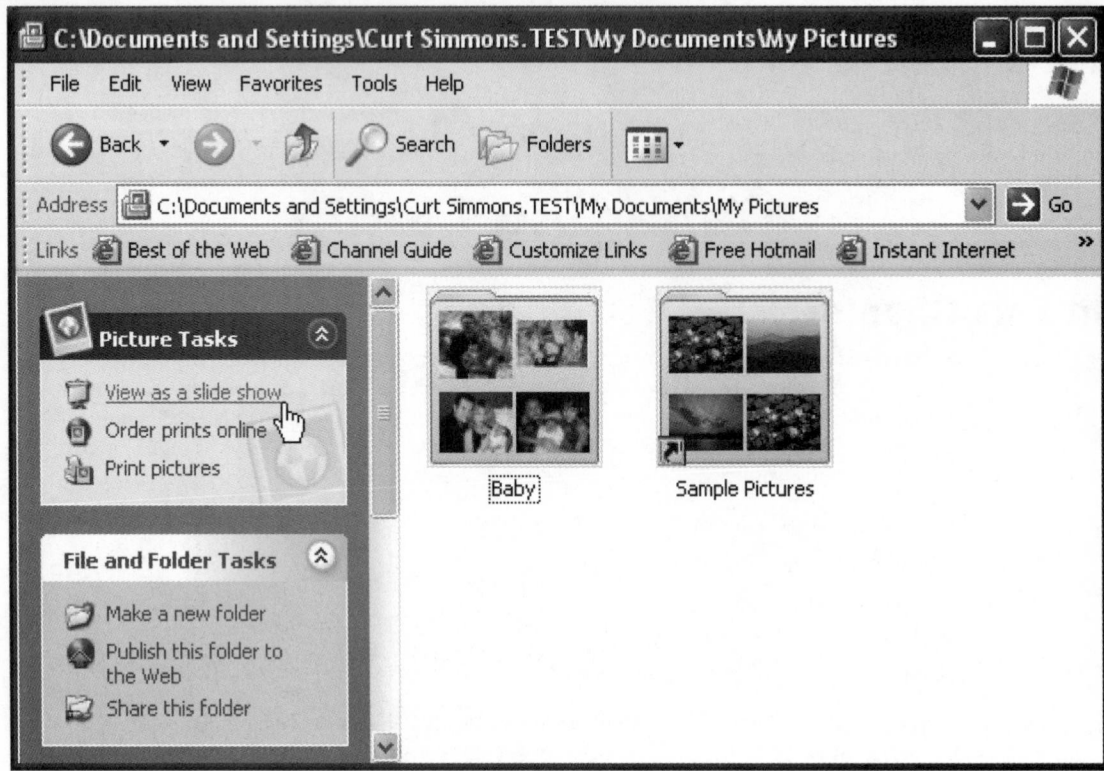

Figure 9-1: Media folders contain specific tasks for that media.

Windows Media Player

Windows Media Player is just that — a tool you can use to play digital media and organize it to meet your needs. As I mentioned, Media Player has seen a lot of improvements during the past couple of years, and it has become a very useful (yet sometimes aggravating) product capable making your media experience more enjoyable and productive. You explore those features in this section, but before getting started, you should open up Media Player and take a look at the default interface if you are not familiar with the product (if you are from NT/2000 land, this may be your first look).

The default Windows Media Player interface uses a Windows XP console view. Regardless of the view (or skin) you choose to use (explored later), the basic functionality of Media Player always remains the same. In many ways, Media Player functions like the MMC. The left pane of the Media Player contains different categories that do different jobs, and the main window displays what you are currently doing. The Now Playing window, as you can see in Figure 9-2, simply shows what is going on at the moment (a music CD in this case). The tracks are displayed, and a graphic visualization dances in the middle of the window (for no other purpose than entertainment). There are a number of button controls, such as show equalizer, turn shuffle on, hide playlist, stop, start, forward, reverse, and related control settings. Just hover your mouse over a button, and an explanation appears.

You also see a Skin Chooser button option that enables you to switch to skin mode. If you click this button, the current skin selected appears, as shown in Figure 9-3. A *skin* is simply an interface overlay that gives Media Player a different look. Skins vary from the tame to the wild, and you have a chance to explore those in more detail later in this chapter.

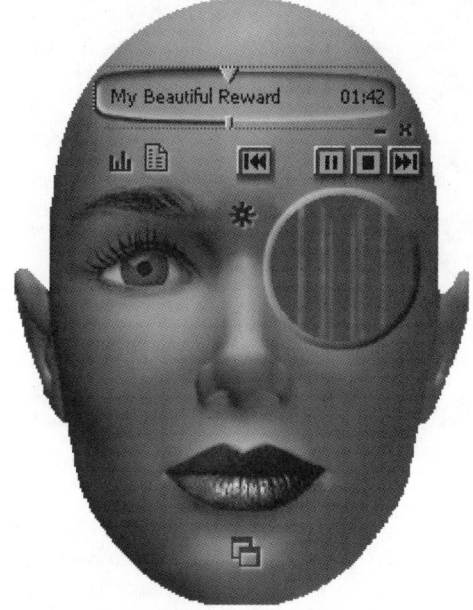

Figure 9-2: Media Player default interface

Figure 9-3: Skin Mode

The Now Playing area presents whatever media you are playing at the moment, whether it is music, a video, or even pictures. The following sections dig you deeper into Windows Media Player, showing you more features and configuration options.

> **SECRET:** Although Windows Media Player can display pictures, it displays only basic Internet types, such as JPEG and GIF files. It does not display all picture file types, such as TIFF. You're better off viewing pictures with Paint or Imaging and leaving Media Player to handle audio and video.

Using the Media Guide

The Media Guide, which sounds really helpful, is basically just a Web site full of media you can download and play on Windows Media Player. It might be better labeled "Media Advertisement." Media Guide connects you to www.windowsmedia.com, where you can check out a number of different music and video categories and find the latest movie trailers. As you can see in Figure 9-4, all you are doing here is accessing a Web site via Media Player and opening files on the site with Media Player. Of course, you can to browse the Web site with IE or Netscape, and if you want to open a file while using your browser, Windows Media Player will automatically open and play the file for you.

Figure 9-4: Windows Media Guide at WindowsMedia.com

Copying music from a CD

If you click the "Copy from CD" option in the left windowpane, you can select any of the desired tracks on the current CD playing and copy those tracks to the My Music folder. The purpose of the copy feature is to enable you to play the tracks you like directly from your computer without having to have the music

CD. You can also combine tracks from different CDs and create a playlist, which you'll explore a little later in this chapter.

As you can see in Figure 9-5, the tracks from the current CD are displayed in the Copy from CD window. Select the tracks you want to copy so that a check mark is beside them, and then click the Copy button. You also see the option Get Names, which retrieves the album and song names from the Internet, and the Album Details button, which gives you more information, including reviews, about the album. You must also be connected to the Internet to use this feature.

SECRET: Although copying a bunch of music to your computer sounds great, the Windows Media Player documentation does not make clear that under the default copy options, a lot of disk space will be consumed. For example, a typical song from a CD may take around 2MB of disk space. As you can see, you can easily consume about 20MB of hard drive space just by copying an entire CD. You may be fine with this if you have a lot of disk space; just keep in mind that media files are not small in terms of megabyte consumption.

Figure 9-5: Copy from CD window, copying in progress

Now you may wonder, how is all of this copying business legal? When you copy a song from a CD to your computer, Windows Media Player attaches a license to the song by default. This means that you are licensed to play the song on your PC, but you cannot send it to someone else or copy the song on someone else's computer — it is for your use alone. When you click the Copy button, a window appears telling you about the licensing feature. At this point, you have the option to turn licensing off, but the window, of course, tells you that it is illegal to send the file to someone else, so you are on your own in terms of copyright infringement. Of course, Windows Media Player has no idea whether the CD you are copying from actually belongs to you, but the idea is that you cannot legally copy music from a CD to your computer and then distribute that music to others.

Legalities now aside, Media Player does give you more control over the copy functions than it might readily seem. If you choose Tools ⇨ Options and then click the Copy Music tab, shown in Figure 9-6, you see some configuration actions you can take to copy music the way you'd like.

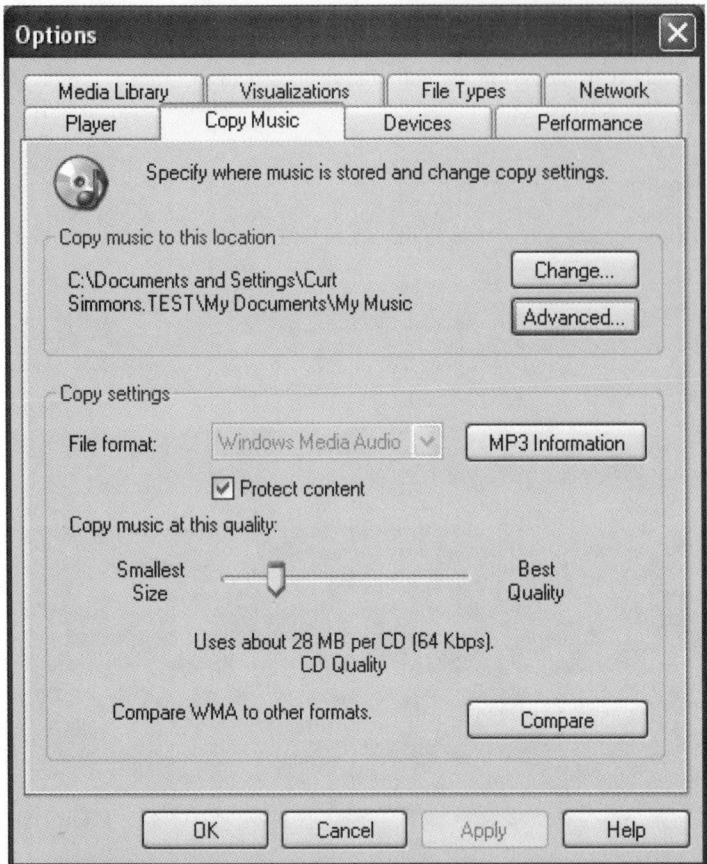

Figure 9-6: Copy Music tab of Media Player Options

The following list points out the actions you can take in each section of this Copy Music tab:

♦ **Copy music to this location** — By default, all music is copied to the My Music folder, but you can change this setting by clicking the Change button. Simply select a new location in the dialog box that appears, and you can even make a new folder from here. If you click the Advanced button, the File Name Options window appears, as shown in Figure 9-7. This window enables you to create a file naming convention for music you copy. By default, the track number and song title are used for the naming convention, but you can include other items, such as artist, album, genre, and bit rate. You can even define the separator value between each item as a space, dash, dot, or underline. Make any desired selections here and click OK.

♦ **Copy settings** — You see that Windows Media Audio (WMA) is the default audio format used for copying content. If you want to copy using MP3, you can click the MP3 Information button to learn more about MP3 from the Internet and how you can option third-party vendor MP3 solutions. Finally, you see the quality settings that determine how many megabytes are consumed when copying takes place. As you can see in Figure 9-6, the default quality is on the lower end, but still consumes 20–30MB per CD. The best quality consumes about 96MB per CD. Ideally, you want to use the best quality you can manage. If you have a huge hard drive with gigabytes of free space, use the highest quality you want. However, if you don't have that kind of space to spare, you need to strike a balance between quality and storage room.

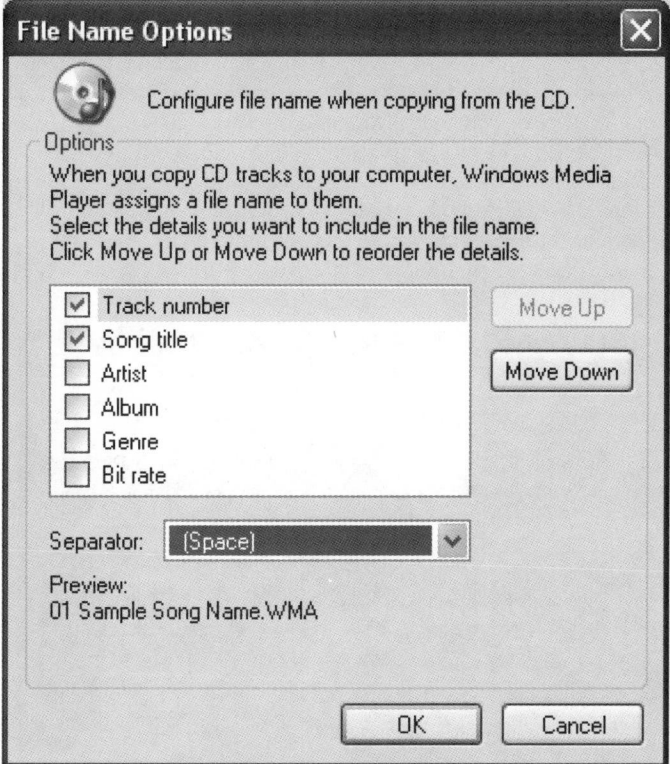

Figure 9-7: File Name Options

TIP: Make sure you delete any music files no longer in use so you can keep as much free disk space available as possible. If you are using a lot of media, it can easily pile up. So, good housekeeping is a must.

While I'm on the subject of copying CD music, I want to spend a bit more time looking at licensing and license management. As I mentioned, a license is created for you when you copy a song from an audio CD to your computer. The license file is generated using information from the CD, and the license determines what you can do with the copied file. Typically, you can play the file only on your computer, but some licenses will allow you copy the file to a portable device. Either way, Windows Media Player will not play a copied song without the proper license that allows you to play it. The same is true for downloaded music. Windows Media Player attempts to acquire a license for you automatically, but there may be fees associated with the license, depending on the content provider. For example, you may be able to download a song for small fee, which provides you with the license to play the song on your computer.

Fortunately Windows Media Player handles licenses for you, but it is recommended that you back up your licenses so that they can be restored in the event of a crash or other problem. If the license is lost for your current songs, Windows Media Player will not play the songs. You can manage the licenses by choosing Tools ⇨ License Management. This presents you with a simple window where you can select a different storage location for your licenses (which is My Documents by default). When you back up your licenses, they are backed up in the current folder in which they are stored. You can then copy the backup file to some other media, such as a floppy or Zip disk. In the event that you need to restore your licenses, Internet access is required because the restore process uses a unique identifier for your computer with a Microsoft service to complete the restore operation. You'll need your backup file, of course, to complete the operation, and you must have the Allow Internet sites to uniquely identify your Player check box option enabled on the Player tab.

Media Library

The Media Library keeps track of the media you use with Media Player. Using the Media Library, you can recall music and videos you've played by title, artist, and genre, and you can even create customized playlists, which is great for those of us who like one or two songs from ten different CDs. Because the Media Library has a tendency to grow over time, it includes a search function to help you find what you are looking for. As you can see in Figure 9-8, the Media Library is organized in a tree structure in the left pane with a display window in the right pane. You can expand any category you want and directly play the items listed there by double-clicking them or right-clicking them and choosing Play. The Media Library also keeps items that you delete in the Deleted Items folder in case you need to retrieve them later.

Figure 9-8: Media Library

The most compelling feature of the Media Library is the ability to create playlists. A *playlist* is simply a collection of media that you put together for Media Player to run. This typically involves audio CD content, but it can be a mixture of songs and videos if you like. The idea is to create a playlist from items that you like so that Media Player can play all of them for you without having to jump from CD to CD. Of course, you'll need to copy that media to your hard drive to use the feature.

Creating a playlist is easy, and playlists are easy to manage. The following steps show you how.

STEPS

Creating a playlist

1. In the Media Library, click the "New playlist" button.

2. Provide a descriptive name for the playlist and click OK. The new playlist now appears under My Playlists.

3. Select the items that you want to add from the Media Library so that they appear in the right pane and then select the individual song or video and click the "Add to playlist" button. Select the desired playlist from the menu that appears.

NOTE: Items must be listed in the Media Library before they can be added to a playlist.

4. Continue this process until you finalize your playlist.

Once the playlist is complete, you can reorganize it by selecting the playlist in the left pane and then individually right-clicking items and choosing Move up or Move down. In the same manner, you can delete items from the playlist.

You can also import and export playlists using the options on the File menu. When you export a playlist to a file, it is saved as a Media Playlist, which can then be imported to another computer using Windows Media Player. Some Web sites also provide playlists that you can download and import using the Import option on the File menu.

TIP: When importing a playlist from a Web page, you must download the playlist first and then use the import feature. You cannot directly import a playlist over the Internet.

SECRET: The documentation on Media Player doesn't make this explicitly clear, but a playlist simply provides an order for items you select in your Media Library. If you import a playlist, you must have those items in your Media Library for the imported playlist to work, and of course, the issue of licensing comes into play once again. The playlist is an organization method — not a way of moving AV files from one PC to the next.

Radio Tuner

The Radio Tuner enables you to listen to radio stations on the Internet — maybe. One of the most common support complaints from new users of Internet radio is that it is choppy and of poor quality. The answer here is simple: if you are using a modem for Internet connectivity, Internet radio does not work well. Although Media Player uses buffering technologies to attempt to correct the problem, the bandwidth is simply not there to produce uninterrupted play. You may experience periods of success, but overall a modem is just too slow. Internet radio works great, however, with broadband connections.

When you click the Radio Tuner option, you are connected to the Internet, and the default Radio Tuner interface appears, as you can see in Figure 9-9. In the left pane, you see featured stations already configured for you, a place where you can add your own stations for easy access, and a list of recently played stations. In the right pane, you can find stations by category, search for them, or access a number of Today's Hits stations. You can easily add any station you find to your My Stations by clicking the radio link provided so that it can be accessed from your list later. The Radio Tuner interface is very intuitive and easy. Spend about five minutes with it, and you'll be a pro.

Figure 9-9: Radio Tuner

Copying to CD or devices

The Copy to CD or Device option provides a simple interface that allows you to select media on your computer and copy it to a CD-RW drive or another storage device, such as a Zip disk. The trick here is that you must have the proper license to copy an item to a device before it will work. So, if you thought you could copy music from a CD and then burn your own CD, guess again. If you want to create custom listening CDs, you can use your CD-RW documentation and perform this action outside of Windows Media Player altogether (which may be easier, but not necessarily legal).

Customizing Media Player

You can customize Media Player in a number of specific ways to meet your needs. The following sections explore your customization options.

Skin Chooser

As I mention earlier in this chapter, you can apply a number of skins to Media Player, which essentially give it an interface overlay so that it looks different. You retain the same functionality using skins, and you can easily switch back to the Full Mode view by clicking the Full Mode button. To change the skin, click the Skin Chooser option in the left pane. This presents you with a list of included skins. When you select a skin, you can see what it looks like in the right pane, shown in Figure 9-10.

Figure 9-10: Skin Chooser

Clicking the More Skins button takes you to www.windowsmedia.com/mg/skins.asp, where you can view a big list of skins that you can download directly from the Web site to Windows Media Player. The downloaded skins appear in the Skin Chooser, where you can begin using them.

TIP: You can also download other skins from third-party Web sites. Check out www.skinz.org.

Default player options

Windows Media Player has some basic settings that are configured on the Tools ⇨ Options, General tab. You can change these settings to meet your needs, of course. The following list outlines the check box options you see on this tab.

- ◆ **Automatic Updates** — Media Player can automatically update itself once a day, once a week, or monthly. This feature works well if you have an always-on Internet connection. The once a month setting is selected by default.

- ◆ **Internet Settings** — By default, both the Allow Internet sites to uniquely identify your Player and Acquire licenses automatically options are selected. You don't have to use these, but you will lose some automatic functionality on the Internet if you do.

- ◆ **Player Settings** — You have a number of self-explanatory settings here, which are as follows:

  - Start player in Media Guide (default)

  - Display on top when in skin mode

  - Display anchor window when in skin mode (default)

- Allow screen saver during playback
- Add items to Media Library when played (not selected by default, but this one is good to use)

Devices

The Devices tab lists the devices on your computer that can hold media, such as your CD-ROM drive, Zip drive, and any related removable media drives on your computer. If you select the drive in the provided dialog box and click Properties, you can adjust some basic settings for the drive, as shown in Figure 9-11. By default, devices are configured for digital playback without using error correction. If you are having problems reading from a particular piece of media, you can change this setting and try analog and error correction. Both of these settings cause performance degradation, so don't use them unless you are having problems.

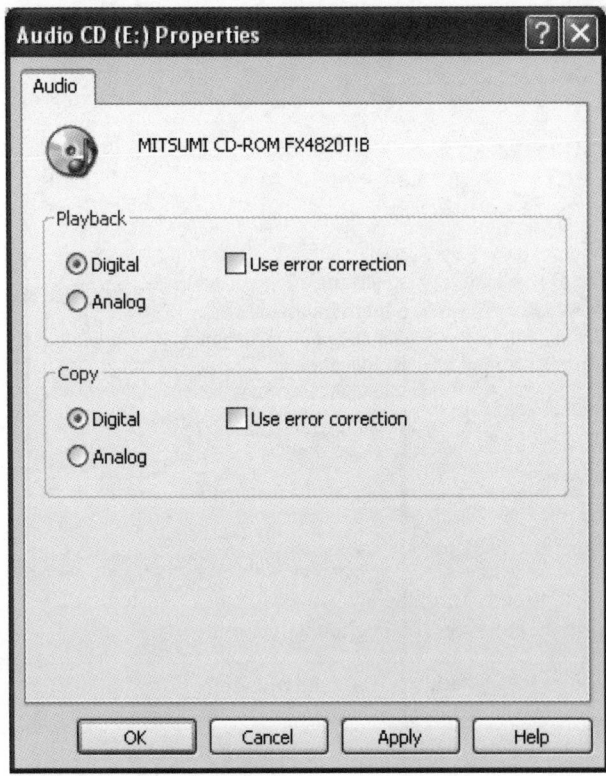

Figure 9-11: Device Properties

Performance

The Performance tab lists performance options for the Media Player. You have categories for Connection Speed, Network Buffering, and Video Acceleration. Under most circumstances, the default selections are the best settings.

Windows Media Player automatically detects the connection speed by default. The only reason to change the connection speed to manual is if you seem to be having problems with transmission. You might try a manual setting fixed slightly lower than your modem capability to resolve the transmission problem.

Under Network Buffering, Windows Media Player uses default buffering by default. You can attempt to use a custom setting that increases or slows buffer speed to tweak performance, but you'll typically see the best results with the default setting.

Under Video Acceleration, the slider bar is set to full by default and all advanced options are selected, with the exception of the full-screen mode switch. These settings take full advantage of your video card and should not be changed unless your system is not able to keep up with the settings, in which case they can be lowered. Such a lowering will degrade performance.

Media Library

The Media Library tab enables you to set rights to media in your media library. By default, all applications on your computer have read-only access to media, while Internet sites have no access. Also by default, music that you purchase and download over the Internet is automatically added to the Media Library. You can change these settings in order to restrict Media Player's Internet usage for security purposes, or in the case of using Media Player behind a corporate firewall where Internet downloads may not be allowed.

Visualizations

Windows Media Player gives you a list of visualizations you can use when playing audio music. On the Visualizations tab, you can see the current collection. You can add new visualizations by downloading them from the www.windowsmedia.com Web site by clicking the Add button (this works basically the same way as skin download). Also, you can tweak the look of visualizations by selecting the one you want and clicking the Properties button.

If you click the Properties button, you see a screen size and buffer size setting option for the visualization, as shown in Figure 9-12. You experiment with these settings by adjusting them. If you don't like what you see, return to this Properties page and change them back or try another setting.

TIP: Not all of the visualizations are adjustable. For the ones that aren't, Media Player doesn't present a Properties sheet.

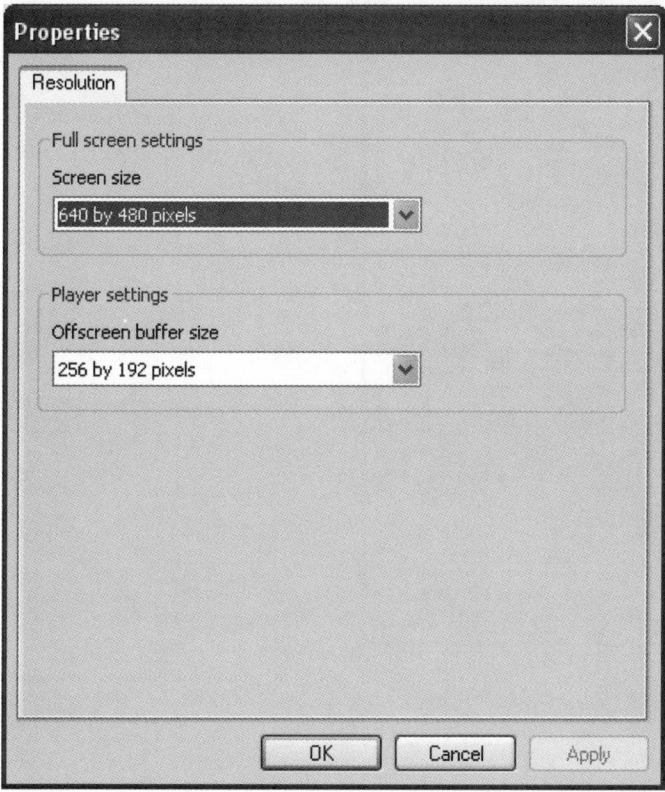

Figure 9-12: Visualizations Properties

SECRET: You cannot delete any default visualizations that ship with Windows Media Player. You can, however, select and delete the ones you download.

File Types

The File Types tab lists the file types that can be read by Windows Media Player. All of these are selected by default, and deselecting them reduces the types of media that Windows Media Player can play. I recommend that you leave all of the file types selected.

Network

If you are connecting to the Internet through a network, such as a proxy server on a corporate network, you may need some additional configuration settings in order for Media Player to work. The Network tab, shown in Figure 9-13, enables you to choose the protocols to use with Media Player and configure proxy settings.

TIP: If you use Media Player on a corporate network that may be protected by a firewall/proxy server, you need to check with your network administrator before changing any of these settings. Some networks may restrict the protocol that can be used, or you may need to configure proxy settings to reroute Media Player through a proxy server

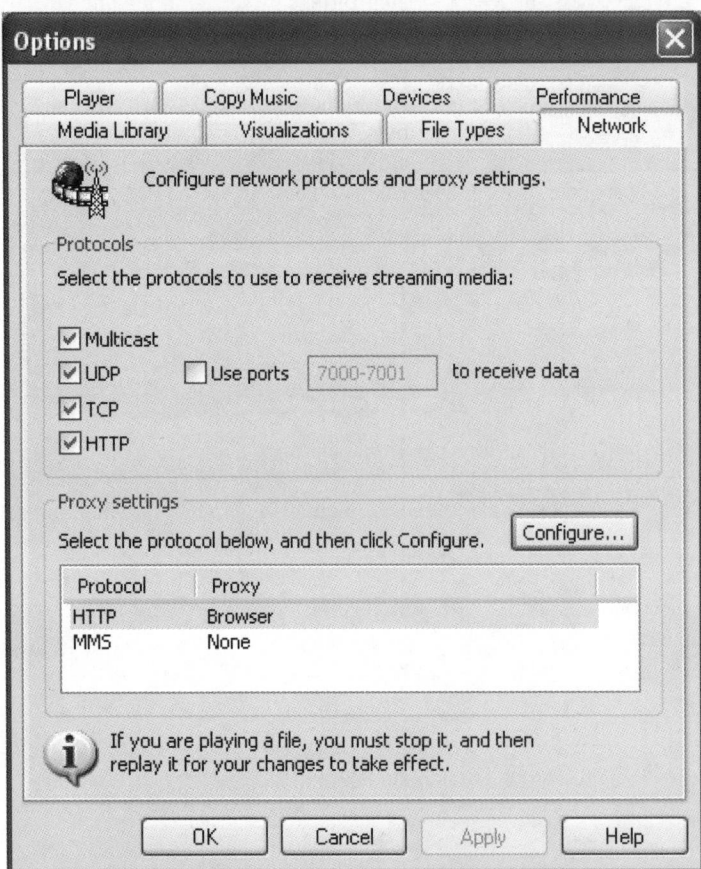

Figure 9-13: Network settings

Windows Movie Maker

Windows Movie Maker is a video-editing tool that enables you to collect either digital or analog video clips and edit them together. Using Movie Maker, you can trim video clips, combine them, provide background music, insert title pages and slides, provide narration, and perform a number of editorial features.

Movie Maker is by far not the best video editor available. If you are serious about video editing, you should consider a software package that will run on Windows XP. Movie Maker is free, though, and included with your operating system, so you can't expect it to be as good as the video editing software packages that often run in excess of $500.

Movie Maker gives you basic video editing functionality and overall is quite easy and intuitive to use. My biggest complaint about Movie Maker is that it generates only WMV (Windows Movie Maker) files; movies generated on Movie Maker run only in Movie Maker or Windows Media Player. In other words, you can't create a movie clip and save it as an MPEG or RAM file so that virtually anyone on the Internet can read it. That's a real drag and forces any sharing that you do to be limited to people using Windows. The Movie Maker documentation makes this sound like a feature, but in fact, it is restrictive. Most other video editing software packages enable you to save your movies in a variety of standard formats supported on any platform, and Movie Maker needs to do the same.

Okay, enough with the griping. To use Windows Movie Maker, you have to get the video clips you want to edit into Movie Maker. I'm using the term *video clip* here to refer to the section of video from your camcorder that you want to put into Movie Maker for editing. Movie Maker also uses the term clip to refer to segment of video that you work with. As you put video into Movie Maker, Movie Maker divides the video into clips of videos so that you can easily work with them. Movie Maker attempts to detect when a scene changes and to create a clip at the time so you have organized pieces of video you can work with.

To get video from a source into Movie Maker, you have a few different options. First, if you use a digital camcorder, you can connect it to your PC and use the Movie Maker's Record feature to record the video. The same is true for analog camcorders or VCRs. Your computer must be outfitted with a capture device of some kind, such as a video card that support S/V jacks like those found on camcorders and VCRs (these kinds of video cards are available at your local computer store for around $150 and up).

TIP: Depending on your device and video card, getting Movie Maker to record from your camera or VCR can be a frustrating experience. See the Movie Maker help files for a number of known issues with various cameras and video cards.

You can choose to record both video and narration, or you can record only video or narration. This feature is good if you want to leave off the movie's dialogue to be replaced with your own narration. When you set up your recording session, just click the Record button when you are ready. You'll see a record window that enables you to choose low, medium, high, or other quality. The medium quality is selected by default, but you can change this setting to meet your needs. Of course, the high quality requires more disk space.

SECRET: If you are having problems recording your video, you can record it using another piece of video editing software and save it in a common file format (such as MPEG). Then you can import it into Movie Maker using the Import feature on the File menu.

The Movie Maker interface

When you first open Movie Maker, which is available in Start ⇨ All Programs ⇨ Accessories, you see right away that the basic Explorer-type interface is used, shown in Figure 9-14.

Figure 9-14: Windows Movie Maker

The Movie Maker interface contains several panes and standard toolbar and menu features. In the very left pane, you see the Collections area. A *collection* is a current work area that contains clips of videos that you have recorded/imported. Collections are saved by Windows Movie Maker so you can continue working with the clips until you create your actual movie.

The next section of the window shows the location of the clips that Windows Movie Maker generates as you record or import video. Movie Maker attempts to divide clips when it senses a change in the video (such as a change from one scene to the next).

SECRET: If you don't want Movie Maker to divide your video stream into clips, choose View ⇨ Options and clear the automatically create clips check box.

The next area of the interface is the preview area where the video is played. You have standard start, stop, pause, fast-forward, rewind, and split-clips buttons here.

The bottom portion of the interface provides you with a clip assembly area, where you drag and drop clips, create transitions, and record narrations. When you finish, you can save the movie. The following sections show you how to perform the various tasks leading to movie creation.

Trimming clips

You can think of the clips in your video area as raw pieces of divided footage. That raw footage may have interesting spots as well as dull spots. Consider my personal example: My wife and I had a baby a few months before writing this book. Making sure I didn't miss anything, I recorded almost everything that happened that day. Watching the video later, we found a lot of boring sections that I wish I could remove. No problem. Using Windows Movie Maker, I simply dumped the video into Movie Maker, trimmed out the parts I did not want, reassembled the good pieces, and then recorded it back to my camcorder. Now, I am left with a video that is interesting and fun to watch.

Before you start trimming clips, you may want to use the Split Clip button on the preview window. If you have a long clip that you need to break into two pieces so that it is easier to work with, simply play the clip and click the Split Clip button where you want to break it. Movie Maker then breaks the clip apart and puts the two clips into the clip window. In the same manner, you can combine two clips if it makes your work easier. Select the first clip, then hold down the Shift key while selecting the second clip. Then, choose Clip ⇨ Combine.

When you are ready to trim a clip, there is one important item that you need to remember. When you trim a clip, you set a beginning and ending trim point. Everything included in the beginning and ending trim point is kept, and everything outside of the trim points is discarded (it's easy to get the concept confused).

> **WARNING:** Keep in mind that clip segments that are trimmed and discarded cannot be retrieved without re-importing them into Movie Maker from the source.

When you are ready to trim a clip, just follow these steps.

STEPS

Trimming a clip

1. In the clip window, drag the clip that you want to trim to the Storyboard/Timeline at the bottom of the window.

2. Select the clip on the Storyboard/Timeline so that the clip appears in the display area.

3. Click Play on the menu and while the clip is playing, choose Clip ⇨ Set Start Trim Point and Clip ⇨ Set End Trim Point at the appropriate locations on the clip.

4. If you like, you can move the start and end trim points automatically by clicking the Timeline button in the lower workspace area. Then, move the trim points as desired and shown in Figure 9-15.

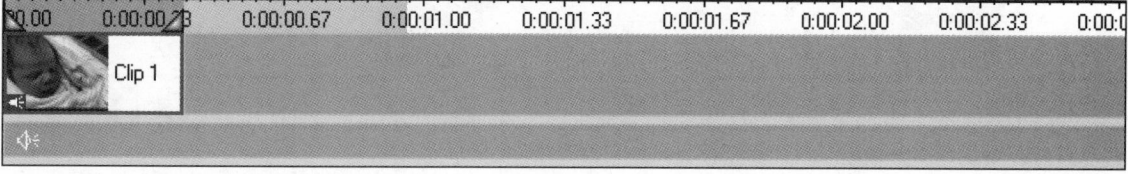

Figure 9-15: Manually set start and end trim points.

Assembling clips

Once you have trimmed the clips that you want to use, your next task is to assemble them on the Storyboard. Click the Storyboard icon on the workspace area and then drag and drop the clips you want to the Storyboard in the order that you want them to be displayed from left to right, shown in Figure 9-16.

Figure 9-16: Assemble clips

Keep in mind that the clips that you place on the storyboard can be video clips, but they can also be pictures. You can import most major picture file formats (JPEG, BMP, GIF, TIFF, and so on) into Movie Maker and mix them into the movie.

TIP: The PNG format is not supported.

You can also create slides in PowerPoint or another application and import those. Essentially, any standard picture type can be imported and displayed. This makes it easy for to you to mix video and still shots, along with title pages or picture/title page combinations.

NOTE: Specifically, Windows Movie Maker supports the following file formats: MPEG, MPG, V1V, MP2, MPA, MPE, ASF, AVI, WMV, WAV, SND, AU, AIF, AIFC, AIFF, WMA, MP3, BMP, JPEG, JPE, JFIF, GIF, DIB.

Creating transitions between clips

If you place your clips on the storyboard and then save your movie, you'll have the clips like you want them, but the transitions between them will be choppy. You can easily create transitions that fade into each other, giving your video a professional feel, by using the Timeline feature.

Click the Timeline button, which changes the Storyboard view to Timeline, and follow these steps.

STEPS

Creating transitions

1. In Timeline view, click the Magnify button on the left of the window so you can more easily see the two clips you want to splice with a seamless transition. You can see the first clip and the amount of time that passes until the second clip begins. Notice the second values above the picture icons, shown in Figure 9-17.

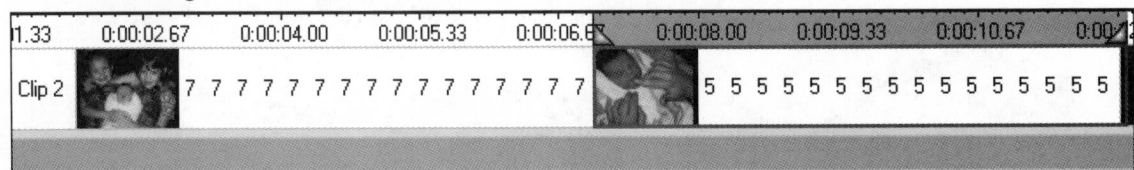

Figure 9-17: Clip duration

2. Click the second clip so that you see the trim marks above the picture. Then drag the left trim clip back over the previous clip. The covered area will take on a grayed-out appearance, as you can see in Figure 9-18. The amount of overlap you create will be a blended fade transition. Three seconds is typically long enough.

3. Repeat this process with other the remaining clips as desired.

TIP: If you make a mistake when working on your storyboard, you can easily drag clips off the storyboard or drag new clips onto the storyboard. You can even drag a new clip in between two existing clips on the storyboard.

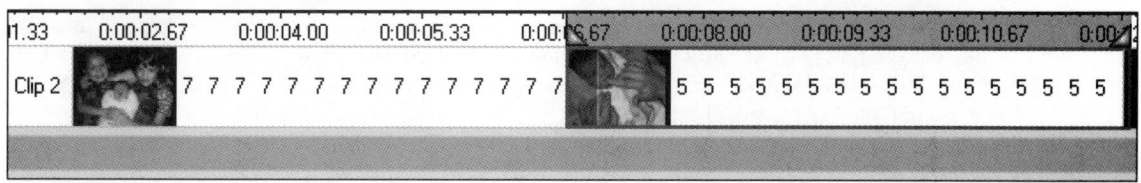

Figure 9-18: Transition effect

4. When you finish, choose Play ⇨ Play Entire Storyboard/Timeline to see how the transitions work. You can then readjust them as desired.

> **SECRET:** By default, still shots are given 5 seconds on the timeline. You can adjust the time to a shorter value by trimming the time while in Timeline View. If you want to standardize a time for all still shots (such as 10 seconds), choose View ⇨ Options and then change the imported photo duration value to a desired time in seconds.

Inserting narration

Once you are finished working on your storyboard, you can choose to insert narration or some kind of other background music. Keep in mind that narration or music does not replace the original audio track that was recorded on the video — the two are just mixed together. If you don't want to use the original audio track, then you need to record the clips into Movie Maker without the audio. When recording, change the Record value that appears on the Record window to "video only."

To record narration for your movie, click the Narration button in the workspace area (looks like a microphone). Of course, you first need to set up a microphone on your computer. Once you click the Narration button, a Record Narration Track dialog box appears, as shown in Figure 9-19.

Figure 9-19: Record Narration Track dialog box

To record the narration, follow these steps.

STEPS

Recording narration

1. On the Record Narration Track window, adjust the Record level as desired. If you need to change devices, click the Change button and select the desired microphone that you want to use. While you are recording, the original video soundtrack will be playing, as well. If you don't want to hear it, click the "Mute video soundtrack" check box option. When you are ready, click Record.

2. While you are recording the timeline moves and runs the video. Speak clearly, and keep in mind the segment of the timeline currently showing in the display window is where the recording of the narration will fit on the track. You must narrate by what you currently see in the display area so that the video and the narration will match.

3. When you finish recording, click the Stop button.

4. The Save Narration Track Sound File window appears. The file will be saved as a WAV audio file. Enter a friendly name and click Save.

5. A narration clip is created and placed in your clips area. Drag the narration clip to the timeline record area (if it doesn't appear there automatically), shown in Figure 9-20. You can now play the timeline and hear the narration.

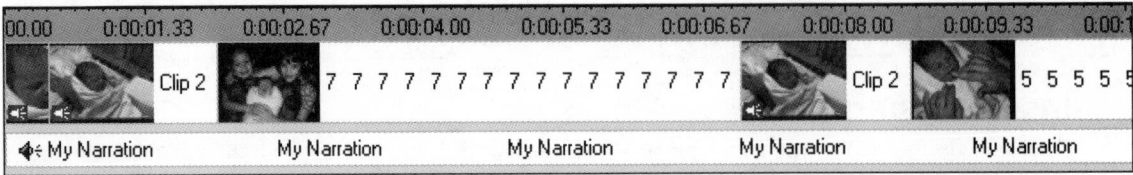

Figure 9-20: Narration track

If you are using the original video soundtrack and narration/music over that soundtrack, you may notice that the narration/music is too loud, or the original video soundtrack is too loud. No problem. In the workspace area, click the Audio Levels button in the left timeline column and adjust the slider bar that appears, shown in Figure 9-21. Moving the slider bar closer to the desired track makes that track louder and the other track softer.

Figure 9-21: Audio levels

SECRET: You noticed that the narration file is saved as a clip, right? Because it is saved as a clip, you can record other bits of narration or sound effects and mix the clips together on the timeline. Just like combining video clips together, you can combine audio clips as well — which opens a new world of sound effect possibilities. Just be creative and see what you come up with.

Saving the movie

When you finish creating clips, editing transitions, and recording any narration that you want, you are ready to save the movie. To save the movie, just click the Save Movie button on the toolbar. This action opens the Save Movie window, as you can see in Figure 9-22.

You need to choose a quality setting for the movie. By default, medium quality is selected and the estimated file size is displayed. You can try different quality settings and compare file sizes to determine which one is right for you. Obviously, if you are going to be e-mailing the file to other people, you want to keep the file size as small as possible. You can, of course, zip the file to help reduce transmission size.

NOTE: On my soapbox again: it will do no good to send the file to people who don't have Windows Movie Maker or Media Player; they will not be able to open it.

Assign a title to the movie, an author, date, and description if you like; you can even assign a rating. Click OK when you finish.

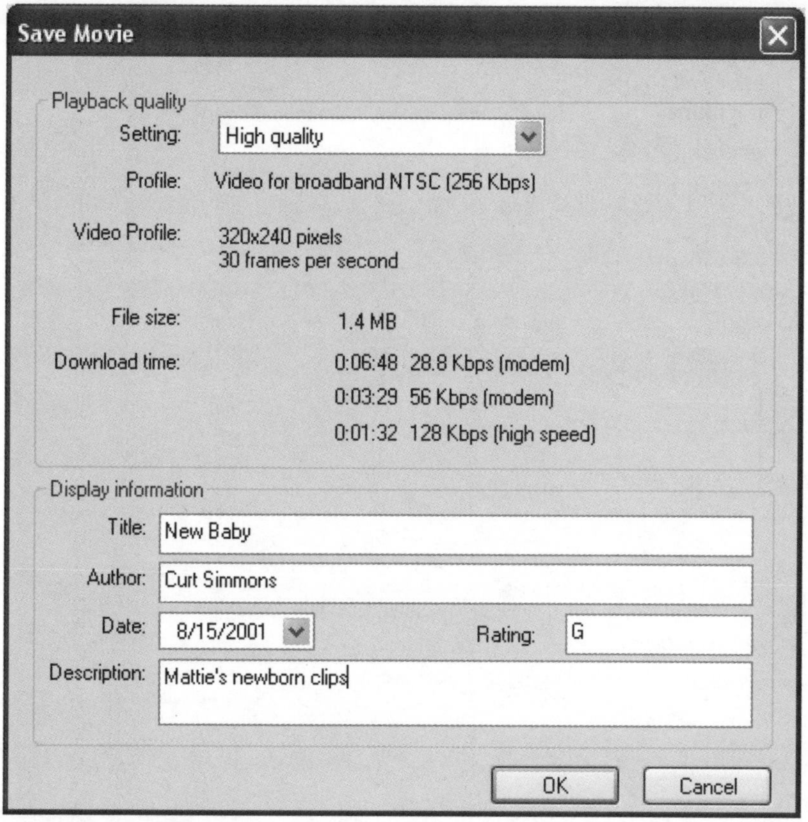

Figure 9-22: Save the movie

The Save As window comes up. Give the video a name, choose a location on your hard drive that you want to save the movie in, and click Save. Depending on the length of your movie and quality setting, it may take a few minutes to create the movie. Once the file is saved, you can play it with Windows Media Player or e-mail it to friends. Windows Movie Maker can even automatically put the video in an e-mail message for you if you click the Send button on the Movie Maker toolbar.

Summary

Windows XP handles digital media better than any previous version of Windows. Using the tools and features of Windows XP, your computer can easily become a personal digital playground in which to view and create information.

♦ Windows XP's default theme makes digital media viewing easier and more organized through the default My Documents folders.

♦ You can easily view media files and even video segments within folders while in the Windows XP theme.

♦ Windows Media Player is a diverse product that enables you to view movies, hear audio, and even look at digital pictures. You can save media files to your hard drive, copy them, listen to Internet radio, and choose from a number of customization options.

♦ Windows Movie Maker is a video editor that allows you to record or import digital or analog video and then edit that video and create your own movie file. Use clips, transitions, narration, still shots, and a host of creative features to make your own movies.

Part IV

Hardware Secrets

Chapter 10

Managing Your Computer with Control Panel

In This Chapter

Control Panel is the tool in Windows XP that allows you to manage and control the operations of your system. Through Control Panel, you can manage all kinds of hardware items and software configurations, and it is your first place of reference to make your system look and behave in a way that is right for you. In this chapter, you explore the new XP Control Panel and see what is available for management of your system with it. I also point out a number of secrets and tips that you can use time and time again to configure your XP system. In this chapter, you learn about . . .

♦ Managing the XP Control Panel view

♦ Customizing the Control Panel

♦ Configuring Control Panel Applets

Getting to Know the XP Control Panel

In an attempt to make things easier for new users, Microsoft has implemented a new Control Panel look in Windows XP. The default XP Control Panel, as seen in Figure 10-1, provides a category view divided by appearance and themes, network connections, programs, and so on. The idea is that the category view helps users find configuration items that they need more quickly and more easily.

Clicking on a category gives you the option to choose a task by clicking an associated link or by selecting a Control Panel icon from which you can configure the item that you want. For example, in Figure 10-2, I have selected the Appearance and Themes link, and I have the task options to change the theme, change the background, choose a screen saver, and change the screen resolution. Or, I can simply open Display, Taskbar and Start Menu Properties, or Folder Options in order to configure these items myself.

The new Control Panel view is great for the new user, but the different categories do not provide access to all that Control Panel offers. In other words, if you use only the category view, several configurable items will hide behind these links and not be viewable to you. For more advanced users, the XP Control Panel Classic view is going to be your best option.

> **TIP:** You can use either the Classic or Category View at any time by simply clicking the provided link, or you can toggle between them as you like. However, Control Panel will always open with the last view you used. In other words, if you only like the Classic View, just switch to that view and Control Panel will always default to Classic unless you change back to Category view at a later time.

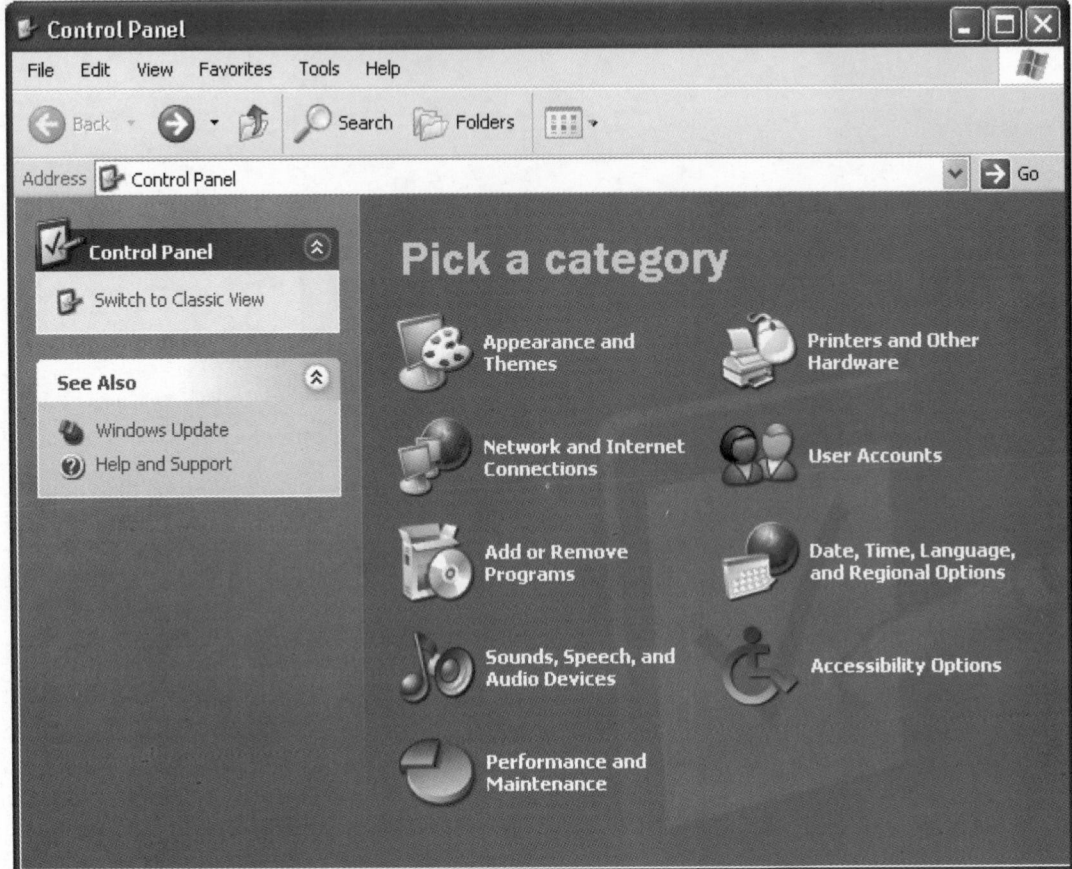

Figure 10-1: XP Control Panel view

By clicking the Switch to Classic View in the left console pane, you see all of the Control Panel applets that are available appear in the right console pane, as shown in Figure 10-3. Obviously, you will not have the task link help in this view, but for many of us, that is perfectly fine.

Customizing Control Panel

Control Panel itself doesn't have a lot of items that you can customize. For the most part, the Category or Classic View is what you use. However, there are a few things that you can do in order to make Control Panel and Control Panel applets more accessible. These options are explored in the following sections.

Changing Control Panel views

First things first — one of the easiest ways in which you can customize Control Panel is by configuring a view that is helpful to you. By default, Control Panel applets are listed by icon under the Classic View and are simply organized alphabetically. You can change these default options, however, to something that is more useful to you.

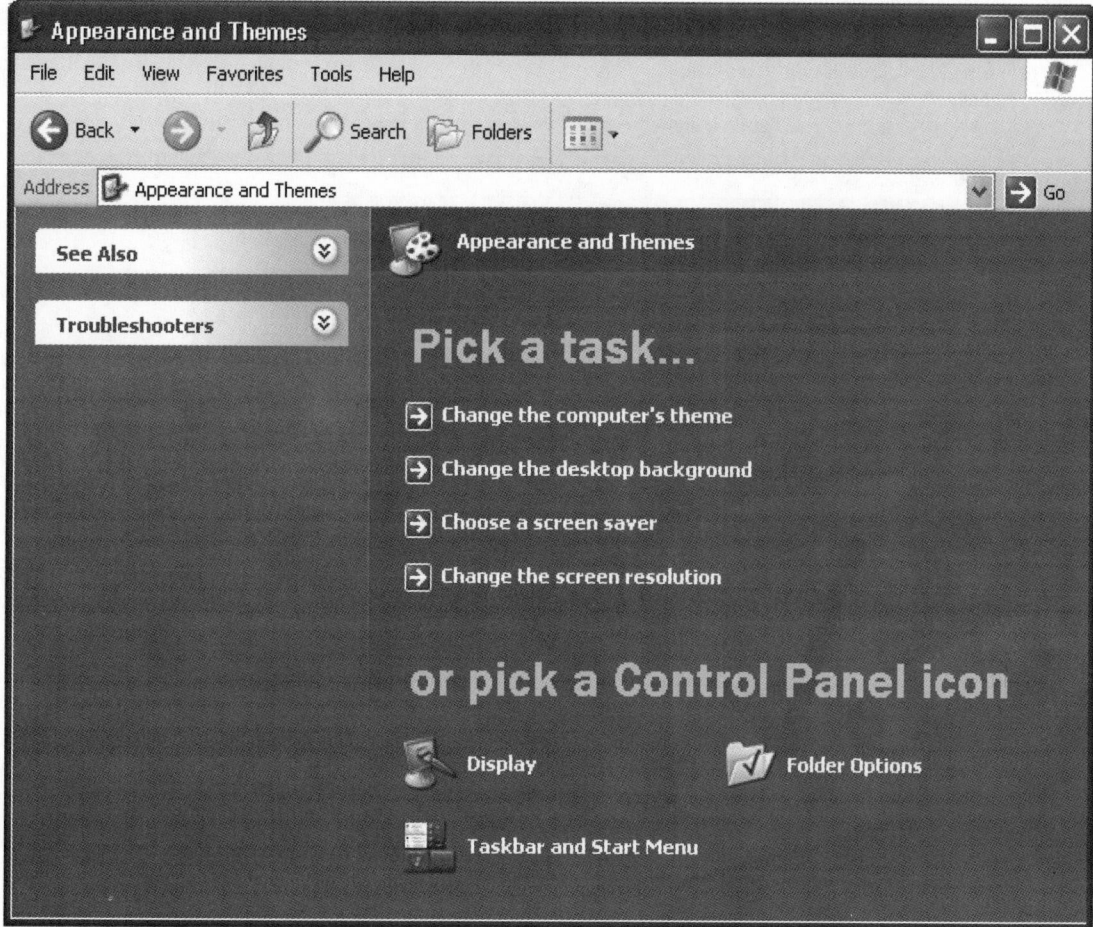

Figure 10-2: Control Panel Task options

To change views, simply click the View menu and select a different option. You can set views based on:

- **Thumbnails** — This option shows larger graphics of each Control Panel item. The problem with this view is that it takes up a lot of room and you cannot see all of the icons in one window.

- **Tiles** — This option uses a smaller graphic than the Thumbnail view, but you still may find this view too large for practical use.

- **List** — This option enables you to easily see all Control Panel items in a list format using a small icon. The list is alphabetized.

- **Details** — This option provides you with a list format, but a comment for each applet is visible. Each comment tells you the basic tasks that are performable with the applet.

- **Arrange Icons By** — This feature enables you to arrange icons by name or comments, or to show them in groups. The Group feature simply organizes the icons in alphabetical order and subdivides them, as you can see in Figure 10-4.

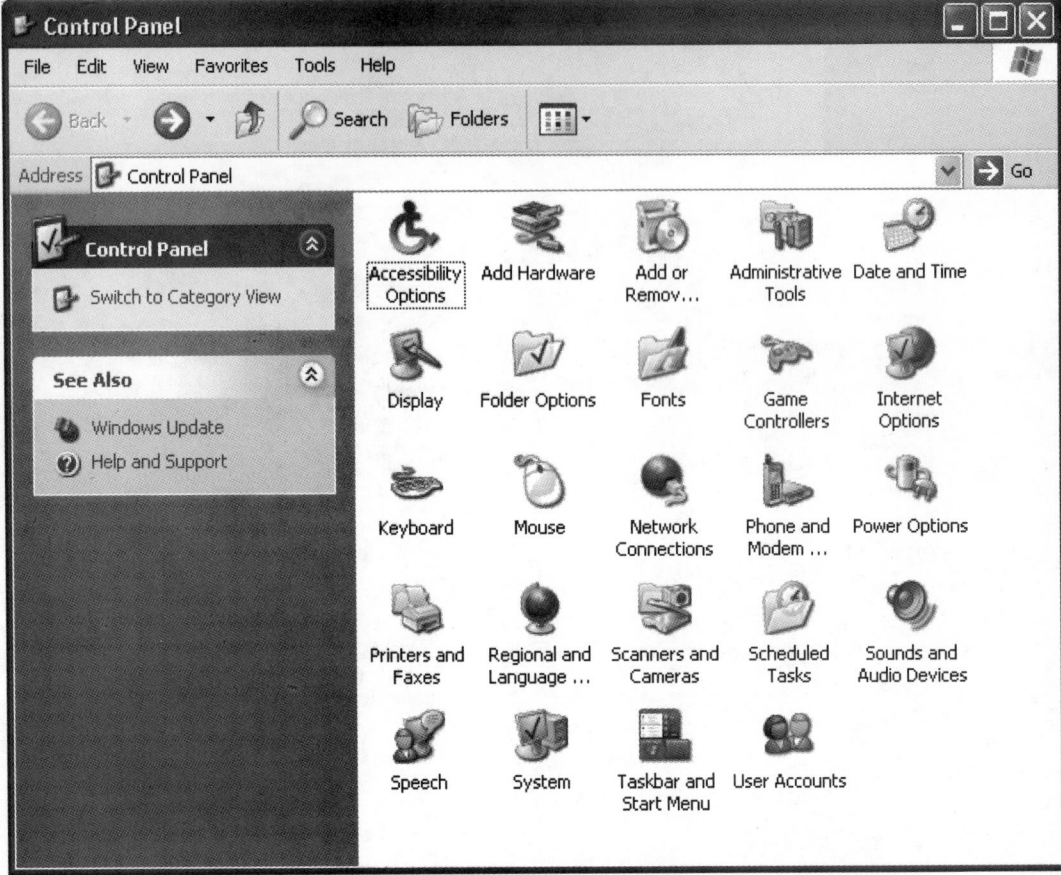

Figure 10-3: Classic Control Panel view

Creating Quick Access shortcuts

You can create a shortcut for any Control Panel applet by simply right-clicking on the applet and clicking Create Shortcut. The shortcut is automatically placed on the desktop. At this point, you can drag the shortcut to any location that you desire, or you can simply leave the shortcut on the desktop.

Another option is to create shortcuts for the Control Panel icons that you most often use, and then drag the shortcuts to the Start Menu. This moves the shortcut to the Start Menu where you can easily access it. However, you should only place applets that you use frequently on the Start Menu in order to reduce clutter.

Another shortcut option to consider is enabling expandable views on the Start Menu. By default, a link to Control Panel is available on the Start Menu. If you enable the expandable view, all Control Panel applets will be visible when you point to Control Panel so that you can directly access the desired applet from the expandable menu.

CROSS-REFERENCE: See Chapter 5 to learn more about Start Menu configuration.

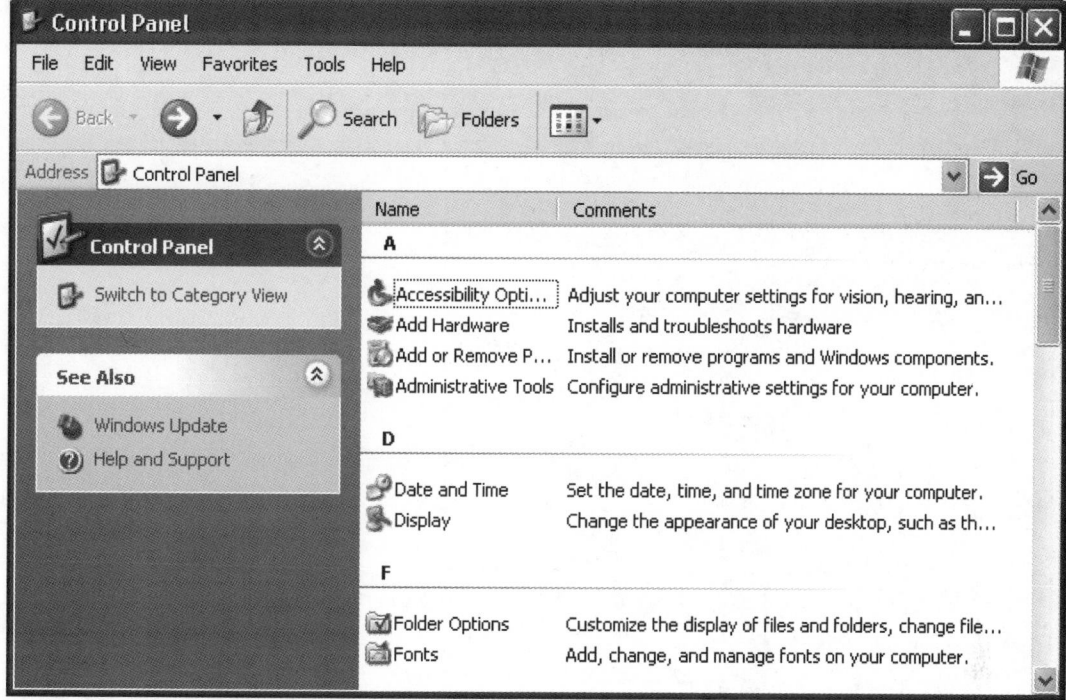

Figure 10-4: Arranged by Groups

Creating a custom Control Panel

Suppose you have eight Control Panel applets that you access on a regular basis. You want to those applets readily available, but you do not want them on the Start Menu because of the space they consume. One alternative is to enable the expandable view option and select them, but you want easier access. What can you do?

A simple solution is to create your own Control Panel. Essentially, you create shortcuts to the items that you want, and then configure a folder to hold those shortcuts. This folder can then be placed on the Start Menu if you like or stored in another easy-to-access location. The following steps show you how to create your own custom Control Panel.

STEPS

Creating your own Control Panel

1. Right-click an empty area of your desktop and click New ⇨ Folder.

2. The new folder appears on the desktop. Type a new name for the folder, such as **My Control Panel**.

3. Open Control Panel and then create shortcuts to the Control Panel applets that you want to use.

4. Drag those shortcuts to your new folder. You can now move the folder to the desired location. For example, as Figure 10-5 shows, My Control Panel now resides on the Start Menu.

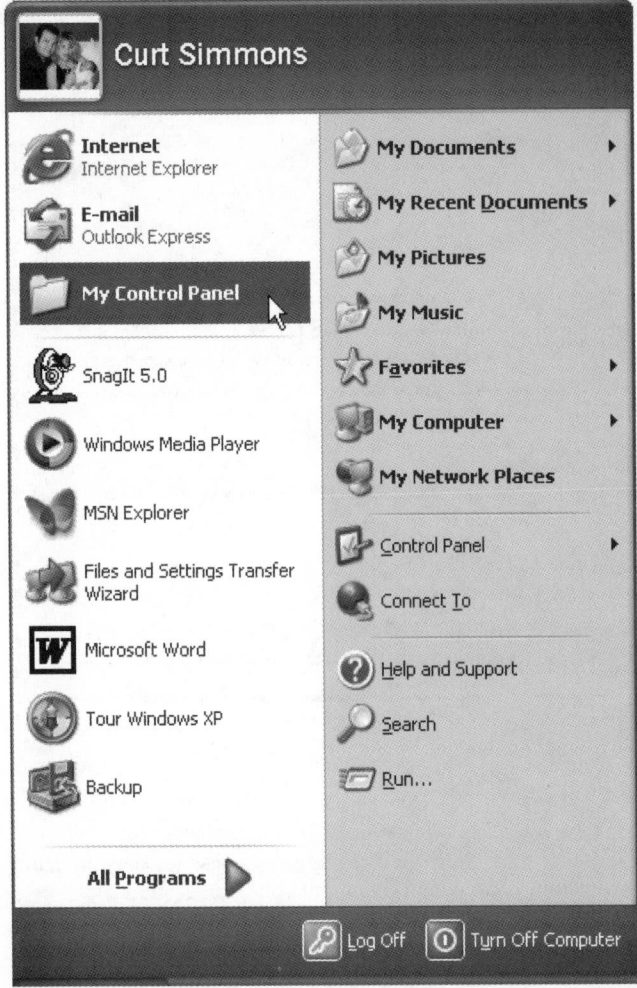

Figure 10-5: Custom Control Panel

SECRET: By default, all shortcuts are named Shortcut to... such as Shortcut to Display, Shortcut to Connections, and so on. You don't have to keep these default names, however. Just right-click the shortcut, click Rename, and rename the shortcut as desired. You can also change the icon by right-clicking the shortcut and clicking Properties. Then, click Change Icon on the Shortcut tab. Simply choose a new icon or browse for one and click OK. You can even use custom icons and pictures that you create.

Configuring shortcut hotkeys

For shortcuts that you create, you can also create a keyboard hotkey so that you can just press the hotkey to open the shortcut. This is a great timesaving tool that allows you to open the item more quickly. Of course, you'll have to remember the keyboard shortcut, but for commonly used items, that won't be a big deal.

To create shortcut hotkey, just right-click the shortcut and click Properties. On the Shortcut tab, click your mouse in the Shortcut key dialog box, and then press the desired keyboard letter that you want to use for a shortcut. Windows automatically configures the shortcut as Ctrl+Alt+*key*. As you can see in Figure 10-6, I am using S for my hotkey to Administrative Tools. When you are done, just click OK to save the hotkey.

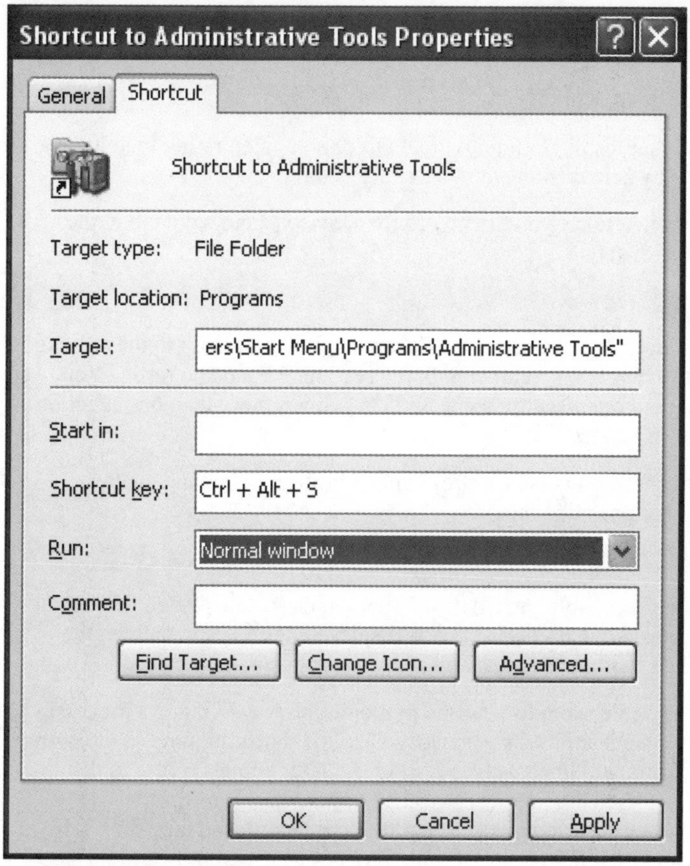

Shortcut to Administrative Tools Properties [?] [X]

| General | Shortcut |

Shortcut to Administrative Tools

Target type: File Folder

Target location: Programs

Target: `ers\Start Menu\Programs\Administrative Tools"`

Start in:

Shortcut key: `Ctrl + Alt + S`

Run: Normal window ▼

Comment:

[Find Target...] [Change Icon...] [Advanced...]

[OK]   [Cancel]   [Apply]

Figure 10-6: Shortcut hotkey

Locating Control Panel files

The Control Panel occupies a special place in the Desktop hierarchy. If you look for Control Panel in the Explorer, it doesn't appear as an icon under the `\Windows\Start Menu` folder, as you might expect. Instead, it appears in the left pane of the Explorer *after* all your floppy drives and hard drives. This implies that Control Panel isn't on any of your disks at all.

This isn't the case, of course. Control Panel is, in reality, a normal executable file stored in your `\Windows\System32` folder. You can verify this by choosing Start ➪ Run and then typing the following command:

```
C:\Windows\System32\Control.exe
```

When you click OK, you see the same Control Panel window appear as you do when you run Control Panel directly from the Start menu.

If you've visited the Control Panel before, you know it includes icons for changing your keyboard, mouse, and modem settings, and for accessing many other functions of your system. The exact complement of Control Panel applets in your Control Panel window depends on the hardware and software you've installed. But the Control Panel holds a lot of secrets beneath its humble exterior. `Control.exe` supports a number of parameters that can dramatically speed up your access to the settings in its applets.

For example, suppose you want to change your dialing properties frequently, perhaps because you travel a lot. You could choose Start ⇨ Run and type the following:

```
C:\Windows\System32\Control.exe Modem.cpl
```

Even better, you can create a command that displays an individual tab of an applet, rather than having to start out at the first one and click your way across to the tab you really want.

For example, you can create a command that takes you directly to the Device Manager, a tab in the System applet. That command looks like this:

```
C:\Windows\System32\Control.exe Sysdm.cpl, System,1
```

This command causes Control Panel to open Sysdm.cpl, the System applet, and jump to the second available tab. (In programmer-speak, the first tab is numbered 0, the second is 1, and so forth.) You need to specify the applet name in this command line because some applets contain more than one function within them.

What the three examples above have in common is the Control Panel's built-in command syntax. Stripped down to skeletal form, the syntax goes like this:

```
Control.exe {filename.cpl} {,applet-name} {,tab#}
```

If you run Control.exe with no parameters, only the Control Panel window is displayed. If you add the correct *filename.cpl*, the first tab of that applet's dialog box is displayed. And if you tack on the correct applet name and tab number, then *that* tab is displayed.

In actual practice (as opposed to theory), there seem to be some quirks in the way Windows processes the tab number for an applet. Some Control Panel applets, particularly Display, dutifully jump to the correct tab when you specify a number in the command line, such as 1, 2, or 3. Other applets refuse to display any tab but the first (tab 0) even if you've used the "correct" syntax. Apparently, some of the programmers at Microsoft didn't know they were supposed to build in this feature, so they didn't. If a particular tab doesn't seem to want to let you "jump to it," the tab may not be programmed to do so.

You can place commands such as these on the Start menu, on your Desktop, or elsewhere, and access them with a mouse click or a hot key.

Table 10-1 shows some of the .cpl files available in most Windows systems, and the applet name you need to jump to a particular tab. (Some applets, such as Main.cpl, contain more than one function; these are listed separately below.)

Table 10-1: Control Panel File and Applet Names

Filename	*Applet Name*
Main.cpl	Fonts
Main.cpl	Keyboard
Main.cpl	Mouse
Main.cpl	Printers
Access.cpl	Accessibility Options
Appwiz.cpl	Add/Remove Programs
Desk.cpl	Display
Fax.cpl	Fax

Filename	Applet Name
Hdwwiz.cpl	Hardware Wizard
Inetcpl.cpl	Internet
Infrared.cpl	Infrared
Intl.cpl	Regional Settings
Joy.cpl	Game Controllers
Main.cpl	Mouse
Mmsys.cpl	Multimedia
Mmsys.cpl	Sounds
Modem.cpl	Modems
Ncpa.cpl	Network
Nusrmgr.cpl	User Manager
Nwc.cpl	Network Connections
Powercfg.cpl	Power Management
Sticpl.cpl	Scanners and Cameras
Sysdm.cpl	System
Sysdm.cpl	Add New Hardware
Telephon.cpl	Telephony
Timedate.cpl	Time and Date

Now that you know the filenames and applet names to use, make sure you never have to type these lines more than once. It's easy to create a shortcut icon on your Desktop that takes you directly to the tab of your choice in a Control Panel applet's dialog box.

Here's how:

STEPS

Creating Control Panel shortcut icons on the desktop

1. Right-click an unoccupied spot on your Desktop.

2. On the context menu that appears, point to New and then click Shortcut.

3. In the Create Shortcut Wizard, type a command line such as the following:

```
C:\Windows\System32\Control.exe Desk.cpl, Display,2
```

4. Click Next. Type a name for your new shortcut, such as **Display Appearance**, and then click Finish. You're done!

You should see a new icon on your Desktop. Click it and you are almost instantly transported to (in this case) the Appearance tab of the Display Properties dialog box.

TIP: Remember that you can change the shortcut's name and icon appearance by right-clicking the icon and accessing the Properties sheets.

Configuring Your Computer with Control Panel Applets

As mentioned earlier in this chapter, Control Panel is your gateway to system configuration. Using Control Panel applets, you can configure Windows XP to look and behave in a way that is pleasing to you. Because a number of Control Panel applets are used to configure specific system components, those applets are discussed in other chapters. For example, the Hardware Wizard is covered in Chapter 11 while Internet options are explored in Chapter 16. Applets that are not covered in other chapters are covered in the following sections. If you don't see the applet you are looking for here, check the book's table of contents or index to help locate it.

Accessibility options

Microsoft includes a number of accessibility features in Windows XP that enable people with certain disabilities to configure XP in a way that makes it easier to use. The accessibility options presented in XP are better than ever and provide several features.

The configuration options for accessibility are rather straightforward, so I hit the high points in the following sections. To configure Accessibility Options, just double-click the applet in Control Panel. Five tabs are available.

Keyboard

The Keyboard tab, shown in Figure 10-7, enables you to configure three primary options for keyboard usage. The options are:

♦ **StickyKeys** — The StickyKeys option enables the keyboard keys to "stick" so that you can press several keys at once using only one hand. For example, this feature is great for commands such as Ctrl+Alt+Delete.

♦ **FilterKeys** — FilterKeys "filter" extra keystrokes. For example, if you accidentally hit a key twice, the second keystroke is not repeated. This setting is helpful for those with motor skill problems.

♦ **ToggleKeys** — This option plays tones when you press Caps lock, Num lock , or Scroll lock.

To configure one (or all) of the options, click the appropriate check box and click Settings. The Settings window tells you which hot key can be used and gives you a few other basic configuration options.

Sound

The Sound tab gives you the option to use two tools: SoundSentry and ShowSounds. SoundSentry gives you visual warnings on the screen for Windows events (which are typically sound warnings), and the ShowSounds options displays captions on the screen for sound events. To enable these options, just click the appropriate check boxes.

Display

The Display tab enables you to use high contrast colors so that the screen is easier to see. You can also configure the size and blink rate of the mouse cursor here as well.

Mouse

This tab enables you to use MouseKeys, which gives you the ability to use the keyboard for mouse movements. If you click the Settings button, you can determine how you want mouse keys to operate.

Figure 10-7: Keyboard Configuration

General

The General tab contains a mixture of other various settings. You can use automatic reset if accessibility options are idle for a period of time; use notifications when accessibility features are turned on; enable SerialKey devices; and set a few basic administrative options. All of these items are self-explanatory.

Date and Time

The Date and Time Properties dialog box enables you to configure the date and time on your Windows XP computer, as shown in Figure 10-8.

You can change the date by choosing the month from the drop-down list, spinning the Year field, and clicking a day. You can change the time by typing a new time or by using the spin control. To change the clock to a 24-hour display (instead of a.m. and p.m.) select it in the time field and use the selection buttons.

You can also set your time zone by clicking the Time Zone tab, as shown in Figure 10-9. Check out the world map. This map used to be pretty cool, because you could click an area to illuminate the whole time zone/daylight savings zone. No longer. Too many political entities with disagreements about borders.

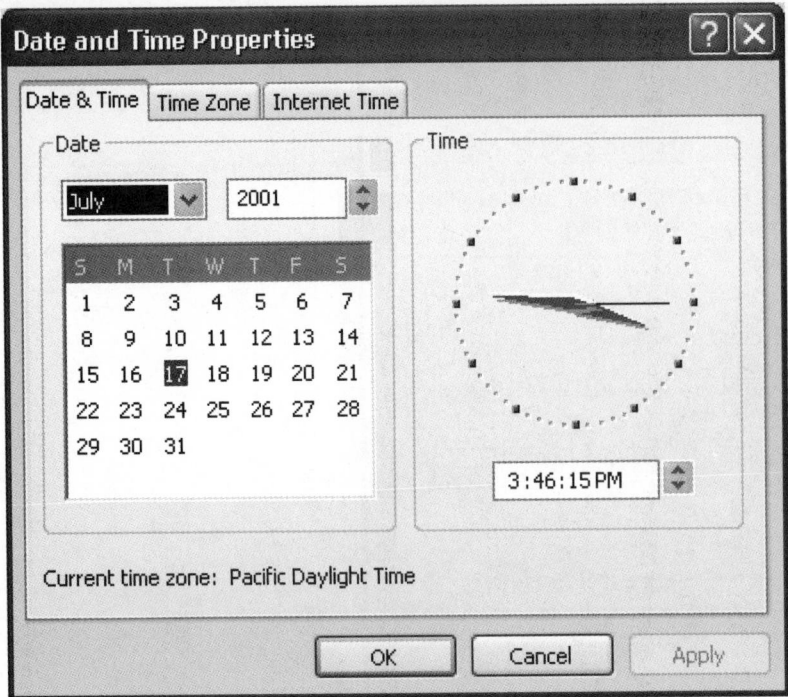

Figure 10-8: The Date and Time Properties dialog box. You can set the date and time by typing new values or by clicking the spin controls in the Date and Time fields.

SECRET: There are 76 separate entries in the list of time zones (in the original version of Windows 95 there were only 51, even though you might assume that there are only 24 unique time zones. Windows keeps track of the daylight savings time rules for various locations, so, for example, there is a unique entry for Arizona (USA) that doesn't honor daylight savings time. There are also separate entries for Darwin and Adelaide (Australia), both of which are plus 9.5 hours from Greenwich Mean Time.

When the first day of daylight savings time arrives, you are asked if you want to have your computer's clock moved an hour ahead.

The time zone value does have something of a practical value. If you are on a network that crosses time zones — say, your own company's WAN — your computers will use this time zone value to get everyone's time synched to a universal standard such as Zulu, Greenwich mean time, or whatever arbitrary one you choose. Your computers can correctly compare files that are time-stamped on the West Coast with files that are time-stamped on the East Coast.

You also see an Internet Time tab, which enables your computer to be synchronized with an Internet time server found at `time.windows.com`. This ensures that your computer has the exact time. Of course, you have to be connected to the Internet for this feature to work, and if you don't want to use it, just clear the check box at the top of the window.

Fonts

The Fonts folder found in Control Panel, and shown in Figure 10-10, lists all of the fonts that are currently available on your computer. There's not a lot for you to do here except to peruse the fonts that are available. If you double-click a font, you'll see how it looks and you can also right-click a font and print a sample. If you download new fonts from the Internet, you can also place them here so that they are available for Windows to use. In the same manner, you can also delete fonts that you detest.

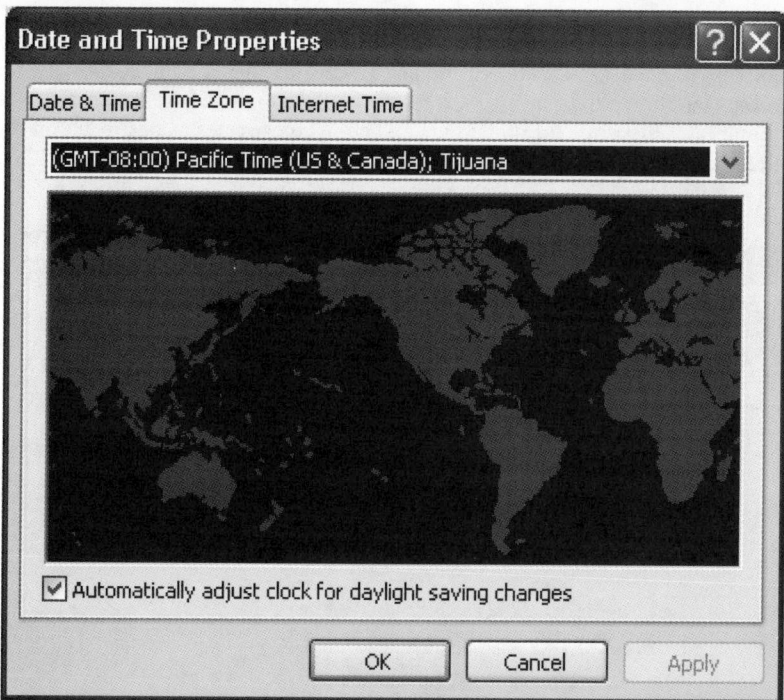

Figure 10-9: The Time Zone map. Click the drop-down list above the map to pick a time zone.

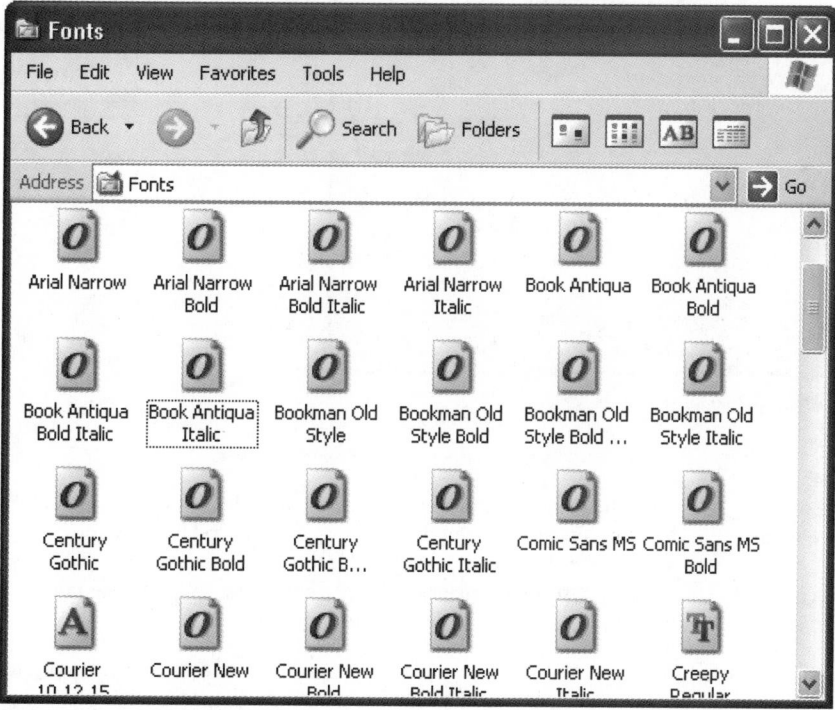

Figure 10-10: Fonts folder

Keyboard

The Keyboard Properties dialog box provides you with a Speed and Hardware tab. The Speed tab provides you with a few slider bars, as shown in Figure 10-11, which you use to configure the repeat delay, repeat rate, and cursor blink rate. Just slide the slider bars and adjust these rates as desired. You might need to experiment with them a bit in order to find the settings you like.

The Hardware tab gives you basic information about the Keyboard and tells you if the keyboard is working or not (duh!). You can click the Properties button to open Device Manager (see Chapter 11) or you can launch the XP troubleshooter if you are having problems with the keyboard.

Figure 10-11: Keyboard Properties, Speed tab

Mouse

Use the Mouse Properties dialog box to set the properties of the mouse and how the mouse behaves. You can use this dialog box to change the responsiveness or speed of the mouse pointer relative to your movements of the mouse. You can switch the function of the right and left mouse buttons for left-handed operation. You can also change the double-click time interval. A longer interval counts two separate mouse clicks that are separated by a longer period of time as a single double-click.

You get to pick from a collection of mouse pointer icons, including animated pointers that correspond to a range of mouse functions. You can turn the hourglass pointer into a spinning world, for example. Because Windows XP uses the same .ani file format as Windows 2000 and Me, you can select from a wide variety of shareware and freeware animated icons available on online services and the Internet. And if you're using an LCD screen, you can add mouse pointer trails by setting the number of ghost images that get left behind (briefly) at the mouse pointer's former location.

The following sections explain how to change the properties of your mouse.

Button configuration

You change the "handedness" of your mouse by clicking the Button configuration check box at the top of the Buttons tab, as shown in Figure 10-12. This action will reverse the left and right mouse keys and is particularly helpful if you are left-handed.

Figure 10-12: The Buttons tab of the standard Mouse Properties dialog box. The Properties dialog box for your particular pointing device may look different, depending on your driver.

Speed

Although Windows lets you use a single-click for many actions that used to require a double-click, there are still times when a double-click is required (selecting a word in text, for example).

To adjust how fast you need to double-click, do the following:

STEPS

Changing double-click speed

1. Move the "Double-click speed" slider to the left to increase the time interval allowed between two mouse clicks that are counted as one double-click. Move the slider to the right to increase the speed with which you must twice click the left mouse button (assuming a right-handed configuration) in order for it to count as a double-click.

2. To test your double-click agility, click twice in the test area. If your two clicks count as one double-click, the jack-in-the-box goes up or down.

> **SECRET:** The range of the slider is between 900 milliseconds (nine-tenths of a second) at the left end and 100 milliseconds (one-tenth of a second) on the right end. This makes the middle of the slider equal to half a second.

ClickLock

If you need to drag items without holding down the mouse key, you can enable ClickLock. This feature allows you to hold down the mouse key momentarily, which turns on the ClickLock feature. Then you can drag the items as desired without holding down the mouse key.

Using different mouse pointers

You can use some of the newer static and animated mouse pointers created for Windows XP/2000. They are a lot of fun and are often better designed than the Windows standard ones. Windows XP has a lot of mouse pointer options that are organized by schemes, as you can see on the Pointers tab. These pointers are stored in the \Windows\Cursors folder. You can easily change the mouse pointers that your XP system uses; the following steps show you how.

> **SECRET:** You must have your video display card driver set to at least 256 colors in order for animated cursors to work. Some cards that can display 256 colors have video drivers that don't work with animated pointers. You need to test your card and driver with an animated pointer to make sure that it works.

STEPS

Changing mouse pointers

1. Click the Mouse icon in the Control Panel, and click the Pointers tab, as shown in Figure 10-13. Starting with Normal Select, scroll down the list of pointer functions and their associated pointers. Try clicking different pointers as you go down the list. When you click a pointer, it appears in the gray box in the upper-right corner of the dialog box, and if the pointer is animated, you see what the animation looks like.

2. Click the Scheme pull-down menu in this tab to see various pointer schemes designed by Microsoft. If you have installed any Themes, you see pointer schemes that relate to those themes. In these pointer schemes supplied by Microsoft, only the Busy and Working in Background pointers are animated. You can use this Schemes menu to choose a new pointer scheme, or to mix and match different pointers from different schemes as desired.

Figure 10-13: The Pointers tab of the Mouse Properties dialog box. Each mouse function has an associated mouse pointer.

3. To use a different mouse pointer for a particular mouse function, click that mouse function and then click the Browse button. In the Browse dialog box, you will see the animated pointers in the \Windows\Cursors folder. Animated pointer files have the ani extension, and static pointers have the cur extension. When you highlight a pointer file, it appears in the Preview box in the lower-left corner of the dialog box.

4. Double-click the pointer that you want to use instead of the existing pointer.

Table 10-2 describes the mouse pointers associated with the different mouse functions.

Table 10-2: Windows XP Mouse Pointers

Pointer	Function
Normal Select	This is the normal mouse pointer for selecting items.
Help Select	When you click the ? button in the upper-right corner of a dialog box, you get this mouse pointer. When you see this pointer, you can click any option in the dialog box to get a brief explanation of what the option does.

Pointer	Function
Working In Background	Windows or a 32-bit multithreaded application is busy but using a background thread, so you can proceed with something else if you want.
Busy	Windows or an application is busy trying to accomplish some task before it can proceed.
Precision Select	This pointer guides your eye to its center to help you select with precision.
Text Select	This pointer is also called the *I-beam*. You use it in word processors to select text.
Handwriting	This pointer appears when you have switched to a mode that is expecting handwritten or ink input from you (in an application that supports handwriting).
Unavailable	When you drag a File icon over an area or application that won't accept the file if you drop it there, this pointer appears to remind you of that fact.
Vertical, Horizontal, Diagonal Resize	The double-headed arrow pointers appear when you position your mouse pointer along the edges of a sizable window.
Move	When you click the Move command in the system menu of a window, this pointer appears. When you see it, you can move the window with your arrow keys.
Alternate Select	The only place I've seen this pointer is in the FreeCell solitaire card game.
Link Select	This pointer appears when you hover over a clickable link, whether in Explorer, in a Help file, or when viewing a Web page.

A very important cursor not included in this list shows the insertion point in text editors and word processors. This cursor, aptly called the *insertion point*, tells you where your text will be inserted if you start typing.

If you use the Display Properties dialog box to change the background color of your windows to something other than the default stark white, you'll need to set the color of the insertion point so that it shows up well on top of the background color.

Changing mouse pointer options

The ratio of mouse pointer movement to mouse movement has already been set by your mouse and video driver. The pointer speed values multiply this ratio so that the mouse pointer moves even faster if you move the mouse faster. Each one of the tick marks in the "Pointer speed" slider, shown in Figure 10-14, corresponds to a different set of values for Mouse Speed and different Mouse Threshold behavior values.

If you move your mouse slowly, the mouse pointer moves slowly. If you move the mouse quickly, the mouse pointer moves even more quickly if the MouseSpeed is greater than zero.

Play with this pointer speed slider a bit to determine what speed you are comfortable with. The optimal setting will vary depending on whether you have a trackball or a mouse, among other things.

Also, try the Snap To and Visibility check box options. Each setting listed on the Pointer Options tab is self-explanatory.

TIP: Think your computer is too slow? Try this: Set all your mouse speed settings to the maximum speed. Allow about half a day to get used to this, and see if it doesn't make your PC feel a lot faster. Many "slow" computers are merely suffering from a "molasses mouse." It may turn out that the default settings were way too sluggish for you, or that the mouse settings may have been made slower than is appropriate for you at some point. If you don't like having your mouse set to the maximum speed, you can always back off a bit later.

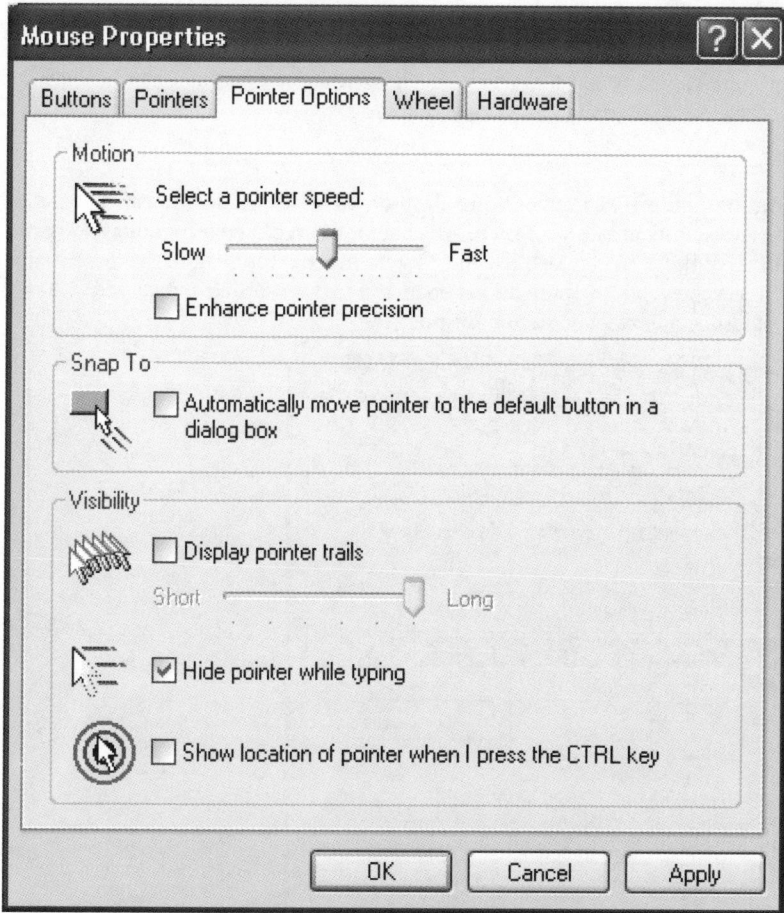

Figure 10-14: The Motion tab of the Mouse Properties dialog box.

Wheel and Hardware

Windows XP includes additional Mouse properties tabs for Wheel and Hardware. The Wheel option enables you to determine how fast wheel movements occur. The default value is 3, but you can try different settings to see if you like the speed difference. The Hardware tab simply provides you information about the mouse hardware. You can click the properties button to learn more in Device Manager.

Power options

If you have a new computer that fully and completely supports the Microsoft-defined Advanced Configuration and Power Interface (ACPI), then you can fully control your computer's standby, disk spin down, monitor turnoff, and power management features. All you have to do is go to your Control Panel and click the Power Management icon.

If you have an older computer whose BIOS supports Advanced Power Management (APM), either APM 1.1 or APM 1.2, you may find that controlling the power management settings is not quite so easy. Your computer's BIOS and the Windows Power Management control panel are fighting to see whose settings should be used. Because you can set the power management features in either location, your computer doesn't know whom to believe.

The odds are quite good, though, that your Windows XP computer supports ACPI because of the demands of the operating system and upgrade options. By accessing the Power Schemes Properties pages in Control Panel, you can configure some options that determine how your XP computer handles power management. The following sections examine the tabs available to you.

Power Schemes

The Power Schemes tab, shown in Figure 10-15, gives you a drop-down menu where you can select a scheme of your choice, or you can simply create your own. All schemes turn off your monitor and hard disks after a certain period of inactivity. You can also use the System hibernation feature that essentially powers down your computer (but keeps current applications open and current settings preserved) when you are away from your computer for an extended period of time.

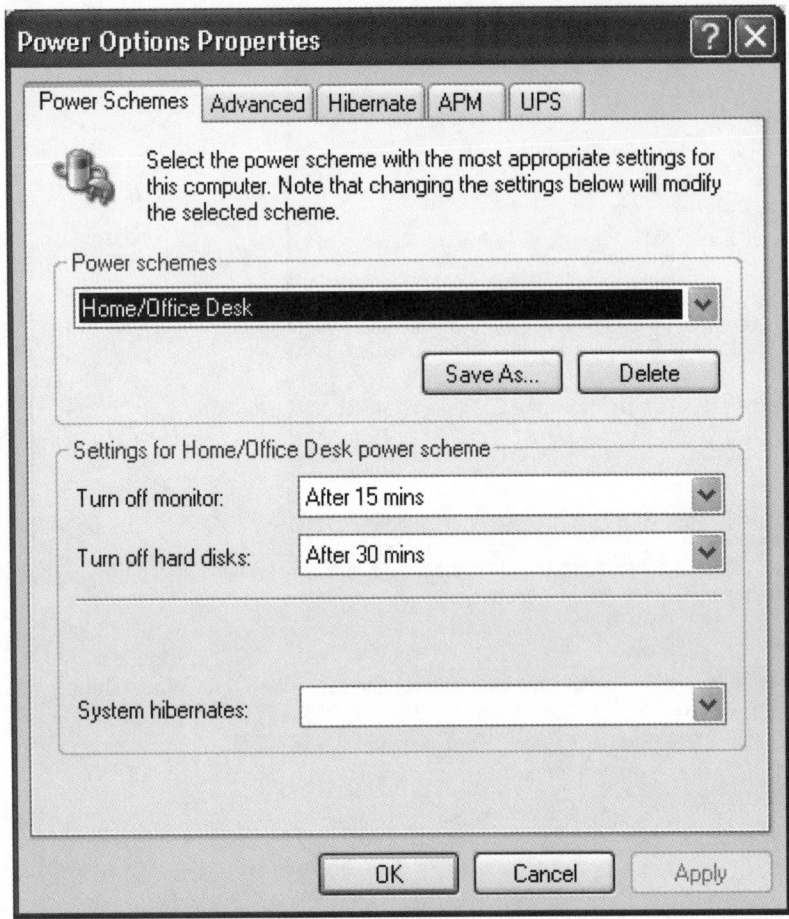

Figure 10-15: Power Schemes

You can easily create your own scheme by simply selecting values for the monitor, hard disks, and system hibernates options, then clicking Save As and giving your personal scheme a name.

Advanced

The Advanced tab, which isn't so advanced, offers two check box options. You can choose to always show a power options icon on the taskbar, and you can have the computer prompt for a password when resuming stand-by. There — that wasn't so advanced, was it?

Hibernate

The XP hibernation feature allows the computer to store information about your operating system on the hard disk before going into a low-energy mode. Essentially, the computer "remembers" everything and shuts down. When it is brought out of hibernation, the computer reads the information from the hard drive and reopens programs or dialog boxes so that your computer is the same as it was when hibernation began. If you want to enable hibernation, simply click the check box found on this window.

APM

If your computer supports Advanced Power Management (APM), this tab, which essentially tells you that APM is enabled on your computer, appears. Most current computer systems support APM, which helps Windows XP manage power more efficiently.

UPS

An Uninterruptible Power Supply (UPS) is a device that attaches to your computer. In the event of a power failure, the UPS can provide the computer with enough power so that you can shut down safely. If you have a UPS device installed on your computer, it is listed here.

Regional settings

Regional settings, as shown in Figure 10-16, enable you to make language, currency, and other regional setting configurations on your Windows XP computer. If you plan to use additional language options, you may need your Windows XP installation CD-ROM to configure the desired options.

As in previous versions of Windows, you can choose a language from a list so that Windows XP will supply the most obvious settings. A look at the choices in locales gives you an idea of the international scope of Windows XP. There are more than 60 locales from which to choose. In the Western European and U.S. language group alone, the choices range from Afrikaans, Basque, and Catalan through Swahili and Swedish, with 13 different English settings alone — Australia through Zimbabwe.

To widen the scope of languages even further, you can add more language groups. In the U.S. version of Windows XP, only the Western European and United States language group is enabled, as shown by the selection in the Location portion of the Regional Options tab shown in Figure 10-16.

Checking the Central European language group adds additional locales, including Polish, Croatian, Slovenian, and Albanian. There are a number of Asian and Middle Eastern languages, as well.

If you choose Polish as your locale from the Regional Options tab and then click Apply, you can then select the Language tab to see that the currency unit is now the zloty, and the date and number settings will be those that are commonly used in Poland. To switch back to U.S. settings, select the Regional Options tab again, select English (United States) as your locale, and then click Apply.

> **TIP:** In addition to currency symbols such as the zloty and the dollar, Windows XP can display the symbol for the Euro — the new monetary unit of the European Monetary Union. If you select the Euro as your currency symbol, and then use Microsoft Excel to format cells as currency, you will see the Euro symbol instead of the dollar symbol.

Multilanguage support

If you use the U.S. English version of Windows XP, you can still work in other languages — such as French or Croatian in your applications. However, application menus, help files, dialog boxes, and tips will still be displayed in English. (There are 24 localized versions of Windows XP. The localized versions — French, for example — display a French user interface, but you still have the ability to work in English or in other languages. A multilanguage version of Windows XP allows users to switch the language both for the user interface and for documents.)

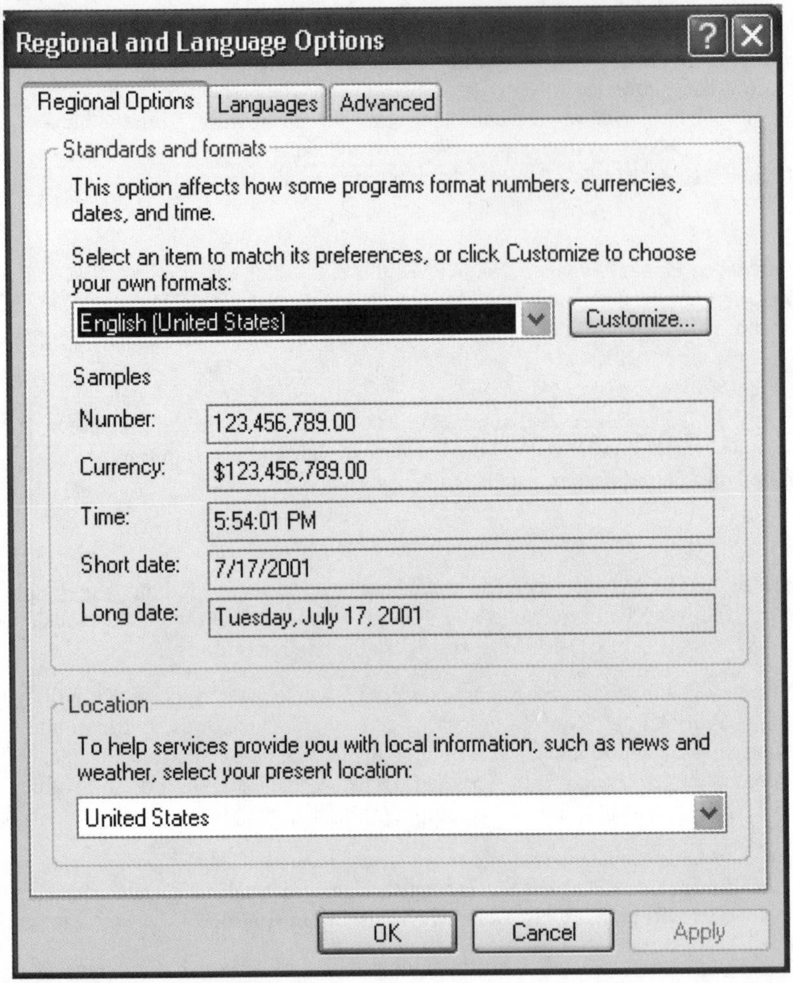

Figure 10-16: Regional settings

Unicode support

Windows XP Professional uses Unicode 2.1 for its base character encoding. This is an international standard that represents the characters commonly used in the world's major languages. Unicode makes sharing data simpler in a mixed platform environment.

Windows XP stores national language support settings in system tables. These tables contain the following data:

♦ **Locale information** — date, time, number and currency format, and localized names for days of week and month

♦ **Character mapping tables** — converts local characters in ANSI or OEM format to Unicode format and back again

♦ **Keyboard layout information**

♦ **Character typing information** — for foreign characters

♦ **Sorting information**

Sounds and Audio Devices

Earlier versions of Windows allowed you to assign specific sounds to play during events and that tradition continues in Windows XP. From the Control Panel, click Sounds and Audio Devices. Then, select the Sounds tab to assign sounds to certain events, as shown in Figure 10-17.

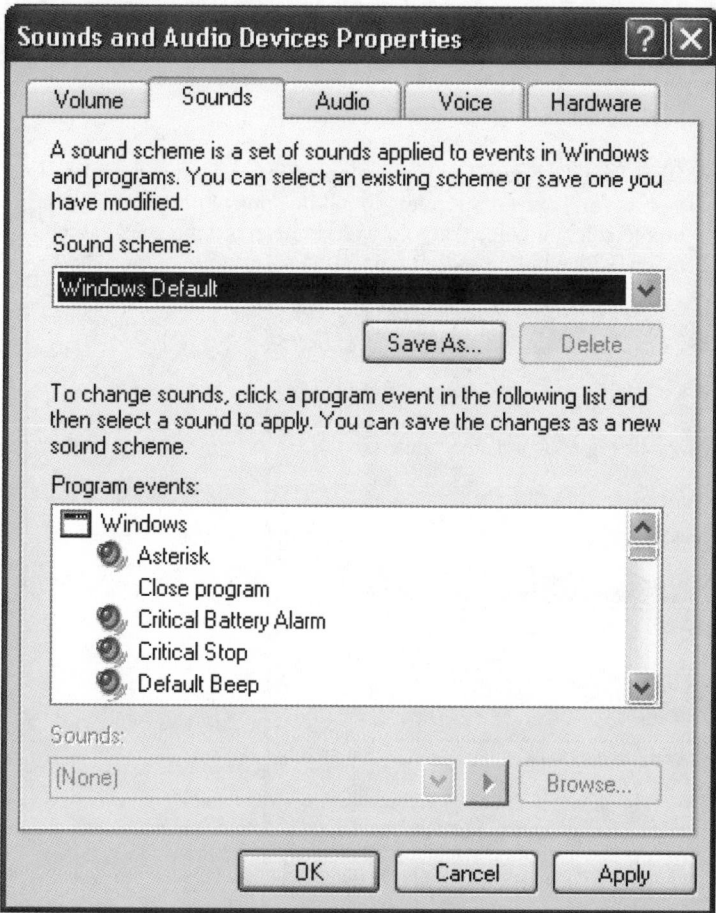

Figure 10-17: Assign sounds to Windows events.

You can assign sounds to Windows XP events, such as when Windows starts or stops, when an error occurs, and so on. When you scroll through the list of sound events in the Program events list box, those events that have an assigned sound event display a loudspeaker icon to the left of the event. To preview a sound, just double-click it.

Other applications often add their events to the Program event list, and they often come configured to use their own sounds based on events within the application. You can change the sounds for these events just as you would for Windows XP events.

TIP: If you make a lot of custom selections to individual event sounds, you can save your selections as your own theme. Click Save As, and then type a name for your sound theme in the dialog box. If you later make changes to your selections, you can always restore your saved theme by selecting it from the list box.

Aside from Sounds configuration, notice that several additional tabs reside on the Sounds and Audio Devices Properties dialog box. These tabs — Volume, Audio, Hardware, and Voice — allow you to make basic adjustments to volume, device selection, speaker types, and related settings. All of these settings are very easy and are self-explanatory.

> **NOTE:** Bored with your sounds? You will find a number of Web sites on the Internet devoted to sound clips, many of which have `.WAV` files that you can download and use for your events. An extensive list of sites is available from Yahoo! at `http://dir.yahoo.com/Computers_and_Internet/Multimedia/Audio/`.

Text To Speech

Windows XP includes a new feature called Text To Speech so that the operating system can read dialog boxes to you. A simple properties dialog box for Text To Speech is found in Control Panel, as shown in Figure 10-18. You can use this dialog box to select a voice that you want to hear and the speed at which the voice speaks. Be sure to use the Preview Voice button as you are testing selections.

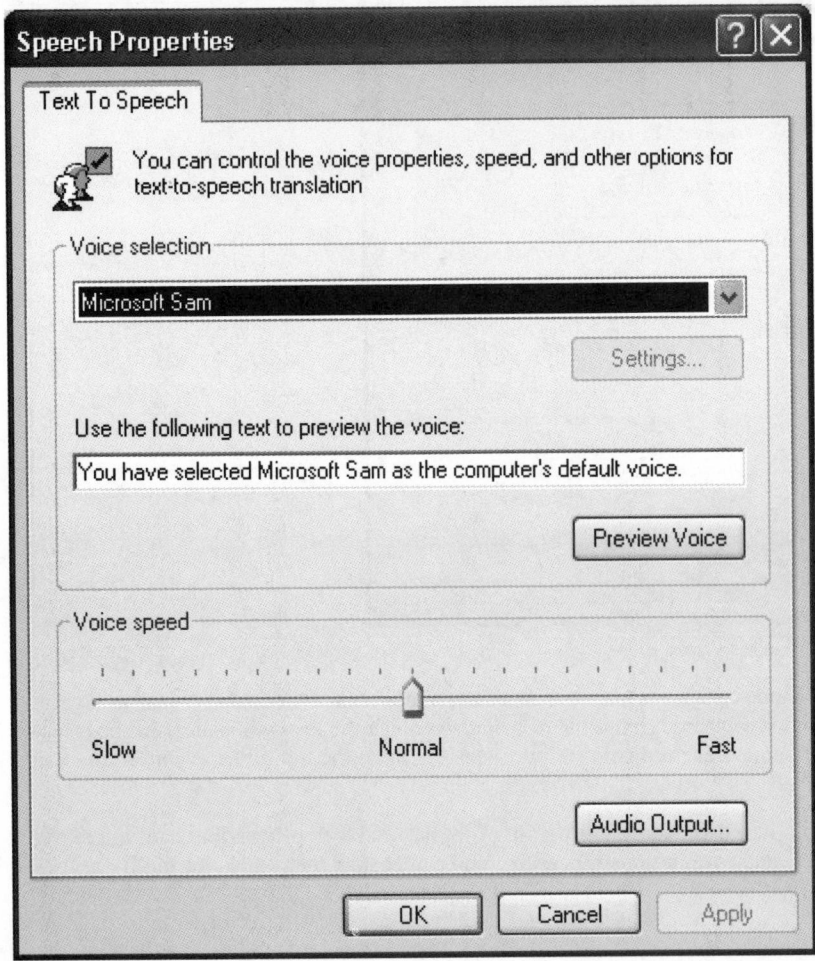

Figure 10-18: Text to Speech

Summary

The Control Panel is your graphical interface for configuring the way Windows XP system components function. Using Control Panel, you can safely configure a number of Windows XP features, including:

◆ Accessibility

◆ Date and time

◆ Fonts

◆ Mouse

◆ Power options

◆ Regional Settings

And there are many more. Keep in mind that many Control Panel options and features are explored in other portions of this book. Refer to the Table of Contents or this book's index to locate the specific item you want to explore.

Chapter 11

Installing and Managing Hardware

In This Chapter

In the not-so-distant past, installing a hardware device and actually getting that hardware device to function on a computer was no easy task. You had to know some things about IRQs and device allocation, plus you had to have a bit of dumb luck. That all began to change in Windows 98 as we saw Plug and Play begin to grow up, and since that time, hardware management has become much, much easier. With improved Plug and Play and an extensive driver database, Windows 98/Me/2000 could automatically install new hardware without intervention from you. Windows XP works the same way — in fact, it is more automated than ever, and device management is easier than it has ever been. In this chapter, you explore the technologies that make hardware a real snap in Windows XP, and then you learn to manage hardware on your XP system. This chapter covers . . .

♦ Installing hardware devices

♦ Configuring and managing hardware

♦ Solving common problems

Living in a Plug and Play World

Plug and Play is a driving force in Windows XP hardware management. With Plug and Play, your Windows XP computer can automatically detect hardware changes and respond to those changes by installing or removing drivers that make the hardware work on your operating system. This installation feat, along with IRQ and resource allocation, is performed automatically, without any input from you — and Plug and Play makes it all happen.

A consortium of hardware manufacturers and software developers agreed, in 1994, to a standard that enables easier installation and tracking of PC hardware independent of the operating system. (Nobody (not even Microsoft) owns the PC's hardware and software standards. Therefore, companies who would like nothing better than to grind each other into the ground have to cooperate with one another to arrive at standards that offer great benefits to the customer.) Windows 95 was the first commercial manifestation of an operating system to completely embrace this standard. Windows 98 continued the trend and Windows 2000 and Windows Me improved the operating system's use of the standard. Windows XP takes Plug and Play even further by making it more stable and more automated. Windows XP contains the most extensive device driver database ever included in an operating system.

Everyone knows it is relatively difficult to set up PC hardware (and accompanying hardware drivers), especially when your computer is filled with cards from different manufacturers. The major difficulties are as follows:

♦ Assigning hardware interrupts, of which there are only 16 — and some of these are used by the basic computer hardware

♦ Assigning nonconflicting I/O addresses so that each add-on card can have its own unique address

♦ Assigning direct memory access (DMA) channels (in non-PCI bus cards) so that there is no conflict

♦ Installing PC Cards (formerly known as PCMCIA cards) that adhere to different standards

- Setting monitor parameters to automatically work with your video card
- Making sure there are no memory blocks used (especially by video and network cards) that conflict with memory assignments, particularly in upper memory
- Recognizing and highlighting conflicts so they can be resolved
- Gracefully handling multiple hardware configurations for one computer — for example, docking stations with portables
- Recognizing when the hardware configuration changes, so that the operating system and Windows-aware application software can take the appropriate action

Microsoft realized that many of its support calls had to do with hardware conflicts of the first three types. Hardware manufacturers realized that it was more difficult to sell add-on devices (in particular multimedia kits) when they were so difficult to install.

The first order of business for Plug and Play was to make it easier to install hardware and to resolve any conflicts with the hardware interrupts, the I/O address, the memory ranges used, and the DMA channel used, if any. Windows solves most of these problems automatically and gives you the tools to solve the rest.

Plug and Play in Windows XP combines the best features of Windows 2000 and Windows Me, making hardware detection and management a real snap. Hundreds of devices that were not supported in Windows 2000 are now supported in Windows XP, and you'll find that USB, IEEE 1394, and PCI devices are better supported than ever before. Windows XP supports digital media devices better than any previous versions of Windows, making XP a true digital media machine.

> **CROSS-REFERENCE:** For more on digital media and Windows XP, see Chapter 9.

Universal Plug and Play

Universal Plug and Play (UPnP) is a new feature that is supported in Windows XP. Whereas Plug and Play refers to a local machine's hardware, Universal Plug and Play provides network device detection and usage. UPnP is much more than an extension of Plug and Play in Windows XP because it enables your XP computer to detect network devices, to install them, and to automatically use them without any intervention from you. In fact, UPnP is basically considered "invisible" because it handles the installation and management of network and local devices without intervention from you.

UPnP is defined by protocols and familiar computer languages, so it is not tied to one operating system. UPnP uses TCP/IP and standard Internet languages, such as XML (extensible markup language), in order to communicate with devices and operating systems. The result is networked devices that can be dynamically detected and installed so that they are ready to use.

UPnP has a number of potential uses including basic network hardware usage, home automation, and printing, as well as several additional applications. Because Windows XP automatically supports UPnP, there is nothing for you to configure on your system; however, you can check to make sure that UPnP is installed on your system. Just follow these steps:

STEPS

Universal Plug and Play

1. Open Control Panel and double-click Add/Remove Programs.
2. Click the Add/Remove Windows Components button.
3. In the Windows Components window, select Networking Services, and then click Details.

4. In the Networking Services window, ensure that Universal Plug and Play is selected, as shown in Figure 11-1. If it is not selected, you can select it and click OK to install it.

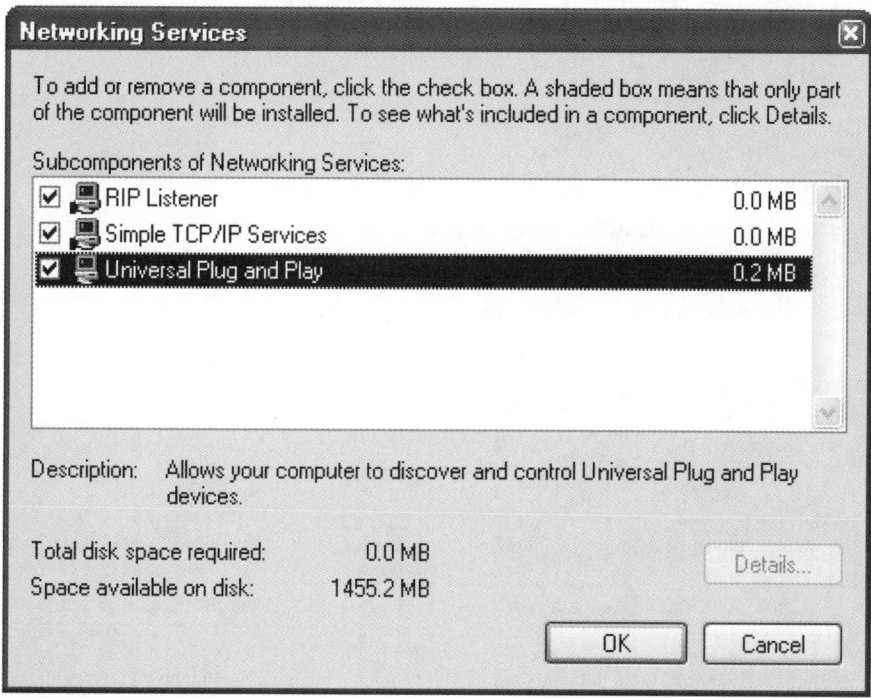

Figure 11-1: Universal Plug and Play

32-bit Drivers

Windows XP is a 32-bit operating system, and one big part of that is its 32-bit drivers. Microsoft has released close to 2000 new 32-bit device drivers in addition to those that initially shipped with the original Windows 95 operating system. All the 32-bit device drivers get loaded into extended memory so they don't take up conventional or upper memory.

Not only are the drivers 32-bit, but they also have lots of new features — features that come about because they have more room to wiggle in extended memory. The Device Manager and the Add New Hardware Wizard install these new drivers for the hardware that they detect. When you run Windows XP Setup, it casts aside 16-bit drivers in favor of the new 32-bit drivers.

SECRET: There is a file in your \Windows folder named Ios.ini that contains the names of the hardware driver files that can be (and are) *safely* replaced by 32-bit drivers in Windows. *Safe* just means that the 32-bit driver implements at least all of the functionality of the 16-bit driver. If you find that your real-mode driver is listed but provides functionality missing from the replacement 32-bit driver, you can delete it from the list and reinstall the 16-bit driver.

New 32-bit drivers are available from the Microsoft Windows Update Web site. If you have an Internet connection, choose Start ⇨ Settings ⇨ Windows Update to get the latest drivers for your hardware. Microsoft has also implemented digital signatures as a part of the system integrity process. Because of this feature, you are notified if an "unsigned driver" is used.

NOTE: There is also a 64-bit version of Windows XP, the first 64-bit operating system designed by Microsoft. The 64-bit version is designed for intense networking functionality and for video production and other types of multimedia that heavily consume system resources.

Plug and Play BIOS and Devices

If you are using Windows XP, your computer uses a Plug and Play BIOS, and it is likely that all of your devices are Plug and Play compliant. Windows enumerates all the Plug and Play devices it recognizes in your computer — including buses such as ISAPNP, PCI, and PCMCIA (PC Card) — each time you start Windows. This also happens when the computer's BIOS sends information that the computer's hardware configuration has changed, and when you click the Refresh button in the Device Manager. This enumeration is different than hardware *detection* (see the next section, "Hardware Detection") because it only applies to Plug and Play devices.

If Windows does not recognize your computer as being Plug and Play, there may be an updated system BIOS available for your particular model that is more fully compliant with the Microsoft Plug and Play standard. You are not likely to encounter this problem unless you are using a pre-PCI system. Check out your computer manufacturer's Web site for more information.

Hardware Detection

Windows Setup detects installed hardware and drivers for a broad range of pre-Plug and Play hardware as well as the new stuff. Detection happens during Windows setup, and when you use the Add New Hardware Wizard. Windows doesn't run the hardware-detection program each time you start Windows. (However, the Plug and Play BIOS flags new hardware and passes the hardware ID information to Windows for driver assignment.)

> **SECRET:** Hardware detection most likely will assign your hard drive, floppy disk drives, and disk controller cards to the generic category, unless you have specific SCSI controllers. You may have manufacturer-specific hard disk driver software, but you shouldn't use it unless it has been updated for Windows XP and is 32-bit.

Windows creates a hardware-detection log called Detlog.txt in the root directory of your boot drive every time hardware detection runs. You can read this to see what hardware is being detected and in what order.

> **SECRET:** The installation files contain a database of existing hardware and drivers. This database is stored in specific inf files and coordinated by the Msdet.inf file. You find these files in the \Windows\Inf folder. (If you don't see the Inf folder, choose View ⇨ Folder Options in the Explorer, and mark Show hidden files and folders in the View tab.) The detection routines are noninvasive and do their best to determine just what you've installed over the years from one of a zillion different manufacturers.

Older IDE drives that are 1GB and larger often came with software that allowed them to be partitioned even in a computer with a BIOS that doesn't understand drives larger than 524MB. Windows works with Ontrack's Disk Manager 6.03 (and later) and other partition software of this nature.

Detecting non-Plug and Play display adapters is probably the most difficult problem for hardware detection because there are so many. Microsoft has written a series of display drivers, and Windows Setup does its best to install the correct one. However, if you are upgrading to Windows XP, XP will try to use the video driver that is working under the current version of Windows (the odds are very good that a Windows 2000 driver will work). However, you might need to download a newer driver for this older hardware from the manufacturer's Web site. You can install an older driver and use it on Windows XP, but you might lose some functionality.

> **SECRET:** Windows Setup checks your BIOS to determine if you have Automated Power Management features compatible with the APM 1.0 and APM 1.1 standards. If you do, a Power Management icon will appear in your Control Panel. You can use this icon to adjust the power control settings of your portable.

Lots of portables have a BIOS that is not really compatible with APM 1.0 or 1.1 (as far as Microsoft is concerned). So, even if you have control of your power-saving configuration through your BIOS settings, you may not have an APM icon in your Control Panel. You just won't have the convenience of power management through Windows. Look in the Device Manager under System Devices for other APM features, which may or may not work on your portable.

> **SECRET:** Hardware detection finds only one keyboard, even if you have a portable with an external keyboard plugged into it. Both keyboards will be live. If your external keyboard is an extended keyboard and the one on the portable is not, you should make sure that the extended keyboard driver is installed (or install it if it isn't).
>
> Windows XP can support multiple mice simultaneously. If you have a trackball built into your portable as well as a serial mouse attached to a serial port, Windows Setup will recognize and install two mouse drivers. Both mice should work. If only one driver is installed, you can install the other after initial setup. The mice will most likely be on different interrupts, so you won't have to do any interrupt conflict resolution. If that is not the case, see the section entitled "The Device Manager" later in this chapter.

Detection after setup

Hardware detection takes place during Windows setup, but you can also force it to happen later, or you can install a driver for a specific device that may or may not be physically installed yet. You use the Add New Hardware icon in your Control Panel, discussed later in this chapter in "Adding New Hardware Drivers," to install new drivers for your devices.

However, if you physically install new hardware without using the Add New Hardware icon and the device is Plug and Play compatible, the device will notify Windows that it has been installed, and Windows will install a driver automatically. A note will appear in your Notification Area (formerly System Tray) to tell you that the device has been installed.

The hardware Registry

Windows keeps information about installed hardware and its drivers in the Registry. The original entries are made during Windows setup. You can use the Registry Editor to view the hardware drivers installed on your computer. To learn how to invoke the Registry Editor, see Chapter 12.

> **SECRET:** You'll find references to your hardware under the HKEY_LOCAL_MACHINE key, specifically under the Enum (enumeration) subkey. It's easy to use the Registry Editor to view the values stored there.

When you start Windows, a dynamic hardware tree is created based on information in the Registry. This tree is stored in RAM (random access memory), and you can view it using the Registry Editor under the HKEY_DYN_DATA\Config Manager\Enum subkey. Looking at this data is not particularly enlightening, as you will quickly see for yourself. It consists of unique keys that enumerate the installed hardware and its current status.

The hardware tree in RAM is updated every time the hardware configuration changes. Microsoft's favorite example is that the tree updates when you plug your portable into a docking station.

It is a much better idea to use the Device Manager to manage your hardware configuration. The Device Manager's user interface is a lot more informative and understandable. You should use the Registry Editor only if the Device Manager is not working for you, and you understand the effect of the changes that you are making to the Registry.

Adding New Hardware Drivers

In a perfect world, you would physically install your new device, such as a printer, in your computer (or perhaps plug it into a port), and the drivers for that device would be automatically installed and the device activated. If you install a Plug and Play–compliant device, this usually happens.

You may need to turn off the computer first so that you don't inadvertently cause any electrical damage when you install a card in a slot (although you can plug in PC Cards without turning off your computer). After you turn your computer back on, you may be asked for a floppy disk or CD-ROM from the device manufacturer that contains the drivers needed to use the device. If the drivers for that device were shipped with Windows, you may be asked to insert the Windows CD-ROM. After Windows installs the new drivers, you'll be able to use your new device.

If the device is pre-Plug and Play, you may need to click the Add New Hardware icon in the Control Panel (as shown in Figure 11-2) to inform Windows that it needs to check for the new hardware and add a new driver.

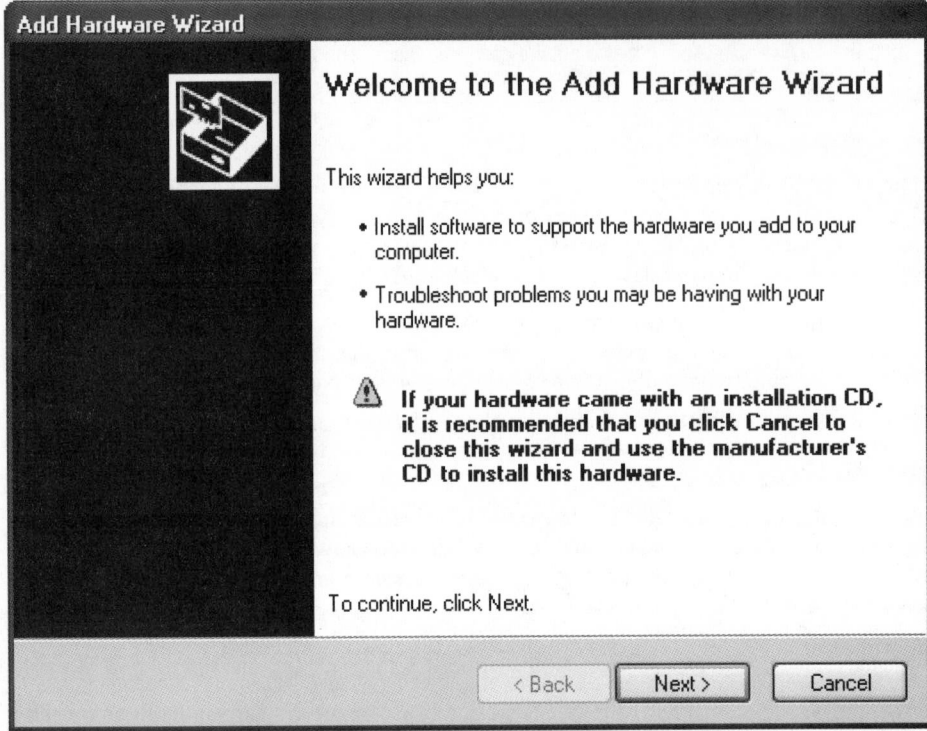

Figure 11-2: The Add New Hardware Wizard invokes the hardware-detection routines to find your pre-Plug and Play device.

This wizard will first run through the Plug and Play enumeration process to make sure that this isn't a Plug and Play device. You can then have the wizard attempt to automatically detect your installed hardware (and thereby find the device that you just installed). Alternately (or afterward if your hardware is not detected), you can direct the wizard to install a specific driver by providing it with a manufacturer and model designation or by pointing it toward an installation floppy disk from the manufacturer (see Figure 11-3).

> **NOTE:** The Add Hardware Wizard is designed to help you install older devices that cannot be automatically installed by Windows XP. This "legacy" approach to hardware is slowly dying, however, and you will find that Windows XP will not be as friendly to older devices as was Windows 9x and Me. Remember that Windows XP is built on the Windows 2000 code base and it expects that you are using up-to-date hardware. If you are, you will have few to no problems, but if you are still trying to use older cards, don't be surprised if XP simply will not work with them.

Device Manager

The Windows Control Panel is filled with icons that let you manage your computer's hardware and drivers. You explored them in Chapter 10. If you have a question about a specific piece of hardware, turn to the chapter that focuses on that hardware.

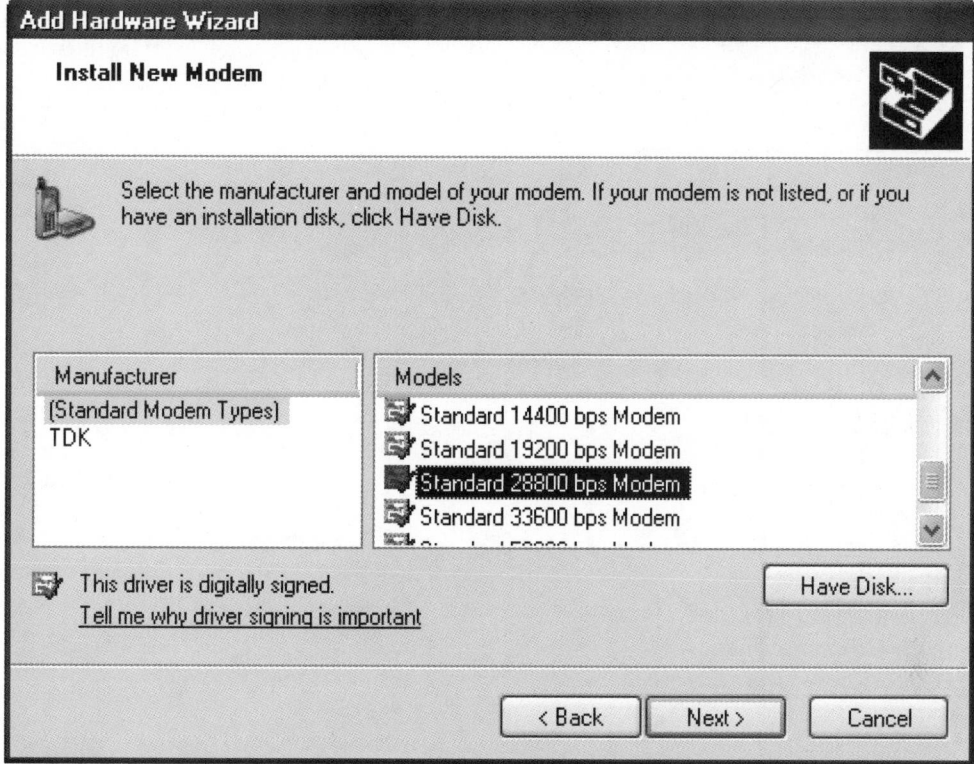

Figure 11-3: You can have the wizard attempt to automatically detect your hardware. If you know what driver you want installed, you can pick the manufacturer and model yourself.

The Device Manager, which you access through the System icon in the Control Panel, or via the Computer Management console, provides a general view of all hardware installed on your computer. Sometimes the Device Manager and the hardware-specific icons overlap in functionality, and sometimes you can do something only in one and not the other.

The Device Manager is a powerful tool. Nothing like this was available before Microsoft released Windows 95, even from third-party software developers that created Windows-specific diagnostic tools. The Device Manager superseded MSD, the Microsoft Diagnostic tool that came with Windows 3.1*x*, but which was never documented by Microsoft. The Device Manager is much easier to use and much more powerful than MSD. The Device Manager is shown in Figure 11-4.

Devices are listed in the Device Manager. Click the plus sign to the left of a device type to see the installed devices. Double-click a particular device name to display its Properties dialog box. You can also highlight a device and click the Properties button.

If you mark the View devices by connection option found on the View menu, the devices are displayed hierarchically by their hardware connection to the motherboard.

If there is a yellow exclamation mark over a device name, it means that there is a problem with the device driver. This mostly likely indicates a resource conflict. You may need to set different jumper settings on a non-Plug and Play device. Use the Device Manager to track down these conflicts.

If you have to hunt for the source of a problem, highlight the Computer icon in the Device Manager and then click the Properties button. In the View Resources tab of the Computer Properties dialog box, successively click the option buttons to check for interrupt, I/O, memory, and DMA channel conflicts.

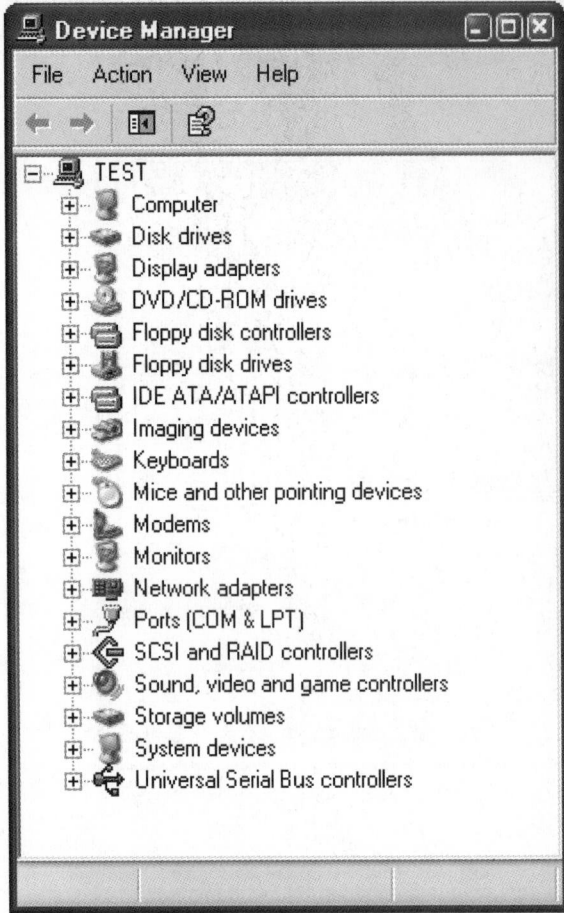

Figure 11-4: Device Manager

The yellow exclamation mark may also indicate a missing device that was previously installed, or a removable device (such as a Zip drive). You can remove the device permanently (until you reinstall it) by highlighting the device and clicking Remove.

If there is a red X over your device, the Device Manager is telling you that this device isn't functioning. Check the installation of the device; it may not have been properly installed. Or, you may need an updated driver.

Choose File ⇨ Print to generate a report of the devices in the computer. You can specify a summary report, a report on a specific device, or a report for all the devices. The report lists your devices, their properties, and the resources they use.

IRQs, I/O, memory addresses, DMA channels

Windows XP automatically handles the gory details of hardware management. Unless you are using a non-Plug and Play device, you should never have to configure any of these settings. However, should there be a problem with a device, Device Manager and System Information make troubleshooting much easier. You can access System Information and view all the IRQ and related hardware settings, or you can view them individually by device in device manager. To access System Information, just choose Start ⇨ Run, type **Msinfo32** and click OK.

NOTE: Even though Plug and Play gives you the ability to be oblivious to hardware configuration and setup, for troubleshooting purposes, it is a good idea to know thing or two about hardware resource assignment, such as IRQs.

To view the specific resource settings for each device and to make changes in the case of conflicts, expand the desired category in Device Manager, select the device, and then click the Properties button. Click the Resources tab, which is shown in Figure 11-5. You can examine the resources here and note whether there are any conflicts; they are reported here also.

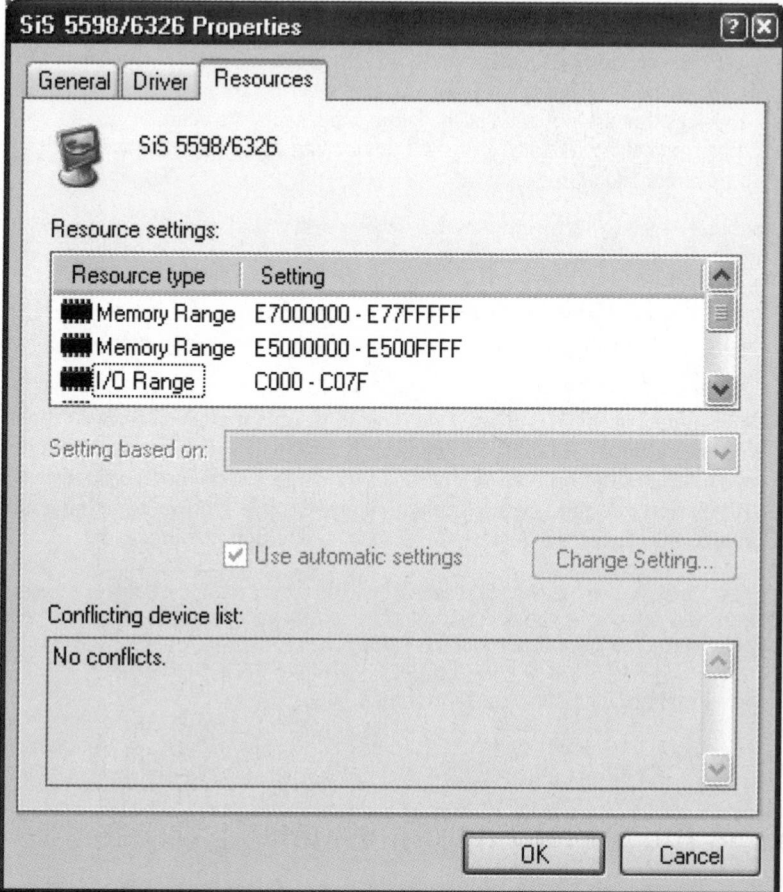

Figure 11-5: Resources tab

If you have Plug and Play devices, you should usually let the hardware-detection routines in Windows determine what the resource settings should be. If you set them manually, the settings become fixed and Windows can't adjust them to avoid conflicts. You can, however, change the resource settings for Plug and Play, as well as for non-Plug and Play, devices. Some devices are flagged and cannot be changed at all, except during startup or enumeration. Others, however, can be edited, but only when the device is inactive, and still others cannot be changed because they must map to established BIOS rules.

Should you need to make resource changes for a device, see the device's Resource tab found on the device's properties dialog box. You'll see the IRQ settings along with memory allocation settings, and you can make changes to the settings (if possible).

If you need to make resource changes, be sure you don't introduce any new resource use conflicts. If you print a copy of the system summary, you have a ready reference on resource use. Also, the Device Manager tracks conflicts and can warn you when you have created them.

If you changed settings in the driver for a non-Plug and Play device, you need to make the same changes to the hardware itself. You may need to either change the jumpers on the device to match the settings that you just made, or, if the hardware device is software configurable, you may need to run the manufacturer's software to reconfigure the hardware. This may require opening a DOS window to run the hardware configuration software.

IRQ conflicts

Windows lets two physical devices share the same interrupt request line (IRQ) under certain circumstances. Many Peripheral Component Interconnect (PCI) devices are capable of sharing IRQs through the use of *IRQ steering* (see the section "IRQ steering"), which can be a big help if you have lots of devices fighting for resources. However, it doesn't work for two devices that are used at the same time, such as a modem and a mouse. Devices that are not used at the same time, such as a scanner and a modem, are much better candidates for sharing IRQs. A non-PCI device can't share an IRQ with a PCI device. Each device still keeps a different I/O address.

IRQ sharing can happen automatically when you install new hardware. You can also set the interrupts for a given piece of hardware using the Device Manager. Double-click a specific device in the Device Manager, click the Resources tab, clear the Use automatic settings check box, and change settings as described in the previous section. If you have problems with IRQ sharing on an older computer, you may need to upgrade the computer's BIOS. You can get an upgraded BIOS from a third-party supplier, or you can go to your computer manufacturer's Web site.

You can also disable a device to eliminate an IRQ conflict. You have to disable it physically first (check the documentation that came with the device to find out how) and then disable it in the Device Manager. If the device is an integrated device that resides on your motherboard (such as a serial port), you also have to disable it in the BIOS. If you don't do this, the next time you power up Windows, the Plug and Play enumeration process will notice the difference, restore the device, and assign resources to it.

> **NOTE:** Aside from an IRQ conflict, there may be any number of reasons that you would want to disable a device. For example, if a driver is giving you problems, you can disable the device for troubleshooting purposes. Also, depending on the device, disabling it can free up more system resources that can used for other purposes.

To completely disable a device and reclaim its resources, follow these steps:

STEPS

Disabling a device in the current configuration

1. Open Device Manager.
2. Click the plus sign next to the type of device you are looking for, and then double-click the device that you want to disable to open its Properties dialog box.
3. Click the General tab, and then choose the Do not use this device option from the drop-down menu. Click OK. (If you have multiple profiles, this applies only to the current one.)
4. Restart your computer.
5. If you are disabling a device that is not integrated on your motherboard, you are finished. If this is an integrated device, you must now disable the device in your computer's BIOS settings. The exact steps for doing this vary from one computer to the next. In general terms, you need to press a key during your computer's power-on self-test to enter your BIOS's setup program, and then set the value in that program to disable the device.

If your computer has a specialized port — for a PS/2 mouse, for example — you may see that device listed in your Device Manager even if you don't have one connected. Sometimes just having the capability on your motherboard to support such a port is enough to make it show up, even if you don't have a physical port. Disabling the device using the steps above may free up these resources, but not in every case.

IRQ steering

Windows XP supports a feature called *IRQ steering* that allows devices to share interrupts. With IRQ steering, Windows can catch messages sent to an IRQ and reroute them to the next available IRQ. This is useful for PCI bus devices in laptops with docking stations. As hardware is added and subtracted (when docking occurs), PCI devices can be dynamically reconfigured to work together. In addition, if two PCI cards are sharing an interrupt, IRQ steering "steers" the request to the correct card. It can also determine whether a PCI card needs an IRQ at all (many don't). If IRQ steering is not enabled, the BIOS handles this routing instead of Windows.

IRQ steering is enabled by default. In Device Manager, expand Computer and select the Standard Computer icon. Click Properties, and then click the IRQ Steering tab. You can see that IRQ Steering is enabled, as shown in Figure 11-6.

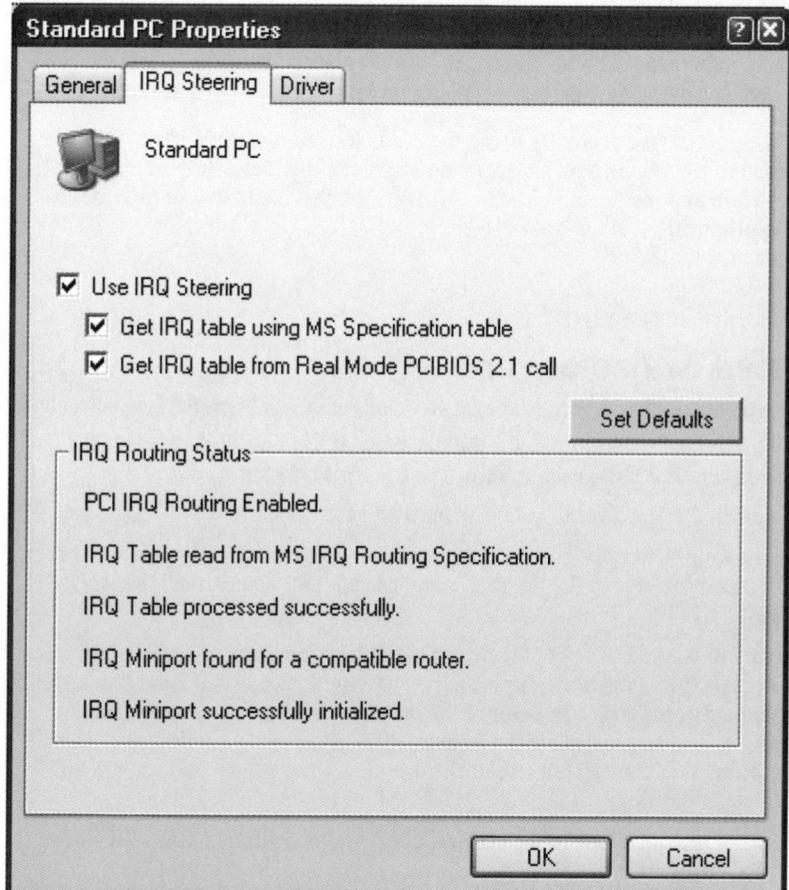

Figure 11-6: IRQ Steering tab

Forced configurations

You can manually assign IRQs, I/O addresses, and DMA channels, and direct Windows to use the ones you assign. After you manually assign a specific configuration to a device, Windows is no longer free to change that configuration if new hardware is added later. This is true even if the device that you configure is Plug and Play compatible.

It is best to allow Plug and Play to assign resources to all your Plug and Play devices. This gives the enumerator maximum flexibility to reconfigure Windows if new devices are added. If you have a Plug and Play BIOS and you force a configuration, Windows will also change the BIOS to match your forced settings if those settings are available to the BIOS.

PC Cards

PC Cards, previously known as PCMCIA cards, are most popular in laptops. They let you swap devices (such as a modem or floppy drive) "on the fly," without turning off your computer. Windows supports many of these products, including many that are not Plug and Play compatible.

If you have trouble installing or using PC Cards, you can access the Windows PC Card Troubleshooter by choosing Start ⇨ Help, and then clicking Troubleshooting in the Contents tab, clicking Windows Troubleshooting, and clicking PC Card.

Updating device drivers

You can install new device drivers over existing ones for some devices by using the Device Manager. You may want to do this when you get a new driver from your hardware manufacturer. Or you might want to check whether Microsoft has made new drivers available on its Windows Update Web site.

You could, of course, install the new device driver by using the Add New Hardware Wizard. However, this wizard is primarily designed to search for new hardware and to install the corresponding driver. If you haven't installed new hardware and just want to update a driver, the Device Manager provides a semantically friendlier starting point.

STEPS

Installing an updated device driver

1. Double-click the specific device in the Device Manager to open the device's properties dialog box.

2. Click the Driver tab in the Properties dialog box for the device, if it has one. If there is no Driver tab, you can't update the driver. The Driver tab is shown in Figure 11-7.

3. Click Update Driver to launch the Hardware Update Wizard and then click Next.

4. The wizard offers to search for a better driver than the one you have or to let you select the driver from a list. If you ask the wizard to search for the driver and click Next, you can tell the wizard where to look (see Figure 11-8).

5. If you told the wizard that you wanted to select the driver in the previous step, it will display a list of the drivers for that device type (modems, for example) that came with Windows. By default, the list is set to Show compatible hardware; you will see only the drivers that Windows knows are compatible with your device. To see a complete list of available drivers for your device type, select the Show all hardware option. You can choose one of the drivers on the list, or you can click Have Disk if you have a new driver on a floppy disk, on a CD-ROM, or on your hard drive.

6. When you've answered all of the questions in the wizard, click Finish, and then click OK in the Driver tab of the Properties dialog box.

7. Restart your computer to enable the new driver to take effect.

Resolving resource conflicts the easy way

There is another way to resolve resource conflicts. Windows Help contains a Hardware Conflict Troubleshooter. It gives you a little background on resource conflicts and then promptly leads you to the exact same places that we just covered. It's kind of cute, though.

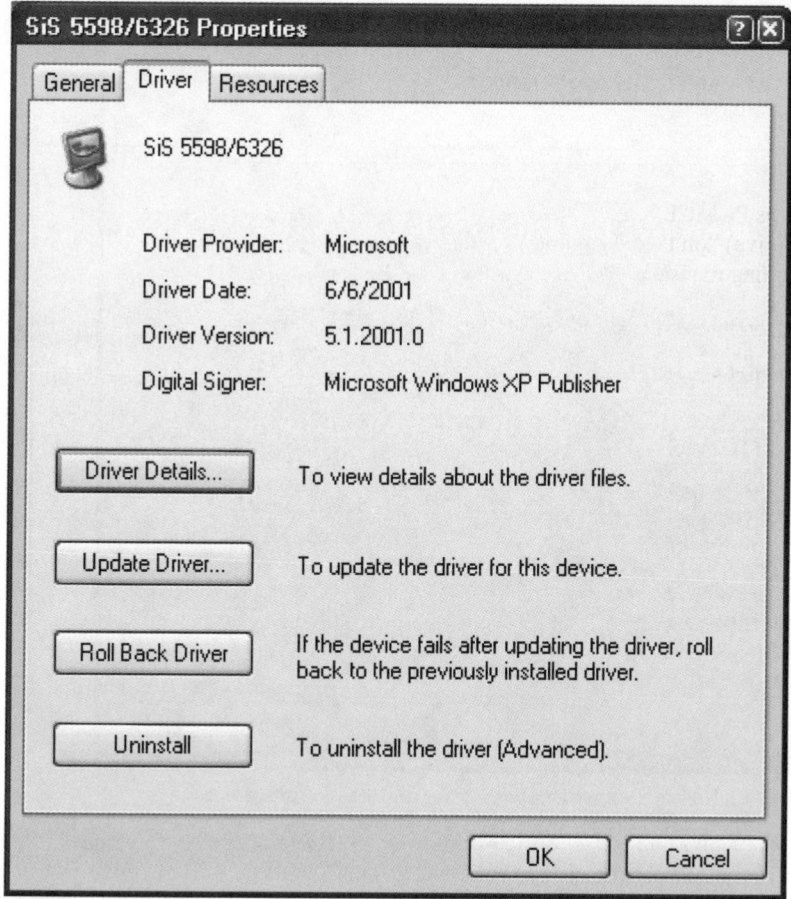

Figure 11-7: Driver tab

STEPS

Starting the Hardware Conflict Troubleshooter

1. Choose Start ➪ Help. The Windows XP Help and Support Center appears.

2. In the main window, click Hardware, and then click Fixing a Hardware Problem in the Hardware section.

3. The Hardware Troubleshooter appears in the right pane, as shown in Figure 11-9.

4. Follow the suggestions and shortcuts to the Device Manager.

Hardware Profiles

We have *hardware profiles* for different hardware configurations on one computer, *user profiles* for different users on the same computer, and *Windows Messaging profiles* (if you have Windows Messaging installed) for different e-mail services. Windows presents us with quite a prolific world.

Windows can automatically load the hardware drivers that it needs based on the hardware it detects and stores in the hardware tree in RAM. Change the configuration (by pulling the portable from the docking station, for example), and Windows reconfigures itself dynamically.

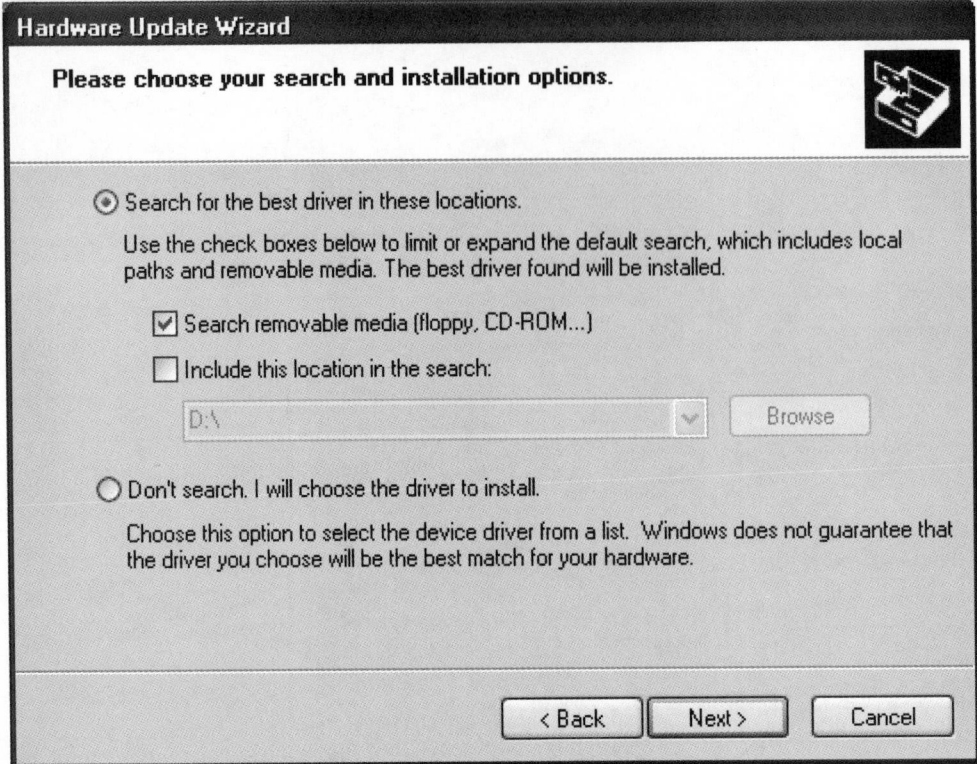

Figure 11-8: The Hardware Update Wizard offers to search for a better driver, and asks you where to look.

The static hardware profiles are a bit of a kludge. A menu comes up in DOS full-screen text mode before the Windows Desktop appears and asks you to choose your current configuration. Still, if you are using a laptop computer that is docked in some cases and not in others, the profile option can make your life easier and save your laptop some hardware confusion.

> **TIP:** You have to set up the hardware profiles manually. You install all the drivers for all the hardware configurations for all the profiles, and then assign the proper set of drivers to each profile. The hardware doesn't have to be installed at the time that you install the drivers. You can just install the drivers, and then make any necessary changes later if there is a difference between the device settings and the resource settings that you chose.

To create multiple hardware configurations, take the following steps:

STEPS

Creating multiple hardware configurations

1. Use the Add New Hardware Wizard to install all the drivers applicable for all your configurations. Tell the wizard what to install if you don't have all the hardware physically installed at the moment. You can run the Add New Hardware Wizard in each hardware configuration and have it search for the installed hardware if you like. This will also build up a base of installed hardware.

2. Click the System icon in the Control Panel, and then click the Hardware tab. Click the Hardware Profiles button. You see that the Original Configuration (or Undocked if you have a portable) is highlighted, as shown in Figure 11-10.

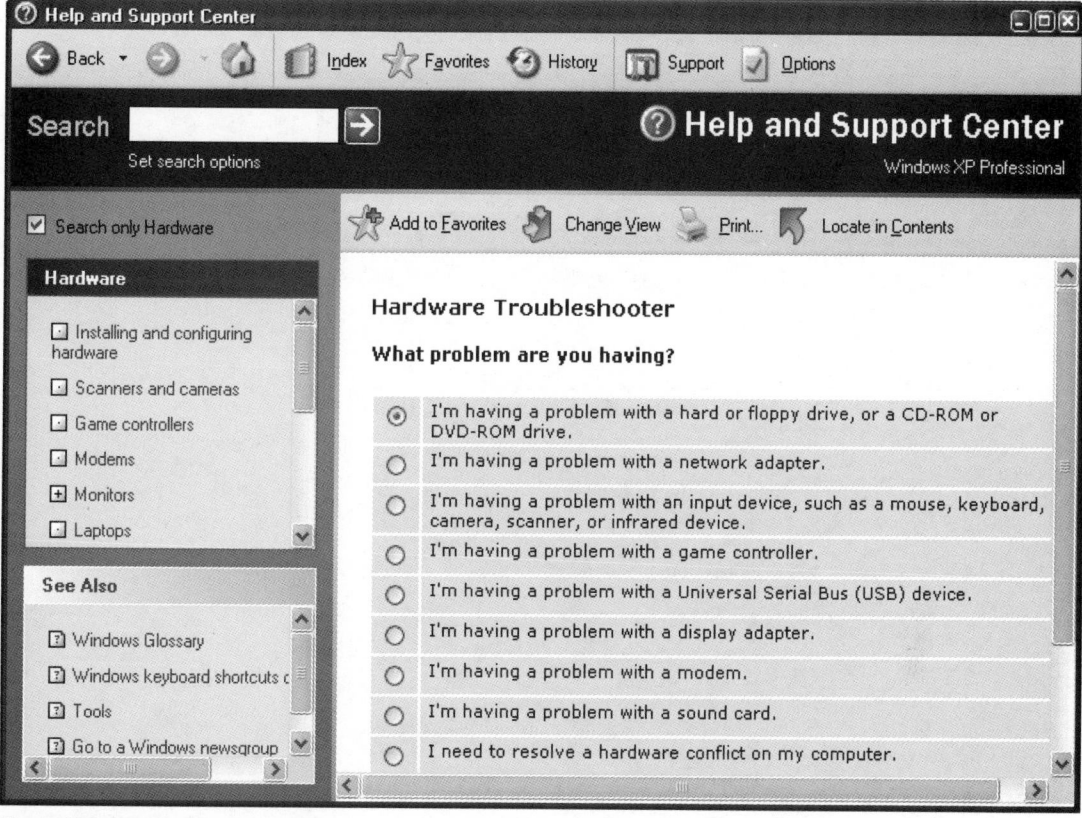

Figure 11-9: Hardware Troubleshooter

3. Click Copy and then type a name for the new profile in the Copy Profile dialog box. When done, click OK. You may want to use the Rename button to give Original Configuration (or Undocked) a more descriptive name as well.

4. Click OK, close the Control Panel, and restart your computer. Before the Windows desktop reappears, you will see a text menu showing the profiles you have set up. Select a profile by typing its number (in this case, choose a profile that you just created). Windows starts up in that profile.

5. Open the Control Panel, click the System icon, and click the Device Manager tab. Double-click each applicable device to display its Properties dialog box. In the Device Usage area of General tab, mark or clear check boxes to disable or remove the device from the profile you are currently in.

6. After completely defining the hardware available for this hardware profile, repeat Steps 4 and 5 for each hardware profile you have created. You must restart your computer each time for the changes in the profile configuration to take effect.

For some devices, you will have an additional option in Step 5, between the check boxes Remove in this hardware profile and Disable in this hardware profile. If you remove a device from one of your profiles and then need to restore it later, the Add New Hardware Wizard may not detect it. Instead of removing a device in the Device Manager, you should normally disable it. To restore a device that was accidentally removed from one profile, you need to remove it from all the profiles. Then run the Add New Hardware Wizard to reinstall the device, and use Steps 4 and 5, detailed previously, to restore the device to each profile.

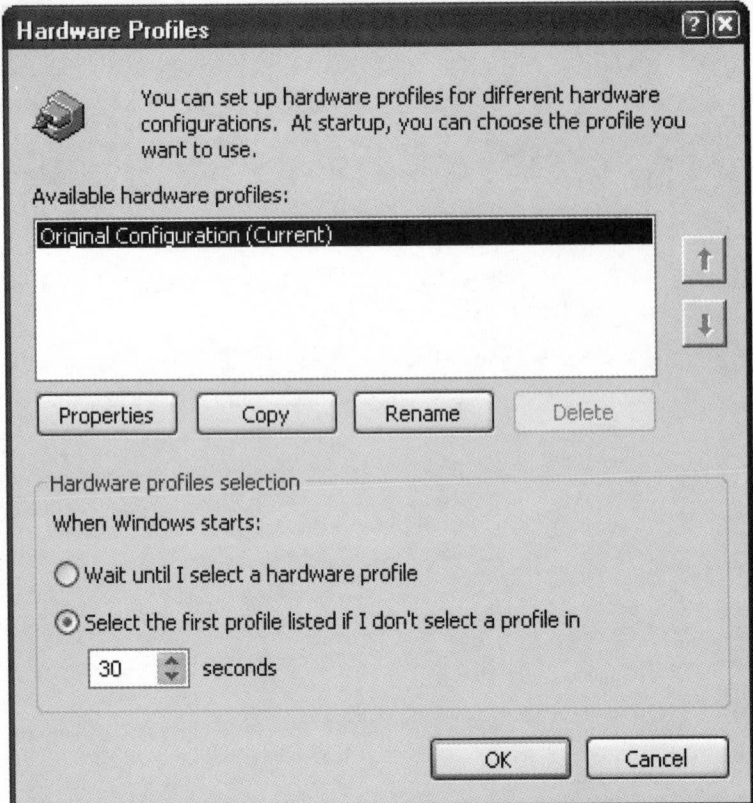

Figure 11-10: Hardware Profiles

LCDs and external monitors

Perhaps you have a portable that uses its built-in LCD screen in one configuration and uses an external monitor in another. You can choose a different monitor for each of the two separate hardware configurations. If the portable is not Plug and Play compatible, you will probably want to do this. Portable computers that aren't Plug and Play compatible can have problems with the Windows video drivers supplied by Microsoft (and developed in cooperation with the video chip and card manufacturers). The video chips inside many portable computers can drive external monitors to greater resolutions than the LCD screen can handle. In some cases, the older generic video drivers that come with Windows are not sophisticated enough to be capable of handling the switch between a lower-resolution LCD screen and a higher-resolution external monitor.

Problems occur when you're attempting to view Windows on the LCD display (or after you've set the portable to feed the video signal to both the external monitor and the LCD display). If the Windows video drivers are set for a resolution above the resolution supported by the LCD display, Windows displays an error message indicating that the video driver settings need to be changed. The Windows Desktop is then displayed at the lower LCD resolution (640×480) and at a reduced color depth of 16 colors.

You can make up for some of the lost functionality of the older, generic Windows video drivers for non-Plug and Play portables. It takes a bit of doing, but you can configure your computer and Windows to let you manually switch between the LCD screen and the external monitor at bootup in a manner that eliminates the Windows video error message, sets the proper resolution, and retains 256-color depth.

The first step is to set your portable's BIOS to output to the external monitor. You need to do this because the Windows video drivers determine the maximum video resolution based on the display that's currently set to receive the video signal, and they will drop to the lower resolution if the video signal is set to feed to the LCD screen or (in some cases) to both screens.

How you change your computer's BIOS settings varies among BIOS manufacturers. Check your computer documentation for specific instructions for accessing BIOS setup.

After you've changed your BIOS settings, you need to create two Windows hardware profiles. Unless you have a Plug and Play external monitor and Plug and Play video chips in the portable, the Windows hardware-detection routines won't be able to tell that you have two displays, so you're going to have to force the issue.

Hot swapping and hot docking

A Plug and Play–compatible computer can notify Windows when the connection with a docking station is made or broken. This triggers a reconfiguration of the hardware tree, which, in turn, makes Windows aware of the new hardware.

> **TIP:** You can plug a device into your SCSI controller card (if you have one), and then use the SCSI device (for example, a SCSI-based Zip drive) without having to restart Windows. Unfortunately, Windows doesn't automatically check that you've installed a new device. You need to give it a hint. To do this, open the Device Manager (click the System icon in the Control Panel and click the Device Manager tab), choose the View devices by connection option button, highlight Computer, and click Refresh. However, due to proper bus termination issues, SCSI devices typically should not (or cannot) be hot plugged.

Look for the new device by opening up the branches in the Device Manager and looking for your SCSI host adapter. Check whether the new device is connected to it.

Sound Cards, CD-ROMs, and LPT Ports

Windows doesn't flag interrupt conflicts between devices such as sound cards and CD-ROMs and the LPT1 and LPT2 ports. LPT1 and LPT2 use interrupts 7 and 5, respectively. Many sound cards and CD-ROMs are also set by default to use these very same interrupts. In spite of this conflict, the Device Manager doesn't inform us that it exists.

The Device Manager is silent on this conflict because printers connected to these parallel ports really don't use these interrupts. In some ways, the IRQs are up for grabs.

The problem is that Direct Cable Connection (DCC) *does* use these interrupts when it is configured to use a parallel cable. DCC is at its fastest when it uses the parallel ports, and it slows by a factor of three if it finds a sound card or CD-ROM drive using these interrupts. The only way you notice this is by testing the speed of communication across these ports. If you notice a problem, change the resource settings in the Device Manager so that the LPT port is set on interrupt 7 and the sound card or CD-ROM is on interrupt 5.

Finding interrupts for new peripherals

It is most unfortunate that we still have only the 16 defined interrupts that came with the original IBM AT hardware. PCI architecture does add interrupt sharing, and Windows XP does support IRQ steering, which allows the interrupts to be shared. Still, there may be times when you could use a few free interrupts.

It is possible to free up hardwired interrupts with a bit of rewiring, or at least reconfiguring, on your part.

If your computer has COM2 enabled, but you are not using this port for a modem or a serial connection, you can disable it. You can do this either in your computer's BIOS or by rearranging jumper connectors on your computer's motherboard or peripheral card. The same is true of any other COM port that is available to be freed up.

Newer computers allow you to disable the serial device in the computer's BIOS. You'll need to restart Windows and press the designated key during power-on self-test to enter the BIOS setup program. Then navigate within the setup menus to find the menu in which you can disable the serial ports. The designated key and the menu structure are different for every BIOS.

> **NOTE:** It is important to note concerning BIOS that some allow you to let one or both COM ports become Plug and Play autoconfigured devices rather than simply legacy or disabled.

If you have an older computer or a card that is configured with jumpers, you need to refer to the manual to correctly change the jumper settings.

After you disable the serial port, remove it from your Device Manager. Restart Windows after making the changes in your BIOS or jumpers. Open Device Manager, highlight the disabled communications port under the Ports (COM & LPT) branch, and click the Disable button (see Figure 11-11). The port that you have disabled should be marked with a yellow exclamation point.

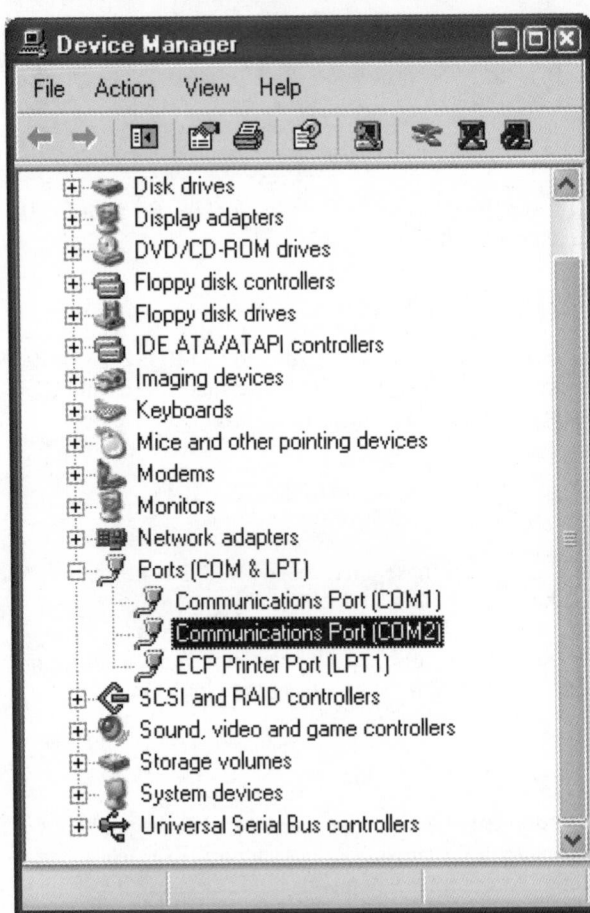

Figure 11-11: Select the port you want to disable.

Some motherboards and chipsets still let Windows see the serial ports even if they have been disabled in the BIOS. In these cases, my recommendations won't work.

If your computer has a dual PCI IDE controller that is used to control only one device (most likely your hard disk), then it is possible to free up one half of the dual controller, which frees up interrupt 15. You need to do this in your computer's BIOS.

Be sure that your computer isn't using the second IDE controller. While your hard disk may be on the first controller, your CD-ROM drive could be on the second. If it is, don't do this. The Device Manager won't tell you directly, nor will Microsoft System Information. You have to check in your computer's BIOS and use your hardware manuals.

After you disable the second controller in your computer's BIOS, restart Windows and go to your Device Manager. The Secondary IDE controller will be marked with a yellow exclamation point. Highlight the device and click Remove. Then click OK.

Finally, you can free up interrupt 7 (or perhaps interrupt 5) by disabling LPT1, your parallel port (again, in your computer's BIOS or with jumpers), and then removing it from the Device Manager. You'll be able to do this and still print to your printer if your parallel port hardware supports ECP (enhanced capabilities port). ECP is an enhanced communication feature that enables bidirectional traffic from the computer and printer, as well as more user management control features. See the following steps.

STEPS

Freeing up IRQ 7 or IRQ 5

1. Start your computer. During the power-on self-test, press the designated key to enter your BIOS setup. Disable your LPT1 parallel port. Exit the BIOS setup, saving your changes.

2. Start Windows. Access Device Manager. Click the plus sign next to Ports (COM & LPT) and highlight your LPT1 port. Click the Disable button, and then click OK.

3. Choose Start ⇨ Turn Off Computer ⇨ Turn Off.

4. Turn off your computer and install the device that is configured to use IRQ 7 (or IRQ 5).

5. Turn on your computer, and let Windows install the new device, using drivers either from the Windows CD-ROM or from the device manufacturer's floppy disks. Go to the Device Manager and make sure that the device is installed. If it is, shut down Windows.

6. Re-enable LPT1 in your BIOS before restarting Windows. Windows should automatically find the LPT port when it restarts.

7. Check in the Device Manager to see if Windows indicates a conflict. Even if there is an exclamation mark next to the LPT1 device, it may work fine.

8. If your parallel port can operate as an ECP port, you can define it to take advantage of these characteristics, and then remove the conflicting LPT1 port. Use the Add New Hardware control panel applet to manually add the ECP port, and then follow the remaining steps.

9. In the Device Manager, click the LPT1 port, click Properties, click the Resources tab, and write down the Input/Output Range memory values. Click Cancel, and then remove the original LPT1 device by clicking the Remove button and OK while the LPT1 port is highlighted.

10. Click the ECP port in the Device Manager, click Properties, and click the Resources tab. Clear the Use automatic settings check box, and display the Setting based on field. Choose a setting (if possible) that matches the previous LPT1 Input/Output Range with no Interrupt Request. Click OK.

11. Shut down Windows and restart. Windows may redetect the LPT1 port. If this happens, you can most likely ignore the yellow exclamation point in your Device Manager regarding the LPT1 port.

With Plug and Play BIOSs, other devices may grab interrupts before your newly installed device has a chance to get the ones that you just freed up. That's fine; there should then be others available and you can use them.

Troubleshooting IRQ steering

If you find that you can't get your IRQ steering to work with your PCI bus, it may be because you don't have the latest patch for your VIA chipset. Of course, this is only true if your motherboard uses the VIA chipset. Check your computer's documentation for more information about the chipset

The cause: IRQ steering is disabled on the Use IRQ Steering check box on the IRQ Steering tab (see Figure 11-12). To get to this dialog box, open Device Manager, expand the Computer category, then right-click the Standard Computer icon and click Properties.

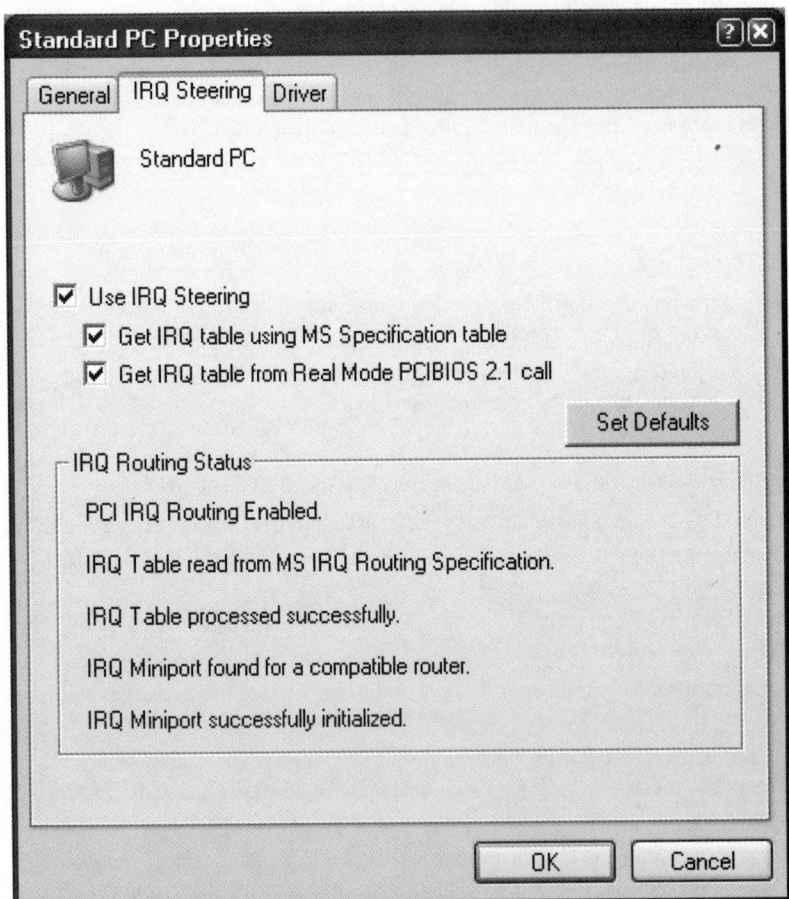

Figure 11-12: The IRQ Steering tab. Use IRQ Steering has been marked.

By default, IRQ Steering should be enabled on your computer, but if it is not, be sure to enable it, as well as the two secondary check box options, here.

Getting enough interrupts for your PCI cards

If you have only PCI cards, and not ISA cards, you want to be sure that all the interrupts are available to your PCI bus. If you have only Plug and Play PCI cards, you have no need for PCI steering. Make sure that your BIOS allocates all of the available interrupts to your PCI bus. This prevents them from being used by Plug and Play ISA cards (I am assuming you don't have any).

You have to go to your Plug and Play BIOS setup by pressing the indicated key during the power-on self-test. Navigate through the menus until you find the interrupt setup screen that enables you to nominate which interrupts are assigned to the PCI bus.

After you have configured your Plug and Play BIOS, install one PCI card at a time, and then confirm in the Device Manager that an interrupt has been assigned to the card. If you have two PCI cards that allow for interrupt sharing, install them last if you have only one interrupt left.

SECRET: If any of your PCI cards are not Plug and Play, you may need to enable PCI steering. Use the steps in the previous section to enable PCI steering, marking the Use IRQ Steering check box. If none of your PCI cards will share an interrupt, install your non-Plug and Play PCI cards last, and you won't have to enable PCI steering. If you have PCI cards that can share interrupts, and you have non-Plug and Play PCI cards, you will have to enable PCI steering.

USB

The Universal Serial Bus (USB) isn't universal yet, but it's available on most new computers. If you don't have a USB device attached to your computer, you can turn off USB support in your BIOS and save the time required to load the USB drivers in Windows. You have to get to your BIOS setup menu before Windows starts (hold down the indicated key during the power-on self-test), find the USB IRQ setup, and disable it.

If later you decide to install a USB device, re-enable this feature in your computer's BIOS. Windows will then automatically detect and install USB functionality.

To determine whether you have a USB port, open your Device Manager and see whether the Universal Serial Bus Controller is listed under Computer. Want to know more about the Universal Serial Bus? Check out the USB Web site at www.usb.org.

Most computers produced since late 1998 include a Universal Serial Bus port. Some include two. These ports provide a new way to connect a device to your computer, and may allow you to connect a device without having to use one of the limited IRQs.

The USB port will probably allow you to connect only one device, not the vaunted 127. If you want to connect more than one device to the USB port, the device either has to incorporate a USB hub (most don't) or you have to purchase a USB hub.

The power provided from the computer's USB port will probably not be enough to support more than one device. If you want to add multiple devices, make sure that the hub that you purchase can be powered by an AC adapter.

TIP: You should also confirm that your computer's BIOS fully supports USB peripherals. Some computers that include USB ports don't have a BIOS that recognizes USB peripherals — including keyboards and mice — on startup. You can go to the support area of your computer manufacturer's Web site to check on its BIOS updates.

Other Hardware Issues

There are a few other hardware issues that you should be aware of. These are not terribly difficult, but they are often overlooked.

Is your computer compatible with Windows XP?

One of the great problems for users and support personnel is attempting upgrades that are simply not compatible with their current computer. In other words, before upgrading a computer to Windows XP, you should make certain that all of the computer's components are compatible with Windows XP. This will save you a world of time and frustration. To find out whether your computer is compatible and can be upgraded to XP, turn to the Windows compatibility list at Microsoft's Web site at www.microsoft.com/hwtest/hcl. You can peruse this list and find out what hardware is compatible with XP. Also, see www.microsoft.com/windowsxp for more hardware compatibility information.

GenuineIntel or AuthenticAMD?

Ever wonder what was up with the single word *GenuineIntel* or *AuthenticAMD* in the General tab of your System Properties dialog box (right-click My Computer, click Properties)? Couldn't they have put a space between *Genuine* and *Intel* and *Authentic AMD*? Maybe there is a secret code?

To find out if there is, take these steps:

STEPS

Checking Out Your Processor

1. Open your Registry editor and navigate to
   HKEY_LOCAL_MACHINE\hardware\DESCRIPTION\System\CentralProcessor\0.

2. Double-click VendorIdentifier in the right pane of the Registry Editor to display the Edit String dialog box and put a space between *Genuine* and *Intel* or between *Authentic* and *AMD*, as shown in Figure 11-13. Click OK and close the Registry Editor.

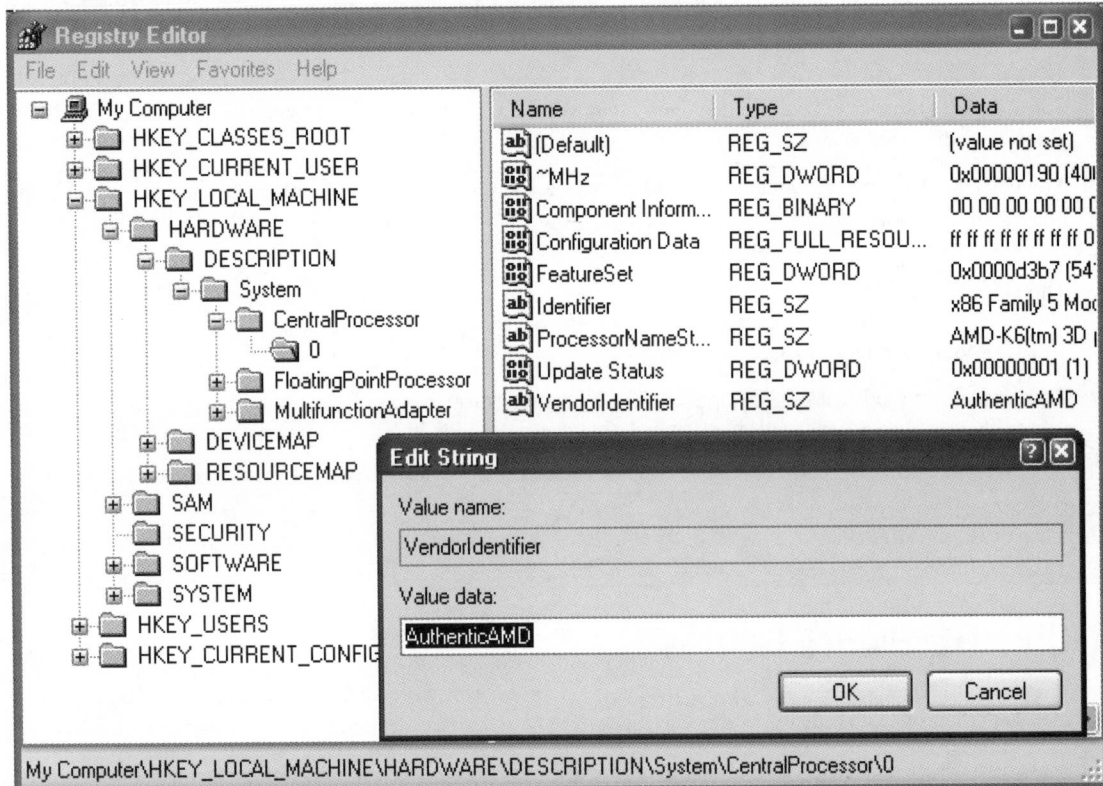

Figure 11-13: Edit the Value data field to add a space.

3. Right-click My Computer, click Properties, and check whether you have an Intel processor (something similar appears for other processors), you will see additional information under Genuine Intel, such as "x86 Family 5 Model 12 Stepping 12."

The next time you restart Windows, this reverts to GenuineIntel, and the additional information disappears. Strange.

Add more memory

If you have empty memory sockets on your motherboard, you can add additional memory — SIMMs or DIMMs — to your computer. The first thing you want to do is take a peek at your motherboard to confirm that you do have some empty memory sockets. If you don't know what they look like, pull out the manual for your computer (or any computer's manual), or check out the support pages at your computer manufacturer's Web site. If neither of these resources is available, review the diagram of a (typical) motherboard at http://www.jegsworks.com/Lessons/lesson4/lessons4-8.htm.

Most computers built in the last few years use either SIMMs (single inline memory modules) or DIMMs (dual inline memory modules). Check your computer's manual to see which kind of memory modules you have in your computer.

You also need to know what type of memory chips you have on the modules — EDO, FPM, and so on — and whether they are nonparity checking (very likely) or parity checking (maybe in a server). Your computer may also display your memory chip type during the power-on self-test. You may be able to see it then, and you might be able to press the Pause/Break key to pause the display and confirm what it says.

Next, you need to know how much memory you can install and how much you are willing to pay for. If you have a couple of banks for SIMM sockets available, you will probably be able to install anywhere from 8MB (what's the point?) to 256MB of memory. Check your computer manual for a chart of possible memory sizes and combinations.

Now, if you have a couple of banks of memory sockets available, you know your memory type and module type, and you know how much you can install, it's time to spec out the memory modules to purchase. You don't necessarily need to purchase the memory from your computer vendor, unless you want to put a little extra change in its pocket.

For example, SIMMs are for the most part packaged in 72-pin modules (although older computers may use 30-pin SIMMs) using EDO nonparity-checking chips. A single module at 16MB would be labeled as 4×32. The 4 stands for 4×4, in other words 16MB. The 32 means nonparity-checking memory. The other option is 36, which stands for parity-checking memory.

After you've purchased the memory modules, putting them in couldn't be easier. The main issue is keeping your hands off of anything but the insulated material. Your computer manual should supply you with instructions on how to push in the new modules, and the memory chips themselves will probably ship to you with instructions.

Real information online about computer hardware and software

No Web site does it all, and you have to search around the Web to get answers to your specific questions. I did find one site though, PC Mechanic, which concentrates on the kinds of questions that people building or buying personal computers need to ask. The site contains lots of good information about drive types (buy IDE and forget SCSI), memory, motherboards, video cards, networking, and monitors. It's definitely geared toward the buyer who wants to specify every component in his or her new purchase.

PC Mechanic also has a nice section on setting up a small network and connecting the network to the Internet. You'll find it at www.pcmech.com. The networking article starts at www.pcmech.com/networking.htm.

Summary

Windows XP is the best operating system Microsoft has ever produced for hardware management. By using Universal Plug and Play, your computer can detect network hardware and automatically adjust the hardware environment as changes are made to your system. Microsoft has made a concerted effort to bring a new level of standardization to the PC world. By providing an extensive list of 32-bit device drivers and giving manufacturers a new model for creating new drivers, it has improved the stability of

Windows and has made hardware installation and configuration easier than ever. In this chapter, you learned that . . .

♦ Windows deals with both existing and Plug and Play hardware, providing a way to track it all.

♦ Hardware-detection routines built into Windows do a robust job of matching your hardware to Windows' needs.

♦ Drivers are easily updated.

♦ The major benefit of Plug and Play is the automatic resolution of hardware conflicts. It isn't automatic with non-Plug and Play hardware, but Windows XP helps make things easier.

♦ If you have multiple hardware configurations, you can direct Windows to the current configuration.

♦ You can make adjustments to hardware configuration by using the Registry Editor.

♦ Most problems can be avoided by simply using hardware that is compatible with Windows XP.

Chapter 12

The Registry

In This Chapter

Ah, the Registry — that storehouse of computer information and settings that truly holds the secrets to Windows XP. The Registry, both friend and foe, has been around since the days of Windows 3.x, and the Registry is alive and well in Windows XP (and rather large). This chapter looks at the Registry, the repository of almost all the settings for your computer, operating system, and much of your software. In this chapter, you discover . . .

♦ The Registry structure and how the Registry stores data

♦ Backing up and restoring the Registry

♦ Exporting and importing Registry keys

♦ Using command-line tools in the Windows XP Support Tools folder to access the Registry

Getting to Know the Registry

The Windows XP Registry is the central repository of configuration information for your installed hardware and software. When you use the Control Panel applets to make changes in your system configuration, when you make changes using the Computer Management Console, or when you install and remove software, those changes are almost always stored in the Registry.

In the days of 16-bit Windows, configuration information was kept in .INI files. Microsoft used WIN.INI and SYSTEM.INI to hold specific information. Third-party software often added their settings to these files, and they often created their own .INI files, either in the Windows directory or in the application's home directory. If you wanted to backup your vital configuration information, the settings were spread all over your computer's hard disk in many different files. The Registry was Microsoft's attempt to bring all this information together into a single place.

> **TIP:** Although the Registry has been around since the days of Windows 3.x, it has grown quite a bit over the years. With the introduction of Windows 2000, it was not uncommon for registries to be greater than 12 MB in size, and you see this trend continue in Windows XP.

One reason for the expanding size of the Registry is because third-party software developers are now using the Registry to store their own settings and preference information, rather than using .INI files. Every time you use the Windows XP Setup program, install additional hardware, or install 32-bit Windows software, data is stored in the Registry. Some programs still use .INI files, however, to save their settings. This is supported by Windows XP to maintain backward compatibility with older applications.

Editing the Registry gives you an immense amount of power over your system's configuration. It also gives you an immense amount of power to wreck your system to the point where a reinstallation is necessary. This is one place where experimentation is *not* in order.

CAUTION: Although this chapter teaches you techniques for editing and manipulating the Registry, it is a good practice to edit the Registry only as a last resort. If you can make configuration changes to your system through a Control Panel applet or through the Management Console, do so there rather than directly in the Registry. It is far safer to use these configuration tools; if you somehow manage to corrupt the Registry, you might disable your computer altogether. It is also important to know how to restore the Registry. If you find that you need to edit your Registry and you have even the slightest hesitation about this potentially dangerous process, you should call technical support at your designated Windows support provider (for many people, this is the computer manufacturer from which they purchased their computer) and insist that they walk you through the procedure. Okay — fair warning!

When disaster strikes

Before we do anything to the Registry, it is important to learn how to recover from the problem of a corrupted Registry. If your computer cannot boot, and you receive an error message that your Registry has been corrupted, you can restore the Registry. Each time Windows XP is able to successfully start, it backs up the last known good version of your Registry files. This way, you have a record of your computer's configuration the last time it started successfully. If you somehow manage to trash your Registry, you can restore the last known good version stored on your system. Also, consider using Windows XP's System Restore feature, which can restore your computer to an earlier configuration time. See Chapter 25 to learn more about System Restore. The following steps show you how to restore the Registry.

STEPS

Restoring the Registry

1. If your computer will not boot, and you see the error message that the Registry is corrupt, shut down your computer.

2. Wait about ten seconds, and then turn on the power again.

3. When you see the following message: "Please select the Operating System to Start," press F8. You will only have a brief amount of time to do this — only a second or two.

4. If you press F8 in time, you will then see the Safe Mode menu. Use your arrow keys to cursor down and select the following choice: "Last Known Good Configuration." Then press Enter.

5. Follow the remaining instructions on your screen.

NOTE: If you made any configuration changes or installed any software since the last known good configuration was saved, those changes will be lost.

The Registry Editor

Windows XP contains a Registry editor called RegEdit. The use of RegEdit can help you find a configuration setting, troubleshoot problems, and make technical changes in Windows XP, as well as in applications that use the Registry to store preferences.

RegEdit does not appear on the default menus in Windows XP. To use it, you must type the name into the Open text box in the Run dialog box, or create a shortcut on your desktop from which to launch the tool. Of course, because this utility is an advanced power tool, you might not *want* it to be easily available. If you use it frequently, however, you'll want it a click away. The following steps run RegEdit.

STEPS

Running RegEdit

1. Choose ⇨ Start ⇨ Run.

2. In the Run dialog box's Open text box, type **regedit**. Click OK.

Figure 12-1 shows RegEdit just after its window has opened and the plus sign to the left of the HKEY_CURRENT_USER key was clicked to expand its contents.

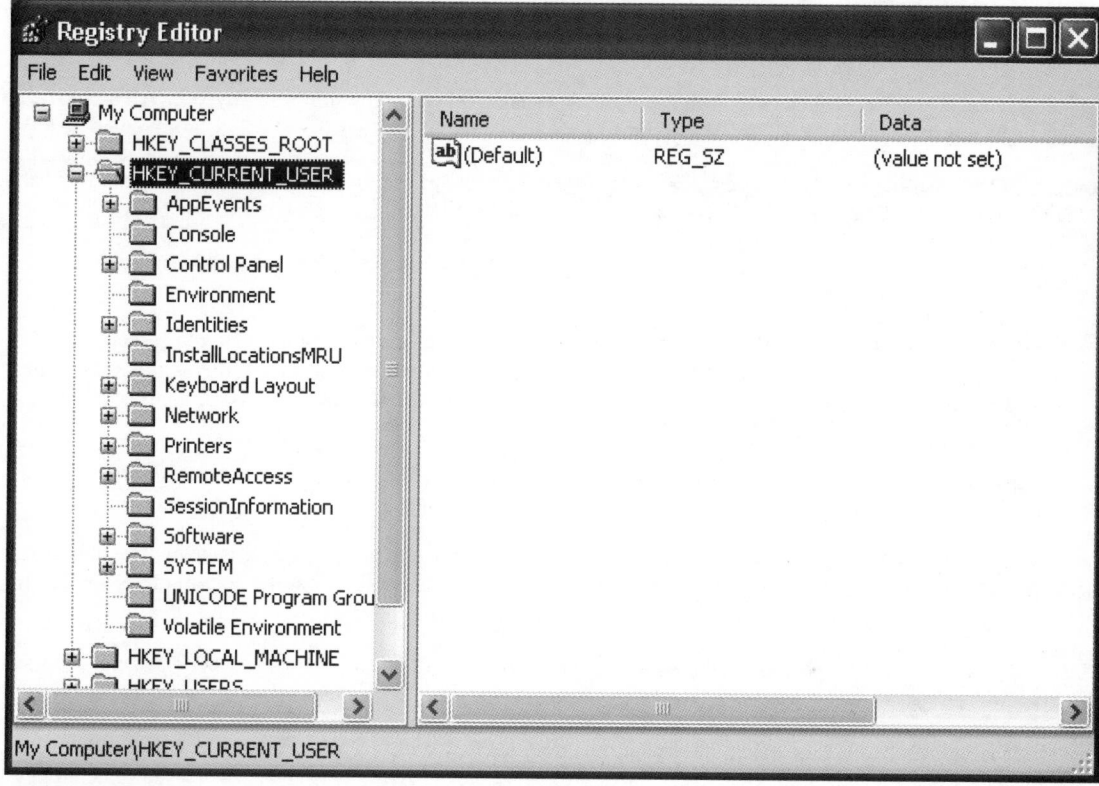

Figure 12-1: RegEdit

At this point, you can expand and explore the following:

- **Keys** — which are shown in the left pane of RegEdit.
- **Value entries** — which are shown in the right pane.

Value entries have three parts:

- **Names** — shown in the right pane define the values contained by a key.
- **Data types** — determine the kind of data allowed in a value. Data types may be one of three styles:
  - **String value** — which may consist of any characters of text
  - **Binary value** — which is actually displayed as a hexadecimal value
  - **DWORD value** — which consists of four 8-bit bytes
- **Values** — are the data associated with a name.

> **SECRET:** Many people don't know that they can quickly expand all the subkeys within an entire major key (or all the subkeys within the entire Registry) by using RegEdit. It's easy to do — just press the undocumented Alt+Keypad Asterisk keyboard combination.

STEPS

Quickly expanding the Registry or a Registry key

1. Run `RegEdit`.

2. In `RegEdit`'s left pane, click the folder icon near the key you want to expand, such as `HKEY_CURRENT_USER`.

3. Hold down the Alt key, and then press the Asterisk (*) key on the numeric keypad. (Alt+Asterisk or Alt+Shift+8 on the main keyboard doesn't work.)

> **SECRET:** In `RegEdt32`, the key combination to expand all subkeys is Ctrl+Asterisk. In this case, you can use the asterisk key either on the numeric keypad or on the main keyboard (Ctrl+Shift+8).

To collapse a key you've expanded in `RegEdit`, double-click the key or press the minus key on the numeric keypad or the main keyboard.

In `RegEdit`, pressing Alt+Keypad Asterisk immediately begins expanding the key you selected — including each subkey beneath the selected key. This is very handy if you don't remember exactly where the key you're looking for is located. It's much faster to press Alt+Keypad Asterisk than to manually click every plus sign to expand keys until you find the spot you want.

Figure 12-2 shows the effect of expanding all subkeys of the `HKEY_CURRENT_USER` Registry key. The subkeys of this key, of course, continue far beyond the limits of the window shown in the figure.

If you first select the My Computer icon before pressing Alt+Keypad Asterisk, this key combination will expand every key and subkey in the entire Registry. This can take a few minutes to complete, so plan to go get a cup of coffee if you choose to expand the entire Registry.

> **SECRET:** If it's taking too long to expand the keys you selected (or if you already see the subkey you want), you can stop the expansion process by pressing Esc.

There is one very mild side effect of expanding every subkey within a key. When you collapse the key and then expand it again, it shows every subkey expanded exactly the way it was when the selected key was collapsed.

You might prefer to collapse a key and then expand it only to the first level of subkeys below it. (This is the original, default behavior when you expand a key.) It's easy to restore the original behavior, no matter how far you've expanded a key, by pressing F5.

STEPS

Restoring the default expansion behavior to a Registry key

1. In `RegEdit`, collapse a key in the left pane by clicking the minus sign to the left of the folder you wish to collapse.

2. Press F5. When you expand this key by clicking its plus sign, the folder expands only to the first level of subkeys.

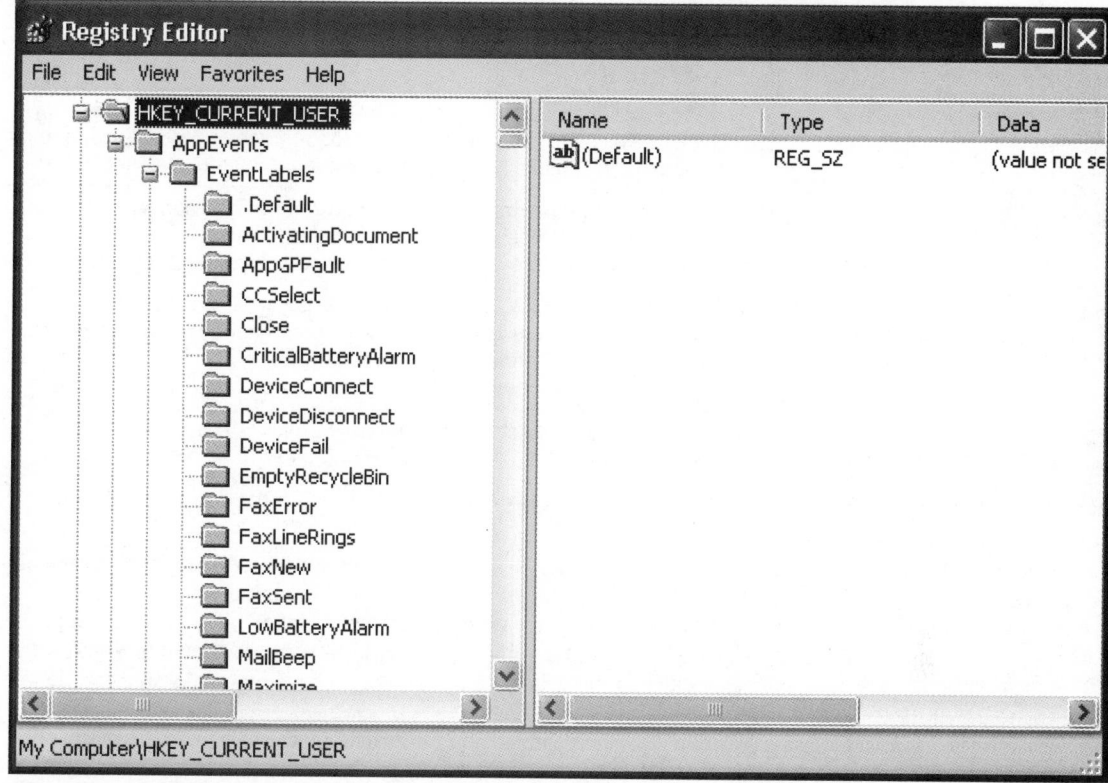

Figure 12-2: The RegEdit window, after pressing Alt+Keypad Asterisk on the HKEY_CURRENT_USER key, and then selecting the AppGPFault key in the left pane

RegEdit is documented by two compiled Windows Help files: RegEdit.hlp and RegEdit.chm. Of the two, RegEdit.chm is, by far, the more informative.

This file contains tips on how to search for a particular key, name, or value; how to add, modify, and delete keys and values; how to connect and edit a Registry across a network; and many other topics.

In Figure 12-2, for example, you can see the AppGPFault subkey within the expanded HKEY_CURRENT_USER key. The AppGPFault subkey contains a default text string that is displayed when something crashes (in other words, when a General Protection Fault occurs). Using the techniques documented in RegEdit.chm to change a value, you could right-click the name Default, click Modify, and then change the string Program error to Microsoft error. (I'm not suggesting that anyone actually do this, of course.)

Registry Structure

The Registry is structured in a top-down fashion, similar to how folders on your hard drive are organized. The Registry consists of five subtrees, each of which is devoted to holding a certain kind of information. Each subtree begins with the word HKEY (see Table 12-1). According to Microsoft, this is a signal to software developers that each is a handle that can be used by a program. The subtrees in Windows XP are the same in name and number as in Windows NT/2000 Registry, less than the subtrees in Windows 95 and 98 (which have six), but more than in Windows NT Server (which has four).

Table 12-1: Windows XP Registry Subtrees

Root Key Name	Description
HKEY_CLASSES_ROOT	Contains the associations between applications and file types (for example, .XLS files belong to Microsoft Excel), Object Linking and Embedding (OLE) Registry information, and file-class associations.
HKEY_CURRENT_USER	Contains the user profile for the individual who is currently logged on. It also contains environment variables, desktop settings, application preferences, network connections, and printer information.
HKEY_LOCAL_MACHINE	Contains information about the local computer system. Settings for hardware and operating system features such as bus type, system, memory, device drivers, and startup control data are located here.
HKEY_USERS	Contains all the actively loaded user profiles. This includes the HKEY_CURRENT_USER and the default Admins profile.
HKEY_CURRENT_CONFIG	Contains the configuration information for the current hardware profile.

Each subtree within the Registry holds individual keys. A key might contain subkeys, or it might actually hold data. Subkeys can, in turn, hold additional subkeys. You expand and navigate in the left pane of RegEdit much like you do in the Windows Explorer. When you select a key or subkey in the left pane, its contents — or value entry — are displayed in the right — or details — pane, as shown in Figure 12-3. A subkey might only have one value entry in the details pane, or it might have many. As an example, expand the HKEY_LOCAL_MACHINE key, and then navigate to Hardware, Description, Central Processor, and then 0. This particular key holds identifying information about the CPU in your computer, including the vendor and model.

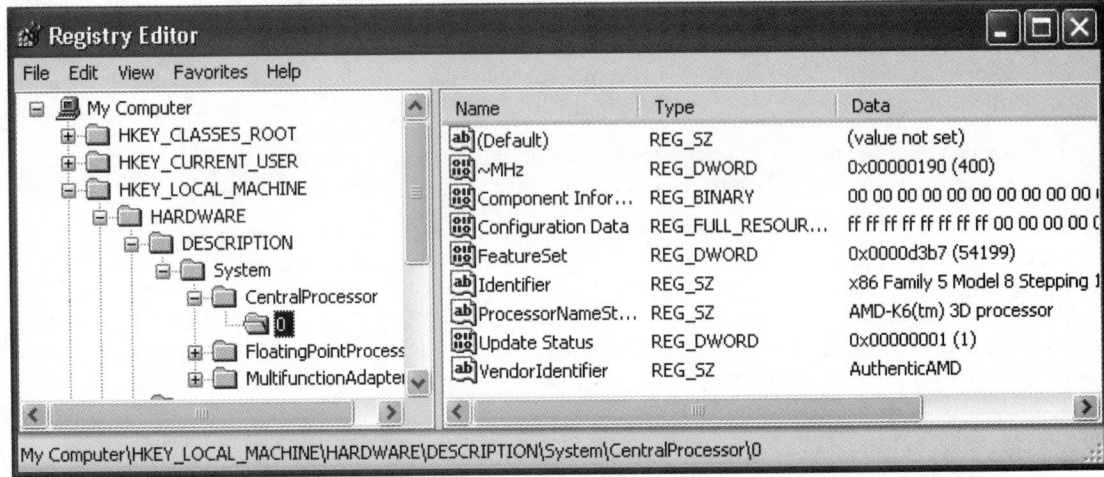

Figure 12-3: There can be many layers of subkeys through which you need to navigate before you reach any actual data in the Registry.

A Registry key's value entry has three parts: The first part is the name of the subkey; the second part is the subkey's data type; and the third part is the subkey's actual value, as you can see by the three columns displayed in the details pane. Table 12-2 describes the six data types.

Table 12-2: Windows XP Registry Data Types

Data Types	Description
REG_BINARY	Raw binary data that will typically be displayed in hexadecimal notation, making it difficult for you to read.
REG_DWORD	A 4-byte long number that is displayed in binary, hexadecimal, or decimal format. This data type is often used for device drivers and services.
REG_EXPAND_SZ	An expandable data string that holds a variable that is replaced when it is called by an application. It often looks similar to %systemroot%, which will be replaced by the actual folder name containing your Windows XP files.
REG_MUTLI_SZ	A multiple string that usually holds a list of values, which will be in a human-readable form, rather than being in binary or hexadecimal notation. The values will be separated by a NULL character.
REG_SZ	A text string, which will be in a human-readable form.

SECRET: You might also see other data types in the Registry, such as REG_FULL_RESOURCE_DESCRIPTOR. Other programs can create their own data types to add to the Registry, but the Registry editors are unlikely to be able to deal with them.

Unlike Windows 95, Windows 98, and Windows NT 3.*x*, which stored the Registry in two files called System.dat and User.dat, the Windows XP Registry is patterned after the Windows NT 4.0 and 2000 Registries. This means that Microsoft switched metaphors in midstream, moving from trees and keys to hives. Microsoft used to discuss the parts of the Registry when looked at with RegEdit as trees and keys. Now, however, when the Registry is saved to disk, it is actually split into many more parts, which are referred to as hives. Officially, a hive is a "discrete body of keys, subkeys, and values rooted at the top of the Registry hierarchy."

Actually, not all of the Registry is stored in hives. Hives are those Registry keys that are permanent components of the Registry (see Figure 12-4), not the dynamic parts, such as HKEY_LOCAL_MACHINE\Hardware, which is built only when Windows XP boots.

Most of the hives are stored in the c:\windows\System32\Config folder. Table 12-3 lists the stored hives.

Table 12-3: Registry Hives in \System32\Config

Part of the Registry	Goes with These Files
HKEY_CURRENT_CONFIG	system, system.alt, system.log, system.sav
HKEY_LOCAL_MACHINE\SAM	sam, sam.log, sam.sav
HKEY_LOCAL_MACHINE\Security	security, security.log, security.sav
HKEY_LOCAL_MACHINE\Software	software, software.log, software.sav
HKEY_LOCAL_MACHINE\System	system, system.alt, system.log, system.sav
HKEY_USERS\.Default	default, default.log, default.sav
HKEY_CURRENT_USER	ntuser.dat, ntuser.log (files for each user profile, within the user profile folder)

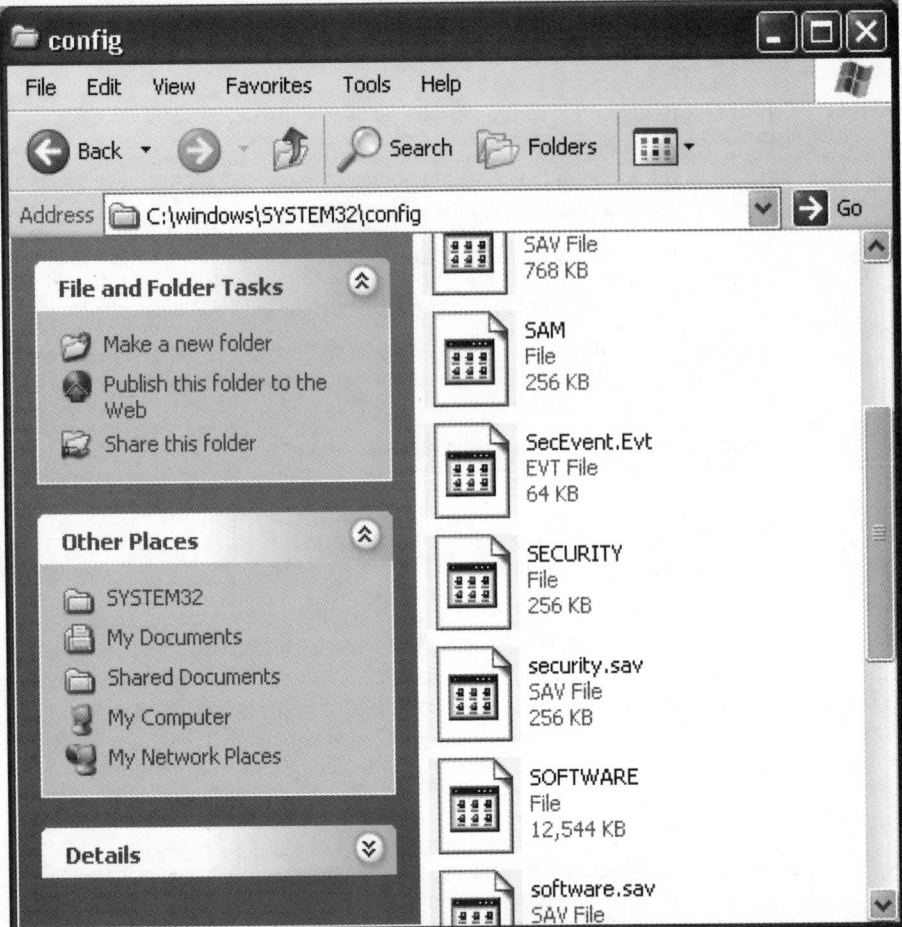

Figure 12-4: The Registry data is split up into a number of files that are called hives.

In addition to those listed in Table 12-3, you will also find `userdiff` and `userdiff.log` files in `System32\Config`. These are not associated with a particular part of the Registry. Instead, they are used when you upgrade your operating system, such as from Windows 2000 or Me to XP (or from one build of Windows XP to another).

As Table 12-3 shows, each hive might have three or four files associated with it. If the file has no extension, it is a copy of the hive. If the file has a `.log` extension, it is a transaction log showing changes to keys and value entries in the hive. The `Software`, `SAM`, `Security`, `System`, and `.Default` hives also have `.sav` files. These are copies of the hive created at the end of the text mode stage of the Windows XP setup. Therefore, they should have file dates that correspond to the date you installed or upgraded Windows XP.

One hive — `HKEY_LOCAL_MACHINE\System` — plays such a critical role that an extra backup is created. Because `HKEY_LOCAL_MACHINE` stores hardware and driver configuration information about the computer, Windows XP would be crippled without it. This backup has the filename `System.alt`. (The other hives do not have `.alt` files.)

SECRET: The Registry contains a list that shows which file goes with which hive. You can find it in the Registry at `HKEY_LOCAL_MACHINE\SYSTEM\CurrentControlSet\Control\hivelist`.

Registry Roadmap

This section examines the Registry subtrees, and shows where within Windows XP you can change these settings.

HKEY_CLASSES_ROOT

The HKEY_CLASSES_ROOT tree holds the information that relates file types to applications, as well as data types and COM (Component Object Model) objects, as shown in Figure 12-5. Given the large number of associations that a computer might have, this subtree is usually quite large when it is first expanded, and it will grow as you install more software onto your computer. This subtree is also where COM object information is stored, which tells Windows XP how to find and run software components.

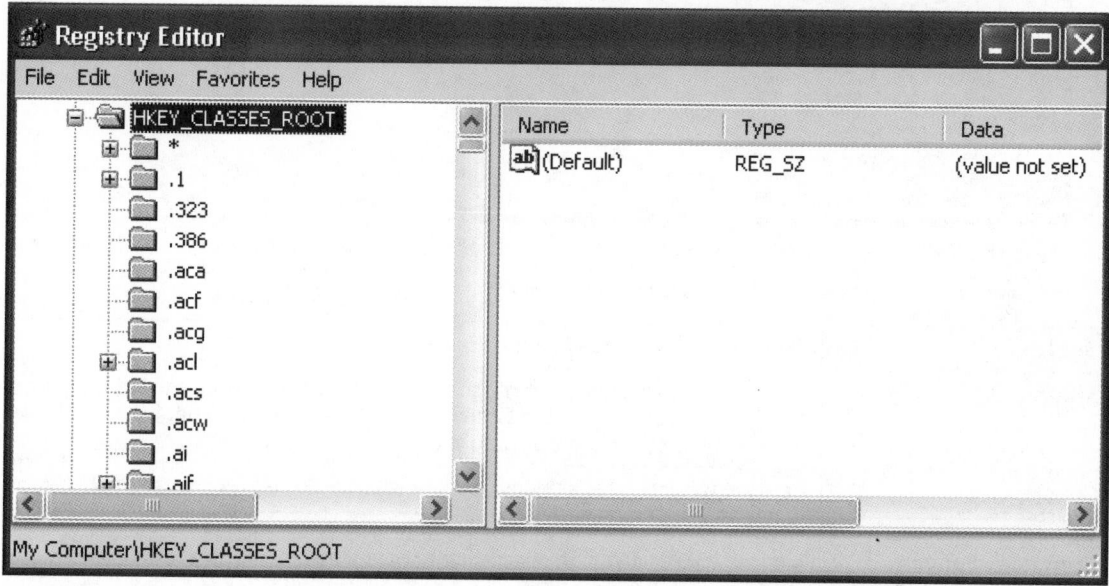

Figure 12-5: HKEY_CLASSES_ROOT is the key in which file association information is stored in the Registry.

HKEY_CURRENT_USER

The HKEY_CURRENT_USER subtree holds the information about the user profile for the person who is currently logged on to the computer. Most of the user interface settings that you set through the Control Panel are stored here (see Figure 12-6).

SECRET: Some settings here are duplicated by settings contained in HKEY_LOCAL_MACHINE key. If there are different settings for the same environment variable between the two subtrees, the choice in the HKEY_CURRENT_USER key is given priority.

When a user logs on to a Windows XP computer, their user profile is taken from the HKEY_USERS key and copied into the CURRENT_USER key. If no user profile exists for the user who is logging on to the computer (for example, a guest or a new user), Windows XP uses the Default User profile.

The subkeys in the HKEY_CURRENT_USER key are typically set from choices you make by using the Control Panel applets, or by adjusting other settings menus. Table 12-4 lists the subkeys located in the HKEY_CURRENT_USER key.

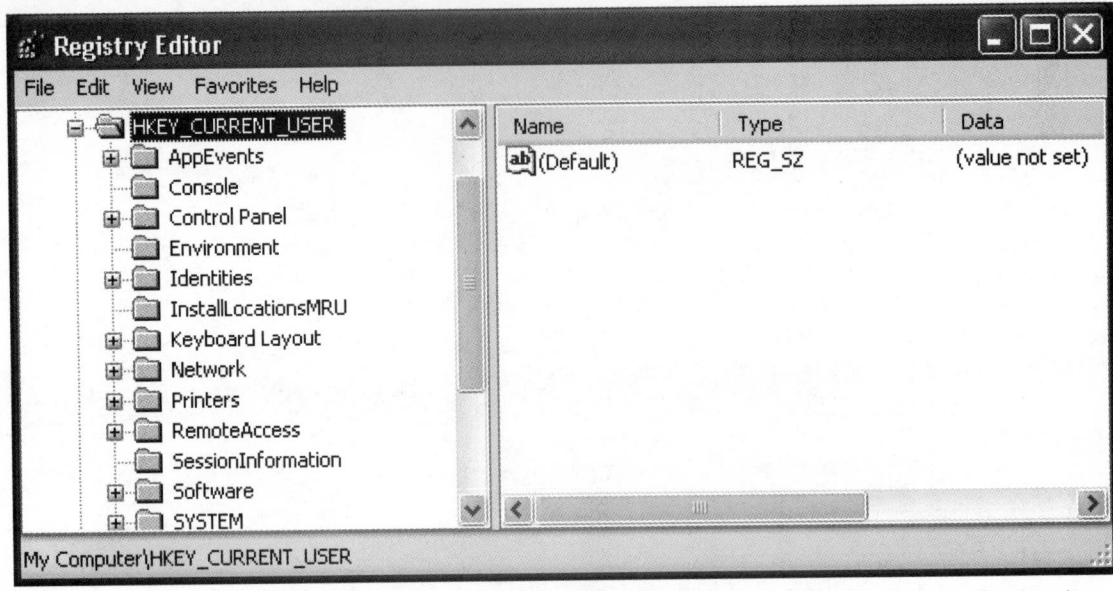

Figure 12-6: The HKEY_CURRENT_USER subtree contains the settings for the user who is currently logged on to the computer.

Table 12-4: HKEY_CURRENT_USER Subkeys

Subkey	What Information the Key Contains
AppEvents	Application events that you assign to certain .WAV sound files using the Sounds and Multimedia applet in the Control Panel. They can be Windows XP events, or they can be events associated with a particular application.
Console	Sets the window size, along with options for any console tools, such as the Windows XP Command Prompt.
Control Panel	Many of the options that you configure using the Mouse, Keyboard, and Display Options applets in the Control Panel are stored in this subkey.
Environment	Environment settings that are set using the System applet in the Control Panel are stored in this subkey. Many of the settings contained here were extracted from the existing AUTOEXEC.BAT file when you installed Windows XP.
Identities	Multiple identities in Outlook Express are stored in this subkey. The user identities will look something like {0771C1B2-F98C-11D2-AB18-005004707D0A}. Under each subkey, you can find the actual user name belonging to the identity.
Keyboard Layout	This subkey stores the keyboard language information relating to the Input Locales you choose in the Regional Options applet in the Control Panel.
Printers	Printer information is stored in this subkey. Information about each physically installed printer can be found here, but there will not be any information contained in this subkey for software-based devices such as fax modems, which you would find in the Software subkey.
Software	Application-specific settings are stored in this subkey. These entries are usually created when you install software. Much of the data here will have a similar structure to the data in the HKEY_LOCAL_MACHINE\Software subkey.
Unicode Program Group	Starting with Windows NT 4.0, this key is no longer used. It is left in place for compatibility reasons.

HKEY_LOCAL_MACHINE

The HKEY_LOCAL_MACHINE key contains the configuration information for your computer. Some of the data in this key is dynamic, meaning that it is created anew each time the computer boots up. The data in this key cannot be edited directly, even using the Registry Editor. There are five subkeys in HKEY_LOCAL_MACHINE, as shown in Figure 12-7.

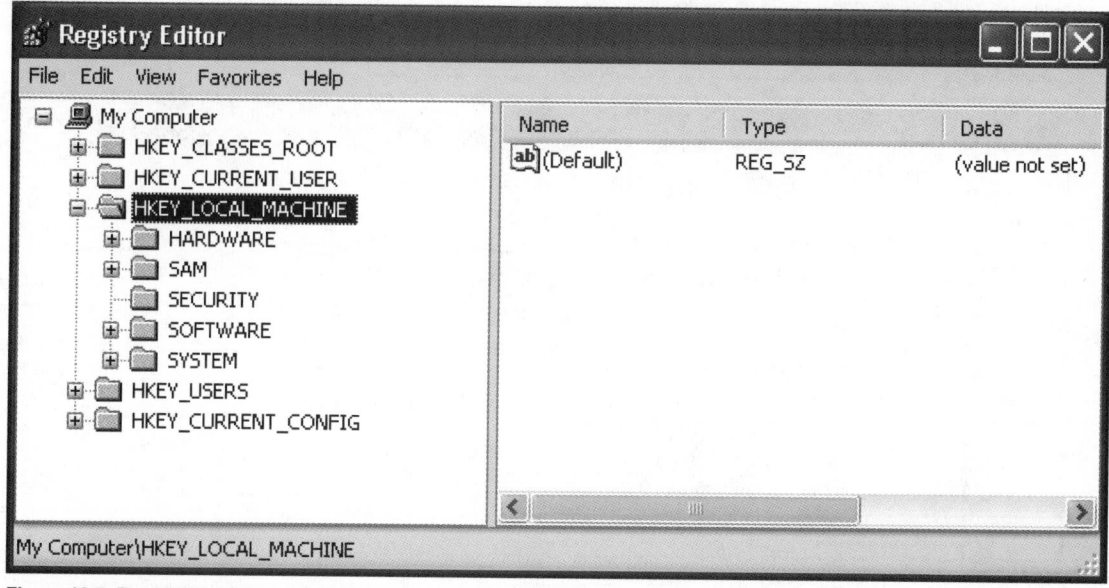

Figure 12-7: The HKEY_LOCAL_MACHINE subtree has five subkeys. Each subkey contains additional subkeys that contain vital system information.

Hardware

The HKEY_LOCAL_MACHINE\Hardware subkey holds the dynamic hardware configuration data for the computer. For example, suppose you install a new modem. The installation data and the driver information about that modem are stored in this subkey; in fact, data about all hardware on your computer can be found in this subkey. This subkey is refreshed each time the computer boots up, and the data is then discarded when the system shuts down (it is not stored in a hive file).

TIP: If you want to see your current hardware configuration, it is easier to open the Computer Management Console and view either the System Information or the Device Manager.

SAM and Security keys

SAM is the Windows XP Security Account Manager. These two keys handle security information, and they play a big role when a Windows XP computer is connected to a Windows XP network server using the new Active Directory services. In a network environment, a Windows XP computer must be authenticated with a Windows 2000 domain controller. The SAM and Security keys hold machine specific identifications and security information that allow Windows XP to support the advanced security features required in today's complex networks.

Software

The data contained in the HKEY_LOCAL_MACHINE\Software subkey is configuration information about the software installed on the computer. The subkeys under this key differ depending on what applications are installed, but there are always common subkeys among computers.

The `Classes` subkey contains another list of file associations similar to those found in the `HKEY_CLASSES_ROOT` key. You also find a lengthy list of Component Object Model (COM) objects here. The Microsoft subkey contains information about all the Microsoft applications that accompany Windows XP.

> **TIP:** The `HKEY_LOCAL_MACHINE\SOFTWARE\Microsoft\MMC\SnapIns` subkey maintains a list of all the snap-ins available on the computer. They are identified by a rather long string of numbers, but if you select a string in the left pane of the Registry Editor, the Details pane on the right will display the plain text name of the snap-in, as shown in Figure 12-8.

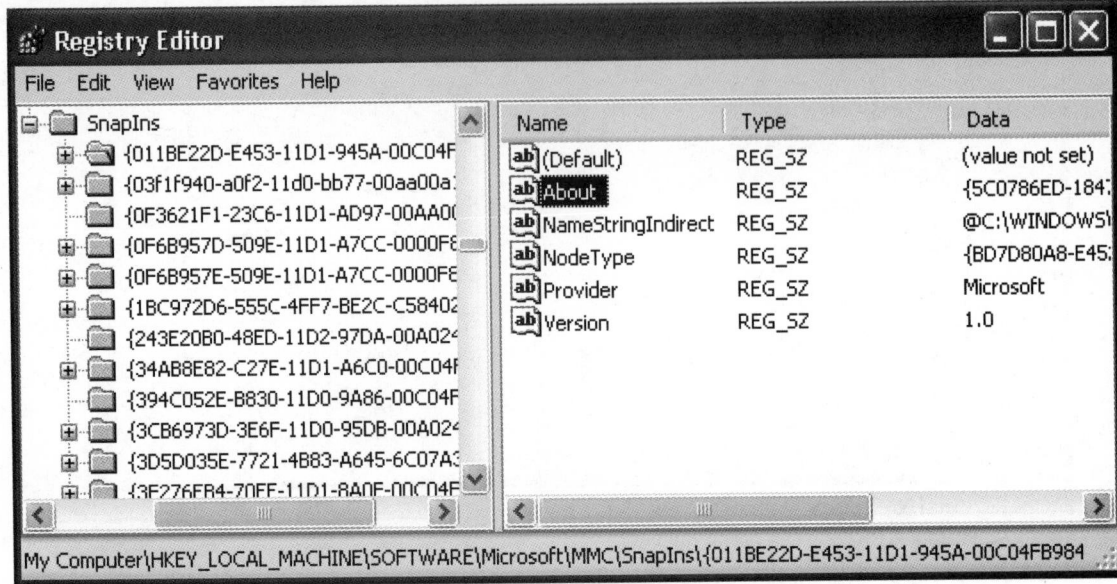

Figure 12-8: A listing of the installed snap-ins that can be used in the Microsoft Management Console

Note that toward the end of the Microsoft subkey is a subkey called `HKEY_LOCAL_MACHINE\SOFTWARE\Microsoft\Windows NT\CurrentVersion`. One might think that the Registry designers never got the memo about the name change to Windows XP. Actually, the name was probably left alone so that there would be a consistent architecture between the Windows NT 4.0 Registry and the Windows XP Registry. This subkey holds information about Windows XP services, as well as information about the installed version of Windows XP.

In addition to the common subkeys discussed above, software that you install creates its own subkeys, and the subkeys are often used to store configuration information specific to the application (in lieu of using `.INI` files).

System

The `HKEY_LOCAL_MACHINE\SYSTEM` subkey holds all the data that Windows needs, but that can't be initialized during the startup process. Instead, the information is stored here in the `System` subkey. Because the system recognizes the importance of this information, this is the one subkey that also has an extra backup file called `System.alt`. This data is crucial to starting the system; if you make changes with unintended consequences, you can back your changes out, because Windows XP automatically keeps a safe backup of this information.

The startup data is kept together in subkeys called *control sets*. Although there can be as many as four control sets — which would be labeled ControlSet001, ControlSet002, and so on — there are usually only two, the current control set plus one backup. This backup is done automatically by the system and normally requires no user intervention. Information on the various control sets is tracked in the

HKEY_LOCAL_MACHINE\SYSTEM\Select subkey, as shown in Figure 12-9. There are four value entries in this subkey that track the following:

♦ **Default** — This is the number of the control set that will be used at the next system startup, unless the LastKnownGood configuration is manually selected (see "When Disaster Strikes," at the beginning of this chapter).

♦ **Current** — This is the control set that started the system for the current session.

♦ **LastKnownGood** — This set is an unmodified copy of the last set that was used to successfully start the system.

♦ **Failed** — This control set was replaced when the LastKnownGood control set was used to start the system.

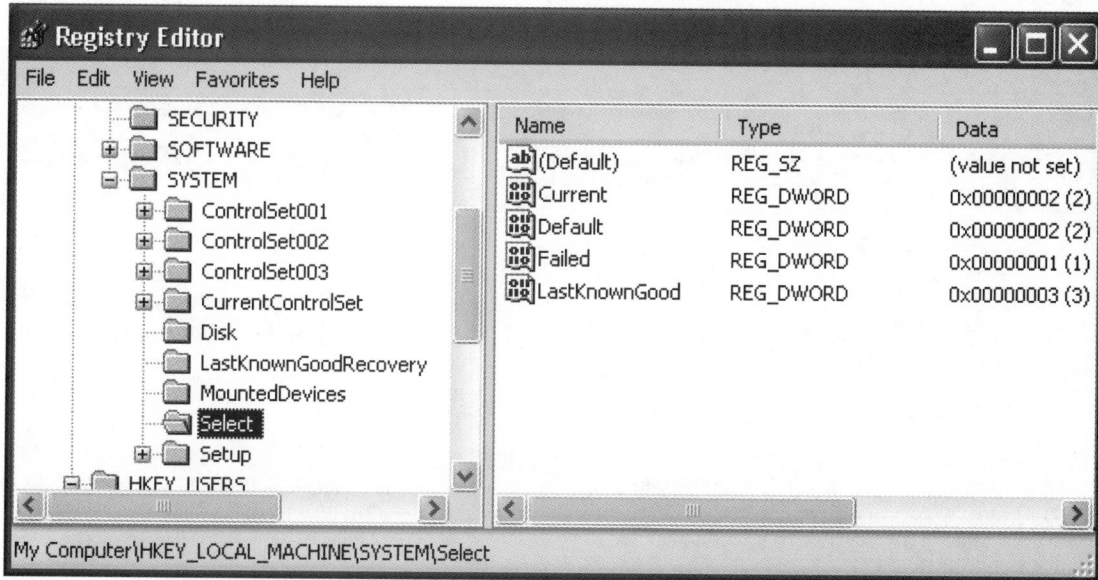

Figure 12-9: The HKEY_LOCAL_MACHINE\SYSTEM\Select subkey keeps track of the control set, or system configuration, that started the computer, as well as the LastKnownGood configuration.

TIP: What determines a "good" system start? Microsoft's definition of good is if there are no severe or critical errors and at least one user is able to successfully log on. You can actually redefine this standard, either to make it more stringent or to remove a particular criterion. However, that is not as simple a procedure as it sounds. You must create an executable program that checks your system start settings for you in order to determine whether your desired conditions have been met. The name of the program with which to verify your startup must be specified in the HKEY_LOCAL_MACHINE\SYSTEM\ControlSet001\Control\BootVerificationProgram key to determine whether the startup was a "good" startup.

If you had a problem starting your computer, the presence of both the bad and the good control set might give you a clue as to what problem occurred. You can view the failed set with the Registry Editor, and then compare it to the functional control set.

CAUTION: Although you can use the Registry Editor to track down the problem, do not use it to change any settings unless you have verified that it is safe to do so. Many of the control set settings are automatically maintained by the system. Presumably, your LastKnownGood control set is working, so you can rely on it to successfully boot your computer.

The control set organizes its data into the subkeys listed in Table 12-5.

Table 12-5: Control Set Subkeys

Subkey	Description
Control	Holds startup parameters for the system. These parameters include the subsystems to load, as well as the environment variables and the paging file information.
Enum	Holds hardware configuration information for devices and drivers.
Hardware Profiles	Holds information that tracks which configuration information is used with various hardware profiles. See Chapter 11 to learn more about hardware profiles.
Services	Holds the information that controls which services are loaded, and in what order.

TIP: If you have created different hardware profiles and you are unsure which numbers correspond to the profile you are running, see the information contained in the `HKEY_LOCAL_MACHINE\System\CurrentControlSet\Control\IDConfigDB` key. The value of `CurrentConfig` displays the currently loaded hardware profile.

HKEY_USERS

The `HKEY_USERS` subtree usually holds two user profiles; the first profile is for the user who is actually logged on to the computer. The key name for the active user shows the Security ID for that user, which looks similar to the following:

```
HKEY_USERS\S-1-5-23-527479835-1964818763-2035704189-520
```

The second profile is the default user profile, located in the subkey `HKEY_USERS\.DEFAULT`, which is in use when no one is logged on to the computer (for example, when the Login prompt is displayed on the Desktop). The structure of the `.DEFAULT` subkey is similar to the structure of the `HKEY_CURRENT_USER` section in the Registry.

HKEY_CURRENT_CONFIG

The `HKEY_CURRENT_CONFIG` key was added to the Windows NT 4.0 Registry — and is also contained in the Windows XP Registry, as well as the Windows 2000 Registry — to achieve compatibility with the Windows 95 Registry. It duplicates the information in the `HKEY_LOCAL_MACHINE\System\CurrentControlSet\Hardware Profiles\Current` subkey, which is the current hardware profile data. According to Microsoft, programs written for Windows 95 (which may look for information in these keys) can run under Windows XP/2000.

Backing Up and Restoring the Registry

The Registry has taken the role of arbitrator of important system settings. It has become even more important as third-party software developers use it more and more as a storehouse for their applications' settings, rather than using .INI files. Now that all our eggs are being kept in one basket, really, really good care must be taken of that basket (and those eggs).

In addition to the automatic backup of the LastKnownGood Registry copy, you can create additional backups. You might want to place a copy of a backup on an alternate backup media (such as a Zip disk or CD-RW), so that all of the backup copies are not stored on the same hard drive. However, to make this backup, you cannot use a regular copy and paste procedure in the Windows Explorer or My Computer, because the Registry files are open while the computer is in use, and you will receive a sharing error.

One way to back up the Registry is to use the Windows XP Backup and Recovery Tools program, a utility that is included with Windows XP. One of the options of the Backup program is to back up the system state. According to the Backup Help file, when you back up the system state, you create backup copies of all the data files relevant to your computer. For Windows XP, this includes the Registry, the boot files needed to start Windows XP (which includes `Ntdlr` and `Ntdetect`), and the COM+ class registration database. (Additional files are backed up if you are using Windows 2000 Server.)

> **SECRET:** When you back up the system state, in addition to backing up the Registry and the files needed to boot the computer, you also back up all the files that Microsoft has labeled as protected. These are the files — mostly DLLs — that can't be overwritten when you install third-party software. On one of my Windows XP computers, backing up only the system state backed up 225MB of data.

To create a system state backup in Windows XP, follow these steps:

STEPS

Create a System State backup

1. Choose Start ⇨ All Programs ⇨ Accessories ⇨ System Tools ⇨ Backup.

2. Select the Backup tab.

3. In the left pane, check the System State option to enable it.

4. In the Backup media or filename text, select the drive to which you want to create your backup (see Figure 12-10). Given the size of the system state data, as shown in the previous Secret icon, the minimum size of your backup media should probably be equivalent to a 100MB Zip disk. You would not want to select a floppy drive as the target unless you have a lot of time to feed disks into the drive. If you have a CD-RW disk, that would work great too.

5. Click Start Backup.

If you need to restore the system state, the procedure is similar to the above steps. However, you will select the Restore in Step 2 instead, and you then select the backup file from which you want to restore your system state.

Using the Registry Editor

As you learned in earlier sections of this chapter, the Registry Editor is the XP tool that enables you to make changes to registry values. Of course, it is, again, important to remember that editing the Registry is serious business. If at all possible, you should make configuration changes using Control Panel applets and other desktop tools before using Registry Editor.

To learn how to edit the registry, it helps to get to a location that has some useful keys, constants, and values. Check out the following steps, which explore editing of the desktop.

STEPS

Editing the Registry

1. Click the plus sign to the left of `HKey_Current_User`. (The name *HKEY* refers to the fact that this is a handle to a key. The Registry is filled with keys that eventually have data attached to them.) Click the plus sign to the left of `Control Panel`, and then the one next to `desktop`.

2. Highlight the `WindowMetrics` name next to its folder icon. Notice that the right pane is now filled with constant names (Name) and values (Data).

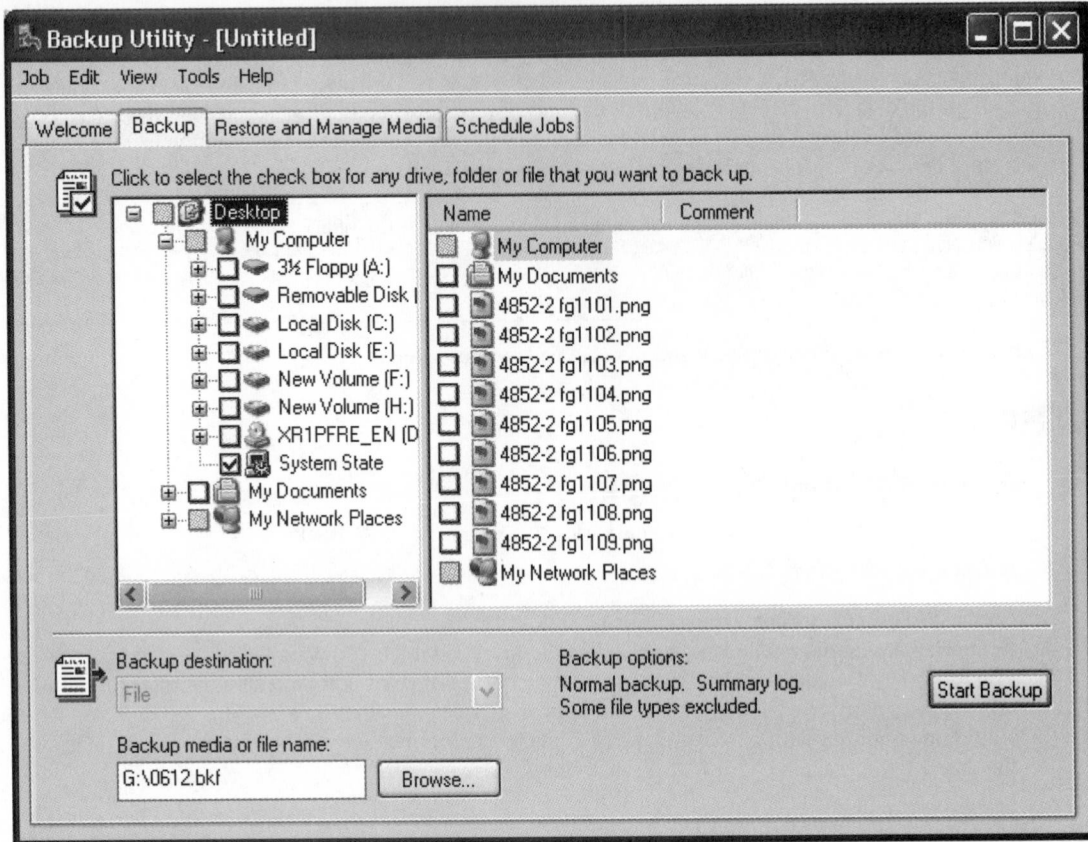

Figure 12-10: You can back up your computer's system state, which includes the Registry, using the Windows XP Backup program.

3. Right-click in the right pane of the Registry Editor (but not on a constant name or value). A New button, as shown in Figure 12-11, appears. Point to the New button, and a menu appears. You can choose to create a key, a string value, a binary value, or a DWORD value. The key and/or any of the constants will be attached to the `WindowMetrics` key.

4. Right-click the `desktop` key in the left pane of the Registry Editor. As shown in Figure 12-12, the context menu will give you the choice of collapsing this expanded branch of the Registry; creating a new key, string value, or binary value; finding a text or numerical string in the local branch; or deleting or renaming the key, among other editorial possibilities.

> **CAUTION:** It is not a good idea to delete or rename a key unless you know exactly what you are doing. Adding a new key or value (actually a constant that has a value, which the Registry Editor refers to as *Data*) may change the way that Windows operates, but it won't do any damage.

5. Right-click a constant in the Name column in the right pane of the Registry Editor. A context menu appears, allowing you to modify the constant's value, delete the constant and its value, or rename the constant.

6. The Edit menu provides similar choices to those that appear on the context menu when you right-click a key or a constant. The Edit menu changes depending on whether you have highlighted a key or a constant. You can't highlight a value (or Data).

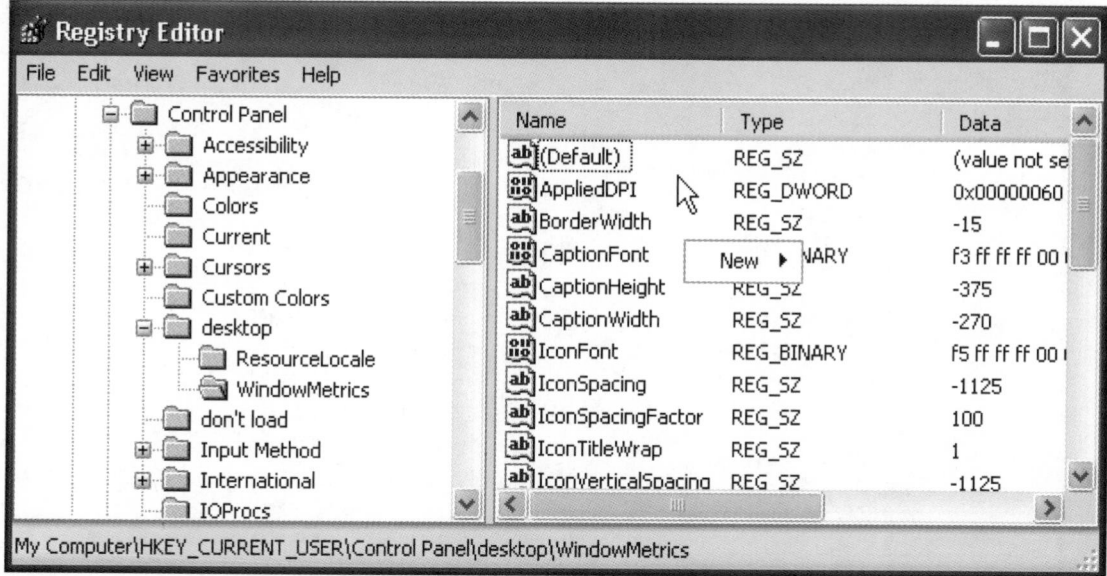

Figure 12-11: Inserting new keys or values in the Registry. Right-click the right pane of the Registry Editor to insert new keys or constants.

Editing the Registry consists of adding or deleting keys, adding new constants and their values to be associated with the keys, and modifying those constants and their values — pretty straightforward. It's knowing what keys, constants, and values to add, rename, or delete that's the trick.

Editing the Registry with .reg files

When you upgrade to Windows XP from an older version of Windows, you may lose some of the little fixes to the Registry you've made. You can get them back if you create registration files (.reg files) that save these changes before upgrading, and then merge them back into your Registry after your upgrade. If you've already upgraded, is it too late for you? Well, your previous registration files are gone, but you can still save any important personal settings you define after your upgrade to Windows XP so that they are available when you upgrade your operating system the next time.

Most often, you edit the Registry by changing settings in dialog boxes, without being directly aware that the changes you make are being recorded in the Registry. Another way that you can switch between Registry settings is to create and use .reg files. With this method, you first choose one of the settings you want in a dialog box. You then export the small branch of the Registry that contains this setting to a text file and save the file with the .reg extension. Next, you use the dialog box to switch to another setting, and then export the updated Registry branch to a second .reg file. If you now place shortcuts to these two .reg files on your Desktop, you can quickly switch back and forth between the settings by clicking these files instead of by interacting with a dialog box.

Help with Registry edits

You can download a help file (Regedit.hlp) that provides a bit of help with Registry edits for Windows Me, Windows 9x, and Windows NT/2000/XP. It includes a Registry FAQ, plus lots of little Registry edits that help out.

It is not a comprehensive Registry help file that thoroughly explains the Registry and its deeper branches, which is disappointing. But it may have information that you wouldn't otherwise have access to.

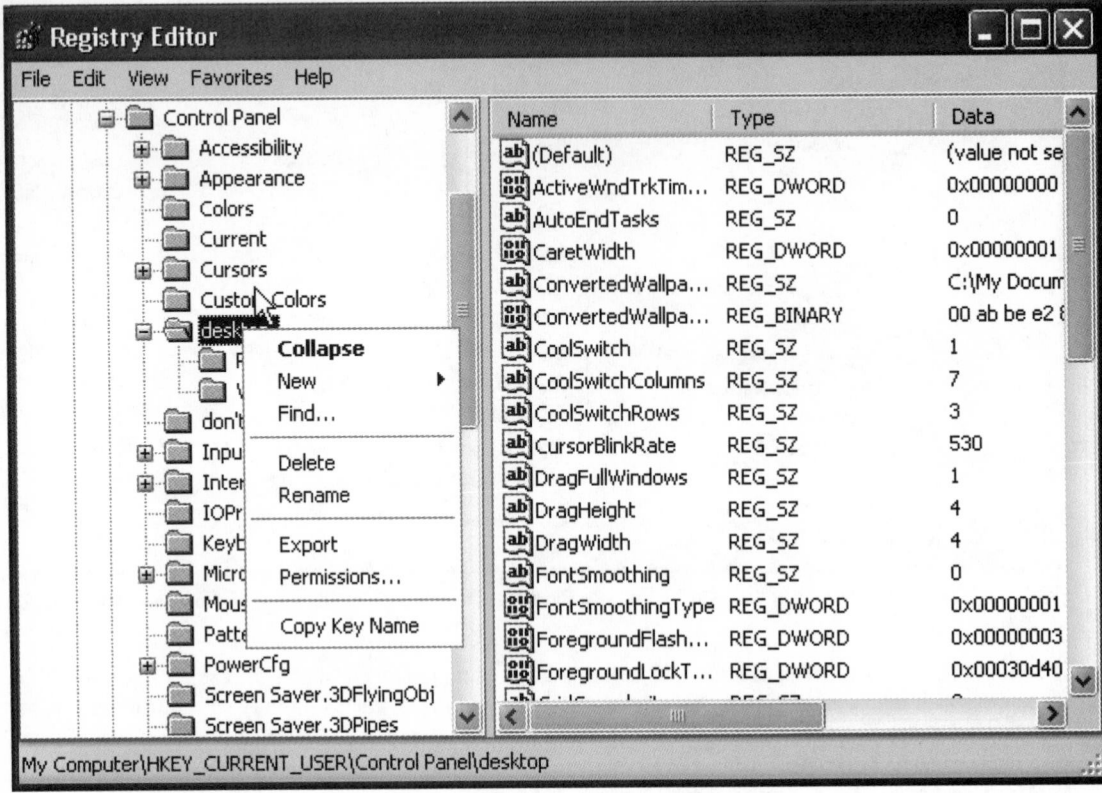

Figure 12-12: Right-click next to a key in the left pane of the Registry Editor to access a context menu.

You can download this help file from `http://www.regedit.com`. Check out the Web site for more information about Registry edits.

Registry Tricks and Secrets

Now that you have seen what and where the Registry is, and some of the tools that you can use with it, it's time to learn some of the tricks and secrets that you can use when there is no other way to accomplish a task.

Exporting and importing Registry files

You can export a branch of the Registry, or the entire Registry, to a text file that can be opened in an editor such as Notepad or WordPad. You might want to do this so that you can search for values or perform some involved editing (to take advantage of the advanced editing tools in WordPad, such as Search and Replace), or to import some of the exported data into another Registry file.

> **CAUTION:** Although you can export the entire Registry, remember that it can be 12MB to 14MB in size, which makes it difficult to work with. Unless you have a specific reason to export the entire Registry, it's probably best to export a branch instead.

STEPS

Exporting the Registry

1. Choose Start ⇨ Run and then type **regedit** in the Open text box. Press Enter or click OK.

2. Navigate to the branch of the Registry that you wish to export. For example, select the `HKEY_CURRENT_USER\Control Panel\Appearance\Schemes` key.

3. Choose File ⇨ Export Registry File. This opens the Export Registry File dialog box, as shown in Figure 12-13.

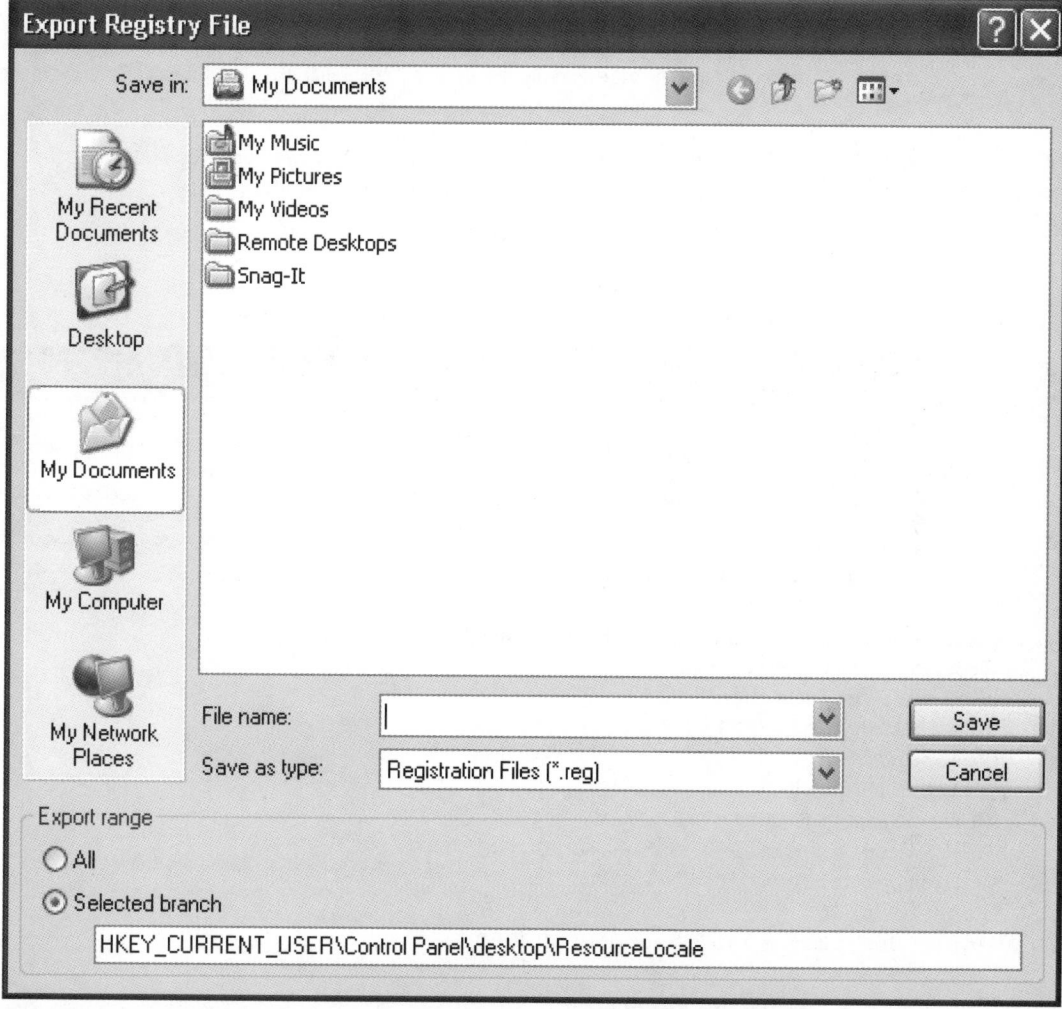

Figure 12-13: Normally, when you export the Registry, you want to export only the current branch, even though you can export the complete Registry if you need to. The default file extension for exported Registry files is .reg.

4. Unless you want to export the entire Registry, choose Selected branch in the Export range section in the lower portion of the dialog box.

5. Choose the subfolder to which you want to save the file, and then provide a name for your file, such as **Schemes**.

6. If you want to be able to import this data back into this or some other Registry file, use the default file extension of `.reg`.

7. Click Save, which saves the file, and then close the dialog box.

After you have exported the Registry branch, any text editor, such as NotePad or WordPad, can read it. You can start WordPad, and then use its File ⇨ Open command to load the file. You also can find the file in the Windows Explorer, and then right-click the file and click the Open With option on the context menu to select a program with which to open the file, such as WordPad or Notepad.

CAUTION: You do not want to click (or double-click) the `.reg` file, nor do you want to select the Open command from the context menu. Doing so will cause the file to be merged back into the Registry.

If you open a `.reg` file with a regular word-processing program such as Microsoft Word or WordPerfect, make sure that you do not save the edited file as a native Word or WordPerfect document. Both Word and WordPerfect files embed data into the headers of the documents, and saving the file in these formats could cause problems with your Registry if you somehow managed to import the saved file.

When the exported Registry file is opened, you see the key name in square brackets, the constants surrounded by quotation marks, and, finally, the value entries, as shown in Figure 12-14.

♦ If the value entries are strings, they are surrounded by quotation marks.

♦ If the value entries are binary, they begin with the word `hex`.

♦ If the value entries are DWORD values, they begin with the word `dword`.

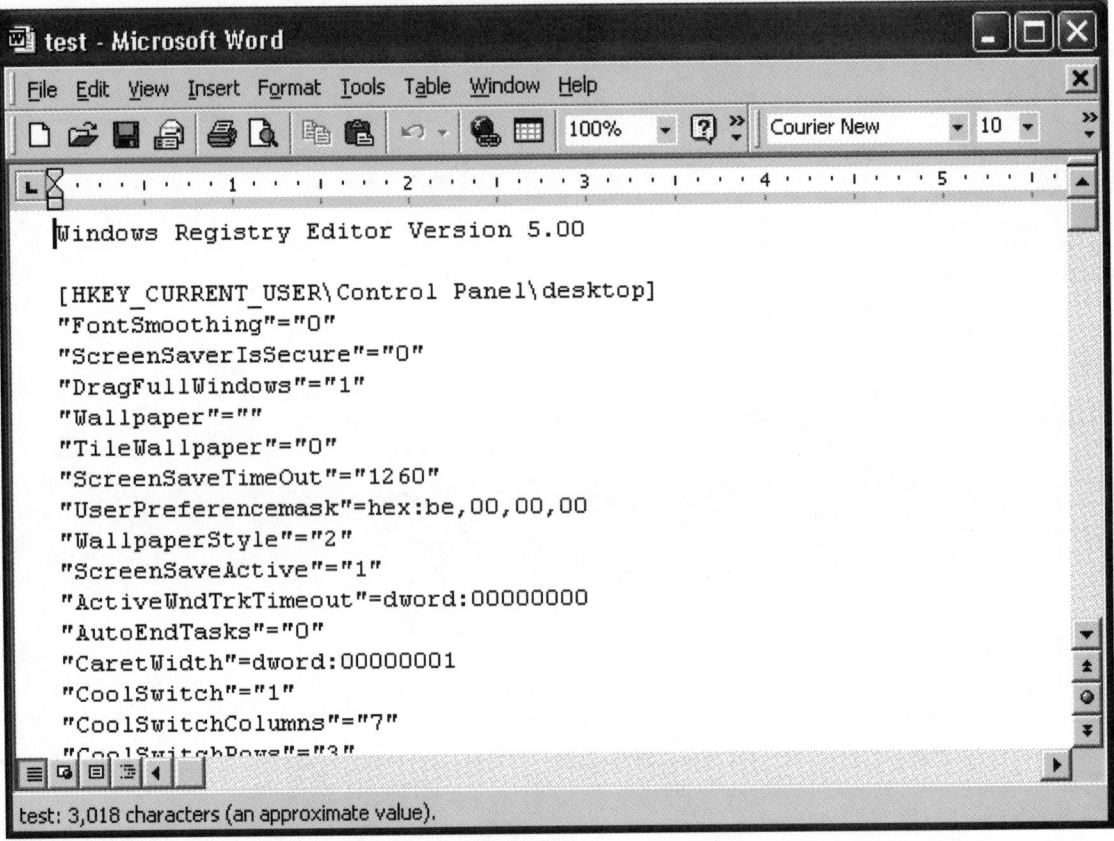

Figure 12-14: When you export a branch of the Registry to a text file, and subsequently open it in a text editor, the key name is seen within square brackets at the top, followed by the value entries.

Importing a display scheme

One reason you might want to export a Registry branch is so that you can import the branch — or a portion of the branch — into another Registry file. This is a lot of trouble to go to for a simple Registry setting or key. If you only had to change one value, it would certainly be easier to use RegEdit to edit the value. Some changes are a lot more complex, however, and it might be easier to import a branch of the Registry than to manually make all the changes.

One situation in which this might be appropriate is with display schemes. You can choose different colors for desktops, title bars, and menus; different spacing for icons; and different fonts and sizes for the menus, among other things. You can make many individual changes to these items, and then save all your changes as a scheme. Someone might have taken a lot of time to tweak those settings to achieve an attractive display, and then saved it as a new scheme.

SECRET: A Desktop scheme created in Windows XP is available only to the user who created it because the data is saved in the HKEY_CURRENT_USER segment of the Registry. This segment is available only to the account with which you log on when you boot your computer. However, you can export and then import that scheme into another user's HKEY_CURRENT_USER key.

Assume you have exported the HKEY_CURRENT_USER\Control Panel\Appearance\Schemes key to a .reg file using the steps outlined in the previous section. You now have to decide whether you want to import all of the schemes, or just the one scheme that interests you. When you import a branch of the Registry, all of the keys and values are imported into the existing branch having the same name. If the key existed in the old Registry, it is overwritten with the new values. If the key is new, it is appended to that branch.

If you import the entire branch, and the user had modified any of the existing Windows XP Desktop schemes, those modifications are overwritten. Therefore, it might be easier to prune the existing schemes out of the exported branch with a text editor, and then import the newly trimmed scheme.

STEPS

Editing and importing a .reg file

1. Open your saved .reg file in WordPad.

2. Scroll through the file until you find the scheme that you want to import. Each scheme name will be enclosed in quotation marks, followed by the word =*hex:* and a long series of numbers.

3. You will need to delete all the other schemes. Return to the top of the file. Leave the subkey name that appears in square brackets, and delete the other scheme names, making sure you delete everything before the desired scheme name, but leave the quotation marks around the desired scheme. If there are additional schemes following the one you want, they must also be deleted.

4. Save the file, making sure it is saved as a plain text file with the extension .reg. Also, if you want other users to be able to read it, it should be saved as a public file.

5. Log off Windows XP, and then log on as the other user.

6. Open the Windows Explorer, and then navigate to the folder to which you saved the .reg file. Right-click the file, and then select Merge from the context menu. You should see a message telling you that the merger has taken place.

7. Right-click the Desktop and choose Display Properties from the context menu. In the Display Properties dialog box, click the Themes tab. The merged scheme should now be available.

TIP: You are not limited to importing a scheme only to another user on the same computer. After you save the .reg file in Step 4, you can copy this file to a floppy disk and move it to another computer, or you can even send it as an e-mail attachment to somebody else, who can then import it into his or her Registry.

Default Registry actions

As I emphasized earlier, making mistakes with the Registry can do very bad things to your computer. If you start working with .reg files, as in the example above, you don't want to mistakenly import the file when you open it. One way to safeguard against inadvertently doing so is to make sure that the default action for .reg files is to edit them and not open them.

STEPS

Checking .reg file behavior

1. Choose Start ⇨ Settings ⇨ Control Panel.

2. Click Folder Options, and then select the File Types tab.

3. Find Reg, or Registration Entries, in the list of File types, and then select it.

4. Click Advanced. In the Edit File Types dialog box, shown in Figure 12-15, Edit should be in bold, and the Set Default button should be grayed out when Edit is selected. If it is, you are all set, and you can click OK twice to exit.

5. If not, select Edit and then click the Set Default button. Click OK twice to exit.

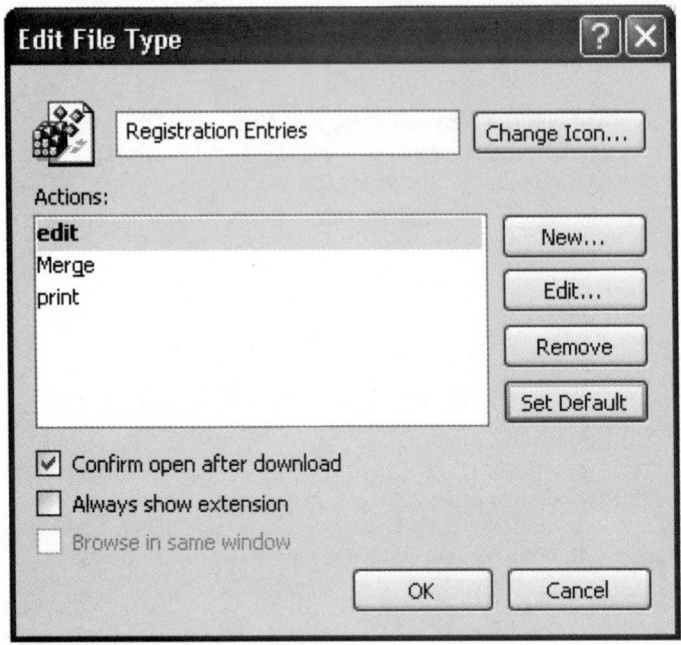

Figure 12-15: Setting the default action for .reg files to Edit makes it difficult to accidentally merge a file into the Registry.

SECRET: When you are in the Edit File Types dialog box, you also can change the program that is used by default for editing .reg files. Make sure that Edit is selected in the list of Actions, and then click the Edit button. The default program used in editing will be shown in Editing action for file type: Registration Entries. If it is Notepad, and you would rather use WordPad, you can change the Application used to perform action text box to WordPad, by replacing the path to Notepad with the path to WordPad. On most systems, WordPad can be found at the following path

```
C:\Program Files\Windows\Accessories\wordpad.exe
```

After supplying the file path, make sure that the argument %1 is still appended, as shown in Figure 12-16.

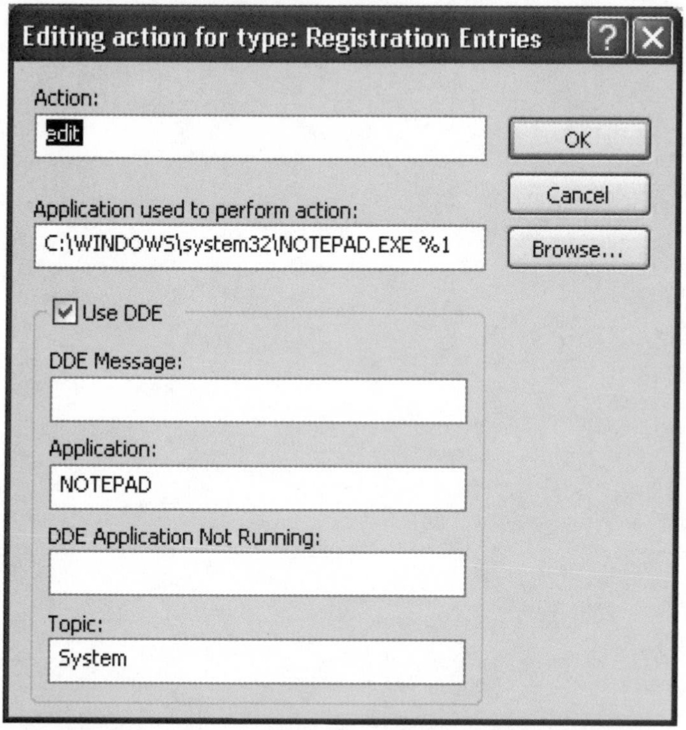

Editing action for type: Registration Entries   [?] [X]

Action:

edit

OK

Application used to perform action:

C:\WINDOWS\system32\NOTEPAD.EXE %1

Cancel

Browse...

☑ Use DDE

DDE Message:

Application:

NOTEPAD

DDE Application Not Running:

Topic:

System

Figure 12-16: Instead of using Notepad as the default editor for .reg files, you can use WordPad. If you use WordPad or some other program that handles multiple file formats, make sure that .reg files are saved as plain-text files.

Summary

If you learn the secrets of the Registry, you have total control of your computer. Even settings that are typically out of your reach when you use Control Panel applets and other system settings are available. In this chapter . . .

♦ You learned how to back up and restore the Registry.

♦ You learned about the structure of the Registry.

♦ You learned where the Registry files are actually stored on your computer.

♦ You looked at a number of tools that you can use to edit, back up, restore, compare, and monitor the Registry.

♦ You saw a number of secret things that you can do only through editing the Registry.

Chapter 13

Configuring Printers, Cameras, and Scanners

In This Chapter

If you have configured printers and related media hardware in Windows 2000 and Windows Me, you are not in for anything new in Windows XP. Indeed, XP takes the best features of Windows 2000 printing and Windows Me easy configuration and combines them in Windows XP. In fact, there hasn't been much change in printing technology for several years now. The Windows printing subsystem has not changed radically since 1992. Windows printer drivers continue to be based on a universal driver that gives printer manufacturers a big head start toward producing specific drivers for their printers. The advantage with Windows XP, however, is better support for many different kinds of printers and easier configuration. In this chapter, you take a look at printer configuration, as well as camera and scanner installation. You learn about . . .

♦ Printing with Windows XP

♦ Installing and configuring printers

♦ Installing and configuring cameras and scanners

Printing with Windows XP

Windows XP makes printing easy. A friendly wizard helps you to set up printers, and the operating system supports more than 1000 different printers and provides drivers for those printers directly from the operating system. On the printer manufacturer's side, printers work better than ever before and typically come equipped with their own installation and management CD. This ease of use does not come without advanced technology improvements, however, and the following sections give you a look at the printing features of Windows XP.

The 32-bit printer driver

Like all the other drivers that come with Windows XP, the printer driver is a 32-bit driver. This means that it spools print jobs as threads, which Windows can preemptively multitask. The 32-bit driver gives the print subsystem more control over the printing process, including bidirectional communication with the printer.

Each printer has its own print queue. You can have multiple printers connected to different ports, all printing at the same time and all managed by a different print-queue manager.

The print-queue managers do a better job of spooling print jobs to the printers than earlier versions of Windows did. They are aware of when the printer is ready for more data, and they don't send it until it is.

Image Color Management

Windows includes Image Color Management (ICM), a utility designed to produce more consistent color among displays, and between your display and your printer. The latter has been a big challenge in desktop publishing, because the way your eye perceives color emitted from a monitor is very different from the way it perceives color reflected from a printed page. Programmers of individual applications, such as Adobe PhotoShop, must include calls in their programs to implement ICM.

The initial ICM version that shipped with Windows in 1995 only supported RGB color, and it was designed to be invisible to you as a user. Newer versions have more powerful features and support more color models, including CMYK (cyan-magenta-yellow-black, the standard for printing on a commercial press). It also lets you set the *rendering intent* — the way you ultimately want the image or document to be seen — from within the application you use to create the document or image.

To set the rendering intent for a program, choose File ⇨ Color Management. Windows offers a choice of four rendering intents:

♦ **Perceptual matching** — best for photographic images

♦ **Saturation matching** — best for graphs and pie charts

♦ **Relative Colorimetric matching** — best for logos and artwork in which a few colors must be matched exactly

♦ **Absolute Colorimetric matching** — best for creating idealized, device-independent images, such those on Web sites

Universal print driver

The universal print driver communicates between printer-specific minidrivers and the rest of the operating system. It supports higher-resolution laser printers, and it can download TrueType outlines to printers that support the PCL language (the HP LaserJet printer control language). This lets the printer rasterize fonts without using the resources of the computer. In other words, the printer can take on more of the tasks of rendering what you see on the printed paged instead of the computer having to do all of the work.

The universal print driver also supports Hewlett-Packard's HPGL/2 plotter language, so CAD and similar applications can send their HPGL output to a printer instead of to a plotter.

Unified printer control interface

In Windows XP, printer configuration, installation, and the print-queue management functions are combined and associated with the individual Printer icons in the Printers folder. Each printer has an icon representing its own print-queue manager and printer driver properties. You set the configuration information for each printer individually and manage each print queue separately and simultaneously.

Spooling EMF, not RAW, printer codes

When you print a document, the document file has to be translated into the printer's codes that instruct the printer on how to print each character. Microsoft refers to these printer codes as the RAW data. (RAW is capitalized because Microsoft capitalizes it in order to contrast it with EMF, or *Enhanced Metafile Format*.)

In Windows XP, both the translation to RAW data and the print spooling are done in the background. You don't have to wait for the lengthy translation to RAW data to finish before you can continue working with your application. Your document is instead translated to EMF, which is a much higher level and more compact format than the RAW data. This reduces the initial translation time and returns you to your application more quickly.

The temporary EMF file is spooled and translated as it is sent to the printer. EMF is built into the Graphic Device Interface (GDI) module of Windows. If you run into problems spooling EMF files, you can switch to the old way of spooling RAW data files instead. You can change this setting on the printer's Properties pages. Click the Advanced tab, and then click the Print Processor button to select RAW.

PostScript printer drivers spool PostScript files to the PostScript printer. There is no EMF translation available for PostScript printers. PostScript is already a high-level page description language like the Enhanced Metafile Format, so there is little or no benefit in translating first to EMF and then from EMF to PostScript. The PostScript printer driver translates your document to a temporary PostScript file, spools this file, and starts sending it to the printer as the driver creates the temporary file.

CROSS-REFERENCE: For more information on PostScript printing, see the PostScript section later in this chapter.

DOS and Windows printing work together

The Windows print subsystem spools DOS print files, so you can print from any DOS application and let the operating system handle the printer. The printer ports are virtualized, which makes the DOS application think it is printing to a real port, when in fact it is printing to the Windows print subsystem. You can turn off DOS print spooling.

DOS print files are not translated into EMF print files. Rather, the translation occurs as the files (as RAW data files) are spooled. This still releases the DOS application faster than it would be released without a spooler.

Offline printing

If you don't have a printer currently hooked up to your computer, you can still create print files. They will be printed automatically the next time you get connected to a printer and use the queue manager to put the printer back online. To do this, you must first install on your computer a printer driver that references a printer connected to a network server or to another computer over a peer-to-peer network. This network can be as simple as the Direct Cable Connection (DCC) program, which lets your laptop computer connect to your desktop computer.

SECRET: Offline (or *deferred*) printing is useful when your computer is not connected to a network printer. Unfortunately, offline printing works only for printing to nonlocal (network) printers. You can't use it with a local printer that, for whatever reason, is not currently connected to your computer. You can pause printing while you reconnect your local printer, if for some reason it was offline when you started printing, but pausing does not save the print jobs for later printing.

Bidirectional communications

For years, users couldn't have cared less what a printer had to say to them. Now all users realize that things are a lot easier when the printer can talk back.

Plug and Play printers can give the Windows printer installation routines all the information they need to set up the printer, without requiring you to answer any questions about manufacturer, model, and so on. Many Plug and Play printers can send status reports to the printer driver reporting such things as paper jam or out of paper. This helps if the printer is down the hall. And some sophisticated Plug and Play printers can supply even more detailed status reports.

Support for Enhanced Parallel Port

The Enhanced Parallel Port (EPP) and Enhanced Capabilities Port (ECP) specifications for parallel ports permit higher speeds and improved bidirectional communication. This is most evident when you use devices that can deal with these higher speeds.

PostScript

Adobe and Microsoft jointly developed the PostScript printer driver for Windows. The fact that Microsoft is willing to credit Adobe with joint development speaks volumes about Adobe's role in PostScript and Microsoft's desire to have a well-respected printer driver.

The same PostScript printer driver is used for all PostScript printers. Windows uses a separate spd (Simplified PostScript printer description) or ppd (PostScript printer description) file to modify the driver to reflect the features of each PostScript printer. These files are stored in the \Windows\System32 folder. The filenames are shortened versions of the printer name.

The Windows PostScript driver includes PostScript Level 2 support as well as numerous incremental upgrades to better handle more complex PostScript documents.

If you have a PostScript printer and are using Adobe Type Manager (ATM), you'll want to make sure you have a fairly recent version of the ATM software. ATM versions 3.01 and earlier do not support Windows' Image Color Management, and this incompatibility can cause your system to crash when you try to print.

Printer shortcuts

Because each printer has its own associated icon in the Printers folder, you can place shortcuts to each printer driver on your Desktop, Start Menu, or in any other folder. When you want to print to the printer, drag and drop your document file onto the shortcut.

If you drag a Printer icon from the Printers folder, Windows assumes you want to create a shortcut when you drop the icon. You don't need to hold down the Ctrl+Shift keys.

Printing without installing printer drivers first

You may have installed a local printer by installing its driver on your computer. You can always print to that printer. If you want to print to another printer on your network, you don't necessarily have to install the driver beforehand. You do need to have a driver for that printer installed on your computer, but the installation process can be automatic. This comes in handy, because there could be all sorts of printers on an extensive network, and it would be a bit of a pain to manually install drivers for all of the 1000+ printers that Windows supports.

If you print to a shared printer on your network that's on a computer running Windows XP, Windows Me, Windows 98, Windows 2000/NT, or Novell NetWare, Windows XP automatically installs the printer driver for that printer on your computer. Microsoft calls this *point and print*.

If the network printer is connected to a Windows computer, all the information about the printer and the location of the files associated with it is stored in the Registry of that computer. Point and print uses this information to change your Registry, copy the appropriate files from the other Windows computer, and install the printer driver on your computer.

Printing and logical port redirection

Windows 3.1x required that you assign a network printer to a specific logical port if you wanted to print to it. This is not necessary in Windows XP, as long as your network supports the universal naming convention (UNC) for naming its server, folders, and printers. When you install a network printer, Windows retains its UNC name and uses it to direct the output to the correct printer — for example, \\Curtsimmons\Laser.

If your network doesn't support UNC (the 16-bit networks that worked with Windows 3.1x do not), you can still redirect printer output to logical ports LPT1 through LPT9 on the Ports tab of the printer properties dialog box. Most DOS programs may require that you print to a logical port and not to a printer through a UNC port name.

The Printers and Faxes Folder

You'll find that most printing functions in Windows are consolidated in the Printers and Faxes folder. The Printers and Faxes folder is found in Control Panel. Feel free to make a shortcut to it so that you can directly access it from the desktop or the Start Menu.

Your Printers and Faxes folder window looks something like the one shown in Figure 13-1. You won't have any icons other than the Add Printer/Fax icon in this folder until you install some printers (or have them installed for you). Each installed printer driver has its own Printer icon in the Printers and Faxes folder.

Figure 13-1: The Printers folder window. This folder contains the Add Printer icon and icons for each of your installed printers.

You can use the Printers and Faxes folder and the icons in it for a variety of purposes. Click the Add a Printer icon to install a new printer. Double-click a Printer icon to view its print queue. Right-click a Printer icon and click Properties to view a printer driver's properties, or click Set As Default to change the default printer. Right-click an empty area of the Printers and Faxes folder and click Server Properties to configure the default behavior of your computer if it is acting as a print server.

You'll find most everything to do with printers in the Printers and Faxes folder. You can:

◆ Install new printer drivers

◆ Delete printer drivers you are no longer using

◆ Change the characteristics of your printer driver

◆ View and manage the print queues (pause and purge print jobs)

◆ Set the default printer

♦ Give LPT*x* names to printers connected to networked servers (redirect logical printer ports to network printers)

Printer driver installation and configuration and print-queue management are combined in Windows XP to make it easier to get at the important printer functions. So, what is outside of the Printers and Faxes folder that relates to printing?

♦ The Fonts folder, where you'll find the fonts that are installed on your computer. See Chapter 10.

♦ Printer and communication port configurations, including the enhanced parallel port, which you will find in the Device Manager under the System icon in the Control Panel.

♦ The Add New Hardware icon in the Control Panel, which you can use to run the Add Printer Wizard. (You can also run this wizard from the Printers and Faxes folder by clicking the Add Printer icon.)

♦ The Network Connections icon in the Control Panel, which lets you enable printer sharing.

♦ Shortcuts to Printer icons. (You can't drag a Printer icon out of the Printers folder, but you can drag to create a shortcut to the Printer icon on the Desktop.)

♦ The Print Preview capability, a system-wide dynamic link library (DLL) that developers can incorporate into their applications. (An example of this type of Print Preview is found in WordPad.)

♦ The common Print dialog box, which developers can use in their applications. (An example of this dialog box is found in WordPad.)

♦ Shared printers attached to servers on your network. You can view shared printers by clicking the servers' icons in the Explorer; they also appear in your Printers folder if you print to them, drag and drop them to the Printers folder, or click them.

> **TIP:** The Device Manager tracks most of the hardware attached to your computer, but it doesn't track your printers. The Properties dialog box associated with a particular printer is the only place that displays the parameters of that printer driver that are stored in the Registry. The Device Manager does track the printer port parameters.

Dragging and Dropping to a Printer Icon

You can drag and drop a File icon from a folder window, the Explorer, or the Desktop, to a printer's icon or its queue window. The printer's icon could be a shortcut on your Desktop, or it could be an icon in the Printers and Faxes folder. With this action, you are telling Windows to invoke the application associated with the print command for this file type and then execute the application's print command.

If you want to quickly print a file or a group of files, this is an easy way to do it. The associated application starts, and you may see the document in the application window on the Desktop while the document is spooled to the printer. The application is closed as soon as the document is completely spooled.

This is the same thing that would happen if you right-clicked a document file and chose Print from the context menu. The actions listed at the top of the context menu are the ones defined for the file type in the Registry and listed in the File Types tab of the Folder Options dialog box.

If you drag and drop a file to a Network Printer icon in a shared folder, and your computer doesn't have that printer's driver installed, you are instructing Windows to start installing the driver on your computer.

Installing a Printer Driver

Windows documentation refers to *installing a printer*. That really means *installing a printer driver* — in other words, installing software. This is confusing, because the intuitive meaning of installing a printer is to physically place a printer next to a computer and connect them with a printer cable. You'll have to do a little translation in your head when you see the words *install a printer*.

If you have a new computer running Windows, or if you get a new Plug and Play printer, chances are you won't have to install a printer driver at all. After you physically connect the printer to the computer, turn on the printer and start Windows, your system detects the new printer, and attempts to identify and install it. Especially with newer equipment, that should be all there is to it.

CAUTION: If you are using a USB printer, you need to check the printer's documentation for installation instructions on Windows XP. You may need to install the printer driver before installing the actual printer or the printer may not work.

On the other hand, you may want to install drivers for printers you don't own. Perhaps your work will be printed at a service bureau, for example, or on a specialized printer at your office. You can use the Add Printer Wizard to easily install drivers for printers that are not connected to your computer.

If you install Windows XP into a directory with an existing, previous version of Windows, Windows XP Setup automatically installs the printer drivers for the printers that you previously installed. On the other hand, if you install Windows XP into a *new* folder on a computer running a previous version of Windows, you will be asked during setup to install a new printer. You'll see the Add Printer Wizard, and you just need to answer the questions.

After Windows is installed, if it does not detect your new printer on startup, you can invoke the Add Printer Wizard (to add a new printer driver) by opening the Printers and Faxes folder and clicking the Add a Printer icon. If your printer is Plug and Play compatible, the Add Printer Wizard can communicate with it, find the correct printer driver, and install the correctly configured printer driver itself.

Otherwise, the Add Printer Wizard asks you for the manufacturer's name and printer model before it proceeds to find the correct files from the Windows CD-ROM. If you have a printer that isn't covered by Windows driver files and you have a printer setup diskette from your printer manufacturer, you can click the Have Disk button in the Add Printer Wizard. This disk has to include a driver file for the new printer.

If Windows cannot find a printer, it gives you the opportunity to choose a printer make and model, as you can see in Figure 13-2. Select the printer model that is attached to your computer, or you use the Have Disk button to install the software from a disk. Once you have made your selection on this screen, Windows can install the printer driver for you.

When the Add Printer Wizard has finished installing the driver, it asks if you want to print a test page. You should do this if you're setting up the printer for the first time. Printing a test page lets Windows check out the printer, and if Windows finds a problem, it leads you to a Windows Help-based print troubleshooter. The troubleshooter asks you questions to help you track down glitches in your printer driver configuration.

You can also invoke the print troubleshooter from the Windows XP Help files if you are having problems.

CROSS-REFERENCE: See "Troubleshooting Printing" later in this chapter for more information on dealing with printing difficulties.

You can install a printer driver for a network printer in the same manner that you install a driver for a local printer. The only difference is that you will be asked for the server and printer name. Type the name using the UNC. Your network must support this convention if you install a network printer this way.

You can install a printer driver on your computer for a printer on a network in a few other ways, a couple of which are a little more automated. It goes without saying that new printers are constantly coming onto the market. If a driver for your printer is not included with Windows, you may want to check Microsoft's Hardware Compatibility List (HCL). This list is constantly updated with the latest available drivers, as well as other information. If you want, you can search the HCL for your printer: Just go to www.microsoft.com/hcl/default.asp, select Printer in the Category list, choose your manufacturer, and click the Search button. The search will tell you the compatibility level of your printer,

and whether a driver is available for download. You may also want to visit the printer manufacturer's
Web site to see if you can locate the proper drivers.

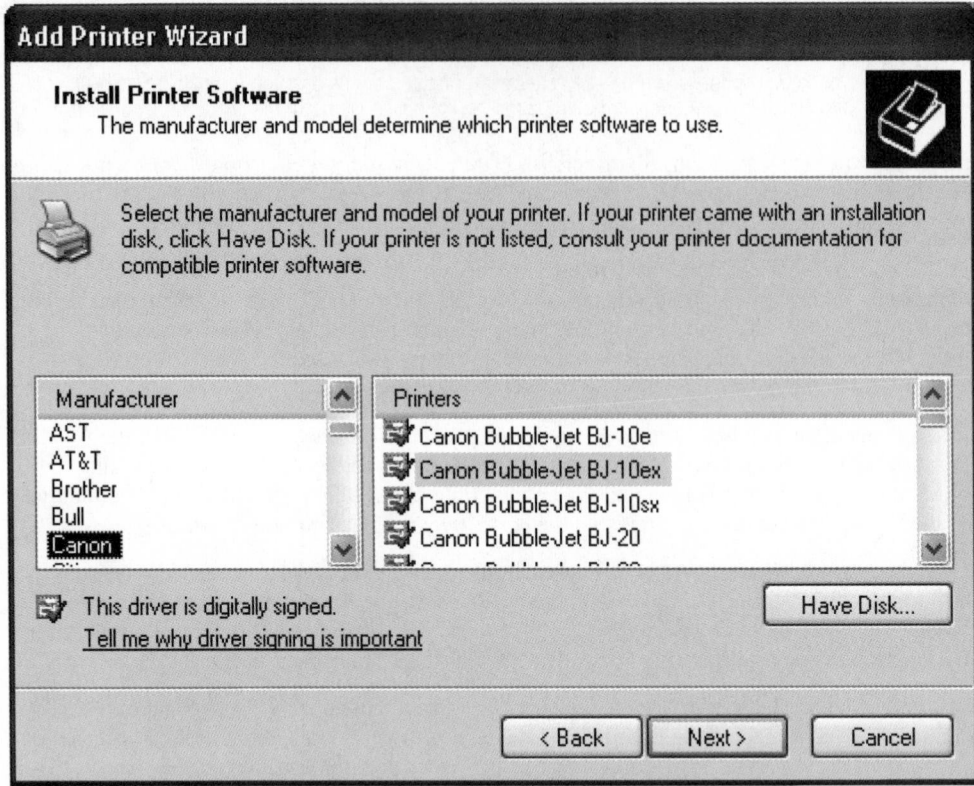

Figure 13-2: Choosing a printer make and model

To get the latest update, you can choose Start ⇨ Settings ⇨ Windows Update. This connects to Microsoft
Windows Update site, which interrogates your computer to see if you have the latest drivers.

Printer Driver Properties

Each printer driver has its own icon in the Printers folder. Attached to each printer icon is a Properties
dialog box that contains numerous properties that you can customize for that printer.

Properties that were previously global for all printer drivers have been moved to each printer driver's
Properties dialog box. For example, you can determine for each printer whether to print directly to the
printer or through a print queue.

Getting to a printer's properties

You get to a printer driver's properties by right-clicking its icon in the Printers and Faxes folder and
clicking Properties in the context menu. You can also highlight a Printer icon in the Printers folder and
choose File ⇨ Properties. If a printer's Print Queue window is open, you can choose Printer ⇨ Properties
in that window.

You can also get to some of a printer's properties through the printer setup options in your application,
usually through the Print or Print Setup command in the File menu. The 32-bit applications can use the
common Print dialog box dll to get to the printer properties. The properties you access through your
applications will not exactly match the ones connected to the printer's icon in the Printers folder. Settings

that you make in the application — the number of copies, for example — override any settings you make in the printer's Properties dialog box, or physically on the printer itself.

Basic printer properties

There are too many printer properties to go through all of them in this book. Besides, I want to focus on the undocumented aspects of printer drivers, not those features that are obvious.

You can find out what the various option buttons and fields in the Properties dialog box do by right-clicking them and then clicking the What's This? button that appears. You can also click the question mark in the upper-right corner of the dialog box and then click an area of interest.

Separator page

The General tab of the Properties dialog box is the same for all printers. One of the options on it lets you print a separator page between print jobs so that you can easily separate them. Separator pages are useful if many different people print to one printer.

The separator page can be blank, or it can contain a graphic that more easily identifies it. The graphic needs to be in the Windows Metafile format (WMF). Files of this type have the extension .wmf.

> **SECRET:** Microsoft doesn't ship any applications with Windows that can produce Windows Metafile files. You have to purchase an application that creates such files if you want to be able to create a separator page with a graphic on it. Paint Shop Pro, a shareware program that is available at almost every shareware site on the Internet, enables you to create WMF files or convert other types of graphics files into WMF files.

After you turn off separator pages, you may still get them when you print from MS-DOS-based programs. This happens when the program is printing to a UNC printer name instead of to a port. To stop the extra pages, capture a specific port for this printer.

Ports

All Windows printer drivers have the same Ports tab, which is shown in Figure 13-3. Select the ports that you want to use with the provided list. You can also add and delete ports and configure ports that are available.

If you want to connect to a different printer, or if your network printer has moved, click the Add Port button. The network path to your already installed network printer will be shown in the list of ports. You can type the path to a network printer for later use. At the bottom of the page, you see the option to enable bidirectional printing, if available, and to enable printer pooling. Printer pooling is useful if your XP computer is acting like a print server with several printers attached. The pool feature makes all of the printers appear to be one printer.

Advanced

The Advanced tab contains a number of different settings that determine how the printer responds. You can change the available time (always available, by default), set a priority, and even update the printer driver from this window, as shown in Figure 13-4.

Print speed is measured in two ways in Windows. One is the length of time it takes to regain control of the system after you issue the Print command (called the *return to application* or RTA speed). The other is the time from when you issue the Print command to when your finished page drops into the printer's paper catch (called *page drop speed*). Both of these speeds are affected by the spool settings in Windows.

You can affect each of these times by setting options in the Spool Settings section of the Advanced tab.

For faster RTA speed, mark the Start printing immediately option button. If this is not a PostScript printer, choose EMF as the spool data format by clicking the Print Processor button and choosing the EMF option.

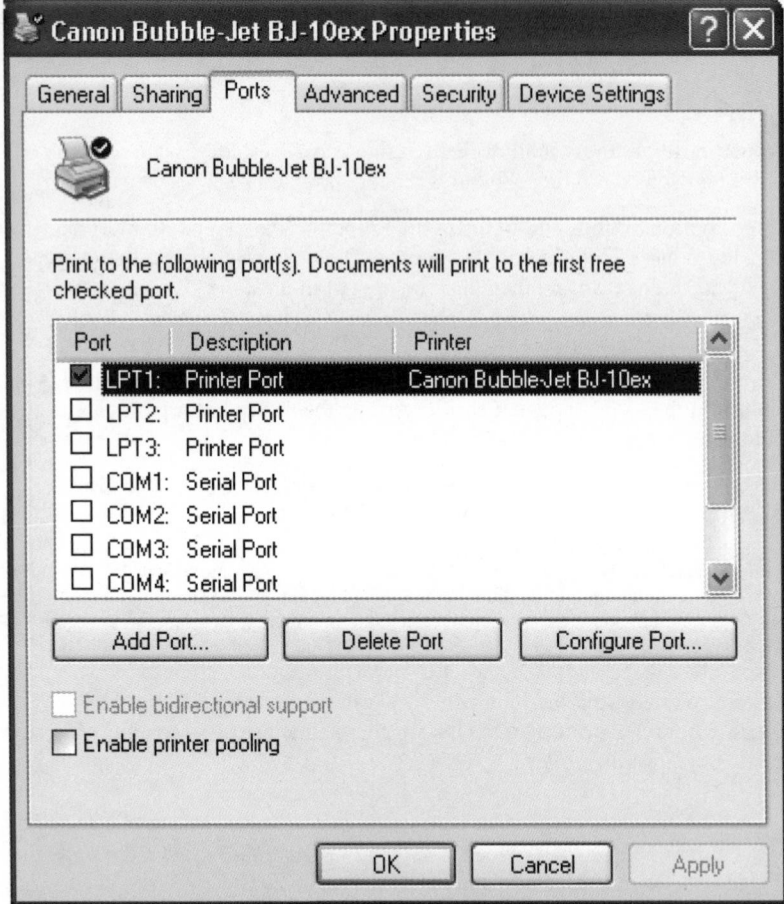

Figure 13-3: The Ports tab of the printer Properties dialog box

For faster page drop speed, mark either the Print directly to the printer option button or the Start printing after last page is spooled option button.

Sharing

One thing that you can't do with a printer driver that is configured to print to a file is share the printer (because there isn't any printer to share). If you have an actual printer connected locally and you've enabled print sharing (using the Network icon in your Control Panel), you have a Sharing tab in the printer driver's Properties dialog box that lets you specify whether or not to share the printer.

You can also get to the Sharing tab by right-clicking a local printer's icon in the Printers folder and clicking Sharing in the context menu. For more details, see the section later in this chapter entitled "Sharing a Printer."

Managing Print Queues

You can change the order in which documents are printed by changing their order in the print queue. To do this, open the Printers and Faxes folder, double-click the Printer icon to open the Print Queue window, and simply drag the documents into the order you want. You can do this only for documents that haven't started printing yet.

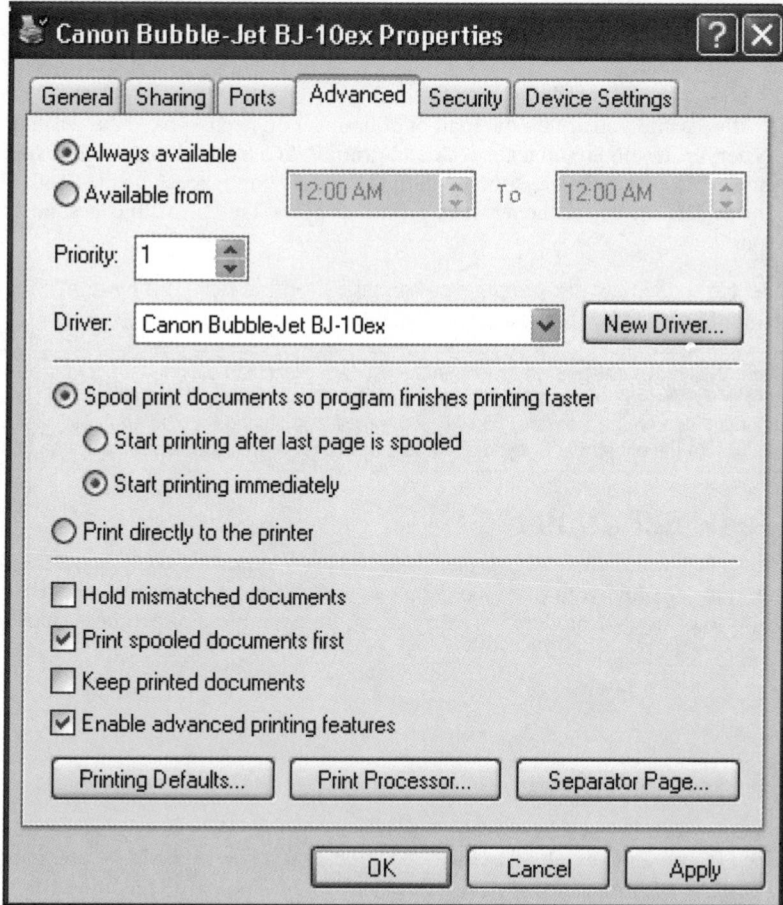

Figure 13-4: Advanced tab

Windows doesn't let you move documents from one printer's queue to that of another. This is because the documents have already been translated into RAW format for that specific printer. Instead, you must remove the document from the old queue and print it again to the other printer.

You can use the Purge Print Documents command in the Printer menu of a queue to remove all documents from the queue (and not print any of them). However, you cannot use your computer to remove documents from the print queue of a network printer.

Deferred Printing

You can print documents using a printer driver for a network printer that isn't currently connected through the network to your computer. The print jobs will be spooled, and you can print them later when you reconnect to the printer through the network. The print jobs are tracked in the print queue for that printer, and when you put the printer online, they are automatically printed. Deferred printing will not work if you have turned off spooling in your printer properties.

One way you can use deferred printing is to create documents on a portable computer, print them to the print queue, and then print them later when you connect your portable to a computer with a printer (perhaps your desktop computer). The portable has to have a printer driver for the desktop's printer installed as a network printer, and the two computers need to be connected with DCC or through another network connection. If you use a docking station, the files you send to the queue while undocked are printed automatically when you redock.

You can also use Dial-Up Networking (DUN) to phone in to the desktop computer from the portable and to print your documents at the office while you are on the road or at home. You need to have the desktop computer configured as a DUN server. If you are on a network and printing to a network printer and you lose the connection to that printer, your print jobs are spooled until the connection is reestablished and you place the printer online. The printer driver for the network printer displays itself as offline as soon as the network connection is broken.

Even if you are presently connected to the network printer, you can take it offline (for you) by right-clicking its icon in your Printers folder and clicking Use printer offline.

SECRET: If you take a network printer offline by right-clicking its icon in the Printers folder and clicking Use printer offline, the icon in the Printers folder is ghosted. If you have a shortcut to that icon on your Desktop, however, it is not ghosted when the printer is offline. If you click the shortcut icon on the Desktop, you will see a message stating that the printer is offline in the title bar of the Print Queue window. To turn the printer back online, click the Use printer offline command again.

Printing with the Task Scheduler

One approach to deferred printing that works on a local printer is to use the Windows Task Scheduler (previously called System Agent) to schedule your print job. You can set it up to print on an as-needed basis, or on a regular schedule — to print your modem log every night, for example. Follow these steps to set up a print job in the Task Scheduler:

STEPS

Scheduling unattended printing

1. If you have the Task Scheduler icon in your tray, double-click it to open the Scheduled Tasks window. You can also open the window by clicking the Scheduled Tasks icon in the My Computer window, or by choosing Start ⇨ All Programs ⇨ Accessories ⇨ System Tools ⇨ Scheduled Tasks.

2. In the Scheduled Tasks window, click the Add Scheduled Task icon to start the Scheduled Task Wizard, and then click Next.

3. From the wizard's list, select the program you used to create the document you want to print — or click Browse if you don't see the one you want. Click Next.

4. Give your task a name, such as **Print Weekly Status Report**, and indicate when you want the task to run (see Figure 13-5). If this is the only time you want to print this file, mark the One time only option button. Click Next. If you choose one of the last two options (When my computer starts or When I log on), skip to Step 6.

5. Enter the time and date when the task should run, and click Next.

6. Enter your username and password and click Next.

7. Mark the Open advanced properties for this task when I click Finish check box. Click Finish.

8. The Task tab of the Properties dialog box for this task will open. In the Run field, add a space after the path for the program you have chosen, and then type the command to print a document, using this syntax: /p "*drive:\foldername\filename*" You must use the quote marks if any of your files or folders have spaces in their names. The command to print a report you wrote in WordPad might look like this: C:\Program Files\Accessories\Wordpad.exe /p "C:\My Documents\Report.txt"

9. Click OK, and then close Task Scheduler.

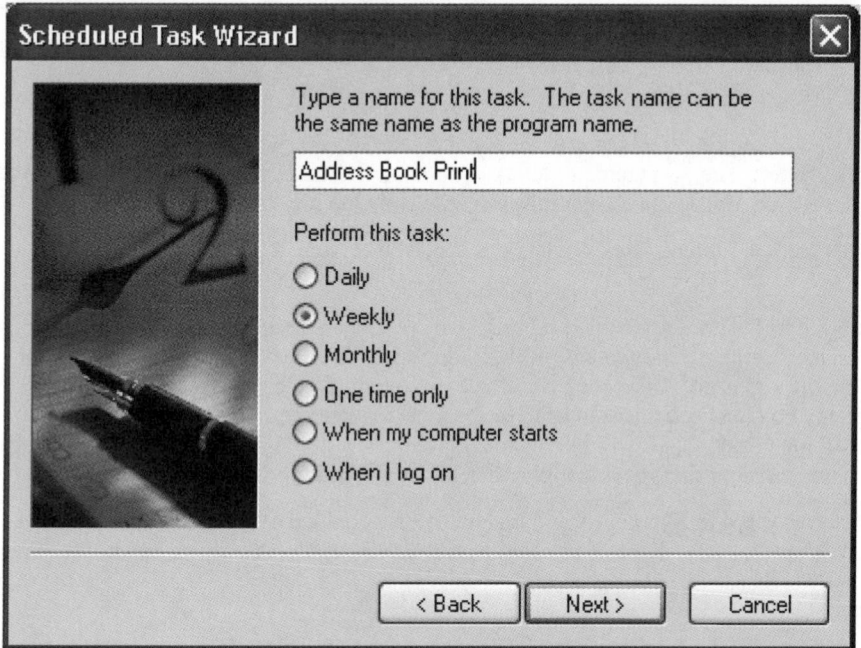

Figure 13-5: The Scheduled Task Wizard lets you name your task and indicate how often it will run.

Although the /p switch for printing is quite common, it is by no means universal. Microsoft Word and Excel are two noteworthy exceptions (Word uses /x and Excel uses /e). The switch is defined for an application by the developers. If you have trouble getting the Task Scheduler to work for your document, you can check the application's syntax for printing. In the Explorer, choose View ⇨ Folder Options, and click the File Types tab. In the list there, highlight the file type that you want to use and click Edit. Highlight Print in the Actions list, and click Edit. Look at the contents of the Application used to perform action field. After the filename of the application (probably ending in .exe), you'll see the appropriate characters needed to carry out the Print action. Use these characters instead of /p in the steps above.

If you want to get back to the Properties dialog box for a task, simply right-click the task in the Scheduled Tasks window and click Properties in the context menu. You can temporarily disable a task without deleting it by clearing the Enabled check box on the Task tab. To change your task's schedule, go to the Scheduled tab and change the contents of the fields there. On the Settings tab, you'll find additional ways to constrain your task — for example, the Power Management settings let you avoid running a task if you're on battery power, or let you tell your computer to "wake up" for tasks that run late at night.

The Task Scheduler also keeps a log, which can be handy if you're troubleshooting. To see the log, choose Advanced ⇨ View Log in the Scheduled Tasks window.

Printing to a file

Printing to a file can be a very effective way to work with a service bureau, because the service bureau won't have to have your application or your fonts to print your file. Printing to a file also lets you design a document at home, and then print it on a specialized PostScript printer at the office or at a copy center. Remember that the file that you produce will often be considerably larger than your original document, especially if you include imported images or print color separations. Perhaps the biggest drawback is that you cannot edit the print file after you create it. If your service bureau finds a mistake, or if you don't want that paper tray after all, you must go back to your original document and print to a new file.

When you later have access to the printer whose driver you chose, you can copy the file to the printer port. You actually need to use the DOS Copy command at the Windows command prompt. You can't drag and drop the print file to the Printer icon. This method would make the most sense (visually), but it doesn't work.

```
command /c copy /b file1.hp lpt2:
```

This command copies the file of print commands to the second parallel port (which could also be redirected to a network printer). The /c parameter tells Command to execute the following command and then return to the DOS prompt. The /b parameter tells Copy to copy the file in binary mode.

Note that if you use this method for a network printer, you'll need to capture a printer port to make it work.

Some people print to a file to generate ASCII text reports — from a database application, for example — which they can read on their computers as well as print. To do this in Windows, make sure to set Spool data format to RAW before you print. (Click the Print Processor button on the Advanced tab of the printer's Properties dialog box to check this setting.) For the most readable results, install the driver for a generic printer (by choosing Generic/Text Only in the manufacturer list of the Add Printer Wizard) with FILE as its port. Then target that printer in your application when you print the report.

The whole point of deferred printing is to get around this tiresome technique of manually copying print files to the printer port. Unfortunately, deferred printing works only for network printers and not for local printers that are presently offline.

Troubleshooting Printing

If you are having trouble printing, you can use the Print Troubleshooter section of the help system to track down the problem. Windows Help is no longer just a semi-meaningless collection of statements of the obvious; it is actually useful in the real world. The print troubleshooter can pinpoint a problem for you, as long as you answer the questions correctly. Choose Start ⇨ Help and Support and then click the Printing and Faxing link in the lower portion of the window.

You can also search the Microsoft Knowledge Base for articles related to your particular printer or problem; the address is http://support.microsoft.com/.

Also, be sure to check the printer documentation. The solutions to many common problems are provided in the manufacturer's documentation or via online support.

If you are having trouble printing, and have established that the printer is connected properly and that its properties are set correctly, try these strategies to isolate your problem:

♦ **Make sure you have enough disk space for spooling** — You should have at least 3MB free on the logical disk drive that contains your \Windows\Temp folder. Although the temporary files in this folder are supposed to be automatically deleted when you shut your computer down, sometimes (after a crash, for example) they remain on your disk and cause problems.

♦ **Try printing from a DOS prompt** — Restart your computer in Safe mode, open a DOS session, and then try printing a test file to LPT1 (or to whichever port you've assigned your printer). To do this, type **copy c:\boot.ini lpt1** (or **copy c:\Windows\System\testps.txt lpt1** if you have a PostScript printer) and press Enter.

♦ **Try printing from Notepad or WordPad** — If you can't print from these two applets, check to make sure the port is set up correctly, and that there are no resource conflicts. To do this, open the Control Panel, click the System icon, and click the Device Manager tab. Click the plus sign next to Ports (COM & LPT), Double-click the port you have assigned to this printer, and click the Resources tab. Look at the Conflicting device list box. If there is a resource conflict, Windows will tell you what the conflicting device is, and which resource the two devices are fighting over. If you *can* print from Notepad or WordPad, click the Print Processor button in the Advanced tab of the printer's Properties dialog box, and try different combinations of spool settings and bidirectional support until you find a combination that works in your other applications.

♦ **Try disabling the ECP port if you have one** — Open the Device Manager, find the ECP port, and double-click it. On the General tab in the Properties dialog box for the port, mark Disable in this hardware profile.

♦ **Try reinstalling the printer port** — Use the Device Manager to select the port assigned to your printer and click the Remove button. Restart your computer. In the Control Panel, click the Add New Hardware icon and let Windows XP detect your hardware and walk you through reinstalling the port.

♦ **Try a different printer driver** — In the Printers folder, click the Add Printer icon and use the Add Printer Wizard to install the Generic/Text Only driver (to determine whether the problem is your driver). If the generic driver works, you may be able to solve the problem by deleting your printer from the Printers folder and reinstalling the driver for your printer's manufacturer and model. If that doesn't work, try installing a driver for a printer that your printer emulates. For example, if you have a PostScript printer, try using the Apple LaserWriter II NTX driver.

Sharing a Printer

You can share your printer over your network so that others can use it to print their documents. There are two basic ways to do this. The first is to configure your computer as a server (either a file server, a print server, or both), as described in the next couple of sections. Your computer can become a file and print server on a peer-to-peer network such as Microsoft Network, or on a server-based network such as a Novell NetWare or Windows NT network.

Enabling print sharing

If you want share your local printer with others on a network, you must first enable print sharing. File and printer sharing must be enabled on your XP computer and you must have general network connectivity. See Chapter 19 to learn more about networking.

Sharing your printer

To share a printer, take the following steps:

STEPS

Sharing a printer

1. Open the Printers and Faxes folder.

2. Right-click the icon of the printer that you want to share, and then click Sharing in the context menu.

3. You'll see the Sharing tab of the Properties dialog box for the printer, as shown in Figure 13-6. Mark the Share this printer option button.

4. If you want to allow earlier versions of Windows, such as 2000, Me, 98, and so on, to use the printer, you need install the "downlevel" drivers in order to support these earlier operating systems. If you want to make downlevel drivers available to other operating systems then click the Additional Drivers button and select the desired drivers from the provided list.

5. Click OK.

Your computer is now a full-fledged print server. If you are using a NetWare network, you can use the Windows computer as a complete print server and offload the extra resource use from your NetWare server. You can access the printer's properties dialog box and click the Security tab to invoke security settings as needed.

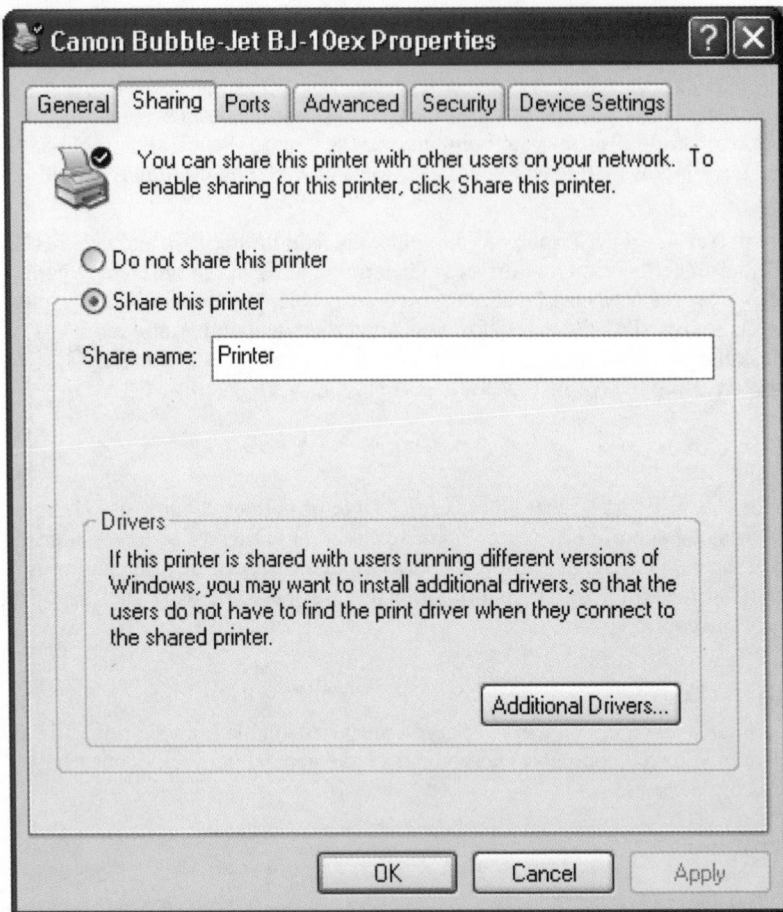

Figure 13-6: The Sharing tab. Click Share this printer button to allow your printer to be used by others. You can provide a name to help others decide whether they want to use your printer and to determine where to find the output.

TIP: Because your Windows XP computer is acting as a print server, you can remove print server features from any "real" servers on your network (such as Windows or NetWare) so that print jobs are handled by the Windows XP computer and the servers can spend their system resources handling other networking and client service tasks.

Using the XP Fax Console

A new feature in the Windows XP Printers and Faxes folder is the Fax Console. The console appears as the Fax icon in the folder, and if you open the Fax console, you'll see a Microsoft Management Console–based window, as shown in Figure 13-7.

TIP: If you don't see the icon, click the Setup Faxing task option in the left window pane, or use Add/Remove Programs — Add/Remove Windows Components to add the service.

The cool thing about the Fax Console is that it works a lot like an e-mail client. You have an inbox, outbox, sent items, and an incoming folder. If you send a lot of faxes using your Windows XP computer, this interface can be very helpful and enables you to easily track all faxes that are sent and received.

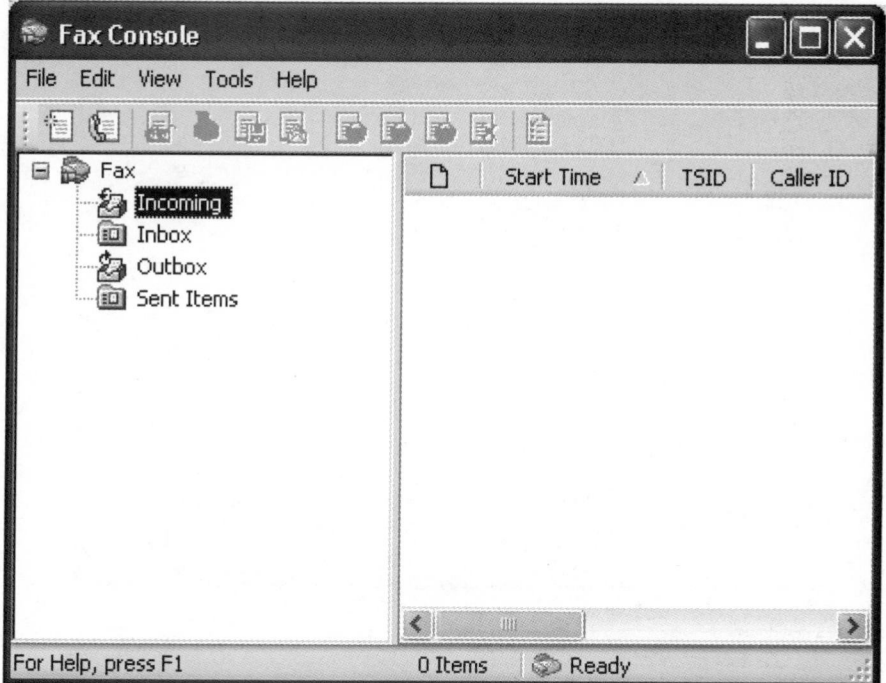

Figure 13-7: Fax Console

You can easily send a fax from this console. Just choose File ⇨ Send a Fax. This opens the new XP Fax Wizard that enables you to easily set up a fax, enter a message, and even determine when the fax should be sent.

TIP: The wizard enables you to send the fax now, when discount rates apply, or at a specific time during the next 24 hours. You cannot schedule revolving faxes or schedule fax transmissions beyond the 24-hour mark.

Overall, the interface is very straightforward and easy to use. The following sections point out the major features and options of the Fax Console.

Importing faxes

You can easily import sent and received faxes into the Fax Console by choosing File ⇨ Import. This feature simply opens a browse window in which you can locate a folder where faxes are stored. Simply select the folder and click OK and the faxes are imported into the Fax Console.

TIP: Imported faxes are not deleted from their original location — rather a copy is imported to the Fax Console.

Add/Remove Columns

The details pane of the Fax Console (right pane) contains a default listing of details about faxes that are being sent or received. By default, you can see icon, start time, recipient name, recipient number, subject, document name, pages, and size. However, if you choose View ⇨ Add/Remove Columns, a window appears, as shown in Figure 13-8, in which you can add new columns that you want to see and remove any columns that you do not want to see. Simply highlight your choice and use the arrow keys to move the selection from available to displayed columns or vice versa.

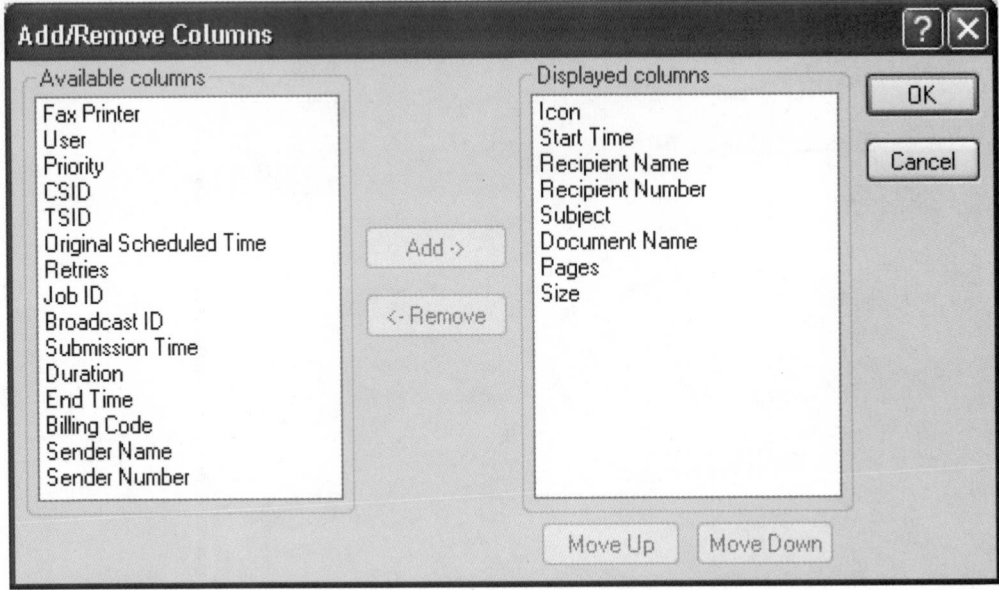

Figure 13-8: Adjust column headings using this window.

Configure Fax

Before using the Fax Console, you should choose Tools ⇨ Configure Fax. This action opens the Fax Configuration Wizard, which simply enables you to enter information about yourself and enables you to select the device that will send and receive faxes (typically, your modem) on the XP computer. After you have completed the wizard, each fax that you send can automatically identify you and your contact information.

Sender Information

You can access a sender information window by choosing Tools ⇨ Sender Information. This self-explanatory dialog box enables you to enter information about yourself that can be used during fax transmissions.

TIP: Be sure not to put any information on this page that you want kept private.

Personal Cover Pages

You can add personal cover pages to the Fax Console by choosing Tools ⇨ Personal Cover Pages. You can create personalized cover pages with any typical word-processing program, such as Microsoft Word, and then list them here so they are available for your use.

Fax Printer Configuration

If you choose Tools ⇨ Fax Printer Configuration, the Fax Properties dialog box appears, as shown in Figure 13-9. You can also access this same properties dialog box by right-clicking Fax in the Printers and Fax folder and then clicking Properties.

The properties sheets you see here are self-explanatory. Check out each tab to change any desired configuration. Be sure to take a look at the Tracking and Archives tabs so you can see how Windows XP tracks and archives faxes that are sent and received. Typically, the default settings are all you need here, but you might want to change some default items as well as the default storage location.

Figure 13-9: Fax Properties

TIP: Also, click the Printing Preferences button on the General tab to set up the default printer settings for fax printing. You can change the paper size, image quality, and orientation, which may help you conserve paper.

Fax Monitor

The Fax Monitor is a handy tool that enables you to answer fax calls, as well as see a listing of calls that were made or received. As Figure 13-10 shows, this is a simple utility to use.

Scanners and Cameras

Continuing the trend started in Windows Me, Windows XP gives you a Scanners and Cameras Control Panel applet. Previously, the icon for this folder appeared only if you had actually installed a camera or a scanner on your system; now it contains a convenient wizard that helps with the installation process.

Like other Control Panel folders, Scanners and Cameras displays the devices you have installed so that you can view and change their properties if needed. To access the properties for other cameras and scanners, just open the Scanners and Cameras folder in Control Panel.

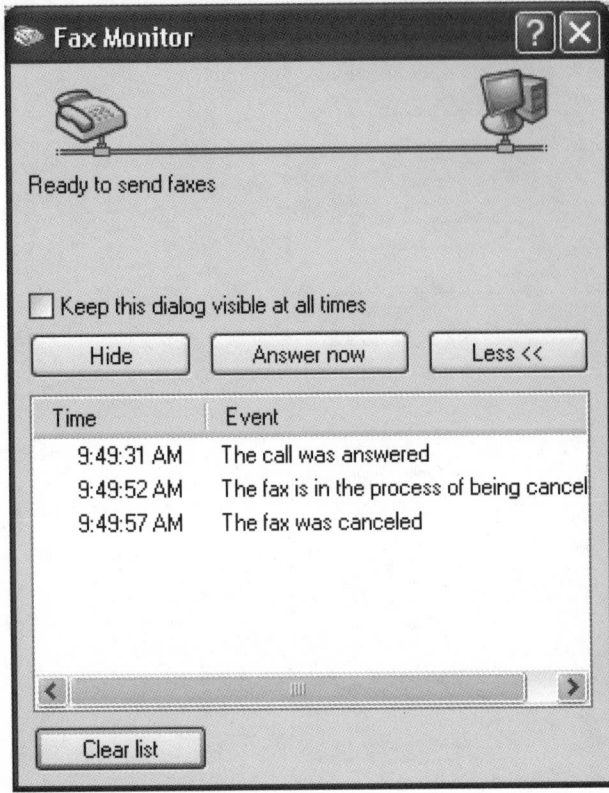

Figure 13-10: Fax Monitor

This folder works a lot like the Printers and Faxes folder. You can add a new imaging device by clicking the icon option, and any installed items are present here. It is possible that some scanners and cameras that are properly installed still may not show up in this interface. If this is the case, you can access the device through Device Manager.

If you are installing a parallel scanner, an older scanner, or a non-USB camera for the first time, you should use the wizard. To launch the Scanner and Camera Installation Wizard, click the Add an Imaging Device icon. Click Next to begin. You will see the list of manufacturers and models as shown in Figure 13-11. If your manufacturer is listed, select it and the model, and then click Next. If your manufacturer isn't listed, click the Have Disk button and follow the directions.

Only USB or Firewire cameras appear on this list (and no scanners); for other devices, you need to have a driver (or download one from the manufacturer's Web site), and then click the Have Disk button and follow the directions. If a driver for your specific model is not listed, try the generic driver for that manufacturer — for example, Olympus Digital Camera or Epson Digital Camera.

In the next screen, select a port to use and click Next. Give your device a name that will appear in the Scanners and Cameras folder, as shown in Figure 13-12.

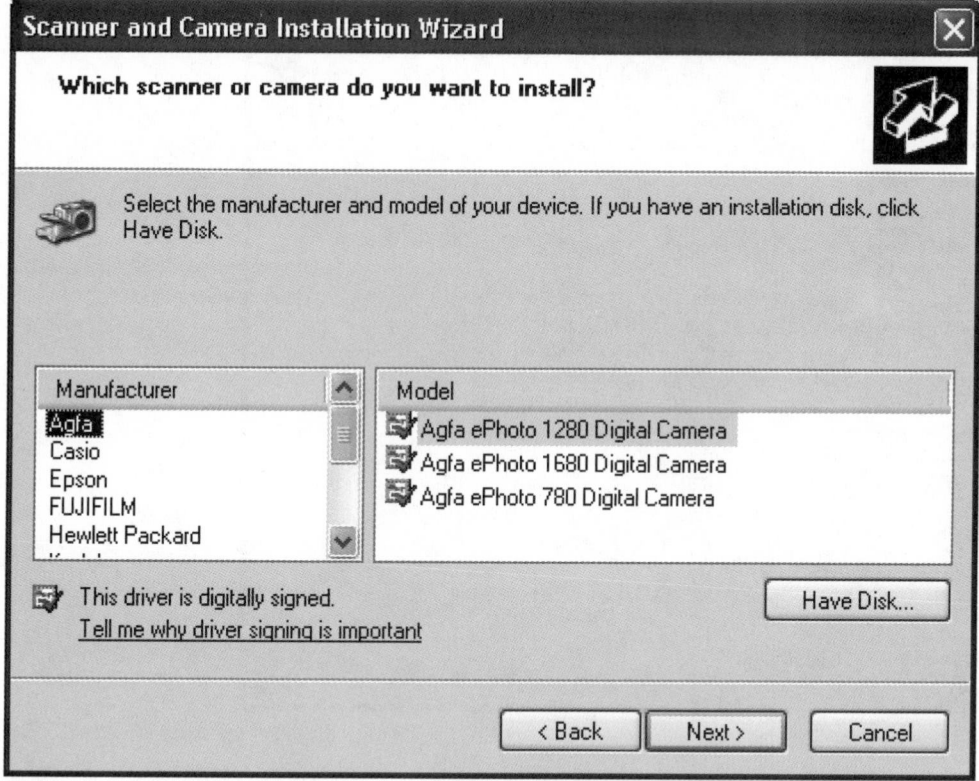

Figure 13-11: The Scanner and Camera Installation Wizard. Select the manufacturer and model of your camera from the list, or click the Have Disk button.

If you have been using a SCSI or USB scanner, a Windows Imaging Architecture (WIA) driver will most likely replace your driver when you update to Windows XP. The WIA drivers, which first appeared in Windows 2000, provider better imaging and image type matching between hardware devices and applications. You will see a new WIA dialog box when you use the device to acquire an image.

Some manufacturers offer more functionality in their own drivers than in the WIA drivers they provided to Microsoft. Check your manufacturer's Web site for a newer WIA driver, follow the instructions on the Web site to download it, then run the Scanner and Camera Installation Wizard using the Have Disk button to install the manufacturer's driver. If you install a non-WIA driver for a Windows XP-supported device, it may not work very well — and Plug and Play will probably reinstall the WIA driver next time you start your computer.

Linking an application to a scanner or digital camera

If your scanner or camera supports the WIA standard, you can link it to an application on your computer. This is similar to what happens when you click a data file in the Explorer — you click the file, the linked application begins automatically, and your file opens. Now you can launch an application with your new image displayed by pressing a button on your camera or scanner. Not all applications work this way, but newer versions of the most popular imaging applications should support WIA functionality.

Figure 13-12: Scanners and Cameras folder

STEPS

Linking your camera or scanner to an application

1. Open the Scanners and Cameras folder in Control Panel.

2. Right-click the scanner or camera you want to use and select Properties. Click the Events tab. (If this tab does not appear, this device does not support linking to an application.)

3. In the Scanner or Camera Events list, click the event that will open the program — for example, pressing the Scan button on your scanner.

4. In the Run an Application list, click the program that you want to start when the event you selected occurs. Click OK.

Taking pictures

After a scanner or camera is installed on your system, you can use the Scanner and Camera Wizard to take photos or make scans. Choose Start ⇨All Programs ⇨ Accessories ⇨ Scanner and Camera Wizard to launch the wizard, or navigate to the My Pictures folder and click Get pictures from a scanner or camera. Select a device from the list and follow the wizard's instructions to crop your picture and change its brightness, then save the new image to your hard drive.

Of course, most scanners and cameras have their own capture and image-editing software. In many cases, the software that ships with your scanner or camera gives you more options, so be sure to check out what is available by reading your camera or scanner documentation.

Summary

In this chapter, you learned about the features and processes of Windows XP printing, faxing, and scanner/camera support, including how . . .

- ♦ Windows XP provides superior printing subsystem features, as well as support for hundreds of different printer makes and models. You can configure a number of printing features, share a printer attached to Windows XP, and even use Windows XP as a print server.

- ♦ Windows XP provides a new fax console utility, which makes sending, receiving, and managing faxes much easier and more streamlined.

- ♦ Windows XP continues to provide support for digital cameras and scanner products.

Chapter 14

Configuring Modems

In This Chapter

In the past, the modem was a great source of headaches for computer users. After all, it is the modem that gives you connectivity to the outside world, but it is also the modem that can be really tricky to configure. Fortunately, modem technology has advanced in the past few years so that modems function better and are easier to work with. Windows XP supports many different kinds of modems and makes installation and configuration much easier than prior Windows operating systems. Still, the modem is a complicated little device, and in this chapter, I explore how to get the best performance from your modem. In this chapter, you learn about . . .

♦ Installing modems

♦ Configuring modems

♦ Troubleshooting modems

Installing Modems

A modem is a piece of hardware that modulates and demodulates data. Basically, the modem enables digital data leaving your computer to travel over analog phone lines. The modem's job is to handle the translation of data between the two formats. It is an important job and one that modems have been doing for a number of years. However, modems tend to be more problematic in their configuration and performance, and Windows XP, like previous versions of Windows, devotes a whole Control Panel icon to them to help make configuration and management easier.

The modem should install on Windows XP like any other piece of hardware — automatically. Plug and Play modems should be detected by the Windows XP system, and a driver for that modem should be installed. However, if you have the modem's actual driver, you may consider installing the factory driver to get better modem performance.

In general, when purchasing a modem and attaching it to your computer, keep the following points in mind at all times:

♦ Modems that are compatible with Windows 9*x*, Me, NT, and 2000 should work fine under Windows XP. If you want to use an older modem, try to get your hands on the driver. The factory driver for the modem may work best.

♦ If you are purchasing a new modem, look for one that explicitly says that it is compatible with Windows XP. Also, check the hardware compatibility list on Microsoft's Web site for a list of compatible modems. You can also view a list of compatible modems using the Windows XP help files (search for modems). You need an Internet connection to retrieve the files list.

♦ If you are installing an internal modem in the computer, make sure you unplug the computer and follow the manufacturer's directions for installation on one of the computer's communication ports.

♦ If the modem is an external modem, turn off the computer, attach the modem, and plug it into a power source, then boot the computer so it can detect the new hardware.

Under most circumstances, a compatible modem that is Plug and Play compliant will automatically install and work just fine under Windows XP. However, there are cases where this does not happen, or if you want to use an older modem that is not Plug and Play compatible, you can attempt to install it on your computer using the New Modem Wizard.

> **TIP:** One of the ways you can seriously avoid modem problems and modem detection in Windows XP is to buy a brand-name modem that is designed to work with Windows XP. This statement is true of all hardware. While you may initially save some money by purchasing a cheap off-brand, you will likely end up spending more money to replace it when it does not work so well.

Open Phone and Modem Options in Control Panel. On the Modems tab, as shown in Figure 14-1, you can see any modems that are currently installed on your computer. If you want to try and install a new modem, you can click the Add button to invoke the Install New Modem Wizard.

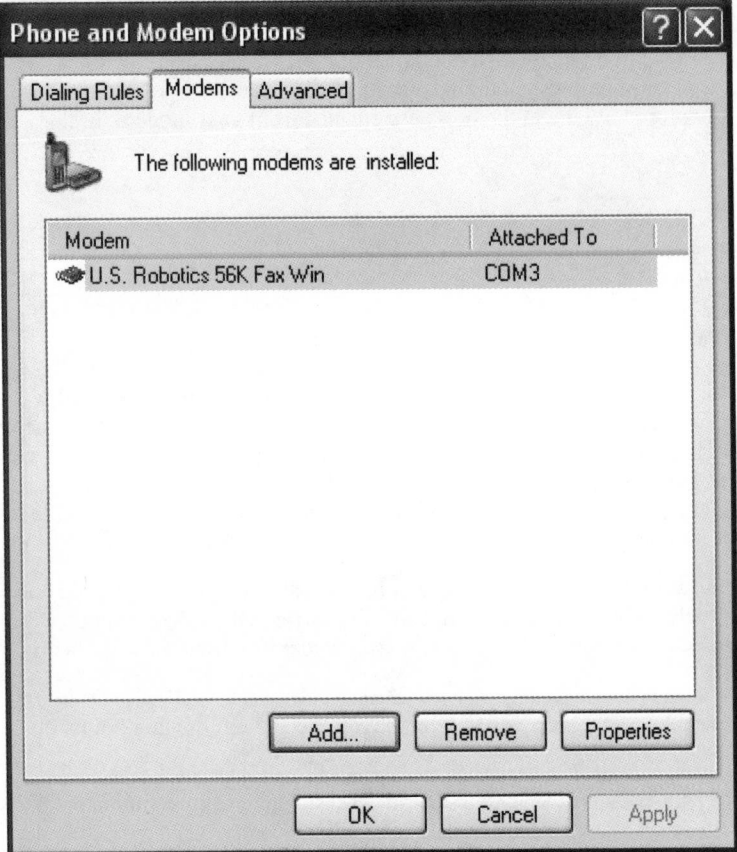

Figure 14-1: Modems tab

The following steps walk you through a modem installation using the Install New Modem Wizard.

STEPS

Installing a modem

1. Open Phone and Modem Options from the Control Panel.
2. Click the Modem tab and click Add.

3. On the Install New Modem welcome screen, you can have Windows try to detect the modem or you can choose the "Don't detect my modem" option so that you can install the modem from a list. If you have an installation disk for the modem, choose this radio button option and click Next. If you want Windows to look for your modem, it will redetect hardware on the system and report any results back to you.

4. If you chose to select your modem from a list or if Windows did not find a modem during hardware detection, a window appears, shown in Figure 14-2, where you can select the modem from a list. If the modem does not appear in the list or if you have an installation disk, click the Have Disk button and install the software from the disk.

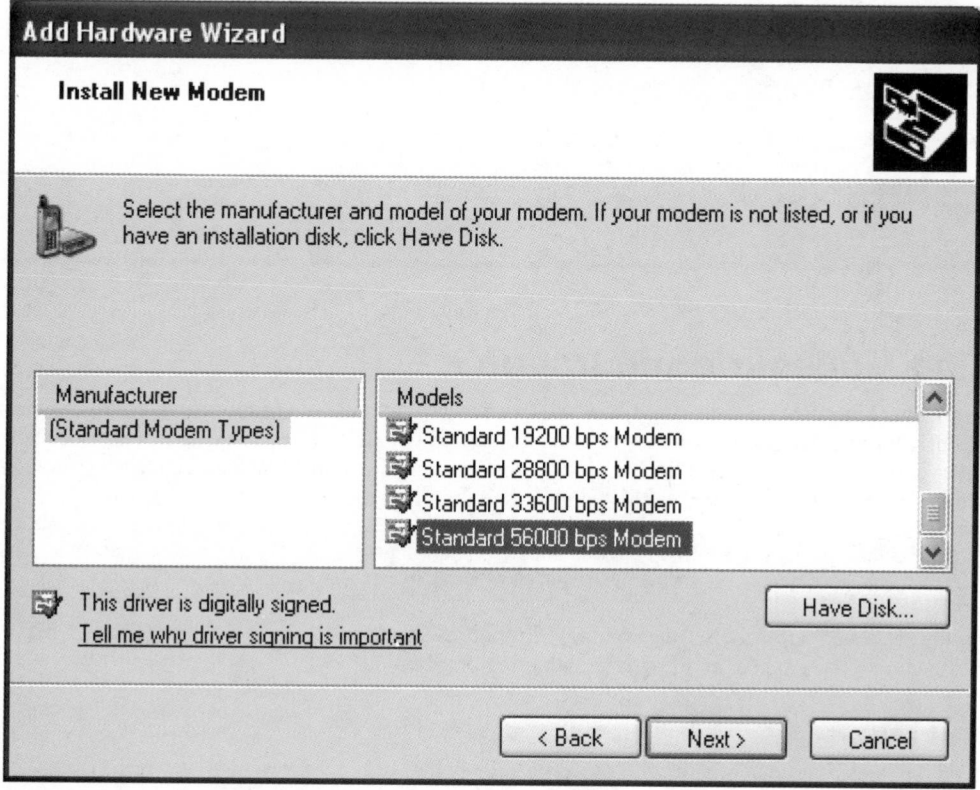

Figure 14-2: Choose the modem from the list or use the Have Disk button.

5. The COM Ports window appears. Select the COM port you want to install the modem on (or select all ports) and click Next.

6. Windows XP installs the modem. Click Finish.

TIP: Modem configuration is stored in an INF file, which is located in the INF folder in Windows. You can open this file with Notepad, but make sure you do not alter any of its contents, as this may cause your modem to stop working. Modem filenames typically begin with *mdm*, and you can see a sample of one in Figure 14-3.

TIP: You can use the Standard modem options only for basic ISA internal or external (COM port connected) modems — not if the internal Plug and Play modem requires a specific driver. If you lose the driver for your internal modem, you will need to disable one of your existing COM ports in order to let the modem have an IRQ, since Windows XP will not let you share an ISA IRQ.

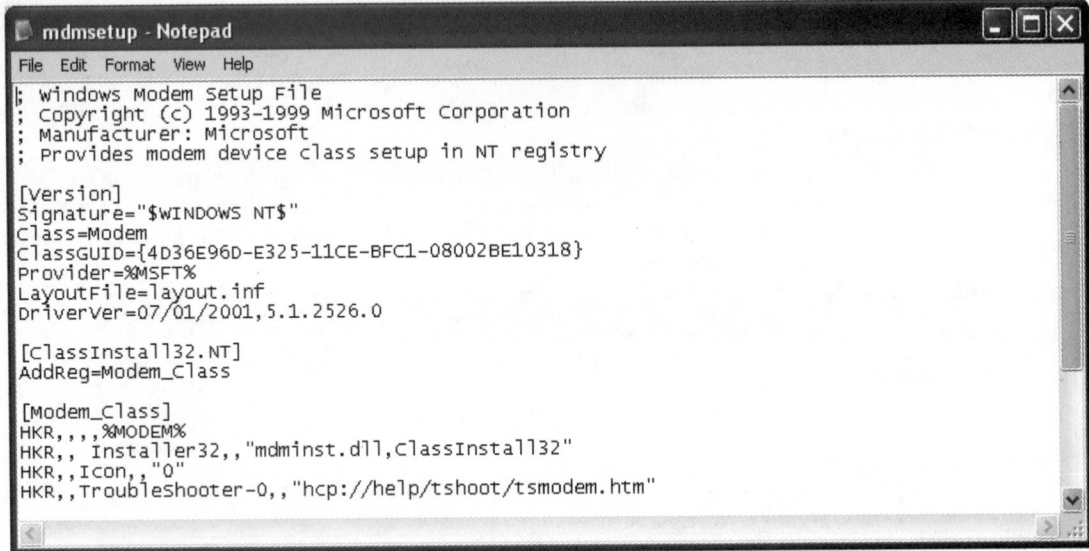

Figure 14-3: Modem INF file

Managing Modem Configuration

Once the modem is installed on your computer, you can access the modem's properties to configure the modem. Configuration involves various settings that can either get the modem working if it is not or help the modem work better. If you open Phone and Modems Options in Control Panel and click the Modems tab, you can select the desired modem in the list and click the Properties button to configure it.

> **SECRET:** The Properties sheets you see here are the same ones that appear under the modem's properties in Device Manager. So, you can easily access the modem's properties in either location.

The following sections review the settings on these Properties sheets and point out the options that may help your modem work better (or at all, if you are having problems).

General tab

The General tab doesn't do much of anything except tell whether or not your modem is working. However, you can use this tab to disable the device using the provided drop-down menu if necessary. You can also click the Troubleshooter button to access the Windows XP help file modem troubleshooter, if you are having problems. If you are having problems, also see the section later in this chapter, "Troubleshooting Modems."

Modem tab

The Modem tab provides three important setting options, which are explained in the following list.

- ♦ **Speaker Volume** — If the modem connection noise is driving you crazy, use the slider bar to adjust it. You can move the volume from Off to High.

- ♦ **Maximum Port Speed** — The default value for maximum port speed is typically 115,200 Kbps. This means that the modem can use the highest port speed available for transmission from programs to the modem. By default, it can be set to four times the speed of the modem as long as the modem supports compression. If you are having transmission problems or problems with connectivity with your ISP, consider taking a look at this setting. You can lower it and see if performance improves.

SECRET: Some modems actually connect and work better if the maximum port speed is set at or near the desired connection speed. For example, if you are using a 28.8 Kbps online data service, set the maximum port speed to 38,400. This prevents the modem from trying to negotiate higher speeds that are not usable

♦ **Dial Tone** — If your phone must have dial tone before dialing, then use this check box. This is enabled by default and typically needs to stay that way. However, if your phone system uses voice mail or other status tones, you may need to disable dial tone detection. Start with the setting enabled, and then work from there.

Diagnostics tab

The Diagnostics tab, shown in Figure 14-4, gives you a place to test the modem. If you click Query Modem, a series of commands are issued from the computer to the modem to check for correct responses. If you choose, you can then view the log file. Also, if you click the Append to Log check box, then one log file is used for queries. By default, the old one is overwritten, but the Append selection causes the new query to be added to the old one. This gives you a full look at query behavior, but it may create a big log file for you to deal with.

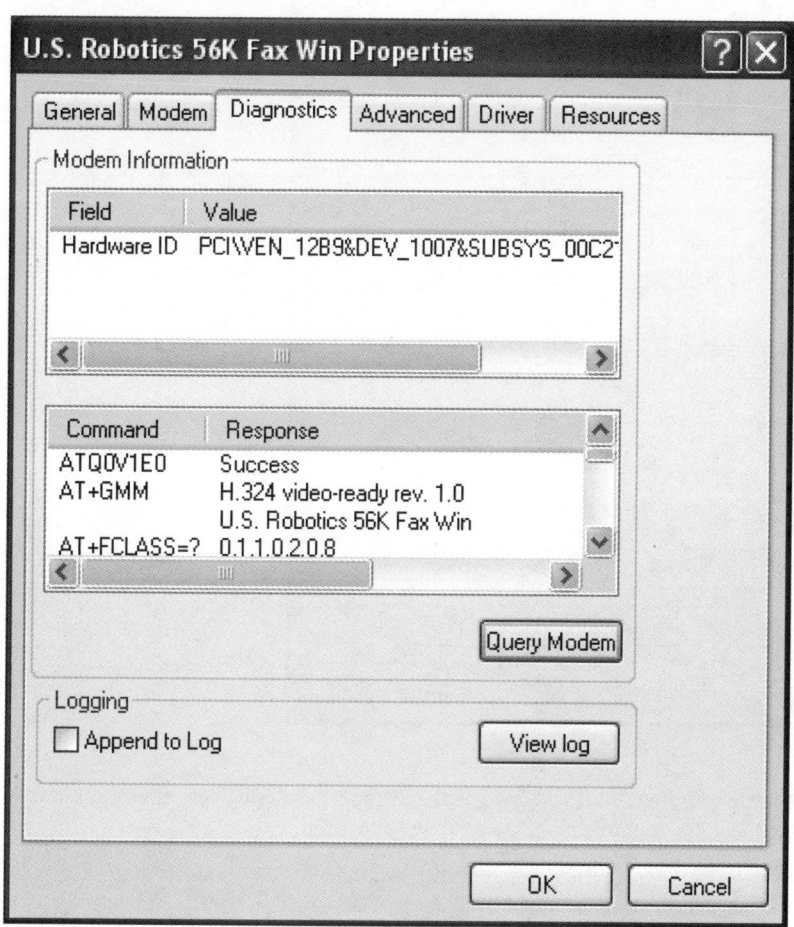

Figure 14-4: Query the modem using the Diagnostics tab.

Advanced tab

The Advanced tab, shown in Figure 14-5, provides you a place to enter extra initialization commands. Under most conditions, it is not necessary to add extra commands here. However, if you are having problems with the modem, check your modem documentation for potential initialization commands you can enter in this dialog box that may help resolve the problem. A number of settings may make your modem work better. For example, you can usually type **S11=35** to speed up the modem's dialing action, and **S10=50** and **S36=7** can help keep your modem working at the fastest speed possible. Once again, though, it is important to check your documentation or the manufacturer's Web site for initialization string details, because their use and effectiveness can vary from modem to modem.

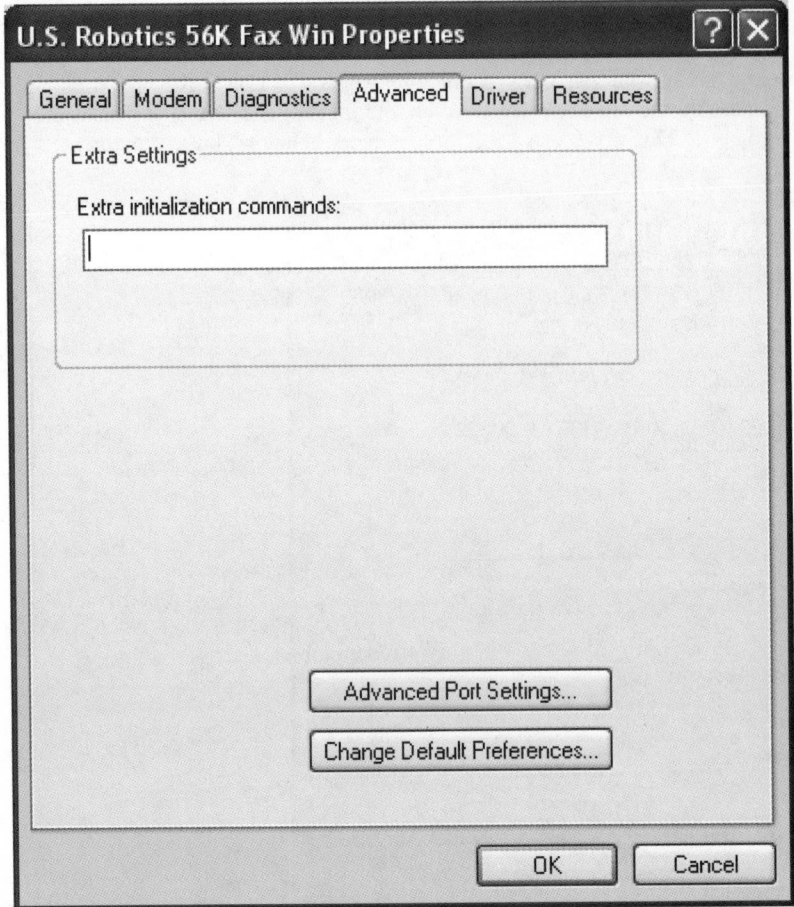

Figure 14-5: Advanced tab

If you click the Change Default Preferences button, a two-tabbed Properties dialog box appears. On the General tab, shown in Figure 14-6, you can make changes to the following:

- **Disconnect a call if idle** — You can enable an automatic disconnect if the modem is idle for certain period of time. This setting is not enabled by default. You can also configure a similar setting per dial-up connection. See Chapter 15 for details.

- **Cancel the call** — By default, the call attempt is cancelled if the connection does not take place within 60 seconds. After the modem cancels the call, your connection can redial the call if it is configured to do (see Chapter 15).

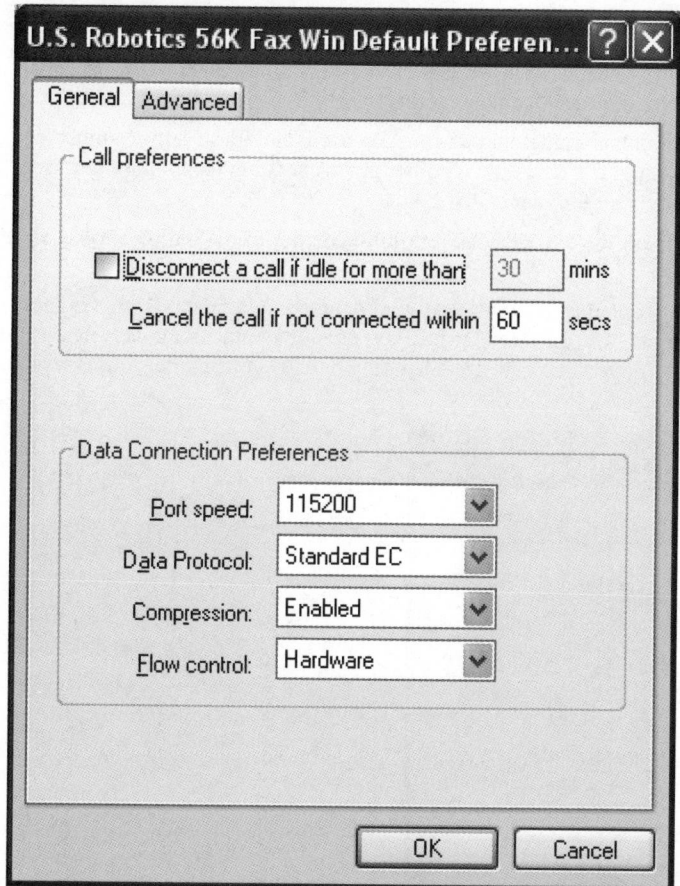

Figure 14-6: General default preferences

- ◆ **Port speed** — This is the same setting that appears on the Modem tab. You can adjust the port speed to a lower value if you are having transmission problems.

- ◆ **Data Protocol** — By default, the standard error correction (EC) setting is used. This setting enables your modem to negotiate with another modem concerning transmission error correction. You can change this setting to disabled or forced EC, but you are likely to experience problems unless the modem you are connected to has these same settings. If it does, you may still experience problems, because line noise and other factors may not leave the modem any negotiating room, thus resulting in a dropped connection.

- ◆ **Compression** — By default, compression is enabled if the modem supports it. You want to leave compression enabled; however, if you are having transmission problems, you can disable compression and see what effect it has on modem transmission behavior.

- ◆ **Flow control** — Flow control handles the flow of data between applications and the modem. Hardware flow control is typically used here by default.

SECRET: Software flow control is the Xon/Xoff setting. If you seem to be having problems with applications communicating with the modem, try the software flow control option. By default, Windows enables hardware flow control so that your modem handles data flow instead of an application. In some cases, however, the application can more accurately handle data flow, and you can experiment with this if a particular application seems to be having problems working with your modem

On the Advanced tab, shown in Figure 14-7, you have some additional hardware settings, which are:

- ◆ **Data bits** — The default setting for connectivity to an ISP or another compute is 8. The data bits determine the number of bits that are used for each character.

- ◆ **Parity** — Parity concerns different data parameters that must be used, and these settings must match the computer you are contacting. It's basically an older error-checking technology not used often anymore. This setting should be set to None.

- ◆ **Stop bits** — A stop bit is used to mark the end of a packet of information. This setting should have a value of 1.

- ◆ **Modulation** — Modulation is the process of converting digital data to analog data. Both modems need to use the same modulation type, which is standard. If you need to contact a modem that uses nonstandard modulation type or V.23, you can change the setting here, if your modem supports the nonstandard option.

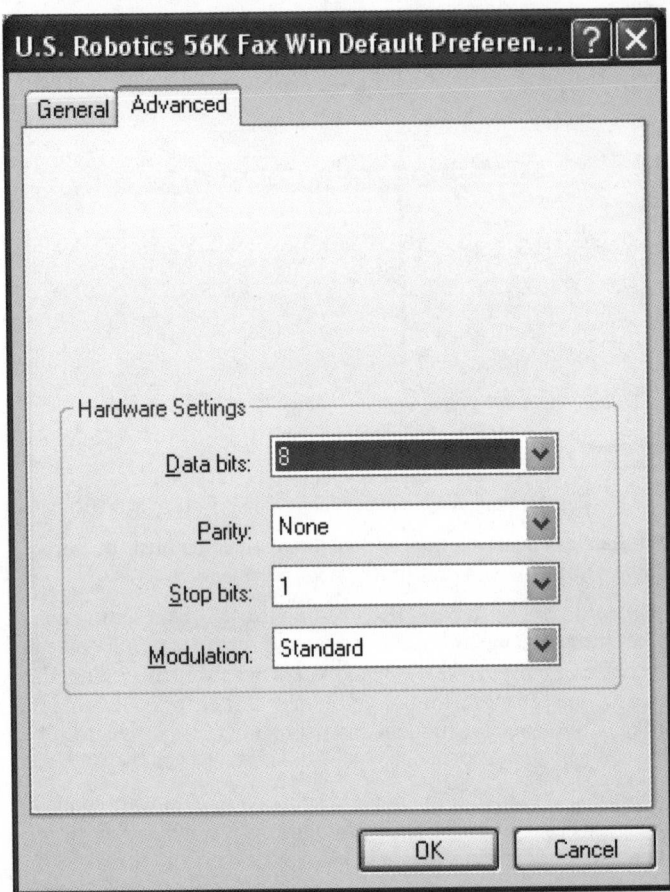

Figure 14-7: Advanced default properties

Driver and Resources tabs

The Driver and Resources tabs are the same tabs that appear on most hardware Properties sheets. Use the Driver tab to update the modem driver and the Resources tab to adjust Plug and Play allocation of resources (which is typically not necessary). See Chapter 11 for more information about these options.

Configuring Dialing Rules

If you click the Dialing Rules tab on the Phone and Modems Options page, you can configure a number of items that determine how your modem dials certain numbers and uses calling cards. For the desktop PC, these settings are fairly straightforward because you don't move around. For laptop users, however, you can configure a number of items that control how calls are made depending on your location.

When you first install Windows XP, you are asked for your area code if the OS detects modem hardware. From this area code, XP creates a default dialing location, as shown in Figure 14-8. This default location can be edited as desired, and you can create multiple locations depending on your needs.

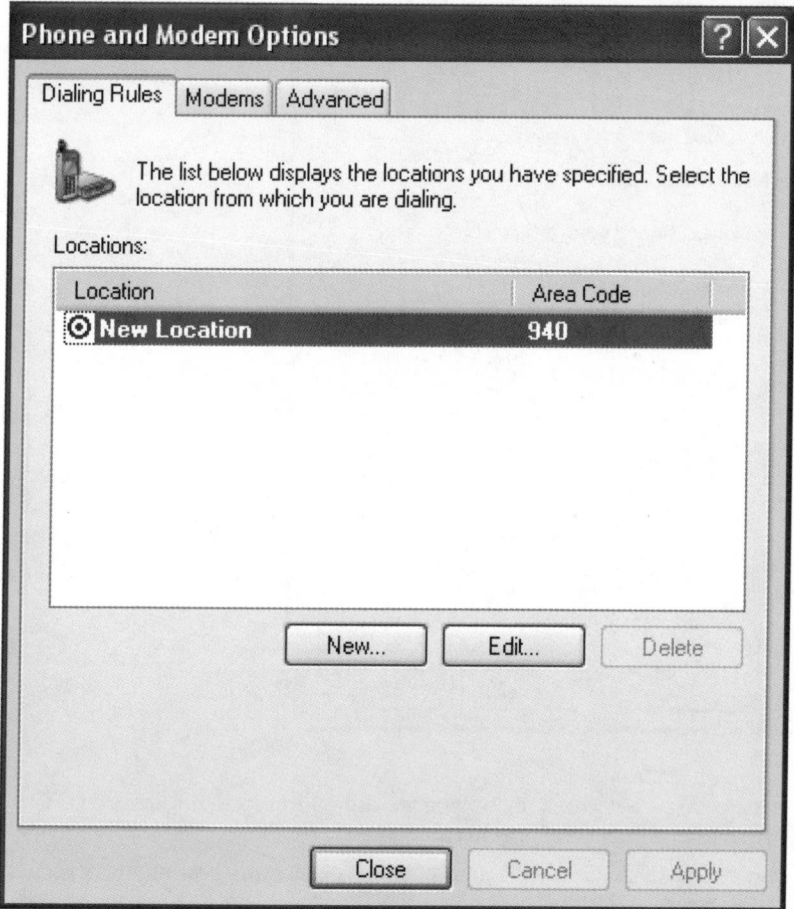

Figure 14-8: Dialing Rules

If you click the New button to create a new location, or if you decide to edit the existing one, a New Location dialog box appears with three tabs that you can configure. The following sections explore the configuration of a location and the options that are available to you.

General tab

The General tab, shown in Figure 14-9, has some standard settings that you need to make for the dialing location. The following list outlines these for you.

 ♦ **Location name** — For easy reference, give the location a recognizable name that has meaning to you or whoever uses that location.

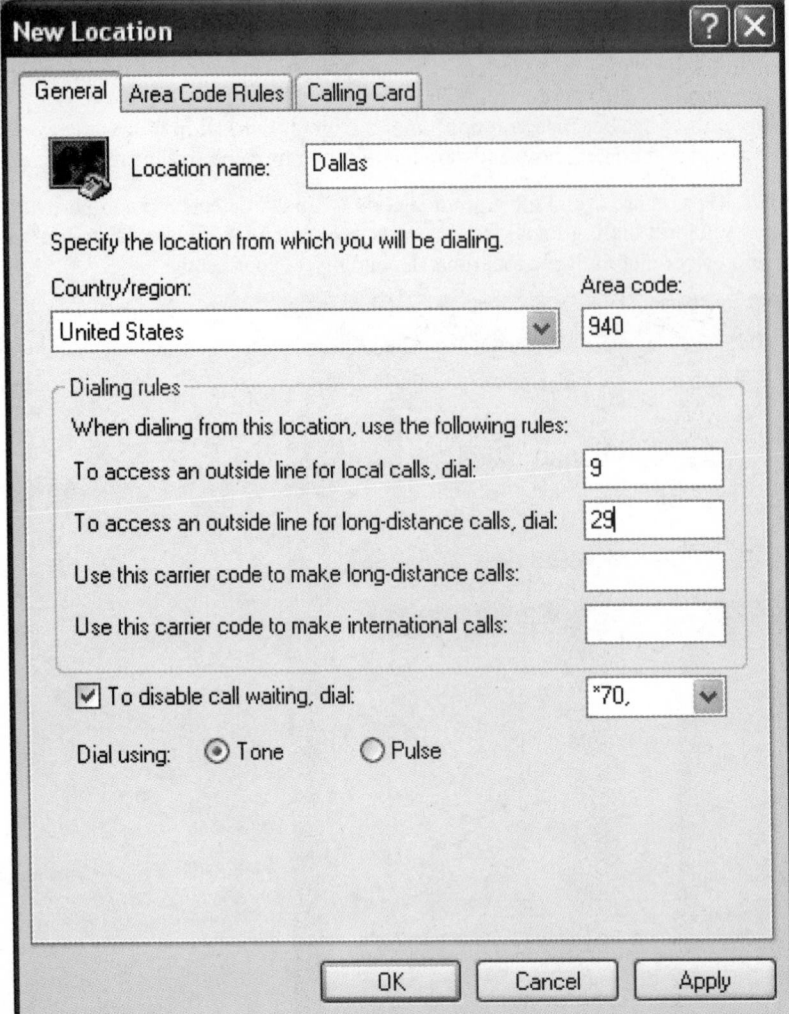

Figure 14-9: New Location General tab

- **Country/region and area code** — Select the region you are calling from and the area code. The rest of the location configuration is based on this information.

- Under **dialing rules**, you can make some general configurations concerning how numbers should be dialed from this location. Specifically, you can:

  - **Access an outside line for local calls** — Enter a required number, if any (such as 9).

  - **Access an outside line for long-distance calls** — If the number is different that for local calls, enter it here.

  - **Carrier code** — If you need to use a long-distance carrier number, enter it here.

  - **Carrier code, international** — If you need to use a long-distance carrier number for international calls, enter it here.

- **Disable call waiting** — Because call waiting can interfere with modem calls, you can disable it by selecting the check box option and using the drop-down menu to select the correct command for your carrier (such as *70).

- **Dial using** — Choose tone or pulse.

Area Code Rules tab

In the past, an area code defined long distance. You could usually place calls within your area code without dialing a 1 in front of the number. In some areas, a 1 might be required for long-distance calls within the same area code, but not the actual area code. Due to the growth of the population and the competition between phone companies, it is not uncommon to have multiple area codes that are all considered local calls. All of this, of course, wreaks havoc on computer dialing systems, as well as on human memory capacities. You use the Area Code Rules tab, shown in Figure 14-10, to determine how calls are handled from the location you are in according to area code. Essentially, you have to define the area code settings here by creating rules that the modem must follow when placing calls.

> **TIP:** It is important to keep in mind that the rules here are based on your current location. In other words, how should calls be handled from your current area code? Because these rules may change if you are in a different location, you can create multiple locations to define them.

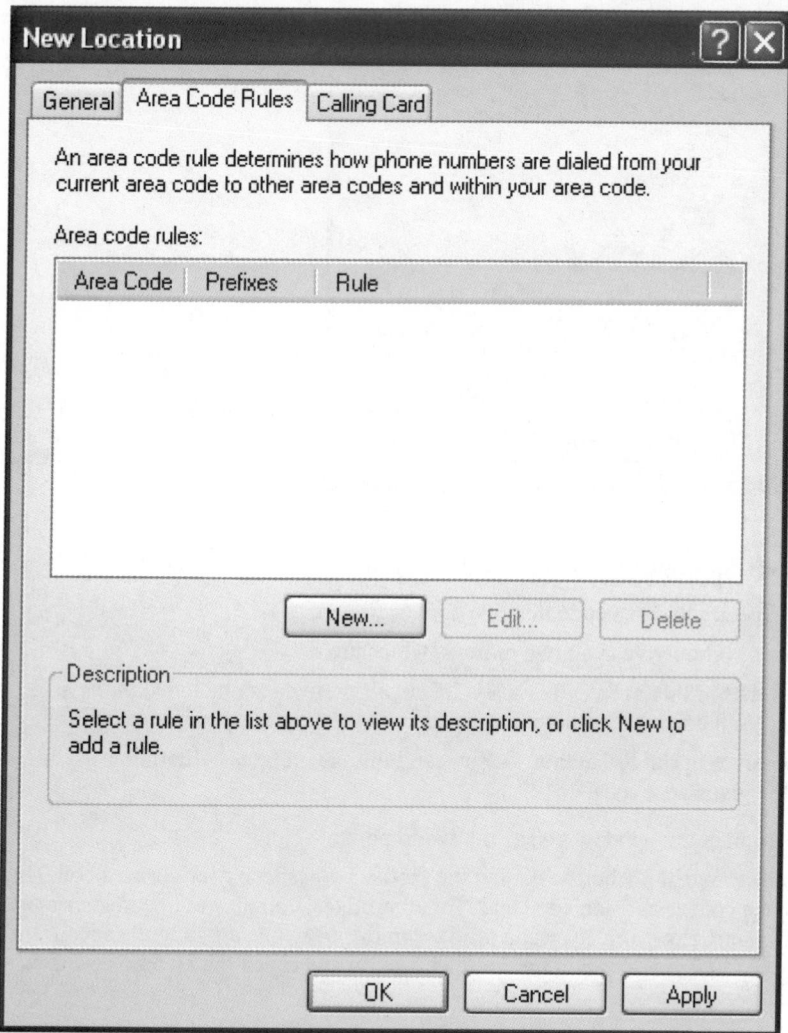

Figure 14-10: Area Code Rules tab

To create a new rule, simply click New. This opens a single New Area Code Rule window, as shown in Figure 14-11.

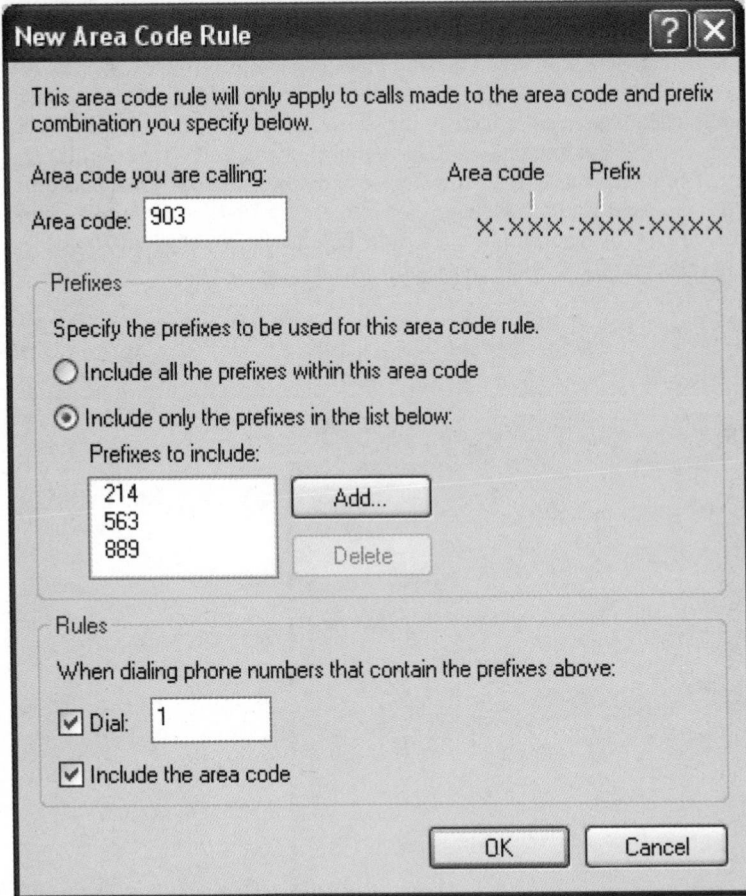

Figure 14-11: New Area Code Rule

The following list outlines the configuration options available to you:

♦ **Area code** — Used to specify the area code this rule applies to.

♦ **Prefixes** — The prefixes section gives you two options, which are:

• **Include all prefixes within this area code** — By default all prefixes are included in the area code. This means that Windows XP assumes any prefix you use belongs to this area code.

• **Include only the prefixes in the list below** — You can limit the prefixes by defining which prefixes belong to the given area code.

♦ **Rules** — The rules portion of the window gives you two important settings:

• **Dial** — Choose whether to dial a 1 before dialing the prefixes you specify for the area code. In other words, if the area code is considered "local" for all prefixes, you may not need your modem to dial a 1 for any of them. However, if certain prefixes in the area code are long distance from your location, you need to define those in the Prefixes section and check the Dial box to place a 1 in front of those numbers.

• **Include the area code** — If you need to include the area code in order to dial the prefix, whether the number is long distance or not, then check this box. Some areas require that the area code always be included, even for numbers within that area code.

TIP: You can easily edit or delete an area code rule by selecting it in the Area Code Rules tab and clicking Edit or Delete.

Calling Card tab

If you are traveling with a laptop, you may need to make long-distance calls to your corporate LAN and charge those calls to a credit or calling card. Like previous versions of Windows, Windows XP enables you to configure this option on the Calling Card tab, shown in Figure 14-12. By default, Windows XP gives you a predefined list of common calling cards. Select the card that you using and the correct access number for the card, then simply enter your account number and PIN so that this information can be transmitted, as you can see in Figure 14-12.

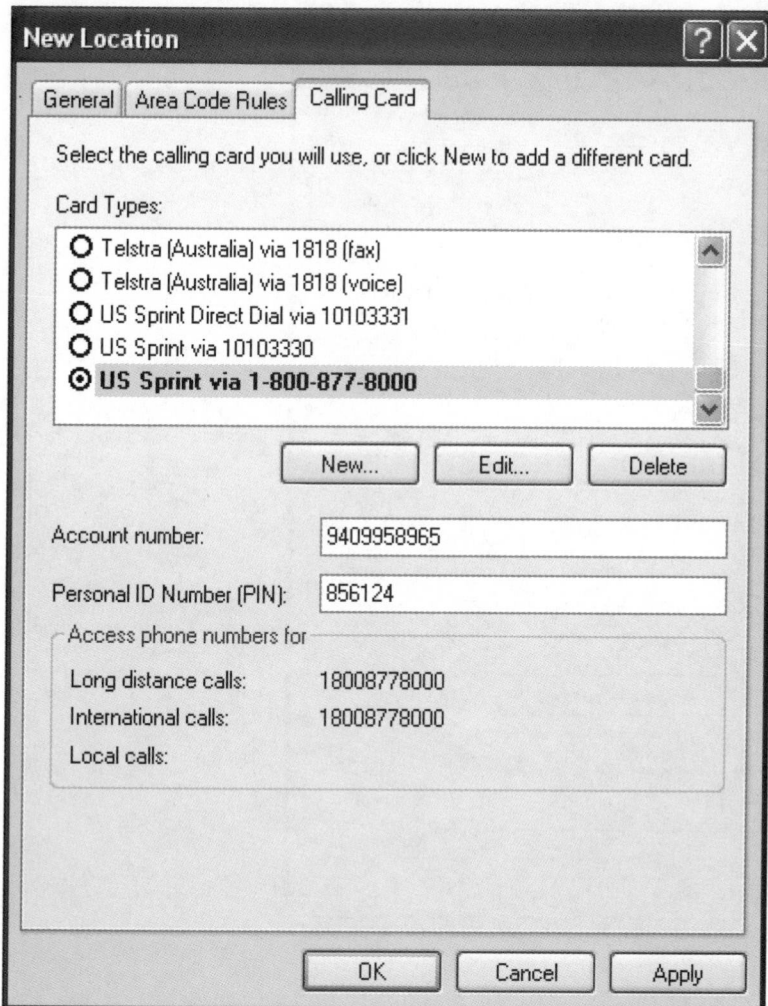

Figure 14-12: Calling Card tab

If your calling card and/or access number is not in the provided list, you can manually enter it by clicking the New button. The following steps show you how to manually configure a calling card option.

STEPS

Creating a new calling card entry

1. Open Phone and Modem Options from the Control Panel.

2. Click the Dialing Rules tab and click New.

3. Click the Calling Card tab and click New.

4. In the New Calling Card window, enter the calling card name, account number, and PIN on the General tab.

5. Click the Long Distance tab, shown in Figure 14-13. Enter the access number for long-distance calls. Then, in the provided dialog box, click the available buttons to list the order in which the card calls should occur. For example, you might choose to dial an access number, wait for the prompt, and enter an account number, in that order. You may need to access your calling card documentation to get this information; you can just make the entries and test them out.

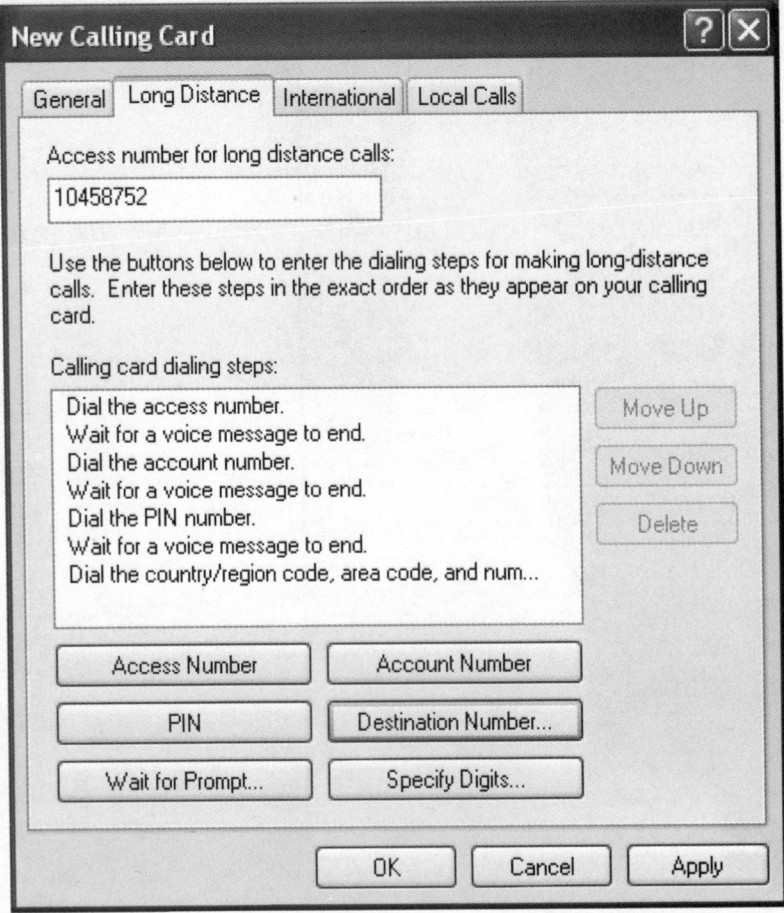

Figure 14-13: Long Distance tab

6. Complete the same information for the International and Local Calls tabs as necessary (these tabs look the same as the Long Distance tab).

7. Click OK when you finish. You can now return to the Calling Card tab and select the new entry you created for the calling card.

Configuring the Advanced Tab Settings

The Phone and Modem Options dialog box has an Advanced tab that lists the telephony providers installed on your Windows XP computer. You don't need to touch anything here as a general rule. However, You can add new telephony providers, which is most often needed for custom applications in corporate settings.

I do want to call your attention to one item, the Microsoft H.323 Telephony Service Provider. The H.323 protocol is for voice, video, and data communications between two computers over a public network, such as the telephone service. The protocol enables these kinds of communications to take place and is used in Microsoft operating systems, so it supports NetMeeting functionality. If you are not using NetMeeting, then you have no reason to configure the service, but if you are attempting to use NetMeeting, select the provider in the list and click Configure. You'll see a single configuration window, shown in Figure 14-14, in which you can invoke the H.323 settings that NetMeeting needs. NetMeeting calls can be placed using an H.323 gateway, a proxy, or a gatekeeper. Although it is beyond the scope of this book to discuss the network configuration of NetMeeting, I note here that you need to configure these settings so that your modem knows how to handle H.323 calls. Refer to the NetMeeting documentation and your network administration team for more information.

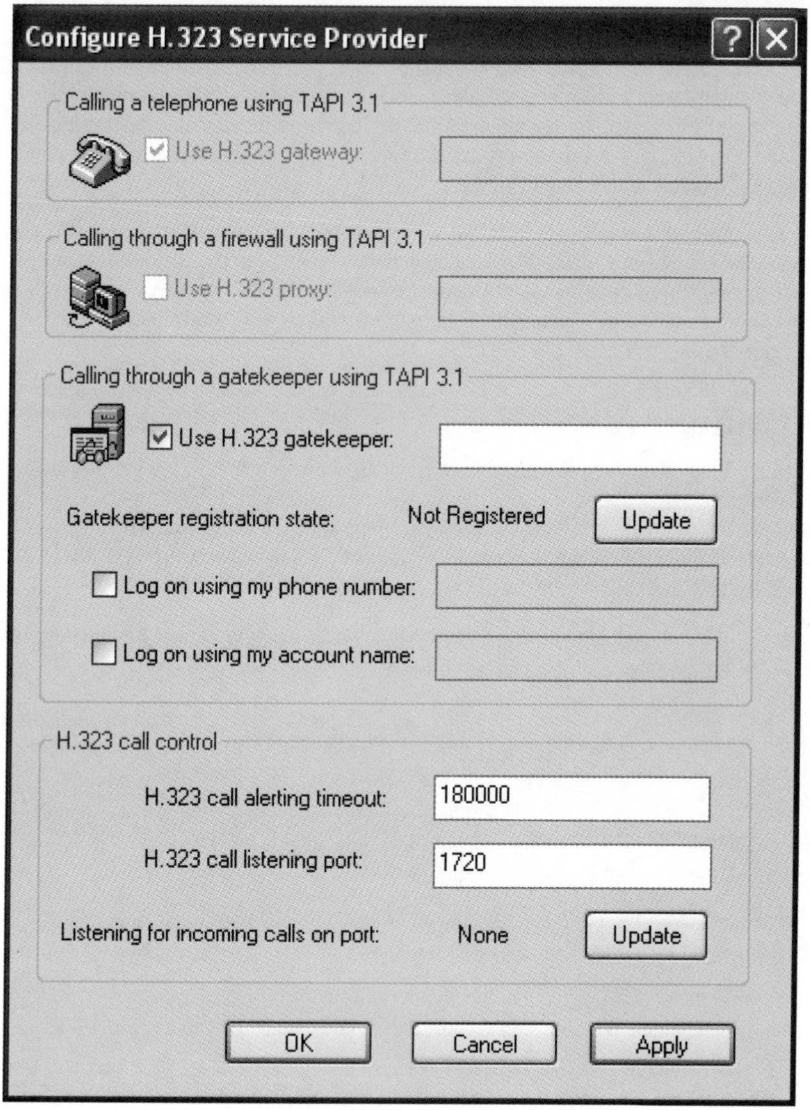

Figure 14-14: Configure H.323 Service Provider window

Tweaking Modem Performance

Modem connection speed and performance are often out of your control, unfortunately. The performance of your modem has a lot to do with the quality of the phone lines between your computer's location and the ISP, as well as the ISP's support of your modem. In order to get the highest bandwidth, your ISP must support 56 Kbps (V.90) service. That sounds simple enough, but many major ISPs have banks of modems that contain older modems and thus older service. Your modem can only go as fast as the modem on the other end. As you are looking for an ISP, it's a good idea to specifically ask if the company supports V.90 communications and if that is the standard for its modem banks.

Aside from your ISP, the phone lines can be a problem concerning speed. Older phone lines, load coils, digital pads, and phone line technologies used to boost voice signal can slow down modem transmissions.

Aside from these issues, however, you can make certain that your modem is in peak working order by checking out its Properties sheets. Check your compression settings and try adjusting the maximum speed as necessary. Also, check out your modem's initialization commands. You may be able to enter additional initialization strings that help boost performance and resolve problems you may be having. Getting the best throughput can require testing and experimentation, but you can make the most of your modem connection by playing with these different settings and finding the ones that work for you.

You can also test your modem's connection speed with bandwidth tests that are available on many Web sites, such as www.msn.com and www.cnet.com. These tests can give you a fairly accurate picture of your available bandwidth. Also, you might consider downloading iSpeed, available as a free trial product, that helps test different speed settings with your modem and helps you make configurations that may boost performance. Check it out at www.hms.com.

Troubleshooting Modems

Because Windows Plug and Play makes modem installation and configuration rather easy, you are not likely to experience major problems with your modem. Your frustration may be in the connection speed, which is often out of your control. However, if you are having problems with transmission or flaky behavior on the modem's part, the answer typically lies in some kind of Properties setting. It is important to review those settings carefully and logically try different settings to resolve the problem.

If you are having problems getting the modem installed, you need to check the physical connection to the computer, make sure the modem is compatible, and try rebooting Windows XP to see if it detects the modem.

In some cases, you may have problems with installation if there is a COM port conflict or problem. You can check the COM port's configuration by following these steps:

STEPS

COM port configuration

1. Choose Start ⇨ Control Panel. Double-click the System icon.

2. Select the Hardware tab and choose Device Manager.

3. Click the plus sign to the left of Ports to see the COM and LPT ports, as shown in Figure 14-15.

4. None of the ports you see should have an error icon (an exclamation point, a red X) on them. If one does, open its Properties sheets and review the Device Status on the General tab, then try to troubleshoot the port.

5. If the port is disabled, enable it by selecting the option "Use this device (enable)" from the Device usage drop-down list box on the lower portion of the dialog box.

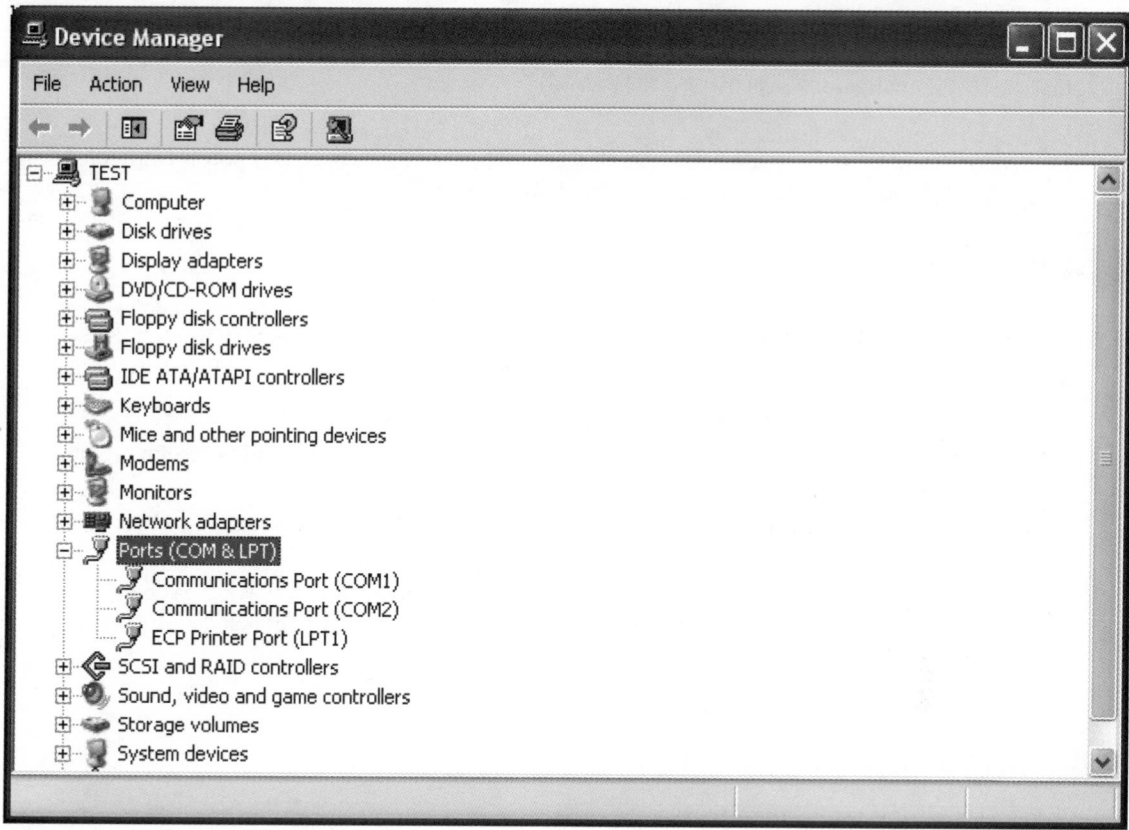

Figure 14-15: COM and LPT ports

6. Select the Resources tab.

7. Review the resources used by the COM port. They should appear similar to those shown in Table 14-1, unless your computer is configured to use different settings.

8. Microsoft recommends that the "Use automatic settings" check box be selected. If you need to change the settings to agree with your modem documentation, clear the check box.

9. Click Change Settings and type the new values. Click OK to close the COM port Properties dialog box, and click OK again to close the Device Manager.

Table 14-1: Standard COM Port Settings

Port	Input/Output Range	Interrupt Request
COM 1	03F8-03FF	04
COM 2	02F8-02FF	03
COM 3	03E8-03EF	04
COM 4	02E8-02EF	03

Be sure to check the modem Diagnostics tab of the modem's Properties sheets. Also, you can view the log file to see if there appear to be any errors. If you continue to have problems, try uninstalling the modem and reinstalling it. This clears up any installation errors or problems that may have occurred. Also, make sure you have the most updated driver from the vendor's Web site. Driver problems are commonly the cause of problems, so always check the driver early in your troubleshooting steps.

If modem diagnostics seem okay but you still cannot make a connection, make sure you check the phone and the phone line connection to the modem. Also, check the dial-up connection you configured and make sure it is configured correctly (see Chapter 15).

If you are using a laptop and are having problems with a PCMCIA modem, you may need to use the Add Hardware Wizard to configure the COM port built in to the card. Once the COM port is configured, you can then install the modem using the modem installation wizard.

Summary

In this chapter, you learned about modem installation and configuration. Because of Windows XP's wide modem support and Plug and Play features, modem installation is typically not that difficult. However, if you have problems with the modem, you can solve most by adjusting the modem's Properties pages.

- ◆ Plug and Play modems are automatically installed by Windows XP.
- ◆ If you are having installation problems, use the New Modem Wizard found on the Phone and Modem Options Properties pages.
- ◆ Configure the modem and dialing rules using the Phone and Modem Options Properties pages, or use Device Manager.
- ◆ You can typically resolve installation and configuration problems by following basic troubleshooting guidelines and checking your modem documentation for help.

Part V

Internet and Dial-Up Communication Secrets

Chapter 15

Configuring Internet Connections

In This Chapter

The Internet is a huge part of today's PCs and the operating systems that Microsoft produces. One of the primary reasons people purchase PCs today is simply to access the Internet. Therefore, it is in Microsoft's best interest to produce operating systems that make Internet connectivity easy, yet robust. To date, Windows XP is the operating system most integrated with the Internet. You can easily access the Internet from any folder, and configuring Internet connections has never been as easy as it is in Windows XP. Also, the advanced XP user can configure a number of powerful options. In this chapter, you will learn about . . .

- ♦ Configuring and managing Internet connections
- ♦ Creating PPPoE connections and connecting through firewalls/proxy servers
- ♦ Solving common Internet connection problems

Understanding Internet Connections

In order for your computer to use applications such as Internet Explorer or Outlook Express on the Internet your computer must connect to the Internet. Without this connection, Web browsers and e-mail clients wouldn't be much good. This seems like a simple statement, yet it is in the connection that users often experience frustrating problems. The good news is that Windows XP is designed to help you configure and manage Internet connections easily. You can configure a variety of Internet connections — from dial-up to broadband — using the available tools in Windows XP. For most people, that simply means that the computer uses a modem to connect to an ISP or a corporate network for gaining Internet access. Although broadband connections are becoming increasingly popular, broadband is typically available only in major cities, which leaves out a lot of the population. So, a connection to the Internet typically means a dial-up connection.

Before looking at connection creation and configuration, I want to quickly consider the components of an Internet connection. Internet connections are built on the following:

- ♦ **Hardware** — Your computer must have some kind of hardware that enables it to connect to the Internet. Typically, this hardware is a modem, but it also includes other types of connection hardware, such as ISDN cards, DSL modems, satellite connection boxes, and so forth. Whatever type of connection you to choose to make on your computer, you must have the required hardware to support the connection.

- ♦ **Software** — Windows XP generally contains all of the software that you need in order to connect to the Internet. You can easily create a dial-up connection and even broadband connections using Windows XP. The provided software configures Windows XP to communicate over the Internet using Transmission Control Protocol/Internet Protocol (TCP/IP) according to the specifications you make during the connection setup.

- ♦ **Connectivity information** — The software you configure uses the XP hardware to attempt a connection to another server, such as an ISP server or a corporate network server. The connectivity information you give Windows XP must be correct before a connection can take place.

♦ **Credentials** — In making a connection with the ISP server or server on your corporate network, Windows XP is required to submit a username and password in order to verify credentials. Windows XP must have a valid username and password, and it must be submitted according to the security requirements of the remote server. For instance, if my ISP requires that my username and password be encrypted, then Windows XP must encrypt the username and password for the connection to be made.

Creating the connection, then, is really about having the right information and using the Windows XP wizards and tools that are available to correctly configure the connection to the Internet. Fortunately, Windows XP streamlines this process and makes it rather easy.

If you use an ISP for Internet connectivity, you need information from the ISP in order to configure the Internet connection. This includes any required dial-up access numbers, usernames and passwords, and related settings that are used to configure mail clients. If you are still shopping for an ISP, spend some time looking at the options and features each one provides in order to find the ISP that is right for you. Windows XP can even try to help you locate an ISP, which I cover later in the chapter.

In order to communicate on the Internet, Windows XP has to configure TCP/IP to function with the particular type of Internet connection you are going to make. This is referred to as "binding" TCP/IP to a particular service. For example, if you have a modem installed on your computer, the binding is generally configured automatically by the system and is visible in TCP/IP properties. With TCP/IP being bound to an adapter (which is a modem in the case of dial-up networking), you can make a connection over that modem, and Windows XP can use TCP/IP on the Internet. You may have another type of connection to the Internet. For example, I use MSN's satellite service, because I do not live close enough to the city for DSL connectivity. The satellite connection installs software on my computer that binds TCP/IP to two different satellite network cards. The point is that TCP/IP must be used on the Internet for connectivity to take place, regardless of what kind of connection hardware you are using.

Dial-Up Connections

A dial-up connection is any kind of connection that dials a number in order to connect to a server. This may include a connection to any ISP that dials a phone number or even a connection to an X.25 network. ISDN connections are classified as dial-up connections in Windows XP. The point is that a number must be dialed to access some kind of network. For most of us, this involves either dialing out to an ISP or a corporate network for access. You create a connection built on the proper phone number and credentials, and Windows XP uses that information to generate a connection to that network.

Dial-up connections are certainly nothing new. (You or people you know may remember surfing the Internet with a 9 Kbps modem back in the early 1990s, which was really cool at the time.). Most standard modems today provide 56 Kbps service (or close), which is still painfully slow with the multimedia-driven nature of the Internet. Nevertheless, the modem is still the main connection hardware used, and I cover modem hardware in detail in Chapter 14.

> **CROSS-REFERENCE:** If you are having problems with your modem or with getting your modem to work properly with Windows XP, see Chapter 14 for details about modem hardware.

Dial-up connections are made in Windows XP using the New Connection Wizard. In fact, most all connections in Windows XP are generated with this wizard. XP presents one wizard that can do everything, avoiding separate wizards for Internet connectivity, network connectivity, and direct cable connections. Overall, the wizard does a good job, and you'll find it easy to use.

> **SECRET:** The Internet Connection Wizard first appeared in Windows 98 and has been a primary tool used to connect to the Internet through Windows. It is still around in Windows XP, although you don't see it at first. Invoking some connection options makes it suddenly jump to life, as you see throughout the chapter. If you love the Internet Connection Wizard, you can still run the entire thing. Just type **icwconn1.exe** at the Run line, and it will appear. By default, the wizard is stored in `Program Files\Internet Explorer\Connection Wizard`.

To create a dial-up connection, gather the information you need from your ISP, corporate network, or connection destination. Then, in Control Panel, open the Network Connections folder. If you configure the Start menu to display Network Connections, you can simply choose Start ⇨ Connect To. Choose to open all connections, and then click the Create a Connection option in the left pane under Network Tasks. The Network Connection Wizard appears and first presents you with a Network Connection Type window, as shown in Figure 15-1.

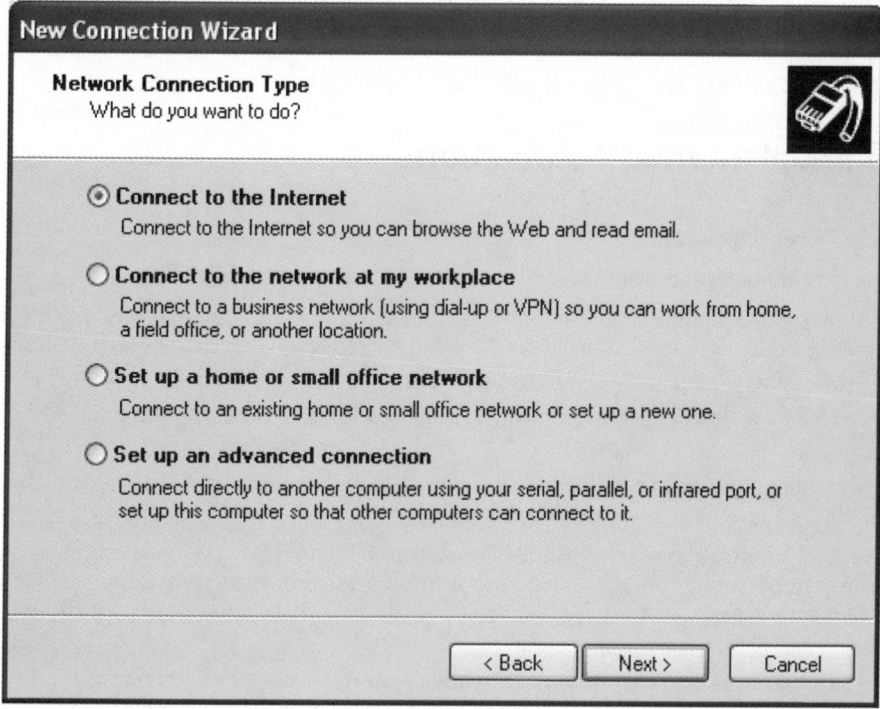

Figure 15-1: Choose a connection type.

Of course, you should "Connect to the Internet" and click Next. At this point, you see three different options from which you can choose. The following three sections explore those options.

Choosing from a list of ISPs

You can use the wizard to help you locate an ISP. If you choose this radio button option and click Next, you are prompted to finish the New Connection Wizard. At this point, the Online Services folder opens, and you can choose to automatically set up an account with CompuServe, EarthLink, or Prodigy. Just open the folder of your choice and follow the instructions. If you don't want to sign up with one of these, you can get help on the Internet from the Microsoft referral service by clicking the "Refer me to more ISPs" shortcut.

SECRET: The Online Services folder is certainly nothing new and has been around since the days of Windows 95, cluttering up our desktops. It's in the background now and resides in the `Program Files\Online Services` folder.

Opening the shortcut opens, as you might guess, the Internet Connection Wizard. The connection wizard dials an access number to Microsoft, where referral information is downloaded to you if any ISPs are available in your area. It is important to remember that the referred ISPs have partnerships with Microsoft and have agreed to tout Internet Explorer. There may be ISPs in your area that are perfectly fine to work with and don't have a contract with Microsoft. The important thing is to shop around. If you want to use one of the ISPs Microsoft recommends, just click the link option you see and follow the instructions for online setup.

Setting up the connection manually

If you have already signed up with an ISP of your choice, your best bet is to set up the connection manually. The wizard presents you with a number of straightforward setup steps. The following steps walk you through the wizard for manual account creation.

STEPS

Creating a manual Internet connection

1. Start the New Connection Wizard and click Next.

2. Choose Internet Connection and click Next.

3. In the Getting Ready window, choose to set up the connection manually and click Next.

4. In the Internet Connection window, choose the type of connection that you want to create. For these steps, I am choosing a dial-up modem connection. I'll address broadband connections later in this chapter. Click Next.

5. In the Connection Name dialog box, enter a friendly, recognizable name for the connection and click Next.

6. Enter the phone number that should be dialed to access the ISP or the corporate dial-up server. Be sure to include the area code here if it is needed for the connection.

7. The Internet Account Information window appears, as shown in Figure 15-2. Using the information from your ISP or your corporate network, enter a username, a password, and a password confirmation. Remember that passwords are case sensitive. You also have a few important check box options:

   - **Use this account name and password when anyone connects to the Internet from this computer** — If your computer is a home or small office computer that many people use to connect to the Internet, you may want to leave this option enabled. However, just remember that your username and password are exposed with this setting, and anyone logged on to the computer can use your account to get onto the Internet.

   - **Make this the default Internet connection** — If you want this connection to be the default connection that applications such as browsers and e-mail clients use to connect, then select this check box.

   - **Turn on Internet Connection Firewall** — If you want to use Windows XP's firewall for the connection, click the check box. This setting is recommended, and you can learn all about the firewall in Chapter 22.

8. Click the Finish button. The connection window appears, as shown in Figure 15-3, so you can test the connection. Notice the password box. The password you configure is hidden but can be changed by clicking in the box. Also notice that you can save the username and password for anyone who uses the computer or just for you. Again, these settings are very helpful when a number of people are using the computer, and multiple Internet connections with multiple usernames and passwords may be used. You can test the connection by clicking the Dial button.

TIP: As in previous versions of Windows, a dial-up connection icon appears in your Notification Area so you can easily disconnect when desired.

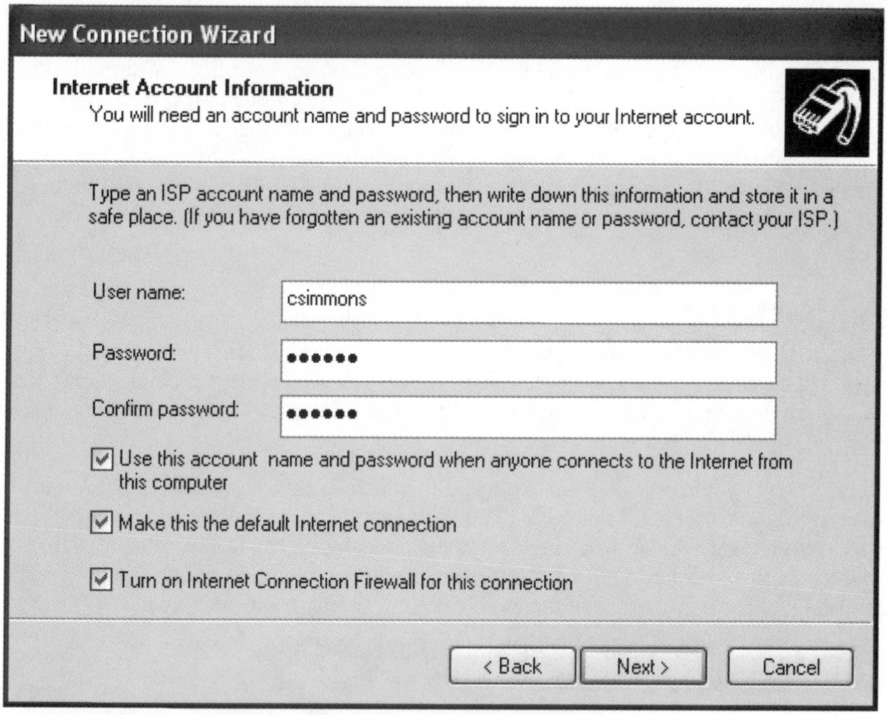

New Connection Wizard

Internet Account Information
You will need an account name and password to sign in to your Internet account.

Type an ISP account name and password, then write down this information and store it in a safe place. (If you have forgotten an existing account name or password, contact your ISP.)

User name: csimmons

Password: ●●●●●●

Confirm password: ●●●●●●

☑ Use this account name and password when anyone connects to the Internet from this computer

☑ Make this the default Internet connection

☑ Turn on Internet Connection Firewall for this connection

< Back   Next >   Cancel

Figure 15-2: Internet Account Information

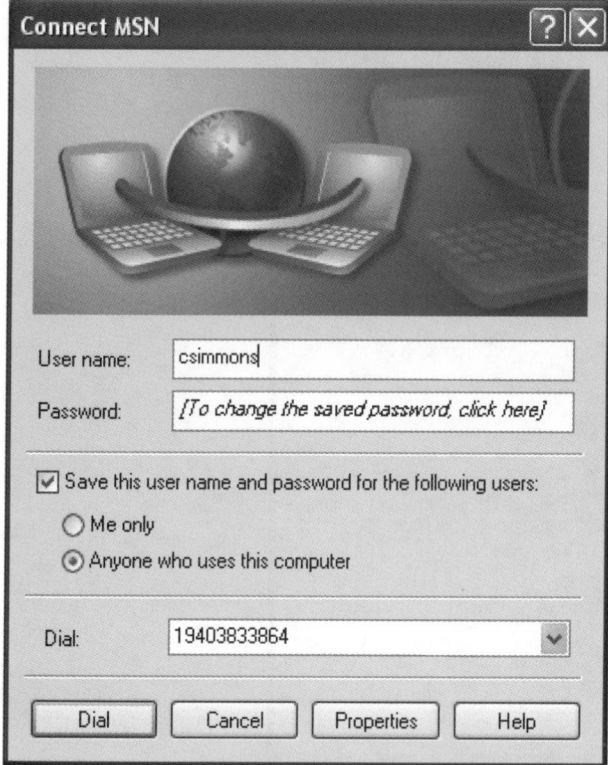

Connect MSN   [?][X]

User name: csimmons

Password: *[To change the saved password, click here]*

☑ Save this user name and password for the following users:

○ Me only

⦿ Anyone who uses this computer

Dial: 19403833864

Dial   Cancel   Properties   Help

Figure 15-3: Connection window

Using the CD

The last connection option presented to you is to use the CD that comes from your ISP. Most major ISPs provide a setup CD that helps configure your system for use with the ISP. In some cases, setup must be run from the CD, and in others you can just as easily set up the connection manually (and avoid a lot of junk that may be automatically installed on your system, such as advertisements and the like). In any case, check out the instructions from your provider. If you want to use the CD, click the wizard radio button option and click Next, and the wizard closes (you don't need it now; just start the CD and run setup from there).

Managing connections

Once you create any desired dial-up connections, they appear in the Network Connections folder, along with any other types of connections for your computer. With the default XP theme, the connections display by category, such as Dial-up and LAN. You can easily change these views, however, with options in the View menu.

You'll notice that your dial-up connections have an icon, and the default connection that you configured has a check mark over it, as you can see in Figure 15-4. You can easily change the default connection to another connection by right-clicking the desired connection and choosing Set as Default Connection. As with typical menu options, you can connect, check out the status of the connection, create a copy, create a shortcut, delete, rename, and access properties of the connection by simply right-clicking it.

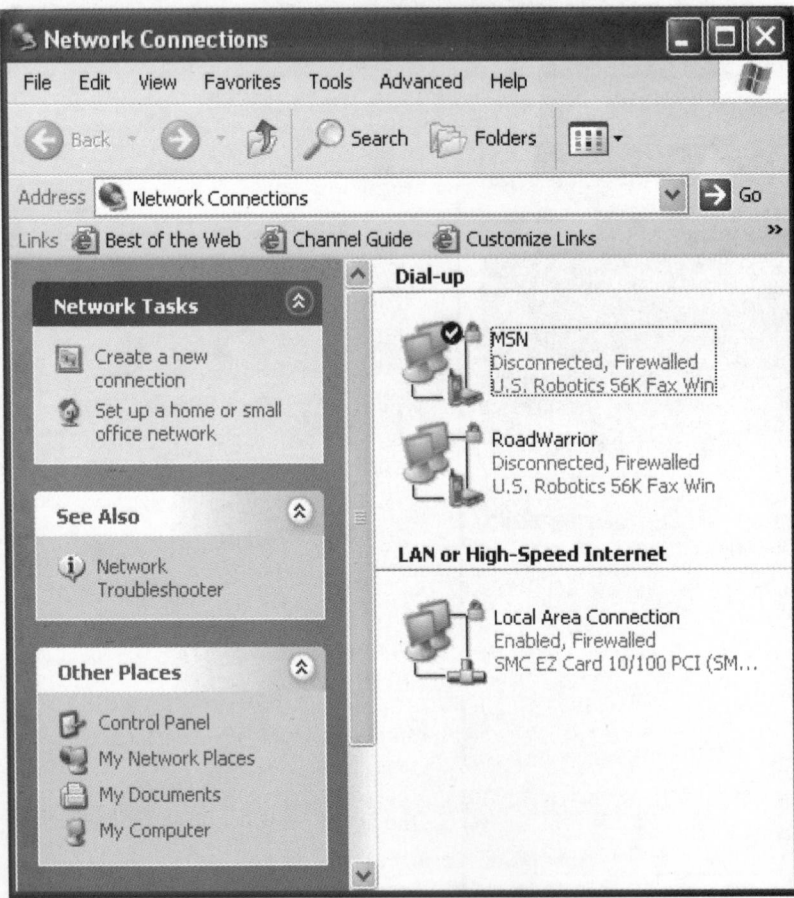

Figure 15-4: Network Connections

The Status option is available only if the connection is active. If the connection is active, the Status option gives you some basic information about the connection, such as speed and bytes sent and received. You can also disconnect from the Status window. If you click the Details tab, shown in Figure 15-5, you can gain some quick and easy information about the connection, such as the IP address your computer is assigned, the server's IP address, and the authentication method used to log in.

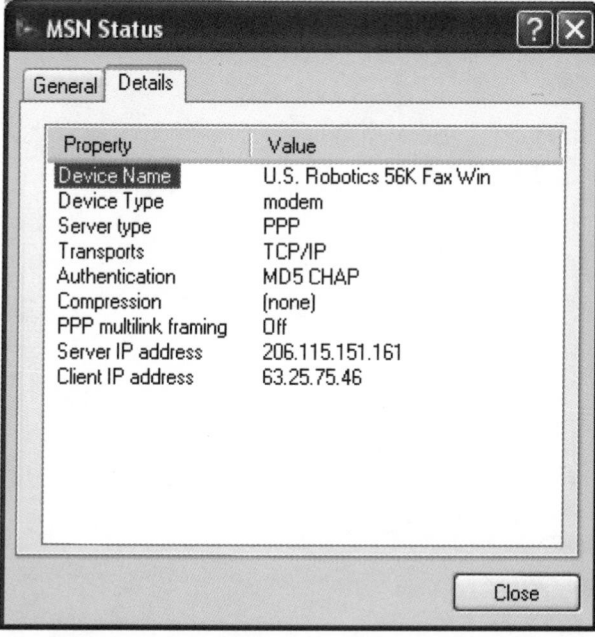

Figure 15-5: Connection details

> **TIP:** If you click the Change the Settings task in the left folder pane found in the Network Connections folder, the properties sheets appear. Although the task features that appear are often helpful to newer users, you can do everything noted in those tasks by simply right-clicking the connection icon and choosing a desired action.

Configuring connection properties

Once you create a connection, it has properties you can edit and configure as needed. These are all important, and incorrect changes can easily cause the connection to fail. The reverse, however, is also true: you can use the properties sheets to resolve problems that may exist with the connection. The next several sections explore each tab of the properties sheets, and I note any potential problems or issues tied to the available settings.

General tab

The General tab provides you quick access to modem properties by clicking the Configure button and the phone number you are dialing. Not much is exciting here, except for the alternate phone numbers, which you can choose after clicking the Alternates button. As you noticed when setting up the connection, the wizard gave you the option of using only one phone number per connection. If your ISP has multiple phone numbers you can choose from (and most do), as well as multiple corporate dial-up numbers, you can add them by clicking Alternates. This opens the Alternate Phone Numbers window, as shown in Figure 15-6. Simply enter the new phone numbers you want or adjust and delete phone numbers by using the Add, Edit, and Delete buttons. Also, note the check boxes at the bottom of the window. If you want the connection to rotate between phone numbers (if the first one fails, use the second one, for example), select the check box option. You also have the option to rotate successful numbers to the top of the list so that the number you have the most success with is always tried first. These options can certainly speed your connection time, especially if your ISP has a tendency to have a lot of busy signals (which is, unfortunately, common).

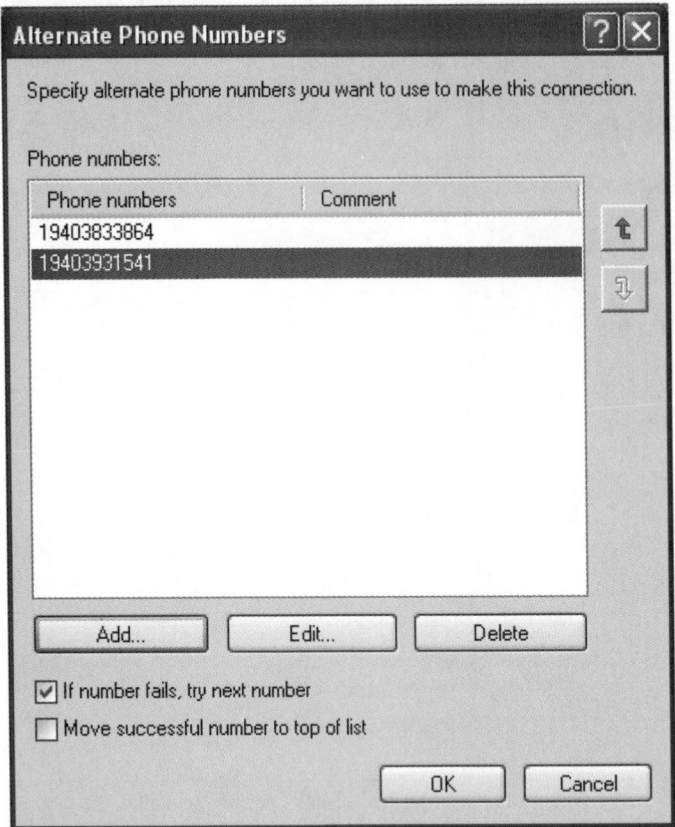

Figure 15-6: Configure alternate phone numbers.

Back on the General tab, you have one last check box option concerning the Notification Area. If you want to see a modem icon, make sure you leave this check box selected. This puts a connection icon in the Notification Area so you can easily access the connection's status or disconnect it when desired.

Options tab

The Options tab, shown in Figure 15-7, gives you several connection options that are important to the connectivity and connectivity behavior of your dial-up connection. The following list outlines the features and problems with these options:

- **Display progress while connecting** — The display progress option simply allows you to see what is happening when you attempt to make a connection. I suggest that you leave this one enabled because if the connection fails, you may be able to pick up clues pointing to the cause of the failure if you can see the progress of making the connection.

- **Prompt for name and password, certificate, etc.** — This option prompts the connection window, where you enter your username and password (which already appear there by default). If you use only one connection, you can clear this check box and save yourself an extra connection step.

- **Include Windows logon domain** — This option is not selected by default, because it is not needed for most ISPs. If you need to log in to your corporate Windows domain to access the Internet, select this check box, and you'll get a domain login option.

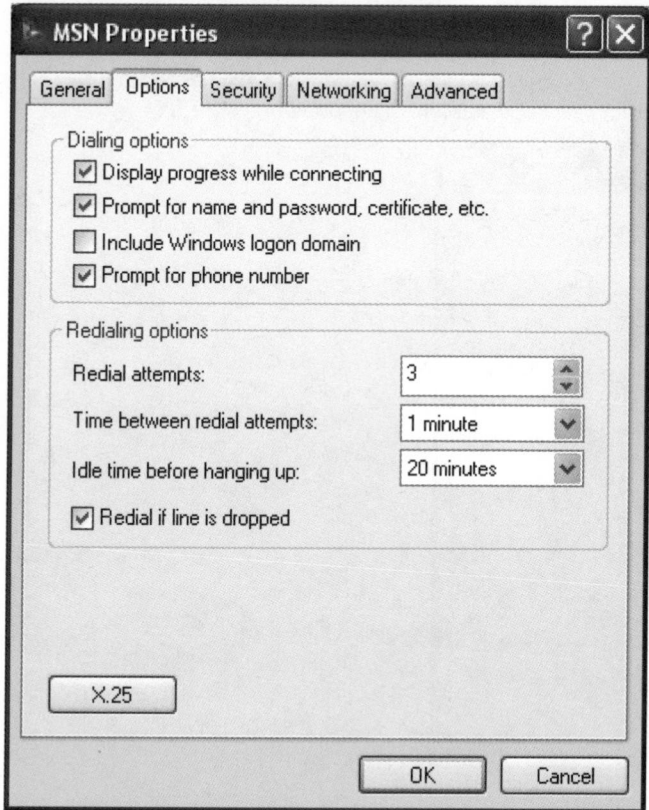

Figure 15-7: Dial-up Options tab

♦ **Prompt for phone number** — This is the same issue as with username and password. If you primarily use one phone number, this setting creates extra work for you. You can safely clear it.

♦ **Redialing options** — These drop-down menus enable you to configure the way redialing is handled, in the case of a busy signal or dropped connection. By default, there are three redial attempts at one-minute intervals, but you can change these to whatever you want. If you do not want the connection terminated every time you step away from your computer for a few minutes, then set the "Idle time before hanging up" setting to Never.

> **TIP:** The idle time setting can be aggravating, but it can also really be helpful if you have coworkers or family members who forget to terminate connections when they are no longer needed. This is especially important if the connection is tying up a primary phone line. Before using the Never setting, just consider whether an automatic disconnect is actually needed if the connection becomes idle.

♦ **X.25** — If you are connecting to an X.25 network, click the X.25 button. You'll see a simple interface where you can configure your X.25 logon settings and related addressing information.

> **NOTE:** X.25 is a network type that transmits data using a packet-switching protocol so that phone lines are bypassed. Obviously, X.25 is not as common as other types of connectivity options, but if you are attempting to connect to an X.25 network, Windows XP can support your need.

Security tab

The Security tab, shown in Figure 15-8, contains a number of settings that determine how your computer logs in to the remote ISP computer or your corporate network. Since security settings can vary from ISP to ISP and certainly between corporate network connections, you need to configure these settings based on documentation from your ISP or corporate administrators. By default, typical settings are used where unsecured passwords are allowed. This essentially allows the connection to match the kind of authentication used by the ISP. You can use the drop-down menu to require secured password authentication or a smart card, but these settings must be explicitly supported by your ISP.

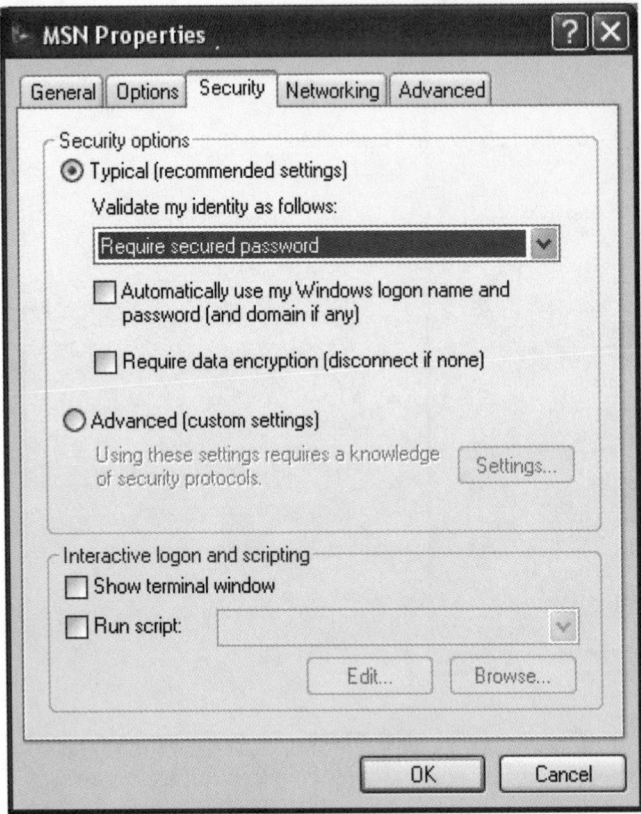

Figure 15-8: Security tab

You can choose to use the Advanced setting option on this tab, but again, your ISP or corporate network must support any settings that are configured here. If you click the Settings button, you can choose from several different encryption, protocol, and logon options, as shown in Figure 15-9. The following list reviews these settings:

♦ **Data encryption** — By default, optional encryption is configured. This means that your connection can use encryption if supported by the ISP, but it is not required for the connection. You can use the drop-down menu and change this setting so that encryption is required or not allowed, or maximum encryption is required. These settings, however, can be a point of connection failure if they are not supported by your ISP. If you choose encryption settings that are too strong, then the server may not connect with you, and if you choose no encryption, the connection may also fail if the server requires encryption. Again, make sure you are using the correct encryption settings for your ISP.

♦ **Use Extensible Authentication Protocol (EAP)** — EAP, an extension of PPP, is a security method that uses a variety of different authentication methods, such as smart cards, digital certificates, and related technologies. EAP must be enabled on the server end in order for you to be able to use it, and if EAP is used, you can further configure the logon credentials and method by clicking the Properties button.

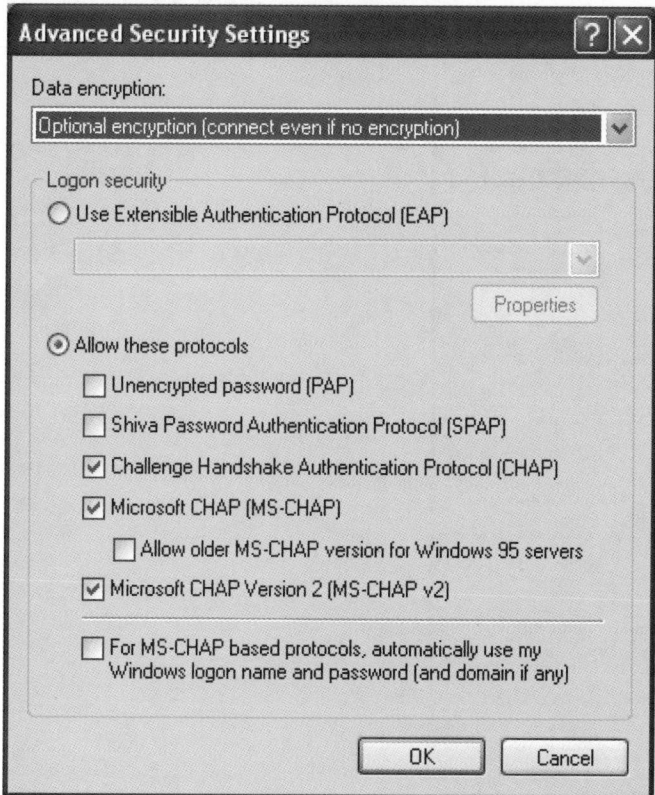

Figure 15-9: Advanced Security Settings

♦ **Password Authentication Protocol (PAP)** — PAP is a basic protocol using unencrypted passwords. PAP usernames and passwords are presented to the server in plain text. This is the most unsecure method of authentication.

♦ **Shiva Password Authentication Protocol (SPAP)** — SPAP uses a simple encryption scheme to encrypt usernames and passwords.

♦ **Challenge Handshake Authentication Protocol (CHAP)** — CHAP is a commonly supported authentication method that uses a challenge-response hash scheme to determine if authentication is valid. This method of authentication is very secure.

♦ **Microsoft CHAP** — This is Microsoft's version of CHAP designed for Windows computers. Version 2 supports tighter encryption standards.

Returning to the Security tab, you can also view interactive logon by having Windows show you a terminal window each time a connection is made. Just click its check box option. Also, you can run any logon script that may be needed. This setting is available for backward compatibility with older systems that use logon scripts.

Networking tab

The Networking tab, shown in Figure 15-10, shows you the components used for this particular connection, such as TCP/IP. You see that the "Type of dial-up server I am calling" drop-down option enables you to connect to any PPP, Windows 95/98/NT 4/2000, or Internet server. This setting is generally all you need, but you can place some restrictions on the setting by selecting a different option.

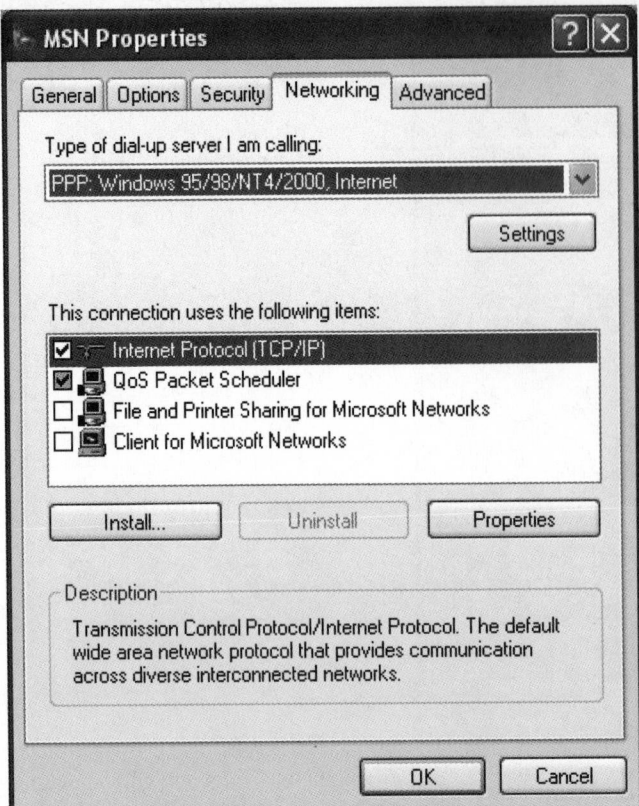

Figure 15-10: Networking tab

The Settings button presents some important options:

- **Enable LCP extensions** — LCP is the Link Control Protocol used to manage PPP connections. It may cause problems, however, if your ISP uses older PPP servers. By default, it is enabled, and you should keep it that way; however, if you are having problems with your connections, you might try clearing the check box option to see if the problem resolves.

- **Enable software compression** — Compression technology reduces the amount of time required to transmit data to and from your computer, but your ISP must support compression for you to use it. Most ISPs do, so this option is enabled by default. However, if you are having problems with connection failure, clear this check box option to see if the problem resolves.

- **Negotiate multilink for single link connections** — *Multilink* combines several modems together to create one logical connection. The idea is to get more bandwidth using the modems together. This connection option enables your computer to act like it has a multilink connection in order to improve audio transmissions from the Internet. Your ISP has to support his feature for it to work, however.

From the Networking tab, you can access the properties for any of the networking components, and I would like to call your attention to TCP/IP. If you select TCP/IP in the window and click the Properties button, you see that your IP addressing and subnet mask settings are configured to obtain them automatically. These settings come from your ISP each time you log on, and they should not be changed unless information from your ISP tells you to do so.

If you click the Advanced button on the TCP/IP properties page, there is an important setting to consider. On the General tab, you see that IP header compression is used for PPP links by default, as shown in

Figure 15-11. For most ISPs, this is fine, but some ISPs may not support header compression. If you are having problems connecting, first remove the compression setting from the Settings window (described in the previous list), and then access the Advanced TCP/IP Settings window and clear the header compression option. This may solve your connection problem.

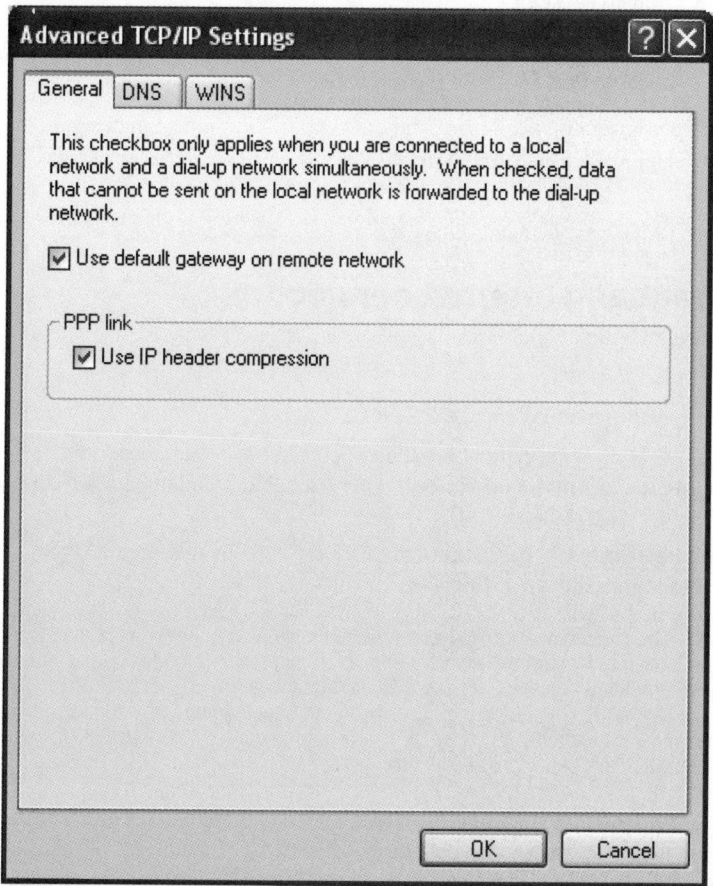

Figure 15-11: Advanced TCP/IP Settings

Advanced tab

The Advanced tab of a connection's properties sheets enables you to configure the Internet Connection Firewall for the dial-up connection. The Internet Connection Firewall is explored in Chapter 22.

Broadband Connections

Windows Me made a strange stab at helping you configure broadband connections by providing an ISDN Setup Wizard (which is strange, considering most people do not use ISDN these days). Windows XP takes the idea much further by helping you set up and configure a variety of broadband connections. I'll be the first to tell you that the broadband configuration options in Windows XP work fine, but in many cases, you'll need to use your broadband provider's documentation and most likely their software as well to get things up and running the way they should. Also, using your provider's software is simply easier. So, use the broadband connection software in Windows XP as needed, but begin with the provider's software.

If you have been stuck in modem land and you are interested in broadband, broadband is simply a general term that refers to variety of connection options that have high throughput. For example, a typical modem theoretically gives you 56 Kbps, while a DSL connection can give you up to 800 Kbps, and a typical cable or satellite connection can give you up to 500 Kbps. Also, these connections are typically "always on" — that is, you don't have to connect to a provider for access, because you are always connected. Of course, this exposes your computer to more risks from the Internet, which is why Windows XP introduces a new Internet Connection Firewall.

Overall, broadband is the way of the future; it's just taking a little time to grow. You can expect future releases of Microsoft Windows to support broadband technology in greater ways.

If you want to use Windows XP to help you set up your broadband connection, you return once again to the connection wizard. The following steps walk you through the process.

STEPS

Creating a manual broadband Internet connection

1. Start the New Connection Wizard and click Next.

2. Choose Internet Connection and click Next.

3. Choose to set up the Internet connection manually and click Next.

4. In the Internet Connection window, choose the type of broadband connection you have — either one that requires you to connect or one that is always on. Refer to your broadband documentation for details.

5. If you choose to connect using a username and password, complete the screens that request this information. If you do not need to log in, the wizard finishes and closes.

> **SECRET:** Okay, here's the deal. Windows XP manages your broadband connection login. If you are required to log in, the wizard creates an icon for you in Network Connections. If your connection is always on and requires no login from you, then the wizard doesn't do anything, because there is nothing Windows XP needs to do to manage the connection. An icon for it may appear under LAN Connections in the Network Connections folder, but you should manage and perform any configuration options according to the provider's instructions. In other words, for an always-on connection, follow the provider's setup instructions and skip XP's attempt to help you with its connection wizard.

If you must log in to connect with your broadband connection, an icon appears in Network Connections. You might notice that this connection is referred to as a WAN Minipot PPPoE. This stands for Point-to-Point Protocol over Ethernet. These types of connections use a broadband "modem" and can be authenticated into high-speed networks that can then service their needs. This type of connection isn't that typical with an ISP account, but a corporate network could implement this solution to give employees network access when they are in a remote location. The properties sheets for the PPPoE connection in Network Connections give you the same configuration options as a dial-up connection, so refer to the "Dial-Up Connections" section earlier in this chapter for tab-by-tab details.

Connecting via a Proxy Server

Corporate networks today are not isolated islands as they once were in the past. Networks cannot be self-contained and leverage the power of the Internet at the same time, so corporate networks are faced with striking a balance between Internet usage and corporate security. After all, even Microsoft has been hacked by Internet intruders.

One of the major ways that corporate networks protect themselves is through a hardware and software solution called a *firewall* or a *proxy server*. As you have seen, Windows XP even includes firewall software that is designed to protect your computer from malicious attacks from the Internet. The firewall software functions at the TCP/IP packet level and can detect typical IP attacks that occur. The same is true at the corporate level: the firewall software and hardware can examine TCP/IP data streams and determine whether certain packets are allowed, and in those packets can be potential attacks. When the firewall picks up threats or questionable packets, they are discarded before they ever enter the private network. The end result is a security system that allows network users to access the Internet, but one that keeps people on the Internet out of the corporate network.

The firewall/proxy server market is rather competitive, and even Microsoft is in the game. Microsoft's Internet Security and Acceleration Server 2000 is designed to provide firewall protection, as well as performance enhancements for network users. ISA Server can cache popular Internet information and return that information to network clients via the cache, which speeds response time. To network clients, it appears as though the computer is directly connected to the Internet, when in fact, the client is connected to the firewall or proxy server. All transmissions to and from the client are filtered through the firewall and proxy server, thus protecting the client and network.

> **CROSS-REFERENCE:** ISA Server 2000 is a complicated networking topic, but if you are interested in the product and firewall protection in general, see *Microsoft ISA Configuration and Administration* also by Curt Simmons, published by Hungry Minds, Inc.

If you are on a corporate network that uses a firewall or proxy server, then you have no connection that you need to configure. However, your browser and mail client will have to be configured in order to connect. Typically this involves changing the networking settings on the browser's connection properties. As you can see in Figure 15-12, the network settings are adjusted to have Internet Explorer contact a particular server for service. In order to configure the settings, you'll need information from a network administrator. Often, these settings are configured automatically through client setup software administered from network technicians or through Windows 2000/XP Group Policy.

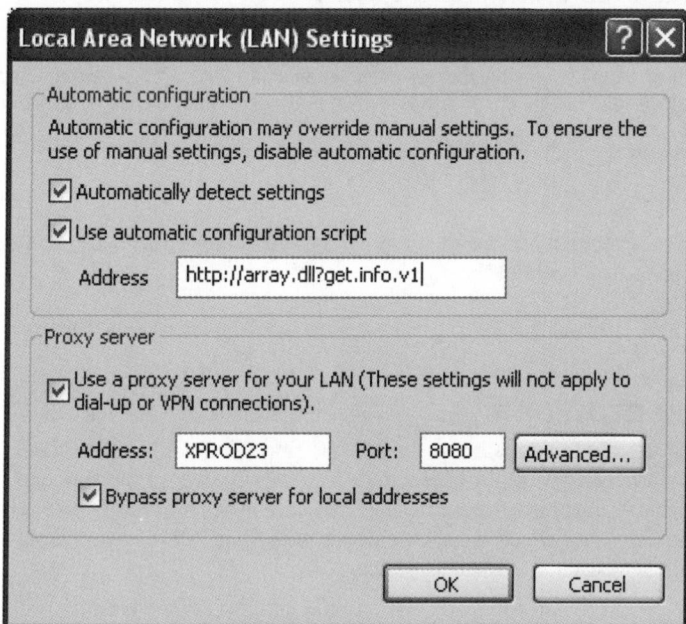

Figure 15-12: LAN Settings for Internet Explorer

> **NOTE:** Internet Connection Sharing (ICS) is alive and well in Windows XP. You can configure a computer to share an Internet connection so that other computers can use that connection. This solution works great for home and small office networks, and you can learn how to set up and use ICS in Chapter 20.

Solving Common Connection Problems

No network is perfect, and the Internet is certainly no perfect place, either. The more you use the Internet, you find that connectivity can be a problem from time to time, and there are a number of reasons why (although a good explanation doesn't reduce the frustration):

♦ **Connection problems** — Incorrect configurations on your end or hardware problems with your computer can halt a connection.

♦ **ISP problems** — Like all of us, your ISP uses computers that are not perfect. They fail, must be upgraded, and sometimes just don't work the way they should. If you can't get connected, the problem may just as likely be on the ISP's side.

♦ **General Internet problems** — If you can connect, but the Internet is slow or some sites are down, just chalk it up to the way things are. Sometimes you'll experience problems with certain Web sites, and there is nothing you can but wait and try again.

> **TIP:** Don't be so technically minded that you forget to check the simple things: Is the phone line connected? Are your username and password correct? What about the phone number? Simplicity is often the answer, so check the obvious before you get into the details.

The good news is that if misery loves company, you are certainly not alone. All of us have had our fair share of "I'm going to pull my hair out" Internet connection problems. The trick to solving these problems is to first inspect your computer and determine if the problem is on your end. If so, you can fix the problem and move forward. If not, you owe your ISP or help desk a call for support. The following sections are designed to identify common problems and help you resolve those problems. Use these sections as a quick reference guide when you are troubleshooting a connection on your Windows XP computer.

> **NOTE:** In the Windows XP online help, search on the string *error messages*. You will be able to find a page that lists many of the error messages you may get with both network and dial-up connections. If you get a specific error message, try looking it up here.

Access is denied

If you attempt to connect and see an "access denied" message, there is probably an incorrect setting on your connection. See the following steps to troubleshoot the problem.

STEPS

Resolving access denial problems

1. If you receive this error when you attempt to connect to your ISP, the first thing you want to check is whether your encryption settings are correct. Right-click your connection, select Properties, and click the Security tab. Make sure that Typical is selected. In the "Validate my identity as follows" option, choose "Allow unsecured password." You also should check with your ISP to ensure that you have set the correct encryption settings.

2. Some ISPs, such as the EarthLink Network and MSN, require a prefix (realm) before your username, such as ELN/*username*. Be sure to add any required prefix before your username. (The ELN part of the username is an example of a realm.)

The port is disconnected

If you are having problems with port disconnects, you can check out the following steps to help you resolve the problem.

STEPS

Error 629: The port was disconnected by the remote machine

1. Request a terminal window, and manually enter your username and password (see Figure 15-13). To open a terminal window, right-click the connection icon and choose Properties, and then click the Security tab. Check "Show Terminal Window."

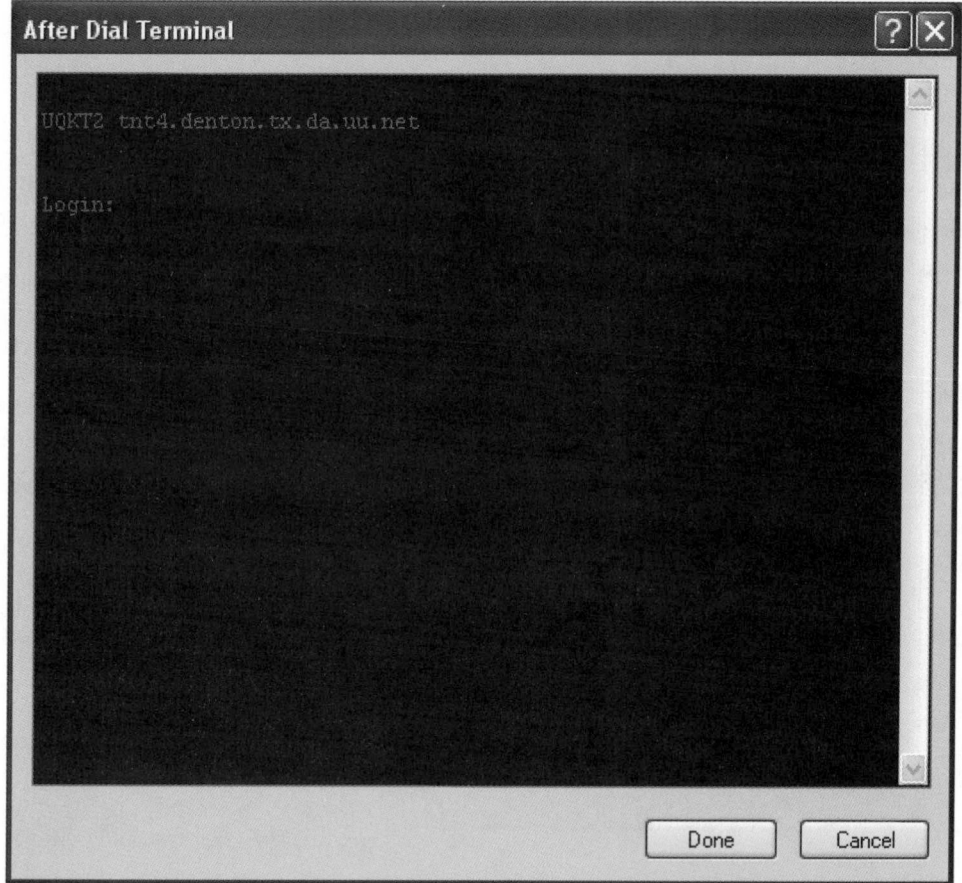

Figure 15-13: The terminal window lets you perform an interactive logon.

2. Check your modem control properties. In the connection's Properties dialog box, select the General tab, and then click Configure. Make sure that "Enable hardware flow control," "Enable modem error control," and "Enable modem compression" are all checked.

3. Right-click the connection's icon and choose Properties, and then select the Networking tab. Click Settings, and ensure that "Enable software compression" is checked.

4. The remote server may not support LCP extensions. Right-click the connection's icon and choose Properties, select the Networking tab, and then click Settings. Clear the "Enable LCP extensions" check box.

NetBIOS error

You may be able to make a connection if you slow down your modem speed. Microsoft suggests dropping the speed to 9600 bps. To do this, follow these steps.

STEPS

Slowing down your modem

1. Open the Network Connections folder.

2. Right-click your connection's icon, and then click Properties.

3. Select the General tab, and then click Configure.

4. Set your modem's maximum speed to 9600 bps, as shown in Figure 15-14.

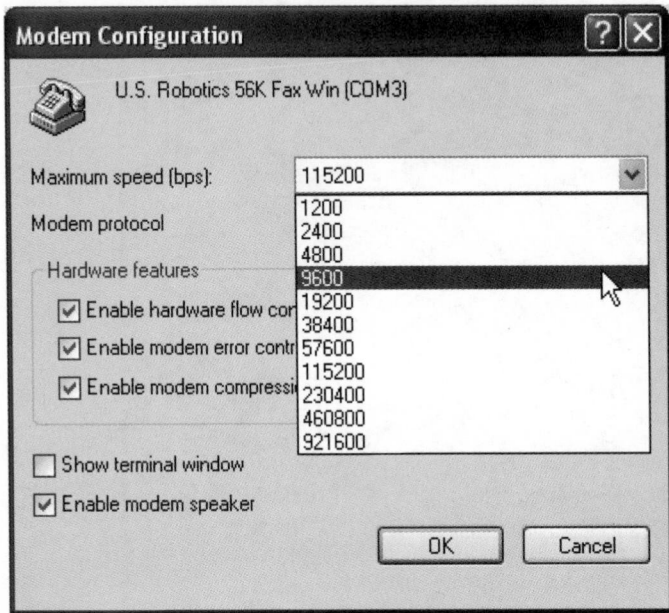

Figure 15-14: Adjust your modem speed.

If this works, you can go back later and try increasing the speed in single-step increments until you reach a speed at which you can't connect. (You don't want to operate at 9600 bps if you can help it.)

Remote PPP peer is not responding

When you receive this error, you might need to manually connect to your ISP; a manual connection attempt also helps you monitor what is happening. You will need to use a terminal window.

STEPS

Opening a terminal window

1. Open the Network Connections folder.

2. Right-click your connection's icon and click Properties.

3. Select the Security tab and check "Show Terminal Window." Then, just start the manual connection process to see the terminal window appear.

TCP/IP utilities do not work

If you make a connection to a server but you can't get TCP/IP utilities like `ping` or `tracert` to work, you may have to turn off IP header compression. To do this, follow these steps.

STEPS

Disabling IP header compression

1. Open the Network Connections folder.

2. Right-click your connection's icon and click Properties.

3. Select the Networking tab.

4. Select Internet Protocol (TCP/IP) from the installed components list and click Properties.

5. Click the Advanced button, and then clear the "Use IP header compression" check box.

No dial tone

Of course, make sure the phone line is connected or not in use by someone else before you jump off the technical deep end. A no dial tone may also mean a physical error with the connection. Make sure that your phone line is connected to your modem and that your modem is correctly configured and connected to the COM port on the back of your computer.

> **CROSS-REFERENCE:** See Chapter 14 to learn more about modem configuration.

Once you are connected

Even after you have a working connection, things can occasionally go bad, break the connection, and leave you unable to reconnect. The first thing to do is wait and try a few minutes later. Your ISP may have had a temporary outage, your initial data transmission may have gotten mangled, or there could have even been sun spot activity. Also, make sure someone else isn't trying to use the phone line.

> **SECRET:** Instead of blaming your software or hardware, maybe it's time to blame the phone company. Noise and static on phone lines may either prevent connections or slow them down. You probably won't get much response from the phone companies, either. Their lines are supposed to be good enough for voice quality, but they aren't required to guarantee the lines for data quality. It's not called POTS (plain old telephone service) for nothing.

Summary

This chapter explored connections in Windows XP. Windows XP provides the software that you need to create and manage connections to the Internet, including dial-up connections and broadband PPPoE connections. In this chapter, you learned about . . .

- ISP selection and connection technology
- Using the Network Connections folder and related wizard to configure connections
- Connecting when a proxy server or firewall is in place
- Troubleshooting connectivity problems

Chapter 16

Configuring Internet Explorer

In This Chapter

Internet Explorer (IE), now in its sixth edition in Windows XP, has long been Microsoft's offering in the browser market. Like IE 5, which was integrated with Windows 98, Me, and 2000, IE continues as an integrated part of the XP operating system. You can't uninstall it and at times, it can be very difficult to hide. However, if you prefer IE to Netscape, there are quite a few configuration options and hidden tweaks that you can use. Because Internet Explorer is a basic product that has been around for quite some time now, I assume you are familiar with the basics. This chapter does not explore browsing, adding favorites, and common surfing tasks. Instead, this chapter focuses on intermediate to advanced configuration issues you may want to employ with IE. In this chapter, you learn about . . .

♦ Configuring and customizing Internet Explorer

♦ Using Internet Explorer tools and features

♦ Securing your computer with IE

♦ Configuring advanced options

Getting Connected

Internet Explorer doesn't do much without an Internet connection — after all, it's through a connection to the Internet that you can use Internet Explorer to access the Web, download Web pages, and do just about everything else you might want to do on the Internet. You can configure connectivity, like many of Internet Explorer's configuration options that are explored in this chapter, in the Internet Options dialog box, which is available both as a Control Panel icon and in Internet Explorer by choosing Tools ⇨ Internet Options. Connectivity is configured specifically on the Connections tab.

It is important to note that Internet Explorer itself doesn't create connections for you. Instead, it uses connections that are already configured on your computer through your Network Connections folder, or it helps you create a new connection by opening the Network Connection Wizard for you.

For example, take a look at Figure 16-1, which shows the Connections tab. If you click the Setup button at the top of the window, the Network Connection Wizard opens, and you can configure a new connection to the Internet. Once a connection(s) is configured, it appears in the Dial-up and Virtual Private Network settings section of the tab. This also includes some cable or DSL connections. If you click the Add button, the New Connection Wizard opens once again. So, you can see that Internet connections are always configured via the Network Connections folder — not directly through Internet Explorer.

If you select a desired connection in the provided window, you can also click Settings to adjust a few properties of the connection, as shown in Figure 16-2. The settings options you see here are helpful if your environment uses a proxy server or automatic configuration sometimes used with proxy servers. You can enable the check boxes under Automatic configuration and Proxy server so that the server updates your connection as necessary. If you are not using IE in an environment like this, you see the Properties and Advanced buttons for the connection's settings. If you click these button options, you are simply taken to the dial-up connection's properties, which is the same thing you see if you right-click the connection icon in Network Connections and choose Properties.

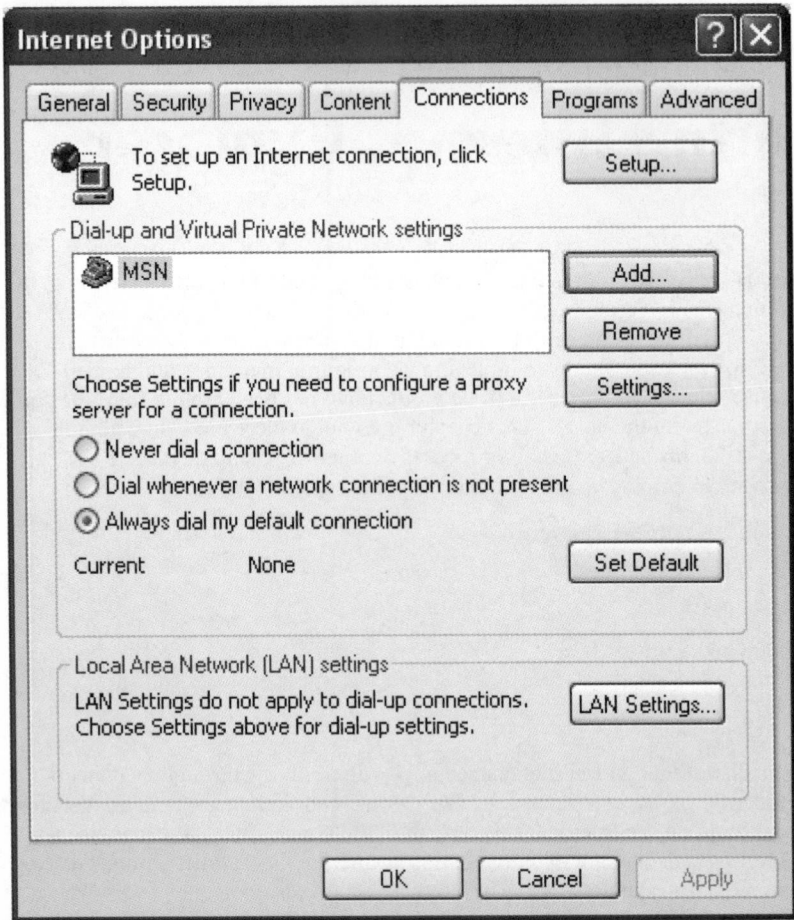

Figure 16-1: Connections tab of the Internet Options dialog box

CROSS REFERENCE: See Chapter 15 to learn all about configuring connections to the Internet.

In the second half of the Internet Options dialog box, you have three radio button options that determine how Internet Explorer can use your connection(s). They are as follows:

♦ **Never dial a connection** — This option keeps IE from automatically dialing a connection when you launch the browser. You have to manually connect to the Internet each time you want to use it.

♦ **Dial whenever a network connection is not present** — If you use IE on a LAN and connect through that LAN, use this option if you also have a dial-up connection configured for backup purposes. IE will use the LAN connection, but if it is unavailable, the browser will automatically dial a connection for you.

♦ **Always dial my default connection** — This option is selected by default. Each time you open IE, it will attempt to dial your default connection.

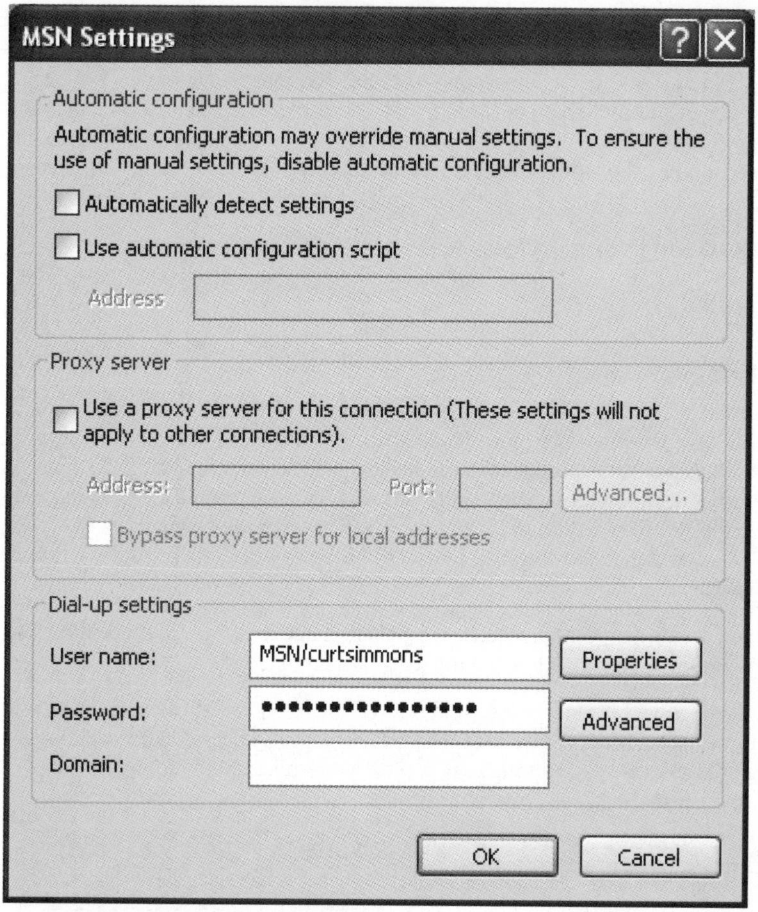

MSN Settings

Automatic configuration

Automatic configuration may override manual settings. To ensure the use of manual settings, disable automatic configuration.

☐ Automatically detect settings

☐ Use automatic configuration script

Address [ ]

Proxy server

☐ Use a proxy server for this connection (These settings will not apply to other connections).

Address: [ ]   Port: [ ]   Advanced...

☐ Bypass proxy server for local addresses

Dial-up settings

User name: MSN/curtsimmons   Properties

Password: ●●●●●●●●●●●●●●●●   Advanced

Domain: [ ]

OK   Cancel

Figure 16-2: Connection settings options

You determine which connection IE uses for the default connection by simply selecting the connection's icon in the provided window and clicking the Set Default button. If you have only one connection, you don't have to worry about this setting.

If you are connecting through a LAN or through certain broadband connections such as satellite, you may need to configure IE to use the LAN or broadband connection by clicking the LAN Settings button. The setting options here enable you to choose a proxy server or set up the browser for automatic detection. You need to get information from your network administrator or broadband documentation to configure these options. Overall, because IE uses Internet connections from the Network Connections folder, your primary configuration tasks are simply selecting the connection(s) that you want to use and configuring how they behave with IE.

Configuring Toolbars

IE 6 provides you with a default interface that has an overall XP feel. The toolbars have been jazzed up, and buttons look different than they did in IE 5. Also, there's more Office 2000/XP integration, including buttons on the toolbar for Office if it is installed. Beyond these differences, the toolbar configuration for Internet Explorer is managed in the same manner as other folders and toolbars on your computer. You can easily customize and remove toolbars as desired so that IE has the look and feel you want.

Use the View menu to add and remove standard toolbar options. If you choose View ⇨ Toolbars, you see options to use standard buttons, the address bar, links, and to lock the toolbar in place. Under View, you also see the option to use the Status bar if you want, and you see several Explorer bar options. The Explorer bar appears in the left pane of Internet Explorer, making it a dual-pane interface. You can place Search, Favorites, Media, History, Folders, and Discuss in the Explorer bar. To find what works best for you, you need to do a little experimenting. Try some of the different toolbar options and Explorer bar views to find what you like best.

You can also rearrange the appearance of IE by moving the toolbars around. Simply drag them to reorganize their appearance. If they don't move, choose View ⇨ Toolbars ⇨ Lock the Toolbars to clear this option.

Customizing toolbars

You can customize the primary toolbar in IE by choosing View ⇨ Toolbars ⇨ Customize. This action opens the Customize Toolbar window, as shown in Figure 16-3. The current toolbar buttons appear in the right pane, and all of the available toolbar buttons appear in the left pane. You can change the buttons that appear on your toolbar by selecting a desired button, then using the Add/Remove buttons, depending on what you want to do. Simply use the Remove button to remove any buttons from the right pane that you do not want displayed on the toolbar, and then use the Add button to move any buttons from the left pane to the right pane that you want to use.

Under the Text options drop-down menu, you can choose icon labels that appear on the right of the icon, under it, or not at all. Under Icon options, you can choose large or small icons.

Also notice the Move Up and Move Down buttons on the right side of the window. These buttons enable you to reorganize the toolbar buttons in an order that is best for you. For example, by default, the Back button appears first on the toolbar. However, you can move it to a different place in the toolbar icon lineup by selecting it in the list and using the Move Down button.

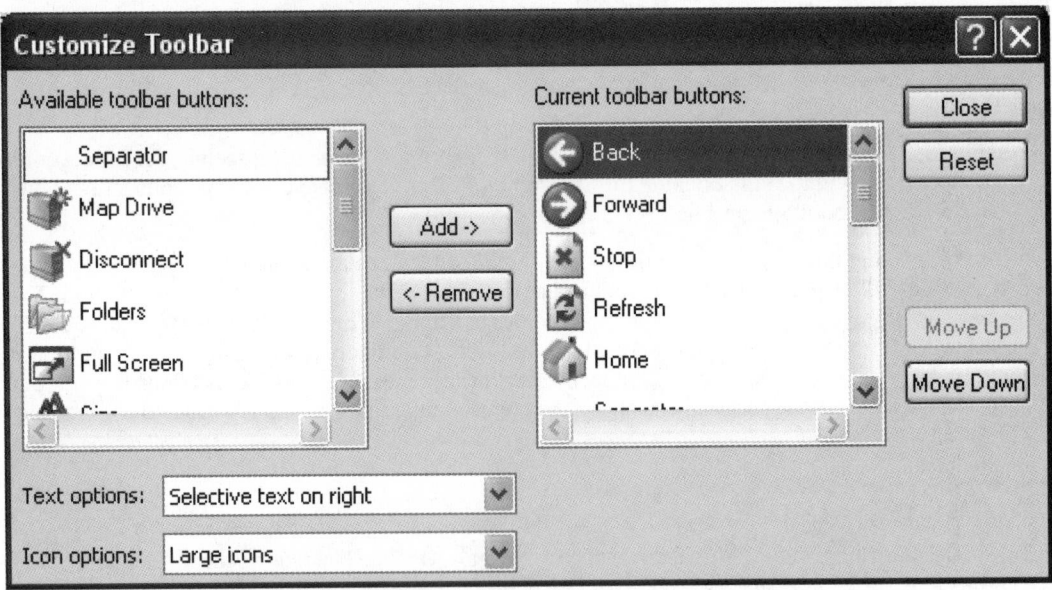

Figure 16-3: Customize Toolbar options

Downloading additional toolbars

You can download additional toolbars from www.microsoft.com/ie. The toolbars currently available are sanctioned for IE 5.5, but by the time you read this, IE 6 toolbars should be available. These toolbars are considered third-party toolbars, in that other vendors developed them. For example, you can install a *New York Times* toolbar for keeping up with live news content. If the IE 5.5 toolbars are still available when you are reading this, you can download them and try them on IE 6, but I had problems getting them to work correctly, so experiment at your own risk.

Adjusting Internet Explorer's Basic Appearance

Aside from toolbar configuration, you can also adjust IE's basic appearance, the languages used, and even accessibility features. All of these options are available in the form of buttons in the Internet Options dialog box, General tab. The buttons appear at the bottom of the tab. These options are relatively easy to configure, and the following sections give you the skinny on each of them.

Colors

If you click the Colors button, a small window appears, as shown in Figure 16-4. You can adjust the colors used for actual IE interface colors as well as hyperlinks. In the left side of the window, you can see that Windows colors are used by default, but you can clear this check box and determine a new color for the text of Web pages and the background. If you want to change these, you can certainly do so, but you will probably need some experimentation to find what you want. On the right side of the pane, you can configure how links appear. By default, visited links appear in maroon, and unvisited links appear in blue. You can also activate a hover color so that links turn yet another color when your mouse is pointing to them. You can change any of these as desired in the Colors dialog box.

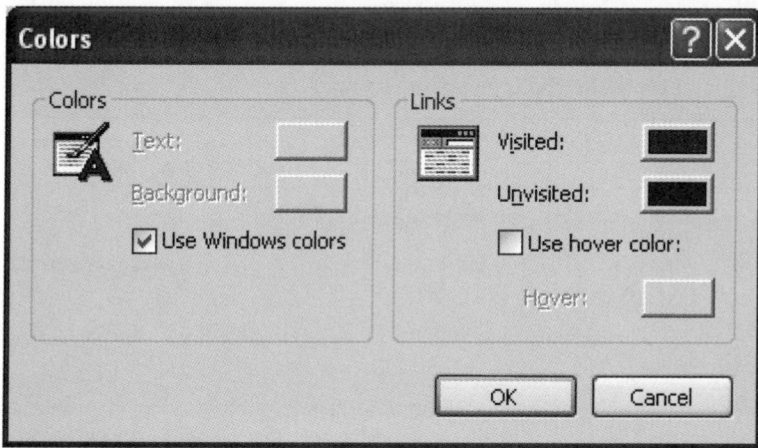

Figure 16-4: Colors window

Fonts

By default, Times New Roman is used as the Web page font and Courier New is used as the plain text font. If you click the Fonts button, a small dialog box appears where you can make changes these defaults as desired. You may need to try several font settings to find what works for you.

Languages

IE has the capability to display Web pages written in languages other than English. If you click the Languages button, you see the current languages available for Internet Explorer to display. You can add more languages by clicking the Add button (you will not need your Windows XP CD).

> **TIP:** Notice that you have a Move Up and a Move Down button here. You should order the languages you make available so that the most commonly used languages are at the top of the list. This will help IE's performance because it will not have to regularly sift through each language option in this list in order to find a match. Keep in mind that IE sees the language options as a list that it runs through in order to find a language match.

Accessibility

You can use the Accessibility button to access a small configuration window with a few check box options. These accessibility features enable IE to override standard Web page graphics and formatting and use the Accessibility formatting options so that the Web pages are easier to read. For example, you can create a style sheet using Accessibility where you specify how documents should be displayed. This style sheet can also apply to Web pages as well. You have the following options:

♦ Ignore colors specified on Web pages

♦ Ignore font styles specified on Web pages

♦ Ignore font sizes specified on Web pages

♦ Format documents using my style sheet

Managing History

IE keeps track of the Web sites you have visited for a period of time and stores them in a folder called History. You can click the History button on the toolbar, and a History menu appears in the Explorer pane. If you want History displayed all of the time, choose View ⇨ Explorer Bar ⇨ History. The History folder is found in `\Documents and Settings\username\Local Settings\History`. You can browse through the History listing and click any item that you have visited. The selected item then appears in the right IE pane. History is a quick and easy way to reaccess Web sites you found but did not add to your Favorites. It is also a good way to check up on the surfing sites of your children (unless they have deleted the history items, which they might know how to do). Overall, though, it's a good way to back up and remember a site that you have visited before you lose track of it.

> **SECRET:** You can expand the History list, then drag a history link (IE icon page) to your desktop, Start menu, or another folder. This automatically creates a shortcut of the item so you can access it quickly from a more convenient location.

You can manage IE's history in a few different ways, all of which are quick and easy:

♦ You can delete any history item from the History list by simply right-clicking it and choosing Delete.

♦ You can more easily delete all history items by choosing Tools ⇨ Internet Options. On the General tab, click the Clear History button.

♦ You can easily search history items with the Search feature that appears in the History explorer bar. You can also reorganize the history listing so that sites appear by date, size, most visited, or order visited. Use the View menu that appears on the History explorer bar to change the options.

♦ Finally, you can determine the number of days that Internet Explorer remembers history listings before they are automatically deleted. By default, history pages are kept for 20 days, but you can alter this setting on the General tab in Internet Options. If you choose a longer period of time, keep in mind that more disk space will be consumed by IE so that the history items can be maintained. As with many configuration options on your computer, you need strike a balance between what is great and what is feasible in terms of hardware usage.

Managing Temporary Internet Files

As you visit a Web site, IE maintains a temporary file for it. For example, suppose you visit www.hungryminds.com. Once you leave the site, you can revisit www.hungryminds.com, and notice that the page seems to load faster. This is because IE has cached the Web page and is retrieving the Web page from the cache so that it loads faster and is available to you more quickly. These cached pages are stored in the Temporary Internet Files folder, a hidden folder stored in `\Documents and Settings\username\Local Settings\Temporary Internet Files`. You can browse the items in this folder, but you can view the items stored there more easily through the General tab under Internet Options.

On the General tab of Internet Options, you see a Temporary Internet Files section. You can choose to delete all items from the folder by clicking Delete Files, and you can click the Settings button to configure IE to handle the cached items for you.

In the Settings window, shown in Figure 16-5, you can select a radio button option to determine how Internet Explorer checks for newer versions of cached Web pages. The options are as follows:

♦ **Every visit to the page** — This option forces IE to check the Web site each time you access the cached page for an updated version. This selection makes sure you have the most current version of the Web page available to you, but it does slow down your browsing because IE has to check the page each time you want to view it. Unless the Web pages you are visiting change very frequently, this option is not suggested because it degrades surfing performance.

♦ **Every time you start Internet Explorer** — When you start IE, the page you want to visit is checked for updates. It is not checked again during your current browsing session. Once you close IE and reopen it, the page is rechecked. This setting enables IE to keep a check on the Web page and update it, but does not require IE to check the Web every time it is accessed.

♦ **Automatically** — This setting is like the previous one, but IE manages the updates based on information it collects about the page. For example, if the page changes every day, IE learns that it needs to update the page each day. For pages that rarely change, IE learns that those pages do not change often and does not check them as often for updates. This is the recommended setting.

♦ **Never** — This option causes IE to always use cached pages and to never check for updates. If you want an updated page, you have to delete the temporary Internet files so IE can recache them or click the Refresh button on individual pages to see if there are updates. This setting is not recommended unless you are regularly accessing sites that never change. However, if you access any sites that do change, they will never be updated under this setting until you delete the items in the temporary Internet files folder so that IE can recache them or until you click the Refresh button for each individual page you want updated.

In the middle of the temporary Internet files Settings window, note that you can adjust the amount of disk space IE uses to store Web pages. As the disk space allotment runs low, cached pages are deleted in the order they were cached (oldest are deleted first). If you want to adjust the amount of disk space used for temporary files, just change it using the slider bar or menu.

Next, you see three button options. You can view objects in the folder or view files in the folder by clicking the desired button. Either way, the Temporary Internet Files folder appears in a new window, where you can see a list of contents. You can directly open items from here, delete them, access properties, and perform any other folder action.

> **SECRET:** You can create shortcuts to the Temporary Internet Files folder and even the History folder and put the shortcuts on your desktop or Start menu for easier access. Just browse to the folders, right-click the desired folder, and click Create Shortcut. Then, drag the shortcut to the desired location.

Finally, you see an option to move the Temporary Internet Files folder. Say you have a second hard drive or a second disk volume that has more room. You can move the folder to that volume or drive to conserve the use of disk space on your primary drive, yet not restrict the use of cached items in order to keep your browsing performance high.

Figure 16-5: Temporary Internet files settings

Moving the Temporary Internet Files folder is easy; just follow these steps:

STEPS

Moving the Temporary Internet Files folder

1. Create a new folder in the desired location. You can call this folder Temporary Internet Files if you like, but you are not required to do so.

2. On the Settings window of Temporary Internet Files, click the Move Folder button.

3. In the Browse for Folder window that appears, shown in Figure 16-6, browse for and select the desired folder you want to use and click OK.

4. Click OK on the Settings window. A message appears telling you that you will be logged off for the file move to continue. Click Yes.

5. The file move occurs, and you are logged back on.

Managing Cookies

A *cookie* is a file that is stored on your computer and generated when you visit certain Web sites at which you enter information and preferences. For example, when I visit www.amazon.com, the site automatically knows who I am, as well as basic information about me. The site originally gathered this information from me and then prompted Internet Explorer to create a cookie file. Now when I visit the site, the cookie is automatically exchanged with the Web server so that the site can recognize me. This process keeps me from having to log in over and over again and configure various preference settings for the site. Overall, cookies are great, but depending on your needs, they can infringe on your privacy and make you want to invoke certain privacy settings.

Figure 16-6: Browse for Folder window

There are few different types of cookies, which you should know about:

♦ **Persistent cookies** — These cookies remain on your computer and are exchanged each time you visit the Web site. The cookie is used to identify you and invoke any preferences you specified during other visits.

♦ **Temporary cookies** — These cookies are generated and used during your current browser session, but are deleted when you close Internet Explorer.

♦ **First-party and third-party cookies** — First-party cookies are those directly generated by you. For example, I visit www.amazon.com and create a profile and preferences. A cookie is generated and sent to www.amazon.com each time I visit the site. A third-party cookie is one that is sent to a different Web site than the one you are viewing. The third-party site may have content on the first-party site, and your cookie is indirectly sent to that site, as well.

SECRET: Have you ever wondered where spam e-mail comes from? One culprit is cookies. Suppose you are visiting a Web site that contains a cookie for you. While on this site, you click a banner ad you find curious. Without your knowledge and consent your cookie for the first-party site is transferred to the third-party site. Now, the third party has your e-mail address, and you suddenly start getting spam e-mail advertising its product. Of course, this third-party company may exchange e-mail addresses with another company, and so on. The good news is you can block third-party access to your cookies, and I show you how later in this section.

♦ **Unsatisfactory cookies** — IE defines an unsatisfactory cookie as one that might allow access to personal information about you (phone numbers, credit card numbers, and so on) without your consent. Settings are available to prevent the use of unsatisfactory cookies, which I explore in a moment.

The cookies IE generates are stored in \Documents and Settings\username\Cookies. Cookies are text files, so you can easily open them and take a look. You can delete any cookie by right-clicking it and choosing Delete, or you can delete all of your current cookies by clicking the Delete option on the Internet Options's General tab. Of course, if you delete all cookies, you'll have reenter information at Web sites that use them. Don't delete all of them unless you have a specific security reason for doing so.

You can also manage cookie usage through the Privacy tab in the Internet Options dialog box, as shown in Figure 16-7.

Figure 16-7: Privacy Tab

TIP: At www.microsoft.com/privacy/safeinternet, you can find a good primer on Internet security and privacy.

On the Privacy tab, you see a slider bar option where you can configure how Internet Explorer handles cookies. Table 16-1 provides you a quick look at the different settings you can employ.

Table 16-1: Internet Privacy Settings

Setting	Description
Accept All Cookies	All cookies are saved on the local hard drive, and any cookies on the computer can be read by Web sites that create the cookies.
Low	Restricts third-party cookies that do not have a compact privacy policy and restricts third-party cookies that use personal information without your consent.

Setting	Description
Medium	Contains the same settings as Low but restricts first-party cookies that use personal information without your implicit consent.
Medium High	Contains the same settings as Medium, but blocks first-party cookies that use personal information without your implicit consent instead of only restricting them.
High	All cookies are blocked that do not use a compact privacy policy and that use personal information without your explicit consent.
Block All Cookies	All cookies are blocked, and any existing cookies on your computer cannot be read.

You can adjust the slider bar to find a setting that is right for you. As a default, the Medium setting is generally all you need, but if you want tighter cookie security, you can use one of the higher settings. Tighter control, however, means more "OKs" from you. For example, return for a moment to my www.amazon.com example. If I use a higher security level, I will receive prompts for me to OK cookie exchange with this site. Also, if I am blocking third-party cookies, I will see similar messages when I click on a banner ad. The security is, of course, great, but make sure you need it because the permission prompts will get old very quickly!

You can also import a cookie setting from another IE 6 browser on another computer by clicking the Import button. See the section "Importing and Exporting" later in this chapter for more information about importing and exploring data.

If you click the Advanced button, you can override all of the automatic settings configured with the slider bar and choose your own. This button opens the Advanced Privacy Settings dialog box, as shown in Figure 16-8. Click the "Override automatic cookie handling" check box, choose to accept, block, or prompt for first-party cookies, and choose a setting for third-party cookies. The most secure setting is to prompt for first-party cookies and block all third-party cookies. This, of course, causes you more prompts and actions while you are surfing, but it puts you in control of cookie generation instead of leaving control to Internet Explorer. You should consider using the session cookie option, which simply means you accept temporary cookies that are deleted once you close IE. However, if you want to maintain the tightest privacy setting, don't enable this option.

Finally, you also have the option to manage cookies on a Web site–by–Web site basis. The following steps show you how.

STEPS

Overriding cookie handling for Web sites

1. On the Privacy tab of Internet Options, click the Edit button under Web Sites.

2. In Per Site Privacy Actions, enter the address of the Web site.

3. Click either the Block or Allow button to block or allow cookies for that particular Web site. Note that the block or allow actions here override any other cookie policy settings you have configured.

4. Repeat Step 3 to add other sites, as shown in Figure 16-9, and click OK when you are finished.

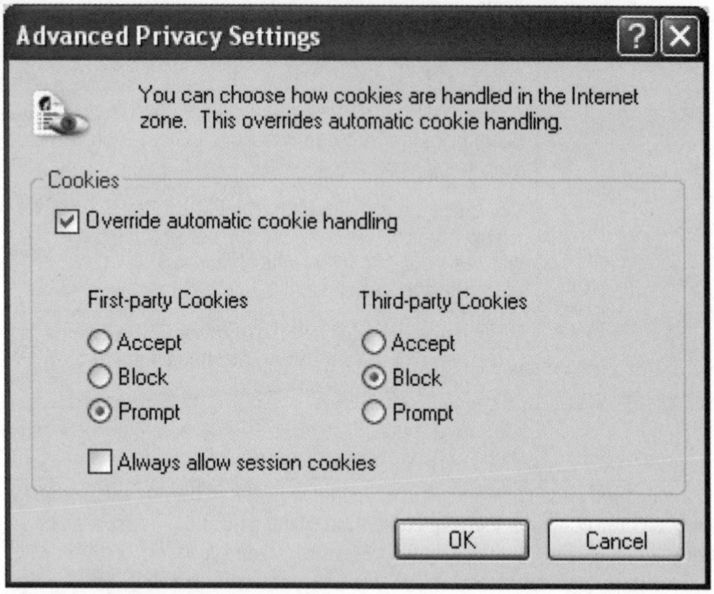

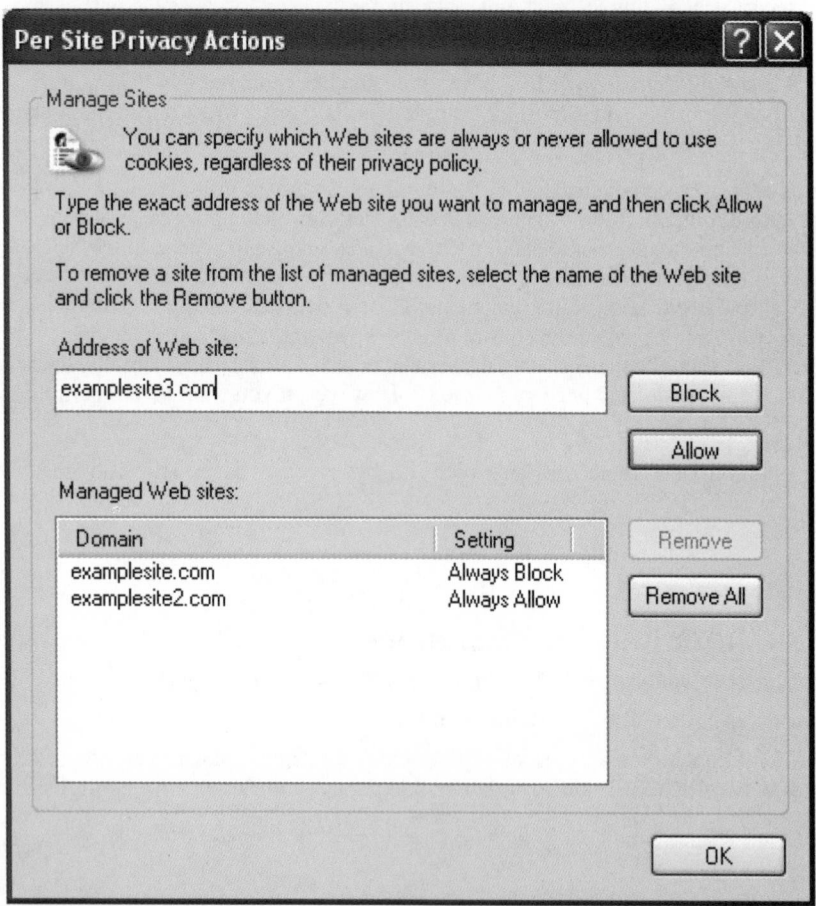

Figure 16-8: Advanced Privacy Settings

Figure 16-9: Per Site Privacy Actions

TIP: You can download a utility called Cookie Pal from www.kburra.com that gives you a finer level of control over cookies. The trial version is free for 30 days and then costs $15. You might also want to a program called Bugnosis, available at www.bugnosis.org, which can analyze Web pages and look for "bugs" that invisibly link you to third-party sites and send tracking info to them.

IE Default Programs

Suppose you have Netscape Navigator installed on your Windows XP computer and prefer to use Netscape over IE. That's no crime, but you'll notice that IE always wants to be your default browser, and it always wants to open Microsoft programs for its default e-mail, HTML editor, and so forth. You can change this behavior by accessing the Programs tab of Internet Options, shown in Figure 16-10.

As you can see, you use each drop-down menu and select the program that you want to use for the HTML editor, e-mail, newsgroups, Internet calls, calendar, and contact list. Even if you are not using IE at the moment, Windows will attempt to use whatever program is selected here. Make your changes by using the drop-down menus, and if you do not want IE to keep prompting you about being the default browser, clear the check box option at the bottom of the window.

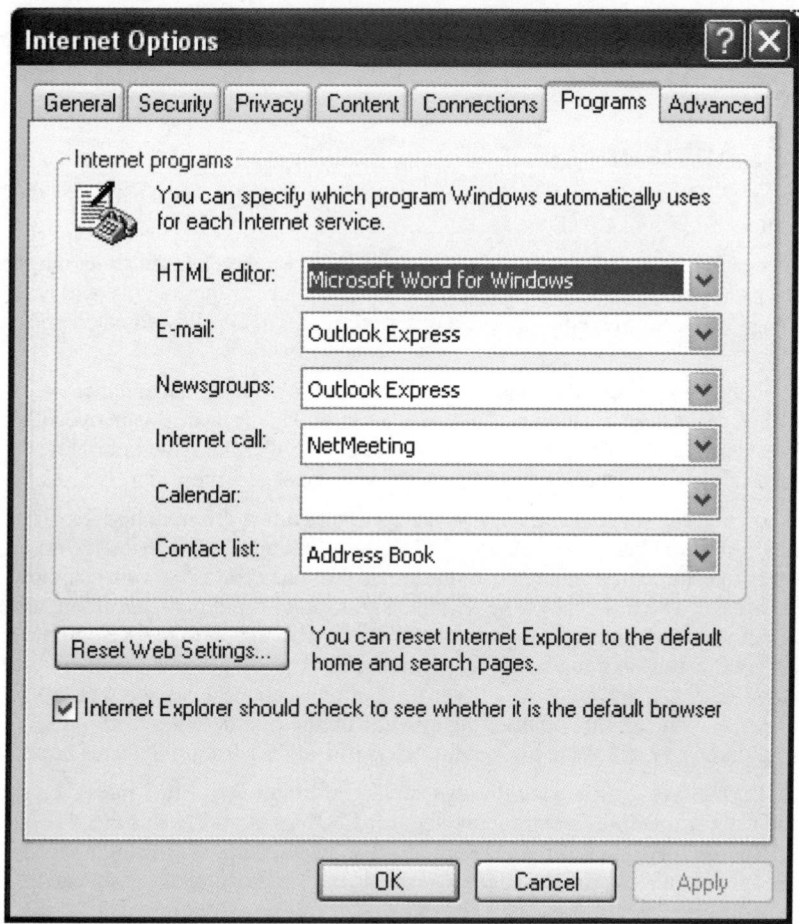

Figure 16-10: IE default programs

Managing Content Advisor and Personal Information

The Content tab in Internet Options contains two important setting options that help you manage content on Internet Explorer. I'll first consider how you can manage content with Content Advisor.

> **CROSS-REFERENCE:** This tab also contains settings for digital certificates, which you can learn more about later in this chapter.

Content Advisor

Content Advisor enables IE to check Web sites for content ratings using standardized rating systems, such as the Recreational Software Advisory Council (RSACi). These standardized rating systems enable Web sites to provide information to the browser and depending on your content rating settings, the browser can refuse to show the material. Although certainly not foolproof, the rating settings are helpful in keeping objectionable material off your computer.

To set up Content Advisor, click the Enable button on the Content tab. This opens a four-tabbed window where you can configure the options you want to use. The following steps walk you through the configuration.

STEPS

Setting Up Content Advisor

1. Click the Enable button for Content Advisor on the Content tab of Internet Options. This opens the properties dialog box you see in Figure 16-11.

2. On the Ratings tab, select each category (language, nudity, sex, violence), then use the slider bar to determine what content is acceptable. Level 0 basically does not allow any of these items, and each level adds permissions to view various levels. You see a description of what is allowed when you move the slider bar.

3. Click the Approved Sites tab. You can use this page to create a list of Web sites that are always viewable or never viewable, regardless of Content Advisor's settings. This is basically an override option you can invoke for desired Web sites. Enter the URL and click either the Always or Never button. The URL is added to the list on this tab, which you can change at any time.

4. Click the General tab, shown in Figure 16-11. Here you can configure a few different options. The first two are check boxes. You can click the check box that allows users to see sites that have no rating, but this may lead to questionable content. Also, the supervisor can type a password to allow users to view restricted content, which is enabled by default. Speaking of the supervisor, if you are a local administrator you can configure these settings so that all users who log on to the XP computer must use them. This is a great feature if you want to invoke these settings on a home computer where children access the Internet. Click the Create Password button to create a password to use with Content Advisor. Finally, you can find other rating systems on the Internet with the Find Rating Systems button, and you can add those to Content Advisor using the Rating Systems button.

5. Click the Advanced tab. If you have downloaded Ratings bureau information or PICS rules, you can use this tab to install and use them. You can learn more about PICS rules at www.safesurf.com and www.rsac.org. Also, use the Find Rating System button on the General tab to automatically get information from the Internet about rating systems and rules you can download (or you can go directly to www.microsoft.com/windows/ie/features/contentadv/default.asp).

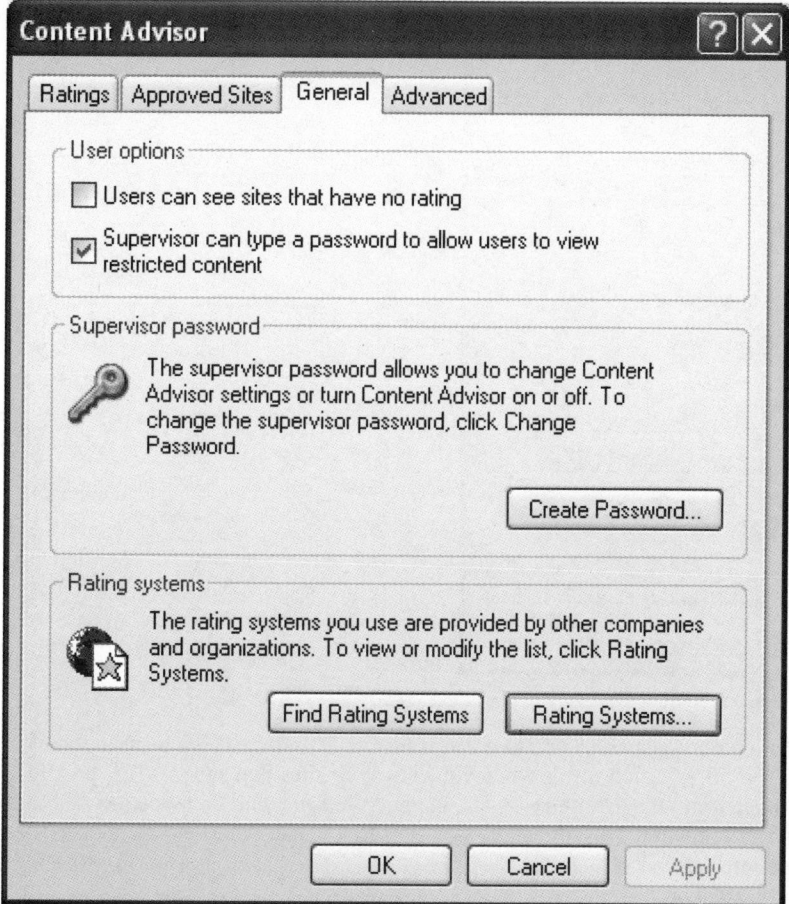

Figure 16-11: Content Advisor, General tab

Personal Information

On the Content tab in Internet Options, the lower portion of the window provides two Personal Information setting options. The first is AutoComplete. AutoComplete remembers frequently accessed Web sites and fields that you have entered on Web pages and attempts to help you by guessing what you are trying to type. Some people like this setting while others find it annoying, but it can help you by finishing URLs for you and even your address, city, and so on in Web forms. To configure AutoComplete, just click the AutoComplete button on the Content tab. This opens the AutoComplete Settings dialog box, shown in Figure 16-12. You have the following setting options:

- ◆ **Web addresses** — AutoComplete attempts to complete Web addresses for you as you type.

- ◆ **Forms** — AutoComplete attempts to complete forms for you as you type.

- ◆ **User names and passwords on forms** — AutoComplete attempts to complete names and passwords on forms for you as you type.

- ◆ **Clear** — You can use the two provided buttons to clear all form content and password content that AutoComplete remembers.

SECRET: The data held in AutoComplete's files is encrypted, so it cannot be viewed by unauthorized Web sites. Also, IE uses an automatic correction feature that can correct common URL typing errors.

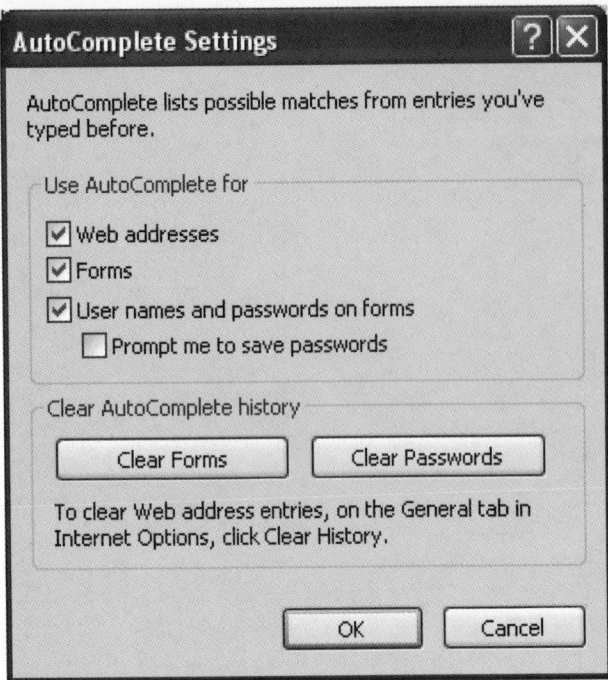

Figure 16-12: AutoComplete Settings

The second Personal Information option enables you to create a profile, which can then be used to help you automatically complete Web registration forms when you visit Web sites that support IE's profile feature. The information you enter into the profile is kept in an encrypted file, and then you are prompted to use the profile information as you want. The advantage to this profile is that you don't have keep manually reentering the same information.

> **TIP:** Web sites must support the IE profile feature for it to work. If you're a Web site administrator interested in including this feature on your Web site or if you are just interested in Web site administration in general, you can learn more at `http://msdn.microsoft.com/workshop/management/profile/profile_assistant.asp`.

To set up a profile, click the My Profile button on the Content tab, then choose to create a new profile in your Address Book. Enter all the desired information in the Main Identity fields and click OK. Click OK again in the Choose Profile window.

> **CROSS-REFERENCE:** See Chapter 17 to learn more about Address Book.

If you want help with Web forms so that you don't have to type the same information over and over, you can use a third-party utility called TypeItIn. This utility places a toolbar on your desktop that you can use to define up to 50 buttons. For example, you can click one button to enter your mailing address, another to enter your state, and so on. Check it out at `www.wavget.com/typeitin.html`.

Getting a Privacy Report

IE 6 includes a new tool that tells you about the cookie settings for a particular Web site and how the site measures up against your cookie settings. For example, if your cookie settings prohibit third-party cookies, the report tells you about any violation the site attempted.

You can easily get the report by accessing the desired Web site using IE, and then choosing View ⇨ Privacy Report. A single window appears, as shown in Figure 16-13, based on the page and linked information. You see a note at the top of the page telling you if any cookies were restricted or blocked.

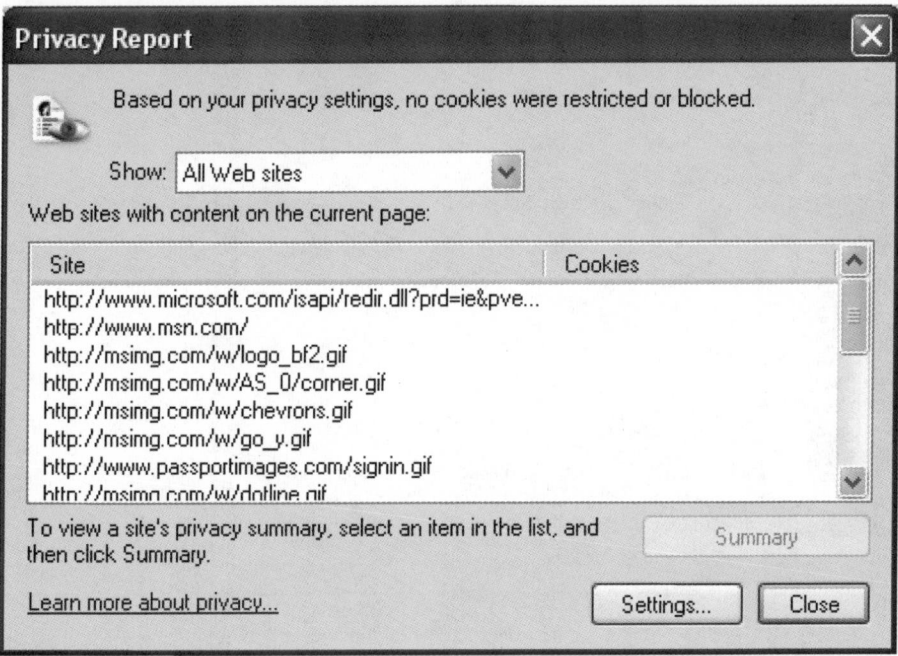

Figure 16-13: Privacy Report

Offline Files

You already know that IE enables you to save Web pages as favorites. Essentially, you create a clickable link in your Favorites folder that retrieves the page from the Internet and displays it for you. But what if you want to download an entire Web site to your hard drive and view it at a later time? IE has the capability to do this by making the Web site available offline. The following steps walk you through the process of making the site available offline after saving it to your hard drive.

STEPS

Making a Web site available offline

1. Connect to the Internet and use Internet Explorer to navigate to a Web page on a Web site that you want to view offline. If you already have this page in your Favorites, you don't need to go online — right-click it in the Favorites menu, choose "Make available offline," and go to Step 4.

2. Navigate to a central page of the Web site that provides links throughout the site to information that you are interested in.

3. Choose Favorites ⇨ Add to Favorites. In the Add Favorite dialog box that appears, mark the "Make available offline" check box, and select a Favorites folder for saving the shortcut. Then click the Customize button.

4. This brings up the Offline Favorite Wizard shown in Figure 16-14. (If you haven't run the wizard before, you will see an introductory screen that tells you about the wizard. You can choose not to show this again.) Click the Yes option button, choose how deep to delve into the Web site by selecting 1, 2, or 3, and click Next.

5. The wizard now asks how often you want to update (synchronize) the Web page/site. Unless you already have a schedule set up, click "Only when I choose Synchronize from the Tools menu," as shown in Figure 16-15. Click Next.

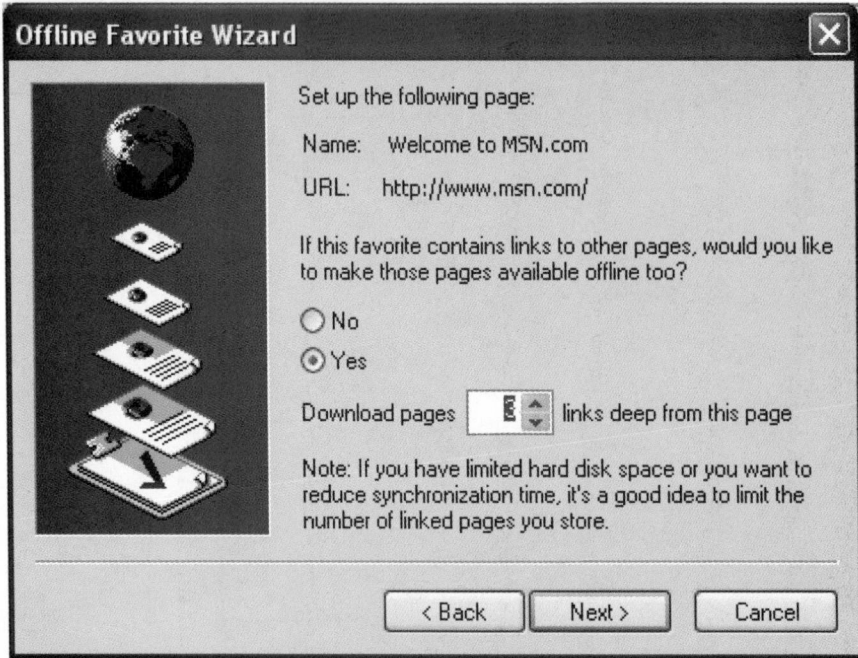

Figure 16-14: The Offline Favorite Wizard

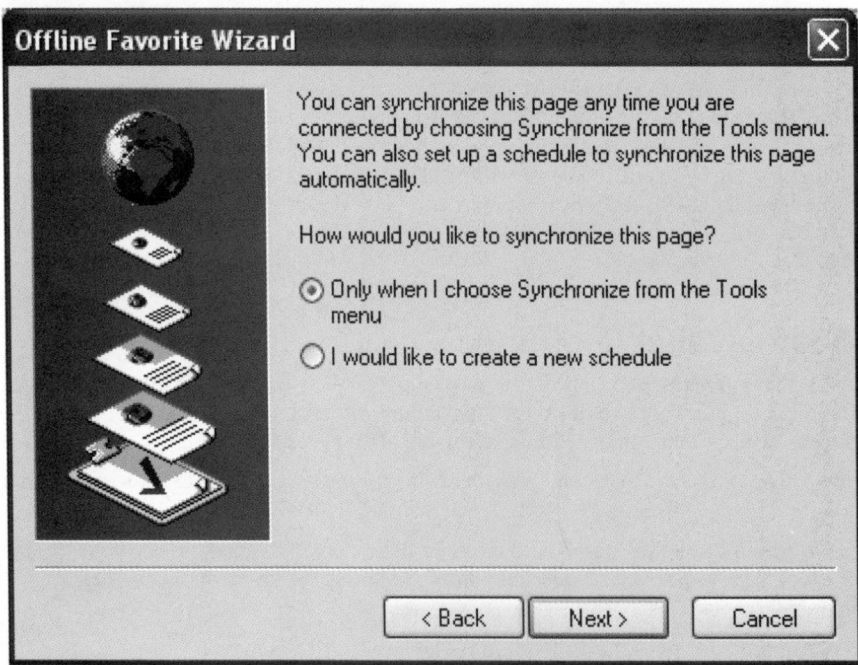

Figure 16-15: Mark the first option button in this Offline Favorite Wizard dialog box unless you have established a schedule for downloading.

6. If the site doesn't require a password, click the Finish button. Otherwise, enter your username and password (twice), click Finish, and then click OK to close the Add Favorite dialog box.

7. Internet Explorer attempts to download (synchronize) the site. You can do this now or wait until after you've refined your synchronization schedule using the remaining steps. To wait until later, click the Stop button shown in Figure 16-16.

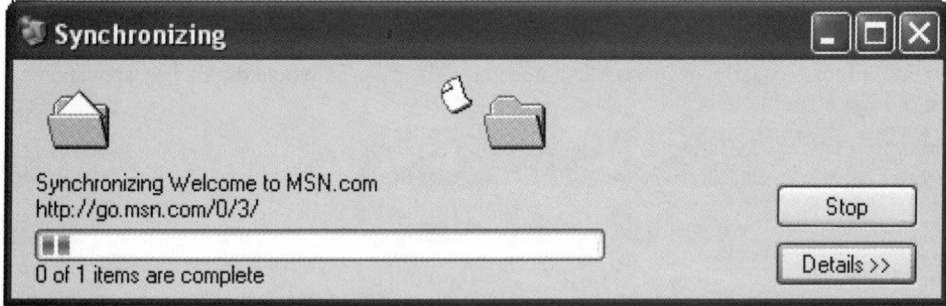

Figure 16-16: Click the Stop button if you want to refine your schedule before synchronizing.

8. If you placed an Offline Web Pages shortcut on your desktop or in your Start menu, you can access the pages directly from that shortcut. Or, navigate to the Offline Files folder found in \Windows\Offline Web Pages. Right-click the shortcut to the offline Web page that you just created, and choose Properties. Click the Download tab in the Properties dialog box, as shown in Figure 16-17.

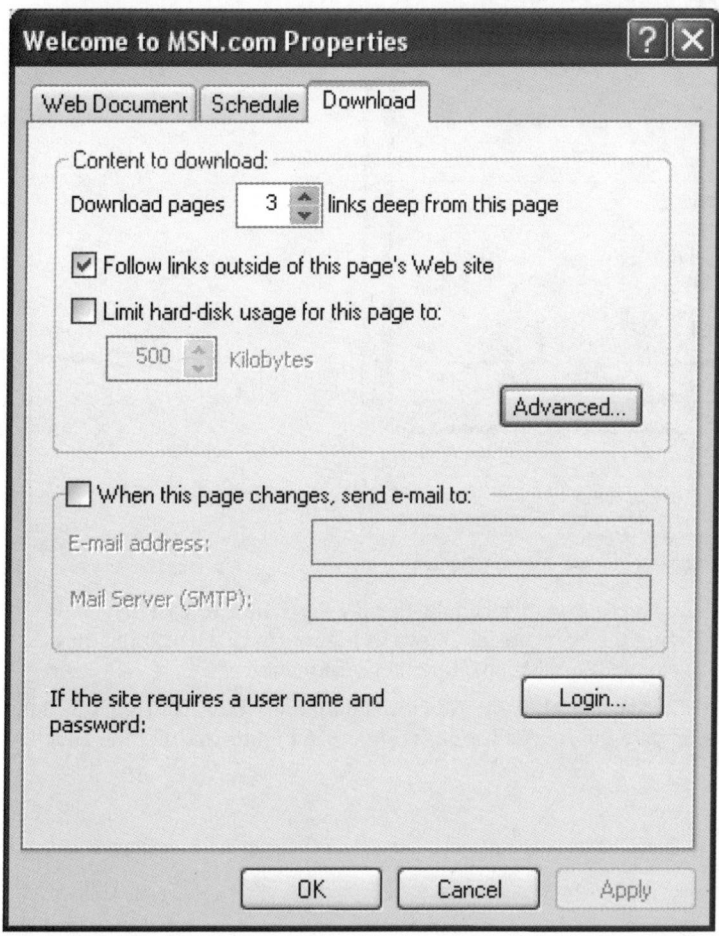

Figure 16-17: The Download tab of the Properties dialog box for MSN.com

9. Adjust any of the parameters in the Download tab. If you want to exclude graphics files, sound, video, ActiveX controls, or Java applets, click the Advanced button.

10. To set up a regular schedule to update your downloaded Web site or page when you're asleep or away from your computer, click the Schedule tab, shown in Figure 16-18. You can select a daily, weekly, or monthly schedule, or create a custom schedule. Highlight the schedule you want and click the Edit button, or click New to create a new one. The New Schedule dialog box appears, as also seen in Figure 16-18.

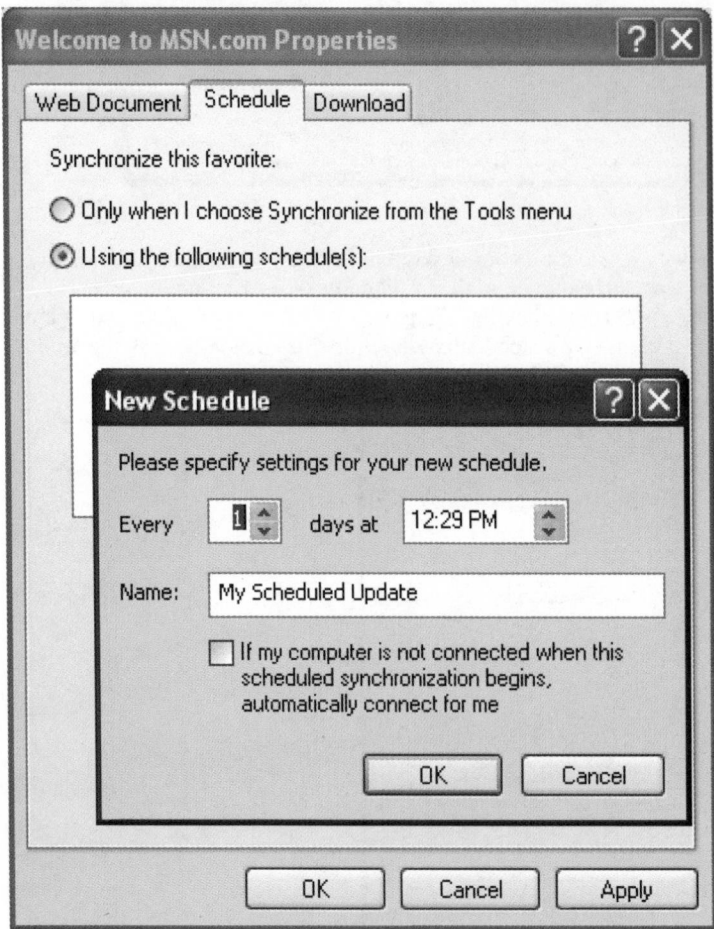

Figure 16-18: Select one of the preset schedules, or set up a custom schedule.

11. Click the Schedule tab in the dialog box for your schedule, display the Schedule Task list, and choose a frequency for synchronizing the Web site, as shown in Figure 16-19. Depending on what you select, you may also need to choose a time or specify other information.

12. If you chose Weekly or Monthly in Step 11, click the Advanced button. In the Advanced Schedule Options dialog box, choose a start date for your schedule, as shown in Figure 16-20. Then click OK twice.

My Scheduled Update
General
Synchronization Items
Schedule
Settings
At 12:29 PM every day, starting 8/14/2001
Schedule Task:
Start time:
Daily
12:29 PM
Advanced...
Daily
Weekly
Monthly
Once
At System Startup
At Logon
When idle
day(s)
Show multiple schedules.
OK
Cancel
Apply

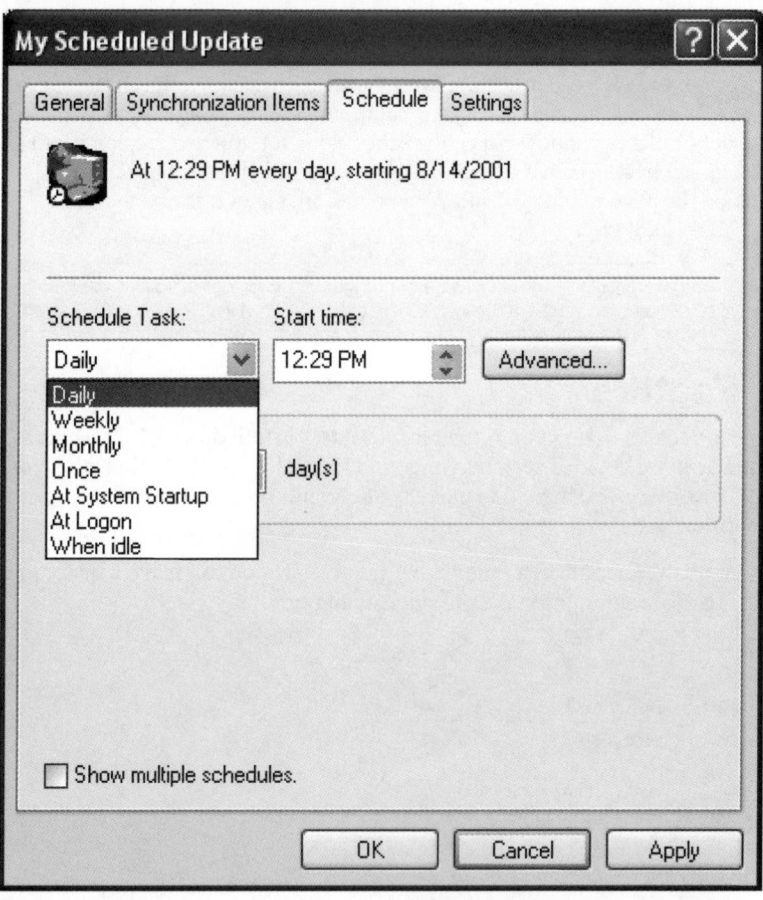

Figure 16-19: Select a frequency for synchronizing from the Schedule Task drop-down list.

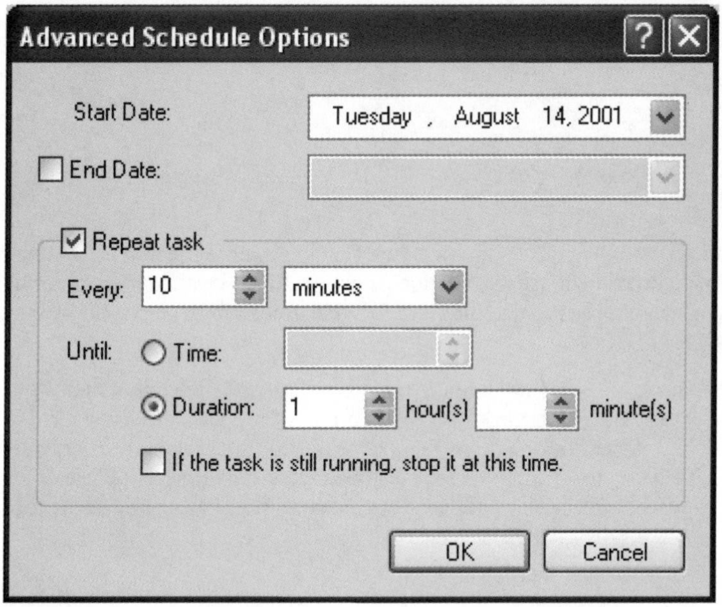

Advanced Schedule Options
Start Date:
Tuesday , August 14, 2001
End Date:
Repeat task
Every:
10
minutes
Until:
Time:
Duration:
1
hour(s)
minute(s)
If the task is still running, stop it at this time.
OK
Cancel

Figure 16-20: You can set your weekly or monthly schedule to start today.

Your Web page/site will now be downloaded at the date and time that you've chosen, as long as you have your computer on at that time. During synchronization, the icon for the Synchronization Manager will appear in your system tray. Later, you can click your Offline Web Pages shortcut on your desktop or in your Start menu, and click the new Web page to view it. If your computer attempts to go online, choose File ⇨ Work Offline in the Internet Explorer window. Once the schedule is set, Internet Explorer will go out on the schedule you have set up to check whether a page has been changed since the last synchronization. It won't download the page to your offline Web page store again if the page hasn't changed.

> **TIP:** Deeper offline viewing is available using a third-party utility called SiteSnagger. It helps you download an entire Web site. Check it out at `http://www.zdnet.com/pcmag/pctech/content/17/04/ut1704.001.html`.

Using IE's Search Feature

The search feature in IE 6 is like the search option you find in most folders in Windows XP. It works better than ever before. You can use more detailed search strings, and IE is more likely to find what you are looking for. Unfortunately Microsoft has attempted to make the Search function so easy that it gets in the way by trying to help you too much.

When you click the Search button on the IE toolbar, as shown in Figure 6-21, you can make a query to a search engine by entering what you are looking for in the provided dialog box.

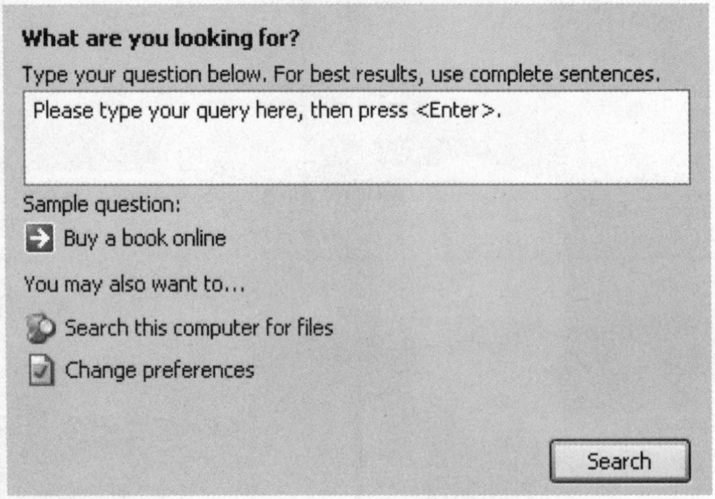

What are you looking for?

Type your question below. For best results, use complete sentences.

> Please type your query here, then press <Enter>.

Sample question:

➡ Buy a book online

You may also want to...

🔍 Search this computer for files

☑ Change preferences

[Search]

Figure 6-21: IE Search

Click the "Change preferences" option and in the next window, click Change Internet Search Behavior. In the Internet Search Behavior window, you can choose to continue using the XP Search Companion or use the Classic Internet search. Also, you can choose the default search engine you want to start with from this location, as shown in Figure 6-22.

Search engines often return far too many results to find the one item you want, and different search engines refine their searches in completely different ways. Now someone is doing more than just complaining about this. Danny Sullivan, the editor of Search Engine Watch, an Internet analysis service, has a goal to bring together major search engine executives so users need learn only one set of search techniques that works across all engines. See `http://searchenginewatch.com/standards` for details.

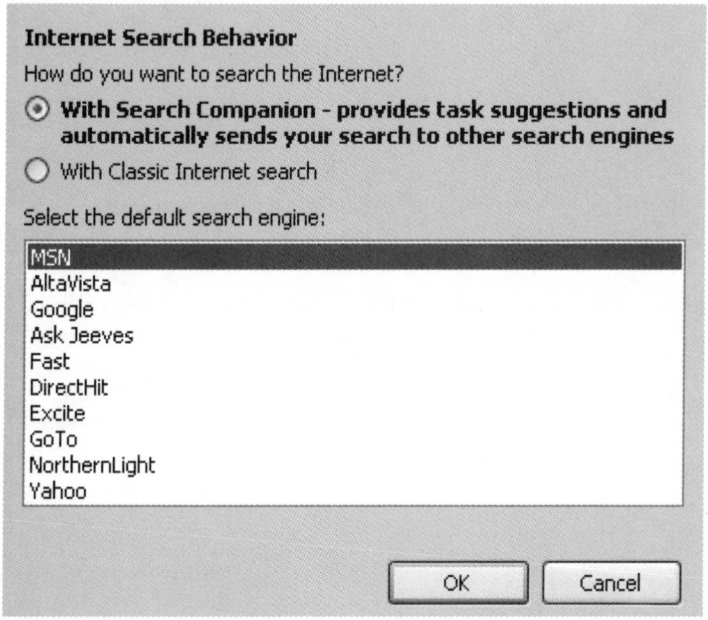

Internet Search Behavior

How do you want to search the Internet?

⦿ **With Search Companion - provides task suggestions and automatically sends your search to other search engines**

◯ With Classic Internet search

Select the default search engine:

MSN
AltaVista
Google
Ask Jeeves
Fast
DirectHit
Excite
GoTo
NorthernLight
Yahoo

[OK] [Cancel]

Figure 6-22: Internet Search Behavior

By "major" search engines, Sullivan means AltaVista, AOL NetFind, Excite, HotBot, InfoSeek/Go, Google, GoTo, LookSmart, Lycos, MSN Search, Netscape Search, Northern Light, Snap, WebCrawler, and Yahoo. All of these engines exist because no single engine can fill all users' needs.

Choosing which engine to use for a particular task is daunting, even for experienced data miners. Sullivan's project to standardize search procedures may help users who must jump from engine to engine to find the information they need.

Most queries return thousands of hits, and narrowing your search becomes a painful but essential step. Fortunately, there are many little-known ways to make fine-tuning easy — and this is exactly where Sullivan's standards project may be able to help.

One fast way to narrow your focus is to search only the titles of Web sites. This eliminates many sites that have mere passing references to your subject. AltaVista, HotBot, InfoSeek, GoTo, MSN, Snap, and Northern Light allow you to do this with the prefix **title:** (as in *title: windows bugs*). But Yahoo uses the prefix **t:** and Lycos makes you go to an Advanced Search page.

If you are still getting too many hits, you can narrow your search to a single Web site that has many relevant pages. The syntax for this type of search is even less standardized, however. AltaVista uses the prefix **host:** (as in *host:infoworld.com windows bugs*). InfoSeek uses **site:**. HotBot, GoTo, MSN, and Snap use **domain:**. Other engines don't yet support this useful refinement (though some do through advanced search pages).

Even the most basic searches, such as *windows bugs*, aren't foolproof. Most engines treat this entry as *windows* OR *bugs*, but HotBot, Lycos, MSN, and Northern Light treat such entries as *windows* AND *bugs*.

CROSS-REFERENCE: For a complete description of all these search engine rules, you can browse to
`http://searchenginewatch.com/facts/powersearch.html`. Further, a handy chart summarizing the rules is available at `http://www.davisstraub.com/secrets/searchenginerules.htm`.

Another Web site, `http://www.searchengines.net`, makes it easy to quickly review different search engines. If you have a Web site and want to place a link on one of your Web pages to a search engine, this site makes that easy. Many search engines provide small forms that you can incorporate into your site, thus allowing your visitors to do a quick, perhaps specialized, search of the Net from your site. You can find all the forms here.

Importing and Exporting

One of the most aggravating things about computing is getting your system "just right." By the time you learn everything there is to know about the operating system and have it configured just the way you want, it's time to either upgrade or invest in a new computer.

Microsoft has recognized this aggravation and provides you with the File and Settings Transfer Wizard (see Chapter 5), so that you can move files and settings easily from one Windows computer to the next. Internet Explorer is no exception to this rule, as XP provides you with ways to retain Internet Explorer settings that are important to you. You can use the Import/Export Wizard to import and export IE's favorites and cookies from one computer to the next. The following steps walk you through the process of using the Import/Export Wizard.

STEPS

Using the Import/Export Wizard

1. In Internet Explorer, choose File ⇨ Import and Export.

2. The Import/Export Wizard appears. Click Next on the Welcome screen.

3. You can choose to import or export favorites or cookies to another browser or a file, as shown in Figure 16-23. Make your selection and click Next.

Figure 16-23: Choose to import or export.

4. If you choose to export favorites, you can select the favorites category and click Next. If you choose the import option, you are prompted for the file to import so that you can browse for the file and complete the wizard. If you are exporting, you are then given a Web browser transfer option, if another browser resides on your computer, or you can export to file and manually import that file on another computer. Make your selection and click Next.

5. Click Finish. If you export to a file, the file is saved in the location you selected as a text file. If you choose to transfer the settings to another browser on your computer, the transfer takes place.

IE Security

Internet Explorer supports various levels of security through predefined zones and through digital certificates. Both of these options, if configured correctly, can give you a safe surfing and downloading experience.

Security zones

Internet Explorer's "security levels" — designed by Microsoft to protect you from the Internet as you surf the Web — have caused consternation among many Windows users. In some ways, the default settings aren't secure enough to be safe. But many people also want to keep security warning messages from popping up every time they move from one Web site to another.

If you know where you're going on the Internet, follow the advice in the next three sections, and you'll see far fewer dialog boxes interrupting your journeys.

Some Web sites also provide extra forms of security. If you see a little padlock on the right side of your status bar, you know that you're on a site that has some sort of security. If you want to know just what sort, hover your mouse over the padlock.

You can check out www.nwnetworks.com/iesc.html for the Unofficial Microsoft Internet Explorer Security FAQ.

In Internet Explorer, choose Tools ⇨ Internet Options, and click the Security tab, shown in Figure 16-24. You see four different security zones defined by Microsoft — Internet, Local intranet, Trusted sites, and Restricted sites. You can select a zone and determine a security level you want to impose on that zone. For Local intranet, Trusted sites, and Restricted sites, you can click the Sites button and define specialized settings for that zone. For example, in Trusted sites and Restricted sites, you can use the Sites button to enter sites that are trusted and those that are explicitly restricted.

For any zone, you can select the zone and move the slider bar to set a desired level of security for the zone. Table 16-2 outlines the differences between the Low, Medium, and High settings. The Medium-Low setting strikes a balance between Medium and Low.

Table 16-2: Internet Explorer's Security Settings

Setting	High	Medium	Low
Run ActiveX controls and plug-ins	Disable	Enable	Enable
Download signed ActiveX controls	Disable	Prompt	Enable
Download unsigned ActiveX controls	Disable	Prompt	Prompt
Script ActiveX controls not "safe"	Disable	Prompt	Prompt

Setting	High	Medium	Low
Java permissions (security level)	High	Medium	Low
Active scripting	Enable	Enable	Enable
Scripting of Java applets	Disable	Enable	Enable
File downloads	Disable	Enable	Enable
Font downloads	Disable	Prompt	Enable
Submit nonencrypted form data	Prompt	Prompt	Enable
Launching applications and files	Disable	Prompt	Enable
Installation of desktop items	Disable	Prompt	Enable
Drag and drop or copy and paste files	Prompt	Enable	Enable

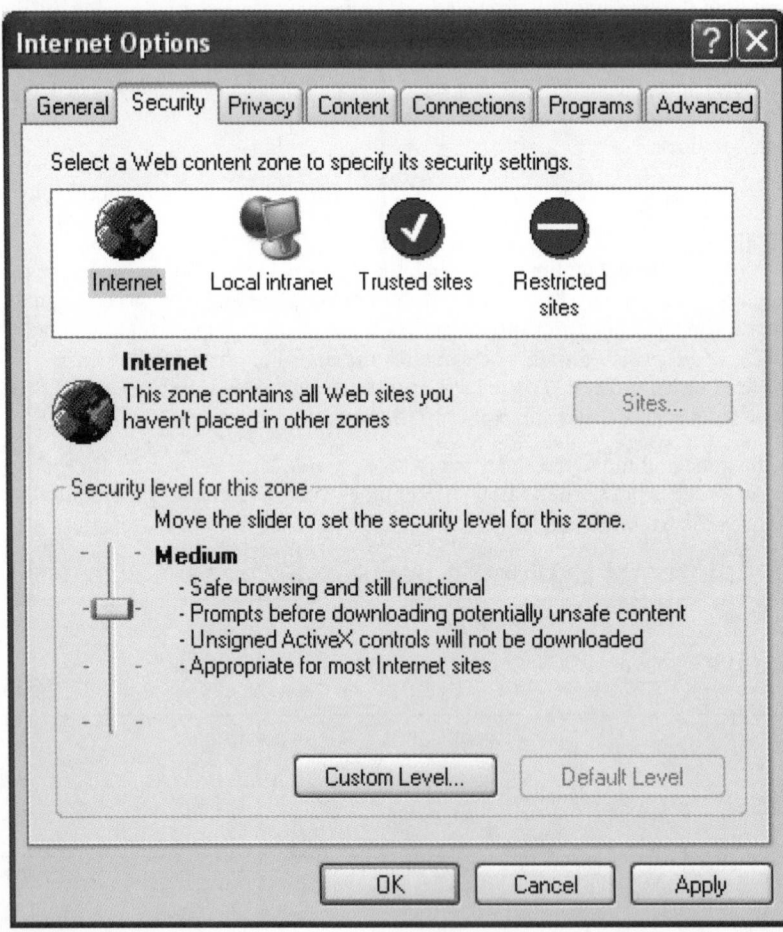

Figure 16-24: Security tab

You can also customize the setting level yourself instead of using the slider bar. Just click the Custom Level button to access the Security Settings window, as shown in Figure 16-25.

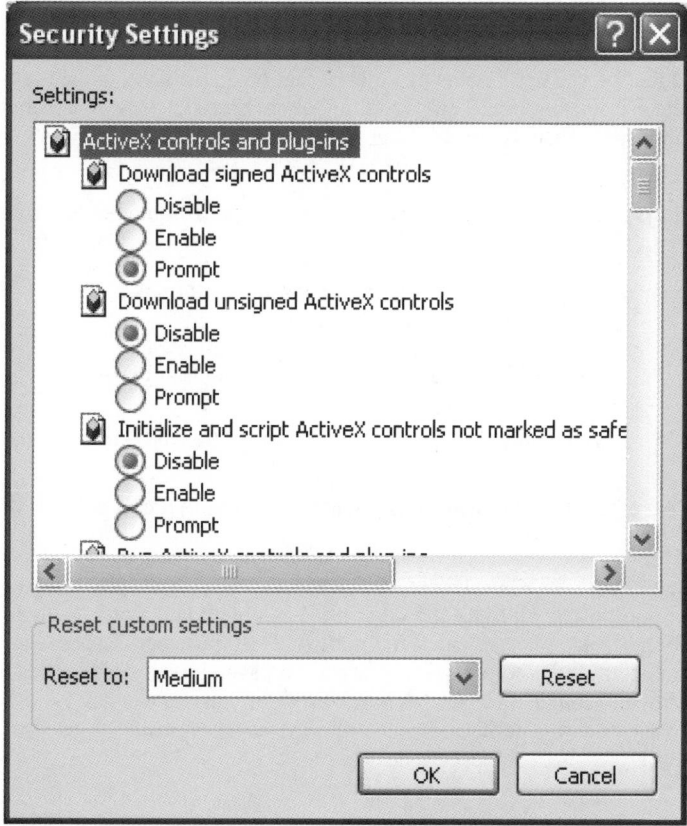

Figure 16-25: Security Settings

In this dialog box, you can see some of the assumptions Microsoft has built into Windows. If you select the Medium default settings, these are the values you get. All types of data are acceptable to Internet Explorer under these defaults, except ActiveX controls that are not "signed" or marked "safe." Simply click the desired radio buttons to invoke the settings you want for that zone.

Generally, you want fairly restrictive rules for sites. But if you feel fairly confident about your ability to notice when a rogue Web site is messing around in files it should not be getting into, you may want to set your security level to Low. This enables all behaviors of Web sites, except that Internet Explorer will still prompt you with a dialog box prior to acting on ActiveX controls and scripts that are unsigned or not marked as safe — the ones that do not carry an "electronic certificate" acting as a kind of Good Housekeeping seal.

You can even turn off the warnings for suspect ActiveX controls by resetting all defaults to Low. To do this, click the Custom Level button, choose Low Security in the Reset to drop-down list, click the Reset button, click Yes, and then choose Enable under "Download unsigned ActiveX controls" and "Initialize and script ActiveX controls not marked as safe." But with these two cases, it makes sense to remain on the Prompt security level, since the whole premise of electronic certificates is to distinguish between ActiveX controls developed by reputable and disreputable sources.

In addition to the security settings in the Security tab, you'll find some options available on the Internet Options Advanced tab, which is explored later in this chapter.

Digital certificates

Digital certificates perform two different functions. First, they provide a signing feature for people on the Internet that essentially says, "I am who I say I am, and here's my proof." The digital certificate proves the authenticity of the site you are using. You most often see this when you are downloading a file. IE may tell you that a digital certificate cannot be verified — this just means that IE doesn't recognize the digital certificate from the site or the site is not using one. The good thing about digital certificates is they let you know that a download is coming from a trusted source — one that is not going to send a virus coursing through your computer's veins.

The second feature of digital certificates is encryption, which scrambles data so that it cannot be decrypted without the correct security key.

With the use of digital certificates, IE can keep your computer safe on the Internet and transmit information safely. Digital certificates are made up of three different components:

- **Public key** — A decryption key that is public. The decryption key works with your private key in order to decrypt data.
- **Private key** — A private decryption key generated from a Certificate Authority, and one that must be kept secret.
- **Certificate Authority (CA)** — An organization that assigns private keys to individuals and organizations, such as VeriSign.

Using these three items, IE can use digital certificates as a means of security. You can configure digital certificates in Internet Explorer by opening Internet Options and clicking the Content tab. You can open Certificates or Publishers and see a listing of current certificates and publishers of those certificates, as seen in Figure 16-26. You don't need to do anything here, because these options are already configured. However, if you purchase a digital certificate from a company such as VeriSign, you can use the Certificates window to install it, or you can add new publishers and authorities as necessary.

Advanced Options

The Internet Options Advanced tab contains a number of different settings you can invoke. The defaults configured here are generally all you need, but you should take a look at them in case there is something you want to change. I include a list of each item in each category for quick reference.

Accessibility

- Always expand ALT text for images — Expands a picture box to ensure that all of the alternate text for an image is displayed.
- Move system caret with focus/selection changes — Accessibility options, such as a magnifier, follow the system caret to magnify what is on the screen. This setting ensures that the caret follows the focus/selection changes so that the magnifier will work.

Browsing

- Always send URLs as UTF-8 — UTF-8 is a standard character format for URLs that can be translated into different languages. This is selected by default.
- Automatically check for Internet Explorer Updates
- Close unused folders in History and Favorites
- Disable script debugging — This option avoids those aggravating warning dialog boxes.
- Display a notification about every script error
- Enable folder view for FTP sites

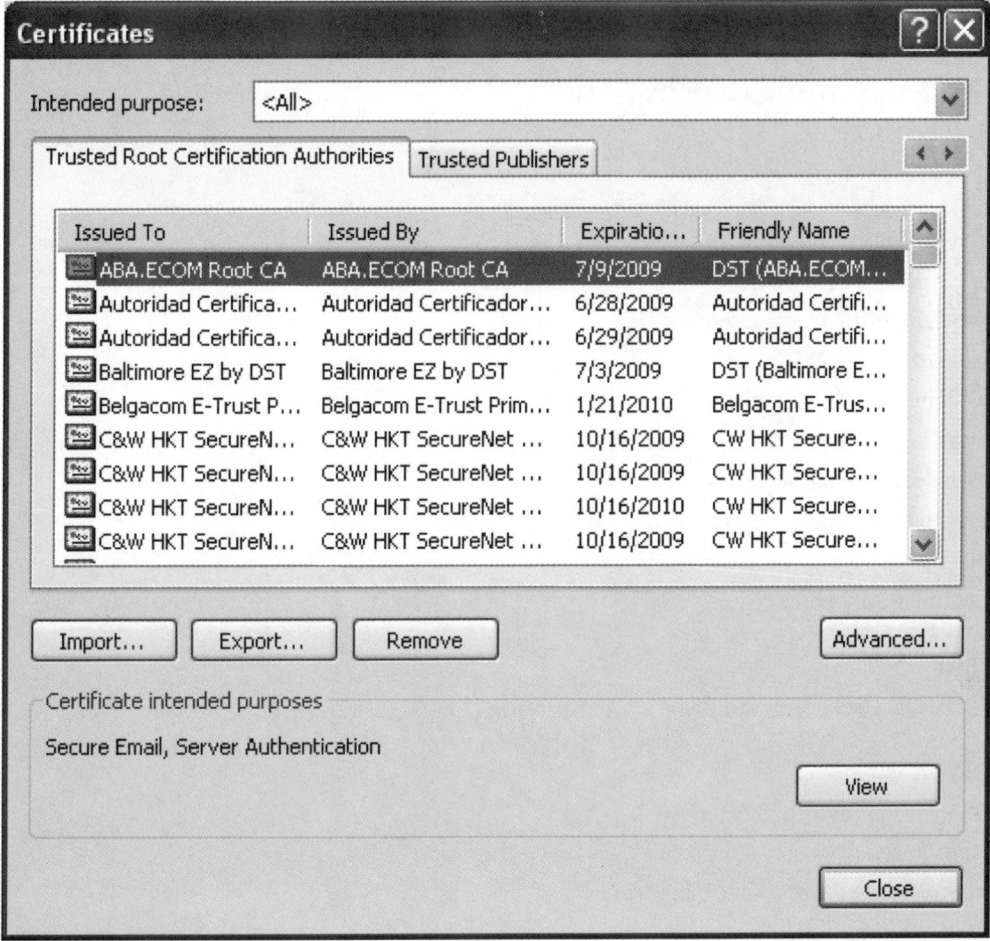

Figure 16-26: Certificates window

- ◆ Enable Install on Demand (IE)
- ◆ Enable Install on Demand (Other)
- ◆ Enable offline items to be synchronized on a schedule
- ◆ Enable page transitions
- ◆ Enable Personalized Favorites Menu
- ◆ Enable third-party browser extensions
- ◆ Enable visual styles on buttons and controls in Web pages
- ◆ Force offscreen compositing even under Terminal Services
- ◆ Notify when downloads complete
- ◆ Reuse windows for launching shortcuts
- ◆ Show friendly HTTP error messages
- ◆ Show friendly URLs
- ◆ Show Go button in Address Bar
- ◆ Enable Smart tabs/show Office XP Smart tabs

- Underline links (always, hover, never)
- Use inline autocomplete
- Use passive FTP (for firewall or DSL modems)
- Use smooth scrolling
- Use HTTP 1.1/through proxy

Multimedia

- Don't display online media content in the media bar
- Enable automatic image resizing
- Enable Image Toolbar
- Play animations in Web pages
- Play sounds in Web pages
- Play videos in Web pages
- Show image download placeholders
- Show pictures
- Smart image dithering

Printing

- Print background colors and images

Search

- Display results and go to the most likely site
- Do not search from the Address bar
- Just display the results in the main window
- Just go to the most likely site

Security

- Check for publisher's certificate revocation
- Check for server certificate revocation
- Check for signatures on downloaded programs
- Do not save encrypted pages to disk
- Empty Temporary Internet Files folder when browser is closed
- Enable Integrated Windows authentication
- Enable Profile Assistant
- Use SSL 2.0
- Use SSL 3.0
- Use TLS 1.0
- Warn about invalid site certificates
- Warn if changing between secure and not secure mode
- Warn if forms submitted are being redirected

As with most setting options, the default configuration is the most common, so there is typically no need for you to make extensive changes on this tab. You may find the browsing, multimedia, and printing options the most helpful because you can control the look and feel of IE and save ink by not printing background images. The best way to use this tab is to identify IE behaviors that you would like to change, and then use the settings on this tab to see if you can make those needs a reality.

Helpful Keyboard Shortcuts

Like with all Windows applications, keyboard shortcuts can help reduce your time working with IE. Some of these shortcuts, listed in Table 16-3, are great timesavers, so be sure to check them out.

Table 16-3: Keyboard Shortcuts for Internet Explorer

Key or Combination	Effect
Enter	Goes to the highlighted link
Backspace and Shift+Backspace	Same as Back and Forward arrow buttons on the Internet toolbar
Alt+left arrow and Alt+right arrow	Same as Back and Forward arrow buttons on the Internet toolbar
Shift+F10 and Ctrl+B	Displays a context menu for a page
F5	Reloads the current page from the server
Esc	Stops downloading a page
Ctrl+O or Ctrl+L	Goes to a new location (URL)
Ctrl+N	Opens a new window
Ctrl+S	Saves the current page
Ctrl+Shift+Tab	Cycles between frames
Tab and Shift+Tab	Cycles between links on a page
Ctrl+D	Adds current Web page to Favorites (immediately and silently)
Ctrl+R	Reloads the current page (F5)
Ctrl+W	Closes the active Internet Explorer window
Alt+D	Jumps to the Address bar
Ctrl+F	Brings up the Find dialog box
Ctrl+P	Brings up the Print dialog box
Ctrl+Tab	Moves forward among frames
F4 (or Alt+down arrow)	Displays the Address bar history
F6	Jumps to the Address bar
F11	Toggles full-screen mode
Page Down	Scrolls down, one screen at a time
Page Up	Scrolls up, one screen at a time
Spacebar	Scrolls down, one screen at a time

IE and Group Policy

If you are the administrator of your Windows XP computer and several other people also use the computer, you can impose a number of Internet Explorer settings on the other users. These management settings enable you to control how IE is used and the actions users can take. You can do this through Group Policy on your local Windows XP computer. Further, you can learn all about Group Policy in Chapter 23.

Summary

In this chapter, you explored the many settings and configuration options provided by Internet Explorer.

- Most configuration options can be configured through the Internet Options interface.
- You can configure the IE toolbar to meet your needs and download additional toolbars from the Internet.
- IE contains a number of personalized settings, such as Content Advisor, Profiles, and AutoComplete.
- You can download entire Web sites to be viewable anytime offline.
- IE supports many security features, such as digital certificates and security zones.
- Use the Advanced tab of Internet Options to configure a number of specific items.

Chapter 17

Outlook Express

In This Chapter

Outlook Express is the default e-mail client in Windows XP, just as it was in previous versions of Windows. Outlook Express, although sometimes ignored by the public at large, has actually grown and developed quite a bit over the past few years. In fact, Outlook Express contains a wealth of functionality and features. It is not as powerful as the full version of Outlook, but for most people, Outlook Express has more than you need to manage e-mail and newsgroups — and best of all, it's free and installed by default on Windows XP. In this chapter, you learn about . . .

♦ Using Outlook Express view options

♦ Using Outlook Express with multiple accounts

♦ Customizing Outlook Express

♦ Accessing newsgroups

♦ Configuring mail and news rules

♦ Configuring the address book

Checking Out the Outlook Express Interface

Outlook Express uses a pane interface that gives you access to folders, contacts, and mail — the three primary components that make up Outlook Express. From this pane-based interface, you can easily send and receive mail, read mail, access contacts, and access Outlook Express default folders, such as Inbox, Outbox, Sent Items, and so forth. As you might guess, the options you find in this interface are configurable and can be adjusted according to your wants and needs. The following sections take a look at the possible choices. Because this book is for intermediate to advanced computer users, I assume you can explore the basics on your own, so the following sections stick to tasks and options that you might not readily see.

Outlook Express folders

The Folders column in the Outlook Express interface, shown in Figure 17-1, provides you with quick access to your inbox, outbox, and other local folders. By selecting a folder, the contents of the folder are displayed in the right pane. If you select a primary folder with subfolders, they expand and appear in the pane, as well.

The Local Folders provide most of what you need, but you can also create your own folders and add them to this list. I use this feature commonly when I am working on a book. For example, in Outlook, I have a folder called "XP Secrets" while I am writing. All e-mail concerning the book is placed in that folder so I can easily access and review it. You might do the same — create folders for specific users or subject matter.

Regardless, all you have to do is right-click Local Folders in the folder list and choose New Folder (or select it and use the File menu). You can also create subfolders under Inbox, Outbox, and so on, if you like. Give the folder a name, click OK, and you are all set.

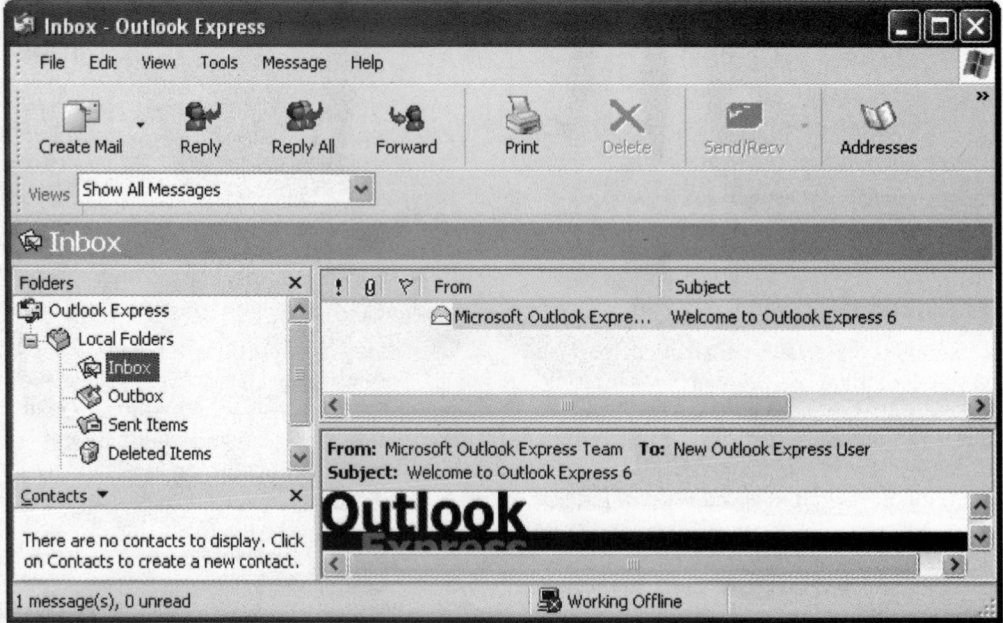

Figure 17-1: Outlook Express folders

If you right-click a folder in the folders list and choose Find, the Find Message dialog box opens, allowing you to search for and open a message from any folder without opening the folder itself. So, for example, if you're reading a large newsgroup, you can search for and read a message in your Sent Items folder without losing your place in the newsgroup. You can also empty the Deleted Items folder by right-clicking its icon in the Outlook Bar and choosing Empty Deleted Items Folder. Right-click and select Properties to see the properties of the folder itself (not the shortcut), with a quick summary of the number of files in that folder, the number unread, and the location where the folder is stored.

Outlook bar

The Outlook bar is another pane that gives you icons for your Inbox, Outbox, Sent Items, Deleted Items, and Drafts, shown in Figure 17-2. Of course, this simply repeats what is already available in your Folder view, and by default, the Outlook bar is not configured to appear on Outlook Express 6. If you want to see it, though, choose View ⇨ Layout and select the Outlook Bar option.

Contacts pane

You'll notice a pane in the lower-left part of the Outlook Express window that displays the entries in your address book. If you prefer not to see the Contacts pane, click the close window (X) button in the upper-right corner of the pane. To get it back, choose View ⇨ Layout and mark the Contacts check box.

To send a message to someone in your address book, simply double-click the name or group, and a New Message window opens. This works even while you are using the newsreader and does not make you lose your place. Although the Contacts pane in the Outlook Express window is handy for quickly picking a name out of your address book, it does not have all the address book features. For example, you do not have the ability to sort other than by first name. The Outlook Express Address Book is a full-featured contact storage and management tool, and I explore it later in this chapter.

While I'm on the subject of the Layout page, shown in Figure 17-3, it's worth noting that you can always access View ⇨ Layout to change most any Outlook Express configuration. Just use the check boxes as you like so that Outlook appears the way you want.

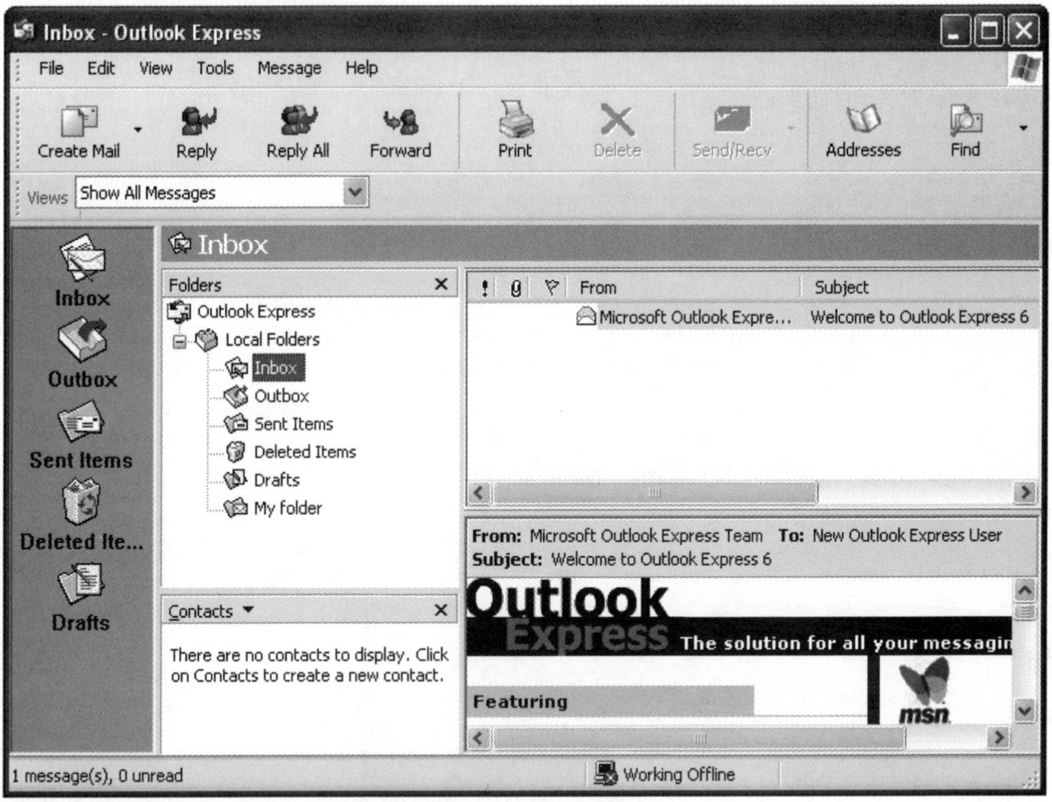

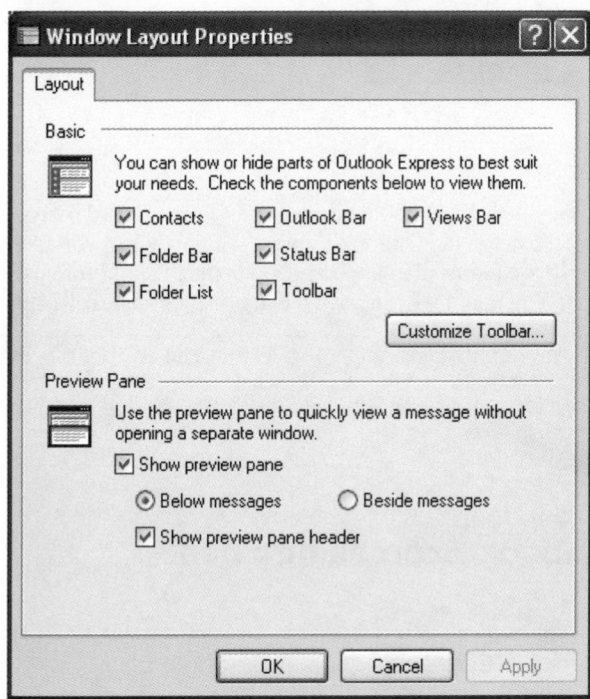

Figure 17-2: The Outlook bar (left column) provides easy access to Outlook features.

Figure 17-3: Outlook Express Layout

Renaming Outlook Express

If you would like to customize the name of Outlook Express, you can do so through the Registry. See the following steps for instructions.

STEPS

Changing the Outlook Express title bar

1. Open your Registry Editor and navigate to `HKEY_CURRENT_USER\Identities\{`*your identity number*`}\Software\Microsoft\Outlook Express\5.0`. If you aren't sure which identity number is the right one, click a number, and you'll see the associated username in the right pane. If you have only one identity set up in Outlook Express, you'll only see one number.

2. If the value WindowTitle doesn't exist in the right pane, right-click the right pane, choose New ⇨ String Value.

3. Give the string value variable the name **WindowTitle**, and press Enter.

4. Double-click WindowTitle. In the Edit String dialog box, type the name you'd like to see in the title bar, as shown in Figure 17-4. Press Enter and close the Registry Editor. The next time you open Outlook Express, it will use your new title in the title bar.

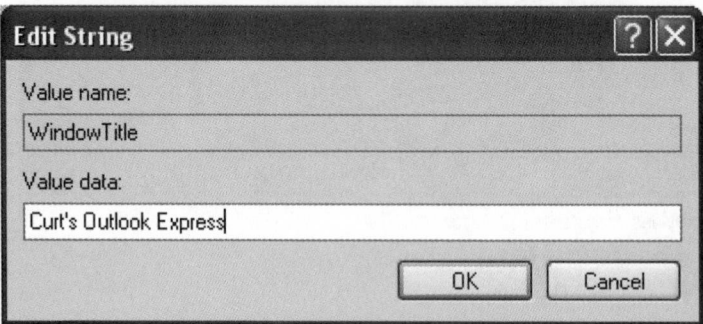

Figure 17-4: Changing the title of Outlook Express

Disabling the Info pane

If you have a "branded" version of Outlook Express — that is, one that carries the logo of a third party such as a computer vendor — you see an additional pane in the Outlook Express window when you first open it. This is called the Info pane. In fact, even if you uninstalled the branded version, the old Info pane may still display when you open Outlook Express. You may feel you have a better use for that real estate.

SECRET: To temporarily disable the Info pane, open Outlook Express, choose View ⇨ Layout, and clear the Info Pane check box. However, when you restart Outlook Express at a later time, the Info pane is likely to reappear. To permanently disable the Info pane, you must edit the Registry, as described in the steps that follow.

STEPS

Permanently disabling the Outlook Express Info pane

1. Start with Outlook Express closed.

2. Open the Registry Editor (`regedit.exe`) and navigate to `HKEY_CURRENT_USER\Identities\{`*your identity number*`}\Software\Microsoft\Outlook Express\5.0`.

3. Find the string called `BodyBarPath` and delete it. Press F5 to refresh your Registry, and close the Registry Editor.

4. Open Outlook Express, and choose View ⇨ Layout. You no longer see the Info Pane check box.

If you are feeling creative, you can also create your own Info pane. Here's how.

STEPS

Creating your own Info pane

1. Create artwork using Microsoft Paint or another pixel-painting application. A good dimension is 720 pixels wide by 72 pixels high. Save your image as a `.bmp` file.

2. Close Outlook Express.

3. Open the Registry Editor and navigate to `HKEY_CURRENT_USER\Identities\{your identity number}\Software\Microsoft\Outlook Express\5.0`.

4. If you already have a string called `BodyBarPath` (because you have a branded version of Outlook Express), double-click it. In the Value Data field, enter the path and filename of the `.bmp` file you created in Step 1 and click OK. If you don't have `BodyBarPath`, right-click the right pane of the Registry Editor, and choose New ⇨ String Value. Rename the value **BodyBarPath**. Then double-click it and in the Value Data field, enter the path and filename of the `.bmp` file you created in Step 1. Click OK.

5. Find the DWORD called `ShowBodyBar` and look at its value. If the last digit is set to 0, double-click `ShowBodyBar`, type **1** in the Value Data Field, and click OK. Close the Registry Editor.

6. Now open Outlook Express. You should see your new image in the Info pane at the bottom of the window. You can change your artwork as often as you like without editing the Registry. Just save it with the same name and path you entered in Step 4. You must close Outlook Express and reopen it to see the change.

The Views bar

Right-click your toolbar and you'll see a Views bar option. Click it to display a handy drop-down list of views. Now you can easily see whether you've chosen Show All Messages, Hide Read or Ignored Messages, or perhaps a custom viewing filter. You can drag the Views bar up to the same row as the menu bar and toolbar. If there's not enough room to display the down arrow to the right of the Views list, you can click the currently selected view to display the list instead.

Setting Up a Mail Account

By default, the Windows XP Internet Explorer uses Outlook Express as the mail tool when you click an e-mail address while viewing a Web page. If you want to use another e-mail client (such as Outlook or Eudora) you can change this default behavior (see Chapter 16 for details). To create a mail account for Outlook Express, choose Tools ⇨ Accounts and then click Add ⇨ Mail. A wizard walks you through the process of setting up your username and password. You will need to know the SMTP/POP3 server names of your ISP's mail server, so check your ISP's documentation for details. Outlook Express uses your default Internet connection, such as your dial-up or broadband connection, configured in Network Connections.

CROSS-REFERENCE: See Chapter 15 to learn all about setting up Internet connections.

You can also configure news and directory service accounts under Tools ⇨ Accounts. Just click Add and choose the type of account that you want to create, and follow the wizard steps to set up the account. Newsgroup usage is covered in more detail later in this chapter.

> **SECRET:** Outlook Express allows you to create multiple e-mail accounts that you can contact through one or multiple Internet connections. You can log on to any Internet service provider where you (or an associate) have an account and get your e-mail from any Internet standard e-mail server on which you have a valid e-mail account.

Outlook Express switches to mail mode when you highlight a mail folder in the Folder List pane or the Outlook bar. The toolbar changes to the mail toolbar, and any changes that you make to the toolbar affect only the mail toolbar. The menu items change also. For example, Catch up (used in newsgroups) does not appear on the Edit menu, and the Tools menu has fewer commands for synchronizing.

If you have multiple e-mail server accounts, you can poll a single account for e-mail manually. Just choose Tools ➪ Send and Receive, and then choose the account from the submenu that appears. You can choose which e-mail accounts are polled when you click the Send and Receive button (which does the same thing as Tools ➪ Send and Receive ➪ All Accounts). Just choose Tools ➪ Accounts, highlight a mail account, click the Properties button, and mark or clear the Include This Account When Receiving Mail or Synchronizing check box. This also works to choose which accounts Outlook Express polls automatically.

Replies to your messages still go to your stated e-mail address (the reply address you indicate in the General tab of each account's Properties dialog box), even though you don't necessarily send your e-mail through the SMTP server at your e-mail address location.

If you have multiple e-mail server accounts, the New Message window gives you the ability to choose which account the message will be delivered through. This is true even if you are replying to a message that was delivered through a different account. Each account has a specific SMTP outgoing mail server. To associate a specific account with a message, use the drop-down menu button at the right end of the From field.

If you don't specify an account, Outlook Express sends the message through your default mail server account. Because each account can have a separate Internet connection and because you can stack mail in your Outbox, it is quite possible to click the Send and Receive button and have Outlook Express call up multiple Internet service providers and send mail through each of them.

> **SECRET:** Many Internet service providers won't let you send e-mail through your e-mail account with them if you are logged on to another service provider. They do this to keep spammers from using their server to send out "offerings." This actually doesn't present you with a problem. You can send e-mail out through the SMTP outgoing mail server provided by the service you are connected to and receive mail through the POP3 incoming mail server at another provider. Just configure each e-mail account to use the SMTP server of the connection it is intended to use.

Outlook Express and E-Mail

When you install Outlook Express, it sets itself up as the default e-mail client. If you install other e-mail clients or somehow mess up your settings, Outlook Express may not appear when you click e-mail addresses embedded in Web pages. To get it back, you'll want to check your system.

Choose Tools ➪ Options and click the General tab. Make sure that the tab says, "This Application is the Default Mail Handler; if not, click the Make Default button." (To do the same for news, click the lower Make Default button.)

You get the same results by right-clicking the Internet Explorer icon on the Desktop, choosing Properties, and clicking the Programs tab. Make sure that Outlook Express is selected in both the Mail and News drop-down lists. This also allows you to click the Mail toolbar button in Internet Explorer to invoke Outlook Express.

Outlook Express is not a full MAPI client. You can't use it to send faxes, for example. It is a simple MAPI client, and if you are willing to disable Windows Messaging or Outlook, you can use it in conjunction with Word, Excel, and PowerPoint. If you choose File ➪ Send in any of these programs, the current document is sent to a new message in Outlook Express as an attachment.

Sending messages to a group

Outlook Express lets you create groups of e-mail recipients from among those listed in your Windows Address Book. It does this to let you send one message to a group of folks.

SECRET: If you just put the name of the group in the To field, then everyone gets a message starting with a long list of names. That's no fun. To keep this from happening, insert the group name in the BCC field of your message and put your own name in the To field (assuming you have your own name in your address book).

Corrupted folders

If you get error messages regarding your Outbox, Inbox, Deleted Items, or Sent Items folder, you're going to have to delete the corrupted folder. Outlook Express will construct a new, clean, empty folder for you if it is one of the standard folders. (If the corrupted folder is one you created, you'll have to create it again.)

First exit Outlook Express. Use your Explorer to navigate to `\Windows\Application Data\Identities\{youridentitynumber}\Microsoft\Outlook Express`. Delete the `.dbx` file associated with the corrupted folder — for example, `Outbox.dbx`. Restart Outlook Express. This deletes all the text of the messages (which essentially means all messages) in your Outbox, so you have to recreate the messages. Although corrupted message folders are not as common as they once were, it is still a good idea to save important messages in a separate local folder and to avoid letting your Inbox fill up with several weeks' worth of messages.

Playing a tune when mail arrives

You can make your computer play a tune (play a `.wav` file) when your mail arrives. To do this, choose Tools ⇨ Options, click the General tab, and mark the Play Sound When New Messages Arrive check box. Setting this makes sense if you have marked Check for New Messages Every [ ] Minute(s) in the same tab.

If you dial in to your Internet service provider, download your mail, and then disconnect, there's no point in setting Outlook Express to play a tune. Outlook Express must be running for the tune to play. (If you receive your mail from the Internet and not an intranet, you have to be connected to the Internet, as well.)

You can, if you like, set your own sound to play when new messages arrive. Find the New Mail Notification event under the Windows events, and choose among the listed `.wav` files or browse for another one.

When Outlook Express is running and you're connected to the Internet (or your intranet), an envelope appears in your system tray when mail arrives. Be sure to turn on your speakers to hear the sound that accompanies the arrival of the mail.

Leaving mail on the server

If you are traveling, you might want to leave mail messages on your mail server until you get back, even if you read them on the road. That way, you can download them to your office computer when you return.

To do this, choose Tools ⇨ Accounts, highlight your mail server, click the Properties button, click the Advanced tab, and mark the "Leave a copy of messages on server" check box, as shown in Figure 17-5.

Converting the mail

You can import Eudora, Netscape, Microsoft Exchange, Windows Messaging, or Outlook e-mail messages into Outlook Express format. In Outlook Express, just choose File ⇨ Import.

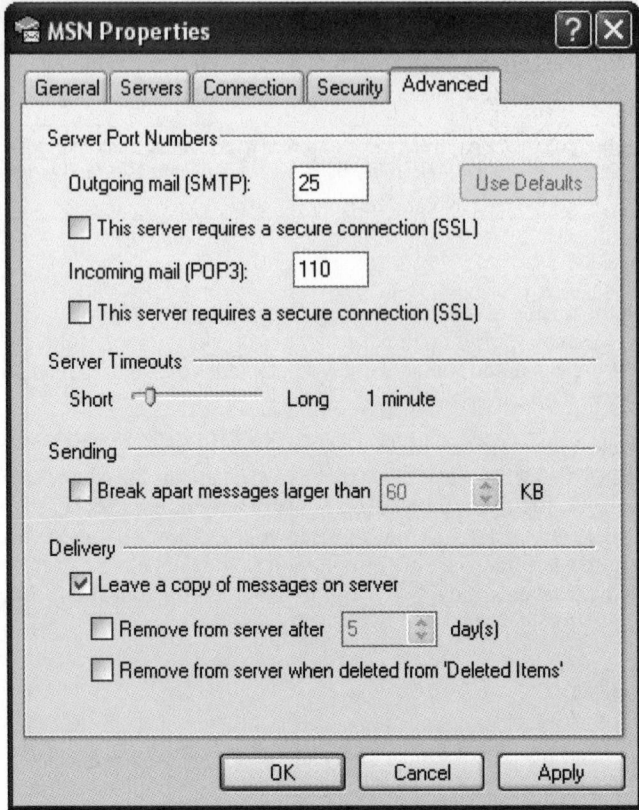

Figure 17-5: Advanced configuration options

To see how to import Pegasus messages, check out Eric Miller's User Tips for Outlook Express at www.okinfoweb.com/moe.

You can find out more about Eudora, which uses the same message format as Outlook Express, at http://mango.human.cornell.edu/kens/MoreFAQ.html. Go to Qualcomm's Web site at www.eudora.com, where you can also download a freeware version of the program.

Reading and managing messages

Electronic messages differ from other types of messages in several ways, but one of the most significant is the ease in composing and sending messages electronically. This ease contributes to the absolute flood of messages that many people send and receive on a regular basis. Fortunately, Outlook Express offers several ways for you to deal with all of these messages — as you'll see in the following sections.

Did the message arrive?

When you send an important letter the old-fashioned way, you can ask the post office to notify you when the letter is delivered. E-mail can work the same way. Actually it's not quite the same, because there's no friendly postal carrier to hand the letter to the addressee and ask him or her to sign the receipt. Still, you can ask to be notified when someone opens a message you have sent. In the New Message window, select Tools ➪ Request Read Receipt. You can set this globally for all messages you send by choosing Tools ➪ Options ➪ Receipts and marking "Request a read receipt for all sent messages." But before you mark this box, consider: Do you really want to clutter your Inbox with all those receipts?

If you receive a message with a receipt request, Outlook Express asks whether you wish to send a receipt. You can set it to "Always send a read receipt" or "Never send a read receipt" by marking the appropriate box on the Receipts tab of the Tools ⇨ Options dialog box. If you decide to always send a receipt, you probably want to make an exception for mailing lists by marking the check box shown in Figure 17-6.

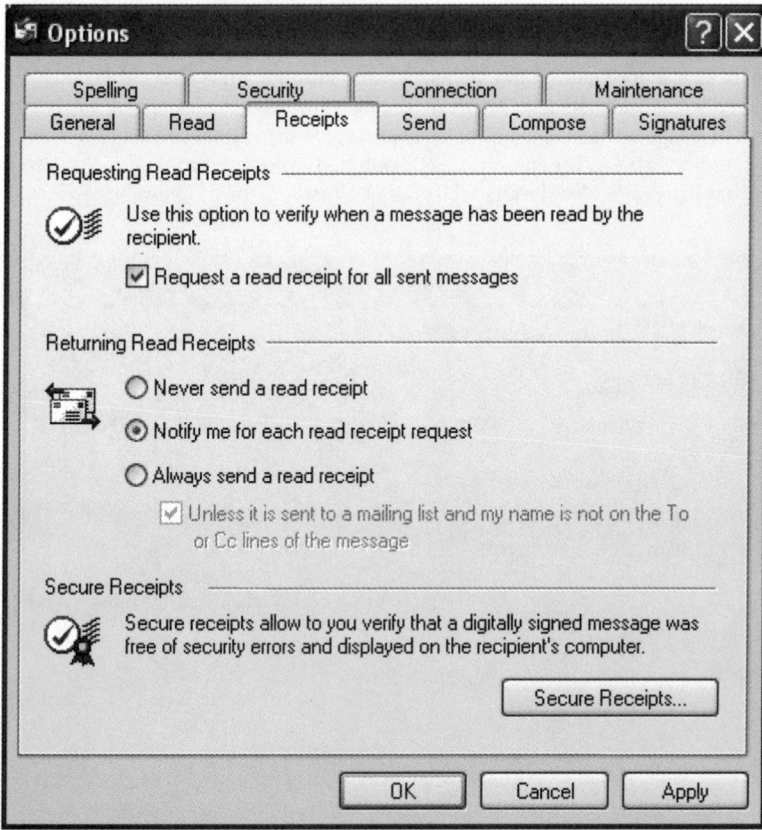

Figure 17-6: The Receipts tab of the Options dialog box. Avoid sending receipts to mailing lists by marking the check box shown.

If you frequently send or receive digitally signed messages, it can be very helpful to verify that the message arrived free of security errors. You set the behavior for secure receipts separately from the nonsecure kind, using the same Tools ⇨ Options ⇨ Receipts dialog box.

Making messages and threads easier to find

You can flag mail and news messages that are important or that you want to find easily later. Either highlight the message header in the Message pane and choose Message ⇨ Flag Message, or simply click next to the message header in the Flag column. A little flag icon appears next to the header of a flagged message, and when you open the message you see a flag icon and the note, "This message is Flagged" in the header.

The Flag column is turned on by default in mail message folders, but in news folders it is turned off. To see the Flag column when you are reading news, right-click a column header button at the top of a column and select Columns. In the Columns dialog box, mark the Flag check box and click OK. The Columns setting can be different for each message folder.

You can also flag a message header that appears in the Find Message dialog box (choose Edit ⇨ Find ⇨ Message), so that you'll be able to locate it later in the Message pane. Just click in the Flag column as you would in the Message pane.

A similar tool for tracking conversations in a newsgroup is the watch/ignore icon (a pair of glasses or a red X), which you can use to mark threads that you want to watch or ignore (see Figure 17-7). To mark or unmark a thread, choose Message ⇨ Watch Conversation or Message, or Message ⇨ Ignore Conversation — or simply click next to a message in the Watch/Ignore column. Your first click marks the thread to be watched, your second click marks it to be ignored, and your third click unmarks it. You have to select and mark only one message to mark the entire thread. As you download headers for new messages in a thread, they will also be marked. When you open a watched or ignored message, you see the glasses or X icon and a note saying either "This message is being Watched" or "This message is being Ignored."

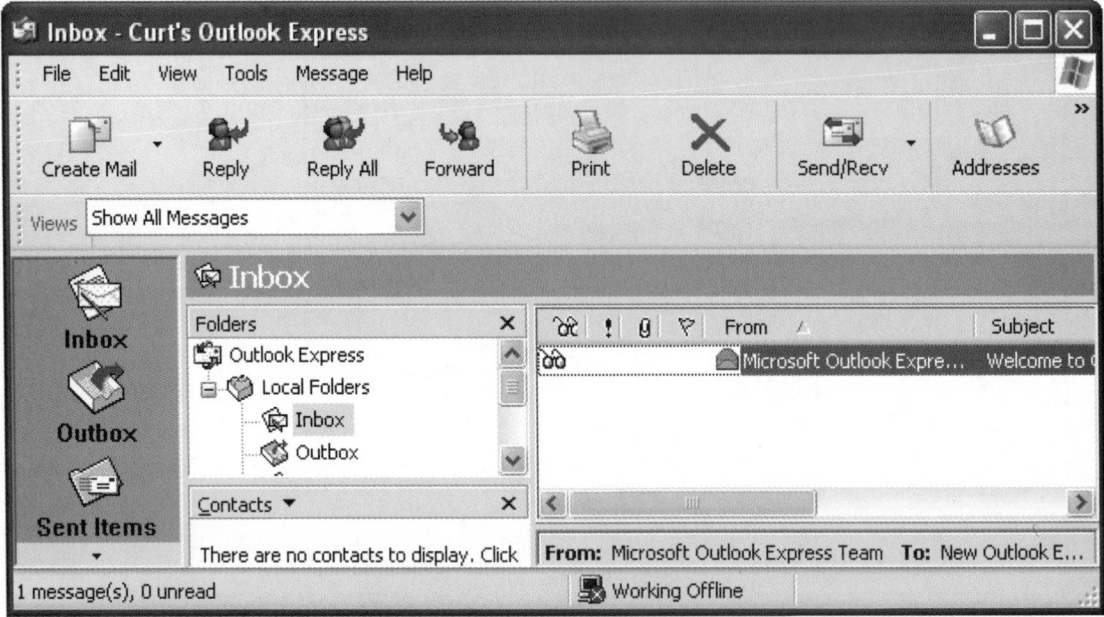

Figure 17-7: You can watch or ignore messages, which is helpful in newsgroups and with message threads.

Threads now function in mail, as well as in news, but the Watch/Ignore column is not turned on by default for message folders. You might want to use this if you save messages in a message folder over a period of time or if you have a very high volume of messages. To turn on the Watch/Ignore column, right-click a column header button at the top of a column and select Columns. In the Columns dialog box, mark the Watch/Ignore check box and click OK.

So that watched threads are highly visible, they are by default highlighted with red. To select a different color, choose Tools ⇨ Options, click the Read tab, and select the color you want from the Highlight Watched Messages with the Color drop-down list. (To turn off color highlighting, select Default from the drop-down list.) Not only will watched threads be highlighted in color, but folders containing unread watched messages will be highlighted in the Folders pane.

A big advantage of flags and watch/ignore icons is that you can sort by them. Just click the column header button (the flag or glasses icon) at the top of the column to bring the flagged or watched messages to the top of the list. While the author sets the priority of a message, the reader gets to flag it or mark it to be watched.

If you have chosen Hide Read Messages in the Views bar (or View ⇨ Current View ⇨ Hide Read Messages), you won't be able to see a message you have read even though you have flagged it or marked it to be watched. But if you have collapsed a thread you're watching so that you see only the first message, that message will appear to be unread as long as there is at least one unread message in the thread.

Depending on your settings, Outlook Express may still download headers for ignored threads, but you can choose not to view them by choosing Hide Read Or Ignored Messages in the Views bar. Outlook Express will download the body of an ignored message only if you select the message header while online.

Managing columns

You can choose which columns to display in the Message pane. To do this, right-click any column header button and click Columns (or choose View ⇨ Columns). In the Columns dialog box, mark the columns you want to see and clear those you don't. Use the Move Up button and the Move Down button to set the order in which columns will appear (or you can drag the column header buttons to position them). Each message folder can have different column settings.

For example, if you find the Flag and Watch/Ignore columns aren't useful and are just taking up space, you can turn them off. While you are still able to flag a message or mark a thread to watch or ignore, you won't see the icons in the Message pane and will be unable to sort by flag or by thread state.

TIP: If you have more than one incoming mail account, you might want to view the Account column. That way, you can easily see where a message came from without bothering with message rules. The Account column can also be very helpful in your Outbox.

Sending Web addresses

You can include Internet URLs in your messages. Outlook Express changes the address's font color and makes it clickable. If you click an address in a message, your Internet Explorer displays that Web page or other resource.

Your Desktop (and other folders) can also display clickable URLs. Instead of changing the font color, Windows designates these URLs as shortcuts and adds an icon to the URL's name.

Windows XP makes it easier to send URLs and shortcuts to URLs to your recipients. They can drag a URL's shortcut to their Desktop for easy access. There are a number of ways to do this.

You'll find a Mail button on the Explorer toolbar when you're viewing a Web site. Click this button and choose Send a Link to mail the URL of the current Web page along with its shortcut. The URL shortcut is sent as an attachment. If you want to send the whole HTML-formatted page instead of just the link to the page, choose Send Page.

If you are viewing a Web page in Explorer, you can right-click anywhere in the Address field and click Copy. Then in Outlook Express, click the New Mail or New Post button, right-click in the body of the message, and click Paste to place the URL in the message. The URL is clickable, but there is no URL shortcut added to the message.

If you want to send one of the URLs from your Favorites list, click the Start button, point to Favorites, navigate to the favorite, and drag and drop it into the body of your new message. The shortcut is added as an attachment to the message.

Viewing the message header

Outlook Express doesn't display much of the message header information in the preview pane or the separate message window. Most of this information is really used only by e-mail clients or newsgroup readers to correctly format the message, and it's not all that useful to us. Nonetheless, sometimes you need this information to help troubleshoot a problem or find out an e-mail address.

To see the complete message header, press Ctrl+F3, or right-click the message header in the message header pane, click Properties, and click the Details tab. If you click the Message Source button, a new window opens up and you can cut and paste text from the complete message.

Install on Demand

With older versions of Outlook Express, if someone sent you a message using a character set that you had not installed — Hebrew, for example — you saw what appeared to be gibberish with no easy way to find out how to fix it. Now, if you open a message that uses a language or other component you don't have, the Internet Explorer Install on Demand dialog box appears and offers to download the components you need.

To download and install the necessary component, click the Download button. Outlook Express initiates a dial-up connection if necessary, downloads the component from Microsoft, and installs it for you. If you don't want to download the component, just click Cancel.

Install on Demand applies not only to languages, but also to other components that you might need to see animation or hear sounds. You no longer need to worry about whether to install everything in advance, because you'll be able to get what you need easily whenever you need it.

Install on Demand should be enabled by default. If it is not, choose Tools ⇨ Options, click the Connection tab, and click the Change button. In the Internet Properties dialog box, click the Advanced tab, and mark Enable Install On Demand, as shown in Figure 17-8.

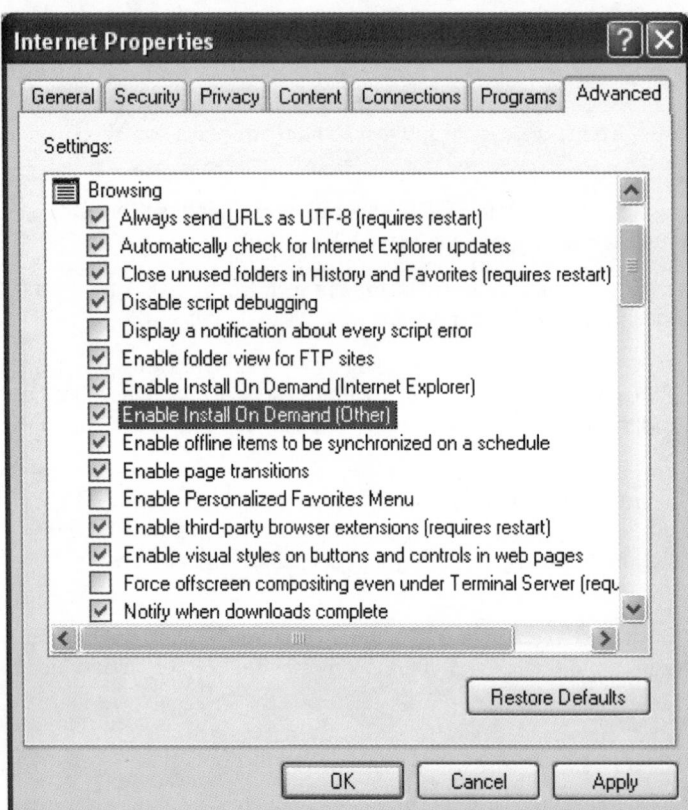

Figure 17-8: Install on Demand

Composing and Sending Messages

Outlook Express 6 offers more flexibility in how you compose and send your messages. Some features are more intuitive than others; here are some suggestions for getting the mail out.

Uuencode or MIME

A basic e-mail client allows you to send messages as plain text — that is, no characters beyond the first 128 (7-bit) ASCII: no underlining, italics, boldface, fonts, pictures, or attachments. Outlook Express, which is quite a bit more than a basic e-mail client, supports HTML formatting of the text in your message. It also lets you include pictures in your message and add attachments to it.

Because the Internet e-mail standard supports only 7-bit ASCII characters, formatted messages and attachments need to be encoded by the e-mail client into ASCII characters and decoded by the recipient's e-mail client when they arrive. Outlook Express supports the MIME and Uuencode encoding and decoding standards.

If you are sending e-mail messages to recipients who have powerful e-mail clients, then you want to select HTML formatting and MIME encoding. This allows you to format your messages to your heart's content.

> **TIP:** If you send messages to recipients with UNIX e-mail readers, to UNIX-based mailing lists or to news servers that don't support formatted messages (which includes most news servers), then you want to ignore MIME altogether and set encoding at Uuencode. (This will not encode the message text but will encode attachments with Uuencode.)

To change your encoding scheme, choose Tools ⇨ Options, click the Send tab, and then click the Settings button for the selected format, HTML or Plain Text. If you choose MIME in the HTML Settings or Plain Text Settings dialog box (the only option with HTML), you can select None, Quoted Printable, or Base 64 from a drop-down list. These options apply only to the text portion of your message and not to the attachments. The attachments are coded in MIME at Base 64. Although useful, these settings may pose some problems for users to whom you send e-mail, such as described in the following Tip and Secret.

> **TIP:** If you choose None, your message is not encoded at all, although any attachments will be encoded in MIME (Base 64). Your message text will be sent as unencoded 8-bit characters. This may cause a problem, because your message has a very slight chance of being forwarded through a machine that can't handle 8-bit characters. The advantage of choosing None is that even a recipient who doesn't have a MIME-capable e-mail client can easily read your text.

> **SECRET:** If you choose Quoted Printable and send your message to a recipient who can't handle MIME, he or she will find equals signs (=) at the end of the lines in your message. This is your clue to stop sending messages formatted with MIME to this recipient.

Outlook Express makes it easy to switch back and forth between sending formatted (HTML) and plain-text messages. You set the default in the Send tab of the Options dialog box. Then when you're composing a message, you can change the setting for just that message by choosing Format ⇨ Rich Text (HTML) or Plain Text in the New Message menu. This lets you set your default for HTML and then switch to plain text when sending to less capable recipients. (For more on HTML-formatted messages, see "Messages Formatted in HTML" later in this chapter.)

> **TIP:** You can also choose to send only plain text to a given recipient by marking the "Send E-mail Using Plain Text Only" check box in the Personal tab of the recipient's Properties dialog box in your Windows Address Book. This is really the best way to be sure that you don't send badly formatted or unreadable text to a mailing list or a recipient with an inadequate e-mail client.

Outlook Express automatically encodes and decodes attachments. It can't decode some types of encoded messages, and you may find that an attachment isn't decoded properly. If this is the case, you can use another program such as WinZip to decode the attachment.

One encoding method that Outlook Express doesn't handle very well is BinHex, a popular Mac standard. Outlook Express will decode some forms of BinHex but not all. You can see if a message or an attachment is encoded with BinHex by right-clicking it and selecting Properties and then Details. You'll need to save the message or attachment as a separate file and then decode it with a BinHex decoder. WinZip can handle BinHex.

You can find encoders and decoders at `ftp://ftp.andrew.cmu.edu/pub/mpack` for munpack (MIME decoding), `www.tucows.com` for Wincode (Uudecoding), and `www.aladdinsys.com` for StuffIt (BinHex).

Associating a message with an account

You can associate a new mail message with a specific account at the time that the message is composed. This is especially helpful if you have multiple users with different accounts on the same computer.

STEPS

Associating a message with an account

1. Open a New Message window by choosing Message ⇨ New Message.
2. Click the down arrow at the right end of the From field to display a list of your accounts.
3. Select the mail account you want to use when sending the message.

Using a draft

The Drafts folder is a place to keep messages that you're not yet ready to send. When you are composing a message and you choose File ⇨ Save, your unfinished message is automatically stored in the Drafts folder. If you close a New Message window without sending the message and click Yes when asked if you want to save it, the message will be stored in Drafts. To finish editing a message stored in the Drafts folder, double-click the message to open it. When you click the Send button, Outlook Express moves it from the Drafts folder to the Outbox.

Quoting in replies and forwards

When you reply to an e-mail message, it's helpful if you can distinguish the text you write from the message text you are replying to. In plain-text messages, the standard is to place a > symbol in front of each quoted line of text. To make this happen automatically, follow these steps.

STEPS

Automatic quoting in plain-text replies

1. Choose Tools ⇨ Options in the Outlook Express window and click the Send tab.
2. Make sure that the Include Message in Reply check box is marked. (This is the default.) If this option is deselected, your replies will be much harder to understand, because they will not include a copy of the original message.
3. On this same tab, click the Plain Text Settings button under Mail Sending Format. Make sure "Indent the original text with [ ] when replying or forwarding" is marked (see Figure 17-9). If you like, you can use the drop-down list to choose : or | as your quote character instead of >.

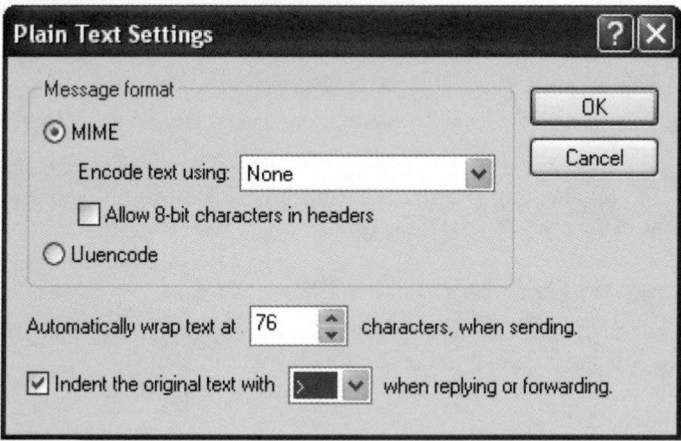

Figure 17-9: Use the Plain Text Settings to insert a quote character.

4. Click OK.

So far so good. But this kind of quoting works only if you are replying to a message sent using plain text. Messages sent using MIME/Quoted Printable (such as HTML-formatted messages) don't insert line endings, so there are no line beginnings for Outlook Express to mark with >. Instead, the text is formatted in paragraphs. Even if you tell Outlook Express to reply in plain text, it will still not place a > at the beginning of quoted lines if they weren't originally composed in plain text.

If you reply in HTML format, you can use the blockquote paragraph tag to mark paragraphs. However, this is not one of the paragraph styles available via the Paragraph Style toolbar button in the New Message window. To be able to use it without editing the HTML source, you must choose Tools ➪ Options and click the Send tab. Click the HTML Settings button under Mail Sending Format, and mark Indent Messages on Reply in the HTML Settings dialog box. Now your quoted HTML text will be indented with a vertical bar along its left side.

> **SECRET:** There is a downside to marking Indent Messages on Reply, however, if you like to intersperse replies with quoted text to simulate a conversation. If you insert your reply after a section of quoted text, you'll find the new text is also indented with the vertical bar. To get rid of the indent and the bar, first place your insertion point in the quoted text where you want to insert your reply text and press Enter. This inserts a line break. Then with your insertion point in the new paragraph, click the Paragraph Style toolbar button and click Normal. Even though the drop-down list shows that the current paragraph is already Normal, this will work. Your new text will be flush left and will not have a vertical bar.

Sending a message as a Web page

You can use Outlook Express to e-mail a Web page from the Internet without having to open your browser.

STEPS

Mailing a Web page from Outlook Express

1. In Outlook Express, choose Message ➪ New Message Using ➪ Web Page (or click the down arrow next to the New Message toolbar button and choose Web Page).

2. In the Send Web Page dialog box, type the address of a Web page and click OK. Outlook Express will initiate a dial-up connection if necessary. The address must start with *http*. Even if the Web page is available offline, you can't send it without actually going to it on the Internet.

3. A New Message window opens, displaying the Web page you have indicated. You can click in the page and insert additional text if you like. You can also do more extensive HTML editing by choosing View ⇨ Source Edit and then clicking the Source tab at the bottom of the page.

4. Address your message, add a subject, and click the Send toolbar button to send it to your Outbox.

You can send an HTML file that resides on your hard drive by opening it in Internet Explorer, saving it in archived Web page (.mht) format, and then sending the .mht file as an attachment. However, if you use this method the Web page will not appear in the body of your message.

Removing hyperlinks from HTML text

While composing a message, if you type a sequence of characters that looks something like an e-mail address or a URL, Outlook Express automatically makes it into a clickable hyperlink. Sometimes, however, what you've typed might not be a real link, or there may be some other reason why you'd rather not have a link associated with that particular text.

To remove a link from an HTML message, click anywhere in the link, and then choose Edit ⇨ Remove Hyperlink. The text remains in your message, but it is no longer highlighted and will not produce a clickable link when the message is sent. The Remove Hyperlink command works only with HTML-formatted messages; it's dim for plain-text messages, even though these messages can still contain links.

Breaking up large messages

You can tell Outlook Express to automatically break apart messages larger than a certain size. This is a courtesy to your recipient and may be necessary depending on your ISP. When Outlook Express receives mail files that have been broken apart, it will combine and decode them automatically. For newsgroup files you must do this by choosing Message ⇨ Combine and Decode.

STEPS

Breaking up large messages

1. In Outlook Express, choose Tools ⇨ Accounts. Highlight the name of the account you use to send large files and click the Properties button. In the Properties dialog box for that account, click the Advanced tab.

2. Under Sending, mark the Break Apart Messages Larger Than [ ] KB box. Enter a file size, or keep the default of 60K, and click OK. Then click Close.

3. Send the large file using the usual method. It will look normal in your Outbox. But when you do a Send and Receive, you will see that the message is being broken into two or more messages.

TIP: Outlook Express often has difficulty combining HTML files, so it's best to send files with big attachments as plain text in MIME/Quoted Printable in case they have to be broken up.

Messages Formatted in HTML

Outlook Express allows you to format your e-mail messages and newsgroup posts using HTML. Choose Tools ⇨ Options and click the Send tab. You'll find the option to set the default format for messages as HTML.

You can always override the default setting for the current newsgroup post or e-mail message. Just choose Format in the New Message window, and click Rich Text (HTML) or Plain Text. If you're using HTML, you get a formatting toolbar that lets you choose the font, font size, font color, and so on.

TIP: Lots of newsgroup and e-mail clients aren't able to display HTML-formatted text. If they can't, your correspondents will see the HTML tags embedded in the text of your messages — something they might not appreciate.

HTML-formatted messages are always sent as MIME-structured, and by default, Quoted Printable encoded messages. For them to display properly, your recipient has to have an e-mail client that can display HTML-formatted messages, and his or her Internet service provider has to have an e-mail server that correctly handles MIME.

If your recipient's e-mail client cannot read HTML but can read MIME documents, then he or she will receive a text version of your message and an attached HTML version that can be read by a browser.

Outlook Express's default setting is to reply to messages using the same format as the message. If you want to use your own settings instead, clear the Reply to Messages Using the Format in Which They Were Sent check box under Tools ⇨ Options ⇨ Send.

TIP: Outlook Express displays all messages using HTML. This is true even if you create a message in plain text, because Outlook Express uses an HTML display engine, so it has to add HTML tags to non-HTML-formatted messages to display them correctly.

You can see this by double-clicking a message header to open a separate message window and then pressing Ctrl+F2. A new window opens to display a plain-text version of the message with its HTML tags.

Outlook Express doesn't include these HTML tags when it sends a message that you have formatted as plain text. It just adds these tags on the fly to allow the message to be displayed correctly. You can see the actual content of the message by pressing Ctrl+F3 or by right-clicking the message header, clicking Properties, clicking the Details tab, and clicking the Message Source button.

Editing HTML messages

Outlook Express has a simple HTML-capable WYSIWYG editor built in. You can set the font, font style (boldface, italic, underline), font size, font color, and background color. You can format paragraphs as bullets or numbered lists and align them left, right, or center. You can insert a .gif picture or use one as a background. Microsoft provides a small selection of .gif files in the \Program Files\Common Files\Microsoft Shared\Stationery folder.

Microsoft also provides a more sophisticated HTML editor/generator called FrontPage 2002. You can edit the body of a message in FrontPage 2002 and insert the HTML text using the Insert ⇨ Text command from the File menu. Because Outlook Express uses the capabilities of Internet Explorer to display its messages (all of which it formats for display using HTML), you can create and receive all manner of multimedia messages. You can learn more about FrontPage 2002 at Microsoft's Web site: www.microsoft.com/frontpage.

Of course, you can send Web pages as attachments, but as long as your recipients have Outlook Express or a similar e-mail client, they can view the page as part of (or all of) the message (just paste it in). They won't have any need to open a separate browser window.

Stationery

The HTML tag BACKGROUND lets you create a stationery-like effect for your messages. You can configure Outlook Express to automatically start a new blank message with your chosen background color, background image, font, and margins. You can choose from among the existing stationery files, create new stationery, create stationery that is just a background color, or download new stationery from Microsoft.

You need to format your message with HTML to be able to use stationery (choose Tools ⇨ Options ⇨ Send, and mark the HTML option button under Mail Sending Format). To pick a default stationery type, choose Tools ⇨ Compose, mark the Mail or News check box under Stationery, and click the Select button. You get to preview the stationery before you select it. Once you have chosen a stationery type, clicking New Mail or New Post opens a New Message window with that stationery already included in the message.

If you want to create a message with something other than the default stationery, click the down arrow to the right of the New Mail or New Post button. You can pick which .htm file to use as stationery or choose no stationery at all.

Choose File ⇨ Save. Your message is saved in the Draft folder. (The Draft folder is used to store messages that you save with the File ⇨ Save command. The messages remain in this folder until you click Send.) Now choose Tools ⇨ Options ⇨ Send, and change the Mail Sending Format to Plain Text. On the same tab, clear the "Reply to messages in the format in which they were sent" check box. Highlight the message header in your Drafts folder in Outlook Express and click the Forward button on the toolbar. You'll see the associated .gif file in the Attach field of the New Message window that appears.

Converting the message to plain text make the attached .gif file apparent. Outlook Express doesn't show this as an attachment as long as you are formatting an HTML-formatted message.

Outlook Express creates stationery by using a very small .gif file and an .htm file that contains at least the BACKGROUND tag and maybe more. You can view the source code for the stationery files that Microsoft includes with Outlook Express by opening the .htm and .gif files in the \Program Files\Common Files\Microsoft Shared\Stationery folder. Check out the Chicken Soup .htm file as an example of a more complicated stationery file (see Figure 17-10).

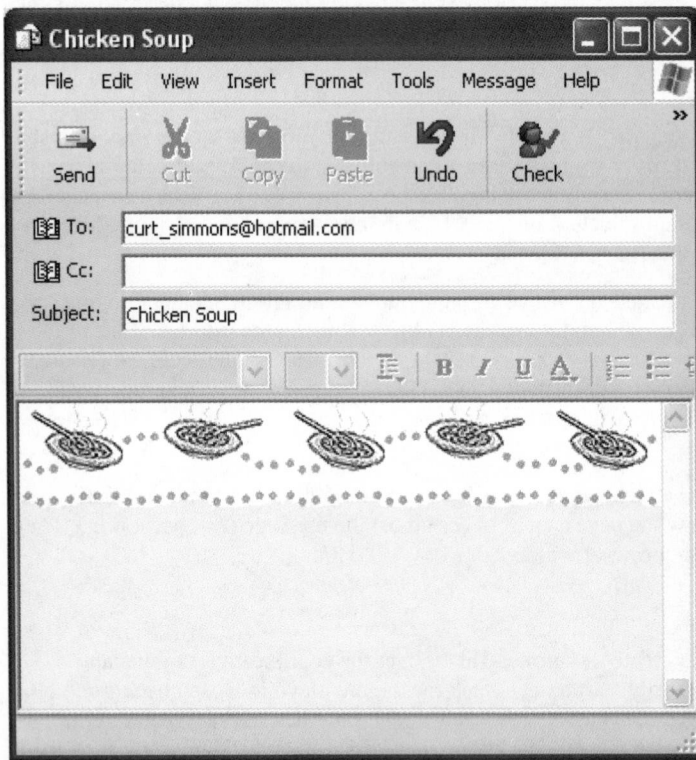

Figure 17-10: The Chicken Soup stationery

SECRET: Stationery files are basic `.gif` files found commonly on Web pages. Outlook Express includes the stationery's associated `.gif` file as an attachment when it sends out a message with stationery. You can verify this by first creating a new test message with stationery.

You can create your own stationery using copies of the `.htm` files and just editing or replacing the `.gif` files. You can also click the Create New button on the Compose tab (choose Tools ⇨ Options) to launch the Stationery Setup Wizard, which walks you through the creation of stationery. To keep your messages small, make sure that you use very small `.gif` files (under 500 bytes) that can be displayed as a repeated pattern on the recipient's computer.

TIP: You can capture stationery from an incoming message. Just double-click the message header and choose File ⇨ Save As Stationery. Despite what *Save As Stationery* sounds like, the whole message is not saved as stationery, just the stationery part of the message.

If you're familiar with HTML, you can make any changes you like in your stationery files, including changes to fonts. You should use a text editor to edit these files. If you reference a font in your stationery that isn't widely found on your recipients' computers, your message will be displayed with their default font (found on their computers in Outlook Express under Tools ⇨ Options ⇨ Read ⇨ Fonts).

Microsoft makes more stationery available at its Web site. Choose Tools ⇨ Options ⇨ Compose ⇨ Download More to see what is available.

Managing Attachments

Obviously, a user can send an attachment with an e-mail, and this attachment can be a picture, a document, a program, or just about any other file imaginable. E-mail attachments are important — I use them every day — but before getting into attachment management, there is one big warning I would like to send your way. E-mail attachments are notorious for harboring viruses. Because attachments can contain viruses, you should always use an antivirus program on your computer, such as Norton or McAfee. Also, avoid opening attachments from people you do not know. With that said, here's how to handle all those incoming e-mail attachments.

Saving attachments

To save an attachment to a message you have received, double-click the message header in the message header pane to display the message in a separate window. Then drag and drop the attachment icon from the Attach field into a folder or onto the Desktop. You can also right-click the attachment icon and choose Save As.

To save an attachment without opening a separate message window, click the message header, and then click the yellow paper clip icon in the upper-right corner of the preview pane (the Show Preview Pane Header check box must be marked in the View ⇨ Layout dialog box). A menu listing the names of the attachments in the message appears. Click the name of the attachment you want to open or save. You can then choose to open it or save it to a folder. If you instead choose Save Attachments from this menu, you can browse to a folder for saving more than one at a time. If, when you click attachments of a particular type, you find that they open automatically and you'd like the option of saving them instead, you need to edit the file type.

You can also just highlight the message header and choose File ⇨ Save Attachments.

You can send graphic files in `.gif` and `.jpg` format (as well as other formats) as attachments to Outlook Express messages. Outlook Express encodes the graphics in Uuencode or MIME format. After you receive a message with a `.gif` or `.jpg` attachment and it is decoded (Outlook Express does this automatically) you can read the file using the helper application with which it's associated. (To check what applications are associated with `.gif` and `.jpg` files, choose View ⇨ Folder Options in the Explorer, click File Types, and look through the Registered File Types list for these file types.)

Reading attachments without opening messages

Sometimes a message is nothing but attachments. For example, some mailing list digests arrive as an empty message with a bunch of text files attached. The easy way to deal with attachments is to use the big paper clip icon that appears at the right end of the preview pane header of the message. If this header isn't visible, choose View ⇨ Layout, and mark Show Preview Pane Header. (You must of course also have Show Preview Pane marked.) Click the paper clip to display a list of all the attachments.

Click an attachment in the list to open it. Alternatively, you can choose Save Attachments at the bottom of the list (or choose File ⇨ Save Attachments) to display the Save Attachments dialog box, and then save any or all of the attachments to disk.

Unfortunately, you can no longer save an attachment by dragging its little paper clip icon out of the Message pane. Now if you do that, you'll save a copy of the whole message.

Strange attachments

Occasionally you may receive attachments that you can't seem to view or open. They may have a `.dat` or `.doc` extension. Usually these are files that were saved in Rich Text Format (RTF), and it's likely that they were sent by someone using Windows Messaging or Outlook 9x. RTF is not an Internet standard and cannot be decoded using Outlook Express. Your only option is to ask your correspondent to resend the attachment as a text file.

On the other hand, Outlook Express can now read many attachments encoded using BinHex, a popular Macintosh format. This decoding is transparent; you shouldn't have to do anything special to read these files. If you do receive one that doesn't open, you can decode it using Wincode, available as shareware on the Internet from `www.jumbo.com`, `www.zdnet.com/downloads`, and many other shareware sites.

Saving messages without attachments

Some people keep copies of all the messages they send for their records. But attachments can take up a lot of hard disk space, especially since you have probably already saved the file somewhere else.

After sending a message, open it from your Sent Items folder, and then use File ⇨ Save As to save it as a `.txt` file. The attachment will be stripped out in the process. You can then delete the message from your Sent Items folder.

Message Helpers

There are lots of tools available online to help you get your message across. Here are a few you might want to check out.

Spelling-checkers

Outlook Express uses the Microsoft Office spelling checker. But what if you don't use Microsoft Office? AutoSpell for Microsoft Internet Products is shareware produced by CompuBridge. It also makes spelling checkers for Microsoft Office and WordPad, and it makes AutoSpell for other e-mail products such as Netscape and Pegasus. A main benefit of AutoSpell is spelling checking in multiple languages, such as Danish, Dutch, French, German, Italian, and Spanish, as well as a couple flavors of English. Also, CompuBridge is promising to support the checking of spelling in the Subject line of Outlook Express messages — a helpful touch.

You can download free evaluation copies of AutoSpell for Microsoft Internet Products from `www.spellchecker.com`.

Talking E-mail

Now you can have a pleasant voice announce the arrival of your e-mail and read your messages to you (up to 30 lines each). Use the Talking E-mail program and choose a friendly, animated cartoon character to do the talking. The registered version of Talking E-mail gives you a choice of characters and voices.

Developed by 4Developers, Talking E-mail is shareware that uses Microsoft's advanced text-to-speech technology. It works with your standard mail account, and leaves messages on your mail server so you can download them later with Outlook Express. No special hardware other than a sound card is required. You can download Talking E-mail at `www.4developers.com/talkmail`.

Resolving Problems in Outlook Express

Occasionally, you may experience some problems with Outlook Express, primarily due to corruption. You may be able to fix these problems with database files and the Registry. The following sections explore these issues.

When Outlook Express won't open

If something in your message store becomes corrupted, you may not be able to open Outlook Express at all. You may see an error message such as:

```
Outlook Express could not be started. The application was unable to open the
Outlook Express Message Store. Your computer may be out of memory or its disk is
full. (0x800C0069, 8).
```

SECRET: This error message means that Outlook Express could not start because the `Msoe.dll` file could not be loaded into memory (probably because it could not be found). Despite the message's wording, lack of memory or a full disk are not probable causes of this problem. A more likely cause is that Outlook Express is not installed correctly. This is a side effect of having everything in one big message store. Still, it's possible to recover.

STEPS

Recovering when Outlook Express won't open

1. In Explorer, create a new temporary folder. Then navigate to the folder that contains your Outlook Express message store. The default location is `\Documents and Settings\username\Application Data\Identities\{your identity number}\Microsoft\Outlook Express`.

2. Move the contents of the message store folder (`.dbx` files) to the temporary folder you created in Step 1. If you have a `.wab` file in the message store folder, leave that where it is.

3. Now open Outlook Express. When it doesn't find your message store files, it will rebuild your Inbox and other system folders. Your mail accounts, news accounts, and other settings should be intact.

4. Choose File ⇨ Import ⇨ Messages to launch the Outlook Express Import Wizard. Choose Microsoft Outlook Express in the first wizard dialog box and click Next.

5. The Import From OE Wizard appears. Click Import Mail from an OE Store directory and click OK.

6. In the Location of Messages dialog box, click the Browse button and navigate to the temporary folder where you moved your `.dbx` files. Select all folders and click Next. After your message store is re-imported into Outlook Express, click Finish.

You may lose the hierarchical structure of your message folders during this process. You will certainly lose all your newsgroup subscriptions and their contents. But at least you will be back in business.

Transferring message rules to a new computer

Message rules, formerly called Inbox Assistant, are a part of Outlook Express designed to help you filter and organize your mail and news, based on rules you set up in advance. To find this feature choose Tools ⇨ Message Rules, then choose either Mail, News, or the Blocked Senders List. The rules that you define are stored in your Registry. You can export the rules branches of the Registry into a text file, which you can then import into the Registry of another computer.

You'll find the Message rules at HKEY_CURRENT_USER\Identities\{*your identity number*}\Software\Microsoft\Outlook Express\5.0\Rules. This branch contains subbranches for View filters, Mail, News, and Junk Mail, so you can select the Rules branch itself to export them all or select only one of these folders. These Registry entries contain values only if you have created some rules.

Notice that each rule is numbered, starting with Rule0000 (if you haven't deleted your first rule previously). You'll want to edit these numbers in the exported text file if they conflict with rule numbers of rules already on the target computer.

First export each of these branches by using RegEdit and choosing Registry ⇨ Export Registry File. Then edit the rule numbers, and import the files into the Registry of the target computer.

Corrupted passwords

You may you find that you are repeatedly asked to enter your account name and password when connecting to a news or mail server. Outlook Express doesn't keep its passwords (which are different than your Internet service provider logon password) in the .pwl file; it keeps them in your Registry. These passwords are encrypted in RSA RC4 format.

The first step in fixing the Outlook Express password problem is to create a new news or mail account and then check to see if Outlook Express remembers the password for it.

STEPS

Repairing Outlook Express password problems

1. Choose Tools ⇨ Accounts ⇨ Add ⇨ News or Mail to invoke the Internet Connection Wizard. Follow the steps in the wizard to create a new account.

2. Check to see if the new password was saved correctly by choosing Tools ⇨ Accounts, highlighting the account name, clicking the Properties button, and clicking the Server tab. Check if there are asterisks in the Password field. If the field is blank, Outlook Express isn't remembering the password to the server.

3. If your Password field is blank, open a DOS window by choosing Start ⇨ Run and typing **command**. Press Enter. At the DOS prompt, type **cd \Windows\System** and press Enter to change directories to your \Windows\System folder.

4. Type **pstores -install** and press Enter. Type **exit** and press Enter to return to Windows.

5. Enter a new password in one of your mail or news accounts. Click the Connect button in Outlook Express to see if you can successfully connect to that server without being asked for your password.

Using Identities

In Outlook Express you can store your personal information — your *identity* — to make using e-mail far easier. The following sections show you how to use identities in Outlook Express.

Signatures

The Signatures tab of the Tools ➪ Options dialog box lets you create several signatures for different uses (see Figure 17-11). You can create signatures for specific mail and news accounts and set up a separate set of signatures for each identity.

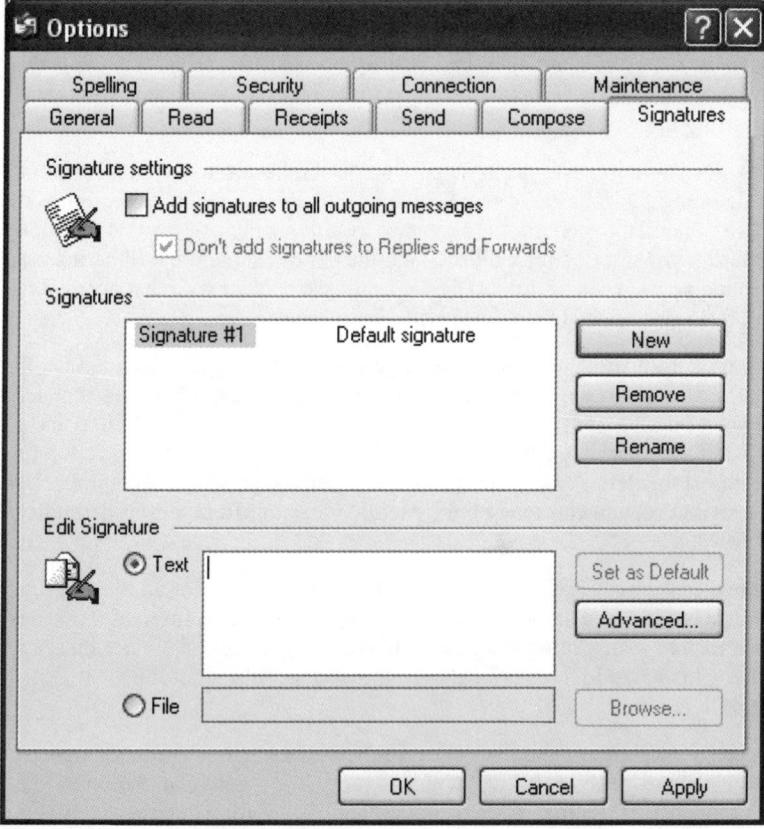

Figure 17-11: The new Signatures tab lets you create and manage multiple signatures.

STEPS

Creating a new signature

1. Choose Tools ➪ Options and click the Signatures tab.

2. In the Signatures area, click the New button. The words *Signature #1* appear in the Signatures list, and your insertion point jumps to the Edit Signature box. You can type the text for your signature in the box, or click the File option button and type or browse to a file that contains your signature. Your signature can be a text file, an HTML file, or an animated .gif file. However, there is a 4K size limit on signature files, so it's best to keep your ego in check.

3. To give your signature a short name so that you'll remember which one it is, click the signature in the Signatures list. Now click the Rename button, type the new name, and press Enter.

4. To set a signature as your default, select it in the Signatures list and then click the Set as Default button next to the Edit Signature box.

5. If you want to associate your signature with an Outlook Express account, select it and click the Advanced button. In the Advanced Signature Settings dialog box, select the account(s) and click OK. You can associate only one signature with a particular account.

6. To automatically insert your signature in all messages, mark the Add signatures to all outgoing messages check box at the top of the Signatures tab. If you prefer to insert your signature at the time you compose a message, clear this check box. Click OK to close the Options dialog box.

To insert a signature in a message as you're composing it, make sure your insertion point is in the text area of the message (not the header), choose Insert ⇨ Signature, and click the one you want. To replace a signature, highlight it before inserting the new one.

If you marked Add signatures to all outgoing messages in Step 6, and if you have multiple mail accounts going into the same Inbox, the signature for your default mail account is the default. The exception is that if you reply to a message sent to a nondefault account, the signature inserted is the one for that account. If you have not associated a signature with your default mail account, the default signature will be inserted. If you are sending a message from a news or IMAP folder, the signature associated with that account is inserted, or the default signature is used if none is associated with that account.

You can add a Signature button to the toolbar of your New Message window (but not to the main Outlook Express toolbar). To do this, start a new message, right-click an empty spot on the toolbar, and choose Customize. In the Customize Toolbar dialog box, double-click the Insert Signature toolbar button and then click Close. You'll need to do this separately for mail and news. After you've added this button to your toolbar, you can click it to insert the default signature (as described in the previous paragraph). If you have created more than one signature, you can select the signature you want from a drop-down list attached to the button.

If you have set up Outlook Express to insert a signature automatically, it will do this for all messages and all accounts, both mail and news. What if you want to sign only newsgroup postings, not mail messages? You can't set up an empty signature and assign it to an account. But you can set up a signature that consists of nothing but one space. This will add a blank line to your message, so it's not the ideal solution, but you might be able to live with it.

In keeping with a generally accepted standard on many newsgroups, Outlook Express precedes signatures in newsgroup messages with two hyphens on a line above, with an empty line above that. You don't need to add the hyphens or the line; Outlook Express inserts them automatically. So, for example, a signature for a news account might look like this:

```
--
Curt
```

This is not the case with signatures in mail messages, however. No hyphens, no extra line. If you want them, you'll have to create a different signature for use in mail messages and put them into that signature yourself.

Using identities

Identities make it a lot easier for several people to use the same computer to get their mail and read their favorite newsgroups. Unlike user accounts or profiles, which affect all of your Windows XP settings, identities affect only Outlook Express. You can easily add or remove identities at any time. Each identity has its own accounts, newsgroup subscriptions and maintenance, signatures, and settings. You have to set up all of these items separately for each identity. When you first install Outlook Express, you have only one identity, called Main Identity, and it is set as the default.

Because it's easy to switch among different identities, you may find it convenient to use multiple identities for yourself. For example, you might use your laptop on a local area network at the office and then take it home to follow your favorite hobby newsgroups on a dial-up account. Or you might have one identity with a password and one without. Maintaining a different identity for each situation makes it easy to globally switch all of the settings that change with each environment.

STEPS

Adding a new identity

1. In the Outlook Express window, choose File ⇨ Identities ⇨ Add New Identity.

2. In the Type Your Name field of the New Identity dialog box, type a name for your identity (different from all other identity names). Click OK, and click Yes in the Identity Added dialog box to switch to your new identity. Outlook Express will close, and after a few seconds it will reopen along with the Internet Connection Wizard.

3. After you have finished or canceled the wizards, Outlook Express closes and reopens at the Welcome screen, with the name of your new identity displayed at the right end of the Folder bar. Choose File ⇨ Identities ⇨ Manage Identities to display the Manage Identities dialog box, as shown in Figure 17-12. If you want to make your new identity the default, highlight it in the Identities Names list and click the Use this identity when starting a program check box.

Figure 17-12: Manage Identities dialog box

4. To always start Outlook Express in your new identity (regardless of whether it is the default), select it in the Use this identity when starting a program list. If you want to be prompted for an identity when you open Outlook Express, choose Ask Me.

5. To add password protection for this identity, click the Properties button, and mark the Ask Me for a Password When I Start check box in the Properties dialog box. Type your password (twice) in the Enter Password dialog box, click OK twice, and click Close in the Manage Identities dialog box.

Adding password protection to your identity is a simple way to protect your e-mail messages and newsgroups from the prying eyes of your coworkers or family members. It does not protect anything on your system outside of Outlook Express, and it offers only a basic level of security — a truly malicious, computer-savvy person could most likely get around it. For more robust security, you'll need a more "corporate" program such as Outlook 2002 (and likely a secure mail server such as Exchange Server).

You are prompted for your password only when you switch identities or log off your current identity before closing Outlook Express. To log off your identity, choose File ⇨ Identities ⇨ Logoff *YourIdentityName*. The next time you open Outlook Express, you will have to enter your password to use this identity.

As you go about your business under this new identity, you will quickly notice that all settings are set to the default, *not* to what you had for your original identity. For example, you'll need to create new signatures for your new identity, you'll need to set up the toolbars and panes the way you like them, and you'll need to set up all new newsgroup accounts. In essence, it's as though you had just installed a new copy of Outlook Express.

Importing messages from another identity

It may seem odd to import messages from one identity to another, because one of the reasons to use identities is to keep one set of messages separate from another. But maybe you've just set up a new identity, and previously your messages were all mixed up with someone else's in the same Inbox. You can move your messages to a different mail folder and then import only that folder from the other identity.

To import messages from another identity, choose File ⇨ Import ⇨ Messages, select Microsoft Outlook Express in the Select Program list, and click Next. Mark the Import Mail from an OE Identity option, select the identity from which you want to import messages (*not* your current identity), and click OK. You will see the message store location for the identity you have chosen; click Next if it is correct. In the Select Folders dialog box, mark the Selected Folders option button and highlight the folder(s) that contain the messages you want to import. Click Next and then click Finish. Your imported folders should now appear in the Folders pane. These folders and messages have not been moved from the other identity, only copied.

Working with Newsgroups

Keeping up with newsgroup messages can be very easy if you let Outlook Express do most of the work for you. The following sections show you how.

Reading news with Outlook Express

Highlight a news server account in your Folder List pane or Outlook bar, and Outlook Express turns into a newsgroup reader. Notice the various changes on your toolbar and in your Tools menu. Outlook Express uses the term *synchronize* to refer to downloading a newsgroup. It's true; you are synchronizing the header list on your computer to the one on the newsgroup server. But all those folks who have wasted time looking for the "download" command are wondering if the change was really necessary. To avoid confusion, though, I'll stick with Microsoft's terminology.

You determine what synchronization entails for each newsgroup in the Synchronization pane for the newsgroup's news server. Highlight the server in the Folders pane or the Folders list to display its Synchronization pane. In the Synchronization pane, highlight a newsgroup or use the Ctrl and Shift keys to highlight several at once and then click the Settings button and select the desired option from the menu that appears. You can change the synchronization settings for a single newsgroup by right-clicking it in the Folders pane or the Folders list and choosing Synchronization Settings. This brings up the same menu as the one that's displayed when you click the Settings button in the Synchronization pane.

Here is a description of the commands in the Settings menu:

♦ **All Messages** — Outlook Express first downloads all of the headers for this newsgroup that aren't already downloaded and then downloads all of those messages. This can take quite a while if there are thousands of messages (often the case).

♦ **New Messages Only** — Outlook Express retrieves the headers and messages for a predetermined number of the newest messages.

♦ **Headers Only** — Outlook Express downloads only the headers. You can then mark the headers that look interesting (right-click the message header and choose either Download message later or Download conversation later — or click in the Mark for offline column if you have it displayed) and download only those messages the next time you synchronize (this will automatically be added to the tasks to be carried out for sending and receiving). A blue arrow appears next to the message in the Mark for offline column if you have this column displayed.

♦ **Don't Synchronize** — Outlook Express skips this newsgroup when it synchronizes the others. (You can also clear the newsgroup's check box in the Synchronization pane.)

To synchronize all of your newsgroups on all news servers, choose Tools ⇨ Synchronize All. This action performs sending and receiving operations for your e-mail at the same time. You'll see all of the tasks listed in the Outlook Express dialog box. Although you can stop the whole process by clicking the Stop button, there's no way to skip a task and continue with the others once the process begins. Put a Synchronize All button on your news toolbar if you use this command a lot.

You can synchronize a single newsgroup or a single news server (which can include numerous newsgroups). To do this, you highlight the newsgroup or account in the Folders pane and then choose Tools ⇨ Synchronize Newsgroup if you've highlighted a newsgroup, or Tools ⇨ Synchronize Account if you've highlighted a server.

Moving around in a newsgroup

When you go to a newsgroup and you're in online mode, Outlook Express automatically tries to download headers. If you don't have a connection, you will be prompted to connect. Select a header, and the message will be downloaded. If you like, you can read the whole newsgroup this way without ever synchronizing.

When you click a newsgroup in the Folders pane or the Outlook bar, Outlook Express takes you to the first unread message. To see the next unread message, conversation, or folder, choose View ⇨ Next and select from the menu. Because this is a bit cumbersome to do constantly, you may want to add a button to your news toolbar for one or all of these commands. Or, just use the keyboard shortcuts shown in the menu: Ctrl+U for the next unread message, Ctrl+Shift+U for the next unread conversation, and Ctrl+J for the next unread folder.

When you reach the bottom of the Message pane, the Next Unread Message command cycles the focus back to the top if there are still unread messages in this newsgroup. If you have read all of the messages and click the Next Unread Message button, you are prompted to go to the next news folder with unread messages.

Working with Message Rules

You can create your own rules for handling messages in Outlook Express. When you do, Outlook Express will apply those rules whenever you receive new messages.

Setting up message rules

The user interface for editing mail message rules is now simpler and more explicit, compared with previous versions of Outlook Express, and you now have a similar dialog box for creating news message rules. If you set up Inbox Assistant rules in an earlier version of Outlook Express, they will be preserved as mail rules and displayed in the Mail Rules tab of the Message Rules dialog box (choose Tools ⇨ Message Rules ⇨ Mail), as shown in Figure 17-13.

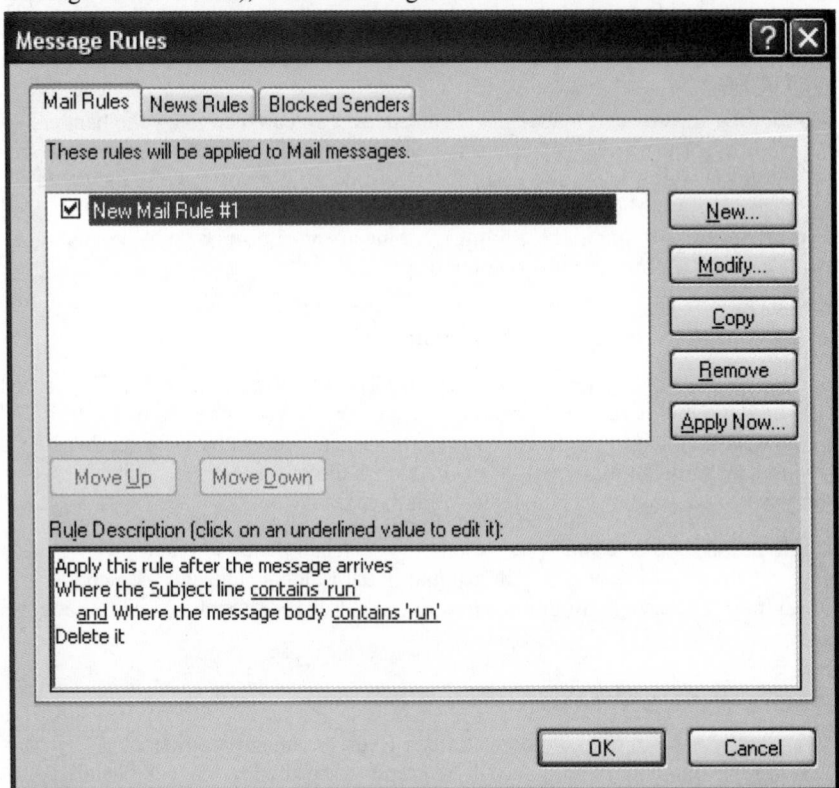

Figure 17-13: The Mail Rules tab of the Message Rules dialog box

To define a new rule that applies to incoming mail messages, use these steps.

STEPS

Designing a new mail rule

1. In Outlook Express, choose Tools ⇨ Message Rules ⇨ Mail. The Mail Rules tab of the Message Rules dialog box appears. Click the New button to open the New Mail Rule dialog box.

2. In the Conditions area, select one or more conditions that will cause this rule to be applied to a message. For example, mark Where the To line contains people if this rule is based on the contents of the To line. Don't worry yet about what the actual content will be (you'll specify it in Step 4). As you select conditions, they appear in the Rule Description area.

3. In the Actions area, mark one or more actions that will be applied to messages that meet the conditions of this rule. For example, you might want the message moved to a specific Outlook Express folder or forwarded to a different address. You can mark more than one action here — both Move it to the specified folder and Forward it to people, for example.

4. In the Rule Description area, you define the specifics. Click each piece of highlighted text to define what it will mean. For example, click the word *people* to enter one or more e-mail addresses in the Select People dialog box. For a folder, click the word *specified,* and you'll see a Move dialog box with a folder tree. Click the phrase *contains specific words* to list one or more keywords in the Type Specific Words dialog box.

5. The Select People dialog box and the Type Specific Words dialog box contain an Options button. Clicking this button displays the Rule Condition Options dialog box, in which you can further refine your selection. You can change your condition in two important ways. The first pair of option buttons lets you select by *exclusion* rather than by *inclusion* — in other words, you can set the rule to act on all messages that do *not* contain the keywords or addresses you have indicated. (The default is inclusion.) The second pair of option buttons (active if you have entered more than one address or keyword) lets you change the OR operator to AND — so that a message must contain all of the keywords or addresses you have indicated in order for the condition to be met. (The default is OR.) Any changes you make in the Rule Condition Options dialog box will affect only that one condition. You don't need to bother with the Options button if you want to use the default settings.

6. If you selected more than one condition in Step 2, a highlighted *and* will connect each condition in the Rule Description area. Click it, and the And/Or dialog box appears, giving you a choice between having messages match *all* of the criteria (AND) or *any* of the criteria (OR). If you don't set up a definition for each highlighted word in the Rule Description area, you will see a warning and the undefined phrases will be highlighted in red.

7. Enter a descriptive name for your rule in the Name field at the bottom of the New Mail Rule dialog box. When you finish defining your rule, click OK. Your new rule appears in the Mail Rules tab. Highlight it and use the Move Up and Move Down buttons to put it in the correct spot. (I address the reasons why rule order matters immediately after these steps and later in this chapter.)

8. If you have messages in your Inbox and you want to apply your new rule to them, click the Apply Now button to open the Apply Mail Rules Now dialog box. Select your new rule and click the Apply Now button, wait for the filter to work, and then click Close. Click OK. You can also use the Apply Mail Rules Now dialog box to apply a rule to a folder other than the Inbox. (In fact, this is the only way you can apply a rule to a folder other than the Inbox.) The settings you apply here are used on a one-time-only basis and do not become part of the rule definition. Outlook Express carries out message rules in the sequence they are listed in the Message Rules dialog box. Since the sequence is run each time, you may see slight performance gains by having the most common rule placed at the top of the list. Giving each of your rules a meaningful name helps you keep them in the correct order.

TIP: You can temporarily disable a rule without deleting it by clearing it in the Message Rules dialog box. Then mark it when you want to enable it again. This can be especially helpful in troubleshooting, when you think one rule might be affecting the rules below it.

To set up rules that apply to newsgroups, choose Tools ⇨ Message Rules ⇨ News. The news rules work in the same way as the mail rules, but you choose from a slightly different set of conditions and actions, as shown in Figure 17-14. For example, you might want to set up a news rule to flag messages from a certain newsgroup member.

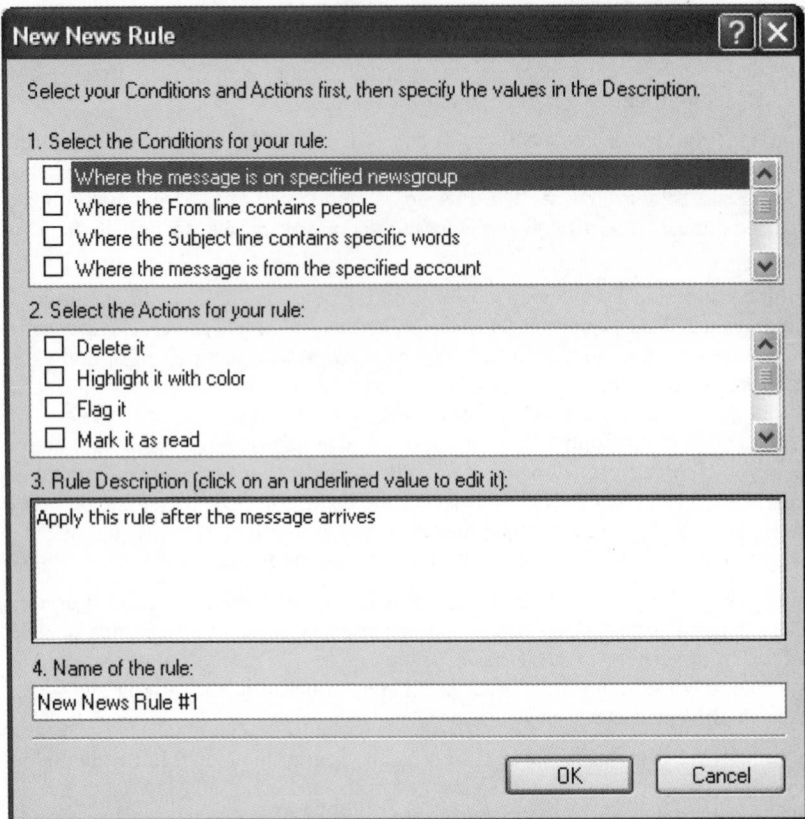

Figure 17-14: Rule conditions and actions

Creating a rule from a message

The easy way to create a new rule with a condition based on the From line is by using a message as an example. This works with both mail and news messages. Simply select the message header and choose Message ⇨ Create Rule from Message.

The New Mail Rule (or New News Rule) dialog box appears with the Where the From line contains condition set to the address of the person who sent the message. Although you may have different criteria in mind, more often than not this at least gives you a helpful head start. Then follow Steps 2 through 8 in the "Setting up message rules" section earlier in this chapter to finish your rule.

Filtering spam

One of the most popular uses for message rules is to filter out unsolicited mail. Because new spam techniques are being invented every day, this is never going to be 100 percent effective. But many people have reasonable success using the principle that most of the unsolicited e-mail you receive has something other than your own address in the To or Cc line.

SECRET: To the delight of many users, the regular message rules now allow for exclusionary searching, which lets you leave the "good" mail in your Inbox where it belongs. You can set the action to send the unwanted mail to a junk mail folder you've created in Local Folders, where it's easy to delete permanently.

To define such an additional rule, follow these steps.

STEPS

Filtering junk mail to a specified folder

1. Choose Tools ⇨ Message Rules and click New.

2. In the Conditions area of the New Mail Rule dialog box, mark Where the To or Cc line contains people.

3. In the Actions area, mark Move it to the specified folder.

4. In the Description area, click the highlighted phrase *contains people*.

5. In the Select People dialog box, enter your own address (or addresses if you have more than one) and click Add, and then click the Options button.

6. In the Rule Condition Options dialog box, mark the Message does not contain the people below option button, and then click OK to return to the Select People dialog box. Click OK. Also in the Description area, click the highlighted word *specified*. In the Move dialog box, highlight the folder where you want to stash junk mail, and click OK.

7. Give your new rule a name, and click OK.

Blocking senders

You don't have to set up a rule just to avoid mail from a specific address. Instead, you can use the Blocked Senders tab of the Message Rules dialog box. The Blocked Senders tab works on both mail and news, so if someone from a newsgroup starts sending you abusive personal mail, you can more or less avoid seeing any of it.

You still can't avoid downloading mail messages or news headers from these addresses. But the mail messages will be moved automatically to your Deleted Items folder, and news messages will be marked as read. To completely avoid seeing blocked mail messages, you should mark Empty messages from the Deleted Items folder on exit in the Maintenance tab of the Tools ⇨ Options dialog box. To avoid seeing headers for blocked news messages, set your current view to Hide read or ignored messages. If you're having a real problem with mail, you might prefer to use a mail rule with the action "Delete it from server" to delete messages from that address. You can't delete a message from a news server, however; you can only tell Outlook Express to ignore it.

Setting up automatic reply rules

You can set up a rule to automatically reply to messages that meet certain criteria. For example, if people send you messages with a certain subject or send messages to a certain address, you can send them an automatic prewritten message or file in response. This is a great way to distribute a Frequently Asked Questions document, a current price list, or your résumé.

STEPS

Setting up an automatic reply rule

1. In Outlook Express, choose Tools ⇨ Message Rules ⇨ Mail. The Mail Rules tab of the Message Rules dialog box appears. Click the New button to open the New Mail Rule dialog box.

2. In the Conditions area, mark Where the Subject line contains specific words.

3. In the Actions area, mark both Reply with message, and Move it to the specified folder (or mark Delete it if you don't want to keep the incoming messages).

4. In the Rule Description area, click the underlined text *contains specific words*. In the Type Specific Words dialog box that appears, type the text that people should put in the subject line of their messages to receive your reply. It doesn't matter whether you use capital letters. Click Add and then click OK.

5. In the same area, click the underlined word *specified*. If you did not mark the action Move it to the specified folder in Step 3, this text won't appear. If that's the case, go on to Step 6. In the Move dialog box that appears, select the mail folder that will be the parent of your new folder, and click New Folder. In the New Folder dialog box, type a name for the mail folder — for example, **Resume Requests**. Click OK and click OK again to close the Move dialog box.

6. Also in the Rule Description area, click the underlined word *message*. The Open dialog box appears to let you browse to the file that you want people to receive as your reply. Double-click to select the file you want to use. You can send news, mail, HTML, or ASCII text files. If you want the file to appear in the body of the reply, choose text or HTML. If you want it to appear as an attachment, choose news or e-mail. Select your file, and click Open.

7. Type a name for your rule in the Name field. When you finish defining your rule, click OK. If you have forgotten to define any values in Steps 4, 5, and 6, the New Mail Rule dialog box stays open, and Outlook Express displays a message box telling you that some information is missing or incorrect and asking you to correct the highlighted items. Click OK. A similar message appears at the top of the Rule Description area, and the problem is highlighted in red. After you enter the information, click OK again, and you'll be back at the Message Rules dialog box.

8. Your new rule appears in the Mail Rules tab. Highlight it and use the Move Up and Move Down buttons to put it in the correct spot in the list. You will probably want to put your automatic reply rules at or near the top of the list, where the other rules can't affect them.

9. If you have messages in your Inbox and you want to apply your new rule to them, click the Apply Now button. In the Apply Mail Rules Now dialog box, select your new rule, click the Apply Now button, and click Close. Click OK.

Now when a message comes in with the word you have specified in its Subject line, a reply message will be created automatically and sent to your Outbox, where it will wait for the Send and Receive command to be issued.

Working with Windows Address Books

The Windows Address Book is a powerful tool that you can use as a part of Outlook Express, but it also stands on its own as an independent application. Address Book enables you to record information about contacts and manipulate that information as needed. The following sections point out the tasks you can do with Address Book.

Merging Windows Address Books

Because you can import and export data from your Windows Address Book, you can merge data from one or more address books into an existing (or new) address book. To merge a Windows Address Book from another computer, take the following steps:

STEPS

Merging a Windows Address Book from another computer

1. Open the address book on one computer, choose File ⇨ Export ⇨ Address Book, select Text File (Comma Separated Values), and click the Export button. In the CSV Export Wizard, set the target file extension as `.csv` and mark every field if you want to export everything in the address book. Then click Finish.

2. Copy the file to a folder holding temporary files on the target computer.

3. Open the address book on the target computer. Choose File ⇨ Import ⇨ Address Book, select Text File (Comma Separated Values), and click the Import button. In the CSV Import Wizard, browse for the exported filename. You can choose which fields to import and where they go. Click Finish.

4. You will be notified of any duplicate names as they are about to be imported, and you will get to choose whether to overwrite the existing names. If you choose not to overwrite, you will end up with multiple entries for the same name. You'll need to go back and remove the redundant entries manually.

> **TIP:** You can also create a new blank Windows Address Book and merge names from other address books into it using these steps. To create a new blank Windows Address Book, choose Start ⇨ Run. Type **wab /New**. Enter the path and filename for the new blank address book.

Adding new entries to your address book

It's easy to add addresses to your Windows Address Book from messages you've received. Just right-click a message in the Message pane and choose Add Sender to Address Book. You can also right-click an address in the body of a message (or in the Preview pane), or in the header of an open message window, and choose Add to Address Book.

> **SECRET:** In the toolbar of an open mail or news message, choose Tools ⇨ Add to Address Book. In the submenu that appears, choose Sender, or Everyone on To List or select individual addressees. The Everyone on To List option is an easy way to capture a whole group of addresses at once. For example, if you get a message that's been circulated to everyone working on a certain project, you can add them all with one command. Unfortunately you can't specify a folder or a group, so if you want to keep the addresses together, you'll have to go into the address book, hunt each address down individually, and drag it into a group or folder.

If you get mail from someone new, you can automatically add him or her to your address book when you send a reply. In Outlook Express, choose Tools ⇨ Options, click the Send tab, and mark "Automatically put people I reply to in my Address Book." If you don't reply to a message, the new address will not be added unless you specifically add it.

The only drawback to using this option is that if you have already entered this person with a slightly different name (Bob instead of Robert, for example), Outlook Express will create a second entry for the new name. If your correspondent has not bothered to enter a "friendly name" in his or her account setup, you will see an e-mail address instead of a name in your address book. You are pretty much forced to live with the name the way your correspondent has it set up or have a lot of duplicates in your address book.

The Nickname field almost gets around this. The Nickname field is shown in Figure 17-15. If you give someone a nickname for which the first few letters are unique in your address book, you can type those letters in the To field, and Outlook Express will enter the e-mail address. But if another entry starts with those letters, you can type the whole nickname, and it will still not insert the person's address. So, for example, in our address book the nickname Goofy works fine as an alias for a contact whose first name is Robert, but Bobby does not work because we already have a couple of other names starting with Bob.

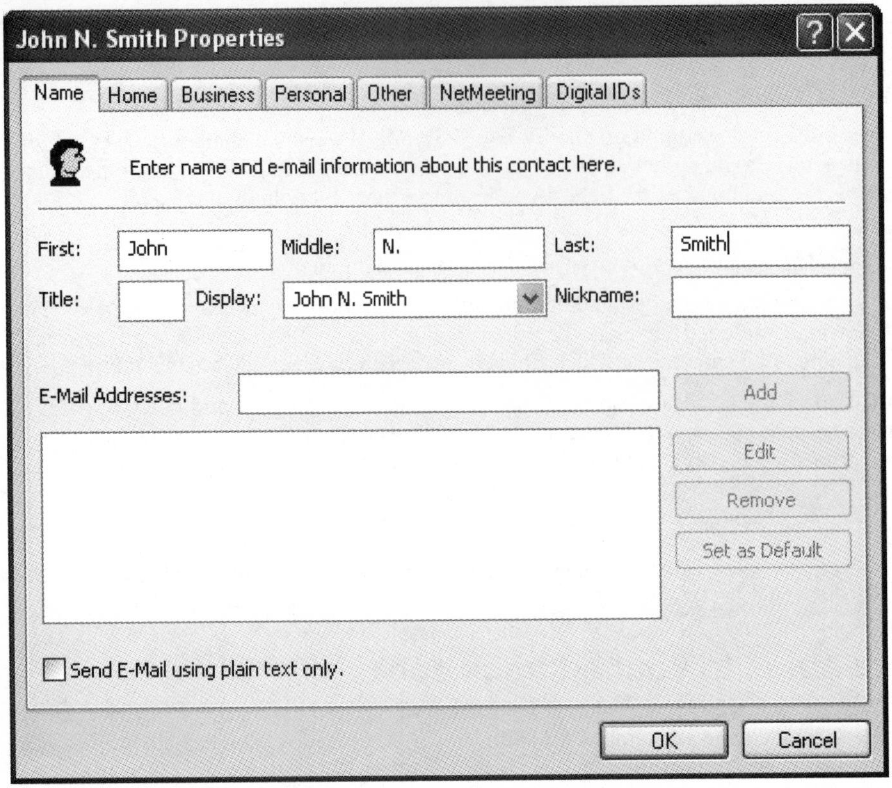

Figure 17-15: You can add a nickname that's different from a contact's name.

Folders and groups

A *group* is a set of pointers to address book entries, not the entries themselves. If you regularly e-mail information to the same people (people in your department at work, distant family members, or fellow hobbyists, for example), you can put all of their addresses into a group. If you do this, you can avoid having to enter each contact individually in the To line every time you send a message to these people. A contact can belong to multiple groups.

A *folder*, on the other hand, is a way of subdividing actual address book entries to make them easier to find and manage. A contact can belong to only one folder. All folders must be part of either the Shared Contacts folder or your identity's main Contacts folder. (I explain these two permanent folders further in the next section.)

SECRET: If you open your address book and don't see any entries, it's most likely because the focus is on the Shared Contacts folder instead of your main Contacts folder. To see your Contacts folder, along with subfolders and groups you have created in the address book, choose View ⇨ Folders and Groups. A left pane opens in the Address Book window.

You can't copy contacts, groups, and folders between folders; you can only move them. You can move a group to another folder without affecting the folder locations of the contacts in the group. You cannot move or copy a folder from one computer to another; if you need this kind of portability, you'll need to create a separate address book.

If you double-click a group to view its Properties dialog box and click Select Members, you will see a list of all the contacts in the main Contacts folder. Add any of these contacts to the group by highlighting them and clicking Select and then OK. To add contacts from another folder to this group you must drag and drop them. (The contacts are copied, not moved.) To remove a contact, highlight the name in the right pane and press your Delete key (the contact will only be removed from the group, not from your address book).

When you right-click an address book folder, you'll notice there's no Rename menu option. Instead, to rename a folder, select Properties. The folder name is the only value in the Properties dialog box. You can't change the name of your main Contacts folder (or remove it, for that matter). This restriction is probably to prevent two identities from accidentally giving their main folders the same name.

You can type a contact directly into a group or a folder. Simply select the group or folder before choosing New ⇨ New Contact. This is different from the behavior of the Contacts pane, where you can add contacts only to your identity's main Contacts folder. You cannot import contacts from another address book directly into a folder or group; you must first import them into your identity's main Contacts folder (choose File ⇨ Import ⇨ Address Book), and then move them to a folder or add them to a group individually.

Sharing an address book

Every address book contains at least two permanent folders — one for each identity, and one called Shared Contacts. No matter how many identities there are for a particular user profile, there is only one default address book (.wab) file, named for the current user. (Remember that profiles are different from identities in that they govern your entire system, not just Outlook Express.) Ordinarily you can see only the entries for your identity's main Contacts folder, plus the Shared Contacts folder.

When you add a contact to your address book — for example, by right-clicking an address and choosing Add to Address Book — that information is stored in the Contacts folder for the current identity. To share a contact or group with other identities, drag the icon for that item into the Shared Contacts folder in the left pane. That contact or group now appears in the Shared Contacts folder (and thus the Contacts pane) of every identity on this computer, instead of in your main Contacts folder. If you use a lot of shared contacts, it's probably worthwhile for you either to keep the Contacts pane open in Outlook Express (choose View ⇨ Layout ⇨ Contacts) or to add the Contacts icon to your Outlook Express toolbar.

Multiple address books

Now that the Windows Address Book can contain multiple folders, the need for multiple address book files is significantly decreased. Address book folders are certainly easier to set up and use. But you can still have multiple address books if you choose, and this may be the best option if you need to move a subset of your address book between computers.

You can have as many .wab files (address books) as you want, but only one default .wab file. The default .wab is the one you see in the Contacts pane, and the one used when you click To in the header of a New Message window. The path to the default .wab is stored in your Registry.

> **TIP:** To create a new address book, choose Start ⇨ Run, type **WAB /New**, and press Enter. Browse to the place where you want to keep your new address book (probably the same folder where you keep your other one). Then type a name for your new address book and click Open. A new, empty address book appears.

You can open the nondefault `.wab` files by clicking them in the Explorer. You can easily make shortcuts to them on your Desktop, on a toolbar, or in the Start menu. Or, you can make shortcuts to Registry files that automatically change the default `.wab`. To see how this is done, take a look at "Using Multiple WABs" on Eric Miller's User Tips Web site, `www.okinfoweb.com/moe/wab/wab_015.htm`.

Printing a phone list

If you click the Print button in the Address Book toolbar, you see a dialog box that enables you to choose print options. What makes it different from a normal Print dialog box is the choice of print styles. The Memo option prints all of the contact information for your contacts, Business Card prints the information on the Business tab, and Phone List produces a nice alphabetized phone list that you can carry with you. With all three print styles, you can print the information for all of the contacts in your address book or only for the selected ones. On the downside, you don't have much control over the layout, and you're stuck with printing on 8 1/2-by-11-inch paper.

Keyboard Shortcuts for Outlook Express

In addition to the standard Windows keyboard shortcuts, there are a number of shortcuts more or less unique to Outlook Express. Most are listed in Table 17-1:

Table 17-1: Keyboard Shortcuts in Outlook Express

Action	Key
Go to Inbox	Ctrl+I
Go to the Newsgroup Subscriptions dialog box	Ctrl+W
Send and Receive	Ctrl+M
Download all (news)	Ctrl+Shift+M
Open a New Message window	Ctrl+N
Forward a message	Ctrl+F
Reply to author	Ctrl+R
Insert signature	Ctrl+Shift+S
Send	Ctrl+Enter or Alt+S
Next message	Ctrl+Shift+>
Previous message	Ctrl+Shift+<
Next unread message	Ctrl+U
Next unread news thread	Ctrl+Shift+U
Next unread newsgroup	Ctrl+J
Mark as read	Ctrl+Enter or Ctrl+Q
Mark all news messages as read	Ctrl+Shift+A
View full header and body	Ctrl+F3
Edit HTML source	Ctrl+F2

Summary

Outlook Express is a powerful e-mail and news client that provides you with many configuration and customization options. This chapter discussed the following:

- ◆ Customizing the Outlook Express interface and using a number of customization features
- ◆ Using Outlook Express with multiple e-mail accounts
- ◆ Managing attachments
- ◆ Troubleshooting Outlook Express problems
- ◆ Configuring identities
- ◆ Creating messaging rules
- ◆ Accessing newsgroups
- ◆ Configuring and using the address book

Chapter 18

Web Publishing with Windows XP

In This Chapter

Windows XP contains a few tools that enable you to make information available on the Internet — and even host an Internet or intranet site from your Windows XP computer. As a general rule, the tools included with Windows XP are somewhat basic, and if you want to create complex Web sites, you'll need some kind of additional Web authoring tool, such as Microsoft FrontPage. But with Windows XP, you can easily post HTML pages, and you can even store information on public Web servers. Using Windows XP Professional, you can host Internet sites using Internet Information Services. In this chapter, you learn about . . .

♦ Using the Web Publishing Wizard

♦ Installing and configuring Internet Information Services

Storing Data on the Internet

Both Windows XP Professional and Home editions provide you with the Web Publishing Wizard, a revamped, yet older, Windows utility that enables you to store information on the Internet both in terms of HTML documents and other types of data. In the past, the Web Publishing Wizard was primarily used as a simple tool to move HTML and related Web files from your computer to a storage location on the Internet. For example, you might have an account with an ISP that gives you a few megabytes of Web space. This Web space can be used to create a small Web site or store other files. Generally, these spots on the Web have been used to set up an HTML home page for that particular user. The home page can be transferred from your computer to that Web space using the Web Publishing Wizard. The ISP may also provide you with a tool to transfer information from your computer to the Internet.

Beyond these simple beginnings, the Web Publishing Wizard still does the same thing: It moves, typically by FTP, documents from your computer to a Web storage location for which you have permission to store information. However, Windows XP adds a new twist. You can set up a section of free Web space at MSN to store information on the Internet. This includes any kind of documents, folders, and files, even those zipped or compressed. The idea here is to give you a storage location away from your computer, thus freeing more of your computer's hard drive space from stuff you don't use but don't want to lose. You can access your stored files with a Web browser and a Microsoft .Net Passport account that you freely create. If you have read about Microsoft's .Net initiative, you can see how this simple idea fits into the grand scheme of complete Internet integration. In the future, many computer software manufacturers envision our documents, applications, and possibly even operating systems stored on the Internet and downloaded to the PC only when they are needed. Of course, to make this happen, broadband connectivity will have to become an ordinary thing in each user's home. The Web Publishing Wizard provides you with a brief introduction to that concept by allowing you to put your own information on the Internet quickly and easily.

Using Web storage

The Web storage feature is very easy to use, and the following steps walk you through the process.

STEPS

Publishing files with the Web Publishing Wizard

1. Open the folder that contains the item you want to publish to the Internet, and select it.

2. In the left File and Folder Tasks pane, click the "Publish this File to the Web" link.

3. The Web Publishing Wizard appears. Click Next on the Welcome screen.

4. In the Change Your File Selection window, as shown in Figure 18-1, you can make adjustments to the files you have chosen to save to the Internet. Make any desired changes on this screen by clicking and clearing the check boxes provided, and click Next.

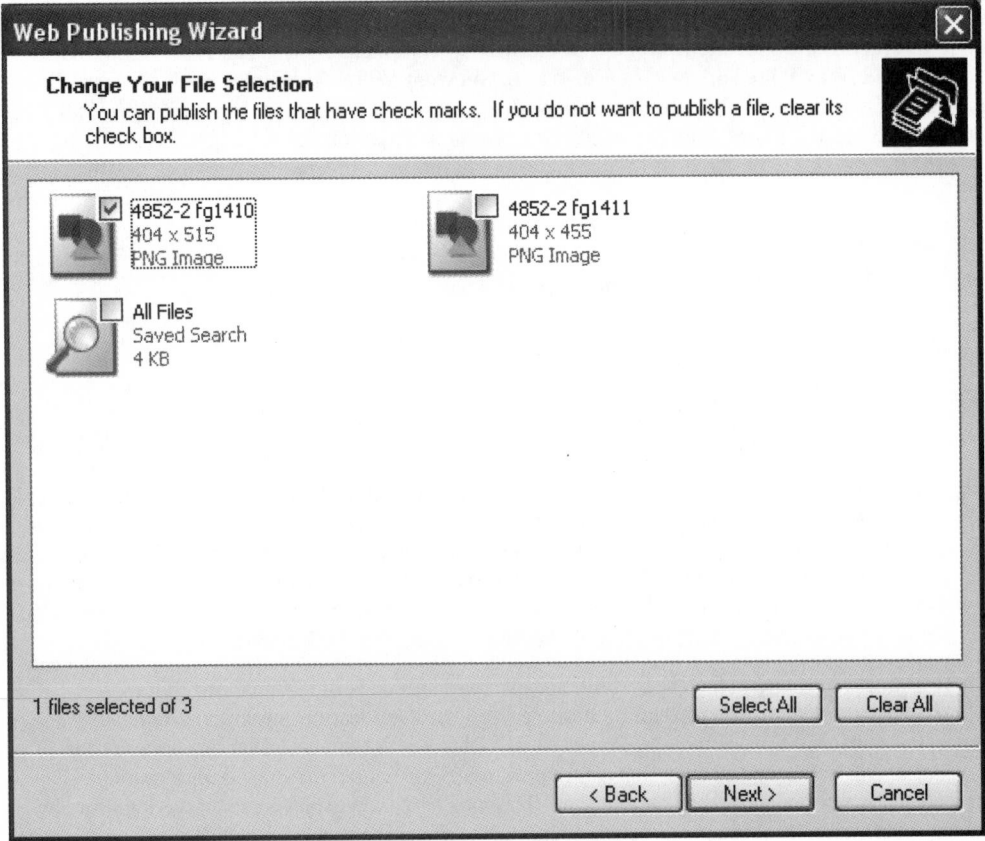

Figure 18-1: Change Your File Selection window

5. If you do not have a direct connection to the Internet (as with dial-up), you are prompted to connect. Once the connection is made, a window appears in which you can select a service provider to host your Web site or save your files. You are likely to see options for MSN or Xdrive, or you may be able to choose a different provider. Make a selection and click Next.

6. Information from the selected provider is downloaded to your computer. Click Next after you review the information.

7. The .Net Passport Wizard appears. In order to use the Web Publishing Wizard, you must have a .Net passport, which is free of charge. Click Next on the Welcome screen.

8. Passports are based on e-mail accounts. You can choose to use an existing e-mail account for your passport, or you can create a new account (such as a Hotmail account) for the passport. Make a selection and click Next.

SECRET: The setup wizard doesn't tell you that you must have an MSN, Hotmail, or Passport e-mail address — others need not apply. The good news is that a Hotmail or Passport account is free, so you'll just have to go through the trouble of setting one up.

9. If you choose to create a new e-mail account, additional steps will appear; simply follow the prompts. If you choose to use an existing account, enter your e-mail address and click Next.

10. Enter the password associated with the account. Your account information will be processed. Simply click Finish to close the .Net Passport Wizard.

11. You now return to the Web Publishing Wizard. You are prompted to create a new account or use an existing one. Choose to create a new account and click Next.

12. Your passport e-mail address appears automatically. Enter your password and click Next.

13. Once you are logged in, a window appears, shown in Figure 18-2, telling you that an online drive will be created for you (typically 25MB of free space where you can store files). Click Next.

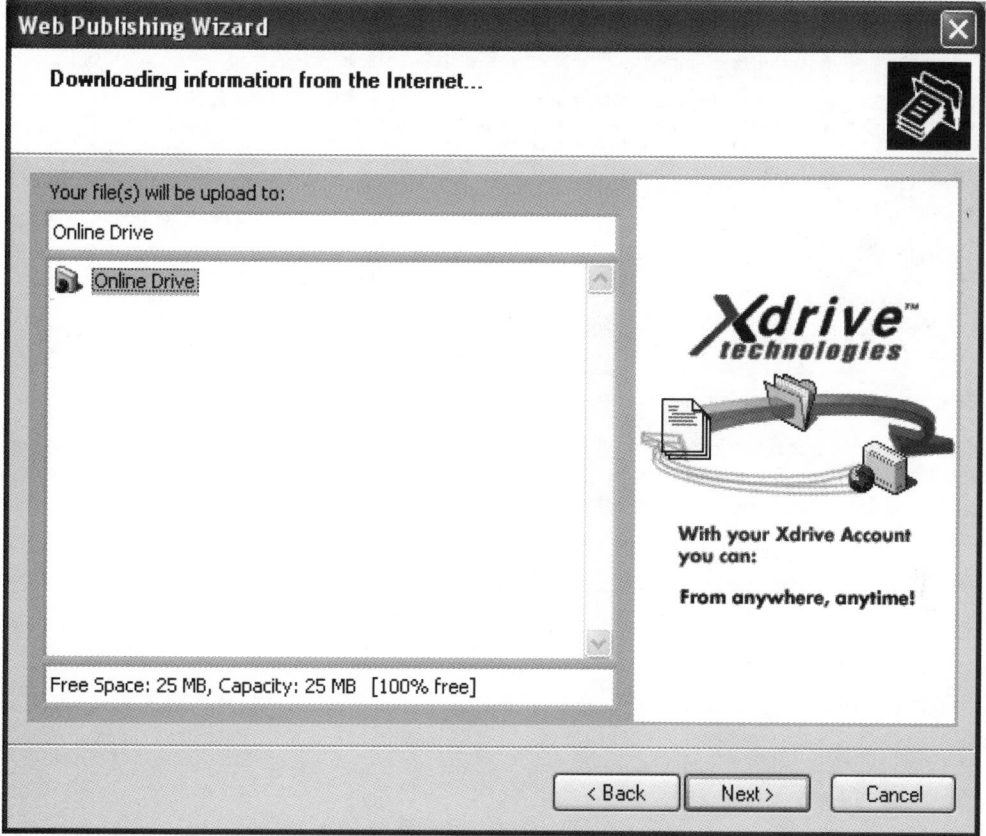

Figure 18-2: Web storage location

14. The uploading of your selected files begins. Once the process is complete, click Next and then Finish.

When you finish, XP places a shortcut to your Web storage location in your Favorites folder in Internet Explorer. You can easily use Internet Explorer to access the storage location assigned by the Web site. From this HTML page, as you can see in Figure 18-3, you can view the contents of your Web storage folder, upload new files, download new files, create folders, view documents, and do anything else you would do with files and folders stored locally on your computer.

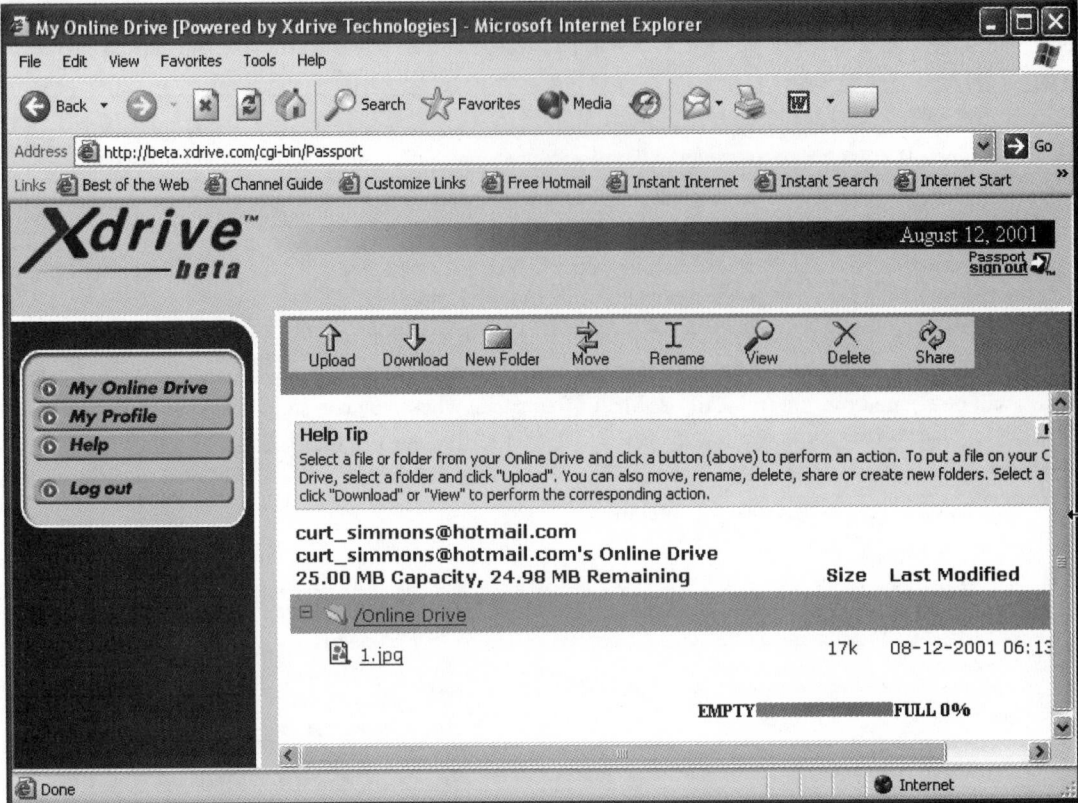

Figure 18-3: Access to storage through Internet Explorer

The good news is that Microsoft does not own the free Web storage market. You can easily access other Web sites via your browser and create accounts, then upload and download files as desired. You can even use free calendars and related tools that are all stored for you on the Internet and can be accessed from anywhere. Check these Web sites to get started:

♦ www.filesanywhere.com

♦ www.zxmail.com

♦ www.mydocsonline.com

♦ www.myspace.com

♦ www.calendarserver.com

Benefits of Web storage

At first glance, the idea of Web storage may not seem that important; after all, if you get only 25MB of storage space, what is the point when most hard drives today are over 12GB? The important aspect of Web storage really isn't the allocated space; it's in fault tolerance and access.

Fault tolerance is a computer business term that concerns the ability of a computer to tolerate a fault. For example, say that your hard drive burns up. What happens to the data? If the computer isn't fault tolerant, the data is lost unless you have backed it up to some other location. Many computer operating systems, including Windows XP, have the ability to tolerate faults if you have at least two hard drives. Information from one drive is copied to the other, and in case of a drive failure, all data can be regenerated from the second drive. (See Chapter 3 to learn more about drive configuration.)

The concept of fault tolerance also encompasses information management on your part. This includes backing up critical data on your computer and storing it in another location. Backup can be used with various kinds of media, including Zip drives, tape drives, CD burners, and even hard drives on another machine. The use of Web storage takes fault tolerance a step further. Suppose that you have a series of critical documents on your XP computer. You know you need to back those documents up, which you do, but why not take a further measure of protection and store those documents on the Web, as well? Since Web sites are protected with fault-tolerant schemes, your documents are safe there. This way, you can maintain a local copy if you like, and you can access those documents on the Web. In the case of a catastrophe in your office or home, the documents are safe because they are stored on the Web.

The second important aspect of Web storage is the concept of access. When you store important information that you need on the Internet, you can access it with your .Net Passport. This means that access is not tied to any single computer. If you have Internet access, you can access your files anywhere from any computer. If you are traveling, there is no need to store important files on your laptop: just grab them from the Internet when you need them. As you can see, Web storage gives you a virtual hard drive that is available on any computer from any location — and depending on your needs, a virtual drive can be very useful.

Publishing Web pages on Web storage

So far, I've approached the use of the Web Publishing Wizard as a way to store files on the Internet. However, you can publish Web pages, as well. You can use the Web Publishing Wizard to upload all of the files for your Web page to the desired site, and you can even upload folders. You can create Web pages for the default storage locations at MSN and Xdrive. The links you create with those HTML documents are preserved upon upload. What Microsoft doesn't expressly tell you, however, is that MSN and Xdrive are not public access sites. In order to access files on your virtual hard drive, you must share the drive with others so that they can virtually log in. Because your virtual drive is protected by a .Net Passport, the sharing feature virtually allows other e-mail addresses to log in using your passport. Your username and password are not given out, however; the login occurs through a link that users can click to access your virtual drive. This feature is great for people who need to give access to a few other people at a time. In most cases, you select the files or folders on your virtual drive that you want to share, and then enable a sharing option. This opens a Web page, as shown in Figure 18-4, where you can enter the e-mail addresses of the people you want to share your drive with. Those people are sent an e-mail message with a link to your virtual hard drive.

SECRET: Depending on your service, the link may remain active for only a week or so; this is not a permanent sharing configuration. Check your storage provider's instructions and fine print for information.

SECRET: You may notice that Windows XP does not provide any default Web page creation tools. If you came to XP from Windows 98, you may be looking for FrontPage Express, which has died a cruel death since the days of Windows 2000. If you want to create Web sites, you'll need an authoring package to create and publish Web pages, unless you want to do it all by hand (writing the HTML yourself). FrontPage is popular, of course, and a number of other software titles are available from various vendors. Check your favorite computer store for more information.

Introduction to Internet Information Services

Windows XP Professional includes software that enables your computer to become a Web server and provide a Web site to users on the Internet or to be used to provide an intranet site on your company network. Internet Information Services (IIS), which as been around since the earlier days of Windows NT, is a robust Web publishing tool. IIS can support multiple Web sites and advanced Web site languages and security. It is a complex product, and entire books are available on the subject alone.

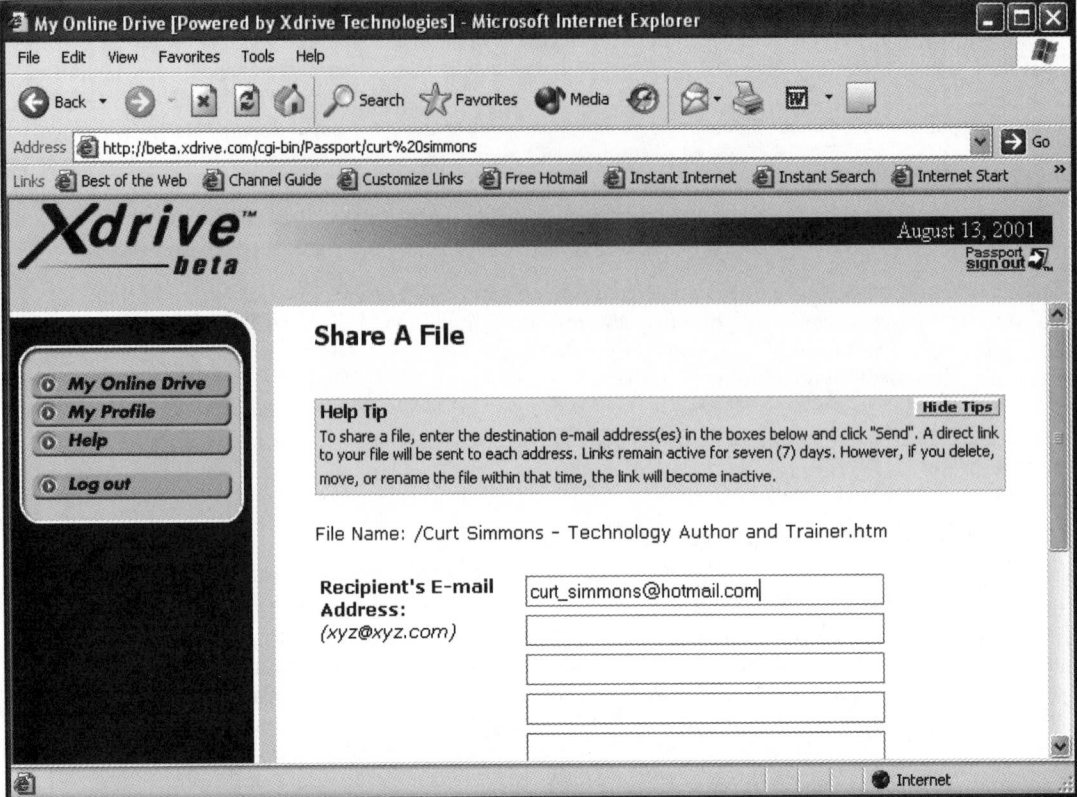

Figure 18-4: Sharing files from virtual storage

The remainder of this chapter explores the features of IIS and helps get you started, but a complete tutorial and instruction manual on IIS are, of course, beyond the scope of this book. Use this section to learn about IIS and determine if it is the right product to meet your needs. If so, you can then purchase an IIS administration book that will get you moving in the right direction.

Also, let me reiterate that IIS is available on Windows XP Professional only. If you are using Windows XP Home Edition, you can safely move on to another topic.

> **CAUTION:** You can install IIS and play around with the software to get familiar with it; however, if you have a persistent Internet connection, such as a DSL or cable connection, IIS may open your computer to attacks from the Internet. This, of course, does not mean that you will get attacked, but you will simply be more vulnerable. If you are experimenting, that 's fine, but I recommend that you uninstall IIS when you are finished.

Getting to know IIS

IIS is a full-featured product that is not installed by default when you install Windows XP. Rather, it can be installed manually if you want to use it, and the next section gives you a quick walkthrough of installation. The first question that comes to mind concerning Web site hosting and publishing concerns the use of Windows XP Professional for the job. After all, shouldn't a Web site be hosted on a server?

Although Windows 2000/XP Server provides a great way to publish Web sites to the Internet, Windows XP Professional contains the same power. By giving XP Professional the necessary software to host Web sites, network administrators have more flexibility. For example, using a Windows XP Professional computer, an intranet site for a company can be placed on the computer, thus freeing up the server to perform more necessary tasks. The operating system is less expensive and easier to maintain. If you lived in the Windows 2000 world, this concept is not new. Many of the jobs typically reserved for a server product can be performed on Windows XP Professional.

I should mention here that IIS on Windows XP is best used in an intranet environment. Due to the amount of traffic on the Internet, most Windows XP computers would not be able to handle the client service load as a Windows 2000/XP server can. IIS provides you some freedom on the corporate network because you can pull intranet content off the servers and provide that content to local network clients through IIS's easy administration tools. The job of an Internet Web site host, however, is best left to Windows 2000/XP Server.

TIP: You can learn more about IIS and access some usage scenarios in the HTML help that becomes available to you when you install IIS. This information can help you evaluate IIS and determine if it is right for your organization.

As I have mentioned, IIS is a full-featured product designed to provide you with the tools and options necessary to host and manage today's complex Web sites. The following list gives you a look at just a few of the important features of IIS:

- ◆ **MMC** — IIS functions as an MMC snap-in for easy management and configuration. The IIS snap-in can even be used remotely from another computer running Windows XP, Windows 2000 Server, or Windows 2000 Professional.

CROSS-REFERENCE: You can learn all about the MMC in Chapter 7.

- ◆ **Internet standards** — IIS supports all Internet standards, providing complete Web site hosting features that are typical on the Internet today. For example, IIS is fully HTTP 1.1 compatible and supports multiple Web sites on one IP address through the use of host headers. IIS also supports full mail and news functionality with applications such as Microsoft Exchange. PICS ratings are also supported, and you can even provide HTTP compression for faster client downloads.

- ◆ **Programming features** — IIS supports all major Web programming formats, including Active Server Pages and Active Directory Services Interface.

- ◆ **Security** — IIS provides the strictest security features available on the Internet today. Advanced Digest authentication, Secure Sockets Layer, Server-Gated Cryptography, and even the government's Fortezza security standard are supported in Windows XP's IIS.

Installing IIS

You can easily install IIS on your Windows XP Professional computer using Add/Remove Programs, Add/Remove Windows Components in Control Panel. You'll need your Windows XP Professional CD-ROM in order to complete the installation. Before doing so, you'll also need make certain that the DNS service is installed on a server on your network, if you will be using IIS for an intranet site. Also, IIS does not provide any Web authoring tools: it is strictly a Web site hosting tool. In order to create the actual Web site, you should use FrontPage. Although you can use a different Web authoring software tool, you'll find the easiest functionality and best integration with IIS if you use FrontPage. IIS provides FrontPage server extensions so you can easily make use of all of the automatic components provided with the FrontPage software.

Installing IIS is rather easy, using the Windows Components Wizard. The following steps show you the process.

STEPS

Installing IIS

1. Open Control Panel and open Add/Remove Programs.
2. Click the Add/Remove Windows Components button.

3. When the Windows Components window appears, as shown in Figure 18-5, select Internet Information Services from the components menu and click Next.

SECRET: By default, the FTP service is not installed with IIS. If you want to make FTP sites available, select Internet Information Services in the Windows Components window and then click the Details button. Check FTP and click OK, then click Next to install it.

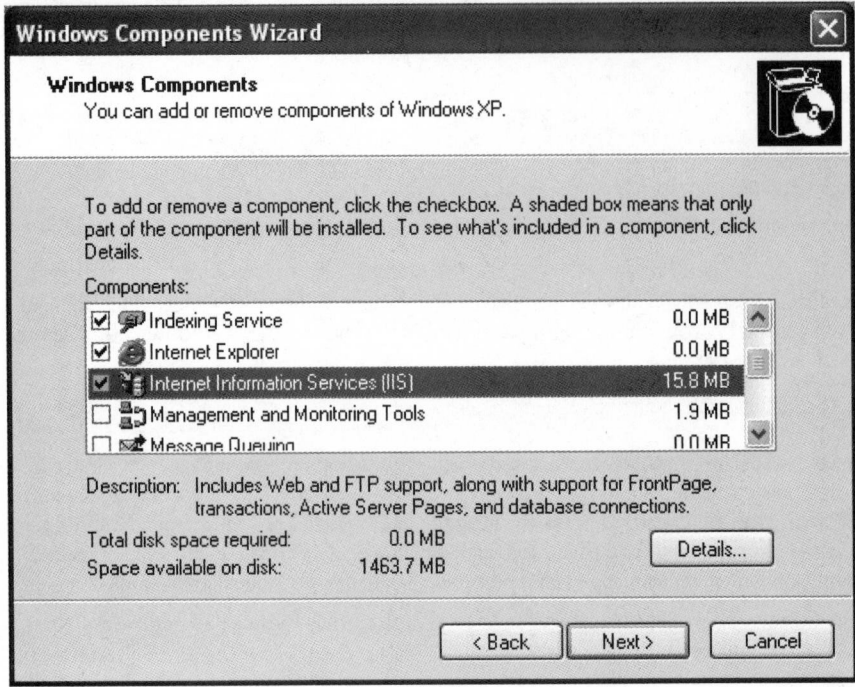

Figure 18-5: Windows Components

4. IIS is installed on your computer. Click the Finish button to exit the wizard.

Exploring IIS

Once IIS is installed, you can open the IIS MMC by double-clicking the option in your Administrative Tools folder in Control Panel. You'll see the familiar MMC interface with an expandable folder structure in the left pane and the contents of the selected item appearing in the right pane, as shown in Figure 18-6.

By default, IIS contains three basic divisions for the local computer — Web Sites, FTP Sites, and Default SMTP Virtual Server. Because the hosting of Web sites is the primary purpose of IIS, I will limit my discussion to this topic.

As you will quickly see, the IIS console organizes Web site information through directories or folders. Under the Web Sites folder, you have a Web site provided for you by default. This default Web site contains the basic Web site components installed with a Web site. You can use this default Web site as a guide, and you can access the HTML help files here, as well. You can use FrontPage to publish the Web site you create to the Web Sites folder. Keep in mind that IIS can host multiple Web sites simultaneously.

As I mentioned, IIS is built on the concept of directories, and there is a home directory found in C:\inetpub\wwwroot (which you can change). This root directory contains "home" directories that serve the Web sites. You don't have to store your Web sites under the root directory, however; you can store them just about anywhere. However, you do have to create a virtual directory that points to the location of the home directory you are using. You can create virtual directories via the Virtual Directory Wizard, available from the Action menu when you select the Web site under the Web Sites folder.

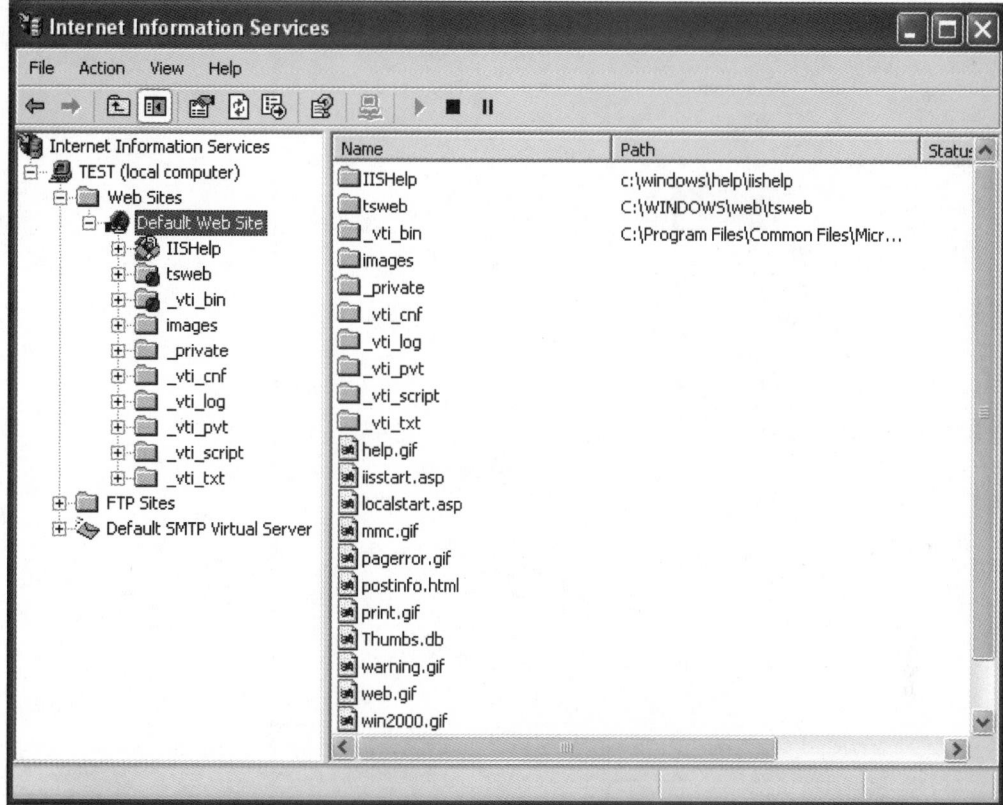

Figure 18-6: IIS console

You can get started with IIS by copying your default.htm page to the \inetpub\wwwroot directory. When users on your intranet type your computer's name in a browser window, the default.htm (or default.asp) file appears as your home page. This, of course, uses the default Web site provided for you. You can create a complete Web site under a new directory using FrontPage or a similar Web authoring tool.

One of the easiest ways to get a handle on how IIS functions is by taking a look at the Web site's properties. The Properties dialog box shows you how the Web site is configured by default and how you can alter the site to meet your needs. The Properties pages are available for any Web site hosted by IIS by simply selecting the Web site's name in the console tree and choosing Action ⇨ Properties. The following sections explore the configuration options you find on the Properties pages.

Web Site tab

The Web Site tab, shown in Figure 18-7, provides you with three configuration options — Web Site Identification, Connections, and Logging. Under Web Site Identification, you can manipulate the description of the Web site, the IP address, and the TCP or SSL port used for the site. You also set connection timeout defaults and logging options. The default settings found here are typically all you need for an intranet site.

ISAPI Filters tab

You can manage the default behavior of a Web site through the use of ISAPI (Internet Server Application Programming Interface) extensions. These are used automatically, but you can generate your own programmatically and install them for the Web site here. You can learn more about programming with ISAPI extensions and filters in the IIS online help files.

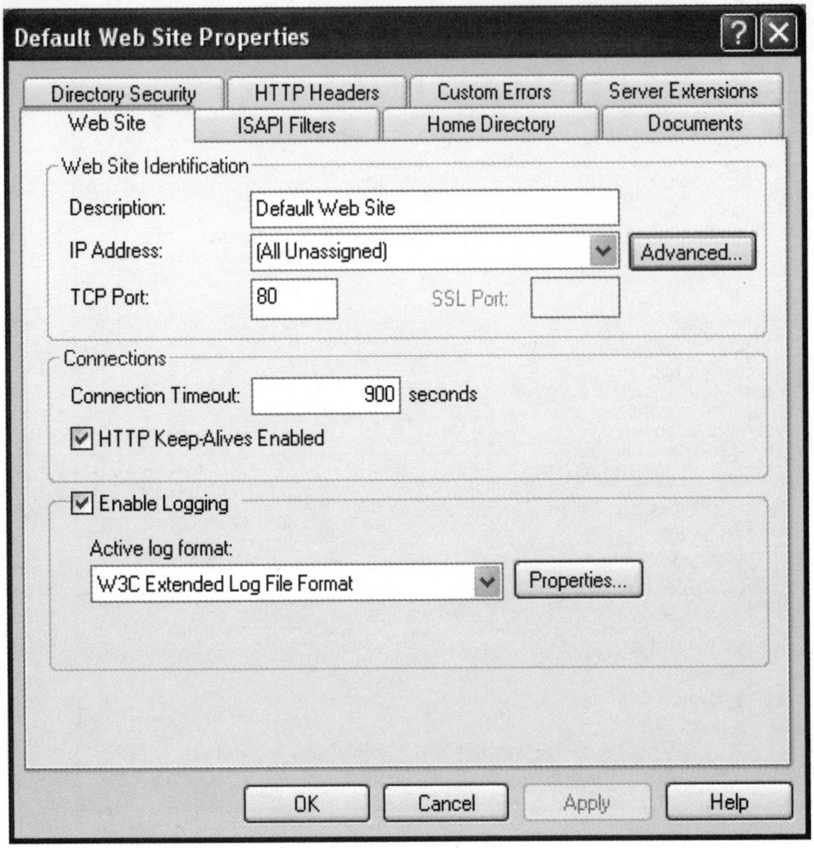

Default Web Site Properties   [?][X]

Directory Security	HTTP Headers	Custom Errors	Server Extensions
Web Site	ISAPI Filters	Home Directory	Documents

Web Site Identification

Description: Default Web Site

IP Address: (All Unassigned)   ▾   [Advanced...]

TCP Port: 80   SSL Port:

Connections

Connection Timeout: 900   seconds

☑ HTTP Keep-Alives Enabled

☑ Enable Logging

Active log format:

W3C Extended Log File Format   ▾   [Properties...]

[OK]   [Cancel]   [Apply]   [Help]

Figure 18-7: Web Site tab

Home Directory tab

The home directory for the Web site tells IIS where the Web site is located. By default, IIS looks for all Web sites in the \inetpub\wwwroot directory. As mentioned previously, you can create a virtual directory that points to an alternate location. When a user attempts to access the Web site, the virtual directory is used to retrieve the Web site information from its actual location. As you can see on the Home Directory tab, shown in Figure 18-8, a home directory redirect can be another URL on the Internet.

In the Local Path section, you see some basic options such as script source access, read, write, and browsing. By default, users who access the Web site can only read the site, log the visit, and index the resource. These are standard options and the most secure ones, but you can give more rights by selecting other check box options.

Finally, you also see some basic application and permission settings. The default options configured for you are all you generally need for most Web sites, but as you can see, you can easily provide additional options.

Documents tab

The Documents tab enables you to determine which documents the Web site supports. By default, the site supports default.htm, default.asp, index.htm, and index.asp. You can add other ones here if necessary.

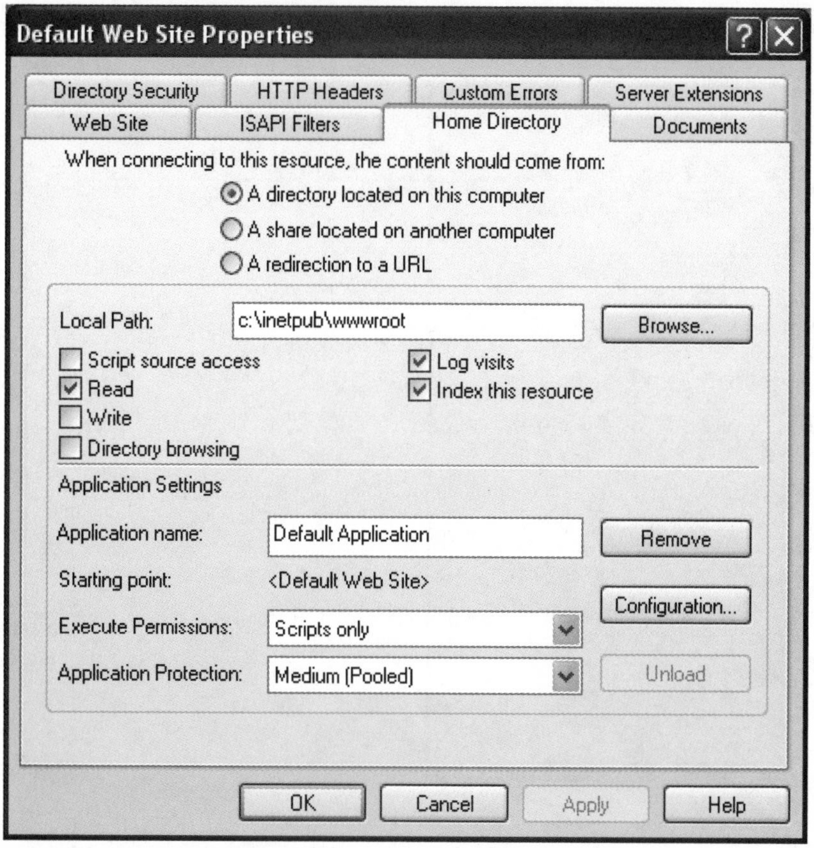

Figure 18-8: Home Directory tab

Directory Security tab

Web site security is always an issue. As a Web site administrator, your security policies and procedures will vary according to the Web site's needs. The idea is to provide the maximum amount of security and usability. That, of course, is a challenging proposition, but regardless of the outcome, IIS can support a number of different security features.

The Directory Security tab provides three basic divisions of configuration, with additional Edit buttons to further configure each option. First, you have anonymous access and authentication control. If you click the Edit button, you can determine whether to include anonymous access for your site and the desired level of access. If no anonymous access is allowed, then users must log in to the site using digest, basic, or integrated Windows authentication, shown in Figure 18-9. Under most circumstances, you should allow anonymous access. However, you might want to set up an intranet site for which only a few select individuals have access to information. In this case, you should disable anonymous access and implement a desired level of security where the users log in to the site. You can configure these options here.

The Directory Security tab also allows you to configure IP address and domain name restrictions for the site, which enables you to grant or deny access to the resource using IP address and Internet domain names. If your Web really needs top-level security, then you can configure the option under Secure Communications on the Directory Security tab. You'll need a server digital certificate to configure this option so that client certificates can be used with the site. See the IIS help files more information about implementing this level of security.

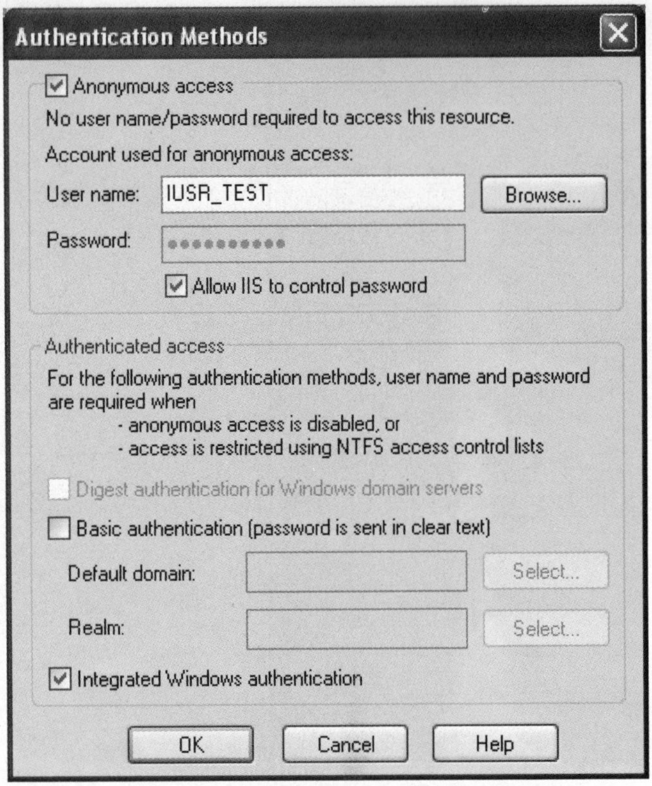

Figure 18-9: IIS Authentication Methods

HTTP Headers tab

The HTTP Headers tab enables you to configure several items you may find important for your Web site, as shown in Figure 18-10. I describe these in the following list:

♦ **Content Expiration** — If your site provides content that expires, you can enable content expiration for the page. Users will see when the page expires and know that that the page needs to be refreshed. If you choose enable content expiration, it can expire immediately, after a certain number of days, or on a specified date.

♦ **Custom HTTP Headers** — HTTP headers provide information to users when a Web page is requested. You can customize the standard HTTP header content that is included by adding custom HTTP headers to the provided field. You can learn more about custom HTTP headers by accessing the IIS help files.

♦ **Content Rating** — The Recreational Software Advisory Council (RSAC) defines a rating system for Web sites based on content. The ratings categories are violence, sex and nudity, language, and chat. If your Web site contains any of this kind of material, you can enable the rating service for the Web site. The rating then appears in the user's browser so that the user knows in advance that the site contains mature content.

♦ **MIME Map** — The MIME map configures various MIME extensions that are included in the HTTP header. You can define additional MIME types here. (MIME is a messaging format that is used to pass e-mail over the Internet. You can read a great overview of it at
`http://mgrand.home.mindspring.com/mime.html`.)

Figure 18-10: HTTP Headers tab

Custom Errors tab

IIS provides a number of default HTTP error messages that appear under various circumstances. For example, if the service is offline, an HTTP 400 "bad request" message is returned to users when they attempt to access the Web site. Many error messages are already configured for you and are viewable on the Custom Errors tab. However, if you need to use a custom HTTP error, you can create the file and add it to the list here, or you can edit an existing HTTP error in order to meet your needs.

Server Extensions tab

The Server Extensions tab provides permissions for authoring, mail settings, and security inheritance settings. You can set different version controls for authoring as well as scripting and configure mail settings for your site.

FrontPage server extensions

As mentioned previously, IIS contains built-in support for FrontPage. FrontPage provides you with an easy-to-use, graphical interface for creating Web pages without knowing HTML formatting. When you create Web sites using FrontPage, you can implement a number of automatic features, such as Web bots, discussion boards, hit counters, chat rooms, and others. You can add these components dynamically to your Web sites with a just a few mouse clicks and without any scripting or programming. However, in order for these components to work, the Web server that hosts the FrontPage site must support FrontPage server extensions. IIS, of course, supports these extensions natively.

When you install IIS, the FrontPage server extensions install automatically. You can determine who will be the administrator of the FrontPage server extensions by right-clicking the desired Web site and choosing New ⇨ Server Extensions Administrator. You can use the All Tasks option to check the server extensions for problems and open the Web site using FrontPage.

> **SECRET:** Technically, these are installed by default because they are selected as an IIS installation option under Details when you use the Windows Components Wizard. You can get rid of them by clearing the check box.

IIS provides a separate MMC snap-in called FrontPage Server Extensions console, which is shown in Figure 18-11. This console is available in your Administrative Tools folder in Control Panel. You can perform basically the same tasks with the FrontPage Server Extensions console that you can perform with the IIS console. You can define a FrontPage administrator for the Web site, create a new subweb to which the extensions will apply, upgrade and delete extensions, recalculate hyperlinks, and perform other actions related to extension management.

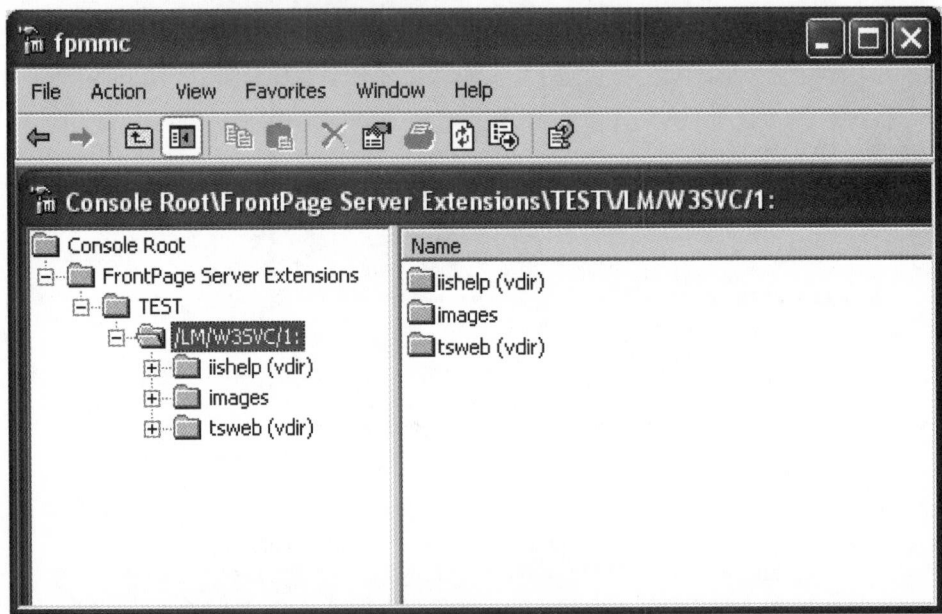

Figure 18-11: FrontPage Server Extensions administration console

You can set the FrontPage server extensions basic properties for the computer and for each individual Web site. For each Web site, just expand the computer name in the FrontPage Server Extensions administration console, then right-click the Web site name and choose Properties. You'll see the same Server Extensions tab that is available from the Web site's properties in IIS. There are some interesting settings you can configure for the entire computer, however. In the FrontPage Server Extensions administrator, right-click the computer name and choose Properties. You see a Server Extensions tab, shown in Figure 18-12, where you can determine the following:

- **General performance** — This drop-down menu enables you to tune IIS for functionality with 100-page service, 100- to 1,000-page service, or 1,000-page service. You can also choose the custom settings option and click Edit to define a desired performance level. Ideally, these settings should reflect the actual amount of access traffic your site is experiencing.

- **Options** — The options section determines how e-mail is handled through this Web site. Click the Settings button and enter the mail server's address, contact address, and SMTP mail server address.

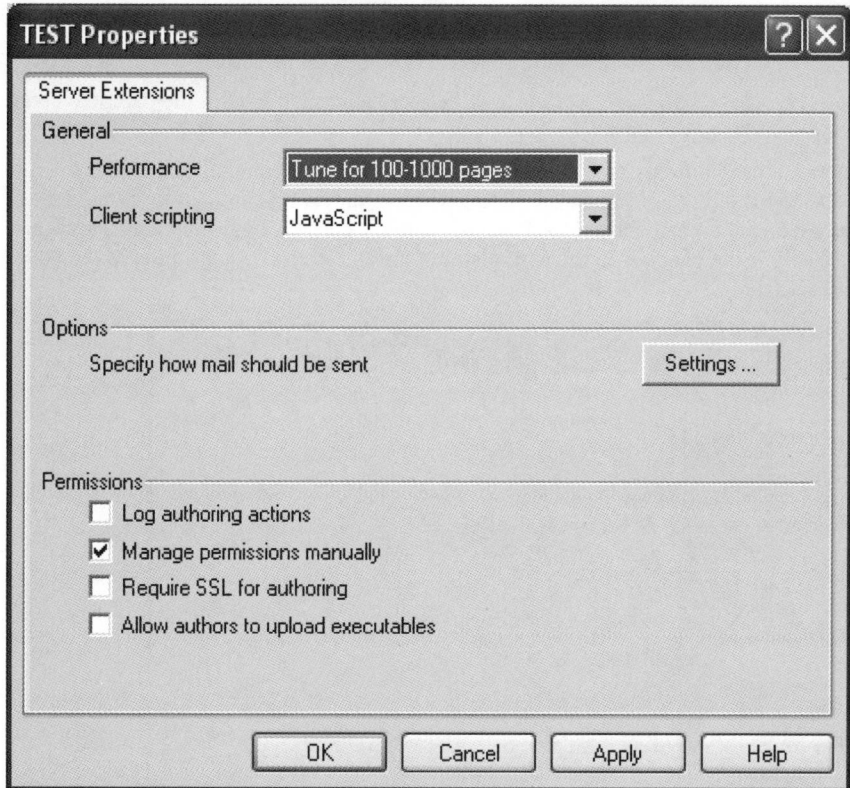

Figure 18-12: Server Extensions options

- ♦ **Permissions** — Under permissions, you have a few options available. You can log authoring actions, manage permissions manually, require SSL for authoring, and allow authors to upload executables. This basically gives you final control if there are numerous authors for the Web site.

Creating subwebs

Mentioned previously in this chapter, IIS enables you to create subwebs under a Web site and apply the FrontPage server extensions to the subweb or configure it as a different site. This feature can be very helpful in a number of situations. For example, suppose that you host a corporate intranet site that allows access to everyone, but you need a new division of that Web site to be made available to only a select few. An easy configuration option is to simply create another Web site, then configure this new site as a subweb of the existing intranet site. You can then create a link from the top-level site for users to access the subweb. You can set security so that the select users enter a username and password to access the site.

IIS provides you with a wizard that helps you create a new subweb. The following steps walk you through the process.

STEPS

Creating a new subweb

1. Right-click the desired Web site name under Web Sites in the console and choose New ⇨ Server Extensions Web.

2. The New Subweb Wizard appears. Click Next on the Welcome screen.

3. Enter a directory name and title for the new subweb in the provided dialog boxes and click Next.

4. In the Access Control window, you can choose to use the same administrator for the parent Web or assign and new administrator to the subweb. Make your selection and click Next.

5. If you choose to create a new administrator for the subweb, the window expands and enables you to choose the desired account, shown in Figure 18-13. By default, a local machine group is created using the Web site's name. You can choose to clear this action if desired, but group configuration will enable you to easily make changes to the administrators of the Web at a later time. Make your selections and click Next.

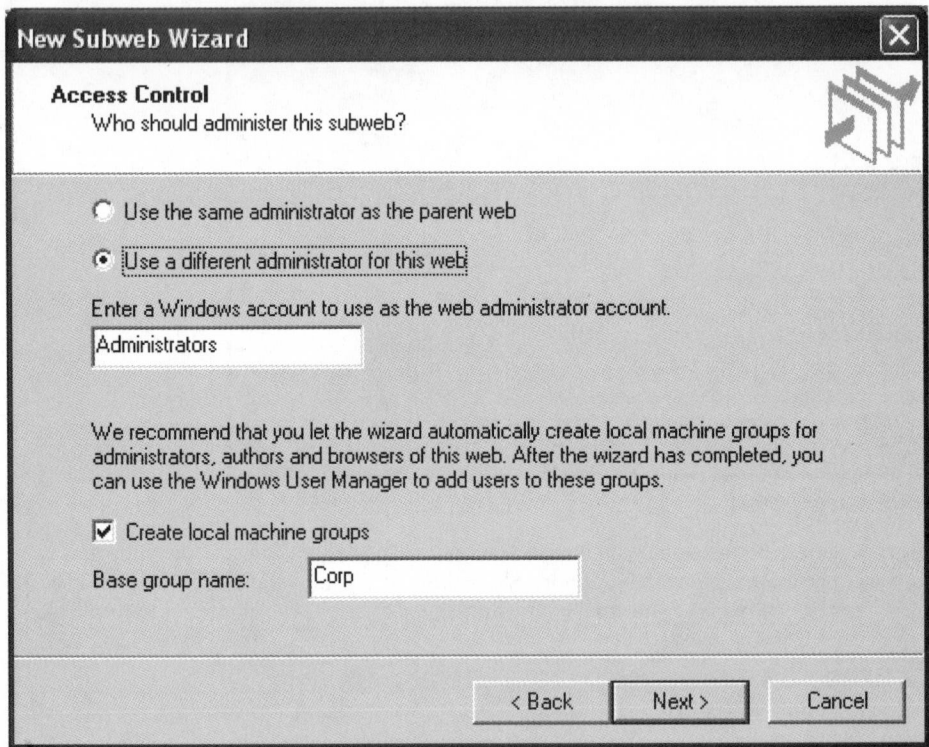

Figure 18-13: Access Control for this subweb

The new subweb is created and now appears under the parent Web directory. You can then administer the new subweb by adding HTML content to the folder.

IIS offers many additional configuration options, and depending on your Web hosting needs, you can configure Web sites, security, e-mail access, and even FTP sites using IIS. IIS on Windows XP provides you a simple way to host corporate Web sites and provide information to others easily and quickly. You can learn more about IIS by reading the HTML help files that are automatically installed when you install IIS, or you can pick up any number of good configuration and administration books on the topic.

Summary

In this chapter, we explored two tools included with Windows XP that enable you to publish content to Web and host Internet and intranet sites on Windows XP:

♦ The Web Publishing Wizard makes publication and storage of files on the Internet quick and easy. You can sign up for a free storage account so that your files can be stored on the Internet, where they are safe and easy to access from any location.

♦ For Windows XP Professional users, Internet Information Services is a diverse Web site hosting tool that can be installed on Windows XP. IIS on Windows XP works best as an intranet server that can help reduce the load from actual servers on your network.

Part VI

Windows XP Networking Secrets

Chapter 19

Windows XP and Networking Concepts

In This Chapter

The world of networking is an ever-changing, constantly evolving animal. As new operating systems such as Windows XP offer new networking services, and as networking hardware grows and develops, networks continue to become more complex, yet more diverse in the services they offer. This chapter is a networking primer that helps you to understand the protocols, services, and hardware that collectively make up networking. In this chapter, you learn about . . .

- ◆ Choosing the best networking type for your business
- ◆ Understanding the different networking topologies and technologies
- ◆ Choosing from the available network cabling and hardware
- ◆ Understanding networking software, including protocols, clients, and adapters

Defining a Network

A network consists of two or more computers — whether they are desktop computers, notebooks or laptops, handheld computers, Macintoshes, or others — connected together so they can share information and peripherals. Networked computers are attached to each other using cables or wires, and it is across those cables that the shared information, commands, and queries pass. You also can attach computers by wireless methods, as described later in this chapter.

In addition to the cables, or the method of connection, there are other pieces of networking hardware you need, such as network interface cards, hubs, and perhaps routers or switches. Additionally, you might attach printers, digital cameras, and other peripherals as part of your network. This equipment can be shared between all of the users on the network.

Computers on a network communicate with each other by sending data and information over the network cables; but as you can imagine, network communication is more complicated than just that.

About packets

The data that transmits over a network might consist of text, images, user authentication, and so on. Before the data can travel from one computer to another, it must be divided into smaller pieces for easier distribution.

> **TIP:** Windows XP, along with previous versions of Windows, has the capability via a network adapter card to convert data into packets and reassemble network data that is received on your computer.

Data is sent over a network in *packets*. Each packet contains not only pieces of the data, but also the name of the sender and the receiver, along with some error-control information, to help make sure the packet reaches its destination in one piece.

> **NOTE:** A packet is also called a *frame* or a *block*. All three terms refer to a unit of transmitted information that includes addresses, data, and error-checking codes.

Packets may be of fixed or variable length. Each packet contains only a portion of the data being sent. Your networking software disassembles the data, places it into packets, and then sends it across the network. (It is the number of packets traveling over the network that makes up the network traffic.) When the packets get to the designated computer, the packets are then reassembled to form the data you sent. Naturally, this is all completed in split seconds.

Multiple packets travel simultaneously. If a packet is lost or becomes corrupted on its journey, the receiving computer notifies the sending computer and the packets must be resent to complete the data.

About transmission

Different topologies and technologies send different types of packets — and provide various error correction and control methods — to make sure the packets are complete when they reach their destination. The topology of the network refers to how you arrange the cables, the networking hardware, and the computers. Technology refers to the type of wiring and hardware you use and the general speed of the network.

Networks can be made up of single or multiple segments. One segment might consist of 10 or 50 workstations and one or two servers connected together to share data and peripherals. A second segment of the network might consist of another server or two, plus 10, 20, or 50 more workstations. The two segments can use the same network operating system or different systems; they might share peripherals and files between them, or they might not.

The topology and technology of the network determines how the network packets are distributed, not only to the computers in one segment, but also in how the packets are distributed to computers in multiple segments.

The ISO/OSI model

For a network to work properly between segments, operating systems, computers, and networking hardware and software, certain standards must be followed. International Standards Organization/Open Systems Interconnect (ISO/OSI) is a set of standards that define network functionality. ISO/OSI sets standards for cabling, network interface cards (NIC), protocols, and so on.

> **NOTE:** The ISO/OSI standards apply to all networking systems, operating systems, and topologies. The purpose of these standards is to define networking components and operations in order to make networks more "open" and less proprietary.

A seven-layer model defines computer-to-computer communications, from the application data to the most basic of the networking hardware. The layers work independently, yet they are connected because each layer builds on the functions of the layers below.

Following is a brief explanation of each layer:

- ◆ **Layer 1** — The Physical layer defines the cabling, hubs, and other equipment that amplifies and carries the electrical signal.
- ◆ **Layer 2** — The Data-link layer controls the flow of data through the network cards, bridges and switches, and other devices that connect the physical layer and the actual data stream. This layer also checks to ensure that all data is received and that it's usable.
- ◆ **Layer 3** — The Network layer defines the protocols for data routing, to ensure that the data gets to the correct destination. Such protocols include IP (Internet Protocol) and IPX (Internet Packet Exchange).

♦ **Layer 4** — The Transport layer defines protocols for error-checking and message formation. If data is too large, the Transport layer divides and numbers the data so that it can transmit the data in smaller pieces. The numbered data helps the layer reassemble the pieces after it gets to the other computer, segment, or other receiving end.

♦ **Layer 5** — The Session layer maintains the connection — or session — for as long as it takes to transmit the packets. It also performs security and administration functions.

♦ **Layer 6** — The Presentation layer identifies the way in which the data is formatted. This layer encrypts and decrypts information, for example, and translates data to ensure that one system can understand the data from another system.

♦ **Layer 7** — The Application layer defines how the applications interact with the network. This layer receives and delivers requests from applications on one computer to those on another computer.

The model's layers work together to send requests from a client to a server, for example. The layers might send a file from the server to the client in answer to a request. When a computer sends a request over the network, it begins on Layer 7, the Application layer, and works its way to Layer 1, the Physical layer. The request then travels across the networking cable to its destination using the network protocol to carry the packets. Figure 19-1 illustrates how the ISO/OSI layers work.

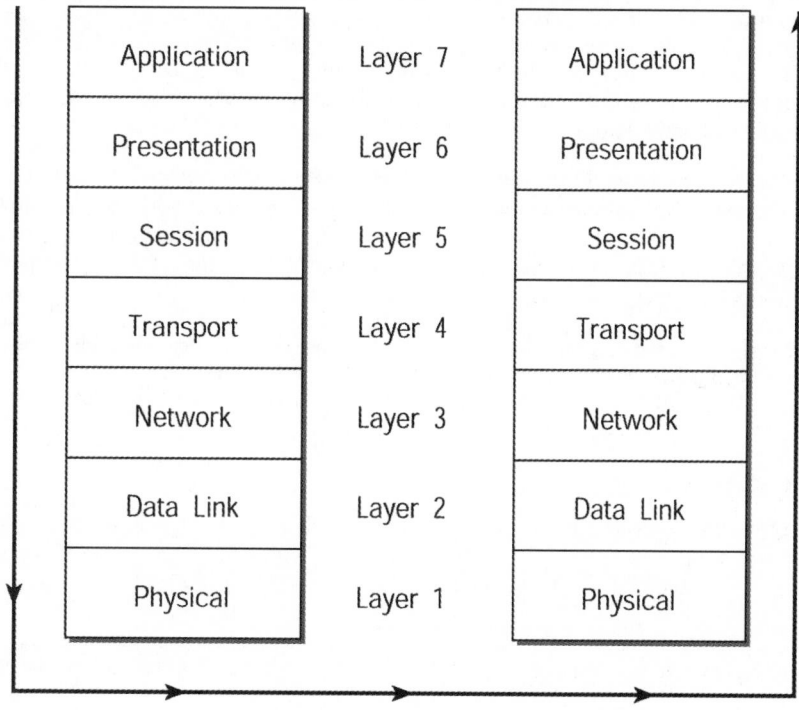

Figure 19-1: The ISO/OSI layers define networking functionality standards.

When the packets reach the remote computer, they enter on Layer 1 and move up to Level 7, the Application layer, where the request is passed on to the process or service responsible for answering the request. Then the cycle starts over again.

The Advantages and Disadvantages of a Network

For the most part, you'll find that networking your computers benefits everyone in your business or your home by enabling them to share files, folders, schedules, expensive printers, and so on. Sharing resources makes your business more efficient and effective, and gives the network users more equipment with which to work.

Networking also presents some disadvantages. The cost can be high, or security issues can be a problem. Fortunately, there are enough options and solutions available with networking as to make the good outweigh the bad.

Considering the advantages

You can connect a small number of computers (usually under 30) in an office or a home in a simple peer-to-peer network that is easy to install, administer, and operate. In larger networks where many client computers are used, a server-based network is typically implemented. The good news is that networking hardware and software is flexible, scalable, and easy to fit to your needs.

You also can expand the network as your needs grow. Adding computers, servers, hubs, and segments when you want to add new users or services is called scalability. Most networking equipment is built for expansion, as are most network operating systems and software.

Windows XP includes the networking software you need to set up any type of network. You can use Windows XP Professional or Home edition on a home or small office network, and Windows XP Professional is capable of functioning on a Windows 2000/XP network. The operating systems include the protocols, clients, services, and drivers for most network interface cards (also called network adapters or NICs). Additional advantages to networking your computers are discussed in the following sections.

TIP: Windows XP Professional not only includes the software you need to set up your network, but it also automatically configures itself to work on a TCP/IP network. All you have to do is install a network card and power up a Windows XP Professional computer; the program locates other computers on the network and configures itself to join the workgroup or domain automatically.

Sharing files

You can share files with everyone on the network. You can share letters, spreadsheets, reports, digital photographs, accounting files, and other business documents with your coworkers. Of course, in many cases, you will want to keep information private, and Windows XP, using NTFS security, enables you to easily do so.

CROSS-REFERENCE: You can learn more about networking and security for files and users in Chapters 20 and 23.

With networking, getting files from one computer to another is quicker across a network than copying them to a removable disk and physically moving them to the other computer. With networking, extremely large files are easier to transfer, as well, especially because it is often impossible to copy some large files to floppy disk. You might transfer or copy application files, large image files, Web documents, and so on from another user's hard drive or from a server. When using the network for these tasks, you can complete the procedure almost instantaneously.

Sharing disk space

Disk space is always at a premium. Graphic and image files, large application files, and data files are getting larger and larger. You can use a network drive or server drive for storing both your large and small files.

In addition to sharing hard drives, you can share file storage drives — tape drives, Zip and Jaz drives, CD-RW drives and even floppy drives. If your computer doesn't have a Zip or CD-RW drive, for example, but someone else on the network does, you can save files to that drive if sharing is enabled. This is a great feature of both larger networks and home networks. After all, if one computer has a storage feature (such as a Zip or CD-RW drive), you can simply share that drive so that it is accessible to all — which is a lot less expensive than buying additional drives! Windows XP makes drive sharing very easy, and you can learn more about sharing devices in Chapter 20.

> **TIP:** Use a Zip disk or CD to back up your important files so that you can access them whenever you need them, even if your files are backed up to a network tape drive. Retrieving files from a Zip disk or CD is much easier than retrieving them from a tape.

You also can share CD-ROM drives across the network. If your computer has a slower CD-ROM drive and another computer on the network has a faster CD-ROM drive, use the faster drive to install software to your computer. The faster CD-ROM drive means the installation process will be faster.

Creating backups

Backing up your data files is important. You should always keep an extra copy of important files in case your hard disk goes bad, a file becomes corrupted, or someone accidentally deletes your work. You can back up all of your data quickly and easily over the network — either to a storage disk or to another hard disk. Restoring that data is also quick and easy over the network.

Peripherals

Expensive peripherals — such as a color inkjet printer or a laser printer — are more affordable if everyone in a network can use them. If a printer isn't networked, only one person has continual use of that piece of equipment. Naturally, others can move to the computer to which the printer is attached; but that may not always be convenient or appropriate. If the printer is attached to the network, however, everyone can make use of it. You save money and time, and you do more with less.

> **TIP:** Keep your old printers — dot-matrix or inkjet, for example — and connect those to individual computers that might be able to make use of them. You wouldn't necessarily want to use a dot-matrix printer over the network because it's slow, noisy, and cumbersome. But if one person can use it to print draft reports or other documents, that takes some of the load off the network printer and eases network traffic.

Considering the disadvantages

Planning and installing a network is a scary proposition. You need to invest time and money. You have to learn about various networking hardware and software. Sharing equipment and files can pose problems, as well. Following are some of the disadvantages to setting up and using a network.

Investing time and money

One obvious problem with installing a network is that you must invest time. When you learn something new, it takes time to understand all the intricacies. Installing hardware and software also takes time. Teaching networking procedures to the office staff might take your time, as well.

> **TIP:** In a networked office environment, you should find the people in your office who understand how computers work and teach them about the network. Then let them teach the others to use the network; also let them be a help desk, of sorts, when users have questions. This will save you time and effort, and it will promote teamwork.

Administering the network will likely take the most time. No matter what type of network you install, you must first configure the networking hardware and software, and you must then maintain the network so that people can use it daily with no problems. You must consider security, backups, printing and file sharing, permissions, and so on. Naturally, the smaller the network, the easier the administration.

Money is another consideration. You might not want to invest a lot of money in your computer system, or you might have the means to install a model network, with all of the bells and whistles. It all comes down to priorities. If a network helps you speed your work and makes you more efficient, you will spend more money, time, and effort in setting up the network.

Fortunately, there are multiple levels of networking from which you can choose. You can purchase a kit, for example, for less than $100 that allows you to set up a small and simple network between two computers and a printer. Even though it might not be the fastest or the most efficient network, it will at least provide simple file and printer sharing with a small investment of time and money.

If you want to install a higher-level network for working with multimedia files, sharing expensive equipment, and providing services for your users, you can install a faster, more efficient network.

Maintaining and troubleshooting the network

Network maintenance includes keeping reliable connections between the computers and peripherals, troubleshooting connection problems between computers, and providing the available services (such as printer or e-mail services) to all computers on the network. The more equipment you connect to the network, and the more services you offer, the more difficult maintaining the network will be.

Network maintenance can often be a huge disadvantage, especially if you must take time to constantly troubleshoot problems. You can avoid some problems with equipment and software by understanding how the network is put together, as explained in this and the next two chapters.

Solving security problems

Another disadvantage to running a network is system security. You don't want just anyone opening payroll files, for example. Customer records, accounting files, reports, inventory, and so on, are just some of the types of files you should protect on the network.

Fortunately, Windows XP Professional offers the option of setting access limits for files, folders, printers, and other resources. You can choose not to share any of your resources with others on the network. You also can set certain limits to those resources to protect them from only certain network users or groups.

> **NOTE:** It is important to note that Windows XP Professional provides more security features and user management options for controlling shared content than Windows XP Home edition. Microsoft assumes that home users are basically friendly with each other, and extensive user management features provided in the Professional edition do not appear in the Home edition.

Sharing equipment and files

When you're sharing your equipment over a network, such as a printer or a Zip drive, you take the chance that the equipment won't be readily available when you need it. For example, if a coworker just sent a 24-page color document to a networked inkjet printer, you have to wait your turn to print, and that could take a while, depending on the network setup, printer speed, and so on.

There are some solutions to these problems. You can speed up your network so that printing and other processes don't take as long. As another example, you might be able to change the order of the documents being printed to rush your job to the front of the line.

> **TIP:** You can use a print server to manage the printing for all users on a network. A print server can be a program or a hardware device that attaches to the network. The print server provides shared access to the printers attached to the network. When a user sends a print job to a network printer, the print server places the job in a queue with other jobs. When a printer is available, the print server sends the next job to the printer.

Considering network traffic

One final disadvantage you might notice when working on a network is a general slowing of all applications and processes. Depending on the type of network equipment, the types of applications installed, and your uses for the network, networking computers can sometimes slow your work considerably. Some methods of networking are built for speed, whereas others are built for simple sharing at a rather slow pace.

SECRET: There are many things you can do to keep your network running smoothly and quickly. For example, consider the quality of your networking hardware; if you use cheap network cards and second-rate cabling, your network performance will suffer. If the cabling is out in the middle of the floor where people trample it, you're putting your network connections at risk. Check the cabling periodically for damage. Check all connectors, routers, hubs, and other devices periodically to make sure connections are secure. Keep backups of your data and, from time to time, test the backups to make sure they're reliable.

Exploring Network Types

The three basic network types are client/server, peer-to-peer, and dial-up networking. The type you choose depends on your networking goals, the equipment you want to install, your experience level, and the time you plan to invest. Each type of network provides distinct advantages and disadvantages.

CROSS-REFERENCE: It is important to note here that networking is certainly not limited to one physical location — indeed, you can even network with the Internet and via the Internet. Windows XP includes Internet Connection Sharing and an Internet Connection Firewall to help you with these matters, and you can learn more about these networking features, as well as virtual private networking, in Chapters 20 and 21.

If this is your first network, or if you only want a small and simple network, you can choose to set up a peer-to-peer network. A peer-to-peer network is simpler to operate and less expensive than a client/server network. After you gain experience, however, you may want to switch over to a client/server network, using your peer-to-peer network as a foundation.

The client/server network provides multiple services for many users. Whereas a peer-to-peer network is typically limited to a handful of computers and users, a client/server network can include hundreds or thousands of users. It is also more difficult to install, administer, maintain, and troubleshoot than a peer-to-peer network.

You might set up a dial-up network to accommodate the needs of only a few users. Telecommuters or home-based workers can easily dial up a computer at the office and transfer files, print, and collaborate with coworkers.

Using a peer-to-peer network

In a peer-to-peer network, all computers share their resources — including files, folders, drives, and printers — with all other computers on the network. Each computer also runs its own local applications and programs; it just has access to additional resources.

A peer-to-peer network usually contains 2 to 20 connected computers. You could include more computers than 20, with the right hardware and software; however, the larger the peer-to-peer network grows, the more difficult it can be to manage.

Figure 19-2 illustrates a peer-to-peer network. Three computers share their files, printers, CD-ROM drives, and other resources.

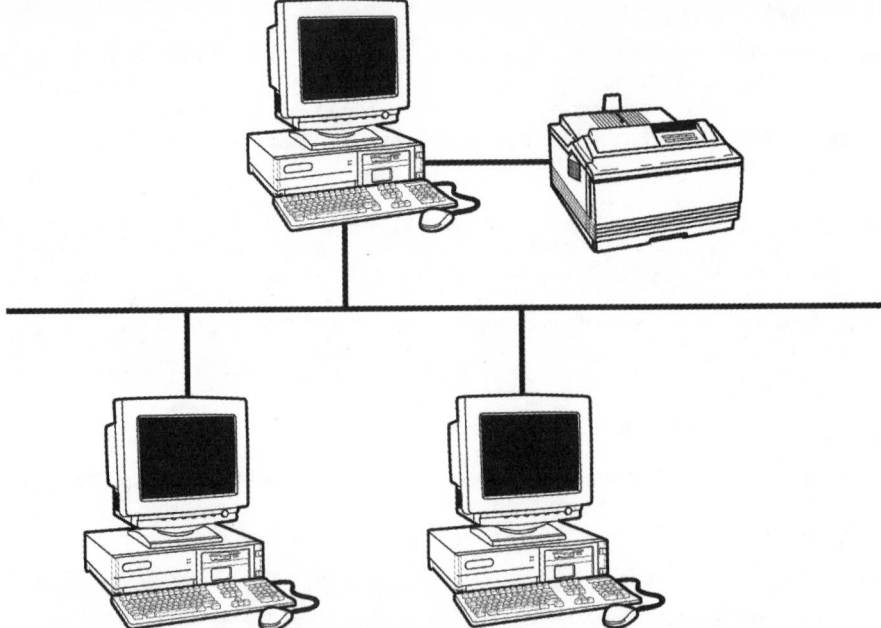

Figure 19-2: Peer-to-peer networking makes all resources available to everyone on the network.

Peer-to-peer networks have several disadvantages. Obviously, using a peer-to-peer computer means the users must trust each other — to be careful of files and programs, to responsibly use printers and other equipment, and to dependably make their computer available to everyone else.

File security can be a problem on a peer-to-peer network. You do, however, have the option of not sharing all your files and folders, and you can set permissions for the use of your resources.

Looking at peer-to-peer networking

A peer-to-peer network is easy to maintain and set up. It's also cost effective, especially for small business and home use. There are a wide range of cabling and networking solutions for a peer-to-peer network. Some solutions provide fast and powerful networking, while others offer slower connections but with reliable service. For home network users, kits are available to help you set up your network, and some of them even use your existing home phone lines for connectivity. See Chapter 20 for more information about home networking.

The computers connected in a peer-to-peer network are called a workgroup. Members of a workgroup usually trust each other to share resources and to responsibly take care of those resources.

It is also possible to have multiple network segments with peer-to-peer networking, and thus set up multiple workgroups. The members of one workgroup share resources with each other. Members of different workgroups generally cannot see each other's computers or share across workgroups.

> **TIP:** If you want to set up multiple workgroups that can share and communicate with each other, within limits, you can set up domains with Windows 2000 Server. Clients can easily cross domain boundaries using trusts, if they have the appropriate permissions and passwords.

The equipment you use when setting up your network defines the speed and efficiency of network communications. You might need only an intermittent connection for file or printer sharing, or you might want to connect to another computer for more routine file and printer sharing. You should decide how you want to use each computer on the network, and how those resources will be shared, before you choose your networking hardware.

The requirements of a peer-to-peer network include:

♦ Two or more computers

♦ A network interface card for each computer

♦ Cabling or alternative equipment to enable the computers to communicate, plus networking hardware when applicable

♦ A compatible (peer-to-peer) operating system — Windows XP, other versions of Windows, and even other operating systems with the right software

♦ Optionally, a printer and other peripherals for sharing

The type of networking equipment you use dictates the performance of your network. You can start out with a fast and efficient network or you can upgrade as necessary. The type of cabling, network cards, and other networking hardware you use dictates the speed of the network.

Assigning computer duties and resources

As you plan your peer-to-peer network, you should think about which computers perform which tasks on the network. Some tasks include file storage, backing up data files, and resource usage. Use the best computer for each job so the entire network will run efficiently and economically.

Items to consider include computer memory, disk space, and specialty hardware for use with attached resources. In addition to using computers that operate efficiently, you might need to add hardware to computers that will perform special network tasks.

To decide how to assign computer duties and resources, follow these steps:

STEPS

Assigning computer duties and resources

1. Determine the duties you expect from your computers. A computer can store files — word processing, database, graphics, application, data, and other files — for any or all of the users on the network. A computer can store backup files for any or all of the computers on the network. The difference between normal file storage and backup file storage not only determines the amount of hard disk space used, but it also influences network traffic.

2. Consider each computer's hard disk space before deciding which computer to use for file storage and backups. A computer with only one or two gigabytes of disk space could comfortably store word processing and spreadsheet documents, but it would not be appropriate for storing multimedia or other large files. Most new computers come with large hard drives now. It's not unusual to see drives that offer 40 or more gigabytes of space.

3. Consider, too, the power and memory of each computer on the network. A very slow machine — a Pentium 120, for example — is inappropriate for storing files that need to be accessed often. A computer that processes slowly slows the rest of the network when accessed frequently. Similarly, computers with less memory react more slowly than those with more memory react.

4. For each resource you add to the network, determine which computer best suits that resource's requirements. Consider the requirements for printers, CD-ROM drives, tape drives, and so on. Remember, too, that when you share a resource, you will experience degraded performance when several users are access the same resource at the same time.

Understanding peer-to-peer limits

Peer-to-peer networks offer many advantages to the office; but you also can experience some real problems with a peer-to-peer network, including:

♦ Peer-to-peer networking can place a strain on individual computers and resources, especially if the requests for services are many.

♦ If network traffic is high, the entire network slows and performance is impaired. This can be a problem on any network, however.

♦ Peer-to-peer networking offers little security to files and data.

♦ . As the peer-to-peer network grows, it can be difficult to manage.

Considering security issues

If you have a small office or home network and everyone gets along well, you won't have to worry much about security issues with your peer-to-peer network. There are, however, a couple of security issues to consider:

♦ First, accidents happen. Someone could accidentally access your hard drive and delete a few files, a folder or two, or even the entire contents of your hard drive. This is a security issue.

♦ Second, someone who fancies himself to be a hacker could get into your computers and cause problems with your network or access files.

♦ Third, if you have an Internet connection, there is always the possibility someone could hack into your system and compromise your data from the Internet.

Windows XP, along with previous versions of Windows, provides some safety measures that can protect your files from access by others on the network. You can choose which files you share and which remain private, and you also can set permissions to both your computer and resources. Also, many third-party applications enable you to control the contents of your computers on the network. As you plan your network, remember the possible problems and solutions and build them into your plan.

Boosting network performance

A peer-to-peer network can be efficient for many networking duties. When only two or three people are using the network, the network traffic should not hamper any one computer's performance. Network traffic encompasses any data sent from computer to computer, as well as to printers and other resources.

However, when more people access resources on the network and traffic increases, or the network tasks become increasingly more complex, individual machine performance may suffer. Computers with minimal power, memory, and disk space not only exhibit slow performance for the user, but also can slow the entire network if multiple people use its resources.

The best way to avoid problems with network traffic is to start your network with computers that are capable of operating efficiently as standalone computers. A Windows XP Professional computer has both minimal and recommended requirements. If you can afford a computer that fits the optimum requirements or better, you'll see much better network performance, as well as general computer performance.

> **CROSS-REFERENCE:** You can learn more about specific networking components found in Windows XP in Chapter 20.

Using a client/server network

A server generally stores all data files, and sometimes applications, and it normally controls the distribution and use of peripherals and resources. Some networks have one server, whereas other networks might have multiple servers. The number of servers depends on the number of clients and the number of services offered. Figure 19-3 illustrates a client/server network.

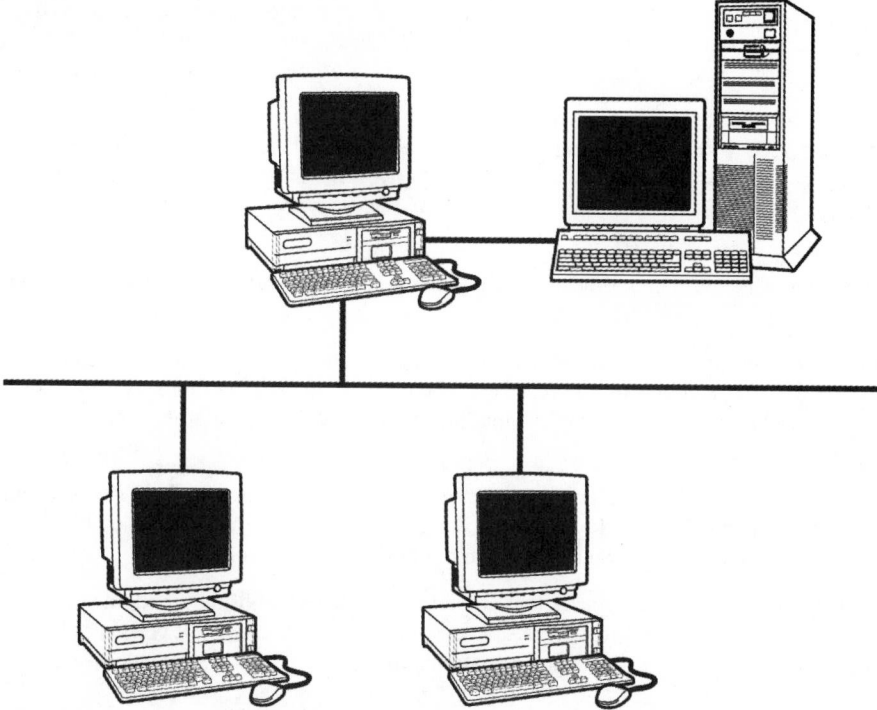

Figure 19-3: The server(s) supply services to the clients.

NOTE: Just as a qualifying statement, the concept of "client/server" network here refers to a server-based network where resources and network management are performed via servers. It does not necessarily refer to client/server application sharing.

Some larger networks have multiple servers to provide a wide variety of services to the clients. In addition to multiple servers, some client/server networks use multiple segments to separate users and resources in manageable groups.

Servers generally use faster processors and have more memory and disk space to perform the management tasks of the network. Servers perform multiple duties, including:

♦ Authenticating users

♦ Allowing access to resources (files, folders, printers, and so on)

♦ Providing Web access

♦ Tracking resource usage

♦ Logging security breaches

♦ Distributing e-mail

♦ Providing application access and data

Understanding client/server

Both the server and the client on the network use an operating system that enables them to communicate. An example of a client operating system is Windows XP Professional. An example of a server operating system (also called a network operating system) is Windows 2000 Server. The client and server operating systems enable the client to request services and the server to grant the requests.

The client/server network is designed for large networks (more than ten clients) and for tasks that require a host computer, such as Internet access or database management. Each network operating system has its own method of organizing users and resources. Windows 2000 Server organizes users into domains.

A domain consists of one or more computers assembled together in a group for naming purposes. The domain of your network affects you when you log on to the network and when you want to access a resource in another network segment. When you log on to the network, Windows asks you for your username, password, and your domain or workgroup (when using peer-to-peer networking).

At least one server in your domain authenticates you as a member of that domain. When the server identifies you as a member of the domain, you can then access the resources in the domain for which you have permissions.

Each domain must have one server that can authenticate users and manage resources. Often, a domain also has a backup server that keeps copies of all records for the domain, in case the first server crashes or has other problems. Domains might also have servers that manage printers, files, Internet access, applications, and so on.

As a network grows in clients, servers, and services, you can add multiple segments to help manage and organize the resources. Each segment added to a network is usually formed into a separate domain for administration purposes, although you can use one domain to contain multiple segments.

Each new domain, or segment, must have a server that authenticates the users within that domain. Users from one domain cannot access the servers in another domain unless they have explicit permission to do so. Two or more domains can, however, create a trust relationship in which the users can access resources when permitted.

Looking at client requirements

The requirements for the clients on a client/server network are similar to those on a peer-to-peer network. For each client computer on the network, you need a network adapter card. Compatible cabling is also necessary, as well as any other networking hardware — a hub, for example.

> **CROSS-REFERENCE:** See "Discovering Other Networking Hardware" later in this chapter for more information on hubs and networking hardware in general.

You can add printers and other resources to the network, as well. When you add resources, you choose whether to attach them to a local computer or to the server computer. For example, you might have a laser printer you attach to the server and let everyone access. You might have a color inkjet or an old dot-matrix printer, on the other hand, that you attach to just one machine for use by that one computer. A network operating system doesn't share resources attached to the clients, only those resources attached to the network or to the server are shared.

In addition to the client and networking hardware, you need to obtain and set up a server computer. Again, it is important to note that only Windows XP Professional is designed to take full advantage of domain-based computing — Windows XP Home edition is designed for small office and home networks.

> **TIP:** You should always use an Uninterruptible Power Source (UPS) on the server, so you can properly shut the server down before a power outage affects it.

Considering server requirements

A server computer must have sufficient processor speed, RAM, and disk space to provide various services to the clients. The server's hardware configuration depends on the type of services it will offer and the number of clients on the network.

TIP: If you decide you need a server, you should also consider a backup server. It doesn't take long for a server to become indispensable, and the data stored there is often irreplaceable. A backup server running a NOS keeps an up-to-date replication of all data on the other server. If the original server crashes, or becomes inoperable for some reason, the backup server can take over without a loss in time, money, or data.

In addition to hardware, the server needs a compatible operating system. You can use a network operating system such as Windows 2000 Server. You also can choose other network operating systems, such as Novell NetWare or Banyan VINES, although additional client software and possibly protocols may be required. A network operating system supplies more management, security, and other features and tools that make operating the network efficient.

NOTE: Throughout this chapter, I have referred to Windows 2000 Server, which is the current version of the Microsoft Server product at the time of this writing. However, Windows XP will be fully compatible with the next release of Windows Server, which is likely to appear sometime in 2002.

TIP: You can purchase server computers, complete with operating system, that are built specifically for the job. These computers have all of the hardware compatible for the chosen operating system. You might want a supercomputer, which is a computer that has massive amounts of RAM, caching, and disk space. Or you might need only a computer with extra memory and disk space for storing files and accessing the Internet.

The hardware you choose for your server must first and foremost be compatible with the network operating system (NOS). You should first choose the operating system you will use, and then purchase the server computer. Each NOS requires specific amounts of memory and disk space, and perhaps certain drive types — such as Small Computer System Interface (SCSI) or Integrated Drive Electronics (IDE) — and other such requirements.

NOTE: IDE, a popular hard disk interface standard that provides only medium to fast data transfer rates, isn't always a good interface for server applications because it's slow and has other limitations in functionality that hamper a server's operations. However, you can use an IDE interface in some server circumstances, depending on the NOS.

On the other hand, SCSI is a high-speed parallel interface. In addition to being fast and extremely practical for server use, SCSI devices are used to connect up to seven peripheral devices at a time to a personal computer using a single port. SCSI devices include hard disks, tape drives, CD-ROM drives, other mass-media storage devices, scanners, and printers.

Examining network operating systems

A NOS is an operating system that is designed specifically for a server. A NOS offers many features and tools that help you manage the network, clients, applications, security, and other facets of the network.

You might want to use a NOS for any of a variety of reasons. Perhaps you have specific networking needs — such as security problems, a home business, or a Web business.

Another reason to choose a particular network operating system is that you're using an application that requires it. For example, Internet Information Server (IIS, a Web server) works best with the NT Server or Windows 2000 Server network operating system. Some vertical-market applications, such as programs for selling and listing real estate or managing an insurance business, might require a specific NOS.

Some of the features found in NOSs are the following:

♦ All NOSs include a tool for naming the users of the network and limiting their access to certain resources. Through user accounts, you can choose which files and folders a user may access, which resources the user may use, and limit the user's access to other computers or servers, as well.

♦ A good network operating system includes some sort of printer management tool. This tool helps you to direct print jobs to the appropriate printer, to cancel and delete jobs, and otherwise to control printing on the network.

◆ Most network operating systems include diagnostic tools for examining the network components, such as protocols and connections. When something goes wrong with a connection, these tools make it easier to find the problem.

◆ Tools and utilities for gathering network data and analyzing it might be important to you. Some NOSs log application errors and security breaches, for example. Others use optimization utilities to help you determine where the network connections are slow.

◆ Some NOSs include Web utilities and support for browsers. You might want to create your own Web server, for example, for displaying company home pages over the Internet.

Some of the most popular NOSs are:

◆ Windows 2000 Server

◆ Microsoft Windows NT Server

◆ Microsoft LAN Manager

◆ Novell NetWare/IntranetWare

◆ IBM LAN Server

◆ IBM OS/2 Warp Server

Looking at dial-up networking from the client's point of view

Remote access defines attaching to a network from another location and accessing resources from the remote computer. For example, you might attach to your work computer from home or from the road in order to access a file or your e-mail. Using remote access, you can access files, programs, printers, and any other resource on your work computer and other computers on the network for which you have permission. Using remote access to keep in touch with the office is called telecommuting.

> **TIP:** Companies often save office space, insurance, and spend less time and money on remote workers than they do on office workers. In addition, the remote worker saves wasted commuting time, sets his or her own schedule, and has better morale than if he or she were stuck in an office all day.

Filling the client's needs

You will need certain equipment in your home or remote office to enable you to work efficiently. Your company might supply the equipment you need, or you might have to purchase it yourself. Generally, you need the following:

◆ Computer and modem

◆ Communications software

◆ A fast connection to the office

◆ Printer

◆ Phone line

◆ Backup media such as Iomega Zip disks, a tape drive, or a CD-RW drive

◆ Virus protection

> **TIP:** If you are on the road and travel a lot with your work, keep a kit with you at all times that contains such things as an extra computer battery, a spare phone cord, a list of support numbers, spare floppy disks, your Windows XP installation CD, and so on.

Establishing the client's duties

Make sure that you understand how your company defines telecommuting and any guidelines it has for use of the equipment. Also, ask about insurance for the equipment, inquire about how upgrades and repairs are to be handled, and so on.

If you are working away from the office, your first responsibility is to stay in touch with your coworkers to make sure everyone is on the same page. You might need to telephone or e-mail daily, for example, to discuss projects, procedures, or other factors affecting you and others who remain in the office.

Understanding Network Topologies and Technologies

Topology describes how the cables, networking hardware, and computers are arranged and located. Technology refers to the type of wiring and hardware you use. Topology and technology are closely related. The topology you choose must use a specific technology.

Defining topologies

Basically, there are three topologies you might choose to use in your business: bus, spanning tree (or star), and ring. When you choose a topology, you also must choose the technology that best suits the topology, plus the connectors, protocols, and hardware that uses that technology.

Examining bus topology

The bus topology connects computers along one length of cable. Bus topology limits the network in that only 30 or so users can be connected to a segment. Another problem with the bus topology is that the network is slow because only one network packet can be sent at a time. Figure 19-4 illustrates the bus topology; computers attach along a single length of cable.

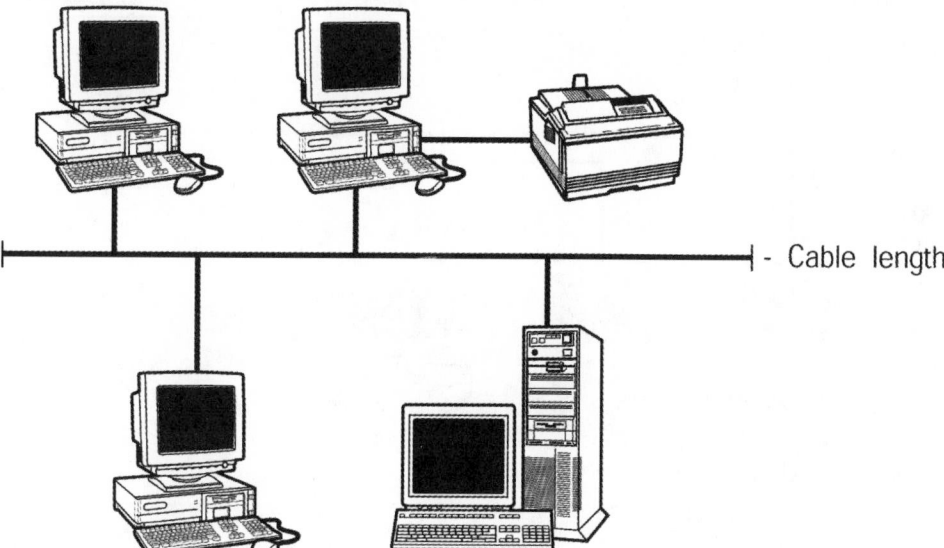

Figure 19-4: The bus topology isn't flexible or scalable.

When there is a problem within the network — say a cable connecting two computers goes bad — the problem cable can be difficult to locate. The entire network must be shut down until the cable is found and fixed. One final problem with the bus topology is that it's not scalable. If you want to expand in the future, it is difficult to add equipment because of the way the network is set up.

Exploring star or spanning tree topology

A spanning tree (also called star) topology connects all computers through a central hub. All packets of data must pass through the hub before they can reach their destination. The hub is a box that contains ports in which to plug networking cables; each computer plugs into the hub with a separate cable. When the hub receives a signal from a computer on the network, it modifies and then distributes the signal to all the other computers on the network.

Figure 19-5 shows a spanning tree network. Hubs make it possible to extend the network so that more workstations can access the resources.

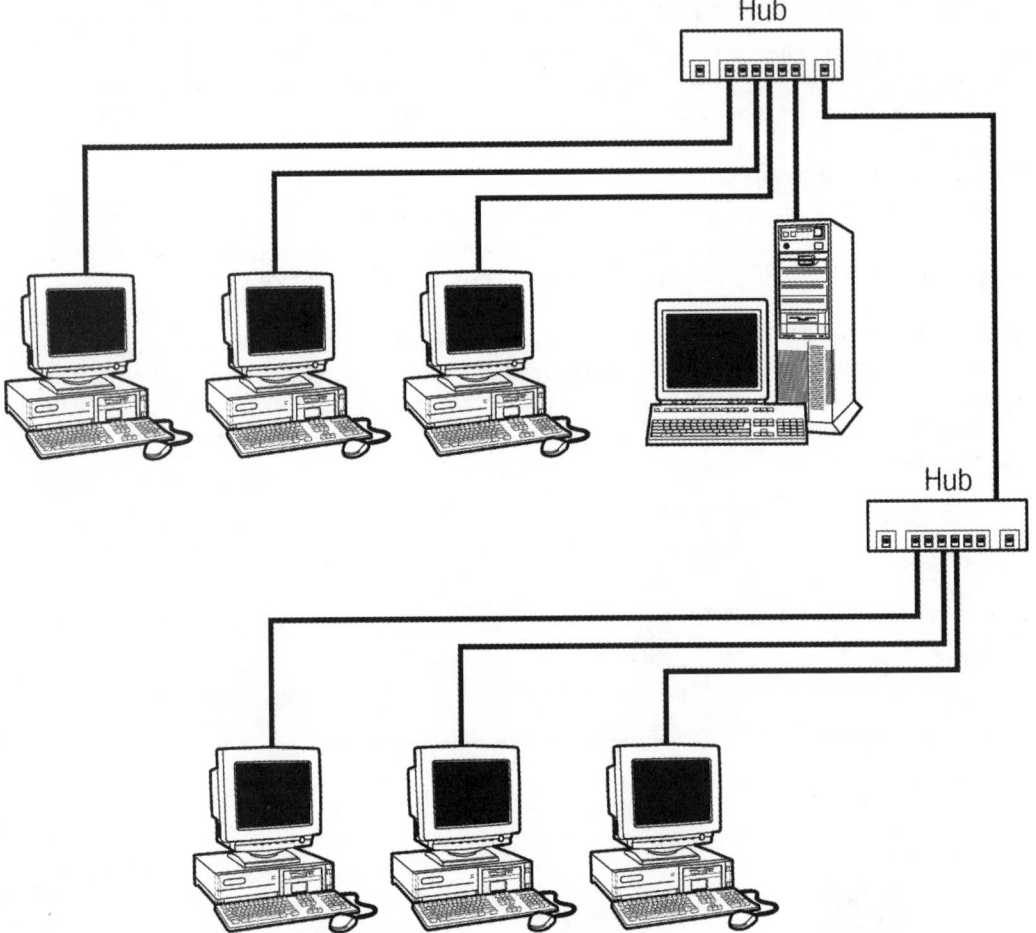

Figure 19-5: A spanning tree network branches out with the use of hubs.

TIP: Spanning tree is the perfect topology for small business offices, but you can grow only to a depth of 3 or 4 hubs You can start with three to seven computers, for example, and keep adding hubs to expand the network as needed. Additionally, spanning tree is the perfect solution for a client/server network; you can add clients and servers on various segments of the network whenever you hire new employees or add to your networking hardware.

Considering ring topology

Ring networks are usually large because the technology can cover great distances. In addition, ring networks often use fiber-optic cable. Figure 19-6 illustrates a simple ring network.

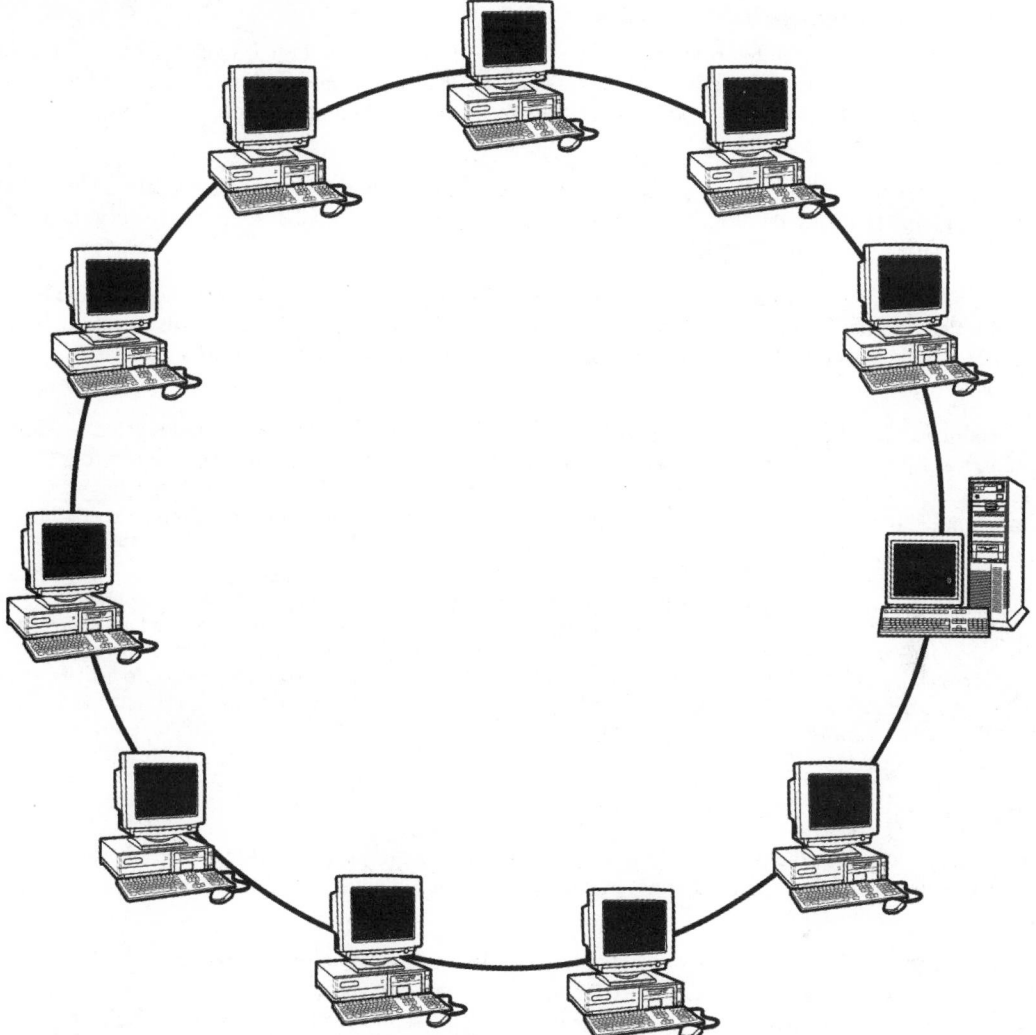

Figure 19-6: A ring network enables token passing from one computer to the next.

The ring topology passes packets from one computer to the next, in one direction only: around a circle (ring). When one computer wants to send data to another, it must first capture a token, which passes around the ring, waiting for someone to transmit information. The token picks up the destination address and the message and then travels around the ring until the destination computer picks it up.

One problem with a ring network is that if a cable or card fails, no data can pass around the network until the problem is corrected.

Defining network technologies

Network technologies refer to the architecture and protocols used on certain networks; Ethernet and Token Ring are two common technologies. The technology you choose governs the speed of the network, the type of cabling you use, and the network cards you install to your computers. Additionally, you must use networking hardware to match the technology you choose.

Identifying Ethernet

Ethernet is a protocol and cabling scheme that can use the bus or the spanning tree topology connected with various cabling types, as described later in this chapter. Ethernet transfers data at the rate of 10 megabits per second (Mbps), which means it can transfer 10 million bits of information per second from one networked computer to another.

An Ethernet packet is variable-length, and a packet consists of a destination address, a source address, the data, and an error-checking mode called cyclic redundancy check (CRC). CRC confirms the accuracy of the data after it's received at its destination.

Common implementations of Ethernet are 10Base2 and 10BaseT. These standards refer to the cable type used with the Ethernet technology. 10Base2 is used with coaxial cable, and 10BaseT is used with twisted-pair cable. See the section, "Regarding Cable and Connections," later in this chapter for more information.

The speed for an Ethernet network is fast and the technology is flexible. Ethernet provides effective data transfer rates for most local area networks (LANs). Realize, however, that the speed of the network (10 Mbps) works in ideal situations. When other issues interfere with the network — such as packet size, degradation of signals, and excess use of the network— the speed and performance of the network varies and degrades somewhat.

> **TIP:** Ethernet is an example of a packet-switched network. Packet switching is a method of delivering packets to their destinations, even if each packet follows a different path. Packets are not received at the same time or in the same order as they were sent, but Ethernet assigns sequence numbers to each packet to help the destination computer reassemble the packets to complete the data. Packet switching is the perfect method of transmission for such data as files, print jobs, surfing the Web, and so on; however, packet switching is not efficient for delivering data such as live audio and video. Circuit switching networks such as Asynchronous Transmission Mode (ATM) are perfect for delivering audio and video applications and files.

Considering Fast Ethernet

Ethernet technology also includes Fast Ethernet. Fast Ethernet's rates are 100 Mbps. Fast Ethernet uses cabling, network cards, hubs, and other networking equipment to match the 100 Mbps speed and works well with the spanning tree topology.

The common standard implementation for Fast Ethernet is 100BaseTX, although 100BaseT4 is growing in the market. 100BaseTX requires Category 5 twisted-pair cabling, and 100BaseT4 can work with either Category 5 or Category 3 twisted-pair. For more information, see the section "Regarding Cable and Connections" later in this chapter.

Fast Ethernet may be a viable choice for your network. You should consider Fast Ethernet if someone on the network plans to regularly use large graphics, audio, or video files, or if you plan to upgrade your network to add more clients, a server or two, and more services. Fast Ethernet provides more bandwidth to your network to accommodate these larger, processor-intensive file types. You also can use Fast Ethernet as a backbone for multiple workstations and servers. Bandwidth is a measurement of the amount of information or data that can pass through any given point on the network: cabling, hub, network cards, and so on — the wider the bandwidth, the more data that can pass through.

> **SECRET:** You can start your network with Ethernet and easily upgrade to Fast Ethernet, if necessary. You can purchase network cards and hubs that work with either a 10 Mbps or a 100 Mbps network, called 10/100 cards. First, buy 10/100 cards for your network. You can use these cards with the cabling and 10 Mbps hubs for a 10 Mbps network. When you can afford the more expensive 100 Mbps hub, simply buy and install it. The 10/100 network cards and the cabling can then be used to create a 100 Mbps network.
>
> Additionally, don't forget about cabling when you perform an upgrade. If you move from a 10BaseT implementation to a 100BaseT implementation, your cabling must be able to support 100 Mbps.

Examining Token Ring

The Token Ring protocol uses the token passing methodology and a ring topology, and it can transmit data at 16 Mbps and 100 Mbps. Token Ring is usually used for larger networks. The networking hardware and wiring is expensive and complicated to install and is, therefore, often used for large client/server networks.

> **TIP:** Token Ring networks have several advantages over Ethernet networks; for example, they support larger packets and therefore more data within a given period of time. Token Ring networks are also very efficient because of the order and method of data transmission. Use Token Ring when you consistently move very large files over the network.

Computers on a Token Ring network take turns sending data. A token (a special network packet) is passed from computer to computer. When a computer has the token, it is that computer's turn to transmit data. The data, plus the token, move to the next computer, and so on.

Problems in a Token Ring network occur when one node — or computer on the network — is down or has connection problems. Unless the ring is maintained, tokens cannot pass through and communications stop until the cable or computer is repaired.

Multistation Access Units (MAUs) are often used to keep the ring working when a workstation fails. MAUs are a series of stacked hubs connected together to bypass the workstation and continue passing the token.

Exploring Fiber Distributed Data Interface

Fiber Distributed Data Interface (FDDI) networks also use the token-passing method of data transmission on the star or ring topology. FDDI most often uses two interconnected rings to create a communications network. The dual rings provide a guarantee that communications continue if one ring fails.

> **TIP:** FDDI uses only one ring; the two rings create a fault-tolerance safeguard.

FDDI uses fiber-optic cabling, although it also can use Category 5 twisted-pair to the desktop. See the section "Regarding Cable and Connections" later in this chapter for more information. FDDI is often used for servers and backbones, as opposed to local area networks.

Looking at backbones

A backbone manages the majority of network traffic. Not all networks need a backbone — only large networks with excessive traffic. Backbones often connect multiple network segments across offices and buildings. Backbones support a high-speed protocol and use different cabling than a LAN, so that masses of data can quickly pass through.

A backbone might provide connections between server rooms and telecommunications closets. Server rooms are a convenient area set off from the rest of the office where multiple servers reside for easier troubleshooting, upgrading, as well as for better security over the equipment. A telecommunications closet is the room or area in which all hubs, routers, and other networking equipment is located for easy troubleshooting and maintenance.

Gigabit Ethernet (also called 1Gbps Ethernet) operates at 1000 Mbps and makes a perfect backbone for a corporate network. The standard implementation for Gigabit Ethernet is 1000BaseSX, which is perfect for a single office or building; 1000BaseSX could, however, be a problem with longer distances.

> **TIP:** Gigabit Ethernet was created to compete with ATM. ATM has been around longer than Gigabit Ethernet, but ATM vendors continue to disagree on standards for the technology; thus ATM hasn't really come into its own.

Gigabit Ethernet runs over fiber-optic cabling, although it can use twisted-pair from servers or telecommunications closets, for example. When used with twisted-pair, Gigabit Ethernet is limited in distance to 70 feet or less. With fiber cabling, the distances range as far as 1600 feet.

ATM can manage live video and audio files, video conferencing, large graphics, and other such data that requires high speed and high performance. With ATM, only one transmission takes place at a time, so large file transfers don't collide with other network traffic.

ATM also uses a fixed cell (packet) size for all data transmission, which makes the network traffic more foreseeable and more easily managed than the variable packet networks, such as Ethernet. In addition, ATM's packet size is nearly three times as large as any Ethernet packet size, resulting in a more efficient transfer of data and fewer bottlenecks.

> **TIP:** A bottleneck is any component on the network that slows the transmission of data. A bottleneck might be the speed difference between the client computer and the server; or it could be a server's slow hard disk transferring only one-half of the packets it receives per second. Applications, image files, RAM, and even the difference between network cards can all cause bottlenecks.

Regarding Cable and Connections

Cabling provides the physical connection between computers. Cabling is used for transmitting and receiving information over the network. You can connect your network with any of various types of cabling, including traditional cabling such as coaxial or twisted-pair, fiber optic, and even radio signals or infrared.

> **TIP:** When preparing to cable your office network, check with your city for any applicable building codes. Some building and commercial codes prohibit laying cable without specific permits and permissions.

The cable you choose must be suited for the distance between your computers. Some cables work better with short distances, while others reach farther between machines. You also choose the type of cabling to match the network cards and other networking hardware.

Network cabling and other equipment have standards that are set by the Institute of Electrical and Electronics Engineers (IEEE) to ensure interoperability of products and services from vendor to vendor. The IEEE 802 series of standards sets computing and electrical engineering standards. Check standards before you buy. The common IEEE (pronounced eye-triple-E) 802 standards defining local area network criteria are:

- 802.1 — Network management and bridging
- 802.2 — LAN data-link protocols
- 802.3 — Ethernet standards
- 802.4 — Bus topology using token passing
- 802.9 — Integrated data and voice networks
- 802.10 — LAN security
- 802.11 — Wireless connections

> **CROSS-REFERENCE:** See Chapter 21 to learn more about Windows XP's support of 802.11.

Using coaxial and twisted-pair cabling

The decision you make on the type of cable depends on the speed you want for your network. Consider how difficult or easy the cable is to install, how expensive the cabling solution is, the distance between computers, and your security issues.

Defining coaxial

Coaxial — or coax — cable is inexpensive to use on a network; however, it is used less frequently today because it is not upgradeable. Don't use coax for your network unless you plan to connect only a few computers and you never expect to upgrade, add computers, or add users.

TIP: Thin coax works well with Ethernet; however, it can't work with Fast Ethernet. If you choose to upgrade your Ethernet to Fast Ethernet later, you'll have to throw out all of your 10Base2 cabling and hardware and start from the beginning to build a faster network.

The cable consists of a plastic jacket surrounding a braided copper shield, plastic insulation, and a solid inner conductor. Coaxial cabling is also called thin net, or thin Ethernet cabling, and it's used with 10Base2 standard implementation. The data-transfer rate for 10Base2 is 10 Mbps over 185 meters. The 185-meter limit (around 607 feet) describes the maximum cable segment length.

Thin Ethernet doesn't require a hub because you can use special connectors for joining two or more computers. You can use T-connectors to attach the thin coaxial cable to a BNC connector on the Ethernet network interface card. However, it is important to note here that Thin Ethernet and BNC connections are rather old and virtually no one is implementing them at this point. I'm mentioning them here for reference purposes, but they represent an older technology that is quickly falling by the wayside.

Defining twisted-pair

Twisted-pair cabling is similar to common phone wire, but it is a higher grade of cabling that enables high-speed data to travel over it. The majority of networks today use twisted-pair because it's relatively inexpensive and it offers high rates of data transfer.

Twisted-pair cable consists of two or more pairs of insulated wires twisted together. In each twisted pair, one wire carries the signal and the other wire is grounded. The cable can either be unshielded twisted-pair (UTP) or shielded twisted-pair (STP).

Shielded twisted-pair cable has a foil shield and copper braid surrounding the pairs of wires. STP provides high-speed transmission for long distances. Unshielded twisted-pair cable also contains two or more pairs of twisted copper wires; however, UTP is easier to install, costs less, limits signaling speeds, and has a shorter maximum cable segment length than STP.

Twisted-pair uses 10BaseT standard implementation over UTP wiring and uses RJ-45 connectors. 10BaseT provides data transfer speeds up to 100 Mbps. You use the star topology with twisted-pair so that each computer on the network connects to a central hub. The maximum cable segment length for twisted-pair is around 100 meters, or 328 feet.

TIP: If you use the 10BaseT cabling scheme, you have to buy network cards that accept 10BaseT, or twisted-pair cabling. You must also buy Ethernet-specific cables. Further, you need to buy a 10BaseT hub — one with jacks for twisted-pair plugs.

There are categories — or levels — of twisted-pair cabling. Each level describes the performance characteristics of the wiring standard. Of the levels of twisted-pair cabling, Category 3 (Cat 3) and Category 5 (Cat 5) are the most common. Cat 3 is less expensive than Cat 5, but its transfer rate isn't as fast.

> **TIP:** Cat 5 works equally well with 10BaseT or with 100BaseTX. You might want to start your network with Cat 5 cabling and 10BaseT hardware — 10Mbps network cards and hub. Then, when you're ready, upgrade to 100BaseTX hardware.
>
> You also can purchase network cards — called 10/100 cards — that operate at both 10 Mbps and 100 Mbps. Use these cards and Cat 5 cabling for a network speed of 10 Mbps. Then, when you're ready, you can upgrade with the purchase of a 100 Mbps hub.

Choosing the right cabling type

Consider the following if you have any doubts as to the type of cabling you want to use in your network:

Choose coaxial cabling if you:

- Have fewer than ten computers
- Don't have any portable computers (laptops, notebooks) on the network
- Plan to never expand the network

Choose 10BaseT cabling with a hub if you:

- Have fewer than ten computers
- The computers are within 328 feet or so of each other
- Have portable computers to connect to the network
- Might, at some point, need to add computers to the network

Choose 100BaseTX (Fast Ethernp) cabling with a hub if you:

- Plan to use large graphic files, streaming audio, and/or video

Using wireless connections

A wireless connection creates a network using technologies other than conventional cabling. Microwave, radio signals, infrared beams, and laser links use electromagnetic signals to create these links. Speeds vary from 1 Mbps to 10 Mbps in wireless networks, although manufacturers are working to increase the speed of their products.

Wireless connections have become a standard for many networks that use desktop computers, as well as with those that use portable computers. Wireless connections provide connection without physical limitations.

Manufacturers have established and adhere to universal standards for connecting computing devices through wireless technologies. Set standards guarantee that hardware from different vendors will be compatible.

On the other hand, interference from the atmosphere, obstacles, and other technologies make wireless connections less predictable than cable connections. Additionally, data transfer rates are slower with wireless than with cable, although new technologies are in the works.

> **TIP:** Even though standards have been set for wireless network connections, not all wireless manufacturers meet those standards. The IEEE standard for wireless network connections is 802.11. Check before you buy.

There are four common methods of communication to wireless networking — infrared, radio signals, microwave, and laser links. The most popular wireless connections for networks are radio signals and infrared connections. Microwave and lasers might have a use in large corporate, educational, or government networks.

> **TIP:** It's common to use wireless connections in conjunction with other cabling methods. You might want to use Cat 5 twisted-pair cabling for the majority of your network, and add a few wireless connections where appropriate, such as for mobile workers or separate buildings.

Understanding infrared

Infrared works similarly to a television's remote control. The connection must be line-of-sight; infrared cannot penetrate obstacles. The cone of the infrared beam is highly directional and ensures that the infrared connection doesn't spill to other nearby devices. The transmission distance for infrared is relatively short.

TIP: When two infrared devices are within range of one another, Windows XP automatically detects the second device and establishes an automatic connection. See Chapter 21 to learn more about wireless networking.

One of the major benefits of infrared transmission is increased bandwidth for each user. Instead of shared bandwidth, as with cables, each user receives dedicated bandwidth. Infrared also provides a safe, invisible light wave for transferring data.

Breaking the cone of infrared light might disconnect the infrared connection, depending on the length and severity of the break. If the data transmission is interrupted however, the protocol resubmits the data repeatedly until the data is successfully transmitted or the limit is exceeded.

Understanding Radio Frequency

Radio Frequency (RF) is the type of wireless communication method used in many wireless networks today. Radio signals are accessible to most users throughout the world. RF is a common method of wireless communication, as implemented in 802.11, and it provides a way to wireless connect computers and peripherals.

Radio signals penetrate many obstacles, such as walls, doors, and ceilings. RF can even pass through thick walls, but the transmission time can be slow.

RF signals are fairly secure against tampering from outside sources. Additionally, spread-spectrum products provide 1 to 2 Mbps data rates at a range of 50 to 1000 feet, depending on the building construction, interference sources, and other factors. Radio frequency systems are generally slower than 10 Mbps Ethernet, and they are often quite expensive.

CROSS-REFERENCE: You can learn more about wireless networking concepts in Chapter 21.

Using fiber-optic cable

Fiber-optic cable is often used as the backbone cable for large networks; however, it might become useful in smaller networks in the near future as data speed requirements increase and the price of fiber drops. Fiber optic cabling is reliable, fast, and expensive. Fiber optic cables are difficult and expensive to install and to repair.

Fiber-optic cabling works by transmitting pulses of light through a glass or plastic core. A plastic shield of PVC protects the fibers. Fiber optic cable can transmit at speeds of 655 Mbps and even 1 Gbps for up to 6562 feet.

All fiber transmissions take place in one direction only; fiber can either send or receive, but it cannot receive while it is sending — or vice versa. However, because the transmission speeds are so great, the direction problem is a minor one.

Discovering Other Networking Hardware

Networking hardware includes network interface cards, hubs, routers, and switches. This is the equipment you use to build your network. You insert network interface cards into each computer. Additionally, for 10BaseT and 100BaseT network segments you must use a hub if you connect three or more computers; 10Base2 or Thin Ethernet coax systems use T-connections at each workstation and special termination plugs at the ends of the cable. You might not use routers and switches in your network; it depends on the size and purpose of your network.

> **TIP:** When choosing networking hardware, make sure it is compatible with the IEEE standards listed earlier in this chapter.

Examining network interface cards

A network interface card (also called a NIC — pronounced "nick" — network card, or network adapter card) is a printed circuit board that plugs into a slot inside the computer and connects the computer to the network. The network card also connects to the network media (cable), which, in turn, connects all of the network interface cards to the network so the computers can communicate.

> **NOTE:** The connections between the network card and the cable depend on the cable type. Coaxial cable uses a BNC connector, whereas twisted-pair cabling uses a RJ-45 connector.

A network card usually comes with a disk that includes any network driver software used to configure the network card. The card translates commands so that it can manage the placement of the flow of data to and from the computer.

> **TIP:** After you purchase a network interface card, go to the card manufacturer's Web site on the Internet and download the most updated software driver for that particular card. Manufacturers are always updating the drivers to make the card work more efficiently. The latest driver will be on the Web, not on the disk that comes with the new card.

Network cards can cause problems upon installation. Depending on the other devices in and software on a computer, it might be difficult to get a card to work. Sometimes it's the brand of the card, and sometimes it's from other problems. Under most circumstances, Windows XP can automatically detect, install, and configure network adapter cards that are attached to you computer. See Chapter 20 to learn more about network adapter cards for home and small office networking, and you can learn more about hardware installation and configuration in Chapter 11.

Determining when to use hubs, bridges, repeaters, switches, and routers

Most networks require a hub, and many networks can make use of switches, bridges, repeaters, and routers. These devices extend services, interpret data, boost performance, and provide other benefits to the network.

Table 19-1 summarizes the uses of each hardware device.

Table 19-1: Hardware Devices and Uses

Device	Use
Hub	Extends the network by adding computers
Bridge	Connects networks that use different protocols
Repeater	Extends the length a network cable can reach
Switch	Connects similar networks to add speed to the network
Router	Connects similar or dissimilar networks to add speed through intelligent addressing

Hubs

A hub is a device that modifies network transmission signals, thereby allowing you to extend the network for additional workstations. There are two kinds of hubs: an active and a passive hub. An active hub amplifies the transmission signals to help extend cable length. A passive hub splits the transmission signal so that another client computer can be added.

> **TIP:** Use hubs with twisted-pair cabling in a star or spanning tree topology. You must also match the hub type with the network technology. For example, if you use 10BaseT twisted-pair cabling and cards, you must also use a 10BaseT hub.

Figure 19-7 illustrates how a hub acts as a central device to which all computers are attached. Signals travel from computer to hub and then to the destination computer.

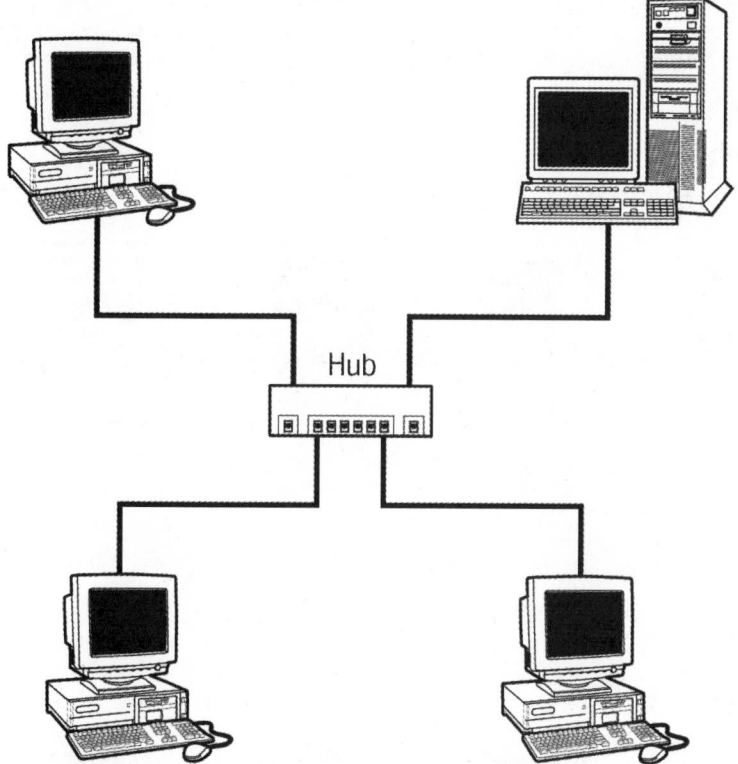

Hub

Figure 19-7: You must use a hub when you connect more than two computers in a 10BaseT or 100BaseT network.

Hubs come with a certain number of ports, including 4, 5, 8, 16, and 24. You plug one computer into each hub. The hub protects other computers on the network so that the other computers aren't hindered by one bad connection.

> **TIP:** Choose a hub with more ports than you think you'll need for your network. Consider doubling the number of ports; for example, if you think you'll only need 12 ports, consider buying a 24-port hub. You'll be surprised how quickly a network can grow.

Stackable hubs are reasonable for most businesses to use. With stackable hubs, you can add a hub as you need it — say as your network grows. One hub stacks on top of the next. You can save money by buying the hub size you need, an 8-port hub, for example. Then, as your network grows, you can add another 8- or 12-port hub and link the hubs together.

> **SECRET:** When buying stackable hubs, consider buying managed — or intelligent — hubs. Managed hubs include software that enables you to communicate with the device and to check the status of the ports, to send out alerts, and so on. This monitoring software makes troubleshooting hub problems easier, and helps you to get back online more quickly. However, smart hubs may cost considerably more than standard hubs, so price comparisons are worth your time and effort.

Bridges

Use a bridge to connect to network segments or LANs that use different protocols or different wiring, in most cases. The bridge examines a packet to see if its destination is on the same network. If the destination is not on the same network, the bridge forwards the packet to another segment. As a bridge monitors messages and reads packets, it learns where each network system is located. It constructs a table of the media access control (MAC) addresses that are accessible by its ports and uses those addresses to regulate the flow of traffic on the network.

NOTE: An Ethernet address is also called a MAC address. It's a number written as 12 hexadecimal digits — 0 through 9 and A through F — as in 0080001021ef. Alternatively, a MAC address might have six hexadecimal numbers separated by periods or colons, as in 0:80:0:2:21:ef. The MAC address is unique to each computer and does not identify the location of the computer — only the computer itself.

Figure 19-8 illustrates how a bridge connects two network segments.

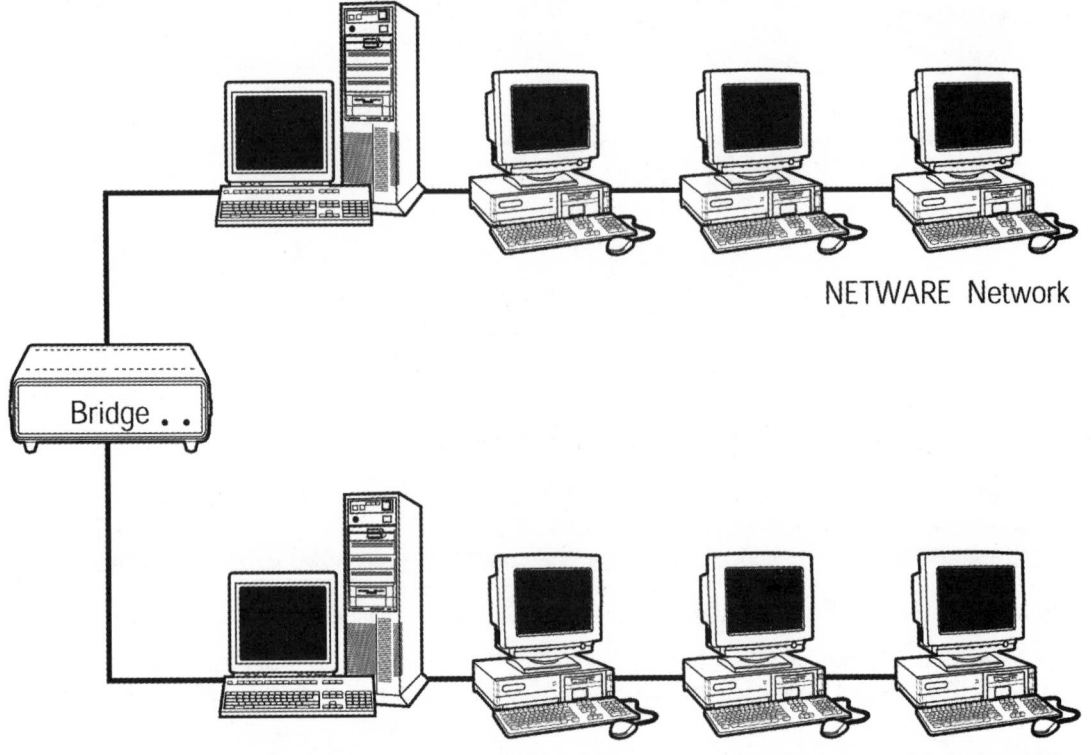

Figure 19-8: A bridge connects network segments using different protocols.

TIP: Translating bridges (Brouters) connect networks with different architectures, such as Macintosh and UNIX.

Bridges can cause traffic problems on large networks because they do forward all packets for which they don't know the destination address. However, bridges are less expensive than routers, and they are also easier to install and configure.

SECRET: Don't use bridges and routers on the same network. Traffic gets jammed because bridges are less discriminating than routers, and packets often must bounce back and forth to reach the appropriate destination.

Repeaters

Use the inexpensive repeater to extend cable lengths. You can double the length of a network cable by positioning a repeater halfway between the cable lengths. You can even use multiple repeaters to extend the distance to the maximum that the specifications allow.

Figure 19-9 shows how a repeater can extend twisted-pair cabling in an Ethernet network.

You use the star topology with twisted-pair so that each computer on the network connects to a central hub. The maximum cable segment length for twisted-pair is around 100 meters, or 328 feet.

Figure 19-9: Repeaters amplify the signal so that it can travel longer distances over the transmission medium.

A repeater is a signal amplifier. Whatever signal the repeater receives, it boosts the signal and sends it on its way. Repeaters don't examine or verify packets; they don't determine data quality. They simply amplify the signals and transmit it to another computer.

Switches

A switch is a cross between a hub and a bridge. Switches connect similar network segments or LANs. Switches filter data and speed the flow between networks by keeping track of the addresses attached to each port, and then routing traffic destined for a certain address.

TIP: To increase bandwidth, use switched hubs instead of shared hubs. Hubs operate on the machine level and cannot discern addresses or errors in packets. Adding a switch to the hub device makes the hub more efficient and speeds traffic on the network.

Routers

A router is an intelligent connecting device that sends packets to the correct LAN or network segment. The router knows the addresses of all computers on the network. When it reads a destination address in a packet, the router can choose the best available path for the packet to travel to get to its destination.

Figure 19-10 shows a router connecting multiple network segments.

Router configuration is complex because it involves setting functions, protocols, hardware interfaces, and parameters. LAN connections are usually easier to configure; Wide Area Network (WAN) connections are a bit harder. With a WAN connection, the line ending is one you don't normally control because the ending is located at, for example, the phone company.

Routers keep track of a packet's movement. That tracking information is stored in the routing table. Each protocol on the network uses its own separate routing table. Also, routers perform error-checking services to make sure bad packets aren't sent through the entire network.

SECRET: Routers are different from bridges in several ways. Routers build tables based on network (IP and other) addresses, whereas bridges build tables based on MAC addresses. You cannot change a MAC address; to alter the address patterns, you have to move computers when you use a bridge. Routers block traffic to unknown addresses but bridges forward it, thus adding to the network traffic. Also, routers block broadcast traffic, while bridges cannot block broadcast traffic. The more broadcast traffic, the more bandwidth used, and the slower the network.

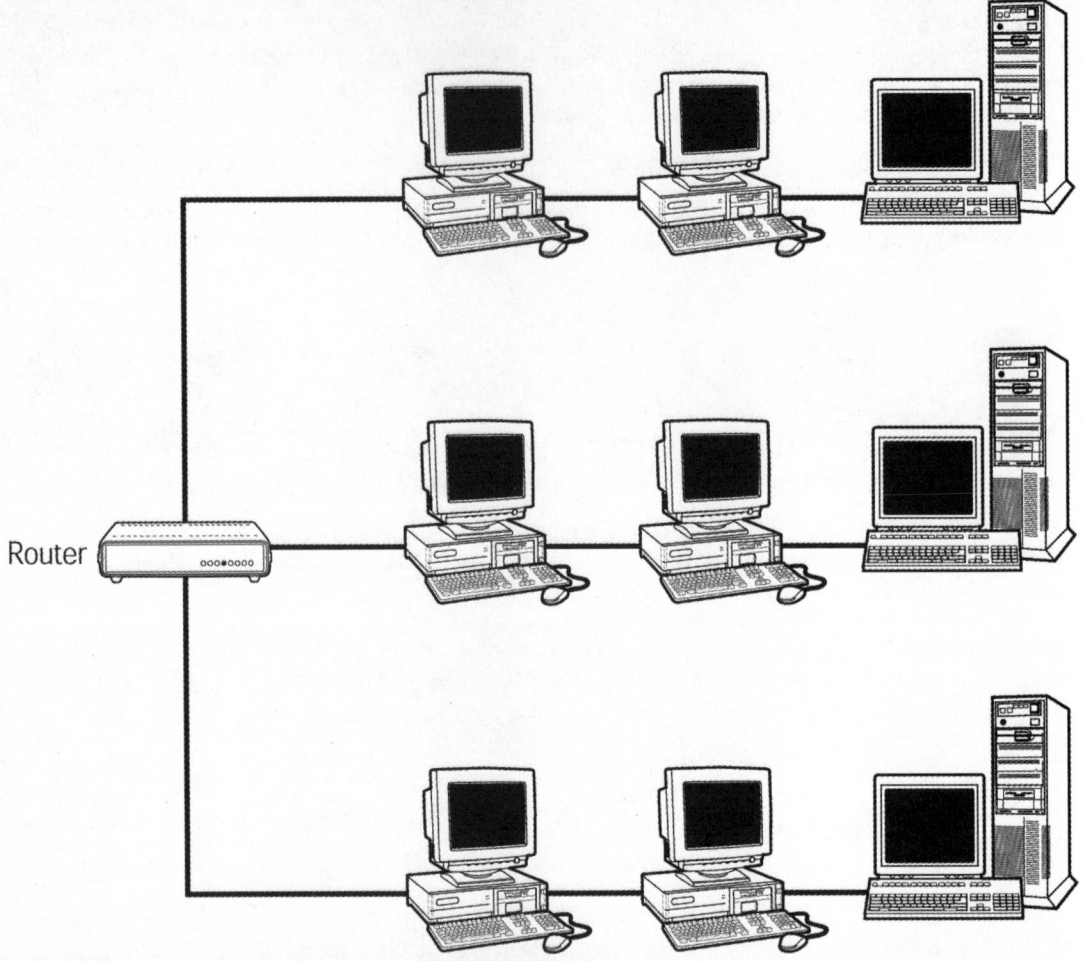

Figure 19-10: Use routers to quickly send the packets to their destinations.

Understanding the Network Software

Even if the pieces of networking hardware — cables, cards, and so on — are attached to your computers, they cannot communicate with each other without networking software. The networking software installed on the computer enables the hardware to do its work.

Windows XP automatically adds a client (Client for Microsoft Networks), protocol (TCP/IP), and services (File and Print Sharing) when it detects a network card in the computer. You can add additional network components and reconfigure components to each network connection, if you want.

> **TIP:** Windows XP automatically sets up the default network connection for you; however, there are times when you might need to change configurations or components in the Networking and Dial-up Connections dialog box. See Chapter 22 for more information.

Defining adapters

In networking, an adapter refers to the software driver that makes the NIC work. Windows locates your adapter and configures it for you; however, you can install a new adapter or change the configuration for an existing adapter in Windows XP.

TIP: When you first turn your computer on after installing a Plug-and-Play network card, Windows detects the card and prompts to install the network driver. You can let Windows install the driver and complete the task. Later, you can add an updated driver, change the driver, or leave the adapter configured as is.

You should always install the latest version of the NIC driver to ensure that the card works efficiently with Windows. It's important to note that the drivers on the manufacturer's disk accompanying the NIC are not necessarily the most recent driver version. For the best solution, check the manufacturer's Web site.

Any time you add a new or change an old device — such as a network card — you can cause your computer to stop working. Each device has it's own settings. If you add another device that tries to take those settings, you have a hardware conflict.

The three settings you must consider are the Interrupt Request (IRQ), Direct Memory Access (DMA), and Input/Output (I/O) addresses. Hardware lines carry a device's signal to the processor. When a device wants to communicate with the processor, it causes an IRQ to gain the processor's attention. The I/O is the means by which data is transferred between the computer and its peripheral devices. DMA is a method of transferring information directly from a hard disk, for example, into memory by bypassing the processor.

TIP: In Windows XP, the IRQ is called the Interrupt Request; the DMA is called the Memory Range; and the I/O is called the Input/Output Range.

IRQs

Most computers have 15 IRQs. Some IRQs are assigned to specific devices, and others are free for cards and devices you install. Following in Table 19-2 is a listing IRQs and some devices that are commonly assigned to specific IRQs.

TIP: To locate the IRQ for your devices, including the network card, check the Device Manager in Windows XP.

Table 19-2: Common IRQ Device Assignments

Interrupt Request	Device
1	Keyboard Controller. IRQ1 is never available to other add-in cards. If there's a conflict with IRQ1, it probably means the system board is bad.
2	Tied to IRQs 9 to 15. Don't use this IRQ if you can help it. IRQs 9 to 15 use it to communicate with the CPU.
3	COM2. Shares IRQ3 with COM4; serial ports use mice, modems, and other such devices.
4	COM1. Shares IRQ4 with COM3, so you cannot assign a device on COM1 and COM3 at the same time.
5	LPT2 or sound card. A secondary printer port; if no secondary printer, then used for sound card. This IRQ may also be open.
6	Floppy disk controller. Not available for other uses if you have a floppy drive.
7	LPT1. First parallel port is used for attached printer. This IRQ may also be open.
8	Clock. Reserved for the internal real-time clock. Never available. If conflict arises, could mean you have a bad motherboard.
9	Cascades from IRQ 2. A high priority IRQ because it talks directly to the CPU. Often used for network cards.

Interrupt Request	Device
10-11	Unused. Open for network cards, sound cards, and other devices.
12	PS/2 mouse. If you use a PS/2 port mouse, this is its IRQ. If you don't use a PS/2 mouse, you can use it for something else.
13	Coprocessor or Numerical Processing Unit (NPU). Never available for anything else.
14	Primary IDE hard disk controller. Not available for other devices.
15	Unused or secondary IDE hard disk controller. Generally not available for other devices.

I/O addresses

I/O addresses refer to locations in a computer's memory map. Addresses are in hexadecimal format, which is a base-16 numbering system that uses the digits 0 to 9 followed by the letters A to F. Hexadecimal numbers represent the binary numbers that computers use internally (they all fit into the 8-bit byte).

Table 19-3 lists common devices that are assigned to certain I/O addresses.

Table 19-3: Common I/O Address Device Assignments

I/O Address	Device
130h	SCSI host adapters
140h	SCSI host adapters
170h	Secondary IDE interface
1F0h	Primary IDE interface
220h	Sound Blaster cards
240h	Sound card alternate
278h	LPT 2 or LPT3 (and generally IRQ 5)
280h	Network interface cards
2A0h	Alternate for NIC
2E8h	COM 4 (with IRQ 3)
2F8h	COM 2 (with IRQ 3)
300h	Network interface cards
320h	Network card, SCSI adapter, or MIDI device
330h	SCSI adapter
340h	SCSI adapter
360h	Network card, unless first parallel printer port is using this address
378h	LPT1 with color systems (with IRQ 7)
3BCh	LPT1 with monochrome systems
3E8h	COM3 (with IRQ 4)
3F8h	COM1 (with IRQ 4)

DMA channels

DMA channels might be an area for hardware conflicts. Plug-and-Play systems use DMAs. The most commonly assigned devices for DMA channels are listed in Table 19-4.

Table 19-4: Common DMA Channel Device Assignments

DMA Channel	Assignment
0	Assigned internally for system board. Not available.
1	No specific assignment; may be used for sound cards and SCSI adapters.
2	Floppy disk drives.
3	No specific assignment; may be used for sound cards, network interface cards, and SCSI adapters.
4	No specific assignment.
5	No specific assignment; may be used for Sound Blaster cards.
6	No specific assignment.
7	No specific assignment.

Defining the network client

The network client is the software that enables your computer to become a member of a network. Each network type — Windows peer-to-peer, NT Server, Novell NetWare, and so on — has its own specific client. You install the client software for the network type to a computer to allow the computer to communicate over the network. Microsoft supplies clients for Microsoft networks, plus clients for NetWare. You also can add a network client.

Novell NetWare also supplies clients for its NOS. If you set up a client/server network with NetWare, you may want to use Novell's client because it offers more features on that particular network than the Windows NetWare client. However, the Novell client also has more compatibility problems with Windows.

Defining Protocols

Protocols are languages that define procedures for transmitting and receiving data over the network. They define the format, timing, sequence, and error checking used on the network. There are many protocols that work on many levels in networking. For example, Ethernet is both a networking technology and a protocol, as is Token Ring. These are communications protocols that guarantee the synchronization and flow of data from computer to computer.

SECRET: Don't install and configure multiple protocols unless you have a specific reason to do so, such as if you're a member of an integrated NetWare and NT network, or you must occasionally communicate with a Macintosh computer. When you install more than one protocol on your workstation, each protocol is checked for every network connection, thus slowing the response time to network transmissions.

Transport protocols send messages and data from one computer to another over the network. The common transport protocols include TCP/IP, Internet Packet Exchange/Sequenced Packet Exchange (IPX/SPX), and Network Basic Input/Output /System Extended User Interface (NetBEUI).

CAUTION: NetBEUI is a fast, non-routable protocol that was heavily used in small Microsoft networks. However, NetBEUI does not provide all of the features and security functions of TCP/IP, and since Windows XP can self-configure its own TCP/IP settings, TCP/IP is now the protocol of choice, even in small office and home networks. See Chapter 20 to learn more about TCP/IP configuration in Windows XP.

NetBEUI

NetBEUI is a Microsoft protocol that you can use with any Windows operating system — Windows for Workgroups, Windows 95, Windows 98, Windows NT, Windows 2000, and Windows XP Professional and Home editions.

NetBEUI is perfect for small networks. It's easy to set up, provides good performance, and is a fast protocol. NetBEUI uses very little memory and also provides good error detection over the network. If you're setting up your first network and you want an easy job of it, use NetBEUI as your networking protocol. NetBEUI is not a routable protocol, so it can work on only one segment of the network. That's why it's best used with small networks of 150 computers or fewer.

Although NetBEUI is easier to use, ICS is designed to function with TCP/IP, so even in small networks, TCP/IP has become the protocol of choice.

> **SECRET:** NetBIOS also works with other protocols and various network types. NetBIOS is an interface for the network protocol; it provides the Transport and Session layer services for the protocol with which it's working. NetBIOS isn't routable, meaning it cannot reach computers located in segments other than its own.

IPX/SPX

IPX/SPX was the protocol used with Novell NetWare networks, at least in the past. Today, most Novell Networks are built on TCP/IP, just as Windows networks are. IPX is used to transfer data between a server and workstations on the network. IPX packets carry the packets used in Ethernet and in Token Ring networks. IPX doesn't guarantee the delivery of data, nor the sequence in which the data is delivered.

SPX is a set of Novell NetWare protocols that adds to the capabilities of IPX. SPX guarantees packet delivery, for example, by requesting verification from the destination computer.

> **TIP:** IPX/SPX supports many of the Windows' features, including NetBIOS and Windows sockets.

IPX/SPX is a routable protocol; however, there are some problems with routing. For example, routing tables are not always accurate because of the way they're built. In addition, routing tables are vulnerable to errors because of the time it takes to circulate packets to other segments.

NWLink IPX/SPX/NetBIOS Compatible Transport Protocol is a Windows XP IPX/SPX-compatible protocol. NWLink supports routing and Novell NetWare client/server applications. In many cases, however, TCP/IP is now used to connect these different clients together.

AppleTalk

AppleTalk is the Apple Computer networking protocol that connects Macintosh clients to an Ethernet network. Windows 2000 Server networks with Macintosh computers attached use the Services for Macintosh feature to enable Macintosh computers to communicate with IBM-compatible computers on the network using the AppleTalk protocol. In addition, the AppleTalk protocol enables file and information shares across an AppleTalk intranet, or a collection of AppleTalk networks.

AppleTalk uses the MAC address to locate computers for packet delivery. The AppleTalk Address Resolution Protocol (AARP) is the protocol that finds MAC addresses by sending out a network broadcast containing the address for which it is searching. When the system replies, AARP adds the MAC address to its mapping table.

DLC

DLC (Data Link Control) uses MAC addresses to provide communications between applications and computer hardware. DLC is not a routable protocol; it works within only one segment.

TCP/IP

TCP/IP is actually a set (stack or suite) of network protocols designed by the government's Advanced Research Projects Agency (hence the name ARPAnet) in the 1970s. Each of the protocols that make up TCP/IP make it an efficient and fast communications language for the Internet and for local and wide area networks.

TCP/IP works with a variety of hardware and software products. You can use it on UNIX, Macintosh, and IBM-compatible computers using Windows, NetWare, OS/2, and more. Many manufacturers and vendors support TCP/IP because it is so widely used.

Some of the protocols in the TCP/IP suite are:

♦ **IP (Internet Protocol)** — IP enables network packets to move data between network segments and to travel across routers. IP is a routing protocol. IP chooses the path the packets take across routers and networks. IP regulates packet forwarding by tracking Internet addresses, recognizing incoming messages, and routing outgoing messages. However, data in these packets (called datagrams) may arrive at the destination in any order or they may not arrive at all.

♦ **TCP (Transmission Control Protocol)** — TCP is a higher-level protocol than IP. It provides continuing connections between programs. TCP also makes IP datagrams smaller and faster. TCP divides datagrams into smaller segments to fit the physical requirements of the servers on the network. Then it uses IP to transmit the segments of data. TCP inserts a header into each segment that is used to track every segment from one port to the other. TCP guarantees that every byte sent arrives and without duplication or loss. After the segments arrive at the target host, TCP checks for errors. If it finds any corrupted data, it discards it and requests the data be transmitted again.

♦ **UDP (User Datagram Protocol)** — UDP is similar to TCP in that it divides some datagrams into segments and sends them over the network using IP. UDP is a primitive version of TCP.

♦ **PPP (Point-to-Point Protocol)** — PPP enables connections between hosts and networks and the nodes (routers, bridges, and so on) in between and is the protocol used to carry TCP/IP across dial-up connections.

♦ **SMTP (Simple Mail Transfer Protocol)** — SMTP is used for exchanging e-mail.

♦ **FTP (File Transfer Protocol)** — FTP is used for transferring files. FTP lets one computer transfer a file to another using TCP.

♦ **SMB (Server Message Block)** — SMB lets a computer use network resources as if they were local.

♦ **NFS (Network File System)** — NFS enables a computer to use files as if they were local.

♦ **TELNET** — This is a terminal emulation protocol that lets you connect to a remote service while in Windows.

♦ **ARP (Address Resolution Protocol)** — ARP translates 32-bit IP addresses into physical network addresses, such as 48-bit Ethernet addresses.

♦ **RARP (Reverse Address Resolution Protocol)** — RARP translates physical network addresses into IP addresses.

♦ **ICMP (Internet Control Message Protocol)** — ICMP helps IP communicate error information about the IP transmissions for routers.

♦ **IGMP (Internet Group Management Protocol)** — IGMP allows IP datagrams to be broadcast to computers that belong to groups.

NOTE: Some of the TCP/IP protocols are also applications. FTP, TELNET, and SNMP, for example, are programs that you can use over the network because they're included with the TCP/IP suite.

An IP address identifies the computer or other node (router, printer, server, or other) on the network. Each IP address on a network must be unique.

An IP address is a binary number that is written in a series of four decimal digits, known as dotted decimal. An IP address is formed by four period-delimited octets, consisting of up to 12 numerals. For example, Microsoft's home page IP address is the dotted decimal number: 207.46.131.137. The numbers represent decimal notations for each of the four bytes of the address; the address identifies the computer.

The IP address is really made up of two parts: the network number and the host number. The network number identifies the general location of the computer on the network, and the host number pins it down to the exact computer. In Microsoft's IP address, 207.46 is the network address. 131.137 represents the host number. Each class of address uses a different manner of dividing the octets. Microsoft is a Class B network.

The highest value in any octet is 255 because of the way the binary format translates to dotted decimal.

IP addressing is divided into five categories, or classes. Three of the classes — Class A, Class B, and Class C — are in use today. The following list describes each of these classes:

- **Class A** is used for large networks. To identify a Class A network address, the first octet uses the numbers from 1 to 126. Class A networks have an 8-bit network prefix; therefore, they are currently referred to as /8s (pronounced slash eights) or just "eights."

- **Class B** is mainly used for medium-sized networks and the first octet values range from 128 to 191. Class B network addresses have a 16-bit network prefix; thus, they are referred to as /16s.

- **Class C** is reserved for smaller networks. To identify a Class C network, the values range from 192 to 223. Class C networks have a 24-bit network prefix and are referred to as /24s.

Universities and corporations have already taken the Class A addresses. Class B addresses are assigned to companies and institutions with a minimum of 4000 hosts. If you apply for an Internet address, you will likely receive a Class C address. Each class defines its own 32-bit address boundaries. In Class C, the first three octets are for the network address; the last octet represents the host address.

A subnet mask is part of the IP addressing system. A subnet mask creates subnetworks that allow a computer in one network segment to communicate with a computer in another segment of the network. The main reason for subnetting (or creating subnets on a network) is to divide a single Class A, B, or C network into smaller pieces.

The subnet mask is a 32-bit address that hides, or masks, part of the IP address so as to add to the number of computers added to the network. All networks must use a subnet mask, even if it doesn't connect to another network. If a network isn't divided into subnets, the default subnet mask is used. The default depends on the IP address class.

- Class A networks use a default subnet mask of 255.0.0.0.
- Class B uses 255.255.0.0.
- Class C uses 255.255.255.0

The gateway is a bridge between two segments of a network. Messages travel between network segments through the gateway. A gateway is a combination of hardware and software; it creates a shared connection between, say, a LAN and a larger network.

There are several IP addresses that are reserved for private use. Following are the three blocks reserved for IP addresses:

- 10.0.0.0 to 10.255.255.255
- 172.16.0.0 to 172.31.255.255
- 192.168.0.0 to 192.168.255.255

You should change numbers only in the last octet of the IP address for a business network. If your corporate network is very large, you can make other changes to the IP addresses, as long as they are consistent.

In addition to IP addresses, you also need a subnet mask. Use the same subnet mask for all computers on the network.

TIP: If all of this information about TCP/IP configuration worries you — don't worry. Windows XP can self-configure its own TCP/IP settings in a small office and home network. See Chapter 20 for details.

Summary

In this chapter, you learned about global networking services, features, and hardware, and about how home, small office, and large networks can meet the needs of both individuals and corporations alike. You explored . . .

♦ How you can choose the type of network that best suits your home or small office.

♦ How, in larger networks, there are a number of networking topologies and technologies that can be implemented.

♦ How Windows XP makes the home and small office network easy to set up and configure.

♦ How various network protocols may be used, although TCP/IP is the protocol of choice in today's small and large networking environments.

Chapter 20

Home and Small Office Networking

In This Chapter

If you reviewed Chapter 19, you learned a thing or two about networking. The concept of networking includes a number of protocols and technologies that make vast, enterprise-scale networks possible. Yet, many of those same technologies apply to a home network of two or more computers, or a small office network consisting of 5 to 20 computers. Because these small networks cannot economically support a server-based design, the workgroup concept is alive and well in homes and small offices everywhere. Microsoft recognizes this fact and includes tools in Windows XP that make home and small office networking simple and easy to configure. In this chapter, you learn to . . .

♦ Set up a home or small office network

♦ Configure network settings

♦ Configure Internet Connection Sharing (ICS)

♦ Share files, folders, and drives

♦ Use connection tools

♦ Use offline folders

Home and Small Office Networking Concepts

Home and small office networking has become very important during the past few years. Although small office networks have been around for quite some time, it has only been in the past three years that home networks have become popular. With the advent of the home PC, families today find themselves upgrading and purchasing new PCs, with the old ones still hanging around for good measure. You can't get any decent money for the older ones at a garage sale, and you don't want to send them to the garbage dump — so what do you do with them? The answer that more people are discovering is to network the computers together. By networking, you can use the resources each computer in your home or small office has to offer. In fact, you can even find entire books on home and small office networking.

The purpose of home and small office networking is to make resources available to users. Simply put, you may have four computers and one printer. Through networking, all of the computers can be connected to that single printer. In home and small office situations, one computer may have files stored on it that are needed by someone on another computer. At home, your children may want to play networked games against each other. Maybe you have a computer in an office and one in your bedroom, but only the office computer is configured with an Internet connection — you can share that, too. In fact, the uses of home networks are quite diverse — access files, share hard drives and CD-ROM drives, run programs, access the Internet, share peripherals, use older computers as file storage servers or even print servers — it's all there with home and small office networking.

The good news is that Windows XP, along with Windows 98, Me, and 2000, make home and small office networking rather simple because Windows can do much of the configuration for you. In fact, in a simple home or small office networking, Windows XP can virtually set everything up without your help. Of course, you can manually set up the network and you can manually adjust settings after it has been set up. I'll explore manual setup a little later in this chapter.

To network computers together, each computer has to be outfitted with a network adapter card of some kind. Typically, this means either an Ethernet card or a Home PNA card that uses your home's phone jacks to network the computers together. Either way, your computer must be outfitted with a network adapter card that can be connected to some kind of cable so that computers in your home can be connected to each other. Using an Ethernet connection, your home network may need a small hub that routes the information between computers. You can learn more about these issues in Chapter 19.

> **NOTE:** If you are unfamiliar with Home PNA, this very user- and small office–friendly type of networking uses typical network cards, but you plug into your home's phone jacks. Using the phone wiring, the computers can communicate with each other. This type of network is typically very handy when you want to network several computers in different rooms in your house — and it doesn't even interfere with phone calls! You can find Home PNA kits at your favorite computer store, often for under $60.

Like Windows Me, Windows XP includes the Network Setup wizard that enables you to create a home or small office network without dealing with TCP/IP configuration. You can also choose to use Internet Connection Sharing, as well as XP's new Internet Connection Firewall (ICF). You can even create connections to computers over the Internet using Remote Desktop connections. The end result is a robust system that can meet your networking needs, regardless of what they might be.

> **CROSS-REFERENCE:** Both ICF and Remote Desktop are covered in more detail in Chapter 22.

In the remaining sections in this chapter, you learn how to set up and configure a home or small office network. I point out relevant technologies along the way, so you know how XP works and what is happening under the hood.

Setting Up a Home or Small Office Network

The Network Setup wizard included with Windows XP is designed to make home and small office network setup a snap. However, it is important to note that the Network Setup wizard is designed for use on home and small office networks only — it is not designed to be used by computers on a Windows 2000/XP domain. If you are on a domain, your computer should be configured for access to a Windows 2000 domain controller, and you can learn more about domain connections in Chapter 21.

In a Windows XP home or small office network, you need one XP computer, preferably the one that has Internet access if you intend to share Internet access with the other computers on your network. This XP computer will be viewed as the central or host unit. The rest of your home or small office network computers can be running Windows XP, Me, 98 SE, or 98 as their operating system. Windows XP will help you generate a disk to set up these clients for network connectivity if necessary. Also, you can connect with computers running other operating systems, such as Windows 95, 2000, Linux, or Macintosh. However, you will have to manually set up these computers for access and sharing files and printers can be difficult, especially on non-Windows computers. If you have a Macintosh or Linux computer that you want to network, you should check out the networking documentation that came with those computers.

> **TIP:** Check out the latest in home networking from your local computer store. Home PNA cards and setup documentation are often sold in inexpensive kits. Also, there are external USB network adapters that save you the hassle of opening up the computer's case.

After you have outfitted the computers with network adapter cards that are physically connected, you are ready to start the setup.

Using the Network Setup Wizard

The Network Setup Wizard helps you to create your home or small office network easily and quickly. It must first run on the XP computer that will serve as the network host. If you are using ICS, the computer that has the Internet connection should be the host computer. After you set up the host, you can then use the Network Setup Wizard to set up the other clients. Make sure all computers, printers, and external modems are turned on.

To set up the Windows XP host computer using the Network Setup Wizard, follow these steps:

STEPS

Setting up the Windows XP host computer

1. On the computer that will be the host computer, choose Start ⇨ All Programs ⇨ Accessories ⇨ Network Setup Wizard.

2. Click Next on the Welcome screen.

3. In the Before You Continue window, review the information on this page about getting ready for installation, and then click Next.

4. In the Select a connection method window, shown in Figure 20-1, choose the radio button that describes your connection method. Because you are setting up the host computer, you should choose the first option as it is your computer that connects to the Internet and other network computers connect to you. If this does not describe what you want to do, click the second option, or click Other.

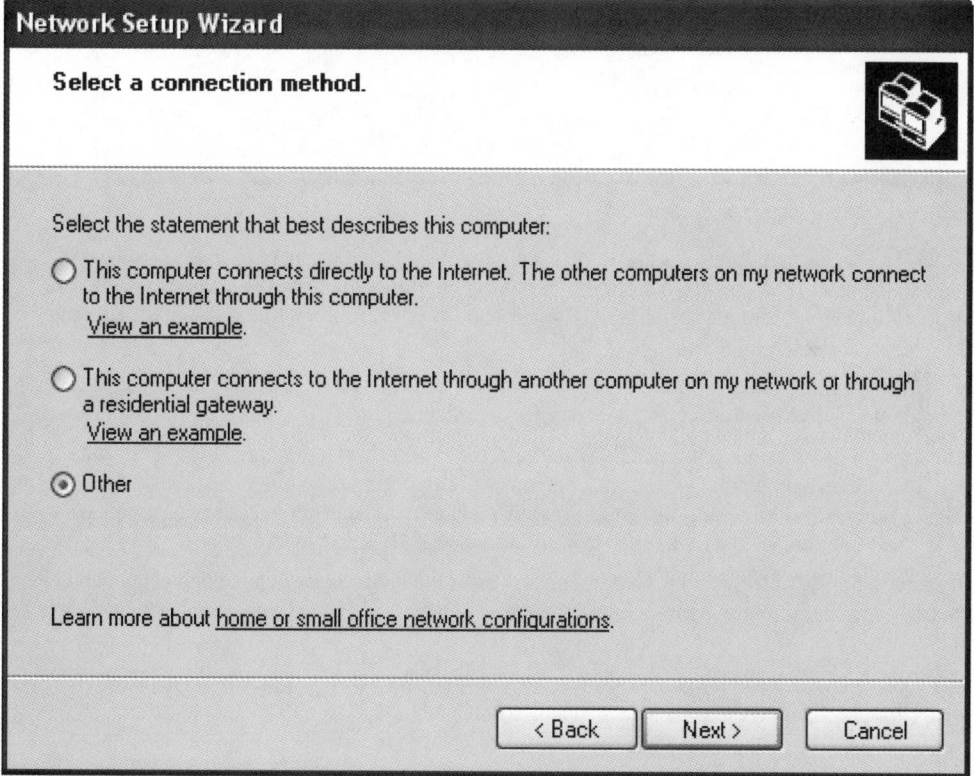

Figure 20-1: Select a Connection method. Click Other if your computer is not currently a host or does not connect to another host.

5. If you chose Other in Step 4, in the Other Internet connections methods window, shown in Figure 20-2, choose a connection that matches your computer description. (This window does not appear if you do not choose Other.) Click Next.

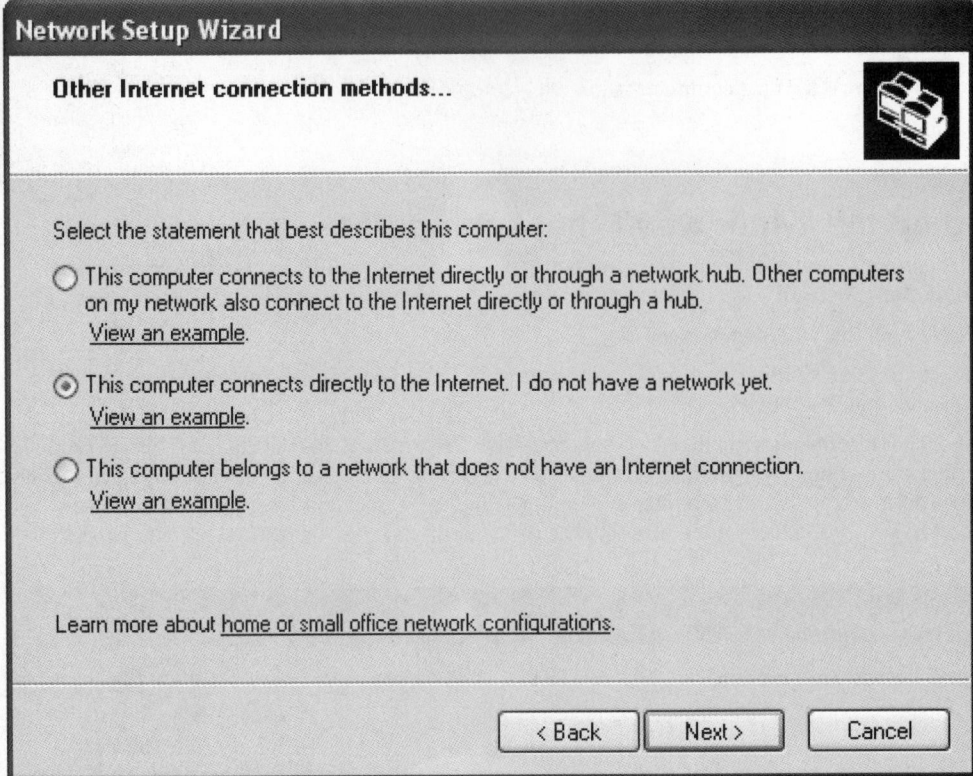

Figure 20-2: Select a different connection method.

6. The Internet Connection window appears. (If the network doesn't connect to the Internet, go to Step 7). Choose the Internet connection from the list of connections that appears. Everything in your Network Connections folder appears here, so just choose your primary Internet connection and click Next.

7. Enter a description of the computer if desired, and you can change the name here. If your ISP or cable modem requires a certain computer name, do not change it. Click Next.

8. The workgroup name window appears. By default, the workgroup is named MSHOME, but you can change it whatever you want. For security reasons, it is a good idea to change this name to something unique. With the default name, it is possible that an Internet hacker can more easily discover your network if it is named the default of MSHOME. Click Next.

9. The "ready to apply" settings window appears. Review the settings you chose and click Next. Your computer is set up with networking components and configured accordingly. This may take a few minutes.

10. If you chose to create a setup disk, as shown in Figure 20-3, click the disk where you want to copy the files (floppy, Zip, CD-RW, or so forth) and click Next.

11. Insert the disk into the drive and click Next.

12. Files are copied to the disk. Click Next to complete the wizard, and then click Finish. You are prompted to reboot your computer.

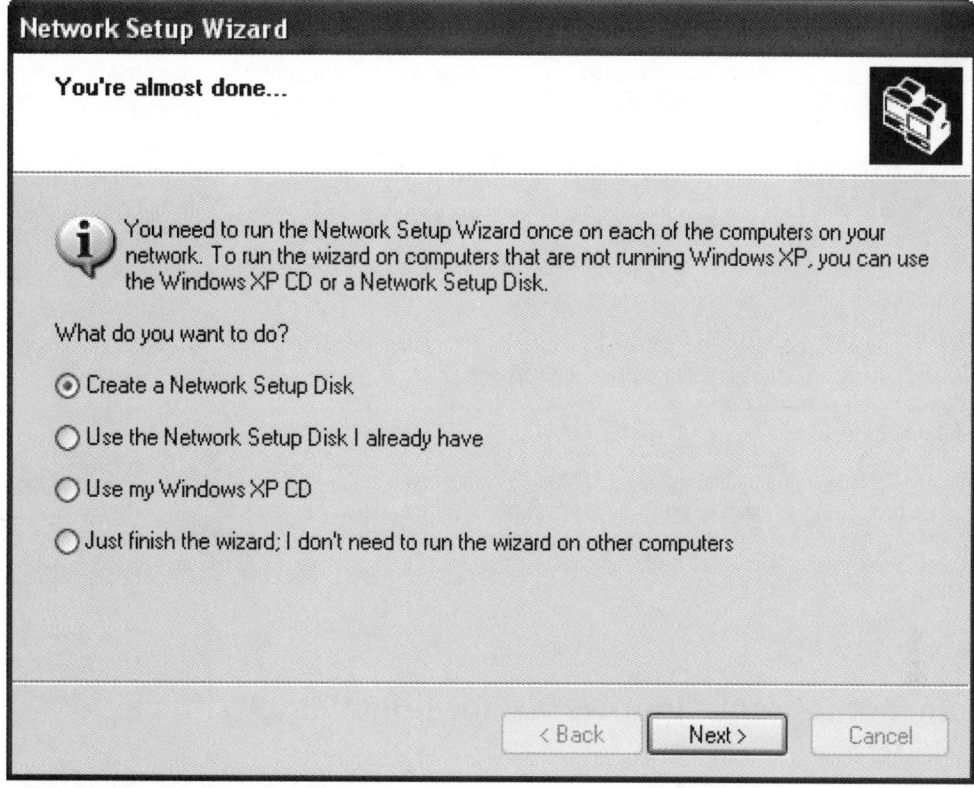

Figure 20-3: Select the client setup method.

What the wizard did . . .

If you are naturally curious, which you probably are, then you want to know what the wizard did to your computer. After all, it's nice that the host computer is now set up for networking, but what, exactly, did the wizard do.

The wizard installed a couple of services and configured your computer to use TCP/IP. In the past, configuring TCP/IP for home and small networking was enough to drive most intermediate to advanced users crazy, but Windows XP automatically sets this up for you. Specifically, Windows XP . . .

♦ Configured your network adapter card as a client for Microsoft Networks.

♦ Configured your network adapter card for file and printer sharing for Microsoft Networks. This enables your XP computer to share files, printers, and other resources on the network.

♦ Assigned your network adapter card a TCP/IP address in what is considered an "automatic, private IP addressing" (APIPA) scheme to automatically assign an IP address to your computer and other computers on your network so that no manual configuration of TCP/IP or subnet masks is required. When APIPA is used, the range is 169.254.0.1 to 169.254.255.254 and the subnet mask is set to 255.255.0.0.

NOTE: The 169 IP address range is reserved by the Internet Assigned Numbers Authority (IANA) and cannot be used on the Internet. The 169 address range is designed for computers that use APIPA.

♦ Installed the ICS service and configured your connection for sharing, if you chose ICS. The ICS service uses a dynamic host configuration protocol (DHCP) allocator to provide automatic address and a domain name system (DNS) proxy for name resolution. When you set up the client computers, they will be configured to contact the host computer for Internet access. ICS also supports Universal Plug and Play for network device management. In the same manner, ICS clients can detect the Internet connection on the network via Universal Plug and Play. Autodial is enabled on dial-up connections so that an Internet connection can be dynamically established when needed.

Manually configuring Windows XP for networking

The Network Setup Wizard is really the best way to configure a home or small office network because it ensures that all settings are collected and configured appropriately. However, you can configure the computer yourself without the wizard. You can also manually set up ICS, which is explored in the "Internet Connection Sharing" section later in this chapter.

To set up Windows XP manually, the network adapter must be installed on your computer. Next, you need to add the Client for Microsoft Networks and File and Printer Sharing for Microsoft Networks services. Finally, you need to configure TCP/IP. The following steps show you how to set up these services and the protocol.

SECRET: Windows XP likes to help you to create a network, but it doesn't seem to help you to remove that network (there's no wizard to help you to do that). However, as you are reviewing these steps, remember that you can stop your XP computer from participating on a network by removing these services. Also, you can right-click the network adapter and click Disable, which is an easier way of stopping all network communication.

STEPS

Manually setting up Windows XP for home/small office networking

1. Open the Network connections folder.

2. Right-click the local area connection and click Properties. If you do not see a local area connection, then your computer has not detected your network card. Refer to Chapter 11 for more information about hardware installation.

3. On the General tab, click Install.

4. In the Select Network Component Type window, choose Client, and then click Add, as shown in Figure 20-4.

5. In the Select Network Client window, select Client for Microsoft Networks and click OK. At the reboot prompt, click No.

6. Click Install again.

7. Click Service and click Add. In the Service window, select File and Printer Sharing for Microsoft Networks and click OK. At the reboot prompt, click No.

8. On the General tab, click TCP/IP and click Properties.

TIP: Typically, TCP/IP is installed by default. If it does not appear on the General tab, choose Install ⇨ Protocol, and select TCP/IP.

---

9. On the General tab, ensure that the Obtain an IP address automatically radio button and the Obtain a DNS server address automatically radio button are selected, as shown in Figure 20-5. If you prefer, you can manually assign the computer an IP address and appropriate subnet mask. Each computer on your network, then, must have an IP address in that range and the same subnet mask for connectivity to be available. Obviously, you need to know a thing or two about IP before making such manual changes. If you do not, then just leave the automatic settings in place.

10. Click the Alternate Configuration tab, as shown in Figure 20-6. Ensure that the Automatic private IP address radio button is selected. Click OK, click Close, and then reboot your computer.

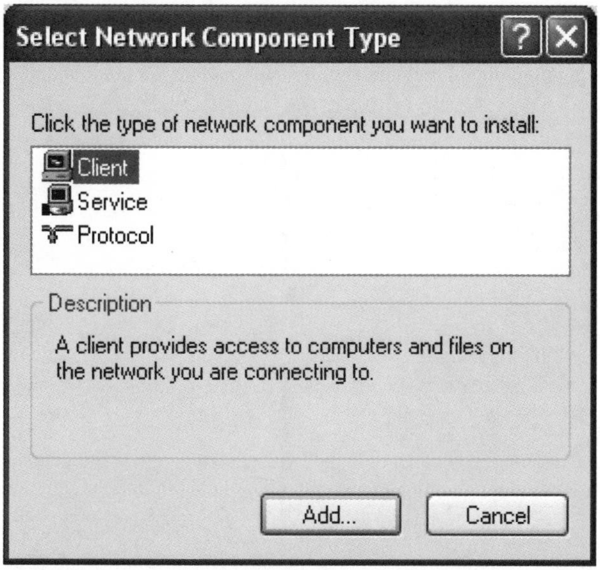

Select Network Component Type ?X

Click the type of network component you want to install:

- Client
- Service
- Protocol

Description

A client provides access to computers and files on the network you are connecting to.

Add... Cancel

Figure 20-4: Network Component Type window

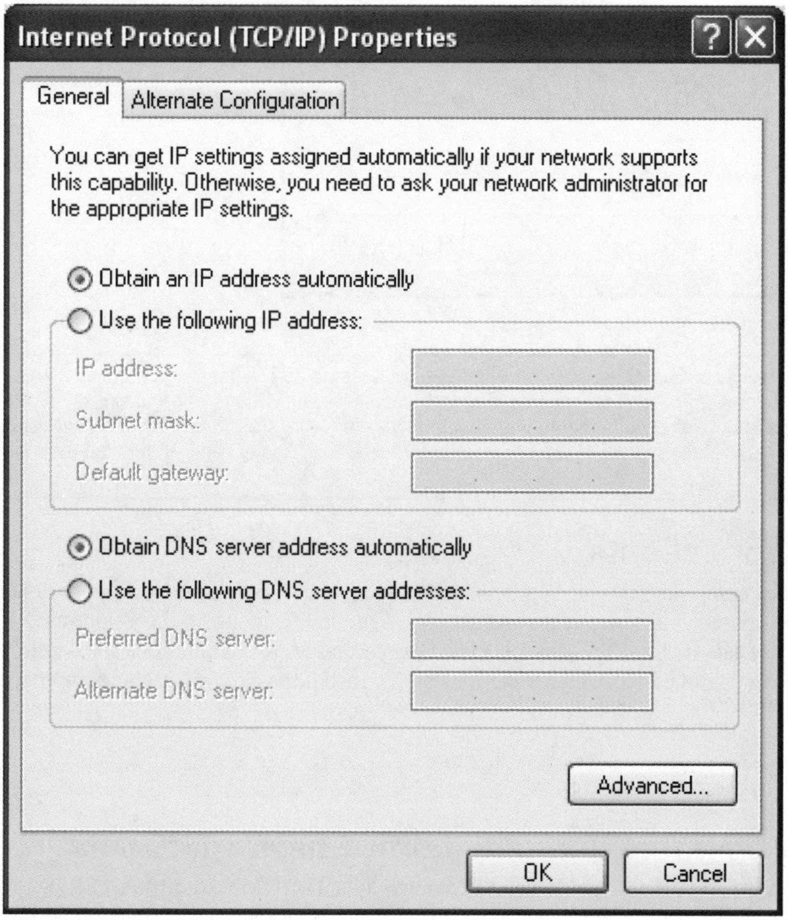

Internet Protocol (TCP/IP) Properties ?X

General | Alternate Configuration

You can get IP settings assigned automatically if your network supports this capability. Otherwise, you need to ask your network administrator for the appropriate IP settings.

○ Obtain an IP address automatically
○ Use the following IP address:

IP address:
Subnet mask:
Default gateway:

○ Obtain DNS server address automatically
○ Use the following DNS server addresses:

Preferred DNS server:
Alternate DNS server:

Advanced...

OK Cancel

Figure 20-5: Internet Protocol (TCP/IP) properties

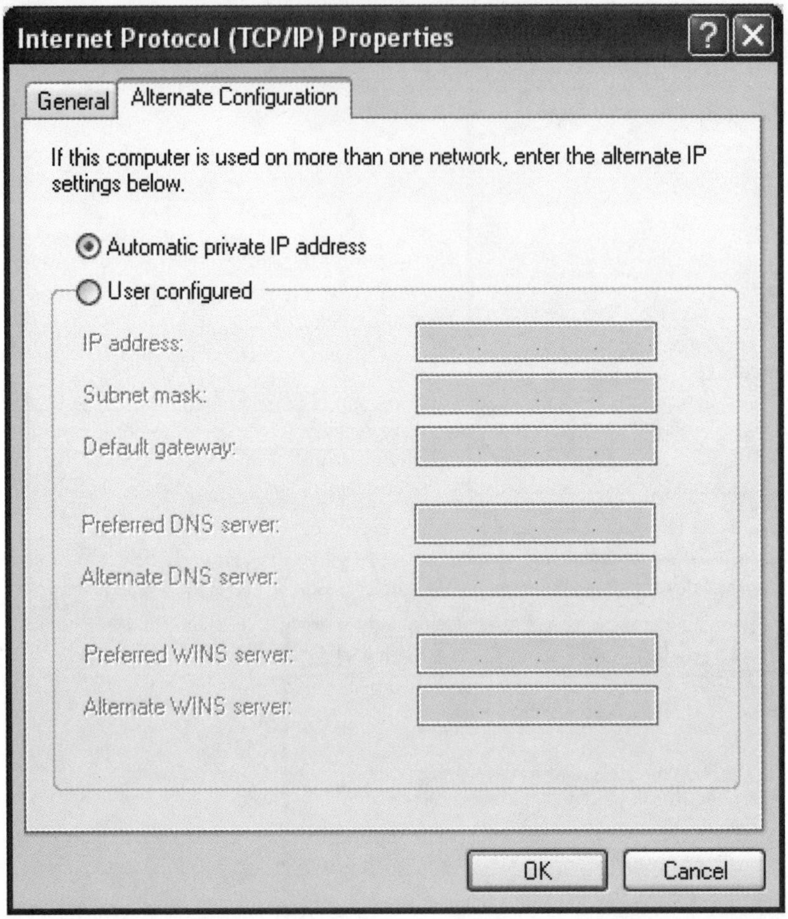

Figure 20-6: Alternate Configuration tab

SECRET: Windows XP Professional is configured to obtain an IP address automatically. This means that the computer first looks for a DHCP server on a Windows 2000/XP network that leases IP addresses. If it does not find one and your IP configuration is checked for automatic, it then checks the setting on the Alternate Configuration tab. If you have manually entered an IP address and subnet mask here, it is used. Otherwise, if the automatic setting is used on this tab as well, the computer assigns itself an automatic IP address in the 169 range.

Configuring network clients

After you have set up the host computer on your Windows XP home or small office network, your next step is to install the other computers with the client software. You can do this by using the Windows XP installation CD or the disk that you made when installing the host computer. Remember that the wizard setup works only on Windows 98, 98 SE, Me, or XP computers. To install the network client computers, follow these steps:

STEPS

Manually setting up home and small office network clients

1. If you are setting up the client computers using the Windows XP CD-ROM, insert the CD-ROM into the client CD-ROM drive and click the Perform Option Tasks option on the screen that appears. On the next screen, click Setup a home or small office network. This starts the Network Setup

wizard. If your computer needs some additional files, the file installation may take place along with a reboot first.

2. If you are installing from a disk, open the disk on the client computer and launch NETSETUP.EXE. Files may be copied and the computer restarted before installation continues.

3. Click Next on the Welcome screen.

4. In the Before You Continue window, review the information on this page about getting ready for installation, and then click Next.

5. In the Select a connection method window, choose the radio button that states that your computer connects to another computer to access the Internet, or if your network does not have Internet connectivity, then choose that option. Make your selection and click Next.

6. Enter a description of the computer if desired; you can change the name here. Click Next.

7. The workgroup name window appears. By default, the workgroup is named MSHOME, but you can change it to whatever you want, as recommended for security reasons. If you do change the name, make sure it matches the workgroup name you assigned when setting up the host computer. If you use different workgroup names, the computers on your network will not be able to "see" each other. Click Next.

8. The "ready to apply" settings window appears. Review the settings you chose and click Next. Your computer is set up with networking components and configured accordingly. This may take a few minutes.

9. Click Finish. You are prompted to reboot your computer. Reboot the computer for the new networking settings to take effect, and your computer should be a part of the network once the reboot is completed.

Internet Connection Sharing

The Network Setup Wizard automatically configures the host computer for ICS and configures client computers to access the host's shared Internet connection. When using ICS, a number of settings are configured by default, and because of these default settings, you cannot change the IP addressing scheme implemented by the Network Setup Wizard. In other words, if you change the address range to a manually configured range, ICS will not work because the IP address range automatically used is the autoassigned range.

ICS, as a general rule, works great and is problem free, assuming that you follow the setup instructions. Again, the easiest way to manage ICS is to use the Network Setup Wizard to configure the host computer first, and then to configure the client computers. After ICS is installed, the autodial feature is turned on and a DHCP allocator service is functional by default. The host computer must, obviously, be configured with a connection to the Internet (dial-up or broadband), and a LAN connection to the other computers on your network. When clients make a request for Internet access, the host computer makes the connection and retrieves the desired information for the client. Used in conjunction with the Internet Connection Firewall, the result is secure Internet access for all clients on your network.

There are, however, a few caveats regarding ICS of which you need to be aware — things are not always as rosy as they seem, and in all networking configuration, you are more likely to have problems with ICS than with any other type of configuration. Table 20-1 outlines some configuration issues of which you should be aware. If you are having problems with ICS, check out these settings and see if you notice any discrepancies.

Table 20-1: ICS Configuration Issues

Issue	Explanation
Domains	ICS is not designed for use with XP computers that are members of Windows 2000/XP domains where DHCP and DNS are used on corporate servers.
Connections	ICS can be used on dial-up, LAN, PPPoE, VPN, and broadband connections.
Browser	You must use IE 5 or later. In the Internet Options properties dialog box (found in Internet Explorer on the Tools menu), you must use the LAN Settings and use the Proxy Server check box option.
Mail Client	Outlook and Outlook Express are supported. The mail client settings must be configured to access mail through the LAN.
Internet Connection Sharing Service	Automatically started after ICS is configured.
DNS Proxy	Enabled.
DHCP Allocator	Assigns IP addresses in the range of 192.168.0.2 to 192.168.0.254 with a subnet mask of 255.255.255.0 to client computers.
IP Address	When ICS is installed on the host computer, it is given a static IP address of 192.168.0.1 and a subnet mask of 255.255.255.0. This is different than the typical 169 address provided if ICS is not used. This is one reason that the use of the Network Setup Wizard is recommended — clients must be aware of this address to query the host for Internet connectivity.

TIP: If you are having problems with ICS, there is an ICS Troubleshooter in the Help and Support center, which may be able to help you.

Windows XP's version of ICS also uses a feature called ICS Discovery and Control. ICS Discovery and Control gives client computers more power over the connection. From a client computer, you can launch a connection, terminate it, and monitor it as needed. The discovery mechanism used from client computers is able to determine whether the Internet connection is available and to give users information about that connection. Basically, ICS Discovery and Control enables clients to view statistics about the shared connection, monitor it, and connect and disconnect. When ICS is installed and configured, client computers see an icon on their Notification Areas/System Trays that enables them to connect and gain information. As Figure 20-7 illustrates, a connection to a Windows XP computer from a Windows Me computer gives me access to information and control for that connection.

Because ICS Discovery and Control enables client computers to discover the presence and condition of a shared Internet connection, the Internet Explorer properties sheets must be configured for this purpose (remember, only IE 5 and later are supported). If you access the Connections tab of Internet Options (found on the Tools menu in Internet Explorer), make sure the dial-up setting is set to Never dial a connection. Click the LAN Settings button and ensure that the Automatically detect settings check box and the Use a proxy server for your LAN check box options are selected, as shown in Figure 20-8.

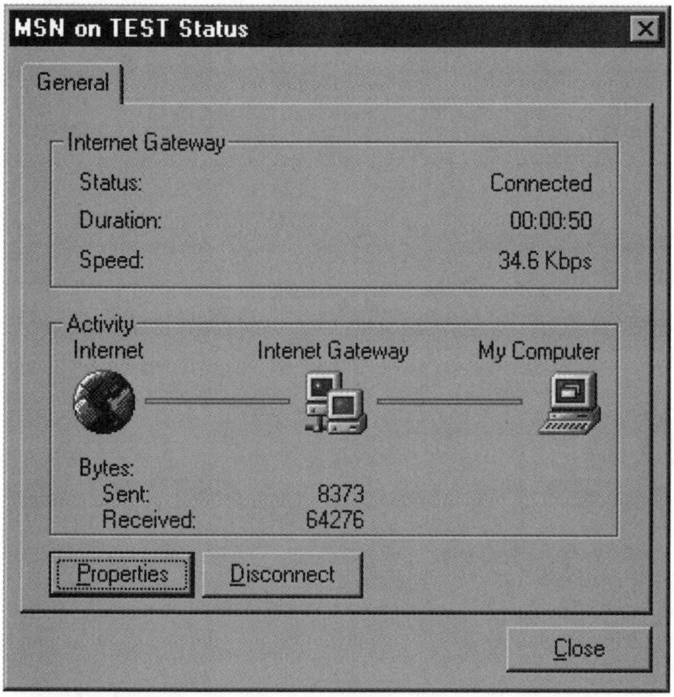

MSN on TEST Status   ✕

General

┌─ Internet Gateway ──────────────────────────┐
   Status: Connected
   Duration: 00:00:50
   Speed: 34.6 Kbps

┌─ Activity ──────────────────────────────────┐
   Internet   Intenet Gateway   My Computer

   Bytes:
      Sent: 8373
      Received: 64276

[Properties]   [Disconnect]

                              [Close]

Figure 20-7: ICS Discovery and Control enables clients to manage and view information about the connection.

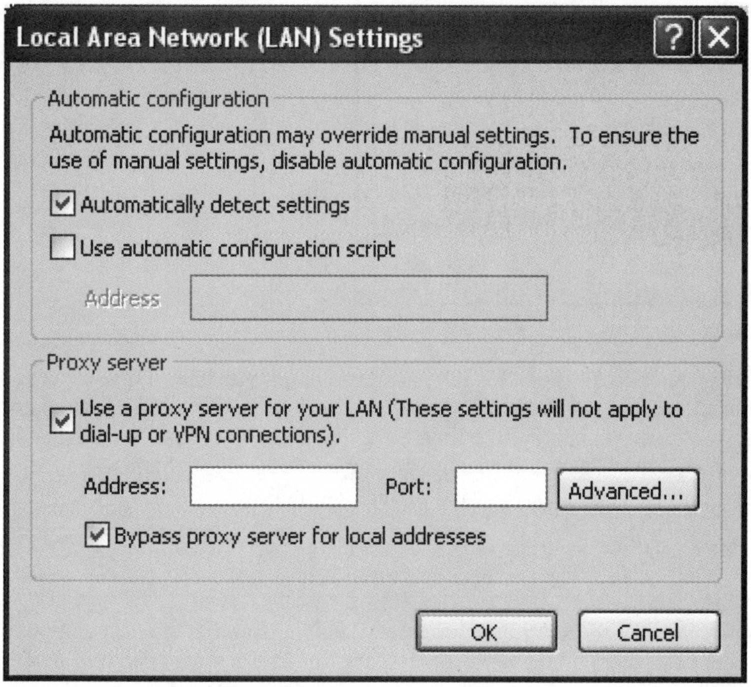

Local Area Network (LAN) Settings   ? ✕

┌─ Automatic configuration ───────────────────────────┐
  Automatic configuration may override manual settings. To ensure the use of manual settings, disable automatic configuration.

  ☑ Automatically detect settings

  ☐ Use automatic configuration script

     Address [   ]

┌─ Proxy server ──────────────────────────────────────┐
  ☑ Use a proxy server for your LAN (These settings will not apply to dial-up or VPN connections).

     Address: [   ]   Port: [   ] [Advanced...]

     ☑ Bypass proxy server for local addresses

                          [OK   ]   [Cancel]

Figure 20-8: IE LAN Settings

If at any time, you want to stop sharing the Internet connection or want to restrict user control over the setting, you can do so by right-clicking the connection, clicking Properties, and then clicking the Advanced tab, shown in Figure 20-9. Under the ICS section, simply clear the Allow other network users check box. This effectively stops ICS from running on this connection. Also, you can stop autodial and the ability of network users to control or disable the shared connection. As a general rule, however, these two settings should be left enabled so that users can connect and disconnect when necessary. Of course, if you are using an always-on broadband connection, this isn't an issue.

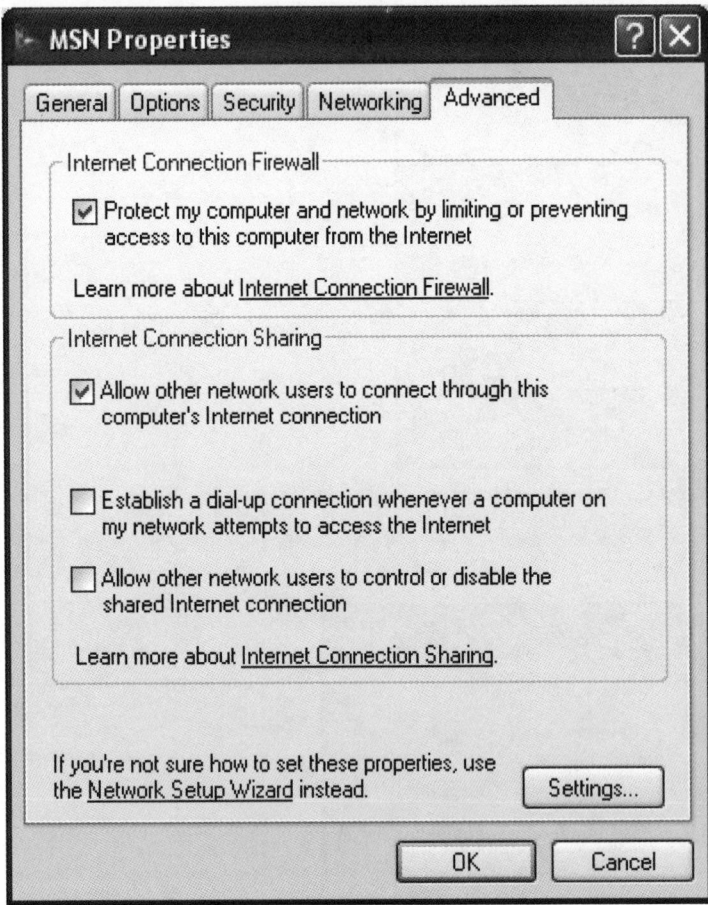

Figure 20-9: Advanced connection settings

At any time, you can also configure other connections for ICS. For example, if you have a dial-up connection and a broadband connection, you can disable ICS on the dial-up connection and enable it on the broadband connection using the Advanced tab. For the most part, the settings are easy to adjust and you are unlikely to have major connection problems. If you are having connectivity problems, see the "Connectivity Tools" section later in this chapter for information on helpful tools.

NOTE: I strongly suggest that you use the Internet Connection Firewall in conjunction with ICS. See Chapter 22 to learn more about ICF configuration.

If you decide that ICS is a hassle because of the sharing requirements and the fact that the host computer always has to be available for other computers on the network to access the Internet, you can turn it off by accessing the Advanced tab of the Connection Properties dialog box and clearing the ICS check boxes. Your network computers will then have to be reconfigured to directly access the Internet as needed.

Using My Network Places

After your XP computer is set up for networking, the My Network Places folder appears on your Start Menu. If you have used Windows 2000 or Windows Me, you are familiar with My Network Places, which was known as Network Neighborhood in previous versions of Windows. There is really nothing new in My Network Places in Windows XP. Basically, My Network Places enables you to connect to Web sites, as well as to other computers on your local network. You can open the Entire Network icon and see the other networked computers. Then, you can browse those computers and look for resources that you want to use. My Network Places appears in Figure 20-10.

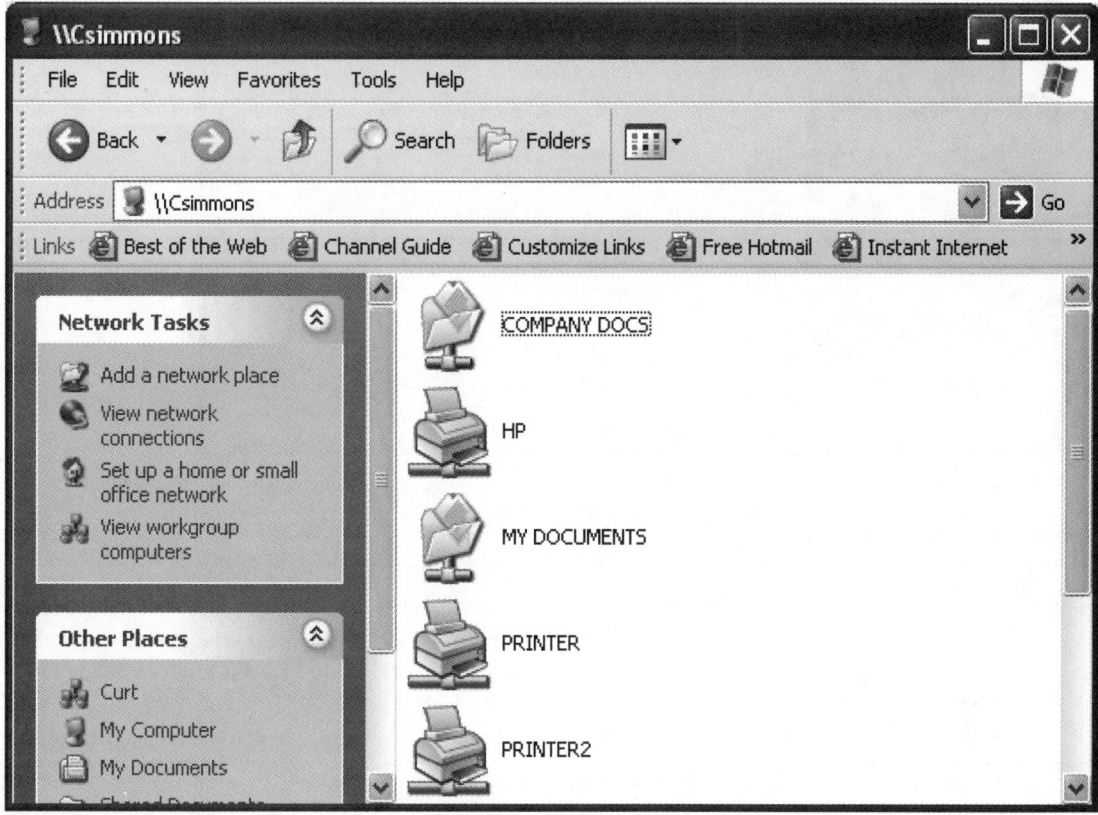

Figure 20-10: My Network Places

You can access computers on the network directly from My Network Places, or you can access them via the Run line by UNC (Universal Naming Convention) path. Also, if you want to map a network drive to another computer so that a particular folder is always available, you can do so using the Tools menu in My Network Places.

In case you are a little rusty on the UNC path, the UNC gives you a way to access computers and shares on your network. The UNC path is represented by *computername**foldername**sharename*. For example, say that a computer named "test" holds a shared folder called Docs with a shared document called MyDoc.txt. By using the UNC path, you can enter \\test\docs\mydoc.txt in the Run line or in the Address bar in any window in Windows XP, which gives you quick, easy access to items on another computer. If you just want to see the folder, just enter the *computername**foldername*\, or if you just want to access the computer, you could type *computername*.

If you want to map a network drive to shared resource so that the resource always shows up in My Network Places, just choose Tools ⇨ Map Network Drive. In the window provided, which is shown in

Figure 20-11, choose a drive letter to represent the mapped drive and enter the UNC path (or you can just browse to it). To make sure the drive is always available, click the Reconnect at logon check box.

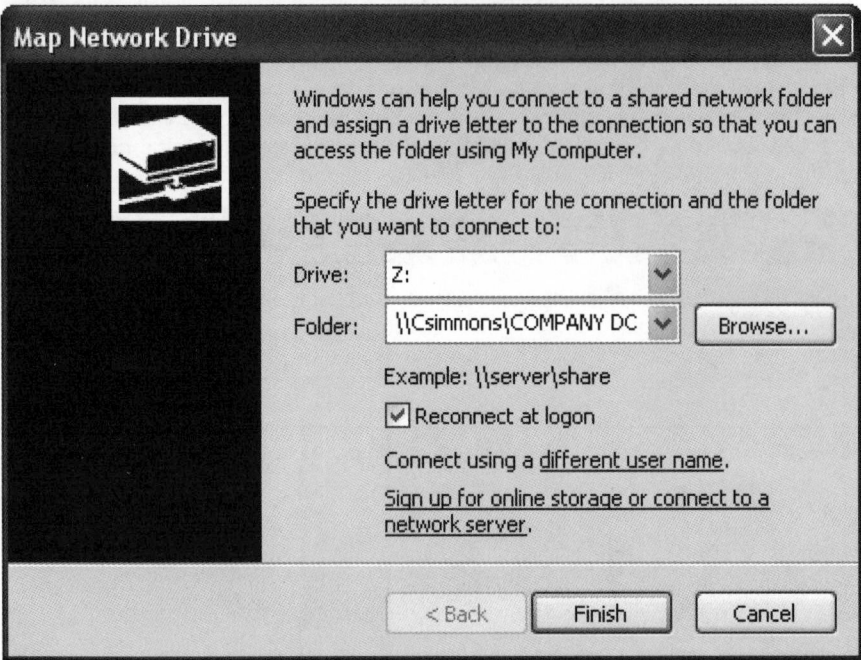

Figure 20-11: Map Network Drive

> **SECRET:** Mapped network drives are essentially shortcuts that locate the data using the UNC path. Of course, you can make your own shortcuts from these items and put them on your desktop, Start Menu, or in any location that can hold a shortcut.

Another option you have in My Documents is the Create Network Place Wizard. The Create Network Place Wizard enables you to connect with an online storage service and to locate a Web page that you want to appear in My Network Places. This gives you easy access to information that is on the Internet. The wizard is self-explanatory and easy to use.

> **SECRET:** For any shared item found under any computer in My Network Places, you can right-click the item and click Properties to see the full UNC path. In case you get lost deep inside of shared folders, this can help you see exactly where you are within the shares.

Connectivity Tools

If you are having problems with your home or small office network, there are a number of tools that you can use that will hopefully help you to discover the problem. Windows XP includes a few additional features that can give you information about connectivity, and you can use command-line tools as well. This section shows you the available tools and how to use them.

Command-line tools

There are two command-line utilities that you can use to check for connectivity and quickly find out about IP configuration on your computer. If you are not already familiar with these tools, you should try them out and commit them to memory because they can be extremely helpful.

Ping

Ping is a command that enables you to test connectivity to another computer or even to test your own network adapter card. Ping works by sending small IP packets to the destination IP address to see if there is a response. To use Ping, you must know the IP address of the computer that you want to test connectivity with. See the next section on Ipconfig to find out how to gain the IP address.

If you cannot access another computer on your network by using My Network Places, then you can use Ping to first test connectivity with your own network adapter and against other computers on your network. To test for connectivity on your network adapter, called a *loopback test*, access the command prompt and type the following:

```
Ping 127.0.0.1
```

127.0.0.1 is an IP address class reserved for loopback testing. By running this command, you can determine whether your computer has connectivity. If the Ping test fails, you know there is a problem with your network adapter card. If the test is successful, reply messages are displayed, such as those shown in Figure 20-12.

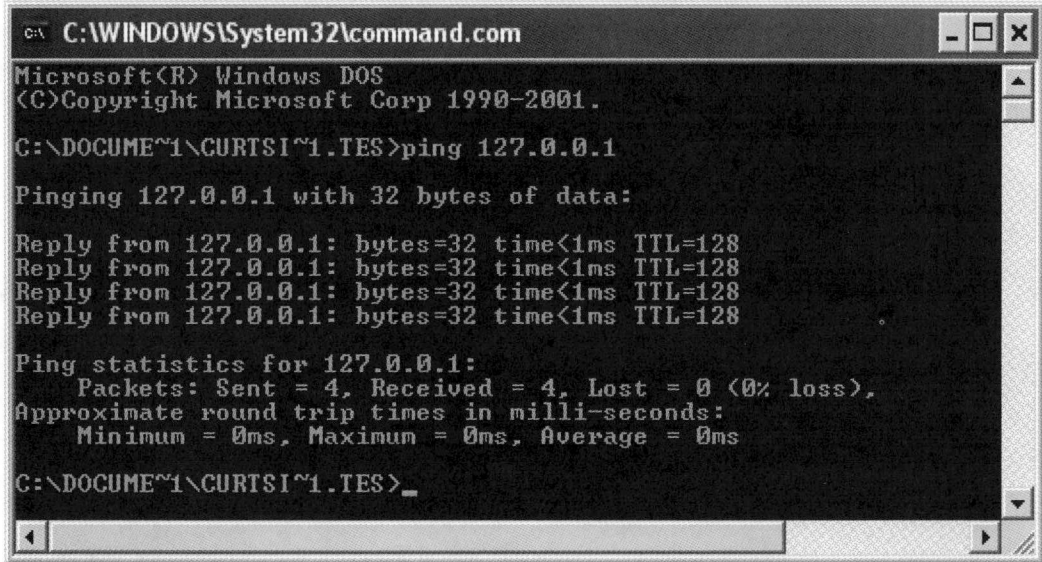

Figure 20-12: Ping success

If the loopback test comes out okay, then you should try pinging the IP address of a computer on your network. If the address is successful, you'll know that you do have lower-level IP connectivity. If the address is not successful, you see an unreachable notice, as in Figure 20-13.

Ipconfig

Ipconfig is a command-line utility that gives you information about the current IP configuration of your computer. Use this tool to find out your IP address and subnet mask, the default gateway, and related settings on your computer. You can Ipconfig with the /all switch, such as:

```
Ipconfig /all
```

This /all switch gives you all the information, including DHCP leases, if that information applies. There are other switches available as well; just type the following command to discover them:

```
Ipconfig /?
```

Ipconfig is shown in Figure 20-14.

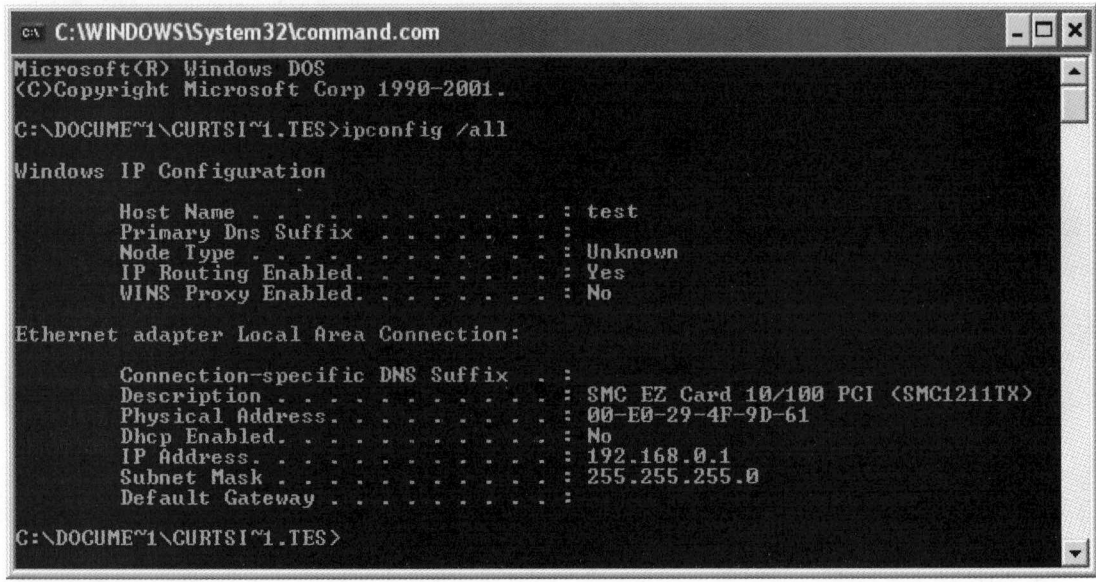

Figure 20-13: Host unreachable message

```
C:\WINDOWS\System32\command.com                              _ □ ×

Microsoft(R) Windows DOS
(C)Copyright Microsoft Corp 1990-2001.

C:\DOCUME~1\CURTSI~1.TES>ipconfig /all

Windows IP Configuration

        Host Name . . . . . . . . . . . . : test
        Primary Dns Suffix  . . . . . . . :
        Node Type . . . . . . . . . . . . : Unknown
        IP Routing Enabled. . . . . . . . : Yes
        WINS Proxy Enabled. . . . . . . . : No

Ethernet adapter Local Area Connection:

        Connection-specific DNS Suffix  . :
        Description . . . . . . . . . . . : SMC EZ Card 10/100 PCI (SMC1211TX)
        Physical Address. . . . . . . . . : 00-E0-29-4F-9D-61
        Dhcp Enabled. . . . . . . . . . . : No
        IP Address. . . . . . . . . . . . : 192.168.0.1
        Subnet Mask . . . . . . . . . . . : 255.255.255.0
        Default Gateway . . . . . . . . . :

C:\DOCUME~1\CURTSI~1.TES>
```

Figure 20-14: Ipconfig /all

Tracert

Tracert (Trace Route) is a simple utility that pings an Internet host and gives you information about that ping and the speed at which is was carried out. The tracert information shows you the number of server "hops," or the route that was used to ping the Internet host. You can then take a look at the tracert information see if the expected speed of your connection is measuring up. For example, a 28.8 Mbps connection typically indicates a consistent 250 millisecond response, while a broadband connection will typically show 10 milliseconds or less. As you can see in Figure 20-15, the route to www.hungryminds.com has been traced.

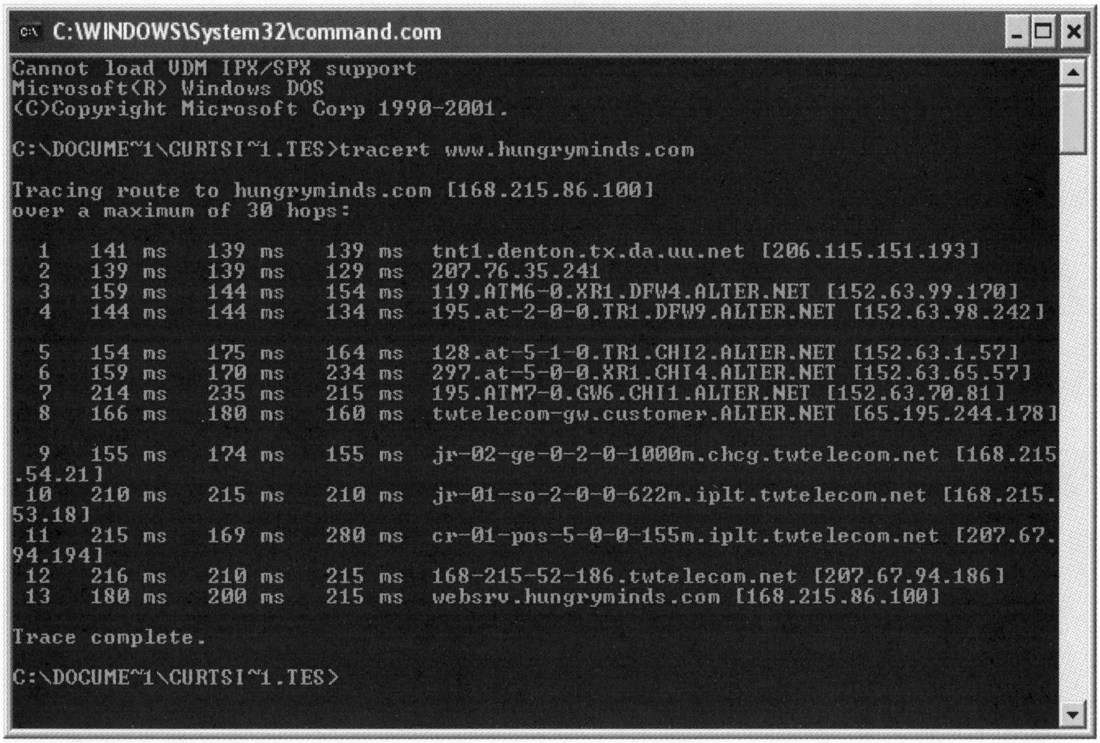

```
C:\WINDOWS\System32\command.com                                    - □ ×

Cannot load UDM IPX/SPX support
Microsoft(R) Windows DOS
(C)Copyright Microsoft Corp 1990-2001.

C:\DOCUME~1\CURTSI~1.TES>tracert www.hungryminds.com

Tracing route to hungryminds.com [168.215.86.100]
over a maximum of 30 hops:

  1    141 ms     139 ms     139 ms  tnt1.denton.tx.da.uu.net [206.115.151.193]
  2    139 ms     139 ms     129 ms  207.76.35.241
  3    159 ms     144 ms     154 ms  119.ATM6-0.XR1.DFW4.ALTER.NET [152.63.99.170]
  4    144 ms     144 ms     134 ms  195.at-2-0-0.TR1.DFW9.ALTER.NET [152.63.98.242]

  5    154 ms     175 ms     164 ms  128.at-5-1-0.TR1.CHI2.ALTER.NET [152.63.1.57]
  6    159 ms     170 ms     234 ms  297.at-5-0-0.XR1.CHI4.ALTER.NET [152.63.65.57]
  7    214 ms     235 ms     215 ms  195.ATM7-0.GW6.CHI1.ALTER.NET [152.63.70.81]
  8    166 ms     180 ms     160 ms  twtelecom-gw.customer.ALTER.NET [65.195.244.178]

  9    155 ms     174 ms     155 ms  jr-02-ge-0-2-0-1000m.chcg.twtelecom.net [168.215
.54.21]
 10    210 ms     215 ms     210 ms  jr-01-so-2-0-0-622m.iplt.twtelecom.net [168.215.
53.18]
 11    215 ms     169 ms     280 ms  cr-01-pos-5-0-0-155m.iplt.twtelecom.net [207.67.
94.194]
 12    216 ms     210 ms     215 ms  168-215-52-186.twtelecom.net [207.67.94.186]
 13    180 ms     200 ms     215 ms  websrv.hungryminds.com [168.215.86.100]

Trace complete.

C:\DOCUME~1\CURTSI~1.TES>
```

Figure 20-15: Tracert utility

Network status

You can view the status of your network card and also find out your IP address and subnet mask on that card by right-clicking the LAN icon in Network Connections and then clicking Status. You see a General tab that shows you the packets sent and received on your network, the current status (connected or not), the amount of time you have been connected, and the speed. You can view this same status information for other kinds of connections as well, such as your dial-up connection, broadband connection, and so on. As you are viewing the status window, you can also disable or enable the connection as well.

If you click the Support tab, which is shown in Figure 20-16, you see your IP address, subnet mask, and default gateway (if one is configured). If you are having problems with the connection, you can click Repair. This enables windows to run a tool that checks the connection and even re-leases a new IP address if you are on a domain-based network. Overall, it's a quick and easy tool to find information that you need.

SECRET: Okay, do you want an even easier way to find the IP address? Just select the local area connection icon in Network Connections, and then scroll down to the Details section in the left pane. You'll see the same Status information listed there as well.

Networking in Task Manager

Task Manager has a Networking tab in Windows XP that gives you a real-time look at network statistics, as shown in Figure 20-17. Use this tab to see what percentage of your network is being used, the link speed, and the network's state. Although this tab will not help you get connected, it will give you a good idea of how much traffic is flowing on your network, and whether there are any traffic issues that you need to address.

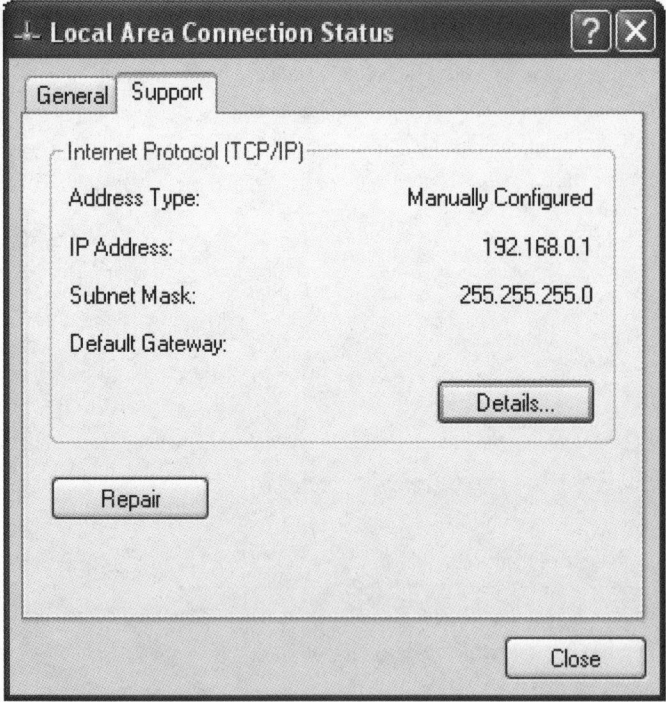

Figure 20-16: Support tab of Status

CROSS REFERENCE: You can also learn more about Task Manager and using it for troubleshooting purposes in Chapters 24 and 25.

SECRET: There are a number of issues that can also cause the networking traffic counter to run high — inadvertent file sharing; peripheral sharing of devices such as CD-ROM drives; background processes, such as auto updates; and even viruses! To protect your computer, make sure that you have a good anti-virus program running, and if your network traffic seems high, you may have to do a little snooping to find the culprit.

Network Bridge

Windows XP includes a service called network bridge, which enables your Windows XP computer to act as a gateway between two networks. This service is typically not needed in a home or small office network, but it is worth mentioning, and it could come in handy in a few situations. Say that you have an office network made up of five Home PNA computers. Suddenly, you want to add 15 more computers, and you decide to begin using Ethernet. You can use Windows XP, outfitted with both an Ethernet card and a Home PNA card, to provide automatic translation between those two networks.

The network bridge enables you to connect two different network segments that use the same network media or different network media. Essentially, the network bridge creates a resolution scheme for the two IP segments so that they appear as one subnet. You can think of the XP computer as the literal bridge that connects the two different segments. Then, through the XP computer, each network segment can communicate with each other seamlessly without extra router hardware and painful TCP/IP configurations. Although not the best solution for corporate networks, the XP bridge feature is a great solution for smaller networks that need to connect two dissimilar segments.

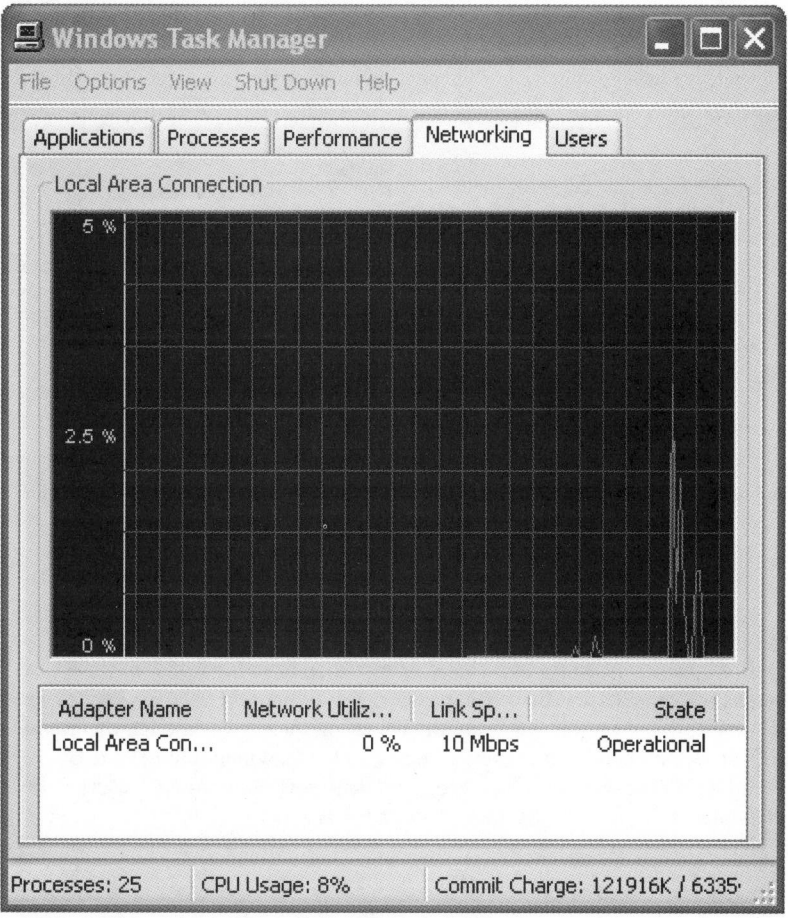

Figure 20-17: Networking tab in Task Manager

You can have only one bridge on a Windows XP computer, but you can use that single bridge to connect as many network segments as the computer can physically accommodate. You can create the network bridge by selecting the two network adapter cards in the Network Connections folder, right-clicking them, and clicking Bridge Connections. Windows XP handles the IP address translation between the two segments.

Overall, network bridging is a simple solution to what can be a major and extensive problem. Discussing it, however, cannot come without a few caveats. The following list notes some important concepts that you should keep in mind:

♦ A network bridge can be used to join Ethernet, Home PNA, IEEE 1394 adapters, or other Ethernet-compatible adapters.

♦ You cannot use ICS or ICF with a network bridge to bridge two LAN segments. If you need to bridge an adapter that has these services configured, you must first disable them.

♦ If you remove one of the network adapters after the bridge has been created, the bridge will no longer function, but it will continue to use system resources. You should disconnect the bridge before removing the adapter.

♦ If you create a network bridge by using a wireless connection or an IEEE 1394 connection, only Internet Protocol version 4 (IPv4) is supported.

♦ Do not create bridges between an Internet connection and a private network connection. Doing so creates an unprotected link between the Internet and your network. This can be prevented with ICF, but this kind of configuration is not recommended due to the security risks involved. Remember, the network bridge feature is designed to be used with two LAN segments — not your LAN and the Internet.

Sharing Information on Your Network

Without a doubt, one of the most important aspects of configuring a home or small office network is the sharing of resources. Without the need for shared resources, there is no reason to connect computers together. With your home or small office network, you can share folders, printers, and drives, and even play network games. Aside from Internet connection sharing, no items on your computer are shared by default. To share an item on the network, you must share that item so that others can use it.

Sharing is easy on an XP network. The following steps show you how to share a folder.

STEPS

Sharing a folder

1. Locate the folder that you want to share, right-click the folder, and click Sharing and Security.

2. The Sharing tab that appears gives you two options, as shown in Figure 20-18. If you want to share the folder only with people who use your computer (local users), then drag the folder to the Shared Documents folder. If you want to ensure that no one can access the folder and that it is kept private, then click the Make this folder private option. To share the folder on the network, click the Share this folder on the network check box and enter a friendly name in the provided dialog box. By default, users are given read-only access to the files in the folder. If you want network users to be able to make changes to the items in the shared folder, click the Allow network users to change my files option.

3. Click OK.

> **TIP:** If you are connected to a domain and not to a home or office network, the Shared Documents folder is not available. You can share each individual folder, and then set permissions on that folder so that you can determine who can access the folder.

Managing shared folder permissions

Once you share the folder, a hand icon appears beneath the folder to indicate that it is shared. Users on your network can now access the shared folder.

However, what do you do if you work in a small office network and one user should have no access to a certain shared folder? What if you have a home network and your children should have no access to a shared folder? By default, simple file sharing is enabled, which just gives you the option to turn on file sharing for a folder, but doesn't allow you to manage who can access the folder. However, you can turn off simple file sharing, and instead set individual permissions for folders that are stored on NTFS drives.

To turn off file sharing, double-click the shared folder to open it. Choose Tools ⇨ Folder Options ⇨ View. Scroll to the bottom of the tab, clear the Use simple file sharing check box, and then click OK (see Figure 20-19).

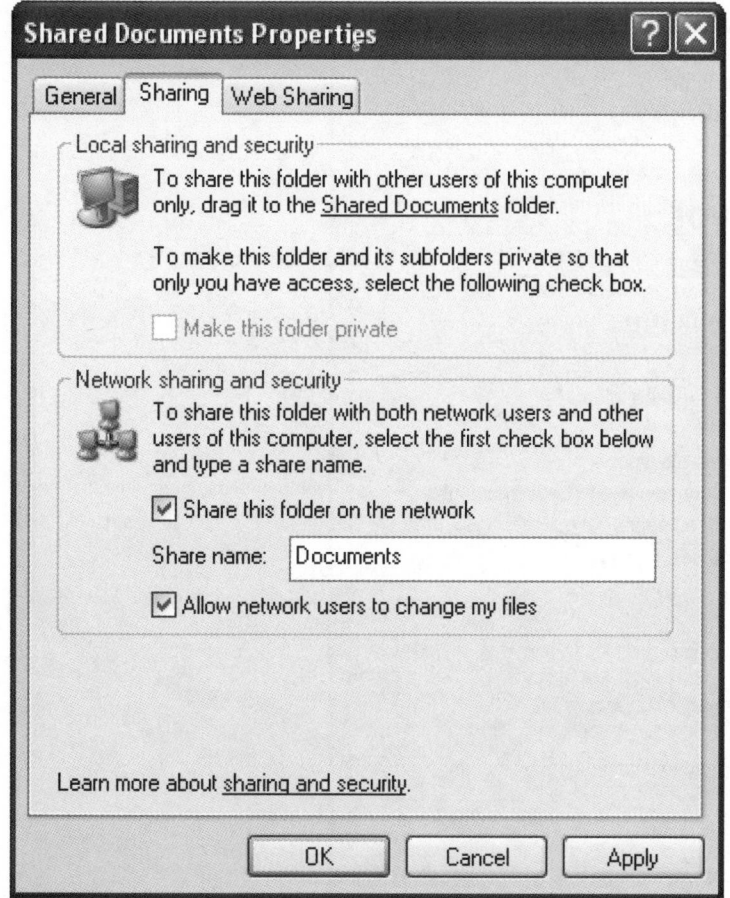

Figure 20-18: Sharing tab

After simple file sharing is turned off, you'll see a Security tab on the folder's properties sheets, which are shown in Figure 20-20. By default, everyone has permission to access the folder. To prevent a user from accessing the folder, you need to clear the Everyone permissions and set them to Deny. Use the Add button to add each desired user, and then select each user and determine the level of permission you would like to assign that user. Some users may have full control, whereas others may have only read control. If you don't want a particular user to have any permission, simply don't do anything for that user's account. Because the Everyone group now has no access, a user will not be able to access the folder unless you assign specific permissions.

TIP: If you are really excited about managing file permissions, you can click the Advanced button and manage more permissions for the file. This feature gives you a very fine level of control over what users can and cannot do with your files and folders. However, do be careful. Permissions can become a dark alleyway full of pitfalls because it is easy to lose track of how they are applied to the user, so remember the basic "less is more" rule. Don't enable any file and folder restrictions unless you are sure they are necessary.

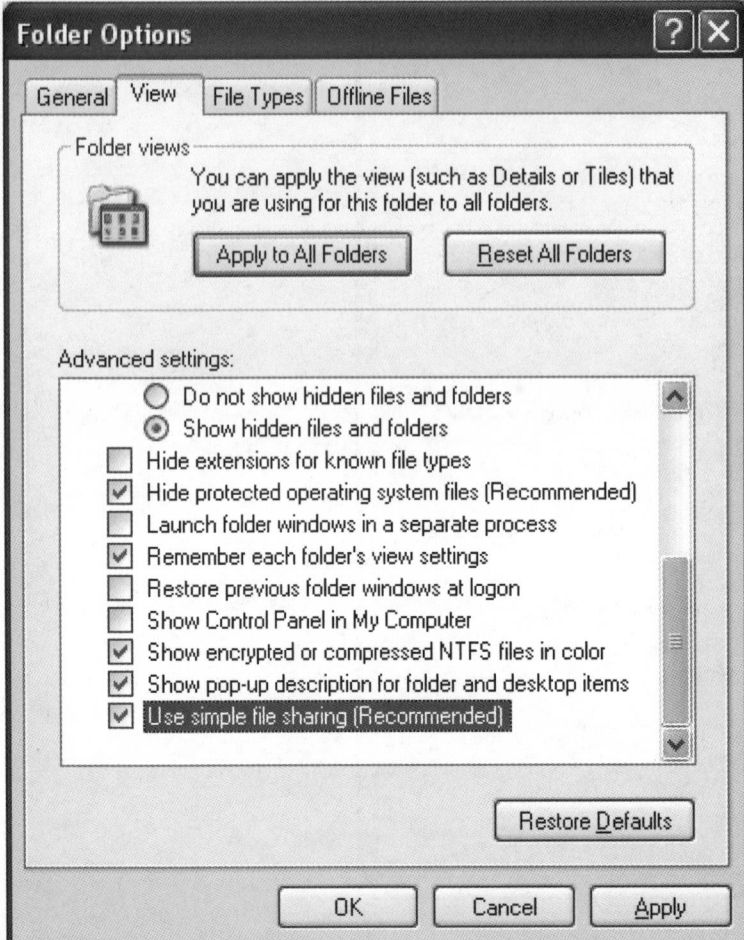

Figure 20-19: Turn off simple file sharing

Sharing other items

Although files and folders tend to get more attention when it comes to sharing, the fact is that you can share just about anything, including CD-ROM drives, Zip drives, your entire hard drive (which is not recommended), and, of course, printers. Sharing these items all works the same way. Access the Shared tab on the properties sheets for the item and make it shared. You can configure advanced permissions for these items as well, by disabling simple file sharing.

As a general rule, you should share only the information or drives that need to be shared. Avoid becoming "share happy." If no one needs it, keep it to yourself — and, of course, if permissions are an issue, feel free to assign them.

Sharing a printer also works the same way. You can set permissions on the share, and in many cases, your printer software also helps you share the printer. See your printer's documentation for details.

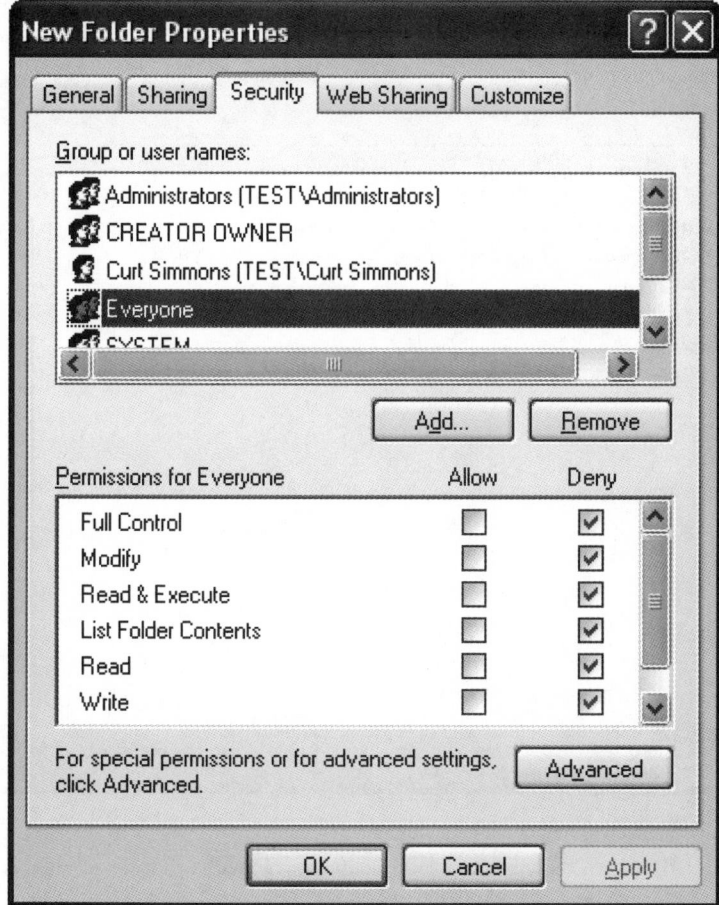

Figure 20-20: Managing permission entries

Shared Folders

If you access the Computer Management console, found in Administrative Tools in Control Panel, you see a Shared Folders option in the list, as shown in Figure 20-21. If you expand Shared Folders, you can see containers for Shares, Sessions, and Open Files. Each of these items gives you information about the status of the shared folder and the number of client connections. If your Windows XP computer is connected to a domain, you have more functionality here, such as deleting shares, disconnecting users, creating new shared folders, and similar management features. If you are not on a domain, you can't do anything here but look at the information given to you (which is sort of a bummer).

Using Offline Files

Offline files enable you to use network documents when you are not connected to the network. For example, suppose that you are working on a document that is officially stored in another computer on your network. You want to leave the office with your laptop for the day, but you want to be able to work on the document. Sure, you can copy the document to your hard drive, but how can you integrate the changes without retyping all of them again?

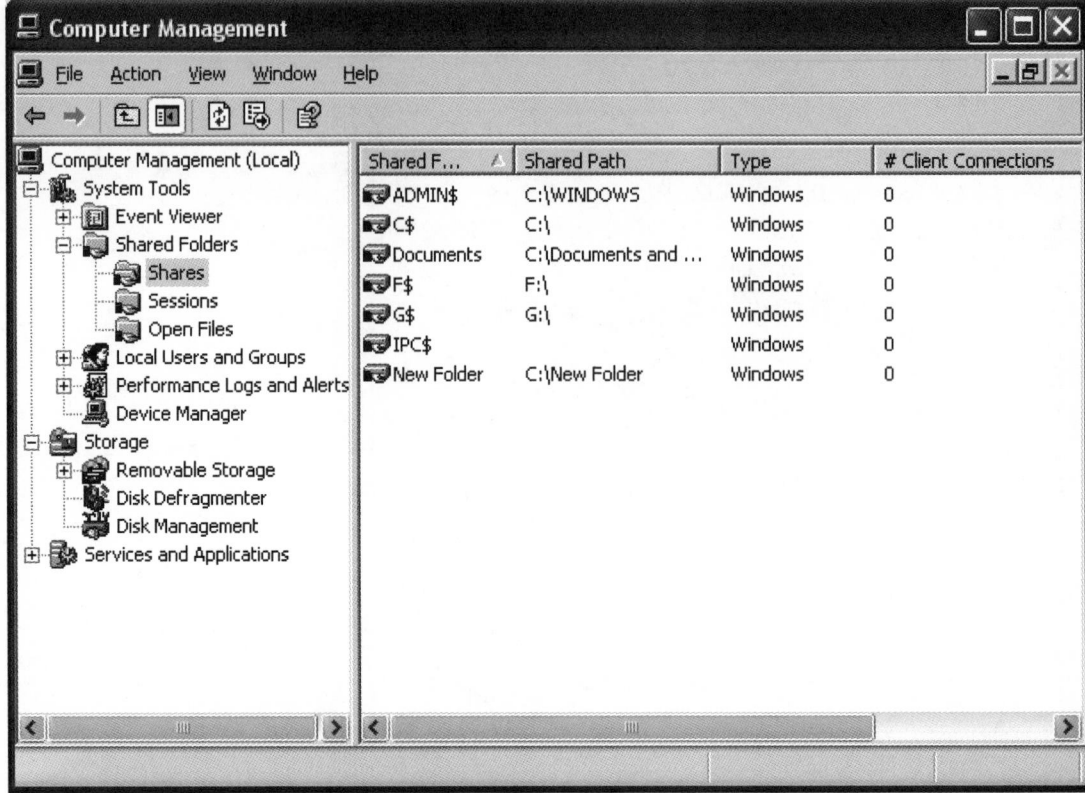

Figure 20-21: Shared folders in Computer Management

The answer is through offline files. Offline files makes files available on your local hard drive so you can work on them when you are not connected to the network. Then, when you reconnect, you can synchronize the files with the actual network copy — it's quick and easy and ensures that there are not multiple copies of the same document floating around the office.

Before using offline files, you have to enable them on Folder Options. Before doing that, however, you must disable fast user switching, if you are using it. Offline files and fast user switching are not compatible, so if you have been wondering why offline files do not seem to work on your computer, now you know.

To disable fast user switching, follow these steps:

STEPS

Disabling fast user switching

1. Open Control Panel ⇨ User Accounts.

2. Under Pick A Task, click Change the way users log on or off.

3. In the Select Logon and Logoff options, clear the Use Fast User Switching check box and click Apply Options.

4. Close User Accounts.

Now that fast user switching is turned off, you can enable offline files by accessing Folder Options in the Control Panel. Click the Offline Files tab, which is shown in Figure 20-22.

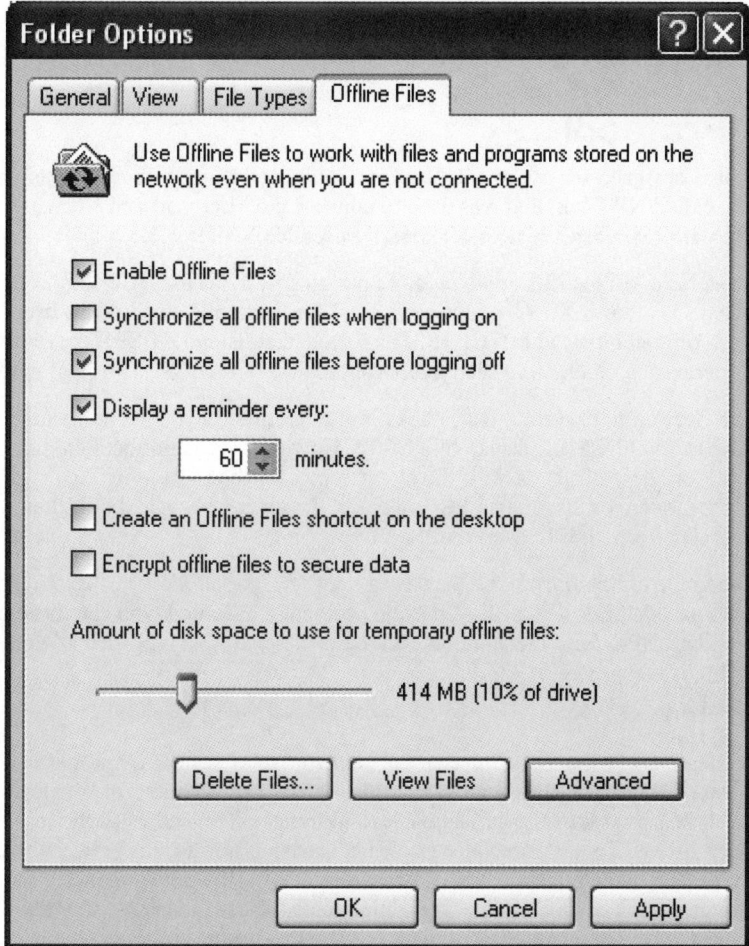

Figure 20-22: Offline Files tab.

To enable offline files, click the Enable Offline Files check box. You also have these options:

♦ Synchronize all offline files before logging on

♦ Synchronize all offline files before logging off

♦ Display a reminder every *x* minutes (60 is the default)

♦ Create an offline files shortcut

♦ Encrypt offline files to secure data

By default, 10 percent of your drive space can be used for offline file storage. You can change this value by using the slider bar. On the Advanced tab, you can determine how your computer behaves when a network connection is lost. By default, you get a notification and your computer begins working offline. Typically this is the best setting. Click OK when you are done, and offline files are now available on your computer.

After your computer is set up and ready for offline files, use My Network Places to browse to the desired network folder or file that you want to use. Select it, and then choose File ⇨ Make Available Offline. Your computer begins a synchronization process that downloads the file to your hard drive. When synchronization occurs again, according to your settings on the Offline Files tab, your changes will be synchronized with the original document, as well as any changes that are made by another person.

Using the IPX/SPX Protocol

IPX/SPX is a default protocol that is designed for use in NetWare environments. Microsoft created its own implementation of IPX/SPX, called NWLink, that was used to connect the Microsoft and NetWare environments together, especially when Microsoft networks primarily used NetBEUI.

Since the passing of those old days, both Microsoft's and Novell's operating systems use TCP/IP, but the IPX/SPX protocol is still available in Windows XP. One area of interest for home and small office users is the use of IPX/SPX as a network protocol instead of TCP/IP. The idea is that using IPX/SPX prevents IP attacks from the Internet, thus creating a much more secure environment.

Although Windows XP contains a firewall to prevent those attacks (not to mention that other software is available, as well), you can choose to use IPX/SPX instead of TCP/IP. However, if the protocol is used, ICS doesn't work because it is built on the TCP/IP stack. If the client computers connect individually to the Internet or through a DSL/cable modem or through an Ethernet hub, then it can be used, but if the typical ICS setup is in use, you need to keep your network built on IP.

To set up IPX/SPX, you need to add the protocol from the local area network adapter's properties sheets. Choose Install ⇨ Protocol and choose NWLink IPX/SPX. After the protocol is installed, you can disable TCP/IP. You can learn more about IPX/SPX from the Windows XP help file or from Microsoft.com.

QoS Packet Scheduler

You may have noticed an item called QoS Packet Scheduler on the General tab of your LAN properties, along with your protocols. QoS stands for Quality of Service, and this feature first appeared in Windows 2000 networks. QoS is able to analyze network traffic and adjust how Windows XP handles traffic in order to accommodate network conditions. This is especially true when transmission speeds between two networks are very different. The speed at which data arrives can cause problems, thus causing the resending of data and network congestion. The QoS Packet Scheduler detects these inconsistencies and takes actions to prevent the inconsistency. There's nothing you can configure for the QoS Packet Scheduler, but it's good to know it is around. You can learn more about it at http://www.microsoft.com/windows2000/library/technologies/communications/default.asp.

Summary

Windows XP provides the best tools ever produced by Microsoft for home and small office networking. You can easily create a network and share Internet connections with the help of a Network Setup Wizard.

♦ The Network Setup Wizard can configure the host computer and the client computers for networking and a shared Internet access point.

♦ Client computers can now manage the ICS connection through the ICS Discovery and Control Feature.

♦ Windows XP includes new tools that help you resolve connection problems with TCP/IP.

- My Network Places makes networking browsing easy and readily accessible.

- Network bridges can be used to automatically connect two dissimilar network segments with Windows XP.

- You can share network folders, drives, and printers. You can also use offline files to work with network documents when you are not connected to the network.

- Shared folders and files can be easily managed, and you can even set advanced permissions on folders so you can control what users can access them and what they can do.

- Windows QoS provides network management services that are provided automatically in Windows XP.

Chapter 21

Other Types of Networks

In This Chapter

Windows XP makes home and small office networking a real snap. You can easily set up a home or small office network and Windows XP will do most of tough networking configuration for you. However, Windows XP Professional also contains a number of additional networking features that enable you to network in a variety of diverse ways. The networking goal for Windows XP is to meet your networking needs — no matter what they might be. This chapter explores those additional networking features and options that may be just right for you. In this chapter, you learn about . . .

♦ Windows XP and the Windows domain

♦ Direct network connections

♦ Receiving dial-up calls

♦ Virtual Private Networking

♦ Wireless networking

♦ Connecting with other networks

Windows XP and the Windows Domain

Windows NT/2000 networks use a domain model, which logically groups computers and network objects in a way that makes administration easier. Although the domain models used by Windows NT and Windows 2000 networks are radically different from each other (and beyond the scope of this book), the idea is to bring as much simplicity as possible to large Windows networks where thousands upon thousands of Windows clients are used. Network administrators manage the Windows NT/2000 servers and clients use a client operating system, such as Windows 9*x*, Me, 2000, or XP. Windows XP Professional (not the Home edition) contains the networking features and support necessary to be an active, integrated part of a Windows domain, and is especially built for Windows 2000 domains.

Windows XP Professional contains all of the security features and advanced networking options that were seen Windows 2000 Professional. Unlike Windows 9*x* and Me, which contain little security features and networking possibilities, Windows XP makes complete use of the Windows 2000 technologies, including Group Policy.

> **CROSS-REFERENCE:** You can learn more about Group Policy in Chapter 23.

In a domain environment, Windows XP logs onto a Windows 2000 server using a valid username and password that you provide. That username and password is checked in the Windows 2000 Active Directory and authenticated by the server. After the XP computer is authenticated, any user-level Group Policy is applied to the computer and your computer becomes active on the network. At this point, you can begin using network resources, depending on the permissions applied to your user account. While on the network, you can publish printers to the Active Directory (if permissions allow), share files and folders, access resources on the network, including applications, and just about anything else a networking environment provides. Because you are in a domain environment, the IT end of things is handled by administrators and you don't have to spend your time worrying about connectivity and security.

If your Windows XP Professional computer needs to reside in a Windows domain, you simply need to make a quick adjustment to Windows XP so that it knows to look for a domain controller. Open System in Control Panel and click the Computer Name tab, shown in Figure 21-1.

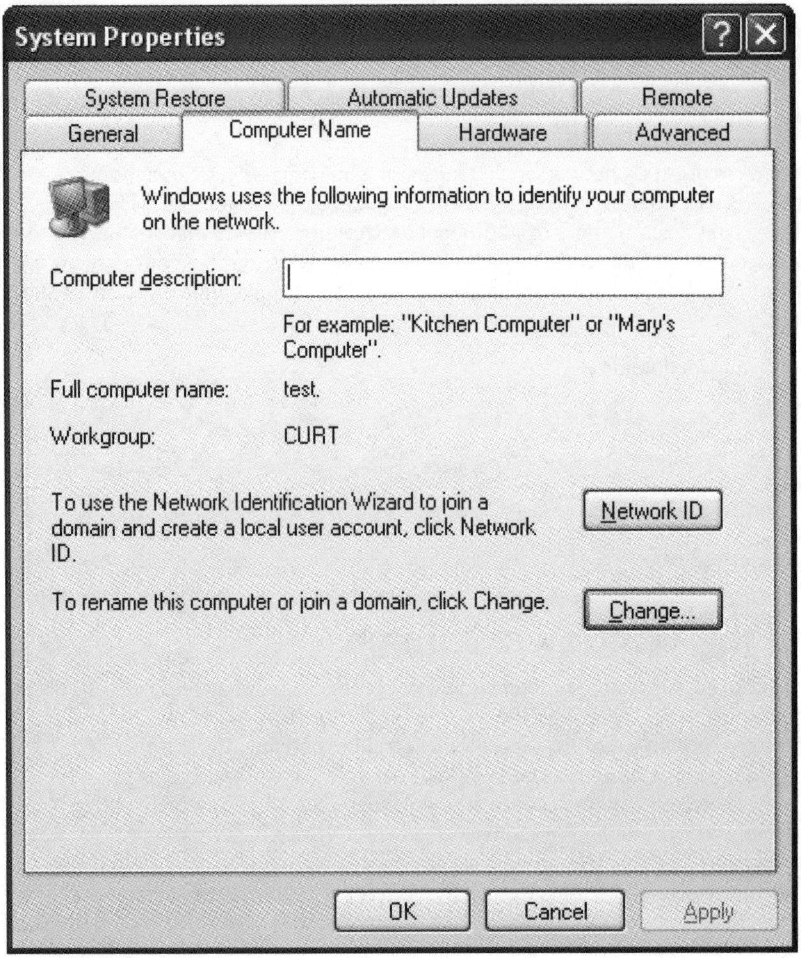

Figure 21-1: Computer Name tab

To join a domain, click the Change button, and then change the Member Of option to Domain and type a name for the domain, as shown in Figure 21-2.

Click OK, and OK again, to apply the changes. When you reboot the computer, a domain logon window appears where you can enter your username and password so that Windows XP can attempt to join the domain.

If you prefer, you can use the Network ID Wizard, found on the Computer Name tab to join the domain. The wizard collects the necessary information from you in order to contact and be authenticated by a domain controller. The following steps walk you through the wizard.

Figure 21-2: Computer Name Changes

STEPS

Using the Network ID Wizard

1. Click the Network ID button on the Computer Name tab and click Next on the Network Identification Wizard Welcome screen.

2. In the How do you use this computer window, click the This computer is a part of a business network, and I use it connect to other computers at work radio button option, and then click Next.

3. In the Connecting to the Network window, choose the My company uses a network with a domain radio button option, as shown in Figure 21-3.

4. In the Network Identification window, review the items you need to complete the wizard, which are primarily the domain name, username, and password. Click Next.

5. In the User Account and Domain Information window, enter your username, password, and the domain name (shown in Figure 21-4), and then click Next.

6. At this point, the Windows XP computer attempts to contact the domain. If successful, you are logged on, and the wizard completes. If not, you may be prompted for your computer name and the computer domain.

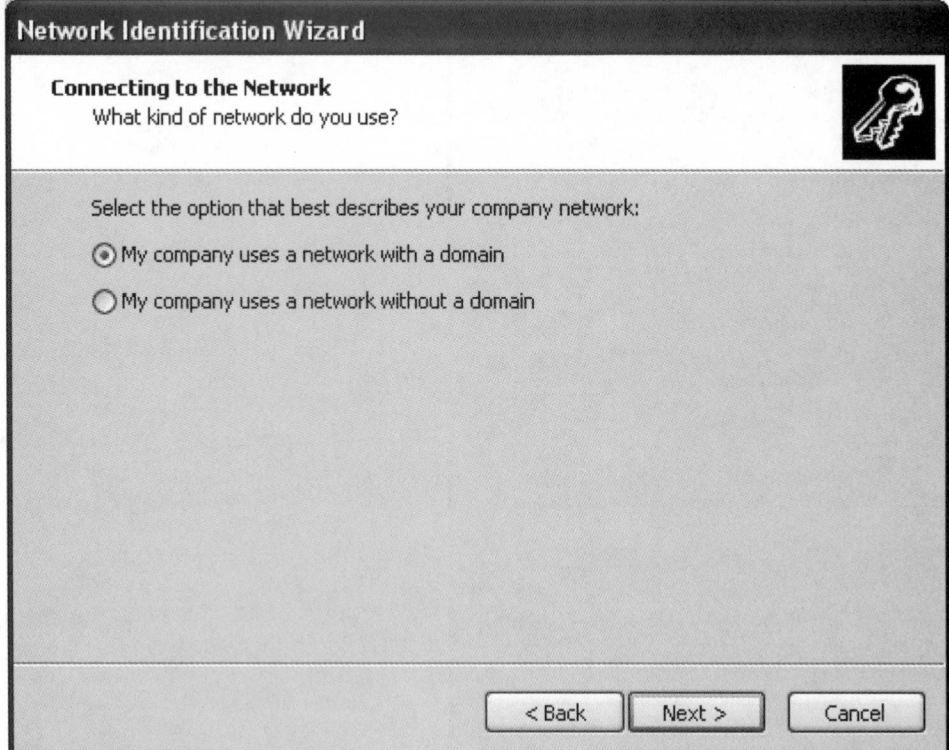

Figure 21-3: Connecting to the network

IP Addressing in a Windows Domain

In a home and small office network, you can use Windows XP's automatic IP addressing feature that enables each Windows XP computer on the network to automatically assign itself an IP address in the 169 address range (191 if Internet Connection Sharing (ICS) is used). This automatic addressing scheme is designed for home and small office networks so that users do not have to know how to configure TCP/IP in order to use a network (or, they can be completely oblivious to the fact that it exists). In larger networks, though, there has to be a mechanism to assign IP addresses to computers. Because each computer on a TCP/IP network must have a unique IP address and a correct subnet mask in order to communicate, the task of manually assigning addresses to computers would be overwhelming and impractical. Just imagine having to manually configure 10,000 XP computers with a unique IP address and subnet mask without making a mistake!

Fortunately, network administrators do not have to worry themselves with this task. Windows 2000 networks use a protocol that automatically assigns and manages IP addresses called the Dynamic Host Configuration Protocol (DHCP). When a Windows computer is booting, it queries the DHCP server for an IP address. A negotiation process occurs and ends with a unique IP address being assigned to the client computer for a period of time. When half of that lease time expires, the client computer begins querying the DHCP server for a renewal of the lease. DHCP is configured on Windows 2000 server(s) on the network, and once configured, the IP lease assignment process is automatic and generally problem-free, which is good news for network administrators who need to focus on other tasks.

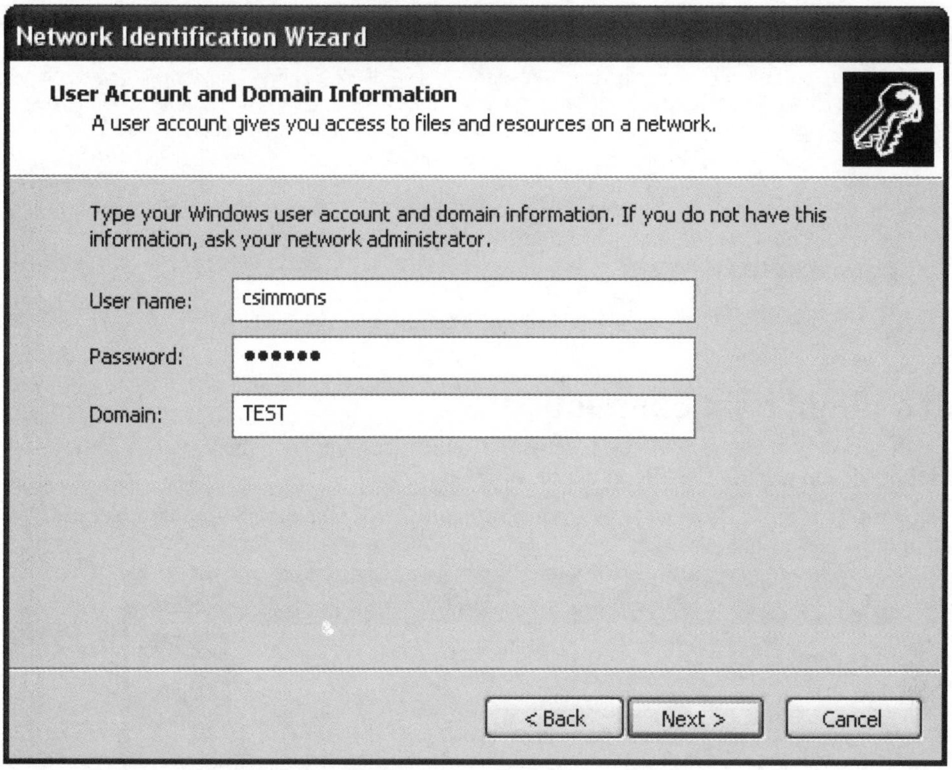

Figure 21-4: User Account and Domain Information

Direct Network Connection

Moving away from the domain model of networking, what can you do if you simply need to connect two Windows computers together for a period of time in order to transfer files from one to the other? If no network is available, you can easily connect two computers together with a direct network connection. You can create a direct network connection using Windows XP Professional or Home edition.

A direct network connection (which is a new name for direct cable connection) enables you to connect two Windows computers together using a parallel cable connecting both computers (using the printer port works great), or through a null modem cable connecting the serial ports on the two computers. You may be able to use other ports that are available as well, such as infrared ports or wireless ports. Cables needed for the connection are readily available at most computer stores and via online retailers. DirectParallel cables are also available and can be used to connect Windows XP computers and Windows 2000 computers. DirectParallel cables use standard and enhanced ECP parallel ports and represent one of the fastest direct cable connection methods. Other types of cables can connect Windows XP with any Windows version.

A direct network connection sets up one computer as the host and one as the guest. The guest computer accesses the host computer for files, but the host computer does not access the guest computer. So, traffic goes one way between the two. You must be logged onto Windows XP with an administrator account in order to set up a host connection, but you can be logged on with any account to set up a guest connection.

> **SECRET:** A direct network connection can be a quick and easy way to transfer files from computer to the next, but depending on your cable type, it can be painfully slow (some under 56 Kbps). Add this to the fact that the transfer direction is one way, and you see that a direct network connection is a temporary solution. If you need to connect two home computers together, I recommend a networking connection kit. If you want to use a Home PNA solution, you can often find these kits for under $60. With a Home PNA kit, you can take full advantage of all Windows XP networking features. See Chapter 20 to learn more about home and small office networking.

After the two computers are physically connected to each other by using the cabling method of choice, you can use the Create a New Connection wizard to create the host network connection. See the following steps for instructions.

STEPS

Creating a direct host connection

1. To create the direct host connection, open Network Connections and open the Create A New Network Connection wizard. Click Next on the Welcome screen.

2. In the Network Connection Type window, shown in Figure 21-5, Click the Set up an advanced connection radio button and click Next.

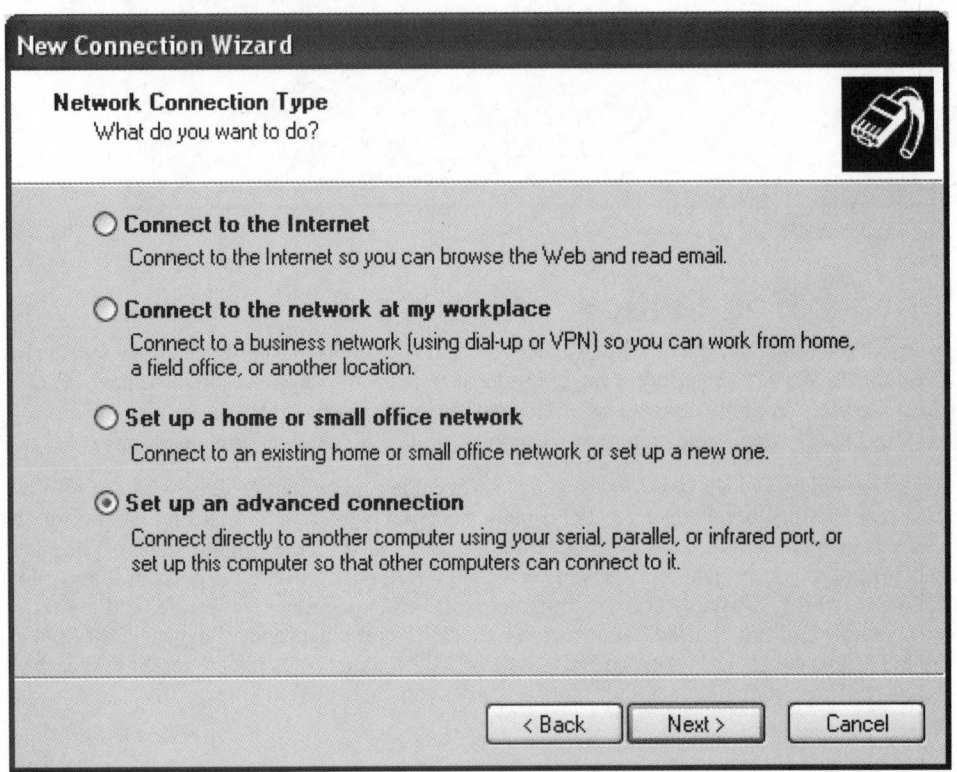

Figure 21-5: Network Connection Type

3. In Advanced Connection properties, choose the Accept incoming connections radio button and click Next.

4. The Devices for Incoming Connections window appears. You see a list of options that are installed on your computer (modem, parallel port, and so on). Select the connection that you want to use and click Next.

TIP: If the port you want to use is not listed, then it is not configured on your system. Configure the port for use first, and then rerun the wizard.

5. The Incoming VPN Connection window appears. Because this is a direct cable connection, you do not want to allow VPN connections. Simply leave the default Do not allow virtual private connections radio button enabled and click Next.

6. In the User Permissions window, shown in Figure 21-6, select the users that are allowed to access the direct connection. You can add and remove users from this interface and reconfigure passwords using the Properties button if necessary. Click the Next button.

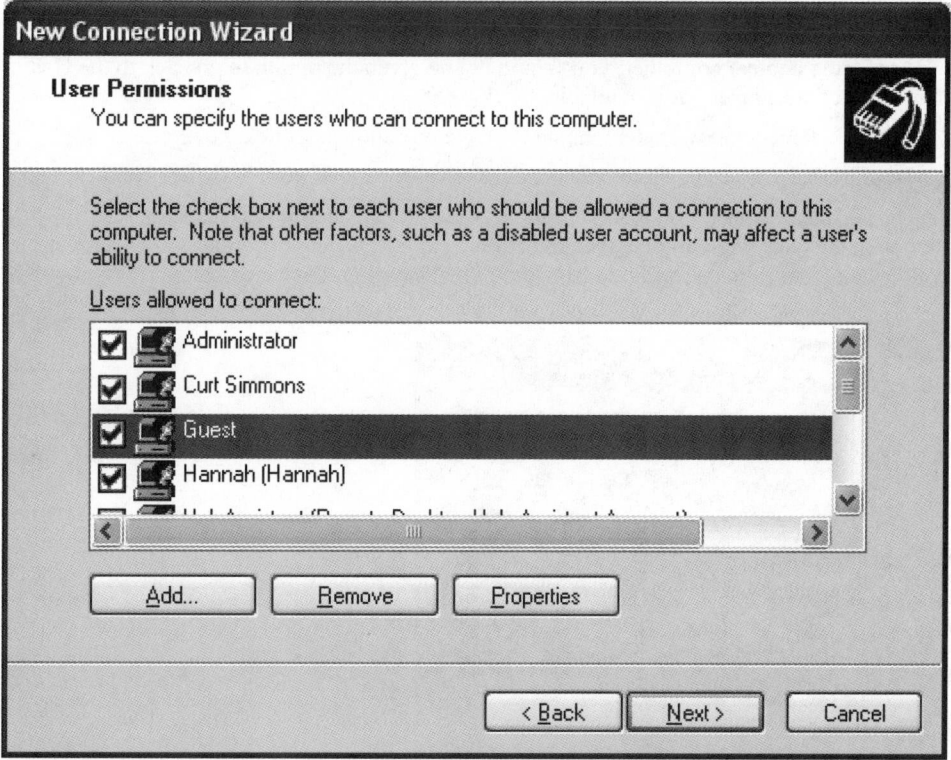

Figure 21-6: User Permissions

7. In the Networking Software, review the software that is selected for use. TCP/IP, File and Printer Sharing for Microsoft Networks, and Client for Microsoft Networks are typically selected by default. For connectivity to occur, these items should remain selected. Click Next.

8. Click Finish to complete the wizard. After the wizard completes the installation, an Incoming Connections icon now appears in the Network Connections folder.

After the incoming connection is established on the Host computer, you must set up the guest computer for connectivity with the host. The following steps walk you through the process of setting up a Windows XP computer to act as a guest. If you are using another version of Windows for the guest, see that operating system's documentation because the setup steps will be different.

STEPS

Creating a direct guest connection

1. To create the direct guest connection, open Network Connections and open the Create A New Network Connection wizard. Click Next on the Welcome screen.

2. In the Network Connection Type window, click the Set up an advanced connection radio button and click Next.

3. Choose the Connect directly to another computer radio button and click Next.

4. The Host or Guest window appears. Notice that you can choose Host or Guest. Choose the Guest radio button. This is one place where the wizard is sort of mixed up. Because you have already chosen to connect to another computer, you should not be given the option to go back to the Host configuration here; nonetheless, it is available. Click Next.

5. In the Connection Name window, enter a name for the connection and click Next.

6. Select a port or device you are using to connection, such as a parallel port, and click Next.

7. Click Finish. The direct connection icon appears in Network Connections. To establish the connection with the Host, double-click the direct connection, enter your username and password in the provided dialog box, shown in Figure 21-7 (you must have permission to access a Windows XP host), and then click Connect.

Figure 21-7: Establishing a direct network connection

Configuring Direct Dial-Up Access

When using a modem, Windows XP can enable remote clients to directly access it via a dial-up connection. Consider an example. Suppose you have a small office network of ten computers. You also have a laptop that you carry with you when you travel. Although the workgroup network does not have a server and advanced connectivity software, such as Windows 2000's Remote Access, you can configure a modem on one of the Windows XP computers to accept incoming connections. With your username and password, the XP computer can authenticate you and give you access to information on your network through the dial-up link. This is a simple and easy way to establish remote access when you are away from the network.

Of course, to establish a direct dial-up configuration, the XP computer needs to have a modem installed and be connected to a phone line that you want to use for direct dial-up access.

CROSS-REFERENCE: See Chapter 14 to learn more about setting up and configuring modems in Windows XP.

When you are ready to configure the dial-up access, you can do so, once again, with the Create a New Connection Wizard. The following steps walk you through the process.

STEPS

Configuring dial-up access

1. To configure dial-up access, open Network Connections and open the Create A New Network Connection Wizard. Click Next on the Welcome screen.

2. Click the Setup and Advanced Connection and click Next.

3. In the Advanced Connection Options, select Accept incoming connections and click Next.

4. In the Devices for Incoming Connections, select your modem (or ISDN line) and click Next.

5. In the VPN window, you can choose to allow VPN connections on the modem or ISDN line if you like. You can learn more about VPN connections later in this chapter.

6. In the User Permissions window, select the users who have access to connect using the remote connection. Users must provide a username and (preferably) a password to make the connection. Click Next.

7. In the Networking Software window, TCP/IP, File and Printer Sharing for Microsoft Networks, and Client for Microsoft Networks are selected by default. You should leave these options enabled so that the user can connect to your network. Click Next.

8. Click Finish. The Incoming Connection is configured and displayed in the Network Connections folder.

After the connection is created, you can right-click the connection in the network connections folder and click Properties. On the General tab, you can select the modem or ISDN connection and click the Properties button to adjust calling options. These are the same options you typically see when configuring a modem connection. For example, you can choose to disconnect the call if it is idle for a certain period time, adjust the port speed, data protocol, compression, flow control, and related settings.

SECRET: If you have the Internet Connection Firewall (ICF) enabled on the modem that will be dialed into, you are likely to have problems or a complete connection failure. You need to disable the firewall on the modem. You can learn more about working with ICF in Chapter 22.

Now that the modem or ISDN line is configured to accept incoming connections, you can create a dial-up connection on the client computer that will be dialing into the network. The following steps walk you through this process.

STEPS

Creating a remote computer/network connection

1. To create a connection to dial-up to a remote computer or network, open Network Connections and click the Create a New Connection Wizard. Click Next on the Welcome screen.

2. On the Network Connection Type window, choose the Connect to the network at my workplace option, and click Next.

> **TIP:** Remember that you are simply setting up a direct remote connection using a dial up (or VPN) to a remote computer that can give you access to the network. It doesn't matter if you are simply dialing up one computer, a home network, or whatever; in each case, you use the Connect to the network at my workplace option in the wizard.

3. On the Network Connection window, choose either dial-up or VPN. Because we are dealing with dial-up connections in this section, choose that option, and see the next section to learn more about VPN connections.

4. Enter a name for the connection and click Next.

5. Enter the phone number necessary to dial the connection and click Next.

6. Click Finish. The icon appears in Network Connections.

> **TIP:** You can make changes to the connection entry at any time by right-clicking the connection in Network Connections and clicking Properties.

To connect to the remote computer, double-click the connection icon. A Connect window appears in which you can enter your username and password and dial the phone number you provided in the wizard.

> **SECRET:** If you need to access a workgroup using the dial-up connection when you are on a remote computer. Make the connection and then access My Network Places. Your computer should attempt all connections with the workgroup via the modem to the connected computer. Also, remember that anything not shared on the network or computer you are calling into cannot be accessed. The dial-up connection gives you rights to the remote system only as provided by shares and your user account.

> **SECRET:** If you dial into a computer that is Internet Connection Sharing (ICS) enabled on a different connection, you can access the Internet over the ICS connection remotely. For example, suppose the host computer for your workgroup uses a modem to allow dial-in access, but is configured with a DSL link for Internet access. Because ICS is used, the connection is shared, and because you are a legal user on the network and of ICS, you can dial-in to the modem, and then access the shared Internet connection, just as you would do if you were locally connected to the network. In the same manner, you can access shared printers and other drives on computers on your network, just as though you were connected locally.

Virtual Private Networking

Virtual Private Network (VPN) is a technology that has been around for some time. Because of its security and potential cost savings, VPN is popular. In response to the increase in VPN usage, Windows XP is capable of using a VPN connection or allowing a VPN connection as the host computer. Either way, VPN functionality is typically easy to set up and to configure.

A Virtual Private Network uses the Internet or any other public network to create a secure "virtual" network link to another computer or a network. Over this link, you can then access and use network resources securely. Consider an example. Say you have a small office network in Houston and one in Seattle. Both networks have accounts with local ISPs where connections are made. From time to time, a computer in Seattle needs to access a computer in Houston to transfer financial records safely and security. You can perform this action using a direct dial-up connection, but the dial-up connection doesn't give you any enhanced security. To transfer that file securely, you can use a VPN connection in which a VPN tunnel is created and data is safely (and inexpensively) transmitted over the network.

When a VPN network is established, a direct tunnel connection is used over the public network. As TCP/IP packets are created to send over the network, they are encapsulated to appear as regular PPP (Point-to-Point Protocol) packets on the public network. The encapsulation process gives the packet a new header so that it can traverse the public network, such as the Internet. Inside the encapsulated packet is the real data, which is encrypted so that it can securely travel the over the public network. On the receiving end, the VPN end point "decapsulates" the data where it can be reconstructed as in a typical connection. This process involves the use of the Point-to-Point Tunneling Protocol (PPTP) or the newer Layer 2 Tunneling Protocol (L2TP), which provides additional security features. Windows XP always attempts to use L2TP instead of PPTP, but L2TP must be supported on both end points. If it is not, then PPTP is used. The good news is you don't have to configure these protocols; they are installed and configured automatically when you configure the VPN connection.

Because the network packets are encapsulated by using PPP, you can use any networking protocol that you like, such as TCP/IP or IPX/SPX. For example, two computers in remote locations on IPX/SPX networks could use a VPN connection over the Internet. The IPX packets are encapsulated and appear as typical PPP packets on the Internet. At the receiving end point, the PPP encapsulation is simply stripped away and you are back to IPX.

You can use a VPN in two primary ways: First, you can access it by using the Internet. By using an account with an Internet Service Provider (ISP), your computer can make the ISP connection first (using PPP), and then a second call is made over the Internet to the VPN host. The VPN tunnel is then negotiated and you can use the VPN tunnel over the Internet at no additional cost to you.

Second, if you have an always-on connection, such as DSL or cable, the VPN connection can be established over the existing Internet connection.

Setting up the VPN connection

The VPN connection works a lot like any other type of connection. You create the connection by using the Create a New Connection Wizard. Like other remote connections, you configure one computer to receive VPN calls, while one is configured to make VPN calls. However, unlike a direct network connection, VPN traffic can be two-way. Simply configure both computers to make and accept VPN calls. The following wizard steps show you how to enable a computer to receive VPN calls.

STEPS

Creating an incoming VPN connection

1. To create an incoming VPN connection, open Network Connections and then open the Create A New Network Connection Wizard. Click Next on the Welcome screen.
2. Click Setup an Advanced Connection and click Next.

3. In the Advanced Connection Options window, click Next. Then select the Accept incoming connections radio button and click Next.

4. In the Devices for Incoming Connections, select your modem (or ISDN line) and click Next.

5. In the VPN window, choose to allow VPN connections on the modem or ISDN line. Click Next.

6. In the User Permissions window, select the users who are to have access to connect using the remote connection. Users must provide a username and (preferably) a password to make the connection. Click Next.

7. In the Networking Software window, TCP/IP, File and Printer Sharing for Microsoft Networks, and Client for Microsoft Networks are selected by default. You should leave these options enabled so that the user can connect to your network. Click Next.

8. Click Finish. The incoming connection is configured and displayed in the Network Connections folder.

In the same manner, you can configure the computer to place VPN connection calls. Just follow these steps.

STEPS

Creating a outgoing VPN connection

1. To create an outgoing VPN connection, open Network Connections and click the Create a New Connection Wizard. Click Next on the Welcome screen.

2. In the Network Connection Type window, choose the Connect to the network at my workplace and click Next.

3. In the Network Connection window, choose the VPN connection option, shown in Figure 21-8. Click Next.

4. Enter a name for the connection and click Next.

5. In the Public Network window, Windows XP can automatically dial the initial connection to the Internet for you before the VPN connection is placed. To have Windows do this for you (recommended), select the Internet connection you want to use from the drop-down list and click Next. If you don't want to use this feature, click the Do not dial the initial connection radio button, shown in Figure 21-9. Click Next.

6. In the VPN server selection window, enter the host name, such as hungryminds.com, or the IP address of the VPN host computer. Click Next.

7. Click Finish. The icon appears in Network Connections.

To connect to the remote computer, double-click the connection icon. A Connect window appears where you can establish the VPN connection.

> **TIP:** If you are connecting to an ISP to reach the VPN host, the ISP connection is first established, and then a VPN Connection window appears where you enter your username and password for the VPN connection. Remember that a VPN connection is just like any other network connection. You can access network folders and other resources according to what is shared and what you have access rights for.

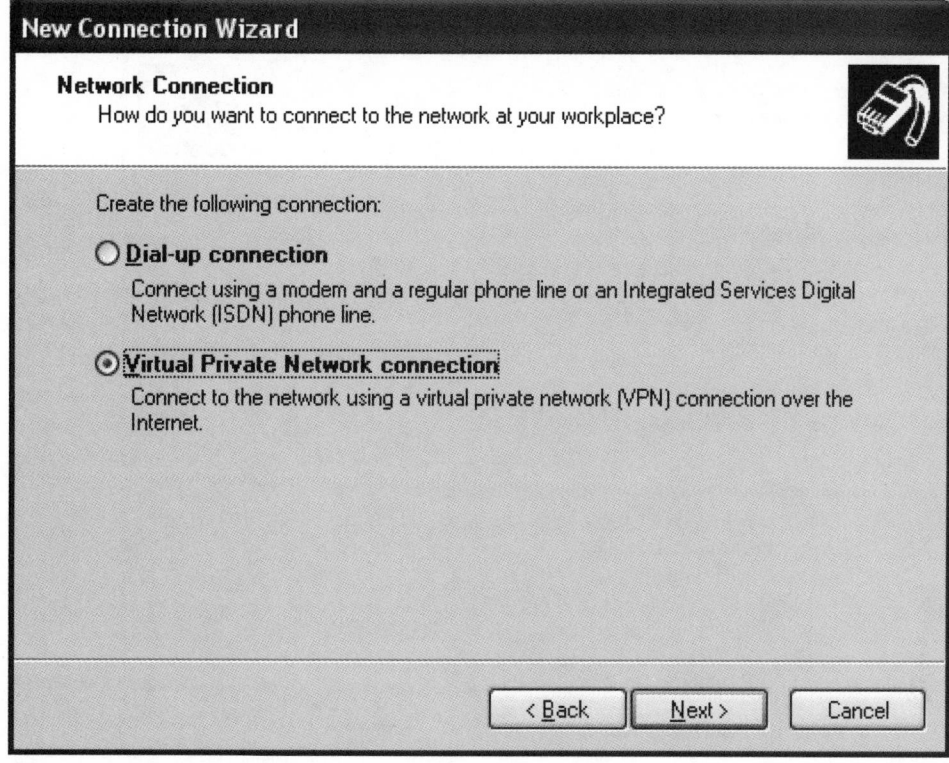

Figure 21-8: Selecting the VPN connection option in Network Connection

Configuring VPN security

Because VPN connectivity is often used to ensure secure transmissions over the Internet, you can determine the level of security that you want to invoke on these connections. You can access the VPN connection's properties, click the Security tab, and then click Advanced Properties to determine what protocol you want to use, as shown in Figure 21-10.

> **NOTE:** If your network is using an internal nonregistered Internet IP address or a private IP address (such as 10.0.0.1), you can still use VPN connectivity because the VPN connection can route through the public IP address given to you by the ISP. The true IP address of the VPN host is protected because all packet data is encrypted and encapsulated in the PPP packet that uses the public IP address. This feature ensures that private IP addresses on your network do not leak to the Internet and that you do not have to reconfigure IP just to use the VPN.

Depending on the level of security that you want to invoke, you can select a minimum standard that represents the least-secure method that clients can use. Doing so requires certain authentication methods and encryption settings to be used in order for the VPN tunnel to be established.

For PPTP and L2TP, the least secure methods that do not require data encryption are CHAP, MS-CHAP, and MS-CHAP v2. If encryption is not available, authentication occurs using CHAP. If you want to require encryption, use MS-CHAP or MS-CHAP v2. If you want to use Smart Card logon with or without encryption, you can use EAP/TLS.

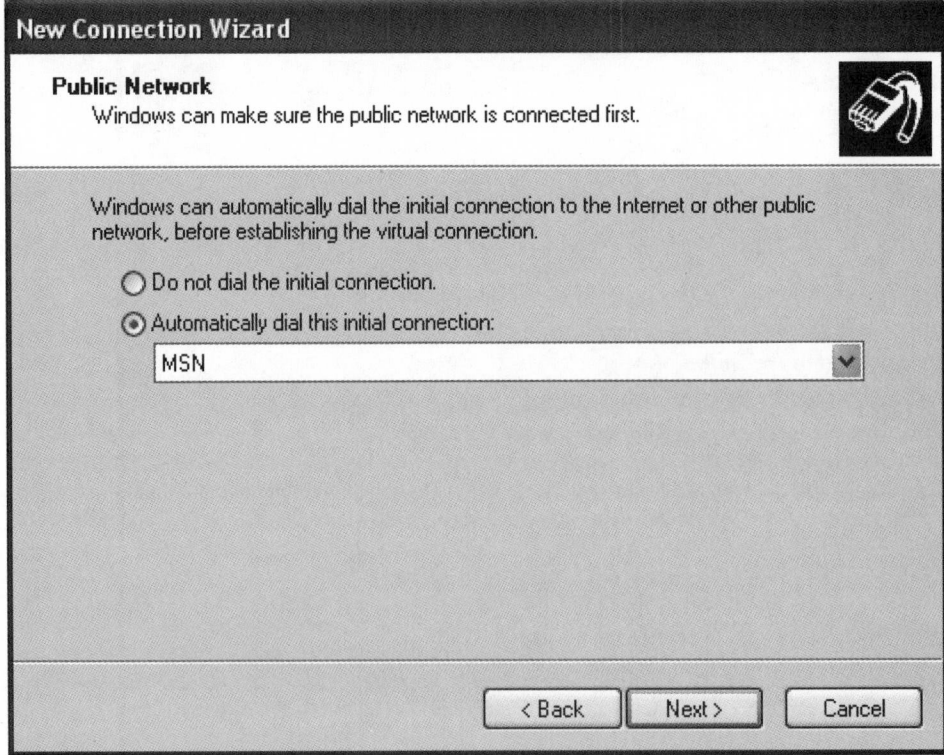

Figure 21-9: Public Network window

L2TP is the preferred protocol because it supports higher security standards. This is done through the Internet Protocol Security (IPSec) feature of Windows XP. With IPSec, data is encrypted and transported over an IP network with much tighter encryption and security features than are supported by standard encryption. This is the discriminating factor between PPTP and L2TP. If PPTP is used, data is encrypted using Microsoft Point-to-Point Encryption (MPPE), which is not as strong as IPSec.

CROSS-REFERENCE: If you want to learn more about L2TP, visit www.l2tp.net. For more information about IPSec and VPN, visit www.vpninsider.com.

The rule of thumb is to provide the highest level of security that can be supported between the VPN client and host, but not so restrictive that connectivity becomes a problem.

Wireless Networking in Windows XP

Over the past year, there has been a big buzz in the IT industry about wireless networking. Wireless networking, in and of itself, is certainly nothing new; in fact, if you use a cellular phone, you are using a wireless network. But wireless networking in the computing area has not been widely adopted because of a number of restrictions and difficulties with configuration. Because of the expense and often-problematic infrastructure, wireless networking has been more of a dream than a reality. For this reason, the Institute of Electrical and Electronics Engineers (IEEE) along with other organizations have been working to provide wireless standards that can make wireless networking more cost effective and reliable.

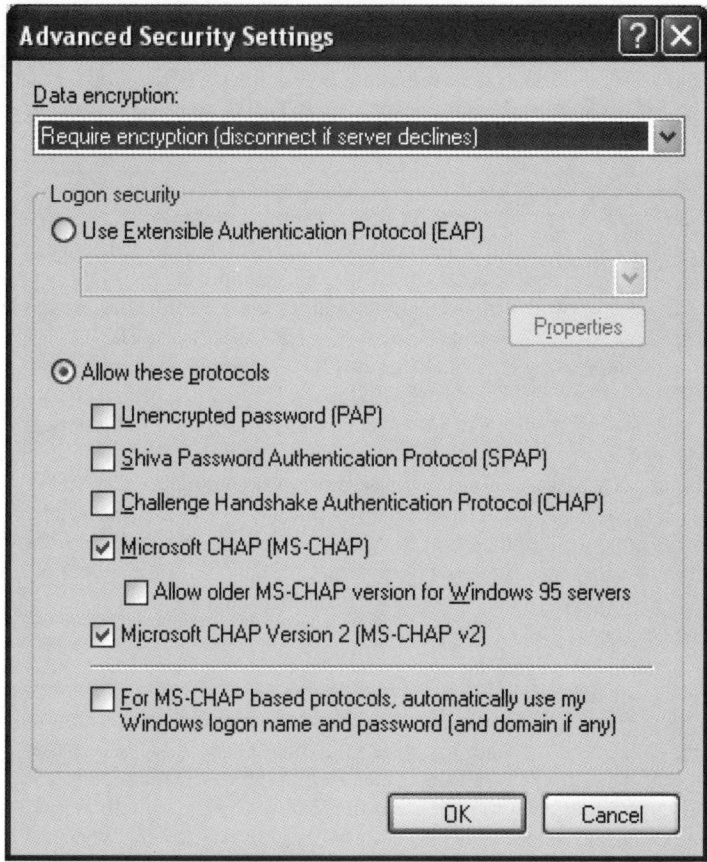

Figure 21-10: VPN Security Settings

Windows XP certainly does not solve the world's wireless networking problems, but it does support a number of wireless networking features. To gain a better understanding of wireless networks and wireless technologies, it is important to differentiate between the different types of wireless networks and the technologies that define them, as prescribed by IEEE. The following list describes these types:

♦ **Wireless Personal Area Networks (WPANs)** — Wireless Personal Area Networks include mobile devices such as cellular phones, PDAs, and laptops. The technology makes use of infrared and Bluetooth, which uses radio waves. The IEEE standardization for WPAN is classified as 802.15.

♦ **Wireless Local Area Networks (WLANs)** — WLAN technologies include wireless computers and devices that connect with each other using radio network adapter cards or external modems. To bridge larger or remote LAN segments, wireless stations and backbones are used. The IEEE standardization is 802.11, which is receiving a lot of attention these days. Data transfer at present is 11 Mbps over a 2.4 GHz frequency band.

♦ **Wireless Metropolitan Area Networks (WMANs)** — WMANs enable users to connect between locations in a metropolitan area. For example, the WMAN enables you to connect to your network while you are in a cab or a different building. The WMAN concept works like the cellular phone where a broadband wireless network services the wireless connectivity. The IEEE standard for WMAN networks is 802.16.

♦ **Wireless Wide Area Networks (WWANs)** — WWANs enable users to make connections over wide area networks through wireless antennas or even satellite. Key technologies fueling the WWAN networks, such as found with the cellular network and wireless Internet, are Global System for Mobile Communications (GSMC), Cellular Digital Packet Data (CDPD), and Code Division Multiple Access (CDMA).

TIP: You can learn more about the IEEE standards at `http://standards.ieee.org/wireless`.

In terms of connectivity with your Windows XP computer, you can use an infrared port to access other computers and printer devices on your workgroup or local area network. This is called an "ad-hoc wireless network" because each device is responsible for connectivity and no central controller is used as is done in typical wireless networks. In terms of WLAN access, Windows XP supports the 802.11 standard, and in an environment that is implementing 802.11, Windows XP can be outfitted with a wireless networking card or wireless external modem for access. Obviously, setup and configuration for this kind of network is dependent on the network's wireless infrastructure and configuration by network administrators, but Windows XP can make that easy because once a wireless network interface card (NIC) is installed, Windows XP automatically searches for the wireless network and identifies it. This process, known as Wireless Zero Configuration Services, presents the availability of the wireless network to the user, and if two wireless networks are detected, then the user can pick the one that the user wants to use. If no 802.11 wireless network is found, then Windows XP will configure the NIC for ad hoc mode so that the user can communicate directly with other wireless devices or printers in that area.

Connecting with Other Networks

As with previous versions of Windows, Windows XP Professional (not Home) provides the support needed to connect in other networking environments. With the wide implementation of TCP/IP as the networking protocol of choice, connectivity is often easier than it has been in the past. Of course, accessing resources can still be a challenge, and you'll not see all of the features provided with Windows XP networking when you use XP on a different vendor network. Still, the option is available when needed and the following sections give you an overview of connectivity issues with UNIX, Linux, and NetWare, three commonly used networks.

Connecting to a UNIX network

Windows XP Professional workstations are no different than any other Windows workstation in a UNIX environment. To communicate with other workstations on the network, Windows XP Professional workstations need to be running the same protocols.

The UNIX network might be running the TCP/IP transport protocol. On top of this, the network might be running the NFS application protocol and Samba, which is based on the Server Message Block application (SMB) protocol. Installing Samba makes the UNIX server look like a Windows 2000 server to Windows XP and 2000 Professional workstations.

Most Windows XP features translate into the Samba-enabled UNIX environment, including the Windows Explorer, Windows shortcuts, drive letter mapping, and My Network Places.

TIP: Recently accessed file shares are automatically stored in My Network Places so you can easily return to the file share you established before without having to map the drive letter.

The first thing you need to do when connecting to a UNIX share is to make sure that your network is configured correctly. If you are using a DHCP server on your network, Windows XP should set up everything you need by default. If you are not using a DHCP server, you need to set up your TCP/IP information manually by assigning an appropriate IP address and subnet mask on your network adapter's properties sheets.

To make drives and the data they contain available to others on the network, you have to map them to the server. There are several ways to do so, as shown in the following steps.

STEPS

Mapping a drive to UNIX server #1

1. Open My Network Places.

2. Choose Tools ⇨ Map Network Drive.

3. In the Map Network Drive dialog box, select the drive letter that you want to map to (this is your own personal preference). You also can specify the folder you are mapping from. The format for this follows UNC (Universal Naming Convention) standards. The format is *SOLARIS_SERVER_NAME**SHARENAME* where *SOLARIS_SERVER_NAME* is the exported name of the Solaris server, and *SHARENAME* is the name of the share to which you want to connect.

STEPS

Mapping a drive to UNIX server #2

1. Open My Network Places.

2. Choose the View Computers option.

3. You can search for the desired server. You are shown a list of computer names that match the name you typed. If you click the name of your Solaris server, you are taken to a window with the list of the shares on that server.

4. Click the share to which you want to connect and select Map Network Drive. All the information should be filled out by default. All you might have to do is change your username and click Finish.

STEPS

Mapping a drive to UNIX server #3

1. Open My Network Places.

2. Click the View Computers option.

3. To connect to a Samba share, click (or double-click) Microsoft Windows Network. This will take you to a list of all known workgroups.

4. Click (or double-click) the workgroup name that your Samba server belongs to, and then click (or double-click) your Samba server name when it comes up. Whether you search for the server or browse the entire contents for it, you are taken to the next screen where you find a list of available shares.

5. Click the share to which you want to connect and select Map Network Drive. All the information should be filled out by default. All you might have to do is change your username and click Finish.

Connecting to a Linux network

Networking Windows XP Professional workstations to a Linux network is virtually identical to networking to UNIX (see above). The main difference is that support for the SMB protocol is native to Linux (as it is to Windows NT and OS/2), so you shouldn't have to install anything additional.

Connecting to a NetWare network

Windows XP Professional workstations connect to Novell NetWare networks pretty much like any other Windows client. To communicate with other workstations on the network, Windows XP Professional workstations need to be running the same protocols. Typically, the NetWare network could be running IPX as the base protocol, with the NCP application protocol for file and print services running on top of that. However, many NetWare networks are now running TCP/IP.

Microsoft has included a Client Service for NetWare Networks in Windows XP, but it won't be very useful to organizations in which NetWare functionality actually matters. Although it does boast a single logon feature for both NetWare and Windows 2000, Microsoft Client Services for NetWare won't work with Novell ZENworks, Novell Distributed Print Services, or Novell Storage Management Services — which makes Microsoft three-for-three in torpedoing major functionality in a competing network.

Fortunately, Novell supplies a NetWare Client for Windows 2000/XP, which is significantly more functional than Microsoft's client — although not without foibles of its own. Check Novell's Web site at www.novell.com for the latest version. If the XP version is not available, the 2000 version should work just fine.

> **TIP:** Windows XP Professional makes it easier to connect to numerous different — even wildly different — networks by means of the Per-Connection Settings feature, which allows every dial-up, VPN, or direct network connection to have completely separate configurations, including networking protocols, scripts, and security.

The first thing you need to do when connecting to a NetWare network is to make sure that your network is correctly configured. Then, you need to install the Novell NetWare client for Windows 2000.

STEPS

Installing Novell's NetWare Client for Windows 2000 on a Windows XP system

1. Open Network Connections.
2. Right-click Local Area Connection and select Properties. This will take you to a list of protocols and services that are installed on the computer, as shown in Figure 21-11.
3. Click the Install button, select Client in the Select Network Component Type dialog box, and then choose Add, as shown in Figure 21-12.
4. Select the NetWare client and click OK.
5. After various files have been extracted and installed and you have rebooted the computer, you should see the NetWare login box that prompts you to press Ctrl+Alt+Delete to log in.

Figure 21-11: Local Area Connection Properties

Now that you are logged into the NetWare server, you can create a network drive mapping for easy future access to the information you need on the NetWare server. Mapping a network drive to a NetWare volume is very similar to mapping a drive to a Windows share and is explained in the following steps.

STEPS

Mapping a drive in NetWare

1. Open My Network Places and choose to Novell Map Network Drive from the Tools menu.

2. If you know the path to the volume, you can just type it in and select Map. If you're not sure, you can click Browse to use the NetWare Resource Browser.

3. Locate the volume you want in the NetWare Resource Browser, and then click OK. This will take you back to the Map Drive dialog box with all the path information filled in.

4. Now you just need to select Map, and you will be able to use the files on the NetWare volume just as if they were on a local drive (provided you have the proper rights).

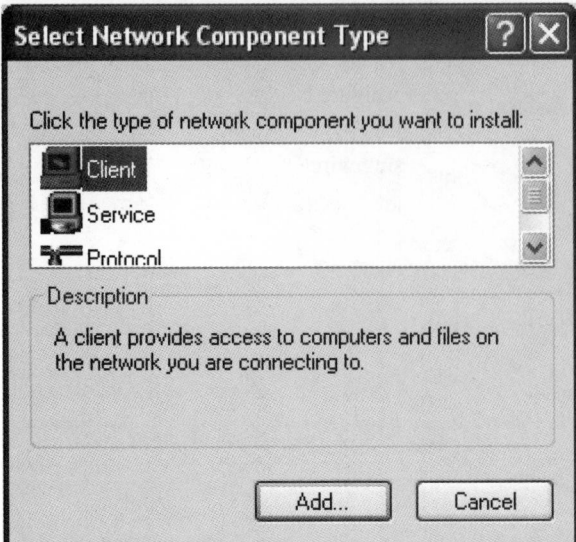

Figure 21-12: Select Network Component Type dialog box with Client selected

If you have successfully connected your Windows XP Professional workstation to a Novell NetWare network using Novell's Client for Windows 2000/XP, you should have a rich range of enhanced printing services available, courtesy of Novell's Distributed Print Services. These enhanced printing services include bidirectional printer communication, single-seat printer administration, and automatic printer driver installation.

STEPS

Installing a network printer in NetWare

1. After the NetWare Distributed Print Services printer has been installed and configured on the NetWare server, the Windows XP workstation finds the printer by browsing My Network Places in the Windows Explorer.

2. Right-click the network printer you want to install and click Connect.

3. The server should now install and configure the printer for the Windows XP Professional workstation so that it is available to it.

As you can see, Windows XP provides you with the ability to connect with different types of networks. Although your best bet for XP functionality and feature usage is to use XP on a Windows-based network, you can easily make these different connectivity solutions work for you, depending on your networking needs.

Summary

In this chapter, you explored some of Windows XP's additional networking features:

♦ Windows XP Professional is fully compatible with Windows 2000 domains and can help you get authenticated on the domain quickly and easily.

♦ Windows XP supports direct network connections where a direct cable or infrared connection can be made between two Windows computers.

- Windows XP can be configured to receive incoming connections over a modem, over an ISDN adapter, and by using VPN.

- VPN features are supported in Windows XP, and you can configure both a host and client. Windows XP also helps you connect to a VPN host via the Internet.

- Wireless networking 802.11 is supported in Windows XP using wireless network adapter cards.

- You can use Windows XP Professional on UNIX, Linux, and NetWare networks and access resources on these types of servers.

Chapter 22

Internet Connection Firewall and Remote Desktop Management

In This Chapter

Security and connectivity are two of the driving forces in networking today, including for the home/small office user. As more and more users upgrade existing dial-up connections to broadband connections, the issue of security becomes more important because the computer is always exposed to the Internet. In the same manner, users want and need more connectivity options to other computers for both work and play. This chapter explores two items that fall under the networking category, both of which are new in Windows XP — the Internet Connection Firewall (ICF), which is available in both Windows XP editions, and Remote Desktop Management, which is available only in Windows XP Professional. In this chapter, you learn about . . .

- ♦ Configuring and using ICF
- ♦ Configuring and using Remote Desktop
- ♦ Configuring and using Remote Assistance

What Is a Firewall?

It wasn't too many years ago that both networks and home computers were isolated islands. Sure, modems have been around for quite some time, but when the Internet was still a baby (a harmless baby) the idea of security really didn't concern most small networks, and it certainly didn't concern home users. On larger LANs, security has always been an issue because of corporate secrets, but security was rather easy to maintain because there was no network connectivity to the outside world.

That all changed over the past few years. As the Internet became more pervasive and more needed, LANs connected to it, giving their users access to the Internet's resources and capabilities. However, this connectivity introduced a number of problems. How can a LAN connect to the Internet, receive e-mail from the Internet, and keep unauthorized users out of the local network? That question is difficult and costly to answer, and remains an issue today. On LANs, the accepted solution is to use a firewall.

A firewall can be either a software or hardware product that sits between a private network and the Internet. The firewall's job is to allow internal traffic to get to the Internet and to allow requested Internet traffic through the firewall and to the network, while keeping out any unauthorized traffic or potential security threats. It is a tough job to do and one that is rather complex. There are products that are actual hardware products — routers of sorts — that act as network firewalls. There are also software solutions. For example, Microsoft Internet Security and Acceleration (ISA) Server is a software firewall solution that runs on Windows 2000 Server. ISA Server provides advanced caching features and policy management so that administrators can carefully manage what their users are allowed to do on the Internet. The firewall portion of the product is able to inspect TCP/IP packets and determine whether they are safe to enter the network. Aside from ISA Server, there are many other firewall products available. All of these products are expensive, and all require IT professionals in order to configure them. However, corporate networks are more than willing to part with hard-earned money to get them up and working.

To break all of this down, you can think firewalls in three primary categories, which are:

♦ **Commercial firewalls** — As mentioned above, commercial firewalls can be hardware or software based and used to protect corporate networks. They are expensive (often several thousand dollars) and require professional IT personnel to configure and operate.

♦ **Routers** — Aside from firewall products, various IP routers, such as those produced by Cisco, can manage IP traffic as it flows in and out of a network. Routers, however, are primarily designed to route traffic — not necessarily to provide security.

♦ **Small office/home solutions** — Personal firewall software, like XP's firewall software, is also available from a number of other vendors, including Symantec and McAfee. These firewalls provide a measure of protection, but are obviously not as capable as corporate products.

Ideally, you want a firewall to do three basic jobs:

♦ The first job of a firewall is to make your PC invisible to the Internet at large while still allowing you to interact with the Internet. If you are invisible, most would-be hackers will leave you alone because they cannot tell if you are on the Internet or not.

♦ The second job of a firewall is to let the right data pass through and ensure that the data you do let through the firewall is indeed the right data, which is more important in protecting your PC against attacks and viruses.

♦ An optional job of a client-side firewall is application control. Of course you want to allow IE, Outlook, and so on to freely access the Internet — but maybe you do not want MediaPlayer to have Internet access (could be a security hole in it), yet you'd like to use it for local file viewing. A client-side firewall can help arrange that.

You may be thinking, "That's great, but what does it have to do with me?" As Internet use has become more commonplace, many small companies and home users are now connecting to the World Wide Web through a broadband connection such as DSL, cable, or satellite. These always-on connections are fast and great, but they expose your computer to the Internet all of the time, unlike a dial-up connection that usually isn't connected unless you are using it. The always-on connection simply gives hackers and other Internet intruders a greater opportunity to hack into your computer to do all kinds of damage. Let there be no mistake — once you are connected to the Internet with an "always-on" connection, you are exposed to the Internet, you are a part of it, and you are open to potential attack. I don't mean to sound fatalistic, but an always-on connection keeps your PC exposed to the Internet at all times, so you must take care to protect yourself.

> **SECRET:** Your ISP may have protection software, but under no circumstances should you assume that protection is the responsibility of your ISP. You are responsible for your own Internet protection. Don't believe me? Not to give away hacking information, but you can download a copy of NetBrute from www.rawlogic.com, choose a Class C subnet range from your DSL provider, and see all of the shared C drives out there! Want to learn more about how big this problem really is? Check out www.sfgate.com/cgi-bin/article.cgi?file=/c/a/2001/08/26/MN209383.DTL

So, why not include a firewall software product that helps protect your computer against such attacks? Windows XP includes such a product; it is called Internet Connection Firewall (ICF). The idea of single computer firewall protection is not new — in fact, other vendors, such as Norton and McAfee, already produce firewall protects, some of which are bundled with their antivirus software. These products are great, and I use Norton's Internet Security product myself, but the ICF software included in Windows XP is also good, and it is already included as part of the operating system. The idea behind ICF is simple — to enable you to use the Internet and all that it has to offer and to keep anyone on the Internet from hacking into your computer.

> **NOTE:** Before I sound like an ICF salesman, let me emphatically say that no consumer level firewall product is foolproof. Sure, ICF can help protect you, but be smart and do not share items that should not be shared. Also, you may consider using a third-party firewall product, such as those offered by Symantec and McAfee, which may give you more protection options than ICF.

How ICF Works

ICF, like all firewall products, works by sifting through TCP/IP packets. When you communicate on the Internet, data that is sent and received from your computer is broken down into tiny pieces called packets. Packets leave and enter your PC through appropriate TCP/UDP ports — for example, HTTP Web pages use port 80. These packets have header information stating where they are from and where they are going. The packets then traverse the Internet until they reach their destination. The destination computer receives the packets and reassembles them to provide you with data of some kind, whether that is a Web page, a file, or an e-mail message.

Because IP traffic is broken down into packets, hackers can send certain kinds of packets to your computer, attempting to get inside. They can even launch attacks against your computer with IP packets that cause the computer to crash or to be overwhelmed with information. Hacker attempts usually begin by scanning your computer's TCP/IP logical ports, which your computer uses for communication on the Internet. These logical ports are used with different TCP/IP protocols and provide you with the vast Internet functionality known today. When a port scan takes place, the hacker can identify an open TCP port on your computer and get through your computer using that port.

ICF's job is to monitor all traffic that leaves your computer and all traffic that arrives at your computer. With arriving traffic, the firewall can monitor the packets' header information and determine whether the packets were requested from the destination address. For example, suppose that I enter www.hungryminds.com in Internet Explorer. ICF creates a table and notes the request in the table. The request is sent over the Internet to www.hungryminds.com, which returns home page information to my computer. As those packets begin arriving, ICF inspects their header information and compares that information with table entries. ICF realizes that the information was requested, and the packets are allowed to enter the computer. No information from the Internet that was not requested by your computer is allowed to enter it — by default anyway (you can adjust that to meet your needs, and I show you how later in this chapter). So, anything you don't request doesn't get through the firewall. When the firewall identifies packets that were not requested, they are simply dropped before they enter your computer. You are not notified or asked if this action is okay — the ICF software just handles it.

> **TIP:** This kind of firewall is called a "stateful" firewall. The ICF software inspects traffic in terms of its communication use with your computer and determines whether that traffic is allowed or not.

ICF works with Internet browsing or with Internet mail. However, some e-mail programs experience problems with ICF. If the e-mail program polls the e-mail server for mail, ICF will work fine because the request was initiated at your local machine. For example, Outlook Express polls the server for mail at timed intervals as configured. Because the mail client is making a request to the server, server traffic is accepted. However, Microsoft Outlook, when connecting to a Microsoft Exchange server, receives RPC (Remote Procedure Call) messages from the server that there is new mail. Because these RPC messages are "unsolicited" by the local computer, they are dropped at the firewall. Outlook can get mail from the server, but you would have to check for it manually.

Beyond the potential mail problem, ICF works easily and in the background. The next section explores how it should be used.

How to Use ICF

ICF was designed with the small office/home network in mind. Although ICF could be used in larger networks, each Windows XP computer would have to have an Internet connection, or share connections with several users. In corporate environments, there is typically one connection to the Internet that is controlled by server. All client requests to the Internet are sent to the server and are handled from there. The server contains the firewall software, or, in the case of a hardware product, the firewall sits in between the Internet connection and the server. In these cases, you don't need to use ICF because you already have firewall protection; in fact, if you enable ICF on your network adapter card, it will cause some network traffic not to reach your computer. The skinny is simply this — don't enable ICF if you are on a LAN unless you are instructed to do so by your network administrator.

With that said, ICF is designed to protect the individual computer or the small network. ICF is configured per connection. In other words, there is not one global configuration for your entire machine. If you have both a dial-up and a broadband connection, you have to configure ICF on each connection individually. Because of this, you need to enable and configure ICF on any connection to the Internet used by your computer.

If you are using Internet Connection Sharing (ICS), the connection to the Internet needs to be protected by ICF. However, the internal network adapters that make up your internal small office or home network should not be protected by ICF — only the external Internet connection needs the firewall. If you firewall internal network adapters, you will have problems with network communication because ICF will drop network communication that is not generated by you. So, the connection to the Internet should be firewalled — but all internal network connections should not be firewalled. If ICS is used and one or more client computers also have a separate connection (such as a backup dial-up connection), then those connections must be firewalled. Try to think of your network as a house. You may have several doors to the outside world, but those doors must be closed in order have solid protection. It doesn't matter how secure the front door is if the back door is open. The same is true with the ICF. You have may have the main ICS connection firewalled, but all backup connections must be firewalled as well, or you have a potential security breach on your hands. The key points to remember are:

♦ ICF can be used with ICS, but the two components do not have to work together.

♦ ICF should be enabled on any Internet connection.

♦ If ICS is used, ICF should be enabled on the ICS host's Internet connection, but not the internal network adapter card or the network adapter cards of the ICS clients.

♦ If ICS is used, any backup Internet connections on the ICS host or clients should be firewalled. For example, if you have a dial-up connection that is sometimes used on one of the clients, then the dial-up connection should also be firewalled. Think of each Internet connection as a door — make sure a lock (firewall) exists on each door that leads out of your local network.

> **CAUTION:** ICF is not designed to work on Virtual Private Network (VPN) connections. ICF software interferes with VPN communications if it is enabled on those connections. Do note, however, that other firewall solutions may work fine with VPN connections.

Configuring ICF

ICF is not difficult to configure, but there are some options that you need to understand so that you can determine which settings are right for you and your network, particularly if you are using ICF in conjunction with ICS. The following sections explore ICF configuration.

Enabling ICF

ICF can be enabled on the Advanced properties tab of any Internet connection. Open the Network Connections folder and right-click the desired Internet connection. Click the Advanced tab, and click the Protect my computer and network by limiting or preventing access to this computer from the Internet check box, shown in Figure 22-1. After you click OK, the firewall is turned on and is active.

TIP: If you are using ICS, the ICS configuration information appears in the bottom portion of the Advanced tab window. As you can see, the two components can work together or independently.

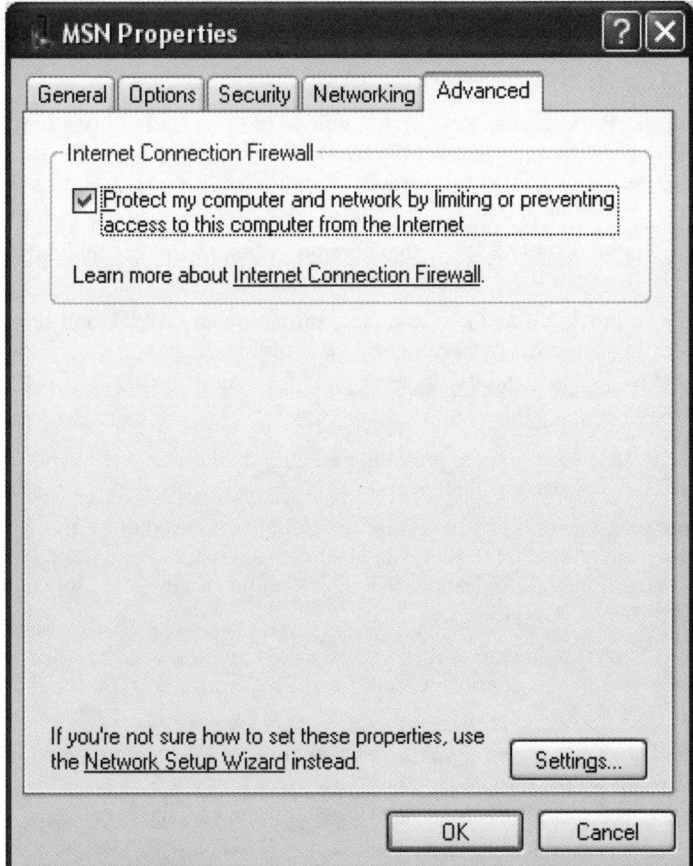

Figure 22-1: Enable ICF

Configuring services

As discussed earlier in this chapter, ICF drops all communication from the Internet that was not initiated by the firewalled computer. This essentially keeps unsolicited communication from entering your computer. However, for a number of services, this kind of configuration will not work. So, ICF enables you to allow certain services that will enable traffic from the Internet to reach your host computer. These services must be defined so that ICF knows what is allowed and how to forward the incoming traffic to your computer. This configuration is called a *service definition*. It defines the service and enables ICF to understand how to handle the Internet protocol (IP) traffic.

You need to take a look at these and enable the ones that are needed, or you can configure your own custom services. However, you should not enable any service that is not absolutely necessary. No firewall is foolproof, and the more services you enable for entry to the private computer, the less secure the connection becomes. So, use what you need to, but don't enable anything that is not expressly needed.

By default, ICF provides preconfigured service definition settings for the following, as shown in Figure 22-2. You can see these options by clicking the Setting button on the Internet connection's Advanced tab.

> **NOTE:** The services listed here enable Internet clients to contact a computer on your network; the services have nothing to do with your access to Internet servers. For example, if you enable the FTP server, the ICF software allows FTP traffic to enter your network in order to access your FTP server. This has nothing to do with your ability to access an FTP server on the Internet — all of the services here control whether or not certain kinds of traffic are allowed to enter *your* computer or network. They don't restrict your access.

- ◆ **FTP Server** — FTP, or File Transfer Protocol, enables users to upload or download information from a Web site. If you have a Web server running on your network that provides FTP to clients, then you could enable this service definition so that Internet clients could contact your FTP server. If you are not providing FTP to Internet clients, don't enable this service.

- ◆ **Internet Mail Access Protocol Version 3 (IMAP3)** — If you are providing an IMAP3 mail server and clients need to access their mail through ICF, you can enable this option.

- ◆ **Internet Mail Access Protocol Version 4 (IMAP4)** — If you are providing an IMAP4 mail server and clients need to access their mail through ICF, you can enable this option.

- ◆ **Internet Mail Server (SMTP)** — If you are providing an SMTP mail server and clients need to access their mail through ICF, you can enable this option.

- ◆ **Post Office Protocol Version 3 (POP3)** — If you are providing a POP3 mail server and clients need to access their mail through ICF, you can enable this option.

- ◆ **Remote Desktop** — If clients on your network, or your computer itself, are allowed to receive a Remote Desktop connection from a client on the Internet, you need to enable the Remote Desktop service here; otherwise, ICF will not allow the connection. See the "Remote Desktop" section later in this chapter to learn more about Remote Desktop.

- ◆ **Secure Web Server (HTTPS)** — If you are hosting a Web site on a computer on your network that uses secure HTTP, you need to enable this service in order for HTTPS traffic to get through ICF.

- ◆ **Telnet Server** — If you are running a Telnet server (which you probably aren't) on your network, enable the service here so that ICF allows the traffic.

- ◆ **Web Server (HTTP)** — If you are providing a Web site via a Web server on your network, enable the Web Server service so that HTTP requests can be passed through the firewall and to the Web server on your network.

You can enable any desired service by clicking the check box next to the service name. When you click a service, a Service Settings window appears, as shown in Figure 22-3. The Service Settings window essentially provides the service definition by providing the following information:

- ◆ **Description of service** — This is a friendly name for the service.

- ◆ **Name or IP address of the computer hosting the service on your network** — This is the only option you must complete. Provide the name or the IP address of the computer on your network that is hosting the service.

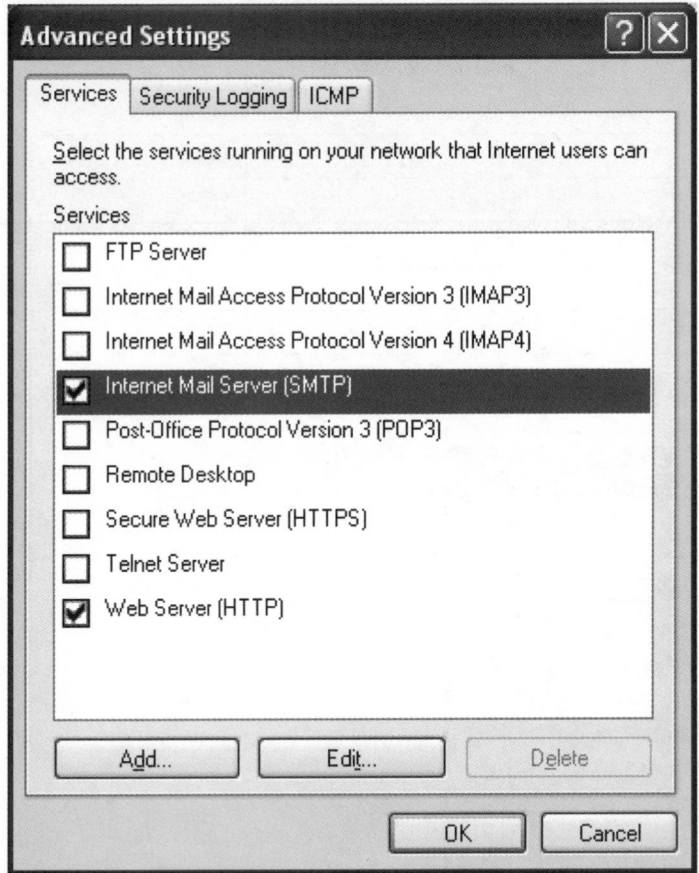

Figure 22-2: ICF Services

♦ **External port** — The TCP/UDP external port that is used for this kind of service traffic.

♦ **Internet port** — The TCP/UDP internal port that is used for this kind of service traffic.

♦ **Protocol** — The protocol used for this kind of service traffic (either TCP or UDP).

SECRET: Notice in Figure 22-3 that the port, protocol, and description information are grayed out. The configured services use Internet standard settings. For example, if you are hosting a Web site, all Web browsers attempt to connect on port 80, which is standard. The standard settings provided here do not need to be changed, and you cannot do so from within ICF. If you need non-standard port configurations, you'll probably want to use a different firewall product that gives you this flexibility.

Table 22-1 provides the settings for each preconfigured service provided by ICF.

Table 22-1: Preconfigured Services

Description	External Port	Internal Port	Protocol
FTP Server	21	21	TCP
IMAP3	220	220	TCP

Description	External Port	Internal Port	Protocol
IMAP4	143	143	TCP
SMTP	25	25	TCP
POP3	110	110	TCP
Remote Desktop	3389	3389	TCP
Secure Web (HTTPS)	443	443	TCP
Telnet Server	23	23	TCP
Web Server	80	80	TCP

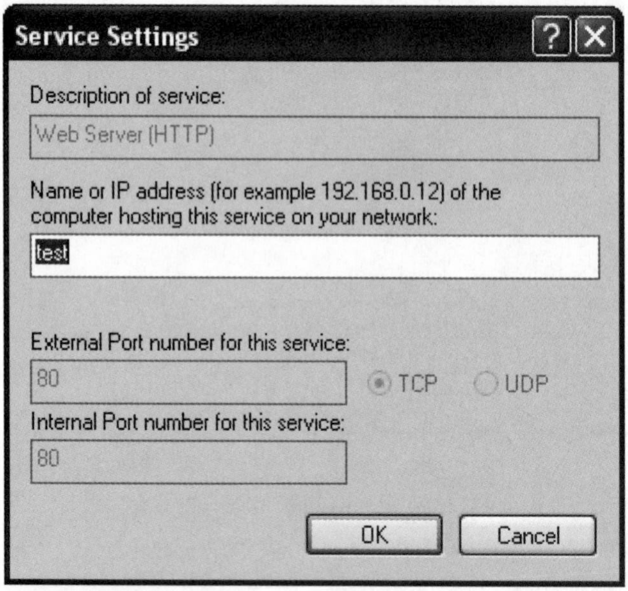

Figure 22-3: Service Settings

About Service Definitions

ICF uses a service definition to allow certain kinds of Internet traffic through the firewall so that it may by received by a server service of some kind. You might wonder, "Is this how the big networks do it?" The answer is both yes and no. Most firewall software programs do use the service definition feature to determine what traffic can enter a firewall and what traffic cannot. However, the larger networks often take much greater pains to insure that the traffic entering the network can go only to the desired server and that the actual server is hidden from the Internet.

When a service request is made, it is done by IP address. Typically, when you access Web server on the Internet using the Fully Qualified Domain Name (FQDN), such as www.hungryminds.com, DNS servers on the Internet resolve your request to an IP address, and then the IP address is actually used to contact the Web server. In firewalled environments, the IP address of the Web server is usually the firewall, masquerading as the Web server. When the HTTP request arrives at the firewall, the firewall inspects it before forwarding the service request on to the actual Web server, which may be using a different IP address. The real IP address of the Web server is never exposed to the Internet, so anyone trying to hack into the Web server by IP address is actually hitting the firewall — not the real Web server.

Some environments that want to make absolutely sure that an Internet intruder doesn't get beyond a Web server (or mail server, FTP server, or whatever), use a tactic known as a Demilitarized Zone (DMZ). In this scenario, the Web, FTP, mail, or other service server is actually contained on a different IP subnet surrounded by firewalls. When a request is made, the request is sent directly to the service by the firewall (using a different IP address). Another firewall sits behind the service server so that no traffic can escape the server and enter the private network, which is actually on a different IP subnet.

As you can see, network architects and administrators go to great lengths to provide service to Internet clients while deploying numerous tactics to keep unauthorized traffic out of the private network. Although ICF doesn't provide all these capabilities to you, the basic principle still works. ICF's job is to statefully examine packet traffic and to determine what traffic can be forwarded to a service server inside your network and what traffic must be dropped.

> **CROSS-REFERENCE:** You learn more about LAN security concepts in *Microsoft ISA Configuration and Administration* by Curt Simmons, which is also published by Hungry Minds, Inc.

Configuring Custom Services

Aside from enabling a preconfigured service, you can also configure your own custom service by clicking the Add button. Before doing so, you need to install the service on the desired computer on your network, and then gather the service name, the ports used, and the protocol used. After you click Add, a Service Settings window appears, shown in Figure 22-4, in which you can enter the desired information. Click OK when you are done, and the new service definition appears in the Services window as a selected item.

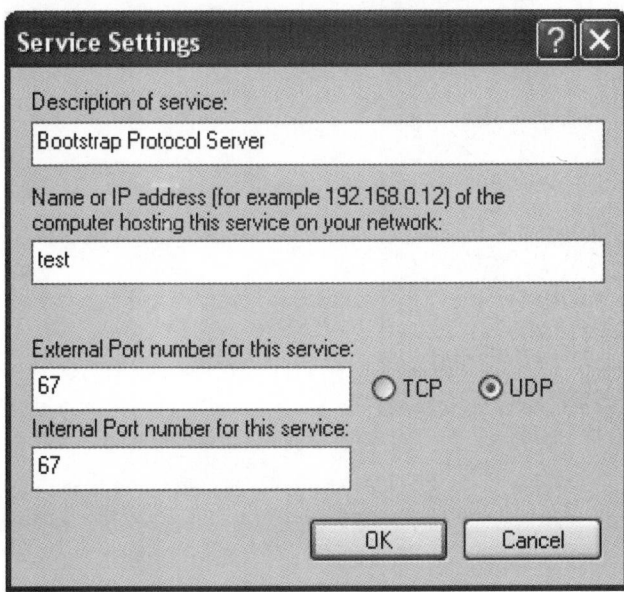

Figure 22-4: Creating a new service definition

> **TIP:** You can only edit or delete service definitions that you create. You cannot edit or delete the preconfigured service definitions.

Security logging

The Security Logging tab, shown in Figure 22-5 enables you to configure security logs for ICF. The security log enables you to log information about dropped packets and successful connections. If you choose to log dropped packets, all packets that are dropped at the firewall are recorded in a log file that you can view. If you choose to log successful connections, obviously, connections to Internet servers that are successful are logged. This log file creates a listing of traffic leaving your network and records what connections have been made. In short, it is a way to record all visits to the Internet and where these visits occurred. If you are using ICS on a home or small office network, this successful connections option gives you a secret way to see what sites users on your network are accessing. Even if the History and Temporary Internet files are cleared in Internet Explorer, you'll still be able to see the visits via the log file.

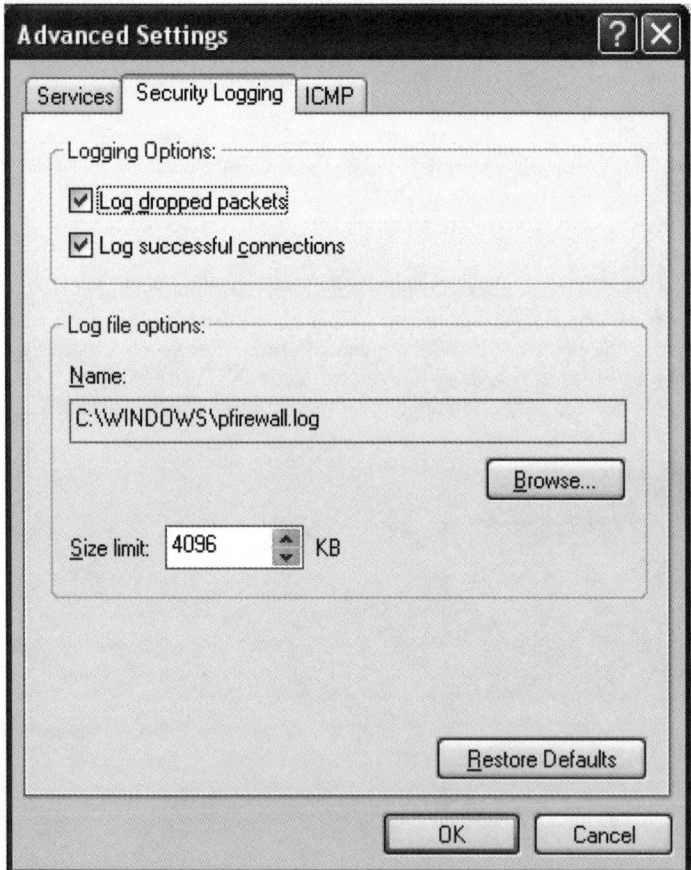

Figure 22-5: Security Logging tab

To enable the log files, simply click one or both options on the Security Logging tab. By default, the log is stored in `C:\Windows\pfirewall.log`. (You can change the name and location if you like, as long as you give the log file a name with a `.log` extension). You also set the file size limit, which is 4096 KB by default. You can lower or raise this level if you like. After your log file begins to run out of room, the log is saved as `pfirewall.log.1` and a new `pfirewall.log` is created. This way, you never lose any information, but you should consider deleting or moving old log files to storage in order to conserve space on your hard disk.

The log file is recorded in the World Wide Web Consortium (W3C) Extended Log File format, which means that the log files are recorded in a text file and organized by header information and data that is collected. The body of the log file contains the data collected from the dropped packets or the successful connections. The data is organized in a left to right field fashion, such as you might see with a database file.

The following fields are used in the log files:

- **Date** — Provides the year, month, and day that the record occurred and is displayed as YY-MM-DD. For example an entry on September 15, 2001 would read 2001-09-15.

- **Time** — Provides the hour, minute, and seconds when the record occurred and is displayed as HH:MM:SS in a 24-hour format. For example, an entry recorded at 1:15 and 29 seconds in the afternoon would read 13:15:29.

- **Action** — Displays the action that occurred, which can be one of the following:

  - **Open** — Connection is opened.

  - **Close** — Connection is closed.

  - **Drop** — Packets are dropped at the firewall.

  - **Info-Events Lost** — Reports that several events occurred that were not recorded in the log.

- **Protocol** — Reports what protocol was used for the connection. The entry can show TCP, UDP, or ICMP (Internet Control Message Protocol).

- **Src-ip** — Reports the source IP address of the connection. The source IP address is the IP address of the computer attempting the connection (your computer or a computer on your network).

- **Dst-ip** — Reports the destination IP address of the connection. The destination IP address is the IP address of the computer that the local computer (your computer or a computer on the network) is making.

- **Src-port** — Reports the source TCP or UDP port of the sending computer. If ICMP is used, there is no port information and a dash (-) is displayed in this field.

- **Dst-port** — Reports the source TCP or UDP port of the destination computer that was connected to. If ICMP is used, there is no port information and a dash (-) is displayed in this field.

- **Size** — Reports the size of the packet in bytes.

- **Tcpflags** — Each IP packet header may contain TCP control flags. These control flags give the computer some instruction about how to handle the packet. See RFC 793 to learn more about Tcpflags. Typical control flags are as follows:

  - **Ack** — Acknowledgment

  - **Fin** — Data is finished

  - **Psh** — Push Function

  - **Rst** — Reset the connection

  - **Syn** — Synchronize sequence numbers

  - **Urg** — Urgent Pointer field significant

- **Tcpsyn** — Provides the TCP sequence number.

- **Tcpack** — Shows the TCP acknowledgment number in the packet.

- **Tcpwin** — Presents the TCP window size (bytes) in the packet.

- **Icmptype** — Shows a number that represents the Type field in an ICMP message.

- **Icmpcode** — Specifies a number that represents the Code field of an ICMP message.

- **Info** — Provides an information entry for the type of action that occurred.

You can open and view the log file at any time (it will open with Notepad or any word processor application). When you open it, you'll see the fields in the upper line and the corresponding data entries beneath the field, as you can see in the log file in Figure 22-6.

```
pfirewall.log - Notepad
File  Edit  Format  View  Help
#verson: 1.0
#Software: Microsoft Internet Connection Firewall
#Time Format: Local
#Fields: date time action protocol src-ip dst-ip src-port dst-port s

2001-08-21 10:10:58 OPEN TCP 63.24.200.49 64.4.13.227 3483 1863 - - -
2001-08-21 10:11:03 OPEN UDP 63.24.200.49 198.6.100.194 3014 53 - - -
2001-08-21 10:11:03 OPEN TCP 63.24.200.49 207.68.171.254 3485 80 - -
2001-08-21 10:11:05 OPEN UDP 63.24.200.49 198.6.100.194 3010 53 - - -
2001-08-21 10:11:06 OPEN TCP 63.24.200.49 207.68.183.190 3486 80 - -
2001-08-21 10:11:06 OPEN TCP 63.24.200.49 207.68.177.126 3487 80 - -
2001-08-21 10:11:07 OPEN UDP 63.24.200.49 198.6.1.194 3014 53 - - - -
2001-08-21 10:11:07 OPEN TCP 63.24.200.49 198.5.146.194 3488 80 - - -
2001-08-21 10:11:07 OPEN TCP 63.24.200.49 207.68.171.254 3489 80 - -
2001-08-21 10:11:07 OPEN UDP 63.24.200.49 198.6.1.194 3010 53 - - - -
2001-08-21 10:11:08 OPEN TCP 63.24.200.49 207.46.179.134 3490 80 - -
2001-08-21 10:11:08 OPEN TCP 63.24.200.49 207.46.179.134 3491 80 - -
2001-08-21 10:11:14 OPEN TCP 63.24.200.49 207.68.177.126 3492 80 - -
2001-08-21 10:11:24 OPEN TCP 63.24.200.49 168.215.86.100 3495 80 - -
2001-08-21 10:11:25 OPEN TCP 63.24.200.49 168.215.86.100 3496 80 - -
2001-08-21 10:11:26 OPEN TCP 63.24.200.49 168.215.86.100 3497 80 - -
2001-08-21 10:11:27 OPEN TCP 63.24.200.49 208.184.29.70 3498 80 - - -
2001-08-21 10:11:27 OPEN TCP 63.24.200.49 208.184.29.70 3499 80 - - -
2001-08-21 10:11:29 OPEN TCP 63.24.200.49 208.184.29.210 3500 80 - -
2001-08-21 10:11:29 OPEN TCP 63.24.200.49 208.184.29.210 3501 80 - -
2001-08-21 10:11:30 CLOSE TCP 63.24.200.49 207.68.183.190 3486 80 - -
2001-08-21 10:11:30 CLOSE TCP 63.24.200.49 207.68.177.126 3487 80 - -
2001-08-21 10:11:30 CLOSE TCP 63.24.200.49 198.5.146.194 3488 80 - -
2001-08-21 10:11:30 CLOSE TCP 63.24.200.49 207.68.177.126 3492 80 - -
2001-08-21 10:11:30 CLOSE TCP 63.24.200.49 168.215.86.100 3495 80 - -
2001-08-21 10:11:30 CLOSE TCP 63.24.200.49 208.184.29.70 3498 80 - -
2001-08-21 10:11:30 CLOSE TCP 63.24.200.49 208.184.29.70 3499 80 - -
2001-08-21 10:11:35 OPEN TCP 63.24.200.49 168.215.86.100 3502 80 - -
```

Figure 22-6: Pfirewall.log sample

As Figure 22-6 shows, the date, time, action, protocol, and IP addresses are displayed, as well as additional, relevant, field information.

SECRET: The log file doesn't record the FQDN of any Web sites that were accessed, but the IP address is present under the `dst-ip` field. If you want to see what a site actually is, just copy and paste the IP address into Internet Explorer's address line and press Enter. IE can access sites via IP address instead of by FQDN, so you can view what users on your network are doing on the Internet (or your children, in the case of a home network). Keep in mind that this information resides in the log file and remains available to you, even if IE's history and Temporary Internet files are deleted. Of course, if the `Pfirewall.log` is deleted, then the information is lost, but keep in mind that you can rename this file and have it stored anywhere on your computer for tighter security.

TIP: You can also download Sam Spade, a cool tool from `www.samspade.org` that gives you a friendly Windows interface for tracking down the owner of an IP address or domain name. You can also run `tracert` and `PING` from this tool in order to identify a potential intruder.

ICMP

ICMP is a simple protocol that enables computers to share connectivity error and status information with each other. By default, ICF does not allow ICMP messages because, again, if you do not request the information, the firewall drops it. To use ICMP with ICF, you must first enable the ICMP actions that you want to allow.

But first, you need to know a little more about ICMP. ICMP can be thought of as a management protocol that computers use to exchange IP messaging information with each other via IP datagrams. It is a simple communication method that gathers information about network errors and network status. ICMP announces network errors, such as destination or host unreachable errors. Announcements concerning network congestion because of buffer overruns are also provided. This kind of congestion generates the ICMP Source Quench message, which tells the source sending the data to slow down. Echo functions are also provided to assist in troubleshooting. You are familiar with the `Ping` command, which is based on the ICMP echo. Also timeouts are announced when the TTL field expires. The `Tracert` tool uses the timeout feature.

As you can see, this protocol provides information, but Internet intruders might take advantage of ICMP to launch attacks against your network. So, you have to weigh the need of using ICMP against the potential threat of being hacked. For this reason, ICF provides the option of using or not using the features of ICMP, depending on the level of security desired. Remember that the firewall prevents ICMP messages from entering your computer, and some of these messages may be important for running your applications. It's a good idea to allow ICMP if you can, but if you are really concerned about security, it's okay not to allow it.

The ICMP tab, shown in Figure 22-7, enables you to place check marks next to the ICMP features that you want to include. These features are as follows:

- **Allow incoming echo request** — An echo request allows the computer that receives the message to respond, similar to a `ping` command. If you enable this check box, someone can ping your machine and get a response. Otherwise, the echo request is dropped.

- **Allow incoming timestamp request** — A timestamp request enables your computer to respond to a request with a timestamp noting when the request arrived. This ICMP message is commonly used with the `Tracert` utility.

- **Allow incoming mask request** — Requests made about the public network to which the request is made. Enabling this feature allows the computer to give information about the public network connection.

- **Allow incoming router request** — A request for information about recognized routers. Enabling this feature allows the computer to give out public router information.

- **Allow outgoing destination unreachable** — Allows an ICMP message to be returned to you when a request for service fails.

- **Allow outgoing source quench** — Allows the computer to send an outgoing source quench message when data is arriving too quickly.

- **Allow outgoing parameter problem** — Allows the computer to respond to an Internet host when IP packets have problematic headers. The packets are dropped and the parameter problem message is sent to the server.

- **Allow outgoing time exceeded** — Provides an outgoing time exceeded message when a data transmission takes more time than is allotted.

- **Allow redirect** — Allows data from the sending computer to be rerouted if the default path changes.

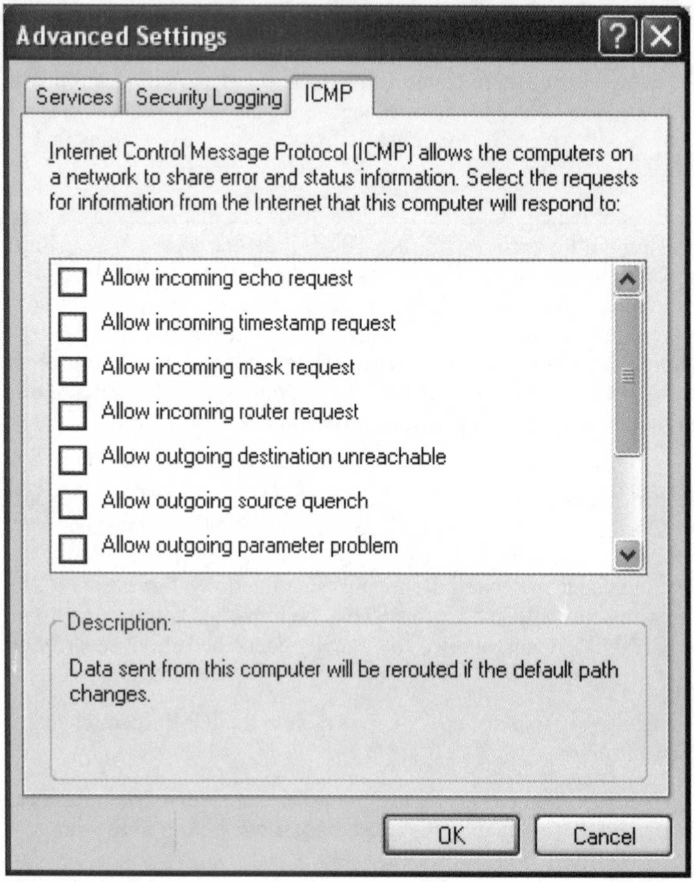

Figure 22-7: ICMP tab

Common Hacker Attacks

The ICF firewall provides an effective defense system against unauthorized communication from the Internet. Because ICF uses tables to determine whether packets have been requested or are allowed, you are generally safe from Internet attacks. This does not mean that attacks cannot happen, but the firewall does provide a high level of security.

In case you are curious about hacker attacks, there are several that are very common. All of these function at the IP packet level and look for ways to cause you problems. These kinds of attacks are generally called Denial of Service (DoS) attacks. The following list outlines some common IP hacker attacks:

♦ **Windows Out-of-Band (WinNuke)** — A DoS attack, and one that is quite common, WinNuke makes use of a security hole in Windows operating systems (for which a patch does exist). A WinNuker needs a client's IP address to launch the attack, but once the attacker has the IP address, he or she connects to port 139 and essentially floods the port with junk IP information. The IP junk data is considered "out of bounds" by the operating system and causes the networking system to crash, bringing the system down. Although typically not harmful to the system, WinNuke causes the client computer to crash or lose Internet connectivity.

♦ **Land Attack** — A Land Attack is another DoS attack that causes a computer to believe it is sending IP packets to itself. This creates a communication loop. With a Land Attack, a hacker gains a source IP address, and then spoofs the address by sending SYN IP packets. The computer reads the SYN IP packet and sees its own address, as if the computer itself sent a packet to itself. The spoofed SYN packet then creates a loop by which the computer is trying to both send and acknowledge its own IP packets. This eventually brings the computer down and causes network connectivity or the entire operating system to crash.

♦ **Ping of Death** — A ping of death attack uses the ICMP echo request packet to flood a computer system with data and to cause it to crash. With this type of attack, a large amount of data is appended to the ICMP echo ping, causing a kernel buffer overflow, which then crashes the system. By default, packets are 64 bytes in size. The ICMP echo ping often sends packets of 65,536 bytes, which overflow the receiving computer. Packets of this size are actually illegal-size packets, but they can be created using "chunks" of data that are reassembled on the receiving computer, which then overflow the buffer. All the attacker needs is the client's IP address to launch a ping of death attack, and such attacks are quite common on the Internet.

♦ **IP Half Scan** — The IP Half Scan attack is used when a remote computer does not issue an ACK packet (acknowledgment). When a session with a remote computer is initiated, a SYN packet is sent to the destination computer. The destination computer should then respond with a SYN/ACK packet so that it can connect to a specified port. If the destination computer is not waiting on the port connection, it sends an RST packet. An IP Half Scan attack then uses the RST packet instead of an ACK packet to probe which ports are open. Because no ACK packet is sent, the computer does not know it is being probed and the attacker learns which ports are open for other attacks. This is why ISA server's ability to dynamically open and close ports when needed is a great security feature.

♦ **UDP Bomb** — This type of attack uses an illegal UDP packet that contains illegal data in some of the UDP fields, which can cause a computer system to crash. Although not as threatening today because of computer security patches, some older computer systems are susceptible to UDP bombs, and ISA supports the detection of the UDP bomb packets for protection purposes.

♦ **Port Scan** — The Port Scan attack attempts to access more than the configured number of IP ports. It is often used in an attempt to probe each port so that the attacker can learn which ports are running which services. The attacker then uses this information to launch other attacks.

TIP: Get more information about Internet security from www.microsoft.com/security.

Remote Desktop

Remote Desktop is a feature, built on Terminal Services, of Windows XP Professional that enables two computers in different locations to connect and to use a virtual desktop. Consider an example: Your company has two building that are connected by a LAN. You have an XP workstation in both buildings. You are working with a number of applications on one desktop, but you have to go the next building for a series of meetings. During breaks between those meetings, you can use an XP workstation in that building and connect with your primary workstation, accessing your applications and documents through the virtual desktop, just as though you are actually at the desktop.

In other examples, you could use Remote Desktop to connect up with your office computer from a home computer over the Internet. You could work on collaborative applications when another user is using your desktop PC. Remote Desktop allows multiple sessions on the same PC.

For Remote Desktop to work, you must have two Windows XP computers (or the Remote Desktop client installed on Windows 9x, 2000, Me, or NT) that are on the same network. Or, you can connect via the Internet or a VPN. You must have appropriate user accounts in order to access the remote machine. The following sections explore Remote Desktop setup and configuration issues.

Enabling Remote Desktop

You can easily enable your Windows XP computer to use Remote Desktop by opening System Properties in Control Panel. Click the Remote tab, and then click the Remote Desktop check box, shown in Figure 22-8, to enable it.

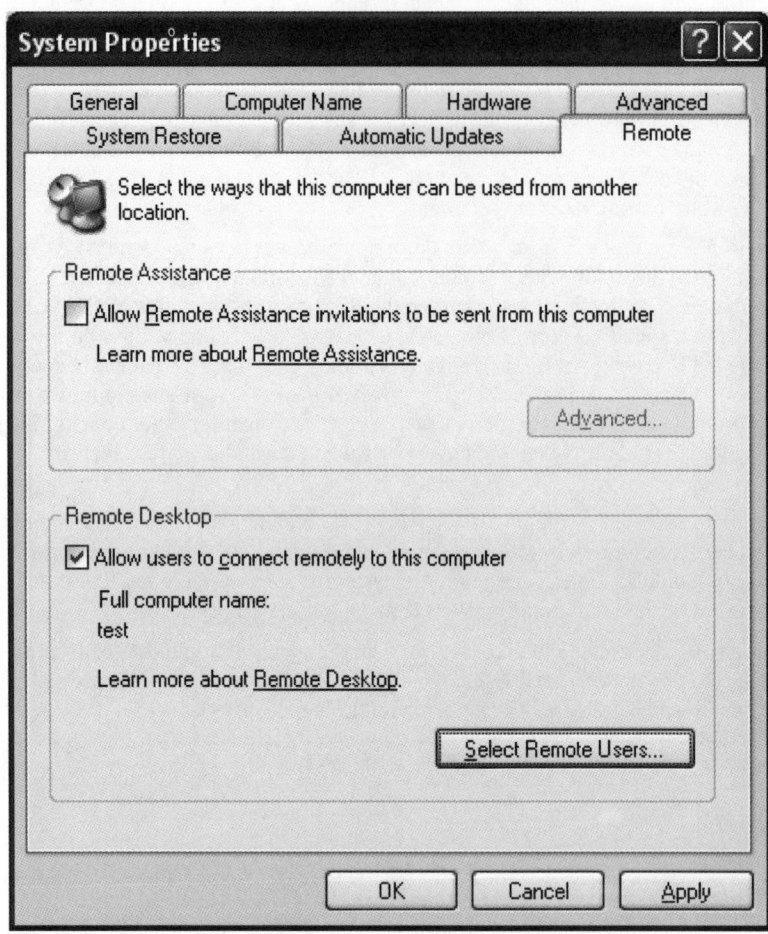

Figure 22-8: Enabling Remote Desktop

When you click the check box to enable Remote Desktop, you may see a message that tells you two important things about enabling the Remote Desktop connection:

♦ Usernames and passwords — If you have users that can only log on to the computer by using a password, then you need to configure passwords for those users or they will not be able to log on.

CROSS-REFERENCE: See Chapter 23 to learn more about user accounts.

♦ If you have ICF enabled, you need to check the Remote Desktop option on the Services tab of the ICF settings so that Remote Desktop communication is allowed to pass through the firewall. See the previous sections of this chapter for more information about ICF.

Enabling user accounts

To make a Remote Desktop connection on your computer, a user must have a valid user account on the computer. Chapter 23 explores user account creation. After you have the accounts created on your computer as desired, you need to enable these accounts for Remote Desktop support. On the System Properties' Remote tab, click the Select Remote Users button. In the provided window, shown in Figure 22-9, click the Add button and enter the desired names. Click Close and then click OK. By default, administrators can always access the computer via Remote Desktop. You do not need to add administrator accounts to this list.

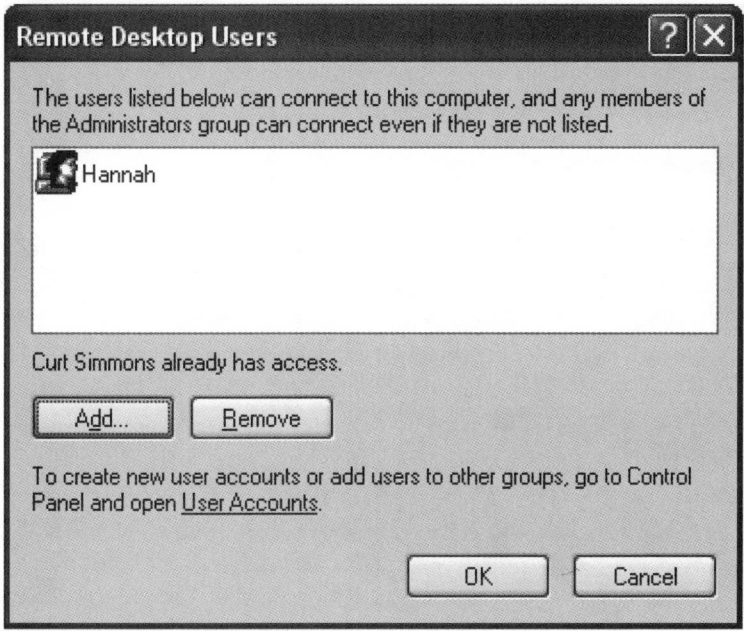

Figure 22-9: Enabling user accounts

Installing Remote Desktop on other clients

You can easily enable the Remote Desktop connection software on any Windows XP computer, but if you want to connect to a computer using an earlier version of Windows, you can use the Windows XP installation CD-ROM to install the Remote Desktop software on those computers. Supported computers are Windows 95, 98, Me, 2000, and NT 4.0. You can also install Terminal Services clients on 16-bit computers and Windows NT 3.5. The following steps show the installation of Remote Desktop on a Windows Me computer.

STEPS

Installing Remote Desktop software on earlier versions of Windows clients

1. Insert the Windows XP CD-ROM into the CD-ROM drive and click the Perform Other Tasks option that appears on your screen. Click Install Remote Desktop.

2. On the installation wizard's Welcome screen, click Next.

3. Review the end-user license agreement and click Next.

4. Enter your username and any desired organization information and click Next.

5. Click Install to begin the installation.

6. After installation is complete, click Finish.

Establishing a Remote Desktop connection

To establish a Remote Desktop connection, you access the Remote Desktop Connection window and enter the necessary information to connect to the computer. You can connect over a network, a VPN connection, or directly over the Internet.

TIP: If you need to establish a Remote Desktop connection to a computer on the Internet, you can create a direct dial-up connection. See Chapter 21 to learn more about direct dial-up access.

To generate the connection, follow these steps:

STEPS

Creating a Remote Desktop connection

1. Choose Start ⇨ All Programs ⇨ Accessories ⇨ Communications ⇨ Remote Desktop.

2. In the Connection window that appears, click Options.

3. On the General tab, shown in Figure 22-10, enter the computer name, username, and password information. You can also choose to connect to the Remote Desktop using an IP address.

Figure 22-10: Connection's General tab

SECRET: For security reasons, you should use highly unique computer names and complex passwords (containing both letters and numbers). This is not the time to use "Sally" as your username and your kid's/pet's names as your password. Keep in mind that Remote Desktop presents some security risks by its nature. This is probably okay for your needs, but just go into the process of using Remote Desktop with your eyes wide open.

4. Click the Display tab. You can adjust the screen size and color settings for the Remote Desktop connection as desired.

5. On the Local Resources tab, shown in Figure 22-11, you can adjust the settings for the remote computer's sound, keyboard, and access to local devices, such as disk drives, printers, and serial ports. Make any desired selections and click the Programs tab.

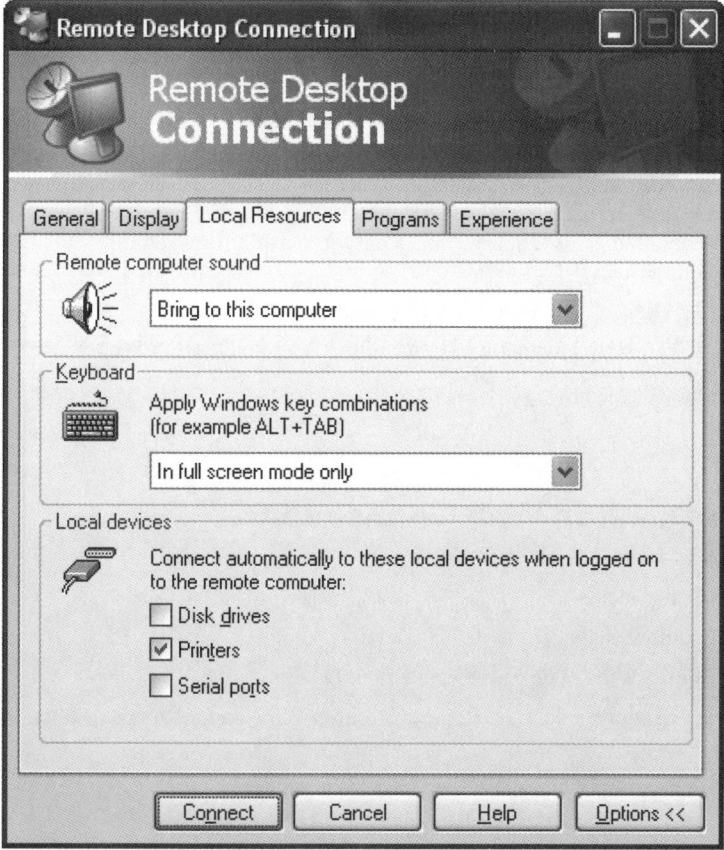

Figure 22-11: Local Resources tab

6. On the Programs tab, you can choose to enter the name of a program that you want to start automatically when you log on.

7. Finally, on the Experience tab, you can adjust any of the available settings to suit your needs, such as desktop background, menu and window animation, themes, and so on.

8. When you are done, click Connect.

When you are finished with the Remote Desktop session, you can choose to close the connection completely, or you can choose to save your work. The next time you want to open a Remote Desktop connection, you can open the Remote Desktop file in order to access the connection. This feature enables you to save a session and then return to it at a later time.

To save your current settings, click the Save As button on the General connection tab and enter a filename and location. The file is saved as an .rdp file, and you can open this file to connect the next time you are ready.

As you use Remote Desktop, keep in mind the following: First, the screen saver used with a Remote Desktop connection is always the blank screen saver. You can't choose a screen saver on the Remote Desktop and have it run on your desktop. Second, if you have a lower bandwidth connection, such as a dial-up connection over the Internet, using the XP interface and desktop background can consume a lot of bandwidth. Third, if Remote Desktop seems to be running slowly, use the connection tabs and remove some of the features you selected, such as background colors, sound, and so on. Finally, if you are having problems with connectivity or staying connected, there are a number of terminal services errors and problems that can cause these problems. See the Windows Help files for possible solutions if errors and disconnects are coming your way.

About Remote Desktop Web Connection

Remote Desktop Web Connection is a Web application made up of an ActiveX control and sample ASPs (Active Server Pages). It is designed to be deployed on a Web server. Once deployed, users on the network can create a Remote Desktop connection to another computer within Internet Explorer, even if the Remote Desktop software is not installed. This feature enables easy, cross-platform remote connectivity that is as easy as connecting to a URL.

To set up and use the Remote Desktop Web Connection, you must be working on a network, such as IIS (Internet Information Server), with a Web server available. To install the Remote Desktop Web Connection, follow these steps:

STEPS

Installing the Remote Desktop Web Connection

1. Open Add/Remove Programs in Control Panel.
2. Click Add/Remove Windows Components.
3. In the Windows Components window, select IIS and click Details.
4. In the Details window, select World Wide Web Service and click Details.
5. In the World Wide Web Service window, select the Remote Desktop Web Connection, as shown in Figure 22-12.
6. Click OK and then click Next. The component is installed on your computer.
7. Click Finish.

After the Remote Desktop Web Connection is active on the Web server, clients can connect, open Internet Explorer, and connect to the Web server and the Remote Desktop Web Connection directory on the Web server using the http://servername/directoryname convention. The Remote Desktop Web Connection page, shown in Figure 22-13, appears. In the Server dialog box, enter the name of the computer to which you want to connect and click Connect. The Remote desktop session will begin within Internet Explorer.

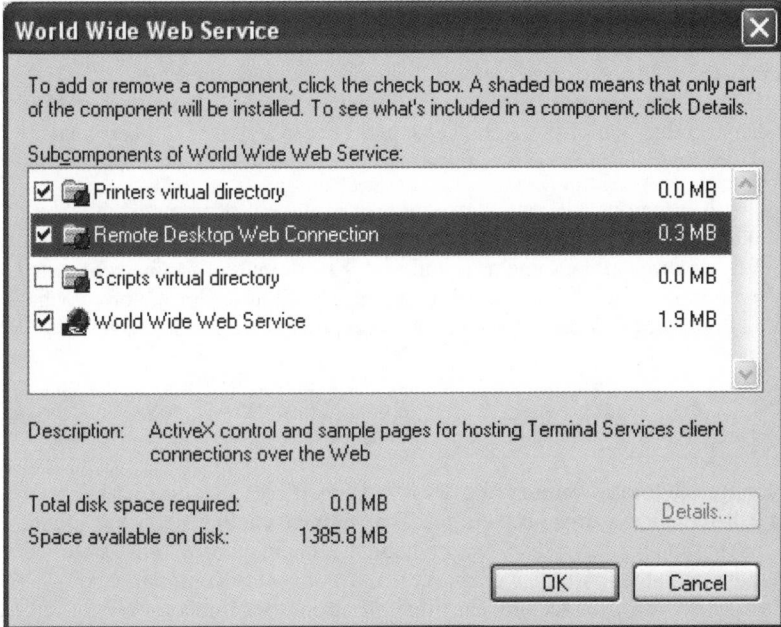

Figure 22-12: Remote Desktop Web Connection

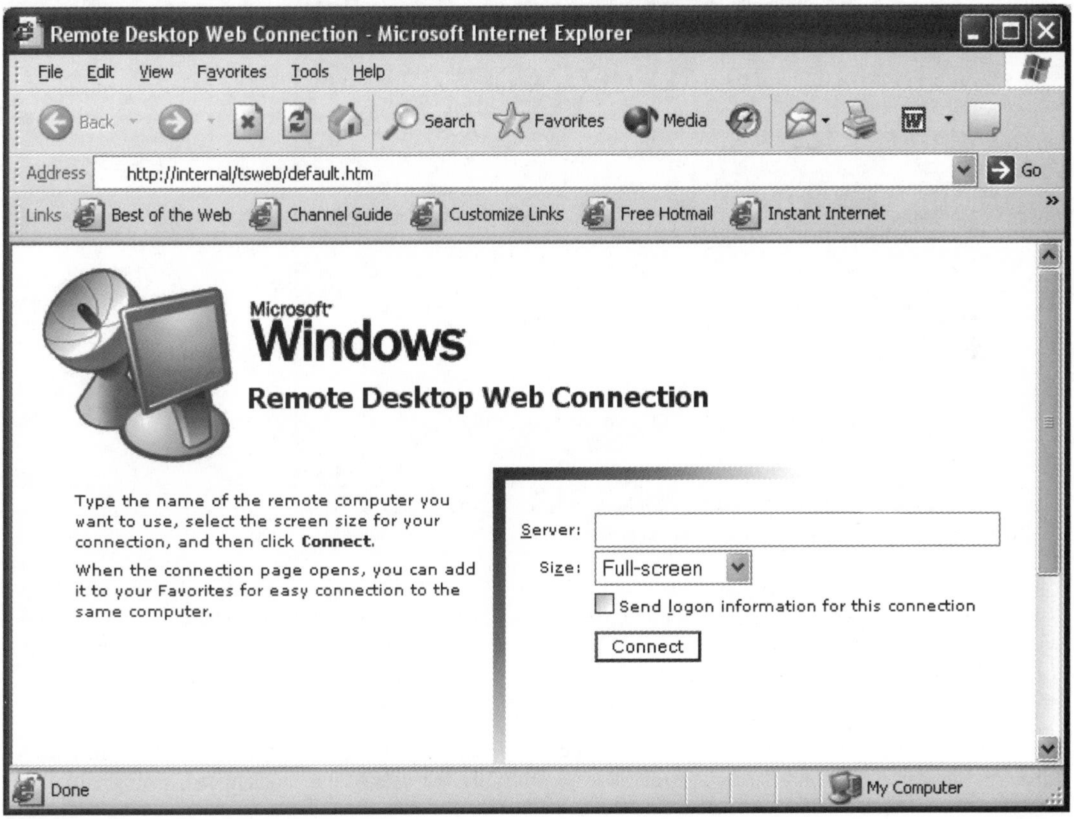

Figure 22-13: Remote Desktop Web Connection

Remote Assistance

Remote Assistance is a feature that allows one user to connect to another user's computer over the Internet, and then provide configuration assistance right in front of the user's eyes. It's a new way of helping people. Remote Assistance greatly simplifies technical support because it uses the Terminal services feature so that you can remote manage the user's system and fix a problem.

Remote Assistance works only with Windows XP computers at this time and both computers must be using Windows Messenger or a MAPI-compliant e-mail account such as Outlook Express or Outlook. You both must be connected to the Internet at the same time and each XP computer must be configured for Remote Assistance. If an invitation is received in another mail client (such as Eudora), you may have to drag and drop the invitation into OE or Outlook — you may also find that Windows Messenger is an easier way to deal with invitations.

TIP: If you are on a LAN, a firewall may prevent Remote Assistance from working. Check with your network administrators to see if Remote Assistance traffic is allowed over your network. Port 3398 must be available for Remote Assistance to work.

To enable Remote Assistance, return to the Advanced tab of System Properties. Click the check box to enable Remote Assistance, and then click the Advanced button. The Settings window, shown in Figure 22-14, enables you to set the maximum number of days that invitations remain open. With Remote Assistance, you send an invitation to another party that enables them to connect to your computer. This prevents the need of having to create a new user account each time that you want someone to connect to your computer. By default, invitations stay open for 30 days, but you can adjust this value if needed.

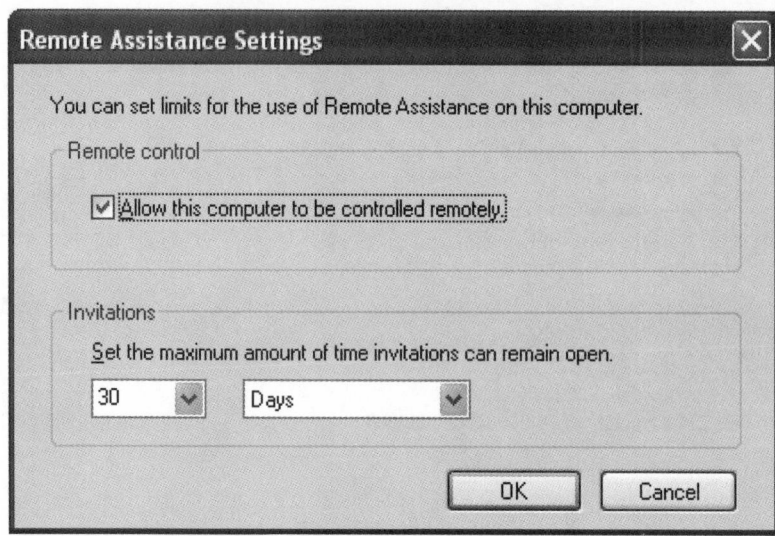

Figure 22-14: Advanced Remote Assistance Settings

If you want to send an invitation to someone for Remote Assistance, choose Start ⇨ All Programs ⇨ Remote Assistance. This opens the Help and Support center. Click the Invite Someone to Help you link where you enter the person's e-mail address. You are prompted to either log in to Windows Messenger or to send the message using the default e-mail program (you can send the invitation using any e-mail program — receiving it and reading it outside of OE or Outlook is the problem).

You can also save the invitation as a file and manually send it to someone. The wizard will walk you through a few steps, and it is recommended that you require the user to use a password, which you can designate.

If you receive an invitation from someone, you can connect to their computer using the invitation and the password given to you. If you receive the invitation via e-mail, the invitation appears as an attachment that you open and click Yes to connect to the remote computer. You see a terminal window appear where you can maneuver through the user's operating system and make configuration changes as needed. At any time, the user may stop the Remote Assistance session by clicking the Stop button in Windows Messenger or by pressing the Esc key on the keyboard.

Summary

Windows XP has several built-in features not found in earlier versions of Windows:

♦ Windows XP provides you with the Internet Connection Firewall in order to protect your Internet connections for Internet hackers.

♦ The firewall functions by examining IP packets and recording data in tables. Any information that you have not requested from the Internet is dropped from the firewall.

♦ You can configure the firewall to allow various service connections, to create log files, and to allow ICMP traffic.

♦ Remote Desktop uses Terminal Services to create Remote Desktop connections to other Windows operating systems. Remote Desktop connections can be made over the Internet or on a LAN.

♦ Remote Assistance provides a way for you to assist other users by connecting to their Windows XP computer over the Internet. You must be invited to participate in a Remote Assistance session, and once you open the connection, you can provide troubleshooting and configuration support.

Chapter 23

User Management

In This Chapter

Windows XP provides all the networking tools and features that you would expect from a Microsoft operating system. In the past, however, user management tools were less than good, and user management was primarily left to network administrators using servers. That all began to change with Windows 2000 and the trend continues in Windows XP. Although Windows XP Professional edition is designed to function in both domains and workgroup environments while Windows XP Home edition is designed for home and small office networks, in both cases Windows XP gives you greater control and management over the local user who logs onto the machine. With these tools, you can easily administer your computer and place rules and restrictions, and even force certain configurations, on other users. In this chapter, you learn about . . .

- ♦ Configuring accounts with Users in the Control Panel
- ♦ Using Computer Management to control users and groups
- ♦ Configuring Group Policy for your local computer

User Management in Windows XP

Before I get started with the tools and features of Windows XP user management, it is important to make some distinctions about user management and how Windows XP handles users. First off, I need to reiterate that user management in this chapter refers to the management of local users on a local machine. For example, say that you use Windows XP at home. You use the administrator's account, but you create other accounts for your children — accounts that do not have the right to format a disk, for example. Or, perhaps the Windows XP machine is used in a small office where three different people access it. The user accounts created for each person enable customized XP settings and a way of keeping one's documents separate from other users. Local users are just that — people who are actually logging on to the computer and using it.

You are also aware that user management can refer to a domain model, where Windows XP Professional (not Home) computers are used in a larger networking environment. In this case, users do not (typically) log on to the local machine; instead, they log on to a Windows 2000/XP Server. The server identifies the user and enables the user to log on to the domain so that network resources can be used. User management in this kind of environment is handled by network administrators who work with Windows 2000/XP server — not the local Windows XP computer. So, in this chapter, user management and users always refer to local user management on your machine.

Because of the need for solid user management, Windows XP organizes itself somewhat differently than did previous versions of Windows, based on the user. User accounts on your Windows XP computer have their own folder, found in `Documents and Settings\username`. Using these profiles, Windows can easily store different configuration settings, files, Internet Explorer Favorites and History, and a number of other items. After a user logs on, the user essentially accesses the information in the user's folders and cannot access information in other users' folders, unless the user is an administrator.

Speaking of administrator, when you install Windows XP, there are two default accounts — administrator and guest. The administrator account is automatically created, and it cannot be deleted or disabled, and it cannot be removed from the Local Administrators group (groups are discussed later in this chapter). The guest account, on the other hand, is designed for people who do not actually have a user account on the computer. The guest account is just that — a user can log on with the guest account, but the user essentially has no rights to do anything. You can disable the guest account if you have no need for it, and in terms of security, I recommend that you do disable it unless you are actively using it.

As a final note about users and groups, it is important to remember that user configuration and group configuration are considered security tactics. In terms of users and groups on the local machine, the reason for using these accounts is to control what other users can and cannot do on the Windows XP computer. The level of control that you want to deploy is, of course, up to you, and the remainder of this chapter shows you how to configure these accounts and leverage the management tools that are available to you in Windows XP.

User Accounts

Windows XP gives you two tools that can be used to set up user accounts on your local computer — Users in Control Panel and Computer Management. For experienced users, Computer Management is faster and easier to use than the sometimes too friendly GUI interface of Users, but there are some important options found in Users that are not presented to you in Computer Management. So, it's worth time to take a look at both.

Users in Control Panel

The Users option in Control Panel presents you with a simple interface, shown in Figure 23-1, for creating and managing user accounts on your computer. You can see the current accounts and the icons associated with those accounts on this screen as well.

You have three different action divisions here — change an account, create a new account, or change the way users log on and log off. The following sections explore these options.

Creating a new account

The Users feature enables you to easily create new accounts with the help of a miniature wizard that appears when you click Create an Account from the main page. When you click Create an Account, you are prompted to enter a username and click Next. The user account name is the name that will appear on the Welcome screen and the Start menu, so you should use the person's real name as general rule — there is no security reason to use usernames other than the user's actual name unless you do not want a user to know who else logs on to the computer, which in a home or small office environment usually isn't an issue.

After you click Next, you are prompted to choose an account type, either computer administrator or limited. Simply select the desired radio button and click Create Account. Before doing so, you have to determine the kind of account you are creating. The computer administrator account gives the user total control over the computer. The administrator can add and remove accounts, configure system components, install programs, format and reconfigure hard drives. The administrator can do anything — he or she has total control over the computer. It's okay to have more than one computer administrator, but you should be very careful who is given this level of control. In a home situation, I don't recommend giving it to inexperienced computer users in your family because they have the potential to wreak havoc on the system by making incorrect configuration changes.

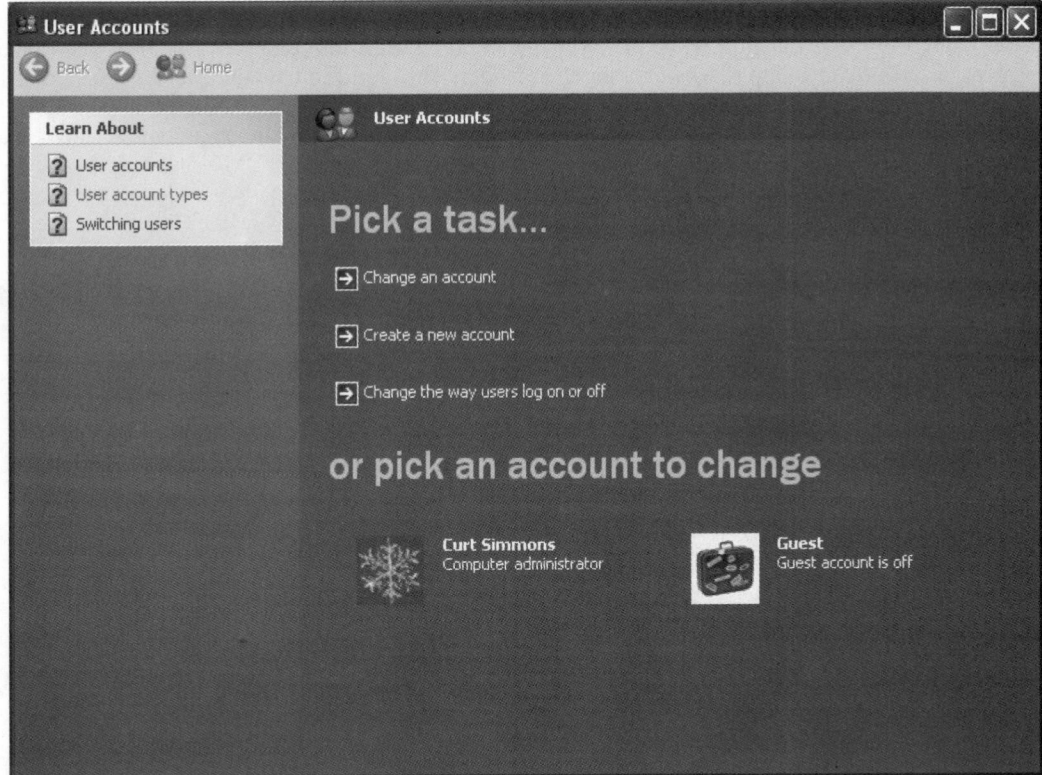

Figure 23-1: Users in Control Panel

The limited account user can change his or her password (if you allow it — see the "Creating user accounts with Computer Management" section later in this chapter) or desktop settings, can create and view files, and can view items in the Shared Documents folder. Limited users may not be able to install programs. Basically, the limited user can *use* the operating system, but can't make any harmful configuration changes to it.

TIP: Some older programs (before Windows 2000) might not work with the limited account. You'll have to do some experimenting to find out whether a particular program works with the limited account, but keep this limitation in mind when working with users and programs.

After you determine the type of account that you want to create, the account is created with a default picture to represent it, and it now appears on the main User page.

Changing an account

After user accounts have been created, you can easily make changes to the user account with the Users interface. Simply select the account on the main User window that you want to change, and then click Change an Account.

A window appears with a list of tasks that you can perform, such as change the name, create a password (delete a password), change the picture, change the account type, and delete the account. As you can see, you can change anything you configured when you created the account.

Windows XP's theme uses pictures to represent user accounts, along with the account name. This may seem silly, but it is actually helpful if you have younger children using the computer. Children who can't recognize their name can still log on by clicking their icon picture. A default, unique picture is assigned to each user. If you click the Change picture option, a window appears, as shown in Figure 23-2, where you can select a new picture icon from the provided list, or you can browse your computer to locate another picture. You can use just about any kind of picture format (JPEG, GIF, BMP, and so on). You might want to use certain company icons, or, in a home setting, you might actually use a photograph of the person to represent the user account. Simply choose a desired picture and click the Change Picture button.

Figure 23-2: Change Picture option

The Create a Password option enables you to create a password for the user. Windows XP gives you the freedom to have users log on with passwords or not to use them. A password ensures that only the person to whom the account belongs logs on to the computer, assuming the password is kept secret. Again, in a very small office or home situation, you may not want to use passwords, but if security for some accounts is a concern, then you need to assign a password. To meet security standards, passwords should be at least seven characters long and should use both letters and numbers. Common names, phone numbers, and related information should not be used.

When you click the password option, a window appears where you can enter the password, reenter it for confirmation, and type a word or phrase as a password hint, as shown in Figure 23-3. The password hint is descriptive text that reminds you of the password, but the hint can be viewed by anyone, so you have to be careful.

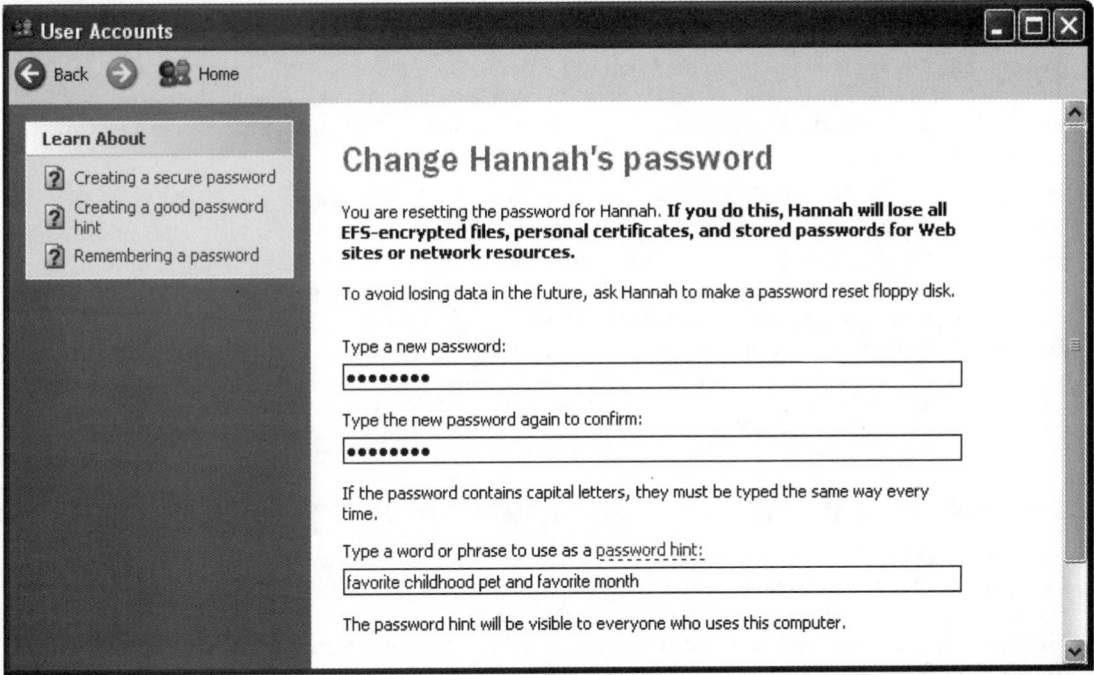

Figure 23-3: Changing a password

TIP: If you are assigning a password to a limited user, and the user has already been using the account, any Encrypting File System (EFS) encrypted files, personal certificates, and stored passwords for Web sites or network locations are lost. You can reset the password on an administrator's account, however, and this data is not lost. Also, if the user changes his or her own password, the data is not lost — this data is only lost when an administrator creates/changes a password for the limited user. If this data loss is going to happen, then the user should create a user reset disk, which is explained in the "User Actions" section later in this chapter.

Finally, you can also delete an account. When you delete an account, Windows saves all of the user's desktop contents and My Documents folder to a folder named with the username on the desktop. This enables you to easily place the contents on a disk and give it to the user who will no longer be accessing the computer. If you want to use this option, just click Keep Files — if not, click Delete Files.

Changing the way users log in or off

The log on and off setting is a global setting that applies to all users. You have only two check box options here, which are as follows:

♦ **Use the Welcome screen** — The Welcome screen provides the accounts created on this computer so that a user can click on his or her account and enter a password if necessary. Essentially, this is just a snazzy logon screen. If you want a more secure environment, turn this feature off. A Windows logon prompt will appear where the user must enter the actual username and password and the user will not be able to see the usernames of the other local users.

♦ **Use Fast user switching** — Fast user switching enables users to quickly change users without closing any programs, which can be really helpful in a collaborative situation in which several people are working on a project together at one PC. The caveat here is that fast user switching is not compatible with offline files, so if you are using offline files, you can't use fast user switching.

User actions

When limited users are logged onto the Windows XP computer, they can perform any of the actions that their account is configured to use. Users cannot access folders that do not belong to them, and they cannot make system-wide setting changes. They can make desktop and appearance changes that are applied to their accounts only.

One item that users can and should do is to access the Users option Control Panel, and under Related Actions, choose to create a password reset disk. This action opens a small wizard that enables them to create a small backup file of their password(s) and basic settings. If the user forgets the password, the account can be recovered, along with the settings tied through that account through the disk. If the disk needs to be used, an option appears to the user when he or she attempts to log on without the correct password. So, this disk is something every user should make and keep handy.

TIP: If you are logging onto a domain, the process is a little different. Attempt to log on at the Windows logon box. When the logon fails, click Reset and put the disk into the disk drive. Follow the instructions that appear.

User Accounts and the Computer Management Console

The Computer Management console also allows you to create and manage user accounts as well as group accounts. With a little experience under your belt, this will probably be the console you prefer to use. You do everything here (and more) that you can do with the Users option in Control Panel, except assign pictures to accounts and choose whether or not to use the Welcome screen and fast user switching. Beyond that, Computer Management is faster and gives you more options for user account configuration.

Computer Management is available in Administrative Tools in Control Panel. If you open Computer Management and expand System Tools, then Expand Local Users and Groups, you can click on Users and see a listing of the user accounts on your computer. As Figure 23-4 shows, some of the accounts that are listed, aside from Administrator and Guest, were not created by you. These accounts are used by Microsoft support, Internet Information Server (IIS) (if it is installed), and for Remote Desktop help assistance.

Creating user accounts with Computer Management

By using the Computer Management console, you can easily create new users and manage existing user accounts. The following steps show you how to create a new user by using the Computer Management console.

STEPS

Creating a new user account

1. Open Computer Management. Expand System Tools and Local Users and Groups. Right-click the Users container and then click New User.

2. The New User window appears, as shown in Figure 23-5. Complete the information dialog boxes. If you want to assign a password, enter and confirm the password and choose a desired check box:

   - **User must change password at next logon** — This option enables you to provide a default password to the user so that the user can log on to the computer, but once logged on, the user must create his or her own password that is used from that point forward.

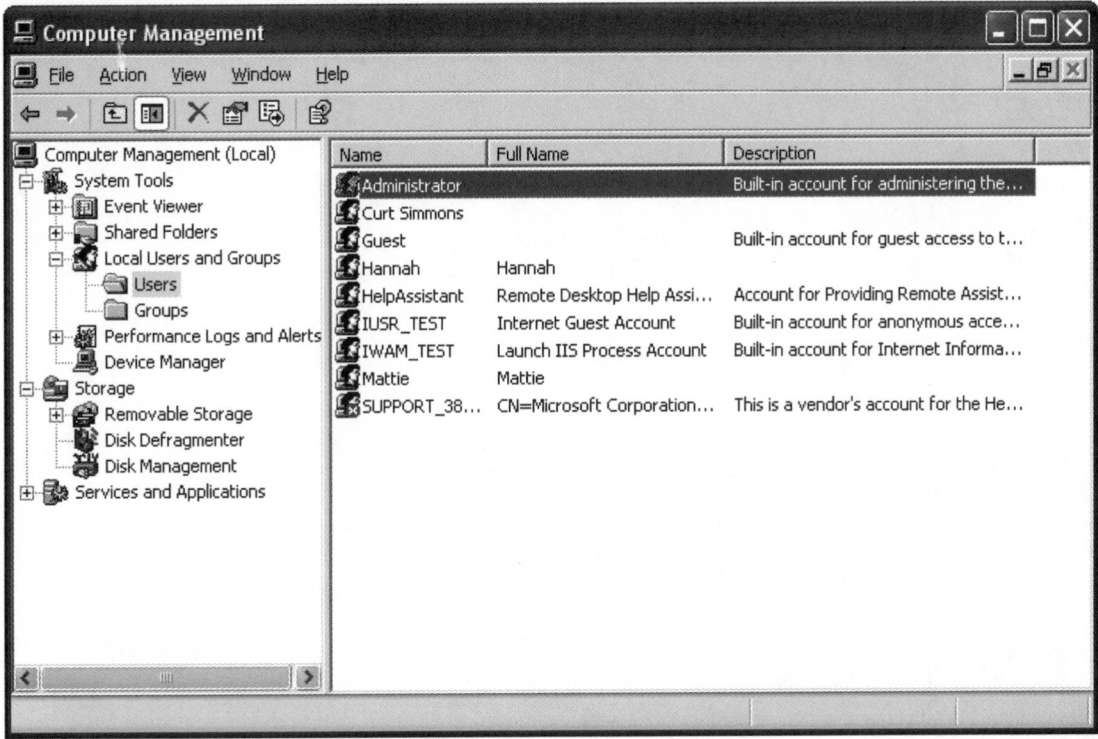

Figure 23-4: Computer Management

- **User cannot change password** — If you prefer to provide passwords instead of allowing the users to create them, choose this option.

- **Password never expires** — If you have Group Policy configured to expire passwords after a certain length of time, you can check this box to override the expiration policy if necessary. See "Using Group Policy" later in this chapter to learn more about Group Policy.

- **Account is disabled** — You can disable an account here if you want to stop the user from logging on with the account, but don't want to delete the account.

3. When you are done, click the Create button. The new account now appears in the Users container.

NOTE: You can't assign administrator or limited user permissions here. However, you can configure the account's properties, which is explored in the next section.

Managing user accounts with Computer Management

Just as you can create a new user account with the Computer Management console, you can easily manage the accounts that you can create. If you select Users in the left console pane, a list of users configured on your computer appears in the right pane. If you select a user in the right pane and right-click the icon (or use the Action menu), you can choose to reset the account's password, in which case a dialog box appears, as shown in Figure 23-6. This action gives the same result as using the Users interface — if you have to reset an account's password, all EFS-encrypted files, Web passwords, and related settings are lost. This is why local users need to create a password backup disk so you do not have to bail them out when they forget their passwords and so they do not lose information.

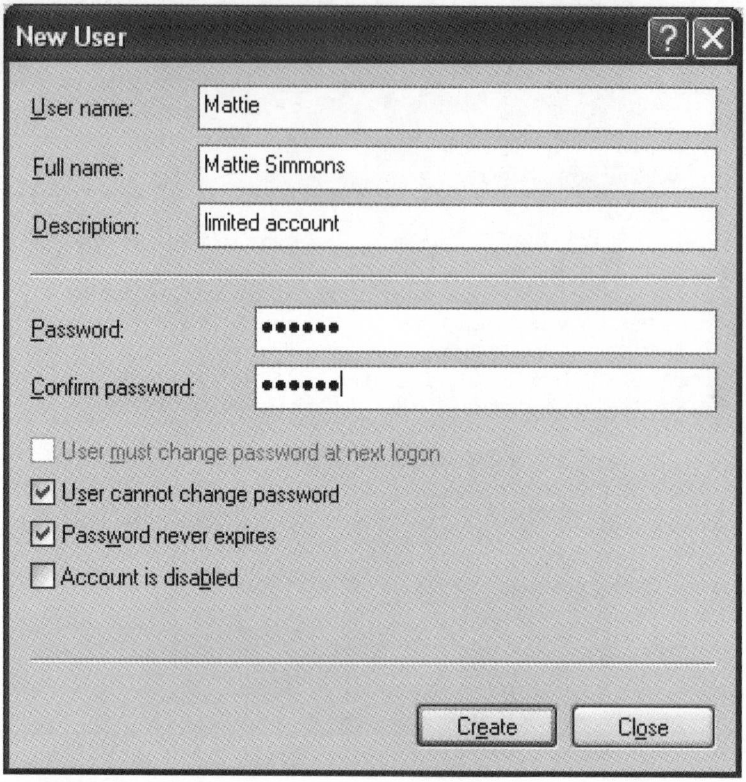

New User

User name:	Mattie
Full name:	Mattie Simmons
Description:	limited account

Password: ●●●●●●

Confirm password: ●●●●●●

☐ User must change password at next logon

☑ User cannot change password

☑ Password never expires

☐ Account is disabled

[Create] [Close]

Figure 23-5: New user creation

Set Password for Hannah

New password: ●●●●●●

Confirm password: ●●●●●●

⚠ If you click OK, the following will occur:

- This user account will immediately lose access to all of its encrypted files, stored passwords, and personal security certificates.

- Any password reset disks the user has created will no longer work.

If you click Cancel, the password will not be changed and no data loss will occur.

[OK] [Cancel]

Figure 23-6: Reset password

Aside from this action, you can Delete and Rename the account and you can click Properties to access the properties sheets.

On the Properties sheets, you see three tabs. On the General tab, you can make the same changes that were presented when you created the account. You can configure the password never to expire, configure it so that the user must change password at next logon, and so on. An additional check box you see here is the Account is locked out option. Depending on Group Policy settings, a user's account may lock after so many unsuccessful password attempts. This is a security feature that keeps someone from trying to break the password by entering guesses over and over. In environments where security is an issue, "three tries and you are locked" is often the policy. You can't lock the user's account here; you can only unlock it if it is locked from failed password attempts.

The Member of tab provides a place to add the user to groups that are configured on your computer. Group membership determines what the user is able to do on the computer (or not do). To add the user to a group, simply click the Add button and select the desired group from the list that appears. You can learn more about the default groups and group usage in the next section.

Finally, you also see a Profile tab. If a profile/logon script is used with the user, you can point to the location of the profile/logon script here. Because you are dealing with the local users, you probably will not use this tab, and most profile information is now configured in Group Policy, which is also explored later in this chapter.

Managing Groups

Windows XP configures several default group accounts for you. The purpose of groups is to organize users so that they have certain permissions. With local user configuration, groups are not such a big deal because your users are typically either administrators or those with limited accounts, which are provided by default. This group structure is the same that network administrators use to organize network users and assign permissions. Obviously, group configuration and assignment can get very complex if you are a server administrator, but for the local computer, you spend little to no time worrying about groups. The important thing to realize is that each user account needs to be assigned to at least one group that has the permissions that you desire.

There are several default groups, with the three primary groups being Administrators, Power Users, and Users. Table 23-1 outlines each of these groups and the other groups that may appear on your system.

Table 23-1: Default Windows XP Groups

Group	Explanation
Administrators	Computer administrators have complete control over the computer. Administrators can add and remove users and groups, configure the system, install and remove hardware, reconfigure hard drives, install applications, and perform any other action that is available under Windows XP.
Power Users	Power users can perform most actions that administrators can perform, but they can only modify and delete accounts that they create. Also, they can only modify group memberships that they have created. They can remove users from Power Users, Users, and Guests groups. They cannot modify the Administrators and Backup Operators groups, take ownership of files, or perform back/restore functions. They cannot change device drivers or manage security or log/auditing.

Group	Explanation
Users	The default "limited" user account. Users can configure the desktop systems and create files, but they cannot make any configuration changes to the system, add/remove accounts, or access other users' folders.
Backup Operators	Backup Operators can back up and restore files on the computer, regardless of which user owns those files. Backup Operators cannot be changed.
Guests	Enables a guest to log on to the computer. Guests can perform basic computing actions, but do not have all of the abilities given to the limited user accounts.
Network Configuration Operators	Provides some basic administrative privileges for the configuration of Windows XP's networking features. Typically, under local usage, the administrator would handle these functions.
Remote Desktop Users	If Remote Desktop is configured, this group is provided for remote desktop users in order to access the remote access connection.
IIS Groups	If IIS is installed, you'll see additional groups, such as administrators for the Web site, authors for the Web site, and so on.
Help Services Group	Provided for the Help and Support Center.

You can also create your own groups. Just right-click the Groups container and click New Group. The New Group dialog box, shown in Figure 23-7, appears. Then, name the new group and add the desired users. This organization enables you to add this new group to the default security groups as provided. Of course, you can simply add individual users to the default security groups, and if only a few people use the Windows XP computer, this is probably your easiest choice. If you double-click a desired group in the console pane, you can see the current members of the group and adjust the members as desired.

Using Group Policy

Group Policy is a powerful policy tool that was first introduced with Windows 2000. Available on both Windows 2000 Server and Windows 2000 Professional, and now on Windows XP Professional (not Home edition), Group Policy is used to invoke certain settings on client computers and to control what users are able to do — from security settings to Internet Explorer settings. On a network, network administrators can use Group Policy to automatically install and manage software on their users' computers, enforce settings, and even automatically remove software when it is no longer needed.

If you have read anything about Group Policy, you may think of it as a network feature. While it is true that the main focus of Group Policy is configuration of network clients by network administrators, you can also use it to administer your local computer so that settings you configure affect the users logging onto the computer. This is a powerful way to standardize certain settings that you want to make sure are used by each user. Obviously, a lot of features of Group Policy that may appear in your console are not designed for the local machine; still, you'll find a number of secrets and nuggets that you can easily invoke on your computer — and ones that might be really useful to you.

Group Policy is not available to you as a tool in any folder, but it is available as a Microsoft Management Console (MMC) snap-in (see Chapter 7 to learn more about the MMC). You can add the snap-in to a new or existing console and begin using Group Policy as a management tool on Windows XP. To use Group Policy, you must be using Windows XP Professional and you must be logged on as an administrator.

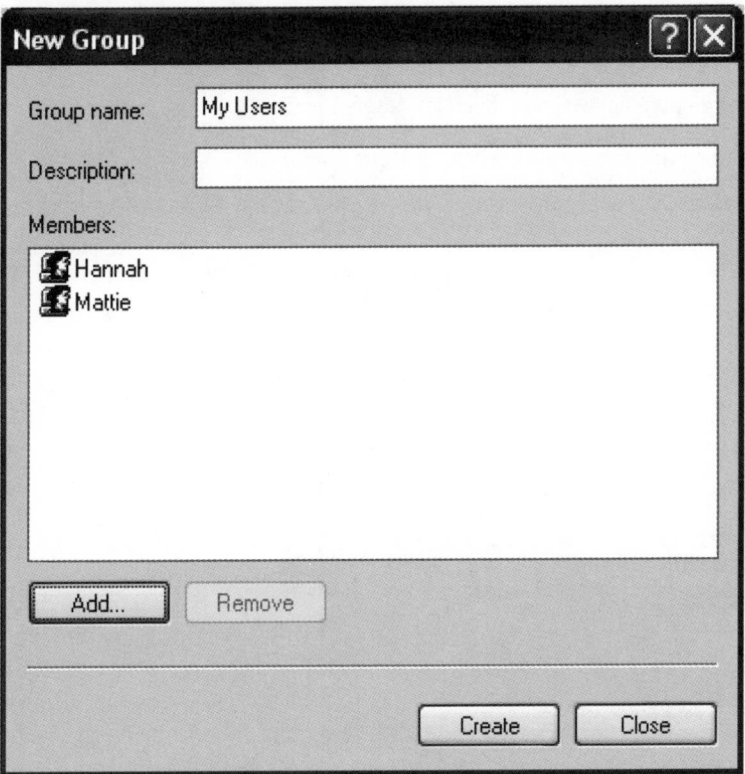

Figure 23-7: New Group dialog box

The following steps show you how to use set up the Group Policy console.

STEPS

Setting up the Group Policy Console

1. Choose Start ⇨ Run. Type **MMC** and click OK.

2. In the MMC console, choose File ⇨ Add/Remove Snap-in.

3. In the Add/Remove Snap-in window, click Add.

4. In the Add Standalone Snap-in window, select Group Policy, as shown in Figure 23-8, and then click Add.

5. In the Welcome to the Group Policy Wizard window, shown in Figure 23-9, leave the default selection to Local Computer set, and then click Finish.

6. Click Close on the Add Standalone Snap-in window and click OK on the Add/Remove Snap-in window.

7. The snap-in appears in the Console. Choose File ⇨ Save As to save the console.

Figure 23-8: Add Standalone Snap-in window

Exploring Group Policy

After you have the Group Policy snap-in loaded, you see the Local Computer Policy node. This expands into the Computer Configuration node and into the User Configuration node. Computer configuration contains settings that you want to impose on the computer system when users log on. For example, you can use the Computer Configuration node to automatically enable disk quotas for users on your computer. On the other hand, the User Configuration node provides you with settings you can apply to the user. If you click through the options in either container, you'll notice that they are largely the same. This is because computer settings apply to a computer, while user settings should apply to the user, regardless of what computer the user is logged onto. Of course, because you are only configuring the local user on the local computer, settings are rather redundant. I help you sift through that later in the chapter.

If you expand each category, you see Software Settings, Windows Settings, and Administrative Templates. Each of these nodes expands into different categories of settings, which categories may also expand into different categories as well, shown in Figure 23-10. After you expand down into a category, the different available settings that you can apply from within that category appear in the details pane. Click one of the settings and the taskpad view gives you some additional information about the setting.

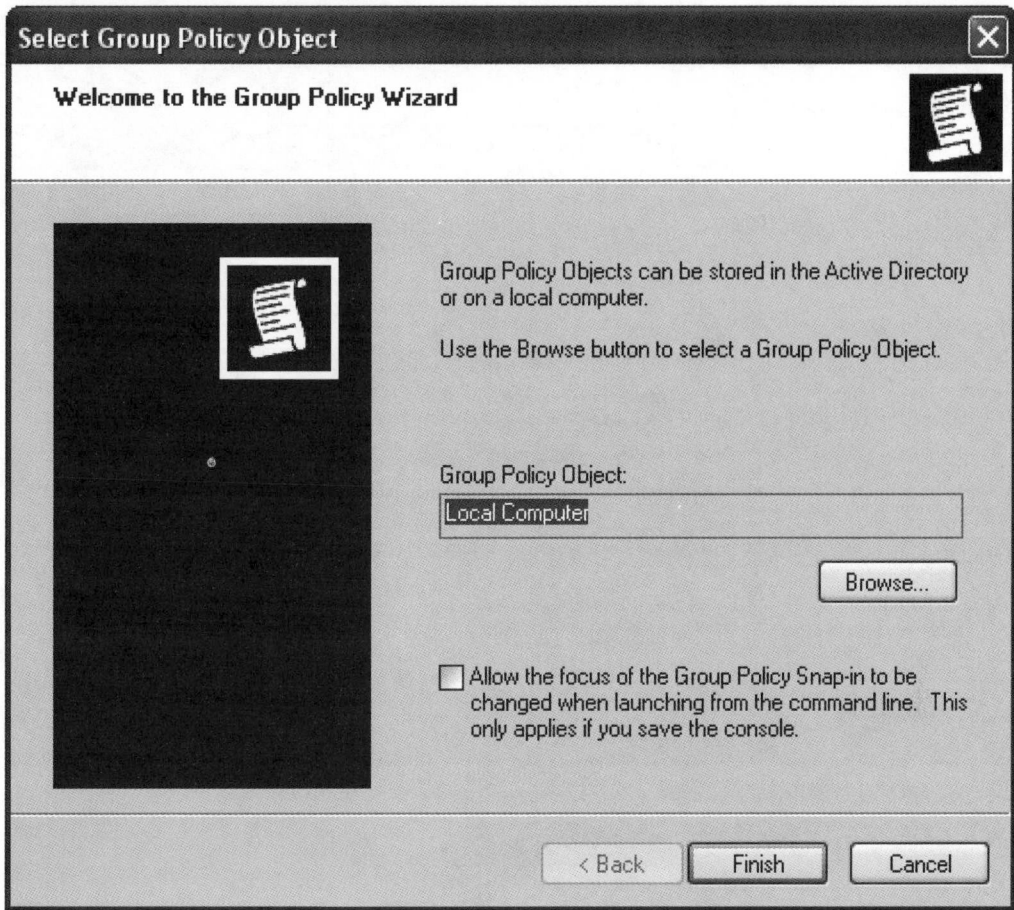

Figure 23-9: Group Policy window

Configuring Group Policy settings

After you use the MMC to drill down into the category that you configure, the settings available in that category appear in the details pane of the console. You can configure a desired setting by double-clicking it to open the category. This opens the setting window for the desired item. For example, you can see in Figure 23-11 that I opened the Enable disk quotas Properties window. At this point, I can use the Setting tab to enable quotas or to disable them, or I can leave them Not configured. If you click the Explain tab, you learn more about the particular entry. The large dialog box that appears in the middle of window may become active, depending on your selection and entry. For example, because I enabled as the Limit Windows File Protection cache size, I need to set what the cache size limit will be in its properties window, shown in Figure 23-12.

At the bottom of each window, you see the Supported on setting, which will tell you if the setting applies to at least Windows 2000 or to at least Windows XP. In later revisions of Windows, this "at least" setting will be more useful because there will be more versions that support Group Policy. You can also navigate through the settings in the category by simply using the Previous Setting and Next Setting buttons.

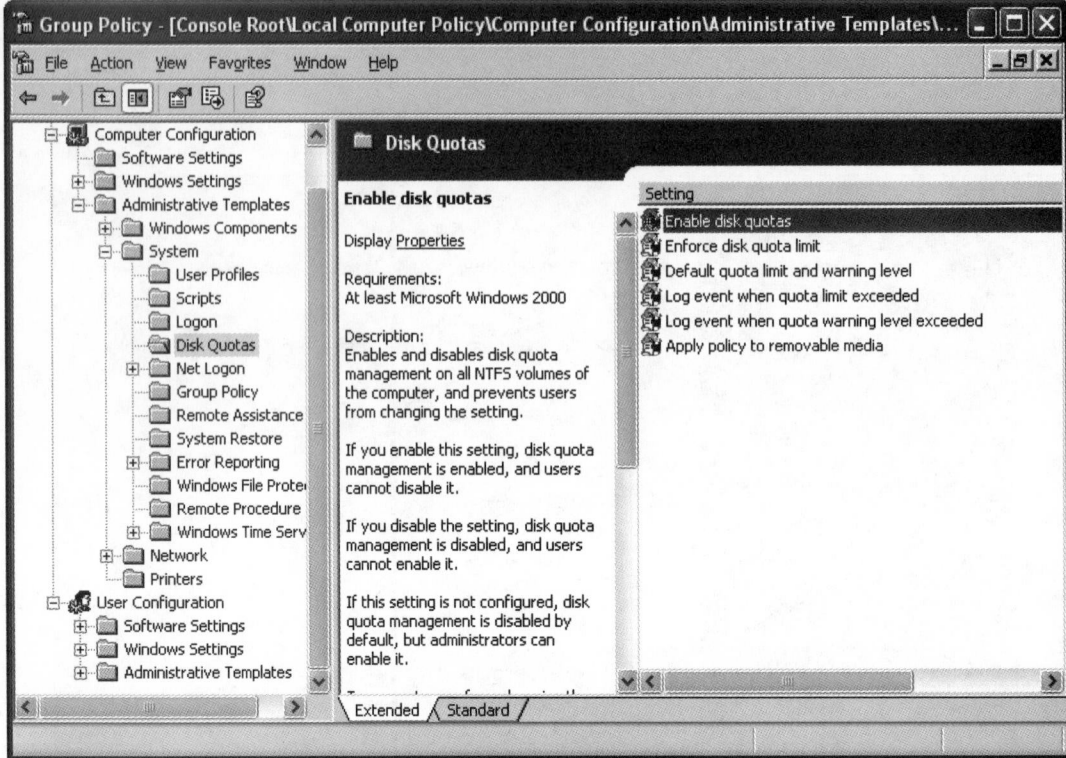

Figure 23-10: Group Policy settings

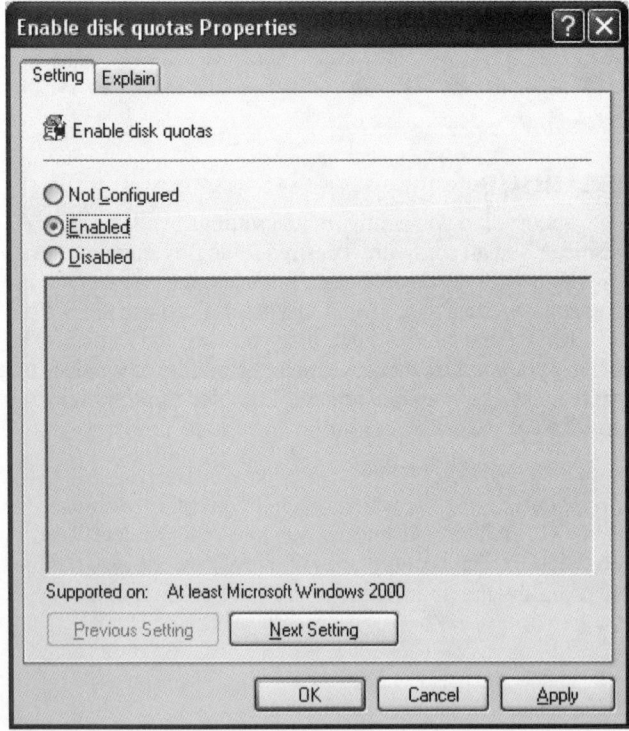

Figure 23-11: Enable Disk Quotas properties

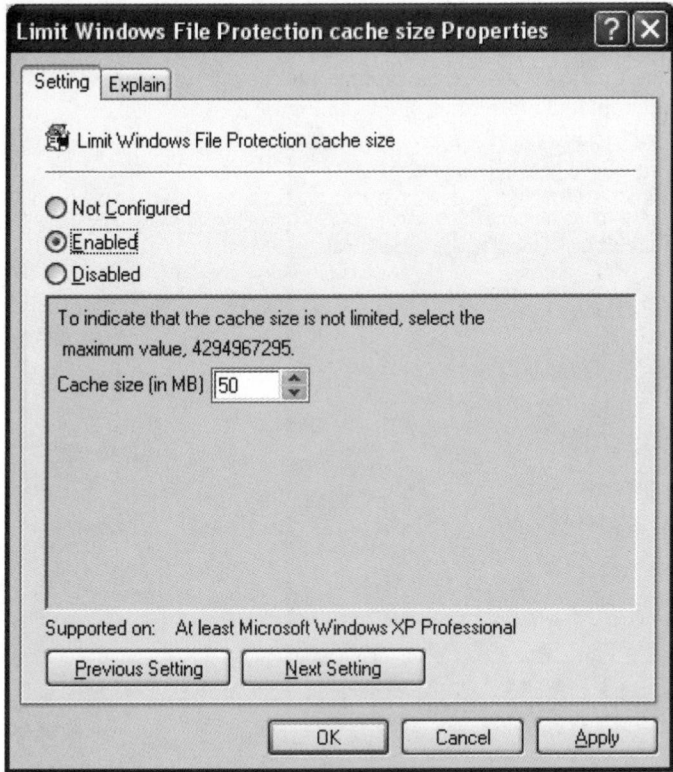

Figure 23-12: In some cases, the dialog box gives you additional setting options that must be configured.

Before using Group Policy, it is important that you have a firm understanding of what the Not Configured, Enabled, and Disabled options that you see mean. To make sure you configure Group Policy to meet your needs, commit these concepts to memory:

♦ **Not Configured** — This setting is simply not configured — in other words, no setting is written to the Registry. Whatever the setting is by default, that is what is used.

♦ **Enabled** — The setting is enabled and written to the Registry.

♦ **Disabled** — The setting is disabled and written to the Registry

Return to the Disk Quotas example I used earlier. In the Disk Quotas window, those settings mean:

♦ **Not Configured** — Nothing is changed and the default setting is used. Disk Quotas are not enabled by default, so they would not be enabled. The user can enable it if the user wants, assuming the user has proper permission to do so.

♦ **Enabled** — Disk Quotas are turned on and functional. Users cannot turn them off.

♦ **Disabled** — Disk Quotas are turned off and not functional. Users cannot turn them on.

The last two settings require Registry entries, whereas the first simply says "Do nothing — the default is OK." As you are configuring Group Policy, it is important to remember that you should not enable or disable any setting that you don't care about — leave the setting Not Configured. Otherwise, you are creating unneeded Registry entries that can bog down the computer's loading time. Enable or disable settings that you want, but leave everything else as Not Configured.

For the most part, the configuration windows you see within Group Policy all look the same as the examples shown here. Depending on setting, some windows look differently. For example, some of the security setting dialog boxes do not use an Enabled/Disabled appearance, but they provide you with a configuration option, such as the logon attempt lockout setting, shown in Figure 23-13.

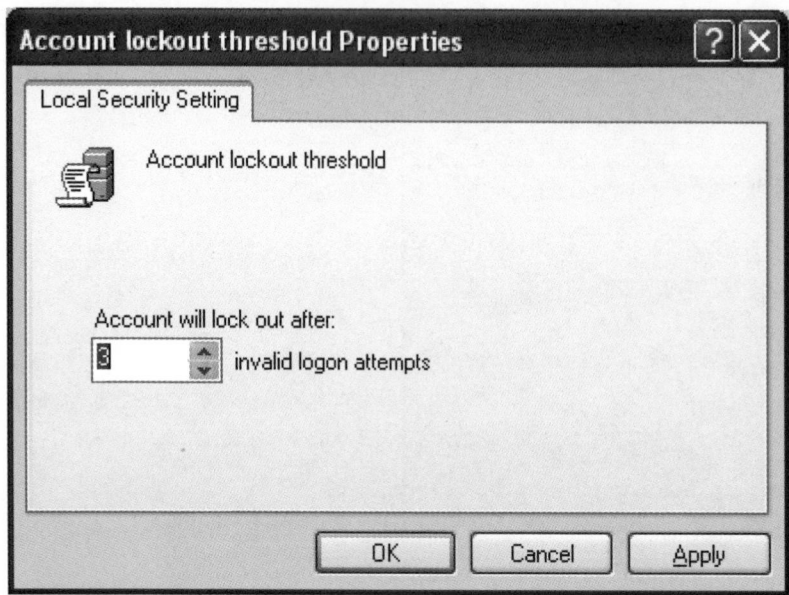

Figure 23-13: Account lockout policy

Regardless, the configuration windows you see in Group Policy are easy and self-explanatory. Configuring Group Policy is as easy as locating the setting that you want to change, adjusting the setting as desired, and clicking OK. When users log on to the Windows XP computer, the settings in Group Policy are applied.

Group Policy Settings

To use Group Policy, you have to find the setting that you want to configure, and then choose an enforcement option to invoke that policy. Locating what you want can be challenging at times because there are so many potential settings to choose from. It is also important to remember that a number of settings that are found in the Group Policy console do not apply to local computer configuration. The Help files are also full of references to Windows 2000/XP domain configurations and other networking issues that do not apply to the local computer. This is because the Group Policy snap-in tool is a global tool that is used on both servers and workstations, and so although you are only using the local computer option, you still see everything — which is a real pain.

So, I sifted through this stuff for you in hopes of making your work with Group Policy easier. In the following section, I review the major settings found in the different nodes and point out in a number of tables those settings that you are most likely to use. You can use this information when you sit down to work with Group Policy as a sort of filter to help you get to the settings you most likely need.

Computer Configuration

The following sections explore the containers found under the Computer Configuration node. Remember that the computer configuration and user configuration, although useful, are designed for networked computers in a domain that allows users to logon to the network at different workstations. The user configuration enables the users to receive the same configuration regardless of the computer they are using, whether there is a computer policy applied or not. Because you are configuring a local computer with local users, most of your configuration is going to be focused in the Computer Configuration node.

Software Settings

The Software Settings container provides a place where network administrators can configure software packages that are delivered to computers on a network. It is a way to automatically rollout software and to manage it from one central location. Because you are configuring a local computer, this setting does not apply to you.

Windows Settings

Windows Settings contains Group Policy objects for startup and shutdown scripts as well as a variety of security settings. If you want to use startup and shutdown scripts with users on your network, you can apply the scripts by opening the startup or shutdown properties window and adding a script to the policy. Then, the script will be used each time the computer is started or shut down.

Under security settings, you see a number of additional containers. The following sections and tables point out setting options you might find useful on your computer.

Account Policies refer to password policy and account lockout policy for users. Table 23-2 reviews the options that you can configure here. I list only the options that apply to the local computer.

Table 23-2: Account Policies

Policy	Explanation
Enforce password history	When enabled, requires Windows XP to remember passwords for users. You can choose the number of passwords that should be remembered.
Maximum password age	The default setting is 42 days. You change it here. Also, if you choose the password never expires setting on a user's account properties, the maximum setting here is overwritten so that it never expires.
Minimum password age	When enabled, this requires that a password be used for a certain amount of time until it is changed. By default, 0 is the setting.
Minimum password length	You can use this setting to enforce a minimum password length, creating more secure user accounts. This setting is set to 0 by default.
Passwords must meet complexity requirements	Disabled by default, this setting requires both numbers and letters in the password.
Account lockout duration	Specifies the amount of time that an account will stay locked after it has been locked because of password failure. This is not configured by default.
Account lockout threshold	Specifies the amount of time a user can attempt to log on before the account is locked. This setting is 0 by default.
Reset account lockout counter	The amount of time that passes before the account lockout counter is reset.

Local Policies include a section of settings concerning audit policy, user rights assignment, and security options. Audit Policy is a container containing a number of individual settings, such as audit account logon events, and audit account management, audit policy change. Some of these apply to the local machine, and some are specific to networking. If you want to enforce auditing on your Windows XP Professional computer, these settings can be enabled so that auditing always occurs.

The User Rights container contains a number of settings showing the groups that have permission to perform a certain action. For example, as Figure 23-14 shows, by default, only administrators and backup operators can perform backup and restore functions. If you wanted to change this policy, you could simply add/remove the desired group.

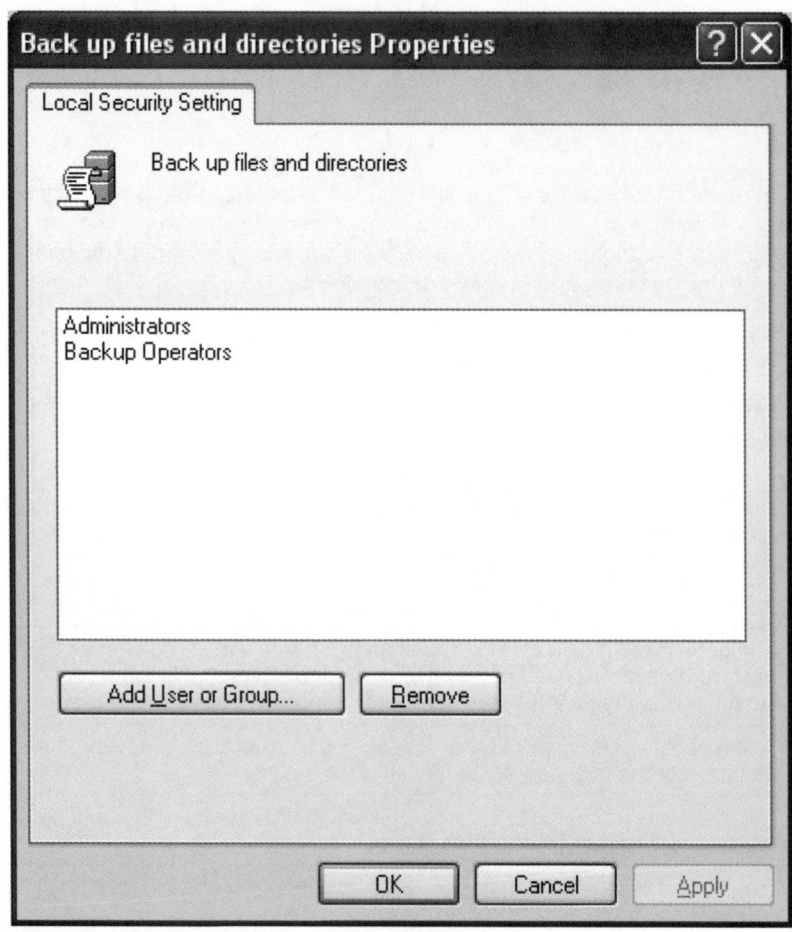

Figure 23-14: Local Security Setting — User Rights.

There are quite a few User Rights settings, and Table 23-3 points out the ones that you are likely to find helpful. The policy and the default setting are listed.

Table 23-3: User Rights Assignment

Policy	Defaults
Backup files and directories	Administrators, Backup Operators
Change the system time	Administrators, /Power Users
Create pagefile	Administrators
Increase scheduling priority	Administrators

Policy	Defaults
Load and unload device drivers	Administrators
Manage auditing and security logs	Administrators
Modify firmware environment variables	Administrators
Perform volume maintenance	Administrators
Profile single processes	Administrators, Power Users
Profile system performance	Administrators
Restore files and directories	Administrators, Backup Operators
Shut down the system	All groups
Take ownership of files and other objects	Administrators

The final container under Local Policies is Security Options. The Security Options container holds individual options for various security options, such as accounts, auditing, and devices. Table 23-4 points out the options under each division.

Table 23-4: Security Options

Policy	Options
Accounts	Provides individual settings for Windows accounts. Configure administrator account status, guest account status, limit local use of blank passwords, rename administrator account, and rename guest account.
Audit	Provides individual settings for auditing permissions. Configure audit access of global system objects, audit the use of Backup and Restore, and shut down the system immediately if unable to log security events.
Devices	Provides individual settings for devices, such as allow undock without logon, allow format and ejection of removable media, prevent users from installing print devices, restrict CD-ROM access to locally logged-on user only, restrict floppy access to locally logged-on user only, and set unsigned driver installation behavior.
Domain Controller	Settings apply to domain controllers, and thus are not applicable in Windows XP Professional since Windows XP cannot be a network domain controller.
Domain Member	Settings for domain members, which are also not applicable in Windows XP Professional.
Interactive Logon	Provides interactive logon settings, such as do not display user last name, do not require Ctrl+Alt+Del, do provide message text for users attempting to logon, and others.
Microsoft Network Client	Provides machine configuration for networking, such as digital signatures and unencrypted password usage.

Policy	Options
Microsoft Network Server	Not applicable in Windows XP Professional.
Network Access	Provides a number of network access settings, including permissions and security models.
Recovery Console	Provides settings for recovery console.
Shut Down	Provides allow system shutdown without logon and clear virtual memory pagefile options.
System Cryptography	Provides Federal Information Processing Standards (FIPS) encryption settings.
System Objects	Provides default owner and internal system settings.

This container holds the Encrypting File System container, which may not contain any settings on your Windows XP computer.

Software Restriction Policies enables you to set a default policy that enables software usage by the group membership of the user, or not at all. By default, the unrestricted setting is configured by default, which you will probably want to use. If there are any additional software restriction rules available, those appear here as well.

If IP Security is used on your network, the default client and server policies reside here. The network administrator typically configures these settings are on an enterprise-wide basis.

Administrative Templates

The final major container in the Computer Configuration node is Administrative Templates. These are a collection of template settings from a number of Windows OS divisions, such as Windows Components, System, Network, and Printers. There are a lot of available settings here, virtually all of which are "not configured." The following sections discuss them one container at a time. Although I do not address each possible configuration option, I do point out those that are more likely to be useful from a local computer perspective.

The Windows Components container provides settings for NetMeeting, Internet Explorer Task Scheduler, Terminal Services, Windows Installer, and Windows Messenger.

Under NetMeeting, your only option is to disable remote Desktop Sharing.

Table 23-5 presents the configuration options available under Internet Explorer.

Table 23-5: Internet Explorer Options

Policy	Description
Security Zones: Use only machine settings	Applies the same zone settings to all users. By default, each user can define his or her own settings.
Security Zones: Do not allow users to change policies	Users cannot change security zone settings.

Policy	Description
Security Zones: Do not allow users to Add/Delete sites	Users cannot add or delete security sites.
Make proxy settings per machine.	Proxy settings are applied to all users — not configured on a user-by-user basis.
Disable automatic install of Internet Explorer components	Prevents IE from automatically installing new components.
Disable periodic check for IE software updates	Disables IE from automatically checking the IE update site for new downloads.
Disable software update shell notifications on program launch	If enabled, users are not be notified when IE updates their programs by using the Microsoft Software Distribution Channel.
Disable showing the splash screen	The IE splash screen does not appear when the user starts the browser.

The next option is Task Scheduler, which contains the setting options listed in Table 23-6.

Table 23-6: Task Scheduler

Policy	If Enabled . . .
Hide Property Pages	Users cannot view or change the properties of an existing task.
Prevent Task Run or End	Users cannot manually stop or start a task.
Prohibit drag and drop	Users cannot add/remove tasks by copying them into the Scheduled Tasks folder.
Prohibit new task creation	Users cannot create new tasks.
Prohibit task deletion	Users cannot delete tasks.
Remove advanced menu	Users cannot change or view the properties of newly created tasks.
Prohibit browse	Users cannot change the schedule program for existing tasks, and limits the task items on the user's Start Menu.

The next section is Terminal Services. If you are using Terminal Services in Windows XP to connect to Windows 2000 terminal servers, your network administrator will configure these settings. You can easily review them if you like, but unless you are a network administrator, you are unlikely to use these settings.

Next, you can invoke settings for Windows Installer. Windows Installer helps you add and remove programs to Windows with ease, but you can force some settings that can help you better control the Windows XP computer. Table 23-7 outlines these options for you.

Table 23-7: Windows Installer

Policy	If Enabled . . .
Disable Windows installer	Disables the use of Windows Installer.
Always install with elevated privileges	Programs are installed with system permissions.

Policy	If Enabled . . .
Prohibit rollback	Stops windows from creating rollback files so that an install can be reversed.
Remove browse dialog box for new source	Disables the Browse button in Windows Installer.
Prohibit Patching	Windows Installer patches cannot be used.
Disable IE security prompt for Windows Installer scripts	Allows Web-based programs to install software on the computer without having to notify the user.
Enable user control over installs	Enables users to change installation options that are normally available to administrators only.
Enable user to browse for source while elevated	Users can search for installation files during privileged installations.
Enable user to use media source while elevated	Allows users to install programs from removable media during privileged installations.
Enable user to patch elevated products	Programs can be upgraded during privileged installations.
Allow admin to install from Terminal Services sessions	Self-explanatory.
Cache transforms in secure location on workstation	Saves copies of transform files on the local computer.
Logging	Determines the kinds of events that Windows Installer logs.
Prohibit user installs	Enables you to prohibit or limit user installs.
Turn off creation of System Restore checkpoints	Stops System Restore from functioning because checkpoints are not created.

Finally, under Windows Message container gives you two options. You can choose to not allow Windows Messenger to be used or to not automatically start Windows Messenger.

The System container contains a number of different containers with settings on a variety of options pertaining the Windows XP system. These settings are easy to use and there are number of interesting controls you can implement, so I suggest that you spend a little time prowling around in this portion of Group Policy. Table 23-8 gets you started.

Table 23-8: System

Policy	Description
User Profiles	Contains user profile settings, such as:
	Do not detect network settings
	Wait for remote user profile
	Prevent roaming profile changes from propagating to the server
	Only allow local user profiles
Scripts	Provides settings for logon and log off scripts

Policy	Description
Logon	Provides logon settings, such as: Always use classic logon Do not process the run once list Do not process the legacy run list Always wait for the network at computer startup
Disk Quotas	Provides disk quotas settings, such as: Enable disk quotas Enforce quota limit Default quota limit and warning level Log event when quota is exceeded Apply policy to removable media
Net Logon	Provides logon settings when logging onto a Windows domain. These setting are typically set on client computers by network administrators.
Group Policy	The Group Policy settings determine how Group Policy is refreshed on client computers and other network administration issues. Most of these settings are used by network administrators for network client computer configuration.
Remote Assistance	Provides two settings where solicited and offer remote assistance can or cannot be used.
System Restore	You can choose to turn off system restore and configuration.
Error Reporting	Provides advanced error reporting settings and error notification.
Windows File Protection	Provides Windows File Protection settings, such as: Hide file scan progress window Limit Windows file protection cache size Specify Windows File Protection cache location
Remote Procedure Calls	Enables RPC troubleshooting state information and propagation of extended error information.
Windows Time Service	You can enable global configuration settings here that apply to all local users.

The Network settings under Administrative Templates provide settings that you may find useful for local user and computer configuration, although a number of these are more appropriately used by network administrators. Table 23-9 reviews these options.

The Printers container holds settings that are configured by network administrators that determine how and if users can publish printers to the Active Directory on a Windows 2000/XP network. There is nothing configurable for the local machine here.

Table 23-9: Network

Policy	Description
DNS Client	Provides DNS client settings. These are typically configured by network administrators.
Offline Files	If users on your computer use offline files, you can enforce a number of settings here, including:
	Allow or disallow offline files
	Prohibit user configuration of offline files
	Default cache size
	Files not cached
	Turn off reminder balloons
	Event logging level
	Encrypt the offline file cache
	Configure slow link speed
Network Connections	Contains settings for ICS and ICF
QoS Packet Scheduler	Provides QoS enforced settings. These are normally configured by network administrators.
SNMP	SNMP (Simple Network Management Protocol) is used and configured by network administrators.

User configuration

As I mentioned earlier, you'll see that many of the settings under user configuration are the same as they are under computer configuration. Remember that on a network, computer configuration applies to a group of computers and user configuration applies to a group of users. Computers receive their policy and users receive their policy — regardless of which computer is logged onto or whether that computer is managed by Group Policy.

There are a number of user-specific settings here that you can invoke. You may find these helpful, especially if you need to tightly control users who log on to your computer (such as your children or coworkers.) I'll not repeat information covered in the previous section, but I do want to point out some of the interesting options available to you.

Internet Explorer

If you expand Windows Settings, you'll see a container for Internet Explorer Maintenance. If you open this up, you'll find a number of fun items. For example, as Figure 23-15 shows, you can create your own custom title for Internet Explorer. You can also access options to create a custom logon and animated bitmaps, and you can even customize the toolbar background. These settings are primarily provided for companies who want to provide company branding on IE, but you can play around with them, too, and create your own custom look for IE.

Additionally, you can use the provided categories under Internet Explorer Maintenance to customize the connection, favorites, home page, security settings, and default programs. Using Group Policy, you can configure most of the items you find on Internet Options so that they are enforced for all users on your computer.

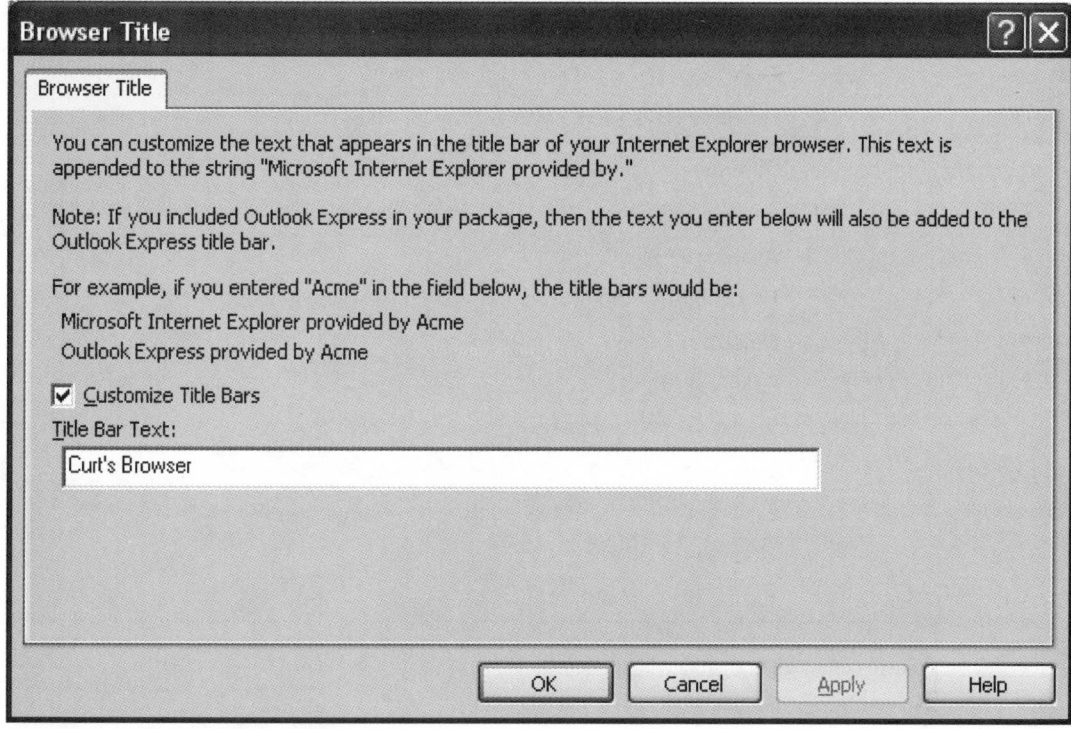

Figure 23-15: IE custom title bar option

Start Menu and Taskbar

You can configure the Start Menu and Taskbar and force desirable configurations on other users. If you expand Administrative Templates, you see the Start Menu and Taskbar node. There are a number of settings here, and the following list points out some of the more interesting ones:

- ♦ Remove links and access to Windows Update
- ♦ Remove My Documents from the Start Menu
- ♦ Remove Programs on the Settings menu
- ♦ Remove Network Connections from the Start Menu
- ♦ Remove Search from the Start Menu (in fact, you can remove just about anything)
- ♦ Add Logoff to the Start Menu
- ♦ Prevent changes to the Start Menu and Taskbar
- ♦ Turn off personalized menus
- ♦ Do not keep history of recently opened documents
- ♦ Prevent grouping of Taskbar items
- ♦ Lock the Taskbar
- ♦ Force Classic Start Menu
- ♦ Remove balloon help
- ♦ Remove and disable the Turn Off Computer button
- ♦ Hide the Notification Area

. . . and the list goes on. As you can see, you can completely customize how the Start Menu and Taskbar look — and then place that configuration on all users of your computer.

Desktop

As with the Start Menu and Taskbar, you can customize the desktop as well. Again, there are a number of configuration options, and the following list points out some of them to you:

◆ Hide and disable all items on the desktop

◆ Remove Recycle Bin from the desktop

◆ Prevent adding, dragging, dropping, and closing of the Taskbar toolbar

◆ Don't save settings at exit

◆ Prohibit adjusting desktop toolbars

◆ Remove the Desktop Cleanup Wizard

Control Panel

Finally, you can customize Control Panel settings and keep users out of configuration areas where they should not be. For example, among other things, you can:

◆ Prohibit access to Control Panel

◆ Hide specified Control Panel applets

◆ Force Classic Control Panel style

◆ Prevent the addition/deletion of printers

◆ Remove Display in Control panel

◆ Hide the Screen Saver tab

◆ Hide Appearance and Themes tabs

◆ Hide desired themes

◆ Remove Add/Remove Programs

◆ Hide Add/Remove Windows Components page

◆ Remove support information

As you can see, there are a number of important settings and a number of management features you can choose to implement. For example, just consider some of the following potential applications of Group Policy:

◆ Hiding Add/Remove Programs and Hide Add/Remove Windows Components pages so that your kids can't install/uninstall software or Windows components.

◆ Preventing other users from reconfiguring Display properties so as not to cause problems with display configuration.

◆ Stopping users from accidentally deleting a printer.

◆ Stopping users from saving any desktop settings. That way, they can use any wild and crazy wallpaper they want, but once they log off, the setting is not changed.

◆ Preventing users from shutting down the computer. This setting can be very important in a home and small office situation where the XP computer is the ICS host. Other users will not be able to access the Internet if this computer is shut down, so this setting prevents that possibility.

There are many more, but these possible uses give you an idea of the amount of management potential Windows XP makes available to you.

Summary

This chapter explored how Windows XP provides advanced tools that help you locally manage users on your Windows XP computer. You can easily add, remove, and manage user accounts with . . .

♦ Users in Control Panel

♦ Computer Management

You can also finely control users with local Group Policy administration. Taken together, these tools make user management in Windows XP much more manageable than it was in previous versions of Windows. Because of the user management tools found in Windows XP, several people can use your computer while maintaining their own settings and documents — a feature that benefits us all.

Part VII

Optimization and Troubleshooting Secrets

Chapter 24

Optimizing Windows XP

In This Chapter

Optimization is the process of configuring and tweaking system functions and features to get the best performance from your operating system. Fortunately, Windows XP does this for you in a number of automatic ways, but there are still many things you can do and tools you can use order to increase Windows XP performance, as well as locate items that are causing performance problems. In this chapter, you learn about . . .

- ♦ Optimizing Windows processes
- ♦ Using Event Viewer
- ♦ Using Task Manager
- ♦ Using Performance Monitor

Optimizing Windows Processes

Before we take a look at the actions you can perform and the tools you can use to manage Windows XP's performance, I first want to consider the ways in which Windows XP attempts to optimize the operating system for you.

Reducing boot time

One of the most aggravating things about using a computer can be a slow boot. It seems as though you wait forever until the operating system is ready for you. Microsoft is aware of this consumer complaint, and it has made constant strides in reducing your wait. Windows Me was faster than any previous version of Windows, and Windows XP typically has a very fast boot time — 30 seconds on average. Of course, the actual time it takes Windows XP to boot may depend on several different factors, including device initialization, reconnection of network drives, and other related services and features. To make booting time faster, Windows XP touts improvements to the Boot Loader so that drivers load more quickly and Registry initialization happens faster. Also, Windows XP improves upon Windows 2000's input/output lengths, which made boot time slower in Windows 2000. Windows XP can prefetch operating system code at the same time that devices are being initialized — essentially performing two different booting jobs simultaneously.

Windows XP also has the ability to speed up booting by watching previous boots. As booting occurs, Windows XP can identify the code and data needed to boot and can optimize the placement of the code and data on the disk to speed up booting. In other words, after the first few boots of Windows XP, the boot time should actually speed up! Finally, Microsoft worked with OEMs and hardware vendors to improve drivers. Drivers that are poorly written or do not function well with Windows XP require more time to load, thus increasing the boot time. By making drivers faster, the operating system loads faster.

You can take two actions to help speed up booting time:

- ♦ Make sure Windows XP–supported drivers are installed with your hardware devices. If you have been using older or generic drivers, do a little Web work and download new ones for the system. Drivers that are enhanced for Windows XP load faster and give you the operating system faster.

♦ Use MSCONFIG to clear the applications that you really do not need at startup. Windows XP has to load every application during startup that is listed on the Startup tab. You may see older applications and stuff you do not want that can be disabled from startup. This will also increase boot time.

CROSS-REFERENCE: See Chapter 25 to learn more about MSCONFIG.

In relation to booting faster, you also have standby and hibernation modes available. When standby occurs, power is reduced to devices so that they are placed in a dormant state. When you bring XP out of hibernation, your devices must be initialized, which can take time. Windows XP uses a feature called "parallelism" that initializes devices not one at a time, but several at a time, including system checks to ensure that initialization does not cause conflicts. Because parallelism enables devices to be initialized faster, your system's boot time is faster as well.

In terms of hibernation, Windows XP writes current memory to the hard disk when hibernation occurs. Hibernation shuts down the computer; the physical memory is written to disk, where it can be read when power is resumed. The speed in recovering from hibernation is found in the compression algorithms used with data written to the physical disk. This speeds the boot process, because the information can be loaded into memory at the same time devices are initializing.

Application optimization

For the most part, Windows XP uses the system resources it needs to boost application performance. In fact, application optimization occurs in much the same way as the boot process, because the same basic technologies are used to make applications launch faster. Windows XP watches the process of starting an application each time you do so to learn what system resources the application needs and how the application can be optimized to boot faster. Once Windows XP "learns" this information, the process of starting an application should occur more quickly, because Windows XP already knows what to expect from the application and makes system requests more quickly and efficiently.

Although Windows XP does a good job of handling application optimization, you can also do your part:

♦ **Install enough physical RAM on your computer.** You can adjust settings, tweak performance, stand on your head, and do just about anything else you want, but the simple fact remains — applications eat memory and system resources. If your computer is not up to par, performance will suffer and possibly even fail. There is no replacement for additional physical RAM on your Windows XP computer, so try to always install enough RAM to run all of the applications that you want to use. See the section "Memory" later in this chapter for a more specific discussion of how much RAM your system might need.

♦ **Make sure your system is optimized for applications, not system processes.** On servers, it is not uncommon for performance to be tuned to system processes and not applications, since the bulk of the server's work is running system processes that meet the needs of users. However, on Windows XP Home or Professional Edition, you want system resources to be optimized for applications so that whenever you launch an application, Windows XP gives it all it can. You may make sure your system is optimized for applications by opening System in Control Panel and clicking the Advanced tab. Under Performance, click the Settings button and then click the Advanced tab, shown in Figure 24-1. Make sure the Processor scheduling and Memory usage settings are set to Programs, not Background services/System cache.

Resource management

Windows XP is able to detect system idle time and perform lower-level processes, such as managing files and directories and cleaning up the hard disk during times of inactivity. In other words, instead of system processes occurring at any given time, regardless of how busy you are using the computer, the system is able to detect when it is busy and when it is idle. It can then run background processes and perform functions that it needs when the system is idle. In the same manner, you can help Windows XP improve performance by scheduling functions, such as disk cleanup, defragmentation, and so on, to run during idle hours, such as in the middle of the night. These processes help keep Windows XP functioning at its peak, and they do not interfere with your work or play.

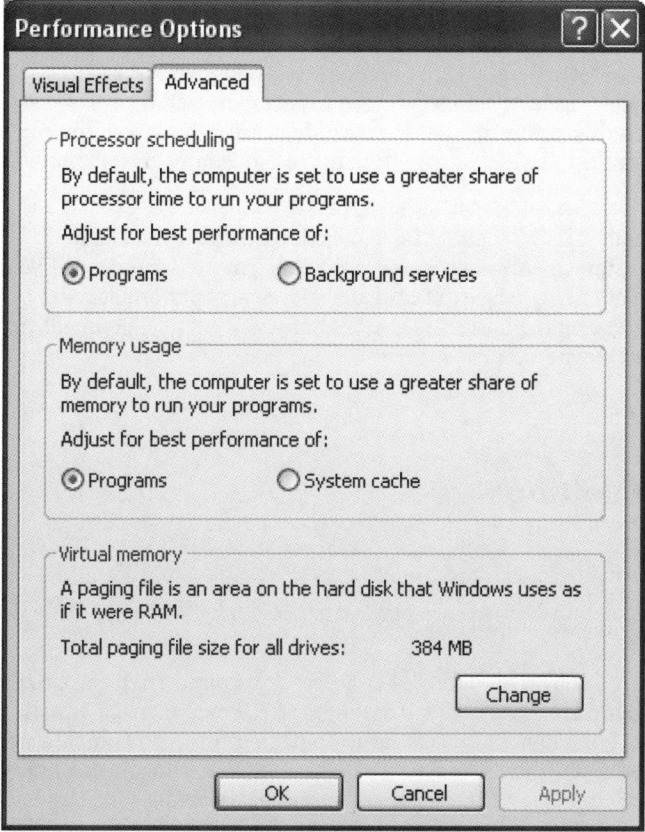

Figure 24-1: Optimize system resources for programs.

TIP: Windows XP also tries to reduce the XP interface graphics if the system resources are not able to handle them well. For example, animated GIFs and other operating system graphics features consume resources and memory. If the computer is low on system resources, Windows XP can automatically disable some of these interface features to conserve system resources.

Memory

Yes, you know; add more RAM. In a nutshell, that is the single most important action you can take if you even think your computer is low on memory. Windows XP tends to be a memory hog, and the more RAM you have installed, the better. Although the recommended amount of RAM is 128MB, having 256MB or more is not at all too much. The amount of RAM that you need has a lot to do with the applications that you plan on running. Graphics-intensive applications and games consume more system resources and particularly more RAM than most other applications, so if you are considering a RAM upgrade, think about what you want to do with the computer and the applications you plan on using, and then buy *more* RAM than you think you will need.

Windows XP uses Virtual Memory like previous versions of Windows and most all other computer operating systems. Virtual Memory enables Windows XP to write memory data to the physical disk on a paging file when designated memory gets too full. Information in memory but not currently being used is written to the paging file and then recalled into physical memory when needed by reading the paging file. Because a combination of physical and virtual memory is used, Windows XP attempts to maximize memory settings for applications by using the best combination of physical and virtual memory. Of course, the more memory there is, the more Windows XP has to work with, and the better results you will have.

The problem is that virtual memory, although very useful and needed, is costly in terms of performance. Input/Output cycles to the physical disk slow down performance, and because Windows XP has to perform this dancing act between physical and virtual memory, you can expect that overall system performance will take a hit. You may not readily notice this hit, but nevertheless it is important to keep in mind that virtual memory has a performance cost. Again, you are back to the old axiom, "Install more physical RAM."

You can adjust the size of the paging file, although Windows XP handles the paging file itself and recommends that you leave paging file adjustments to Windows XP. Still, you can try tweaking it if you like to attempt performance gains. You are not likely to see radical gains in memory performance by doing this and again, you return to the need for more physical RAM. Still, if you want to experiment with these settings, the following steps show you how.

STEPS

Adjusting Virtual Memory settings

1. Open System in Control Panel.

2. Click the Advanced tab. Under Performance, click the Settings button.

3. In the Performance Options dialog box, click the Advanced tab, and then click the Change button under Virtual Memory.

4. The Virtual Memory window appears, as shown in Figure 24-2. Select the desired drive and enter a desired initial size (MB) and a maximum size. You can also enable the System to manage virtual memory on its own by selecting the radio button, or you can have no paging file at all (which is not recommended). The recommended settings appear at the bottom of the window, and you can use those as a guide. If you need to squeeze more power out of the paging file, you can try increasing the maximum size of the paging file, but you need to make sure you have enough room on the disk for this action. When you finish, just click OK to invoke the settings.

TIP: The paging file minimum size recommended on the Virtual Memory tab is 1.5 times the amount of physical RAM installed on the computer. You should at least set this amount. A lower configuration may adversely affect performance. Also, if you have two drives, consider assigning the paging file to the fastest drive.

SECRET: How you do know if your paging file is large enough? You can monitor it with Performance Monitor to gain an accurate look. See the Performance Monitor section later in this chapter for details.

Optimizing other system components

You have a few other system components and performance tweaks you can implement to squeeze the best possible performance out of your system.

SECRET: For the best speed, use the fastest DMA100 or Ultra/Wide SCSI hard disk you can — you will see tremendous performance improvements.

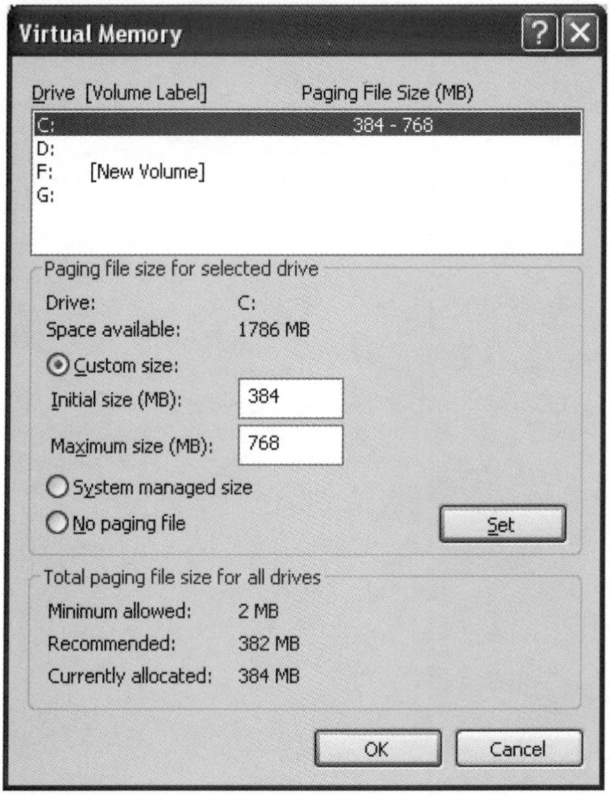

Figure 24-2: Virtual Memory window

Defragmenting hard disks

First of all, concerning hard disks, you should run defragmentation regularly, especially if you use your computer a lot. Every few weeks is not too much, and although disk defragmentation doesn't completely defragment the entire disk, it can increase system performance. You can also schedule disk defragmentation using scheduled tasks to run automatically at off-peak times so that you aren't sitting there, twiddling your thumbs.

CROSS-REFERENCE: See Chapter 3 to learn more about hard drive configuration and management.

Controlling visual effects

The Windows XP interface is demanding on the computer system because of the graphics used in the default Windows XP theme. This theme places more demands on system processes, because the graphics it uses must be rendered. However, you can tweak the performance of visual effects in order to boost system performance. Although you will lose some of the appearance features of Windows XP if you do so, this may be just what you need to get a little more power from the system.

To boost performance, access System Properties and click the Advanced tab. Under Performance, click Settings. On the Visual Effects tab, shown in Figure 24-3, change the radio button to "Adjust for best performance." When you make this setting, you see that most of the check box options presented are cleared. You can review this list and see what you are losing. If you want to strike a balance between appearance and performance, try the custom setting and clear the check boxes of the items that you can live without.

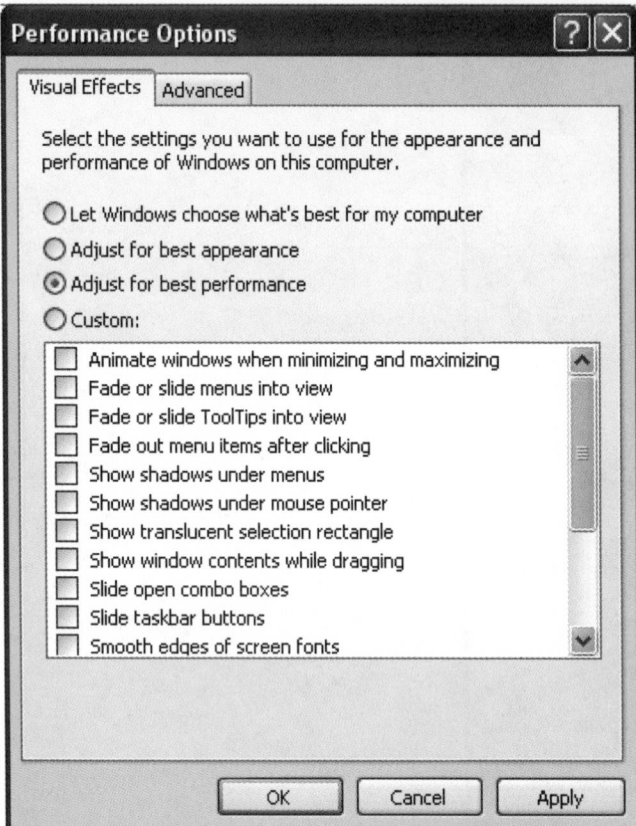

Figure 24-3: Visual Effects tab

TIP: Remember, Windows XP attempts to manage these settings for you if you have the "Let Windows choose what's best for my computer" setting enabled. However, you can try to boost system performance by choosing the performance setting yourself instead permitting Windows XP to perform the balancing act it uses by default.

Performing clean installations

You may not want to hear this, but the fact remains — clean-install systems perform better than upgrades do. Consider this scenario: Your computer used Windows Me until you upgraded to Windows XP. Although the upgrade to Windows XP works well, Windows Me does not support NTFS. Therefore, you had to convert FAT disks to NTFS. Converting also works well, but cluster sizes found on the disk are not as optimized as they would have been during a clean install when the disk was formatted and installed with NTFS. Of course, the choice to wipe down the computer and completely reinstall Windows XP may not be practical, and you may not see enough performance gains to really matter, but this an important tip to tuck in the back of your mind for future use. When possible, choose a clean installation over an upgrade.

Configuring startup and recovery

As mentioned earlier in this chapter, Windows XP startup is configured to start faster and come out of standby and hibernate modes faster. However, if you are using a dual-boot system, you can make a few adjustments to settings that can help you. Also, if there is a system failure, you can configure the actions that Windows XP should take. Both startup and recovery settings can be configured on the Startup and Recovery window. On the Advanced tab of System Settings, click the Settings button under Startup and Recovery to access the Startup and Recovery window, as shown in Figure 24-4.

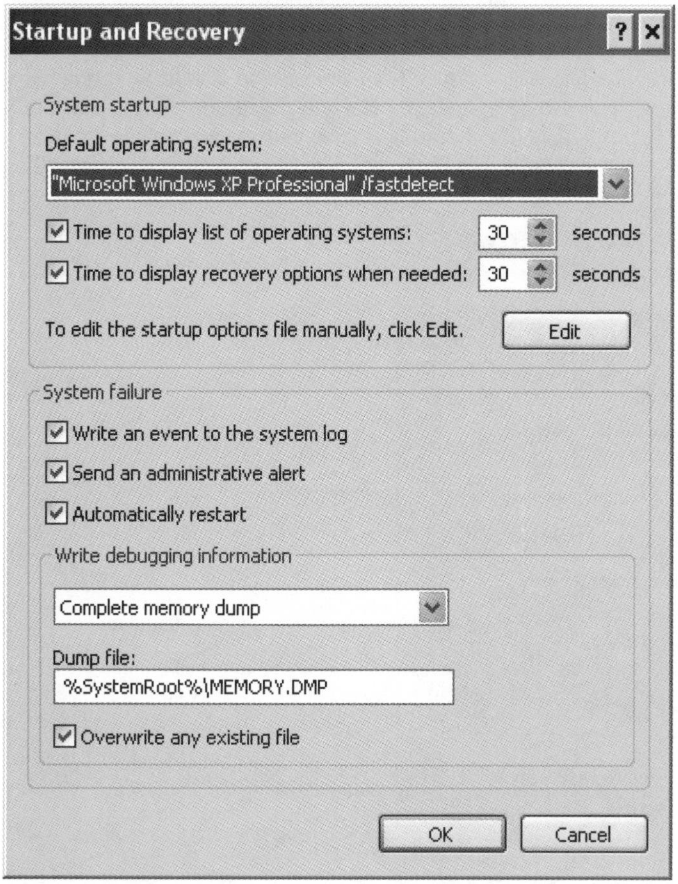

Figure 24-4: Startup and Recovery window

Note that if you are using a dual- boot system, you can choose the default operating system that will be selected during a boot, unless you make a change using the menu. Say you are booting Windows XP and Windows 98, but you use Windows XP most all of the time. You can save time by selecting Windows XP from the drop-down menu and then changing the time value for the Startup menu to a much lower value, such as 5 seconds instead of the default of 30. If you click the Edit button, you can actually edit the Boot.ini file from this location, as well.

Under System failure, by default, an event is written to the system log, an administrative alert is sent, and the computer is automatically restarted. You should leave these options selected because they may be able to help you resolve problems. By default, debug information is written in the Memory.DMP file, and this file may be helpful when troubleshooting problems with Microsoft technical support (it's cryptic and not any help to you without phone support personnel).

Editing environment variables

Environment variables comprise a list of information about your computer that is used to determine how Windows runs and where temporary folders are located. Environment variables are tied to your user account, and they can be edited and even deleted if necessary. Under most circumstances, you don't need to change any of these variables, but if you are having problems, you can inspect the file path locations for each variable and ensure that they are correct. Users can change environment variables tied to the user's account, but only administrators can change the System variables in Windows XP.

The Environment Variables window, shown in Figure 24-5, contains both the user variables and system variables for the operating system. If you select a desired variable and click Edit, you see that the variable is basically a path, shown in Figure 24-6. Like I said, you typically do not need to change anything here, but if a path to an environment component seems to be wrong, you can edit the information on this tab. For example, suppose that you are having problems with operating system paths. You can choose that environment variable, click Edit, and directly make changes to the OS paths. Again, this is not something you would normally need to do, but keep in mind that these variable settings are here.

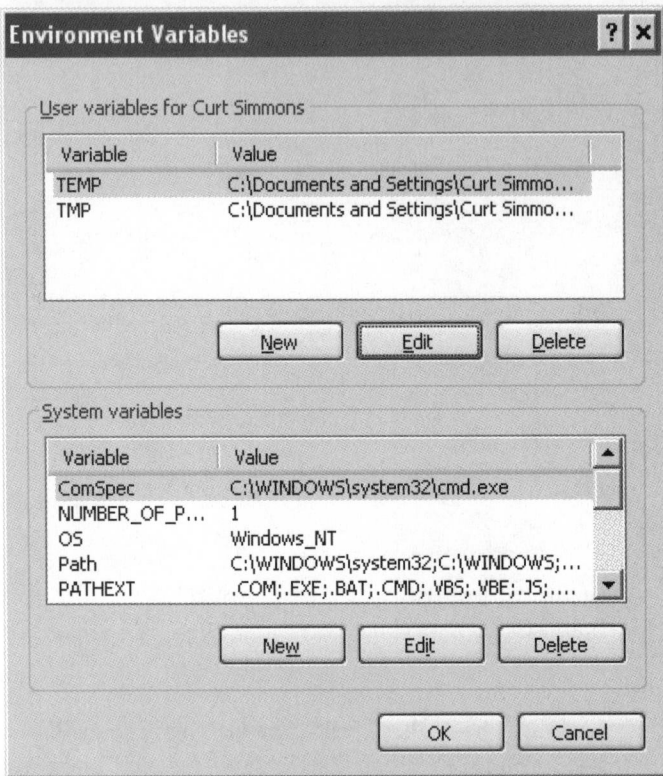

Figure 24-5: Environment Variables window

Figure 24-6: Edit User Variable window

SECRET: If you are not too worried about keeping things private, you can store your temp file to an out of the way drive or volume, which can free up more primary disk space and reduce fragmentation or your C: drive.

Configuring internal services

Windows XP configures a number of internal services to start either automatically or manually, depending on the service itself. As a general rule, Windows XP does a good job of managing these services, but it is important to remember that any background service running consumes system resources, so if you can configure some services to start manually instead of automatically, you can save resource consumption. Of course, you have to be careful because you don't want to turn off a service that the operating system needs to run or perform correctly, and as a general rule, the services configured to automatically start are necessary for Windows operations. However, there may be instances where you want to manually start a service when necessary instead of having Windows use system resources to automatically start it. For example, in Figure 24-7, you see that the Fast User Switching Compatibility service is started automatically. If you know that you do not need fast user switching capabilities, you can stop that service so that it is not automatically started each time you boot the computer. You should get familiar with the available services and what their default settings are so that you can change them if necessary.

You can access the services by opening Computer Management, expanding Services and Applications, and selecting Services. The services appear in the right console pane, shown in Figure 24-7.

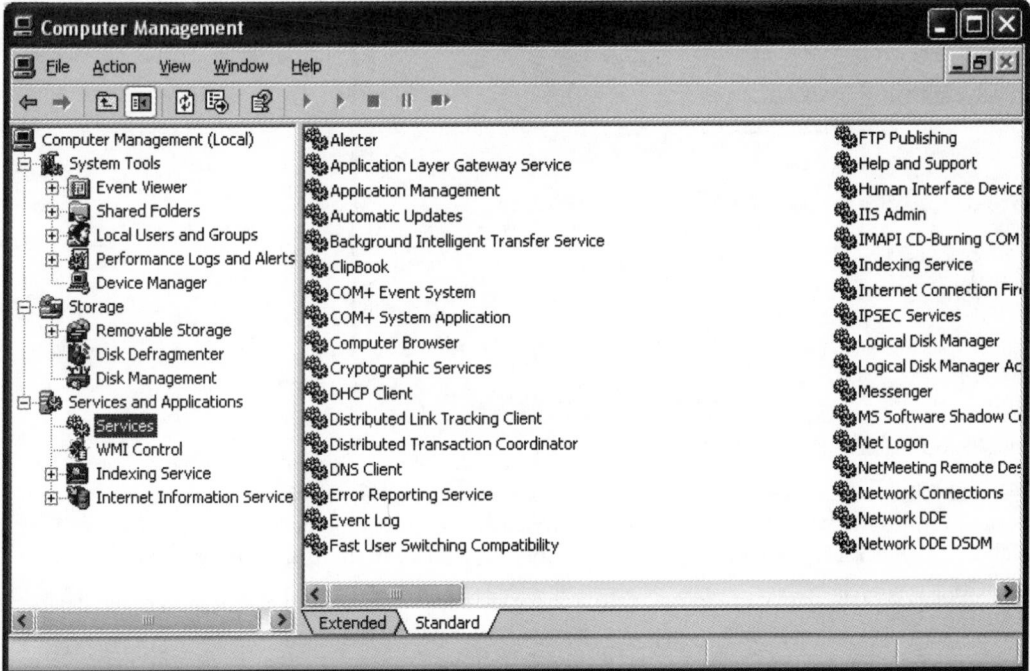

Figure 24-7: Services in Computer Management

If you double-click a service in the right console pane, you see the properties sheets for the service. I describe the notable properties in the following sections.

On the General tab, shown in Figure 24-8, you see the name, description, path, and startup type of the service. A service can start up either manually or automatically. Manual startup means that Windows XP can start the service when it is needed, or you can start it yourself using the Start button. You see the current service status of the service, as well. If you identify services that are starting automatically that you really do not need, you can stop the service and change the startup type to manual.

The Log On tab describes how the service is started by log on. For most services, the service is started by the Local System account, but you can tie a particular service to a designated account if necessary. For the example, if want to the service to only be started by a particular user's log on. Normally, the "local system account" option selected is all you need.

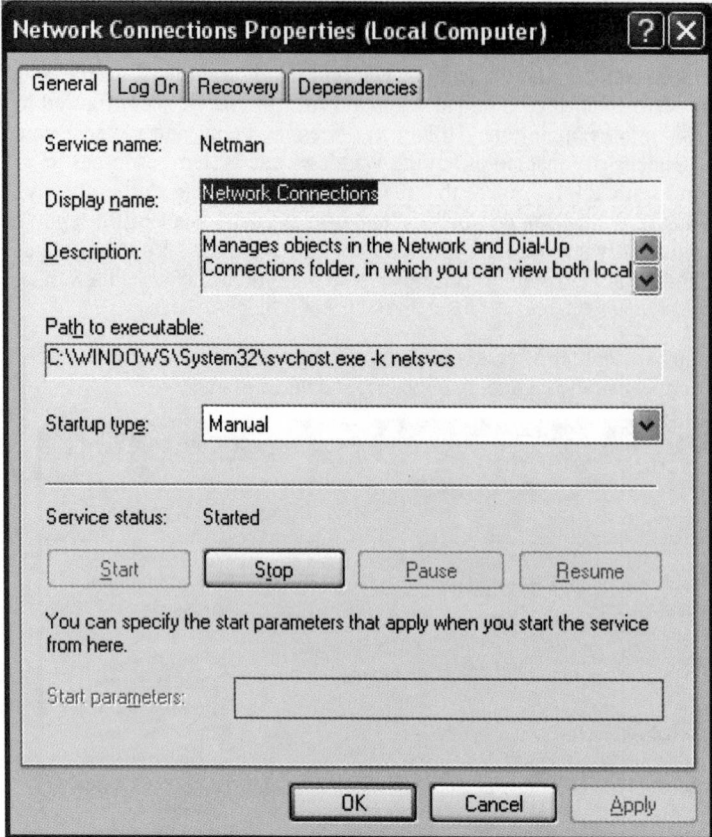

Figure 24-8: General tab

If a service fails, you can use the Recovery tab, shown in Figure 24-9, to specify how recovery should work. Use the drop-down menus to select any desired actions that should occur after each failure. The available actions are Take No Action, Restart the Service, Run a Program, and Restart the Computer.

The Dependencies tab, shown in Figure 24-10, is one you should pay careful attention to if you decide to stop a service. The tab shows you what other services this service depends on and what service depends on this service. For example, as you see in Figure 24-10, if you stop the Network Connections service the ICF and ICS services will not run. Before stopping a service, always check this tab so you will know the full impact of your actions and how stopping the service may halt other services.

Event Viewer

Windows XP gives you a few tools to troubleshoot optimization problems. The first is Event Viewer, and you can learn more about two other tools, Task Manager and Performance Monitor, in the following two sections.

Network Connections Properties (Local Computer)
General
Log On
Recovery
Dependencies
Select the computer's response if this service fails.
First failure:
Restart the Service
Second failure:
Restart the Service
Subsequent failures:
Restart the Computer
Reset fail count after:
0
days
Restart service after:
1
minutes
Run program
Program:
Browse...
Command line parameters:
Append fail count to end of command line (/fail=%1%)
Restart Computer Options...
OK
Cancel
Apply

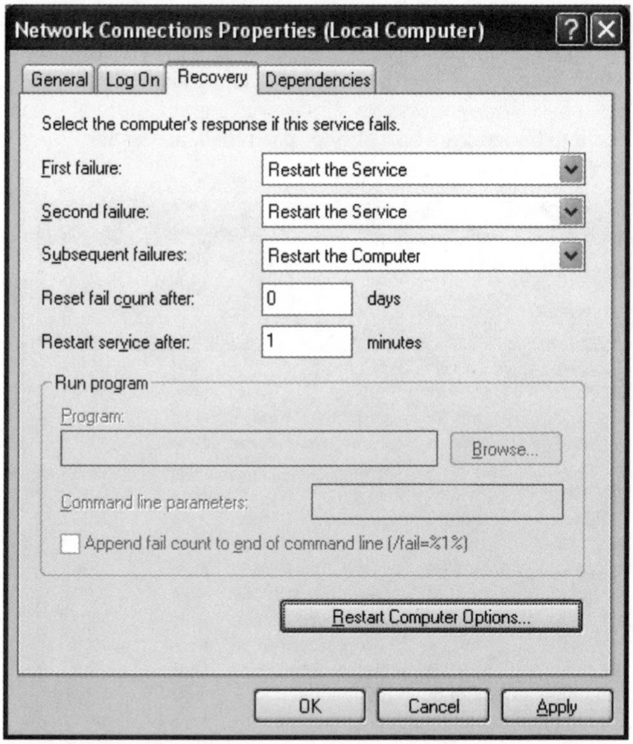

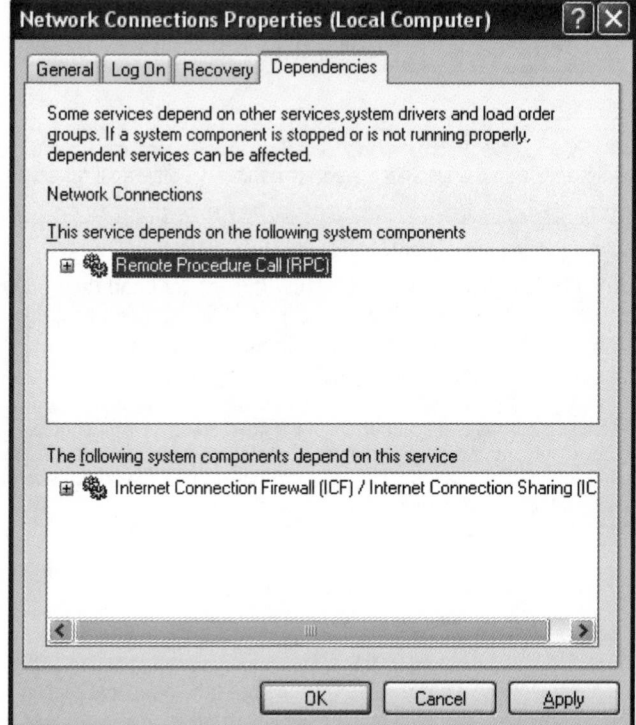

Figure 24-9: Recovery tab

Network Connections Properties (Local Computer)
General
Log On
Recovery
Dependencies
Some services depend on other services,system drivers and load order groups. If a system component is stopped or is not running properly, dependent services can be affected.
Network Connections
This service depends on the following system components
Remote Procedure Call (RPC)
The following system components depend on this service
Internet Connection Firewall (ICF) / Internet Connection Sharing (IC
OK
Cancel
Apply

Figure 24-10: Dependencies tab

Event Viewer enables you to view events that are written to various Windows XP log files, namely the Application, Security, and System logs. When application, security, or general system events error, they are written to these log files. The log files, which are viewable with Computer Management, typically provide error messages, information messages, and warning messages. If a service, application, or some other component of Windows XP does not seem to be working correctly or has failed, access the appropriate log and look for an event about that item, as shown in Figure 24-11.

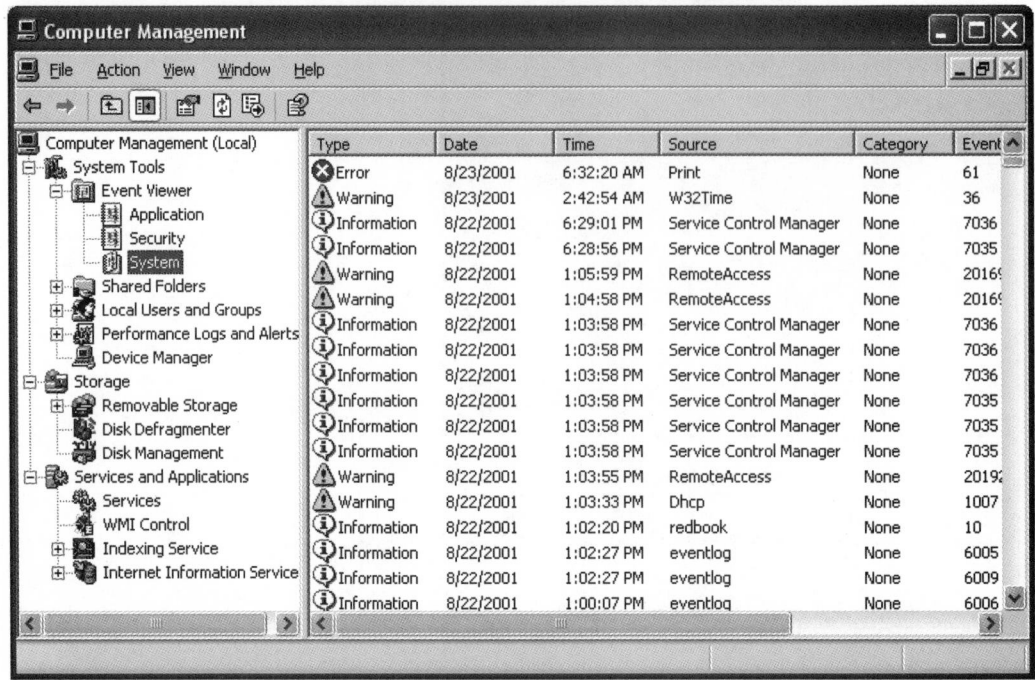

Figure 24-11: Event Viewer

> **TIP:** You can right-click the desired log in the Computer Management console and click Properties to manage the log. You can clear the existing events, determine how long events remain in the log, filter events, and change other related settings. These options are self-explanatory.

If you double-click an event, you can learn more about it. For example, in Figure 24-12, you see that a document has failed because of an error returned by the print processor. Using this event, I can then begin to troubleshoot the printer system and find what is causing the problem. Aside from error messages, the warning and information messages all have the same basic appearance and structure, but can give you valuable information about potential problems.

> **SECRET:** In some cases, you may also see an on-screen error message about a service not starting when it should. This is a good time to check the Event log for an explanation about why the service did not start. Often, some dependency may call on a service that must be manually started, hence the cause of the error message. When you see these "not starting" messages, always check Event Viewer first for clues about what has happened.

Task Manager

The Windows Task Manager, which is available by pressing Ctrl+Alt+Del, provides you with information about the applications that are running, network connections, processes, and general system performance. You can learn more about it in Chapter 25 and about the Networking tab specifically in Chapter 20. The two tab options that give you performance and optimization information are Processes and Performance.

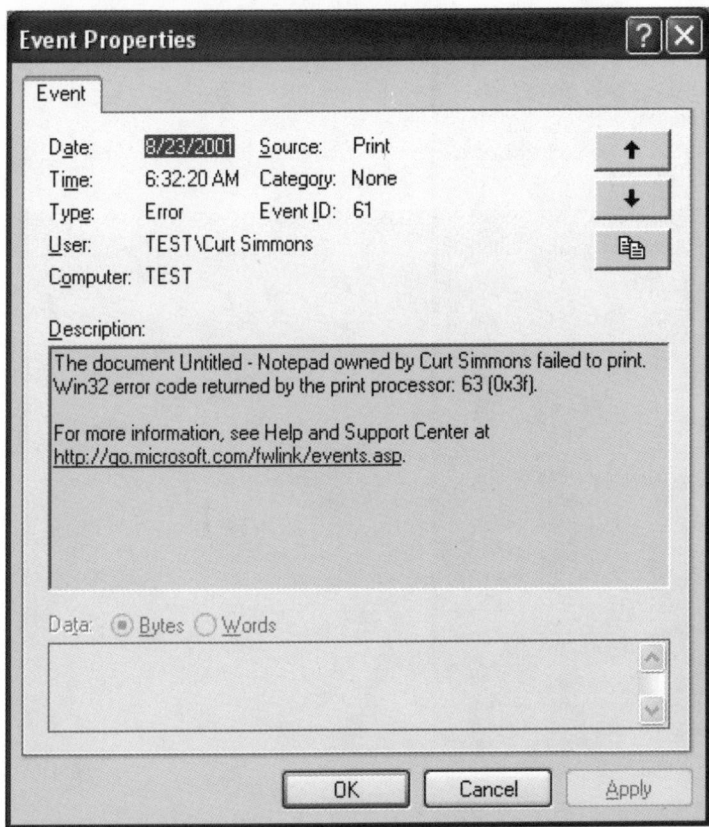

Figure 24-12: Event Properties

The Processes tab, shown in Figure 24-13, shows you all of the processes that are currently running on the system. You can see how much CPU usage and memory usage is occurring per process. If you are using Windows XP and it suddenly seems to slow down, the odds are good that some service or application is hogging a lot system resources. You can open this tab, locate the process, and click the End Process button to kill the process. This is a quick and painless way to get control of your operating system and stop processes that are not needed but are taking up resources.

SECRET: Have you ever tried to start an application and nothing happens? The odds are good that the application is somehow hung up in the system. Access the Processes tab, locate the application you tried to start, and use the End Process button to stop it. You can then try to start the application again as you normally would.

The Performance tab, shown in Figure 24-14, gives you simple graphic information about the percentage of the CPU cycles you're currently using. You also see the page file (PF) usage by the amount of megabytes currently being used. In the bottom of the window, you see divisions for Totals, Physical Memory, Commit Charge, and Kernel Memory. If you are experiencing performance problems, this tab gives you a quick place to view information about CPU and memory usage. Used in conjunction, the Processes and Performance tabs can often help you identify the problem and correct it.

SECRET: If you double-click a graph on the Performance tab, you get a larger image, as shown in Figure 24-15.

TIP: As you are looking at the graph, keep in mind that as a rule of thumb, spikes in CPU usage and memory usage are normal. Consistently high graph values usually indicate that something is taking up too many system resources. Your job at that point is to play detective and figure out what is causing that problem.

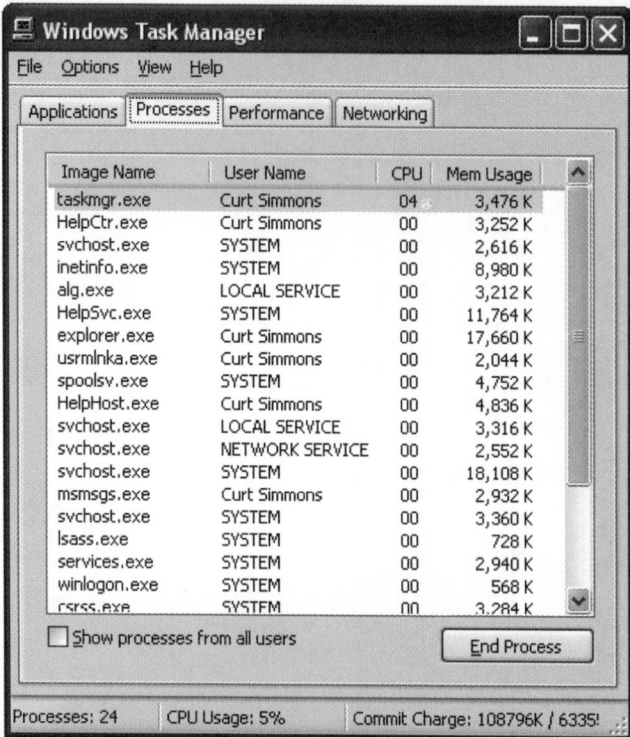

Figure 24-13: Processes tab of Windows Task Manager

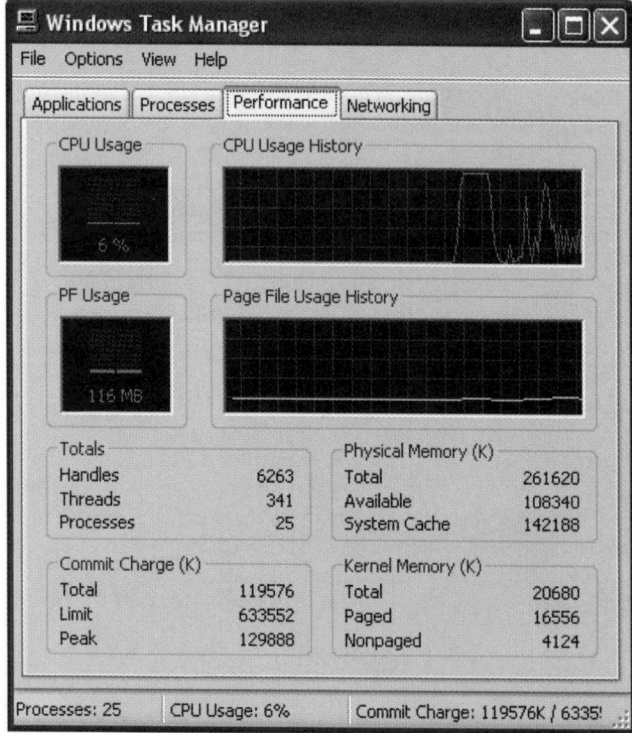

Figure 24-14: Performance tab

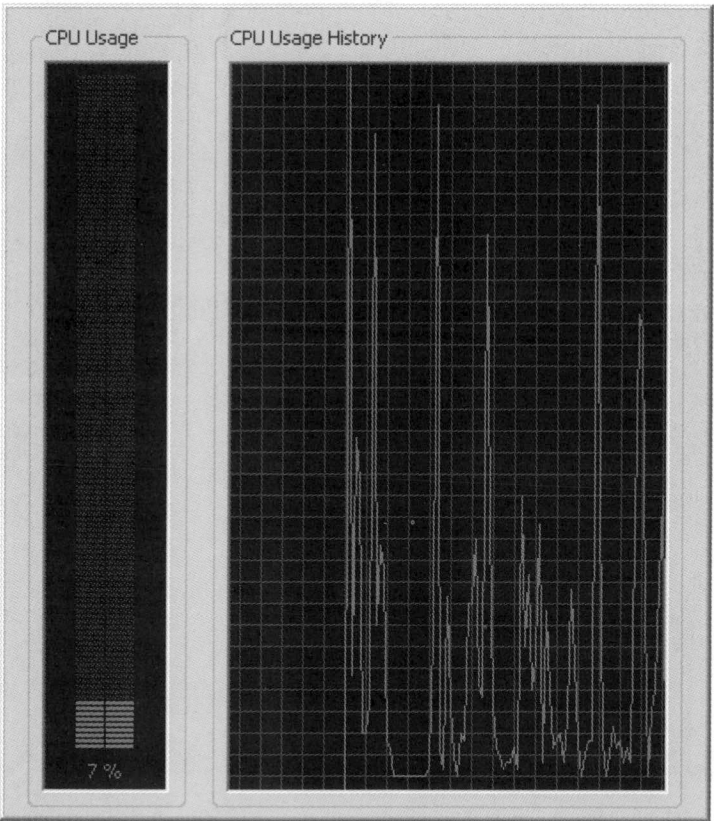

Figure 24-15: Large graph

Performance Monitor

Performance Monitor is a graphical analysis tool that enables you to monitor the real-time performance of various system processes. Performance Monitor has been around since the days of Windows NT, and it remains a vital tool that can help you isolate and solve performance problems. With Performance Monitor, you can chart various counters and see if the various system components are performing as they should. You can see how the processor is handling the system load, how well RAM is performing, how well network objects are performing, and much more. Before getting into the details of Performance Monitor's use, I'll want to give you a brief overview of the Performance Monitor interface, shown in Figure 24-16. If you have never used Performance Monitor, it is important that you spend some time using it so you can learn how it works. The interface is easy and with just a little practice, you'll have it down in no time. Performance Monitor is available in the Administrative Tools folder in Control Panel.

Performance Monitor works by creating charts, graphs, or reports for counters that you select. A *counter* is a particular Windows XP component or service that can be monitored. By adding counters to the console, you can view information about the performance of that particular component or service.

The Performance Monitor interface is a basic MMC interface with Performance Monitor functioning as a snap-in. (For more on the MMC see Chapter 7.) The left console pane contains the System Monitor node and the Performance Logs and Alerts node. However, you primarily interact with Performance Monitor by using the right console pane. This pane has three basic divisions, starting at the top, which are:

◆ **Toolbar** — The toolbar contains icons you use regularly to generate the types of charts and information that you want. The toolbar contains the following button options, seen from left to right: New Counter Set, Clear Display, View Current Activity, View Log File Data, View Chart, View Histogram, View Report, Add Counter, Delete, Highlight, Copy Properties, Paste Counter List, Properties, Freeze Display, Update Data, Help. You use the toolbar to manage Performance Monitor as needed.

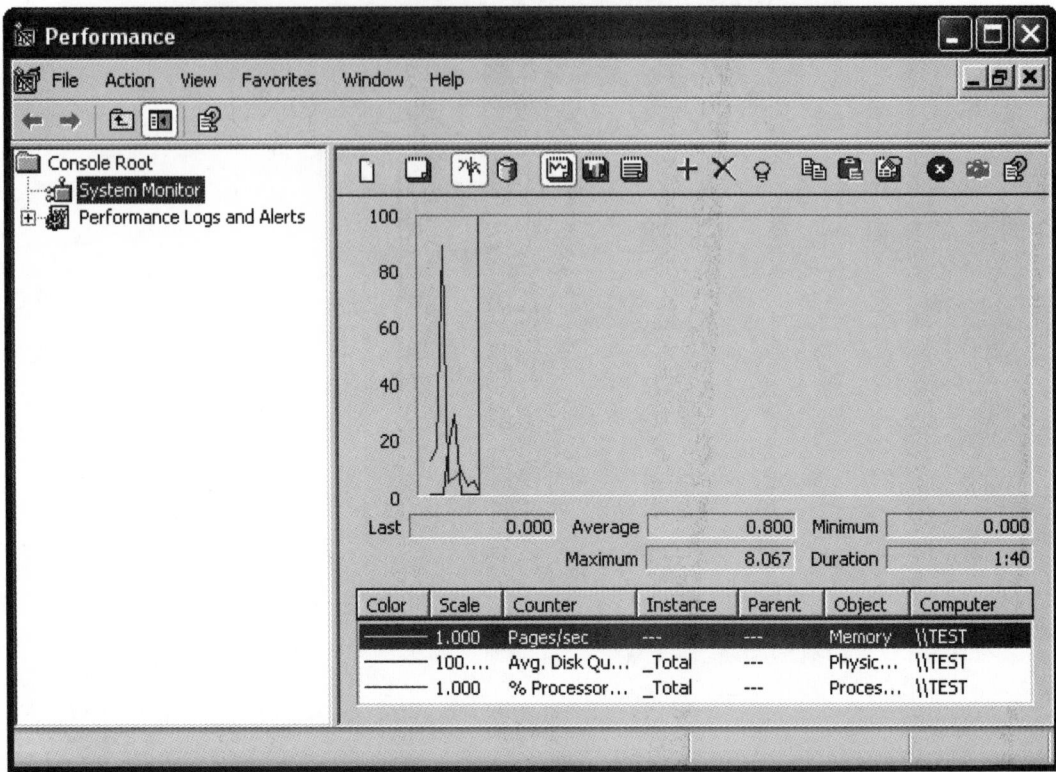

Figure 24-16: Performance Monitor

- ◆ **Information area** — The Information area contains the chart, histogram, or report that you want to view. Just click the desired button on the toolbar to view counter information in the desired format.

- ◆ **Counter list** — The bottom portion of the window contains a Counter list. All of the counters displayed in this list are currently being reported in the Information area. You can easily remove or add counters to the list using the toolbar. Each counter in the Counter list is given a different color for charting and histogram purposes.

The primary functionality of Performance Monitor is through counters. Without counters, there is no way to break down performance information to view various components and services. As you might guess, there are a number of different counters under many different Performance objects. The counters define the object itself. For example, the Processor object contains several counters such as % Processor Time, % Interrupt Time, Interrupts/sec, and a number of others.

You can use Performance Monitor to gain valuable data so that you can make decisions about performance and optimization in your environment. You can monitor activity for a period of time, then save the data to a log file. You can even set up logs and alerts so that data is gathered on a periodic basis automatically, and you are alerted if certain values fall below a baseline that you determine.

Your first action is to determine the manner in which you want to view information — either in chart, histogram, or report view. The type of counters you choose to view may also impact your choice, but once you make the decision, you can add the desired counters to the chart, histogram, or log. Managing counters is rather easy, and the following steps show you how.

STEPS

Creating a chart

1. Open Control Panel ⇨ Administrative Tools ⇨ Performance Monitor.

2. On the Performance Monitor toolbar, click the New Counter Set button, and then select the type of view you want (chart, histogram, or report). In this example, I am creating a chart.

3. Click the New Counter button. The Add Counters window appears, shown in Figure 24-17.

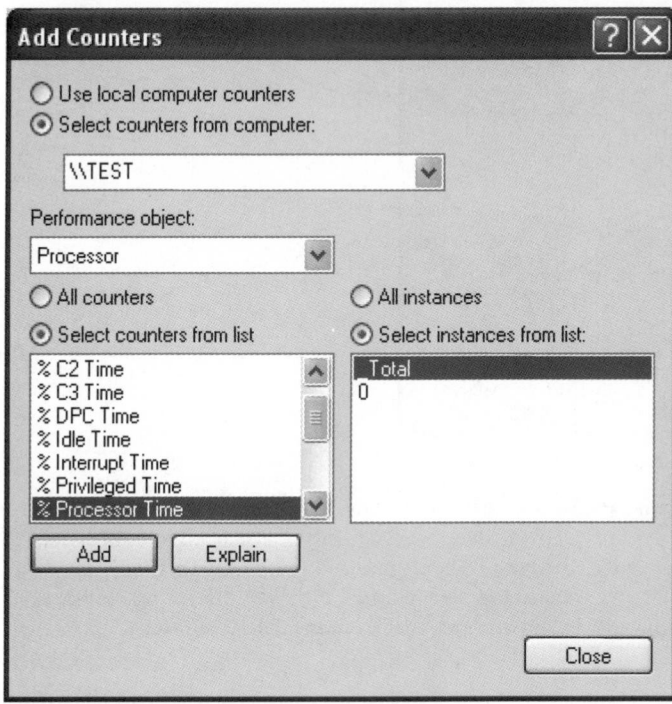

Figure 24-17: Counter list in Add Counters window

4. Click the Performance object drop-down menu and select the desired performance object, such as Processor, Memory, Paging File, and so on.

5. Select the desired counters by clicking the counter and clicking the Add button. If you want an explanation of the counter, just select it and click the Explain button. Also, notice that you can click the All Counters radio button to select all counters. For some counters, you can select an instance from the list that appears in the right dialog box. For example, as you can see in Figure 24-18, I have selected Network Interface with the Bytes Total/sec option selected. In the instances window, I can select to monitor the TCP Lookback interface or my network card.

6. The counters you selected are now added to the window and are charted (or reported, depending on your selection). You can change charting or reporting views at any time, and you can remove counters from the console by selecting the counter and clicking the Delete button.

7. If you want to save the data you are currently charting, you can right-click the chart and save it as an HTML file.

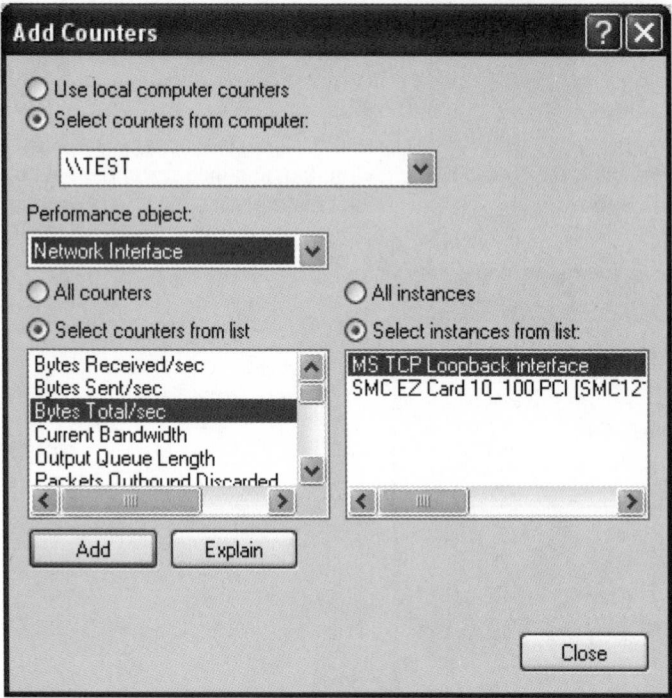

Figure 24-18: Instance options in the Add Counters window

Aside from the live collection of data, you can also set up a counter log so that desired counters are recorded and logged at the intervals you specify. This feature is very handy if you need to collect data over a period of time but do not manually wish to do so. To configure counter logs, you simply create a new counter log and add the counters that you want to log, then configure the additional log elements. Configuration is rather easy and self-explanatory, and you can check out the following steps.

STEPS

Configuring performance logs

1. Open Performance Monitor in the Administrative Tools folder.

2. In the left console pane, expand Performance Logs and Alerts. Right-click Counter Logs and choose New Log Settings. Enter a name in the dialog box that appears and click OK.

3. The Log File Settings window appears with three tabs. On the General tab, shown in Figure 24-19, you see the log name and the location where it will be stored (C:\PerfLogs by default). Click the Add button to add the desired objects and counters that the log will record.

4. Click the Log Files tab, shown in Figure 24-20. You can make changes on this tab to the manner in which the log file is saved and its maximum size. The setting options here are self-explanatory.

5. Click the Schedule tab. Use this tab to determine when logging should start and stop. The settings on this tab are self-explanatory. Click OK to save your changes.

Performance Monitor also provides a performance alert feature you can use to configure a counter to be monitored and a baseline of performance. Then, if the performance measured by that counter falls below that configured baseline, a certain action or actions can be carried. Performance Monitor supports the actions of logging an event to the Application Event log, sending a network message, starting a performance data log, or running a program for Performance alerts.

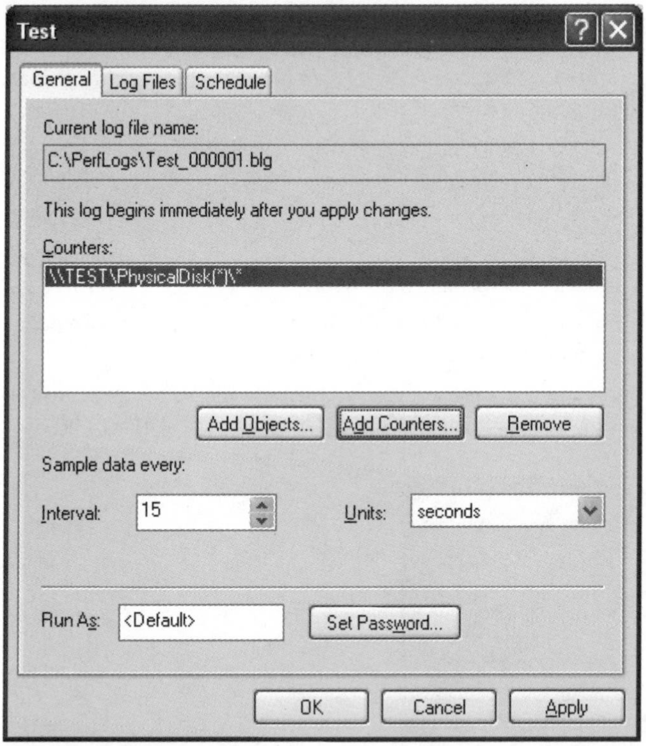

Figure 24-19: Log file settings

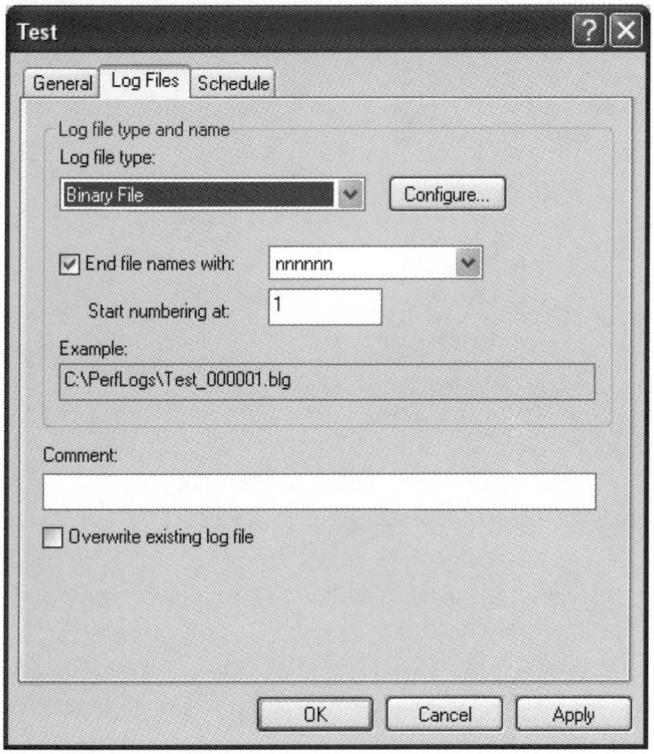

Figure 24-20: Log Files tab

You should configure alerts only for items that are very important. With too many alerts, you may end up with too much information that is difficult to sort through. So, determine what counters and baselines for which you absolutely want some action performed when baseline levels are not met; then configure those alerts accordingly.

STEPS

Configuring alerts

1. Open the Administrative Tools folder and start Performance Monitor.

2. In the left console pane, expand Performance Logs and Alerts. Right-click Alerts and choose New Alert Settings. Enter a name in the dialog box that appears and click OK.

3. On the General tab, use the Add button to add a desired counter(s); then use the Value and Limit dialog boxes to create a baseline. When performance falls below the baseline, the alert will be triggered, as shown in Figure 24-21.

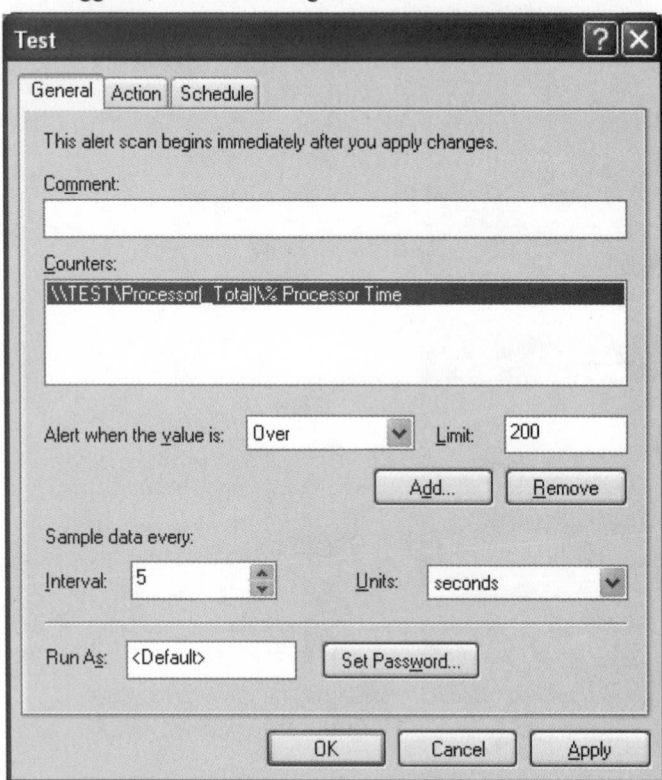

Figure 24-21: Alert General tab

4. Click the Action tab, shown in Figure 24-22. Select the desired action(s) and configure the necessary options.

5. Click the Schedule tab. Configure the options to start and stop the scan at the desired times. Click OK to save the alert.

Overall, Performance Monitor is an easy tool to use, and it is a great way to see if your current settings and optimization tactics are really paying off. As you use Performance Monitor, you'll see that many different options are available to you.

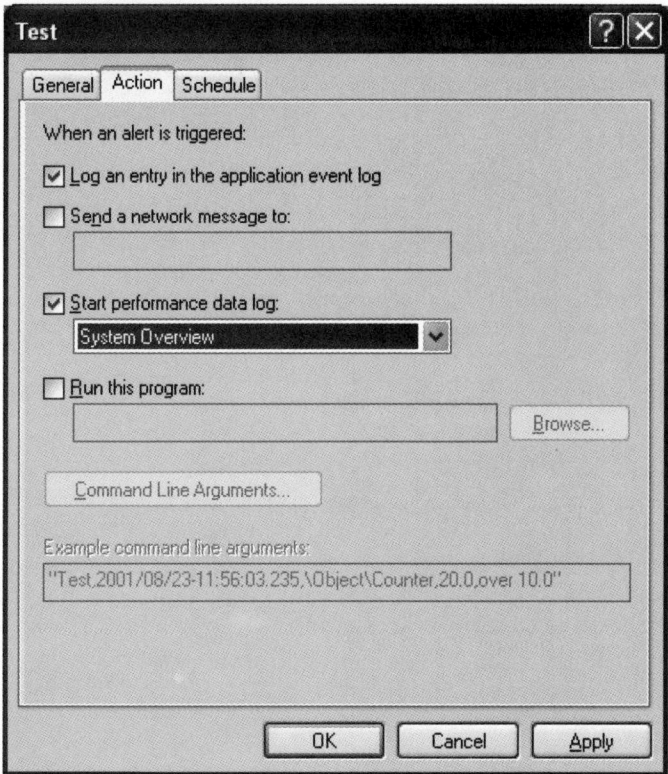

Figure 24-22: Action tab

What counters and objects you need to use are, of course, a matter of personal need, but I'll give you a few of my favorites:

- ◆ **Memory** — the Memory object gives you a number of different counters that can tell you how well your computer's memory is handling the load placed on it. This is a good one to watch to see if your system's memory is providing what you really need.

- ◆ **Paging File** — Along with Memory, check out the Paging File object counters to see how well the paging file is being utilized (or overutilized).

- ◆ **PhysicalDisk** — the PhysicalDisk object gives you a number of counters so that you can view the usage of the computer's physical disk. High readings often tell you there are read/write problems.

- ◆ **Processor** — Use the Processor object counters to see how well your computer's processor is handling the workload placed on it.

Summary

In this chapter, you explored the tools and features of Windows XP that enable you to optimize system performance and resolve performance problems:

- ◆ Use the System Properties Advanced tab to manage virtual memory, interface graphics usage, environment variables, and related performance issues.

- ◆ Use Computer Management to manage system services and view events recorded in the Event Log.

- ◆ Task Manager is a handy tool that you can use to view basic performance data and end processes.

- ◆ Use Performance Monitor to identify areas of performance problems that can be resolved.

Chapter 25

Troubleshooting Tools in

Windows XP

In This Chapter

In the days of Windows 95/NT/98, Microsoft began to realize that users needed and wanted computers that at least attempted to take care of themselves. In other words, users needed and wanted systems that were aware of problems, could identify them, and could solve them — rather than giving some cryptic message or a simple "blue screen of death." Although Windows XP hasn't arrived at that goal of effortless computing, it does move closer to the goal. If you have used Windows Me, there are no differences in the troubleshooting tools and features in Windows XP — this is one area where Microsoft did not make any new improvements this time around. The good news is that you are much less likely to have problems in the first place, which of course, is always the best solution. In this chapter, you learn about the following tools and features to help you troubleshoot your system . . .

- ◆ System Restore
- ◆ Recovery Console
- ◆ Safe mode
- ◆ Automated System Recovery (ASR)
- ◆ Device Driver Rollback
- ◆ Task Manager
- ◆ MSCONFIG
- ◆ MSINFO32

System Restore

Perhaps the best new feature presented in Windows Me was System Restore. It continues to live in Windows XP and rightly so. I have used System Restore on several different test machines that I have broken both on purpose and accidentally, and it has not failed me yet. If you are new to System Restore, I'll give you a little information about how it works before walking you through the System Restore tasks you can perform.

System Restore is a Windows XP feature that creates "restore points" automatically on your computer, recording system configuration information. The restore point is a snapshot of how your computer looks and how it is configured. If you run into problems with Windows XP that you cannot seem to solve, you can simply roll your computer back to an earlier date — a *restore point* — and Windows XP reconfigures the computer like it was at that time, essentially reversing your problem and putting you back to where you need to be.

Consider my personal example: I installed a program from the Internet on Windows XP that was questionable at best. Although the program installed, it continued to crash and consume system resources. In the meantime, it seemed that some of my other programs started acting strange, as well. Sure, I could have manually troubleshot the problem and tried to resolve it, but I know that application at least carried a lot of blame for my difficulties. So, I simply used System Restore to return the computer to previous day's configuration. This took only a few minutes and immediately solved my problem — without any effort on my part.

Or consider another example. You update some drivers on your computer, and now the computer does not boot correctly. No problem; you can boot into safe mode (covered later in this chapter) and access System Restore to resolve the problem.

As you can see, System Restore takes you out of the driver's seat and enables the operating system to automatically repair configuration problems. As a general rule, you want to be in XP's driver's seat, but this is one circumstance in which letting the operating system fix itself is a great time and stress saver.

You should keep the following points in mind about System Restore:

♦ Restore points are created daily by the system, or when a major configuration change occurs, such as new hardware or driver installation. You can, however, create your own restore points, which I cover later in this chapter.

♦ System Restore does not affect your personal files and data files. E-mail, documents, history, passwords, and basically all other personal files are unaffected. In fact, everything in My Documents is unaffected. During a System Restore, Windows XP does not affect any common file formats that are used with user documents, such as .doc or .xls.

SECRET: If you need to run System Restore and you are unsure what effect the restore process will have on a file or folder, just drag it to My Documents. Nothing stored in My Documents is affected by System Restore.

♦ Applications that you have installed since the last restore point was created may, and probably will, be removed during the restore process. For example, if a restore point was created yesterday at noon and you install a new application this morning, System Restore will probably remove the application so that your computer and applications are configured in the same manner they were yesterday at noon. This feature helps you get rid of offending applications.

SECRET: Although System Restore may remove the program from your system, it may not remove all files associated with that program. You should use Add/Remove Programs in Control Panel to fully remove the program from your computer.

♦ Even if an application is removed in the restore process, no documents or files that you have already created with the application will be removed. You simply need to reinstall the application once restoration is complete so that you can use the files again.

♦ By default, System Restore keeps restore points for about one to three weeks. The more activity there is on your system, the more restore points are made and the less time System Restore will keep restore points. The amount of disk space you have allocated for System Restore also affects this setting, and I show you how to adjust it later in the chapter.

♦ The actual number of restore points varies. For example, if you do not use your computer for one day, there may be no automatic restore points generated for that day. If you use your computer a lot in one day, there may be several restore points. Typically, there is at least one per day; this setting varies according to your computer usage. The more your system changes or is reconfigured, the more restore points System Restore creates.

♦ Suppose you run a restoration, and it does not fix the problem or you find that you need to use an earlier restore point. No problem; restorations are completely reversible. If a restoration fails, you are automatically returned to the settings your operating system was using before you ran the restore.

♦ Encrypted files are never restored to a decrypted state. This ensures that that running System Restore does not present a security breach.

♦ System Restore does not restore the contents of redirected folders or any settings with roaming user profiles.

Types of restore points

Several different types of restore points are created during certain circumstances or when certain Windows XP utilities run. The following list describes each of them:

♦ **Initial system checkpoints** — When you first upgrade to Windows XP or start a new computer with Windows XP the first time, an initial system checkpoint is created. In the event that a restoration is needed, the system can be returned to its first boot state. However, any documents created in the meantime are not affected by this kind of restore.

♦ **System checkpoints** — These are the typical type of restore points. They are system snapshots taken, under typical circumstances, at least every 24 hours. If your computer is turned off for more than 24 hours, a restore point is created when you boot the computer.

♦ **Program name installation restore points** — If a program is installed using the Windows XP Professional installer or InstallShield, a restore point is created. These restore points enable you to return the system to a state just before you installed the program should the program give you problems.

♦ **Automatic update restore points** — If you are using automatic updates, System Restore creates a restore point before installing any downloaded updates. If problems occur due to the update installation, you can simply take your computer back to the time before the installation occurred.

> **TIP:** An automatic update restore point is created only when you start the installation process of the updates — not when they are downloaded.

♦ **Unsigned device driver restore points** — If System Restore detects that you are installing an unsigned driver, a restore point is created. If the unsigned driver then gives you problems, you can simply roll back to the restore point created just before you installed the driver.

♦ **Backup utility recovery restore points** — If you start to perform a backup recovery of data, a restore point is created before the backup process begins. If you have problems after the backup recovery is run, you can use System Restore to correct the problem.

Configuring System Restore

Before you can use System Restore, it has to be configured to work on your computer and to monitor the desired disks that you want System Restore available on. Depending on your computer, System Restore may already be enabled and configured, but you can adjust that configuration to meet your needs. To configure System Restore settings, just follow these steps.

STEPS

Configuring System Restore

1. Right-click My Computer and choose Properties, and then click the System Restore tab.

2. On the System Restore tab, if System Restore is not available, you can enable it with the provided check box, as shown in Figure 25-1. Notice that you can monitor one or more drives on your computer. As you can see in Figure 25-1, I am monitoring drives C, G, and F. If you want to make changes to a drive, select drive in the dialog box and click the Settings button.

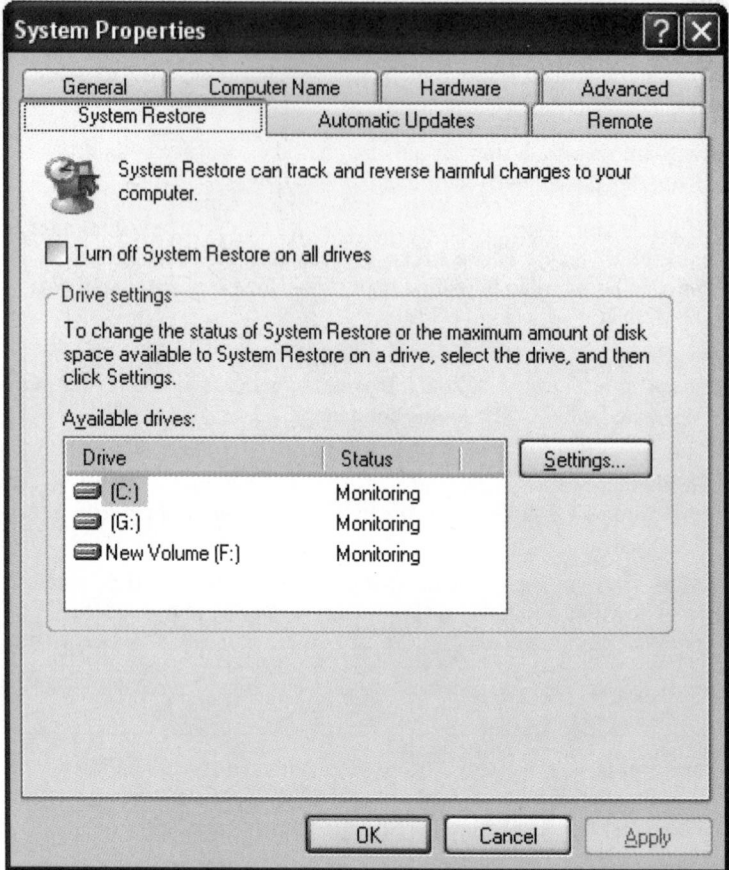

Figure 25-1: System Restore tab

3. The Settings window, shown in Figure 25-2, is set to use 12 percent of the disk's space for System Restore. The actual megabyte amount reserved is shown on the tab under the slider bar. If you do not want to use this much space, simply move the slider bar down to a desired level. If you want to turn off System Restore so that it is not used on this drive, click the check box option.

> **SECRET:** You cannot turn off System Restore on your %systemroot% drive (such as C:) without turning off System Restore on the main tab. In other words, you can turn off monitoring on all drives except your C: drive using the Settings dialog box. If you want to stop using System Restore altogether, you have to disable it on the System Restore tab.

4. Click OK when you finish.

Running System Restore

In the event that you need to run System Restore, you can do so from a booted operating system or within safe mode. If you boot using safe mode, the Help and Support center automatically opens and provides you with the ability to run System Restore. If you can boot and are booted, you can simply access the System Restore tool from Start ⇨ All Programs ⇨ Accessories ⇨ System Tools ⇨ System Restore.

> **TIP:** If the computer is bootable, just run System Restore in normal mode: there is no advantage to using safe mode with System Restore if you can boot normally.

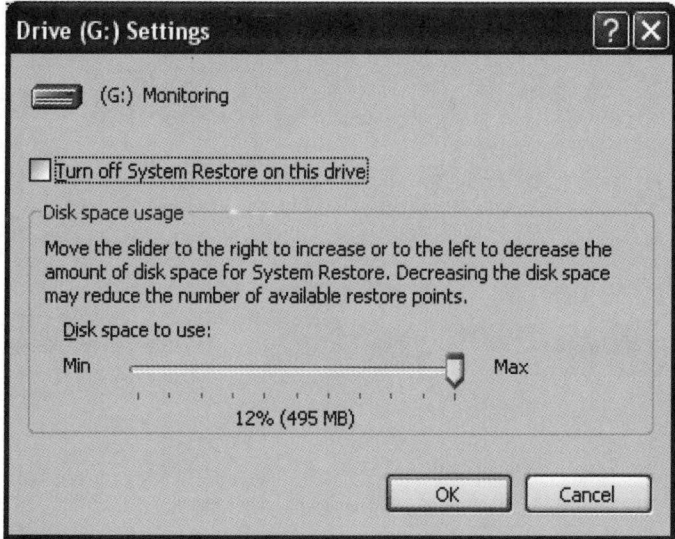

Figure 25-2: Drive Settings dialog box

The following steps walk you through the process of performing a System Restore.

STEPS

Performing a System Restore

1. Open System Restore found in your System Tools folder. If you are booted into safe mode, choose the Restore option presented to you.

2. The System Restore window appears. You have the option to restore your computer to an earlier time, create a restore point, or undo a restoration. Choose the Restore my computer to an earlier time radio button and click Next.

3. The Select a Restore Point window appears, shown in Figure 25-3. The calendar displays the days that have restore points in bold. Select a desired date, and then select a restore point in the provided dialog box. Click Next.

> **SECRET:** You'll notice that System Restore sometimes calls them checkpoints and sometimes restore points. Any difference in meaning between these two is ill defined, so whenever checkpoint and restore point are used, they are both referring to the same thing.

4. If System Restore detects the changes that will be made, a window appears listing those changes. Click OK.

5. A window appears listing the restore point you selected and instructing you to close all programs before clicking next. Follow these instructions and click Next.

6. The restore process takes place. Your computer reboots automatically once restoration is complete, and a message appears telling you that restoration has completed successfully. At this point, your computer should appear and respond as it did when the restore point was created.

Creating a restore point

As you have learned, System Restore automatically creates restore points every 24 hours (assuming the computer is turned on), and during times of major configuration changes. There may, however, be a time when you want to manually create a restore point.

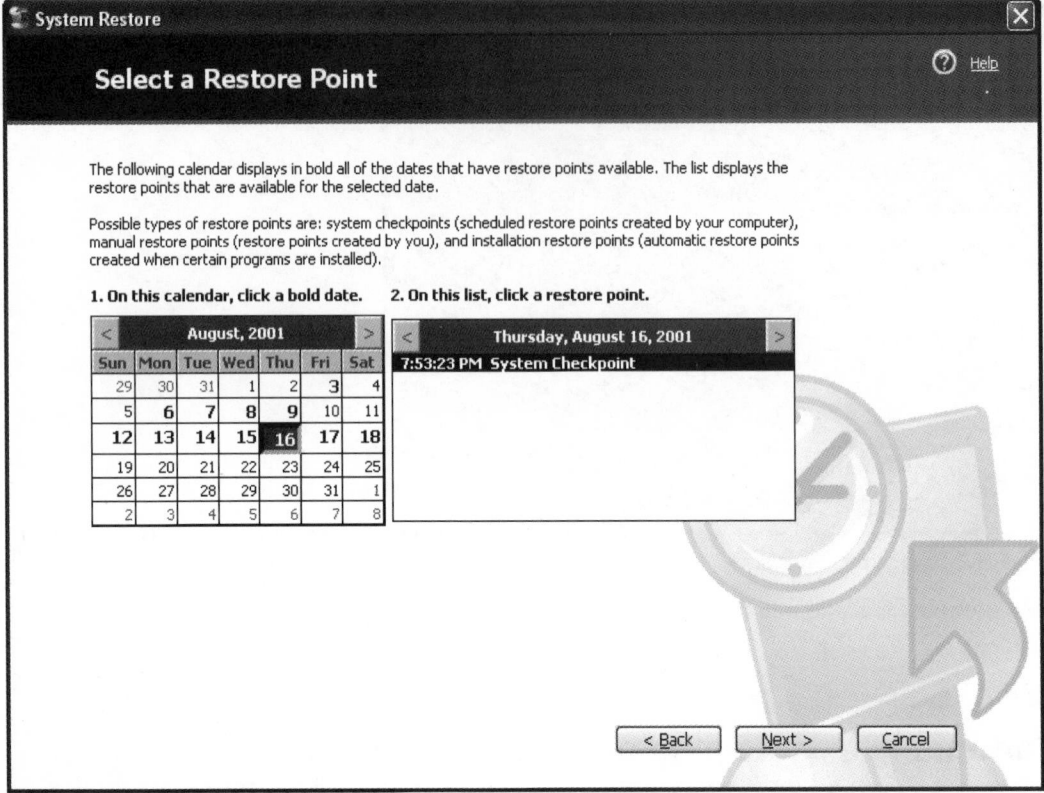

Figure 25-3: System Restore's restore point selection

Why? As an answer, consider this example. Suppose that your XP system creates a restore point at 6:30 a.m. You may then make a number of configuration changes to your system, such as the use of a new theme, desktop settings, and even some folder options changes. You want to make sure nothing happens to these new settings because once configured, you like what you see. However, you want to install an application that has been troublesome in the past. The only way you can be assured of not losing your new settings is to wait for a new restore point to be created, which could take until the next day.

For this reason, Windows XP gives you the ability to create your own restore points. This enables you to create the point at this moment in time and name the restore point so you can keep track of it. The following steps show you how to create a new restore point.

STEPS

Creating a restore point

1. Open System Restore. On the initial screen, choose the Create a restore point radio button and then click Next.

2. In the Create a Restore Point window, shown in Figure 25-4, enter a name for the restore point and click the Create button. The name, or description, should give you a reminder of why the restore point was created. The date and time of the created restore point appear automatically. After the restore point is created, click Close.

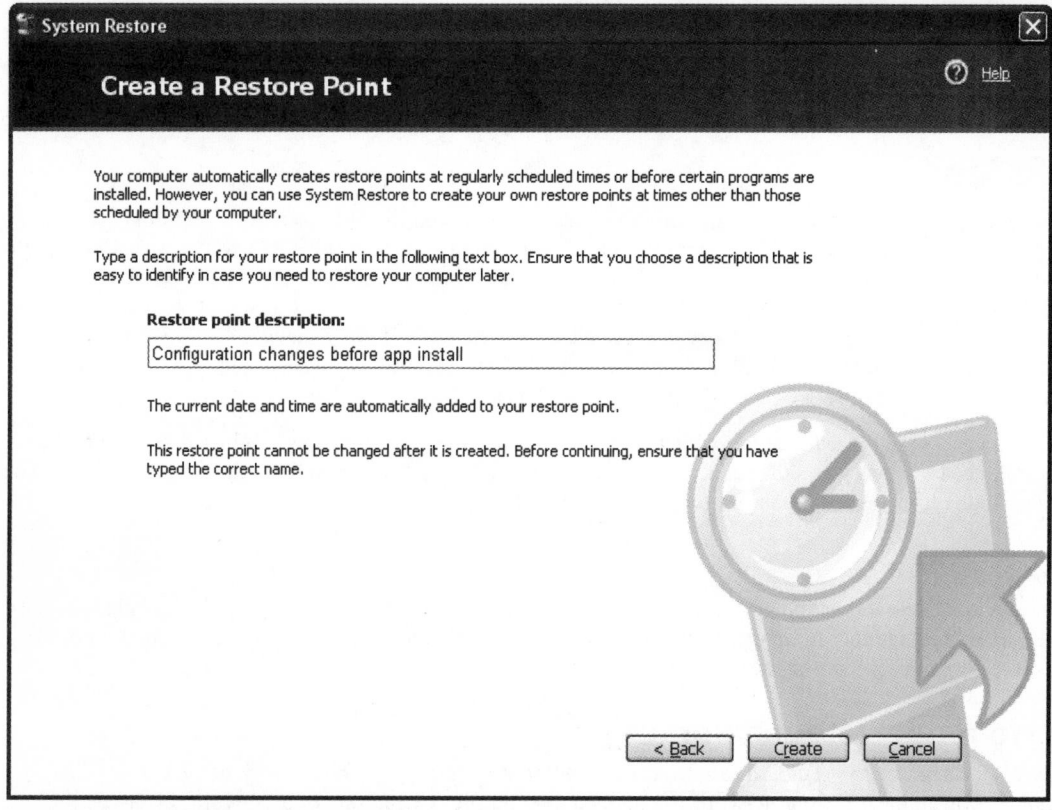

Figure 25-4: Create a Restore Point window

> **SECRET:** You cannot create any restore points while you are booted in safe mode. Because no restore points are created in safe mode, you cannot undo a restoration that was performed while in safe mode. In other words, use System Restore while in safe mode when you must, but no restore points are created, and you can't undo the restoration once it is complete.

Undoing a restoration

In some cases, a restoration doesn't complete as it should, or you realize that the restore point you selected was not the correct one. If you are not careful, you can end up in a "restoration land" where one restoration after another are placed on top of each other, which can lead to new configuration problems. If you realize that a restore point was incorrect or the restoration did not seem to complete properly, you should undo that restoration before trying another restore point, because should a restoration fail, any configuration changes made during that restoration attempt remain on your computer. Then, the next restoration attempts to return the computer a previous time and remove changes made by the previously failed restoration. Although you can recover from all of this, multiple failures tend to create more problems, so undoing a failed restoration is always your best step.

Fortunately, undoing a restoration is automated and simple. Just follow these steps.

STEPS

Undoing a restoration

1. Open System Restore. On the initial screen, choose the Undo my last restoration radio button, and then click Next.

2. A dialog box appears, showing what configuration changes will be undone. Click OK.

3. A window appears telling you to close all applications. Close any open applications and click Next.

4. The restoration is undone, and the computer automatically reboots.

Safe Mode

Safe mode, which has been around since Windows 95, gives you the ability to boot Windows XP with a minimal number of drivers and services. Often, if you cannot start Windows XP, you can boot using safe mode so that your computer can be started. Safe mode in Windows XP provides you with the same options that are found in Windows 2000's safe mode. You have a number of different startup options that can help you resolve problems and even access data on a network if necessary. Like most computer users, I have used safe mode on a number of occasions and it has the ability to get you out of a number of jams, so it is important that understand all that safe mode has to offer.

You can access the Startup menu, which contains your safe mode options, by holding down the F8 key on your keyboard when your computer starts. You will see the variations of safe mode available to you. The following sections discuss your options.

Safe mode

The standard safe mode option is what you should use most of the time. This option boots Windows XP with a minimal number of drivers required to start your computer. Once XP boots, you can attempt to resolve system problems or use System Restore.

Safe mode with networking

This is the same as the standard safe mode option, but it adds support for network connections. This enables you connect to your network if you need to copy files or call on other network resources.

Safe mode with command prompt

This option boots Windows XP to a command prompt only. You will not have access to the GUI, but you can use command-line utilities to attempt solve problems. See "Recovery Console" later in this chapter to learn more about the command-line utilities available.

Enabling boot logging

The boot logging option performs a normal Windows XP startup, keeping a log of all of the drivers and services loaded during the boot process (including details about those having problems). If Windows XP does not start normally, it will probably not start when you use this option, but hopefully you can view the information during boot and discover what is causing the problem. You then need to start Windows XP in safe mode and attempt to resolve the problem.

Enabling VGA mode

If you just upgraded your video driver and Windows XP no longer starts, the problem may be the new driver. This command starts a full Windows XP startup using a basic VGA driver, the same basic driver that is used when you boot in safe mode. If Windows XP starts, you should reinstall your previous driver.

Last Known Good Configuration

The Last Known Good Configuration is good to use if you experience problems during hardware installation. Windows XP keeps a backup copy in the Registry of the Last Known Good Configuration. If you get into trouble, you can try booting into Last Known Good to see if Windows XP can resolve the problem by using the backup Registry copy. Since the backup is made when you last shut down the computer, any changes that you have made since your previous startup are lost when you use Last Known Good.

> **TIP:** Last Known Good does not repair or replace drivers.

Debugging mode

The Debugging mode option sends debug information to another computer through a serial cable connection. Under most circumstances, debugging mode is not used unless you need to dump the debug information to another computer so that it can be sent to technical support for review. Beyond that, this mode is not very helpful to you.

> **NOTE:** You may see other startup options, especially if the Recovery Console has been installed or if you have Remote Installation Services (XP Professional only) installed.

Recovery Console

The Recovery Console is a powerful command-line tool that enables you to essentially operate on Windows XP when it will not start. The Recovery Console has a lot of power, so be careful with it. You can even format your C: drive with the Recovery Console, so be forewarned.

With this power come a lot of commands that you can use to fix problems on your system. See Chapter 2 for Recovery Console installation instructions. Once the Recovery Console is installed, it appears as a Startup menu option when you hold down the F8 key.

As I mentioned, the Recovery Console has a number of available tools. The following sections highlight those tools. You might consider booting into Recovery Console and getting used to the command-line interface, in the event that you need to use it someday.

> **TIP:** You cannot copy files from folders to a floppy disk using the Recovery Console. This is why a solid backup plan is so important in order to make sure you do not lose files. See Chapter 3 to learn more about Windows XP Backup.

CHDIR (or CD) — Change Directory

This command changes the current folder to the one given in the command. The syntax is:

```
c:\cd {/d} [drive:][path]
```

The `{/d}` parameter changes to a different drive, which is specified in the `[drive:]` parameter. If you omit the `/d` parameter, the command changes to the specified folder on the current drive. You can substitute three special symbols for the `[path]` parameter:

```
cd..
```

will return you to the parent folder of your current folder (up one folder level), and

```
cd\
```

will take you to the root folder of the current drive. This will be your only means of navigating between folders if you are using the Recovery Console or command prompt.

```
cd..\
```

takes you to the another subfolder of the same level as the current folder, but still beneath the parent folder. For example, you can type `cd..\system` at the `c:\winnt\applog` folder prompt to change to the `c:\winnt\system` folder.

CHKDSK — Check Disk

CHKDSK is a troubleshooting tool that checks a disk for errors, optionally fixing errors if specified. The syntax and options for CHKDSK at the Recovery Console, shown in Table 25-1, are different than the parameters for the regular CHKDSK command used at the command prompt.

```
chkdsk drive: {options}
```

Table 25-1: Recovery Console CHKDSK Options

Option	Meaning
none	If there are no options given, the status of the current drive will be displayed.
/p	This performs an exhaustive check of the drive but does not make changes to it.
/r	This finds bad sectors on the drive and recovers information from them. Giving the /r command implies giving the /p command.

CLS — Clear Screen

This command clears the screen. As you type commands at the Recovery Console or the command prompt, the commands you type, along with their results, stay on the screen until they scroll off the top. This can make the display appear somewhat cluttered.

COPY

If you find a damaged or missing file — or if you just want to copy a file from one location to another — use the Copy command. The syntax is:

```
copy source  destination
```

Both *source* and *destination* can be any combination of drive letter, path, and/or filename. If the drive letter or path is omitted, the default is the current drive and folder. If the destination filename is omitted, the existing filename will be used at the destination. The source directory can be any directory within the system directories of the Windows installation, the root directory of any drive, local installation sources, the Cmdcons directory, or removable media. The destination drive can be the same locations as the source directory, except for removable media.

ERASE (or DEL or Delete)

This command deletes a specified file. The syntax is:

```
c:\del [drive:] [path] [filename]
```

If the drive and path are omitted, the current directory is used. Another DEL command that can be used at the command prompt has additional options. Those options do not apply at the Recovery Console. You will be able to use the DEL command only in the system directories of the current Windows installation, the root directory of any hard disk partition, the local installation sources, and removable media.

DIR — Directory

This command will show you the files and subfolders in a given directory. The syntax is:

```
c:\dir [drive:] [path] [filename]
```

Each line in a DIR command represents a single file. You see the date and time stamp, the size of the file, its short (MS-DOS) filename if necessary, and its long (Windows) filename. At the top of the display, you see the path name of the folder; at the bottom of the display, you see the size of the folder and the amount of free space on the drive. You also see the file attributes, if any, for a file. These attributes are shown in Table 25-2.

Table 25-2: File Attributes

Abbreviation	Attribute
a	A file ready for archiving
c	A compressed file
d	A directory
e	An encrypted file
h	A hidden file
p	A reparse point
r	A read-only file
s	A system file

The DIR parameters and switches are listed in Table 25-3.

Table 25-3: DIR Parameters and Switches

Parameter	Description
drive: path	The folder for which you want to see a directory listing. If you omit the drive letter, the current drive is displayed. If you omit the path name, the current folder is displayed.
filename	Returns information only for the file specified, rather than showing all the files in the folder. You can use wildcards for filenames.

You also can use wildcard characters in place of the *filename* specification. If you type the following command:

```
c:\dir f*.*
```

it will return all of the files in the current directory beginning with the letter *f*.

The DIR command can be especially useful if you are having problems starting your computer. Often startup problems happen because a crucial file gets erased or overwritten, although System File Protection is supposed to prevent this. You can either look for the file or check its attributes to see if it has somehow been changed. For instance, many of your system files should have a time stamp matching the date that the operating system was installed. If they all suddenly have today's date, you know something has happened.

DISABLE

This command can be used only at the Windows XP Recovery Console; it can't be used from the command prompt. If your computer isn't starting correctly because of a service or driver, you can disable the culprit using the following command:

```
disable [service] | [device driver]
```

where *[service]* is the specified service, and *[device driver]* is the specified driver that you want to disable or turn off.

When you disable a command, a message is displayed stating the startup type for the service. You need to remember this information if you are going to later use the ENABLE command to again enable the service.

ENABLE

The ENABLE command is the companion to the DISABLE command. It works only from the Windows XP Recovery Console, not from the command prompt. To start a specific service or driver, type the following command:

```
enable [service] | [device driver] {startup type}
```

There are five driver startup types. The first three are similar to the startup options you find in the Services Console in the Computer Management Console (see Chapter 7). These five types are as follows:

- ♦ SERVICE_AUTO_START — Same as Automatic
- ♦ SERVICE_DISABLED — Same as Disabled
- ♦ SERVICE_DEMAND_START — Same as Manual
- ♦ SERVICE_BOOT_START — Starts when the computer boots up
- ♦ SERVICE_SYSTEM_START — Starts when Windows XP boots up

EXIT

This command closes the Windows XP Recovery Console and restarts your computer. It is not available from the command prompt. (To close the command prompt, close its window.)

EXPAND

Sometimes a file gets corrupted or deleted. The EXPAND command is used to retrieve a driver from a cabinet (.cab) file, or from a compressed file on the Windows XP CD. The syntax of the command is

```
expand {options}source | source.cab /F:filename {destination}
```

The parameters and options for the EXPAND command are shown in Table 25-4.

Table 25-4: EXPAND Parameters and Switches

Parameter	Meaning
source	You specify this if your source file is a single file you need to extract from.
source.cab /F:filename	Use this if you need to extract from a cabinet file, using the filename to specify which file to extract. You can use wildcards for the filename.
destination	Shows where you want the extracted file to go.
{Options}	
/d	This lists only files that are stored in a cabinet, without extracting any.
/y	This option suppresses the warning when you are overwriting a file.

FIXBOOT

Normally, when your computer starts, it looks for a particular segment of one hard drive — often called the system drive — for its boot files. These files are generally stored in the boot sector. The FIXBOOT command either changes this to a different drive or, if there is no parameter, writes a new partition boot sector to the current drive. Type the following command:

```
fixboot [drive:]
```

where [drive:] is a specific drive letter. This command works only from the Windows Recovery Console.

FIXMBR — Fix Master Boot Record

This is another command that is available only from the Windows Recovery Console. It writes a new master boot record to the specified hard drive. Type the following command:

```
fixmbr [device]
```

where [device] is the name of the device — and not the drive letter — of the drive to which you want to write the new master boot record. You can use the MAP command to determine the device name of your drive, which may look something like \Device\HardDisk0. The MAP command is available only on Intel-based computers.

FORMAT

The FORMAT command prepares your disk to accept data. The FORMAT command available from the Windows Recovery Console has only a subset of the parameters available from FORMAT run from the command prompt. From the Recovery Console, the command syntax is

```
format drive: {/q} {/fs:filesystem}
```

The drive parameter indicates what drive to format. From the Recovery Console, you are not able to format a floppy disk. The optional /q does only a quick format and does not scan the drive for bad sectors, so you should use this switch only if you know this drive is good. With the /fs: switch, you indicate which file system to use when formatting, FAT, FAT32, or NTFS. If you omit this, the existing file format is used.

LISTSVC

This command, which has no optional parameters, shows what services and drivers are available on this computer. It can be used only from the Recovery Console.

LOGON

From the Windows Recovery Console, this command searches the network for any instances of Windows XP/2000/NT. It lists all that it finds, and it then asks you for the administrator password.

MAP

This maps — or shows the relationship — between drive letters and physical device names on your computer. You might need to run this utility to determine the device names before using the FIXBOOT, FIXMBR, or FDISK commands. The command syntax is as follows:

```
MAP {arc}
```

If you use the optional {arc} switch, MAP shows the Advanced RISC Computing device names. By default, it shows the Windows XP device names. This command is available only from the Windows Recovery Console.

MKDIR (or MD) — Make Directory

This command creates a new folder (directory). The syntax for this command is as follows:

```
mkdir {drive:} path
md {drive:} path
```

If you don't specify a drive on which to create a new folder, the new folder is created on the current drive. Path will be the location and name of the new folder.

If you type just the new folder name as the sole argument, as in the following example:

```
md newdir
```

a subfolder named *newdir* will be created in the current folder.

MORE

When you are at the Windows XP Recovery Console, you might want to view the contents of a text or log file. You can type the following command:

```
type filename.txt
```

If this file is large, it will quickly scroll off the top of the screen before you can read it. The MORE command allows you to see a screen load (approximately 24 lines) at a time. The syntax is as follows:

```
type | more filename
```

If you are using the MORE command on an NTFS drive, then any filename that has spaces must be enclosed in quotation marks. There is another MORE command that can be used at the command prompt that has a different set of options.

RMDIR (or RD) — Remove Directory

This command removes a folder (directory). The syntax is as follows:

```
rmdir {drive:path} directory
rd {drive:path} directory
```

If no drive or path is specified, the folder specified is deleted. This command can be used only on an empty directory. It also works only in the system directories of the Windows installation, on removable media, in the root directory of any hard disk partition, or on local installation sources. There is an alternative RMDIR that can be used at the command prompt.

RENAME (or REN)

This command renames a file, which can be handy when troubleshooting. You might want to replace a driver or a configuration file, while still keeping the original file available as a fallback. You can rename the original file using the following syntax:

```
Rename {drive:path} oldfilename newfilename
Ren {drive:path} oldfilename newfilename
```

If you do not specify a drive and path, the current folder is searched by default. You must place the newly named file in the same directory; you cannot specify a new location for it during the rename process.

SET

You can use the SET command to modify certain environment settings. It can be very useful to circumvent certain built-in limitations of some of the Recovery Console commands. From the Recovery Console, the syntax of the command is

```
set variable=string
```

The variables that can be set from the Recovery Console are shown in Table 25-5.

Table 25-5: Environment Variables at the Recovery Console

Environment Variable	Meaning
AllowWildCards	This lets you use wildcards with commands, such as DEL.
AllowAllPaths	This lets you access all files and directories on the system.
AllowRemovableMedia	This lets you copy files to removable media, such as CD-Rs, CD-RWs, Zip disks, and floppy disks.
NoCopyPrompt	This turns off the warning given before you overwrite a file.

SYSTEMROOT

This command is available only from the Windows Recovery Console. It makes the current folder the systemroot folder, which is the folder in which the Windows XP system files are located. Although this is normally the C: drive, you can switch it to another drive. You might want to change the systemroot folder if for some reason your Windows XP files get hopelessly mangled and you want to install a fresh copy on another drive or in another partition.

TYPE

Displays the specified file on your screen. The syntax is as follows:

```
type {drive:path} filename
```

If no drive or path name is specified, the current folder is used. The TYPE command is often combined with the MORE command, discussed earlier, to examine a long file on a screen-by-screen basis.

If you are having problems starting Windows XP, one troubleshooting step you can try is to boot into safe mode and then enable boot logging to track all the devices and services that are loaded — or that fail to load. Enabling logging will write the information to the ntbtlog.txt file in your Windows directory. If you can't boot into safe mode and land instead in safe mode command prompt mode , you can type the following commands at the command prompt:

```
c:\cd winnt
c:\type ntbtlog.txt |more
```

This displays a screen-by-screen view of the log file, which you then can examine for any errors in services or drivers to provide clues as to why Windows XP is not starting.

Automated System Recovery

Automated System Recovery (ASR) is available as a part of Windows XP Backup. It is a tool that creates startup disks so you can boot and recover Windows XP in the event that it will not start. Because ASR performs a data restoration from backup, note that ASR should be used only if you have tried all other recovery methods, such as safe mode. When you need to use ASR, you can start Windows XP and hold down the F2 key. You'll need the backup disk you created with the ASR Preparation wizard to recover the system.

CROSS-REFERENCE: See Chapter 1 for more information about creating an ASR disk.

Device Driver Rollback

It is not uncommon for bad device drivers to cause problems with devices and even the operating system. Because driver problems are so common, Windows XP includes a device driver rollback feature, which is found on the Driver tab of the device's properties in Device Manager, shown in Figure 25-5.

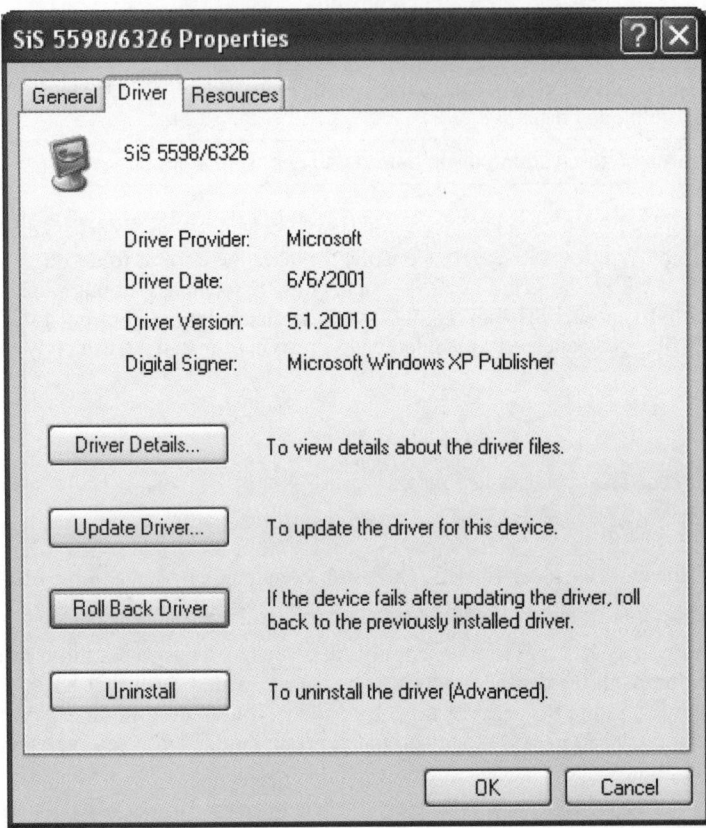

Figure 25-5: Device driver rollback

When you install an updated driver, Windows XP keeps a copy of the old driver so that a rollback to the previous driver can occur. Of course, you will have had to update a driver in order to roll back to the old one. If you are having problems with a new driver, simply click the Roll Back Driver button option and follow the instructions that appear.

Task Manager

Task Manager is certainly nothing new in Windows, and Windows XP includes Task Manager with a few new bells and whistles. You can access Task Manager by pressing Ctrl+Alt+Del on your keyboard, or you can right-click the taskbar and click Task Manager. You'll see four tabs. You can learn about the Performance tab in Chapter 24 and the Networking tab in Chapter 20. For application and process management, you can use the Applications and Processes tab.

On the Applications tab, you can see a list of applications that are currently running. If an application is not working, the status will read, "stopped." You can shut down an offending application by selecting it and choosing End Task. This is the easiest way to get an unruly program under control when you cannot shut it down using the conventional methods. You can also switch to a task by selecting the task in the window and choosing Switch to, and you can start a new task by clicking New Task and entering the application's name.

The Processes tab, shown in Figure 25-6, shows you the processes running on your computer, including system processes and applications. If your computer seems to be sluggish, access this tab and find the application or process that seems to be consuming most of your system resources. You can kill the process by selecting and clicking End Process.

TIP: You should not end any processes here unless absolutely necessary. Killing internal Windows XP processes may cause you even more problems and a reboot.

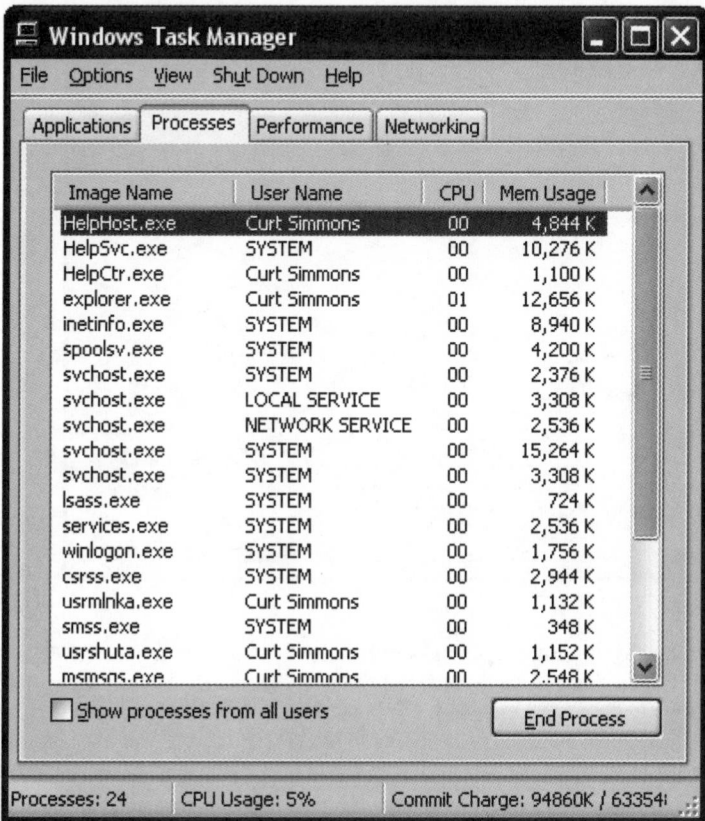

Figure 25-6: Processes tab on Windows Task Manager

MSCONFIG

The MSCONFIG utility, or System Configuration utility, is still around in Windows XP. Using System Configuration, you can manage a number of different system components, primarily startup functions. MSCONFIG is a great utility to use if you want to tweak system startup and the services that load on startup. The following steps show you the options available to you.

STEPS

Using MSCONFIG

1. To open MSCONFIG, choose Start ⇨ Run and type **MSCONFIG**. Click OK.

2. On the General tab of MSCONFIG, shown in Figure 25-7, you can choose a startup selection. By default, of course, Normal Startup is used. However, you can choose to launch a Diagnostic Startup in which basic drivers and services are loaded (basically the same as safe mode). You can also choose a Selective Startup option where you can make the startup configuration. For example, suppose you want to boot using no startup items or with a modified boot.ini file. You can make these choices here. Essentially, these options can help you troubleshoot startup.

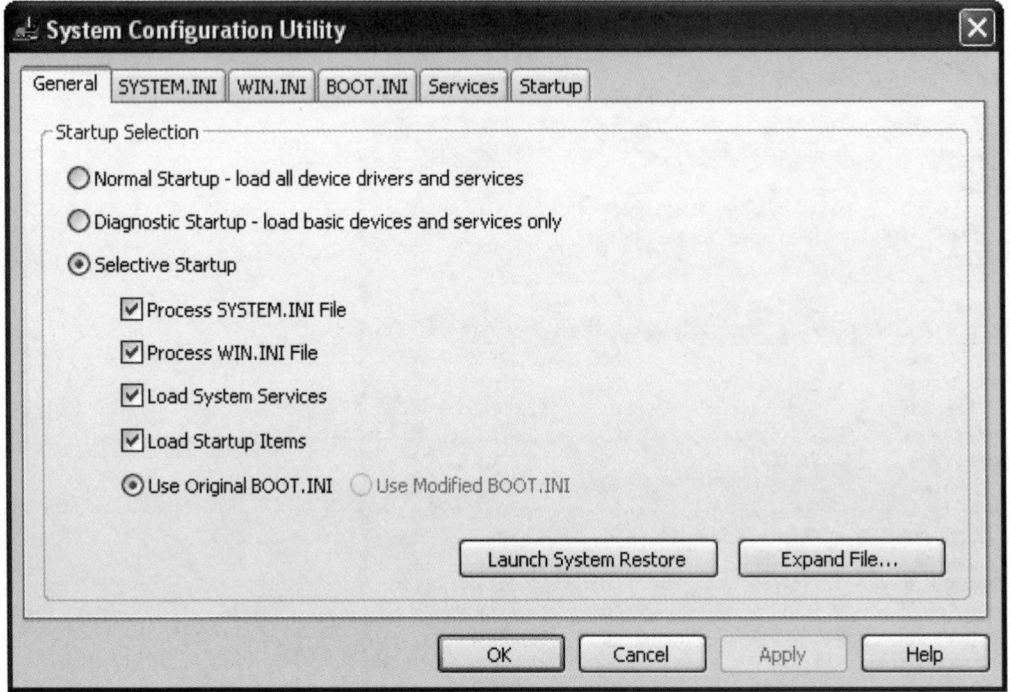

Figure 25-7: MSCONFIG General tab

3. On the System.ini and Win.ini tabs (System.ini is shown in Figure 25-8), you can use MSCONFIG to modify the contents of these files. You can adjust the order of the file, disable items, edit items, create new items, and make other file changes as needed. Obviously, you should have a specific plan in mind before making configuration changes here. You can also learn more about System.ini and Win.ini in the Windows help files.

4. On the Boot.ini tab, you see the contents of the Boot.ini file, shown in Figure 25-9. You can edit this file as needed, such as in a dual-boot scenario (see Chapter 2 for details). You can invoke some boot options. You can also Check All Boot Paths and even access a few advanced options that enable you to manage memory usage and debugging. If you need to work with Boot.ini and startup options, definitely take a look at this tab. The boot options you can invoke, which are the same safe mode startup menu options, are as follows:

- SAFEBOOT — Safe mode
- NOGUIBOOT — Command prompt
- BOOTLOG — Boot logging
- BASEVIDEO — VGA mode
- SOS — Debugging

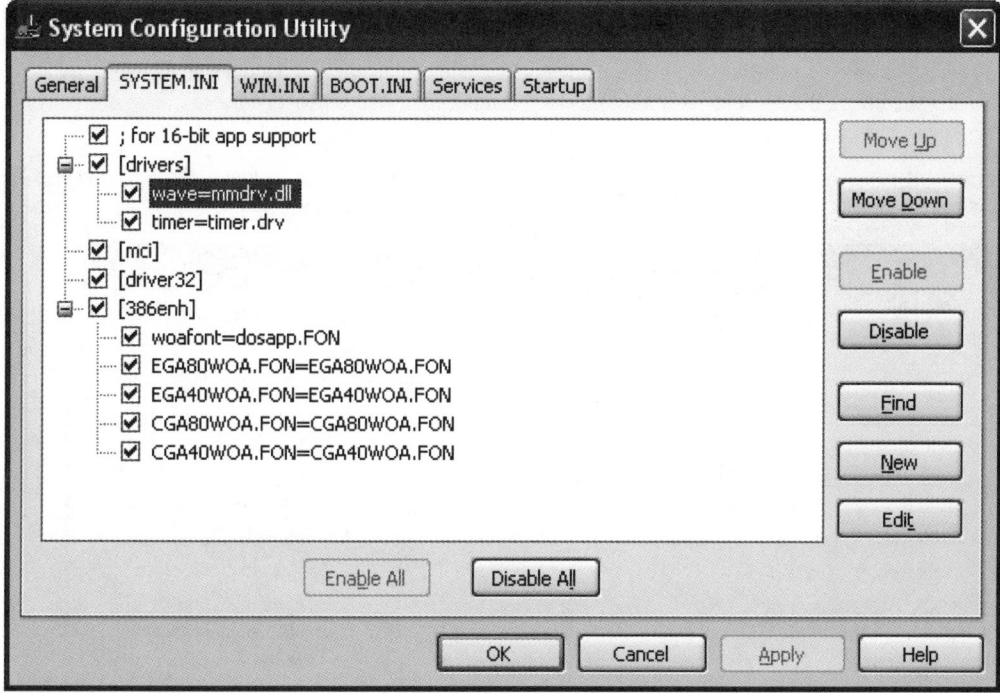

Figure 25-8: System.ini tab

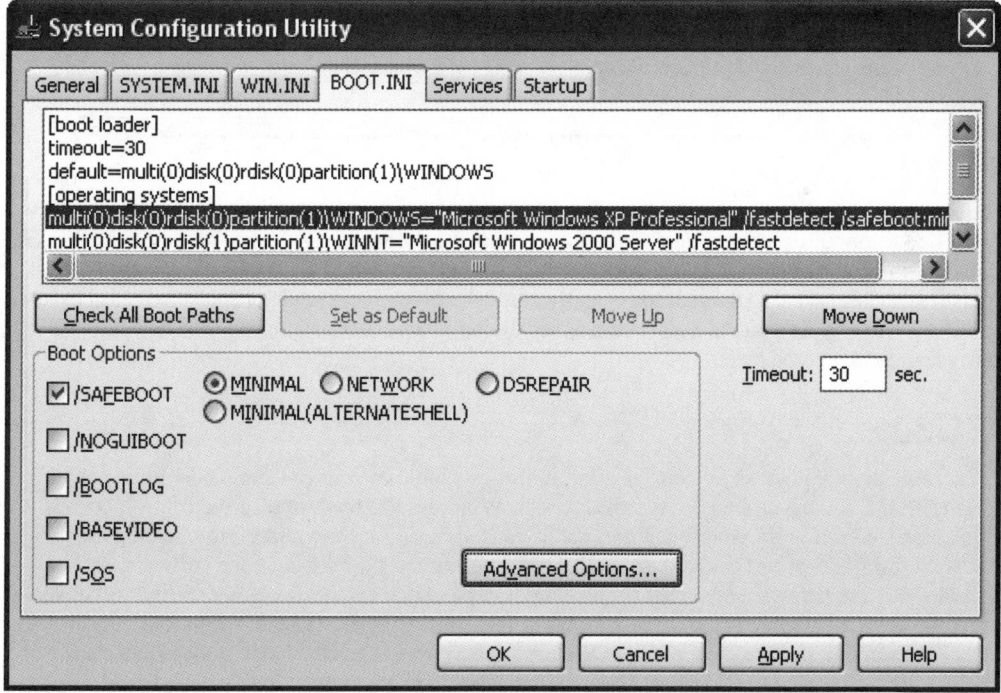

Figure 25-9: Boot.ini tab

5. The Services tab lists all of the services that start on your computer at boot up. As seen in Figure 25-10, essential services are marked as such, and you'll probably see a bunch of services that may not be needed. You can greatly improve startup time and general system resource performance by clearing the check boxes next to items that you do not use or need. Most of these are written in plain English and are easy to understand.

TIP: Don't clear the check boxes of essential services, and proceed with caution when clearing others. You should know what the service is and what it does before disabling its startup.

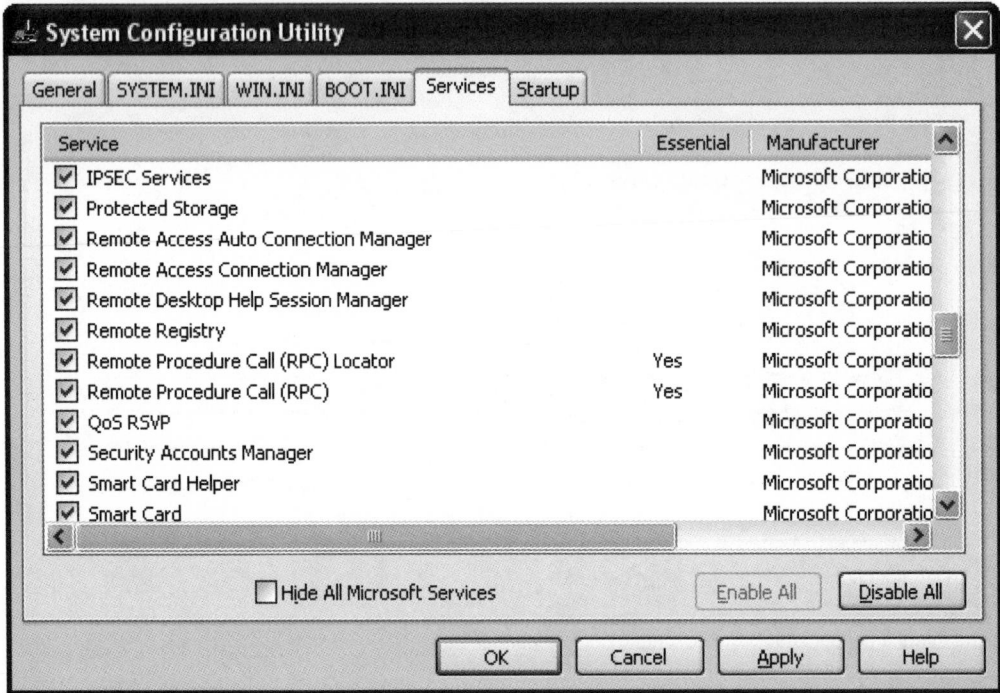

Figure 25-10: Services tab

6. The Startup tab lists commands that are run at startup. You can disable any that are not necessary, but again, do not disable these unless you know what they are starting. You'll see applications here that start up when the system starts, such as Microsoft Office. Feel free to clear those application items if you don't want to them automatically start. Once you have made changes here, XP detects the changes and gives you the Selective Startup dialog box at boot as a reminder that you have left the system in an altered state.

MSINFO32

MSINFO32, otherwise known as System Information, is available in your System Tools folder or by typing **MSINFO32** at the Run line. First introduced in Windows 98, System Information is a central storage location for configuration information about your system. As shown in Figure 25-11, you can access System Information and find out about hardware resources, components, the software environment, Internet settings, and applications. Under expandable categories, you can find out a wealth of information that can help you resolve problems. In fact, MSINFO32 can even point out conflicts and problems. For example, if there is an IRQ conflict on your system, you can see in under Hardware Resources in Conflicts/Sharing. Conflicts and problems are displayed in the details pane in red.

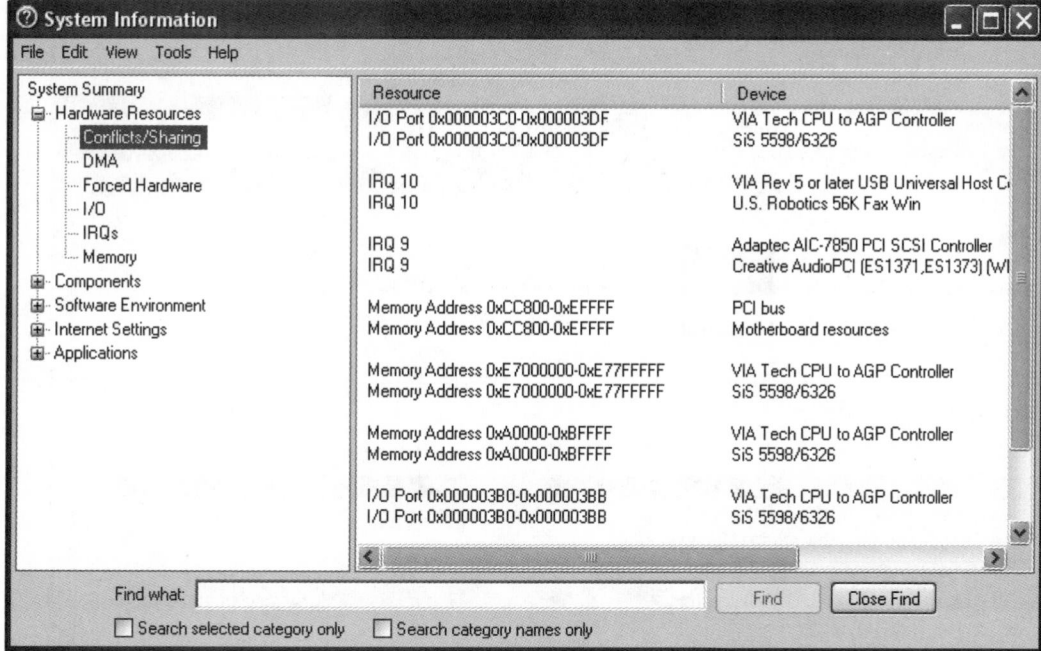

Figure 25-11: MSINFO32

You can access a few additional tools under the Tools menu from within System Information. The following sections give you an overview of these and how they can help you.

Net Diagnostics

Net Diagnostics scans your system and gathers information about hardware, software, and network connections. It's a good "overall" tool that enables you to get a good look at your system. As the name implies, Net Diagnostics primarily checks network connections, applications, and network hardware issues. If you choose Tools ⇨ Net Diagnostics, you can click the Set Scanning options link and run a system scan.

The system scan connects you to the Internet and tests your Internet connections by running different utilities, such as `ping`. Once the scan is complete, you see a report generated, as shown in Figure 25-12, that gives you information about success and failures. You can then troubleshoot the problems on your system. Overall, this one is good to use: it's quick and easy, and it provides information that can be helpful to you.

File Signature Verification Utility

The File Signature Verification Utility runs a check on your system files to ensure that all critical files on your system are digitally signed. When you click the option on the Tools menu, a small window appears where you can start the test. If you like, you can click the Advanced button to scan certain folders only and to create a log file if you want. Once you are ready to run the test, just click Start. Once the test has completed, you are notified of any files that are not digitally signed.

NOTE: Keep in mind that digitally signed files ensures that files have come from a particular vendor. This security feature helps protect your system from viruses and other malicious attacks.

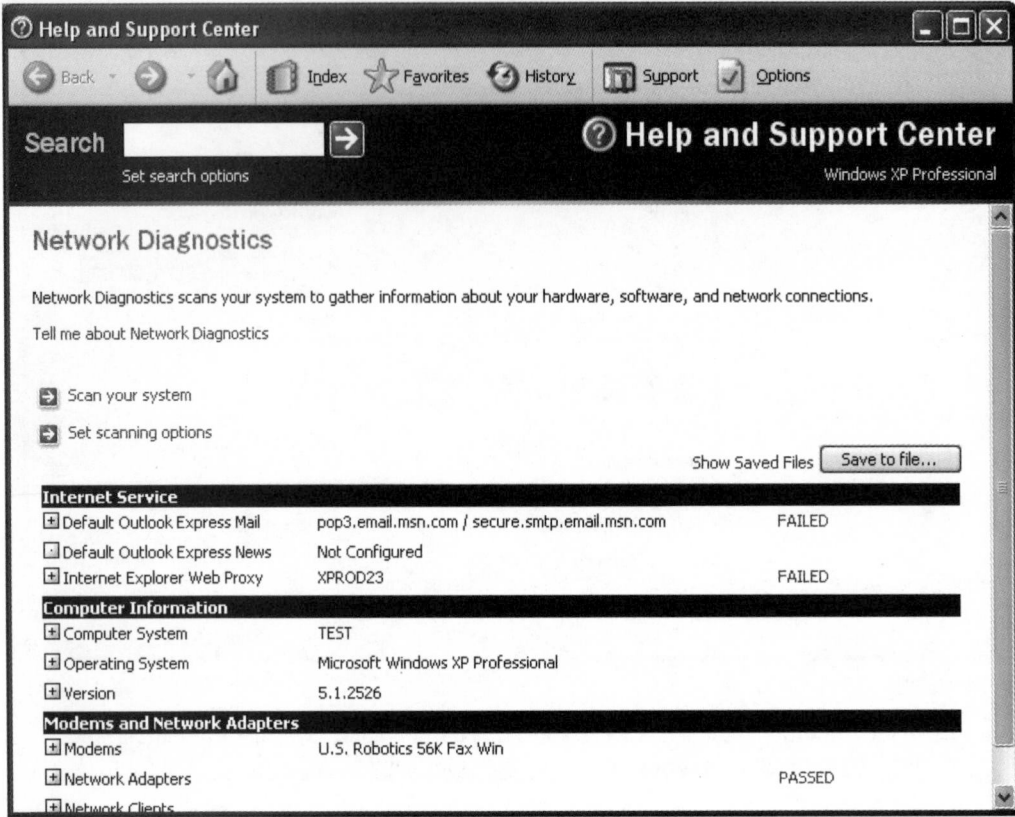

Figure 25-12: Net Diagnostics report

DirectX Diagnostic Tool

DirectX is a graphics and sound tool that enables your Windows XP computer to play games and provide additional graphics and sounds. If you are having problems with DirectX or getting DirectX error messages, you can access the DirectX Diagnostic Tool, as shown in Figure 25-13, to test and troubleshoot DirectX. You can view DirectX files and version information; run display, sound, and music tests; and even access additional help. The tabs provided are easy to use and explanatory, so keep this tool in the back of your mind should DirectX ever become a problem on your system.

Dr. Watson for Windows

Dr. Watson is an older tool that has been around in Windows operating systems for several years now. In a nutshell, Dr. Watson can be used to create log files about system processes so that support personnel can analyze the log files. The log files created require debugging software to read, so this tool isn't directly helpful to you, but it can be used by technical support if you're experiencing severe problems.

Help and Support

Finally, Windows Help and Support is available on the Start menu. Help and Support provides an HTML interface, troubleshooters, guides, articles, and even support via the Internet; you should check out the Help and Support tool if you are having problems that you cannot seem to resolve.

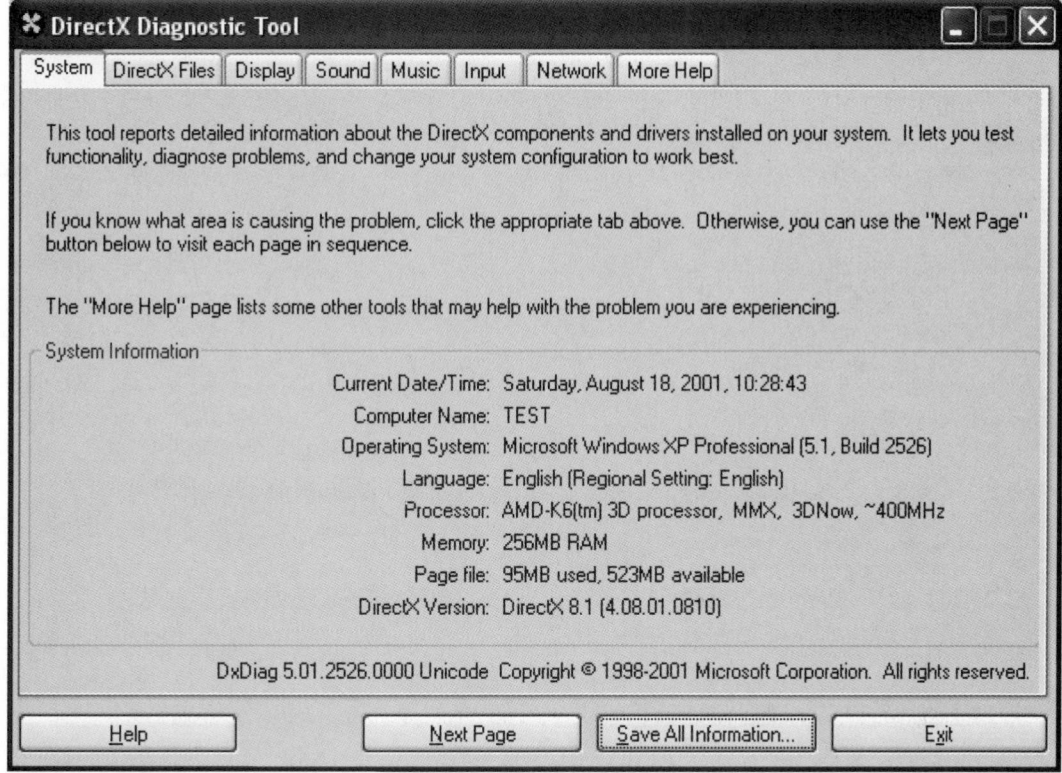

Figure 25-13: Use the DirectX Diagnostic Tool to resolve problems with DirectX.

Other Tools

Naturally, Microsoft does not own the troubleshooting tools world, even for its own Windows products. You may be able to find a number of potentially helpful third-party tools that can keep Windows XP running in tip-top shape. Symantec makes a number of helpful products under the Norton name, and you may consider checking those out at `http://symantec.com` or at www.amazon.com. Also, you'll find related products by other vendors, such as McAfee, Final Data, and Executive software, all of which can be reviewed at www.amazon.com or a related software site.

Summary

Windows XP contains a number of tools that can help you resolve problems on your system. These tools are easy to use and can often give you the information you need to identify and resolve a problem:

- ◆ System Restore restores your system to an earlier time by using restore points.
- ◆ Safe mode helps if you cannot boot Windows normally.
- ◆ The Recovery Console is a powerful tool that is used to repair and manage Windows when you cannot boot.
- ◆ The Automated System Recovery (ASR) feature helps you start Windows and retrieve data from backup.
- ◆ Device Driver Rollback helps you remove a new driver that is not working properly.
- ◆ MSCONFIG enables you to manage the boot and startup processes.
- ◆ MSINFO32 provides system information and provides additional support tools.

Index

O